# Health Care

# Fraud *and* Abuse:

## Practical Perspectives

**Second Edition**

**Publications From BNA Books on Related Topics**

*Managed Care Litigation*

*Health Care Fraud and Abuse: Practical Perspectives*

*Prosecuting and Defending Health Care Fraud Cases*

*E-Health Business & Transactional Law*

*Pharmaceutical Law: Regulation of Research,
   Development, and Marketing*

*Supreme Court Practice, Eighth Edition*

*BNA's Directory of State and Federal Courts,
   Judges and Clerks, 2007 Edition*

*Medical Ethics: Analysis of the Issues Raised by the
   Codes, Opinions, and Statements*

*Medical Ethics: Codes, Opinions, and Statements*

*Occupational Safety and Health Law*

*Codes of Professional Responsibility: Ethics Standards in
   Business, Health, and Law*

For details on these and other related titles, please visit BNA Books Web site at **bnabooks.com** or call **1-800-960-1220** to request a catalog.  All books are available on a 30-day free examination period.

# HEALTH CARE

# FRAUD *and* ABUSE:

## Practical Perspectives

## Second Edition

*Editor-in-Chief*

Linda A. Baumann
*Arent Fox LLP*
*Washington, D.C.*

**The American Bar Association**
**Health Law Section**

BNA Books, A *Division of* BNA, Arlington, VA

**Library of Congress Cataloging-in-Publication Data**

Health care fraud and abuse : practical perspectives / editor-in-chief, Linda
A. Baumann. -- 2nd ed.
    p. cm.
  Includes bibliographical references and index.
  ISBN 978-1-57018-662-2 (alk. paper)
  1.  Insurance, Health--Law and legislation--United States--Criminal
provisions. 2.  Medical care--Law and legislation--United States--Criminal
provisions. 3.  Medicare fraud. 4.  Medicaid fraud.  I. Baumann, Linda A.

  KF3605.H43 2007
  345.73'0263--dc22

                                                                    2007044848

The materials contained in this work represent the opinions of the individual
authors and should not be construed to be those of either the American Bar
Association (ABA) or the ABA Health Law Section, or any other person or
entity.  The authors expressly reserve the right to freely advocate other
positions on behalf of clients. Nothing contained herein is to be considered the
rendering of legal advice for specific cases, and readers are responsible for
obtaining such advice from their own legal counsel. These materials are
intended for educational and informational purposes only.

Published by BNA Books
1801 S. Bell Street, Arlington, VA. 22202
*bnabooks.com*

ISBN 978-1-57018-662-2
*Printed in the United States of America*

# Contributing Authors

Linda A. Baumann
*Arent Fox, PLLC*
*Washington, D.C.*

Thomas S. Crane
*Mintz, Levin, Cohn, Ferris,*
*Glovsky, and Popeo, P.C.*
*Boston, Massachusetts*

Robert Salcido
*Akin, Gump, Strauss,*
*Hauer & Feld, L.L.P.*
*Washington, D.C.*

Patric Hooper
*Hooper, Lundy & Bookman, Inc.*
*Los Angeles, California*

Amanda S. Abbott
*Hooper, Lundy & Bookman, Inc.*
*San Diego, California*

Dennis M. Barry
*Vinson & Elkins, LLP*
*Washington, D.C.*

Christine C. Rinn
*Crowell & Moring, LLP*
*Washington, D.C.*

Barbara H. Ryland
*Crowell & Moring, LLP*
*Washington, D.C.*

Leigh Walton
*Bass, Berry & Sims, PLC*
*Nashville, Tennessee*

Angela Humphreys
*Bass, Berry & Sims, PLC*
*Nashville, Tennessee*

Clevonne Jacobs
*Bass, Berry & Sims, PLC*
*Nashville, Tennessee*

William W. Horton
*Haskell Slaughter*
*Young & Rediker, LLC*
*Birmingham, Alabama*

Monty G. Humble
*Vinson & Elkins, LLP*
*Dallas, Texas*

Larri A. Short
*Arent Fox, PLLC*
*Washington, D.C.*

Richard S. Liner
*Arent Fox, PLLC*
*Washington, D.C.*

Carol A. Poindexter
*Shook, Hardy & Bacon LLP*
*Kansas City, Missouri*

# Foreword

The American Bar Association (ABA) Health Law Section is proud to continue its book series with the publication of the Second Edition HEALTH CARE FRAUD AND ABUSE: PRACTICAL PERSPECTIVES, published in cooperation with BNA Books, a Division of The Bureau of National Affairs, Inc.

HEALTH CARE FRAUD AND ABUSE: PRACTICAL PERSPECTIVES was our first venture into the production of a major treatise for the benefit of practitioners of all experience levels and different settings. In many ways it has set the standard to which we aspire in each of our books. We hope that you will agree that each chapter of this Second Edition contains valuable resources and up-to-date insights to this dynamic and crucially important area affecting the health care industry.

On behalf of the Section we wish to express continuing appreciation to Editor-in-Chief Linda A. Baumann, who has shepherded a talented group of contributors through the Second Edition as well as the original production of this work and five annual supplements. Many others have given dedicated service to this effort, including Jim Fattibene and Elizabeth Turqman at BNA Books and, particularly, the authors, who have given of their time and expertise for the benefit of the profession. You are all to be commended for a job well and faithfully done.

We are confident that readers will continue to find this book to be a useful and practical reference source. We welcome your thoughts as to how the Section's BNA Books series can further address your practice needs.

ANDREW J. DEMETRIOU
SECTION CHAIR

VICKIE YATES BROWN
CHAIR-ELECT

MICHAEL E. CLARK
CHAIR
PUBLICATIONS COMMITTEE
HEALTH LAW SECTION
AMERICAN BAR ASSOCIATION

December 2007

# Preface to the Second Edition

In the five years since publication of the first edition of this book in 2002, there have been a tremendous number and variety of new legal developments related to health care fraud and abuse. With regard to applicable laws, there have been several important statutory changes that impact health care fraud and abuse, such as the creation of the new prescription drug benefit program, Medicare Part D; the enactment of the Sarbanes-Oxley Act; and the promulgation of numerous new state false claims acts as a result of the provision in the Deficit Reduction Act of 2005 encouraging the adoption of state laws comparable to the federal civil False Claims Act. Regulatory changes in certain areas have been equally extensive and far-reaching, such as the long-awaited publication of the Stark II/Phase II regulations in 2004, followed just recently by the issuance of the Stark Phase III regulations as well as numerous Stark (and other) regulatory changes in the 2008 Proposed Physician Fee Schedule. During the intervening years, important regulations related to health information technology also have been issued creating new safe harbors under the Anti-Kickback Statute and new Stark Law exceptions.

Many of these laws and regulations, like those already on the books, are extremely complex and leave numerous "gray" areas. Frequent lawsuits result, some initiated by the government and others by whistleblowers under the *qui tam* provisions of the False Claims Act. However, in this unique area of the law, few health care providers can afford to have their day in court and challenge allegations of fraud, because of the government's broad discretionary powers to exclude individuals and entities from participation in federal health care programs, a virtual financial death sentence. As a result, there continue to be relatively few cases providing legal precedents, and few opportunities to have an independent third party resolve the issues in question.

In the absence of case law, providers and other companies doing business in the health care industry must rely heavily on manual provisions and other guidance documents. Perhaps for this reason, there has been a steadily increasing stream of guidance materials emanating from the Centers for Medicare and Medicaid Services, the Office of Inspector General of the Department of Health and Human Services (OIG), and other government and private entities: everything from Compliance Program Guidance documents for most segments of the health care industry to Special Advisory Bulletins to advisory opinions to trade association codes of conduct. On occasion, new guidance materials have been issued on particular substantive issues, ranging from the OIG's Voluntary Disclosure Protocol to hospital charges for uninsured patients to patient assistance programs. There also have been a growing number of settlements and corporate integrity agreements, which seasoned fraud and abuse lawyers often scrutinize, seeking additional guidance on what behavior will trigger government allegations of fraud or abuse.

Government enforcement priorities also have been changing over time. While it is difficult to generalize, in 2002 when the first edition of this book was published, much of the fraud and abuse enforcement activity seemed to focus on hospitals and nursing homes. Prior enforcement efforts against home health agencies and durable medical equipment (DME) providers continued but at a seemingly slower pace. In the subsequent five years we have seen an explosion of cases in the pharmaceutical industry (primarily focusing on kickbacks and pricing), increased activity in quality of care cases and an expanded number of cases against individual physicians. Most recently, there appears to be a renewed focus on DME providers as a result of sting operations in several states.

Due to the lack of bright line guidance in many areas and the fact that standards often are revised, it can be extremely challenging, as a lawyer, to counsel health care clients. Fraud and abuse issues are potentially inherent in virtually every claim or transaction, yet they can be extremely difficult to identify, let alone to analyze and resolve with any degree of certainty. The risks of failure to do so are staggering: clients may have to enter civil settlements for hundreds of millions of dollars or face criminal penalties or imprisonment or some combination of these sanctions. Moreover, lawyers themselves are at risk, as most recently exemplified by the civil False Claims Act case brought against a former general counsel of Tenet.

This book originally was developed in 2002 as a resource for attorneys dealing with these types of issues. Based on the tremendously positive response that the book has received, it seems clear that the need for this type of publication continues to grow. The 2007 edition has been expanded and updated throughout, and is designed to serve as a desk reference for experienced health law practitioners as well as for the relative novice (who may find it helpful to read the first chapter, "An Introduction to Health Care Fraud and Abuse," before delving into the other chapters). For this reason, the book includes an extensive collection of appendices that contain many of the laws, regulations and guidance documents that are critical to addressing fraud and abuse issues in the health care context. Because of the growing volume of the appendices, and in light of the benefits of being able to search documents electronically, the appendices in the 2007 edition are being provided on a CD Rom.

The topics covered in each chapter reflect the types of issues that health lawyers frequently face in practice. It has been particularly valuable to have different authors for each chapter who can bring their unique expertise to these issues. As a result, certain topics may be covered in more than one chapter, and I encourage you to review the different analyses and perspectives that each author brings to the topic. Moreover, because the authors are experienced health lawyers, they bring an invaluable real world perspective and practical advice to each chapter. Please note, however, that the content of this book is designed for general information purposes only, and should not be construed as legal advice or an opinion on any specific facts or circumstances. The views expressed in the chapters are those of the individual authors, and do not reflect the views of the authors' firms, the firms' clients, my views, or the views of the other authors of this volume.

The book has evolved, along with this rapidly changing field. Accordingly, the 2007 edition contains 10 chapters as indicated below, as well as the appendices:

Chapter 1: An Introduction to Health Care Fraud and Abuse, Linda A. Baumann

Chapter 2: Federal Physician Self-Referral Restrictions, Thomas S. Crane

Chapter 3: The False Claims Act in Health Care Prosecutions: Application of the Substantive, *Qui Tam,* and Voluntary Disclosure Provisions, Robert Salcido

Chapter 4: Practical Considerations for Defending Health Care Fraud and Abuse Cases, Patric Hooper & Amanda S. Abbott

Chapter 5: Legal Issues Surrounding Hospital and Physician Relationships, Dennis M. Barry

Chapter 6: Managed Care Fraud and Abuse: Risk Areas for Government Program Participants, Christine C. Rinn and Barbara H. Ryland

Chapter 7: Corporate Compliance Programs, Linda A. Baumann

Chapter 8: Potential Liabilities for Directors and Officers of Health Care Organizations, Leigh Walton, Angela Humphreys, and Clevonne Jacobs

Chapter 9: The Disclosure Dilemma: How, When, and What to Tell Stockholders and Stakeholders About Your *Qui Tam* Suit or Investigation, William W. Horton, & Monty G. Humble

Chapter 10: Controlling Fraud, Waste, and Abuse in the Medicare Part D Program, Larri A. Short & Richard S. Liner

Appendices: Carol Poindexter, Appendix Editor

Each of the chapters has been updated to be current through May 2007. However, individual authors may have updated their chapters beyond this date in order to reflect major new developments. In this regard, I am very pleased that Tom Crane was able to create a special addendum to his chapter on the Stark Law in order to reflect the new Stark III regulations that were just issued in Sept. 2007.

I would like to take this opportunity to thank the many people who so generously contributed to the success of this book. It has been an honor to work with the chapter authors, experts in the field, who have taken innumerable hours away from their busy practices. My special thanks to those authors who have responded so graciously for each of the past five years: Dennis Barry, Tom Crane, Patric Hooper, and Robert Salcido. I also am very appreciative of those authors who have joined the team, enriching the book by bringing unique perspectives and covering new topics: Bill Horton, Monty Humble, Carol Poindexter, Angela Humphries, Larri Short, Richard Liner, Amanda Abbott, Christine Rinn, Leigh Walton, and Clevonne Jacobs. In addition, I would like to express my thanks and appreciation to Jim Fattibene and Elizabeth Turqman from BNA Books for their exceptional expertise and guidance. This book also would not have been possible without the support of the leaders and staff of the ABA Health Law Section, including Paul DeMuro, Andy Demetriou, Michael Clark, and Jill Peña. Last, but not least, I would like to thank my family, including my sons Greg, Doug, and Daniel Faron, for their patience, under-standing and appreciation of the final product.

On behalf of the authors and publishers, we hope that the 2007 edition of *Health Care Fraud and Abuse: Practical Perspectives* will help readers un-derstand these complex, continually evolving legal issues. Further, we hope the practical perspectives each author provides will help you effectively address these issues as they may arise in your legal practice, reducing the risks for you, as well as for your clients.

LINDA A. BAUMANN
EDITOR-IN-CHIEF
Arent Fox LLP
Washington, DC

December 2007

# Preface to the First Edition

It is change, continuing change, inevitable change, that is the dominant factor in society today. No sensible decision can be made any longer without taking into account not only the world as it is, but the world as it will be.... This, in turn, means that our statesmen, our businessmen, our everyman must take on a science fictional way of thinking.

—Isaac Asimov, *Asimov on Science Fiction*.

Change often makes accepted customs into crimes.

—Mason Cooley, *City Aphorisms*.

It goes without saying that lawyers, too, must take on Asimov's "science fictional" way of thinking. The law is constantly evolving and, in recent times, the field of health care law seems to change more than most. Even the names of various divisions and other entities affiliated with the U.S. Department of Health and Human Services (HHS) are being changed. The Health Care Financing Administration (HCFA), which plays a primary role in government health care reimbursement (and thus is integrally involved in initiatives related to health care fraud and abuse), has been renamed the Centers for Medicare and Medicaid Services (CMS).[1] Similarly, the concept of health care "fraud and abuse" continues to evolve. For example, initially enforcement efforts focused on government overpayments due to improper conduct such as upcoding or billing for services that were never provided. More recently, the fraud and abuse laws are also being used in connection with claims that involve care of inadequate quality or quantity.

Some of these changes have created a situation where practices and customs, long accepted as legitimate in many industries, may now be characterized as "crimes" in the health care context. To give just one example, paying billing companies or salesmen a percentage of the revenues they generate has long been a standard business practice. This method of compensation helps align the interest of both parties in maximizing business revenues. However, under certain circumstances in the health care field, the government may interpret this type of payment as an attempt to induce improper behavior and a violation of the anti-kickback statute, which can lead to criminal penalties including fines and up to 5 years' imprisonment.

What explains this disparate treatment of the health care industry? In large part, the sheer amount of money involved and the perceived abuses of the past

---

[1]Because HHS plans to convert references from "HCFA" to "CMS," for purposes of consistency, this book will do likewise.

likely account for this situation. Other contributing factors include the huge and growing market for health care services as scientific advances create more and better treatments to prevent and cure disease and the percentage of the population over the age of 50 steadily increases. In fact, more than $1 trillion is spent on health care in the United States each year; approximately 15 percent of the gross national product. Moreover, many of these health care products and services will be paid for, at least in part, by federally funded health care programs such as Medicare and Medicaid. However, the HHS Office of Inspector General (OIG) has estimated that over 10 percent of these expenditures, or over $100 billion annually, are lost to fraud and abuse.

As a result, it is not surprising that the government and private industry are continually devoting additional resources to identifying, redressing, and preventing such perceived fraud and abuse.[2] These efforts have led to an explosion in the volume of laws, regulations, and other materials regulating the health care industry and its business partners. The information technology revolution has further contributed to the rapid pace at which these changes occur. The consequences of failure to fully comply with all applicable laws and regulations can be frightening. The penalties range from imprisonment to treble damages to exclusion from participation in federal health care programs, which has been characterized as a "financial death sentence" for a health care provider. Under these circumstances, it is critically important for individuals and organizations involved in the health care industry to be thoroughly familiar with the applicable law. Typically, a health care provider or other business entity will turn to legal counsel for the requisite in-depth knowledge of the laws and regulations, and how they are being enforced.

Interpretive guidance is particularly critical here where the applicable laws are often ambiguous, leaving large "gray" areas and few "bright lines." However, although many documents are available on-line, knowing how to access and interpret them can be a challenge, particularly since the traditional tools of legal research may not be sufficient in this area. There is relatively little case law relating to many of these issues although certain types of guidance materials are sometimes available from other sources. Where there is such a scarcity of precedent and other interpretive materials, practical experience with the issues can be an invaluable asset. In other areas, such as the civil False Claims Act, the volume of relevant case law can be overwhelming. Here too, advice from experienced practitioners can be extremely helpful.

This book is designed to help address these problems by providing practical guidance for those who are new to the field as well as for those who have expertise in this area. The authors of each of the chapters are leading health care practitioners who offer their professional perspectives on a wide range of issues. While these eight chapters do not purport to be a comprehensive analysis of all aspects of health care fraud and abuse, they can provide valuable insights into many of the issues an attorney is likely to face when representing a client

---

[2]While certain government resources have been shifted in light of the events of September 11, 2001, it is still to early to tell whether there will be a significant decrease in health care fraud enforcement efforts. On the contrary, there are numerous indications that health care fraud and abuse remains a major government priority.

involved in the health care industry. There is some overlap among the chapters. However, because various issues arise in different contexts, the unique perspective each author brings to his or her analysis should be valuable.

The first chapter, which I have written, "An Introduction to Health Care Fraud and Abuse" (Chapter 1), is designed for those who are starting with more limited experience in this area. It provides a brief summary and overview of some of the more important topics in health care fraud and abuse, focusing on the statutory and regulatory framework; particularly, those laws not covered extensively in other chapters of the book. This chapter also describes other guidance documents and resources that may assist an attorney in advising his or her clients on how to reduce exposure under the fraud and abuse laws. This introductory chapter may facilitate review of the subsequent chapters in the book, each of which address a specific aspect of health care fraud and abuse.

Tom Crane's chapter on "Federal Physician Self-Referral Restrictions" (Chapter 2) provides a comprehensive analysis of the federal Stark law and its complex regulations, as well as a detailed examination of the exceptions available to help protect transactions that otherwise implicate the statute.

Robert Salcido's chapter on "The False Claims Act in Health Care Prosecutions: Application of the Substantive, *Qui Tam*, and Voluntary Disclosure Provisions" (Chapter 3) contains an extensive discussion of the False Claims Act and interpretive cases focusing on the substantive elements of the statute as well as the *qui tam* (whistleblower) provisions. The discussion of the public disclosure jurisdictional bar to *qui tam* actions may help attorneys defend their clients from such lawsuits. The chapter also contains insights into the use of the OIG's Voluntary Disclosure Program.

Patric Hooper's chapter on "Practical Considerations for Defending Health Care Fraud and Abuse Cases" (Chapter 4) provides background on the development of the fraud and abuse laws; an overview of the enforcement agencies, their weapons and strategies; as well as specific, practical approaches to consider when developing a defense strategy.

Dennis Barry's chapter on "Legal Issues Surrounding Hospital and Physician Relationships" (Chapter 5) examines the myriad of issues that must be considered in the context of physicians' varied relationships with hospitals, including implications of tax, anti-trust, and corporate practice of medicine requirements as well as the prohibitions against kickbacks, self-referrals, and gainsharing. The chapter will be particularly helpful to practitioners because it addresses these issues in the context of many common arrangements between hospitals and physicians.

Robert Roth and Alicia Palmer's chapter on "Managed Care Fraud and Abuse: Risk Areas for Government Program Participants" (Chapter 6) explains how fraud and abuse issues differ when they arise in the managed care (as opposed to the fee-for-service) setting, and provides an in-depth discussion of the role of compliance programs in the managed care context; emphasizing prompt payment and denial of care compliance issues as well as marketing practices.

The chapter by Nancy Jones, Nora Liggett, and Michelle Marsh on "Corporate Compliance Programs" (Chapter 7) describes the advantages of implementing a corporate compliance program, particularly under the U.S. Sentencing Guidelines, and what elements and practical issues should be addressed.

The chapter also summarizes the more important aspects of the various compliance program guidance documents that the OIG has published for different types of health care providers.

Finally, the chapter I co-authored with George McDavid on "Potential Liabilities for Directors and Officers of Health Care Organizations" (Chapter 8) examines the various types of civil and criminal liability that directors and officers may face, with particular emphasis on the evolving *Caremark* doctrine, and measures that may help reduce exposure.

The Appendices contain a ready source for many of the more important documents in the field of health care fraud and abuse. Appendices A through J include not only the texts of relevant statutes and regulations but also contain various guidance documents necessary for analysis of these issues (but whose existence and availability are not uniformly well-known). The Appendices include materials concerning the

- Anti-kickback statute and safe harbor regulations
- Stark law and regulations
- False Claims Act
- Civil monetary penalties and exclusions laws and regulations
- Selected statutes relating to private payer fraud
- Special Fraud Alerts and Special Advisory Bulletins
- Advisory opinions relating to the anti-kickback statute and the Stark law
- OIG Provider Self-Disclosure Protocol
- OIG Compliance Program Guidance for hospitals and for individual and small group physician practices, and the corporate integrity agreement with Vencor, Inc.
- Contract for Participation in Medicare+Choice Program.

Appendices A through E are reprinted and located at the end of this volume. Appendices F through J are provided on the CD-ROM that accompanies this volume.

This book was designed in order to provide a desk reference for members of the health law bar and other attorneys who counsel clients involved in the health care industry. The materials contained in the eight substantive chapters are current through June 2001.

Due to the constant changes in this subject, as discussed above, this book will be updated annually. The supplemental volumes will not only update the material in the "core" chapters but may also add new chapters as various "hot" topics arise. Finally, the reader should remember that the content of this book is designed for general informational purposes only, and should not be construed as legal advice or opinion on any specific facts or circumstances. The views expressed in the chapters are those of the individual authors, and do not reflect the views of their firm or its clients, myself, or the other authors of this volume.

It has been a privilege to work with the many people who have helped bring this book to fruition, and I would like to extend my personal thanks to all of them. The chapter authors have devoted a tremendous amount of their time and shared a great deal of their invaluable professional knowledge. Many members of the leadership in the American Bar Association (ABA) Health Law Section have also made a substantial contribution of their time and energy, as described in more detail in the Foreword. In addition, BNA Books has provided very helpful guidance and assistance throughout the process. Their continuing support and dedication to this project has been essential to its completion.

On behalf of all those who have contributed to this volume, we hope these materials will help the reader counsel his or her clients on this ever-changing area of the law.

LINDA A. BAUMANN
EDITOR-IN-CHIEF
Reed Smith LLP
Washington, D.C.

December 2001

# The American Bar Association Health Law Section 2007–2008 Officers & Council

**Chair**
Andrew J. Demetriou
Los Angeles, CA

**Secretary**
Linda A. Baumann
Washington, DC

**Chair-Elect**
Vickie Yates Brown
Louisville, KY

**Budget Officer**
David L. Douglass
Washington, D.C.

**Vice Chair**
David W. Hilgers
Austin, TX

**Immediate Past Chair**
Paul R. DeMuro
San Francisco, CA

## Council Members at Large

Michael E. Clark
Houston, TX

Daniel A. Cody
San Francisco, CA

Shelley K. Hubner
San Francisco, CA

David H. Johnson
Albuquerque, NM

Alexandria Hien McCombs
Dallas, TX

Kathleen Scully-Hayes
Baltimore, MD

## Section Delegates to the House of Delegates

Gregory L. Pemberton
Indianapolis, IN

Howard T. Wall
Brentwood, TN

**Young Lawyers Division Liaison**
Conrad Meyer
New Orleans, LA

**Law Student Division Liaison**
Katie Rose Fink
St. Louis, MO

**Board of Governors Liaison**
Roderick B. Mathews
Richmond, VA

**Publications Chair**
Michael E. Clark
Houston, TX

**Chair, Editorial Board**
Charles M. Key
Memphis, TN

**Section Director**
Jill C. Peña
Chicago, IL

# About the Authors

**Linda A. Baumann (Chapter 1: An Introduction to Health Care Fraud and Abuse; Chapter 7: Corporate Compliance Programs)**

Linda Baumann serves as editor-in-chief of this volume and also is the author of two of the chapters. Ms. Baumann is a partner at Arent Fox LLP in Washington, D.C., and has extensive experience on a wide range of health care transactions and regulatory matters, particularly those relating to fraud and abuse and reimbursement. She has worked with clients throughout the industry ranging from Fortune 50 companies to community providers, including hospitals, skilled nursing facilities, pharmaceutical companies, distributors, rehabilitation companies, clinical laboratories, DME suppliers, management companies, and many other types of entities involved in the health care industry. She helps clients develop strategies to promote business objectives while ensuring compliance with applicable laws and regulations, and has designed corporate compliance programs, handled government investigations (from the initial audit through negotiation and settlement), and served as outside counsel on a wide variety of legal issues. She has been named one of the 12 Outstanding Fraud and Compliance Lawyers in the country by Nightingale's *Healthcare News* for the past several years, and is listed in numerous *Who's Who* publications. She has experience in the federal government, in private practice, and in academia, having taught at Princeton University. She frequently speaks before national groups, and has published numerous articles on various health care topics. Ms. Baumann also serves as an officer of the ABA Health Law Section, and a liaison to the ABA Commission on Women in the Profession. She also serves as Chair of the Part D Task Force for AHLA. She received her J.D. from Columbia University, where she was an editor of the *Columbia University Law Review* and an International Fellow. She received her undergraduate degree, magna cum laude, from Brown University.

**Thomas S. Crane (Chapter 2: Federal Physician Self-Referral Restrictions)**

Tom Crane is a Member at Mintz, Levin, Cohn, Ferris, Glovsky and Popeo P.C., where he co-coordinates the firm's Health Care Fraud and Abuse and Corporate Compliance practice group. He is a nationally recognized authority on fraud and abuse. He provides comprehensive fraud and abuse services in defending clients against false claims, whistleblower, and anti-kickback allegations, with this work including internal investigations, voluntary disclosures, negotiating settlements, and Corporate Integrity Agreements. He has appeared before numerous offices of U.S. Attorneys, the FBI, and OIGs around the country. He served as counsel to a hospital executive and his management company in *United States v. Jones* (5th Cir. Jan. 16, 2007), a criminal related-party cost report fraud case reversing a district court's sentencing and restitution order based on a failure of the government's proof. He also assists clients in structuring complex transactions to comply with the anti-kickback and Stark laws as well as other regulatory requirements. He received his undergraduate degree from Harvard College (1972), a masters degree in health administration from the University of Michigan (1976), and his law degree from Antioch School of Law in Washington, D.C. (1983).

### Robert Salcido (Chapter 3: The False Claims Act in Health Care Prosecutions: Application of the Substantive, *Qui Tam*, and Voluntary Disclosure Provisions)

Robert Salcido is a partner at Akin, Gump, Strauss, Hauer & Feld, L.L.P., in its Washington, D.C., office. Mr. Salcido has practiced extensively in the area of the False Claims Act (FCA), having previously been a trial attorney with the Civil Fraud Unit of the Civil Division of the U.S. Department of Justice (DOJ), which has nationwide jurisdiction over FCA actions. At the DOJ, he prosecuted actions under the FCA, handled actions under the FCA's voluntary disclosure provisions, and specialized in whistleblower actions brought under the *qui tam* provisions of the FCA. Mr. Salcido is the author of the books *False Claims Act & The Healthcare Industry: Counseling & Litigation* (Amer. Health Lawyers 1999), and *False Claims Act & The Healthcare Industry: Counseling & Litigation: November 2000 Supplement* (Am. Health Lawyers 2000). He is a graduate of Harvard Law School and received his Bachelor of Arts degree summa cum laude from Claremont McKenna College.

### Patric Hooper (Chapter 4: Practical Considerations for Defending Health Care Fraud and Abuse Cases)

Patric Hooper is a founding principal of Hooper, Lundy & Bookman, Inc., a health law specialty firm with a national practice. Mr. Hooper has practiced in the health law field for more than 30 years, and has been involved in many high-profile health law cases. In addition to his involvement in resolving disputes, Mr. Hooper regularly advises nonprofit and for-profit health care organizations regarding reimbursement, certification, and licensure issues associated with business transactions and combinations. He continuously advises health care providers on Medicare, Medicaid, and Tricare fraud and abuse issues and on state anti-kickback and referral issues. Mr. Hooper is a frequent writer and lecturer on fraud and abuse issues and was the first chairman of the Fraud and Self-Referral interest group of the American Bar Association (ABA) Health Law Section. He received his J.D. from the University of San Diego in 1973 and his A.B. from the University of California, Los Angeles in 1970.

### Amanda S. Abbott (Chapter 4: Practical Considerations for Defending Health Care Fraud and Abuse Cases)

Amanda S. Abbott is an associate with the San Diego office of the health care law firm Hooper, Lundy & Bookman, Inc. Since joining the firm in 2005, her work has included advising a variety of health care providers regarding Medicare and Medicaid reimbursement, state and federal regulatory compliance including HIPAA compliance, licensing and certification of health care providers, managed care litigation, *qui tam* false claims defense, fraud and abuse administrative agency appeals, and real estate and contract disputes. Ms. Abbott serves on HLB's health care technology practice and pro bono committees. She is a 2003 graduate of the University of California, Davis, School of Law and received her Bachelor of Science in Nursing, cum laude, from the University of Pennsylvania in 1998. Ms. Abbott is a registered nurse and serves on the bioethics committee of a regional hospital.

### Dennis M. Barry (Chapter 5: Legal Issues Surrounding Hospital and Physician Relationships)

Dennis Barry is a partner in the Washington, D.C., office of Vinson & Elkins L.L.P. He leads his firm's health care practice. His practice deals exclusively with health care clients whom he represents on a broad range of issues, and he spends the majority of his time on Medicare payment and compliance issues. Since 1989, Mr. Barry has served as the editor and principal author of *Dennis Barry's Reimbursement Advisor*, a monthly newsletter published by Aspen Publishing. Mr. Barry is a past chair of the Medicare & Medicaid Institute, an annual three-day program sponsored by the American Health Lawyers Association (AHLA), and is a member of the Board of Directors of the AHLA. Mr. Barry is listed in *Best Lawyers in America*. He has been active in a number of professional associations including the Healthcare Financial Management Association, and he has received the Follmer, Reeves, Muncie, and Medal of Honor awards from that organization. He received his J.D. from the University of Virginia in 1975.

### Christine C. Rinn (Chapter 6: Managed Care Fraud and Abuse: Risk Areas for Government Program Participants)

Christine Rinn is a partner in the Health Care Group at Crowell & Moring LLP, in Washington, D.C. Ms. Rinn focuses her practice exclusively on managed care law issues with an emphasis on state and federal health care programs including Medicare Advantage Program, the Medicare Prescription Drug Benefit, Federal Employees Health Benefits Program, and Medicaid managed care. Ms. Rinn advises clients on rating and payment, provider reimbursement, audit, fraud and abuse, and compliance issues. She also assists managed care organizations and other health care firms in obtaining and maintaining state and federal licenses, contracts and approvals, and in joint ventures and contracting matters. Ms. Rinn received her undergraduate degree from The George Washington University and her Juris Doctor degree from The American University Washington College of Law.

### Barbara H. Ryland (Chapter 6: Managed Care Fraud and Abuse: Risk Areas for Government Program Participants)

Barbara H. Ryland is a Counsel in Crowell & Moring LLP's Washington office. As a member of the Health Care Group, Ms. Ryland's expertise lies in the areas of managed care business relationships and transactions; pharmacy benefit management; fraud and abuse compliance and investigations; confidentiality and privacy; and general business and regulatory issues in the health care industry. She also has represented clients in litigation matters involving contract disputes and antitrust issues. Ms. Ryland graduated from Duke University Law School in 1987, where she was an editor of *Law & Contemporary Problems*. She received her undergraduate degree in 1983 from the University of Virginia. Prior to her employment at Crowell & Moring, she clerked for the United States Court of Appeals for the Fourth Circuit, and was an associate in the tax and employee benefits practice at Miller & Chevalier Chrtd., and a principal at Michaels & Bonner, P.C. Ms. Ryland is a member of the District of Columbia and Maryland bars. She is the coauthor of *A Guide to Health Care Financial Ventures* and has recently edited an ABA treatise on health care joint ventures and antitrust law.

### Linda A. Baumann (Chapter 7: Corporate Compliance Programs)

See entry for Linda A. Baumann at Chapter 1, above.

### Leigh Walton (Chapter 8: Potential Liabilities for Directors and Officers of Health Care Organizations)

Leigh Walton is a member of the Nashville law firm of Bass, Berry & Sims, PLC, concentrating her practice in corporate, securities, and health law matters. She received her B.A. degree, magna cum laude, from Randolph-Macon Woman's College in Lynchburg, Virginia, and her J.D. degree from Vanderbilt University, where she was a member of Order of the Coif and the National Moot Court Team. She is active in the American, Tennessee, and Nashville Bar Associations, serving as the Vice Chair of the ABA's Committee on Negotiated Acquisitions and as a member of its Corporate Practice Committee. She lectures annually at the ABA's *Annual Mergers and Acquisitions Institute* and at the Practicing Law Institute's *Nuts and Bolts of Securities Laws* and participates in many other seminars and programs on corporate, securities, and health care matters. Ms. Walton served as a lecturer at Vanderbilt University Law School from 1980–1987. She is a fellow of the Tennessee Bar Foundation and serves on the Metropolitan Development and Housing Agency of Metropolitan Davidson County. Ms. Walton was selected by her peers and clients as one of the *Best Lawyers in America 2007*, is included in *Chambers USA America's Leading Lawyers for Business 2007* and in *The International Who's Who of Business Lawyers 2008* and *The International Who's Who of Corporate Governance Lawyers 2007*, and as one of the *Lawdragon 500* and *Lawdragon Dealmaker Selection 2007* leading lawyers in America.

### Angela Humphreys (Chapter 8: Potential Liabilities for Directors and Officers of Health Care Organizations)

Angela Humphreys is a partner at Bass, Berry & Sims, PLC, in Nashville, Tennessee, and is a member of the Corporate and Securities and Healthcare Industry Practice Areas. Her practice includes the representation of health care companies in mergers and acquisitions, the creation of joint ventures, public debt and equity offerings, private placements of securities and corporate governance, and public company disclosure matters. Ms. Humphreys graduated from the University of Tennessee summa cum laude with a B.S. in Accounting in 1991. She graduated from the University of Tennessee College of Law and received her J.D. summa cum laude in 1996, where she was recognized as the College of Law's top graduate and was elected to the Order of the Coif. In addition, she served as research editor for the *Tennessee Law Review* and received its Editing Award. Ms. Humphreys is a member of the American, Tennessee, and Nashville Bar Associations, the Tennessee Society of Certified Public Accountants, and the American Health Lawyers Association. She serves on the board of directors of the Nashville Healthcare Council's Leadership Health Care and also serves on its Membership and Marketing Committee. Ms. Humphreys also serves on the First Tennessee Health Care Advisory Council. In addition to her professional affiliations, Ms. Humphreys is active in nonprofit and community service. She serves on the Board of Directors of the Lupus Foundation of America–Mid-South Chapter and serves on the Board of Directors and as President of the Tennessee CASA Association. She also serves on the steering committee of the Nashville Chamber Orchestra's Promoters. She has also been listed in the *Lawdragon 500 New Stars, New Worlds* and the *Nashville Business Journal's* Best of the Bar for 2006.

### Clevonne Jacobs (Chapter 8: Potential Liabilities for Directors and Officers of Health Care Organizations)

Clevonne (Vonne) Jacobs is a senior associate at Bass, Berry & Sims, PLC, in Nashville, Tennessee, and is a member of the firm's Healthcare Industry Practice Area. Her practice includes transactional, operational, and regulatory work for a broad range of health care providers, including hospitals and health systems, physician organizations, and specialty care providers, with a specific focus on representing health care companies in mergers and acquisitions, the creation of joint ventures, and private placements of health care entity securities. Ms. Jacobs has written and lectured on issues of interest to health care providers, such as fraud and abuse, structuring transactions, and other health care related issues. Most recently, Ms. Jacobs was a coauthor, with Cindy Reisz, of *No Double Dipping: Legal Implications of Physician Reimbursement for Split Interpretations of Cardiac CT and Coronary CT Angiography Studies*, published in the 2007 edition of the *Health Law Handbook*, a Thomson/West publication edited by Alice G. Gosfield. Ms. Jacobs graduated from Furman University in 1999 with a B.A. in Business Administration. She received her law degree from Duke University School of Law in 2002, where she was the South Carolina Law Alumni Scholar. Ms. Jacobs is a member of the American Bar Association and the American Health Lawyers Association. She is also a member of the Nashville Healthcare Council's Leadership Health Care.

### William W. Horton (Chapter 9: The Disclosure Dilemma: How, When, and What to Tell Stockholders and Stakeholders About Your *Qui Tam* Suit or Investigation)

Bill Horton is Chair of the Transactional Practice Group of Haskell Slaughter Young & Rediker, LLC, in Birmingham, Alabama. His practice focuses on the representation of health care enterprises and other businesses in securities and corporate finance matters, mergers and acquisitions, corporate governance, and general health care and corporate matters. Mr. Horton has served as lead counsel on some of the largest corporate finance and acquisition transactions in the health care services industry. He has held leadership positions for several years with the American Bar Association's Health Law Section and the American Health Lawyers Association, and he is a frequent speaker and author on health care law, corporate and securities law and professional responsibility. A graduate of Vanderbilt University and the Duke University School of Law, Mr. Horton served in 1985–1986 as a law clerk to United States District Judge James H. Hancock (Northern District of Alabama), and was general counsel of HEALTHSOUTH Corporation, one of the nation's largest health care services providers, from 1994 through 2003. He is listed in *The Best Lawyers in America*® (Health Care Law and Corporate Governance and Compliance Law).

### Monty G. Humble (Chapter 9: The Disclosure Dilemma: How, When, and What to Tell Stockholders and Stakeholders About Your *Qui Tam* Suit or Investigation)

Monty Humble is a partner in the Dallas, Texas, office of Vinson & Elkins, LLP. His practice is focused on public debt offerings and other business transactions, particularly those related to the health care industry. He devotes a substantial portion of his time to representing borrowers and underwriters in connection with public offerings of tax-exempt bonds. He also provides advice and counsel in other areas related to finance, such as acquisitions and reorganizations. Mr. Humble is listed in *Best Lawyers in America* and *Texas Super Lawyers*. He has been active in a number of professional associations, and is a past president of the National Association of Bond Lawyers; he is a Fellow of the Dallas Bar Foundation and the Texas Bar Foundation. He received his J.D. from The University of Texas School of Law with honors in 1976.

### Larri A. Short (Chapter 10: Controlling Fraud, Waste, and Abuse in the Medicare Part D Program)

Larri Short is a partner in the Health Law Group at Arent Fox LLP in Washington, D.C., and serves as Co-Chair of the firm's Life Sciences Taskforce. Ms. Short counsels clients on health care regulatory matters, focusing extensively on Medicare and Medicaid reimbursement, Medicaid and state supplemental drug rebate programs and other state reporting obligations, and fraud and abuse compliance issues facing pharmaceutical and medical device manufacturers, prescription drug distributors, and physician practices. Ms. Short has obtained a number of Advisory Opinions from the Office of Inspector General for clients, including two relating to Patient Assistance Programs. She has represented health care provider and pharmaceutical clients in *qui tam* actions filed under federal and state False Claims Acts and is involved in the defense of pharmaceutical clients facing follow-on litigation from insurers, consumer groups and state attorneys general. She received a J.D. with High Honors from the University of North Carolina School of Law in 1992. Ms. Short also has a Masters in physiology from Duke University (1973) and she received a B.S. with High Distinction from the University of Michigan in 1969.

### Richard S. Liner (Chapter 10: Controlling Fraud, Waste, and Abuse in the Medicare Part D Program)

Richard Liner is a senior associate in the Health Law Group at Arent Fox LLP and serves as Co-Chair of the Arent Fox Hospital Task Force. Mr. Liner represents pharmaceutical and medical device manufacturers, individual and institutional health care providers, health plans, and DME suppliers in connection with a variety of regulatory matters. Mr. Liner's practice focuses on assisting clients in their effort to operate in compliance with federal and state health care fraud and abuse laws, health information privacy rules, licensure and certification requirements, and Medicare coverage policies. Mr. Liner works with clients to develop and implement compliance policies in these areas, structure compliant business relationships, and investigate and assess compliance risks under existing business operations and relationships. Mr. Liner routinely counsels clients through fraud and abuse investigations carried out by government enforcement agencies, such as the Office of Inspector General and the Department of Justice, as well as benefit integrity audits conducted by Medicare contractors and commercial insurers. Mr. Liner received his J.D., magna cum laude, from Boston University School of Law (1998) and his undergraduate degree, magna cum laude, from Tufts University (1995). He also has a Masters in Public Health from the Harvard School of Public Health (2002), where he concentrated on health care economics and health policy.

### Carol A. Poindexter (Appendix Editor)

Carol is a partner at Shook, Hardy & Bacon LLP, in Kansas City, Missouri, where she is Chair of the firm's Business Law Division, Co-Chair of the firm's Health Law Industry and a member of the Government Enforcement, Corporate Responsibility and Compliance Group. Carol's practice focuses on entities in the health care and life sciences industries with particular focus on: advising and defending organizations in federal and state civil, criminal, and administrative health care fraud investigations and False Claims Act litigation; negotiating Corporate Integrity Agreements; providing compliance advice and training; conducting internal investigations; assisting pharmaceutical manufacturers, medical institutional providers, long-term care facilities, and managed care companies in managing fraud and abuse risks. Carol represents a wide range of health care and life science organizations from Fortune 50 corporations and national chains to community health care providers, including: pharmaceutical, medical device, and biotech manufacturers; medical device distributors, hospitals; ambulatory surgery centers; academic medical centers; physicians and physicians groups; and other organizations doing business within the health care industry. Carol has published numerous articles and is a frequent speaker before national audiences on corporate compliance, fraud, and abuse, the Stark Law, and various other health law topics. Carol is active in the American Bar Association (ABA), the American Health Lawyers Association (AHLA), and the Kansas City Metropolitan Bar Association. She is Vice-Chair of the ABA Health Care Fraud Section's Fraud & Compliance Interest Group, a Member of the AHLA Fraud & Practice Group Enforcement Panel, and a member of the AHLA Corporate Governance Task Force. She also serves on the Health Care Law Committees of the Missouri Bar Association, the Kansas Bar Association, and the Kansas City Metropolitan Bar Association and is a past-President and CLE Liaison of the Health Law Committee of the Kansas Bar Association. Carol received her J.D. in 1996 from the University of Missouri (Kansas City) where she served as Editor-in-Chief of the *UMKC Law Review*.

# Summary Table of Contents

# Detailed Table of Contents

# 1

# An Introduction to Health Care Fraud and Abuse*

*Linda A. Baumann, Arent Fox LLP, Washington, D.C. The author gratefully acknowledges the assistance of Anthony Choe and Christopher Esseltine, Arent Fox LLP, in preparing this chapter.

# I. INTRODUCTION

Health care fraud and abuse has become a growth industry. For the past several years, numerous state and federal government agencies have increased the amount of staff, time, and resources they dedicate to investigating and prosecuting it. All types of health care providers, practitioners, and suppliers have been affected including hospitals, nursing homes, home health agencies, renal dialysis facilities, hospices, rehabilitation facilities, clinics, physician practices, and durable medical equipment (DME) suppliers. Pharmaceutical and device manufacturers, distributors, pharmacy benefit managers (PBMs), and pharmacies also have been involved in numerous high profile fraud and abuse cases. Other types of organizations that happen to do business with individuals or entities in the health care industry also have felt the effects of the explosion of laws and regulations in this area. Individuals at all levels may face potential liability, from employees and independent contractors up through management to the board of directors. Almost every health care attorney already has or will have to address the fraud and abuse laws in the context of what used to be considered a routine corporate transaction. Litigators representing health care clients are finding that reimbursement cases often contain additional allegations of health care fraud that can lead to far more serious consequences than the original overpayment in question. Other attorneys who do not frequently represent health care clients will begin to structure a commercial arrangement along terms and conditions that are standard in other industries only to find that the proposed transaction could create exposure under one or more of the health care fraud and abuse laws. As a result, attorneys who represent clients involved in the health care industry are well advised to develop some degree of familiarity with the fraud and abuse laws in order to protect their clients, and themselves, from exposure.

There has been a tremendous increase in the number and complexity of laws, regulations, and other subregulatory guidance materials relating to this area over the past decade. The range of topics being addressed and the level of detail with which they are regulated are similarly expanding. Even experts in health care fraud and abuse frequently comment on how difficult it is to keep up with so many diverse developments. The intricacy of the laws and regulations can be daunting, particularly for those who do not have to deal with these issues on a regular basis. The situation is exacerbated by the fact that there are so few bright lines, and thus many issues fall within a "gray area." Despite having spent years in the field, health care attorneys sometimes have difficulty providing clients with definitive guidance because the laws and regulations are often ambiguous.

## A. The Potential Risks

Nevertheless, it is essential to be fully informed about any potential issues because the liabilities can be enormous. Health care fraud and abuse likely will be a high-priority issue for the federal government for the foreseeable future because billions of dollars have been recovered as a result of numerous investigations, prosecutions, and settlements with various individuals, health care providers, and other entities. The Department of Health and Human Services (HHS) and the Department of Justice (DOJ) announced that in fiscal year (FY) 2005, the federal government won or negotiated more than $1.47 billion in judgments, settlements, and administrative impositions in health care fraud cases. In addition, federal prosecutors opened 935 new criminal health care fraud investigations involving 1,597 potential defendants, filed 382 criminal indictments, and secured the convictions of 523 defendants. There also were 778 new civil cases filed with a total of 1,334 civil matters pending at the end of FY 2005. During this same year, HHS excluded 3,804 individuals and entities from participating in federal health programs and continued to monitor more than 370 corporate integrity agreements (CIAs).[1]

These figures do not reflect various settlement agreements reached in FY 2006 that are reported by the HHS Office of Inspector General (OIG) to include $1.6 billion in investigative receivables.[2]

In addition to government investigations, there is a tremendous incentive for private citizens to look for health care fraud, become whistleblowers/relators, and file suit under the *qui tam* provisions of the federal civil False Claims Act (FCA). Even if the case never goes to trial, whistleblowers can receive millions of dollars as part of an FCA settlement.[3] Several state statutes have similar incentives as described later in this chapter.

---

[1]U.S. DEP'T OF HEALTH & HUMAN SERVS. & DEP'T OF JUSTICE, HEALTH CARE FRAUD AND ABUSE CONTROL PROGRAM ANNUAL REPORT FOR FY 2005, at 19, 25 (Aug. 2006), *available at* http://www.usdoj.gov/dag/pubdoc/hcfacreport2005.pdf [hereinafter 2005 HHS/DOJ REPORT].

[2]U.S. DEP'T OF HEALTH & HUMAN SERVS., OFFICE OF INSPECTOR GEN., SEMIANNUAL REPORT APR. 1, 2006–SEPT. 30, 2006, *available at* http://www.oig.hhs.gov/publications/docs/semiannual/2006/Semiannual%20Final%20FY%202006.pdf [hereinafter SEMIANNUAL REPORT APR.–SEPT. 2006].

[3]The civil False Claims Act is described more fully in Chapter 3 (Salcido, The False Claims Act in Health Care Prosecutions: Application of the Substantive, *Qui Tam*, and Voluntary Disclosure Provisions).

The federal government has implemented several additional programs to encourage beneficiaries to report potential fraud; however, any subsequent prosecutions likely would be undertaken by the government.[4] Moreover, there is always the risk that shareholders, disgruntled by falling stock prices or other corporate problems, will try to use the fraud and abuse laws in connection with a derivative or class action lawsuit filed against the directors and officers of a company.[5]

As indicated above, the financial implications of a fraud and abuse case can be staggering. In addition to sizable criminal penalties applicable in certain cases, depending on the applicable law, the government can invoke statutory provisions that allow it to collect several thousand dollars per improper claim as well as treble damages. In the health care industry, where hundreds and even thousands of claims may be filed by a single provider on a single day, it is easy to see how the volume of monetary damages can escalate dramatically. Even if the case never goes to court, the settlement amounts are usually very high because the government is generally unwilling to discuss settlement for less than double damages in an alleged fraud case. The settlement can be significantly reduced if the provider is able to show that there was no fraud involved. In such cases, return of any overpayment may suffice. However, despite frequent government statements that inadvertence or negligence will not result in civil or criminal claims for penalties,[6] it can be extremely difficult to convince the government that there was no fraudulent behavior.

Government enforcement activities related to health care fraud and abuse have continued to accelerate in recent years, and the dollar amounts of the settlements have generally increased substantially, especially now that the government has targeted the pharmaceutical industry. The statistics tell part of the story. In September 2005, HHS and the DOJ announced that, as a result of the Health Care Fraud and Abuse Control Program (HCFACP) created under the Health Insurance Portability and Accountability Act of 1996 (HIPAA),[7] the federal government won or negotiated more than $1.47 billion in judgments, settlements, and administrative impositions in health care fraud cases in 2005.[8] The HCFACP returned almost $8.85 billion to the Medicare Trust Fund from its inception in 1997 to 2005.[9]

---

[4]One such program involves the creation of the Medicare Fraud Hotline. By 2000, the hotline had received 1.5 million calls since its inception leading to recoveries of over $38 million. *See* U.S. DEP'T OF HEALTH & HUMAN SERVS., OFFICE OF INSPECTOR GEN., SEMIANNUAL REPORT OCT. 1, 1999–MAR. 30, 2000 (June 19, 2000), *available at* http://oig.hhs.gov/semann/ 00fsemi/pdf. The Deficit Reduction Act of 2005, Pub. L. No. 109-171, §6032 (2006), also created a requirement that any entity that receives or gives at least $5 million in annual Medicaid payments must establish written policies for all employees, contractors, and agents that provide detailed information on the federal and state FCAs, including whistleblower rights and the entity's policies and procedures to prevent waste, fraud, and abuse.

[5]Issues of director and officer liability are discussed in Chapter 8 (Walton, Humphreys & Jacobs, Potential Liabilities for Directors and Officers of Health Care Organizations).

[6]*See, e.g.,* OIG Compliance Program Guidance for Individual and Small Group Physician Practices, 65 Fed. Reg. 59,434, 59,436 (Oct. 5, 2000), *available at* http://oig.hhs.gov/authorities/ docs/physician.pdf; for text of guidance, see Appendix I-2 on the disk accompanying this volume.

[7]Section 1128C of the Social Security Act (Pub. L. No. 104-191).

[8]2005 HHS/DOJ REPORT.

[9]*Id.*

Health fraud cases resolved during 2000 through the first quarter of 2007 affected all types of health care providers including hospitals, nursing homes, physicians, and pharmaceutical manufacturers. Most cases involved settlements with substantial payments and multiyear CIAs. While many cases resulted from government or whistleblower-initiated investigations, there were a few voluntary disclosures and cases involving private payor fraud. Some of the significant developments during this period include the following:

- Pharmacia & Upjohn Co., a subsidiary of Pfizer, Inc., pleaded guilty to offering kickbacks in relation to an outsourcing contract for the administration and distribution of Genotropin. The company agreed to pay a criminal fine. Pharmacia & Upjohn Co., a separate Pfizer subsidiary, entered into a deferred prosecution agreement for the off-label promotion of Genotropin. Together, the companies agreed to pay a total of $34.7 million.[10] (2007)
- Raritan Bay Medical Center (RBMC) agreed to pay $7.5 million to settle allegations that it defrauded the Medicare program. Allegedly, RBMC intentionally inflated its inpatient and outpatient care costs to obtain Medicare outlier payments. As part of the settlement, RBMC also entered a CIA with the OIG.[11] (2007)
- East Tennessee Heart Consultants (ETHC), a cardiology practice, agreed to pay $2.9 million and enter a five-year CIA to settle allegations that it violated the FCA and a state false claims statute. Allegedly, the practice had a policy to retain overpayments received from government health care programs and not pay refunds unless specifically requested. The government claimed that ETHC had submitted false claims because it had knowingly submitted claims while aware of its legal obligation to return overpayments on prior claims.[12] (2007)
- RightCHOICE Managed Care, Inc., agreed to pay $975,000 to settle allegations that it overcharged the Federal Employees Health Benefits (FEHB) Program. Allegedly, the plan paid higher fees to physicians serving FEHB program patients rather than patients enrolled in other health plans.[13] (2007)
- Bristol Myers Squibb Co. (BMS), the DOJ, and the Office of the U.S. Attorney for the District of Massachusetts reached an agreement in principle to settle several long-running investigations of the company's

---

[10]Press Release, U.S. Attorney's Office, District of Massachusetts, *Pfizer Subsidiary Agrees to Plead Guilty for Offering Kickback and Pay $19.68 Million Criminal Fine; Second Subsidiary Agrees to Pay Additional $15 Million Penalty to Resolve Allegations of Illegal Promotion of Human Growth Hormone* (Apr. 2, 2007), *available at* http://www.usdoj.gov/usao/ma/Press%20Office%20-%20Press%20Release%20Files/Apr2007/Pharmacia-Information.html.

[11]Press Release, U.S. Dep't of Justice, *New Jersey Hospital to Pay United States $7.5 Million to Resolve Allegations of Defrauding Medicare* (Mar. 15, 2007), *available at* http://www.usdoj.gov/opa/pr/2007/March/07_civ_150.html.

[12]*Tennessee Settlement Shows Failure to Refund Overpayments Can Be A Crime*, 11 HEALTH CARE FRAUD REP. (BNA) 174 (Feb. 28, 2007).

[13]Press Release, U.S. Dep't of Justice, *RightCHOICE Managed Care to Pay United States $975,000 to Resolve False Claims Act Allegations* (Jan. 31, 2007), *available at* http://www.usdoj.gov/opa/pr/2007/January/07_civ_062.html.

drug pricing, sales and marketing activities. The agreement provides for civil fines and penalties of $499 million and requires BMS to enter into a CIA with the OIG. Final settlement is contingent upon the terms of the CIA and approval of the DOJ.[14] (2006)

- Omnicare, Inc., a prescription drug provider, entered into a settlement with the DOJ and 43 states to resolve claims that it switched Medicaid patients to more expensive drugs to increase payments. Omnicare agreed to pay $9.5 million and enter a five-year CIA. The government's investigation of Omnicare was the first time a U.S. attorney's office engaged in a joint health care fraud investigation with the National Association of Medicaid Fraud Control Units.[15] (2006)

- A jury returned a $48 million verdict against Amerigroup Illinois and Amerigroup Corporation after finding both companies guilty of Medicaid fraud.[16] (2006)

- InterMune, a California-based pharmaceutical company, entered into a deferred prosecution agreement with the DOJ and agreed to pay $36.9 million to resolve criminal charges and civil liabilities for alleged illegal promotion of its drug Actimmune. The government alleged that the company knowingly caused the submission of false and fraudulent claims by illegally promoting the drug for off-label uses. The company also entered a five-year CIA with the OIG as a condition of the settlement.[17] (2006)

- A district court held that Peter Rogan, owner and CEO of Edgewater Medical Center, was liable, individually and in conspiracy with others, for violating the FCA by presenting fraudulent Medicare and Medicaid claims. The court concluded that Rogan, through his control of the hospital and the hospital's management company, had knowingly entered into referral arrangements that violated the anti-kickback statute and the Stark law. Because Rogan knew that Edgewater had submitted claims in violation of these laws, the court reasoned that Rogan was liable under the FCA for his false cost report certification. The court ordered Rogan to pay $64.2 million.[18] (2006)

- Medco Health Solutions, the second largest PBM in the country, agreed to pay $155 million and enter an extensive CIA to settle complaints involving violations of the FCA and anti-kickback statute. The government alleged that Medco destroyed valid patient prescriptions, soli-

---

[14]News Release, *Bristol-Myers Squibb Announces Agreement In Principle to Settle Federal Investigation Into Pricing, Sales And Marketing Practices* (Dec. 21, 2006), *available at* http://newsroom.bms.com/index.php?s=press_releases&item=226.

[15]Press Release, U.S. Dep't of Justice, *Omnicare, Inc. to Pay $49.5 Million to United States and 43 States to Settle Medicaid Prescription Drug Fraud Allegations* (Nov. 14, 2006), *available at* http://www.usdoj.gov/usao/iln/pr/chicago/2006/pr1114_01.pdf.

[16]The judge in the case imposed a total $334 million verdict including compensatory damages, treble damages, and civil penalties. *United States ex rel. Tyson v. Amerigroup Ill., Inc.,* 488 F. Supp. 2d 719 (N.D. Ill. 2007).

[17]Press Release, U.S. Dep't of Justice, *Biopharmaceutical Firm Intermune to Pay U.S. Over $36 Million for Illegal Promotion and Marketing of Drug Actimmune* (Oct. 26, 2006), *available at* http://www.usdoj.gov/opa/pr/2006/October/06_civ_728.html.

[18]United States v. Rogan, 459 F. Supp. 2d 692 (N.D. Ill. 2006).

cited kickbacks from pharmaceutical manufacturers to favor their drugs, and paid kickbacks to health plans to obtain business.[19] (2006)

- Schering-Plough Sales Corporation and Schering-Plough Corporation paid a combined total of $435 million to resolve criminal and civil charges in connection with alleged illegal sales and marketing practices, including improper off-label promotion and falsifying best prices. Schering Sales Corporation pleaded guilty to one count of criminal conspiracy to make false statements to the government and paid $180 million, while Schering-Plough Corporation paid $255 million and agreed to an addendum to its existing CIA.[20] (2006)

- Tenet Healthcare Corporation, which operates the nation's second largest hospital chain, entered a five-year CIA and agreed to pay more than $900 million to settle charges that it engaged in unlawful billing practices in violation of the FCA. The alleged unlawful behavior included receiving inflated outlier payments, paying kickbacks to physicians, and upcoding.[21] (2006)

- Intrepid U.S.A. agreed to pay $8 million and enter into a five-year CIA to settle allegations that it submitted false claims to Medicare, Medicaid, and TRICARE/CHAMPUS. The government alleged that the home health chain used non-qualified individuals to provide services, improperly coded claims, and failed to maintain the necessary documentation to support its claims, including physician orders, plans of care, documentation of the patient's homebound status, and Outcome Assessment and Information Set (OASIS) evaluations.[22] (2006)

- Life Care Centers of America (Life Care) agreed to pay $2.5 million and enter a five-year CIA.[23] Federal and state attorneys had charged a Life Care-affiliated skilled nursing facility (SNF) in Georgia with violating the federal FCA by billing for services that were not provided and by furnishing inadequate care to its residents. Specifically, the government alleged that the SNF provided deficient quality care through an inef-

---

[19]Press Release, U.S. Dep't of Justice, *U.S. Announces $155 Million Settlement of Medco False Claims Case* (Oct. 23, 2006), *available at* http://www.usdoj.gov/usao/pae/News/Pr/2006/oct/MedcoPressReleaseUpdated10.20.06.pdf.

[20]Press Release, Schering-Plough, *Schering-Plough Reaches Agreement With U.S. Attorney's Office for District of Massachusetts and U.S. Department of Justice* (Aug. 29, 2006), *available at* http://www.sch-plough.com/schering_plough/news/release.jsp?releaseID=900092.

[21]Press Release, U.S. Dep't of Justice, *Tenet Healthcare Corporation to Pay U.S. more than $900 Million to Resolve False Claims Act Allegations* (June 29, 2006), *available at* http://www.usdoj.gov/opa/pr/2006/June/06_civ_406.html.

[22]Press Release, U.S. Dep't of Justice, *Minnesota-Based Home Health Care Chain Pays U.S. $8 Million to Settle Civil Fraud Allegations* (Feb. 9, 2006), *available at* http://www.usdoj.gov/opa/pr/2006/February/06_civ_072.html. Although some lawyers questioned the legal viability of the government's outlier theory and allegations, St. Barnabas Corporation, a large New Jersey health system, also agreed to pay $265 million to settle outlier allegations. Press Release, U.S. Dep't of Justice, *Largest Health Care System in New Jersey to Pay U.S. $265 Million to Resolve Allegations of Defrauding Medicare* (June 15, 2006), *available at* http://www.usdoj.gov/opa/pr/2006/June/06_civ_373.html.

[23]News Release, U.S. Attorney's Office, Northern District of Georgia, *Lawrenceville Nursing Home to Pay $2.5 Million to Settle Allegations of Gross Neglect of Residents* (Dec. 22, 2005), *available at* http://www.usdoj.gov/usao/gan/press/2005/12-22-2005.html.

fective medical director, high staff turnover, severe understaffing, insufficient staff training, poor nursing documentation, and insufficient budgetary allowances. (2005)

- Harbor Healthcare & Rehabilitation Center (Harbor), a skilled nursing home in Delaware, agreed to pay $150,000 and entered a CIA to settle allegations that it had violated both the state and federal FCAs by billing the Medicaid program for services that were substandard. Allegedly, Harbor had not properly trained its staff to furnish care to children who were in a persistent vegetative state.[24] (2005)

- Drug manufacturer Serono paid $704 million and entered a five-year CIA to settle criminal and civil charges that it illegally marketed the drug Serostim and paid kickbacks to physicians and pharmacies. As part of this settlement, Serono Labs (a non-operational subsidiary) pleaded guilty to criminal fraud charges and agreed to exclusion from all federal health care programs for at least five years.[25] (2005)

- GlaxoSmithKline (GSK) agreed to pay $150 million and amend its existing CIA to require accurately reporting average sales prices (ASP) and average manufacturer's prices (AMP) for drugs covered by federal health care programs. The government alleged that GSK had maintained fraudulent and inflated prices for Zofran and Kytril and had marketed the spread between the actual price paid by providers and the government reimbursement rate for these drugs. The government also alleged that GSK promoted a "double dipping" billing arrangement pursuant to which its customers would pool leftover vials of Kytril to create an additional dosage that would be administered to the patient and billed to federal health care programs.[26] (2005)

- AdvancePCS, a Caremark, Inc., subsidiary, paid $137.5 million to settle allegations that it received kickbacks from pharmaceutical manufacturers in the form of excessive administrative fees and rebates for heavily used drugs in return for marketing certain drugs to providers.[27] AdvancePCS also allegedly paid kickbacks to health plan customers to ensure that it was selected as the plan's PBM. AdvancePCS entered both a five-year CIA with the OIG and a Consent Order with the United States. The government's novel use of 18 U.S.C. §1345, which authorizes the use of an injunction against fraud, reportedly led AdvancePCS

---

[24]Press Release, U.S. Attorney's Office, District of Delaware, *Harbor Healthcare Settlement Reached* (Nov. 10, 2005), *available at* http://www.usdoj.gov/usao/de/press/2005/11_10_2005_healthcare.pdf.

[25]Press Release, U.S. Dep't of Justice, *Serono to Pay $704 Million for the Illegal Marketing of AIDS Drug* (Oct. 17, 2005), *available at* http://www.usdoj.gov/opa/pr/2005/October/05_civ_545.html. Note, however, that Serono Labs is a nonfunctioning corporate entity. As a result, the company's actual operations will not be significantly affected by the exclusion.

[26]Press Release, U.S. Dep't of Justice, *GlaxoSmithKline Pays $150 Million to Settle Drug Pricing Fraud Case* (Sept. 20, 2005), *available at* http://www.usdoj.gov/opa/pr/2005/September/05_civ_489.html.

[27]Press Release, U.S. Attorney's Office, Eastern District of Pennsylvania, *AdvancePCS to Pay $137.4 Million to Resolve Civil Fraud and Kickback Allegations* (Dec. 22, 2005), *available at* http://www.usdoj.gov/usao/pae/News/Pr/2005/sep/PCS.html.

to agree to the stringent Consent Order, which went beyond the usual scope of a CIA by imposing numerous obligations and restrictions on the company's day-to-day operations and business relationships.[28] (2005)

- Abington Memorial Hospital paid $4.2 million, entered a five-year CIA, and agreed to implement specific compliance obligations, including hiring a new compliance team, to settle allegations that it unbundled, upcoded, and double billed laboratory services.[29] (2005)

- PharMerica, Inc., and its subsidiary, PharMerica Drug Systems Inc., agreed to pay $5.975 million and entered a comprehensive five-year CIA to resolve allegations of illegal kickbacks paid in violation of the Civil Monetary Penalty (CMP) statute. The OIG alleged that PharMerica paid an excessive amount of money for a small Virginia pharmacy in return for a commitment from the seller to refer its Medicaid and Medicare pharmacy business for the next seven years.[30] (2005)

- HealthSouth Corporation paid $325 million and entered a five-year CIA to settle allegations that it submitted false claims. The government alleged that HealthSouth submitted false claims for outpatient physical therapy services, committed accounting fraud, and submitted unallowable costs on its cost reports.[31] (2004)

- Gambro Healthcare (Gambro) paid over $350 million to settle allegations of civil and criminal health care fraud. The government alleged that Gambro provided equipment and supplies to home dialysis patients through a "shell" durable medical equipment company, thus obtaining a higher rate of reimbursement than if it had directly billed Medicare. Further, the government claimed that Gambro violated the anti-kickback statute by entering into unlawful joint venture arrangements with its physician partners and by compensating the medical directors of its clinics based on the number and volume of patient referrals. In addition, the government alleged that Gambro submitted claims for ancillary medications and services that were not medically necessary. As part of this

---

[28]*Id.*; *see* United States v. AdvancePCS, Nos. 02-CV-9236 & 03-CV-5425 (E.D. Pa. Consent Order of Court for Injunction and Settlement filed Sept. 2005); News Release, U.S. Attorney's Office, Eastern District of Pennsylvania, *Justice Department Recovers $1.4 Billion in Fraud & False Claims in Fiscal Year 2005; More Than $15 Billion Since 1986* (Nov. 7, 2005), *available at* http://www.usdoj.gov/opa/pr/2005/November/05_civ_595.html.

[29]News Release, U.S. Attorney's Office, Eastern District of Pennsylvania, *U.S. Announces Settlement with Abington Hospital to Settle False Claims* (May 23, 2005), *available at* http://www.usdoj.gov/usao/pae/News/Pr/2005/may/AbingtonSettlement.html; U.S. Dep't of Health & Human Servs., OIG Semiannual Report, Apr. 1, 2005–Sept. 30, 2005, at 20 (2005), *available at* http://oig.hhs.gov/publications/docs/semiannual/2005/SemiannualFall05.pdf [hereinafter OIG Sept. 2005].

[30]Press Release, U.S. Dep't of Health & Human Servs., *OIG Settles Largest Ever Kickback Civil Monetary Action Against Pharmerica* (Mar. 29, 2005), *available at* http://oig.hhs.gov/publications/docs/press/2005/032905release.pdf.

[31]Press Release, U.S. Dep't of Justice, *HealthSouth to Pay United States $325 Million to Resolve Medicare Fraud Allegations* (Dec. 30, 2004), *available at* http://www.usdoj.gov/opa/pr/2004/December/04_civ_807.htm.

settlement, Gambro Supply Corporation, a wholly owned subsidiary, pleaded guilty to criminal felony charges, paid a $25 million fine, and agreed to permanent exclusion from Medicare.[32] (2004)

- Augustine Medical, Inc. (AMI), was sentenced by a federal district court to pay a $5.2 million fine and to a five-year period of probation. AMI had previously paid a $7.5 million civil penalty and Arizant, Inc., AMI's successor corporation, entered a five-year CIA with the OIG. The court also sentenced four former AMI executives, including the CEO and the general counsel, to probation and individual fines, ranging from $100,000 to $2 million. AMI's former reimbursement consultant was also fined $515,000 and sentenced to 10 months' imprisonment. AMI had pleaded guilty to conspiracy to commit fraud against Medicare.[33] (2004)

- Rite Aid Corporation paid $7 million and entered a four-year CIA to resolve its civil and administrative liability regarding the submission of claims to Medicaid and other government health care programs for partially filled prescriptions for drugs that were not delivered to the beneficiaries and, in some instances, were ultimately returned to stock. Rite Aid also entered into settlements with 28 states and the District of Columbia to resolve alleged liability for Medicaid damages.[34] (2004)

- Warner-Lambert Company LLC (Warner-Lambert) and its Parke-Davis division agreed to pay $430 million based on allegations that Warner-Lambert submitted false claims to Medicaid as a result of (1) paying illegal remuneration to doctors to induce them to promote and prescribe the drug Neurontin for off-label uses; and (2) making/disseminating false statements about Neurontin in presentations and marketing literature provided to doctors.[35] (2004)

- Community Residences, Inc., a nonprofit provider of community-based physical disability, mental health, and mental retardation services in Virginia, self-disclosed to the OIG that it had engaged an excluded individual as the medical director for two of its facilities, and was able to resolve the matter for $25,000.[36] (2003)

- Integrated Health Services, Inc. (IHS), a nationwide chain of nursing homes, long-term care hospitals, and providers of ancillary services

---

[32]Press Release, U.S. Dep't of Justice, *Gambro Healthcare Agrees to Pay Over $350 Million to Resolve Civil & Criminal Allegations in Medicare Fraud Case* (Dec. 2, 2004), *available at* http://www.usdoj.gov/opa/pr/2004/December/04_civ_774.htm. Note, however, that Gambro Supply Company is a nonfunctioning corporate entity. As a result, Gambro Healthcare's actual operations likely were not significantly affected by the exclusion.

[33]News Release, U.S. Attorney's Office, Southern District of Illinois, *Augustine Medical Sentenced to $5,249,910 Fine* (Sept. 8, 2004), *available at* http://www.integriguard.org/corp/newsevents/pressreleases/2004/2004-09-08.html; U.S. DEP'T OF JUSTICE, CRIMINAL DIVISION, FRAUD SECTION, ACTIVITIES REPORT FISCAL YEARS 2004 AND 2005, *available at* http://www.usdoj.gov/criminal/fraud/actrp0405.pdf.

[34]U.S. DEP'T OF HEALTH & HUMAN SERVS., OIG SEMIANNUAL REPORT, APR. 1, 2004–SEPT. 30, 2004, at 25 (2004), *available at* http://www.oig.hhs.gov/publications/docs/semiannual/2004/SemiannualFall04.pdf [hereinafter OIG SEPT. 2004].

[35]*Id.* at 24–25.

[36]U.S. DEP'T OF HEALTH & HUMAN SERVS., OIG SEMIANNUAL REPORT, OCT. 1, 2003–MAR. 31, 2004, at 18 (2004), *available at* http://oig.hhs.gov/publications/docs/semiannual/2004/SemiannualSpring04.pdf [hereinafter OIG MAR. 2004].

entered into a global settlement to resolve FCA liability and adminis-trative claims. Because IHS was in bankruptcy and unable to pay more, the chain agreed to pay $19.1 million. The settlement covered five whistleblower lawsuits and two other fraud cases involving numerous allegations, including billing for unnecessary services or services never provided and wrongfully depreciating equipment on its cost report. The company also agreed to enter into two five-year CIAs—one for its long-term care division and one for its mobile diagnostic division (both of which were to be sold to other companies as part of the IHS bankruptcy reorganization).[37] (2003)

- Good Samaritan Hospital in Nebraska agreed to pay the government $1.2 million and entered a five-year CIA to settle alleged violations of the Stark law and the federal anti-kickback statute. The hospital alleg-edly provided a cardiologist with inducements, including underwriting a loan, paying practice consultants, and providing free or reduced-price drugs and medical equipment, in exchange for patient referrals. The cardiologist had been previously sentenced to one year in prison for health care fraud.[38] (2003)

- Abbott Laboratories and Abbott's Ross Products Division entered into a global criminal, civil, and administrative settlement totaling $615 mil-lion with a five-year CIA as a result of the "Operation Headwaters" sting. The settlement resolved allegations that Ross paid kickbacks to purchasers of enteral nutrition items and services by conditioning the sale of enteral nutrition sets on the purchase of enteral nutrition feeding pumps; failing to collect rental payments for the sets and pumps; and paying "conversion bonuses" that bore no relation to the actual cost of converting from one manufacturer to another. As part of the settlement, CG Nutritionals, Inc., an Abbott (non-operational) subsidiary, pleaded guilty to obstructing a health care fraud investigation and agreed to be permanently excluded.[39] (2003)

- HCA, Inc. (HCA), formerly known as Columbia/HCA Healthcare Cor-poration, paid a total of $1.362 billion to settle various fraud and abuse claims. In 2003, HCA agreed to enter into a $631 million settlement to resolve allegations that HCA knowingly submitted false cost reports to Medicare, entered into improper referral arrangements with physicians that violated the anti-kickback statute and the Stark law, and submitted false claims for wound care services provided at 56 HCA hospitals. HCA also agreed to pay the government $5 million to resolve its civil and ad-ministrative liability related to allegations concerning claims for patients transferred to other facilities. In a separate administrative settlement, HCA agreed to pay the Centers for Medicare and Medicaid Services (CMS)[40]

---

[37]*Id.* at 24.

[38]*Id.*

[39]*Id.* at 20.

[40]On June 14, 2001, the former Health Care Financing Administration (HCFA) was re-named the Centers for Medicare and Medicaid Services (CMS). For purposes of this chapter, references will be to CMS.

$250 million to resolve administrative overpayments in connection with its cost reports. Previously, in December 2000, HCA paid approximately $840 million in criminal fines, civil restitution, and penalties to resolve a separate set of allegations and entered into a comprehensive eight-year CIA.[41] The total amount of criminal, civil, and administrative sanctions and penalties imposed on HCA as a result of these investigations represented the largest health care fraud recovery ever obtained by the government from a single provider.[42] (2003)

- Beverly Enterprises, Inc. (Beverly), the nation's largest nursing home chain, and a subsidiary corporation paid the government $175 million to resolve criminal and civil issues, and entered a CIA. This multimillion-dollar settlement resolved allegations that Beverly engaged in a scheme to defraud Medicare of approximately $400 million by inflating nursing costs charged to the program. Beverly will pay $170 million under the terms of the civil settlement. A Beverly subsidiary, which also pleaded guilty to criminal charges, will pay $5 million in criminal fines and divest itself of 10 nursing homes.[43] (2000)

- Fresenius Medical Care Holdings, Inc. (Fresenius), the nation's largest provider of kidney dialysis products and services, under which three subsidiaries pleaded guilty, agreed to pay $486 million to resolve the criminal and civil aspects of the case. The alleged misconduct involved kickbacks, submission of false claims for dialysis-related nutrition therapy services, improper billing for laboratory services, and false reporting of credit balances by National Medical Care, a nationwide dialysis company and various of its subsidiaries, prior to a 1996 merger with Fresenius. Fresenius was also required to enter an extensive, eight-year CIA.[44] (2000)

---

[41]Press Release, U.S. Dep't of Justice, *HCA—The Health Care Company & Subsidiaries to Pay $840 Million in Criminal Fines and Civil Damages and Penalties* (Dec. 14, 2000), *available at* http://www.usdoj.gov/opa/pr/2000/December/696civcrm.htm. The government had brought civil claims alleging that HCA had: (1) engaged in illegal outpatient laboratory billing practices, e.g., laboratory tests that were not medically necessary, and not ordered by physicians, as well as other billing violations such as upcoding, (2) illegally claimed nonreimbursable marketing and advertising costs it had disguised as community education, (3) charged Medicare for nonreimbursable costs incurred in the purchase of certain home health agencies and an elaborate scheme to hide these costs in reimbursable "management fees" paid to third parties, and (4) billed federal health care programs for home health visits for patients who did not qualify to receive them, or that were not performed, and for committing other billing violations. As part of its settlement, HCA agreed to exclude two subsidiaries from participating in Medicare and other federal health care programs and to divest one hospital.

[42]OIG Mar. 2004, at 22.

[43]U.S. Dep't of Health & Human Servs., Office of Inspector Gen., Semiannual Report Oct. 1, 1999–Mar. 30, 2000, at ii (June 19, 2000), *available at* http://oig.hhs.gov/reading/semiannual/2000/00ssemi.pdf.

[44]U.S. Dep't of Justice, *Fresenius Settlement Agreement and Release* (2000), *available at* http://www.usdoj.gov/civil/foia/elecread/2000/Fresenius%20Medical%20Care,%20et%20al.%202000.pdf.

Numerous other settlements are listed on the OIG's Web site and indicate the wide range of government enforcement efforts.[45] It is important to note that investigations do not always end with a total or simple government victory. The *Alvarado* case is one example. In *United States v. Weinbaum*,[46] Tenet Healthcare's (Tenet's) Alvarado Medical Center (Alvarado), and Barry Weinbaum, the former CEO of the hospital, were charged with using physician relocation agreements as kickbacks to induce patient referrals. The jurors deadlocked and the judge declared a mistrial.[47] A new trial in the case began on May 10, 2005, and resulted in a second hung jury in April 2006.[48] Despite two juries' reluctance to convict, a month later, the OIG notified Tenet that it intended to exclude Alvarado.[49] By May 17, 2006, the OIG announced that it had reached an agreement with Tenet to divest Alvarado and pay $21 million to settle civil claims.[50]

Defendants scored a more dramatic victory in one part of the TAP Pharmaceutical Products, Inc. (TAP) case. In October 2001, TAP agreed to pay $875 million to settle certain criminal and civil liabilities. The company pleaded guilty to conspiring to violate the Prescription Drug Marketing Act (PDMA) and agreed to pay a $290 million fine to resolve these criminal charges. The settlement also included $560 million in connection with civil FCA claims and $25.5 million relating to state civil claims. The alleged false claims included fraudulent pricing schemes, sales and marketing misconduct, failure to provide TAP's best price to the government under the Medicaid rebate program, and falsely advising customers to report inflated prices rather than their real discounted price for the drug Lupron. In addition, according to prosecutors, certain TAP sales and account managers defrauded Medicaid and Medicare in the late 1990s by conspiring to have doctors bill free samples of the drug Lupron to the

---

[45]Previous significant settlements include a 2001 settlement with Vencor, a nationwide nursing home chain, for $219 million involving quality of care allegations, and an $87 million settlement with Quorum Health Group, Inc., the owner and manager of numerous hospitals, concerning "reserve" cost reports. *See* U.S. Dep't of Health & Human Servs., OIG Semi-annual Report Apr. 1, 2001–Sept. 30, 2001, at 4, 13 (2001), *available at* http://oig.hhs.gov/publications/docs/semiannual/2001/01fallsemi.pdf [hereinafter OIG Sept. 2001].

[46]No. 03CR1587-MLJ (S.D. Cal. filed July 17, 2003).

[47]United States v. Weinbaum, No. 03CR1587-MLJ (S.D. Cal. Feb. 22, 2005).

[48]*Retrial of Tenet San Diego Hospital Begins in Alleged M.D. Relocation Kickback Scheme*, 14 Health L. Rep. (BNA) 636 (May 12, 2005), *available at* http://www.ama-assn.org/amednews/2005/03/07/bisc0307.htm. A retrial of the case resulted in a second hung jury in April 2006, *Federal Jury Deadlock in Second Tenet Trial over Kickbacks Leads to Mistrial Declaration*, 10 Health Care Fraud Rep. (BNA) 303 (Apr. 22, 2006), *available at* http://www.medicalnewstoday.com/medicalnews.php?newsid=41086.

[49]OIG News, *OIG Notifies Tenet of Potential Exclusion of Alvarado Hospital* (May 8, 2006), *available at* http://oig.hhs.gov/publications/docs/press/2006/Alvarado%20MW%20Press%20Release%205.8.06].pdf.

[50]OIG News, *Tenet Agrees to Divest Alvarado Hospital* (May 17, 2006), *available at* http://oig.hhs.gov/publications/docs/press/2006/051706Tenet.pdf; *see also* Press Release, Tenet Healthcare Corporation, *Tenet Announces Civil Settlement in San Diego Hospital Case* (May 17, 2006), *available at* http://www.tenethealth.com/TenetHealth/PressCenter/PressReleases/ Tenet+Announces+Civil+Settlement+in+San+Diego+Hospital+Case.htm.

government for reimbursement. These individuals also allegedly offered illegal inducements, including free samples, consulting fees, educational grants, travel, forgiveness of debt, and entertainment to persuade doctors to prescribe TAP products.[51] Nevertheless, a federal jury acquitted eight current and former TAP employees of all charges that they defrauded the federal government and paid kickbacks to promote the sale of the company's drugs.

## B. Exposure for Attorneys

Lawyers themselves also are at risk as demonstrated by a number of cases described below, beginning with the indictment of two experienced health care counsel in connection with the *LaHue* case.[52] In the *LaHue* case and its related proceedings, doctors and hospital executives were indicted under allegations that they engaged in a criminal scheme to receive remuneration from various hospitals in return for the referral of Medicare patients.[53] Attorneys for the hospital were charged with conspiracy in connection with the indictment.[54] Although the attorneys' motion for acquittal was later granted,[55] the charges were a sobering reminder to all attorneys that representing clients in the health care industry can be a high-risk endeavor.

In addition, in June 2001 the OIG issued a Special Advisory Bulletin on Practices of Business Consultants. While acknowledging the integral role that consultants can play in improving the integrity of the health care system, the OIG warned that certain "questionable practices" could expose both providers and their consultants to legal liability. The practices identified as suspect include (1) making illegal or misleading representations; (2) offering promises or guarantees that are unreasonable or improbable; (3) encouraging abusive practices such as advising "a client to adopt a patently unreasonable interpretation of a reimbursement law, regulation, or rule to justify substantially greater reimbursement"; and (4) discouraging compliance efforts including making "blanket statements that a client should not undertake certain compliance efforts (such as retrospective billing reviews) or cooperate with payor audits, regardless of the client's circumstances."[56] Because attorneys were specifically identified as one of the types of consultants the OIG was addressing in this Special Advisory Bulletin, attorneys can expect the OIG to scrutinize their actions as well as those of their clients.

In 2004, a federal court sentenced the executives of Augustine Medical, Inc. (AMI), including its CEO and general counsel, to probation and individual fines, ranging from $100,000 to $2 million. AMI's former reimbursement

---

[51]*See, e.g.,* United States v. MacKenzie, No. 01-CR-10350 (D. Mass. acquitted July 14, 2004).

[52]United States v. LaHue, 998 F. Supp. 1182 (D. Kan. 1998), *aff'd*, 170 F.3d 1026 (10th Cir. 1999).

[53]United States v. Anderson, 85 F. Supp. 2d 1047, 1052 (D. Kan. 1999).

[54]*Id.*

[55]*See* United States v. McClatchey, 217 F.3d 823, 828 (10th Cir.), *cert. denied*, 531 U.S. 1015, 121 S. Ct. 574 (2000).

[56]OIG Special Advisory Bulletin, Practices of Business Consultants, *available at* http://oig.hhs.gov/fraud/docs/alertsandbulletins/consultants.pdf.

consultant was also fined $515,000 and sentenced to 10 months' imprisonment. The general counsel pleaded guilty to aiding and abetting others in withholding material facts from a distributor regarding their right to Medicare payment.[57]

In March 2007, the U.S. Attorney for the Southern District of Florida, in conjunction with the FBI and the OIG, announced that Benjamin Metsch, a Miami attorney, pleaded guilty to conspiring to commit Medicare fraud. From October 2002 through August 2004, Metsch conspired with another individual to facilitate the fraudulent sale of 67 South Florida DME companies. Metsch and his accomplice used legal documents to facilitate nominee or "straw" purchasers of the companies, thus concealing the true buyers. This prevented Medicare from receiving timely notification of the changes in ownership, which in turn impaired Medicare's ability to oversee the companies' activities. Metsch agreed to pay $103,000 in restitution to Medicare—the exact amount his law firm had profited from the fraudulent transactions.[58] Although Metsch was eligible for up to a ten-year prison term and a $250,000 fine, he was sentenced to three years of probation and ten months of home confinement with an electronic monitoring device. The court also ordered Metsch to pay $3,100 in addition to the $103,000 restitution.[59]

Later in 2007 the Justice Department filed a civil FCA complaint against the former general counsel of Tenet Healthcare Corporation.[60] The complaint alleged that Christi Sulzbach, Tenet's associate general counsel and corporate integrity program director at the time, falsely stated in certifications furnished to HHS that Tenet was in material compliance with all federal program legal requirements, to the best of her knowledge and belief. According to the complaint, Sulzbach learned that a Tenet hospital in Florida, North Ridge Medical Center, had billed Medicare for referrals from physicians whose employment contracts violated the Stark Law, i.e., the physicians' compensation reflected the volume or value of their referrals and exceeded fair market value. Tenet was operating under the terms of a CIA imposed on a predecessor entity, National Medical Enterprises, Inc. (NME), which required Tenet to report any credible evidence of misconduct that management had reasonable grounds to believe constituted a material violation of the law governing federally funded health care programs, and to take appropriate corrective action. Although Tenet's outside counsel reportedly confirmed the Stark Law violations, Sulzbach allegedly signed off on the false certifications. Further, the various contracts at issue allegedly were not terminated, in some cases, for more than two years.[61]

---

[57]News Release, U.S. Attorney's Office, Southern District of Illinois, *Augustine Medical Sentenced to $5,249,910 Fine* (Sept. 8, 2004), *available at* http://www.integriguard.org/corp/ newsevents/pressreleases/2004/2004-09-08.html; U.S. Dep't of Justice, Criminal Division, Fraud Section, Activities Report Fiscal Years 2004 and 2005, *available at* http:// www.usdoj.gov/criminal/fraud/docs/reports/2004-05/actrp0405.pdf.

[58]Press Release, U.S. Dep't of Justice, *Attorney Pleads Guilty to Medicare Fraud Conspiracy Involving Medical Equipment Company Sales* (Mar. 8, 2007), *available at* http:// www.usdoj.gov/usao/fls/PressReleases/070308-01.html.

[59]United States v. Metsch, No. 07-20022-CR (S.D. Fla. May 22, 2007).

[60]United States v. Sulzbach, No. 07-61329 (S.D. Fla. complaint filed Sept. 18, 2007).

[61]*Id.*

Attorneys who represent publicly traded health care companies also have additional obligations under the Sarbanes-Oxley Act of 2002 (Sarbanes-Oxley),[62] which required the Securities and Exchange Commission (SEC) to adopt rules prescribing minimum standards of professional conduct for attorneys appearing or practicing before the SEC, in any way, in the representation of public companies.

On February 6, 2003, the SEC published final rules codified in 17 C.F.R. Part 205. These rules apply to all attorneys providing legal advice to an issuer,[63] and who have notice that documents they are preparing, or assisting in preparing, will be filed with or submitted to the SEC. The regulations contain numerous new standards for such attorneys, including:

- Evidence of a material violation of an applicable federal or state securities law, a material violation of fiduciary duty, or a similar material violation of federal or state law, determined according to an objective standard, must be reported "up-the-ladder" to the issuer's chief legal counsel or the chief executive officer or equivalent;[64]
- If the chief legal counsel or the chief executive officer of the company does not respond appropriately to the evidence, the attorney must report the evidence to the audit committee, another committee of independent directors, or the full board of directors;[65]
- An attorney may, without the consent of an issuer client, reveal confidential information related to his or her representation to the SEC to the extent the attorney reasonably believes it necessary: (1) to prevent the issuer from committing a material violation likely to cause substantial financial injury to the financial interests or property of the issuer or investors; (2) to prevent the issuer in an SEC investigation or administrative proceeding from committing perjury, suborning perjury, or committing an act likely to perpetrate a fraud upon the SEC; or (3) to rectify the consequences of a material violation by the issuer that caused, or may cause, substantial injury to the financial interest or property of the issuer or investors in which the attorney's services have been used;[66] and

---

[62]Sarbanes-Oxley Act of 2002, Pub. L. No. 107-204, 116 Stat. 745 (2002) [hereinafter Sarbanes-Oxley].

[63]Sarbanes-Oxley defines "issuer" as an "issuer (as defined in section 3 of the Securities Exchange Act of 1934 (15 U.S.C. §78c)), the securities of which are registered under section 12 of that Act (15 U.S.C. §78l), or that is required to file reports under section 15(d) (15 U.S.C. §78o(d)), or that files or has filed a registration statement that has not yet become effective under the Securities Act of 1933 (15 U.S.C. §77a *et seq.*), and that it has not withdrawn." *See* Sarbanes-Oxley §2(a)(7).

[64]"Evidence of a material violation" is defined as "credible evidence, based upon which it would be unreasonable, under the circumstances, for a prudent and competent attorney not to conclude that it is reasonably likely that a material violation has occurred, is ongoing, or is about to occur." SEC Standards of Professional Conduct, 17 C.F.R. §205.2(e).

[65]If an issuer establishes a "qualified legal compliance committee" (QLCC), an attorney could satisfy his or her obligation by reporting evidence of a material violation to the QLCC. 17 C.F.R. §205.3(b)(7).

[66]*See* 17 C.F.R. §§205.3(d)(2)(i)–(iii).

- An attorney supervising or directing another attorney who is appearing and practicing before the SEC must make reasonable efforts to ensure that the subordinate attorney conforms to the regulations and must comply with reporting requirements when the subordinate attorney reports evidence of a material violation.[67]

The SEC regulations generally preempt state laws except that a state may impose on attorneys more rigorous obligations that are not inconsistent with the federal rules.[68] However, the regulations further clarify that these regulations do not create a private cause of action, and authority to enforce compliance is vested exclusively with the SEC.[69]

The scope of liability for attorneys and the companies they represent that are not subject to Sarbanes-Oxley is less clear. To minimize the risk of exposure, numerous organizations are adopting some form of "best practices" based on Sarbanes-Oxley, which may indirectly help protect attorneys to a certain extent. Lawyers also should be alert to applicable and evolving standards in the American Bar Association (ABA) Model Rules and state rules of professional conduct,[70] some of which contain provisions concerning client confidentiality that appear difficult to reconcile with the SEC regulations.

## C. Likelihood of Increased Enforcement Efforts in the Future

In addition to the multimillion-dollar recoveries discussed above, the government also points to the role of the OIG and CMS in correcting systemic vulnerabilities. These "corrections" led to $11.8 billion in savings for Medicare and Medicaid in 1999 because funds were not spent for improper or unnecessary care.[71] Such policy and procedural changes, along with aggressive enforcement, are credited with preserving the solvency of the Medicare Trust Fund until 2018. From 2003 through 2006, the government received approximately $13 for each dollar it spent on enforcement efforts.[72]

---

[67] *See* 17 C.F.R. §205.4.

[68] *See* 17 C.F.R. §205.1.

[69] *See* 17 C.F.R. §205.7. Note that foreign attorneys who are not admitted in the United States, and who do not advise clients regarding U.S. law, would not be covered by these regulations. Nevertheless, foreign attorneys who provide legal advice regarding U.S. law would be covered to the extent they are appearing and practicing before the SEC, unless they provide such advice in consultation with U.S. counsel. *See* 17 C.F.R. §205.2(j) for a definition of nonappearing foreign attorney.

[70] *See, e.g.,* ABA Task Force Final Report on Corporate Responsibility, *available at* http://www.abanet.org/buslaw/corporateresponsibility/home.html. These issues are discussed in more detail in Section V. in Chapter 8 (Walton, Humphries, and Jacobs, Potential Liabilities for Directors and Officers of Health Care Organizations).

[71] A Message From the Secretary, in U.S. Dep't of Health & Human Servs., Office of Insepector Gen., Semiannual Report, Oct. 1, 1999–Mar. 30, 2000, at 9 (June 19, 2000), *available at* http://oig.hhs.gov/semann/00fsemi.pdf.

[72] Dep't Health & Human Servs., Office of Inspector General, Hearing Before the House Ways & Means Committee (Mar. 8, 2007) (statement of Daniel R. Levinson, Inspector General, U.S. Dept. of Health & Human Servs.), *available at* http://oig.hhs.gov/testimony/docs/2007/030807tmy.pdf; Jack Meyer, Fighting Medicare Fraud: More Bang for the Federal Buck (July 2006), *available at* http://www.taf.org/FCA-2006report.pdf (suggesting a $15 to $1 return on investment).

In light of these many "successes," government support for health care fraud and abuse enforcement is likely to continue, and the federal mechanism for funding such efforts makes it likely that the amount of money available for enforcement will increase.[73] HIPAA[74] set up a Health Care Fraud and Abuse Control Account (Health Care Fraud Account) within the Federal Hospital Insurance Trust Fund. Proceeds from enforcement of federal health care cases are generally deposited in the Health Care Fraud Account and made available to finance additional fraud investigations and prosecutions. In 2005, $160 million was jointly allotted to HHS and the OIG from this account, which represented approximately 80 percent of HHS' overall Health Care Fraud Account allocation.[75]

In 2006, Congress boosted its funding for the OIG's fraud control efforts. Title I of the Tax Relief and Health Care Act of 2006 updated funding for the OIG's Health Care Fraud Account through 2010. This was the first increase to the Health Care Fraud Account, the OIG's primary funding source, since 2003. The OIG was expected to receive between $163 million and $166 million in 2007, up from $160 million.[76]

HIPAA also provided funding to the Federal Bureau of Investigation (FBI) for health care fraud enforcement. The FBI is the primary investigative agency involved in the fight against health care fraud that has jurisdiction over both the federal and private insurance programs. As a result, health care fraud investigations are considered a priority within the FBI's White Collar Crime Program Plan. In 2005, the FBI received $114 million, which it used in large part to fund 466 agents and 340 support positions.[77] Through FY 2006, the FBI had investigated 2,423 health care fraud cases, resulting in 588 indictments and 534 convictions. Numerous cases are pending plea agreements and trials. In FY 2006 alone, the FBI had $373 million in restitutions, $1.6 billion in recoveries, $172.9 million in fines, and $24.3 million in seizures.[78]

The FBI indicated that it would work to address the activity of organized crime in medical clinics, independent diagnostic testing facilities, DME companies, and other health care facilities. The bureau also focused on fraud involving hospitals, physicians, DME, chiropractors, home health agencies, pain management, physical therapists, drug diversion, prescription drugs, and beneficiary-sharing.[79] The FBI also planned to continue to work with various or-

---

[73]There was some concern after the events of September 11, 2001, that the government would turn its attention away from health care fraud to terrorism. However, as the statistics cited in Section I.A., above, make clear, health care fraud remains an important law enforcement priority.

[74]Pub. L. No. 104-191, 110 Stat. 1936 (1996).

[75]2005 HHS/DOJ REPORT at 19.

[76]Tax Relief and Health Care Act of 2006, Pub. L. No. 109-432, 120 Stat. 2922.

[77]2005 HHS/DOJ REPORT at 39.

[78]*Financial Crimes Report to the Public Fiscal Year 2006*, FEDERAL BUREAU OF INVESTIGATION, *available at* http://www.fbi.gov/publications/financial/fcs_report2006/financial_crime_2006.htm#Health. The FBI has indicated that the Medicare Part D program will be an area of increasing focus and concern and has established a Part D work group with representatives from CMS, DOJ, HHS-OIG, FDA, DEA, U.S. Postal Inspection Services, and the Federal Trade Commission.

[79]*Id.*

ganizations, including the National Health Care Anti-Fraud Association, the National Insurance Crime Bureau, the BlueCross BlueShield Association, AARP, and the Coalition Against Insurance Fraud. The FBI also launched its Internet Pharmacy Fraud Initiative and Outpatient Surgery Center Initiative.[80]

In early 2007, the White House proposed a FY 2008 budget allocating $200 million for combating fraud and improving program integrity in the Medicare and Medicaid programs.[81] This included a new $183 million discretionary funding stream for the Health Care Fraud Account to be distributed to CMS, the OIG, DOJ, and the FBI. In addition to this discretionary funding, the OIG and DOJ would each receive an additional $17.5 million, while the Medicaid and State Children's Health Insurance Program would receive an additional $10.1 million, and the Medicare Integrity Program would get an additional $137.8 million.

In addition, a new recovery audit contractor (RAC) program by the Medicare Prescription Drug Improvement and Modernization Act (MMA)[82] was created to accelerate enforcement. The program was pilot tested for three years in Florida, New York, and California. The new contractors were authorized to conduct post-payment audits of Part A and Part B claims, and were expected to initially focus on inpatient claims errors such as noncovered services, inaccurate coding (including Diagnosis Related Group (DRG) miscoding and overstated complications), and duplicate services. While the contractors were asked to identify underpayments as well as overpayments, the program was particularly controversial because contractors would be paid a contingency fee, i.e., a percentage of their overpayment recoveries.[83] Preliminary findings, published in November 2006, indicated that the RACs already had identified more than $300 million in net improper payments.[84] CMS stated that it intended to expand this program by adding states to each of the three existing RAC jurisdictions. In addition, CMS intended to have four permanent regional RACs in place by 2010 in accordance with Section 302 of the Tax Relief and Health Care Act of 2006.[85] A request for information and a draft statement of work was released on March 16, 2007, to start the bidding process.[86]

---

[80] *Id.*

[81] *Program Integrity, Fraud Fighting Slated for $200 Million Increase in FY 2008 Budget,* 12 HEALTH CARE DAILY REP. (Feb. 7, 2007). *See also* Dep't Health & Human Servs., FY 2008 Budget in Brief, *available at* http://www.hhs.gov/budget/08budget/2008BudgetInBrief.pdf.

[82] Pub. L. No. 108-173, 117 Stat. 2066 (2003).

[83] *See* Press Release, CMS, *Demonstration to Work Toward Assuring Accurate Medicare Payments* (Mar. 28, 2005), *available at* http://www.cms.hhs.gov/apps/media/press/release.asp?Counter=1405.

[84] CMS RAC Status Document FY 2006 (Nov. 26, 2006), *available at* http://www.cms.hhs.gov/RAC/Downloads/RACStatusDocument–FY2006.pdf.

[85] CMS, Expansion Strategy for Recovery Audit Contractors, *available at* http://www.cms.hhs.gov/RAC/10_ExpansionStrategy.asp#TopOfPage; Tax Relief and Health Care Act of 2006, Pub. L. No. 109-432, 120 Stat. 2922.

[86] CMS Request for Information (and draft Statement of Work), *available at* http://www.fbo.gov/spg/HHS/HCFA/AGG/Reference%2DNumber%2DRFI%2DCMS%2D70445RAC/listing.html. Notably, on March 5, 2007, the AMA's Practicing Physicians Advisory Council, a CMS advisory panel, recommended that RAC audits of physicians be discontinued because of the "demonstrated insignificant amount of overpayments recovered from physicians." PRACTICING

Other new government contractor programs added in 2006, such as the Medicare Drug Integrity Contractors (MEDICs) program to monitor Part D for fraud, waste, and abuse, were created to expand health care fraud enforcement efforts.[87] Further, the appointment of Inspector General Daniel Levinson was expected to affect enforcement priorities, particularly because several previous inspector generals had relatively short tenures.[88] However, it is worth noting that a few of the government's enforcement tools were significantly limited. Specifically, Deputy Attorney General Paul McNulty issued a memorandum in 2006[89] (McNulty Memorandum) that imposes stringent limits on the government's ability to require a corporation to waive its attorney-client privilege and work-product protections in order to demonstrate the cooperation needed to qualify for certain benefits, such as immunity or a reduced charge. The McNulty Memorandum further directs prosecutors generally not to take into account whether a corporation advances attorneys' fees to employees or agents under investigation or indictment. Note, however, that the McNulty Memorandum seems to be limited to criminal prosecutions.[90]

Various ongoing efforts to collaborate among federal and state agencies and private payors also increase the likelihood that the number, type, and scope of health care fraud investigations will continue to escalate.[91] Under these circumstances, an expanded focus on health care fraud and abuse seems a virtual certainty for the foreseeable future.

## 1. Pharmaceutical Fraud

Current enforcement efforts seem to be heavily focused on the pharmaceutical industry. The DOJ's budget request for FY 2006 included $2 million

---

PHYSICIANS ADVISORY COUNCIL, REP. NO. 55 TO THE SECRETARY OF HHS RE: PHYSICIAN QUALITY REPORTING INITIATIVE, TRANSPARENCY INITIATIVE, NATIONAL PROVIDER IDENTIFIERS, PHYSICIANS REGULATORY ISSUES TEAM UPDATE, RECOVERY AUDIT CONTRACTS, HOSPITAL CONDITIONS OF PARTICIPATION, AND OTHER MATTERS, at 10 (Mar. 5, 2007), *available at* http://www.cms.hhs.gov/FACA/03_ppac.asp ("Claims from physicians, ambulatory clinics, and laboratories combined accounted for only 6 percent of improper payments, while claims from hospitals and skilled nursing facilities made up 78 percent of improper payments.")

[87]CMS, Chapter 9–Part D Program to Control Fraud, Waste and Abuse, Prescription Drug Benefit Manual, Section 30 (Apr. 25, 2006), *available at* http://www.cms.hhs.gov/Prescription DrugCovContra/ownoads/PDBManual_Chapter9_FWA.pdf.

[88]On June 16, 2005, Daniel R. Levinson was sworn in as the HHS Inspector General. Levinson had been the acting inspector general for almost a year after being named to replace Dara Corrigan, who was Principal Deputy Inspector General for one year after Janet Rehnquist resigned in June 2003. *See Senate Confirms Levinson as HHS IG,* 14 HEALTH L. REP. (BNA) 821 (June 16, 2005); *President Nominates Daniel Levinson, GSA Official, to Inspector General Post,* 13 HEALTH L. REP. (BNA) 1083 (July 22, 2004).

[89]Memorandum from Deputy Attorney General Paul McNulty to U.S. Attorneys *re* Principles of Federal Prosecution of Business Organizations (Dec. 13, 2006), *available at* http://www.usdoj.gov/dag/speeches/2006/mcnulty_memo.pdf; the memorandum is also included as Appendix C-4 on the disk accompanying this volume.

[90]Benham v. Inspector General, Dep't of Health & Human Servs., No. 2042 (A-06-54) (Departmental Appeals Board Sept. 14, 2006), *available* at http://www.hhs.gov/dab/decisions .dab2042.htm.

[91]A 1999 report stated that collaboration increased through 1999 with the creation of the National Health Care Fraud Task Force chaired by the deputy Attorney General, joint training, and heightened data sharing. U.S. DEP'T OF HEALTH & HUMAN SERVS. & DEP'T OF JUSTICE, HEALTH CARE FRAUD AND ABUSE CONTROL PROGRAM ANNUAL REPORT FOR FY 1999 (Jan. 2000), *available at* http://oig.hhs.gov/press/hipaa2.htm.

for seventeen attorneys to handle over 125 health care fraud matters involving pharmaceutical manufacturers and related entities. DOJ also sought $3 million for 13 attorneys to supplement U.S. attorney resources in criminal and civil prosecutions of pharmaceutical fraud.[92]

Large settlements in pharmaceutical fraud cases since 2002 include the following:

- The Bristol Myers Squibb Company, the DOJ, and the Office of the U.S. Attorney for the District of Massachusetts reached an agreement in principle to settle several long-running investigations of the company's drug pricing and sales and marketing activities. The agreement provides for civil fines and penalties of $499 million and requires Bristol to enter a CIA with the OIG. Final settlement is contingent upon the terms of the CIA and the approval of the DOJ.[93] (2006)

- InterMune entered into a deferred prosecution agreement with the DOJ, agreeing to pay $36.9 million and accept a CIA to resolve criminal and civil liabilities for alleged off-label promotion of its drug Actimmune.[94] (2006)

- King Pharmaceuticals paid over $124 million and entered a CIA to resolve allegations that it underpaid Medicaid rebates and overcharged various federal and state entities for its products, in violation of AMP and best-price reporting requirements.[95] (2005)

- Serono paid $704 million to settle criminal and civil charges that it engaged in off-label promotion and paid kickbacks to physicians and pharmacies to encourage the use of its drug Serostim.[96] (2005)

- GlaxoSmithKline settled for over $150 million to resolve allegations related to fraudulent drug pricing and marketing of two anti-emetic drugs, Zofran and Kytril.[97] (2005)

- PharMerica, Inc., and its subsidiary settled for $5.975 million in connection with alleged kickbacks for future referrals paid through an inflated purchase price for a pharmacy.[98] (2005)

---

[92]*News Briefs*, REPORT ON MEDICARE COMPLIANCE (Apr. 18, 2005).

[93]News Release, *Bristol-Myers Squibb Announces Agreement In Principle to Settle Federal Investigation Into Pricing, Sales And Marketing Practices* (Dec. 21, 2006), *available at* http://newsroom.bms.com/index.php?s=press_releases&item=226.

[94]Press Release, U.S. Dep't of Justice, *Biopharmaceutical Firm Intermune to Pay U.S. Over $36 Million for Illegal Promotion and Marketing of Drug Actimmune* (Oct. 26, 2006), available at http://www.usdoj.gov/opa/pr/2006/October/06_civ_728.html.

[95]Press Release, U.S. Dep't of Justice, *King Pharmaceuticals to Pay U.S. $124 Million for Medicaid Rebate Underpayments & Overcharging for Drug Products* (Nov. 2005), *available at* http://www.usdoj.gov/opa/pr/2005/November/05_civ_581.html.

[96]Press Release, U.S. Dep't of Justice, *Serono to Pay $704 Million for the Illegal Marketing of AIDS Drug* (Oct. 17, 2005), *available at* http://www.usdoj.gov/opa/pr/2005/October/05_civ_545.html. Also see Section I.A., above.

[97]Press Release, U.S. Dep't of Justice, *GlaxoSmithKline Pays $150 Million to Settle Drug Pricing Fraud Case* (Sept. 20, 2005), *available at* http://www.usdoj.gov/opa/pr/2005/September/05_civ_489.html. Also see Section I.A., above.

[98]*See* HHS OIG Web site, Fraud Prevention and Detection Enforcement Actions, *available at* http://oig.hhs.gov/fraud/enforcement/administrative/cmp/cmpitems.html#3. Also see Section I.A., above.

- Rite Aid Corporation paid $7 million to federal and state governments to settle claims alleging that it submitted false (partial fill) prescription claims.[99] (2004)
- Warner-Lambert agreed to pay $430 million to resolve criminal charges and civil liabilities in connection with the Parke-Davis division's promotion of unapproved uses for one of its drug products.[100] (2004)
- Schering Corporation, Schering-Plough Corporation, and Warrick Pharmaceuticals Corporation paid the United States and the state of Texas $27 million to settle allegations that Warrick, a division of Schering-Plough, submitted false pricing information and caused providers to submit fraudulently inflated reimbursement claims to the Texas Medicaid program.[101] (2004)
- Bayer Corporation (Bayer) paid $257 million as part of a global criminal and civil settlement related to its sales of Cipro and Adalat to a health maintenance organization. Bayer pleaded guilty to a violation of certain FDA reporting requirements. The settlement also resolved allegations that Bayer significantly underpaid its Medicaid drug rebates and overcharged 340B program covered entities for the drugs because the company failed to report accurate best prices. Bayer agreed to a three-year extension of an earlier CIA.[102] (2003)
- SmithKline Beecham Corporation, doing business as GlaxoSmithKline (GSK), agreed to pay $88 million and enter a comprehensive CIA to settle claims that it violated Medicaid drug rebate program requirements in connection with two of its drugs, Flonase and Paxil. GSK allegedly failed to report accurate best-price information, resulting in allegedly underpaid Medicaid rebates and overcharges to Section 340B program covered entities.[103] (2003)
- Pfizer Corporation and its subsidiaries, Warner-Lambert and Parke-Davis, paid $49 million to settle allegations that the company violated the FCA by not fully paying the required Medicaid rebates for the cholesterol-lowering drug Lipitor.[104] (2002)

---

[99] Press Release, U.S. Dep't of Justice, *Rite Aid to Pay $7 Million for Allegedly Submitting False Prescription Claims to Government* (June 25, 2004), *available at* http://www.usdoj.gov/opa/pr/2004/June/04_civ_445.htm.

[100] Press Release, U.S. Dep't of Justice, *Warner-Lambert to Pay $430 Million to Resolve Criminal & Civil Health Care Liability Relating to Off-label Promotion* (May 13, 2004), *available at* http://www.usdoj.gov/opa/pr/2004/May/04_civ_322.htm. Also see Section I.A., above.

[101] Press Release, U.S. Dep't of Justice, *Schering-Plough to Pay U.S. & Texas $27 Million to Settle Medicaid Fraud Allegations* (May 13, 2004), *available at* http://www.usdoj.gov/opa/pr/2004/May/04_civ_292.htm.

[102] U.S. Dep't of Health & Human Servs., OIG Semiannual Report, Apr.–Sept. 2003, at 19–20 (2003), *available at* http://oig.hhs.gov/publications/docs/semiannual/2003/03fallsemi.pdf [hereinafter OIG Sept. 2003].

[103] *Id.* at 20.

[104] Press Release, U.S. Dep't of Justice, *Drug Giant Pfizer & Two Subsidiaries to Pay $49 Million for Defrauding Drug Medicaid Rebate Program* (Oct. 28, 2002), *available at* http://www.usdoj.gov/opa/pr/2002/October/02_civ_622.htm.

## 2. *Medicare Part D*

The sweeping MMA[105] expanded prescription drug coverage under the Medicare Part D program[106] modified payments to virtually every type of Medicare provider, replaced the Medicare+Choice program with the Medicare Advantage program offering additional health plan options, established a controversial demonstration project to test direct competition between managed care plans and traditional fee-for-service plans, and instituted administrative reforms to improve Medicare program operations, among many other provisions. The MMA also was notable because it gave the OIG, rather than CMS, responsibility for conducting studies and becoming directly involved in certain payment issues pertaining to DME and drugs, particularly those for cancer and end-stage renal disease (ESRD) patients.

Because the Part D benefit involves hundreds of millions of dollars, government concerns about the potential for fraud and abuse are high, and increased enforcement in this area is inevitable. For example, before the MMA's discount drug card program began on June 1, 2004, the government announced steps it was taking to prevent drug card fraud,[107] and also issued guidance addressing payment arrangements between discount drug card sponsors and their network pharmacies in connection with education, outreach, and enrollment[108] because of concerns under the anti-kickback statute. Moreover, the MMA created new authority to impose civil monetary penalties (CMPs) against endorsed sponsors under the Medicare prescription drug discount card program that: (i) knowingly engage in false or misleading marketing practices; (ii) overcharge program enrollees; or (iii) misuse transitional assistance funds.

Final regulations implementing this authority were issued on December 14, 2004.[109] Interestingly, HHS divided the sanction authority between CMS and the OIG in this area. As a result, the OIG is responsible for violations that involve misleading or defrauding a beneficiary, and/or the misuse of transitional funds. CMS has sanction authority in connection with noncompliance with operational requirements not directly related to beneficiary protection.[110]

There were several other indications that the government's focus on pharmaceutical fraud would continue to accelerate. For example, months before the Medicare Part D drug benefit went into effect on January 1, 2006, the OIG Work

---

[105]Medicare Prescription Drug, Improvement, and Modernization Act of 2003, Pub. L. No. 108-173, 117 Stat. 2066 (2003).

[106]Various aspects of fraud and abuse related to Medicare Part D are discussed in more detail in Chapter 10 (Short and Liner, Controlling Fraud, Waste, and Abuse in the Medicare Part D Program).

[107]*See* Press Release, CMS, *OIG Protecting Drug Card Program from Fraud* (May 18, 2004), *available at* http://www.cms.hhs.gov/apps/media/press/release.asp?Counter=1051.

[108]U.S. DEP'T OF HEALTH & HUMAN SERVS., EDUCATION AND OUTREACH ARRANGEMENTS BETWEEN MEDICARE-ENDORSED DISCOUNT DRUG CARD SPONSORS AND THEIR NETWORK PHARMACIES UNDER THE ANTI-KICKBACK STATUTE (Apr. 8, 2004), *available at* http://oig.hhs.gov/fraud/docs/alertsandbulletins/2004/FA040904.pdf.

[109]*See* OIG Civil Money Penalties Under the Medicare Prescription Drug Discount Card Program, 69 Fed. Reg. 74, 451 (Dec. 14, 2004).

[110]Note, however, that beneficiaries were permitted to enroll in the Medicare drug discount card program until Dec. 31, 2005, although they could continue using their card for a short time thereafter. *Id.* Accordingly, these CMPs will be relevant for a limited period.

Plan for 2006 contained a lengthy list of Part D issues the OIG planned to study in order to prevent waste, fraud, and abuse.[111] Moreover, on April 13, 2006 (less than four months after the program became effective), Senators Grassley and Baucus sent a letter to CMS Administrator Mark McClellan complaining that CMS had yet to fully implement its Part D anti-fraud program.[112]

CMS and OIG resources initially focused on the development and implementation of the Part D program. As a result, relatively few Part D enforcement actions had been taken by August 2007. For example, in January 2007, the OIG released an audit report finding that CMS had overpaid a Part D sponsor by more than $500,000, and that the sponsor had not complied with a requirement to pass discounts and rebates on to beneficiaries.[113] The OIG recommended that the sponsor reimburse CMS. In March 2007, Daniel Levinson, the HHS inspector general, told a congressional committee that the "OIG has developed and is implementing a strategic plan to fight fraud, waste, and abuse in Part D and to protect the health and welfare of its beneficiaries . . . [and has] ongoing investigations of Medicare Part D cases, along with audits and evaluations underway."[114] Consequently, as the program becomes more institutionalized, enforcement is expected to accelerate.

Part D plan sponsors are required to implement a compliance program to "detect, correct and prevent" fraud, waste, and abuse.[115] In April 2006, CMS issued a new Chapter 9 in the Prescription Drug Benefit Manual (PDBM Chapter 9) on "Part D Program to Control Waste, Fraud and Abuse" that contains guidance for Medicare Part D prescription drug plans (PDPs) related to the compliance programs the plans must adopt in order to participate in the Part D program. PDBM Chapter 9 also suggests that PDPs adopt numerous other recommended compliance practices as well.[116] Further, PDBM Chapter 9 identifies various high risk areas for PBMs, pharmacies, prescribers, wholesalers, pharmaceutical manufacturers, and Medicare beneficiaries. Other fraud and abuse "vulnerabilities" identified in PDBM Chapter 9 include (i) coordination with patient assistance programs (PAPs); (ii) counterfeit and abused drugs; (iii) drugs excluded from Part D coverage; and (iv) inappropriate duplicate drug coverage between Medicare Parts B and D.[117]

---

[111] See the discussion in Section IV.B., below.

[112] Letter from Senators Chuck Grassley and Max Baucus to Mark B. McClelland (Apr. 13, 2006), *available at* http://grassley.senate.gov/index.cfm?FuseAction=PressReleases.Detail& PressRelease_id=5038&Month=4&Year=2006.

[113] DEP'T HEALTH & HUMAN SERVS., OFFICE OF INSPECTOR GENERAL, REPORT ON THE MEDICARE DRUG DISCOUNT CARD PROGRAM SPONSOR COMPUTER SCIENCES CORPORATION, No. A-06-06-00112 (Dec. 2006), *available at* http://oig.hhs.gov/oas/reports/region6/60600112.pdf.

[114] Dep't Health & Human Servs., Office of Inspector General, Hearing Before the House Ways & Means Committee (Mar. 8, 2007) (statement of Daniel R. Levinson, Inspector General, U.S. Dept. of Health & Human Servs.), *available at* http://oig.hhs.gov/testimony/docs/2007/030807tmy.pdf.

[115] 42 C.F.R. §423.504(b)(4)(vi)(H).

[116] CMS, Chapter 9–Part D Program to Control Fraud, Waste and Abuse, Prescription Drug Benefit Manual (Apr. 25, 2006) [hereinafter PDBM Chapter 9], *available at* http://www.cms.hhs.gov/Prescription DrugCovContra/ownoads/PDBManual_Chapter9_FWA.pdf.

[117] PDBM Chapter 9 is discussed in more detail below in Chapter 6 (Rinn and Ryland, Managed Care Fraud and Abuse: Risk Areas for Government Program Participants), Chapter 7 (Baumann, Corporate Compliance Programs), and Chapter 10 (Short and Liner, Controlling Fraud, Waste, and Abuse in the Medicare Part D Program).

PDBM Chapter 9 is very similar to the OIG Compliance Program Guidance (CPG) documents that previously were issued for various types of providers,[118] but is more detailed and stringent in several areas. This distinction is likely due to the fact that the OIG's CPG documents are not legally binding whereas PDBM Chapter 9 carries more legal weight since it has been incorporated into a CMS manual. Moreover, a number of the PDBM Chapter 9 requirements are directly based on specific provisions in the law or regulations.

Another new government initiative that is likely to increase enforcement in this area involves the creation of the MEDICs program to assist CMS with audit, oversight, and related fraud and abuse efforts in connection with the Part D program. MEDIC responsibilities and activities are described in considerable detail in Exhibit 1 of PDBM Chapter 9.

### 3. State Enforcement

In recent years, various states have increased their enforcement actions related to state fraud laws. For example, in January 2007, the Illinois Attorney General intervened in a whistleblower lawsuit against several radiology centers. These centers had allegedly entered into sham lease agreements with referring physicians, violating the state Consumer Fraud and Deceptive Business Practices Act as well as the state anti-kickback law and the Insurance Claims Fraud Prevention Act.[119] In December 2006, the Texas Attorney General announced that the state will receive more than $15 million from one of the nation's largest pharmaceutical companies to settle claims of best-price violations. Forty-nine other states have made similar allegations.[120] In October 2006, the New York Attorney General and the New York Medicaid Inspector General's office uncovered a Medicaid fraud ring involving a doctor, pharmacists, several city pharmacies, millions of dollars in fraudulent Medicaid charges, and large money transfers to Pakistan. Sixteen persons and five corporations have been indicted, and the state seeks recovery of $22 million stemming from civil charges against twenty more individuals.[121] In June 2006, the New Jersey Attorney General successfully prosecuted a pharmacy for submitting false claims to Medicaid and paying illegal kickbacks.[122] In May 2006, Alaska prosecuted its largest Medicaid fraud case against a home health agency for $1.3 million where Medicaid was double-billed and billed for services that were not rendered.[123] Also in May 2006, the Michigan Attorney General charged the

---

[118]The OIG's Compliance Program Guidance documents are discussed in detail in Chapter 7 (Baumann, Corporate Compliance Programs).

[119]Press Release, Illinois Attorney General, *Madigan Joins Suit Against Radiology Centers over Illegal Payment of Kickbacks to Doctors* (Jan. 17, 2007), *available at* http://www.illinois attorneygeneral.gov/pressroom/2007_01/20070117.html.

[120]Press Release, Texas Att'y General, *Attorney General Abbott Recovers $15.7 Million in Medicaid Costs Under National Settlement* (Dec. 7, 2006), *available at* http://www.oag .state.tx.us/oagnews/release.php?id=1862.

[121]*Major Medicaid Fraud Ring Dismantled*, NORTH COUNTRY GAZETTE (Oct. 25, 2006), *available at* http://www.northcountrygazette.org/articles/102506MajorFraud.html.

[122]*Essex County Pharmacy Employees Sentenced for Medicaid Fraud*, U.S. STATE NEWS (June 5, 2006), *available at* 2006 WLNR 9643891.

[123]Anne Aurand, *Trial Set in Record Medicaid Fraud: State Charges That Company Billed $1.3 Million for Services Not Performed*, ANCHORAGE DAILY NEWS (May 23, 2006), at B1.

CEO of a nursing home with embezzlement and submitting false claims to the Medicaid program.[124] In another Michigan case, the attorney general entered a settlement and CIA with a nursing home chain to resolve civil charges related to allegations that certain facilities provided inadequate care and failed to comply with applicable federal and state law, including Medicaid requirements.[125] Further, in 2005 the Michigan Attorney General filed a civil lawsuit, seeking over $3.5 million in damages, against a home health/nursing care company, alleging that the company committed Medicaid fraud by billing for services that were never provided.[126]

Moreover, the federal government has taken steps to encourage certain states to increase their enforcement of Medicaid fraud. In one example, despite several prior high-profile health care fraud prosecutions by then-New York Attorney General Eliot Spitzer, a June 2006 CMS report chastised the New York State Department of Health for its waning enforcement of Medicaid anti-fraud rules. In recent years, the department had submitted only fifty cases annually to the New York attorney general for legal action—far fewer than states with smaller Medicaid programs.[127] In any event, enforcement actions in New York were expected to increase when James Sheehan, formerly the Associate U.S. Attorney for Civil Programs in the Eastern District of Pennsylvania and one of the most active prosecutors of health care fraud and abuse cases, became the New York State Medicaid Inspector General.[128]

Further, in a May 2006 speech, HHS Inspector General Levinson emphasized that the OIG would be reaching out to Medicaid Fraud Control Units (MFCUs) and state attorneys general to assist with enforcement efforts, especially those related to kickbacks and nursing home quality of care.[129] MFCUs had obtained $709 million in restitution, fines, and civil settlements in FY 2005, and excluded 1,267 providers in FY 2004–FY 2005.[130] MFCUs are also likely to move beyond their traditional focus on long-term care facilities, and it has been reported that MFCUs are beginning to evaluate payments for specialized motorized vehicle transportation, claims for work performed by unlicensed or excluded providers, DME, and the quality of care.[131]

---

[124]*Attorney General Cox Charges Former Nursing Home Chief Executive Officer with Medicaid Fraud, Embezzlement*, U.S. STATE NEWS (May 18, 2006), *available at* 2006 WLNR 8622801.

[125]*Attorney General Cox Announces Corporate Integrity Agreement with Metron Nursing Home Chain*, *available at* http://www.michigan.gov/ag/0,1607,7-164—143978—,00.html.

[126]*Michigan AG Files Medicaid Fraud Law Suit Against Detroit Home Care/Nursing Company*, 9 HEALTH CARE FRAUD (BNA) 614 (Aug. 3, 2005).

[127]Michael Lueo and Richard Perez-Pena, *U.S. Assails Albany's Efforts on Medicaid Fraud*, N.Y. TIMES, June 6, 2006, at A1.

[128]Press Release, NEW YORK STATE GOVERNOR, *Governor Eliot Spitzer and Lieutenant Governor David Paterson Nominate New York State Medicaid Inspector General* (Apr. 6, 2007), *available at* http://www.ny.gov/governor/press/0406071.html.

[129]*HHS OIG 'Keen' on Curbing Part D Fraud, Giving More Help to States, Levinson Says*, 10 HEALTH CARE FRAUD 403 (BNA) (May 24, 2006).

[130]2005 HHS/DOJ REPORT.

[131]*MFCUs Recoup Record Amounts, Exclude More Providers in FY '05*, MEDICARE COMPLIANCE ALERT, Vol. 3, No. 20 (Oct. 16, 2006), at 3.

Finally, as discussed later in Section III., below, federal law now provides financial incentives to states that enact their own false claims acts and requires many companies to educate certain personnel about the applicable federal and state false claims laws and the opportunities for whistleblowers. Consequently, states are increasingly likely to pursue fraud and abuse cases related to health care programs.

### 4. Private Enforcement

Private payors have followed the government's lead in pursuing fraud and abuse. For example, the BlueCross BlueShield Association (BSBCA) now maintains a national anti-fraud department that coordinates with the antifraud units of each of its member plans. Together, the BSBCA and its plans have more than 600 employees engaged in anti-fraud efforts.[132] In 2005, the BCBSA reported over $249 million in recoveries, an 11 percent increase from recoveries made in 2004.[133]

## II. The Federal Fraud and Abuse Laws

There are many federal laws specifically designed to address health care fraud and abuse including the anti-kickback statute,[134] the Stark law prohibiting physician self-referrals,[135] the FCA,[136] various CMP provisions,[137] and mandatory and permissive exclusion authorities.[138] Many of these laws focus on fraud and abuse affecting various federally funded health care programs such as Medicare, Medicaid, and veterans health care programs, although other statutes address fraudulent practices affecting nongovernmental payors as well.[139]

There are also numerous other federal statutes that do not specifically address any type of health care program but may be used to prosecute fraud and abuse in the health care industry, including the Racketeer Influenced and Corrupt Organizations Act (RICO),[140] the Anti-Kickback Enforcement Act of 1986,[141] and money-laundering prohibitions.[142] In addition, various other laws

---

[132]What the Blues are Doing, *available at* http://www.bcbs.com/betterknowledge/anti-fraud/what-the-blues-are-doing.html.

[133]*Blue Cross and Blue Shield Plans' Anti-Fraud Savings and Recoveries Increased 11 Percent in 2005*, BCBSA News (Aug. 28, 2006), *available at* http://www.bcbs.com/news/bcbsa/bcbsa-antifraud-recoveries.html.

[134]42 U.S.C. §1320a-7b(b); see Appendix A-1 on the disk accompanying this volume.

[135]42 U.S.C. §1395nn; see Appendix B-1 on the disk accompanying this volume.

[136]31 U.S.C. §3729; see Appendix C-1 on the disk accompanying this volume.

[137]42 U.S.C. §1320a-7a; see Appendix D-1 on the disk accompanying this volume.

[138]42 U.S.C. §1320a-7; see Appendix D-3 on the disk accompanying this volume.

[139]See the discussion in Section II.F., below. The historical development of the federal health care fraud and abuse laws is discussed in more detail in Chapter 4 (Hooper and Abbott, Practical Considerations for Defending Health Care Fraud and Abuse Cases).

[140]18 U.S.C. §§1961 *et seq.*

[141]41 U.S.C.A. §§ 51 *et seq.*

[142]18 U.S.C. §1956. *See also, e.g.*, 18 U.S.C. §§286 (conspiracy to defraud the government), 287 (submission of fraudulent claims), 371 (conspiracy to defraud), and 1001 (false statements).

including certain provisions of the tax code, such as those relating to private inurement, may also be implicated by some of the same transactions that potentially implicate the fraud and abuse laws. However, it is critical to remember that the factors (e.g., community benefit) that may protect an arrangement from violating certain Internal Revenue Code provisions will not necessarily protect an arrangement under the fraud and abuse statutes.

## A. The Anti-Kickback Statute

### 1. The Prohibitions

The federal anti-kickback statute establishes criminal penalties with respect to any person who knowingly and willfully offers, pays, solicits, or receives any remuneration to induce or in return for: (1) referring an individual to a person for the furnishing or arranging for the furnishing of any item or service payable in whole or in part under a federal health care program; or (2) purchasing, leasing, ordering, or arranging for, or recommending purchasing, leasing, or ordering any good, facility, service, or item payable under a federal health care program. Remuneration is defined broadly to include the transfer of anything of value, in cash or in kind, directly or indirectly, overtly or covertly.[143]

Violation of the anti-kickback statute constitutes a felony punishable by a maximum fine of $25,000, imprisonment up to five years, or both. Conviction will also lead to automatic exclusion from Medicare, Medicaid, and other federally funded health care programs. Exclusion from these programs may also be sought by HHS through an administrative proceeding, irrespective of any criminal charges. In addition, under the Balanced Budget Act of 1997,[144] violations of the anti-kickback statute are also subject to CMPs of up to $50,000 and damages of up to three times the amount of the illegal kickback.

The anti-kickback statute is expansive in scope and clearly prohibits payments for patient referrals. The applicability of the statute becomes less clear, however, as applied to arrangements that do not simply involve a payment per patient referral, but instead contemplate investment or business relationships between two or more individuals or organizations. The courts have interpreted this prohibition broadly. In 1985, in *United States v. Greber*,[145] the Third Circuit established the "one purpose" test, holding that the anti-kickback statute was violated where one purpose of the payment in question was to induce referrals, irrespective of the existence of other legitimate purposes. Over the years, this approach has been adopted by three other circuits.[146] Further, in *United States v. Bay State Ambulance & Hospital Rental Service*,[147] the court held that simply giving a person an opportunity to earn money may be an inducement to that person to channel Medicare payments toward a particular recipient in violation of the anti-kickback statute. However, in a recent Tenth Circuit case, *United*

---

[143]42 U.S.C. §§1320a-7b(b)(1), (2).

[144]Pub. L. No. 105-93, 111 Stat. 251 (1997).

[145]760 F.2d 68 (3d Cir. 1985).

[146]*See, e.g.*, United States v. Davis, 132 F.3d 1092, 1094 (5th Cir. 1998); United States v. Kats, 871 F.2d 105 (9th Cir. 1989); United States v. McClatchey, 217 F.3d 823 (10th Cir. 2000), *cert. denied*, 531 U.S. 1015 (2000).

[147]874 F.2d 20, 29 (1st Cir. 1989).

*States v. McClatchey*,[148] the court stated that the mere hope or expectation that referrals may result from remuneration designed for entirely different purposes is not a violation, and that there must be an actual offer or payment of remuneration to induce referrals. Moreover, "the intent to gain such influence must, at least in part, have been the reason the remuneration was offered or paid."[149]

In addition, although cases have interpreted the concept of inducement quite broadly, judicial guidance with respect to the criminal intent that must be shown in order to prove a violation of the anti-kickback statute has been inconsistent. For example, the Ninth Circuit and some other courts have suggested that a defendant must violate a known legal duty.[150] However, the federal district court in *United States v. Neufeld*[151] refused to adopt the Ninth Circuit's definition of "willful," but at the same time hesitated from "embarking on an exact definition of the scienter requirement...."[152] In 1998 the Eleventh Circuit found, in *United States v. Starks*,[153] that "willfully" meant an act "committed voluntarily and purposely, with the specific intent to do something the law forbids, that is, with a bad purpose, either to disobey or disregard the law."[154] Further, the court noted that the anti-kickback statute was not analogous to other highly technical laws, and thus knowledge of the specific law was unnecessary.[155]

In *United States v. McClatchey*,[156] the Tenth Circuit used the same language as the *Starks* court to define "willfully." A jury had convicted McClatchey, a hospital executive, of violating the anti-kickback statute but the district court had granted a motion for acquittal, concluding that no reasonable jury could find that McClatchey deliberately intended to violate the statute. On appeal, the Tenth Circuit held that a jury might reasonably have found that McClatchey specifically intended to violate the anti-kickback statute because he renegotiated, rather than terminated, a contract with physicians (1) who had not performed substantial services required under prior contracts, (2) whom staff did not want to perform certain services at the hospital, and (3) who made referrals that were important to the hospital's financial health. The court stated that under these circumstances, a jury could have determined that McClatchey's very reason for negotiating a new contract was to induce continuing referrals.

The Tenth Circuit dismissed McClatchey's claims that he did not have improper intent because he directed legal counsel to remedy the physicians' prior failure to provide services. The appellate court closely examined the underlying facts in the case, noting that hospital staff did not want or need some of the services the physicians were to provide, and stating that a jury might have found McClatchey's directions to counsel were a subterfuge to ensure the contract appeared on its face to constitute a legal arrangement. Further, the

---

[148]217 F.3d 823 (10th Cir.), *cert. denied*, 531 U.S. 1015 (2000).

[149]*Id.* at 834.

[150]*See, e.g.*, Hanlester Network v. Shalala, 51 F.3d 1390 (9th Cir. 1995). The *Hanlester* case was also the first judicial decision to specially address the application of the anti-kickback statute to joint venture arrangements.

[151]908 F. Supp. 491 (S.D. Ohio 1995).

[152]*Id.* at 497.

[153]157 F.3d 833 (11th Cir. 1998).

[154]*Id.* at 837.

[155]*Id.*

[156]217 F.3d 823, 829 (10th Cir.), *cert. denied*, 531 U.S. 1015 (2000).

court pointed out that McClatchey was directing counsel on certain matters, and not vice versa; and did not always follow the advice of counsel when he received it.

In sum, given the undetermined state of the law, judicial inquiry into intent may frequently involve an objective and detailed examination of the facts, circumstances, and structure of each transaction, especially the financial effects of the relationships and arrangements.

## 2. *Exceptions and Safe Harbors*

Because of the broad sweep of the anti-kickback prohibitions, Congress created a number of statutory exceptions to protect legitimate business arrangements including the following:

- properly disclosed discounts or other reductions in price;
- payments to bona fide employees;
- certain payments to group purchasing organizations;
- waivers of coinsurance for Medicare services for individuals who qualify for certain Public Health Service programs; and
- certain risk-sharing and other arrangements with managed care organizations.[157]

In addition, Congress authorized HHS to establish further "safe harbors" by regulation.[158] The OIG has created a number of regulatory safe harbors over the years, and in November 1999 the OIG clarified a number of the existing safe harbors and added several new ones. Note, however, that safe harbor protection is only available if the arrangement fulfills *all* the regulatory criteria. Several safe harbors also have been added since 1999. Currently there are safe harbors covering the following types of arrangements:[159]

- investments in certain large or small[160] entities;
- investments in entities in underserved areas;[161]
- space rentals;[162]
- equipment rentals;[163]
- personal services and management contracts;[164]
- sales of physician practices in health professional shortage areas to hospitals or other entities;[165]
- sales of practices by one practitioner to another;[166]
- referral services;[167]

---

[157]42 U.S.C. §1320a-7b(b)(3).

[158]42 U.S.C. §1320a-7b(b)(3)(E).

[159]See Appendix A-2 on the disk accompanying this volume for full text of the anti-kickback safe harbor regulations.

[160]42 C.F.R. §§1001.952(a)(1), (a)(2).

[161]42 C.F.R. §1001.952(a)(3).

[162]42 C.F.R. §1001.952(b).

[163]42 C.F.R. §1001.952(c).

[164]42 C.F.R. §1001.952(d).

[165]42 C.F.R. §1001.952(e)(2).

[166]42 C.F.R. §1001.952(e)(1).

[167]42 C.F.R. §1001.952(f).

- warranties;[168]
- discounts;[169]
- bona fide employment arrangements;[170]
- group purchasing organizations;[171]
- coinsurance and deductible waivers;[172]
- increased coverage, reduced cost-sharing amounts, or reduced premium amounts offered by health plans;[173]
- price reductions offered to health plans;[174]
- practitioner recruitment activities in underserved areas;[175]
- subsidies for obstetrical malpractice insurance in underserved areas;[176]
- investments in group practices;[177]
- cooperative hospital service organizations;[178]
- investments in ambulatory surgical centers (ASCs);[179]
- referral arrangements for specialty services;[180]
- price reductions for eligible managed care organizations;[181]
- price reductions offered to managed care organizations by contractors with substantial financial risk;[182]
- ambulance replenishing;[183]
- items and services related to electronic prescribing;[184]
- items and services related to electronic health records;[185] and

---

[168] 42 C.F.R. §1001.952(g).

[169] 42 C.F.R. §1001.952(h). This safe harbor contains various differing requirements for buyers, sellers, and offerors depending on the types of parties involved.

[170] 42 C.F.R. §1001.952(i).

[171] 42 C.F.R. §1001.952(j).

[172] 42 C.F.R. §1001.952(k).

[173] 42 C.F.R. §1001.952(l).

[174] 42 C.F.R. §1001.952(m).

[175] 42 C.F.R. §1001.952(n).

[176] 42 C.F.R. §1001.952(o).

[177] 42 C.F.R. §1001.952(p).

[178] 42 C.F.R. §1001.952(q).

[179] 42 C.F.R. §1001.952(r). This safe harbor has different criteria for four types of ASCs.

[180] 42 C.F.R. §1001.952(s).

[181] 42 C.F.R. §1001.952(t).

[182] 42 C.F.R. §1001.952(u).

[183] 42 C.F.R. §1001.952(v).

[184] 42 C.F.R. §1001.952(x). Specifically, this safe harbor protects certain arrangements involving hospitals, group practices, and prescription drug plan sponsors and Medicare Advantage organizations that provide to specified recipients certain nonmonetary remuneration in the form of hardware, software, or information technology and training services necessary and used solely to receive and transmit electronic prescription information.

[185] 42 C.F.R. §1001.952(y). This safe harbor protects certain arrangements involving the provision of nonmonetary remuneration in the form of electronic health records software or information technology and training services necessary and used predominantly to create, maintain, transmit, or receive electronic health records. Safe Harbors for Certain Electronic Prescribing and Electronic Health Records Arrangements Under the Anti-Kickback Statute, 71 Fed. Reg. 45,110 (Aug. 8, 2006), available as Appendix A-3 on the disk accompanying this volume. The OIG also has proposed new safe harbors relating to the waiver of Medicare SELECT beneficiary coinsurance and deductibles arrangements, 67 Fed. Reg. 60,202 (proposed Sept. 25, 2002), and to Federally Qualified Health Centers, 70 Fed. Reg. 38,081 (proposed July 1, 2005).

- cost-sharing waivers for beneficiaries who qualify for the low income subsidy under Part D.[186]

A common theme that runs through these safe harbors is the intent to protect certain arrangements in which commercially reasonable items or services are exchanged for fair market value compensation. While the statute does not contain a general definition of the term, "fair market value" is defined in the space and equipment rental safe harbors. For example, under the space rental safe harbor, fair market value means the value of rental property for general commercial purposes, but should not be adjusted to reflect the additional value that one party would attribute to the property as a result of its proximity or convenience to sources of Medicare or Medicaid business or referrals.[187] The term "commercially reasonable business purpose" is discussed in the preamble to the 1999 safe harbor regulations, which indicates that in the space and equipment rental, and personal services and management contracts safe harbors, the term means that the space, equipment, or services involved must have "intrinsic commercial value" to the lessee or purchaser.[188]

In addition, several of the frequently used safe harbors, including those for space or equipment rentals, and personal services or management contracts, require that *aggregate* compensation be set in advance.[189] Many of the safe harbors require a one-year written agreement, signed by the parties. A number of the safe harbors added or clarified in 1999 focus on medically underserved areas and populations, although the criteria for determining whether an area is underserved vary depending on the particular safe harbor involved.[190]

While each of the safe harbors have numerous criteria, the regulations confirm that the safe harbors do not broaden the scope of the statute.[191] Further, in Advisory Opinion No. 98-4, the OIG emphasized that compliance with a safe harbor is not mandatory. Rather, the safe harbors set forth specific threshold requirements that, if fully met, will assure the entities involved that they will not be prosecuted for the arrangement. In other words, while the safe harbors provide protection from liability under the statute, failure to comply with these regulations does not mean that the activity is illegal. Moreover, in the 1999 safe

---

[186]42 U.S.C. §1320a–7b(b)(3)(G).

[187]42 C.F.R. §1001.952(b). The term is also defined in the Stark law and regulations as discussed in Section II.B., below. However, the requirements of the two statutes differ in various respects, and thus such definitions may not be used interchangeably.

[188]*See* Clarification of the Initial OIG Safe Harbor Provisions and Establishment of Additional Safe Harbor Provisions Under the Anti-Kickback Statute, 64 Fed. Reg. 63,518, 63,525 (Nov. 19, 1999).

[189]42 C.F.R. §§1001.952(b)(5), (c)(5), (d)(5).

[190]Some safe harbors involve health professional shortage areas (HPSAs), while others involve medically underserved areas and populations. The definition of these various concepts is somewhat uncertain at this time pending the issuance of final regulations. *See, e.g.*, GAO REPORT TO CONGRESSIONAL COMMITTEES, HEALTH PROFESSIONAL SHORTAGE AREAS: PROBLEMS REMAIN WITH PRIMARY CARE SHORTAGE AREA DESIGNATION SYSTEM (Oct. 2006), *available at* http://www.gao.gov/new.items/d0784.pdf. For further discussion of this subject, see Linda Baumann, *Navigating the New Safe Harbors to the Anti-Kickback Statute*, THE HEALTH LAW. (Feb. 2000), at 8–9.

[191]*E.g.*, Clarification of the Initial OIG Safe Harbor Provisions and Establishment of Additional Safe Harbor Provisions Under the Anti-Kickback Statute, 64 Fed. Reg. 63,518, 63,521 (Nov. 19, 1999); OIG Anti-Kickback Provisions, 56 Fed. Reg. 35,952, 35,954 (July 29, 1991).

harbor regulations, the OIG went further and stated that failure to comply with a safe harbor does not necessarily mean that an arrangement is "suspect."[192]

The OIG defined the safe harbors very narrowly, using numerous criteria, in order to prevent any risk of fraud or abuse. Therefore, many common arrangements in the health care industry will at least potentially implicate the anti-kickback statute, and will not fully qualify for protection under the safe harbors. Nevertheless, even when an arrangement cannot satisfy all the criteria of a safe harbor, it is generally advisable to meet as many of the requirements as possible. However, under these circumstances, it becomes necessary to examine the arrangement under the terms of the statute with particular reference to the intent of the parties. As noted above, the anti-kickback statute may be violated if only one purpose of the arrangement is to induce referrals. Therefore, when the anti-kickback statute is implicated, and a safe harbor is not fully applicable, the arrangement should be analyzed in light of the Special Fraud Alerts and other relevant materials described below that may help assess a transaction's legality.

A safe harbor that would expand the existing safe harbor for certain waivers of beneficiary coinsurance and deductibles to Medicare SELECT policyholders was proposed in 2002 and is still under consideration by the OIG.[193] However, a proposed safe harbor for transfers of remuneration between entities under common ownership or control was rejected by the OIG in favor of considering such arrangements on a case-by-case basis.[194] Also, although a proposed safe harbor for the payment of Medicare Part B or Medigap premium payments for financially needy ESRD patients was proposed by the OIG, the OIG subsequently determined that it would not promulgate that proposed regulation.[195]

### 3. Special Fraud Alerts and Special Advisory Bulletins

Special Fraud Alerts, which the OIG issues periodically, provide further insight into the OIG's views on the application of the anti-kickback statute to various types of arrangements. These documents cannot create new law but may influence judicial decisions.[196] They often contain descriptions of specific features that the OIG considers "suspect" or "questionable," and arrangements that contain such features are more likely to be subject to further government review. Nevertheless, it is important to remember that even "suspect" arrangements are not necessarily illegal.

---

[192]64 Fed. Reg. 63,518, 63,521 (Nov. 19, 1999).

[193]Proposed Rule: Safe Harbor Under the Anti-Kickback Statute for the Waiver of Medicare SELECT Beneficiary Coinsurance and Deductible Amounts, 67 Fed. Reg. 60,202 (Sept. 25, 2002), *available at* http://www.oig.hhs.gov/fraud/docs/safeharborregulations/MedicareSELECTNPRMFederalRegister.pdf.

[194]OIG Sept. 2003, at 92.

[195]*See* Medicare and State Health Care Programs: Fraud and Abuse; Civil Money Penalty Exception to Protect Payment of Medicare Supplemental Insurance and Medigap Premiums for ESRD Beneficiaries, 67 Fed. Reg. 72,896 (Dec. 9, 2002).

[196]*See* Polk County, Tex. v. Peters, 800 F. Supp. 1451, 1455 (E.D. Tex. 1992).

The OIG has issued Special Fraud Alerts on the following topics:

- Telemarketing by Durable Medical Equipment Suppliers;[197]
- Rental of Space in Physician Offices by Persons or Entities to Which Physicians Refer;[198]
- Physician Liability for Certifications in the Provision of Medical Equipment and Supplies and Home Health Services;[199]
- Fraud and Abuse in Nursing Home Arrangements With Hospices;[200]
- Fraud and Abuse in the Provision of Services in Nursing Facilities;[201]
- Home Health Fraud;[202]
- Fraud and Abuse in the Provision of Medical Supplies to Nursing Facilities;[203]
- Joint Venture Arrangements;[204]
- Routine Waiver of Medicare Part B Copayments and Deductibles;[205]
- Hospital Incentives to Referring Physicians;[206]
- Prescription Drug Marketing Practices;[207] and
- Arrangements for the Provision of Clinical Laboratory Services.[208]

The OIG primarily has used the "Special Advisory Bulletin" format in recent years and has issued the following:[209]

- Gainsharing Arrangements and CMPs for Hospital Payments to Physicians to Reduce or Limit Services to Beneficiaries;[210]

---

[197]U.S. Dep't of Health & Human Servs., Special Fraud Alert, Telemarketing by Durable Medical Equipment Suppliers (Mar. 2003), *available at* http://oig.hhs.gov/fraud/docs/alertsandbulletins/Telemarketingdme.pdf. This Special Fraud Alert reemphasized the statutory prohibition on making unsolicited telephone calls to Medicare beneficiaries regarding the furnishing of a covered item except in specific situations, and stated that the prohibition could not be circumvented by engaging third-party marketing companies. The Special Fraud Alert also emphasized a DME supplier's duty to ensure that a third-party marketer does not engage in prohibited activity on the supplier's behalf, noting that both the DME supplier and the marketer could be subject to criminal, civil, and administrative penalties under the FCA if a claim, generated by a prohibited solicitation, were submitted.

[198]*See* 65 Fed. Reg. 9274 (Feb. 24, 2000).

[199]*See* 64 Fed. Reg. 1813 (Jan. 12, 1999).

[200]*See* 63 Fed. Reg. 20,415 (Apr. 24, 1998).

[201]*See* 61 Fed. Reg. 30,623 (June 17, 1996).

[202]*See* 60 Fed. Reg. 40,847 (Aug. 10, 1995).

[203]*Id.*

[204]*See* 59 Fed. Reg. 65,372 (Dec. 19, 1994). Because there are many joint ventures in the health care industry and little available guidance, this Special Fraud Alert is often consulted, and recommends analyzing a joint venture in terms of three key areas:
- the manner in which investors are selected and retained;
- the nature of the business structure (i.e., is it a "shell" or "sham" arrangement); and
- financing and profit distributions.
These Special Fraud Alerts are available at http://oig.hhs.gov/fraud/fraudalerts.html and in Appendix F on the disk accompanying this volume.

[205]*See* http://oig.hhs.gov/fraud/fraudalerts.html and in Appendix F on the disk accompanying this volume.

[206]*Id.*

[207]*Id.*

[208]*Id.*

[209]Special Advisory Bulletins are available at http://oig.hhs.gov/fraud/fraudalerts.html#2 and at Appendix F on the disk accompanying this volume.

[210]OIG Special Advisory Bulletin on Gainsharing Arrangements and CMPs for Hospital Payments to Physicians to Reduce or Limit Services to Beneficiaries, 64 Fed. Reg. 37,985 (July

- The Effect of Exclusion from Participation in Federal Health Care Programs;[211]
- Patient Anti-Dumping Statute;[212]
- Practices of Business Consultants;[213]
- Offering Gifts and Other Inducements to Beneficiaries;[214]
- Contractual Joint Ventures;[215] and
- Patient Assistance Programs for Medicare Part D Enrollees.[216]

---

14, 1999), and at Appendix F-15 on the disk accompanying this volume. The subject of gain-sharing is addressed in more detail in Chapter 5 (Barry, Legal Issues Surrounding Hospital and Physician Relationships), Section IV.J.

[211]OIG Special Advisory Bulletin on the Effect of Exclusion From Participation in Federal Health Care Programs, 64 Fed. Reg. 52,791 (Sept. 30, 1999), and at Appendix F-14 on the disk accompanying this volume; see the discussion at Section II.E., below.

[212]OIG/HCFA Special Advisory Bulletin on the Patient Anti-Dumping Statute, 64 Fed. Reg. 61,353 (Nov. 10, 1999), and at Appendix F-13 on the disk accompanying this volume.

[213]OIG Special Advisory Bulletin, Practices of Business Consultants, 66 Fed. Reg. 36,583 (July 12, 2001), and at Appendix F-12 on the disk accompanying this volume.

[214]OIG Special Advisory Bulletin, Offering Gifts and Other Inducements to Beneficiaries (Aug. 2002), *available at* http://oig.hhs.gov/fraud/docs/alertsandbulletins/SABGiftsandInducements.pdf, and at Appendix F-18 on the disk accompanying this volume.

[215]OIG Special Advisory Bulletin, Contractual Joint Ventures (Apr. 2003), *available at* http://oig.hhs.gov/fraud/docs/alertsandbulletins/042303SABJointVentures.pdf, and at Appendix F-20 on the disk accompanying this volume. The OIG focuses on those arrangements where a health care provider (the Owner) expands into a related health care business by contracting with an existing provider or supplier of the item or service (the Manager/Supplier). According to the OIG, the following characteristics potentially indicate a suspect arrangement, including:

- *New Line of Business.* The Owner typically seeks to expand into a health care service that can be provided to its existing patients;
- *Captive Referral Base.* The new business predominantly serves the Owner's existing patients, making little effort to expand the business to serve new customers;
- *Little or No Bona Fide Business Risk.* The Owner's primary contribution to the venture is referrals, rather than a financial or other investment. The Owner delegates the operation of the venture to the Manager/Supplier while retaining profits generated from its referral base;
- *Status of the Manager/Supplier.* The Manager/Supplier normally would compete with the Owner because it has the ability to provide virtually identical services and bill insurers and patients under its own name;
- *Scope of Services Provided by the Manager/Supplier.* The Manager/Supplier often provides a "turn key" type operation, which often includes the provision of: (1) day-to-day management, (2) billing services, (3) equipment, (4) personnel and related services, (5) office space, (6) training, and (7) health care items, supplies, and services;
- *Remuneration.* The practical effect of the arrangement is to provide the Owner the opportunity to bill for business otherwise provided by the Manager/Supplier. The Owner's profits from the venture take into account the value and volume of business the Owner generates; and
- *Exclusivity.* The parties may adopt a noncompete clause prohibiting the Owner from providing items or services to patients other than those referred by the Owner, and/or barring the Manager/Supplier from providing services in its own right to the Owner's patients.

Joint ventures that contain one or more of the suspect factors listed in the Contractual Joint Venture Bulletin are not necessarily illegal, nor are Owners (such as hospitals) prohibited from establishing and funding their own new independent subsidiary businesses in certain cases. Nevertheless, arrangements containing "questionable" characteristics, as identified in the Contractual Joint Venture Bulletin, may be subject to increased OIG scrutiny. This Bulletin also contains an important warning that even if various component agreements individually fit all the criteria of various safe harbors, the overall arrangement may, nevertheless, violate the anti-kickback statute.

[216]OIG Special Advisory Bulletin, Patient Assistance Programs for Medicare Part D Enrollees, 70 Fed. Reg. 70,623 (Nov. 22, 2005), *available at* http://oig.hhs.gov/fraud/docs/alertsandbulletins/2005/PAPAdvisoryBlletinFinal-Final.pdf, and at Appendix F-21 on the disk

### 4. *Office of Inspector General Advisory Opinions*

In 1996 Congress directed the OIG to establish a process to enable members of the public to request advisory opinions on whether individual transactions might violate the anti-kickback and certain other statutes. Under the OIG's implementing regulations, advisory opinions may address the following issues:

- what constitutes prohibited remuneration;
- whether an arrangement fits an exception or safe harbor;
- what constitutes inducement to reduce or limit services; and
- whether the activity described would constitute grounds for the imposition of sanctions.[217]

However, the OIG will not address in an advisory opinion what constitutes fair market value or whether a person is a bona fide "employee."[218]

The OIG does not accept requests for advisory opinions on abstract questions. The request must involve an actual, or intended, business arrangement. If the request involves a proposed business arrangement, the requestor must certify that it intends, in good faith, to undertake the arrangement or that it will undertake the arrangement if a favorable advisory opinion is issued.[219] Moreover, advisory opinions are only legally binding with regard to the parties that requested the opinion, although the reasoning of the opinion provides guidance on the OIG's likely approach to similar arrangements in the future. Detailed requirements for the submission of an advisory opinion request are set forth in regulations[220] and in other OIG guidance documents.[221]

Issues that the OIG has addressed in its past advisory opinions include the following:

---

accompanying this volume. This bulletin highlighted the agency's concerns about arrangements in which a pharmaceutical manufacturer PAP directly or indirectly subsidizes Part D cost-sharing amounts. The bulletin does not directly address other potential risk areas, including the FCA or PAPs established by PDPs. According to the OIG, such PAPs "present heightened risks under the anti-kickback statute." However, a manufacturer can contribute to a bona fide independent charity PAP that is not affiliated with the manufacturer under certain circumstances. The OIG also describes other types of arrangements for cost-sharing subsidies that may present reduced risk if properly structured. This issue was subsequently addressed in additional guidance, CMS Perspective on Pharmaceutical Company Patient Assistance Programs (Jan. 25, 2006), *available at* http://www.cms.hhs.gov/PrescriptionDrugCovGenIn/Downloads/PAP Info_01.24.06.pdf, and in several advisory opinions described in Section II.A.4., below. PAPs are discussed in more detail in Section II.B. of Chapter 10 (Short and Liner, Controlling Fraud, Waste, and Abuse in the Medicare Part D Program). Previously, the OIG had opined on PAPs that were found to violate the anti-kickback statute in relation to Medicare Part B. *See* OIG Advisory Op. Nos. 02-13 and 03-3.

[217] 42 C.F.R. §1008.5(a).

[218] 42 C.F.R. §1008.5(b).

[219] 42 C.F.R. §1008.38(b).

[220] *See* 42 C.F.R. §§1008.1–1008.40; *see* Appendix G-1 on the disk accompanying this volume.

[221] *See, e.g.*, Preliminary Checklist for Advisory Opinion Requests, *available at* http://oig.hhs.gov/advopn/precheck.htm, and in Appendix G-3 on the disk accompanying this volume.

- advertising;[222]
- ambulance arrangements;[223]
- ambulatory surgery centers (ASCs);[224]
- beneficiary inducement;[225]
- discounts;[226]
- donations and free goods or services;[227]
- employment of an excluded individual;[228]
- gainsharing;[229]
- joint ventures;[230]
- leasing arrangements;[231]
- malpractice insurance;[232]
- managed care arrangements;[233]
- management agreements;[234]
- percentage compensation arrangements;[235]
- physician recruitment;[236]
- physician consultations;[237]
- patient assistance programs;[238]
- swapping;[239]

---

[222]*E.g.,* OIG Advisory Op. Nos. 02-12, 04-03, and 06-16. The OIG advisory opinions are available at http://www.oig.hhs.gov/fraud/advisoryopinions/opinions.html, and summaries and a topical index of anti-kickback advisory opinions are available at Appendix G-2 on the disk accompanying this volume.

[223]*E.g.,* OIG Advisory Op. Nos. 97-6, 98-7, 98-13, 98-14, 00-9, 01-10, 01-11, 01-12, 01-18, 02-2, 02-3, 02-08, 02-15, 03-09, 3-11, 03-14, 04-02, 04-06, 04-10, 04-12, 04-13, 04-14, 05-07, 05-09, 05-10, 06-06, 06-07, 06-11, and 06-12.

[224]*E.g.,* OIG Advisory Op. Nos. 01-17, 01-21, 02-9, 03-02, and 03-05.

[225]*E.g.,* OIG Advisory Op. Nos. 97-4, 98-9, 99-9, 99-11, 00-3, 00-5, 00-7, 00-10, 01-7, 01-11, 01-14, 01-15, 01-18, 02-1, 02-12, 02-14, 03-4, 03-10, 04-04, 06-01, 06-04, 06-08, 06-09, 06-13, 06-20.

[226]*E.g.,* OIG Advisory Op. Nos. 98-2, 98-5, 98-15, 99-2, 99-3, 99-12, 99-13, 01-8, 02-6, 02-7, 02-8, 02-10, and 03-10.

[227]*E.g.,* OIG Advisory Op. Nos. 01-2, 01-05, 01-09, 01-19, 02-11 (academic medical center), 02-12, 02-14, 03-04, 03-06, 03-07, 03-14, 04-04, 04-05, 04-07, 04-16, 04-18, 05-08, 05-11, 06-01, 06-05, 06-20, and 07-01.

[228]*E.g.,* OIG Advisory Op. Nos. 01-16 and 03-01.

[229]*E.g.,* OIG Advisory Op. Nos. 01-1, 05-01, 05-02, 05-03, 05-04, 05-05, 05-06, and 06-22.

[230]*E.g.,* OIG Advisory Op. Nos. 97-5, 98-12, 98-19, 01-17, 01-21, 03-02, 03-05, 03-12, 03-13, 04-17, 05-12, and 06-02.

[231]*E.g.,* OIG Advisory Op. No. 04-08.

[232]*E.g.,* OIG Advisory Op. Nos. 04-11 and 04-19.

[233]*E.g.,* OIG Advisory Op. Nos. 01-13, 01-15, 01-16, 02-12, and 06-15.

[234]*E.g.,* OIG Advisory Op. Nos. 03-08, 06-03, and 06-17.

[235]*E.g.,* OIG Advisory Op. Nos. 98-1, 98-2, 98-4, 98-10, 99-3, 06-02, 06-17; *see* 03-08.

[236]*E.g.,* OIG Advisory Op. No. 01-4.

[237]*E.g.,* OIG Advisory Op. No. 04-09.

[238]*E.g.,* OIG Advisory Op. Nos. 02-01, 02-13, 03-03, 04-15, 06-03, 06-04, 06-08, 06-14, 06-19, and 06-21.

[239]*E.g.,* OIG Advisory Op. Nos. 99-3, 01-8, 02-12, and 04-16.

- waivers of deductibles, copayments, or premiums;[240] and
- warranties.[241]

It should be noted that while there is no "de minimis" exception to the anti-kickback statute, several advisory opinions indicate that the OIG may use its discretion not to impose sanctions on certain arrangements for this reason.[242]

The statutory authority for the OIG to issue advisory opinions expired on August 22, 2000. However, its authority has been indefinitely extended under the Medicare, Medicaid, and SCHIP Benefits Improvement and Protection Act of 2000.[243]

## 5. Other Guidance

Additional guidance documents from the OIG relating to the anti-kickback statute (and other fraud and abuse laws) include Medicare Advisory Bulletins, Medicare Fraud Alerts, informal advisory letters, and management advisories. Such other guidance documents include a Medicare Advisory Bulletin on "Questionable Practices Affecting the Hospice Benefit,"[244] a "National Medicare Fraud Alert on Billing for Services Not Rendered; Upcoding on Billings for Powered Wheelchairs and Delivering Scooters and/or (POVs),"[245] and an OIG Management Advisory Report on "Financial Arrangements Between Hospitals and Hospital-Based Physicians."[246] Other miscellaneous guidance has been issued on the following topics:

- *Malpractice Insurance Subsidies.* In January 2003, the OIG issued a letter addressing a hospital corporation's medical malpractice insurance assistance program subsidizing the malpractice insurance premiums of its staff physicians.[247] Although the letter did not opine on whether the particular proposal would be subject to penalties under the anti-kickback statute, it did note some features of the arrangement that would be considered to be "safeguards."
- *Charges for the Uninsured.* Class action lawsuits were filed against hospitals nationwide alleging that the rates charged, and other measures taken in regard to underinsured or uninsured patients, were illegal based on several legal theories. Most of these cases have been dismissed from

---

[240]*E.g.,* OIG Advisory Op. Nos. 98-5, 99-1, 99-6, 99-7, 00-5, 01-10, 01-11, 01-12, 01-14, 01-15, 01-18, 02-1, 02-7, 02-8, 02-13, 02-15, 02-16, 03-03, 03-09, 03-10, 03-11, 04-01, 04-02, 04-06, 06-07, 06-09, 06-10, and 06-13.

[241]*E.g.,* OIG Advisory Op. Nos. 01-8 and 02-6.

[242]*See, e.g.,* OIG Advisory Op. No. 98-12. The OIG specifically found that there was minimal risk that the return on investment would be a disguised payment for referrals in part because the estimated revenues from Medicare beneficiaries were only 5 percent of the total anticipated revenues of the venture. *See also* OIG Advisory Op. Nos. 00-5 and 00-11.

[243]This statute was enacted by the Omnibus Consolidated and Emergency Supplemental Appropriations Act for Fiscal Year 2001, Pub. L. No. 106-554, 114 Stat. 2763.

[244]Publication of the Medicare Advisory Bulletin on Hospice Benefits, 60 Fed. Reg. 55,721 (Nov. 2, 1995).

[245]HCFA Medicare Fraud Alert 98-02 (June 9, 1998).

[246]OEI-09-89-00330 (Jan. 1991).

[247]Letter from Lewis Morris, Chief Counsel to the Inspector Gen., Dep't of Health & Human Servs. (Jan. 15, 2003), *available at* http://oig.hhs.gov/fraud/docs/alertsandbulletins/MalpracticeProgram.pdf.

federal court. Hearings on this issue, however, were held in Congress, and several cases were filed in state court and resulted in settlement.[248] Moreover, in February 2004, the OIG issued three documents emphasizing a hospital's ability to take various measures, including the provision of discounts or the waiver of copayment amounts, for underinsured or uninsured patients under certain circumstances, without violating the federal fraud and abuse laws. Useful guidance on related topics such as collection efforts, criteria for indigency determinations, and treatment as bad debt are also discussed.[249]

- *Concierge Physician Practices.* In response to the new and increasing creation of "concierge physician practices," an OIG alert was issued on March 31, 2004, warning physicians that charging Medicare beneficiaries more than the Medicare-authorized coinsurance and deductible amounts can potentially lead to a violation of the assignment regulations.[250]

- *Discount Drug Card Programs.* In response to perceived abuses arising in connection with the implementation of the MMA's Discount Drug Card Program, the OIG issued a guidance document on "Education and Outreach Arrangements Between Medicare-Endorsed Discount Drug Card Sponsors and their Network Pharmacies." The OIG indicates that these arrangements should be reviewed carefully because payment arrangements between drug card sponsors and their network pharmacies in connection with education, outreach, and enrollment services may raise concerns under the anti-kickback statute.[251] The OIG also issued regulations implementing new CMPs related to fraud and abuse in connection with the drug discount card program.[252]

- *Physician Investments in Medical Device Manufacturers and Distributors.* In October 2006, the OIG advised that physician investments in device manufacturers, distributors, and group purchasing organizations would be subject to close scrutiny under the fraud and abuse laws. The OIG further indicated that its guidance on physician investments should be consulted by all industry stakeholders in connection with joint venture

---

[248]*See, e.g.*, Tenet Healthcare Cases II Settlement Web site, *available at* http://www. tenetclassaction.com/tes; Sutter Health Uninsured Pricing Cases, No. JCCP 4388 (Cal. Super. Ct. settlement approved Dec. 12, 2006).

[249]*See* U.S. Dep't of Health & Human Servs., Hospital Discounts Offered to Patients Who Cannot Afford to Pay Their Hospital Bills, *available at* http://oig.hhs.gov/fraud/docs/ alertsand bulletins/2004/FA021904hospitaldiscounts.pdf; *see also* U.S. Dep't of Health & Human Servs., Centers for Medicare & Medicaid Servs., Questions on Charges for the Uninsured (Feb. 17, 2004), *available at* http://www.cms.hhs.gov/AcuteInpatientPPS/downloads/FAQ_ Uninsured .pdf; *see also* Letter from Tommy G. Thompson, Secretary of Health & Human Servs., to Richard J. Davidson, President, American Hospital Ass'n, Concerning Charges for the Uninsured (Feb. 19, 2004), *available at* http://www.hhs.gov/news/press/2004pres/20040219.html.

[250]*See* Press Release, Dep't Health & Human Servs., Office of Inspector General, *OIG Alerts Physicians About Added Charges for Covered Services* (Mar. 31, 2004), *available at* http:// oig.hhs.gov/fraud/docs/alertsandbulletins/2004/FA033104AssignViolationI.pdf.

[251]U.S. Dep't of Health & Human Servs., Education and Outreach Arrangements Between Medicare-Endorsed Discount Drug Card Sponsors and Their Network Pharmacies Under the Anti-Kickback Statute (Apr. 8, 2004), *available at* http://oig.hhs.gov/fraud/docs/alertsandbulletins /2004/FA040904.pdf.

[252]OIG Civil Money Penalties Under the Medicare Prescription Drug Discount Card Program, 69 Fed. Reg. 74,451 (Dec. 14, 2004). See the discussion in Section I.C., above.

arrangements. The OIG also confirmed that, if a substantial portion of a joint venture's gross revenues is derived from investor-driven referrals, this would be considered an indicia of a problematic joint venture.[253]

There also have been numerous informal letters issued by the OIG relating to subjects such as the provision of free items or services and discounts. Most of these and other federal government documents related to health care fraud and abuse can be located at or through the OIG's Web site, http://www.oig.hhs.gov/fraud.html. For the reader's convenience, many of these documents are contained in Appendix F on the disk accompanying this volume.

OIG audit reports often indicate topics the OIG intends to investigate further in the future. For example, dozens of audit reports related to the provision of outpatient cardiac rehabilitation services at hospitals across the country were published in 2003 through 2005.[254] During this same period, there were also numerous audits on various issues related to rebates paid to states by manufacturers of pharmaceuticals.[255] The OIG has continued to evaluate a broad array of entities and issues. For example, in 2006–2007, the OIG audited medical centers to determine whether wage data were accurately reported on their cost reports,[256] drug discount card program sponsors to determine their compliance with transitional assistance limits,[257] providers for their compliance

---

[253] *See* U.S. Dep't of Health & Human Servs., *Response to Request for Guidance Regarding Certain Physician Investments in the Medical Device Industries* (Oct. 6, 2006), *available at* http://oig.hhs.gov/fraud/docs/alertsandbulletins/GuidanceMedicalDevice%20(2).pdf.

[254] *See, e.g.,* U.S. Dep't of Health & Human Servs., Review of Medicare Outpatient Cardiac Rehabilitation Provided by Hospitals, Report No. A-05-03-00102 (Aug. 18, 2005), *available at* http://oig.hhs.gov/oas/reports/region5/50300102.htm; U.S. Dep't of Health & Human Servs., Review of Cardiac Rehabilitation Services at Community Memorial Healthcare, Inc., Marysville, Kansas, Report No. A-07-03-00156 (Feb. 4, 2004), *available at* http://oig.hhs.gov/oas/reports/region7/70300156.htm; U.S. Dep't of Health & Human Servs., Review of Cardiac Rehabilitation Services at Spencer Municipal Hospital, Spencer, Iowa, Report No. A-07-03-00158 (Jan. 30, 2004), *available at* http://oig.hhs.gov/oas/reports/region7/70300158.htm; U.S. Dep't of Health & Human Servs., Review of Outpatient Cardiac Rehabilitation Services at the Cooley Dickinson Hospital [Northampton, Massachusetts], Report No. A-01-03-00516 (Dec. 26, 2003), *available at* http://oig.hhs.gov/oas/reports/region1/10300516.htm.

[255] *See, e.g.,* U.S. Dep't of Health & Human Servs., Follow-up Audit of the Medicaid Drug Rebate Program in Colorado, Report No. A-07-05 04048 (Nov. 17, 2005), *available at* http://oig.hhs.gov/oas/reports/region7/70504048.htm; U.S. Dep't of Health & Human Servs., Multistate Review of Medicaid Drug Rebate Programs, Report No. A-06-03-00048 (Jul. 06, 2005), *available at* http://oig.hhs.gov/oas/reports/region6/60300048.htm; U.S. Dep't of Health & Human Servs., Final Region VIII Rollup Report for 6-State Review of Medicaid Drug Rebate Collections, Report No. A-07-04-04030 (Feb. 26, 2004), *available at* http://oig.hhs.gov/oas/reports/region7/70404030.pdf; U.S. Dep't of Health & Human Servs., Results of Our Self-Initiated Audits of Medicaid Drug Rebate Programs Operated by the State Agencies of Arkansas, Louisiana, New Mexico, and Oklahoma, as Well as the Texas State Auditor's Report on the Texas Medicaid Drug Rebate Program, Report No. A-06-03-00043 (Jan. 30, 2004), *available at* http://oig.hhs.gov/oas/reports/region6/ 60300043.htm.

[256] *See, e.g.,* U.S. Dep't of Health & Human Servs., Review of University of California, San Francisco Medical Center's Reported Fiscal Year 2004 Wage Data, Report No. A-09-05-00039 (Sept. 20, 2006), *available at* http://oig.hhs.gov/oas/reports/region9/90500039.pdf.

[257] *See, e.g.,* U.S. Dep't of Health & Human Servs., Report on the Medicare Drug Discount Card Program Sponsor Medco Health Solutions, Report No. A-06-05-00066 (Sept. 25, 2006), *available at* http://oig.hhs.gov/oas/reports/region6/60500066.pdf.

with Part B reimbursement requirements,[258] and hospitals to review potential overpayments for air ambulance services.[259]

## 6. Enforcement

There are some reported decisions in recent years that relate to the anti-kickback statute.[260] However, it is more often the case that anti-kickback allegations are settled without a trial, often under the rubric of FCA allegations.[261] Further, on April 24, 2006, HHS Inspector General Daniel Levinson issued an Open Letter to Health Care Providers[262] announcing a new OIG initiative to promote its Provider Self-Disclosure Protocol[263] to resolve CMP liability for hospital-physician financial arrangements that violate the Stark and anti-kickback laws. Under this initiative, the OIG would allow for lower CMP damage calculations.[264]

## B. The Stark Law

### 1. The Prohibitions

The Stark law, as amended, prohibits physicians from referring Medicare and Medicaid patients to an entity for the furnishing of certain designated health services (DHS) if the physician (or an immediate family member) has a financial relationship with the entity.[265] In addition, the entity generally may not present, or cause to be presented, a claim for payment for services furnished pursuant to a prohibited referral.[266] While the original law, Stark I, pertained solely to clinical laboratory services, Stark II added 10 other categories of DHS, including inpatient and outpatient hospital services, as well as radiology services; radiation therapy services and supplies; physical therapy services; occupational therapy services; DME and supplies; parenteral and enteral

---

[258]*See, e.g.*, U.S. DEP'T OF HEALTH & HUMAN SERVS., *Review of Medicare Part B Services Rendered by a New Jersey Urologist* (A-02-04-01036) (Sept. 15, 2006), *available at* http://www.oig.hhs.gov/oas/reports/region2/20401036A.pdf.

[259]*See, e.g.*, U.S. DEP'T OF HEALTH & HUMAN SERVS., *Review of Medicare Claims for Air Ambulance Services Paid to Allegheny General Hospital* (A-03-04-00014) (June 12, 2006), *available at* http://www.oig.hhs.gov/oas/reports/region3/30400014.pdf.

[260]United States v. Jackson, 220 Fed. Appx. 317 (5th Cir. 2007); United States v. Rogan, 459 F. Supp. 2d 692 (N.D. Ill. 2006); United States *ex rel.* Perales v. St. Margaret's Hosp., 243 F. Supp. 2d 843 (C.D. Ill. 2003); United States *ex rel.* Pogue v. Diabetes Treatment Ctrs. of Am., Inc., 238 F. Supp. 2d 258 (D.D.C. 2002); United States *ex rel.* Obert-Hong v. Advocate Health Care, 211 F. Supp. 2d 1045 (N.D. Ill. 2002).

[261]*See, e.g.*, Press Release, U.S. Dep't of Justice, *Grand Rapids' Metropolitan Hospital & Related Entities to Pay U.S. $6.25 Million to Resolve False Claims Allegations* (Dec. 10, 2003), *available at* http://www.usdoj.gov/opa/pr/2003/December/03_civ_679.htm (the anti-kickback allegations involved compensation and leases to, and purchases of practices from, referring physicians that were not commensurate with fair market value and commercial reasonableness).

[262]Open Letter to Health Care Providers (Apr. 24, 2006), *available at* http://www.oig .hhs.gov/Fraud/openletters.html.

[263]OIG's Provider Self-Disclosure Protocol, 63 Fed. Reg. 58,399 (Oct. 30, 1998).

[264]See a full discussion on the self-disclosure protocol at Section IV.D.1., below.

[265]42 U.S.C. §1395nn(a)(1)(A).

[266]42 U.S.C. §1395nn(a)(1)(B). The term "referral" has a specific meaning in this context and the definition in both the statute and the regulations should be reviewed.

nutrients, equipment, and supplies; prosthetics, orthotics, and prosthetic devices and supplies; home health services; and outpatient prescription drugs.[267]

The Stark law defines a "financial relationship" as an ownership or investment interest in, or a compensation arrangement between, the physician (or an immediate family member) and an entity. In turn, an "ownership or investment interest" is defined to encompass "equity, debt, or other means and includes an interest in an entity that holds an ownership or investment interest in any entity providing the designated health service."[268] A "compensation arrangement" is broadly defined as "any arrangement involving any remuneration between a physician (or an immediate family member of such physician) and an entity . . . other than certain specifically noted kinds of remuneration."[269] Both types of financial relationship can trigger the Stark law whether they are direct or indirect, although the Stark II final regulations have defined indirect ownership and indirect compensation arrangements rather narrowly.[270]

The Stark law is a strict liability statute; unlike the anti-kickback statute, improper intent is not required for a violation. The penalties for violation of the Stark self-referral prohibitions include a range of civil sanctions, such as nonpayment for the relevant services, CMPs, and exclusion from the Medicare and Medicaid programs. There is also a penalty of up to $100,000 for a circumvention scheme.[271]

Final regulations relating to Stark I were issued in 1995.[272] Phase I of the Stark II regulations was finalized in early 2001, and became effective in 2002.[273] Phase II of the Stark II regulations was published and became effective in 2004.[274]

The Phase II regulations provided a great deal of additional guidance and much-needed additional flexibility in a number of respects. This more pragmatic approach was welcomed by providers because enforcement of the Stark statute, both by whistleblowers and the government, began to increase after the Phase II regulations were promulgated.

In summary, the Phase II regulations:[275]

- Revise and/or clarify several key definitional terms, including:
  - "set in advance";
  - "same building";
  - "consultation"; and
  - "referral";
- Clarify the meaning of direct and indirect ownership and affirm that common ownership of an entity does not create an ownership interest by

---

[267]42 U.S.C. §1395nn(h)(6).

[268]42 U.S.C. §1395nn(a).

[269]42 U.S.C. §1395nn(h)(1)(A).

[270]66 Fed. Reg. 856, 958 (Jan. 4, 2001) (codified at 42 C.F.R. §411.354).

[271]42 U.S.C. §1395nn(g).

[272]42 C.F.R. §§411.350 *et seq.*

[273]66 Fed. Reg. 856 (Jan. 4, 2001).

[274]Physicians' Referrals to Health Care Entities With Which They Have Financial Relationships (Phase II), 69 Fed. Reg. 16,054 (Mar. 26, 2004), effective July 26, 2004.

[275]*See generally* Linda Baumann, *Learning to Live with Stark II/Phase II Regulations,* REIMBURSEMENT ADVISOR (June 2004).

one investor in another (although an indirect compensation analysis still must be performed);

- Explain the relationship between the definition and the exception for indirect compensation arrangements and the related "volume or value" and "other business generated" standards;
- Provide several types of additional flexibility for rural arrangements;
- Limit a provider's ability to require referrals;
- Add flexibility to standards in various exceptions by allowing "without cause" termination of contracts under certain conditions;
- Ease the Stark law's reporting requirements to eliminate mandatory annual data submission;
- Create new Stark "safe harbors" with regard to physician compensation and academic medical centers;
- Eliminate the proposed restrictions on productivity bonuses; and
- Modify various designated health services (DHS), including lithotripsy[276] and those that are defined by current procedural terminology (CPT-4) code.

Another important change in Phase II involved the acceptance of the legality of certain common percentage compensation arrangements that previously had been prohibited by the definition of "set in advance" in Phase I.[277]

The Phase III regulations were published on September 5, 2007.[278] In brief, the Phase III regulations significantly curtail a physician's ability to rely on the more flexible indirect compensation analysis developed under the Phase II regulations. Nevertheless, Phase III provides some additional flexibility in certain other exceptions, including those for physician recruitment and retention, personal services arrangements, nonmonetary compensation, compliance training, professional courtesy, and intra-family rural referrals. The fair market value exception is ostensibly extended, but in a manner that will make it more difficult to rely on the exception for payments by a physician (which is one of the easiest Stark exceptions to satisfy). In addition, Phase III provides guidance and various clarifications on a number of other issues including "incident to" services, the exception for academic medical centers, the definition of "rural" areas, and the exceptions for space and equipment rentals.

While waiting for Phase III's release, several post-Phase II modifications to the Stark regulations were implemented in other ways. For example, see (1) the Physician Fee Schedule final rule for calendar year 2006 that, inter alia,

---

[276]In the Phase I regulations, CMS stated that lithotripsy was a DHS. This position was rejected by a federal district court in *American Lithotripsy Society v. Thompson*, 215 F. Supp. 2d 23 (D.D.C. 2002), *appeal dismissed*, 2003 WL 115257 (D.C. Cir. Jan. 10, 2003) (not for publication). In the Phase II preamble, CMS conceded that lithotripsy itself is not a DHS. *See* 69 Fed. Reg. 16,054, 16,106 (Mar. 26, 2004).

[277]Although Phase I largely went into effect on January 4, 2002, implementation of part of the "set in advance" provision was delayed repeatedly through issuance of interim final rules, and ultimately was eliminated in the Phase II regulations.

[278]72 Fed. Reg. 51,011 (Sept. 5, 2007). The 89-page regulation, which is reviewed in the Addendum to Chapter 2 (Crane, Federal Physician Self-Referral Restrictions), was released just before press time and will be addressed more thoroughly in the next Supplement. The Federal Register document is provided as Appendix B-4 on the disk accompanying this volume, and the complete, merged regulation is provided as Appendix B-5.

made nuclear medicine services and supplies a DHS,[279] (2) the new Stark exceptions for electronic prescribing and health records,[280] and (3) the Medicare Part D regulations that revised the Stark law's definition of "outpatient prescription drugs" to include drugs covered under the Part D benefit.[281] Various significant changes to the Stark regulations also are likely to result from the Physician Fee Schedule proposed rule for calendar year 2008 (2008 PFS Proposed Rule).[282] In the 2008 PFS Proposed Rule, CMS requested comments that ultimately could lead to far-reaching changes in the in-office ancillary services exception, and the analysis (and implementation) of indirect compensation arrangements. In addition to changing the Stark law's definition of "entity" so as to broaden the reach of the self-referral prohibitions, the 2008 PFS Proposed Rule also proposed regulatory changes that would prohibit or restrict various common arrangements in the health care industry, e.g., by limiting the use of certain percentage compensation arrangements, prohibiting the use of "per-click" compensation in space and equipment leases, and restricting certain "under arrangements" operations. Among other issues, the 2008 PFS Proposed Rule also sought comments on expanding the exception for obstetrical malpractice insurance subsidies, and on developing an alternative methodology to allow entities to comply with certain Stark exceptions when there has been a technical failure to satisfy a minor procedural criterion in the exception. Because of the importance of the Stark law, and the length and complexity of the regulations, a subsequent chapter has been devoted to these issues.[283] This chapter presents only a brief overview of this subject.

## 2. The Exceptions

Because the Stark law is a strict liability statute, referrals for DHS cannot be made once the statute is implicated, unless the arrangement qualifies for an exception. Some of the statutory exceptions are applicable to ownership arrangements, others are applicable to compensation arrangements, and some apply to both types of financial relationships. Exceptions applicable to ownership arrangements include the following:

- rural providers;
- hospitals in Puerto Rico;
- hospital ownership;[284] and

---

[279]70 Fed. Reg. 70,283 (Nov. 21, 2005). The Phase II regulations originally took the position that nuclear medicine was not a DHS. However, CMS recently reversed this interpretation and added nuclear medicine services and supplies to the DHS categories of "radiology and certain other imaging services" and "radiation therapy services and supplies." *See* Revisions to Payment Policies Under the Physician Fee Schedule for Calendar Year 2006 and Certain Provisions Related to the Competitive Acquisition Program of Outpatient Drugs and Biologicals Under Part B, 70 Fed. Reg. 70,116 (Nov. 21, 2005). As a result, referrals for positron emission tomography (PET) scans and other nuclear medicine procedures triggered the Stark law's prohibitions effective January 1, 2007.

[280]71 Fed. Reg. 45,140 (Aug. 8, 2006), provided as Appendix B-6 on the disk accompanying this volume.

[281]70 Fed. Reg. 4194 (Jan. 28, 2005).

[282]72 Fed. Reg. 38,122 *et seq.* (July 12, 2007).

[283]See Chapter 2 (Crane, Federal Physician Self-Referral Restrictions).

[284]42 U.S.C. §1395nn(d).

- ownership of or investment in publicly traded securities and mutual funds.[285]

Statutory exceptions applicable to compensation arrangements include those related to:

- office space or equipment rentals;
- bona fide employment relationships;
- personal service arrangements;
- remuneration unrelated to the provisions of DHS;
- physician recruitment;
- isolated transactions;
- certain group practice arrangements with a hospital; and
- payments by physicians.[286]

The statutory exceptions for both ownership and compensation arrangements include the exceptions for:

- physicians' services;
- in-office ancillary services; and
- prepaid plans.[287]

In addition, several new exceptions were published in 2001 as part of the Phase I regulations. The Phase I exceptions, applicable to both ownership and compensation relationships, are:

- clinical laboratory services furnished in an ASC, end-stage renal disease (ESRD) facility, or by a hospice;
- academic medical centers;
- implants in an ASC;
- Erythropoietin and other dialysis-related outpatient prescription drugs furnished in or by an ESRD facility;
- preventive screening tests, immunizations, and vaccines; and
- eyeglasses and contact lenses following cataract surgery.[288]

The Phase I compensation exceptions are:

- nonmonetary compensation up to $300;[289]
- fair market value compensation;[290]
- medical staff incidental benefits;[291]
- risk-sharing arrangements;[292]

---

[285]42 U.S.C. §1395nn(c).

[286]42 U.S.C. §1395nn(e).

[287]42 U.S.C. §1395nn(b). The exception for in-office ancillary services is very commonly used but has numerous complex requirements. See Chapter 2, Section VIII.B. (Crane, Federal Physician Self-Referral Restrictions) for additional information.

[288]66 Fed. Reg. 856, 959 (Jan. 4, 2001) (codified at 42 C.F.R. §411.355).

[289]*Id.* at 961 (codified at 42 C.F.R. §411.357).

[290]*Id.*

[291]*Id.* at 962 (codified at 42 C.F.R. §411.357).

[292]*Id.*

- compliance training;[293] and
- indirect compensation arrangements.[294]

A Phase I general exception to the statutory prohibition allows payment to certain entities for DHS referrals that would otherwise implicate the Stark law, if the entity did not have actual knowledge of, and did not act in reckless disregard or deliberate ignorance of, the identity of the physician who made the DHS referral, and the claim otherwise complies with all applicable federal laws, rules, and regulations.[295]

In some of the pre-Phase II decisions applying the Stark law, federal district courts in Michigan and Illinois provided guidance or discussed the application of the "fair market value" requirement contained in many of the exceptions to the Stark law,[296] as well as the physician recruitment exception.[297]

Phase II interprets the Stark statutory exceptions that were not previously addressed and revises some exceptions in response to comments received on Phase I. Some of the more significant revisions/clarifications relate to the exceptions for:

- Ownership in publicly traded securities;
- In-office ancillary services;
- Academic medical centers;
- Hospital ownership;
- Physician recruitment;[298]
- Personal services;
- Space and equipment leases;
- Risk sharing arrangements;
- Isolated transactions;
- Payments made by a physician;
- Remuneration unrelated to the provision of DHS;
- Compliance training;
- Nonmonetary compensation up to $300 and medical staff incidental benefits; and
- Erythropoietin (EPO) and other dialysis-related drugs furnished in or by an ESRD facility.

In addition, Phase II creates several new exceptions to protect certain practices, including those related to:

---

[293]*Id.*

[294]*Id.*

[295]*Id.* at 958 (codified at 42 C.F.R. §411.353).

[296]*See* United States *ex rel.* Goodstein v. McLaren Reg'l Med. Ctr., 202 F. Supp. 2d 671 (E.D. Mich. 2002).

[297]*See* United States *ex rel.* Obert-Hong v. Advocate Health Care, 211 F. Supp. 2d 1045 (N.D. Ill. 2002).

[298]This exception's applicability to arrangements that predate the effective date of the Phase II regulations was confirmed in an FAQ on the CMS Web site. *See* Answer ID #3163, *available at* http://questions.cms.hhs.gov.

- Arrangements involving temporary noncompliance (a general exception);
- Intra-family referrals in rural areas (applicable to both ownership compensation arrangements);
- Retention payments in underserved areas (compensation exception);
- Professional courtesy (compensation exception);
- Charitable donations by a physician (compensation exception);
- Community-wide information systems (compensation exception);
- Referral services (compensation exception); and
- Obstetrical malpractice insurance subsidies (compensation exception).

In August 2006, CMS finalized its exception for certain nonmonetary remuneration related to electronic prescribing technology and electronic health records technology.[299]

Each exception has a number of very specific criteria that must be met, including the requirement in numerous exceptions that compensation be set in advance, be consistent with fair market value,[300] and not be determined in a manner that takes into account the volume or value of any referrals or other business generated between the parties. However, unlike the requirement in several anti-kickback safe harbors, aggregate compensation need not be set in advance.

The preambles to both the Stark II regulations and the anti-kickback safe harbors emphasize that the two statutes overlap in areas but do not necessarily have the same requirements. At the present time, several of the criteria for protection under one statute seem inconsistent with the requirements under the other (e.g., the physician recruitment safe harbor and Stark exception). On the other hand, there are a number of areas of convergence (e.g., where a Stark exception requires compliance with the anti-kickback statute,[301] where the anti-kickback safe harbor incorporates requirements from the Stark law,[302] or where a Stark law exception replicates an anti-kickback safe harbor[303]). Many of the other laws and regulations impacting physicians are discussed in a later chapter.[304]

### 3. Advisory Opinions

The Stark law and its implementing regulations are extremely complex. Theoretically, some additional guidance is available from CMS.[305] Advisory

---

[299]Medicare Program; Physicians' Referrals to Health Care Entities With Which They Have Financial Relationships; Exceptions for Certain Electronic Prescribing and Electronic Health Records Arrangements; Final Rule, 71 Fed. Reg. 45,140 (Aug. 8, 2006), *available at* http://www.cms.hhs.gov/PhysicianSelfReferral/Downloads/CMS-1303-F.pdf.

[300]"Fair market value" is defined in the Stark law, 42 U.S.C. §1395nn(h)(3), and in the Phase I regulations, 42 C.F.R. §411.351.

[301]*E.g.*, 66 Fed. Reg. 856, 959 (Jan. 4, 2001) (codified at 42 C.F.R. §§411.355(e), (g)); *id.* at 961–962 (codified at 42 C.F.R. §§411.357(k), (l), (m), (n), and (p)).

[302]*E.g.*, 42 C.F.R. §1001.952(p).

[303]42 C.F.R. §§ 411.357(q), (r).

[304]See Chapter 5 (Barry, Legal Issues Surrounding Hospital and Physician Relationships).

[305]*See, e.g.*, CMS advisory opinions relating to physician referrals, 42 C.F.R. §411.370; procedure for submitting a request, 42 C.F.R. §411.372; certification, 42 C.F.R. §411.373; fees for the cost of advisory opinions, 42 C.F.R. §411.375; expert opinions from outside sources, 42 C.F.R. §411.377. See Appendix G-4 on the disk accompanying this volume for these and other regulations applicable to advisory opinions under the Stark law.

opinions regarding whether a business arrangement constitutes a "financial relationship" as defined in the Stark law and whether an exception applies may be submitted to CMS pursuant to 42 C.F.R. §411.370 *et seq.* As of August 2007, CMS had issued only four advisory opinions not related to specialty hospitals.[306]

No Stark law advisory opinions were issued from November 1998 until June 2004. However, in implementing MMA provisions imposing a temporary moratorium on physician ownership of certain new specialty hospitals, CMS suggested that specialty hospitals trying to determine whether they were subject to the moratorium should submit advisory opinion requests.[307] Accordingly, since June 2004, CMS has issued fifteen advisory opinions addressing whether a particular hospital was subject to the specialty hospital moratorium described more fully in Section II.B.4.,[308] below.

In August 2005, CMS issued its first Stark law advisory opinion since 1998 (other than advisory opinions on specialty hospitals). In Advisory Opinion No. CMS-AO-2005-08-01, CMS concluded that the stock held by physician-stockholders in a nonprofit, tax-exempt corporation operating a large group medical practice did not constitute an ownership or investment interest for purposes of the Stark law.[309] In November 2006, in Advisory Opinion No. CMS-AO-2006-01, CMS concluded that a proposed arrangement in which a hospital and a physician practice would jointly use financial incentives to recruit a physician would meet the physician recruitment exception. The specific question involved whether a physician could relocate a practice served by the hospital if the physician spent 10 to 20 percent of his or her time practicing medicine outside of the geographic area served by the hospital. CMS noted that the physician recruitment exception did not require the recruited physician to spent 100 percent of his or her time serving patients in the hospital's geographic area. However, CMS cautioned that a different conclusion could be reached if the recruited physician spent substantially more time outside of the hospital's geographic area.[310]

It is worth noting that a number of the new provisions in the Phase III regulations include a requirement that the parties obtain a CMS advisory opinion to qualify for certain exceptions.[311] In the past, such exceptions often have been difficult and/or time consuming to obtain.

---

[306]CMS Advisory Op. No. 98-001 discusses a proposed ambulatory surgical center. CMS Advisory Op. No. 98-002 addresses whether the partners and physician employees of a proposed partnership may refer patients for eyeglass prescriptions under the in-office ancillary services exception.

[307]*See* Press Release, CMS, *CMS Issues Guidance for Exceptions to Specialty Hospital Moratorium* (Mar. 19, 2004), *available at* http://www.cms.hhs.gov/apps/media/press/release .asp?Counter=982.

[308]*See* http://www.cms.hhs.gov/PhysicianSelfReferral/07_advisory_opinions.asp#TopOf Page.

[309]*See* CMS Advisory Op. No. CMS-AO-2005-08-01, *available at* http://www.cms .hhs.gov/PhysicianSelfReferral/Downloads/CMS-AO-2005-08-01.pdf.

[310]*See* CMS Advisory Op. No. CMS-AO-2006-01, *available at* http://www.cms.hhs.gov/ PhysicianSelfReferral/Downloads/CMS-AO-2006-01.pdf.

[311]72 Fed. Reg. 51,011 (Sept. 5, 2007).

## 4. Specialty Hospitals

The MMA modified the Stark law by providing that for an 18-month period beginning on December 8, 2003, a provider would not qualify for the Stark law's rural provider or "whole hospital" exceptions if it was a "specialty hospital." The MMA restrictions were implemented in the Phase II regulations, which defined a specialty hospital as a hospital that is primarily or exclusively engaged in the care and treatment of patients: (i) with a cardiac condition; (ii) with an orthopedic condition; (iii) receiving a surgical procedure; or (iv) receiving any other specialized category of services designated by the Secretary of HHS.[312] The definition of "specialty hospital" did not include a hospital in operation before or "under development" on November 18, 2003, as long as the hospital has not increased the number of physician investors, changed the categories of specialty services provided, or increased the number of beds on the hospital's main campus by more than 50 percent of the number of beds as of November 19, 2003, or by five beds, whichever is greater.

Subsequently, the MMA specialty hospital moratorium expired on June 8, 2005, and Congress did not enact further legislation on this issue. However, CMS announced the next day that it would take six months (through January 2006) to review its procedures for enrolling specialty hospitals in the Medicare program and to reform Medicare payments that may provide specialty hospitals with an unfair advantage over other providers. During the review period, CMS instructed its regional offices not to issue new specialty hospital provider agreements or authorize an initial survey for a new specialty hospital. Medicare fiscal intermediaries were instructed not to process new provider enrollment applications for specialty hospitals until further notice, with certain limited exceptions.[313]

In February 2006, the Deficit Reduction Act (DRA)[314] extended the CMS suspension of specialty hospital enrollment in Medicare until August 8, 2006, when CMS' submission of its final report on a Strategic Plan Regarding Physician Investment in Specialty Hospitals caused the moratorium to lapse.[315]

## 5. Enforcement

Few Stark law decisions have been issued, but in September 2006 the United States brought an action against Peter Rogan, owner and CEO of Edgewater Medical Center, for violating the FCA individually and in conspiracy with others. The court found that Rogan had paid referring physicians, through a variety of loans and contracts (e.g., for medical services, teaching, recruiting physicians, and medical director services) above fair market value for

---

[312]No additional categories of specialty hospital were specified in Phase II and the MMA's legislative history stated that certain types of hospitals, such as long-term acute care, rehabilitation, psychiatric, cancer, and children's hospitals, were not "specialty" hospitals for these purposes. Medicare Prescription Drug, Improvement, and Modernization Act of 2003, CONF. REP. No. 108-391 to H.R. 1 (Nov. 21, 2003), at 658.

[313]*Id.*

[314]Deficit Reduction Act of 2005, Pub. L. No. 109-171, 120 Stat. 4 (2006).

[315]*Id.* at §5006; CMS, FINAL REPORT TO CONGRESS IMPLEMENTING THE DRA PROVISIONS AFFECTING SPECIALTY HOSPITALS (Aug. 8, 2006), *available at* http://www.cms.hhs.gov/PhysicianSelfReferral/06a_DRA_Reports.asp.

the services furnished. The court held that Rogan knowingly violated the Stark law and the anti-kickback statute and knowingly submitted false claims when he certified Edgewater's cost reports as Edgewater's CEO. The court ordered Rogan to pay $64.2 million.[316]

There have been a number of alleged Stark law violations that have resulted in settlements in the context of FCA litigation. For example, Tenet Healthcare Corporation agreed in 2004 to pay the United States $22.5 million to resolve allegations that one of its facilities improperly billed Medicare for referrals provided by doctors with whom the hospital had prohibited financial arrangements.[317]

In May 2006, the Inspector General announced its settlement and five-year CIA with Lincare Holdings, Inc., and its subsidiary Lincare, Inc., for paying illegal kickbacks and for violating the Stark law.[318] Specifically, the OIG alleged that Lincare violated the Stark law by accepting referrals from parties pursuant to unlawful consulting and medical director agreements. In addition, the government alleged that Lincare had furnished referring physicians with sports and entertainment tickets, gift certificates, rounds of golf, golf equipment, fishing trips, meals, advertising expenses, office equipment, and medical equipment. To date, the $10 million settlement constitutes the largest CMP award imposed by the OIG.

In October 2005, the OIG settled with Erlanger Medical Center and the Erlanger Health System for alleged violations of the Stark law, the anti-kickback statute, and federal and state false claims acts. Erlanger entered into a five-year CIA[319] and paid a total of $40 million ($37 million to the United States and $3 million to the State of Tennessee).[320] Specifically, the government alleged that Erlanger violated the Stark and anti-kickback statutes by providing direct and indirect remuneration to physician practices through the formation of a faculty practice plan and through medical director contracts, recruiting agreements, joint venture agreements, and leases with several large physician groups practicing in the area.[321]

In May 2005, the OIG entered a settlement agreement with St. Joseph's Mercy-Oakland (St. Joseph) for $4 million based on self-disclosed conduct involving Stark law and anti-kickback violations. The settlement was based on allegations that St. Joseph had improper financial arrangements with numerous

---

[316]United States v. Rogan, 459 F. Supp. 2d 692 (N.D. Ill. 2006).

[317]Press Release, U.S. Dep't of Justice, *Tenet Healthcare to Pay U.S. $22.5 Million for Improperly Billing Medicare* (Mar. 24, 2004), *available at* http://www.usdoj.gov/opa/pr/2004/March/04_civ_183.htm; *see also* HHS OIG CMP settlements related to physician self-referral, *available at* http://oig.hhs.gov/fraud/enforcement/administrative/cmp/cmpitems.html#3.

[318]*See* Press Release, HHS, OIG, *OIG Settles Largest Ever Civil Monetary Penalty Case*, *available at* http://oig.hhs.gov/publications/docs/press/2006/Lincare051506.pdf.

[319]Corporate Integrity Agreement Between the OIG and Chattanooga-Hamilton County Hospital Authority D/B/A Erlanger Medical Center and Erlanger Health System (Oct. 24, 2005), *available at* http://oig.hhs.gov/fraud/cia/agreements/chattanooga_hamilton_county_hospital_10242005.pdf.

[320]Richard Simms, *Erlanger to Pay $40 Million Fine* (Oct. 24, 2005), *available at* http://www.newschannel9.com/engine.pl?station=wtvc&id=2418&template=breakout_story1.shtml.

[321]Erlanger Settlement Agreement with the State of Tennessee, *available at* http://www.erlanger.org/media/Current_Press_Releases/settlement/settlement.htm.

physicians and group practices involving office management, equipment, loans, income guarantees, and leases.[322]

In December 2002, Rapid City Regional Hospital settled with the United States for $6 million and entered a five-year CIA with the OIG.[323] The Justice Department claimed that the hospital had violated the Stark law by billing Medicare for referrals from a physician practice that had an improper financial relationship with the hospital.[324] In addition, the government claimed that the physician practice had violated the federal FCA by using the wrong billing code for office visits.

More Stark law settlements became likely after Inspector General Levinson issued an April 24, 2006, Open Letter to Health Care Providers (Open Letter) that announced a new OIG initiative to promote its Provider Self-Disclosure Protocol[325] to resolve CMP liability for hospital-physician financial arrangements that violate both the Stark and anti-kickback laws. According to the Open Letter, the OIG would consider using a lower CMP damage calculation methodology in these cases.[326]

## C. False Claims Statutes

### 1. The False Claims Act

There are several federal statutes that impose criminal or civil penalties for the submission of false claims to the government or others. These statutes can create substantial exposure for health care providers, suppliers, and others involved in the industry. Perhaps the most well-known of these federal laws is the civil FCA.[327] In recent years, particularly after the 1986 amendments to the statute, government enforcement actions have increased dramatically. Similarly, lawsuits brought by private plaintiffs, known as "relators" or "whistleblowers," under the *qui tam* provisions of the FCA have proliferated steadily. For example, in 1987, 33 *qui tam* cases were brought resulting in $355,000 in recoveries. In 1999, 483 *qui tam* suits led to $458 million in recoveries.[328] In 2006, the DOJ announced that *qui tam* suits across all industries had brought in $1.3 billion in recoveries during FY2006 alone.[329] The reason for this increase is

---

[322]*See* HHS OIG Web site, Fraud Prevention and Detection Enforcement Actions, *available at* http://oig.hhs.gov/fraud/enforcement/administrative/cmp/cmpitems.html.

[323]Corporate Integrity Agreement Between the OIG and Rapid City Regional Hospital (Dec. 18, 2002), *available at* http://oig.hhs.gov/fraud/cia/agreements/rapid_city_regional_hospital_1202.pdf.

[324]Press Release, U.S. Dep't of Justice, *Justice Department Announces Settlements with South Dakota Hospital and Doctors for $6,525,000* (Dec. 20, 2002), *available at* http://www.usdoj.gov/opa/pr/2002/December/02_civ_739.htm.

[325]OIG's Provider Self-Disclosure Protocol, 63 Fed. Reg. 58,399 (Oct. 30, 1998).

[326]For a full discussion on the Open Letter, see Section IV.D.3., below.

[327]31 U.S.C. §§ 3729–3733.

[328]Marc S. Raspanti, *Qui Tam Practice and Procedure* 6–7 (2000), presented at American Health Lawyers Association Annual Meeting, *available at* http://www.ahla.org/gsms/gsm_00_ann.pdf.

[329]Press Release, U.S. Dep't of Justice, *Justice Department Recovers Record $3.1 Billion in Fraud and False Claims in Fiscal Year 2006* (Nov. 21, 2006), *available at* http://www.usdoj.gov/opa/pr/2006/November/06_civ_783.html.

readily apparent because those who bring a successful case under the FCA are entitled to a percentage of the recovery, and thus may themselves be awarded millions of dollars. As a result, the number of FCA cases is likely to continue to increase in the future.

Due to the frequency with which the FCA is invoked and the magnitude of the recoveries that often result, an entire chapter of this book is devoted to it.[330] Consequently, this chapter will provide a brief summary of this statute, as well as some of the other laws prohibiting false claims.

The FCA is a Civil War–era statute originally aimed at corrupt military contractors. Among other acts, the FCA prohibits knowingly submitting, or causing to be submitted, false or fraudulent claims for payment, or knowingly making, using, or causing to be made or used, false records or statements to conceal, avoid, or decrease an obligation to pay or transmit money or property to the government.[331]

Because the FCA is not a criminal statute, it offers the government a more favorable burden of proof (i.e., the civil standard of "preponderance of the evidence" rather than the criminal standard of "beyond a reasonable doubt"). The statute requires specific intent, that is, the defendant must have acted knowingly, or in deliberate ignorance, or with "reckless disregard" for the truth or falsity of the submission. However, the government is not required to prove a specific intent to defraud.[332]

The penalties under the FCA are potentially quite large. The law provides for treble damages, plus an additional penalty of $5,500 to $11,000 for each "false claim" filed.[333] The statute of limitations allows false claims actions to be brought within 6 years after the date of the violation, or within 3 years after the date when material facts are or should have been known by the government, but in no event later than 10 years after the date the violation was committed.[334]

The FCA has been used by the OIG, working with the DOJ, to launch several nationwide projects to recover alleged overpayments (plus penalties and interest) incurred in connection with specific types of improper claims. The Physicians at Teaching Hospitals (PATH) initiative involved reimbursement to physicians at teaching hospitals and focused on compliance with Medicare rules concerning payment for physician services provided by residents and teaching physicians. This initiative was premised on the requirement under Medicare Part B that a teaching physician can receive a separate payment for a service rendered to a patient only if he or she personally provided the service or was present when the resident furnished the care. If the resident alone performed the service, the government pays through Medicare Part A's graduate medical education and indirect medical education programs. According to the govern-

---

[330]See Chapter 3 (Salcido, The False Claims Act in Health Care Fraud Prosecutions: Application of the Substantive, *Qui Tam*, and Voluntary Disclosure Provisions).

[331]*See* 31 U.S.C. §3729(a).

[332]31 U.S.C. §3729(b).

[333]The penalties under the FCA were originally $5,000 to $10,000 per claim but were increased pursuant to the 1996 Debt Collection Improvement Act, Pub. L. No. 104-134, 110 Stat. 1321 (1996). *See* 64 Fed. Reg. 47,099 (Aug. 30, 1999). These increased penalties apply to violations occurring after September 29, 1999.

[334]31 U.S.C. §3731(b).

ment, if the teaching physician submits a claim for reimbursement for the same service, the physician is submitting a duplicate claim that may lead to liability under the FCA. Under the PATH initiative, as of September 2000, seven institutions had settled with the government for $76 million, and two other institutions were allowed to simply return overpayments to the appropriate carrier. No problems were found after review at four other institutions.[335] The OIG has stated that the PATH initiative is ongoing but will be limited to those institutions that received clear guidance before December 30, 1992, from their Part B carrier as to the applicable Medicare reimbursement requirements. Nevertheless, PATH-type settlements continue to occur.[336]

The "72-Hour Rule" Project involved payments made to hospitals for certain non-physician services provided to patients within 72 hours of their admission to the hospital.[337] Reimbursement for these services is included in Medicare's Prospective Payment System (PPS) payment to the hospital, and billing separately for them can result in a duplicate payment. This project was coordinated by the U.S. Attorney's Office for the Middle District of Pennsylvania and resulted in 2,799 settlements as of March 31, 2001.[338]

The Hospital Outpatient Laboratory Project began in Ohio and related to claims submitted for hematology and automated blood chemistry tests by hospital outpatient labs. Under Medicare guidelines, such labs are required to bill certain groups of tests together using a bundled code. (The payment for the panel is substantially less than payment for each test individually.) The project also involved lab billing for certain tests that were not medically necessary. The Ohio Hospital Association settled a major case related to the Hospital Outpatient Laboratory national project in *Ohio Hospital Association v. Thompson.*[339]

The PPS Patient Transfer Project involved payments to hospitals when patients are transferred between two PPS hospitals. Medicare regulations provide that the receiving hospital may receive payment based on the DRGs while the transferring hospital is to receive a per diem amount based on the patient's length of stay as well as the DRG.

Another national project involved pneumonia upcoding. Under Medicare regulations, hospital stays are reimbursed on the basis of the DRGs assigned, which in turn result from the diagnosis and procedure codes assigned by the hospital. Most pneumonia cases are grouped into one of four DRGs, and one of these DRGs pays substantially more than the others. The OIG, believing that

---

[335]Six investigations that involved reimbursement for teaching physicians that were not part of the PATH national initiative have also resulted in FCA settlements and CIAs. U.S. DEP'T OF HEALTH & HUMAN SERVS., OFFICE OF INSPECTOR GEN., SEMIANNUAL REPORT OCT. 1, 1999– MAR. 30, 2000 (June 19, 2000), at 9, *available at* http://oig.hhs.gov/semann/00fsemi.pdf.

[336]*Johns Hopkins University Will Pay $800,000 to Resolve Medicare Fraud Case,* OIG NEWS (Feb. 14, 2003), *available at* http://oig.hhs.gov/publications/docs/press/2003/021403release.pdf.

[337]The Medicare statute stipulates that certain outpatient services performed by a hospital or an entity wholly owned or operated by the hospital, within 72 hours of an inpatient admission, are reimbursed as part of the diagnosis related groups (DRGs) and may not be separately billed. 42 U.S.C. §1385ww(a)(4).

[338]U.S. DEP'T OF HEALTH & HUMAN SERVS., OFFICE OF INSPECTOR GEN., SEMIANNUAL REPORT OCTOBER 1, 2000–MARCH 31, 2001, *available at* http://www.dhhs.gov/progorg/oig/semann/index.htm.

[339]No. 1:96 CV 2165 (N.D. Ohio settlement agreement Aug. 6, 2001).

certain hospitals improperly assigned the higher paying DRG to a number of pneumonia cases, has been investigating pneumonia coding at hospitals for the past several years.[340]

The manner in which these national initiatives were conducted caused considerable concern in the health care industry as well as in Congress, and there were allegations that providers were being penalized unfairly and threatened with liability under the FCA for making inadvertent mistakes or billing errors. Various lawsuits were brought challenging these national projects, but generally were dismissed on procedural grounds (e.g., as not ripe for review).[341] Efforts to amend the FCA in 1997–1998 did not succeed, but the OIG[342] and the DOJ[343] issued guidelines on the use of the FCA in civil health care matters to help defuse the situation.

The DOJ implemented new procedures with regard to national health care fraud initiatives in the "Holder memorandum," which directs DOJ attorneys not to allege violations of the FCA in connection with a national initiative or otherwise unless there is sufficient legal and factual predicate for alleging that the provider submitted false claims to the government *and* such false claims (or false statements) were submitted with "knowledge" of their falsity as defined in the FCA.[344] When determining whether false claims exist, DOJ attorneys are to do the following:

- examine relevant statutory and regulatory provisions and interpretive guidance;
- verify the data and other evidence; and
- conduct necessary investigative steps.[345]

In order to determine whether the provider "knowingly" submitted false claims, DOJ attorneys are directed to consider numerous factors, including:

- whether the provider had actual or constructive notice of the rule or policy on which the case is based;
- whether it is reasonable to conclude, under the circumstances, that the provider understood the rule or policy;[346]

---

[340]For example, in February 2006, a central Illinois hospital agreed to a $300,000 settlement and a three-year CIA to settle FCA allegations that it used improper billing codes to receive Medicare reimbursement for patients with pneumonia, sepsis, and renal failure. *See Illinois Hospital Agrees to Pay $300,000,* 12 HEALTH CARE DAILY REP. (BNA) (Feb. 7, 2007).

[341]*See, e.g.,* Greater N.Y. Hosp. Ass'n v. United States, No. 98 Civ. 2741 (RLC), 1999 WL 1021561 (S.D.N.Y. Nov. 9, 1999); Association of Am. Med. Colls. v. United States, 34 F. Supp. 2d 1187 (C.D. Cal. 1998); New Jersey Hosp. Ass'n v. United States, 23 F. Supp. 2d 497 (D.N.J. 1998). *But see* Ohio Hosp. Ass'n v. Shalala, 978 F. Supp. 735 (N.D. Ohio 1997), *aff'd in part, rev'd in part,* 201 F.3d 418 (6th Cir. 1999), *cert. denied,* 531 U.S. 1071 (2001). This case was ultimately settled.

[342]Memorandum from June Gibbs Brown to Deputy Inspector General for Investigations *re* National Project Protocols—Best Practice Guidelines (June 3, 1998).

[343]Memorandum from Eric H. Holder, Jr., to All U.S. Attorneys *re* Guidance on the Use of the False Claims Act in Civil Health Care Matters (June 3, 1998) [hereinafter Holder memorandum]; for text of the Holder memorandum, see Appendix C-2 on the disk accompanying this volume.

[344]Holder memorandum at 2.

[345]*Id.*

[346]This is a particularly important consideration in light of the well-known ambiguity of numerous Medicare regulations.

- the pervasiveness and magnitude of the false claims (e.g., do they support an inference that they resulted from deliberate ignorance or intentional or reckless conduct?);
- compliance measures implemented by the provider including the existence of and adherence to a compliance program and steps taken to comply with the particular billing rules at issue;
- past remedial efforts;
- prior guidance requested from or provided by the program agency (e.g., did the provider furnish all material information when requesting guidance and did it reasonably rely on the guidance provided?); and
- whether the provider had prior notice of similar billing concerns.[347]

The Holder memorandum also directs DOJ attorneys to use "contact letters" to initiate a discussion of the issues before making a demand for payment. Moreover, in determining how to respond to a particular situation, they are to consider issues such as the provider's ability to pay, the impact of an enforcement action on the community (e.g., access to adequate health care), minimizing burdens imposed on providers during the investigation (which might entail accepting results from a sample audit rather than insisting on a complete audit), and provider cooperation.[348]

The OIG subsequently has issued numerous letters offering assurances that health care providers, practitioners, and suppliers will not be subject to the FCA (or the CMP prohibitions) for billing errors, honest mistakes, or negligence. According to these letters, law enforcement efforts are to focus on improper claims made intentionally, with reckless disregard for the truth or with deliberate ignorance of the truth. Moreover, "in almost all cases, reckless disregard or intentional filing of false claims is proved by establishing a pattern of conduct."[349] Nevertheless, despite the complexity of Medicare laws and regulations, the lack of clear written guidance on many issues, and the frequent inability to obtain oral guidance from the government, it can be very difficult, as a practical matter, to convince the government that certain practices did result from inadvertence or honest mistake. Toward this end, if a provider is able to obtain oral guidance from the government or one of its agents, it is essential that such advice be documented. While some government employees or agents may be reluctant to provide "official" advice, a provider may be able to obtain a written response if a written inquiry is submitted. While such a response does not have the force of law, it can help document the provider's (or other entity's) intention to comply with the law, thus undercutting any claim of improper intent in violation of the FCA or other statutes with similar scienter requirements.

After publication of the Holder memorandum, the national project model fell from favor, although government investigations and settlements continue to be reported in connection with various "national project" topics including pneumonia upcoding and reimbursement to PATH. Nevertheless, even without

---

[347]Holder memorandum at 3–4.

[348]*Id.* at 5–6.

[349]Letters from June Gibbs Brown, Inspector General, to Marilou King, Executive Vice President, American Health Lawyers Ass'n, and to William Coughlan, President and Chief Executive Officer, National Ass'n for Medical Equipment Services (Aug. 5, 1998).

the national project template, FCA investigations, prosecutions, and settlements continue on a wide range of issues ranging from cases involving billing for items or services not rendered to quality of care to the waiver of coinsurance or deductibles.

There are ongoing efforts to use the FCA in connection with violations of other laws such as the anti-kickback statute or the Stark law.[350] Although *United States ex rel. Goodstein v. McLaren Regional Medical Center*[351] was dismissed on other grounds, various other parties have sought to use the Stark law as the basis for an FCA violation,[352] at times resulting in a judgment against the defendant,[353] other times leading to substantial settlements.[354]

In addition, courts continue to address in more traditional FCA cases, "implied certification" and other "quality of care" theories put forth by DOJ and *qui tam* relators in health care FCA cases. Many of these certification theories seek to impose FCA liability where payment is sought for goods or services that were delivered or rendered in a manner that violated applicable statutes or regulations notwithstanding an implicit or general certification to the contrary. Courts have begun to grapple with these theories and generally have allowed for FCA liability only in situations where the alleged regulatory violation has a specific and direct impact on the government's reimbursement decision.[355] In the past the majority of quality of care cases arose in the nursing home context.[356] However, the first case charging a hospital under the FCA with quality of care violations (i.e., the alleged improper use of physical and chemical restraints in violation of Medicare's conditions of participation) was settled in July 2005.[357]

---

[350]*See, e.g.,* United States v. Solinger, 457 F. Supp. 2d 743 (W.D. Ky. 2006); Klaczak v. Consolidated Med. Transport, 458 F. Supp. 2d 622 (N.D. Ill. 2006); United States v. McLaren Reg'l Med. Ctr. (dismissed on other grounds); United States *ex rel.* Pogue v. American Healthcorp., 914 F. Supp. 1507 (M.D. Tenn. 1996); United States *ex rel.* Thompson v. Columbia/ HCA Healthcare Corp., 938 F. Supp. 399 (S.D. Tex. 1996), *aff'd in part, vacated in part,* 125 F.3d 899 (5th Cir. 1997).

[351]202 F. Supp. 2d 671 (E.D. Mich. 2002).

[352]*See, e.g.,* United States v. Solinger, 457 F. Supp. 2d 743 (W.D. Ky. 2006); United States *ex rel.* Schmidt v. Zimmer, Inc., 386 F.3d 235 (3d Cir. 2004); United States *ex rel.* Perales v. St. Margaret's Hosp., 243 F. Supp. 2d 843 (C.D. Ill. 2003); United States *ex rel.* Pogue v. Diabetes Treatment Ctrs. of Am., Inc., 238 F. Supp. 2d 258 (D.D.C. 2002).

[353]United States v. Rogan, 459 F. Supp. 2d 692 (N.D. Ill. 2006).

[354]*See, e.g.,* Press Release, United States Attorney for the Northern District of Georgia, *Northside Hospital and Doctors' Groups Pay $6.37 Million to U.S. to Settle False Claims Act Suit* (Oct. 20, 2006), *available at* http://www.usdoj.gov/usao/gan/press/2006/10-20-06b.pdf.

[355]*See, e.g.,* United States *ex rel.* Cooper v. Gentiva Health Servs., No. 01-508, 2003 WL 22495607 (W.D. Pa. Nov. 4, 2003) (not for publication) (setting forth federal court treatment of implied certification and other quality of care issues); United States *ex rel.* Swan v. Covenant Care, Inc., 279 F. Supp. 2d 1212 (E.D. Cal. 2002) (rejecting implied certification theory in nursing home setting because regulations that were purportedly violated were conditions of participation, not conditions of payment). This is a very complex topic. For more detail on implied certification in the FCA context, *see* Chapter 3 (Salcido, The False Claims Act in Health Care Prosecutions: Application of the Substantive, *Qui Tam*, and Voluntary Disclosure Provisions).

[356]*See, e.g.,* Press Release, U.S. Attorney's Office, District of Connecticut, *Nursing Home Agrees to Pay $750,000 to Settle Allegations Under the False Claims Act* (May 18, 2005), *available at* http://www.usdoj.gov/usao/ct/Press2005/20050518.html.

[357]*Failure-of-care Case Against Pa. Hospital a Landmark*, MODERN HEALTHCARE (online) (July 25, 2005).

On a related topic, in 2003 the U.S. Supreme Court definitively answered the question of whether municipal corporations and other local entities could be subject to suit under the FCA. In *Cook County, Illinois v. United States ex rel. Chandler*,[358] the Court resolved a circuit split: the Seventh Circuit had held that local governments, like state governments, were immune from suit under the FCA, while the Third and Fifth Circuits had held that those entities enjoyed no immunity. The Supreme Court reversed the Seventh Circuit in *Chandler*, and held that municipal corporations and other entities were "persons" for purposes of the FCA, and therefore were subject to suit.

### 2.  *Other Statutes Prohibiting False Claims*

Various other statutes may also be invoked by the government in connection with false claims, including several provisions imposing criminal liability. Under Section 1128B of the Social Security Act, various types of false statements, made knowingly and willfully, are criminal offenses. For example, it is a felony to knowingly and willfully make, or cause to be made, a false statement of material fact in any application for payment or in determining the right to such payment under a federal health care program.[359] Presenting, or causing to be presented, a claim for a physician's services for payment under a federal health care program knowing that the individual furnishing the services was not licensed as a physician is also a felony under this statute.[360] There is also criminal liability for concealing or failing to disclose an event affecting an individual's initial or continued right to a benefit or payment if done with intent to fraudulently secure the benefit or payment, when no such benefit or payment is authorized or in a greater amount than is due.[361] Making, inducing, or seeking to induce the making of any false statement of a material fact regarding the conditions or operation of certain institutions, facilities, or entities in order that they may qualify for certification or recertification, including a hospital, skilled nursing facility, nursing facility, or home health agency, or with respect to information required under 42 U.S.C. Section 1320a-3a, also is a felony.[362]

HIPAA added several additional criminal penalties for the use of false statements or false pretenses in connection with any health care benefit program, thus making these prohibitions applicable to statements made to private payors as well as to federal health care programs.[363]

A criminal false claims statute provides for fines and imprisonment of up to 5 years for filing fraudulent claims with the government, and up to 10 years for conspiring to file fraudulent claims.[364] Various other general criminal prohibitions also may be used in connection with false or fraudulent representations made in the health care context, including provisions relating to mail

---

[358]538 U.S. 119 (2003).

[359]42 U.S.C. §§1320a-7b(a)(1), (2).

[360]42 U.S.C. §1320a-7b(a)(5).

[361]42 U.S.C. §1320a-7b(a)(3).

[362]42 U.S.C. §1320a-7b(c).

[363]*See* 18 U.S.C.§§1347 and 1035 and the discussion at Section II.3.F., below.

[364]*See* 18 U.S.C. §286.

or wire fraud,[365] RICO,[366] money laundering,[367] conspiracy to defraud,[368] and submission of fictitious or fraudulent claims.[369] Common law causes of action and state statutes may also be used in connection with a false claims case.

State false claims statutes are proliferating in large part as a result of incentives in the DRA.[370] For further information on these laws, see Section III.

## D. Civil Monetary Penalties

### 1. The Prohibitions

The OIG has the authority to impose CMPs on any person (including an organization or other entity, but excluding a beneficiary) who knowingly presents, or causes to be presented, to a state or federal government employee or agent certain false or improper claims.[371] Section 1128A of the Social Security Act authorizes imposition of CMPs up to $10,000 per item or service in most cases, and in certain cases up to $50,000 per act, as well as treble damages.[372]

The basic prohibitions to which the CMPs apply include knowingly filing claims for:

- services that were not provided as claimed (e.g., upcoding);
- medical or other items or services that are fraudulent;
- services of a physician or services provided "incident to" a physician's service if the physician:
  —was not licensed as a physician;
  —obtained his or her license through misrepresentation; or
  —falsely represented to the patient at the time the service was furnished that he or she was certified by a medical specialty board;
- medical or other items or services furnished during a time in which the person was excluded from participation in the program under which the claim was made; or
- a pattern of medical or other items or services that a person knows or should know are not medically necessary.[373]

Additional grounds for imposition of CMPs include the following:

- knowingly presenting or causing to be presented claims in violation of certain assignment agreements or participating provider agreements;[374]

---

[365] 18 U.S.C. §§1341, 1343.

[366] 18 U.S.C. §§1961 *et seq.*

[367] 18 U.S.C. §§1956–57.

[368] 18 U.S.C. §§286, 371.

[369] 18 U.S.C. §287.

[370] *See* Section 6032 of the DRA, Pub. L. No. 109-171, 120 Stat. 4 (2006).

[371] *See* 42 U.S.C. §1320a-7a(a). A "beneficiary" is defined as an individual eligible to receive items or services for which payment may be made under a federal health care program, but excludes a provider, supplier, or practitioner. 42 U.S.C. §1320a-7a(i)(5).

[372] 42 U.S.C. §1320a-7a(a). The OIG considers various factors when determining the CMP amount to impose. *See* 42 C.F.R. §1003.106. Persons who violate certain CMPs may also be subject to exclusion from federal health care programs. See the discussion at Section II.E., below.

[373] 42 U.S.C. §1320a-7a(a)(1).

[374] 42 U.S.C. §1320a-7a(a)(2).

- knowingly giving or causing to be given false or misleading information about Medicare coverage of inpatient hospital services that could reasonably be expected to influence the decision when to discharge a patient from the hospital;[375]
- individuals excluded from Medicare or Medicaid and who
  —retain a direct or indirect ownership or control interest in an entity participating in these programs and know or should know of the action constituting the basis for exclusion; or
  —are officers or managing employees of such an entity;[376]
- offering to transfer or transferring remuneration to a beneficiary to influence such beneficiary to order or receive from a particular provider, or supplier, items or services that may be reimbursed, in whole or in part, under Medicare or Medicaid;[377]
- arranging or contracting with an individual or entity that the person knows, or should know, is excluded from participating in federal health care programs[378] for the provision of items or services that may be reimbursed under such programs;[379]
- direct or indirect payment as an inducement by certain hospitals to physicians to limit or reduce services to Medicare or Medicaid beneficiaries who are under the direct care of the physician;[380]
- false certifications by physicians of a patient's eligibility for home health services;[381]
- violations of the anti-kickback statute;[382] or
- violations of the Stark self-referral prohibitions.[383]

Intent is an important element in CMP cases. The statute creates liability for actions taken "knowingly" and/or where the individual "knows or should know" of the falsity of the claim. "Should know" is defined to mean that the individual acts in deliberate ignorance, or reckless disregard, of the truth or falsity of the information. No proof of specific intent to defraud is required.[384] Moreover, principals may incur CMP liability or exclusion as a result of the actions of their agents.[385]

---

[375]42 U.S.C. §1320a-7a(a)(3). The OIG's regulations provide for CMPs of up to $15,000 for each person with respect to whom false information was provided. 42 C.F.R. §1003.103(b).

[376]42 U.S.C. §1320a-7a(a)(4).

[377]42 U.S.C. §1320a-7a(a)(5).

[378] "Federal health care programs" are defined as "any plan or program that provides health benefits, whether directly, though insurance, or otherwise, which is funded directly, in whole or in part, by the United States Government" (excluding the Federal Employees Health Benefits Program). 42 U.S.C. §1320a-7b(f). Medicare, Medicaid, Tricare, and veterans' programs are the most significant federal health care programs.

[379]42 U.S.C. §1320a-7a(a)(6).

[380]42 U.S.C. §1320a-7a(b)(1). The statute initially prescribed a CMP of $2,000 per occurrence. This penalty was increased to $10,000 for acts occurring on or after January 1, 1997, by Pub. L. No. 104-191. 42 C.F.R. §1003.103(a).

[381]42 U.S.C. §1320a-7a(b)(3).

[382]42 U.S.C. §1320a-7a(a)(7).

[383]42 C.F.R. §1003.102(a)(5).

[384]42 U.S.C. §1320a-7a(i)(7). This is the same intent requirement applicable under the FCA. *See* 31 U.S.C. §3729.

[385]42 U.S.C. §1320a-7a(*l*).

The OIG's implementing regulations (contained in Appendix D-4 on the disk accompanying this volume) largely reiterate the above cited statutory bases for CMPs, and list a number of additional conditions under which CMPs may be imposed. They include, but are not limited to, the following:

- failure to report
  —payments made under insurance policies, self-insurance, or otherwise, for the benefit of a health care practitioner in settlement or satisfaction of a medical malpractice claim, and as required by law or regulation; or
  —other adverse actions required to be reported to the Healthcare Integrity and Protection Data Bank;[386]
- improper use or disclosure of, or access to, information reported in accordance with the requirements for the National Practitioner Data Bank;[387]
- use of letters, symbols, or emblems that falsely imply that an advertisement, solicitation, or other item was authorized, approved or endorsed by HHS or CMS;[388]
- contracting organizations that fail to comply with certain requirements;[389]
- failure to refund, on a timely basis, amounts collected for DHS provided as the result of a referral prohibited under the Stark law or other attempts to circumvent the Stark law;[390]
- offering, paying, soliciting, or receiving remuneration in return for referral of federal health care program business;[391]
- an excluded individual retaining a direct or indirect ownership or controlling interest of 5 percent or more, or is an officer or managing employee, in an entity that participates in Medicare or a state health care program;[392]
- offering or transferring remuneration to any individual eligible for benefits under Medicare or a state health care program to influence that person to obtain Medicare or state health care program services and items;[393]
- a physician certifying that a Medicare beneficiary requires home health services when the physician knows the beneficiary does not satisfy the eligibility requirements;[394]
- a Part D sponsor knowingly misrepresenting outreach material provided to a program enrollee;[395]
- a Part D sponsor knowingly charging an enrollee in violation of the terms of its endorsement contract with Medicare;[396] and

---

[386]42 C.F.R. §1003.102(b)(5). The CMP for this violation has been increased to $11,000, pursuant to the Federal Civil Monetary Penalty Inflation Adjustment Act of 1990. 42 C.F.R. §1003.103(c), n.1.

[387]42 C.F.R. §1003.102(b)(6).

[388]42 C.F.R. §1002.103(b)(7). Under certain circumstances, a CMP may be imposed despite the use of a disclaimer of affiliation with the federal government or HHS or its programs. *See* 42 C.F.R. §1003.102(b)(7)(i).

[389]42 C.F.R. §1003.102(b)(8).

[390]*See* 42 C.F.R. §1003.102(b)(9)–(10).

[391]42 C.F.R. §1003.102(b)(11).

[392]42 C.F.R. §1003.102(b)(12).

[393]42 C.F.R. §1003.102(b)(13).

[394]42 C.F.R. §1003.102(b)(14).

[395]42 C.F.R. §1003.102(b)(17).

[396]42 C.F.R. § 1003.102(b)(18).

- certain Emergency Medical Treatment and Active Labor Act (EM-TALA) violations.[397]

## 2. Beneficiary Inducement

Many arrangements could potentially implicate the CMP for beneficiary inducement; however, the law and regulations have clarified the scope of the restriction, to a certain extent. Remuneration under this CMP includes the transfer of items or services for free or other than fair market value and the waiver of coinsurance and deductible amounts except under certain, narrowly defined circumstances. Such copayment waivers are not included in the definition of remuneration if

- they are not offered as part of any advertisement or solicitation;
- the person does not routinely waive coinsurance and deductible amounts; and
- the person
  —waives the coinsurance and deductible amounts after determining in good faith that an individual is in financial need; or
  —fails to collect the coinsurance and deductible after making reasonable collection efforts.[398]

In addition, remuneration generally does not include (1) practices protected by the exceptions or safe harbors to the anti-kickback statute, (2) certain differentials in coinsurance and deductible amounts as part of a benefits plan design, (3) incentives given to individuals to promote the delivery of preventive care, and (4) reductions in the copayment amount for certain outpatient services for the aged and disabled (OPD services).[399]

"Preventive" care is defined in regulations as a prenatal service or postnatal well-baby visit or a specific clinical service described in the current U.S. Preventive Services Task Force's Guide to Clinical Preventive Services that is reimbursable in whole or in part by Medicare or Medicaid.[400] Moreover, the regulations clarify that permissible preventive care incentives cannot be tied (directly or indirectly) to the provision of other services reimbursed, even in part, by Medicare or Medicaid. Permissible incentives may include the provision of preventive care itself but may not include (1) cash or instruments convertible to cash; or (2) an incentive whose value is disproportionately large in relation to the preventive care service (e.g., the value of the service itself or the future health care costs reasonably expected to be avoided as a result of the preventive care).[401]

---

[397] *See* 42 C.F.R. §1003.102(c). The penalties for these types of violations are set forth at 42 C.F.R. §1003.103(e). Also note that under the Program Fraud Civil Remedies Act, 31 U.S.C. §3802, CMPs may be imposed for making, presenting, or submitting a claim that the person knows, or has reason to know, is false, fictitious, or fraudulent.

[398] 42 U.S.C. §1320a-7a(i)(6)(A).

[399] 42 U.S.C. §§1320a-7a(i)(6)(B)–(D). "Covered OPD services" are defined at 42 U.S.C. §1395l(t)(1)(B).

[400] 42 C.F.R. §1003.101.

[401] *Id.*

The preamble to the regulations specifically states that preventive care involves services provided to *asymptomatic* individuals and does not apply to tertiary preventive care (i.e., preventive care that is part of the treatment and management of persons with existing clinical illnesses).[402] The regulations decline to expand this exception to cover disease management programs or other services designed to prevent the deterioration of or complications from an acute or chronic illness. Moreover, there cannot be any tie between the provision of an exempt, covered preventive care service and a nonpreventive covered service.[403] The regulations do provide considerable flexibility with regard to the type and value of permissible preventive care exceptions, noting that blood sugar screening and cholesterol tests, as well as gift certificates to encourage beneficiaries to obtain preventive care, may be permissible. Moreover, despite their continuing concern with routine copayment waivers, the OIG specifically allows providers to waive copayments as an incentive to promote the delivery of preventive care.[404] In addition, preventive care incentives do not have to be of nominal value or offered to all similarly situated individuals in a given community.[405]

Items of nominal value are not prohibited under this CMP because their value is minimal and unlikely to influence a beneficiary's choice of provider. The OIG interprets "nominal" to be no more than $10 per item or $50 in the aggregate per year.[406] Finally, the OIG notes that incentives that are not advertised or otherwise disclosed to a beneficiary before he or she selects a provider do not come within the statutory proscription because the beneficiary is not being influenced in his or her choice of provider.[407]

There are some areas of similarity between the CMP provisions and the anti-kickback statute. For example, the OIG will use the advisory opinion process to respond to inquiries as to what constitutes prohibited remuneration under the anti-kickback statute as well as to whether an arrangement constitutes grounds for sanctions under the CMP (or exclusion) provisions.[408] Numerous advisory opinions have specifically addressed the CMP for beneficiary inducement. Further, in May 2000, the OIG had proposed a new safe harbor from the beneficiary-inducement CMP to provide protection for independent dialysis facilities that pay premiums for Supplementary Medical Insurance (Medicare Part B) or Medicare Supplemental Health Insurance policies (Medigap) for financially needy Medicare beneficiaries with ESRD.[409] The OIG subsequently withdrew this proposed safe harbor on December 9, 2002.[410]

---

[402] 65 Fed. Reg. 24,400, 24,408 (Apr. 26, 2000).

[403] *Id.*

[404] *Id.* at 24,409.

[405] *Id.* at 24,410.

[406] *Id.* at 24,411.

[407] *Id.* at 24,409.

[408] *See* 42 C.F.R. §1008.5(a).

[409] *See generally* 65 Fed. Reg. 25,460 (May 2, 2000).

[410] *See generally* 67 Fed. Reg. 72,896 (Dec. 9, 2002).

### 3. *Special Advisory Bulletin on Beneficiary Inducement*

In August 2002, the OIG provided further guidance on this topic in its Special Advisory Bulletin, "Offering Gifts and Other Inducements to Beneficiaries."[411] In the Special Advisory Bulletin, the OIG confirmed its position that providers may not offer any gifts or "free" services to beneficiaries that exceed $10 per item (with a $50 annual limit) unless the incentives fit within a statutory or regulatory exception or are the subject of a favorable advisory opinion. Nevertheless, the OIG officially acknowledged for the first time that incentives offered by drug manufacturers in connection with product selection generally are exempt from the statutory prohibition unless the manufacturers own or operate, directly or indirectly, other entities that file Medicare or Medicaid claims.

In addition, the OIG noted that it may solicit public comment on the possibility of creating regulatory "safe harbors" for certain complimentary local transportation and for free goods and services provided in connection with government-sponsored clinical trials. However, these safe harbors would apply only to the CMP provisions. The OIG also noted that arrangements that do not violate the CMP requirements may nevertheless implicate the anti-kickback statute under certain circumstances.

The Bulletin contains definitions and interpretations of key concepts within the CMP provisions, which bars offering remuneration to Medicare or Medicaid beneficiaries where the person offering the remuneration "knows or should know" that the "remuneration" is likely to influence the beneficiary to order or receive items or services from a particular provider. The OIG noted that the term "remuneration" has been broadly interpreted to include "anything of value" in the context of various health care fraud and abuse statutes and affirms this broad definition in connection with the beneficiary inducement prohibition. The "should know" standard is met if a provider acts with deliberate ignorance or reckless disregard; no proof of specific intent is required.

The "inducement" element encompasses any offer of valuable goods and services as part of a marketing or promotional activity, regardless of whether the marketing or promotional activity is active or passive. Thus, even if a provider does not directly advertise or promote the benefit to beneficiaries, exposure can result from indirect marketing or promotional efforts or informal channels of disseminating information, such as "word of mouth" promotion by practitioners or patient support groups. The OIG further considers providing free goods or services to existing customers who have an ongoing relationship with a provider as conduct that is likely to influence those customers' future purchases. Thus, the practice, common in other industries, of rewarding customers for their loyalty can violate the law in the health care context under certain circumstances.

With respect to the "beneficiaries" covered by the provision, the OIG states that inducements may not be offered to Medicare and Medicaid

---

[411]OIG Special Advisory Bulletin, *Offering Gifts and Other Inducements to Beneficiaries* (Aug. 2002), *available at* http://oig.hhs.gov/fraud/docs/alertsandbulletins/SABGiftsandInducements.pdf; *see* 42 U.S.C. §1320a-7a(a)(5).

beneficiaries, regardless of the beneficiary's medical condition. The OIG noted that some specialty providers offer valuable gifts to beneficiaries with specific chronic conditions. However, the OIG states that there is no meaningful basis under the statute for creating an exemption based on a beneficiary's medical condition or the condition's severity, particularly because providers have more incentive to offer gifts to chronically ill beneficiaries who, as a result of their condition, are likely to generate substantially more business. Moreover, the prohibition applies regardless of whether the incentive provides therapeutic as well as financial benefits to the beneficiary. Similarly, the OIG finds no statutory basis for an exemption based on the financial need of a category of patients, because Congress expressly included the Medicaid program within the prohibition and created only a narrow exception for nonroutine waivers of copayments and deductibles based on individual financial need.

The OIG also discussed the application of the CMP to providers, practitioners, and suppliers. The OIG has interpreted this element to exclude health plans that offer incentives to Medicare and Medicaid beneficiaries to enroll in a plan, although incentives provided to influence an already enrolled beneficiary to select a particular provider, practitioner, or supplier within the plan are subject to the statutory proscription (other than copayment differentials that are part of a health plan design).

The OIG stated that it will apply the beneficiary inducement CMP according to certain principles, including the following:

- Medicare or Medicaid providers may offer beneficiaries inexpensive gifts (other than cash or cash equivalents) or services without violating the statute.
- Providers may offer beneficiaries more expensive items or services that fit within one of the five statutory exceptions: (1) waivers of cost-sharing amounts based on financial need; (2) properly disclosed copayment differentials in health plans; (3) incentives to promote the delivery of certain preventive care services; (4) any practice permitted under the federal anti-kickback statute pursuant to 42 C.F.R. Part 1001.952; or (5) waivers of hospital outpatient copayments in excess of the minimum copayment amounts.
- The OIG will continue to accept requests for advisory opinions related to the prohibition on inducements to beneficiaries, although favorable opinions will likely be limited to situations involving practices that are very close to an existing statutory or regulatory exception.

The Bulletin also discussed the OIG's interpretation of the CMP, establishing an important exception that permits valuable services or other remuneration to be furnished to financially needy beneficiaries by an independent entity, even if the benefits are funded by providers, as long as (1) the independent entity makes an independent determination of need; and (2) the beneficiary's receipt of the remuneration does not depend, directly or indirectly, on the beneficiary's use of any particular provider.[412]

---

[412] A large number of advisory opinions have addressed this, and related Patient Assistance Programs, particularly in the Part D context. See Section II.A.4., above.

Finally, although the OIG indicated that it did not expect to propose additional regulatory exceptions related to unadvertised waivers of copayments and deductibles, the agency encouraged providers to bring such situations to the OIG's attention through the advisory opinion process.

Subsequently, in December 2002, the OIG issued a letter clarifying the provision of complimentary local transportation for program beneficiaries.[413] The letter states that local transportation valued at no more than $10 per trip and $50 per patient in the aggregate on an annual basis is permissible under the beneficiary inducement/CMP statute. However, because the OIG has under consideration a safe harbor for such transportation that is worth more than $10 per trip and $50 per patient in the aggregate on an annual basis, the OIG states that it will not impose administrative sanctions on such a transportation program if it is hospital-based and meets the following criteria: (i) the program was in existence prior to August 30, 2002; (ii) transportation is offered uniformly and without charge or at reduced charge to all patients of the hospital or hospital-owned ambulatory surgical center (ASC) (and may also be made available to their families); (iii) the transportation is only provided to and from the hospital or a hospital-owned ASC and is for the purpose of receiving hospital or ASC services (or, in the case of family members, accompanying or visiting hospital or ASC patients); (iv) the transportation is provided only within the hospital's or ASC's primary service area; (v) the costs of the transportation are not claimed directly or indirectly on any federal health care program cost report or claim and are not otherwise shifted to any federal health care program; and (vi) the transportation does not include ambulance transportation.

Subsequently, the OIG published various advisory opinions further interpreting and applying the beneficiary inducement prohibitions. For example, in March 2006, the OIG also concluded that a home health care agency's proposal to provide certain free preoperative home safety assessments could be subject to civil monetary penalties.[414] Although the requestor noted that the telephonic assessments proposed cost less than $10 to provide, the OIG noted that they likely had a value to the recipient in excess of that value. As a result, the OIG concluded that these assessments were not of a nominal value and were likely to influence beneficiaries to select the requesting home health agency to provide items and services that would be paid for by a federal health care program.[415]

### 4. Gainsharing

One CMP applies to direct or indirect payment by certain hospitals to physicians as an inducement to limit or reduce services to Medicare or Medicaid beneficiaries who are under the direct care of the physician.[416] Despite strong OIG language questioning the legality of gainsharing arrangements in a

---

[413]Letter from Kevin McAnaney, Chief, Industry Guidance Branch, to OIG (2002), *available at* http://oig.hhs.gov/fraud/docs/alertsandbulletins/LocalTransportation.pdf.

[414]OIG Advisory Op. No. 06-01 (Mar. 27, 2007).

[415]*Id.*

[416]42 U.S.C. §1320a-7a(b). This prohibition is also discussed in Section II.D.1., above.

Special Advisory Bulletin,[417] the OIG stated that it would not impose sanctions on the arrangements described in Advisory Opinion No. 01-01, indicating that not all gainsharing arrangements violate the anti-kickback statute or the applicable CMP. Nevertheless, a federal district court case in New Jersey involved a challenge to a CMS demonstration project in New Jersey to test the efficacy of a "gainsharing" arrangement, whereby physicians would receive incentive payments to help contain hospital costs.[418] In an unpublished opinion the court found that the demonstration project did not violate the anti-kickback statute and that the Stark law was inapplicable in this context. The court granted the requested enjoinment of the demonstration project based on finding that it violated the CMP statute absent further proceedings to cure its defects, such as receipt of a favorable advisory opinion from the OIG. However, the OIG's subsequent discussion of gainsharing in the OIG Draft Supplemental Compliance Program Guidance for Hospitals[419] emphasized the fact that gainsharing arrangements could implicate the anti-kickback statute and the Stark law[420] as well as the CMP statute.

From 2005 into 2007, the OIG began to take a more positive approach to gainsharing. In a series of advisory opinions, the OIG approved seven gainsharing arrangements between hospitals and physicians.[421] These opinions are based on a similar model and involved a hospital sharing savings that resulted from a physician group's implementation of certain cost reduction measures.

The OIG stated that the cost saving arrangements implicated the CMP, because payments were to be made to physicians to insure a reduction of items or services to federal beneficiaries. However, it would not seek sanctions under the CMP statute because of the safeguards built into the arrangements, including:

- specific cost saving actions and resulting savings were clearly and separately identified;
- credible medical support indicated that the arrangements would not adversely impact patient care;
- payments to physicians would be based on all procedures performed, regardless of the payor, and would be subject to a payment cap for federal health care program procedures, and federal health care program beneficiaries would not be disproportionately affected;
- objective historical and clinical data would be used to set baselines beyond which no savings could accrue to the physician group;
- the same selection of devices would be available for physician use as before;

---

[417]*See* Dep't Health & Human Servs., Office of Inspector General, Special Advisory Bulletin, *Gainsharing Arrangements and CMPs for Hospital Payments to Physicians to Reduce or Limit Services to Beneficiaries* (July 1999), *available at* http://oig.hhs.gov/fraud/docs/alertsandbulletins/gainsh.htm, included as Appendix F-15 on the disk accompanying this volume.

[418]*See* Robert Wood Johnson Univ. Hosp., Inc. v. Thompson, Civil Action No. 04-142 (JWB), 2004 WL 3210732 (D.N.J. Apr. 15, 2004) (not for publication).

[419]OIG Draft Supplemental Compliance Program Guidance for Hospitals, 69 Fed. Reg. 32,012, 32,024 (June 8, 2004).

[420]The OIG did not comment on the Stark law implications of the arrangement.

[421]The seven opinions, designated Advisory Op. Nos. 05-01 through 05-06 and Advisory Op. No. 06-22, are available at http://oig.hhs.gov/fraud/advisoryopinions/opinions.html.

- the hospital and the physicians would provide written disclosures to affected patients about the gainsharing arrangements;
- financial incentives under the arrangements would be limited in duration and amount; and
- any incentive for an individual physician to generate disproportionate savings would be mitigated because group profits would be distributed to member physicians on a per capita basis.

The advisory opinions also identified certain features that would heighten the risk that the arrangements would lead to inappropriate reductions or limitations in services. With regard to the anti-kickback statute, the OIG concluded that it would not impose sanctions, despite the fact that the arrangements could result in illegal remuneration, for three primary reasons:

- participation in the arrangements would be limited to physicians already on the hospital's medical staff, potential savings from federal health care program patients would be capped, the contract term was limited to one year, and admissions would be monitored for changes in severity, age, or payor;
- the composition of the participating physician group would be limited, and profit distributions would be made on a per capita basis; and
- the action that would generate cost savings for a participating physician entails some increased liability risk for which the physician would be entitled to additional compensation.[422]

Other support for gainsharing came in a March 2005 report to Congress on physician-owned specialty hospitals, in which MedPAC recommended that Congress grant authority to HHS to allow certain gainsharing arrangements.[423] This recommendation was premised on a belief that gainsharing encourages physicians and hospitals to work together to lower costs and improve care. However, like the OIG advisory opinions, MedPAC cautioned that gainsharing should only be permitted when appropriate safeguards are in place.[424]

The DRA required HHS to establish a demonstration program to evaluate certain gainsharing arrangements by November 2006. To qualify, the arrangements had to meet specified criteria, including the following:

- The hospital's remuneration to the physician must come from savings that directly resulted from a collaboration between the hospital and physician;
- A written agreement must be submitted to the HHS Secretary that outlines how the arrangement will improve quality and efficiency;
- The hospital must notify patients that it is involved in this demonstration project;

---

[422]*See id.*

[423]*See* MEDPAC, REPORT TO THE CONGRESS: PHYSICIAN OWNED SPECIALTY HOSPITALS, *available at* http://www.medpac.gov/publications/congressional_reports/Mar05_SpecHospitals .pdf.

[424]For a more detailed discussion of this topic, see Section IV.J.1. in Chapter 5 (Barry, Legal Issues Surrounding Hospital and Physician Relationships).

- The project must measure and maintain the quality and efficiency of patient care;
- The project must be reviewed by an independent organization; and
- The project cannot reward the physician on the basis of referral volumes or the dollar value of referrals to the hospital.[425]

In September 2006, CMS announced a three-year demonstration program to determine whether gainsharing arrangements improve the quality of patient care without increasing costs.[426] Authorized under Section 646 of the MMA, the demonstration was scheduled to begin in 2007.

## 5. CMP Enforcement

CMPs can be imposed by the Secretary, initially without a hearing. Accordingly, there have been numerous OIG enforcement actions under various types of CMPs, including those related to false and fraudulent claims,[427] kickbacks and self-referrals,[428] managed care,[429] patient dumping (violations of EMTALA),[430] and overcharging beneficiaries.[431]

In one major case, the Inspector General announced its settlement and CIA with Lincare Holdings, Inc., and its subsidiary Lincare, Inc., for paying illegal kickbacks and for violating the Stark law.[432] As of August 2007, the $10 million

---

[425]Deficit Reduction Act of 2005, Pub. L. No. 109-171, §5007 (2006).

[426]Press Release, CMS, *Details for: CMS Demonstration Program Supports Physician-Hospital Collaborations to Improve Quality of Care While Getting Better Value* (Sept. 6, 2006), *available at* http://www.cms.hhs.gov/apps/media/press/release.asp?Counter=1957. The DRA demonstration was designed to examine the short-term effects of gainsharing on quality and efficiency of care. In contrast, this demonstration will test the long-term effect of gainsharing across an entire episode of care across a health care delivery system. CMS FAQ ID #7984, *available at* http://questions.cms.hhs.gov.

[427]*E.g.,* physicians submitting claims for services provided by an unlicensed person, hospitals employing or contracting with excluded persons, DME suppliers not having adequate documentation for claims such as physician signatures or determinations of medical necessity, clinics billing for services not furnished at the indicated location, and physicians billing for services not rendered. *See* http://oig.hhs.gov/fraud/enforcement/administrative/cmp/cmpitems.html#2.

[428]*E.g.,* physicians accepting gifts and entertainment from DME suppliers in exchange for patient referrals, a hospital leasing space to a surgeon at below fair market value, and paying physician employees more than fair market value for on-call services the surgeon should have paid for, nursing facilities billing for services referred by a medical director of the nursing facility in violation of the Stark law, physicians receiving lease payments from hospitals for unused space, physicians billing for free drug samples, physicians receiving greater than fair market value payments for the lease of a lithotripter, swapping arrangements between an ambulance company and a hospital, loans to physicians in return for referrals, termination of nonreferring physicians, and free devices from DME suppliers to physicians. *See* http://oig.hhs.gov/fraud/enforcement/administrative/cmp/cmpitems.html#3.

[429]*See, e.g.,* http://www.oig.hhs.gov/fraud/enforcement/administrative/cmp/cmpitems.html#4.

[430]*See, e.g.,* http://www.oig.hhs.gov/fraud/enforcement/administrative/cmp/cmpitemspd.html.

[431]*See, e.g.,* http://www.oig.hhs.gov/fraud/enforcement/administrative/cmp/cmpitems.html#5.

[432]*See* Press Release, HHS OIG, *OIG Settles Largest Ever Civil Monetary Penalty Case* (May 15, 2006), *available at* http://oig.hhs.gov/publications/docs/press/2006/Lincare051506.pdf.

settlement constituted the largest CMP imposed by the OIG. The Inspector General also issued an Open Letter to Health Care Providers in 2006 announcing an initiative to use the OIG's Provider Self-Disclosure Protocol to resolve certain types of CMP liability.[433]

## E. Exclusion Authorities

One of the most severe sanctions results from the OIG's ability to exclude individuals and entities from participation in federal health care programs, including Medicare and Medicaid.[434] Exclusion is mandatory in some cases, and permissive in others, left to the OIG's discretion. The potential impact of exclusion, which can be a financial death sentence for a provider, provides significant leverage to the government in settlement negotiations.

### 1. Mandatory Exclusion

The law mandates exclusion from federal health care programs of individuals or entities convicted of the following offenses:

- a criminal offense related to the delivery of an item or service under Medicare or Medicaid;
- a criminal offense related to the neglect or abuse of a patient in connection with the delivery of a health care item or service;
- any felony relating to fraud, theft, embezzlement, breach of fiduciary responsibility, or other financial misconduct under federal or state law relating to health care fraud for an offense that occurred after August 21, 1996; and
- any felony conviction under federal or state law occurring after August 21, 1996, relating to the unlawful manufacture, distribution, prescription, or dispensing of a controlled substance.[435]

Mandatory exclusion is for a minimum five-year term,[436] which increases to 10 years for repeat convictions that occur after August 5, 1997.[437] Exclusion can become permanent for multiple convictions.[438] There are limited exceptions to mandatory exclusions available under certain circumstances for sole community health care providers where a state program requests an exception.[439]

---

[433]An Open Letter to Health Care Providers (Apr. 28, 2006), *available at* http://www.oig.hhs.gov/fraud/docs/openletters/Open%20Letter%20to%20Providers%202006.pdf. See also the discussion at Section IV.D.2., below.

[434]There are various other sanctions available to the government, including asset freezes and payment suspensions. For text of the exclusion statute and regulations, as well as a table of exclusion authorities, see Appendix D-3, Appendix D-5, and Appendix D-2 on the disk accompanying this volume.

[435]42 U.S.C. §1320a-7(a). For text of the exclusion statute, see Appendix D-3 on the disk accompanying this volume.

[436]42 U.S.C. §1320a-7(c)(3)(B).

[437]42 U.S.C. §1320a-7(c)(3)(G)(i).

[438]42 U.S.C. §1320a-7(c)(3)(G)(ii).

[439]42 U.S.C. §1320a-7(c)(3)(B).

"Conviction" includes (1) judgments entered by state, federal, or local courts (regardless of whether an appeal is pending or the records have been expunged); (2) findings of guilt by state, federal, or local courts; (3) pleas of guilty or *nolo contendere* accepted by the courts; or (4) when the individual or entity is participating in a first offender or similar program where judgment of convictions has been withheld.[440]

## 2. Permissive Exclusion

The OIG has discretionary or "permissive" authority to exclude individuals and entities on the basis of the following:

- convictions for offenses under federal or state law occurring after HIPAA's enactment (August 21, 1996) for:
  —criminal misdemeanors related to health care program fraud, theft, embezzlement, breach of fiduciary responsibility, other financial misconduct, or other programs operated or financed in whole or in part by a state, federal, or local government agency;
  —obstruction of justice in health care investigations; and
  —certain misdemeanors related to the unlawful manufacture, distribution, prescription, or dispensing of controlled substances;
- revocation or suspension of an individual or entity's license to provide health care, including surrender of a license pending a disciplinary hearing for reasons relating to the individual's professional competence, performance, or financial integrity;
- suspension or exclusion under any federal program involving the provision of health care, or state health care program, for reasons related to the individual or entity's competence, performance, or financial integrity;
- submission of claims for items or services furnished substantially in excess of the individual or entity's usual charges, without good cause; provision of unnecessary or substandard services; failure of a medical plan to offer necessary services required by law or contract that adversely affects Medicare or Medicaid beneficiaries; or failure of an entity to provide medically necessary items and services required for individuals covered under a risk-sharing contract, if the failure adversely affected those individuals;
- activities involving fraud or kickbacks;[441]
- any entity controlled by a person convicted of various program-related abuses, or who has been excluded from Medicare or Medicaid or had a CMP imposed against him or her;[442]

---

[440]42 U.S.C. §1320a-7(i).

[441]42 U.S.C. §1320a-7(b).

[442]42 U.S.C. §1320a-7(b)(8). A sanctioned individual is deemed to "control" an entity where the individual has a direct or indirect ownership or control interest of 5 percent or more in the entity, or is an officer, director, agent, or managing employee. The prohibition also applies if such a person held an ownership interest, but transferred it to an immediate family member or household member in anticipation of, or following, a conviction, assessment, or exclusion. *Id.*

- individuals controlling a sanctioned entity (i.e., having a direct or indirect ownership or control interest in a sanctioned entity) in which the person knew or should have known of the action constituting the basis for the conviction or exclusion, or being an officer or managing employee of such an entity;[443]
- any entity's failure to disclose certain required information;
- a disclosing entity's failure to supply requested information on ownership of certain subcontractors or failure to supply information as to significant business transactions between the entity and any wholly owned supplier, or between the entity and any subcontractor, for the five-year period ending on the date of the request;
- failure to supply certain payment information;
- failure to grant immediate access to a facility, records, or documents on reasonable request by the HHS, OIG, a state agency, or a state Medicaid Fraud Control Unit;
- failure by a hospital to take corrective action required by HHS with regard to improper hospital admission practices; and
- default on education loans or scholarship obligations in connection with health professions education made or secured, in whole or in part, by HHS.[444]

Initially, the OIG took the position that it would only apply the exclusion authority to so-called "direct providers" of medical items and services (e.g., physicians and pharmacists). However, on September 2, 1998, the OIG published a final rule that reversed this policy, extending exclusion authority to "indirect providers" of services, such as manufacturers of drugs, medical devices, and other medical supplies.[445] The exclusion would apply to all of a manufacturer's items and services, even those unrelated to the item or practice that formed the basis for the exclusion.[446] However, OIG stated in the preamble to these regulations that it intended to exercise its sanction authority "prudently" and would entertain requests for waivers in certain cases.[447]

### 3. Special Advisory Bulletin on Exclusion

The OIG interpreted its exclusion authority even more expansively in the Special Advisory Bulletin on The Effect of Exclusion From Participation in Federal Health Care Programs (Exclusion Special Advisory Bulletin), particularly with regard to the CMP provision that prohibits arranging or contracting

---

[443] 42 U.S.C. §1320a-7(b)(15)(A). A "sanctioned entity" is one that has been convicted of various program-related abuses or has been excluded from Medicare or Medicaid participation. 42 U.S.C. §1320a-7(b)(15)(B).

[444] 42 U.S.C. §1320a-7(b).

[445] 63 Fed. Reg. 46,676, 46,677 (Sept. 2, 1998) (codified at 42 C.F.R. pts. 1000, 1001, 1002, 1005). The final rule became effective October 2, 1998. While the HHS appropriations bill for FY 1999 directed the OIG to reexamine this issue, no change has been made in the OIG's interpretation. Omnibus Consolidated and Emergency Appropriations Act, 1999, Pub. L. No. 105-277, 112 Stat. 2681 (1998).

[446] See definition of "exclusion" at 42 C.F.R. §1001.2.

[447] 63 Fed. Reg. 46,676, 46,679 (Sept. 2, 1998).

with an individual or entity that the person knows or should know is excluded from participation in federal health care programs.[448] The Exclusion Special Advisory Bulletin asserts that no federal program funds can be used to cover an excluded individual's salary, expenses, or fringe benefits, regardless of whether they provide direct patient care. Moreover, the prohibition can extend to payment for administrative and management services not directly related to patient care if they are a necessary component of providing items and services to federal health care program beneficiaries. Therefore, although an excluded individual can provide items and services to non-federal health care program beneficiaries, such excluded individuals can only be paid with private funds or other nonfederal sources. As a result, according to the OIG, an excluded individual or entity is effectively precluded from being employed by, or under contract with, *any* practitioner, provider, or supplier to furnish *any* items or services reimbursed by a federal health care program.

The OIG provides several examples of the types of items and services that can subject an employer or contractor to possible CMP liability if they are furnished by excluded parties, including the following:

- services performed for program beneficiaries by excluded individuals who sell, deliver, or refill orders for medical devices or equipment reimbursed by a federal health care program;
- services performed by an excluded administrator, billing agent, accountant, or claims processor that are related to and reimbursed, directly or indirectly, by a federal health care program; and
- items or equipment sold by an excluded manufacturer or supplier, used in the care of beneficiaries and reimbursed, directly or indirectly, by a federal health care program.

The prohibition applies regardless of whether federal reimbursement is based on itemized claims, cost reports, fee schedules, or PPS; and the prohibition applies even when payment is made to an individual or entity that is not excluded. Moreover, items and services furnished at the medical direction or prescription of an excluded physician are not reimbursable when the individual or entity furnishing the services knew or should have known of the exclusion. Toward this end, the OIG asserts that providers and contracting entities have an affirmative duty to check program exclusion status before entering into arrangements with individuals or entities.[449] As a practical matter, the OIG claims that these sanctions will likely prevent any entity receiving federal health care program funds, directly or indirectly, from hiring an excluded individual in any capacity.

Individuals sanctioned under the CMP and exclusion authorities may request a hearing before an administrative law judge (ALJ)[450] and may appeal to

---

[448]42 U.S.C. §1320a-7a(a)(6). The Exclusion Special Advisory Bulletin is contained in Appendix F-14 on the disk accompanying this volume.

[449]The OIG recommends periodically checking its Web site for the list of excluded individuals/entities with regard to both prospective and current employees and contractors (http://oig.hhs.gov). However, there may be numerous practical difficulties inherent in using the list to identify all excluded individuals and organizations.

[450]*See* 42 C.F.R. §§1005.2–1005.19. The regulations contain detailed rules concerning these proceedings.

the Departmental Appeals Board.[451] The ALJ may hold a hearing, issue subpoenas, review evidence, and examine witnesses. The parties have the right to counsel, to conduct discovery as permitted, and to submit written briefs.[452] The ALJ may modify the sanction,[453] but may not review the OIG's exercise of discretion to impose permissive exclusion or a CMP.[454]

## F. Federal All-Payor Statutes

There are several statutory provisions that apply broadly to all payors, not just federal health care programs. These include, by way of example, prohibitions on knowingly and willfully falsifying or concealing material facts or making materially false statements in matters involving a health care benefit program.[455] There is also a federal statute making it a crime to knowingly and willfully execute, or attempt to execute, a scheme or artifice to defraud any health care benefit program, or obtain through false representations or pretenses any money or property owned or under the custody or control of any health care benefit program.[456] "Health care benefit program" is defined as any public or private plan or contract, affecting commerce, under which any medical benefit, item, or service is provided to any individual, and includes any individual or entity who is providing a medical benefit, item, or service for which payment may be made under the plan or contract.[457] Violation of the statute can lead to a fine or imprisonment for up to 10 years. However, if the violation results in serious bodily injury, the violator may be fined and/or imprisoned up to 20 years. If the violation results in death, the violator may be imprisoned for any number of years, or for life.[458]

It is particularly important to note that although various federal statutes specifically apply to federal health care programs, attempts to "carve out" Medicare or Medicaid beneficiaries from an arrangement may be viewed with suspicion by the OIG[459] and result in increased scrutiny. The OIG may consider such "carve-outs" as an attempt to swap discounts or other benefits provided in connection with private payor patients as an inducement to obtain referrals for other business that will be reimbursed by federal health care programs.

---

[451]The Departmental Appeals Board may decline to review the case. 42 C.F.R. §1005.21(g).

[452]42 C.F.R. §1005.3.

[453]42 C.F.R. §10005.20.

[454]42 C.F.R. §1005.4.

[455]18 U.S.C. §1035. For text of §1035, see Appendix E-1 on the disk accompanying this volume.

[456]18 U.S.C. §1347. For text of §1347, see Appendix E-2 on the disk accompanying this volume.

[457]18 U.S.C. §24. For text of §24, see Appendix E-3 on the disk accompanying this volume.

[458]18 U.S.C. §1347.

[459]*See, e.g.,* Advisory Op. Nos. 98-15, 00-1, 05-12, and 06-02, *available at* http://oig.hhs.gov/fraud/advisoryopinions/opinions.html.

### III. STATE LAWS

Most states have fraud and abuse prohibitions, some of which are quite similar to their federal counterparts.[460] However, there can be diverse variations, so any applicable state laws should be closely examined. Generally, states are likely to have an anti-kickback statute(s) and a law restricting physician self-referrals. Many states also have fee-splitting prohibitions, commercial bribery statutes, deceptive trade practice laws, and/or consumer protection statutes that may apply in the health care context. Some states have legislation prohibiting providers from waiving coinsurance or deductible amounts while case law in other states indicates that such practices would constitute fraud under state law. As discussed in more detail below,[461] a number of states have enacted laws similar to the federal FCA, and some of the state versions are more stringent than their federal counterpart. Finally, there are state insurance fraud statutes that may also be used to prosecute certain types of health care fraud.

Some state laws may be limited to fraud and abuse affecting the Medicaid program, but many state fraud and abuse laws apply to all payors. Thus, transactions that may be acceptable under federal law because Medicare and Medicaid beneficiaries are not affected by the arrangements might still violate state law. Even state laws that are generally based on their federal counterparts can vary in subtle, but significant, ways. Unlike the federal Stark law, which applies only to physicians, state self-referral prohibitions may apply to other types of health care practitioners.[462] Similarly, state self-referral laws may apply to different types of services, not the 11 DHS listed under federal law.[463] Some state self-referral prohibitions apply only to ownership, but not to compensation relationships. Self-referral prohibitions are often extended to family members of physicians, but the type of "family member" implicated by the statute can vary. Violations can be subject to a variety of penalties, including professional discipline and/or CMPs. In other cases, there is no violation of the self-referral prohibition as long as the affected physician discloses his or her financial relationship as required by the applicable law.[464]

Another major difference between federal and state law may involve the anti-kickback prohibitions. The federal anti-kickback statute is an intent-based statute, and there can be no violation absent knowing and willful action. In contrast, numerous state laws do not contain such a qualification within the language of the statute. Many state anti-kickback laws also contain far fewer exceptions or safe harbors. As a result, in Florida, in March 2004, the Third

---

[460]Even before the Stark II regulations were finalized, some states largely incorporated the Stark law and regulations into their own statutes. *See* KY. REV. STAT. ANN. §205.8461 (2006); MONT. CODE ANN. §45-6-313 (2005); *see also* MICH. COMP. LAWS ANN. §333.16221 (2006); TEX. HEALTH & SAFETY CODE §142.019 (2006).

[461]See the discussion in this section, below.

[462]*E.g.*, MD. CODE ANN., HEALTH OCC. §1-301(g) (2006).

[463]FLA. STAT. ANN. §456.053 (2007); N.Y. PUB. HEALTH LAW §238-a(1) (2007); VA. CODE ANN. §54.1-2410 *et seq.* (2006).

[464]*E.g.*, ARIZ. REV. STAT. ANN. §32-1401(27)(ff) (2006); HAW. REV. STAT. ANN. §431:10C-308.7(c) (2006).

District Court of Appeals held in *State v. Harden*[465] that the state's Medicaid provider fraud statute implicitly conflicted with the federal anti-kickback statute, and thus was preempted under the Supremacy Clause of the Constitution. The opinion reasoned that the Florida statute, which generally had the same objectives as the federal anti-kickback statute, was an obstacle to the execution and accomplishment of the objectives and purpose of the federal statute. This decision was good news for providers, because numerous state kickback laws ostensibly contain more stringent prohibitions than their federal counterpart because state law fraud and abuse laws often (1) do not require improper intent for a violation; (2) contain few, if any, exceptions or safe harbors; and (3) provide little additional guidance.[466] In 2004, the *Harden* decision was limited by a separate panel of the Florida Third District Court of Appeals in *Florida v. Wolland*,[467] which held that the federal FCA did not preempt the Florida Medicaid provider fraud law because both laws' provisions regarding false claims were "in harmony in purpose and effect." However, in December 2005, the Florida District Court of Appeals in *State v. Rubio* disagreed with *Wolland*, concluding that the Florida Medicaid provider fraud statute was unconstitutional. Finally, in May 2006, the Florida Supreme Court affirmed the holding in *State v. Harden* that the federal anti-kickback statute preempted the state Medicaid anti-kickback statute, thus making the latter unconstitutional under the Supremacy Clause.[468]

In other states there may be case law, attorney general opinions, or regulatory board decisions providing further guidance on the interpretation of these seemingly inflexible anti-kickback laws. However, many times no further guidance is available and it becomes necessary to analyze the particular facts at issue very carefully within the context of the statutory language.

Fee-splitting statutes often prohibit kickbacks or similar remuneration arrangements. Some states interpret these laws broadly to prohibit physicians from paying a percentage of their revenues to a management company, particularly when the management company will be performing any type of marketing activity.[469]

State deceptive trade practices and consumer protection statutes often can be used both by the government and private citizens to challenge certain arrangements involving self-referrals and kickbacks. Like the *qui tam* provisions of the federal FCA, private litigants who prevail in cases brought under these statutes may be eligible to receive large damage awards. Similarly, some state statutes prohibit filing false claims with private insurers and may further provide insurance companies with a private right of action to recover compensatory

---

[465] 873 So. 2d 352, 355 (Fla. Dist. Ct. App. 2004).

[466] *Id.*

[467] 902 So. 2d 278 (Fla. Dist. Ct. App. 2005).

[468] *See* State v. Harden, 938 So. 2d 480 (Fla. 2006).

[469] *E.g.*, FLA. STAT. ANN. §458.331(l)(i), §817.505 (2007). *See also* Gold, Vann & White, P.A. v. Friedenstab, 831 So. 2d 692 (Fla. App. 4 Dist. 2002) (management services agreement between physician and medical management company was an illegal fee splitting arrangement); *In re* Petition for Declaratory Statement of Magan L. Bakarania, M.D., 20 FALR 395 (Fla. Bd. of Med. 1997). *Cf. In re* Petition for Declaratory Statement of Rew, Rogers & Silver, M.D.'s, P.A., 21 FALR 4139 (Fla. Bd. of Med. 1999) (distinguishing *Bakarania*).

damages or penalties.[470] In some states the waiver of copayment amounts may be a false claim under regulations[471] or case law.[472] In some cases, the result has depended on the language of the insurance policy at issue.[473]

Because of the wide variation among state laws, it is essential to review all applicable provisions. Particularly if an arrangement involves more than one state's law, a helpful starting point may be the CMS Web site,[474] which provides a listing of many state fraud and abuse laws. Because there often is little case law or other guidance available in many jurisdictions, it may be advisable to contact the appropriate regulatory boards for further guidance. Some states also have mechanisms for obtaining formal advisory opinions on particular issues. While some states have been actively enforcing their fraud and abuse laws, there has been less evidence of enforcement in other states. However, state enforcement activities will likely increase due to increased resources, collaboration, and encouragement being provided by the federal government.

Other states have enacted state false claims laws with whistleblower provisions, including California,[475] Delaware,[476] the District of Columbia,[477] Hawaii,[478] Illinois,[479] Indiana,[480] Louisiana,[481] Massachusetts,[482] Michigan,[483] Nevada,[484] New Hampshire,[485] New Mexico,[486] Tennessee,[487] Texas,[488] and Virginia.[489] Arkansas also has a state false claims law; however, there is no provision allowing for a private individual to file a *qui tam* action.[490]

A significant number of states have enacted state false claims laws for their Medicaid programs due to the financial incentives contained in the DRA.[491]

---

[470] 18 PA. CONS. STAT. ANN. §4117(g) (2006).

[471] *See* FLA. ADMIN. CODE ANN. r. 69B-153.003 (2007).

[472] Feiler v. New Jersey Dental Ass'n, 489 A.2d 1161 (N.J. Super. Ct. App. Div.), *cert. denied*, 491 A.2d 673 (N.J. 1984).

[473] Kennedy v. Connecticut Gen. Life Ins. Co., 924 F.2d 698 (7th Cir. 1991).

[474] The CMS Web site relating to state fraud statutes is http://www.cms.hhs.gov/apps/mfs/citation_info.asp.

[475] CAL. GOV'T CODE §12650 *et seq.* (2007).

[476] 6 DEL. CODE. ANN. §1201 *et seq.* (2007).

[477] D.C. CODE ANN. §2-208.03 *et seq.* (2006).

[478] HAW. REV. STAT. §661-25 (2006).

[479] 740 ILL. COMP. STAT. ANN. §175/1 *et seq.* (2006).

[480] IND. CODE §5-11-5.5 (2006).

[481] LA. REV. STAT. ANN. §46:439.1 *et seq.* (2006).

[482] 12 MASS. ANN. LAWS §§5A–5O (2007).

[483] MICH. COMP. LAWS ANN. §400.601 *et seq.* (2006).

[484] NEV. REV. STAT. §357.010 *et seq.* (2005).

[485] N.H. REV. STAT. §167:61-b (2006).

[486] N.M. STAT. ANN. §27-14-1 *et seq.* (2006).

[487] TENN. CODE ANN. §71-5-181 *et seq.* (2006).

[488] TEX. HUM. RES. CODE §§36.001–36.117 (2006).

[489] 19.1 VA. STAT. §8.01-216.1 *et seq.* (2006).

[490] ARK. CODE. ANN. §20-77-901 *et seq.* (2006).

[491] Deficit Reduction Act of 2005, Pub. L. No. 109-171, §6032 (2006). Some states may have decided not to take advantage of this DRA program since it may result in a net loss to state coffers. Under the DRA-required FCA laws, in some cases a state may have to pay a larger percentage of monies recovered to the whistleblower than the increased amount the state will receive from the federal government.

Since January 1, 2007, the DRA has offered states with qualifying false claims legislation an additional 10 percent of recoveries from Medicaid false claims. To qualify, the state's false claims law must: (1) create liability to the state for claims that are prohibited under the federal FCA; (2) have provisions at least as effective as those in the federal FCA to facilitate and reward *qui tam* whistle-blowers; (3) require that the action be filed under seal for 60 days with review by the state Attorney General; and (4) contain a civil penalty not less than the amount authorized under the federal FCA.

In January 2007, in its first evaluation of state FCAs under the DRA provisions, the OIG notified five states—Hawaii, Illinois, Massachusetts, Tennessee, and Virginia—that they qualified for the financial incentives offered under the DRA because their FCAs met the rigorous required specifications.[492] The DRA also created a requirement that any entity that receives or makes at least $5 million in annual Medicaid payments must establish written policies for all employees, contractor employees, and agents that provide detailed information on the federal and applicable state FCAs, including whistleblower rights, and the entity's policies and procedures to prevent waste, fraud, and abuse.[493] Because of this increased education, the likelihood of enforcement actions may increase due to the creation of a new generation of potential whistleblowers.

CMS also sought to furnish additional guidance on the DRA requirements. On December 13, 2006, CMS issued State Medicaid Director Letter #06-024.[494] Because this letter was directed to state Medicaid directors, it did not address many of the concerns that existed throughout the Medicaid provider community. Consequently, in March 2007, CMS issued a FAQ responding to over 70 requests for clarification.[495]

## IV. OTHER RESOURCES

There are a number of other documents published by the federal government that may be helpful to the practitioner trying to eliminate, or at least minimize, his or her client's exposure to the fraud and abuse laws. Most of these can be accessed through the OIG's Web site.[496]

The CMS Web site[497] also contains numerous guidance materials that can help clarify the agency's underlying regulations, in turn helping to prevent the errors that can lead to subsequent allegations of fraud and abuse. In particular, the CMS Quarterly Provider Update is an excellent source of information on changing Medicare requirements.[498] Moreover, because CMS is the agency

---

[492]OIG Web site, Specific State Laws Reviewed by OIG, *available at* http://oig.hhs.gov/fraud/falseclaimsact.html#1.

[493]DRA §6033 (2006).

[494]This letter is available at http://www.cms.hhs.gov/smdl/downloads/SMD121306.pdf.

[495]CMS Frequently Asked Questions, DRA 6032–Employee Education About False Claims Recovery (Mar. 20, 2007), *available at* http://www.cms.hhs.gov/smdl/downloads/SMD032207Att1.pdf.

[496]The OIG Web site is http://oig.hhs.gov.

[497]The CMS Web site can be found at http://www.cms.hhs.gov.

[498]*Available at* http://www.cms.hhs.gov/QuarterlyProviderUpdates/.

charged with implementing the Stark law, guidance materials relating to this statute may often be located on the CMS Web site rather than the HHS OIG Web site.

In those instances where the OIG resolves allegations against an entity by settlement, the corporate integrity agreements that address the perceived regulatory issues are available for general review and may provide useful guidance.[499]

## A. Compliance Program Guidance

The OIG had developed and released 12 final compliance program guidance (CPG) documents for 11 types of entities by August 2007: clinical laboratories;[500] hospitals;[501] home health agencies;[502] third-party billing companies;[503] the durable medical equipment, prosthetics, orthotics, and supply industry;[504] hospices;[505] Medicare+Choice (now Medicare Advantage) organizations that offer coordinated care plans;[506] nursing homes;[507] individual and small group physician practices;[508] ambulance service providers;[509] and pharmaceutical manufacturers (Pharma CPG),[510] as well as a supplemental CPG for hospitals (Supplemental Hospital CPG).[511] On November 28, 2005, the OIG published for public comment its Draft OIG Compliance Program Guidance for Recipients of PHS Research Awards.[512]

---

[499] *See* http://oig.hhs.gov/fraud/cias.html.

[500] 63 Fed. Reg. 163 (Aug. 24, 1998).

[501] 63 Fed. Reg. 8987 (Feb. 23, 1998). For text of this guidance, see Appendix I-1.1 on the disk accompanying this volume.

[502] 63 Fed. Reg. 42,410 (Aug. 7, 1998). All of the OIG compliance program guidance documents are available at http://oig.hhs.gov/modcom/index.htm.

[503] 63 Fed. Reg. 70,138 (Dec. 18, 1998).

[504] 64 Fed. Reg. 36,368 (July 6, 1999).

[505] 64 Fed. Reg. 54,031 (Oct. 5, 1999).

[506] 64 Fed. Reg. 61,893 (Nov. 15, 1999).

[507] 65 Fed. Reg. 14,289 (Mar. 16, 2000).

[508] 65 Fed. Reg. 59,434 (Oct. 5, 2000). For text of this guidance, see Appendix I-2 on the disk accompanying this volume.

[509] OIG Compliance Program Guidance for Ambulance Suppliers, 68 Fed. Reg. 14,245 (Mar. 24, 2003).

[510] *See* 68 Fed. Reg. 23,731 (May 5, 2003), available at Appendix I-3.1 on the disk accompanying this volume. This CPG discusses numerous key compliance issues affecting the pharmaceutical industry, including the relationship between pharmaceutical manufacturers and PBMs, the practice of "preceptorship" or shadowing and other consulting arrangements, and manufacturer influence on formulary decisions. Further, the OIG notes that the compliance program elements and potential risk areas "may have application to manufacturers of other products that may be reimbursed by federal health care programs, such as medical devices and infant nutritional products." *Id.* at 23,742 n.5. The Pharma CPG is discussed in more detail in Section III.B.11. in Chapter 7 (Baumann, Corporate Compliance Programs). It is also discussed in MICHAEL E. CLARK, PHARMACEUTICAL LAW: REGULATION OF RESEARCH, DEVELOPMENT, AND MARKETING (BNA 2007).

[511] 70 Fed. Reg. 4858 (Jan. 31, 2005), available at Appendix I-1.2 on the disk accompanying this volume. Additional detail on the Supplemental Hospital CPG is available in Section III.B.1. in Chapter 7 (Baumann, Corporate Compliance Programs).

[512] Draft OIG Compliance Program Guidance for Recipients of PHS Research Awards, 70 Fed. Reg. 71,312, 71,313 (Nov. 28, 2005), available at Appendix I-5 on the disk accompanying

It is important to remember that these compliance program guidance documents are not legally binding. Rather, they have often been described as the OIG's "wish list." However, they contain descriptions of "high-risk" areas that the government is likely to scrutinize and thus should be carefully monitored by health care providers and other entities. Moreover, implementing a corporate compliance program can have various other tangible benefits for health care providers.

It is also important to note that the OIG expects providers to be familiar with and consider relevant provisions from any potentially applicable CPG. Towards this end, all health care companies should review the Supplemental Hospital CPG, which provides considerable new guidance, particularly on auditing to ensure compliance program efficacy.[513]

The Supplemental Hospital CPG supplements the OIG's prior Hospital CPG, which was issued in 1998.[514] The Supplemental Hospital CPG emphasizes risk areas that have emerged since 1998, and it specifically highlights numerous aspects of outpatient procedure coding, admissions and discharges, supplemental payment considerations, and the efficient use of information technology.[515] There is a detailed discussion of various fraud and abuse topics including gainsharing, joint ventures, compensation arrangements with physicians, malpractice insurance subsidies, recruitment practices, cost-sharing waivers, gifts and gratuities, and the offer of free transportation to federal health care program beneficiaries. In addition, the Supplemental Hospital CPG provides advice regarding areas of recent concern to hospitals, including discounts to uninsured patients, preventive care services, and professional courtesy practices. The Supplemental Hospital CPG contains an important new discussion on how to evaluate the effectiveness of a compliance program. In particular, the OIG emphasizes the importance of periodically reviewing the compliance program as a whole, rather than simply focusing on individual audits. This material is relevant to all individuals and entities because the OIG will likely use these criteria to assess all providers' compliance programs, e.g., when deciding whether to impose a CIA in connection with a fraud and abuse settlement.[516]

---

this volume; see also Section III.B.12. in Chapter 7 (Baumann, Corporate Compliance Programs). This guidance is directed toward the recipients of National Institutes of Health extramural research grant and cooperative agreement awards. The draft guidance identified three principal risk areas: (1) the accurate reporting of research time and effort; (2) the proper allocation of charges to multiple research awards; and (3) the reporting of financial support from other sources. Further, this guidance added an eighth element to the previous seven basic components of a compliance program; i.e., that a compliance plan define roles and responsibilities within an organization and ensure the effective assignment of oversight responsibilities.

[513]*See* 70 Fed. Reg. 4858.

[514]OIG Compliance Program Guidance for Hospitals, 63 Fed. Reg. 8,987 (Feb. 23, 1998), available at Appendix I-1.1 on the disk accompanying this volume.

[515]70 Fed. Reg. 4858.

[516]Similarly, it also may be helpful to review Chapter 9 of the Prescription Drug Benefit Manual on Part D Program to Control Fraud, Waste and Abuse, CMS. Chapter 9–Part D Program to Control Fraud, Waste and Abuse, Prescription Drug Benefit Manual (Apr. 25, 2006), *available at* http://www.cms.hhs.gov/Prescription. Unlike the CPGs, many of the manual provisions contained in this chapter are based on legal requirements. Nevertheless, the chapter provides insight into recent government expectations on legal requirements and compliance programs.

These and numerous other issues related to compliance programs are discussed in further detail in a subsequent chapter.[517]

Various other government publications also can be helpful in identifying issues where government enforcement is particularly likely and can provide further guidance as to how federal authorities are interpreting certain requirements. Reviewing such documents can help the attorney assist his or her client in taking a proactive stance to reduce the risk of exposure rather than simply reacting to problems after they arise. In this connection, it may be helpful to review documents such as the OIG's annual Work Plan, the Semiannual Report, and the HHS/DOJ Annual Health Care Fraud and Abuse Control Program Report. In addition, CMS's program manuals and program memoranda may contain relevant material and should be consulted.

## B. The OIG Work Plan

The OIG Work Plan[518] summarizes the major projects the OIG intends to pursue in the coming year in each of HHS's major operating areas. For FY 2007, the report listed numerous projects under such categories as hospitals, home health care, nursing home care, hospice services, physician services, DME supplies, Part B drug reimbursement, Part D administration, other Medicare services, Medicare managed care, Medicare contractor operations, Medicaid services, investigations, and legal counsel. Within each of these and other areas, the OIG listed numerous issues planned for review.[519]

For 2007, with regard to Medicare hospitals, the Work Plan list included the following items, among others:

- Hospital Capital Payments;
- Inpatient Rehabilitation Facility Classification Criteria;
- Adjustments for Graduate Medical Education Payments;
- Payments for Observation Services Versus Inpatient Admission for Dialysis Services;
- Nursing and Allied Health Education Payments;
- Inpatient Prospective Payment System Wage Indices;
- Inpatient Rehabilitation Facility Compliance With Medicare Requirements;
- Inpatient Rehabilitation Payments–Late Assessments;
- Organ Procurement Organizations;
- Inpatient Hospital Payments for New Technologies;
- Inpatient Psychiatric Facilities;
- Long Term Care Hospital Payments;
- Long Term Care Hospital Admissions;
- Long Term Care Hospital Classification;

---

[517] *See* Chapter 7 (Baumann, Corporate Compliance Programs).

[518] The OIG Work Plans are on the OIG Web site, *available at* http://oig.hhs.gov/publications/workplan.html. The most recent version is OFFICE OF INSPECTOR GEN., U.S. DEP'T OF HEALTH & HUMAN SERVS., WORK PLAN, FISCAL YEAR 2007, *available at* http://oig.hhs.gov/publications/docs/workplan/2007/Work%20Plan%202007.pdf [hereinafter WORK PLAN FY 2007].

[519] WORK PLAN FY 2007, at I, iii–iv.

- Critical Access Hospitals;
- Rebates Paid to Hospitals;
- Outpatient Outlier and Other Charge-Related Issues;
- Outpatient Department Payments;
- Unbundling of Hospital Outpatient Services;
- "Inpatient Only" Services Performed in an Outpatient Setting;
- Medical Appropriateness and Coding of Diagnosis Related Group Services;
- Medicare Rural Hospital Flexibility Program;
- Inappropriate Payments for Interpretation of Diagnostic X-rays in Hospital Emergency Departments; and
- Oversight of Specialty Hospitals.[520]

Medicaid hospital issues for review in 2007 included:

- Outlier Payments; and
- Disproportionate Share Hospital Payments.[521]

Home health issues included home health outlier payments, enhanced payments for home health therapy, cyclical noncompliance in Medicare home health agencies, accuracy of data on the home health Compare Web site, accurately coding claims for Medicare home health resource groups, and home health rehabilitation therapy services.[522]

Hospice care issues included hospice payments to nursing facilities as well as plans of care and appropriate payments.

With regard to Medicare nursing homes, the OIG intended to review several issues, including those related to:

- Skilled Facility Rehabilitation and Infusion Therapy Services;
- Skilled Nursing Facilities' Involvement in Consecutive Inpatient Stays;
- Enforcement Actions Against Noncompliant Nursing Homes;
- Skilled Nursing Facility Payments for Day of Discharge;
- Skilled Nursing Facility Consolidated Billing;
- Nursing Home Residents' Minimum Data Set Assessments and Care Planning;
- Imaging and Laboratory Services in Nursing Homes;
- Implementation of Medicare Part D in Nursing Facilities;
- Submission of Skilled Nursing Facility No-Pay Bills; and
- Inappropriate Psychotherapy Services in Nursing Facilities.[523]

Medicaid long term and community care issues for review included:

- Billing for Medicaid Nursing Home Patients Transferred to Hospitals;
- Community Residence Claims;
- Assisted Living Facilities;
- Targeted Case Management;

---

[520] *See id.* at 1–5.

[521] *See id.* at 26.

[522] *Id.* at 6.

[523] *Id.* at 7.

- Home and Community Based Services Administrative Costs; and
- Home and Community Based Services: Erroneous Medicaid Payments After a Beneficiary's Death or Institutionalization.

Issues related to physicians and other health professionals included:

- Billing Service Companies;
- Physician Pathology Services;
- Cardiography and Echocardiography Services;
- Physical and Occupational Therapy Services;
- Payment to Providers for Initial Preventive Physical Examination;
- Part B Mental Health Services;
- Wound Care Services;
- Evaluation of "Incident to" Services;
- Potential Duplicate Physical Therapy Claims;
- Eye Surgeries;
- Place of Service Errors;
- Review of Evaluation and Management Services During Global Surgery Periods;
- Psychiatric Services Provided in an Inpatient Setting;
- Medicare Reimbursement for Polysomnography;
- Long Distance Physician Claims Associated with Home Health and Skilled Nursing Facility Services;
- Violations of Assignment Rules by Medicare Providers; and
- Advanced Imaging Services in Physician Offices.[524]

Added to the DME reviews were DME payments for beneficiaries receiving home health services, Medicare payments for therapeutic footwear, Medicare payments for DME claims with ZX, KX, and KS modifiers, medical necessity, and Medicare pricing of equipment and supplies.[525]

In connection with Medicare Part B drug reimbursement, the OIG planned to examine the computation of ASP, the Part B drug reimbursement methodology, Medicare payments for oral antiemetic medications, payments to independent dialysis facilities for Epogen, Botox treatments, monitoring ASP to widely available market prices and to AMP, duplicate payments for Part B drugs under the CAP, the adequacy of reimbursement for drugs under the ASP, and the Medicare reimbursement and availability of intravenous immune globulin.[526]

Issues of concern related to the administration of Medicare Part D, the fastest growing portion of the Work Plan, included:

- Third Party Liability Safeguards;
- Comparisons of Part D Drug Pricing;
- Medicare Part D: Drug Access Through Prior Authorization and Exceptions;
- Monitoring Drug Prices of Medicare Part D Drug Plans;
- Part D Dual-Eligible Demonstration Project;

---

[524]*Id.* at 9–12.
[525]*Id.* at 12–13.
[526]*Id.* at 13–15.

- Dually Eligible Hospice Patients;
- Medicare Part D Duplicate Claims;
- Coordination and Oversight of Medicare Parts B and D to Avoid Duplicate Payments;
- Allocation of Employer Premiums Under the Retirement Drug Subsidy Program;
- Allowable Costs Under the Retirement Drug Subsidy;
- Actuarial Value of Retiree Prescription Drug Coverage;
- Rebates in the Retirement Retiree Drug Subsidy Program;
- Tracking Beneficiaries True Out-of-Pocket (TrOOP) Costs for Part D Prescription Drug Coverage;
- Prescription Drug Plan Marketing Materials;
- Medicare Prescription Drug Benefit Pharmacy Access in Rural Areas;
- Rural Pharmacy Drug Purchases;
- Medicare Part D Drug Benefit Payments;
- State Contribution to Drug Benefit Costs Assumed by Medicare; and
- Medicare Part D Risk-Sharing Payments and Recoveries.[527]

The OIG's review of other Medicare services in 2007 addressed: laboratory services furnished during an inpatient stay, therapy services provided by comprehensive outpatient rehabilitation facilities (CORFs), emergency health services for undocumented aliens, Medicare reimbursement for ESRD drugs, separately billable laboratory services under the ESRD program, Medicare pricing of laboratory services, and Medicare duplicate claims.[528]

The OIG also planned to evaluate various Medicare managed care areas, such as: administrative costs, the accuracy of payments, managed care encounter data, enhanced managed care payments, duplicate Medicare payments to cost-based plans, Medicare capitation payments after a beneficiary's death, Medicare Advantage regional plan concerns such as availability, physician participation and beneficiary enrollment in rural areas, and Medicare Advantage lock-in provisions.[529]

It may be advisable to review the entire Work Plan each year, at least briefly, because topics of interest may appear under various headings. For example, numerous other relevant OIG reviews may be listed under Medicaid topics including Medicaid Mental Health Services, Medicaid Prescription Drugs, and other Medicaid Services. Even categories such as Medicaid Administration, Information Systems Controls, and Investigations and Legal Counsel may contain useful information on which issues will be subject to OIG scrutiny in the coming year.

## C.  The OIG Semiannual Report

While the OIG Semiannual Report ostensibly documents prior initiatives and enforcement actions, it also provides insight into issues likely to be of

---

[527]*Id.* at 15–19.
[528]*Id.* at 19–20.
[529]*Id.* at 21–22.

continuing concern to the OIG. For example, in the OIG Semiannual Report, April 1, 2006–September 30, 2006,[530] the OIG noted that it would "continue to be involved in hurricane [Katrina]-related investigations" of health care fraud, quality-of-care lapses and other issues. This Semiannual Report also suggested that the OIG would continue to develop partnerships with states to monitor the Medicaid program.[531] Similarly, the OIG had indicated in its Semiannual Report, October 1, 2005–March 31, 2006, that it would continue "to focus on Medicaid activities, including Medicaid prescription drug fraud."[532] Further, the numerous topics discussed in each OIG semiannual report may indicate areas the OIG is likely to investigate in other settings during subsequent time periods.[533]

## D. Enforcement Resources

### 1. The Provider Self-Disclosure Protocol

Relatively few providers used a pilot self-disclosure program implemented by the OIG in 1995 due to numerous inherent limitations. As a result, the program was modified to a certain extent when the Provider Self-Disclosure Protocol (Self-Disclosure Protocol) was published in 1998.[534] The Self-Disclosure Protocol is open to all health care providers (individuals and entities) throughout the industry. Even providers currently subject to a government investigation or audit may be eligible to participate. The Self-Disclosure Protocol is specifically designed for matters that may violate federal criminal, civil, and administrative laws, and the OIG emphasizes that overpayments should be handled by the appropriate government contractor instead (although the contractor ultimately may refer the matter to the OIG).

The Self-Disclosure Protocol specifies certain detailed information, investigative procedures, and a certification that the disclosing party is to furnish. While the OIG suggests that using the Self-Disclosure Protocol may be advantageous to the provider, the OIG specifically declines to "make firm commitments as to how a particular disclosure will be resolved or the specific benefit that will inure to the disclosing entity."[535] However, providers using the Self-Disclosure Protocol likely can expect to be more favorably viewed by the OIG (in the numerous areas where the OIG has tremendous discretion in enforcing the fraud and abuse laws). In addition, the requisite investigation may

---

[530]U.S. DEP'T OF HEALTH & HUMAN SERVS., OFFICE OF INSPECTOR GEN., SEMIANNUAL REPORT APR.–SEPT. 2006, *available at* http://oig.hhs.gov/publications/docs/semiannual/2006/Semiannual%20Final%20FY%202006.pdf.

[531]*Id.* at 18.

[532]U.S. DEP'T OF HEALTH & HUMAN SERVS., OFFICE OF INSPECTOR GEN., SEMIANNUAL REPORT OCT. 1, 2005–MAR. 31, 2006, at i, *available at* http://oig.hhs.gov/publications/docs/semiannual/2006/SemiannualSpring2006.pdf [hereinafter SEMIANNUAL REPORT OCT. 2005–MAR. 2006].

[533]All OIG semiannual reports are available at http://www.oig.hhs.gov/publications/semiannual.html.

[534]63 Fed. Reg. 58,399 (Oct. 30, 1998), *available at* http://oig.hhs.gov/authorities/docs/selfdisclosure.pdf.

[535]*Id.* at 58,400.

be less intrusive, and the provider generally may have more control over how the facts are presented to the government when using the Self-Disclosure Protocol. On the other hand, using the Self-Disclosure Protocol can entail certain significant risks, e.g., documents prepared in connection with the internal investigations required under the Self-Disclosure Protocol may lose their privileged status, the investigation may alert and activate potential whistle-blowers, and the investigation may educate the OIG about other potential problems.

After balancing these and other considerations, voluntary disclosure may be a beneficial option in certain cases. However, most providers continue to be reluctant to use this procedure. As a result, in subsequent years, the OIG has taken additional measures to make the Self-Disclosure Protocol a more attractive option.

## 2. *The Inspector General's Open Letter on the CIA Process*

On November 20, 2001, Inspector General Janet Rehnquist issued an Open Letter to Health Care Providers announcing several new initiatives intended to modify various aspects of the corporate integrity agreement (CIA) process and terms.[536] A Summary of New CIA Claims Review Procedures and Frequently Asked Questions Regarding the OIG's New Corporate Integrity Agreement (CIA) Claims Review Requirement were attached to the open letter. These materials indicate several important developments, including the fact that resolution of a FCA case now may proceed separately from resolution of the provider's permissive exclusion liability. In addition, when determining whether to require a CIA, the OIG has indicated that it will consider the following factors:

- whether the provider self-disclosed the alleged misconduct;
- the monetary damage to federal health care programs;
- whether the case involves successor liability;
- whether the provider is still participating in federal health care programs or is still in the line of business that gave rise to the fraudulent conduct;
- whether the alleged conduct is capable of repetition;
- the age of the conduct;
- whether the provider has an effective compliance program and would agree to limited compliance or integrity measures and would annually certify such compliance to the OIG; and
- other circumstances, as appropriate.

The new CIA claims review procedures contained several notable features:

- full statistically valid random samples are now required only when initial claims review (the discovery sample) reveals a high error rate;
- discovery samples will consist of 50 randomly selected paid claims from each relevant universe and may be validated by the OIG;

---

[536] An Open Letter to Health Care Providers, Janet Rehnquist, Inspector General (Nov. 20, 2001), *available at* http://oig.hhs.gov/fraud/docs/openletters/openletter111901.htm. *See also* http://oig.hhs.gov/fraud/cias.html for various other guidance documents related to CIAs.

- no further audit work for the year is required if the error rate in the discovery sample is below five percent;
- the error rate is calculated by dividing net overpayments by the total dollar amount associated with sample items;
- if the error rate is five percent or more over the reimbursement received for all sampled claims, an independent review organization (IRO) must conduct a statistically valid random sample (SVRS) (90 percent confidence/25 percent precision level) for that time period;
- identified overpayments must be repaid pursuant to payor policies;
- providers must conduct a systems review related to the identified errors in the discovery sample concurrently with the SVRS;
- providers currently operating under a CIA may be allowed to use the new claims review requirements; existing CIAs will be reviewed on an individual basis;
- IROs will still be required for certain billing reviews if required under an existing CIA; and
- compliance engagement requirements may be waived.

In her CIA open letter, Inspector General Rehnquist also indicated that the OIG is exploring ways to increase reliance on providers' internal audit capabilities and provide more flexibility related to employee training.

### 3. 2006 Open Letter to Health Care Providers

On April 24, 2006, Inspector General Levinson issued an Open Letter to Health Care Providers announcing a new OIG initiative to promote the use of the Self-Disclosure Protocol.[537] to resolve CMP liability for hospital-physician financial arrangements that violate both the Stark and anti-kickback statutes. The new initiative is intended to supplement the Self-Disclosure Protocol by indicating how certain types of self-disclosures are likely to be resolved. However, the initiative is limited to conduct involving a financial benefit knowingly given to a physician by a hospital that could lead to CMP liability under both the Stark law and the anti-kickback statute in the provider's reasonable assessment.

The OIG noted that it had the authority under the CMP laws to calculate damages under the Stark law based on the number and dollar value of improper claims, while kickback CMP damages are calculated based on the number and dollar value of the improper remuneration. Providers using the Self-Disclosure Protocol in cases that qualify under this initiative will likely face damages falling toward the lower end of the continuum; i.e., a multiplier of the financial value of the benefit given to the physician(s) by the hospital. Participation under the Self-Disclosure Protocol requires "full cooperation and complete disclosure of the facts and circumstances surrounding the violation," and the degree of cooperation will affect the terms of the settlement. The provider's compliance program will be evaluated when the OIG determines whether a CIA or a (less onerous) Certification of Compliance Agreement also will be required.

---

[537] OIG Provider Self-Disclosure Protocol, 63 Fed. Reg. 58,399 (Oct. 30, 1998).

Finally, the OIG acknowledged that participation in the Self-Disclosure Protocol and the resulting agreements with the OIG are not binding on DOJ.

## E. Miscellaneous

Several other resources are available to assist lawyers trying to counsel their health care clients. Notably, speeches by government officials can provide guidance as to likely agency interpretation of particular regulatory provisions or indicate changing enforcement priorities. OIG officials' testimony before Congress can often be found on the OIG Web site.[538] Other speeches are frequently given at conferences and seminars sponsored by various organizations across the country. As a practical matter, it is not feasible to attend all these meetings, and there is usually no way to know in advance exactly which topics will be addressed. Fortunately, the trade press is aware of the government's propensity to use these venues and generally reports on important new developments.

The speakers often preface their remarks by noting that they are expressing their personal views and, in any event, such semiofficial pronouncements cannot make new law. Nevertheless, in light of all the complexities and ambiguities in the laws and regulations, these comments can provide helpful guidance.

CMS periodically holds Open Door Forums on a wide range of topics that also furnish guidance on regulatory issues. It usually is possible to participate in person or by conference call.[539] Such guidance can be critical in the fraud and abuse context because regulatory violations often are the basis for subsequent fraud allegations. In addition, materials published by trade associations and others in the industry, although not legally binding, can be helpful. For example, the Code on Interactions with Healthcare Professionals, published by the Pharmaceutical Research and Manufacturers of America (PhRMA Code)[540] was referenced in the OIG's Pharmaceutical Compliance Guidance, which recommended using the PhRMA Code standards as a minimum baseline in order to achieve compliance with the fraud and abuse laws.[541]

## V. Conclusion

Simply identifying the applicable health care fraud and abuse requirements in what appears to be a typical commercial transaction can be a challenge, particularly for those who do not specialize in health care law. This book

---

[538] *See* http://oig.hhs.gov/reading/testimony.html.

[539] *See* http://www.cms.hhs.gov/OpenDoorForums for more information.

[540] Pharmaceutical Research & Mfrs. of Am., PhRMA Code on Interactions with Healthcare Professionals (July 1, 2002), *available at* http://www.phrma.org/files/ PhRMA%20Code.pdf. The PhRMA Code is reprinted as Appendix I-3.2 on the disk accompanying this volume. For further information, *see* PhRMA's Web site at http://www.phrma.org.

[541] OIG Compliance Program Guidance for Pharmaceutical Manufacturers, 68 Fed. Reg. 23,731, 23,737 (May 5, 2003). Other trade associations have also issued industry codes that help demonstrate company/individual compliance with industry standards. *Also see, e.g.,* Advanced Medical Technology Association (AdvaMed) Code of Ethics on Interactions with Health Care Professionals, *available at* http://www.advamed.org/publicdocs/coe.html.

is intended both to serve as a useful starting point and to provide more advanced, practical guidance for any attorney handling arrangements that could implicate one or more of the various laws and regulations relating to health care fraud and abuse. This chapter is directed at those with less background in this area, and has endeavored to provide an overview of many of the more important subjects, references, and resources in the field. The subsequent chapters, which address a number of related subjects in considerable detail, will be particularly helpful for the experienced health care attorney as well as for those whose expertise lies in other areas.

As the statistics and other data in this chapter indicate, all those individuals and entities involved in the health care industry, as well as their attorneys, potentially face a significant degree of exposure if they fail to comply with any one of the complex laws and regulations relating to health care fraud and abuse. While many of these laws cannot be violated absent improper intent, other statutory schemes impose a form of strict liability.

Various government agencies now have extensive funds and personnel available to investigate and prosecute those who fail to fully comply with these provisions, and the penalties can be enormous. However, the government is also making efforts to help the industry come into compliance through initiatives such as the issuance of advisory opinions, special advisory bulletins, compliance program guidance documents, and other supplemental materials.

Fraud and abuse enforcement actions are not likely to diminish significantly at any time in the foreseeable future. In fact, state agencies and private payors seem to be getting more actively involved in health care fraud audits, investigations, and prosecutions. Virtually every segment of the health care industry has been subject to criticism for fraudulent or abusive practices over the past decade, including hospitals, nursing homes, hospices, therapy providers, DME suppliers, physicians, GPOs, distributors, and pharmaceutical manufacturers. There are indications that other types of entities such as device manufacturers and Part D plans will face increasing review in the future. Moreover, government focus on quality-of-care cases also seems likely to increase.

The best protection for any health care entity, and for those who do business with them, is to be sure their attorney is very well informed about the current laws, regulations, and interpretations relevant to this area. This in-depth knowledge is also essential for the attorney involved in a health care transaction or case, so he or she will not face exposure.

# 2

# Federal Physician Self-Referral Restrictions*

*Thomas S. Crane, J.D., M.H.S.A. The author gratefully acknowledges the substantial assistance provided by his colleagues, Theresa C. Carnegie, J.D.; Io C. Cyrus, J.D.; David L. Cusano, J.D.; Brian P. Dunphy, J.D.; Garret G. Gillespie, J.D.; Karen S. Lovitch, J.D.; Sarah L. Whipple, J.D.; and Jennifer E. Williams, J.D.

The views expressed in this chapter are the personal, professional views of the author and do not represent the formal position of Mintz, Levin, Cohn, Ferris, Glovsky and Popeo, P.C., any other individual attorneys at the firm, or any of its clients. The author expressly reserves the right to advocate freely other positions on behalf of clients.

# I. Introduction

For more than two decades, the Social Security Act has criminalized physician self-referral through the federal health care program anti-kickback statute.[1] Congress's original concern in enacting the anti-kickback statute was to prevent fraud and abuse that might result from a variety of business and professional arrangements involving individuals in a position to influence patient referrals. In 1989, however, Congress developed another approach to the problem by enacting a sweeping, targeted federal restriction on physician self-referrals. Specifically, the federal Medicare/Medicaid self-referral statute prohibits a physician from referring Medicare/Medicaid patients for designated health services (DHS) to entities with which the physician (or an immediate

---

[1] Social Security Amendments of 1972, Pub. L. No. 92-603, 86 Stat. 1329 (1972) (originally codified at 42 U.S.C. §1395h (1972); presently codified at 42 U.S.C. §1320a-7b(b) (1987)). See Appendix A-1 on the disk accompanying this volume for full text of the anti-kickback statute.

family member) has a financial relationship, unless the relationship is permitted by one of the enumerated exceptions to the statute.[2]

From its inception to the present, the federal Medicare/Medicaid self-referral statute has undergone considerable change and has been subject to volumes of interpretative writings. Proponents of self-referral restrictions maintain that physicians' medical judgments as to where and when to refer patients are corrupted, however subtly, by their financial relationships with referral sources, thereby negatively affecting the quality and price of health care services and patient care. Among the many deleterious effects of self-referral, according to these proponents of restrictions, is that physicians with financial arrangements will order unnecessary services that result in increased costs to third-party payors.

Conversely, critics of restrictions on physician self-referral argue that self-referral arrangements may improve the quality of patient care because the financial arrangement fosters a stronger working relationship between the physician and the entity providing the item or service. This relationship works to ensure that the entity provides superior health care services because entities with a reputation for providing substandard services are likely to lose money. In addition, critics argue that prohibiting a physician from referring patients to an entity may make physicians hesitant to invest their own time and money in certain projects. Accordingly, certain necessary medical items and services may not become available, and a vital source of funding no longer will be available in the health care market. Regardless of this ongoing debate, the federal Medicare/Medicaid self-referral statute will continue to have a significant impact on the delivery and structure of health care in the United States.[3]

The author's approach in this chapter has been to discuss various sections of the statute and its implementing regulations thematically and to devote separate sections to important exceptions. For example, Section VI. groups together all of the exceptions that relate to physician compensation even though, in some cases (for example with group practices and academic medical centers), only the compensation provisions of those exceptions are discussed, leaving the discussion of other aspects of these exceptions for other sections. Next, Section VII. covers the exception for indirect compensation, which is combined with a discussion of the definition of that term.

Even a brief reading of this chapter will make abundantly clear the complex nature of the Medicare/Medicaid self-referral statute and its implementing regulations. This chapter is intended to aid providers and their counsel in obtaining a preliminary overview of the issues raised in the Medicare/Medicaid self-referral statute and the implementing regulations, but **none of the information or analysis contained herein should be construed as providing legal advice. Readers should consult counsel familiar with the statute when questions arise.**

---

[2]Omnibus Budget Reconciliation Act of 1989 (OBRA 1989), Pub. L. No. 101-239, §6204, 103 Stat. 2106 (1989), *codified at* 42 U.S.C. §1395nn. See Appendix B-1 on the disk accompanying this volume for full text of the physician self-referral statute.

[3]In addition, certain states have enacted laws that prohibit or restrict physician self-referrals. These state laws are outside the scope of this chapter. Because these laws vary considerably as to their scope and penalties, however, practitioners need to review them closely.

## II. Historical Background

### A. Self-Referral Studies

Congress recognized the need for the federal Medicare/Medicaid self-referral statute after reviewing the findings of numerous studies regarding financial arrangements between physicians and health care entities.

### 1. *Medicare Catastrophic Coverage Act of 1988*

In 1988, Congress enacted the Medicare Catastrophic Coverage Act of 1988.[4] Although subsequently repealed by Congress,[5] the Catastrophic Coverage Act would have expanded Medicare coverage of intravenous (IV) drug therapies while simultaneously prohibiting home IV providers from providing services to Medicare or Medicaid beneficiaries referred by physicians who had ownership interests in, or received compensation from, the home IV provider. The Catastrophic Coverage Act also required the Office of Inspector General (OIG) of the Department of Health and Human Services (HHS) to perform a study of ownership or compensation arrangements between physicians and entities providing Medicare covered services (the OIG Study). The conference report for the Catastrophic Coverage Act revealed that Congress sought the OIG Study to address concerns regarding physician self-referral arrangements that might have existed beyond the scope of home IV therapy benefits.[6]

### 2. *The OIG Study*

The OIG Study was issued on April 30, 1989, and it contained findings on numerous issues, including the variety and scope of self-referral arrangements and the potential for such arrangements to lead to overutilization of health care services.[7] After providing an overview of several other studies regarding physician ownership,[8] the OIG Study focused on physician investments in

---

[4]Medicare Catastrophic Coverage Act of 1988, Pub. L. No. 100-360, 102 Stat. 683 (1988).

[5]Medicare Catastrophic Coverage Repeal Act of 1989, Pub. L. No. 101-234, 103 Stat. 1979 (1989).

[6]H.R. Conf. Rep. No. 100–661 (1988), *reprinted in* 1988 U.S.C.C.A.N. 923.

[7]Office of Inspector Gen., U.S. Dep't of Health & Human Servs., Report to Congress, *Financial Arrangements Between Physicians and Health Care Businesses,* No. OA-12–88–01410, *reprinted in* Medicare & Medicaid Guide (CCH) ¶37,838, at 19,925–19,938 [hereinafter OIG Study].

[8]*Id.* at 19,927. The OIG Study cited to the following studies: Mich. Dep't of Social Servs., Med. Servs. Admin., *Utilization of Medicaid Laboratory Services by Physicians With/Without Ownership Interest in Clinical Laboratories: A Comparative Analysis* (June 9, 1981) (finding that Michigan Medicaid recipients referred by physician-owners averaged 41% more tests than those referred by nonowners); Division of Health Standards & Quality, Region V, Health Care Fin. Admin., Dep't of Health & Human Servs., *Diagnostic Clinical Laboratory Services in Region V,* #2–05–2004–11 (May 1983) (finding that patients of practice-related laboratories have a higher incidence of service per patient than patients of nonpractice-related laboratories); Med. Affairs Div., Blue Cross & Blue Shield of Mich., *A Comparison of Laboratory Utilization and Payout to Ownership* (May 9, 1984) (finding that laboratories owned by physicians provided 20% more services than the average for all laboratories and 40% more services than nonphysician-owned laboratories).

independent clinical laboratories, independent physiological laboratories, and durable medical equipment (DME) suppliers. Overall, the OIG Study found that 12 percent of the physicians who billed the Medicare program had ownership or investment interests in entities to which they made patient referrals.[9] The OIG Study found a prevalence of physician investments in a wide range of health-related businesses other than the independent clinical and physiological laboratories and DME suppliers that were the focus of the OIG Study, including home health agencies, hospitals, nursing homes, ambulatory surgical centers, and health maintenance organizations.[10] Moreover, the OIG Study found that, nationally, at least 25 percent of independent clinical laboratories, 27 percent of independent physiological laboratories, and 8 percent of DME suppliers were owned in whole or in part by referring physicians.

Regarding utilization, the OIG Study stated that patients of physician-owned independent clinical laboratories received 45 percent more clinical laboratory services than all Medicare patients in general.[11] The OIG estimated that this increased utilization of clinical laboratory services by patients of physician-owners cost the Medicare program $28 million in 1987. Patients of physician-owned independent physiological laboratories received 13 percent more physiological laboratory services than the national Medicare average. Patients of physicians who owned or invested in DME suppliers, however, did not use any more DME than all Medicare patients in general.

Of note is that neither the OIG Study, nor the vast majority of subsequent studies, attempted to evaluate the effects of physician ownership on the quality of care or outcomes. However, many researchers used the utilization variable as a proxy for quality. Thus, an inference exists that quality of care may be suspect where utilization disparities appear to be explained only by self-referral. Of course, such inferences may well be rebutted by other patient care measures.

In what remains the only reported study that examines self-referrals related to compensation arrangements, as opposed to ownership interests, the OIG Study also found that 8 percent of Medicare physicians had compensation arrangements with entities to which they referred patients.[12] These compensation arrangements varied from space rental agreements and consulting agreements to management service contracts. The OIG did not attempt to examine the effects of such compensation arrangements on the utilization of services.

Based on the results of the OIG Study, the OIG recommended that the Health Care Financing Administration (HCFA), now the Centers for Medicare and Medicaid Services (CMS),[13] pursue the legislative and regulatory changes necessary to require entities billing Medicare to disclose to the program the names of physician-owners and -investors, and to require claims submitted by

---

[9]OIG Study at 19,931.

[10]*Id.* at 19,931–32.

[11]*Id.* at 19,933–34.

[12]*Id.* at 19,932.

[13]As of July 1, 2001, the former Health Care Financing Administration (HCFA) was renamed the Centers for Medicare and Medicaid Services (CMS). For the purposes of this chapter, references will be to CMS.

all entities providing services under Medicare Part B to include the names and provider numbers of referring physicians.[14] To address overutilization problems by physician-owners and -investors, the OIG Study also urged legislators and administrators to pursue the following six options:

1. Implement a post-payment utilization review program by carriers directed at physicians who own or invest in other health care entities.
2. Require physicians to disclose financial interests to patients.
3. Improve enforcement of the federal health care programs anti-kickback statute.
4. Institute a private right of action for anti-kickback cases.
5. Prohibit self-referral arrangements involving specific types of health care entities in which physicians have a financial interest.
6. Prohibit physicians from referring to any entity in which they have a financial interest.

### 3. The Florida Study

In the same year that the OIG Study was released, the Florida legislature required the Florida Health Care Cost Containment Board (HCCB) to conduct a special study of joint venture arrangements between health care providers. The Florida legislature required the HCCB to conduct specific studies that would identify, analyze, and evaluate the impact of ownership and compensation interests on referrals by persons who provide health care. Moreover, the HCCB was required to submit recommendations that would work to strengthen enforcement of Florida anti-kickback laws and coordinate interagency regulation of joint venture relationships in the health care industry. The HCCB issued a series of three final reports detailing the results of its study (collectively, the Florida Report).[15]

In 1991, Volume I of the Florida Report stated that "[o]f the eight states covered by the [OIG] study, Florida had the highest percentage of physicians involved in joint ventures. Medicare patients of physician owners in Florida received 40 percent more lab tests and 12 percent more diagnostic imaging tests, and utilized 16 percent more durable medical equipment than the general population of Florida Medicare beneficiaries."[16] In general, the HCCB's findings revealed that physician ownership of health care businesses providing diagnostic testing or similar ancillary services was common in Florida. The HCCB reported:

> [M]ore than three-fourths of the responding ambulatory surgical facilities and about 93 percent of the diagnostic imaging centers are owned either wholly or in part by physicians. Almost 80 percent of the responding radiation therapy centers, more than 60 percent of the responding clinical laboratories and nearly 40 percent of the responding physical therapy and/or rehabilitation facilities also report physician owners. Furthermore, about 20 percent of the responding durable

---

[14]OIG Study at 19,936–37.

[15]Fla. Health Care Cost Containment Bd., Joint Ventures Among Health Care Providers in Florida, Vol. I (Jan. 1991), Vol. II (Sept. 1991), Vol. III (Oct. 1991).

[16]*Id.*, Vol. I, at iv–v.

medical equipment businesses, as well as close to 13 percent of the home health agencies, are owned by physicians.[17]

The HCCB also reported that a high percentage of patients who were referred to a physician-owned health care facility were sent there by the physician-owner. As a result of its findings, the HCCB recommended that the Florida legislature consider prohibiting physician owners from referring patients to the four specific facility types that the HCCB identified as being problematic—clinical laboratories, diagnostic imaging centers, physician therapy/rehabilitation centers, and radiation therapy centers.[18]

## B. Legislative History

On August 10, 1988, Congressman Fortney "Pete" Stark (D-Cal.) addressed the issue of physician self-referrals by introducing a bill, H.R. 5198, "to amend Title XVIII of the Social Security Act to provide civil monetary penalties (CMPs) and other remedies for certain improper referral arrangements for services provided under the Medicare program."[19] This bill would have barred physician referrals for all Medicare covered services; the bill ultimately formed the basis for the Ethics in Patient Referrals Act of 1988, which was introduced by Congressman Stark and enacted on December 19, 1989.[20] Partially as a result of the OIG Study that found elevated numbers of referrals only for clinical laboratory services, subsequent congressional negotiations in 1989 narrowed the scope of the legislation to apply only to referrals for clinical laboratory services.

In his remarks to the House of Representatives in 1988, when his original bill was introduced, Congressman Stark described his frustration with the failure of the anti-kickback statute to stop physician self-referrals even though the anti-kickback statute is a "sweeping law prohibiting payment of kickbacks for patient referrals under Medicare . . . [that] is clear on its face[.]"[21] He noted that providers of medical services, despite the anti-kickback statute, had continued to develop and promote "a variety of new forms of business organization specifically intended to secure patient referrals from physicians."[22] With respect to joint ventures with physicians, in particular, Congressman Stark complained that "lawyers advising health care clients have recognized that joint ventures with physicians are potentially within the scope of Medicare's anti-kickback law, but have argued that such ventures are nonetheless permissible if

---

[17]*Id.*

[18]*Id.,* Vol. III, at 23. The Florida legislature subsequently enacted the Florida Patient Self-Referral Act of 1992, which prohibits a health care provider from referring a patient for "designated health services" (clinical laboratory services, physical therapy services, comprehensive rehabilitative services, diagnostic imaging services, and radiation therapy services) to an entity in which the health care provider is an investor or has an investment interest. *See* FLA. STAT. ANN. §456.653.

[19]Ethics in Patient Referrals Act of 1988, H.R. 5198, 100th Cong. (1988).

[20]OBRA 1989, Pub. L. No. 101-239, §6204, *codified at* 42 U.S.C. §1395nn.

[21]134 CONG. REC. E2724–02 (daily ed. Aug. 11, 1988) (statement of Rep. Stark).

[22]*Id.*

(i) there is no explicit requirement that physician investors make referrals and (ii) dividend payments do not vary in proportion to the number of referrals made by the physician investor."[23]

Finally, in support of the bill, Congressman Stark explained the two major shortcomings of the anti-kickback statute as being "the enormous difficulty involved in proving to the satisfaction of a judge in a criminal or civil enforcement action that a particular arrangement is deliberately structured to induce referrals[,]"[24] and the OIG's inability to adequately enforce the anti-kickback statute due to a severe lack of resources and shortage of investigators.

Congressman Stark's solution was the Ethics in Patient Referrals Act. On introducing the bill in 1998, he remarked that

> what is needed is what lawyers call a bright-line rule to give providers and physicians unequivocal guidance as to the types of arrangements that are permissible and the types that are prohibited. If the law is clear and the penalties are severe, we can rely on self-enforcement in the great majority of the cases.
> [My bill] provides this bright-line rule.[25]

As a result of Congressman Stark's dedication to the issue of physician self-referral, the federal Medicare/Medicaid self-referral statute is commonly referred to as the "Stark law," and the initial legislation enacted in 1989 became known as "Stark I."[26] Stark I provided that, for services furnished on or after January 1, 1992, a physician who has a financial relationship with an entity that furnishes clinical laboratory services (or a physician with an immediate family member who has such a relationship) may not make a referral to that entity for clinical laboratory services that are reimbursable by Medicare unless certain exceptions are met.

In 1993, Congress significantly amended the Stark law as part of the Omnibus Budget Reconciliation Act of 1993 (OBRA 1993),[27] and the legislation became known as "Stark II." Specifically, Stark II expanded the scope of Stark I to cover referrals for numerous DHS in addition to clinical laboratory services, and included referrals for services payable under the Medicaid program. In addition, Stark II significantly amended many of the statutory definitions and exceptions enacted in Stark I.

Stark II, applicable to DHS other than clinical laboratory services, generally went into effect for referrals made after December 31, 1994. The effective date for those provisions of Stark II that amended the definitions and exceptions contained in Stark I, however, was generally made retroactive to January 1, 1992.

---

[23] *Id.*

[24] *Id.*

[25] *Id.*

[26] Stark I was amended by §4207(e) of the Omnibus Budget Reconciliation Act of 1990 (OBRA 1990) to clarify certain definitions and reporting requirements regarding physician ownership and referral and to provide an additional exception to the prohibition. *See generally* Pub. L. No. 101-508, 104 Stat. 1388 (1990).

[27] Omnibus Budget Reconciliation Act of 1993 (OBRA 1993), Pub. L. No. 103-66, §13562, 107 Stat. 312 (1993).

## C. Regulatory History

### 1. Sanctions

The OIG is delegated with the authority to impose CMPs under the Stark law. The regulations implementing these provisions were issued by the OIG on March 31, 1995.[28]

### 2. Stark I

HCFA, now CMS, published a proposed regulation implementing Stark I on March 11, 1992.[29] The final Stark I regulation was published on August 14, 1995, and became effective on September 13, 1995.[30]

### 3. Stark II Proposed Rule

On January 9, 1998, CMS issued a proposed rule (Proposed Rule), Medicare and Medicaid Programs: Physicians' Referrals to Health Care Entities With Which They Have Financial Relationships.[31] On January 9, 1998, CMS also published a final rule to implement the Stark law advisory opinion process.[32] This rule was promulgated pursuant to the Balanced Budget Act of 1997 (BBA), which required the Secretary of HHS to issue written advisory opinions regarding whether a particular referral relating to a DHS (other than clinical laboratory services) is prohibited by the Stark law.[33] The BBA directed the Secretary to apply to the Stark advisory opinion process, to the extent practicable, the rules governing advisory opinions interpreting the anti-kickback, CMP, and Medicare exclusion statutes promulgated by the OIG pursuant to the Health Insurance Portability and Accountability Act of 1996[34] in February 1997.[35]

### 4. Stark II Final Rules

#### a. Phase I and II

CMS implemented Stark II in two phases. All final regulations are now codified at 42 C.F.R. part 411, subpart J (Sections 411.350–411.361) (collectively, the Final Rules).

---

[28]Civil Money Penalties for Referrals to Entities and for Prohibited Arrangements and Schemes, 60 Fed. Reg. 16,580 (Mar. 31, 1995), *codified at* 42 C.F.R. §1003.102(a)(5) (2004).

[29]Medicare Program; Physician Ownership of, and Referrals to, Health Care Entities that Furnish Clinical Laboratory Services, 57 Fed. Reg. 8588 (Mar. 11, 1992), *codified at* 42 C.F.R. pt. 411 (2004).

[30]Medicare Program; Physician Ownership of, and Referrals to, Health Care Entities that Furnish Clinical Laboratory Services, 60 Fed. Reg. 41,914 (Aug. 14, 1995), *codified at* 42 C.F.R. pt. 411.

[31]63 Fed. Reg. 1659 (Jan. 9, 1998), *codified at* 42 C.F.R. pts. 411, 424, 435 & 455 (2004).

[32]Medicare Program; Physicians' Referrals; Issuance of Advisory Opinions, 63 Fed. Reg. 1646 (Jan. 9, 1998), *codified at* 42 C.F.R. §§411.370–.389.

[33]Pub. L. No. 105-33, §4314, 111 Stat. 251, *codified at* 42 U.S.C. §1395nn(g)(6).

[34]Pub. L. No. 104-191, §205, 100 Stat. 1936, *codified at* 42 U.S.C. §1320a-7d(b).

[35]Medicare Program; Physicians' Referrals; Issuance of Advisory Opinions, 63 Fed. Reg. 38,311 (July 16, 1998), *codified at* 42 C.F.R. pt. 1008.

Phase I was published on January 4, 2001, as an interim final rule subject to notice and comment (Phase I Final Rule).[36] The Phase I Final Rule provided a comprehensive review of the statutory history of the Stark law and implemented (1) the general statutory prohibition on referrals; (2) statutory and regulatory definitions, including definitions of direct and indirect ownership or investment interests, direct and indirect compensation arrangements, and group practice; (3) the statutory exceptions for ownership and compensation arrangements, including in-office ancillary services; (4) new regulatory exceptions for ownership and compensation arrangements, such as academic medical centers; and (5) new regulatory compensation exceptions, for example, for fair market value and indirect compensation arrangements.[37] This rule only addresses the applicability of the Stark law to the Medicare program.

The Phase I Final Rule did not address the statutory Sections 1877(c), (d), and (e) providing exceptions for ownership and compensation (e.g., the employee and personal services exceptions), as well as Section 1877(f) related to reporting requirements.

On March 26, 2004, CMS released the second phase of the final regulation (Phase II Final Rule), providing responses to comments and changes to the Phase I Final Rule and implementing the remaining statutory exceptions and new regulatory definitions and exceptions as well as the reporting requirements of the law.[38] The Phase II Final Rule also implemented the moratorium on physician ownership of specialty hospitals enacted as part of the Medicare Prescription Drug, Improvement, and Modernization Act of 2003 (MMA).[39] But this rule did not implement Stark II related to Medicaid services.

CMS issued the Phase II Final Rule as an interim rule with comments, and will issue a subsequent rule (Phase III) responding to these comments.

The Health Law Section of the American Bar Association filed detailed comments on both phases of the final rule.[40]

### b. Annual Rulemaking Cycle

In August 2006, CMS for the first time used the annual rulemaking cycle of the physician fee schedule rules to target one of the issues raised in the Stark II Final Rule related to so-called "pod labs" and the In-Office Ancillary Services exception. These proposed changes are discussed more fully in Section VIII.B.2., below.

---

[36]Medicare and Medicaid Programs; Physicians' Referrals to Health Care Entities With Which They Have Financial Relationships (Phase I), 66 Fed. Reg. 856 (Jan. 4, 2001), *codified at* 42 C.F.R. pts. 411 & 424.

[37]According to CMS, these provisions implement subsections (a), (b), and (h) of the statute. 66 Fed. Reg. at 856.

[38]Medicare and Medicaid Programs; Physicians' Referrals to Health Care Entities With Which They Have Financial Relationships (Phase II), 69 Fed. Reg. 16,054 (Mar. 26, 2004), *codified at* 42 C.F.R. pts. 411 & 424.

[39]Medicare Prescription Drug, Improvement, and Modernization Act of 2003 (MMA), Pub. L. No. 108-173, §507, 117 Stat. 2066 (2003).

[40]Andrew B. Wachler et al., *Stark II Phase II: The Final Voyage,* 16 HEALTH LAW. (No. 4) (Apr. 2004) (Special Edition); Patricia T. Meador et al., *ABA Health Law Section Comments to Stark II, Phase I,* 14 HEALTH LAW. (Sept. 2001) (Special Edition).

Practitioners should anticipate that CMS will use the annual fee schedule updates as a future vehicle to amend these regulations, thus enabling it to avoid the cumbersome process used to date of omnibus rulemaking. This trend was seen in CMS's July 12, 2007, publication of its 2008 proposed Medicare Physician Fee Schedule, containing several potentially important changes to CMS's Stark law regulations.[41] Because this rulemaking only represents CMS's proposals, they will not be discussed further. However, practitioners should closely watch these developments.

### c. Phase III Rule

CMS's Phase III rule finalizes those areas remaining open after the 2004 Phase II Final Rule. Pursuant to a new requirement of the MMA, CMS was obliged to publish Phase III by March 26, 2007, i.e., three years from the promulgation of Phase II, "except under exceptional circumstances."[42] On March 23, 2007, CMS announced a delay of up to one year.[43] Although it appeared that CMS could lawfully proceed to finalize those issues raised in the Phase II Final Rule, in *Renal Physicians Ass'n v. Department of Health and Human Services*, the United States Court of Appeals for the District of Columbia Circuit indicated there were questions about "the continued viability" of issues raised in the 1998 Stark II Proposed Rule, but not yet addressed in any of the final rules, and found that with respect to the Phase II Final Rule: "CMS restarted the rulemaking process from scratch but waived publication of a notice of proposed rulemaking."[44] Thus, any issues CMS may have wanted to revisit from earlier rulemakings would need to be raised as a proposed rule.

**Editor's Note:** On September 5, 2007, CMS published the Phase III rule.[45] Although the Phase III rule came out too late to update this chapter, see the Addendum immediately following Chapter 2 for a thoughtful discussion of the rule, which reprints the author's September 26, 2007, analysis for BNA's Health Care Fraud Report, *Stark Phase III Regulation—Analysis and Commentary*.[46]

### d. CMS's Approach to Drafting the Final Rules

In drafting the Final Rules, HHS clearly sought to re-examine the Stark law's statutory language and legislative history, to reconsider the Proposed Rule, and to respond to the industry's concerns about the Phase I Rule, the Proposed Rule, and the Stark law itself. HHS stated that it wanted to "reduce the burden and prescriptive nature"[47] of the Stark law and to avoid the "undue

---

[41]72 Fed Reg. 38122 (July 12, 2007).

[42]42 U.S.C. §1395hh(a)(3)(B).

[43]72 Fed. Reg. 13,710 (Mar. 23, 2007).

[44]489 F.3d 1267, 1270 (D.C. Cir. 2007).

[45]72 Fed. Reg. 51,012 (Sept. 5, 2007). The final rule is reproduced as Appendix B-4 on the disk accompanying this volume. The full, updated Stark rules are reproduced as Appendix B-5 on the disk accompanying this volume.

[46]Health Law Section of Mintz, Levin, Cohn, Ferris, Glovsky and Popeo, P.C., *Stark Phase III Regulation—Analysis and Commentary*, 11 HEALTH CARE FRAUD REP. (BNA) No. 19 (Sept. 26, 2007).

[47]69 Fed. Reg. at 16,055.

disruption" of common financial arrangements, yet not adversely impact the delivery of services to Medicare beneficiaries.[48] In addition, CMS used its limited statutory authority to create new exceptions, but only where it determined that there was "no risk of abuse."[49] CMS also sought to balance the provider community's need for clear "bright line" rules against the competing need for flexibility and practicality in application of the statute's restrictions. Toward these goals, HHS tried to interpret the prohibitions narrowly and the exceptions broadly, focusing on financial relationships that may result in overutilization.[50] By interpreting the Stark law in this manner, HHS interpreted the Stark law's reach as narrowly as possible, consistent with the statutory language and congressional intent.

Of note, although not publicly acknowledged, is that the OIG provided substantial technical assistance to CMS in drafting the Final Rules, as evidenced by the fact that they contain many indications of OIG policies and enforcement concerns. The OIG's role became even clearer during the implementation of the physician recruitment exception from the Phase II Final Rule. In a July 14, 2004, posting on CMS's Web site, published in response to frequently asked questions, CMS addressed various issues of concern raised about the physician recruitment exception, and stated that "[i]nquiries with respect to the [Stark law] should be directed to the Office of Inspector General."[51]

Taken together, the Final Rules inject a substantial dose of common sense and an understanding of the realities of the Stark law's effect on the enormously complex health care market. On balance, HHS appears to have taken providers' concerns into account and has introduced a variety of adjustments and amendments offering greater clarity and, in several instances, increased protections for legitimate arrangements.

Finally, practitioners must bear in mind that, when researching a particular Stark law issue, one often must review both the Phase I and Phase II Final Rules unless confident that the particular issue at hand is addressed in only one of these rulemakings. The general rule as stated by CMS is to read the two rules "together as a unified whole."[52]

## 5. *Effective Dates*

On the one hand, the Stark law provides generally that it covers referrals for clinical laboratory services made on or after January 1, 1992, and referrals for all other covered services made after December 31, 1994.[53] On the other hand, the Phase I Final Rule provides an effective date of January 4, 2002,

---

[48]66 Fed. Reg. at 860.

[49]42 U.S.C. §1395nn(b)(4).

[50]66 Fed. Reg. at 860.

[51]No. 3163 of the Frequently Asked Questions posted on CMS's Web site on July 14, 2004, *available at* http://www.cms.hhs.gov/faqsearch/faqfull.asp?faq_id=3163.

[52]69 Fed. Reg. at 16,056.

[53]OBRA 1993, Pub. L. No. 103-66, §13562(b)(1).

except for one section relating to physician referrals to home health agencies, which became effective February 5, 2001.[54] In addition, in several subsequent notices, CMS extended the effective date of the Phase I Final Rule regulating percentage compensation arrangements until the promulgation of the Phase II Final Rule.[55] The Phase II Final Rule became effective on July 26, 2004.[56]

Practitioners may be faced with determining which of these three dates is the applicable effective date. The problem may arise in the context of an enforcement action under the *qui tam* provisions of the False Claims Act (FCA)[57] where the services at issue were rendered sometime between January 1, 1995, and July 26, 2004. For example, in a September 29, 2000, letter to Congressman Stark, the Department of Justice (DOJ) announced that it had more than 50 matters under investigation involving possible violations of the Stark law that were brought by whistleblowers under the FCA. Presumably, such actions are premised on the theory that Stark II became effective in January 1998.

In determining whether liability should be imposed for referrals made prior to the effective date of the Phase II Final Rule, CMS provided the following useful guidance in the frequently asked questions section of its Web site. It stated that although it believes providers have had an obligation to comply with the Stark law as of its statutory effective dates, "[i]n the absence of final regulations for a particular exception, parties must have complied with a reasonable interpretation of the statute."[58] This common-sense statement comports with notions of fair play and the fundamental tenets of the Administrative Procedures Act (APA) that matters addressed in "legislative" or substantive rules become effective only prospectively.[59]

The foregoing amply demonstrates that this massive regulatory history is a clear indication of the failure of the promise for clear, bright-line rules, and that many issues have only been resolved through the rulemaking process.

## III. HIGHLIGHTS OF THE FINAL RULES

The two rules taken together make important contributions to one's understanding of the Stark law. To ease in the identification of specific issues, the highlights of each rule are discussed in turn.

---

[54] 66 Fed. Reg. at 856.

[55] *See, e.g., id.* at 959; Medicare and Medicaid Programs; Physicians' Referrals to Health Care Entities With Which They Have Financial Relationships: Partial Delay of Effective Date, 66 Fed. Reg. 60,154–55 (Dec. 3, 2001), *codified at* 42 C.F.R. pt. 411.

[56] 69 Fed. Reg. at 16,054.

[57] The False Claims Act is discussed extensively in Chapter 3 (Salcido, The False Claims Act in Health Care Prosecutions: Application of the Substantive, *Qui Tam,* and Voluntary Disclosure Provisions). The *qui tam* provisions appear at 31 U.S.C. §3730. See Appendix C-1 on the disk accompanying this volume for full text of the False Claims Act.

[58] No. 3163 of the Frequently Asked Questions posted on CMS's Web site on July 14, 2004, *available at* http://www.cms.hhs.gov/faqsearch/faqfull.asp?faq_id=3163.

[59] Administrative Procedures Act, ch. 324, 60 Stat. 237 (1946) (codified as amended in scattered sections of 5 U.S.C.).

## A. Phase I Final Rule Highlights

### 1. Significant Interpretations/Exceptions

The Phase I Final Rule contained several new provisions or revised interpretations of the Stark law, including four significant interpretations and/or exceptions that, taken together, provide significant relief and flexibility to providers.

- HHS introduced a knowledge standard that limits the enforcement of the Stark law to "knowing" violations as defined in the final rule.[60] This standard prevents unfair enforcement of the statute where noncompliance with an exception is de minimis or unintended. The consequence of this approach is to introduce uncertainty because an examination of intent is now required. Ironically, HHS has determined that Congressman Stark's promise of clear, bright-line rules appears to be illusory and ultimately not achievable.[61] (See Section IV.C.7., below.)
- In a sweeping new interpretation, HHS determined that a "referral" does not take place when physicians refer patients for services the physicians personally perform.[62] This elimination of "pure self-referrals" can apply to services physicians perform anywhere, e.g., in their offices or as part of the professional component of a hospital service. (See Section IV.C.1., below.)
- HHS introduced a fair market value exception and related definition that generally allows (under certain guidelines) payments based on a per-use, per-service, per-click, or per-time-period basis, but does not permit many common percentage compensation arrangements because they violate the requirement that payments be set in advance.[63] In addition, the requirements for this exception were significantly relaxed from the Proposed Rule. (See Sections VI.C. and D., below.)
- HHS also defined "indirect compensation arrangements" and created a related exception.[64] The concept of indirect compensation could apply to a large number of arrangements that must be analyzed to determine compliance with the definition and the exception. (See Section VII., below.)

### 2. New Exceptions

The Phase I Final Rule also created regulatory exceptions in the following areas (see Sections IX., X., XI.B., and XIV.C., below):

- managed care;
- academic medical centers;

---

[60]66 Fed. Reg. at 864–65, 958–59; *see also* 42 C.F.R. §411.353(e).
[61]66 Fed. Reg. at 864–65.
[62]42 C.F.R. §411.351 (definition of "referral").
[63]*Id.* §411.354(d).
[64]*Id.* §411.354(c)(2).

- erythropoietin (EPO) or other prescription drugs furnished by end-stage renal disease (ESRD) facilities; and
- noncash gifts or benefits of minimal value.

*3. Key Statutory Terms*

The Phase I Final Rule also addressed key statutory terms and definitions of DHS including the following (see Sections IV.C. and V., below):

- A person or entity is generally considered to be furnishing DHS if it is the person or entity to which CMS makes payment for the DHS.[65]
- Unexercised stock options and unsecured loans are not ownership interests.[66]
- "Under arrangement" services provided by physician-owned providers need only comply with the compensation exceptions.[67]
- Under certain rules, a compensation arrangement may be conditioned on referrals.[68]
- Many DHS are clearly defined by Current Procedural Terminology (CPT) or CMS Common Procedure Coding System (HCPCS) codes.[69]
- Included within radiology and other imaging services are the technical and professional components of the service, but excluded are invasive procedures.[70]
- Outpatient prescription drugs include all such drugs covered under Medicare Part B.[71]

## B. Phase II Final Rule Highlights

*1. Significant Interpretations/Exceptions*

- CMS attempted to dissipate confusion regarding the interplay of the indirect compensation definition and time- or unit-based compensation arrangements by making clear that even if a time- or unit-based arrangement meets the special rules for such arrangements, the arrangement is nevertheless an indirect compensation arrangement that must meet an exception. (See Section VII., below.)
- CMS took significant steps toward minimizing the differences in the various rules applicable to physician compensation arrangements and modified these rules so as to more accurately reflect industry practices. (See Section VI., below.)
  - CMS expanded the definition of fair market value to include a provision deeming hourly compensation for a physician's personal services

---

[65]*Id.* §411.351 (definition of "entity").

[66]*Id.* §411.354(b)(3).

[67]*Id.* §411.354(c).

[68]*Id.* §411.354(d)(4).

[69]*Id.* §411.351 (definition of "list of CPT/HCPCS codes").

[70]*Id.* §411.351 (definition of "radiology and certain other imaging services").

[71]*Id.* §411.351 (definition of "outpatient prescription drugs").

to be fair market value if the hourly payment is established using one of two specified methodologies.

○ In the wake of a great deal of controversy regarding CMS's interpretation of the term "set in advance" in the Phase I Final Rules, CMS modified this definition to permit certain percentage compensation arrangements.

○ CMS clarified the circumstances under which the exception for group practice profit shares and productivity bonuses apply.

○ DHS entities can only direct referrals from physicians under significantly narrow circumstances.

## 2. Statutory Exceptions

• For purposes of the in-office ancillary service exception, CMS introduced a clearer, more flexible test for determining whether services are furnished in the "same building," and, further, created three new alternative tests that are available to solo practitioners as well as group practices. All three tests require the office to be open for a specified number of hours each week with the referring physician regularly practicing medicine at the site. (See Section VIII., below.)

• CMS implemented the moratorium for ownership of specialty hospitals adopted in the MMA, which essentially modifies the so-called "whole hospital" exception to the prohibition on physician ownership. (See Section XII.B.3., below.)

• CMS significantly eased the requirements for structuring arrangements to fit within the space and equipment rental exceptions. (See Section XIII.A., below.) The following are now permitted:

○ termination without cause provisions within one-year lease terms;

○ month-to-month holdovers for up to six months;

○ subleases; and

○ capital leases.

• CMS implemented the Stark law exception for physician recruitment arrangements. (See Section XIII.B., below.)

○ Recruitment payments from federally qualified health centers are now permitted.

○ Hospital residents and new physicians need not relocate to qualify for the exception.

○ Indirect payments to medical groups are permitted, but under tight restrictions; for example, requiring both the group and recruited physician to sign the agreement and *not permitting*:

— A group's costs under an income guarantee to be allocated to the recruited physician for amounts above the group's "actual incremental costs"; and

— The group to impose additional requirements on the recruited physician, such as a noncompete clause.

These requirements, where payments flow to the existing medical practice, will likely require a significant number of existing physician recruitment arrangements to be renegotiated.

## 3. New Exceptions

- Based on comments received from the Phase I rulemaking, in Phase II CMS revised some of the regulatory exceptions it created, including those under the Academic Medical Centers (AMC) exception. CMS liberalized the rules for the components of a qualifying AMC and for the requirements to document the affiliations among the components of the AMC, expanded the rules for the teaching hospital to meet the admissions and faculty requirements, created deeming rules for the requirement that the referring physician devote substantial time to academic services or teaching, and eliminated the requirement that faculty practice plans be tax-exempt. (See Section X., below.)
- CMS created new additional regulatory exceptions not tied to any of the exceptions based in the statute. (See Sections IV.B., XI.E., and XIV., below.) CMS requires compliance with the anti-kickback statute as a condition for qualifying under certain exceptions. In addition, two of these exceptions (for referral services and obstetrical malpractice insurance subsidies) base qualification under the exception exclusively on complying with an OIG anti-kickback statute safe harbor.
  - Arrangements that have temporarily fallen out of compliance with a Stark law exception due to events beyond the provider's control;
  - Intra-family referrals in rural areas;
  - Charitable donations by physicians;
  - Referral services;
  - Obstetrical malpractice insurance subsidies;
  - Professional courtesy;
  - Retention payments to physicians practicing in:
    - health practitioner shortage areas (HPSA), and
    - areas of "demonstrated need" as determined on a case-by-case basis through an advisory opinion. Of note, this advisory opinion process is the first indication by CMS that it will allow this process to be used like the OIG's advisory opinion program to permit arrangements determined to be of low risk of abuse, and either innocuous or beneficial, but not otherwise permitted by the statute or regulation. With CMS soon to be arbitrating on community need for services, this suggests the federal health planning program may be rising again like the Phoenix, after being presumed dead and buried since the early 1980s.
  - Community-wide health information systems.

## 4. Key Statutory Terms

- As a result of enactment of MMA, CMS indicated that it would revisit the definition of "outpatient prescription drug" in a future rulemaking, and stated that it was interested in receiving comments regarding potential approaches for expanding the definition to reflect the MMA's definition of "covered Part D drug." (See Section V.D., below.)

## 5. Other

- CMS eased the reporting requirements imposed on providers with a reportable financial relationship and indicated that it does not intend to issue reporting forms. (See Section XV.A., below.)
- CMS clarified that, under the Stark law, physicians are not liable for payment recoupments for claims submitted in violation of the statute, but are liable only for CMPs and only where the government can prove the physicians acted with knowledge of the violation. (See Section XV.B., below.)
- Regarding the relationship between the anti-kickback statute and the safe harbors to the Stark law, CMS maintained its position that the two statutes are distinct, and thus a separate analysis is required to determine compliance with each. (Section XVI., below.)

## IV. General Prohibition and Key Statutory Terms

### A. The General Prohibition

The Stark law[72] provides that, unless certain enumerated exceptions are met:

> if a physician (or an immediate family member of such physician) has a financial relationship with an entity specified in paragraph (2) [of the Stark law], then—
>
> (A) the physician may not make a referral to the entity for the furnishing of designated health services for which payment otherwise may be made under [the Medicare program], and
>
> (B) the entity may not present or cause to be presented a claim under [the Medicare program] or bill to any individual, third-party payer, or other entity for designated health services furnished pursuant to a referral prohibited under [this provision].[73]

The Stark law further specifies that:

> a financial relationship of a physician (or an immediate family member of such physician) with an entity specified in this paragraph [(2)] is—
>
> (A) except as provided in [the exceptions applicable to both ownership and compensation arrangements and to only ownership or investments interests], an ownership or investment interest in the entity, or
>
> (B) except as provided in [the exceptions applicable to compensation arrangements], a compensation arrangement ... between the physician (or an immediate family member of such physician) and the entity.

---

[72]Unless otherwise noted, all references will be to the Stark law as currently enacted. Practitioners must note that if they are analyzing physician relationships with clinical laboratory service providers, for which the Stark I regulation is final and binding, they may need to consult the provisions of the Stark I law. This analysis is especially important if the conduct in question occurred prior to 1995. If the conduct occurred subsequent to January 1, 1995, practitioners may want to analyze the arrangement under both the Stark I regulation and the Stark II law and regulation.

[73]42 U.S.C. §1395nn(a)(1).

> An ownership or investment interest . . . may be through equity, debt, or other means and includes an interest in any entity that holds an ownership or investment interest in an entity providing the designated health service.[74]

## B. Temporary Noncompliance Exception

In response to commenters' requests for a "grace period" to accommodate temporary noncompliance with the Stark law, the Phase II Final Rule created a regulatory exception to the general referral prohibition in Section 411.353 for entities that temporarily fall out of compliance with the statute due to events beyond their control. The exception provides that an entity that is not currently in compliance with the Stark law may nonetheless submit claims for DHS provided three conditions are met.[75]

First, the financial relationship between the entity and the referring physician must have fully complied with an exception under the statute for at least 180 consecutive calendar days immediately prior to the date on which the financial relationship became noncompliant with the applicable exception.[76]

Second, the financial relationship must have fallen out of compliance with the exception due to reasons beyond the control of the entity, and the entity must promptly take steps to rectify the noncompliance.[77]

Third, the financial relationship must not violate the anti-kickback statute, and the claim or bill for services must otherwise comply with all applicable federal and state laws, rules, and regulations.[78]

An entity may avail itself of this exception only during the period of time it takes the entity to rectify the noncompliance, which may not exceed 90 consecutive calendar days following the date on which the financial relationship became noncompliant with the exception.[79] For instance, if a provider's geographic area is reclassified from rural to nonrural, the rural provider ownership exception will continue for 90 days, giving the entity time to restructure its financial arrangement or take other measures so as not to disrupt the continuity of patient care.

Finally, an entity may seek protection under this exception only once every three years with respect to the same referring physician. This limitation does not apply to an entity that falls out of compliance with the nonmonetary compensation or the medical staff incidental benefits exceptions because these exceptions are renewed annually.[80]

## C. Key Statutory Terms

The Stark law contains a definitions section that further clarifies many statutory terms and provides special definitional rules. This section includes the

---

[74] *Id.* §1395nn(a)(2).

[75] 42 C.F.R. §411.353(f)(1).

[76] *Id.* §411.353(f)(1)(i).

[77] *Id.* §411.353(f)(1)(ii).

[78] *Id.* §411.353(f)(1)(iii).

[79] *Id.* §411.353(f)(2).

[80] 42 C.F.R. §411.353(f)(3) & (4).

terms "referral," "entity," "financial relationship," "ownership or investment interest," "compensation arrangement," and "remuneration."[81] In addition, CMS introduced a "knowledge" or scienter element.

### 1. Referral

The term "referral" is broadly defined. A referral can be direct or indirect, meaning that physicians would be considered to have made referrals if they caused, directed, or controlled referrals made by others.[82] A referral can be in any form, including—but not limited to—any written, oral, or electronic means of communication. A referral can also be made in a plan of care and does not require that physicians send patients to particular entities or indicate in a plan of care that DHS should be performed by particular entities.[83]

Although the term "referral" generally includes services performed by physicians' employees and group practice members, CMS determined that the term "referral" or "referring physician" excludes services personally performed by the referring physician, and referrals to a physician's wholly owned professional corporation.[84] (Similarly, CMS revised the definition of "entity" to clarify that the referring physician is not an entity for purposes of the statute.)[85] Because there are so many situations where one component of a referral involves a pure self-referral for services personally performed by the referring physician, this interpretation removes a substantial amount of conduct from the ambit of the Stark law. For example, any personally performed service a physician provides in his or her office or at a hospital is not covered by the Stark law under this interpretation. Examples of personally performed services at a hospital include the professional component of cardiac catheterization and lithotripsy. For the most part, these services are physician services, although, as discussed below, the professional component of a radiology service is deemed to be a DHS. Referrals still take place when physicians refer patients to other members of their group practices or to other entities for DHS, including technical components of radiology services or hospital services themselves.

The definition of "referral" includes DHS provided in accordance with a "consultation" with another physician, including DHS performed or supervised by the consulting physician or any DHS ordered by the consulting physician.[86] However, certain requests pursuant to a "consultation" by pathologists, radiologists, and radiation oncologists are statutorily excluded from the definition of "referral."[87] To accommodate concerns raised by consulting physicians in group practices, and by radiation oncologists who furnish services that are ancillary and integral to radiation therapy services, the Phase II Final Rule allowed DHS to be supervised by a pathologist, radiologist, or radiation on-

---

[81] *See generally* 42 U.S.C. §1395nn(h).
[82] 42 C.F.R. §411.351.
[83] *Id.*
[84] *Id.*
[85] *Id.*
[86] *Id.*
[87] 42 C.F.R. §411.351.

cologist in the same group practice as the consulting pathologist, radiologist, or radiation oncologist, and includes those services that are necessary and integral to a course of radiation therapy treatment within the definition of "consultation."[88]

### 2. Entity

To fall within the scope of the Stark law, a referral must be to an "entity" furnishing DHS. An "entity" is the party to which CMS makes payment for the DHS, either directly, upon assignment on the patient's behalf, or upon reassignment pursuant to CMS's reassignment rules. Neither medical device manufacturers nor drug manufacturers are "entities" for purposes of the statute because they do not furnish prescription drugs. However, a pharmacy that delivers outpatient prescription drugs directly to patients would be an entity for such purposes.[89]

### 3. Financial Relationship

A "financial relationship" can occur through either a direct or indirect ownership or investment interest, or a direct or indirect compensation arrangement.[90] Surprisingly, CMS took the position that an ownership or investment interest is a subset or type of compensation arrangement.[91] However, a financial arrangement qualifying under an ownership exception need not also qualify under a compensation exception. Both ownership interests and compensation arrangements may be either direct or indirect.[92]

### 4. Ownership or Investment Interest

#### a. Direct Ownership or Investment Interest

An ownership or investment interest may be through equity, debt, or "other means," and includes an interest in an entity that holds an ownership or investment interest in any entity that furnishes DHS.[93] However, an ownership or investment interest in a subsidiary is neither ownership nor investment in the parent company or in any other subsidiary, unless the subsidiary company itself holds an interest in the parent or such other subsidiary. An ownership or investment interest also includes stock, partnership shares, and limited liability company memberships as well as loans, bonds, or other financial instruments that are secured by an entity's property or revenue.

Ownership or investment interests do not include interests in retirement plans, stock options and convertible securities received as compensation until the options are exercised or the securities converted to equity, unsecured loans,

---

[88] *Id.*
[89] *Id.*
[90] *Id.* §411.354(a).
[91] 66 Fed. Reg. at 870.
[92] 42 C.F.R. §411.354(a).
[93] *Id.* §411.354(b).

or "under arrangements" contracts between a hospital and an entity owned by a physician or physician group.[94] Many of these are defined as compensation arrangements.

The Phase II Final Rule makes clear that common ownership does not establish an ownership or investment interest by one common investor in another common investor.[95]

### b. Indirect Ownership or Investment Interest

In the Final Rules, CMS substantially revised its approach to indirect financial relationships. The Final Rules articulated tests for when an indirect relationship will trigger the Stark law prohibition. The Final Rules also established a limited knowledge requirement to avoid unfair application of the statute's sanctions when an entity has no reason to know that a DHS referral is tainted. The final rule provides:

(i) An indirect ownership or investment interest exists if—

    (A) Between the referring physician (or immediate family member) and the entity furnishing DHS there exists an unbroken chain of any number (but no fewer than 1) of persons or entities having ownership or investment interests; and

    (B) The entity furnishing DHS has actual knowledge of, or acts in reckless disregard or deliberate ignorance of, the fact that the referring physician (or immediate family member) has some ownership or investment interest (through any number of intermediary ownership or investment interests) in the entity furnishing the DHS.

(ii) An indirect ownership or investment interest exists even though the entity furnishing DHS need not know, or act in reckless disregard or deliberate ignorance of, the precise composition of the unbroken chain or the specific terms of the ownership or investment interests that form the links in the chain.

(iii) Notwithstanding anything in this paragraph (b)(5), common ownership or investment in an entity does not, in and of itself, establish an indirect ownership or investment interest by one common owner or investor in another common owner or investor.

(iv) An indirect ownership or investment interest requires an unbroken chain of ownership interests between the referring physician and the entity furnishing DHS such that the referring physician has an indirect ownership or investment interest in the entity furnishing the DHS.[96]

### 5. Compensation Arrangement

A "compensation arrangement" is any arrangement involving remuneration, direct or indirect, between a physician (or an immediate family member) and an entity.[97] Thus, the definition of a compensation arrangement is very

---

[94] *Id.* §411.354(b)(3).
[95] 69 Fed. Reg. at 16,061.
[96] 42 C.F.R. §411.354 (b)(5).
[97] *Id.* §411.354(c).

broad, and virtually any exchange of remuneration between a physician and an entity qualifies.

Many of the Stark law compensation arrangement exceptions require that the compensation be "set in advance" (the "set in advance" test), not take into account the "volume or value of referrals" (the "volume or value" test) and, in some cases, not take into account "other business generated between the parties" (the "other business generated" test). CMS clarified the meaning of these often-used phrases in a section of the regulations entitled "Special Rules on Compensation." In Section VI., below, we discuss direct compensation arrangements, these three tests, and the rules that apply where compensation is conditioned on referrals. In Section VII., below, we discuss the definition of "indirect compensation arrangement" together with the indirect compensation exception.

### 6. Remuneration

Remuneration is broadly defined as "any payment or other benefit made directly or indirectly, overtly or covertly, in cash or in kind."[98] The following, however, are excepted from this definition: the forgiveness of amounts owed for inaccurate or mistakenly performed tests or procedures or the correction of minor billing errors; the furnishing of items, devices, or supplies used solely to collect, transport, process, or store specimens for the entity furnishing the items, or to order or communicate the results of tests or procedures for the entity; and certain payments made by insurers or self-insured plans, or subcontractors of the insurers or plans, to physicians.[99]

### 7. Knowledge Standard

CMS recognized the draconian effect of denying payments when there were unintentional or technical violations of one of its complicated rules. For example, a minor compensation arrangement with a referring physician could require a hospital to repay *all* Medicare revenues related to that physician's admissions or services for the period of noncompliance. Consequently, the Final Rules include a scienter or knowledge requirement applicable in limited situations. Payment may be made for a service provided pursuant to an otherwise prohibited referral if the entity did not have actual knowledge or act in reckless disregard or deliberate ignorance of the identity of the referring physician, and the claim otherwise complies with all applicable laws.[100] Similar knowledge standards are imposed elsewhere in the Final Rules to prevent the application of the statute unless the person or entity submitting the claim knew or should have known of the identity of the referring physician.[101] CMS

---

[98]*Id.* §411.351 (definition of "remuneration").
[99]*Id.*
[100]*Id.* §411.353(e)(1).
[101]*Id.* §§411.354(b)(5) & (c)(2).

clarified that the knowledge element used in the statute is the same as in the False Claims Act (FCA) and the CMP law.[102]

This knowledge standard generally does not impose an affirmative obligation on providers, absent some information that would alert a reasonable person to inquire or investigate whether an indirect financial relationship with a referring physician exists. Instead, providers are required to make reasonable inquiries when possessing facts that could lead a reasonable person to suspect the existence of an indirect financial relationship. The reasonable steps to be taken, the Phase I Final Rule contends, will depend on the circumstances.[103]

Many practitioners hope that as the Stark law is enforced, the addition of this knowledge standard will provide welcome, albeit limited, relief by preventing the law from being applied unfairly. Nonetheless, the knowledge standard represents the ultimate repudiation of Congressman Stark's original promise of regulating physician self-referrals throughout the health care landscape with bright-line rules. However alluring such a concept might have been, CMS appears to have recognized that bright-line rules could bring arbitrary enforcement with significant financial consequences to providers. In contrast, most will agree that CMS's approach preserves the underlying principles of the statute, and will achieve more effective enforcement, although at the expense of bright-line rules, in that Stark law compliance analysis will involve subjective inquiry into the parties' state of mind.

## V. DEFINITIONS OF DESIGNATED HEALTH SERVICES

### A. Listed Designated Health Services

The Stark law lists the following DHS:

1. clinical laboratory services;
2. physical therapy, occupational therapy, and speech-language pathology services;
3. radiology and certain other imaging services;
4. radiation therapy services and supplies;
5. durable medical equipment and supplies;
6. parenteral and enteral nutrients, equipment, and supplies;
7. prosthetics, orthotics, and prosthetic devices and supplies;
8. home health services;
9. outpatient prescription drugs; and
10. inpatient and outpatient hospital services.[104]

---

[102] 69 Fed. Reg. at 16,062. The knowledge or scienter requirement is expressed in both the False Claims Act, 31 U.S.C. §§3729, 3733 and the Civil Monetary Penalty Law, 42 U.S.C. §1320a-7a(a), as "knows or should know." See Appendix C-1 on the disk accompanying this volume for full text of the False Claims Act, 31 U.S.C. §§3729, 3733; and see Appendix D-1 on the disk accompanying this volume for full text of the Civil Monetary Penalty Law, 42 U.S.C. §1320a-7a(a).

[103] 69 Fed. Reg. at 16,062.

[104] 42 C.F.R. §411.351 (definition of "designated health services").

## B. General Principles

CMS defines the entire scope of a number of DHS according to the CPT and HCPCS codes that are commonly associated with those DHS and are familiar to the provider community.[105] Those DHS that are defined by CPT and HCPCS codes are clinical laboratory services, physical therapy, occupational therapy, and speech-language pathology services, radiology and certain other imaging services, and radiation therapy services and supplies.[106] The specific list of CPT and HCPCS codes that qualify as DHS are updated annually. Since the publication of Phase I Final Rule, CMS has provided these updates as part of the annual physician fee schedule regulations. The remaining DHS are not amenable to definition through codes.

Certain DHS definitions, such as the definition of "radiology and certain other imaging services," specifically include both the professional and technical components of a service.[107] Other DHS definitions, such as those for inpatient and outpatient hospital services, specifically exclude the professional component,[108] whereas services such as physical and occupational therapy are inherently professional in nature.

## C. Radiology and Certain Other Imaging Services

Providers have continued to advocate for special exceptions for certain radiological procedures, claiming either that the specified procedures were subject to little or no overutilization or abuse, or that beneficiaries would benefit from the exception. However, CMS declined the opportunity to create any new exceptions.[109] In the Phase II Final Rule, CMS noted its belief that the definition of "referral" and the exceptions for in-office ancillary services and physician services sufficiently address many of the commenters' concerns.[110] CMS continues to exclude nuclear medicine procedures, despite concerns raised by commenters that excluding this service increases the risk of program abuse.[111] CMS also stated that it will continue to consider the application of the Stark law to nuclear medicine procedures.

Excluded from this DHS term are X-ray, fluoroscopy, and ultrasound services that are themselves invasive procedures and integral to a nonradiology procedure, such as cardiac catheterizations and endoscopies requiring insertion of a needle, catheter, tube, or probe.[112] Because invasive radiologists are often referring physicians, this exclusion effectively removed this subspecialty from the ambit of the Stark law.

---

[105]*Id.* (definition of "list of CPT/HCPCS codes").

[106]*Id.*

[107]*Id.* (definition of "radiology" and "certain other imaging services").

[108]*Id.* (definition of "inpatient hospital services" and "outpatient hospital services").

[109]69 Fed. Reg. at 16,103–05.

[110]*Id.* at 16,103.

[111]*Id.* at 16,104.

[112]42 C.F.R. §411.351.

## D. Outpatient Prescription Drugs

In the Phase II Final Rule, CMS noted that due to enactment of the MMA, as of January 1, 2006, many additional outpatient prescription drugs will be covered under Medicare Part D and indicated that it therefore will revisit the definition of "outpatient prescription drugs" in a future rulemaking.[113] CMS stated that it is interested in receiving comments regarding potential approaches to expanding this definition to reflect the definition of "covered Part D drug" in the MMA. CMS also clarified that drugs administered in the physician office setting fall within the definition of "outpatient prescription drugs" and noted that, typically, such drugs either will fall within the in-office ancillary services exception or will not constitute a referral when administered personally by the referring physician.

## E. Inpatient and Outpatient Hospital Services

Referencing the "unique legislative history" surrounding the application of the Stark law to lithotripsy, CMS stated in the Phase II Final Rule that, although it is not revising the regulatory definition, it no longer considers lithotripsy an "inpatient or outpatient service" for purposes of the Stark law. This change follows an opinion of the U.S. District Court for the District of Columbia, where the court held that the legislative history of the Stark law demonstrated that Congress never regarded lithotripsy as part of the self-referral problem and has consistently acted to exclude it from the regulation of self-referrals.[114] CMS noted however, that contractual arrangements between hospitals and physicians or physician practices regarding lithotripsy nevertheless constitute a "financial relationship" for purposes of the Stark law.[115] As such, these contractual arrangements must comply with an exception if the physician will refer Medicare patients to the hospital for services that otherwise fall within the definition of "inpatient or outpatient hospital services" or another DHS. This approach serves to undermine any gains that providers of lithotripsy thought they may have made based on the district court's opinion, because the lithotripsy contract still must satisfy one of the exceptions if the physicians refer any other patients to the hospital.

## VI. EXCEPTIONS RELATED TO PHYSICIAN COMPENSATION

### A. Introduction

There is no better example of the reach of the Stark law than its regulation of physician compensation. In the Phase II Final Rule, CMS attempted to

---

[113] 69 Fed. Reg. at 16,106.

[114] *See* American Lithotripsy Soc'y & Urology Soc'y of Am. v. Thompson, 215 F. Supp. 2d 23 (D.D.C. 2002).

[115] 69 Fed. Reg. at 16,106.

minimize the differences among the various rules applicable to physician compensation arrangements. Although a number of differences still exist, depending on whether the physician is an employee, member of a group practice, or independent contractor, CMS narrowed these differences in the Phase II Final Rule. In addition, CMS attempted to simplify any analysis of physician compensation arrangements by inserting into the Phase II Final Rule a chart summarizing the various compensation rules.[116] This CMS chart follows as Table 2-A.

Despite CMS's attempts at simplifying the requirements for those physician compensation arrangements that do not violate the Stark law, legal practitioners providing advice on physician compensation arrangements still must review carefully the special rules on compensation and the individual exceptions for employees, personal services, fair market value, and academic medical centers, as well as the rules for group practices and the definitions of fair market value and physician incentive plans.

## B. Volume or Value, Other Business Generated, and Set-in-Advance Tests

Numerous exceptions under the Stark law provide that compensation paid to a referring physician must be "set in advance" and must not take into account "the volume or value of referrals or other business generated between the parties." We discuss below each of these special rules on compensation.

### 1. Volume or Value of Referrals

The Stark law regulations provide guidance as to what types of payment methodologies do not take into account the volume or value of referrals:

> Unit-based compensation (including time-based or per unit of service based compensation) will be deemed not to take into account the "volume or value of referrals" if the compensation is fair market value for services or items actually provided and does not vary during the course of the compensation agreement in any manner that takes into account referrals of DHS.[117]

The Final Rules permit per-click or unit-of-service payments, even when the physician receiving the payment has generated the payment through a DHS referral, as long as the individual payment is set at fair market value at the inception of the arrangement and does not subsequently change during the term of the arrangement in any manner that takes into account *DHS referrals*. Thus, a physician may lease equipment to a hospital and receive "per use" rental payments, even on procedures performed on patients referred by the physician-owner, provided that the per use rental payments are fair market value, do not vary over the term of the lease, and meet the other requirements of the lease exception.

---

[116]*Id.* at 16,067–68.
[117]42 C.F.R. §411.354(d)(2).

TABLE 2-A (Source: CMS)

| TERMS OF EXCEPTION | Group Practice Physicians [Social Security Act §1877(h)(4); 42 C.F.R. §411.352] | Bona Fide Employment [§1877(e)(2); §411.357(c)] | Personal Service Arrangements [§1877(e)(3); §411.357(d)] | Fair Market [§411.357(l)] | Academic Medical Centers |
|---|---|---|---|---|---|
| Must compensation be "fair market value"? | No | Yes—§1877(e)(2)(B)(i) | Yes—§1877(e)(3)(A)(v) | Yes—§411.357(l)(3) | Yes—§411.355(e)(1)(ii) |
| Must compensation be "set in advance"? | No | No | Yes—§1877(e)(3)(A)(v) | Yes—§411.357(l)(3) | Yes—§411.355(e)(1)(ii) |
| Scope of "volume or value" restriction | DHS referrals—§1877(h)(4)(A)(iv) | DHS referrals—§1877(e)(2)(B)(ii) | DHS referrals or other business—§1877(e)(3)(A)(v) | DHS referrals or other business—§411.357(l)(3) | DHS referrals or other business—§411.355(e)(1)(ii) |
| Scope of productivity bonuses allowed | Personally performed services and "incident to," plus indirect—§1877(h)(4)(B)(i) | Personally performed services—§1877(e)(2) | Personally performed services—§411.351 ("referral") and §411.354(d)(3) | Personally performed services—§411.351 ("referral") and §411.354(d)(3) | Personally performed services—§411.351 ("referral") and §411.354(d)(3) |
| Are overall profit shares allowed? | Yes—§1877(h)(4)(B)(i) | No | No | No | No |
| Written agreement required? | No | No | Yes, minimum one-year term | Yes (except for employment), no minimum term | Yes, written agreement(s) or other document(s) |
| Physician incentive plan (PIP) exception for services to plan enrollees? | No, but risk-sharing arrangement exception at §411.357(n) may apply | No, but risk-sharing arrangement exception at §411.357(n) may apply | Yes, and risk-sharing arrangement exception at §411.357 may also apply | No, but risk-sharing arrangement exception at §411.357(n) may apply | No, but risk-sharing arrangement exception at §411.357(n) may apply |

## 2. Other Business Generated

In addition to the volume or value standard, some compensation arrangement exceptions require that compensation meet the "other business generated" test. The final rules set forth the test as follows:

> Unit-based compensation (including time-based or per unit of service based compensation) will be deemed to not take into account "other business generated between the parties" as long as the compensation is fair market value for items and services actually provided and does not vary during the course of the compensation arrangement in any manner that takes into account referrals or other business generated by the referring physician, including private pay health care business (except for services personally performed by the referring physician, which will not be considered "other business generated" by the referring physician).[118]

Thus, where an exception requires compliance with the other business generated test (as in the fair market value exception), the compensation (including any per service payments) may not vary over the term of the agreement in any manner that takes into account *referrals or other business generated by the referring physician, including private pay health care business.*[119] CMS does not consider "other business generated" to include personally performed services, but the technical component corresponding to a physician's personally performed service is considered to be other business generated for the entity in certain circumstances.[120] Note that the other business generated restriction applies only to those exceptions in which it expressly appears.

## 3. Set-in-Advance Test

### a. Percentage-Based Compensation and Productivity Bonuses

The personal services, fair market value, and AMC exceptions have provided invaluable protection to physicians and those entities to which they refer, especially hospitals. All three exceptions require that the physician's compensation meet the "set in advance" test in addition to the volume or value and other business generated tests.

Despite CMS's efforts in the Phase I Final Rule to interpret the exceptions broadly and to avoid the "unintended disruption of common financial relationships,"[121] the Phase I Final Rule generated a great deal of controversy with its interpretation of the "set in advance" requirement, especially as applied to percentage based compensation. The Phase I Final Rule provided that percentage compensation arrangements in which compensation is based on fluctuating or indeterminate measures, or in which the arrangement results in the seller receiving different payment amounts for the same services from the same purchaser, do not constitute compensation that is set in advance.[122] Just prior to

---

[118]*Id.* §411.354(d)(3).

[119]*Id.* §411.354(d)(2) & (3).

[120]69 Fed. Reg. at 16,068.

[121]66 Fed. Reg. at 860.

[122]*Id.* at 959.

the January 2002 effective date of the Phase I Final Rule, CMS delayed the effective date of this percentage compensation provision. On three additional occasions, CMS further delayed the effective date of this provision. Finally, as part of the Phase II Final Rule, CMS responded to the criticism voiced by physicians and the entities with which they contract and eliminated this controversial provision. In doing so, CMS agreed that its original position was "overly restrictive." Now, under the personal services, fair market value, and AMC exceptions, physicians can be paid a percent of revenues for personally performed services or receive a productivity bonus.

### b. Specific Formula

Compensation will be considered "set in advance" if the aggregate compensation, a time-based or per unit of service-based (whether per-use or per-service) amount, or a specific formula for calculating the compensation is set in advance in sufficient detail in the initial agreement between the parties so that the amount can be objectively verified.[123] The payment amount must be fair market value compensation for services or items actually provided, not taking into account the volume or value of referrals or other business generated by the referring physician at the time of the initial agreement or during the term of the agreement.

## C. Fair Market Value Definition

The overarching principle running through most of the Stark law physician compensation rules is that the compensation must be consistent with fair market value. The Stark law regulations define "fair market value" as the value in an arm's-length transaction that is consistent with the price that would result from bona fide bargaining between well-informed parties who are not otherwise in a position to generate business with each other. The definition also specifies that the fair market price usually will be the price at which other, similar bona fide sales have been consummated in the same market.[124]

The preamble to the Phase I Final Rule made clear that the contracting parties bear the burden of establishing the fairness of any agreement.[125] That stated, CMS is willing to accept any commercially reasonable valuation method. A list of comparable transactions in the marketplace or an appraisal from a qualified independent expert should be satisfactory. CMS noted, however, that the fair market value standard indicates that compensation may not take into account the volume or value of referrals or other business between the parties. CMS asserted that this volume or value restriction may preclude the use of comparables involving entities or other physicians in a position to refer patients or generate business. As a practical matter, this restriction would seem to prohibit using almost all comparables from the health care industry. Thus, at least

---

[123]42 C.F.R. §411.354(d)(1).

[124]*Id.* §411.351.

[125]66 Fed. Reg. at 944–45.

in the case of rural communities, CMS recognized that this restriction may require the use of alternative valuation methodologies.[126]

Fair market value in the context of a lease of office space or equipment is defined as the value of rental property for general commercial purposes without taking into account the intended use of the property.[127] The definition further specifies that a lease of office space may account for the lessor's cost of developing, upgrading, or maintaining the property, but may not take into account any potential additional value that may result from the proximity between the lessor and lessee and the resulting convenience of making patient referrals from the lessor to the lessee. Although CMS did not change the definition of fair market value to exclude space leases, the preamble takes the unusual position that the term "items and services" does not include space leases. This exception therefore is not available for such arrangements.[128] Although the practical effect of this interpretation may not be important, CMS's interpretation of this term is new and not consistent with the OIG's definitions.

Responding to requests to provide more bright-line rules, in the Phase II Final Rule CMS added to the definition of fair market value a provision deeming hourly compensation for a physician's personal services to be fair market value if the payment is established using either of two specified methodologies.[129] The first is tied to the average hourly rate for emergency room physician services in the relevant market, and the second is tied to the average compensation level for physicians in the same specialty area using established national physician compensation surveys that are listed in the rule itself. To qualify for deemed status, payment must be for the physician's personal services and not for services performed by the physician's employees, contractors, or others. The Phase II Final Rule makes clear that these are merely deeming standards, not mandatory requirements.[130]

## D. Fair Market Value Exception

The fair market value compensation exception, which was created under HHS's statutory authority to promulgate new exceptions that do not pose a risk of program abuse, is very valuable to physicians and entities seeking to set up a business relationship.[131] The exception itself is relatively straightforward, and incorporates the volume or value, other business generated, and "set in advance" tests discussed in Section VI.B., above. As with several other Stark law exceptions, the arrangement must involve a transaction that is commercially reasonable.

Under the fair market value compensation exception, the parties must enter into a written contract, the form of which need not be for one year, as long as the parties enter into only one arrangement for the same items or services

---

[126]*Id.* at 944.

[127]42 C.F.R. §411.351.

[128]69 Fed. Reg. at 16,107.

[129]*Id.*

[130]*Id.* at 16,092.

[131]42 C.F.R. §411.357(*l*).

during the course of the year. An arrangement made for less than one year may be renewed any number of times if the terms and compensation do not change.[132] Additionally, the fair market value exception requires parties to ensure anti-kickback compliance either by meeting a safe harbor, by receiving specific approval under an advisory opinion, or by otherwise not violating the statute.[133] Considering the narrowness of the safe harbors and the stringent rules for obtaining a favorable advisory opinion, most arrangements seeking the protection of this or other exceptions requiring anti-kickback compliance will need to be subjected to a full analysis under the anti-kickback statute, particularly in regard to the parties' intent.

It is noted that the Renal Physicians Association (RPA) challenged this exception as violating the notice and comment requirements of the APA and as arbitrary and capricious, but the court ruled that RPA lacked standing and therefore did not rule on the merits of this challenge.[134]

### E. Commercially Reasonable

Several of the compensation exceptions, including the fair market value exception, require that an arrangement be "commercially reasonable." Responding to concerns that CMS was injecting too much subjectivity into the term "commercially reasonable," the preamble to the Phase II Final Rule noted that "an arrangement will be considered 'commercially reasonable' in the absence of referrals if the arrangement would make commercial sense if entered into by a reasonable entity of similar type and size and a reasonable physician . . . of similar scope and specialty even if there were no potential DHS referrals."[135]

### F. Directed Referrals

The Final Rules contained a series of special compensation rules, one of which was for compensation arrangements that are conditioned on the physician's referral of patients to a particular provider or supplier where the compensation is paid by a bona fide employer or under a managed care or other contract.[136] As a result of changes in the Phase II Final Rule, such arrangements must meet the following conditions:

    a. the arrangement must be in writing;
    b. the compensation must be set in advance and consistent with fair market value;
    c. the arrangement must comply with an exception for ownership/investment interests or compensation arrangements;
    d. the referral requirement may not apply when the patient expresses a different choice of provider, the patient's insurance determines the

---

[132]*Id.* §411.357(*l*)(2).

[133]*Id.* §411.351 (definition of "does not violate the anti-kickback statute").

[134]*Renal Physicians Ass'n v. Department of Health & Human Servs.*, 422 F. Supp. 2d 75 (D.D.C. 2006); *aff'd*, 489 F.3d 1267 (D.C. Cir. 2007).

[135]69 Fed. Reg. at 16,093.

[136]42 C.F.R. §411.354(d)(4).

provider, or the referral in the physician's judgment is not in the best medical interest of the patient; and

e.   the directed referrals must relate *solely* to the physician's services under his or her employment or the contract and must be reasonably necessary to "effectuate the legitimate business purposes of the compensation relationship."[137]

These Phase II changes are a logical attempt to close what appeared to be a large loophole from Phase I that permitted a direct link of payment and referrals, raising serious questions regarding potential anti-kickback statute violations.

## G.  Compensation to Physicians in a Group Practice

The Stark law provides group practices with greater latitude than other entities furnishing DHS in determining how to allocate or divide revenues among their physicians. Under the statute, group practices receive favored treatment with respect to physician compensation in that group practices may pay their physicians both productivity bonuses and shares of profits.[138]

Based on the unique status of group practices under the statute, CMS created special compensation rules in these areas.[139] The Phase II Final Rule made clear that a group practice may pay a productivity bonus or profit share not *directly* related to the volume or value of referrals of DHS. Based on CMS's determination regarding personally performed services not constituting a referral, a group may compensate its physicians *directly* based on personally performed services.

Responding to inquiries about whether a group practice may pay profit shares and productivity bonuses to employees and independent contractors, CMS reiterated in the Phase II Final Rule that a group practice may do so provided that the employee or independent contractor qualifies as a "physician in the group practice."[140] Otherwise, to protect referrals from an independent contractor to a group practice, another exception must be met. This important change narrowed much of the distinction found in Phase I between members of a group and physicians in a group.

The Final Rules provide examples or deeming rules for permissible profit shares and productivity bonuses.[141] In the Phase II Final Rule, CMS clarified that these safe harbors serve as deeming provisions, that group practices are not required to use these compensation formulae, and that other methods are acceptable provided they meet the fundamental requirements that the bonuses and shares are reasonable, objectively verifiable, and not directly related to referrals.[142] The group practice must maintain, and make available to the Secretary

---

[137]*Id.*

[138]42 U.S.C. §1395nn(h)(4)(B)(i).

[139]*Id.*

[140]69 Fed. Reg. at 16,077–78.

[141]42 C.F.R. §411.352(i)(2) & (3).

[142]69 Fed. Reg. at 16,077.

upon request, supporting documentation regarding the methodology used to calculate productivity bonuses and profit shares.[143]

In the Phase II Final Rule, CMS clarified that there is nothing in the statute or regulations that would prohibit or restrict group practice bonuses or incentives based on criteria that do not take into account the volume or value of DHS referrals.[144]

As a result of the Phase II Final Rule changes to the "set in advance" and "other business generated" requirements, the rules for physician compensation outside the group practice context now more closely resemble the broad rules for productivity bonuses in the group practice setting with one key distinction. Unlike physicians in a group practice, physician employees, physician independent contractors, and AMC physicians (who must be employees of a component of the AMC) may receive a productivity bonus based on personally performed services only, and not based on "incident to" services. In addition, such nongroup practice physicians may not receive an overall profit share. Allowable compensation for each type of physician is discussed in greater detail below.

## H. Compensation to Physician Employees

### 1. The Bona Fide Employment Exception

The Stark law permits bona fide employment arrangements with physicians using familiar concepts previously discussed. The arrangement must be in writing and meet the requirements and tests for fair market value, volume or value, and commercial reasonableness.[145] In addition, the Stark law contains special rules allowing DHS entities to pay productivity bonuses to its employees as long as the bonus is based on services personally performed by the physician, including personally performed DHS. The Final Rules track the statutory exception almost word for word.[146] Of note, elsewhere in the Final Rules, CMS takes the position that personally performed services are not referrals for purposes of the Stark law.[147] As to referrals for DHS services that are not personally performed services, such as supervision services, these payments must meet the fair market value exception.[148] CMS is concerned that payments for supervision services "may merely be a proxy for having generated the DHS being supervised . . . [and] could mask improper cross-referral or circumvention schemes."[149]

### 2. Leased Employees

CMS has consistently refused to expand the definition of the term "employee" to include leased employees as defined by state law. CMS's concern is

---

[143]42 C.F.R. §411.352(i)(4).

[144]69 Fed. Reg. at 16,081.

[145]42 U.S.C. §1395nn(e)(2).

[146]42 C.F.R. §411.357(c).

[147]*Id.* §411.351 (definition of referral); *see also* 69 Fed. Reg. at 16,087.

[148]69 Fed. Reg. at 16,088. Note that the exception does not preclude a productivity bonus based solely on personally performed supervision of services that are not DHS, because the bonus would not take into account the volume or value of DHS referrals. *See id.* at 16,087.

[149]*Id.* at 16,088.

that incorporation of state law definitions of employment would be inconsistent with the statute, which is based on the Internal Revenue Service (IRS) definition of employee.[150] However, to the extent that a leased employee is a bona fide employee of the DHS entity under IRS rules, remuneration paid to that employee would be eligible under the bona fide employment exception.[151]

## I. Compensation to Physician Independent Contractors

For physicians who are not employees or part of a group practice, the statutory personal services exception is one of the most commonly used.[152] As implemented by CMS in the Final Rules, the arrangement must be in writing and meet the requirements and tests for fair market value, set in advance, and, except for permissible physician incentive plans (see discussion below), volume or value of referrals or other business generated.[153] This exception also has a slightly differently worded commercially reasonable standard in that the aggregate services under the agreement must be reasonable and necessary for the legitimate purposes of the arrangement. Other provisions of the exception are discussed below.

CMS notes that this exception is the applicable exception for most foundation-model physician practices.[154] The Phase II Final Rule changes to the "set in advance" requirements, the definition of referral as excluding personally performed services, and the fair market value definition for hourly payments for physicians, all discussed above, will give physicians and providers more flexibility when crafting an arrangement to fit within the personal services exception. Nevertheless, because of some of the statutory restrictions in this exception, practitioners may find the fair market value exception to be more flexible and easier to meet.

### 1. Termination

Due to Phase II Final Rule changes, the personal services exception now grants providers more leeway with regard to termination of contracts prior to the end of the required one-year term. The term of the arrangement must still be at least one year, but the parties can meet the requirements of the exception even if the arrangement is terminated during the term with *or without* cause, as long as the parties do not "enter into the same or substantially the same arrangement during the first year of the original term of the arrangement."[155]

### 2. Master List of Contracts

The personal services exception also requires that the arrangement cover all of the services to be furnished by the physician to the entity.[156] A contract

---

[150]*Id.* at 16,087.

[151]42 C.F.R. §411.351 (definition of "employee" and definition of "member of a group").

[152]42 U.S.C. §1395nn(e)(3).

[153]42 C.F.R. §411.357(d).

[154]69 Fed. Reg. at 16,090.

[155]42 C.F.R. §411.357(d)(1)(iv).

[156]*Id.* §411.357(d)(1)(ii).

can meet this requirement if all separate arrangements between the entity and the physician incorporate each other by reference or if they cross-reference a master list of contracts.[157] This master list of contracts must be maintained and updated centrally and be available for review by the Secretary upon request.

### 3. "Furnishing Services"

In the Phase II Final Rule, CMS added another clarification to the personal services exception that goes a long way toward acknowledging the practical realities of a physician's practice. Under the personal services exception, physicians can "furnish" services through locum tenens and a wholly owned entity, in addition to furnishing services through employees.[158]

### 4. Physician Incentive Plan Exception

The personal services exception's requirement that the compensation not take into account the volume or value of any referrals or other business generated between the parties does not apply to a physician incentive plan (PIP).[159] To meet the PIP exception, no payments can be made as an inducement to reduce or limit medically necessary services.[160] In addition, where a physician or physician group is at substantial financial risk, the PIP must comply with the general PIP regulations promulgated by CMS.[161] The Phase II Final Rule expanded the definition of a PIP to include arrangements involving downstream subcontractors of the entity.[162]

## J. Compensation to Physicians in Academic Medical Centers

Although an AMC physician must be an employee of a component of the AMC, this exception permits the academic physician to receive compensation from all components of the AMC, and the focus of the analysis is on the total compensation rather than on each form of remuneration from the AMC components.[163]

One of the principal nagging issues facing CMS from Phase I was how to deal with the "set in advance" rules regarding percentage-based compensation arrangements, especially in the context of faculty practice plans. The Phase II Final Rule changes to the definitions of fair market value and set in advance discussed above relate equally to AMCs, because the AMC exception requires that compensation be fair market value and set in advance. Accordingly, like bona fide employees and independent contractors, AMC physicians may receive productivity bonuses based solely on personally performed services.[164]

---

[157] *Id.*
[158] *Id.*
[159] *Id.* §411.357(2).
[160] *Id.* §411.357(2)(i).
[161] *Id.* §411.357(2)(iii).
[162] *Id.* §411.351.
[163] *Id.* §411.355(e)(i)(C) & (ii).
[164] 69 Fed. Reg. at 16,066–67.

Importantly, in the Phase II Final Rule CMS also clarified that when an AMC is examining salary comparables to determine fair market value, it is free to look at salary information for either academic physicians or private practice physicians.[165] This change removes any lingering questions regarding whether an AMC is allowed to match a private practice salary offer in order to retain a top-level physician.

Finally, CMS clarified in the Phase II Final Rule that any monies paid by an AMC to a physician for research under this exception may also be used for teaching and must be consistent with the grant purposes, but may not be used for indigent care or community service. In all likelihood, other exceptions would be available for such expenditures.[166] See the discussion of other provisions of the AMC exception found at Section X., below.

## VII. INDIRECT COMPENSATION DEFINITION AND EXCEPTION

One of the more significant features of the Final Rules is CMS's recognition that the Stark law either does not reach or does not adequately protect indirect compensation arrangements. As a result, under its rulemaking authority under the Stark law, CMS created an exception for indirect compensation, as well as a parallel definition of this term.

### A. Definitions of Indirect Compensation, Volume or Value, and Other Business Generated

The definition of indirect compensation contains a three-part test: (1) there is an unbroken chain of financial arrangements (either ownership or compensation) linking the referring physician to the entity furnishing DHS; (2) when focusing on the last financial arrangement in the chain that involves a direct payment to the physician, the *aggregate* compensation paid to the referring physician varies with, or otherwise takes into account, the volume or value of referrals to, or business generated for, the DHS entity; and (3) the DHS entity has knowledge that the *aggregate* compensation varies in this manner.[167]

### 1. Unbroken Chain Test

The first element requires, as between the referring physician and the entity furnishing DHS, "an unbroken chain of any number (but not fewer than one) of persons or entities that have financial relationships between them."[168] This first element is met if there is an unbroken chain of any type of financial relationship from the DHS entity to the referring physician, regardless of the form or purpose of the payments or their relationship to the DHS referrals.

---

[165]*Id.* at 16,110.

[166]*Id.*

[167]42 C.F.R. §411.354(c)(2).

[168]*Id.* §411.354(c)(2)(i).

## 2. Volume or Value or Other Business Generated Test

The second element in the definition is the volume or value or other business generated test, which reads:

> The referring physician . . . receives aggregate compensation from the person or entity in the chain with which the physician . . . has a direct financial relationship that varies with, or otherwise reflects, the volume or value of referrals or other business generated by the referring physician for the entity furnishing the DHS, *regardless of whether the individual unit of compensation satisfies the special rules on unit-based compensation.* . . . If the financial relationship between the physician . . . and the person or entity in the chain with which the referring physician . . . has a direct financial relationship is an ownership or investment interest, the determination whether the aggregate compensation varies with, or otherwise reflects, the volume or value of referrals or other business generated by the referring physician for the entity furnishing the DHS will be measured by the nonownership or noninvestment interest closest to the referring physician. . . . (For example, if a referring physician has an ownership interest in company A, which owns company B, which has a compensation arrangement with company C, we would look to the aggregate compensation between company B and company C for purposes of this paragraph[]).[169]

The focus of this second test is the direct financial relationship with the referring physician, i.e., the last financial relationship in the chain. The only exception occurs when the direct financial arrangement with the referring physician is an ownership or investment interest; in that case the analysis moves up the chain until the first compensation arrangement is found. In the example of a group practice's medical director contract with a hospital, one must first look to the direct financial arrangement with the physician, in this case the physician's financial interest in the group practice. If that relationship is an ownership interest, the analysis moves upstream to the hospital's compensation arrangement with the group practice.[170]

Once the reference point of the direct financial arrangement is found, the next step in the analysis is to determine whether that compensation arrangement involves aggregate compensation that varies with or otherwise reflects the volume or value of referrals or business otherwise generated. If total payments under the arrangement rise or fall based on the volume or value of referrals, and the other definitional elements are met, it is an indirect compensation arrangement that will trigger the referral prohibition. The italicized part of this rule was added in the Phase II Final Rule to clarify that with respect to time-based or unit-of-service compensation (such as "per click" fees), the aggregate compensation always takes into account the volume or value of referrals, irrespective of compliance with these special rules, and so an indirect compensation arrangement exists that would require compliance with one of the exceptions.

---

[169] *Id.* §411.354(c)(2)(ii) (emphasis added).

[170] Similarly, in the case of "under arrangement" services between hospitals and physician-owned service providers, the analysis is of the compensation between the hospital and the service provider. The regulation elsewhere makes clear that physician-owned "under arrangement" providers do not have an ownership interest in the hospital, and need only comply with a compensation exception.

CMS also made clear in the Phase II Final Rule that a physician stands in the shoes of his or her professional corporation if the physician is the sole owner, and therefore such arrangements appear to be direct compensation.

### 3. Knowledge

The third element is a knowledge requirement similar to the one that applies to the overall regulation. For an indirect compensation relationship to exist, the entity furnishing DHS must have "knowledge" that the referring physician's compensation "varies with, or otherwise reflects, the value or volume of referrals or other business generated by the referring physician for the entity furnishing the DHS."[171] CMS's intent with this third element is to prevent the unfairness of imposing what would be draconian sanctions when the DHS provider is not aware of the nature of the indirect compensation arrangement. As noted above, the knowledge element here does not impose an affirmative duty on providers to investigate.[172] CMS maintains, however, that the DHS entity must make a reasonable inquiry when it has reason to suspect a financial relationship exists. The nature of such an inquiry is undefined, but CMS suggests that reasonable inquiry by the DHS entity may include obtaining, in good faith, a written assurance from the referring physician or the entity from which the referring physician receives direct compensation, that the physician's aggregate compensation is not based on the volume or value of referrals to the DHS entity.[173]

### B. Exception for Indirect Compensation Arrangements

If an arrangement constitutes an indirect compensation arrangement under the indirect compensation definition, the arrangement must satisfy the indirect compensation exception. This regulation-created exception generally requires that (1) the compensation must be set at fair market value not taking into account the volume or value of referrals or business generated, (2) the arrangement must be a signed written agreement specifying the services covered, and (3) the compensation does not violate the anti-kickback statute.[174] See the discussion of the Stark law's relationship to the anti-kickback statute in Section XVI., below.

Under this exception a fair market value indirect compensation arrangement is permitted if the compensation (not necessarily the aggregate compensation) does not take into account the volume or value of referrals or business generated, and the other standards discussed above are met. It is important to note that although some exceptions contain the standard requiring that the compensation must be set in advance (as discussed in Section VI.B above), this exception does not include such a standard.

---

[171]42 C.F.R. §411.354(c)(2)(iii).
[172]66 Fed. Reg. at 866.
[173]*Id.*
[174]42 C.F.R. §411.355(d)(4).

## VIII. Definition of Group Practice and Exceptions for In-Office Ancillary Services and Physician Services

The in-office ancillary services exception and the related definition of a group practice are among the most difficult provisions to understand and to apply, and yet they are among the most important. The importance of the in-office ancillary services exception lies in the fact that it permits arrangements that may be barred under other exceptions, most notably, the ownership exceptions. Because the definition of group practice is relevant to the physician services exception, we will discuss that exception in this section as well.

### A. Group Practice Definition

The Stark law requires a group practice to meet five requirements, as well as a predicate, definitional requirement. The Stark law defines a group practice as "a group of 2 or more physicians legally organized as a partnership, professional corporation, foundation, not-for-profit corporation, faculty practice plan, or similar association" in which each group physician:

- provides substantially the full range of services that he or she routinely provides utilizing the resources of the group;
- provides, bills, and collects for substantially all services through the group;
- shares expenses and income from the practice, which are distributed in accordance with pre-determined methods;
- does not receive, directly or indirectly, compensation based on the volume or value of the physician's referrals, except through a permitted profit-sharing or productivity bonus arrangement;
- personally conducts at least 75 percent of the group's physician-patient encounters; and
- meets other regulatory standards.[175]

These requirements fall into six functional categories, as discussed below.

### 1. Single Legal Entity

A group practice must consist of a single legal entity formed primarily for the purpose of being a physician group practice.[176]

The entity may be organized by physicians, health care entities, or other persons or entities (including, but not limited to, physicians individually incorporated as professional corporations).[177] Thus, although hospitals may organize a group practice, they must do so through a separate group entity. A group of hospital-employed physicians does not otherwise qualify as a group practice because, in CMS's view, such an interpretation would allow the exception to protect virtually all hospital services and contravene Congress's

---

[175]42 U.S.C. §1395nn(h)(4); *see also* 42 C.F.R. §411.352.

[176]42 C.F.R. §411.352.

[177]*Id.* §411.352(a).

intent. Where hospitals merely employ physicians, such arrangements need to be structured to fit within the employment exception.

CMS also clarified in the Phase II Final Rule that a physician practice consisting of multiple legal entities operating in more than one state may qualify as a single legal entity, but only if certain conditions are met.[178] First, the states of operation must be contiguous as a whole (but each need not be contiguous to the other). Second, the legal entities must be absolutely identical as to ownership, governance, and operation. Third, the operation of multiple entities must be necessary under the applicable jurisdictional licensing laws.

The entity may not be organized or owned by another medical practice that is an operating physician practice, even if the medical practice otherwise meets the requirements for a group practice.[179] However if a medical group is defunct or no longer furnishing medical services it can own or operate a group practice. Furthermore, a single legal entity does not include informal affiliations of physicians formed to share profits for referrals, or separate group practices under common ownership or control through another entity.

The single-legal-entity test also includes entities owned by a single physician, provided, however, that the group must have at least two physicians who are members, whether as employees or as direct or indirect owners.[180]

In the Phase II Final Rule CMS addressed a concern raised by a number of commenters regarding the Phase I requirement that the single legal entity be formed primarily for the purpose of being a physician group practice.[181] CMS agreed with commenters that the relevant inquiry is not the group's intent at the time of formation, but rather whether the group is currently operating primarily for the purpose of being a physician practice. CMS also clarified that an entity with any substantial purpose other than operating as a physician practice, such as running a hospital, cannot meet this standard.

CMS also has noted that many foundation-model practices do not meet the single legal entity test and therefore need to rely on the personal services arrangement exception.

### 2. Members of the Group

The term "members of the group" is a component of various group practice prerequisites, one of which requires a group practice to have at least two physicians who are "members of the group."[182] Physicians employed part-time may qualify as members of the group for purposes of the two or more physicians requirement.[183]

Significantly, in the Phase II Final Rule, CMS modified the definition of employee to include a leased employee if he or she is a bona fide employee under IRS rules.[184]

---

[178] *Id.* §411.352(a)(1)–(3).
[179] *Id.* §411.352(a).
[180] *Id.* §411.352(b).
[181] 69 Fed. Reg. at 16,076–77.
[182] 42 C.F.R. §411.352(b).
[183] *Id., citing* 42 C.F.R. §411.351 (definition of "employee").
[184] 42 C.F.R. §411.351 (definition of "member of the group").

Although independent contractor physicians may supervise tests performed in a group, they do not qualify as group practice members. CMS expressed its view that to allow nonmember physicians to qualify under the "two or more physicians" test would expand the group practice definition to groups that have no physician members, a result that would be entirely inconsistent with the statutory language and would render meaningless many of the provisions relating to group practices.[185]

### 3. The "Full Range of Services" Test

The "full range of services" test requires each member of the group to furnish substantially all of the full range of patient services that the physician routinely furnishes through the joint use of shared office space, facilities, equipment, and personnel.[186] Patient care services include all services a physician performs that address the medical needs of specific patients or patients in general or benefit the group practice.[187] This test measures whether a member of a group practice provides substantially the same scope of patient care services within the group context as he or she would outside of that group; it does not require absolute identity of services.[188] If donated services are within the same scope of services that are provided as part of the group, then the group still should meet the full range of services test as well as the "substantially all" test, which is discussed below. A group practice may structure the donated services so that they are billed through the group even though the group need not actually send or collect on the bill.

### 4. The "Substantially All" Test

The "substantially all" test requires that 75 percent of the patient care services provided by members of the group must be furnished through the group and billed under the group's billing number, and payments must be treated as receipts of the group.[189] This test does not apply to group practices located in HPSAs or to services provided in HPSAs (irrespective of the location of the group practice). The Final Rules establish criteria for measuring compliance. In the Phase II Final Rule, CMS provided a number of other clarifications and changes in response to numerous comments it received.

In response to comments pointing out that the addition of a new physician can jeopardize group practice status because of delays in obtaining Medicare billing numbers, CMS added a 12-month grace period for group practices to come into compliance with this requirement where a recruited physician has relocated his or her practice.[190] This grace period applies only if the new member has relocated a medical practice as defined in the physician recruitment exception (see Section XIII.B.), the group practice otherwise meets the "sub-

---

[185]69 Fed. Reg. at 16,077.
[186]42 C.F.R. §411.352(d).
[187]*Id.* §411.351 (definition of "patient care services").
[188]66 Fed. Reg. at 955.
[189]42 C.F.R. §411.352(d).
[190]*Id.* §411.352(d)(6)(i)(A).

stantially all" test, and the new members' employment with or ownership interest in the group is documented at the inception of the relationship. Contrary to commenters' suggestions, however, the grace period will not apply in the event of reorganization.

Group practices with members who provide substantial patient care services at AMCs must still meet the "substantially all" test.[191] To the extent such groups have difficulty doing so, they may arrange to bill the care through the group and treat amounts received as group receipts. CMS cautioned that although a medical school group practice may qualify for the in-office ancillary services exception, it may use the exception to protect referrals within the group practice, but not referrals to other components of the AMC.

In addition, CMS explained that a physician who provides substantial services through an independent practice association does not necessarily jeopardize the group's compliance with the "substantially all" test.[192] Again, this arrangement does not pose a risk for the group as long as patient care services provided through the independent practice association are not governed by an employment or contractual arrangement unrelated to the group. CMS further declined to adopt the commenter's suggested test that would only count fee-for-service (excluding managed care services) or Medicare and Medicaid services as "patient care services," on the grounds that this test was too narrow to achieve the purpose of the "substantially all" test.[193]

CMS also declined to accept a commenter's suggestion that it allow group practices to elect to treat independent contractors as members of the group for purposes of the "substantially all" and the physician-patient encounters tests.[194] CMS opined that such a change is unnecessary and infeasible and contrary to the expressed desire for ease of compliance, and instead expressed its preference for the current bright-line tests. Instead, CMS suggested that the group restructure its hiring practices to integrate the physicians into the group as employees or owners or to fit into another, separate exception. Also of note, CMS agreed with a commenter that independent contractor physicians in a group practice, similar to group practice members, are in a position to make referrals of DHS to a group practice, provided that an exception applies for those referrals, such as the personal services or fair market value exceptions.[195]

CMS further declined to amend both the "substantially all" and the "full range of services" tests to exclude volunteer patient services provided in a free clinic by physicians in HPSAs.[196] As explained above, donated services would not prevent a group from qualifying for the exception under the "full range of services" test. Similarly, to the extent that the physician donates services that are different from those he or she provides for the group, the donated services would not hinder the group from satisfying the "substantially all" test.

---

[191]69 Fed. Reg. at 16,079.
[192]*Id.*
[193]*Id.* at 16,080.
[194]*Id.* at 16,078.
[195]*Id.* at 16,078–79.
[196]69 Fed. Reg. at 16,079.

Finally, CMS rejected a commenter's claim that the documentation requirement under the substantially all test is actually a "back door attestation requirement."[197] In response, CMS pointed to the distinction between a documentation requirement and an attestation, and upheld the requirement.

### 5. The Unified Business Test

To meet this test, a group practice must also be organized and operated on a bona fide basis as a single integrated business enterprise with legal and organizational integration.[198] Essential elements are (1) centralized decision-making by a body representative of the practice that maintains effective control over the group's assets and liabilities, and (2) consolidated billing, accounting, and financial reporting.

The Final Rules generally permit a group practice to use cost-center and location-based accounting with respect to services that are not DHS, provided that the compensation formulas with respect to DHS revenues otherwise meet the requirements of the Stark law.[199]

The group's overhead expenses and income must be distributed in accordance with methods "previously determined." The Final Rules treat the distribution method as "previously determined" (or determined in advance) if it is determined prior to receipt of payment for the services giving rise to the overhead expense or the production of income.[200] This approach permits groups to adjust their methodologies prospectively as often as they deem appropriate. A compensation method that directly relates to the volume or value of DHS referrals, or is retroactively adjusted, violates the statute.

In the Phase II Final Rule, CMS responded to a concern of a commenter seeking clarification regarding the need for the test's requirement that a body representative of the group practice that maintains control over the group's assets and liabilities be responsible for the decisionmaking within the group practice. Specifically, the commenter asked whether the test could be satisfied when individual group practice locations devise their own budgets and submit them to the board for approval. In response, CMS clarified that the "unified business" test is not supposed to dictate specific business practices, but instead is intended to be flexible in order that it may accommodate a variety of group practice arrangements.[201] However, CMS cautioned that substantial group level management and operation must occur. In other words, those responsible for maintaining control over the group's assets and liabilities cannot simply "rubber stamp" decisions based on the various cost centers or locations.

### 6. Profit Shares and Productivity Bonuses

The rules for compensating group practice physicians are discussed in Section VI., above.

---

[197] *Id.* at 16,080.
[198] 42 C.F.R. §411.352(a).
[199] *Id.* §411.352(f).
[200] *Id.* §411.352(e).
[201] 69 Fed. Reg. at 16,080.

## B. In-Office Ancillary Services Exception

Under the Stark law, certain DHS services are excluded from the in-office ancillary services exception. The exception itself imposes requirements on supervision, location (building requirements), and billing.

### 1. Scope of DHS That Can Be In-Office Ancillary Services

The Final Rules permit certain DME, specifically crutches, canes, walkers, folding manual wheelchairs, and blood glucose monitors to be furnished, provided they meet certain conditions.[202] Blood glucose monitors include a starter set of strips and lancets if the practitioners furnish outpatient diabetes self-management training to patients receiving such monitors. In addition, CMS allows external ambulatory infusion pumps (other than pumps that are PEN equipment or supplies) to be provided under this exception. CMS also explained that a physician billing Medicare for the DME at issue must have a supplier number from the National Supplier Clearinghouse.

### 2. Building Requirements

Generally, in-office ancillary services must be furnished in either the "same building" where the referring physician or his or her group practice provides professional services, or in a "centralized building" used to provide off-site DHS.[203] Although group practices may have more than one centralized facility, the group practice must have full-time, exclusive ownership or occupancy of the centralized space.[204] According to CMS, this requirement helps to ensure that DHS qualifying for the exception are truly ancillary and are not provided as part of a separate business enterprise.[205]

On August 22, 2006, CMS targeted one issue from the Phase II Final Rule by proposing to close a perceived loophole that permitted a proliferation of pod labs. CMS tried to fix this problem with several modifications to the definition of "centralized building," including requiring that the space must be a minimum of 350 square feet and contain on a permanent basis the necessary equipment to perform substantially all of the DHS performed at that site.[206] The purpose of the proposed square footage requirement is to prevent abusive arrangements, such as pod labs, while not disqualifying legitimate small stand-alone physician offices.[207] CMS had not acted on this proposal as of August 2007.

In the Phase II Final Rule, CMS significantly revised the "same building" requirement. CMS introduced three new alternative tests—available to both

---

[202]42 C.F.R. §411.355(b)(4).

[203]*Id.* §411.355(b)(2).

[204]*Id.* §411.351 (definition of "centralized building").

[205]69 Fed. Reg. at 16,072.

[206]Proposed Changes to Reassignment and Physician Self-Referral Rules Relating to Diagnostic Tests, 71 Fed. Reg. 48,981, 49,054–58 (Aug. 22, 2006).

[207]*Id.* at 49,057.

solo practitioners and group practices—for determining whether services are furnished in the "same building."[208] CMS believes that these tests are more flexible, permitting many arrangements to qualify now that previously did not, as well as continuing to allow virtually all arrangements that previously complied with the Phase I test.[209] However, CMS noted that the few arrangements that previously qualified under Phase I, but do not qualify now, must be restructured or unwound before the effective date of Phase II.

The first new test generally describes a building where a physician or group's primary place of practice is located. Under this test, the office normally must be open at least 35 hours per week to patients, and it must be used regularly by the referring physician or by one or more members of his or her group practice to practice medicine and to furnish physician services at least 30 hours per week.[210] Additionally, "some" of the 30 hours of physician services must be unrelated to DHS.

The second test takes a different approach, requiring that the patient receiving the DHS at the site usually receives services from the referring physician or the referring physician's group practice. This test is met if the office is normally open at least eight hours per week for patients, and is used regularly by the referring physician to practice medicine and to furnish physician services at least six hours per week.[211] The six hours per week must consist of "some" physician services unrelated to the furnishing of DHS.

The requirements for the third new test are similar to the second in requiring that the office be open at least eight hours per week, and that it be used at least six hours per week by the referring physician or by his or her group practice member to furnish services, not all of which may be DHS services.[212] However, this test differs from the second in that, instead of requiring that the patient usually receive services from the referring physician or his or her group member, it requires that the referring physician be present and order the DHS during a patient visit in the office, or that the referring physician or a member of his or her group be present when the DHS is provided on the premises.

All three tests require the office to be open for a specified number of hours each week with the referring physician regularly practicing medicine at the site. CMS noted that it is possible to satisfy these tests even if there are occasional weeks when the offices are open for fewer hours (such as during a vacation), or the offices have open appointments, cancellations, or other occasional gaps in the furnishing of services.[213] Despite certain objections, CMS retained, as the closest thing to a bright-line rule, the post office street address test to determine whether DHS is being provided in the same building.

CMS also declined to set a particular threshold for the requirement that "some" of the physician services must be unrelated to the furnishing or ordering of DHS. Rather, CMS stated that it will interpret "some" according to its

---

[208]42 C.F.R. §411.351 (definition of same building); §411.355(b)(1) & (b)(2).

[209]69 Fed. Reg. at 16,072.

[210]42 C.F.R. §411.355(b)(2)(i)(A).

[211]*Id.* §411.355(b)(2)(i)(B).

[212]*Id.* §411.355(b)(2)(i)(C).

[213]69 Fed. Reg. at 16,073.

"common sense meaning."[214] However, in interpreting the meaning of "physician services unrelated to the furnishing of DHS," CMS retained its Phase I interpretation, requiring that the services be neither federal nor private pay DHS. Commenters pointed out the difficulty in satisfying this requirement for radiology and oncology practices, and CMS suggested that these specialty practices should be able to meet the lower threshold of "some unrelated to DHS services."

There are special rules for physicians who primarily treat patients in their private homes to allow these physicians, who do not actually practice in a building, to meet the exception's building requirement. Under the Final Rules, services are generally designated to be "furnished" under the exception in the location where the service is actually performed on the patient or when an item is dispensed to a patient in a manner that is sufficient to meet Medicare billing and coverage rules.[215] To accommodate this special situation, these physicians can meet the same building test if the DHS are provided in a private home contemporaneously with a physician service that is not DHS. The rule does not apply to services provided in a nursing, long term care, or other facility or institution, but does apply to services provided in a private home within an independent living or assisted living facility. CMS explained that such a residence qualifies as a private home if the patient owns or leases the residence and has the right to exclude others from the premises. However, to fall within the special rule, these assisted living facilities may not share a common examination room.[216]

Finally, CMS clarified that loading docks that are not part of the building do not fall under the definition of "same building" to ensure that mobile vans are not permitted under this exception.[217] However, where the mobile services do not qualify under the exception, physicians and group practices may still purchase and bill for the technical components of mobile services under the purchased diagnostic testing rules.

### 3. Direct Supervision

To qualify under the exception, DHS must be provided personally by the referring physician, a physician who is a member of the same group practice as the referring physician, or an individual supervised by the referring physician or another physician in the referring physician's group practice.[218] The supervision requirement is met by complying with the supervision requirements applicable under Medicare and Medicaid payment and coverage rules for the specific services at issue. The supervision requirement does not require the referring physician to be part of a group practice. In addition, a solo practitioner can provide DHS through a shared facility if the exception's other requirements concerning supervision, location, and billing are met. (This means, among other things, that the shared facility may not bill for the services.)

---

[214]*Id.*

[215]42 C.F.R. §411.355(b)(5).

[216]69 Fed. Reg. at 16,074.

[217]42 C.F.R. §411.351 (definition of "same building").

[218]*Id.* §411.355(a).

In the Phase II Final Rule, CMS responded to requests for clarification about the level of supervision required for physical therapists working in a physician office, stating that all services that are billed "incident to" will require that level of supervision that is applicable under the Medicare and Medicaid payment and coverage rules governing "incident to" services.[219]

### 4. Billing Requirements

The Stark law's billing standard for in-office ancillary services requires that the DHS be billed by one of the following:

- the physician performing or supervising the service;
- the group practice in which such physician is a member;
- with respect to services performed or supervised by the supervising physician, the group practice if such physician is a physician in the group practice; or
- an entity that is wholly owned by the referring or supervising physician or the referring or supervising physician's group practice.[220]

For purposes of this requirement "wholly owned" does not include joint ventures between group practices and individual group practice physicians or joint ventures that include other providers or investors that do not qualify as wholly owned entities. The billing number used for billing must be "assigned to the group," and groups "may have, and bill under, more than one Medicare billing number, subject to any applicable Medicare program restrictions."[221] Finally, specific rules are provided for groups using third-party billing companies.

In the Phase II Final Rule, CMS made no substantive changes to the exception's billing requirements. In response to one comment, CMS clarified that compliance with this billing requirement is only a threshold condition for meeting the exception's requirements, and that all other applicable payment and coverage rules therefore still apply. Finally, CMS clarified that physical therapists employed by a physician practice cannot bill using the physical therapist's provider number, but must instead bill through the performing or supervising physician, an entity wholly owned by the performing or supervising physician, or the group practice using a number assigned to the group. Alternatively, the billing requirement would be met if the physical therapist reassigned his right to payment to the group and the group billed for the services using its provider number.

### C. Exception for Physician Services

The Stark law allows an exception for physician services[222] provided personally by, or under the personal supervision of, another physician in the

---

[219]69 Fed. Reg. at 16,071–72.

[220]42 C.F.R. §411.355(b)(3).

[221]*Id.* §411.355(b)(3)(v).

[222]The term "physician services" means professional services performed by physicians, including surgery, consultation, and home, office, and institutional calls. 42 U.S.C. §1395x(q); 42 C.F.R. §411.355(a).

same group practice as the referring physician.[223] This exception is of "limited application."[224] The exception covers services provided by physicians only, not services performed by nonphysicians, even when furnished under physician supervision, such as ancillary services that are "incident to" a physician service.

## IX. MANAGED CARE PREPAID PLANS AND RISK-SHARING EXCEPTIONS

The Stark law also provides an exception for services furnished to enrollees of certain types of prepaid health plans,[225] and CMS has created a parallel risk-sharing exception.[226]

In its analysis of the statutory prepaid health plan ownership and compensation exception in the Phase I Final Rule, CMS was faced with two principal problems in trying to avoid the unintended disruption of many physician arrangements with health maintenance organizations (HMOs) or managed care organizations (MCOs). First, CMS wanted to ensure that it generally permitted physician ownership of network-type HMOs or MCOs, provider-sponsored organizations (PSOs), and independent practice associations (IPAs).[227] Second, the statutory prepaid health plan exception does not protect physician arrangements involving commercial or employer-provided group plans—typically the so-called commercial product paralleling the Medicare MCO product—that include some Medicare retiree members.[228] CMS resolved the first major problem by more clearly defining the party that is furnishing DHS. CMS resolved the second major problem by creating a compensation risk-sharing exception.

### A. The Prepaid Plan Exception

The prepaid health plan exception protects ownership and compensation arrangements for "services furnished by an organization (or its contractors or subcontractors) to enrollees of one of the [designated] prepaid health plans (not including services provided to enrollees in any other plan or line of business offered or administered by the same organization)."[229] The protected health plans include certain Medicare+Choice (now Medicare Advantage) plans, health care prepayment plans, demonstration project MCOs, Medicaid managed care plans, and Public Health Service Act–qualifying HMOs.

In defining the term "entity," the Final Rules provide that the entity that will be deemed to be furnishing DHS, as a general matter, is *not* the HMO, MCO, PSO, IPA, or similar entity under contract with other entities directly

---

[223]*See* 42 U.S.C. §1395nn(b)(1); *see also* 42 C.F.R. §411.355(a).

[224]66 Fed. Reg. at 879.

[225]42 U.S.C. §1395nn(b)(3).

[226]42 C.F.R. §411.355(c).

[227]66 Fed. Reg. at 912.

[228]*Id.* at 913.

[229]*Id.* at 960; 42 C.F.R. §411.355(c).

furnishing DHS. Rather, a person or entity is considered to be furnishing DHS if it is the person or entity to which Medicare payment is made for the DHS, directly or upon assignment on the patient's behalf.[230] Thus, a prepaid health plan, or an MCO, PSO, or IPA with which the health plan contracts directly or indirectly for services to plan enrollees, will be considered to be furnishing DHS only when the services are provided directly through an employee or otherwise, so that Medicare payment is made to the plan for DHS directly, upon assignment on the patient's behalf, or pursuant to a valid reassignment under Medicare reassignment rules; or when services are provided by a supplier employed by the plan or the plan operates a facility able to accept reassignment from the supplier under Medicare reassignment rules.[231] CMS stated that this change makes it possible for physicians to hold ownership interests in most types of network IPAs and MCOs, because most do not provide DHS directly, but rather contract with others for the delivery of services to enrollees.[232] However, in limited situations in which the prepaid health plan will be deemed to be the DHS provider, CMS noted that physicians with an ownership interest in the prepaid health plan would be prohibited from referring patients to that entity for DHS absent an applicable exception.

The Final Rules provide that this exception protects providers, suppliers, and other entities—the "downstream providers"—that provide, either under direct or indirect contract, DHS to enrollees of protected Medicare prepaid health plans.[233] Thus, a physician may refer a patient for DHS covered by the protected Medicare prepaid health plans to an MCO that has a Medicare managed care contract or to any entity, provider, or supplier furnishing the services under a contract or subcontract with the MCO. As noted above, this exception and the explicit language of the final rules only protect services furnished to enrollees of one of the protected prepaid health plans. It does not, however, protect "pull through" patients, i.e., other Medicare beneficiaries served by that prepaid health plan or provider pursuant to a commercial product.

## B. Regulation-Created Exception for Risk-Sharing Compensation Arrangements

Because there are so many commercial or employer-provided MCO arrangements that serve Medicare beneficiaries, CMS determined that additional protection was needed for managed care incentive compensation (for example, withholds, bonuses, and risk pools not protected by either the employment or personal services exceptions).[234] Therefore, the Final Rules create a risk-sharing compensation exception for compensation pursuant to a risk-sharing arrangement (including, but not limited to, withholds, bonuses, and

---

[230]42 C.F.R. §411.351.

[231]*Id.* §411.351 (definition of "entity"—see subsections (1)(ii) & (2)).

[232]66 Fed. Reg. at 913.

[233]42 C.F.R. §411.351(c).

[234]66 Fed. Reg. at 912–13.

risk pools) between an MCO or an IPA and a physician (either directly or indirectly through a subcontractor) for services provided to enrollees of a health plan.[235]

Although CMS defined the term "health plan" in the same manner as the federal anti-kickback statute safe harbor, the Final Rules do not define the term "risk sharing," and the preamble of the Phase I Final Rule made clear that this term was specifically intended to be broader than the same term used in the federal anti-kickback statute risk-sharing safe harbors.[236] The arrangement, however, may not violate the federal anti-kickback statute or any law or regulation governing billing or the submission of claims, and, as with the prepaid health plan exception, the "pull through" of nonenrollees (i.e., traditional Medicare fee-for-service patients) is not protected.

In the Phase II Final Rule, CMS clarified that this exception is intended to cover all risk-sharing compensation paid to physicians by any downstream entity, provided that the terms of the exception are met.[237] CMS declined to define the term "managed care organization" to maintain maximum flexibility and to expand the exception to include referrals to entities owned by a managed care organization even if the patients are not enrollees.[238]

## X. Exception for Academic Medical Centers

CMS's Phase I AMC exception specified requirements for the various components of an AMC and its relationship with faculty physicians and other referring physicians, all of which will be discussed in this section.[239] The AMC exception also contains requirements for the compensation paid to the referring physician, which are discussed separately in Section X.B., below.

CMS created an AMC exception whose principal benefit is that it protects all payments from within a qualifying AMC to a referring physician who is a bona fide employee of one component of the AMC as long as the standards of the exception are met. CMS appears to have recognized that academic physicians often receive compensation from various sources within the organization, such as from the faculty practice plan; the teaching hospital for administrative, supervision, and teaching (AS&T) services; the medical school; and perhaps an affiliated research organization. Under the AMC exception an analysis is only required of the aggregate compensation, for example, to make sure it is set at fair market value and is not related to referrals.

Although AMCs will likely find this exception to be of significant benefit, depending on the facts of a particular situation, it may be worth considering whether the requirements of other exceptions, such as for employees or indirect compensation, are easier to meet.

---

[235]42 C.F.R. §411.357(n).

[236]66 Fed. Reg. at 914.

[237]69 Fed. Reg. at 16,114.

[238]*Id.*

[239]42 C.F.R. §411.355(e).

## A. Teaching Hospital

The AMC exception permits an academic organization to qualify as an AMC without having an affiliated medical school.[240] The teaching hospital component of the AMC can qualify as an "accredited academic hospital" if (1) it sponsors four or more approved medical education programs (either alone or in conjunction with other parts of the AMC), (2) a majority of its medical staff are faculty members, and (3) a majority the hospital's admissions are made by faculty members.[241]

In the Phase II Final Rule, although CMS did not change the requirements that a majority of the hospital's medical staff must be faculty physicians and that a majority of the admissions must come from faculty physicians, it made the following accommodations to facilitate compliance with those two 50 percent rules:

- The faculty physician may be on the faculty of the medical school or one or more of the educational programs of the accredited academic hospital (AAH).[242] This means that both the faculty of the medical school and the AAH may be counted.
- Any faculty member may be counted, whether or not the physician is an employee, meaning that courtesy or volunteer faculty can be included in the count.
- Residents and nonphysician professionals should not be counted.[243]

## B. Referring Physician

The AMC exception covers payments to referring physicians who meet the requirements of the exception. Although the referring physician must be a faculty member, as discussed above, he or she must *also* be a bona fide employee (at least on a substantial part-time basis) of a component of the AMC.[244] Thus, although volunteer faculty will be counted for the purposes of determining whether the hospital qualifies as a component of the AMC, payments to such physicians are not permitted under this exception, but must qualify under another exception. The exception allows the parties, in determining whether the referring physician provides *substantial* academic services or clinical teaching, to use any "reasonable and consistent" method for calculating these services. In the Phase II Final Rule, CMS also created a deeming standard for compliance with this AMC service requirement: 20 hours per week or at least 20 percent of the physician's professional time. CMS made clear that this standard was not a formal requirement, and that failure to meet either of these standards did not preclude the parties from showing in other ways that the referring physician provided substantial academic services or clinical teaching services.[245]

---

[240] *Id.* §411.355(e)(2).

[241] *Id.*

[242] *Id.* §411.355(e)(2)(iii).

[243] *Id.*

[244] *Id.* §411.355(e)(1)(i).

[245] 69 Fed. Reg. at 16,110.

Importantly, whereas many compensation exceptions require the arrangement with the physician to be in writing, this is not required by the AMC exception, which therefore permits various informal, unwritten arrangements that typically exist in academic settings.

CMS does require that the compensation be "set in advance." Although this requires the compensation to be objectively verifiable, it should be noted that the prohibition on mid-year adjustments to the compensation formula only applies when the adjustment takes into account referrals or business generated.[246] This raises the larger question of why CMS has retained the "set in advance" requirement. As one commenter noted in a publication of the American Health Lawyers Association:

> Notwithstanding the relative ease of complying with the set-in-advance requirement, the question must be raised again as to what abuse CMS believes it is cutting out by imposing this requirement on AMCs. The statutory context for this requirement is found in the personal services exception, yet a requirement of the AMC exception is that the referring physician be an employee of a component of the AMC. Therefore, the academic physician's employment salary could be protected under the employment exception or in many cases under the even broader group practice requirements if the physician is an employee of a faculty practice plan qualifying as a group practice. Importantly, both of these exceptions do not require the physician's salary to be set in advance. Because the AMC exception covers all compensation from any component of the AMC, the only plausible abusive flow of money that the set-in-advance requirement would serve to snare is the other non-employee-related compensation of the academic physician, such as for AS&T services paid by the teaching hospital. The problem for CMS's reasoning in imposing this set-in-advance requirement is that these rules only appear to be related to salary-type compensation, such as restricting certain percent of revenue formula. Consequently, given the requirement the referring physician be an employee of the ASC, no abusive compensation is likely to be controlled by requiring that the non-employee compensation be set in advance.[247]

## C. Faculty Practice Plans

In addition to a teaching hospital, an AMC must have one or more faculty practice plans. In the Phase II Final Rule, CMS eliminated the requirement that the faculty practice plan must be tax exempt.[248]

## D. Other Components and Requirements of an AMC

CMS clarified that the supporting documentation necessary to show the affiliation between components of the AMC need not be in a written agreement, but may be in a series of documents. The preamble to the Phase II Final Rule states that the evidence of an affiliation may be "a clearly established course of

---

[246]42 C.F.R. §411.354(d)(1).

[247]Thomas S. Crane, *Letter to the Editor: Stark II, Phase II*, 8 HEALTH LAW. NEWS 2, 2–4 (Aug. 2004).

[248]69 Fed. Reg. at 16,109.

conduct that is appropriately documented."[249] An AMC may consist of a single legal entity, in which case the documentation may be financial reports documenting the transfer of funds. Finally, a nonprofit support organization may be included as a component of an AMC, thereby protecting the transfers of funds from that entity as long as the primary purpose of the support organization is supporting the teaching mission of the AMC.[250]

## XI. OTHER EXCEPTIONS RELATED TO BOTH OWNERSHIP AND COMPENSATION

In addition to the ownership and compensation exceptions discussed above,[251] the Final Rules also include five additional exceptions.[252] These exceptions created by regulation are for (1) ambulatory surgery center (ASC) implants; (2) EPO and other dialysis-related drugs; (3) preventive screening tests, vaccinations, and immunizations; (4) eyeglasses or contacts following cataract surgery; and (5) intra-family rural referrals. The so-called "composite rate" exception found in the Phase I Final Rule was deleted in the Phase II Final Rule.[253]

### A. Implants Furnished in Ambulatory Surgery Centers

The Final Rules create an exception to permit referring physicians or members of the referring physician's group practice to implant certain prosthetic devices in Medicare-certified ASCs. The exception applies to implants including, but not limited to, cochlear implants, intraocular lenses, and other implanted prosthetics, implanted prosthetic devices, and implanted DME that meet the following conditions:

- The implant is furnished by the referring physician or a member of the referring physician's group practice in a Medicare-certified ASC with which the referring physician has a financial relationship.
- The implant is implanted in the patient during a surgical procedure performed in the same ASC where the implant is furnished.
- The arrangement for the furnishing of the implant does not violate the federal anti-kickback statute.
- Billing and claims submission for the implants complies with all federal and state laws and regulations.

This exception does not apply to any financial relationships between the referring physician and any entity other than the ASC in which the implant is furnished to and implanted in the patient.[254]

---

[249]*Id.* at 16,110.

[250]42 C.F.R. §411.355(e)(1)(i).

[251]The statutory exceptions for physician services, in-office ancillary services, and managed care are discussed in Sections VIII. and IX.; the regulation-created exception for AMCs is discussed in Section X.

[252]*See generally* 69 Fed. Reg. at 16,071–81.

[253]69 Fed. Reg. at 16,111.

[254]42 C.F.R. §411.355(f).

CMS created this exception to protect surgeons who refer patients needing implantable devices to an ASC in which the surgeon has an ownership interest. In the absence of a special rule, no other existing exception applies in this situation because many of these devices are billed outside of the bundled ASC rate. CMS believed that the exclusion of these implants would not increase the risk of overutilization beyond what was already presented by the surgeon's Part B physician fee. CMS also noted that, as a practical matter, the absence of an applicable exception allowing implantation of these items at ASCs would result in these procedures moving to more costly hospital settings.[255]

This exception is limited to its explicit terms; it does not protect items implanted in other settings. As to implants provided in other settings or those that otherwise do not meet the conditions of this exception, other exceptions may still apply.

## B. EPO and Other Dialysis-Related Outpatient Prescription Drugs

CMS created this exception for EPO and other dialysis-related outpatient prescription drugs based on its determination that these end-stage renal disease (ESRD) services are less vulnerable to abuse than other financial arrangements for two reasons: (1) they are performed in conjunction with other services paid for by Medicare under a composite rate; and (2) the composite services are, in turn, subject to strict utilization and coverage criteria.[256] Of note, only ESRD facilities can qualify under this exception.

The Phase I Final Rule established a list of dialysis-related treatments, identified by CPT and HCPCS codes, that qualify for an exception. The Phase II Final Rule expands this list to include certain other drugs, including certain outpatient drugs furnished by the ESRD facility that do not dialyze, but that promote the efficacy of the dialysis treatment, such as thrombolytics for de-clotting catheters.[257] CMS declined commenters' requests to add other drugs to the list where it determined the drug was already included in the Medicare composite rate for their accompanying procedures, and therefore do not constitute DHS.

## C. Preventative Screening Tests, Vaccinations, and Immunizations

The Final Rules include an exception for certain legislatively mandated preventive screening and immunization services that are subject to CMS-imposed frequency limits; however, the fee schedule requirement for reimbursement found in the Phase I Final Rule was deleted in the Phase II Final Rule. Preventive screening tests, immunizations, and vaccines that are covered by Medicare and identified by CPT and HCPCS codes meet this exception if the following conditions are satisfied:

---

[255] 66 Fed. Reg. at 934.
[256] 69 Fed. Reg. at 16,117–18; 42 C.F.R. §411.455(g).
[257] 69 Fed. Reg. at 16,117–18; 42 C.F.R. §411.455(g).

- The preventive screening tests, immunizations, and vaccines are subject to CMS-mandated frequency limits (however, the fee schedule requirement for reimbursement has been deleted at Phase II).
- The arrangement for the provision of the preventive screening tests, immunizations, and vaccines does not violate the federal anti-kickback statute.
- Billing and claims submission for such tests, immunizations, and vaccines complies with all federal and state laws and regulations.
- The preventive screening tests, immunizations, and vaccines must be covered by Medicare and must be listed on the CMS Web site and in annual updates.[258]

## D. Eyeglasses and Contact Lenses Following Cataract Surgery

The Final Rules create an exception for eyeglasses and contact lenses that are prescribed after cataract surgery. The exception applies when the following conditions are met:

- The glasses or contact lenses are provided in accordance with Medicare coverage and payment provisions set forth in 42 C.F.R. Sections 410.36(a)(2)(ii) and 414.228.
- The arrangement for the furnishing of the glasses or contact lenses does not violate the federal anti-kickback statute.
- Billing and claim submission for the eyeglasses or contact lenses complies with all federal and state laws and regulations.[259]

CMS created this exception in response to comments urging the exclusion of eyeglasses and contact lenses from the definition of prosthetic devices. CMS noted in the Phase I Final Rule that Medicare coverage of eyeglasses and contact lenses is unique in that it is limited to one pair of either item after each cataract surgery and is available to any patient who has had this surgery. In addition, the Medicare-approved amount of payment does not vary based on the cost of a particular pair of glasses or contact lenses.[260] Accordingly, CMS created this exception because it sees little opportunity or incentive for a physician either to underutilize or overutilize these items in the Medicare program.

## E. Intra-Family Referrals in Rural Areas

The Phase II Final Rule contains a new regulatory exception under which a physician can refer a patient living in a rural area to an entity in which the physician's immediate family member has either an ownership or compensation interest.[261] This exception is similar to the ownership exception for rural providers (see Section XII.B.2., below), but contains certain differences, most importantly

---

[258]42 C.F.R. §411.355(h).
[259]*Id.* §411.355(i).
[260]66 Fed. Reg. at 936.
[261]42 C.F.R. §411.355(j).

that this exception protects compensation arrangements. This exception applies only if there is no other entity within 25 miles of the patient's home, or otherwise available to furnish DHS in a timely manner based on the patient's condition.[262]

Theoretically, both the referring physician and the entity could be located in an urban area and still avail themselves of the exception. CMS emphasized that, unlike other location-based exceptions, this exception is based on where the DHS services are provided, rather than the location of either the referring physician or the DHS entity.[263] This provision has the unique effect of excepting some, but not all, of the patients referred to an entity by a particular physician. For example, a physician may have both patients who live within 25 miles of another DHS and patients who do not, but only the latter can be referred to the DHS connected to the physician's family member. Accordingly, providers who utilize this exception should be aware of which patients qualify for the exception and which do not. Those providers should also track their patients' rural or urban geographical classification, and stay abreast of any changes to urban or rural boundaries as defined by the regulations.[264]

This exception recognizes that neither the referring physician nor the immediate family member has an obligation to inquire as to the availability of persons or entities located farther than 25 miles from the patient's residence.[265] However, the physician must make reasonable inquiries as to the availability of other persons or entities within 25 miles of the patient's residence. Moreover, the preamble to the Phase II Final Rule states that if the physician is aware of another person or DHS entity outside the 25-mile radius that is willing to provide the service, he or she may not refer the patient to a family member.[266] Note that this narrow exception does not allow a physician to consider the quality of services rendered. Rather, the focus is on the timeliness of the DHS, given the patient's condition. Presumably, if the physician is aware of another entity that is outside the 25-mile radius but could not serve the patient in a timely manner appropriate to the patient's condition, the physician may still refer the patient to the family member.

## XII. Ownership and Investment Interest Exceptions

The Stark law, at its heart, is a ban on referrals where the physician has an ownership interest. However, Congress at the same time recognized that there are legitimate investments that need to be protected through ownership exceptions. CMS implemented these exceptions in the Phase II Final Rule. The discussion of the definition of an ownership or investment interest and financial holdings excluded from that definition, such as certain stock options, is found at Section IV.C.4., above.

---

[262] *Id.* §411.355(j)(1)(ii).

[263] 69 Fed. Reg. at 16,084.

[264] At this time, it is unclear whether patients living in so-called "micropolitan" statistical areas would be considered rural area patients for the purposes of this exception. CMS states that this issue will be resolved in a forthcoming regulation not related to the Stark law.

[265] 42 C.F.R. §411.355(j)(2).

[266] 69 Fed. Reg. at 16,084.

## A. Publicly Traded Securities and Mutual Funds

The first of these statutory exceptions is for ownership of publicly traded securities or mutual funds. In identifying whether an ownership interest meets the exception for publicly traded securities, the Final Rules apply the following three-part test.

First, the securities owned by the physician or his or her family member "must be securities that may be purchased on terms generally available to the public."[267] Such investments include shares or bonds, debentures, notes, or other debt instruments. CMS interpreted this provision to mean the ownership interest must be in securities that are "generally available to the public *at the time of the DHS referral.*"[268] Under this interpretation, securities acquired by a referring physician or his or her family member prior to a public offering will fit within the exception (assuming other conditions in the exception are satisfied) if, at the time of the DHS referral, the securities are available to the public.

Second, to satisfy the exception, the securities owned by physicians must either be (1) listed for trading with an exchange whose quotes are published daily, such as NYSE or ASE; or (2) traded under an automated inter-dealer quotation system operated by the National Association of Securities Dealers.[269]

Third, an investment will not constitute a prohibited financial interest as long as the securities are "in a corporation that had shareholder equity exceeding $75 million at the end of the corporation's most recent fiscal year or on average during the previous three fiscal years."[270] Similarly excepted are investments in mutual funds, as defined in Section 851(a) of the Internal Revenue Code, that have total assets exceeding $75 million at the end of the most recent fiscal year, or on average during the previous three fiscal years.[271]

## B. Specific Providers

### 1. Hospital Ownership in Puerto Rico

The Stark law exempts an ownership or investment interest in a hospital located in Puerto Rico, and the Phase II Final Rule tracks this statutory language.[272]

### 2. Rural Providers

The Stark law's rural provider exception allows ownership or investment interests in providers that furnish DHS in rural areas.[273] Under the Stark law, as amended by the Medicare Prescription Drug, Improvement, and Modernization

---

[267]42 C.F.R. §411.356(a).

[268]69 Fed. Reg. at 16,081 (emphasis added).

[269]42 C.F.R. §411.356(a)(1)(i) & (ii).

[270]*Id.* §411.356(a)(2).

[271]*Id.* §411.356(b).

[272]*Id.* §411.356(c)(2).

[273]*Id.* §411.356(c)(1).

Act of 2003 (MMA),[274] such rural providers may not be a specialty hospital (see the discussion in the next section) for the 18-month period beginning December 8, 2003. Further, under the Phase II Final Rule, a "rural provider" is an entity that furnishes at least 75 percent of its total DHS to residents of a rural area and is not within an urban area.[275] A rural area must therefore be a region outside of a Metropolitan Statistical Area.

In addition, the Phase II Final Rule creates a limited exception for referrals by a physician to a DHS entity with which his or her immediate family member has a relationship when the patient lives in a rural area. This exception is referred to as the "intra-family exception" and is discussed in more detail at Section XI.E., above.

### 3. *Hospital Ownership*

The Stark law, as amended by MMA and implemented in the Phase II Final Rule, protects a physician's ownership interest in an entire hospital[276] as long as (1) the referring physician is authorized to perform services at the hospital; (2) the hospital is not a specialty hospital for the 18-month period beginning December 8, 2003 (specialty-hospital moratorium); and (3) the ownership interest is in the hospital as a whole, not merely a department or subsection.[277]

Specialty hospitals include hospitals primarily or exclusively engaged in the care and treatment of patients with a cardiac or orthopedic condition, or patients receiving a surgical procedure.[278] A physician may still refer to a specialty hospital in which he or she has an ownership interest if that hospital was "under development" as of November 18, 2003, as determined by Section 507 of the MMA, or alternatively, by an advisory opinion from CMS.[279] Such referrals are also permitted to specialty hospitals that were in operation as of November 18, 2003, as long as the hospitals do not subsequently (1) add more physician investors; (2) furnish additional specialized services; or (3) add more beds, other than to the main campus of the hospital, and if so, not by more than five beds or 50 percent of the number of beds as of November 18, 2003. This specialty hospital moratorium also applies to ownership of such hospitals in rural areas that would otherwise be permitted under the rural exception.[280]

Previously, CMS interpreted the words "provided by the hospital" to mean that the services have been provided by a "hospital" under Medicare's

---

[274]Pub. L. No. 108-173, §507(c)(1)–(2), 117 Stat. 2066 (2003).

[275]*Id.*

[276]On May 3, 2007, CMS issued a proposed rule to amend 42 C.F.R. part 489, Provider Agreements and Supplier Approval, to define "physician-owned hospital" as any participating hospital in which a physician or physicians have an ownership interest or investment. 72 Fed. Reg. 24,679, 24,816 (May 3, 2007). Under this proposed rule, CMS would require a "physician-owned hospital" to give notice to patients of physician ownership, and to provide a written list of physician owners upon a patient's request. *Id.*

[277]42 C.F.R. §411.356(c)(3).

[278]*Id.* §411.351 (definition of "specialty hospital").

[279]For full text of the Stark law advisory opinions, see the CMS Web site at http://www.cms.hhs.gov/PhysicianSelfReferral/07_advisory_opinions.asp.

[280]42 C.F.R. §411.356(c)(1).

conditions of participation, and not by a hospital-owned entity, such as a skilled nursing facility or home health agency.[281] Additionally, a physician can maintain an ownership or investment interest in a hospital through holding an interest in an organization that owns a chain of hospitals, such as a health system, because the statute does not require that the physician have a direct interest in the hospital.[282]

### a. Background

The Stark Law contains an exception for physician ownership of a whole hospital, but not of a subdivision of a hospital—known as the "whole hospital" exception.[283] However, the MMA modified this exception by placing an 18-month moratorium on physician referrals to new specialty hospitals in which they have an ownership or financial interest.[284] The moratorium remained in effect from December 8, 2003, to June 7, 2005, except for hospitals "under development" as of November 18, 2003.[285] During the moratorium period, Congress required the Medicare Payment Advisory Committee (MedPAC) and the Secretary of HHS (Secretary) to study physician-owned hospitals.[286]

In the absence of further statutory guidance, CMS declined to extend the moratorium once it expired on June 7, 2005. Instead, on June 9, 2005, CMS suspended for six months the processing of Medicare enrollment applications (CMS-855As) submitted by specialty hospitals.[287]

### b. Additional Congressional Action

Despite letting the original moratorium lapse, Congress, as part of the Deficit Reduction Act of 2005 (DRA), extended the CMS enrollment suspension effective February 8, 2006.[288] In the DRA, Congress chose not to amend the Stark Law regarding specialty hospitals. Instead, Congress directed the Secretary to develop a strategic and implementing plan during the suspension period.[289] The suspension remained in effect until the earlier of (1) the date the Secretary submits a final report, or (2) August 8, 2006, unless the Secretary extended the deadline for two additional months.[290]

---

[281]69 Fed. Reg. at 16,084.

[282]*Id.*

[283]Social Security Act §1877(d)(3)(C) (*codified at* 42 U.S.C. §1395nn(d)(3)(C)).

[284]*Id.* §1877(d)(3)(B) (*codified at* 42 U.S.C. §1395nn(d)(3)(B)).

[285]*Id.* §1877(h)(7)(B)(i)(II) (*codified at* 42 U.S.C. §1395nn(h)(7)(B)(i)(II)).

[286]MMA, Pub. L. No. 108-173, §507(c)(1)–(2), 117 Stat. 2066 (2003).

[287]A letter to State Survey Agency Directors from Director, Center for Medicaid and State Operations/Survey and Certification Group (June 9, 2005).

[288]Deficit Reduction Act of 2005, Pub. L. No. 109-171, §5006(c)(1), 120 Stat. 4 (2006).

[289]*Id.* §5006(a)(1), 120 Stat. 4 (2006).

[290]*Id.* §5006(a), 120 Stat. 4 (2006). See Section XII.B.3.d., below, for a discussion of Congress's failure to extend the suspension.

### c. Several Agencies Have Reported on Specialty Hospital Issues

Several agencies have weighed in on the debate over specialty hospitals.[291] The General Accounting Office (GAO)[292] issued a report in October 2003[293] and made several findings. First, the report indicated that specialty hospitals are geographically concentrated. Second, specialty hospitals are less likely to have emergency departments. Third, specialty hospitals tend to perform financially as well as general hospitals on Medicare inpatient business. Fourth, they outperform general hospitals when considering costs for all lines of business.[294]

In the MMA, Congress identified several issues related to specialty hospitals and directed MedPAC and HHS to report on these issues during the 18-month moratorium.[295] The MedPAC report[296] made several findings. First, physician-owned specialty hospitals do not have lower costs for Medicare patients than do community hospitals, although their patients have a shorter length of stay. Second, specialty hospitals generally treat patients with less severe cases and concentrate on particular diagnosis related groups (DRGs), which are relatively more profitable than community hospitals. Third, specialty hospitals have lower shares of Medicaid patients than do community hospitals. Fourth, differences in profitability across and within DRGs that create financial incentives for patient selection can be reduced by improving Medicare's inpatient prospective payment system for acute care hospitals.

The MedPAC report also made five recommendations: First, the Secretary should improve payment accuracy in the hospital inpatient prospective payment system. Second, Congress should amend Medicare to give the Secretary authority to adjust the DRG relative weights to account for differences in the prevalence of high-cost outlier cases. Third, Congress and the Secretary should implement the case-mix measurement and outlier policies over a transitional period. Fourth, Congress should extend the current moratorium on specialty hospitals until January 1, 2007. Fifth, Congress should grant the Secretary the authority to allow gainsharing arrangements between physicians and hospitals and regulate the agreements to protect the quality of care and minimize financial incentives that could affect physician referrals.

---

[291]U.S. GENERAL ACCOUNTING OFFICE, SPECIALTY HOSPITALS: GEOGRAPHIC LOCATION, SERVICES PROVIDED, AND FINANCIAL PERFORMANCE (Oct. 2003) [hereinafter GAO OCTOBER 2003 REPORT]; MEDICARE PAYMENT ADVISORY COMM'N: REPORT TO THE CONGRESS, PHYSICIAN-OWNED SPECIALTY HOSPITALS (Mar. 2005) [hereinafter MEDPAC MARCH 2005 REPORT]; CENTERS FOR MEDICARE AND MEDICAID SERVICES: STUDY OF PHYSICIAN-OWNED SPECIALTY HOSPITALS REQUIRED IN SECTION 507(C)(2) OF THE MEDICARE PRESCRIPTION DRUG, IMPROVEMENT, AND MODERNIZATION ACT (2005) [hereinafter HHS/CMS 2005 REPORT]; CENTERS FOR MEDICARE AND MEDICAID SERVICES, STRATEGIC PLAN REGARDING PHYSICIAN INVESTMENT IN SPECIALTY HOSPITALS SECTION 5006 OF DEFICIT REDUCTION ACT INTERIM REPORT (May 2006) [hereinafter CMS MAY 2006 INTERIM REPORT].

[292]The GAO was renamed the Government Accountability Office in 2004. Pub. L. No. 108-271, 118 Stat. 811 (2004).

[293]GAO OCTOBER 2003 REPORT.

[294]*Id.*

[295]Pub. L. No. 108-173, §507(c)(1), 117 Stat. 2066 (2003).

[296]MEDPAC MARCH 2005 REPORT.

A 2005 HHS/CMS report[297] made several findings regarding specialty hospitals using a sample of 11 physician-owned specialty hospitals. First, there was no consistent pattern of preference in referral patterns. Second, specialty hospitals provided high quality of care/patient satisfaction. Third, specialty hospitals' share of uncompensated care was small. Fourth, specialty hospitals paid taxes whereas community hospitals did not.

In the DRA, Congress directed the Secretary to develop a strategic and implementing plan.[298] Congress defined several issues for the plan to address, including (a) proportionality of investment return; (b) bona fide investment; (c) annual disclosures of investment information; (d) provision by specialty care hospitals of (i) care to patients eligible for medical assistance, and (ii) charity care; and (e) appropriate enforcement.[299] CMS issued an interim report in 2006[300] that made several recommendations. First, payment rates for inpatient hospital services should be reformed by refining DRGs. Second, payment rates for ASCs should also be reformed. Third, CMS would more closely scrutinize whether specialty hospitals meet the definition of hospital contained in Section 1861(e) of the Social Security Act. Finally, CMS would review procedures for specialty hospital approval and participation in Medicare.

### d. CMS Declined to Extend the Suspension, Clearing the Way for New Specialty Hospitals

The CMS Administrator, in testimony to the Senate Finance Committee,[301] indicated that CMS would not extend the moratorium on new physician-owned specialty hospitals beyond the statutorily specified expiration date of August 8, 2006. For all practical purposes this action opened the door again for development of new specialty hospitals, and closed the door on efforts to prohibit physician ownership of these institutions.

CMS issued a final report to Congress in August 2006 declining to extend the moratorium and providing a comprehensive review of the evidence on specialty hospitals and a strategic and implementing plan as required by the DRA.[302]

---

[297] HHS/CMS 2005 REPORT.

[298] Deficit Reduction Act of 2005, Pub. L. No. 109-171, §5006(a), 120 Stat. 4 (2006).

[299] *Id.* §5006(a)(2).

[300] CMS MAY 2006 INTERIM REPORT.

[301] Physician Owned Specialty Hospitals: Profits Before Patients?: Hearing Before the Comm. on Finance, 109th Cong. (2006) (statement of The Honorable Mark. McClellan, Administrator, Centers for Medicare and Medicaid Services), *available at* http://finance.senate.gov/sitepages/hearings.htm.

[302] CMS, Final Report to the Congress and Strategic and Implementing Plan Required under Section 5006 of the Deficit Reduction Act of 2005 (Aug. 8, 2006), *available at* http://www.cms.hhs.gov/PhysicianSelfReferral/06a_DRA_Reports.asp. *See also* CMS Fact Sheet, *Final Report to Congress Implementing the DRA Provision Affecting Specialty Hospitals, available at* http://www.cms.hhs.gov/apps/media/press/release.asp?Counter=1941.

## XIII. Statutory Compensation Exceptions

The Phase II Final Rule addresses the statutory compensation exceptions for the first time. We have already discussed the statutory compensation exceptions for employment and personal services arrangements in Sections VI.H. and VIII.C., above.

### A. Rental of Office Space and Equipment

Virtually all of the exceptions for lease arrangements for office space and equipment contain the same conditions and therefore will be discussed together. The Stark law and Final Rules require the following for both of these exceptions:

- The agreement must be in writing, signed by the parties, and specify the premises or equipment covered.
- The agreement term must be at least one year.
- The rental charges over the term of the agreement must be set in advance and consistent with fair market value and not be determined in a manner that takes into account the volume or value of referrals or other business generated between the parties.
- The agreement would be commercially reasonable even if no referrals were made between the parties.
- The equipment or space rented or leased does not exceed that which is reasonable and necessary for the legitimate business purpose of the lease or rental and is used exclusively by the lessee when being used by the lessee and is not shared with or used by the lessor or any person or entity related to the lessor.
- A holdover month-to-month rental for up to six months immediately following an agreement of at least one year that met the conditions set out above may fall within these exceptions, provided the holdover rental is on the same terms and conditions as the immediately preceding agreement.[303]

Space and equipment rental arrangements have generated a number of specific issues that CMS has addressed in the final rules.

### 1. Termination Provisions

Under the one-year-term rule, lease or rental agreements may contain termination provisions with or without cause, provided that the parties do not enter into a new agreement during the original term.[304] CMS determined that there is little risk of abuse for month-to-month holdovers that proceed on the same terms and conditions as the original lease or rental terms, as long as the holdover is for a limited duration.[305] Therefore, holdovers that follow a

---

[303]42 C.F.R. §411.357(a)(1)–(7).

[304]*Id.* §411.357(a)(2).

[305]69 Fed. Reg. at 16,086.

lease agreement meeting all of the exception's requirements are permitted for up to six months.

## 2. Subleases

The Final Rules permit subleases as long as the lessor does not share— meaning use concurrently—space or equipment with the lessee.[306] In the Phase II Final Rule, CMS revisited its interpretation of "exclusively" and found that Congress did not intend for the exclusive use provisions to prohibit sublease arrangements, but intended only that these restrictions prevent concurrent shared use between the lessor and lessee.[307]

For example, the Preamble explains that "exclusively" means that if a physician practice rents examination rooms to a DHS entity, the physician practice may not then use the rooms while the lessee or a sublessee is using them or renting them.[308] However, as a means of preventing referring physicians or group practices from evading the rule by establishing separate real estate holding companies or subsidiaries to act as the "lessor," the Phase II Final Rule modifies the rule to prohibit the sharing of rented space with the lessor or any person *or entity* related to the lessor. Related entities would include, but not be limited to, group practices, group practice physicians, or other providers owned or operated by the lessor.[309]

With respect to space rental arrangements, the Final Rules permit the sharing of common rooms, but only if a specific formula is used.[310] The cost allocated to the lessee for common areas cannot exceed its pro rata share of these expenses based on the percentage of exclusive space used by the lessee compared to the total exclusive space used by all other tenants.

CMS cautions that although the exception now permits sublease arrangements, such arrangements could also create indirect compensation arrangements that would need to fit within the indirect compensation exception to be acceptable.

## 3. "Per Click" or Per Use Leases

The final rules permit "per click" rental payments, provided that they are fair market value and do not take into account the volume or value of the physician's referrals or other business generated by the referring physician.[311] Alternatively, under certain circumstances, equipment rental leases may fit within the new fair market value exception, as discussed at Section VI.D. However, CMS states that because this fair market value exception is limited to items and services provided by physicians, it does not apply to space leases.[312]

---

[306] 42 C.F.R. §411.357(a)(3); 42 C.F.R. §411.357(b)(2).

[307] 69 Fed. Reg. at 16,086.

[308] *Id.*

[309] *Id.* §411.357(a)(3).

[310] *Id.*

[311] 42 C.F.R. §411.351 (definition of "fair market value"); 42 C.F.R. §411.354(d)(2); 69 Fed. Reg. at 16,085.

[312] 69 Fed. Reg. at 16,086.

## 4. Capital Leases

Reversing the Proposed Rule's interpretation that the space and equipment lease exceptions apply to operating leases only, the Phase II Final Rule establishes that the exceptions apply to any kind of bona fide lease arrangement, including capital leases.

## B. Physician Recruitment

The physician recruitment exception to the Stark law protects remuneration provided by a hospital to a physician for the purpose of inducing the physician to relocate to the geographic area served by the hospital in order to become a member of the hospital's medical staff, if certain conditions are met.[313] Specifically, the physician may not be required to refer patients to the hospital; and the amount of the remuneration under the arrangement may not be determined in a manner that takes into account, directly or indirectly, the volume or value of any referrals by the referring physician. In addition, CMS is authorized to impose other requirements to protect against program or patient abuse.

This exception is implemented in the Phase II Final Rule along with a new exception created by regulation for retention payments to physicians practicing in certain underserved areas, as described in Section XIV.H., below.

### 1. Providers Subject to the Rule

Tracking closely the statutory exception, the Final Rules generally only permit recruitment payments made by a hospital directly to the recruited physician. The two exceptions are for Federally Qualified Health Centers (FQHCs) and "seeding arrangements."

FQHCs are permitted to make recruitment payments to physicians on the same basis as hospitals, provided that the arrangement does not violate the anti-kickback statute or other federal or state laws or regulations governing billing or claims submission.[314] In addition, as discussed more fully below, CMS permits, under very stringent rules, so-called "seeding arrangements" whereby the recruited physician is placed in an existing practice. CMS otherwise declined to extend the exception to other DHS entities, such as nursing homes and home health agencies, or recruitment payments made by physician practices, due to a perceived risk of abuse in these types of arrangements.

### 2. Unavailability of Other Exceptions

In the Proposed Rule, CMS had suggested that physician recruitment payments to hospital residents living in the area and indirect payments to a physician practice could fit, as an alternative, within the fair market value exception.[315] In the Phase II Final Rule, CMS determined that recruitment

---

[313] *See generally* 42 U.S.C. §1395nn(e)(5).

[314] 42 C.F.R. §411.357(e)(4)(vii).

[315] 69 Fed. Reg. at 16,094.

payments cannot fit within the fair market value compensation exception because there is no exchange of services.[316] It is partly as a result of this rationale that CMS created specific rules for seeding arrangements.

Notwithstanding CMS's stated position—that because there is no exchange of service and therefore other exceptions do not apply—practitioners may wish to make their own evaluation. In particular, it seems that strong arguments can be made that most physician recruitment arrangements have two components to the remuneration. The first component involves direct recruitment-related expenses, such as recruitment fees, travel expenses for interviews, and moving expenses. The second component involves expenses related to start-up salary and practice expense subsidies for the recruited physician. In some cases, these expenses may involve an income guarantee to an independent contractor physician or an employed physician. Difficult analytic issues may need to be addressed in each situation. But one example is relatively straightforward. It is difficult to understand CMS's position that other exceptions do not apply in the case of a hospital recruiting a physician to become an employee, where it seems that both components of the expenses could be structured to fit within the employment exception.

### 3. Relocation Requirement

Instead of abandoning the relocation requirement as some commenters had urged, CMS has refined it. CMS explained the necessity of the relocation requirement to prevent against abusive recruitment arrangements, such as cross-town recruiting of an established physician practice by a competitor hospital.[317] Under the Final Rules, satisfying this requirement hinges on the location of the physician's practice, rather than the location of the physician's residence as suggested under the Proposed Rule.[318]

To meet the relocation requirement, the relocated physician must either (1) have relocated the site of his practice by at least 25 miles; or (2) derive at least 75 percent of his or her revenues (including inpatient services revenue) from new patients, meaning that the physician has not seen those patients at his prior medical practice site within the past three years.[319] To meet the 75 percent revenue test, the physician has the choice of being tested at the end of the calendar year or the fiscal year.[320] Finally, CMS created special rules for the initial start-up year that permits physicians to measure the start-up year revenue according to whether it is reasonable to expect that the physician will meet the 75 percent test.[321]

Additionally, for the first time, CMS defined the hospital's "geographic area" in which the recruited physician must be placed as the lowest number of

---

[316] *Id.* at 16,095.
[317] *Id.*
[318] 42 C.F.R. §411.357(e)(2).
[319] *Id.* §411.357(e)(2)(i) & (ii).
[320] *Id.* §411.357(e)(2)(ii).
[321] *Id.* §411.357(e)(2).

contiguous postal zip codes from which the hospital draws at least 75 percent of its inpatients.[322]

CMS also waived the relocation requirement for hospital residents and physicians who have been in practice for less than one year. CMS based this special rule on its view that hospital residents and physicians in practice less than a year do not have an established practice to relocate. The only location requirement for these physicians is that they must establish their practice in the hospital's service area.

### 4. Referral Considerations

Under the Final Rules, the arrangement may not be conditioned on the recruited physician's referrals to the sponsoring hospital, but the physician is expected to join the medical staff of that hospital.[323] In addition, the physician must be allowed to join the medical staff of and refer patients to other hospitals, except where required referrals are permitted under the Final Rules.[324] The Phase II Final Rule indicates, however, that credentialing restrictions on physicians becoming competitors of a hospital would not violate this condition.[325]

### 5. Seeding Arrangements

Seeding arrangements are the most common form of recruitment arrangements for a variety of practical and strategic reasons. These include the natural desire to make sure the physicians do not practice alone and that the physician is a good fit with the existing group practice. This necessarily means that the existing group needs to be actively involved in the recruitment and committed to the successful start-up of the new practice.

Although CMS seems to recognize this reality by creating special rules for such seeding arrangements, on closer examination CMS's rules are very narrow and permit few of the common seeding arrangements. It is in this one critical area that CMS does not hold true to its stated promise to avoid "undue disruption" of common financial arrangements.

CMS's narrow approach to seeding arrangements is first seen in the structure of the rule, which protects only hospital recruitment arrangements "paid directly" to the recruited physician, with additional requirements imposed where the payments are made indirectly through the existing group.[326] These additional requirements apply even where the payments are made directly to the recruited physician if that physician joins a group practice. In other words, these rules apply in virtually all cases except in the unlikely event that the physician practices alone. Because of its stated concern about potential abuse, the rules require the following:

---

[322] *Id.*

[323] 42 C.F.R. §411.351(e)(1)(ii).

[324] *Id.* §411.351(e)(1)(iv).

[325] 69 Fed. Reg. at 16,095.

[326] 42 C.F.R. §411.357(e)(1) & (e)(4).

- the agreement is signed by the group, the hospital or FQHC, and the recruited physician;
- with the exception of actual costs incurred by the group in recruiting the physician, the remuneration must pass directly through to, and remain with, the recruited physician;
- in determining overhead costs for the new physician as part of an income guarantee, the group may allocate only those "actual additional incremental costs" attributable to the recruited physician;
- records of the actual costs and the costs passed through to the group must be retained for a period of at least five years and made available to CMS upon request;
- the "volume or value" restriction on the remuneration applies also to the volume or value of actual or anticipated referrals of the existing group;
- aside from quality conditions, the group may not impose additional practice restrictions, such as a noncompete agreement, on the recruited physician; and
- the arrangement does not violate the anti-kickback statute and other federal or state laws or regulations governing billing and claims submission.[327]

Although some of these provisions are relatively straightforward, a few require further elaboration.

### a. Flow of Funds

This part of the rule permits the group to pay the "actual costs incurred . . . in recruiting the new physician,"[328] but aside from those expenses, the remuneration from the hospital must be passed through directly to the recruited physician or remain with that physician if paid directly to him or her. This language raises a number of issues for practitioners.

First, it appears not to permit the group practice to hold and distribute the funds. Arguably, however, the group would be permitted to do so as long as the remuneration eventually flowed to the recruited physician. Second, and more troubling, it is not at all clear what CMS means by the words "actual costs." Does CMS mean merely the recruitment-specific costs, or does it include the practice start-up subsidies? This language could be read not to permit any overhead to be paid to the group for the costs it incurs in supporting the physician's practice. However, this is an illogical reading, and conflicts with other provisions that appear to permit such overhead payments, at least when made as part of an income guarantee. In any case, as discussed above, if the recruited physician became an employee of the group, such overhead would clearly be permitted under the employment exception. Accordingly, it is difficult to understand why this provision would be read to prohibit such start-up subsidy payments.

---

[327]*Id.* §411.357(e)(4).
[328]*Id.* §411.357(e)(4)(ii).

### b. Overhead Payments

For reasons that are not made clear, the literal language of the exception seems to permit overhead payments only in the context of income guarantees. Importantly, because of CMS's desire to curb perceived abuse, the exception permits such overhead costs to be picked up by the hospital only to the extent they do not exceed the "actual additional incremental costs" attributed to the recruited physician.[329] This stringent standard prohibits the common form of overhead calculation whereby the group has an allocation formula that applies to the entire group, and that formula is applied to the recruited physician. These formulae vary among groups, but generally apply certain costs (for example, corporate and billing costs) on a pro rata basis; other costs (such as rent and equipment expenses) on a site-specific basis; and still other costs (such as salary expenses) directly to the physician.

These overhead formulae are typically applied to the recruited physician for a number of reasons, including that the existing physicians in the group have a natural expectation that a new physician will help share the load and that special rules applicable only to newly recruited physicians raise complications and can be difficult to apply. The Final Rules, however, require the parties to create and agree on a formula as to what constitutes the "actual additional incremental costs."

It is difficult to understand what abuse CMS seeks to curb by prohibiting a group practice from using a preexisting overhead formula it applies to all existing group practice members. Moreover, there may well be situations where the requirements of this provision of the Final Rules lead to the hospital paying *more* than it would otherwise pay. Take for example a situation where the group practice needs to build out space in order to take in a new physician. Under the group's pre-existing rules, the cost of that new space might be allocated pro rata to the entire group or to the physician members who practice at that location, but in any case through some type of averaging methodology. In this example, the recruited physician would pick up only the average cost of this new space. However, under CMS's methodology, the entire actual additional incremental cost of this new space would be allocated to the recruited physician, and subject to financial support by the hospital.

CMS has provided guidance, clarifying that although the provisions of the recruitment exception regulation went into effect with other parts of the Phase II Final Rule on July 26, 2004, "past payments under an income guarantee need not be recalculated so long as, at the time they were paid, the arrangement complied with a reasonable interpretation of the statute."[330]

### c. Practice Restrictions

The Final Rules broadly prohibit the group practice from imposing "additional practice restrictions" that are unrelated to quality.[331] The preamble

---

[329]*Id.* §411.357(e)(4)(iii).

[330]No. 3163 of the Frequently Asked Questions posted on CMS's Web site on July 14, 2004, *available at* http://www.cms.hhs.gov/faqsearch/faqfull.asp?faq_id=3163.

[331]42 C.F.R. §411.357(e)(4)(vi).

to the Phase II Final Rule cites a noncompetition agreement as one type of impermissible practice restriction.[332] This restriction raises numerous questions, some of which turn on the meaning of the word "additional" in this context.

On the one hand, these words could be read to prohibit even the basic requirement that the physician remain in the service area for a specified number of years after the support payments end. On the other hand, the principal purpose of the payments under the exception is to permit the physician to relocate to a new area. Under this reading, perhaps CMS would view a requirement that the physician remain in the service area as not an "additional" practice restriction, but one designed to implement the fundamental purposes of the exception. It is less clear how to analyze a requirement that the recruited physician accept Medicare and Medicaid patients. Although it is difficult to see how or why CMS would want to prohibit such a provision in recruitment agreements, it is even less clear how a textual reading of the exception would permit such requirements.

This provision is another example of the problems CMS has caused by appearing not to permit the employment exception to apply. Where state law permits noncompetition agreements, it would seem permissible under the employment exception for a group practice to include such agreements in their employment contracts.

In any case, as discussed above, CMS appears to prohibit in recruitment agreements common formula and contract provisions that group practices apply to all of their members. It is difficult to see the abuse that CMS seems to think exists and needs to be stopped if all group practice members as well as the recruited physicians live under the same rules.

## 6. Anti-Kickback Compliance

Implicit in the requirement that all recruitment arrangements comply with the anti-kickback statute is that if there is an intent to unlawfully induce referrals from the physician practice whose recruitment the hospital underwrites, this Stark law compensation exception would not apply. A more detailed discussion of the implications of requiring anti-kickback compliance is found at Section XVI., below.

## 7. Other Issues

The Final Rules are starkly silent[333] in two areas that most practitioners consider important for complying with other laws. The recruitment exception does not require that the recruited physician fill a community need. Such community-need analysis, with appropriate documentation, is required by the IRS under its exempt organization rules for tax-exempt hospitals. Many practitioners also consider such community-need analysis important for compliance with the anti-kickback statute.

---

[332]69 Fed. Reg. at 16,096–97.
[333]Pun intended.

Also missing under the Final Rules is any requirement that the recruitment payments meet a fair market value test. Thus, the amount of the payments is irrelevant for Stark law compliance, as long as such payments are not based on the volume or value of referrals. Again, such a fair market value test is required by the IRS, and deemed important for compliance with the anti-kickback statute.

### C. Isolated Transactions

Consistent with the statutory exception, the Final Rules permit isolated transactions, such as the one-time sale of a property or medical practice, as long as the transaction is consistent with fair market value, meets the volume or value and other business generated standards, and is commercially reasonable even if no referrals are made.[334] In the Phase II Final Rule, CMS provides additional requirements and several useful interpretations.

First, CMS defines the term isolated "transaction" to include "integrally related installment payments," provided that the total aggregate payment amount is established before the first payment is made and does not take into account referrals or other business generated.[335] To curtail the incentive of assuring payments through continued referrals, the Final Rules also require that the payments be immediately negotiable if any outstanding balance is guaranteed by a third party, secured by a negotiable promissory note, or subject to a similar mechanism that assures payment.

Second, the parties may not conduct any additional transactions within six months following the sale, unless the arrangements fit within one of the other exceptions.[336] CMS declined to substitute a maximum number of such allowable transactions.

Third, the Final Rules permit post-closing adjustments made within six months of the date of sale, as long as they are commercially reasonable even in the absence of other referrals or generated business.[337] CMS clarified in the Phase II Final Rule that the prohibition applies to all transactions, because any type of financial relationship—not only those involving DHS—can create a prohibited financial relationship between a DHS entity and a referring physician.[338]

### D. Remuneration Unrelated to the Provision of Designated Health Services

The Stark law creates an exception for remuneration by a hospital that is unrelated to the provision of DHS.[339] In the Phase II Final Rule, CMS interprets this exception very narrowly.[340] Specifically, the remuneration must be

---

[334]42 C.F.R. §411.357(f).
[335]*Id.* §411.351 (definition of "transaction").
[336]*Id.* §411.357(f)(3).
[337]*Id.* §411.357(f)(2).
[338]69 Fed. Reg. at 16,018.
[339]42 U.S.C. §1395nn(e)(4); 42 C.F.R. §411.357(g).
[340]42 C.F.R. §411.357(g).

"wholly unrelated" to the provision of DHS. The Phase II Final Rule establishes that remuneration is *not* "wholly unrelated" to the provision of DHS if it (1) is any item, service, or cost that could be allocated in whole or in part to Medicare or Medicaid under applicable cost-reporting principles; (2) is given directly or indirectly, explicitly or implicitly, in a selective, targeted, preferential, or conditional manner to medical staff or other physicians who are in a position to make or influence referrals; or (3) otherwise takes into account the volume or value of referrals or other business generated.

In the preamble to the Phase II Final Rule, CMS commented that payments for the rental of residential property are the type of unrelated remuneration contemplated by the exception, but that payments for malpractice insurance and medical devices would be construed as related to the provision of DHS.[341] Similarly, CMS warned that it would view a loan from a hospital to a physician to finance the physician's purchase in a limited partnership that owns the hospital as related to DHS. Likewise, a hospital's lease of office space in a nearby medical building to physicians in a position to refer to the hospital would be related to DHS.

Viewing any item, service, or cost that could be allocated to Medicare or Medicaid as related to DHS, CMS withdrew its interpretation in the Proposed Rule that administrative and utilization review services are not related to DHS.[342] Further, the Phase II Final Rule explains that under the "wholly unrelated" test, even if the remuneration is not covered by cost-reporting principles, the remuneration may relate to DHS by being given to medical staff who are in a position to make referrals.

CMS declined to extend the exception to cover remuneration from a hospital to a physician's immediate family member. Further, the Phase II Final Rule states that CMS will apply a presumption that payments above fair market value for services unrelated to the provision of DHS are actually related to such services.[343] Responding to the contention that CMS lacked the authority to impose an additional requirement that the payments be at fair market value, CMS stated that payments exceeding that threshold will be carefully scrutinized. CMS also rejected the suggestion that entities other than hospitals should be able to make unrelated DHS payments and qualify for the exception. Finally, despite recognizing that covenants not to compete are not necessarily equivalent to an obligation to make referrals, the Phase II Final Rule clarified that such agreements clearly relate to DHS and, consequently, need to fall within another exception to be acceptable.

### E.  Certain Group Practice Arrangements With Hospitals

The Phase II Final Rule adopts, with minimal modification, the Stark law exception for group practice arrangements with hospitals in which the group furnishes DHS and the hospital bills for these services.[344] The statute and Final

---

[341] 69 Fed. Reg. at 16,093–94.

[342] *Id.*

[343] *Id.* at 16,094.

[344] 42 U.S.C. §1395nn(e)(7); 42 C.F.R. §411.357(h).

Rules require that the arrangement with the group must have been in effect without interruption since the date of enactment of Stark I (December 19, 1989), and that certain other prophylactic provisions be in place, including that the agreement be in writing, with the compensation at fair market value and meeting the volume or value, other business generated, and commercially reasonable tests. Finally, the statutory exception requires that, with respect to "under arrangement" agreements, substantially all of the services furnished to patients of the hospital be furnished by the group under arrangement. In the Phase II Final Rule, CMS interprets "substantially all" to mean that at least 75 percent of the DHS is covered under the arrangement.[345]

## F. Payments Made by a Physician for Items and Services

This statutory exception protects payments by a physician either to a laboratory in exchange for the provision of laboratory services, or alternatively, to an entity as compensation for other items or services, when these are furnished at a price consistent with fair market value.[346] In the Phase II Final Rule, CMS extends the exception to cover payments by a referring physician's immediate family member. In addition, CMS interprets the term "other items or services" to mean any kind of items or services that a physician might purchase, but not including clinical laboratory services. CMS abandoned the controversial requirement in the Proposed Rule that the amount of the discount would have to be passed on in full to patients or their insurers and could not in any way benefit the physician.[347] The Phase II Final Rule explains that further consideration of this discount exception led CMS to conclude that legitimate discounts would fall within the range of values that is "fair market value."[348]

Finally, in an attempt to narrow the apparent breadth of this statutory exception, CMS requires that allowable compensation for other items and services must not be specifically excepted under another exception.[349] In other words, CMS is allowing this exception to be used only where no other exception could apply. Although it is understandable why CMS would want to narrow the availability of this exception, there is little textual support for this interpretation, and it does not appear that Congress gave CMS explicit authority to create other regulatory protections for this exception as it did under other exceptions, such as for physician recruitment, or under its authority to grant new ownership and compensation exceptions where CMS finds no risk of program or patient abuse.

---

[345] 42 C.F.R. §411.357(h)(3).
[346] *Id.* §411.357(i).
[347] *Id.*
[348] 69 Fed. Reg. at 16,099.
[349] 42 C.F.R. §411.357(i)(2).

## XIV. Compensation Exceptions Created by Regulation

### A. Introduction

In addition to the regulation-created exceptions related to both ownership and compensation arrangements, the Phase I Final Rule also established six regulatory exceptions specific to compensation arrangements. Three of these, including the fair market value, indirect compensation, and risk-sharing exceptions, are discussed above in Sections VI.D., VII., and IX., above. The remaining three, including nonmonetary compensation or gifts, compliance training, and medical staff incidental benefits, as well as six new compensation exceptions promulgated in the Phase II Final Rules, are discussed below in the order they appear in the Final Rules. To help practitioners locate the relevant preamble previsions, we have noted if the exception appears first in Phase I (in which case the exception was modified in Phase II) or Phase II.

### B. Charitable Donations by Physicians (Phase II)

In the Phase II Final Rule, CMS reassured commenters that a charitable contribution from a referring physician to a DHS entity will not violate the Stark law.[350] Although CMS could have simply excluded charitable contributions from the definition of remuneration, it has instead chosen to craft a regulatory exception, based on its reasoning that such a payment would constitute remuneration as defined in the statute.[351] For a contribution to qualify for the exception, the recipient of the contribution must be a tax-exempt organization, and the donation from the physician must not be solicited, nor made in any manner that takes into account the volume or value of referrals or other business generated between the physician and the tax-exempt entity.[352] For example, the exception permits contributions made to a broad-based fund-raising campaign that reaches physicians and nonphysicians alike.

### C. Nonmonetary Compensation (Phase I)

The nonmonetary compensation exception applies to gifts or benefits provided by a referral recipient to a physician. To comply with the exception, the gift or benefit (1) must not be in cash or a cash equivalent; (2) must not exceed an aggregate of $300 per year; (3) must not be determined to take into account the volume or value of referrals or other business generated by the referring physician; (4) must not be solicited by the physician or the physician's practice; and (5) must not violate the federal anti-kickback statute.[353] In the

---

[350] 69 Fed. Reg. at 16,116.
[351] *Id.*
[352] 42 C.F.R. §411.357(j).
[353] *Id.* §411.357(k)(1).

Phase II Final Rule, CMS revised this exception to add that the $300 limit will be adjusted each calendar year based on inflation.[354]

## D.  Medical Staff Incidental Benefits (Phase I)

Phase I created an exception for incidental benefits, other than cash or cash equivalents, provided by a hospital to a member of its medical staff.[355] The types of benefits that might fall within this exception include reduced or free parking, free computer/Internet access, and meals. In general, this exception requires that the benefits must be used on the hospital's campus and offered to all medical staff members without regard to the volume or value of referrals. In addition, the benefits must be offered only during the periods when staff members are making rounds or performing other hospital or patient-related duties, and must be reasonably related to the hospital's medical services.

Responding to the Phase I version of this exception, commenters voiced concern that referring physicians are often involved in patient care while physically remote from the DHS entity, and urged CMS to modify the exception to include incidental benefits that facilitate these exchanges.[356] In response to these concerns, in the Phase II Final Rule, CMS maintained the so-called "on campus rule," but modified the rule to accommodate the use of electronic or Internet services from a remote site. Accordingly, a DHS entity may provide a physician with a device such as a two-way pager or Internet connection to be used off-site, as long as the usage relates to services or activities that benefit the hospital or its patients (e.g., communication during urgent patient care situations).[357] The Phase II Final Rule also expanded the scope of the exception beyond hospitals to include any DHS entity that has a bona fide medical staff, and eliminated the requirement that incidental benefits be comparable to those offered at hospitals in the same region. The benefits offered must not exceed $25 per occurrence and, similar to the nonmonetary compensation exception, this $25 limit will be adjusted each calendar year for inflation. In addition, as with many other exceptions, the compensation arrangement must not violate the federal anti-kickback statute.

The exception does not apply if the physician would already employ the technology for his or her own practice, as when, for instance, the physician already had an Internet connection in his or her own office.[358] The referring physician's use of a DHS entity's health information system is addressed in a separate exception discussed below.

## E.  Compliance Training (Phase I)

The compliance training exception applies to compliance training provided by an entity to a referring physician who practices in the entity's local

---

[354]*Id.* §411.357(k)(2).

[355]*Id.* §411.357(m).

[356]69 Fed. Reg. at 16,112.

[357]42 C.F.R. §411.357(m)(3).

[358]*Id.*

community or service area, or to the physician's office staff, and requires that such training be held in the local community or service area.[359] Training held outside the entity's service area does not come within the exception, ostensibly because travel to what could be a vacation resort could confer an additional benefit upon the referring physician.

Such training must cover the basic elements of a compliance program, specific requirements of federal and state health care programs, or other federal, state, or local laws, regulations, or rules governing the conduct of the party for whom the training is provided.[360] Thus, a qualifying general training program can focus on training-related policies and procedures, training of staff, or internal monitoring and reporting, whereas a qualifying specific program should focus, for example, on such requirements as billing, coding, medical necessity, and unlawful referral arrangements.

The exception does not include continuing medical education (CME); however, CME may be covered under the nonmonetary compensation exception, depending on the cost of the program.[361]

## F. Referral Services and Obstetrical Malpractice Insurance Subsidies (Phase II)

In the Phase II Final Rule, CMS carved out two new regulatory exceptions for conduct that complies with two safe harbors of the anti-kickback statute. The first of these exceptions includes any arrangement that fits within the safe harbor for referral services and the second applies to arrangements complying with the obstetrical malpractice insurance subsidies safe harbor.[362]

Unfortunately, because the safe harbor for subsidies for obstetrical malpractice applies only to HPSAs,[363] support arrangements outside of HPSAs will not qualify under this Stark law exception, thereby making it difficult for most such subsidies to continue. See Section XVI., below, for a discussion of the interrelationship of the anti-kickback statute and its safe harbors to the Stark law.

## G. Professional Courtesy (Phase II)

The Final Rules also exempt professional courtesies from the compensation prohibition. This common and long-standing practice, whereby the DHS entity furnishes medical services at no cost or at a reduced cost to referring physicians and their family and staff, is permitted where (1) the courtesy is offered without regard to the volume or value of referrals generated between the parties; (2) the items or services are of a type routinely provided by the DHS entity; (3) the DHS entity maintains a professional courtesy policy which is set out in writing and approved by the entity's governing body; (4) the professional courtesy is not offered to a physician who is a federal health care program

---

[359] *Id.* §411.357(o).
[360] *Id.*
[361] 69 Fed. Reg. at 16,115.
[362] 42 C.F.R. §411.357(q) & (r).
[363] *Id.* §1001.952(o).

beneficiary unless there has been a good faith showing of financial need; and (5) the arrangement does not violate the federal anti-kickback statute.[364] If the professional courtesy involves any whole or partial reduction in any coinsurance obligation, the insurer must be informed in writing of the reduction. As noted above, the professional courtesy policy must be approved by the entity's governing body in order to qualify for this exception.

## H. Retention Payments in Underserved Areas (Phase II)

In response to commenters' concerns about physician turnover in underserved areas, the Phase II Final Rule provided a new exception for retention payments from a DHS entity hospital or FQHC to a referring physician, irrespective of the physician's specialty.[365] To qualify for the exception, the physician must currently practice within an HPSA, or, as explained below, obtain an advisory opinion from the Secretary confirming that there is a demonstrated need for the physician in the area. The physician must also have a bona fide written recruitment offer, including salary, from another hospital or FQHC. Except as explained below, the offer must require the physician to relocate his or her practice at least 25 miles *and* outside of the current hospital's service area. Further, CMS requires the usual prophylactic rules, for example, that the arrangement must be set out in writing and signed by the parties, cannot be conditioned on the physician's referral of patients to the hospital, must allow the physician to establish staff privileges at any other hospital except as restricted under an allowable separate employment or services contract, and must not violate the anti-kickback statute.

CMS limits the amount of the retention payment to the lesser of (1) the difference between the physician's current income from physician and related services and the income proposed in the recruitment offer, calculated over no more than a 24-month period using a consistent methodology; or (2) the reasonable costs the hospital or FQHC must expend to recruit a new physician as a replacement.[366] Any retention payment is subject to the same obligations and restrictions, if any, on repayment or forgiveness of indebtedness as the bona fide recruitment offer. A hospital or FQHC may offer retention payments to a particular physician no more frequently than once every five years. Retention payments paid indirectly to the physician through a physician practice are not permissible.

Finally, the regulation gives CMS the authority to determine on a case-by-case basis, through advisory opinions, whether the physician is serving in areas with a demonstrated need that do not qualify as HPSAs. Additionally, the Secretary may waive, through an advisory opinion, the relocation requirement for a physician practicing in an HPSA or other underserved area.[367]

Both of these advisory opinion processes are new in the Phase II Final Rule and mark the first time that CMS is following the OIG process of case-by-case

---

[364]*Id.* §411.357(s).

[365]*Id.* §411.357(t).

[366]*Id.* §411.357(t)(1)(iv)(A) & (B).

[367]*Id.* §411.357(t)(2).

exceptions. Previously, CMS limited its advisory opinions to answering questions about whether a particular arrangement was prohibited by the Stark law. It will be very interesting to follow how many providers avail themselves of this process and how freely CMS creates exceptions. Although CMS indicated in the preamble to the Phase II Final Rule that it will use this authority sparingly to grant health manpower-need exceptions, it may well be faced with the reality that the hospital will lose the physician in question and then pay more money for a new recruit without needing to show a demonstrated need to CMS.

## I. Community-Wide Health Information Systems (Phase II)

In addition to the incidental benefits exception described above permitting payments for certain portable technologies, the Phase II Final Rule also added a separate exception for hardware and software that enable a referring physician to access the DHS entity's health information infrastructure.[368] CMS does not consider this to be remuneration, because it confers a benefit upon the DHS entity and facilitates patient care. A community-wide health information system meets this exception if it (1) is available to all practitioners, (2) allows for sharing of electronic health care records, (3) does not replace hardware or software that the physician would purchase for his or her own practice, (4) does not take into account the volume or value of referrals, and (5) does not violate the anti-kickback statute.

## J. Electronic Health Records Exception

On August 8, 2006, CMS established an exception to the compensation prohibition for certain arrangements involving the donation of electronic health record (EHR) technology and related services (EHR Final Rule).[369]

CMS defines a electronic health record as "a repository of consumer health status information in computer processable form used for clinical diagnosis and treatment for a broad array of clinical conditions."[370] Central to this exception is that the EHR technology must be interoperable as defined in the regulation.[371] EHR items and services that are capable of only communicating within a limited health care system or community will not be considered interoperable.[372] Further, the donor cannot restrict the use or compatibility of the donated items with other EHR systems.[373] Although EHR items are deemed to be interoperable if certified, the regulation does not mandate certification.[374]

---

[368] *Id.* §411.357(u).

[369] 71 Fed. Reg. 45,140 (Aug. 8, 2006) (codified at 42 C.F.R. §411.357(w) (2007)); provided as Appendix B-6 on the disk accompanying this volume. At the same time, CMS promulgated a similar exception for support for electronic prescribing items and services that have substantially similar requirements to those set forth in the EHR exception. 42 C.F.R. §411.357(v) (2007).

[370] 42 C.F.R. §411.351 (2007).

[371] *Id.*

[372] *Id.*

[373] *Id.* §411.357(w)(3).

[374] *Id.* §411.357(w)(2).

CMS permits nonmonetary remuneration for EHR items and services in the form of software or information technology and training services that are necessary and are used predominately to create, maintain, transmit, or receive electronic health records.[375] In the preamble, CMS notes that the exception excludes the donation of hardware, staffing of physician offices, and software used primarily to conduct personal business or business unrelated to physician's medical practice.[376] The preamble further indicates that EHR items and services do include interface and translation software, connectivity services, training and support services, intellectual property rights and licensing, clinical support and information services related to patient care, maintenance services, and secured messaging.[377]

Donations of EHR items and services may be provided by any entity that furnishes designated health services to any physician.[378] Entities, such as pharmaceutical and device manufacturers, are prohibited donors, and group practices are prohibited recipients.[379] Physician recipients must pay 15 percent of the donor's costs for the items and services provided prior to the receipt of such items.[380]

The EHR exception has certain fraud and abuse protections as well. For instance, the receipt of a donated EHR item may not be a condition of the donor doing business with the recipient.[381] Reflecting the importance to the health care system of diffusing EHR technology, CMS took the unique step of only prohibiting a donor from *directly* taking into account the volume or value of referrals generated between the parties.[382] This is the only exception created by CMS that permits remuneration to a referral source that can indirectly take into account the volume or value of referrals. Further, the final EHR rule enumerates seven methodologies for selecting recipients and determining the amount of donated EHR items or services, including the size of the recipient's medical practice, the total number of hours that the recipient practices medicine, whether the recipient is a member of the donor's medical staff, and the level of uncompensated care provided by the recipient.[383] These methodologies are not required but will be deemed acceptable without more elaborate compliance supporting documentation. Finally, donated EHR items must be necessary, and therefore are not protected if the donor has actual knowledge of, or acts in reckless disregard or deliberate ignorance of, the fact that the recipient possesses or has obtained items or services equivalent to those provided by the donor.[384]

---

[375] *Id.* §411.357(w).

[376] 71 Fed. Reg. at 45,151.

[377] *Id.*

[378] 42 C.F.R. §411.357(w)(1).

[379] 71 Fed. Reg. at 45,157.

[380] 42 C.F.R. §411.357(w)(4).

[381] *Id.* §411.357(w)(5).

[382] *Id.* §411.357(w)(6).

[383] *Id.*

[384] *Id.* §411.357(w)(8).

## XV. Reporting Requirements and Sanctions

Inadvertently, CMS omitted provisions explaining the reporting requirements from the preamble of the Phase II Final Rule. CMS issued a technical correction on April 6, 2004, with these preamble sections.[385]

### A. Reporting Requirements

Under the Stark law, all entities that provide items or services payable under Medicare must comply with the reporting requirements. Under the Final Rules, CMS may collect information on the unique physician identification number (UPIN) of the referring physician with a financial relationship, and the covered items and services provided by the DHS entity.[386] The reporting requirements are waived for DHS entities providing 20 or fewer Part A or B services during a calendar year or for DHS provided outside the United States. For physicians with a reportable financial relationship as defined in the Final Rules (see discussion below), CMS may collect information on the nature of the financial relationship as evidenced in records that the entity knows or should know about "in the course of prudently conducting business." This information would include, but is not limited to, records that the entity is already required to retain to comply with IRS, Securities Exchange Commission, and Medicare and Medicaid program rules.

A reportable financial relationship includes any ownership or investment interest or any compensation arrangement, except ownership arrangements meeting the exceptions for publicly traded entities and mutual funds.[387] This means that DHS entities whose shares or debt instruments are so traded and meet these exceptions need not keep track of whether its referring physicians own an interest in the entity. The Phase II Final Rule clarified that this exemption only applies to shareholder information, and that DHS entities must report other financial relationships with referring physicians who are shareholders, such as personal service arrangements.[388]

The regulatory history of the reporting requirements illustrates the evolving understanding of CMS of the complications of interpreting and enforcing the Stark law. The Stark I regulation provided that entities must submit the requisite information on a form prescribed by CMS within 30 days of the request, and that all changes to that information must be submitted to CMS within 60 days from the date of the change.[389] Specifically, HCFA Form 96, effective January 1, 1992, and entitled "Clinical Laboratory Financial Relationships with Physicians," was a Medicare carrier survey requiring disclosure of the financial relationships between entities furnishing clinical laboratory services and physicians. Similarly, HCFA Form 97, also effective January 1,

---

[385]Medicare Program; Physicians' Referrals to Health Care Entities With Which They Have Financial Relationships (Phase II); Correction, 69 Fed. Reg. 17,933 (Apr. 6, 2004).

[386]42 C.F.R. §411.361(c).

[387]*Id.* §411.361(d).

[388]69 Fed. Reg. at 17,934.

[389]*Id.* at 17,933; 42 C.F.R. §411.361.

1992, was a Medicare fiscal-intermediary survey requiring disclosure of financial relationships between physicians and hospital and facility-based clinical laboratories. Although both forms contained a box indicating that a form was to have been used to update previous information, and indeed the instructions to these forms indicated that such updating is required, CMS informally had indicated that it would not require providers of clinical laboratory services to update these forms as financial relationships change.

In the Stark II Proposed Rule, CMS acknowledged that it was still in the process of developing the statutorily prescribed reporting process and the necessary forms, and that until it completed this process, physicians and entities were not required to report.[390] CMS proposed to amend the reporting regulations in three ways: (1) by specifying that entities would need only to report changes to the requested information once a year, instead of within 60 days of the date of the change; (2) by specifying that all financial relationships would need to be reported, even if those relationships satisfy an exception to the Stark law; and (3) by developing a streamlined reporting system that would not require entities to retain and submit large quantities of data.[391]

In the Phase II Final Rule, CMS appeared to have backed off completely any requirement for the regular submission of such information with updates as financial relationships change. CMS indicated that it did not intend to issue any reporting forms at all.[392] But in August 2006, CMS stated that it would require hospitals to report information on a periodic basis related to their investment and compensation relationships with physicians.[393] In order to obtain a more accurate and complete understanding of physician investment in specialty hospitals, CMS issued a voluntary survey instrument to specialty and competitor hospitals.[394] But 290 hospitals did not respond to the survey.

On May 18, 2007, pursuant to the Paperwork Reduction Act, CMS issued a notice and comment of a proposed information collection regarding a new form called the Disclosure of Financial Relationships Report (DFRR).[395] The initial purpose of the form is to send it to the hospitals that failed to properly complete the 2006 survey. CMS further stated that, once finalized, it will send the DFRR to an additional 210 hospitals.[396] The DFRR will be used by CMS to evaluate investment interests and compensation arrangements between hospitals and physicians, and hospitals will be required to disclose the following: (i) direct ownership information of each owner/investor for each class of stock, equity, or secured debt (this includes both investment reconciliation and loans and loan

---

[390]63 Fed. Reg. at 1703.

[391]*See generally id.* at 1703–04.

[392]69 Fed. Reg. at 17,934; 42 C.F.R. §411.361(e).

[393]Final Report to the Congress and Strategic and Implementing Plan Required under Section 5006 of the Deficit Reduction Act of 2005.

[394]Centers for Medicare and Medicaid Servs., FINAL REPORT IMPLEMENTING THE DRA PROVISION AFFECTING SPECIALTY HOSPITALS, app. 1, *Scope & Methodology*, at v (Aug. 8, 2006).

[395]Agency Information Collection Activities: Proposed Collection; Comment Request, 72 Fed. Reg. 28,056 (May 18, 2007), *available at* http://www.cms.hhs.gov/PaperworkReduction Actof1995/PRAL/itemdetail.asp?filterType=none&filterByDID=99&sortByDID=2&sortOrder=descending&itemID=CMS1199195&intNumPerPage=10.

[396]*Id.*

guarantees from hospital to physician-owners); (ii) an ownership percentage calculation for each owner/investor; (iii) all lease or "under arrangements" with physicians; and (iv) compensation arrangements with physicians including space and equipment rentals, personal service arrangements, and recruitment as well as nonmonetary compensation arrangements.[397] In many cases, CMS is requesting the information be provided by individual physician, including the physicians' national provider identifier (NPI) or UPIN number. Detailed supporting documentation is also required. For example, hospitals will be required to furnish their audited financial statements, and for each of the categories of compensation arrangements for which disclosures are required, all written agreements in effect in 2006 must be submitted. In addition, hospitals will need to submit any explanation of all charitable donations by physicians, including each physician's name and NPI or UPIN.

The DFRR will need to be signed by the hospital's chief executive officer or chief financial officer, and a completed DFRR must be submitted to CMS within 45 days of its receipt by the hospital.[398]

CMS also made clear this initial limited use of the DFRR "is the first step toward implementing a regular financial disclosure process that would apply to all Medicare participating hospitals." Thus, once the Office of Management and Budget (OMB) clears this DFRR form, CMS may use it for this wider purpose. But CMS does not explain why it is limiting this form to hospitals when all providers that furnish DHS are subject to the Stark law. So CMS's final step might be to use this or a similar form to verify compliance by all DHS providers.

## B. Sanctions

Violations of the prohibition on physician self-referrals may result in either Medicare's nonpayment of claims for DHS provided as a result of a prohibited referral, an obligation to refund payment amounts, or, for a knowing violation, a CMP of up to $15,000 per violation or $100,000 per arrangement.[399]

Because there is a violation each time an entity submits a claim for DHS resulting from a prohibited referral, the $15,000 per violation CMP, coupled with the denial of payment sanction, can lead to substantial amounts even for limited infractions of the rules. Significantly, in the Phase I Final Rule, CMS made clear that under the Stark law physicians are not liable for payment recoupments for claims submitted in violation of the law, but are liable only for CMPs, and only where the government has shown the physicians acted with knowledge of the violation.

The Phase II Final Rule made no changes to the existing sanction provisions under subsection (g) of the Stark law. These regulations implementing the civil money penalty provisions were issued by the OIG on March 31, 1995.[400]

---

[397] *Id.*

[398] *Id.*

[399] 42 U.S.C. §1395nn(g).

[400] Civil Money Penalties for Referrals to Entities and for Prohibited Arrangements and Schemes, 60 Fed. Reg. 16,580 (Mar. 31, 1995), *codified at* 42 C.F.R. §1003.102(a)(5) (2004).

## XVI. Differences Between the Stark Law and the Federal Anti-Kickback Statute

Although the Stark law and the anti-kickback statute are intended to combat the same perceived harms, the two provisions must be analyzed separately. In enacting Stark I congressional conferees stated:

> The conferees wish to clarify that any prohibition, exemption, or exception authorized under this provision in no way alters (or reflects on) the scope and application of the anti-kickback provisions in section 1128B of the Social Security Act. The conferees do not intend that this provision should be construed as affecting, or in any way interfering with, the efforts of the Inspector General to enforce current law, such as cases described in the recent Fraud Alert issued by the Inspector General. In particular, entities, which would be eligible for a specific exemption, would be subject to all of the provisions of current law.[401]

Two of the most significant differences between the two laws are the differences in the required proof of intent and the need to comply with exceptions or safe harbors. First, a violation of the Stark law occurs without proof of illegal intent, and thus it is a strict liability offense.[402] In other words, if there is a financial relationship between an entity and a physician, and the physician refers Medicare or Medicaid patients to the entity for designated services, then the arrangement *must* fall within one of the exceptions to avoid violating the self-referral prohibition. By contrast, the anti-kickback statute is a criminal statute requiring proof of criminal intent to induce referrals. Violations are punishable by fines, imprisonment, or both.

Second, the exceptions and safe harbors operate very differently under each statute. One of the confusions between the Stark law and anti-kickback statute is that many of the Stark law exceptions were modeled after the anti-kickback statute's safe harbors. In both cases, the fundamental objective is the same: to create a set of prophylactic rules that dissipate any potential influence of money on referral decisions. However, the anti-kickback statute's regulatory safe harbors are made for certain business conduct the government has determined is innocuous or beneficial even if there is a possible taint of money and referrals. If a provider meets all of the standards of a particular safe harbor, the conduct is immune from prosecution. Failure to comply fully with a safe harbor, however, has no legal effect; rather if the government objects to the arrangement it must still prove illegal intent to induce referrals. By implication, if an arrangement substantially—but not fully—complies with a safe harbor, there is no penalty; it merely means that the parties will not be fully protected by that safe harbor. In contrast, the failure to comply *fully and completely* with a Stark law exception means that the entire financial arrangement is not in compliance with the statute.

Other significant differences are set forth below:

---

[401]H.R. Conf. Rep. No. 386, at 856 (1989).

[402]As discussed in Section XV.B., above, regarding sanctions, CMPs are assessed under the Stark law only on proof of a knowing violation.

- The Stark law applies only to prohibited referrals under the Medicare and Medicaid programs, whereas the anti-kickback statute applies to all federally funded health care programs.[403]
- The Stark law regulates conduct within a physician's own practice, whereas the anti-kickback statute has never been interpreted by a court to apply to a referral to oneself.
- The Stark law regulates physician compensation, whereas the anti-kickback statute generally does not, with the exception that the safe harbors specify that compensation must be at fair market value.
- The Stark law prohibits paying bona fide employees for referrals unless the directed referrals exception is met, whereas the anti-kickback statute does not.
- The Stark law applies only to relationships between physicians and entities, whereas any two parties may violate the anti-kickback statute.
- The Stark law prohibits only referrals, whereas the anti-kickback statute prohibits wider forms of misconduct, including, inter alia, arranging for and/or recommending the purchase of items or services.
- The principal remedy under the Stark law is denial of payment, whereas the anti-kickback statute is principally a criminal felony prohibition.
- The principal remedy of denial of payment under the Stark law applies only to the provider billing for the service rendered pursuant to a prohibited referral under the Stark law, whereas both parties to an illegal kickback arrangement are equally vulnerable.

Clearly, in some of these cases the ambit of the Stark law is broader than that of the anti-kickback statute, and in other cases it is narrower. Because of these significant differences, it is imperative that practitioners conduct a separate analysis of the applicability of both statutes to a financial relationship.

CMS confuses the supposed distinction between the two statutes in two ways. First, there are several Stark law exceptions (such as physician recruitment, fair market value, and indirect compensation arrangements) that are conditioned on compliance with the anti-kickback statute as defined in the Final Rules.[404] Second, in response to Phase I comments, CMS promulgated two exceptions in Phase II for arrangements that comply with the safe harbors for referral services and obstetrical malpractice insurance subsidies. Each of these exceptions is discussed in detail in Section XIV.F., above.

We find troubling CMS's continued reliance on anti-kickback statute compliance as a condition for qualifying under certain Stark law exceptions. This approach introduces intent as an element of the Stark law analysis, which is inconsistent with CMS's goal of providing clear, bright-line rules. We are also not satisfied with CMS's explanation that this approach is required by the statute's dictate that any exceptions created by regulation must pose "no risk of abuse." The OIG has had close to 15 years of drafting safe harbors, and has sufficient experience in developing prophylactic rules that minimize abuse,

---

[403] 42 U.S.C. §1320a-7b(b).

[404] 42 C.F.R. §411.351 (definition of "does not violate the anti-kickback statute").

without resorting to an analysis of whether there is unlawful intent to induce referrals as a condition of complying with the Stark law.

Although conceptually there is merit in certain circumstances to tie safe harbor compliance with compliance with Stark exceptions, the exception for malpractice subsidies demonstrates the pitfalls. The narrowness of the parallel safe harbor for malpractice subsidies combined with the incorporation of that safe harbor into the Stark law renders it difficult for most such subsidies to continue.

We believe, however, that there is an important need to harmonize the compliance provisions of both statutes. We disagree with CMS's position that full compliance with a Stark law exception is irrelevant to compliance with the anti-kickback statute. Rather, the guiding principle should be (i) as long as an arrangement is covered by the Stark law, (ii) there is no agreement or condition for referrals that does not comply with the final rules' directed referrals exception, and (iii) the arrangement complies with a Stark law exception, the OIG should grant it safe harbor protection as well.

## XVII. Stark Law Advisory Opinion Final Rule

In 1989, the House of Representatives voted as part of its consideration of Stark I to authorize an advisory opinion process that would permit case-by-case review of arrangements where providers can demonstrate that the services would otherwise be unavailable, more convenient based on reduced travel time, and provided at a lower unit charge and lower overall cost to the Medicare program than comparable services.[405] This approach was rejected by the conferees and lay dormant until 1996—despite commentary urging action[406]—when Congress authorized advisory opinions under the anti-kickback statute.[407] The OIG's implementing regulation in 1997 adopted just such a case-by-case approach.[408]

The BBA extended the advisory opinion process to the Stark law in response to the health care industry's justifiable confusion concerning the parameters of the self-referral prohibition. The advisory opinion final rule established a process for seeking guidance as to whether existing or proposed arrangements violate the Stark law.[409] At the same time, CMS also imposed what could be very difficult criteria for the requests, certain risks, and somewhat onerous burdens on the parties seeking advisory opinions.

In general, based on the congressional directive in the BBA, CMS has patterned the advisory opinion final rule after the OIG anti-kickback advisory

---

[405]H.R. Conf. Rep. No. 386, at 847–48.

[406]*See, e.g.,* Thomas S. Crane, *The Problem of Physician Self Referral Under the Anti-Kickback Statute: The* Hanlester Network *Case and the Safe Harbor Regulation,* 268 JAMA, 85, 90 (1992).

[407]42 U.S.C. §1320a-7d(b).

[408]42 C.F.R. pt. 1008.

[409]*See generally* 63 Fed. Reg. at 1646. *See also* Medicare Program; Physicians' Referrals to Entities With Which They Have Financial Relationships (Phase II), Correcting Amendment, 69 Fed. Reg. 57,226 (Sept. 24, 2004), *codified at* 42 C.F.R. §§411.370–.389.

opinion regulations, including similar limitations, timing, and procedural rules.[410] The most significant difference between the two advisory opinion processes is that in the anti-kickback advisory opinion process the OIG has adopted a case-specific approach whereby it is free to waive certain safe harbor standards or impose additional requirements on a particular transaction. In contrast, with the exception of the advisory opinions authorized for physician retention payments (see discussion at Section XIV.H., above), the advisory opinions to be issued under the Stark law will analyze merely whether a transaction falls within the statute and, if so, whether it also satisfies the criteria for one of the exceptions. Thus, the advisory opinions under the Stark law are likely to be much narrower and have less utility than those issued under the anti-kickback statute. Given the clear congressional mandate to follow the OIG's process, CMS's rigid approach in the advisory opinion final rule appears to fall well short of fulfilling its statutory mandate.

A Stark law advisory opinion is available only for existing or soon-to-be-consummated arrangements. A party submitting a request must certify that all of the information provided is true and correct, and that it intends in good faith to enter into the arrangement if it does not already exist.[411] CMS will not provide an opinion regarding hypothetical or generalized arrangements. Once the advisory opinion is issued, it is binding upon the Secretary and the requesting party. Although the Secretary retains the authority to revoke an opinion after its issuance, the requesting party does not have any recourse if it is not satisfied with the result. In addition, there is a risk of sanctions following any adverse advisory opinion. CMS has indicated that it will use the information disclosed in the process against the requesting party and others in subsequent civil, criminal, or administrative actions.

Despite a lack of explicit statutory authority, the advisory opinion final rule specifies that CMS will charge a fee equal to the costs incurred in responding to the request, and CMS is not obligated to estimate these costs in advance.[412] CMS estimated that the cost will be approximately $75 per hour, and that the total cost of an opinion will depend on the complexity of the arrangement and the quality of the submission.[413] The advisory opinion final rule provides that CMS will generally issue an opinion within 90 days after the request has been formally accepted, unless the request involves complex legal issues or highly complicated fact patterns; in that case, CMS will respond to the request "within a reasonable time period."[414] By contrast, the anti-kickback advisory opinion authority requires the OIG to issue an opinion not later than 60 days after receiving a request.[415]

---

[410]*See generally id.* For regulations on the Stark law advisory opinion process, see Appendix B-3 on the disk accompanying this volume. For full text of the advisory opinions, see the CMS Web site at http://www.cms.hhs.gov/PhysicianSelfReferral/07_advisory_opinions.asp. Summaries of the advisory opinions and a topical index are included as Appendix G-2 and G-3 on the disk accompanying this volume.

[411]42 C.F.R. §411.370(a); 42 C.F.R. §411.373(a).

[412]42 C.F.R. §411.375(b).

[413]63 Fed. Reg. at 1652.

[414]42 C.F.R. §411.380(c)(1).

[415]42 U.S.C. §1320a-7d(b)(5)(B).

Once a Stark law advisory opinion has been issued, it will be made available promptly for public inspection, but will be legally binding only on the HHS and the requesting party, and only with respect to the specific conduct of the requesting party.[416] CMS will not be bound with respect to the conduct of any third party, even if the conduct of that party appears similar to the conduct that is the subject of the opinion.

## XVIII. Conclusion

The Stark law is the natural child of the budget reconciliation process of the 1980s, where Congress saw excesses in the health care business environment and an executive branch it believed needed to be micromanaged. The result was a sweeping per se prohibition of most then-existing forms of self-referral based on ownership interests, coupled with the regulation of physician compensation relationships with outside referral sources, referrals within physicians' practices, and physician compensation in virtually any setting. All of this was set in motion in Stark I and II with little discretion granted to the executive branch to modify by regulation onerous requirements or requirements rendered meaningless by the sweeping changes in the health care system since the statute's enactment. Although the Final Rules attempt to inject common sense into the Stark law in many areas (with the notable exception of the highly restrictive rules for physician recruitment), the outcome of self-referral enforcement is a long way from being final, and Congressman Stark's promise of "clear bright-line rules" remains elusive.

---

[416]42 C.F.R. §411.384(b); 42 C.F.R. §411.387.

# Addendum to Chapter 2

## Stark Phase III Regulation—Analysis and Comment*

*By the Health Law Section of Mintz, Levin, Cohn, Ferris, Glovsky and Popeo, P.C. Authors are Thomas S. Crane, Stephen Bentfield, Ellen Janos, Margaret D. Kranz, Karen Lovitch, Stephen Weiner, Heather Westphal, Sarah Whipple, and Nili Yolin. All views expressed herein are the personal views of the authors and do not represent the formal positions of Mintz, Levin, Cohn, Ferris, Glovsky and Popeo, P.C., any of its clients, or other attorneys at the firm. The authors expressly reserve the right to advocate freely other positions in other forums or settings. Reproduced with permission from 11 HEALTH CARE FRAUD REP. No. 19 (Sept. 20, 2007). Copyright ©2007 by the Bureau of National Affairs, Inc. (800-372-1033), http://www.bna.com.

# I. Introduction

On September 5, 2007, the Centers for Medicare & Medicaid Services (CMS) published the third and final phase in a rulemaking under the Medicare physician self-referral prohibition, known as the Stark law (72 Fed. Reg. 51,012). We call this regulation Stark II, Phase III, or the Phase III Final Rule, or simply Phase III for short. It is properly called Stark II because this is a rulemaking under the 1993 amended Stark law.[1] This rulemaking cycle spans nine years and close to 300 *Federal Register* pages. The proposed rule appeared on January 9, 1998 (63 Fed. Reg. 1659).

---

[1] We do not discuss Stark I applicable to clinical laboratory services or the rulemaking thereunder.

Because of the scope of the rulemaking, CMS decided to issue the final rule in two phases, the first of which was promulgated on January 4, 2001, that partially implemented Stark II, known as Phase I (66 Fed. Reg. 856). Phase II followed on March 26, 2004 (69 Fed. Reg. 16,054).

At the time of Phase II's publication, CMS realized there were numerous issues warranting further attention and generating concern by providers, and so it published this rule, like Phase I, as an interim final rule with comment. This leads us to Phase III, which CMS published without a comment period, thereby finally bringing this rulemaking cycle to an end.

The Phase III Final Rule is in many ways a clean-up exercise to address continuing questions, concerns, and ambiguities in the regulatory scheme. Because Phase III addresses the entire rule, CMS took the extra step of re-publishing the rule in its entirety, even though most of it did not change. CMS also provided readers with an informal redline, which is available on its Web site, comparing the current rule with Phase II.[2] In addition, readers should watch for a technical corrections notice in the *Federal Register* that will fix many of the small problems individuals have brought to CMS's attention. We have been advised that this technical corrections notice will not include substantive changes.

Our approach in this article to the presentation of the materials attempts to follow the statutory and regulatory structure, but with some major exceptions. In sections IV–VIII, we address separately several significant themes that are important to providers, irrespective of where they appear in the regulation. These include (1) the indirect compensation definition and exception, including CMS's new concept of "stand in the shoes"; (2) the definition of group practice and the in-office ancillary services exception; (3) exceptions related to various forms of physician compensation that commonly arise in physician transactions; (4) physician recruitment and retention; and (5) the exception for academic medical centers.

As noted above, while CMS republished the entire Stark rule, much of it is unchanged. Specifically, Phase III does not discuss the exceptions for electronic prescribing items and services or electronic items and services, both of which were enacted in 2006. (42 C.F.R. §§ 411.357(v) and (w)). If we do not discuss a provision of the regulation, whether a definition or exception, it means that CMS makes no changes or had no meaningful comments that need to be included in this summary.

Finally, although not the specific topic of this article, but relevant to some of the topics covered, on July 12, 2007, CMS proposed many significant changes to the Stark regulations as part of the 2008 Medicare Physician Fee Schedule Proposed Rule (the "2008 PFS Proposed Rule") (72 Fed. Reg. 38,122). Because of the impact this proposed rule will have on Phase III if promulgated as proposed, in several places below we briefly discuss the interplay between the Phase III Final Rule and the 2008 PFS Proposed Rule.

---

[2] *See* http://www.cms.hhs.gov/PhysicianSelfReferral/Downloads/Unofficial_Redlined_411_ 350.pdf.

## II. Summary Comments and Highlights of Phase III

### A. Summary Comments

On August 11, 1988, when Rep. Fortney "Pete" Stark (D-Calif.) introduced legislation that would come to be known by his name, he confidently predicted his bill would provide a clear, "bright-line rule."

Now, 19 years later, we can state with equal confidence that our search for such bright-line rules continues.

In one respect, as noted above, Phase III marks the end of an era because this rule contains no comment period. So it closes the door on omnibus-style regulation packages with rolling comments, which had the effect of keeping uncertainty alive. Instead, CMS has clearly moved its Stark rulemaking agenda to the annual physician fee schedule rulemaking cycle.

This approach makes sense because it allows CMS and the provider community to take digestible bites at the various open issues that remain outstanding. The down-side, though, is the internal pressure under which CMS operates in that these annual fee schedule cycles gives little time for CMS to step back and fully think through the issues at hand, creating on-going possibilities for unintended consequences, a concern to which CMS is obviously acutely sensitive.

Indeed, while not to dismiss the importance of the Phase III rule— especially the "stand in the shoes" rule, one of the more striking observations is how few changes it contains, especially in light of the very significant proposals CMS has offered in the 2008 PFS Proposed Rule.

Indeed, there is almost a disconnect between the two preambles, with CMS suggesting in the 2008 PFS Proposed Rule there are several areas of serious potential fraud that call for more tightened rules; by comparison the Phase III preamble seems more like a modest fine-tuning exercise. We suggest that if CMS adopts all of its proposals contained in the 2008 PFS Proposed Rule without change, that rule will have a substantially greater impact on providers than will Phase III.

We also emphasize the challenges the Stark Law continues to pose for providers and counsel seeking to comply with its provisions. This regulatory scheme is not for the faint of heart. Even experienced counsel may not remember that an important term can be defined in the applicable exception, the definitions section, or elsewhere.

For example, some of the most important statutory terms or conditions are contained in Section 411.354 ("Financial relationship, compensation, and ownership or investment interest"). Who would guess that this section contains a set of rules that permit a provider to condition compensation on the physician's referrals to the provider?

Making compliance even more challenging is the need for a thorough understanding of the various preamble commentaries contained in the 2008 PFS Proposed Rule, Phase I, Phase II, and Phase III. Although preamble statements are not legally binding, they provide critical guidance enabling providers to have a complete understanding of CMS's thinking and how it is likely to apply the rule's requirements. Phase III is important, not so much for what changed in the regulation itself or not, but for the extensive preamble commentary that manifests thinking that cannot meaningfully be gleaned from the text of the regulation itself.

More problematic, of course, are the areas we discuss in this article where the regulation text does not track the stated intent in the preamble and as a result CMS has created unintended problems.

A final cautionary note: Perhaps one of CMS's most understated comments in Phase III is the following: "Phases I, II, and III of this rulemaking are intended to be read together as a unified whole." This means that a critical interpretation of a provision that counsel may be researching could be found in any one of the preamble commentaries, and even then, one cannot stop the research once one passage is located. Counsel may find the passage he/she is reviewing was later rescinded or significantly modified in another phase of the rulemaking.

So the old Hill Street Blues watch-word still applies: "Be careful out there."

## B. Highlights and Issues

We highlight here both the significant provisions of the Phase III Final Rule and its preamble, as well as our comments and concerns.

Indirect Compensation and the "Stand in the Shoes" Rule

- The Phase III Final Rule establishes that a physician has a direct compensation arrangement with a DHS entity if the only intervening entity between the physician and the DHS entity is his or her "physician organization." In essence, physicians "stand in the shoes" of their group practice for purposes of evaluating whether they have a direct or indirect compensation arrangement with a DHS entity.
- A physician who "stands in the shoes" of his or her physician organization is deemed to have the same compensation arrangements, with the same parties and on the same terms, as the physician organization itself.
- The "parties" include the DHS entity and the physician organization, including all of the physician organization's members, employees or independent contractor physicians.
- CMS creates a grandfathering provision, subject to a sunset, for arrangements currently in place that will not satisfy the new "stand in the shoes" rule. CMS will not require restructuring of such arrangements during their original term or the current renewal term as long as they existed and complied with the indirect compensation exception as of September 5, 2007.
- We identify several ambiguities and concerns about the unintended consequences of the application of this new "stand in the shoes" rule.
- We have sufficient questions and concerns that we suggest CMS consider providing additional guidance and/or delaying the effective date of this provision until at least January 1, 2009. Such a delay would allow for another physician fee schedule rulemaking cycle, in which CMS could receive and consider comments from providers on this provision. The potential impact of this rule change is too significant for CMS not to get it right.

Exceptions Related to Various Forms of Physician Compensation
*Fair Market Value*

- In its definition of "fair market value," Phase II contained a "safe harbor" provision for hourly payments for a physician's personal services. But in Phase III CMS eliminates that safe harbor.
- In the exception for "fair market value" compensation arrangements, CMS now applies the exception to compensation paid by a physician to an entity as well as compensation paid by an entity to a physician. Previously the exception applied only to compensation paid by a DHS entity to a physician. The effect of this expansion in the scope of the fair market value exception is to *eliminate* the availability of the "payments by a physician" exception for such payment arrangements. We anticipate this change will have a very significant impact and could require a significant number of arrangements to be restructured.

*Bonus Compensation*

- Phase III makes clear that productivity bonuses may be based directly on "incident to" services that are incidental to the physician's personally performed services, even if those "incident to" services are otherwise DHS referrals. But CMS also has withdrawn its Phase II statement that overall profit shares could relate directly to "incident to" services.

*Independent Contractors and Physicians in the Group*

- CMS modifies the definition of "physician in the group practice" to require that a physician who is an independent contractor must contract *directly* with the group practice, as distinct from a contract running through a staffing company or his or her employer. This change is potentially far reaching, requiring many arrangements to be restructured.
- In the Phase III preamble, but not in the Final Rule itself, CMS states that a leased employee is not considered to be a physician in the group practice.

Physician Recruitment and Retention

- Despite some liberalization, Phase III continues, in large measure, CMS's resistance to use of physician recruitment assistance by hospitals to existing practices. Most arrangements that were commonplace prior to Phase II were rendered unlawful under that rulemaking and will remain so with adoption of the Phase III Final Rule. CMS is sending a clear message that hospitals should continue to integrate horizontally and to employ physicians.
- For the majority of hospitals seeking to recruit physicians to practices not located in a rural area or an HPSA, using an income guarantee as a recruitment incentive will continue to be problematic because of the limitations on overhead allocation.
- CMS agrees that categorically prohibiting physician practices from imposing non-compete provisions may make it more difficult for hospitals to recruit physicians.
- CMS's clarifications regarding practice restrictions and relocation criteria are welcome and quite helpful. These changes will serve to facilitate

hospital efforts to assist existing practices with their recruitment efforts by allowing practices to impose certain non-compete clauses and other commercially well-accepted requirements on the recruited physician.

- CMS makes clear that a recruited physician must be a signatory to the recruitment assistance agreement entered into between the hospital and the physician practice, and that it is insufficient to allow the recruited physician to sign a one-page acknowledgement agreeing to be bound by the terms of the recruitment agreement. This clarification will likely require a large number of recruitment agreements to be reformed, although it is not clear how CMS expects providers to make the needed changes.

- CMS amends the retention payment exception to allow retention payments on the basis of a written certification by the physician that the physician has a *bona fide opportunity for future employment* that would require a move of his or her medical practice at least 25 miles and outside the service area of the current hospital.

- The interplay between the "stand in the shoes" rule and the physician recruitment exception needs to be thought through more completely. If CMS truly intends to apply the logic behind the "stand in the shoes" concept to physician recruitment agreements, hospitals would not need to be concerned about the agreement between the group and the physician and many of CMS's stated concerns would not be relevant, thereby creating a vastly simplified, more realistic exception for physician recruitment activities.

Academic Medical Centers Exception

- CMS appears to have created a problem for academic medical centers it did not likely intend related to the "set in advance" requirement. The exception now specifies: "The total compensation paid by *each* academic medical center component to the referring physician is set in advance." (Emphasis added).

- Previously, under Phase II, "each" was "all." Under Phase II, AMCs needed only to make sure that the total compensation from *all* components of the AMC was set in advance. But, under the change introduced by the Phase III Final Rule, it appears that this approach is no longer sufficient. As written, it appears that, to meet this exception, AMCs *must* assure that the compensation from each component meets the "set in advance" requirement. The preamble strongly suggests that CMS did not mean to impose such a requirement. We hope CMS fixes this problem in an upcoming technical corrections notice.

- CMS makes a clarifying change to the AMC exception relating to the requirement that a majority of a teaching hospital's medical staff must be academic faculty. The exception is amended so that, in making this determination, a teaching hospital may either include or exclude all physicians with the same class of privileges, for example, courtesy staff.

- Many AMCs have arrangements that do not qualify under the AMC exception. AMCs with such non-qualifying payments to a physician for his or her services will likely be particularly hard-hit by the "stand in the shoes" rule. Most such arrangements did not qualify as indirect compensation because the physician's aggregate compensation was not based on referrals, and consequently no further analysis of that arrangement was warranted. These arrangements will need to be analyzed for compliance with a direct compensation exception and perhaps restructured. It is also not clear whether such arrangements qualify for the grandfathering provision described above.

## Statutory Compensation Exceptions

### *Rental of Office Space and Equipment*

- Regarding office sharing arrangements, CMS expands on the "exclusive use" language in the exception, stating that the language effectively requires that space and equipment leases "be for established blocks of time." CMS's hard line on shared lease arrangements that do not include block-time provisions could be one of the more important clarifications in Phase III.

- Shared lease arrangements should be restructured to include block-time. Even with such a provision, providers need to pay careful attention to make certain they are providing appropriate supervision of the shared service.

### *Personal Services*

- CMS now permits a six-month holdover period for personal service arrangements similar to those permitted following the expiration of space and equipment leases under those exceptions, as long as the holdover personal service arrangement is on the same terms and conditions as the immediately preceding agreement.

- With respect to the exception applicable to PIPs, CMS amends its terms to refer consistently to the term "downstream contractor," a newly defined term. In doing so, CMS clarifies that the PIP exception applies equally to the individual or entity contracting directly with the managed care organization ("MCO") to provide or arrange for items and services and to the individual or entity that subcontracts directly or indirectly to provide or arrange for items and services covered by an agreement between the MCO and the first tier contractor.

### *Certain Group Practice Arrangements with Hospitals*

- CMS received no comments on the exception allowing certain group practice arrangements with hospitals, and made no changes in the Phase III Final Rule. However, in the 2008 PFS Proposed Rule, CMS is seeking to eliminate protection for physician-owned entities furnishing services to hospitals under arrangements that do not meet this exception. These proposed changes are very significant and readers should consult the Proposed Rule, and the final rule when published.

## Compensation Exceptions Created By Regulation

### *Non-Monetary Compensation*

- CMS adds a deeming provision to the non-monetary compensation exception found at Section 411.357(k). If a DHS entity inadvertently exceeds the non-monetary compensation limit by no more than

50 percent, and the physician who receives the compensation returns the excess amount by the earlier of (1) the end of the calendar year in which he or she receives it or (2) 180 consecutive calendar days from receipt, then the compensation is deemed to be within the limit.

- A DHS entity may only rely on this deeming provision once every three years with respect to the same referring physician.

## III. General Prohibition and Key Statutory Terms

CMS did not substantively alter the general prohibition against physician self-referrals set forth in section 411.353, and made only minor modifications to the definitions of "ownership or investment interest" in section 411.354. (Note that in Section IV we discuss the definition of compensation arrangement and the amendment to section 411.354 related to the "standing in the shoes" concept.)

Nevertheless, in the preamble, CMS addresses several commenters' concerns related to the temporary non-compliance exception, which is intended to obviate the potentially severe consequences of inadvertent violations of the prohibition. In addition, as discussed more fully below, CMS clarified that an ownership interest in a DHS entity does not include a security interest taken by a physician in equipment sold to the entity and financed with a loan by the physician to the entity, but rather such security interest is considered a compensation arrangement.

Key statutory terms such as "entity," "radiology and certain other imaging services," and "referral" were not redefined in Phase III, but CMS offers a number of clarifications as to definitions of these terms.

Readers should note that in the 2008 PFS Proposed Rule, CMS is seeking several changes that relate to the general prohibition. It seeks comments on specifying the period of disallowance — or statute of limitations — for non-compliant financial arrangements. It proposed an alternative method for Stark Law compliance that requires, among other things, self-disclosure. And CMS proposes to change the definition of "entity" furnishing DHS. Readers should read this part of Phase III in the context of the PFS Proposed Rule.

### A. Temporary Noncompliance Exception

In Phase II, CMS created a temporary "grace period" for entities that briefly fall out of compliance with the statute due to events beyond their control. This exception, set forth in Section 411.353(f), permits a DHS entity to submit claims and receive payment for DHS furnished during a 90-day period of noncompliance if: (1) the arrangement was fully compliant for at least 180 consecutive days prior to date on which it became noncompliant; (2) the financial relationship became noncompliant for reasons beyond the entity's control; and (3) the financial relationship does not violate the anti-kickback statute and otherwise complies with all federal and state laws, rules and regulations. While Phase III makes no substantive changes to this section—indeed, CMS notes that commenters generally were pleased with the protections it offers—CMS proffers various reasons as to why it is not modifying certain of the exception's requirements.

For example, some commenters requested that the 90-day window start to run from the date of noncompliance until 30 or 90 days after the date on which the noncompliance was discovered, rather than simply 90 days from the date on which the financial relationship became noncompliant. CMS rejected this "discovery-based" proposal on the grounds that Stark is a strict liability statute and therefore any discovery or knowledge-based rule would contradict the statutory scheme. Furthermore, CMS indicated that such a rule would create substantial enforcement problems since it may be difficult to establish the date on which the noncompliance was discovered by the parties. Finally, CMS states that any extension of the 90-day period is simply not warranted or necessary, since all parties are obligated to self-monitor their arrangements to ensure compliance with applicable requirements and exceptions

Just as some commenters hoped that CMS would extend the 90-day window discussed above, other commenters recommended entirely eliminating the requirement of "180 consecutive days of compliance" that must precede the date of noncompliance. CMS likewise rejected this proposal, stating that the requirement is necessary to ensure that the temporary noncompliance exception is not abused.

## B. Entity

The general prohibition against self-referrals under the Stark law applies only to those referrals made to an "entity" that furnishes DHS. After the close of the Phase II comment period, the Medicare Payment Advisory Commission (MedPAC) recommended that the definition of "entity" be expanded to include not only an entity that actually furnishes DHS, but an entity that derives a substantial portion of its revenue from the provision of services, such as leased space, equipment, or management services, to an entity that furnishes DHS. According to MedPAC, physician-ownership of entities that provide administrative support and services to DHS entities creates a financial incentive for the physician-owner to refer patients to the DHS entities with which they do business. Thus, an expansion of the term "entity" would help ensure that referrals from the physician-owned entity to the DHS entity are based on clinical, rather than financial, considerations.

While noting that these arrangements are already subject to the self-referral prohibition in that they constitute an indirect compensation arrangement with a DHS entity, CMS agrees that they raise significant fraud and abuse concerns and advises that it intends to review and further monitor such arrangements before they are addressed in a separate rulemaking subject to public comment. Much of this portion of the preamble tracks similar concepts contained in the 2008 PFS Proposed Rule, in which CMS seeks significant changes designed to curtail physician-owned entities furnishing under arrangement services to hospital patients. For a more complete understanding of CMS's thinking, readers should consult the 2008 PFS Proposed Rule.

## C. Radiology and Certain Other Imaging Services

The definition of "radiology and certain other imaging services" was clarified in Phase II to exclude radiology procedures that are integral to the performance of a non-radiological medical procedure and performed during or immediately following the non-radiological procedure to confirm placement of an item inserted during the procedure. Although several commenters advocated for other special exceptions, CMS declines to create any in Phase III.

Notably, one commenter asked that CMS exclude ophthalmic A-scans from the definition of "radiology and certain other imaging services," which CMS had refused to exclude in Phase II. The commenter argued that A-scans are not diagnostic in nature because they indicate *how* surgery will be performed, not whether it will be performed. Moreover, the commenter stated that, even though the scan is not part of the cataract surgery, it is integral to the surgery and is only performed if the surgery has already been prescribed. As such, the commenter maintained, the procedure raises little risk of abuse or overutilization.

While acknowledging that A-scans are integral to cataract surgery, CMS refused to exclude them from the definition of "radiology and certain other imaging services" because they are not performed either during or immediately after the surgery to confirm the placement of an item inserted during the procedure. CMS did point out, however, that, in the CY 2008 Outpatient Prospective Payment System proposed rule, it proposed to exclude from the definition of "radiology and certain other imaging services" radiology procedures that are "covered ancillary services" as defined in Section 416.164(b), which includes certain radiology procedures that are integral to, and performed on the same day as, an ambulatory surgical procedure.

### D. Referral

The Stark law defines "referral" as a request by a physician for an item or service for which payment may be made under Medicare Part B, including a request for a consultation or establishment of a plan of care. In the Phase I Final Rule, the term "referral" excluded services personally performed by the referring physician, but included DHS provided by the physician's employees or contractors or by other members of the physician's group practice. In Phase II, CMS confirmed that a referral includes services that are performed "incident to" a physician's personally performed services, as well as DHS provided in accordance with a "consultation" with another physician, including DHS performed or supervised by the consulting physician or any DHS ordered by the consulting physician. However, certain requests pursuant to a "consultation" by pathologists, radiologists, and radiation oncologists were statutorily excluded from the definition of "referral." CMS makes no changes to this definition in Phase III, but several commenters' suggestions were addressed by CMS in the preamble.

The preamble provides CMS's views as to the circumstances in which a physician might be personally furnishing DME. For example, CMS states that, as a general matter, there would be few if any situations where a physician would personally furnish DME. But if a physician were to seek such protection from the reach of the Stark law by claiming to furnish DME personally, he or she would need to enroll as a DME supplier and comply with all program rules, including but not limited to the supplier standards of Section 424.57(c). Nevertheless, CMS does concede that a physician might personally refill an implantable pump.

In response to one commenter's suggestion that a "referral" not include "incident to" services requested by a physician and performed by an employee or contractor of the physician, unless the employee or contractor performing the services is licensed to provide the service without physician supervision and could bill for the service separately, CMS states that in-office ancillary services exception would provide protect this situation, and that it was going to adhere to its original interpretation that a "referral" includes "incident to" services.

CMS further states that, although the regulatory text of the "referral" definition was not revised to exclude ancillary services that are necessary to the provision of radiation therapy, it believes that the change made to the CY 2006 Physician Fee Schedule Final Rule was sufficient to effectuate this exclusion.

CMS also addresses several commenters' requests that it expand the consultation exception to include "walk-in patients" (i.e., patients that are not referred by another physician). Finding generally that such self-referrals are rare, CMS states that the consultation provision was intended to create a "narrow exception for a small subset of services provided or ordered by certain specialists in accordance with a consultation request by another physician," and that, depending on the circumstances, the in-office ancillary services exception should permit DHS referrals for walk-in patients. Thus, CMS declines to broaden the consultation provision to include walk-in patients.

### E. Ownership or Investment Interest

In response to Phase II modifications made to Phase I definitions of the various financial arrangements set forth in Section 411.354, CMS received several comments to the ownership interest provision, one of which led CMS to determine that a substantive change to Section 411.354 was necessary.

In Phase III, CMS clarifies, and the text of Section 411.354 is modified to state, that a security interest in the equipment of a hospital held by a physician who sold and financed its purchase through a loan to the hospital no longer constitutes an "ownership or investment interest" as that term is defined in Section 411.354(b). This modification is made in response to a commenter's contention that, when a physician sells equipment to a hospital, the contract for sale typically includes a security interest in the equipment to protect against a default on a payment. According to the commenter, this security interest would create an ownership interest in part of a hospital, and thus create a prohibited financial relationship, which he argued was effectively inconsistent with CMS's position in Phase II that a one-time sale of equipment using installment payments protected by a security interest could be eligible for the isolated transaction exception in Section 411.357(f). The commenter maintained that the arrangement described in the comment should instead be viewed as a compensation arrangement so it too could potentially qualify for the isolated transaction exception.

CMS agrees with the commenter, and modifies the text of Section 411.354(b)(3) accordingly. However, CMS cautions that, where a physician-seller refers DHS to the hospital, the transaction must be analyzed as a compensation arrangement and satisfy the requirements of an applicable exception. Further, CMS confirms that it still considers loans or bonds secured by a portion of a hospital's revenue (such as revenue from a particular department) to be an ownership interest in a part of a hospital that would not qualify for protection under the whole hospital exception in Section 411.356(c)(3) (discussed in Section X.C, below).

## IV. INDIRECT COMPENSATION DEFINITION AND EXCEPTION AND "STAND IN THE SHOES" RULE

### A. The New "Stand in the Shoes" Rule

Since CMS created a definition and parallel exception for indirect compensation arrangements in Phase I, commenters have raised various questions and concerns about the meaning and application of these concepts. In Phase III, CMS attempts to address many of these issues by making clear that physicians "stand in the shoes" of their group practice for purposes of evaluating whether they have a direct or indirect compensation arrangement with a DHS entity. These changes expand upon a clarification provided in Phase II that a physician "stands in the shoes" of his or her solely owned professional corporation.

It should be noted that CMS is considering taking an additional significant step to narrow the applicability of the indirect compensation exception in the 2008 PFS Proposed Rule by seeking to apply the "stand in the shoes" concept to arrangements by which one entity owns or controls another entity. In all such circumstances the effect of applying the "stand in the shoes" concept is to change an indirect compensation arrangement to a direct one. This means that, in such circumstances, it is unnecessary to analyze whether an arrangement fits the complicated definition of indirect compensation and, by implication, providers cannot seek the protection of the indirect compensation exception when the "stand in the shoes" concept is applicable.

Previously, when a group practice had a direct link to a physician in a chain of financial relationships between a referring physician and a DHS entity, the rules required a two-part analysis. First, counsel needed to analyze whether the conditions to create an indirect compensation arrangement were met. If not, the arrangement was protected because it was deemed not to be a financial arrangement under the Stark law. If yes, then counsel needed to make sure the arrangement met the terms of the indirect compensation exception in Section 411.357(p).

According to CMS, this situation posed two problems. First, it required an additional, unnecessary step when conducting a Stark analysis. As pointed out by commenters, if the referring physician "stands in the shoes" of the group, the analysis need focus only on whether the arrangement between the DHS entity and the group practice meets a direct compensation exception. Second, some parties may have construed the definition too narrowly and therefore concluded that the Stark law did not apply, especially in the case of arrangements between DHS entities and group practices. CMS is seeking to close this "unintended loophole" with the "stand in the shoes" requirement.

CMS therefore amends the definitions of direct and indirect compensation arrangements through what CMS calls "a commonsense understanding of the relationship between group practices and their physicians." The Phase III Final Rule establishes that a physician has a direct compensation arrangement with a

DHS entity if the only intervening entity between the physician and the DHS entity is his or her "physician organization."

This is one of two new terms defined in Section 411.351 and means "a physician (including a professional corporation solely owned by the physician), a physician practice, or a group practice that complies with the" Stark regulations' requirements for a group. Unfortunately, CMS provides no guidance as to what it means by a "physician practice."

The important analytical principle that CMS establishes is that a physician who "stands in the shoes" of his or her physician organization is deemed to have the same compensation arrangements, with the same parties and on the same terms as the physician organization itself. This means that these "stand in the shoes" arrangements must be analyzed under one of the compensation exceptions applicable to direct compensation arrangements.

We note that, if the arrangement is for personal services, then the likely applicable exceptions are personal services (Section 411.357(d)) or fair market value (Section 411.357(l)). While space does not permit a complete analysis of the differences in these provisions and the indirect compensation exception, we note they both require the compensation to meet the "set in advance" requirements, which is not required in the indirect compensation exception.

In considering the importance of meeting the "set in advance" requirement, consideration should also be given to CMS's proposal in the 2008 PFS Proposed Rule: "Percentage based compensation, other than compensation based on revenues directly resulting from personally performed physician services (as defined in section 410.20(a)), is not considered set in advance."

A second important difference between the personal services and fair market value exceptions on the one hand and the indirect compensation exception on the other hand is that the latter contains very liberalized rules if the physician is a bona fide employee.

However, because the analysis now focuses on the relationship between the DHS entity and the physician organization, it appears that the exception for bona fide employment relationships (Section 411.357(c)) is not available.

Finally, when evaluating the application of the Stark exceptions, the "parties" include the DHS entity, the physician organization, and all of the members, employees, or independent contractor physicians of the physician organization.

## B. The Sun-Setting Grandfather

CMS creates a limited grandfathering provision that sunsets. The "stand in the shoes" provisions will apply as of Phase III's effective date, with one important exception.

Recognizing that many arrangements with a physician organization interposed between a DHS entity and a referring physician may have been properly structured under the Phase II indirect compensation arrangements exception, CMS will not require restructuring of such arrangements during their original term or the current renewal term as long as they existed and complied with the indirect compensation exception as of September 5, 2007.

However, CMS does not state if it will afford the same protection to arrangements that do not need to meet the indirect compensation exception because the arrangement did not qualify as a matter of definition as an indirect compensation arrangement. Presumably, CMS would have no reason not to provide similar grandfathering protection to such arrangements, but a close reading of the rule suggests otherwise.

Arrangements involving any intervening entity other than a physician organization (such as a management company) or multiple intervening entities will continue to require analysis under the rules for indirect compensation arrangements and the indirect compensation arrangements exception. CMS invites comments on how to apply the "stand in the shoes" rules to these types of relationships.[3]

Like Phase II, Phase III included no substantive changes to the indirect compensation exception. CMS addresses many of the comments related to this exception by implementing the "stand in the shoes" provisions described above.

## C. Comments

CMS has taken a significant step in closing a loophole in its narrow definition of indirect compensation arrangements. In so doing, many relationships that formerly would have constituted indirect compensation arrangements (or even fallen from the purview of the Stark law because the arrangement did not qualify as indirect compensation) now qualify as direct compensation arrangements and are therefore subject to the more rigorous requirements of the direct compensation exceptions.

Not only is the impact of this provision far-reaching, but there appear to be a large number of ambiguities and unintended consequences in CMS's approach that require further consideration and clarification. For example, itself recognizing the need for further guidance, CMS in the Phase III Final Rule seeks comments on one element—how to apply the "stand in the shoes" provision when there are multiple intervening entities.

An instance of another concern with the rule change arises because CMS is imputing the relationship between a DHS entity and a physician organization to a physician who may have had no role in negotiating the agreement and no referral incentives thereunder. For example, the physician who now "stands in the shoes" of his or her group may be an employed member of the group with no incentives under the arrangement to refer to the DHS entity.

A benefit of the Phase II indirect compensation definition was its recognition that a potentially non-compliant relationship between a DHS entity and what is now known as a physician organization could be "cleansed," as long as the physician was not being paid based on the volume or value of referrals.

That approach made sense and reflected reality because all that should matter is whether the referring physician himself or herself is corrupted by the financial arrangement with a DHS entity.

CMS's change appears to create an additional problem with respect to the common example of a physician member of a group practice whose services are

---

[3]The invitation for comments is somewhat odd given that the regulation does not have a comment period.

contracted for by a hospital through the group. In that situation, the physician should not lose his or her status as an employee by requiring that the arrangement be examined only as between the group and the hospital.

It does not make sense, and we are not sure CMS intended, to prohibit the hospital from paying its proportionate share of the physician's bonus compensation that he or she earns as a member of the group. As noted above, one of the benefits of the indirect compensation exception was its recognition that there should be more liberal rules where the compensation arrangement is for bona fide employment. That favored treatment for employee compensation appears now not to be available in this example.

In our judgment a position that would be truer to the statutory intent of the Stark law would be, as under the indirect compensation definition, to focus on the direct financial relationship with the physician, i.e., his or her arrangement with the group practice. That analysis is now irrelevant, and providers will need to focus on the compensation relationships between the DHS entity and physician organization.

As noted above, with respect to personal services arrangements, it appears the two applicable exceptions are the personal services or fair market value exceptions. These are very different exceptions in scope and application. In particular they both require that the compensation be set in advance. Time will tell if CMS's new approach represents an appropriate policy advance.

The "stand in the shoes" rule also contains a number of ambiguities that CMS should clarify before the rule becomes effective. These include—

- CMS appears to have used overly broad language regarding the parties to "stand in the shoes" arrangements. CMS takes the position that all of the group practice's members, employees, and independent contractors are parties to the arrangement. One reading of this provision is that, if the arrangement between a physician group practice member and a DHS entity does not comply with the Stark law, *all* of the referrals from the group practice's physicians (including independent contractor physicians) are illegal. Obviously there may be a situation in which the financial arrangement with the group practice relates to the entire group, for example, where the group practice rents its office space from a hospital. In such a situation, CMS's position as to the real parties in interest is understandable. However, it is doubtful that CMS means its new position to apply so broadly, for example, in the case in which a hospital enters into an agreement with a group for the medical director services of a particular physician member and the agreement does not meet an exception. It would appear to us illogical, and likely unintended, for CMS to take the position that all referrals by other members of that group practice are tainted.
- CMS's interpretation of the parties in interest could be of even more concern to independent contractor physicians, who could find themselves parties to arrangements in which they have only a tangential interest.
- CMS's interpretation of the parties in interest raises the question of who is required to sign agreements where an exception requires the parties to have a signed, written agreement. We doubt CMS intended to require

everyone who is a "party" under the "stand in the shoes" rule to sign the agreements.

- CMS does not define what it means by the term "physician practice" in the new defined term "physician organization."
- Does CMS intend to grandfather current arrangements that do not qualify as indirect compensation arrangements and therefore do not need to meet the indirect compensation exception?

Because of the number of ambiguities and potential unintended consequences associated with CMS's "stand in the shoes" approach, we suggest that it consider providing additional guidance and/or delaying the effective date of this provision until at least January 1, 2009.

Such a delay would allow for another physician fee schedule rulemaking cycle, in which CMS could receive and consider comments from providers on this provision. The suggested delay would afford CMS the opportunity to consider in a comprehensive manner the entire "stand in the shoes" concept, including the provisions in Phase III as well as the proposal contained in the 2008 PFS Proposed Rule.

The potential impact of this rule change is too significant for CMS not to get it right.

## V. DEFINITION OF GROUP PRACTICE AND IN-OFFICE ANCILLARY SERVICES EXCEPTION

### A. Definitions

#### 1. Definition of Employee

Rejecting one commenter's suggestion, CMS does not alter the definition of an "employee." One commenter had asked CMS to strengthen the definition to clarify that a group practice must exercise control over the employee, i.e. the group practice must control how the work is done and have hiring and firing authority in order for that person to qualify as an "employee."

CMS declines to alter the definition, but emphasizes that it will focus on the actual relationship of the parties, using various factors, including those used by the IRS, to determine whether an employee relationship exists.

#### 2. Group Practice Definition—Productivity Bonuses and Profit Shares

Phase III makes only one small substantive change to the group practice definition at Section 411.352 related to incident to services. Because this change relates to physician compensation, it is discussed in Section VI.B.2, below.

#### 3. Single Legal Entity

CMS clarifies that a separate corporation formed by a hospital to employ physicians can constitute a single legal entity for the purposes of the group practice definition, provided that the specialty divisions are not separate legal entities and the arrangement otherwise satisfies the requirements of the group practice definition.

## 4. Unified Business Test

To qualify as a group practice, the practice must be a "unified business" with a centralized decisionmaking body representative of the group practice that maintains control over the practice's assets and liabilities. CMS responds to one commenter's request for clarification concerning the interplay of this requirement and the IRS rules that require that a majority of the board of a tax-exempt, nonprofit corporation must be composed of disinterested community representatives.

CMS explains that there is nothing in the regulations that would preclude a tax-exempt, nonprofit group practice from having a majority of its board be composed of disinterested community representatives, as long as the board maintains effective control over the group's assets and liabilities and is representative of the group practice, as is required under the group practice definition.

## 5. Foundation-Model Group Practices

One commenter questioned whether a medical group that contracts with a nonprofit medical foundation that operates a nonprofit health care clinic could qualify as a group practice if the medical foundation bills and collects for the professional services of the medical group using a provider number assigned to the foundation.

CMS suggests that, while this arrangement does not necessarily disqualify the medical group as a group practice, the fact that professional services provided by the medical group's physicians are being billed under the foundation's provider number instead of the group's, pursuant to a reassignment agreement, may affect the ability of the group to satisfy the "substantially all" test of the group practice definition, which requires that "substantially all" (meaning at least 75 percent) of the patient care services of the physician members of a group practice are provided through the group and billed under the group number.

However, CMS notes that, if the professional services are provided to a foundation's clinic pursuant to a services contract between the group practice and the foundation, a group practice may count these services as being provided through the group.

Finally, CMS adds that, if a foundation-model practice qualifies as a group practice, it may be able to avail itself of the in-office ancillary services or physician services exceptions for DHS referrals if the group practice is furnishing and billing for the DHS (referrals for DHS billed by the foundation would not so qualify).

CMS declines another commenter's suggestion that it make a determination that medical foundations should automatically qualify as group practices. Instead, CMS clarifies that depending on the particular facts and circumstances, if a foundation-model practice meets the group practice definition, it may qualify for the in-office ancillary services exception.

Alternatively, CMS suggests that foundation-model practices may qualify for other exceptions, including exceptions for indirect compensation arrangements, personal services arrangements, and the new "stand in the shoes" direct compensation arrangements discussed in Section IV.

## B. In-Office Ancillary Services Exception

The in-office ancillary services exception permits a physician or group practice to order and provide DHS (except for most DME) in the office or physician practice, as long as the DHS is truly ancillary to the medical services furnished by the physician or group practice.

Generally, to meet this exception, the services must be furnished personally by the referring physician, a member of the referring physician's group practice, or an individual who is supervised by the referring physician or a physician in the same group practice as the referring physician.

The services also must be furnished in either the "same building" in which the referring physician or his or her group practice provides professional services or in a "centralized building" used to provide off-site DHS.

Despite acknowledging that it received numerous comments on the in-office ancillary services exception, CMS is not making any substantive changes to this exception in Phase III. However, in the 2007 and 2008 physician fee schedule proposed rules, CMS sought comments on several potential ways to narrow the exception and eliminate perceived abuse.

### 1. Same Building Test

In Phase II, CMS established three new alternative tests to determine whether services are furnished in the "same building." Under each of these tests, the office must be open for a certain number of hours per week with the referring physician regularly practicing medicine at the site.

In addition, each of these tests require that "some" of the services provided in the same building be unrelated to the furnishing of DHS. In Phase II, CMS had declined to clarify the meaning of "some" and instead stated that it would interpret "some" according to its "common sense meaning."

Again in Phase III, CMS declines to provide a quantitative measure for the requirement that "some" of the services provided in the same building be unrelated to DHS. CMS does provide more clarification, however, and states that the critical factor in meeting this prong of the test is that the premises are used for the regular provision of the group practice's physician services, even if only part-time.

CMS further explains that in evaluating whether "some" non-DHS services are performed in the building, it will look at the operation of the arrangement, not its form on paper. This examination would include looking at the nature of the group's overall practice (e.g., the specialties of the group's physicians), and the referring physician's full range of practice.

CMS cautions that creating a satellite office to provide non-DHS services as a "sham arrangement," under which few or no such services are actually contemplated or provided, in an effort to satisfy the "same building" test will result in claims denial.

CMS also explains that it does not consider physicians providing services to patients via telemedicine to be in the same location as the patient for the purposes of satisfying the "same building" test. CMS elucidates that the physician's time providing telemedicine services would count as time spent at the location at which the physician is physically present.

However, if the physician is a member of a group practice, time spent by other physician members of the group practice at the patient's location would count toward the "same building" requirement.

For the benefit of one commenter who had inquired whether physicians could use the facilities simultaneously and share costs and administration of the DHS without separate leases, CMS clarifies that the in-office ancillary services exception requires that a physician sharing a DHS facility in the same building must control the facility and staffing (e.g., supervision of the services) at the time that the DHS is furnished to the patient.

In CMS's view, this means that a block lease arrangement for the space and equipment used to provide the DHS will likely be required and that common per-use fee arrangements are unlikely to satisfy the supervision requirements of the exception and "may implicate the anti-kickback statute." These statements manifest a clear intent by CMS to curtail so-called pod labs.

### 2. Clarification of Interplay of In-Office Ancillary Services Exception and Reassignment and Purchased Diagnostic Tests

In Phase III, CMS amends Section 411.350 to state explicitly that nothing in the physician self-referral statute alters a party's obligation to comply with the rules regarding claim reassignment, purchased diagnostic tests, payment for services and supplies "incident to" a physician's professional services, or any other applicable Medicare law, rule, or regulation.

The purpose of this change is to make clear that although the reassignment regulations now permit an independent contractor to reassign the right to payment even if the services are furnished off the premises, an independent contractor still must furnish services on-site to meet the in-office ancillary services exception.

CMS also states unequivocally that compliance with the physician self-referral rules does not affect a party's obligations under the reassignment and purchased diagnostic test rules. In CMS's view, even where an independent contractor physician furnishes DHS in a centralized building of a group practice in compliance with the in-office ancillary services exception, the anti-mark-up rules still would apply to any purchased diagnostic tests.

### 3. Billing for DHS Services

The in-office ancillary services exception also requires that the ancillary services provided must be billed by any of: (1) the physician performing or supervising the service; (2) the group practice in which the physician is a member under the group's billing number; (3) the group practice if the supervising physician is a "physician in the group practice" as defined at Section 411.351; (4) an entity wholly owned by the performing or supervising physician or by that physician's group practice under the entity's own billing number or under a billing number assigned to the physician or group practice; or (5) an independent third party billing company acting as agent of the physician, group practice or wholly-owned billing entity under a billing number assigned to the physician, group practice or billing entity.

Responding to one commenter, CMS clarifies that, if the services are billed using a billing entity, the billing entity must be wholly owned by the supervising physician, the referring physician or the group practice, and the claims must be submitted under a billing number assigned to the entity or to the physician or group practice.

An arrangement under which a billing entity that is wholly owned by group members as individuals, not by the group, would not satisfy the requirements of the in-office ancillary services exception, and would also not comply with CMS's rules on reassignment.

## VI. EXCEPTIONS RELATED TO VARIOUS FORMS OF PHYSICIAN COMPENSATION

This section discusses a number of the myriad facets of the Stark law related to the requirements for physician compensation. For the most part, the revisions made in Phase III amount to fine tuning, grammatical, and stylistic edits, although CMS does acknowledge that some of the changes are substantive (e.g., the "fair market value" exception now applies to payments made by the entity to the physician; previously it had applied only to payments by the physician to the entity).

In this section, we summarize the key changes that CMS made in Phase III to the physician compensation requirements, as well as several that CMS declined to make.

### A. Fair Market Value Definition and Exception

In its definition of "fair market value," Phase II contained a "safe harbor" provision for hourly payments for a physician's personal services. However, in Phase III, CMS eliminates that safe harbor, although CMS will continue to scrutinize "fair market value" as an "essential element" of many of the exceptions contained in the regulations.

The Phase II safe harbor put forth two methodologies for determining protected fair market value. One was based on emergency room physician compensation in at least three competing hospitals. The other was based on use of at least four of six specified national compensation surveys.

CMS agreed with the commenters that the surveys might not be readily available, or might not be available at all, and that hourly rates for emergency room physicians might not be publicly available. Accordingly, Phase III eliminates this safe harbor.

However, although that safe harbor is eliminated, "fair market value" as an essential standard lives on. In its commentary, CMS acknowledges that parties who are negotiating an hourly rate for a physician's services are free to use "any commercially reasonable methodology that is appropriate under the circumstances" to calculate fair market value, noting that fair market value is a function of facts and circumstances.

Echoing the reality that "fair market value" is, indeed, a function of facts and circumstances, CMS also notes that "fair market value" for clinical services may be different from "fair market value" for administrative services.

In Phase I, CMS created an exception for "fair market value" compensation arrangements (§ 411.357(l)) that cover "compensation from a DHS entity to a physician, an immediate family member of a physician, or a group of physicians for the provision of items or services by the physician or group to the DHS entity."

CMS notes that, in Phase III, it made one substantive change and one clarifying change, the fair market value compensation exception. The substantive change is to apply the exception to compensation provided to an entity by a physician as well as compensation paid to a physician by an entity.

Previously, the exception applied only to compensation paid by a physician to an entity. The effect of this change is significant and relates to the interplay between this exception and the "payments by a physician" exception found at Section 1877(e)(8) as implemented in Section 411.357(i).

This statutory exception is very broad with very few requirements. In an attempt to narrow its reach, CMS's regulation only allows this exception to be available for compensation by a physician for items or services to the extent another exception did not apply. Until Phase III, the fair market value exception did not apply to items or services provided by a DHS entity to a physician, but CMS now has closed this loophole.

The "clarifying change" is to make it explicit that the fair market value exception is not applicable to leases for office space. Rather, the exception for leases of office space is that one set forth in Section 411.357(a).

*Comment.* We anticipate that CMS's change in the fair market value exception to cover items paid by a physician will have a very significant impact and could require a significant number of arrangements to be restructured.

## B. Set in Advance and Incident to Services and Supplies

### 1. Set in Advance

Several Stark exceptions require compensation to be set in advance. CMS's first interpretation of this concept dates back to Phase I, which provided that compensation would be considered "set in advance" if the aggregate compensation or a time-based or per-unit of service-based amount is established in advance in the written agreement in sufficient detail so that it can be verified effectively.

Phase II modified this definition to provide that, if the parties set forth the specific formula for calculating the compensation in an agreement prior to furnishing the items or services, then the arrangement would be considered "set in advance." The formula would still have to be in sufficient detail to permit effective verification, and it could not be changed during the course of the agreement in any way that would reflect or take into account the volume or value of any referrals or other business generated.

Although the Phase III revisions to the "set in advance" standard are, for the most part, linguistic nuances, the standard has now been amended so that it explicitly includes contracts for personal services. In its commentary, CMS acknowledges that percentage-based compensation arrangements can be considered "set in advance."

However, the methodology must be fixed at the outset of the contract with "sufficient specificity," and it cannot be changed during the term of the agreement in a manner that would reflect the volume of referrals or other business.

However, CMS allows the agreement to be amended during its first year as long as the amendment is a bona fide amendment that is not related to the volume or value of any referrals or other business generated between the parties.

In discussing percentage of collections and percentage of revenue compensation methodologies, CMS reiterates its "depending on the facts" qualifier. Such arrangements still must meet the other terms of a relevant exception, such as "volume or value of referrals" and "other business generated between the parties."

Although unit-based compensation may in some circumstances be based on a percentage of collections or percentage of revenues methodology, CMS declined to revise the "Special Rules on Compensation" section to reference percentage-based compensation arrangements.

It should be noted that, in the 2008 PFS Proposed Rule CMS is seeking to narrow the ability to treat percentage based compensation as "set in advance" to compensation arrangements based on revenues directly resulting from personally performed physician services.

### 2. Group Practice Productivity Bonuses Related to "Incident to" Services and Supplies

Group practices may pay profit shares or productivity bonuses to their physicians in ways that otherwise are prohibited to DHS entities. In Phase III, CMS focuses on profit shares or productivity bonuses related to referrals to services furnished "incident to" a physician's personally furnished services.

"Incident to" services and supplies are those that do not have their own independent and separately listed statutory benefit category. In fact, in the exception relating to physician services, CMS deleted a provision that "[a]ll other 'incident to' services (for example, diagnostic tests, physical therapy)" would be outside the scope of the exception as being redundant and incorrectly suggesting that diagnostic tests may be billed as "incident to" services.

To provide consistency with other Medicare rules, the scope of "incident to" services is defined by cross-reference to Section 1861(s)(2)(A) of Act, the "incident to" billing rule and several CMS manual provisions. In addition, CMS expands the definition in the Stark regulation of "incident to" services to include supplies (including drugs), a change that CMS characterizes as a clarification.

Phase III makes clear that productivity bonuses may be based directly on "incident to" services that are incidental to the physician's personally performed services, even if those "incident to" services are otherwise DHS referrals. The "incident to" services do not need to be personally performed by the referring physician. CMS also explains that it is not permissible for productivity bonuses to be directly related to any other DHS referrals, such as diagnostic tests or hospital admissions.

CMS also has withdrawn its Phase II statement that overall profit shares could relate directly to "incident to" services. In Phase III, CMS now concludes that such an interpretation is "inconsistent with the clear statutory language" that authorizes reliance on "incident to" services only as a basis for a productivity bonus, and not for a profit share. Therefore, in Phase III, CMS modifies the special compensation rules for group practices to require that profits be allocated in a manner that does not relate directly to DHS referrals, including any DHS billed as an "incident to" service.

For purposes of profit sharing, CMS requires that the group, or any profit-sharing component thereof, must consist of at least five physicians. In Phase III, CMS declines to change this requirement, noting that its concern is that "smaller components increase the risk of over-utilization of DHS and other abuse by strengthening the ties between an individual physician's compensation and his or her referrals."

## C. Compensation to Physician Independent Contractors and Physicians in the Group

The defined term, "physician in the group practice" is significant with regard to two exceptions: the physician services exception and the in-office ancillary services exception. In general, under the Stark rules physicians in the group providing services to the group may receive the same compensation incentives as members of the group.

CMS creates two significant changes to the requirements for physicians in the group. First, CMS modifies the definition of "physician in the group practice" to require that a physician who is an independent contractor must contract *directly* with the group practice as opposed to the contract running through a staffing company or his or her employer.

Second, in the Phase III preamble, but not in the regulation, CMS states that a leased employee is not considered to be a physician in the group practice. CMS notes that "an independent contractor must have 'a contractual arrangement with the group practice' " to qualify as a "physician in the group practice."

Because group practices receive favorable treatment under the Stark law with respect to physician compensation, the group practice's physicians must have "a strong and meaningful nexus" with the group practice. Contractual privity promotes such a nexus, while employees leased from a staffing company do not.

CMS expresses concern about potentially abusive arrangements, and identifies, as an example, a situation where a physician is leased by a staffing company to a number of group practices each of which would want to consider the physician to be "a physician in the group practice." Therefore, leased employees are not recognized as "physicians in the group practice."

CMS also expresses a number of concerns about physicians in the group. As background, Section 952 of the Medicare Prescription Drug, Improvement, and Modernization Act relaxed the reassignment provisions of the Act so that CMS may make payments to an entity that has received reassigned payments pursuant to a contractual arrangement.

However, the arrangement must meet program integrity and other safeguards. In various rulemakings, including Phase III, CMS has made clear that its statutory authority to recognize certain reassignments does not mean that it is required to do so, especially with regard to reassignments that CMS believes are "potentially abusive."

Accordingly, CMS declines to include as services of the group practice—and therefore not eligible for protection under the in-office ancillary services exception—the services an independent contractor physician furnishes if performed off the group practice's premises.

Limiting the inclusion of the independent contractor as part of the group practice to those instances in which he or she is performing services at the group practice's premises gives the relationship "a clear and meaningful nexus with the group's medical practice."

CMS expresses other concerns that some group practices may try to rely on the in-office ancillary services exception when they:

- nominally comply with the centralized building requirements,
- contract with independent contractor physicians in the centralized building as "physicians in the group practice,"
- accept reassignment of the right to payment from the independent contractor physicians, and
- realize profits based on the services they refer to the independent contractor physicians in the group practice stationed in the centralized building.

The last of these enumerated items is at the core of CMS's concern. In the 2007 physician fee schedule proposed rule, CMS proposed changes to the reassignment rules and to the definition of "centralized building" to address this concern. Although no changes were enacted last year, CMS is revisiting these issues in the 2008 PFS Proposed Rule.

*Comment.* CMS's new requirement that physicians in the group must contract directly with the group practice is potentially far reaching, requiring many arrangements to be restructured.

With its focus on leased employee arrangements with staffing companies, CMS appears to have overlooked the not uncommon arrangement of a group practice leasing one of its physicians to another group. By eliminating leased employees from qualifying as physicians in the group, such physicians' referrals to the group or from the group would not qualify under the in-office ancillary services exception. So CMS appears to be saying that such an arrangement may only include bonus compensation as permitted in the employment exception. Added to the complexity in the analysis is the application of the "stand in the shoes" concept to this situation where a group leases a physician-employee member to another group. Under the "stand in the shoes" concept, the analysis focuses exclusively on the arrangement between the two groups. It is not at all clear if CMS is suggesting that the arrangement cannot include any bonus compensation that would flow down to the leased physician. Or perhaps CMS would permit the arrangement to include such compensation if the aggregate compensation remains consistent with fair market value.

## VII. PHYSICIAN RECRUITMENT AND RETENTION

Recruiting and retaining qualified medical staff to meet a community need remains a high priority for hospitals. Therefore, we discuss separately here the two exceptions found at Sections 411.357(e) and (t) that protect certain of these activities. While Phase III clarifies in some significant respects the rules governing physician recruitment activities by hospitals, in other important ways

CMS fails to address adequately the constraints imposed by the Phase II regulations on physician recruitment activities. CMS takes a similarly cautious approach in its tweaking of the retention exception.

## A. Physician Recruitment

### 1. Income Guarantees and Allocated Costs

Prior to the Phase II regulations, a typical recruitment incentive included an income guarantee for a physician recruited into an existing practice. Income guarantees are among the most important recruitment tools used by hospitals. To calculate the physician's expenses for purposes of determining the guarantee amount, practices often used a pro rata or per capita method of allocating overhead costs.

Typically, this methodology was the same as that which applied to existing physicians in the group. The Phase II regulations sharply reduced the ability of a hospital to provide an income guarantee to a physician who joins an existing practice. It limited the costs allocable by the physician practice to the recruited physician to the *actual additional incremental costs to the practice attributable to the recruited physician.*

Using this methodology, certain practice expenses such as rent and IT costs, which may not necessarily increase with the addition of a new physician, cannot be used as part of the recruited physician's overhead costs. This limitation prompted hospitals to look for other ways to bring needed doctors into the community. Approaches include hospitals again employing physicians or locating employed physicians in an existing practice and entering into a fair market value space and services agreement with that practice.

Phase III loosens this restriction—but only slightly. If the existing practice is located in a rural area or an HPSA, and the physician is recruited to replace a physician who retired, relocated, or died within the previous 12-month period, then the overhead allocation can be based on the lower of a per capita allocation, 20 percent of the practice's aggregate costs, or the actual additional incremental costs attributable to the recruited physician.

But CMS refuses to extend this new allocation method beyond practices located in a rural area or an HPSA because of concerns that, without this restriction on a hospital-subsidized income guarantee, physician practices will inappropriately shift overhead costs to the hospital to which the physician practice refers.

### 2. Practice Restrictions

Under the Phase II regulations, a physician practice may not impose additional practice restrictions on the recruited physician other than conditions related to quality of care. The preamble to the Phase II regulations stated that CMS considered a non-compete clause, which is a standard provision in employment contracts, to be a practice restriction and not a condition related to quality of care. Since the Phase II regulations, hospitals and physician practices have been uncertain as to whether other commonplace provisions, such as a requirement to accept Medicare and Medicaid patients or a restriction on moonlighting, were practice restrictions other than those related to quality of care.

In the Phase III preamble, CMS agrees that categorically prohibiting physician practices from imposing non-compete provisions may make it more difficult for hospitals to recruit physicians. It also notes that it never intended to prevent practices from restricting the recruited physician from moonlighting or prohibiting the solicitation of patients or employees. It simply wanted to be sure that practice restrictions did not frustrate the purpose of the exception, which is to bring needed physicians into the community.

Therefore, CMS amends the exception by deleting the prohibition on conditions other than those related to quality of care and replacing it with the following: "The physician practice may not impose on the recruited physician practice restrictions that unreasonably restrict the recruited physician's ability to practice medicine in the geographic area served by the hospital."

### 3. Relocation

The statutory exception covering recruitment activities excepts remuneration provided by a hospital to a physician to induce the physician to *locate* to the geographic area served by the hospital. The Phase II regulations detailed what it means to relocate: the physician's office must relocate a minimum of 25 miles or at least 75 percent of the physician's revenues must be derived from services provided to new patients. The Phase III Final Rule makes only some minor wording changes to the Phase II definition.

The Phase II regulations also provided that residents and physicians who have been in medical practice for less than one year will not be considered to have an established practice and, therefore, not subject to the relocation limitations. Phase III keeps this intact, but adds some additional, albeit limited, exemptions to the relocation rules for physicians who were employed on a full time basis for at least two years immediately prior to the recruitment arrangement by (1) the federal or a state bureau of prisons; (2) the Department of Defense or Department of Veterans Affairs; or (3) facilities of the Indian Health Service. In addition to these exemptions, if the Secretary in an advisory opinion determines that the physician does not have an established medical practice that serves or could serve a significant number of hospital patients or potential hospital patients, then that physician also will not be subject to the relocation limitations.

### 4. Geographic Area Served by the Hospital

While CMS makes few changes to the relocation provisions, it makes considerable changes to the definition of geographic area served by the hospital. Phase II defined geographic area served by the hospital as "the lowest number of zip codes from which the hospital draws at least 75% of its inpatients." CMS reacted favorably to the comments relating to this requirement, many of which complained that it was unreasonably restrictive and prevented hospitals from recruiting physicians into outlying parts of their services areas.

Therefore, CMS makes several changes to the definition of geographic service area and includes special rules for rural hospitals. Under Phase III, the geographic area may include one or more ZIP codes from which the hospital draws *no* inpatients, provided that such ZIP codes are surrounded by ZIP codes from which the hospital draws at least 75 percent of its inpatients.

For those hospitals that draw fewer than 75 percent of its inpatients from all of the contiguous ZIP codes from which it draws inpatients, the geographic area served by the hospital will be deemed to be the area composed of *all* of the contiguous ZIP codes from which the hospital draws its inpatients.

Rural hospitals are given even more latitude when defining the geographic area served by the hospital for purposes of the recruitment exception. Under Phase III, a rural hospital may determine its geographic service area using the lowest number of contiguous ZIP codes from which the hospital draws at least 90 percent of its inpatients. Alternatively, if the hospital draws fewer than 90 percent of its inpatients from all of the contiguous ZIP codes, then its service area may include certain noncontiguous ZIP codes.

## 5. Written Agreement Signed by All Parties

CMS put to rest any lingering doubt as to whether a recruited physician is required to be a signatory to the recruitment assistance agreement entered into between the hospital and the physician practice. CMS has rejected, with little comment, a suggestion by a commenter to allow the recruited physician to sign a one-page acknowledgement agreeing to be bound by the terms of the recruitment agreement executed by the hospital and the physician practice.

## 6. Rural Health Clinics

Persuaded that expanding the physician recruitment exception to cover rural health clinics does not pose a risk of program abuse, CMS amends this exception so that the exception covers rural health clinics in the same manner as it covers hospitals and federally qualified health centers.

## B. Retention Payments in Underserved Areas

Phase II recognized that retention of physicians in certain underserved communities is as important as the initial recruitment of those physicians. Therefore, Phase II created a new exception for retention payments by a hospital in an HPSA to a physician who receives a bona fide, firm, written offer that would require the physician to move at least 25 miles and outside the geographic area served by the hospital seeking to retain the physician.

Many criticized that hospitals do not always prepare written offer letters or, by the time a physician has received a written offer letter, it is too late to convince the physician to remain in the area served by the current hospital. In response, in Phase III, CMS amends the retention payment exception to allow retention payments on the basis of a written certification by the physician that the physician has a *bona fide opportunity for future employment* that would require a move of his or her medical practice at least 25 miles and outside the service area of the current hospital. Under Phase III, the written certification also must contain, among other things:

- details regarding the steps taken to effectuate the employment opportunity;
- details of the employment opportunity; and
- sufficient information so that the hospital can verify the information in the certification.

Phase III further expands the retention exception for a physician whose current medical practice is in a rural area or HPSA by the addition of "or where at least 75% of the physician's patients reside in a medically underserved area or are members of a medically underserved population."

CMS rejects suggestions by commenters to broaden the retention exception to permit tax exempt organizations to make retention payments if the payments comply with the IRS rules governing tax exempt organizations. CMS continues to take a narrow view of physician shortage areas and is not convinced that compliance with IRS rules by a tax exempt organization necessarily would prevent retention payments from being abused to reward high referring physicians.

## C. Comments

Despite some liberalization, Phase III continues, in large measure, CMS's resistance to hospital use of physician recruitment assistance by hospitals to existing practices. Most arrangements that were commonplace prior to Phase II were rendered unlawful under that rulemaking and will remain so following Phase III. CMS is sending a clear message that hospitals should continue to integrate horizontally and to employ physicians.

Although on its face a simple clarification, CMS's statement that physicians must sign the recruitment agreement itself will likely require a large number of recruitment agreements to be reformed. In the case of existing agreements that need to come in compliance with this "clarification," we assume CMS recognizes that it does not make sense to re-write agreements completely where all payments have been made and the only remaining requirement is for the physician to remain in the service area. Yet it is not clear what CMS expects in the way of a reformed agreement.

For the majority of hospitals seeking to recruit physicians to practices not located in a rural area or an HPSA, using an income guarantee as a recruitment incentive will continue to be problematic because of the limitations on overhead allocation. Most physicians in a group have a natural expectation that a newly recruited member will help shift some of the overhead burden. This is one of many reasons why it was so common that group practices allocated overhead to new physicians on a per capita basis.

CMS's insistence on the "actual incremental cost" model not only removes commonsense incentives within a group to recruit a new physician, but continues an illogical outcome in some recruitment arrangements by permitting more overhead costs to be allocated than otherwise would be the case if new space is acquired or built out or new personnel added.

In these situations, CMS permits 100 percent of the new "actual incremental costs" for such new space or personnel to be allocated. Finally, CMS's approach to allocation may require a practice to keep two sets of books: one for the recruited physician and another for the other physicians in the practice.

CMS's clarifications regarding practice restrictions and relocation criteria are welcome and quite helpful. While there is likely to be some debate over what is meant by practice restrictions that "unreasonably restrict the physician's right to practice in the geographic area served by the hospital," the change to the regulatory language is important and will serve to facilitate hospital efforts to assist existing practices with their recruitment efforts by allowing practices to impose certain non-compete clauses and other commercially well-accepted requirements on the recruited physician.

Further, allowing case-by-case advisory opinions is a practical way for CMS to consider when a physician does not have an established practice and can therefore be exempt from the relocation limitations. Note that we continue to believe that CMS's authority to issue case-by-case advisory opinions is much broader than the agency admits to because Congress clearly stated its intention to give CMS the same authority as the Department of Health and Human Services' Office of Inspector General.

Perhaps one of the more puzzling aspects of the physician recruitment exception is its interplay with the new "stand in the shoes" requirement applicable to agreements between physician groups and DHS entities, such as hospitals. Under Phase III the recruited physician stands in the shoes of his or her group. This "stands in the shoes" concept collapses the three-part arrangement between a hospital, the group, and the physician, with the only required analysis being of the arrangement between the hospital and the group.

If CMS truly intends to apply this approach to physician recruitment agreements, hospitals would not need to be concerned about the agreement between the group and the physician and many of CMS's stated concerns would not be relevant, thereby creating a vastly simplified, more realistic exception for physician recruitment activities.

## VIII. Exception for Academic Medical Centers

The exception specifically crafted in Section 411.355(e) for the unusual and complex arrangements found in academic medical centers (AMCs) and their affiliated foundation and faculty practice plans was first promulgated in Phase I and amended in Phase II. In general, it protects payments to bona fide employed medical faculty from the various sources within a qualifying AMC, including, among other components, an affiliated hospital (or teaching hospital) that meets certain requirements. In Phase III, CMS addresses a number of AMC issues.

Because the AMC exception protects payments from all sources within an AMC to bona fide employed faculty, in Phase III CMS revises the regulation itself to clarify that the exception does not require *each* such payment to be set at fair market value as long as the aggregate compensation meets this requirement.

CMS appears, however, to have created a glitch, probably unintended, regarding another aspect of the individual payments that are collectively protected under this exception. The following comment and response sets the stage:

> *Comment*: One commenter asked that we clarify that the condition in §411.355(e) (1) (ii), which requires that the total compensation to referring physicians be set in advance, does not require that the actual amount of the compensation be set in advance. The commenter also asked that we confirm its understanding that our use of "total" compensation was intended to reflect that faculty physicians in an academic medical center setting may be paid by more than one component of the academic medical center and that each such payment arrangement must meet each of the requirements of the exception, namely that the compensation be set in advance. . . .

*Response*: The commenter is correct that the actual dollar amount of the referring faculty physician's compensation need not be set in advance. It is sufficient if the contribution of *each* component of the academic medical center to the aggregate compensation uses a methodology that qualifies under §411.354(d).

This response appears to suggest that, while the fundamental test is whether the aggregate compensation is set in advance, AMCs would have the option to determine whether the contribution of each AMC component is set in advance. If this was all that CMS accomplished, AMCs would surely welcome such flexibility.

The problem is that the Phase III Final Rule text of Section 411.355(e) (ii)(A) reads: "The total compensation paid by *each* academic medical center component to the referring physician is set in advance." (Emphasis added). Under Phase II, "each" was "all". This means that, until now, AMCs needed only to make sure that the total compensation from *all* components of the AMC was set in advance. But under the change that was made in Phase III, it appears that this approach is no longer sufficient. As written, it appears that, to meet this exception, AMCs *must* assure that the compensation from each component meets the "set in advance" requirement. We hope CMS fixes this problem in an upcoming technical corrections notice.

The second significant clarifying change to the AMC exception relates to the requirement that a majority of a teaching hospital's medical staff must be academic faculty. The exception is amended so that, in making this determination, a teaching hospital may either include or exclude all physicians with the same class of privileges, for example, courtesy staff.

CMS clarifies the concerns raised by a number of commenters that the AMC exception does not permit research funds to be used to pay AMC faculty for indigent care or community service. While CMS does not retreat from this restriction, it states that other sources of funding within the AMC can be used for this purpose.

CMS reiterates at several places that the AMC exception is an optional additional exception that an AMC may choose to use, or, in the alternative, it is free to use any other applicable exception.

CMS uses this rationale to turn aside requests to broaden the exception, for example, to eliminate the requirements that aggregate compensation be "set in advance" and that a majority of teaching hospital physicians must come from academic faculty.

CMS uses the same reasons to deny a request that newly affiliated teaching hospitals be allowed a transition period before being expected to meet all of the applicable requirements in the exception.

*Comment.* Most AMCs are complex organizations with a myriad of financial arrangements with physicians. Many arrangements do not qualify under the AMC exception. One of the more common reasons is that a referring physician does not qualify as an academic physician under the regulation either because he or she is clinical faculty or a community physician.

AMCs with non-qualifying payments to a physician for his or her services are likely to be particularly hard-hit by the "stand in the shoes" rule discussed above at Section IV because the vast majority of payment arrangements are made through a faculty practice plan, foundation, or other type of group.

Payments via such routes trigger the "stand in the shoes" provision. In Section IV we discussed our concerns, which we will not repeat here. But a particular problem for AMCs with non-qualifying arrangements is that most such arrangements did not qualify as indirect compensation because that physician's aggregate compensation was not based on referrals, and consequently no further analysis of that arrangement was warranted.

It is not clear if such arrangements are grandfathered, and, even if so, at some point restructuring will be required. Also as noted in Section IV, one of the components of the restructuring is that *each* compensation arrangement will need to meet the requirements for "set in advance" criteria.

## IX. EXCEPTIONS RELATED TO BOTH OWNERSHIP AND COMPENSATION

Phase III makes no major regulatory changes to Section 411.355. However, the Phase III preamble clarifies certain issues. Note that in Section III.E above we discussed the change to eliminate certain equipment security interests from the definition of the term "ownership and investment interest."

### A. Physician Services

Phase III does not make any substantive modification to the physician services exception. Phase III does make a clarifying change, however, and deletes Section 411.355(a)(3) because CMS believes that it incorrectly suggested that diagnostic tests are "incident to" services and, in CMS's view, subsection (a)(3) is repetitive of subsection (a)(2). CMS also re-clarified its position set forth in the 2003 Physician Fee Schedule final rule that any diagnostic service that has its own benefit category cannot be billed as an "incident to" service.

Rejecting one commenter's suggestion that CMS clearly prohibit referrals within a group practice to independent contractor pathologists who perform services for the group in offsite "pod labs," CMS reiterates that, while professional services performed by a member of the group practice may be performed onsite or offsite under this exception, an independent contractor physician must perform the services in the group's facilities to qualify for the exception.

CMS states that it does not believe it is appropriate to ban group practices from referring to any independent contractor physician, and thus would not make the recommended change, but it notes that the provision of offsite services by group practices raises significant concerns under the anti-kickback statute and would continue to be monitored by CMS.

### B. Implants Furnished by an Ambulatory Surgery Center

In Phase I, CMS established a new exception for implants furnished by an ambulatory surgery center (ASC) when acting as a new entity furnishing DHS. This exception was created to give ASCs not in rural areas the ability to order and perform surgeries that include implantation of DME prosthetics or prosthetic devices that are not part of the composite ASC payment rate.

CMS does not make any changes in Phase III to this exception, but clarifies that the exception does not apply if the ASC furnishes and submits the claim for the implant procedure and the physician furnishes and submits the claim for the device.

According to CMS, Medicare payment policy requires that, whenever an implant is performed during an ASC procedure, the ASC must bill for the implanted item.

## C. EPO and Other Dialysis-Related Outpatient Prescription Drugs

In Phase III, CMS declines one commenter's suggestion to broaden significantly the list of end-stage renal disease (ESRD) drugs under Section 411.355(g) to include all drugs furnished as part of dialysis treatment, whether at home or in a facility.

CMS responds that the annually updated list of ESRD drugs is complete and that CMS has already created a broad exception to the statutory exclusion of outpatient drugs as DHS for those drugs that are administered at the time of dialysis and are required "for the efficacy of dialysis."

CMS recommends that individuals or organizations contact CMS if they believe that certain drugs should qualify for the exception because they are required for the efficacy of dialysis and must be administered at the time of dialysis.

## D. Intra-Family Referrals in Rural Areas

In Phase II, CMS created a new exception for certain referrals from a referring physician to his or her immediate family member or to a DHS entity with which the physician's immediate family member has a financial relationship, when the referrals are made for patients who reside in a rural area and are unable to obtain the services elsewhere in a timely manner.

Under Phase II, the timeliness of available alternatives was measured solely in terms of distance from the patient's residence, where no other person or entity could be available to furnish the services in a timely manner within 25 miles from the patient's residence.

Phase III modifies the exception to include an alternative distance test based on transportation time from the patient's residence. Under Phase III, no other entity may be available within 25 miles or within 45 minutes transportation time from the patient's residence. CMS also clarifies that the referring physician and the immediate family member do not have any obligation to inquire as to the availability of other persons or entities located beyond this 25-mile or 45-minute radius.

CMS provides an example of how an intra-family referral may be permitted during winter months because of snow and winter conditions, but not permitted during summer months when the roads are clear and a non-family member physician is available to provide the needed DHS within 45 minutes travel time.

CMS also recommends that physicians using this 45-minute transportation time test document the information used in determining the transportation time required, and consult available Web sites for travel times and weather conditions.

In Phase III, CMS rejects several commenters' suggestions to broaden the exception to allow referrals to immediate family members if the referring physician receives no economic benefit from the referral, or if the immediate family member has an excepted financial arrangement and does not receive remuneration that takes into account the volume or value of referrals.

CMS explains that its authority to create exceptions is limited to those situations in which there is no risk of program or patient abuse, and broadening this exception as suggested could create a risk of program abuse.

CMS also rejects one commenter's suggestion that, in determining availability of alternative care providers, the exception should consider quality of care issues. CMS declines this suggestion because it states that it is not possible to create an objective test that allows for such quality considerations.

## X. Ownership and Investment Interest Exceptions

The Phase III Final Rule makes no changes to the exception related to ownership and investment interests set forth in Section 411.356. However, the preamble provides helpful guidance on several issues.

### A. Publicly Traded Securities and Mutual Funds

The Stark law contains an ownership exception for certain publicly traded securities and mutual funds that may own DHS entities. One requirement of this exception is that the securities must be purchased on terms available to the general public. In Phase II, CMS made clear that, to satisfy this test, the ownership interest must be in securities that are available to the public "at the time of the DHS referral." In Phase III, CMS further clarifies that the determination of whether a physician or DHS entity is in compliance with this requirement turns on "objective facts that are readily ascertainable" to the physician or DHS entity.

### B. Rural Providers

Another ownership exception is for a financial relationship with a DHS entity if substantially all of the DHS are furnished by the entity to individuals residing in a rural area. In Phase II, "rural area" was defined as an area not considered to be an urban area pursuant to Section 412.62(f), i.e., an area outside of a Metropolitan Statistical Area (MSA). In Phase III, CMS has declined to adopt any alternative or additional criteria for determining or defining "rural area," but offered several points of clarification on this issue.

First, CMS states that a rural area is defined by reference to the current list of MSAs and cities, towns, and counties contained in each, located on the Office of Management and Budget's Web site. Second, CMS clarifies that a Micropolitan Statistical Area is defined as an area containing a single urbanized core population of at least 10,000 but less than 50,000, and therefore is considered a rural area for purposes of physician self-referral rules. Finally, CMS cautions that, when a physician invests in an entity that furnishes DHS in a rural area, he does so at his or her own risk that the area may subsequently be classified as urban.

In other words, there is no protection for arrangements in which a re-classification causes a once-permitted ownership interest to become a violation of the self-referral rules.

## C. Whole Hospital Ownership

A physician's ownership interest in a hospital will not be considered a financial relationship under the Stark law if: (1) the referring physician is authorized to perform services at the hospital; (2) the ownership interest is in the hospital as a whole, and not merely in a subdivision or department of the hospital; and (3) the hospital is not a specialty hospital for the 18-month period beginning December 8, 2003.

With respect to the requirement that ownership be in a "whole hospital," in Phase III CMS clarifies that this includes a security interest in the hospital itself, but not a security interest in equipment sold to a hospital and financed with a loan to the hospital (*see* discussion above in Section III.E that such equipment security interests constitute compensation arrangements).

CMS declines to expand this exception to protect referrals from a physician who has, by virtue of a security interest in the hospital, an ownership interest in DHS entities owned by a hospital. CMS also makes no changes to the provisions related to specialty hospitals.

However, as discussed in Section XI below, CMS will soon implement a data gathering effort to better understand the issues related to physician ownership of hospitals, including specialty hospitals.

## XI. STATUTORY COMPENSATION EXCEPTIONS

The Stark regulations at Section 411.357 contain compensation exceptions derived from the statute itself as well as others that CMS created under authority contained in Section 1877(b)(4) of the Act. Because of the different origins of these compensation exceptions, we discuss them separately, starting with the statutory compensation exceptions.

In Phase III, CMS makes some substantive changes to the regulation's text. It also provides critical guidance in the preamble. Of note, CMS makes substantive changes to the exceptions applicable to personal service arrangements and physician incentive plans (PIPs). Note that, because of the importance of the exception for physician recruitment, we have discussed that exception separately, at Section VII above.

## A. Rental of Office Space and Equipment

CMS's Phase III preamble guidance on these exceptions relates to lease amendments, office sharing arrangements, subtenants' use of common areas, and holdover tenants.

In the preamble, CMS describes certain circumstances that potentially could jeopardize compliance with the exception where the parties to a rental agreement elect to amend its terms.

As a general matter, parties are free to amend a lease or rental agreement as long as the amended agreement complies with the core requirements for the exception, i.e., the rental charge is set in advance consistent with fair market value, is not determined in a manner that takes into account the volume or value of referrals or other business generated between the parties, and is for a term of no less than one year.

Parties risk noncompliance with the exception when they amend the actual rental charges (including the mechanism for calculating such charges), and/or change other terms that are material to the rental charge (e.g., the amount of space rented). The former risks noncompliance with the "set in advance" requirement, while the latter risks noncompliance with the fair market value and volume or value of referral requirements.

Practically speaking, if the parties wish to change the charges set forth in a rental agreement, they must terminate the original agreement and enter into a new agreement, and then only after the first year of the original term of the agreement.

Regarding office sharing arrangements, CMS expands on the "exclusive use" language in the exception, stating that the language effectively requires space and equipment leases "be for established blocks of time."

Commenters argued that office sharing arrangements were extremely common among individual physicians and group practices and that the exception should be modified to permit physicians and/or groups to share facilities and some limited equipment without any exclusivity requirement.

But CMS emphasizes that exclusive use means just that—the lessee must have exclusive use of the rented space or equipment during an established block of time.

Similarly, CMS reiterates its position that common areas (including some limited equipment that may be shared that is located in common areas and is not usually separately leased) may be shared, provided that the rental payment is appropriately prorated among the lessees. Examples include foyers, central waiting rooms, break rooms, and vending areas. Exam rooms do not constitute common areas for purposes of the exception.

Finally, CMS concludes that a lessor could enforce a rental premium charged to a holdover tenant under certain circumstances and not run afoul of the exception.

Specifically, a rental premium is permissible as long as it is set in advance at the time of execution and the rental rate (including premium) remains consistent with fair market value and does not take into account the volume or value of referrals or other business generated between the parties.

In addition, CMS reinforces its position that the six-month holdover period is reasonable despite one commenter's suggestion that the period should be extended indefinitely provided that the lessor is continually taking steps to evict the lessee.

> *Comment.* CMS's hard line on shared lease arrangements that do not include block-time provisions could be one of the more important clarifications in Phase III. Many had held a good-faith belief that such arrangements could be structured if careful attention was paid to the supervision requirements, so that the service provided in the shared space could properly be considered to be furnished by the referring physician.
>
> In light of CMS's clear position in Phase III, these shared lease arrangements should be restructured to include block-time. Even with such a provision,

providers need to pay careful attention to make certain they are providing appropriate supervision of the shared service.

The Phase III Final Rule does not represent CMS's current thinking on the issue of unit-of-service-based payment arrangements (so-called "per click" payments) under the space and equipment rental exceptions. The 2008 PFS Proposed Rule includes a significant change to per click rental arrangements to prohibit per click rental charges to the extent such payments reflect services provided to patients referred by the lessor-physician. If this change is adopted, many—if not most—per click lease arrangements will need to be restructured. Of note, this proposed change actually reflects CMS's original position on the matter in the proposed Stark II Rule published in 1998, which was subsequently dropped from the Stark II Phase I Final Rule published in 2001.

## B. Personal Services

The exception applicable to personal service arrangements is one of the few statutory compensation exceptions that CMS amends in Phase III.

Specifically, CMS agrees with commenters' recommendations to permit a six-month holdover period for personal service arrangements similar to those permitted following the expiration of space and equipment leases under those exceptions, as long as the holdover personal service arrangement is on the same terms and conditions as the immediately preceding agreement.

With respect to the exception applicable to PIPs, CMS amends its terms to refer consistently to the term "downstream contractor," a newly defined term under Section 411.351 that encompasses both a first-tier contractor, as defined in 42 C.F.R. §1001.952(t)(2)(iii), or a downstream contractor, as defined in 42 C.F.R. §1001.952(t)(2)(i). In doing so, CMS clarifies that the PIP exception applies equally to the individual or entity contracting directly with the managed care organization ("MCO") to provide or arrange for items and services, and the individual or entity that subcontracts directly or indirectly to provide or arrange for items and services covered by an agreement between the MCO and the first tier contractor.

CMS provides additional guidance concerning other aspects of the personal services exception, including PIPs. It declines to permit DHS entities to provide incentives to physicians for their services in connection with fee-for-service patients, provided that the incentives "fit the general structure of the [personal service arrangements] exception" due to the risk of program or patient abuse.

Limiting the PIP exception to managed care arrangements, which, by their nature, limit the volume of care provided or ordered by a "gatekeeper" physician, protects Congress's statutory intent to permit certain PIP payments that otherwise would run afoul of the general prohibition on compensation determined in a manner that takes into account the volume or value of referrals or other business generated between the parties.

PIPs that base physician compensation on factors such as patient satisfaction or other quality measures that are unrelated to (i) the volume or value of business generated by the referring physician and (ii) reducing or limiting services would be permitted as long as the other requirements of the exception are met.

In addition, CMS clarifies the use of a master list to comply with the provision requiring a written agreement covering all of the services to be furnished to the entity by the physician (or immediate family member of the physician) or group practice. Specifically, CMS states that an entity may, but is not required to, use a master list. However, if the entity elects to do so, then it must include *all* personal service arrangements that entity has with any physician, family member, or group practice.

Finally, in response to comments concerning amendments to personal service agreements and the addition of the six-month holdover period, CMS notes that parties could take such steps under terms similar to those applicable to the rental of office space and equipment exceptions.

## C. Isolated Transactions

Although CMS makes no changes to this exception, it emphasizes in the preamble that, if the parties elect to use an installment payment mechanism, they must assure the physician makes the required payments even in the event of a default by the purchaser or obligated party. To this end, the regulations permit the parties to select from several options, including immediately negotiable payments or payments guaranteed by a third party, or payments secured by a promissory note.

CMS also addresses issues concerning the six-month post-closing adjustment period. Commenters raised a variety of issues, including whether an adjustment based upon a breach of warranty should be considered a post-closing adjustment, and whether the period permits sufficient time for a buyer to complete a full audit cycle to examine financial statements and confirm the seller's representations and warranties. CMS responds that such adjustments do not, in fact, constitute post-closing adjustments, but rather are considered part of the original transaction. As such, a breach of warranty claim or an adjustment premised upon seller's representations can occur at any time without jeopardizing compliance with the exception.

## D. Remuneration Unrelated to the Provision of Designated Health Services

Hospital trade associations in particular objected to the exception for remuneration that is wholly unrelated to the provision of DHS as adopted in the Phase II rulemaking, asserting that it was inconsistent with the statute and congressional intent. CMS strongly disagrees with the general assertion that hospitals are free to provide any remuneration to physicians provided that the amount of remuneration is not *directly* related to the provision of DHS. CMS adds that, if a bona fide compensation arrangement relates in any way to furnishing DHS, it should be structured to fit squarely within another exception to the general prohibition.

In Phase III, CMS also addresses concerns regarding the issue of whether a particular item, service, or cost could be allocated in whole or in part to Medicare or Medicaid under the applicable cost reporting principles. The preamble explains that, where a hospital does not know, and could not reasonably be expected to know, whether such cost reporting principles apply, CMS would not consider the item, service, or cost to relate to furnishing of DHS under the exception. Hospitals, however, still must meet the additional criteria under the exception to qualify for its protections.

### E. Certain Group Practice Arrangements With Hospitals

CMS received no comments on the exception allowing certain group practice arrangements with hospitals, and made no changes in the Phase III Final Rule. However, in the 2008 PFS Proposed Rule, CMS seeks to eliminate protection for physician-owned entities furnishing services to hospitals under arrangement that do not meet this exception. These proposed changes are very significant and readers should consult that proposed rule and the final rule when published.

### F. Payments Made by a Physician for Items and Services

This statutory exception protects payments by a physician either to a laboratory in exchange for the provision of clinical laboratory services or to any entity as compensation for other items or services when these are furnished at a price consistent with fair market value and are not specifically addressed by another exception. Although the Phase III final rule makes no changes to this exception, CMS does amend the exception for fair market value compensation discussed in Section VI.A to provide that the exception covers compensation from a physician, provided that all other conditions of the exception are satisfied. This expansion of the fair market value exception to compensation paid to DHS entities by physicians will require parties to use that exception going forward.

## XII. COMPENSATION EXCEPTIONS CREATED BY REGULATION

In Phase II, CMS adds a number of regulatory compensation arrangement exceptions. All of these exceptions were promulgated under the authority of Section 1877(b)(4) of the Act, which requires CMS to determine that the exception "does not pose a risk of program or patient abuse."

Because of the relatively narrow circumstances under which CMS may promulgate these additional exceptions, in Phase I when CMS first promulgated exceptions under this authority, it made a policy decision to require that all such exceptions not violate the anti-kickback statute. In Phase III, CMS rejects the many comments it received asking it, in one way or another, to modify this position.

Although CMS does not add any new regulatory compensation arrangement exceptions in Phase III, the agency clarifies the provisions of several of these exceptions, and made substantive changes to the exceptions for charitable donations by physicians, nonmonetary compensation, compliance training, and professional courtesy.

Note that, because of the importance of the exceptions for indirect compensation, fair market value, and physician retention, we discuss them separately above at Sections IV, VI.A and VII.

## A. Charitable Donations by Physicians

CMS makes one revision to the exception for charitable donations by a physician found at Section 411.357(j). This exception now permits such donations as long as the donation is made to a tax exempt entity, is neither solicited nor *offered* in any manner that takes into account the volume or value of referrals or other business generated between the parties, and does not violate the anti-kickback statute or any other federal or state law governing billing or claims submission.

The addition of a prohibition on offering a donation in a manner that takes into account the volume or value of referrals is a change from both the past regulation (which prohibited only soliciting) and the proposed regulation (which only would have protected donations that were neither solicited, offered, nor "made, in any manner" that takes into account the value or volume of referrals).

By deleting "made, in any manner" from the proposed rule, CMS recognizes that the receiving entity cannot be expected to know a donor's intent in making the donation if that intent is not so stated.

## B. Nonmonetary Compensation

CMS adds a deeming provision to the nonmonetary compensation exception found at Section 411.357(k).

If a DHS entity inadvertently exceeds the nonmonetary compensation limit by no more than 50 percent, and the physician who received the compensation returns the excess amount by the earlier of (1) the end of the calendar year in which he or she received it or (2) 180 consecutive calendar days from receiving the excess compensation, then the compensation is deemed to be within the limit. A DHS entity may rely on this deeming provision only once every three years with respect to the same referring physician.

Another change in Phase III permits a DHS entity that has a formal medical staff to hold one local medical staff appreciation event per year (such as a holiday party) without counting that event toward the nonmonetary compensation limit, provided that the event is open to the entire medical staff. However, any gifts or gratuities given in connection with the event must be counted toward the limit.

CMS also makes the clarifying change that the timeframe for nonmonetary compensation limits is the calendar year.

## C. Medical Staff Incidental Benefits

CMS rejected the many requests from the provider community that the medical staff incidental benefits exception found at Section 411.357(m) be broadened to include off-campus benefits. Related to this position, CMS clarifies that the scope does not extend to the provision of electronic devices that would enable physicians to access patients who are at home or work, or personnel who are off the hospital campus. The on-campus requirement permits a hospital to pay for a device that the physician can use off-campus to access on-campus patients and information, but not the other way around.

CMS also comments on questions about hospital referral services by noting that the arrangement could potentially qualify under this exception or under the exception for referral services at Section §411.357(q).

## D. Compliance Training

Section 411.357(o) protects certain compensation arrangements for compliance training. CMS now permits such compliance training to include programs for which physicians may receive Continuing Medical Education (CME) credit.

However, compliance training must be the primary focus of the program and not just incidental to a CME program. In addition, Internet-based compliance training may qualify under this exception if the physician accesses the online training while in the entity's local community or service area and all other elements of the exception are satisfied.

## E. Obstetrical Malpractice Insurance Subsidies

As with the exception for referral services, the compensation exception for obstetrical malpractice insurance subsidies found at Section 411.357(r) mirrors the requirements of the anti-kickback safe harbor.

Although there is no change to this regulation in Phase III, in the 2008 PFS Proposed Rule CMS expressed concern that the requirement is too restrictive and sought comments regarding the difficulty in accessing obstetrical care and recommendations regarding how to make the exception more flexible without creating a risk for program or patient abuse.

## F. Professional Courtesy

In Phase III, CMS makes certain clarifications to the professional courtesy exception found at Section 411.357(s), and deletes the requirement that the entity extending professional courtesy notify the insurer in writing of the reduction of any coinsurance obligation on the part of the recipient of the professional courtesy. Although CMS removed this requirement, it continues to urge DHS entities to provide such notification.

CMS clarifies that this exception, which permits an entity to offer professional courtesy to a physician or a physician's immediate family member or office staff, is only available to entities with "a formal medical staff." One of the requirements of the exception is that the entity must have a professional courtesy policy set out in writing and approved by the entity's governing body. CMS closes the door on an interpretation offered by some commenters that, if the entity does not have a formal professional courtesy policy, then it does not need to comply with the exception at all. It is now clear that a written formal policy is a prerequisite to compliance with this exception.

## XIII. REPORTING AND RECORDKEEPING REQUIREMENTS

### A. Regulatory Requirements

Surprisingly, both CMS and providers have paid little attention to the reporting and recordkeeping requirements of Section 1877(f) of the Act and Section 411.361. As with most parts of Phase III, although CMS makes no substantive changes to this rule, its preamble guidance is important.

Most importantly, CMS rejects all comments to loosen the reporting and recordkeeping requirements because of their associated burdens. In particular, for the reasons stated in Phase II, CMS does not allow financial arrangements that a provider determines to meet an exception to be exempt from these requirements. Specifically, CMS requires providers to retain information about all such arrangements in order to review such arrangements for itself to determine whether they comply with an exception.

Finally, CMS states that while information providers submit under its reporting obligations is typically exempt from disclosure to third parties under the Freedom of Information Act and Trade Secrets Act, CMS must evaluate these exemption determinations on a case-by-case basis, and so CMS cannot make categorical statements that all provider submissions will be exempt.

### B. Disclosure of Financial Relationships Report

On September 14, 2007, CMS published a request for comments on its Disclosure of Financial Relationships Report (DFRR). 72 Fed. Reg. 52,568.[4] CMS intends to use the DFRR to implement a requirement under Section 5006 of the Deficit Reduction Act (DRA), enacted on February 8, 2006, directing the Secretary of the Department of Health and Human Services (HHS) to develop a "strategic and implementing plan" to address certain issues relating to physician investment in specialty hospitals.

CMS intends to issue this DFRR to 500 hospitals, which will be required to complete the form accompanied by a certification executed by the hospitals' chief executive officer or chief financial officer. The DFRR seeks a significant amount of information about hospitals' ownership and compensation arrangements and will assist CMS in determining these hospitals' compliance with the Stark law.

Hospitals not targeted to receive the DFRR and other providers should nevertheless understand its importance because it represents a significant shift in CMS's monitoring of Stark law compliance and therefore could signal heightened risk.

CMS makes clear that this form will ultimately have a much wider use than for the specific congressionally mandated report under the DRA. CMS states that it intends to use this form as a "regular financial disclosure process that would apply to all Medicare participating hospitals."

Again, be careful out there.

---

[4]*See also* http://www.cms.hhs.gov/PaperworkReductionActof1995/PRAL/list.asp#Top OfPage; http://www.cms.hhs.gov/PhysicianSelfReferral/05a_Disclosure.asp#TopOfPage. This information was first published on May 18, 2007. 72 Fed. Reg. at 28,056.

# 3

# The False Claims Act in Health Care Prosecutions: Application of the Substantive, *Qui Tam,* and Voluntary Disclosure Provisions*

*Robert Salcido, Akin, Gump, Strauss, Hauer & Feld, L.L.P., Washington, D.C.

# I. Introduction

Over the past two decades, the health care community has witnessed dramatic changes in the government's efforts to enforce its fraud and abuse laws. For example, fraud alerts regarding prohibited kickback arrangements[1] and the expansion of the Stark law[2] have demonstrated the government's com-

---

[1]*See, e.g.,* 59 Fed. Reg. 65,372 (Dec. 19, 1994); 60 Fed. Reg. 40,847 (Aug. 10, 1995); 61 Fed. Reg. 30,623 (June 17, 1996).

[2]*See* 42 U.S.C. §1395nn. For extensive discussion of the Stark law restrictions, see Chapter 2 (Crane, Federal Physician Self-Referral Restrictions); for full text of the Stark law, see Appendix B-1 on the disk accompanying this volume.

mitment to policing health care transactions. The most dramatic development, however, measured by dollars recovered, has been the government's enforcement of the False Claims Act (FCA).

The FCA is the government's "primary litigative tool for combating fraud."[3] The FCA empowers both the Attorney General and private persons to institute civil actions to enforce the Act.[4] The FCA imposes liability on those who, inter alia, "knowingly" present, or cause to be presented, "a false or fraudulent claim for payment."[5] "Knowingly," at a minimum, is defined to mean that the provider acted in "deliberate ignorance" or in "reckless disregard" of the truth or falsity of the information.[6]

Under the *qui tam* provisions of the FCA, private persons, known as relators, may enforce the Act by filing a complaint, under seal, setting forth allegations of fraud committed against the government.[7] The government, while maintaining the complaint under seal, investigates the allegations.[8] If the government determines that the allegations have merit, the Department of Justice (DOJ) intervenes in the action, unseals the complaint, and assumes primary responsibility for prosecuting the claim.[9] If the government believes the claim lacks merit, it declines to intervene, in which case the *qui tam* plaintiff may elect, but is not obligated, to prosecute the action.[10] If the government intervenes and prevails on the merits, it is awarded treble damages plus a $5,000 to $10,000 penalty for each false claim submitted;[11] the relator receives, under most circumstances, 15 to 25 percent of the government's recovery (depending on his or her contribution to the action) plus reimbursement of reasonable legal fees and expenses.[12] If the government does not intervene in the action, the relator's statutory recovery is between 25 to 30 percent of the

---

[3]United States *ex rel.* Kelly v. Boeing Co., 9 F.3d 743, 745 (9th Cir. 1993) (quoting Senate Judiciary Committee, False Claims Amendments Act of 1986, S. Rep. No. 99-345 (1986), *reprinted in* 1986 U.S.C.C.A.N. 5266).

[4]31 U.S.C. §3730. The False Claims Act is codified at 31 U.S.C. §§3729–3733. See Appendix C-1 on the disk accompanying this volume for full text of the Act.

[5]31 U.S.C. §3729(a)(1).

[6]31 U.S.C. §3729(b).

[7]31 U.S.C. §3730(b)(2). *Qui tam* "is an abbreviation for *qui tam pro domino rege quam pro seipso*, which means 'he who is as much for the king as for himself.' " United States *ex rel.* Springfield Terminal Ry. v. Quinn, 14 F.3d 645, 647 n.1 (D.C. Cir. 1994) (emphasis added) (citation omitted).

[8]31 U.S.C. §3730(b)(3).

[9]31 U.S.C. §3730(b)(4) and (c)(1).

[10]31 U.S.C. §3730(b)(4)(B).

[11]For violations committed on or after Sept. 29, 1999, the defendant is liable for treble damages plus penalties ranging from $5,500 to $11,000 per claim. *See* Civil Monetary Penalties Inflation Adjustment, 64 Fed. Reg. 47,099, 47,103–104 (1999) (codified at 28 C.F.R. pt. 85). However, the statute also contains voluntary disclosure provisions under which a provider's exposure to liability is limited to double the government's damages and civil penalties.

[12]31 U.S.C. §§3729(a) and 3730(d)(1). Under §3730(d)(1), if the relator's action is primarily based upon specified types of information, his or her recovery is capped at 10 percent.

government's recovery plus reimbursement of reasonable legal fees and expenses.[13]

Before 1986, the FCA languished in relative disuse.[14] In 1986, outraged by scandals plaguing the Department of Defense (DOD), Congress revamped the FCA by expanding the scope of its scienter standard.[15] Congress also modernized FCA penalty provisions to increase the government's recovery amounts, allowing from double to treble damages and from $2,000 per claim to $5,000 to $10,000 per claim in civil monetary penalties.[16] Congress also liberalized the FCA's *qui tam* provisions by eliminating the broad jurisdictional bar, increasing the amount of the whistleblower's bounty, and expanding the relator's right to participate in the action.[17]

As a result of Congress's expansion and liberalization of the FCA, the government's recoveries under the FCA have skyrocketed, totaling more than $18 billion since the statute was amended in 1986.[18] The health care industry has been especially hard hit, with every sector—hospitals,[19] fiscal agents,[20]

---

[13] 31 U.S.C. §3730(d)(2).

[14] *See, e.g.*, S. Rep. No. 99-345 at 4 n.10, *reprinted in* 1986 U.S.C.C.A.N. at 5269 (pointing out that in fiscal year 1984 the DOJ received 2,850 fraud referrals, but had filed only 21 complaints based on those referrals).

[15] At the time of the 1986 amendments, the rule of the Fifth, Sixth, Ninth, and Eleventh Circuits was that to establish an FCA violation the government must prove that the defendant acted with specific intent to defraud the government. *See* United States v. Davis, 809 F.2d 1509, 1512 (11th Cir. 1987); United States v. Aerodex, Inc., 469 F.2d 1003, 1007 (5th Cir. 1972); United States v. Mead, 426 F.2d 118 (9th Cir. 1970); United States v. Ueber, 299 F.2d 310 (6th Cir. 1962). Conversely, the Seventh, Eighth, and Tenth Circuits and the Court of Claims had held that an intent to deceive was not necessarily a requisite element of proof under the pre-1986 Act. *See* United States v. Hughes, 585 F.2d 284, 287–88 (7th Cir. 1978); United States v. Cooperative Grain & Supply Co., 476 F.2d 47, 56 (8th Cir. 1973); Fleming v. United States, 336 F.2d 475, 479 (10th Cir. 1964); Miller v. United States, 550 F.2d 17, 23 (Ct. Cl. 1977). In 1986, Congress clarified that "no proof of specific intent to defraud" was required to establish a violation of the statute—and that liability extended to those whose acted with "reckless disregard" or in "deliberate ignorance" of the truth or falsity of the information. 31 U.S.C. §3729(b).

[16] *See, e.g.*, United States v. Hill, 676 F. Supp. 1158, 1165–68 (N.D. Fla. 1987) (describing Congress's 1986 amendments to the FCA).

[17] *See* United States v. Northrop Corp., 59 F.3d 953, 964–69 (9th Cir. 1995) (describing Congress's goals in amending the *qui tam* provisions of the FCA); *see generally* Evan Caminker, *The Constitutionality of* Qui Tam *Actions*, 99 Yale L.J. 341 (1989); *see* Robert Salcido, *Screening Out Unworthy Whistleblower Actions: An Historical Analysis of the Jurisdictional Bar to* Qui Tam *Actions Under the False Claims Act*, 24 Pub. Cont. L.J. 237 (1995) (setting forth the history underlying the 1986 amendments to the *qui tam* provisions of the FCA) [hereinafter Salcido, *Screening Out Unworthy Whistleblower Actions*].

[18] *See* http://www.usdoj.gov/opa/pr/2006/November/06_civ_783.html.

[19] *See, e.g.*, United States *ex rel.* Dhawan v. New York Med. College, 252 F.3d 118 (2d Cir. 2001); United States v. Texas Tech Univ., 171 F.3d 279 (5th Cir. 1999); Hindo v. University of Health Scis./The Chicago Med. Sch., 65 F.3d 608 (7th Cir. 1995); Covington v. Sisters of the Third Order of St. Dominic of Hanford, Cal., No. 93-15194, 1995 U.S. App. LEXIS 20370 (9th Cir. July 13, 1995); United States *ex rel.* Obert-Hong v. Advocate Health Care, No. 99 C 5806, 2001 U.S. Dist. LEXIS 3767 (N.D. Ill. Mar. 27, 2001); United States *ex rel.* Goodstein v. McLaren, No. 97-CV-72992-DT, 2001 U.S. Dist. LEXIS 2917 (E.D. Mich. Jan. 3, 2001); United States *ex rel.* Amin v. George Washington Univ., 26 F. Supp. 2d 162 (D.D.C. 1998); United States *ex rel.* Thompson v. Columbia/HCA Healthcare, 20 F. Supp. 2d 1017 (S.D. Tex. 1998); United States *ex rel.* Cox v. Iowa Health Sys., 29 F. Supp. 2d 1022 (S.D. Iowa 1998).

[20] *See, e.g.*, United States *ex rel.* Stinson, Lyons, Gerlin & Bustamante, P.A. v. Prudential Ins., 944 F.2d 1149 (3d Cir. 1991).

peer review organizations,[21] physicians,[22] researchers,[23] laboratories,[24] home health agencies,[25] long-term care facilities,[26] and suppliers and billing services,[27] among others—having been the target of an FCA action.

This chapter discusses three areas of FCA jurisprudence that those within the health care community are likely to confront.

- Section II examines the FCA's substantive elements. By reviewing these elements, a provider may ascertain the likelihood that its practices will be subject to FCA liability.
- Section III addresses the *qui tam* provisions of the FCA, focusing specifically on the public disclosure jurisdictional bar defense to *qui tam* actions. This jurisdictional bar has spawned a remarkable diversity of case law and presents those accused of a violation with a potential defense.
- Section IV covers the Department of Health and Human Services (HHS), Office of the Inspector General (OIG), Voluntary Disclosure Program, which offers people who may have violated the FCA a significant opportunity to limit their exposure to liability for penalties.

---

[21]*See, e.g.*, United States *ex rel.* McCoy v. California Med. Review, Inc., 723 F. Supp. 1363 (N.D. Cal. 1989).

[22]*See, e.g.*, United States *ex rel.* Hochman v. Nackman, 145 F.3d 1069 (9th Cir. 1998); United States *ex rel.* Bidani v. Lewis, No. 97 C. 6502, 2001 U.S. Dist. LEXIS 260 (N.D. Ill. Jan. 11, 2001); United States v. Cabrera-Diaz, 106 F. Supp. 2d 234 (D.P.R. 2000); United States v. Krizek, 859 F. Supp. 5 (D.D.C. 1994), *aff'd in part, rev'd in part*, 111 F.3d 934 (D.C. Cir. 1997), *on remand*, 7 F. Supp. 2d 56 (D.D.C. 1998), *remanded*, 192 F.3d 1024 (D.C. Cir. 1999).

[23]*See, e.g.*, United States *ex rel.* Cantekin v. University of Pittsburgh, 192 F.3d 402 (3d Cir. 1999); United States *ex rel.* Berge v. Trustees of Univ. of Ala., 104 F.3d 1453 (4th Cir. 1997); United States v. University of Tex. M.D. Anderson Cancer Ctr., 961 F.2d 46 (4th Cir. 1992).

[24]*See, e.g.*, United States *ex rel.* LaCorte v. SmithKline Beecham Clinical Labs., 149 F.3d 227 (3d Cir. 1998); United States *ex rel.* Downy v. Corning, Inc., 118 F. Supp. 2d 1160 (D.N.M. 2000); United States *ex rel.* Kneepkins v. Gambro Healthcare, Inc., 115 F. Supp. 2d 35 (D. Mass. 2000); United States *ex rel.* Ramona Wagner v. Allied Clinical Lab., 1995 Medicare & Medicaid Guide (CCH) ¶43,142 (S.D. Ohio 1995).

[25]*See, e.g.*, United States *ex rel.* Russell v. Epic Healthcare Management Group, 193 F.3d 304 (5th Cir. 1999); United States v. Estate of Rogers, No. 1:97CV461, 2001 WL 818160 (E.D. Tenn. June 28, 2001); United States *ex rel.* Waris v. Staff Builders, Inc., No. 96-1969, 1999 U.S. Dist. LEXIS 15247 (E.D. Pa. Oct. 4, 1999); United States *ex rel.* Joslin v. Community Home Health of Maryland, Inc., 984 F. Supp. 374 (D. Md. 1997); United States v. American Health Enters., Inc., No. 94-CV-450-RCF, 1996 U.S. Dist. LEXIS 7494 (N.D. Ga. Apr. 29, 1996).

[26]*See, e.g.*, United States v. NHC Healthcare Corp., 115 F. Supp. 2d 1149 (W.D. Mo. 2000); United States *ex rel.* Swan v. Covenant Care, Inc., No. C-97-3814, 1999 U.S. Dist. LEXIS 15287 (N.D. Cal. Sept. 21, 1999).

[27]*See, e.g.*, United States *ex rel.* Glass v. Medtronic, Inc., 957 F.2d 605 (8th Cir. 1992); United States *ex rel.* Franklin v. Parke-Davis, 147 F. Supp. 2d 39 (D. Mass. 2001); United States v. Gericare Med. Supply, Inc., No. 99-0366-CB-L, 2000 U.S. Dist. LEXIS 19661 (S.D. Ala. Dec. 11, 2000); United States *ex rel.* Trim v. McKean, 31 F. Supp. 2d 1308 (W.D. Okla. 1998); Luckey v. Baxter Healthcare Corp., 2 F. Supp. 2d 1034 (N.D. Ill. 1998), *aff'd*, 183 F.3d 730 (7th Cir. 1999).

## II. Construction of the "False" and "Knowing" Elements of the False Claims Act

There are several contexts in which a potential FCA action can arise: a person may receive a contact or demand letter from the DOJ;[28] a person may be the subject of a *qui tam* action; or a person may identify a practice that has resulted in the erroneous submission of claims. No matter what the context, however, the person will need to evaluate the elements underlying the FCA to determine its potential liability.

To establish a violation of the FCA, the plaintiff generally must establish a number of elements. Specifically, the plaintiff generally must prove that:

1. the "person";[29]
2. "present[ed]" or "cause[d] to be presented";[30]
3. "a false or fraudulent";

---

[28] Historically, the DOJ's letters to persons reflecting its belief that a provider may have violated the law were known as "demand" letters because the DOJ often demanded payment in exchange for not filing a lawsuit. As a result of Congress's concern regarding the DOJ's abusive use of the FCA, the DOJ has promised to modify its approach and simply notify the provider regarding its possible breach of the FCA (rather than demand payment) and invite the provider to respond to the DOJ's inquiry. These letters are now known as "contact" letters. *See, e.g.,* Memorandum from Eric H. Holder, Jr., Deputy Attorney General to All United States Attorneys, All First Assistant United States Attorneys, All Civil Health Care Fraud Coordinators in the Offices of United States Attorneys and All Trial Attorneys in the Civil Division, Commercial Litigation Section (June 3, 1998). (For text of the Holder Memorandum, see Appendix C-2 on the disk accompanying this volume.)

[29] According to the Senate Judiciary Committee's report on its bill, the word "person" is to be construed broadly:

> The False Claims Act reaches all parties who may submit false claims. The term "person" is used in its broad sense to include partnerships, associations, and corporations—*United States v. Hanger One, Inc.*, 563 F.2d 1155, 1158 (5th Cir. 1977); *United States v. Nat'l Wholesalers, Inc.*, 236 F.2d 944 (9th Cir. 1956)—as well as States and political subdivisions thereof. *Cf. Ohio v. Helvering*, 292 U.S. 360, 370 (1934); *Georgia v. Evans*, 316 U.S. 153, 161 (1942); *Monell v. Dep't of Soc. Serv. of N.Y.*, 436 U.S. 658 (1978).

*See* S. Rep. No. 99-345 at 8, *reprinted in* 1986 U.S.C.C.A.N. 5266, 5273. In Vermont Agency of Natural Res. v. United States, 529 U.S. 765 (2000), the Supreme Court ruled that in *qui tam* actions in which the United States does not intervene, states are not "persons" and therefore cannot be subject to liability. For a discussion of the case law, see Robert Salcido, False Claims Act & the Healthcare Industry: Counseling & Litigation §2:01 (American Health Lawyers Ass'n 1999) [hereinafter Salcido, False Claims Act Counseling]; *see also* Robert Salcido, False Claims Act & the Healthcare Industry: Counseling & Litigation: Oct. 2003 Supp. §2:01 (American Health Lawyers Ass'n 2003) [hereinafter Salcido, False Claims Act Counseling: Oct. 2003 Supp.].

[30] Generally, if an individual did not direct or authorize the submission of a claim, a court will not find the individual liable for presenting or causing the submission of a false claim under the FCA. *See, e.g.,* United States *ex rel.* Shaver v. Lucas Western Corp., 237 F.3d 932, 933 (8th Cir. 2001) (the court found that the relator, who alleged that the defendant employer had been ordered by a state worker's compensation board to pay the relator's medical bills but failed to do so which resulted in those claims being submitted to the Social Security Administration and Medicare, did not state a cause of action because the relator "did not allege that [the defendant] affirmatively instructed [the relator] to submit his medical bill claims to the government; he alleged merely that [the defendant] refused to pay the bills. Even assuming the truth of [the relator's] allegation that [the defendant] 'knew' [the relator] would submit such bills to Medicare, [the defendant] cannot be said to have 'caused' [the relator's] medical bill claims to be submitted to the government."); United States *ex rel.* Kinney v. Hennepin County Med. Ctr., 2001 WL 964011 at *9–10 (D. Minn. Aug. 22, 2001) (when emergency room physicians did not

4. "claim,"[31] "record or statement";
5. "knowingly";
6. to "the United States [g]overnment";[32] that was
7. "material"[33] to the government's determination to pay.[34]

---

instruct or control the representations that a medical center made regarding claims for ambulance transport fees, the physicians could not have "caused" the submission of false claims under the FCA); United States *ex rel.* Piacentile v. Wolk, Medicare & Medicaid Guide (CCH) 1995 ¶43,028 (E.D. Pa. 1995). However, a person will "cause" another to submit a false claim if she instructs the person to do so. *See, e.g.*, United States v. Mackby, 261 F.3d 821, 828 (9th Cir. 2001) (where defendant had instructed office manager and billing service to use an inaccurate provider identification number on claim forms, "he caused the claims to be submitted with false information" and hence the "causation element was established by a preponderance of the evidence"). For a discussion of the case law, see SALCIDO, FALSE CLAIMS ACT COUNSELING, at §2:02.

[31] The word "claim" generally is construed to be a demand for money or property of the United States that results in the United States suffering immediate financial detriment. *See, e.g.*, United States v. McNinch, 356 U.S. 595 (1958); United States *ex rel.* Windsor v. Dyncorp, Inc., 895 F. Supp. 844 (E.D. Va. 1995). For a discussion of the case law, see SALCIDO, FALSE CLAIMS ACT COUNSELING, at §2:04.

[32] The FCA requires that the claim be submitted to "an officer or employee of the United States Government or a member of the Armed Forces of the United States." The Senate Judiciary Committee stated that the provision applies whenever payment will result in a loss to the United States government:

> A claim upon any Government agency or instrumentality, quasi-governmental corporation, or nonappropriated fund activity is a claim upon the United States under the act. In addition, a false claim is actionable although the claims or false statements were made to a party other than the Government, if the payment thereon would ultimately result in a loss to the United States. United States v. Lagerbusch, 361 F.2d 449 (3rd Cir. 1966); Murray & Sorenson, Inc. v. United States, 207 F.2d 119 (1st Cir. 1953). For example, a false claim to the recipient of a grant from the United States or to a State under a program financed in part by the United States, is a false claim to the United States. *See*, for example, United States *ex rel.* Marcus v. Hess, 317 U.S. 537 (1943); United States *ex rel.* Davis v. Long's Drugs, 411 F. Supp. 1114 (S.D. Cal. 1976).

S. REP. No. 99-345 at 10, *reprinted in* 1986 U.S.C.C.A.N 5266, 5275.

[33] *See, e.g.*, United States *ex rel.* Harrison v. Westinghouse Savannah River Corp., 176 F.3d 776 (4th Cir. 1999). In *Harrison*, the relator alleged that the defendant had submitted claims that were not authorized under the terms of its contract with the federal government, but the defendant pointed out that the government had a copy of the contract and could best judge whether its work was unauthorized. The court agreed with the defendant and dismissed the relator's claim. Specifically, the court pointed out that the government "was aware of the terms of the contract—it could have objected to the inclusion of procedure development costs if it had believed that such work was not authorized. [The relator] does not allege that [the defendant] tried to conceal the nature of the work. Thus, [the relator's allegations] do not involve any material falsity, if any falsity at all." *See also* United States *ex rel.* Lamers v. City of Green Bay, 168 F.3d 1013, 1019 (7th Cir. 1999) (holding that even if defendant's representation "was an outright lie," the lie would be immaterial if defendant's practices had conformed (unbeknownst to defendant) with the underlying regulation); United States *ex rel.* Berge v. Trustees of Univ. of Ala., 104 F.3d 1453, 1461–62 (4th Cir.) (rejecting the relator's claim that the defendant had made false representations to the government to obtain federal grant funds by identifying the relator as a post-doctoral graduate student when in fact she was a doctoral candidate because such a misrepresentation would not be material to the government's decision of whether to fund a multimillion dollar grant since the government would be interested in the internationally respected scientists working on the project and not an unknown graduate student), *cert. denied*, 522 U.S. 916 (1997); United States v. Robbins, 207 F. Supp. 799, 807 (D. Kan. 1962) (finding that the government cannot charge that it was defrauded by the false representations of another party where it has made an independent investigation prior to paying any money to defendants); United States v. Goldberg, 158 F. Supp. 544, 548 (E.D. Pa. 1958) (same); *cf.* United States v. Board of Educ. of Union City, 697 F. Supp. 167 (D.N.J. 1988). For a discussion of the case law, see SALCIDO, FALSE CLAIMS ACT COUNSELING, at §2:07; *see also* SALCIDO, FALSE CLAIMS ACT COUNSELING: OCT. 2003 SUPP., at §2:07.

[34] Specifically, courts have found subsection (a)(1), the prohibition on false claims, to have the following elements: that a claim for payment or approval was presented or caused to be

Two elements are discussed in detail in this chapter: the "false or fraudulent" and the "knowing" elements. These two elements of the substantive provisions of the FCA have produced the most litigation. Also set forth below is a discussion of defenses to the charge that a claim is false or fraudulent and that the defendant knew the claim was false.

## A. Defining "Falsity" Under the FCA

To establish liability under the FCA, the government or whistleblower must establish that the claim was false or fraudulent. Although the FCA does not define what constitutes a false claim, general case law provides some parameters. Discussed below are cases in which courts found that a defendant did submit a false claim and cases in which courts found that there was no falsity. These cases offer some guidance to companies in determining whether their practices may fairly be characterized as false or fraudulent.

---

presented to the government; that the claim was false or fraudulent; and that the defendant knew that the claim was false or fraudulent. *See, e.g.,* United States v. Mackby, 261 F.3d 821, 826 (9th Cir. 2001); Luckey v. Baxter Healthcare Corp., 2 F. Supp. 2d 1034, 1044 (N.D. Ill. 1998), *aff'd,* 183 F.3d 730 (7th Cir. 1999); United States *ex rel.* Mikes v. Straus, 84 F. Supp. 2d 427, 432 (S.D.N.Y. 1999) (adding additional element that "the United States suffered damages as a result"). To establish a violation of subsection (a)(2), the prohibition on false statements, the government or whistleblower must prove that the defendant presented or caused a third party to present a claim for payment or approval, that the claim was false or fraudulent, that the defendant presented or caused the claim to be presented knowing it was false or fraudulent, and that the defendant made or used a false statement that the defendant knew to be false and that was causally connected to the false claim. *See* United States *ex rel.* Aakhus v. Dyncorp, Inc., 136 F.3d 676, 682 (10th Cir. 1998); *but see* United Techs. Corp., 51 F. Supp. 2d at 195–96 (adding additional element that "the United States suffered damages as a result"); *Straus*, 84 F. Supp. 2d at 432 (same). To prove a violation of subsection (a)(3), the plaintiff must prove that the defendant conspired with one or more persons to get a false or fraudulent claim allowed or paid by the United States, that one or more conspirators performed any act to effect the object of the conspiracy, and that the government suffered losses as a result of the claim. United States *ex rel.* Durcholz v. FKW Inc., 997 F. Supp. 1159, 1173 (S.D. Ind. 1998), *aff'd,* 189 F.3d 542 (7th Cir. 1999); United States v. Hill, 676 F. Supp. 1158, 1173 (N.D. Fla. 1987); *see also* Blusal Meats, Inc. v. United States, 638 F. Supp. 824, 828 (S.D.N.Y. 1986), *aff'd other grounds,* 817 F.2d 1007 (2d Cir. 1987); *Straus*, 84 F. Supp. 2d at 432; *but see* United States *ex rel.* Wilkins v. North Am. Constr. Corp., 101 F. Supp. 2d 500, 525–26 n.14 (S.D. Tex. 2000) (refusing to find that the elements of a conspiracy violation under the FCA require proof of damages, noting that it was "clear" that "the damages element of the *Blusal Meats* test is erroneous" and that the "better rule has two elements ... the plaintiff must show: (1) the defendant conspired with one or more persons to get a false or fraudulent claim allowed or paid by the United States; and (2) one or more conspirators performed any act to effect the object of the conspiracy") (citation omitted); United States *ex rel.* Atkinson v. Pennsylvania Shipbuilding Co., No. 94-7316, 2000 U.S. Dist. LEXIS 12081 at *27 (E.D. Pa. Aug. 24, 2000) (same). Finally, to establish a violation of subsection (a)(7), the plaintiff must prove that there is a record or statement, that is false, is "known" to be false, and is used to "conceal, avoid, or decrease" an "obligation to pay or transmit money or property." *See, e.g., Dyncorp, Inc.,* 136 F.3d at 681–82; United States *ex rel.* Lamers v. City of Green Bay, 998 F. Supp. 971, 996–97 (E.D. Wis. 1998), *aff'd on other grounds,* 168 F.3d 1013 (7th Cir. 1999); *cf.* United States v. Raymond & Whitcomb, 53 F. Supp. 2d 436, 444–45 (S.D.N.Y. 1999) (adding additional element that the government suffer damage). *See generally* SALCIDO, FALSE CLAIMS ACT COUNSELING: OCT. 2003 SUPP., at §§2:04, 2:08, 2:09.

## 1. Cases Establishing Falsity

There are two general types of health care claims that the government considers false. One type includes claims in which the person furnishes inaccurate or misleading information to the government to obtain payment or approval of a claim. These claims include upcoding, claiming payment for services not rendered, or explicitly certifying compliance with specific rules with which the provider did not in fact comply. The second type concerns instances in which a person omits information from a claim or "implicitly" certifies compliance with rules, but does not actually adhere to those rules. Both types of cases are addressed below.

### a. Literal Falsity

*United States v. Lorenzo*[35] and *United States ex rel. Thompson v. Columbia/HCA Healthcare*[36] present situations in which courts found health care claims or statements to be literally false.

In *Lorenzo*, a dentist performed a cancer examination of the oral cavity of the head and neck as part of a general examination. The dentist billed the service to Medicare as a "limited consultation" although the Medicare statute and regulations generally preclude persons from billing for routine examinations and from billing for dental services that are limited to the treatment of the teeth. The court held that the dentist's claims were false because they "were prepared in such a way as to disguise a routine dental checkup as a limited consultation consisting of 'a cancer examination of the oral cavity [of the] head and neck.'"[37]

In *Columbia/HCA Healthcare*, a hospital explicitly certified that the services in its cost report complied with Medicare laws, regulations, and program provisions, including the provisions outlawing kickbacks. The relator alleged that the hospital violated the anti-kickback statute. The court held that the hospital's certification was false if the hospital in fact breached the

---

[35]768 F. Supp. 1127 (E.D. Pa. 1991).

[36]20 F. Supp. 2d 1017, 1046–47 (S.D. Tex. 1998).

[37]768 F. Supp. at 1131. *See also* United States v. Mackby, 261 F.3d 821 (9th Cir. 2001). There the Ninth Circuit ruled that the defendant clinic had submitted a false claim when, in providing physical therapy, it inserted the provider identification number (PIN) of a physician who did not perform or supervise the service rather than the physical therapist in independent practice who did perform the service. Specifically, the court reasoned: "While the purpose of box 24k [on the HCFA-1500 claim form] is not specified on the form itself, Medicare bulletins sent to the . . . Clinic state that the box is to be used for the PIN of the performing physician or supplier. Placing [the doctor's] PIN in box 24k indicated that [the doctor] was the performing physician or supplier and therefore constituted a false statement. Box 33 is clearly labeled as requiring the PIN or group number of the physician or supplier providing the treatment, and [the doctor] was neither of these. Therefore, placing his PIN number in this box was a false statement as well." *Id.* at 826–27. Moreover, the court rejected the defendant's contention that the claims were not false because the underlying services were actually rendered because "a claim may be false even if the services billed were actually provided, if the purported provider did not actually render or supervise the service." *Id.* at 826 (citation omitted).

anti-kickback law.[38]  Courts have also invoked the false certification theory to apply the FCA to alleged violations of the Stark law. Specifically, courts have found that defendants have either breached the FCA because their certification is false when they have certified compliance with the law or, alternatively, that they "caused" another to submit a false certification or, as will be discussed later, submitted a false claim because they had "impliedly" certified compliance with the Stark law when they submitted a claim.[39]

When a person submits expressly false information to the government, the person clearly may be subjected to FCA liability. Literal falsity cases, like those discussed above, are relatively straightforward. To state a cause of action, the government or whistleblower must demonstrate that some information is false. In determining whether the information is in fact false, there must be a comparison made to some benchmark. For example, the services of the dentist in *Lorenzo* were found to be false when compared to the rules and regulations governing the Medicare program because the services were not consultations, but were instead general examinations. Similarly, in *Columbia/HCA*, the representation that the hospital complied with the rules and regulations governing

---

[38]20 F. Supp. 2d at 1046–47. *See also* United States *ex rel.* McNutt v. Haleyville Medical Supplies, 423 F.3d 1256, 1259 (11th Cir. 2005) (finding that where defendants executed a provider agreement certifying that they would adhere to the anti-kickback statute and the defendants' compliance with the provider agreement is a condition of payment, defendants are liable under the FCA because "[w]hen a violator of government regulations is ineligible to participate in a government program and that violator persists in presenting claims for payment that the violator knows the government does not owe, that violator is liable, under the Act, for its submission of those false claims"); United States *ex rel.* Barlett v. Tyrone Hosp., 234 F.R.D. 113, 126–27 (W.D. Pa. 2006) (stating that allegation that hospital's request for payment contained in Uniform Bill (UB)-92s and submission of cost reports could constitute false claims if contrary to the certifications on those forms the defendants violated the anti-kickback statute) (dicta).

[39]20 F. Supp. 2d at 1047 (rejecting defendants' contention that there was no violation of the Stark law that resulted in a violation of the FCA; defendants had argued that the services they provided were proper and would have been furnished by others and hence the federal fisc was not injured by the defendants' alleged practices, but the court held that the defendants' claims for payment were submitted contrary to the express prohibition in the Stark law and therefore were actionable under the FCA because "payments to improper claimants that know they are statutorily ineligible and prohibited from seeking such payments from the government constitute injury to the treasury"). *See also* United States *ex rel.* Goodstein v. McLaren, No. 97-CV-72992-DT, 2001 U.S. Dist. LEXIS 2917 at *16–17 (E.D. Mich. Jan. 3, 2001) (holding that although health care entities did not directly present certifications or claims to the government, because the government alleged that these entities caused defendant hospital to make false certifications to the government by allegedly engaging in a prohibited financial relationship under the Stark law, the government stated a cause of action under the FCA); Gublo v. Novacare, Inc., 62 F. Supp. 2d 347, 355 (D. Mass. 1999) ("A number of courts . . . have recognized that the submission of a false certification of compliance with the Stark law in order to qualify for Medicare reimbursement can constitute a false claim under the FCA") (citations omitted); *see generally* United States v. Solinger, 457 F. Supp. 2d 743, 754 (W.D. Ky. 2006) ("Although neither the Stark nor Anti-kickback statutes provide for a right of private enforcement . . . , Courts have permitted plaintiffs to bring FCA claims based on similar alleged false cost certifications that violate the Stark and Anti-kickback statutes.") (citations omitted); United States v. Rogan, 459 F. Supp. 2d 692, 717, 724 (N.D. Ill. 2006) ("Falsely certifying compliance with the anti-kickback statute, 42 U.S.C. §1320a-7b(b), and Stark Statute, 42 U.S.C. §1395nn, in a Medicare cost report is actionable under the FCA" and further, although the UB-92 health care claim form does not contain the same express certification that exists in the cost report, the "submission of UB-92s in violation of the Stark Statute constitutes a violation of the FCA.").

the program was false when the facts, if proven, demonstrated the opposite.[40] Inevitably, the government or whistleblower proves falsity by showing an objective gap between the representation that was submitted and what the representation would have been if it were truthful. Thus, for example, if the government contends that a Current Procedural Terminology (CPT) code a physician claims is false, the government must identify what code the physician should have used to properly represent the services furnished to the patient. Similarly, if a provider certifies compliance with a rule or regulation, the government must show that the provider did not in fact comply with the pertinent rule or regulation. As is noted in detail below, when the plaintiff cannot prove the existence of such a gap—because, for example, the defendant complied with all regulatory guidance or contractual provisions in submitting the claim, or the regulatory guidance is so amorphous that no gap between what was claimed and what should have been claimed can be demonstrated—the plaintiff's claim must necessarily fail because it cannot demonstrate falsity.

### b. Falsity by Implicit Certification

Various courts have struggled to define when a specific claim can be "false or fraudulent" under the FCA when the representations on the claims are accurate. The Second Circuit considered this issue at length in 2001 in *United States ex rel. Mikes v. Straus*.[41] This case is important because, in the health care context, it limits the circumstances under which a court will find an implicit false certification to those instances where the rule or regulation the defendant breaches expressly conditions payment on compliance. The basis for the court's narrow

---

[40]*But see* United States *ex rel.* Scott v. Dr. Eugene, No. 99-117 DOC (Eex) (C.D. Cal. Dec. 19, 2000). In *Scott*, the relator alleged that a defendant hospital had submitted false cost report certifications because, contrary to its representation that it had adhered to all program rules and regulations, it had in fact breached the anti-kickback law. The court rejected the relator's contention and questioned whether, because of its breadth, a cost report certification could serve as a predicate to an FCA action. Specifically, the court reasoned: "[I]t is not clear that the cost reports are relied on by the government to the extent required for a FCA allegation. The compliance certification is quite broad, requiring the signer to state that the report is in compliance with all the many and complex laws and regulations governing Medicare. This compliance certification may be so broad that it cannot stand as a basis for a false claim act allegation. Without reliance, the Cost-Report cannot serve as a basis for an FCA claim, even if false." *Id.* at 9. *Cf.* United States *ex rel.* Sharp v. Consolidated Medical Transport, Inc., No. 96 C 6502, 2001 U.S. Dist. LEXIS 13923 (N.D. Ill. Sept. 4, 2001). In *Consolidated Medical Transport*, the district court ruled that the relators could predicate an FCA claim based upon a violation of the anti-kickback act only if they could adequately plead that the United States would have refused to tender payment had it known of the violation. *See id.* at *29–30 ("plaintiffs must plead (and ultimately prove) that had the government known about the kickback scheme, it would have refused payment of the claims and, further, that the defendants were aware that this was the case when they engaged in their fraudulent conduct. It does not make sense to the court to hold, as relators suggest, that defendants that certify compliance with the Medicare laws while secretly maintaining a kickback arrangement, automatically violate the FCA. If the certification in question has no bearing on the government's decision to pay the claims, there is no reason why it should trigger liability under the FCA. However, if the relators can show that the alleged scheme is in fact an illegal kickback scheme, and that the government would have barred claims had it known of the existence of the underlying scheme, a violation of the FCA would be proven. Under these circumstances, the alleged facts would constitute a fraudulent scheme materially bearing on the government's decision to pay the claims submitted to it.").

[41]274 F.3d 687 (2d Cir. 2001).

construction of the FCA is to ensure that the federal government and whistle-blowers do not invoke the FCA in quality of care cases to second-guess medical judgment and to use the FCA to supplant the role of state, local, and private medical agencies, boards, and societies in monitoring quality of care issues.

In *Straus,* the relator, a pulmonologist, alleged that the defendants sub-mitted false reimbursement requests to the federal government for spirometry services.[42] Spirometry is an "easy-to-perform pulmonary function test used by doctors to detect both obstructive (such as asthma and emphysema) and re-strictive (such as pulmonary fibrosis) lung diseases."[43] The defendants' spi-rometers measure "the pressure change when a patient blows into a mouth-piece, thereby providing the doctor with on-the-spot analysis of the volume and speed by which patients can exhale."[44]

The relator alleged that the defendants submitted false Medicare reim-bursement claims for spirometry procedures because these procedures were not performed in accordance with the relevant standard of care.[45] Specifically, the relator alleged that American Thoracic Society (ATS) guidelines recommend daily calibration of spirometers by use of a three-liter calibration syringe, the performance of three successive trials during test administration, and the ap-propriate training of spirometer technicians.[46] The relator contended that the defendants' performance of spirometry did not conform to the ATS guidelines and thus would yield inherently unreliable data.

In evaluating whether the defendants submitted false claims to the gov-ernment, the court pointed out that the statutory term "false or fraudulent" is not defined in the FCA. In giving content to the phrase, the court reasoned:

> A common definition of "fraud" is "an intentional misrepresentation, conceal-ment, or nondisclosure for the purpose of inducing another in reliance upon it to part with some valuable thing belonging to him or to surrender a legal right." *Webster's Third New International Dictionary* 904 (1981). "False" can mean "not true," "deceitful," or "tending to mislead." *Id.* at 819. The juxtaposition of the word "false" with the word "fraudulent," plus the meanings of the words comprising the phrase "false claim," suggest an improper claim is aimed at extracting money the government otherwise would not have paid. *See* Clarence T. Kipps, Jr. *et al., Materiality as an Element of Liability Under the False Claims Act,* A.B.A. Center for Continuing Legal Educ. Nat'l Inst. (1998), WL N98CFCB ABA-LGLED B-37, B-46 ("[A] claim cannot be determined to be true or false without consideration of whether the decisionmaker should pay the claim—that is, a claim is 'false' only if the Government or other customer would not pay the claim if the facts about the misconduct alleged to have occurred were known.").[47]

---

[42] *Id.* at 693.

[43] *Id.* at 694.

[44] *Id.*

[45] *Id.* at 696.

[46] *Id.* at 694.

[47] *Id.* at 696; *accord* United States *ex rel.* Quinn v. Omnicare Inc., 382 F.3d 432, 438 (3d Cir. 2004); *cf.* United States *ex rel.* Riley v. St. Luke's Episcopal Hosp., 355 F.3d 370, 380 (5th Cir. 2004) (" 'False' can mean 'deceitful,' or 'tending to mislead,' and a 'false claim' is one 'grounded in fraud which might result in financial loss to the Government.' ") (citation omitted).

In evaluating whether the defendants' spirometry claims were false, the court found that there are two types of falsity that could trigger liability under the FCA: (1) false express certification, which represents compliance with a federal statute or regulation or a prescribed contractual term; or (2) false implied certification, under which a defendant implicitly represents entitlement to payment notwithstanding the breach of some rule or regulation that is not referenced in the certification. The court found that neither type of falsity was present under the facts and circumstances in the *Straus* action.

First, as to the relator's claim that the defendants tendered a false certification to the United States, the court evaluated the standard form that physicians submit to obtain Medicare reimbursement, the CMS-1500, which contains various certifications to which the physician must attest.[48] In formulating its rule regarding whether the defendants' claim for payment for the spirometry on the CMS-1500 breached the FCA because the defendants tendered a false certification, the court held that it would "join the Fourth, Fifth, Ninth, and District of Columbia Circuits in ruling that a claim under the Act is legally false only where a party certifies compliance with a statute or regulation as a condition to governmental payment."[49] Under this test, two separate elements must be satisfied: (1) the party must certify compliance with a specific statute or regulation, and (2) the party's certification and compliance with the statute or regulation must be a precondition of governmental payment.

In *Straus,* the court found that the second element was clearly satisfied. Both the CMS-1500, which provides that "[n]o Part B Medicare benefits may be paid unless this form is received as required by existing law and regulations,"[50] and the Medicare Regulations[51] state that certification is a precondition to Medicare reimbursement. However, the court found that the first element was not satisfied because the CMS-1500 did not contain any express certification regarding the quality of the spirometry services.

---

[48]For example, a physician, on the CMS-1500 form, will set forth, among other things, the pertinent CT Code representing the service supplied to the patient and certify that the services set forth on the form are "medically indicated and necessary for the health of the patient and were personally furnished by [the physician] or were furnished incident to [his or her] professional service by [his or her] employee...." The form also contains the following "NOTICE":

> Any person who knowingly files a statement of claim containing any misrepresentation or any false, incomplete or misleading information may be guilty of a criminal act punishable under law and may be subject to civil penalties.

*See* CMS-1500, *reprinted in* Medicare & Medicaid Guide (CCH) ¶10,261.

[49]274 F.3d at 697 (citing United States *ex rel.* Siewick v. Jamieson Sci. & Eng'g, Inc., 214 F.3d 1372, 1376 (D.C. Cir. 2000); Harrison v. Westinghouse Savannah River Co., 176 F.3d 776, 786–87, 793 (4th Cir. 1999); United States *ex rel.* Thompson v. Columbia/HCA Healthcare Corp., 125 F.3d 899, 902 (5th Cir. 1997); United States *ex rel.* Hopper v. Anton, 91 F.3d 1261, 1266–67 (9th Cir. 1996)). According to the court, its holding "is distinct from a requirement imposed by some courts that a false statement or claim must be material to the government's funding decision." *Id.* (citation omitted). It reasoned that a "materiality requirement holds that only a subset of admittedly false claims is subject to False Claims Act liability" and "that not all instances of regulatory noncompliance will cause a claim to become false." *Id.* (citation omitted). Consequently, the court declined to "address whether the Act contains a separate materiality requirement." *Id.*

[50]*See* CMS-1500, *reprinted in* Medicare & Medicaid Guide (CCH) ¶10,261.

[51]*See* 42 C.F.R. §424.32.

Specifically, as the court pointed out, a person certifies on the CMS-1500 that "the services shown on this form were *medically* indicated and *necessary* for the health of the patient and were *personally furnished* by [the person] or were furnished incident to [the person's] professional service by [the person's] employee under [the person's] immediate personal supervision."[52] The court ruled that the relator could establish neither that the services lacked medical necessity nor that the physician did not personally furnish the service.

As to medical necessity, the court found that the relator's objections to the defendants' spirometry tests did not implicate the standard set out in the CMS-1500 form that the procedure was dictated by "medical necessity" because the medical necessity standard relates to the level of service provided, not its quality.[53] Specifically, the court reasoned:

> The term "medical necessity" does not impart a qualitative element mandating a particular standard of medical care, and [the relator] does not point to any legal authority requiring us to read such a mandate into the form. Medical necessity ordinarily indicates the level—not the quality—of the service. For example, the requisite level of medical necessity may not be met where a party contends that a particular procedure was deleterious or performed solely for profit, *see United States ex rel. Kneepkins v. Gambro Healthcare, Inc.,* 115 F. Supp. 2d 35, 41–42 (D. Mass. 2000) (procedures chosen solely for defendants' economic gain are not "medically necessary" as required by claim submission form), or where a party seeks reimbursement for a procedure that is not traditionally covered, *see Rush v. Parham,* 625 F.2d 1150, 1156 (5th Cir. 1980) (upholding state's exclusion of experimental medical treatment from definition of "medically necessary" services under Medicaid).
>
> This approach to the phrase "medically necessary"—as applying to ex ante coverage decisions but not ex post critiques of how providers executed a procedure—would also conform to our understanding of the phrase "reasonable and necessary" as used in the Medicare statute, 42 U.S.C. §1395y(a)(1)(A) (1994) (disallowing payment for items or services not reasonable and necessary for diagnosis or treatment). *See New York ex rel. Bodnar v. Sec'y of Health & Human Servs.,* 903 F.2d 122, 125 (2d Cir. 1990) (acknowledging Secretary's authority, in determining whether procedure is "reasonable and necessary," to consider type of service provided and whether service was provided in appropriate, cost-effective setting); *Goodman v. Sullivan,* 891 F.2d 449, 450–51 (2d Cir. 1989) (per curiam) (affirming exclusion of experimental procedures from Medicare coverage pursuant to requirement that procedures be "reasonable and necessary"); *see also Friedrich v. Sec'y of Health & Human Servs.,* 894 F.2d 829, 831 (6th Cir. 1990) (noting that the Health Care Financing Administration, when determining whether a procedure is "reasonable and necessary," considers the procedure's safety, effectiveness, and acceptance by medical community).[54]

The court concluded that, "[i]nasmuch as [the relator] challenges only the quality of defendants' spirometry tests and not the decisions to order this procedure for patients, she fails to support her contention that the tests were not medically necessary."[55]

---

[52] 274 F.3d at 698 (emphasis added).

[53] *Id.*

[54] *Id.* at 698–99.

[55] *Id.* at 699.

Finally, as to the defendants' representation on the certification that services are "rendered under the physician's immediate personal supervision by his/her employee," which the court noted covers the medical assistants' performance of spirometry at the defendants' direction, the court ruled that the relator did not tender "evidence to support an allegation that the defendants did not 'personally furnish' the spirometry tests as required by the [CMS]-1500 form."[56] Hence, the court held that the "plaintiff's cause of action insofar as it is founded on express false certification is without merit."[57]

As to the second type of falsity alleged by the relator, the court turned to the relator's contention that the defendants, in submitting the CMS-1500, made an implied false certification. The court pointed out that under some case law authority a certification can be implicitly false based on the notion that "the act of submitting a claim for reimbursement itself implies compliance with governing federal rules that are a precondition to payment."[58]

However, the court specifically declined to expand this doctrine into the health care context because such an expansion would cause the FCA to conflict with local or private regulation of medical issues concerning the standard of care:

> [T]he False Claims Act was not designed for use as a blunt instrument to enforce compliance with all medical regulations—but rather only those regulations that are a precondition to payment—and to construe the impliedly false certification theory in an expansive fashion would improperly broaden the Act's reach. Moreover, a limited application of implied certification in the health care field reconciles, on the one hand, the need to enforce the Medicare statute with, on the other hand, the active role actors outside the federal government play in assuring that appropriate standards of medical care are met. Interests of federalism counsel that the regulation of health and safety matters is primarily, and historically, a matter of local concern.
>
> Moreover, permitting *qui tam* plaintiffs to assert that defendants' quality of care failed to meet medical standards would promote federalization of medical malpractice, as the federal government or the *qui tam* relator would replace the aggrieved patient as plaintiff. *See* Patrick A. Scheiderer, Note, *Medical Malpractice as a Basis for a False Claims Action?,* 33 Ind. L. Rev. 1077, 1098–99 (2000). Beyond that, we observe that the courts are not the best forum to resolve medical issues concerning levels of care. State, local or private medical agencies, boards and societies are better suited to monitor quality of care issues.[59]

Because of the poor fit of the FCA implied certification theory in the health care quality of care context, the court ruled that the "implied false certification is appropriately applied only when the underlying statute or regulation upon

---

[56] *Id.*

[57] *Id.*

[58] *Id.* (citation omitted). Specifically, the court cited to Ab-Tech Constr. Inc. v. United States, 31 Fed. Cl. 429 (Fed. Cl. 1994), *aff'd,* 57 F.3d 1084 (Fed. Cir. 1995) (unpublished table decision).

[59] 274 F.3d at 699–700 (citations and internal quotations omitted).

which the plaintiff relies expressly states the provider must comply in order to be paid."[60] Accordingly, "[l]iability under the Act may properly be found therefore when a defendant submits a claim for reimbursement while knowing—as that term is defined by the Act (*see* 31 U.S.C. §3729(b))—that payment expressly is precluded because of some noncompliance by the defendant."[61]

---

[60]*Id.* at 700 (citation omitted). *Accord In re* Genesis Health Ventures, Inc., 272 B.R. 558, 570 (Bankr. D. Del. Jan. 24, 2002) ("The notion of implied false certification is appropriately applied only when the underlying statute or regulation upon which the plaintiff relies expressly states that the provider must comply in order to be paid. . . . No specificity regarding the provision of credits for returned drugs to Medicaid as a condition of payment to a provider [exists]. Therefore, the claimant's cause fails under the 'legally false certification' theory.") (citation omitted). Similarly, at a more general level, courts have continued to rule that if the government or relator cannot demonstrate any breach of a governmental rule or regulation in the first instance, there is no violation of the FCA as a matter of law. *See, e.g.,* United States *ex rel.* Quinn v. Omnicare Inc., 382 F.3d 432, 438 (3d Cir. 2004) (affirming dismissal of relator's action alleging that defendant pharmacy violated the FCA when it resold returned medication and only credited Medicaid 50% of what Medicaid had paid because "there is no regulatory requirement of the reversal of a claim once a medication has been returned" and hence "if there is no requirement to adjust the claim, there is no liability for a failure to do so"); United States *ex rel.* Bondy v. Consumer Health Found., No. 00-2520, 2001 U.S. App. LEXIS 24238, at *13–15 (4th Cir. Nov. 9, 2001) (relator could not establish falsity because relator did not demonstrate that "HCFA disapproved of [the apportionment statistic] method [the defendant used on its cost report] or that the method chosen was not in accordance with HCFA's established procedures"); United States v. Medica-Rents Co., 285 F. Supp. 2d 742, 770–71 (N.D. Tex. 2003) (noting that "Medicare regulations are among the most completely impenetrable texts within human experience," and finding that the defendants' use of a Healthcare Common Procedure Coding System Code was not false or fraudulent when they were instructed by the regional carrier to bill under that code) (citations and internal quotation omitted); United States *ex rel.* Perales v. St. Margaret's Hosp., 243 F. Supp. 2d 843, 855 (C.D. Ill. 2003) (rejecting relator's claim because he could not show any falsity based on an alleged breach of the Stark law because "there is nothing illegal per se about a hospital acquiring a physician's practice, the existence of a non-compete agreement, or entering into a subsequent employment contract with that hospital; something more is required to make this conduct illegal, and it is evidence of this something more that is absent here"); United States *ex rel.* Obert-Hong v. Advocate Health Care, 211 F. Supp. 2d 1045 (N.D. Ill. 2002) (because the relator could not establish that defendants' practices breached the Stark law or anti-kickback statute, the relator could not establish a violation of the FCA); United States *ex rel.* Goodstein v. McLaren Reg'l Med. Ctr., 202 F. Supp. 2d 671 (E.D. Mich. 2002) (no violation of FCA because government could not establish violation of Stark law). This same principle has been applied in criminal cases alleging false statements. *See* United States v. Whiteside, 285 F.3d 1345, 1352, 1353 (11th Cir. 2002) (reversing defendants' convictions because "[n]either the regulations nor administrative authority clearly answer the dilemma the defendants faced here. As the FI [fiscal intermediary] testified, under current law, reasonable people could differ as to whether the debt interest was capital-related. The testimony indicates that the experts disagreed as to the validity of the theory of capital reimbursement suggested by the government. This contradictory evidence lends credence to defendants' argument that their interpretation was not unreasonable. Here, competing interpretations of the applicable law [are] far too reasonable to justify these convictions. . . . As such, the government failed to meet its burden of proving the *actus reus* of the offense—actual falsity as a matter of law.") (citation and internal quotation omitted). However, when a court finds that a defendant's practices did not conform to rules and regulations governing the government's program or that the defendant's interpretation of the rule or regulation is irrational, the plaintiff may prove falsity. *See* United States *ex rel.* Humphrey v. Franklin-Williamson Human Servs., 189 F. Supp. 2d 862, 873 (S.D. Ill. 2002) (rejecting defendant's FED. R. CIV. P. 12(b)(6) motion because "it appears that [the defendant's] billing practices did not comply with Medicaid statutes and regulations [regarding a person's spend down obligation]," and therefore the relator "may be able to prove that [the defendant] 'knew' that its billing practices were improper and that the statements they [sic] prepared and claims they [sic] made were false or fraudulent").

[61]274 F.3d at 700.

Under this interpretation of an implicit false certification, the court found that the relator's claim could not survive. The relator had asserted that compliance with Sections 1395y(a)(1)(A) and 1320c-5(a) of the Medicare statute is a precondition to a request for federal funds and that submission of a CMS-1500 form attests by implication to the providers' compliance with both of those provisions.[62] Section 1395y(a)(1)(A) of the Medicare statute states that "*no payment may be made* under [the Medicare statute] for any expenses incurred for items or services which . . . are not *reasonable and necessary* for the diagnosis or treatment of illness or injury or to improve the functioning of a malformed body member."[63] Because this section contains an express condition of payment—that is, "no payment may be made"—it explicitly links each Medicare payment to the requirement that the particular item or service be "reasonable and necessary."

The court rejected the relator's theory because the "reasonable and necessary" test did not address the quality of a service that was provided. Specifically, the court reasoned that, consistent with its analysis of the relator's express certification claim,

> The requirement that a service be reasonable and necessary generally pertains to the selection of the particular procedure and not to its performance. . . . While such factors as the effectiveness and medical acceptance of a given procedure might determine whether it is reasonable and necessary, the failure of the procedure to conform to a particular standard of care ordinarily will not.[64]

Accordingly, because the relator had only contended that the "defendants' performance of spirometry was qualitatively deficient, her allegations that defendants falsely certified compliance with §1395y(a)(1)(A) may not succeed."[65]

Similarly, the court rejected the relator's claim of an implicit false certification regarding Section 1320c-5(a) of the Medicare Act. That section provides:

> It shall be the obligation of any health care practitioner . . . who provides health care services for which payment may be made . . . to assure, to the extent of his authority that services or items ordered or provided by such practitioner . . .
>
> (1) will be provided economically and only when, and to the extent, medically necessary;
>
> (2) will be of a quality which meets *professionally recognized standards of health care;* and
>
> (3) will be supported by evidence of medical necessity and quality . . . as may reasonably be required by a reviewing peer review organization in the exercise of its duties and responsibilities.[66]

The relator had contended that the ATS guidelines constitute a "professionally recognized standard of health care" for spirometry and that the

---

[62]274 F.3d at 700.

[63]42 U.S.C. §1395y(a)(1)(A) (emphasis added).

[64]274 F.3d at 701 (citations omitted).

[65]*Id.*

[66]42 U.S.C. §1320c-5(a) (emphasis added).

defendants had implicitly certified compliance with that standard when they submitted CMS-1500 forms for spirometry tests. However, the court concluded that the relator's "allegations cannot establish liability under the False Claims Act because—unlike §1395y(a)(1)(A)—the Medicare statute does not explicitly condition payment upon compliance with §1320c-5(a)."[67] Specifically, the court found that this statutory provision simply authorizes the peer review organization to recommend sanctions after reasonable notice and the opportunity for corrective action by the provider. Furthermore, if HHS agrees that sanctions should be imposed and further finds the provider unwilling or unable substantially to comply with its obligations, HHS may exclude the provider from the Medicare program or mandate the repayment of the cost of the non-compliant service to the United States "as a condition to the continued eligibility" of the health care provider in the Medicare program.[68] Accordingly, the court ruled that because Section "1320c-5(a) does not expressly condition payment on compliance with its terms, defendants' certifications on the [CMS]-1500 forms are not legally false. Consequently, defendants did not submit impliedly false claims by requesting reimbursement for spirometry tests that allegedly were not performed according to the recognized standards of health care."[69]

Finally, on policy grounds, the court concluded that its interpretation of what constitutes an implicitly false claim conformed the FCA to the Medicare Act. Specifically, the court reasoned:

> Our holding—that in submitting a Medicare reimbursement form, a defendant implicitly certifies compliance with §1395y(a)(1)(A), but not §1320c-5(a)—comports with Congress' purpose.... Section 1395y(a)(1)(A) mandates that a provider's choice of procedures be "reasonable and necessary"; it does not obligate federal courts to step outside their primary area of competence and apply a qualitative standard measuring the efficacy of those procedures. The quality of care standard of §1320c-5(a) is best enforced by those professionals most versed in the nuances of providing adequate health care.[70]

Although the Second Circuit did not reject altogether the view that FCA claims can somehow be "implicitly" false, the court struck an appropriate balance by restricting such assertions to only those occasions in which the defendants knew that the submission of the claim would breach a rule or regulation that would result in denial of the claim. By striking this balance in a

---

[67] 274 F.3d at 701.

[68] *Id.* at 702.

[69] *Id.*

[70] *Id.* For a general discussion of the link between implicit falsity and materiality, see United States *ex rel.* Stebner v. Stewart & Stevenson Servs., Inc., 305 F. Supp. 2d 694 (S.D. Tex. 2004), *aff'd,* 144 Fed. Appx. 389 (5th Cir. 2005). In *Stebner,* the district court opined that "parties should not attempt to split hairs over whether an implied or express certification exists" because notwithstanding "any additional promises or certifications, a contractor's mere request for full payment inherently represents that he has tendered a complete and conforming performance." Given that, the court reasoned that a request for payment becomes "a material misrepresentation when the Government does not receive the benefit of its bargain." *Id.* at 700–01. Alternatively, as the court pointed out, "FCA liability does not exist if the alleged fraudulent act had no bearing on the Government's payment decision." *Id.* at 698.

quality of care case, the court has appropriately prevented the FCA from becoming a federal malpractice statute and federal courts from becoming specialized medical panels that evaluate whether the care provided could have somehow been better, while appropriately penalizing those who knowingly seek to obtain payment for funds that they are prohibited from receiving.

## 2. Cases in Which Courts Refused to Find That Defendant Submitted False or Fraudulent Claims or Statements

There are several discrete categories of cases in which courts generally will find that the defendant's claims are not false. For example, if the provider's practices conform with the regulations or cannot be shown to be objectively false, the FCA plaintiff cannot prove falsity as a matter of law and its claim must be dismissed.

### a. Literal Compliance

In *United States ex rel. Cox v. Iowa Health Systems*,[71] the relator, an air ambulance pilot, alleged that by converting nautical miles to statute miles various health care entities falsified the number of miles flown to yield a higher number and hence higher reimbursement. The defendants contended that no rule or regulation required medical care providers to measure air ambulance mileage in nautical miles rather than statute miles. The court held that the relator could not state a cause of action because the relator failed to "identify any law, regulation, or other source suggesting federal medical programs expected air ambulance mileage claims to be in nautical miles rather than statute miles."[72]

Of course, whenever a defendant's practices conform to the rules and regulations of a government program, the defendant's submission of claims and statements cannot be false or fraudulent as a matter of law.[73] In this sense,

---

[71]29 F. Supp. 2d 1022 (S.D. Iowa 1998).

[72]*Id.* at 1026.

[73]United States *ex rel.* Crews v. NCS Healthcare of Ill., Inc., 460 F.3d 853, 858 (7th Cir. 2006) (where relator could not point to any breach of a regulatory duty, there was no violation of the FCA as a matter of law); United States *ex rel.* Quinn v. Omnicare Inc., 382 F.3d 432, 438 (3d Cir. 2004) (affirming dismissal of relator's action alleging that defendant pharmacy violated the FCA when it resold returned medication and only credited Medicaid 50 percent of what Medicaid had paid because "there is no regulatory requirement of the reversal of a claim once a medication has been returned" and hence "if there is no requirement to adjust the claim, there is no liability for a failure to do so"); United States *ex rel.* v. Southland Mgmt. Corp., 326 F.3d 669, 674–75 (5th Cir. 2003) ("[W]hether a claim is valid depends on the contract, regulations, or statute that supposedly warrants it. It is only those claims for money or property to which a defendant is not entitled that are 'false' for purposes of the False Claims Act.") (en banc); United States *ex rel.* Hochman v. Nackman, 145 F.3d 1069, 1073–74 (9th Cir. 1998) (no falsity when defendants' acts conformed with VA payment guidelines); United States *ex rel.* Lindenthal v. General Dynamics Corp., 61 F.3d 1402, 1412 (9th Cir. 1995) (whistleblower's FCA claims for payment based on work that satisfied contractual obligations "could not have been 'false or fraudulent' within the meaning of the [False Claims Act]"); United States *ex rel.* Glass v. Medtronic, Inc., 957 F.2d 605, 608 (8th Cir. 1992) (a statement cannot be false or fraudulent under the FCA when the statement is consistent with regulations governing program); United States v. Prabhu, 442 F. Supp. 2d 1008, 1026 (D. Nev. 2006) ("Claims are not 'false' under the FCA unless they are furnished in violation of some controlling rule, regulation or standard."); United States *ex rel.* Conner v. Salina Reg'l Health Ctr., 459 F. Supp. 2d 1081, 1090 (D. Kan. 2006) (dismissing FCA action alleging a violation of the anti-kickback law when the alleged remuneration—requiring physician to provide

providers that institute comprehensive compliance programs should achieve substantial cost savings because implementing measures to ensure that their practices conform to the law should dramatically minimize the risk that they will become the subject of a successful FCA lawsuit.

### b. Non-Objective False Claims

A company in *Luckey v. Baxter Healthcare Corp.*[74] certified that it would use test methods that provide accurate and reliable results. The relator contended that the company's testing procedures were scientifically unsound and should be improved. The court ruled that the relator could not demonstrate that the company's certification was false because the relator could not point to any contract or regulation that required a specific type of testing and because "[c]ourts have consistently declined to find that a contractor's exercise of scientific or professional judgment as to an applicable standard of care falls within the scope of the FCA."[75]

In *United States v. Estate of Rogers*,[76] the government contended that the defendants had submitted false cost reports and claims seeking reimbursement

---

his own operating room staff—was permitted by law); United States *v.* Medica-Rents Co., 285 F. Supp. 2d 742, 770–71 (N.D. Tex. 2003) (noting that "Medicare regulations are among the most completely impenetrable texts within human experience" and finding that the defendants' use of a Healthcare Common Procedure Coding System Code was not false or fraudulent when they were instructed by the regional carrier to bill under that code); United States *ex rel.* Ben-Shlush v. St. Luke's-Roosevelt Hosp., No. 97 Civ. 3664 (LAP), 2000 U.S. Dist. LEXIS 3039 (S.D.N.Y. Mar. 10, 2000) (the court rejected the relator's contention that the defendant had falsely certified to the government that it had an adequate written plan of discharge for plaintiff because "a review of the regulations cited by plaintiff does not support his position" in that plaintiff did not cite "any regulations mandating certification to HHS regarding discharge planning" or "specify any information to be included in such a plan" and thus "plaintiff's allegations do not support a False Claims Act claim"); United States *ex rel.* Swafford v. Borgess Med. Ctr., 98 F. Supp. 2d 822, 827 (W.D. Mich. 2000) (the court rejected the relator's allegation that defendant physicians breached their certification that the services they provided were "personally furnished" by them or by an "employee under [their] personal direction" when they billed for interpreting venous ultrasound studies by merely rewording the vascular technologist's worksheet summary when the technologist reported the results as either negative or negative with abnormality (and did not review the technologist's hard copy data [video tape results]) because no regulations mandated that the physicians must review the hard copy data to bill for the interpretations); United States *ex rel.* Gathings v. Bruno's Inc., 54 F. Supp. 2d 1252 (M.D. Ala. 1999) (the court rejected the relator's allegation that the defendants, which were pharmacies, defrauded the government by charging lower dispensing fees for Blue Cross-Blue Shield patients than they did for Medicaid patients contrary to a contractual provision mandating that the Medicaid program be charged the same amount as the general public because the defendants' practice did not breach any Medicaid standard regarding the amount of the dispensing fees); United States *ex rel.* LaCorte v. SmithKline Beecham Clinical Labs., No. 96-1380 *et al.*, 1999 U.S. Dist. LEXIS 13036 (E.D. La. Aug. 20, 1999) (the court dismissed relator's allegation that defendant submitted false claims when it billed the government for a price higher than it billed its best customers because the relator could not point to any "statute or regulation imposing the obligation it asserts defendant has breached" and the "statute does not state that providers must charge Medicare the lowest rate billed to anyone"); United States *ex rel.* Joslin v. Community Home Health, 984 F. Supp. 374, 379 (D. Md. 1997) (where defendants' practices conformed with the law "any representation to the Federal Government . . . is correct . . . and did not violate the FCA"); United States *ex rel.* Milam v. Regents of the Univ. of Cal., 912 F. Supp. 868, 883 (D. Md. 1995) ("as a matter of law . . . False Claims Act liability cannot be imposed on the basis of a literally true statement").

[74]2 F. Supp. 2d 1034 (N.D. Ill. 1998), *aff'd*, 183 F.3d 730 (7th Cir. 1999).

[75]*Id.* at 1047–48.

[76]No. 1:97CV461, 2001 WL 818160 (E.D. Tenn. June 28, 2001).

for management fees that were not properly reimbursable costs because the defendant home health agencies were related to the defendant management company within the meaning of Medicare's rules and regulations. The defendants claimed that the government could not predicate an FCA action on Medicare's related-party rules because they had acted within a reasonable interpretation of those rules. Specifically, the defendants claimed that the Medicare "related party" rules and regulations are complex, subjective, and difficult to understand and apply and that the FCA was not enacted to punish persons for merely disagreeing with the federal government over the meaning of administrative regulations. The court rejected the defendants' contention. The court ruled that with "regard to the specific element of falsity under the FCA, it is immaterial whether the defendants did or did not make reasonable interpretations of the applicable HCFA rules and regulations governing the related-party issues. . . . [T]he defendants' contention that they made a reasonable interpretation of HCFA's related-party rules and regulations only goes to the scienter element and whether the defendants acted 'knowingly' as defined in 31 U.S.C. §3729(b). The factual issue of scienter is a matter for the jury to determine at trial."[77]

As noted earlier, to establish falsity under the FCA, it is not sufficient to demonstrate that the person's practices could have or should have been better. Instead, the plaintiff must demonstrate that an objective gap exists between what the defendant represented and what the defendant would have stated had the defendant told the truth. At times, it is difficult to establish that such a gap exists because the government certification, contract, or guidelines call for the person to exercise discretion. For example, in *Luckey v. Baxter Healthcare Corp.*, the government rule to which the company certified compliance mandated the use of testing methods that provide accurate and reliable results. There is a wide spectrum involving subjective judgment between adopting perfect test procedures and minimally compliant procedures. As long as the defendant's practices were anywhere along that spectrum, it could not be deemed to have submitted false certification because its certification would satisfy its legal duty. Accordingly, under such circumstances, courts will rule that the defendant's claim or statement is not false or fraudulent.[78] However, as the *Rogers* case

---

[77]In *Estate of Rogers*, the district court adopted the reasoning the Ninth Circuit had applied in United States *ex rel.* Oliver v. Parsons Corp., 195 F.3d 457 (9th Cir. 1999), *cert. denied*, 530 U.S. 1228 (2000). There the Ninth Circuit held that the falsity element could not be bypassed by merely demonstrating that the underlying contractual provision is ambiguous or that defendant acted in accordance with a reasonable interpretation of the regulation. *See* 195 F.3d at 463 n.3 (noting that the "amicus brief submitted by the Government correctly points out the potential problem created by embracing a 'reasonable interpretation' exception to the 'falsity' of a claim. A defendant could submit a claim, knowing it is false or at least with reckless disregard as to falsity, thus meeting the intent element, but nevertheless avoid liability by successfully arguing that its claim reflected a 'reasonable interpretation' of the requirements").

[78]*See, e.g.*, United State*s* *ex rel.* Will v. A Plus Benefits, Inc., 139 Fed. Appx. 980, 982 (10th Cir. 2005) ("At a minimum the FCA requires proof of an objective falsehood."); United States *ex rel.* Lamers v. City of Green Bay, 168 F.3d 1013, 1018 (7th Cir. 1999) (holding that "errors based simply on faulty calculations or flawed reasoning are not false under the FCA . . . [a]nd imprecise statements or differences in interpretation growing out of a disputed legal question are similarly not false under the FCA"); Hagood v. Sonoma County Water Agency, 81 F.3d 1465, 1477 (9th Cir. 1996) ("How precise and how current the cost allocation

illustrates, where the rule or the regulation does not call for an exercise of discretion and can be determined with judicial precision, then the court in the first instance will determine whether the claim is false as a matter of law and, if the defendant's acts are inconsistent with the legal requirements underlying the government's program, a jury will determine whether the defendant acted with the requisite intent to submit the false claim or statement.

## B. The FCA "Knowing" Standard

Falsity alone is insufficient to impose FCA liability; the provider must have "knowingly" submitted the false claim. The FCA defines "knowing" and "knowingly" to mean that a person: "(1) has actual knowledge of the information; (2) acts in deliberate ignorance of the truth or falsity of the information; or (3) acts in reckless disregard of the truth or falsity of the information."[79] The FCA further provides that "no proof of specific intent to defraud is required."[80]

---

needed to be in light of the [Water Supply Act's] imprecise and discretionary language was a disputed question within the [government]. Even viewing [the relator's] evidence in the most favorable light, that evidence shows only a disputed legal issue; that is not enough to support a reasonable inference that the allocation was *false* within the meaning of the False Claims Act") (emphasis added); United States *ex rel*. Anderson v. Northern Telecom, Inc., 52 F.3d 810, 815–16 (9th Cir. 1995); Wang v. FMC Corp., 975 F.2d 1412, 1421 (9th Cir. 1992) ("Proof of one's mistakes or inabilities is not evidence that one is a cheat.... Without more, the common failings of engineers and other scientists are not culpable under the Act.... The Act is concerned with ferreting out 'wrongdoing,' not scientific errors.") (citation omitted); United States v. Prabhu, 442 F. Supp. 2d 1008, 1032–33 (D. Nev. 2006) (defendant's "claims are not false ... because his documentation practices would fall within the range of reasonable medical and scientific judgment regarding how to document the medical necessity of pulmonary rehabilitation services.... To establish falsity under the FCA, it is not sufficient to demonstrate that the person's practices could have or should have been better. Instead, plaintiff must demonstrate that an objective gap exists between what the Defendant represented and what the Defendant would have stated had the Defendant told the truth.... Accordingly, because, at a minimum, reasonable minds may differ regarding whether the documentation underlying [defendant's] claims satisfied some undefined standard, the Government has not establish[ed] falsity as a matter of law") (citations and footnote omitted); United States *ex rel*. Burlbaw v. Orenduff, 400 F. Supp. 2d 1276, 1288 (D.N.M. 2005) ("Where disputed legal issues arise from vague provisions or regulations, a contractor's decision to take advantage of a position can not result in his filing a knowingly false claim."); United States *ex rel*. Bettis v. Odebrecht, 297 F. Supp. 2d 272, 294–95 (D.D.C. 2004) ("even if plaintiff could suggest a better methodology than was used by defendant, there is no basis for imposing FCA liability based on faulty or mistaken engineering judgments"), *aff'd*, 393 F.3d 1321 (D.C. Cir. 2004); United States *ex rel*. Swafford v. Borgess Med. Ctr., 98 F. Supp. 2d 822, 831–32 (W.D. Mich. 2000) (where the relator had contended that, in order to bill for an "interpretation or reading" of the "results of the test" of ultrasound studies, the defendant physicians must do more than merely rely upon the findings of the technologist by independently reviewing the supporting data from which the technologist arrived at his conclusions, the court rejected the relator's claim because it found that those terms were undefined and ambiguous and that the relator's position "devolves to a dispute over the meaning of the terms governing the delivery of the professional component of physicians services" and that such a "legal dispute is ... insufficient" to establish FCA liability because "a defendant's decision in the face of a dispute over the requirements of governing regulations is insufficient, without more, to constitute falsity"), *aff'd*, 24 Fed. Appx. 491 (6th Cir. 2001); United States *ex rel*. Roby v. Boeing Co., 100 F. Supp. 2d 619, 625 (S.D. Ohio 2000) ("At a minimum, the FCA requires proof of an objective falsehood.... Expressions of opinion, scientific judgments, or statements as to conclusions about which reasonable minds may differ cannot be false."); United States *ex rel*. Milam v. Regents of the Univ. of Cal., 912 F. Supp. 868 (D. Md. 1995); United States *ex rel*. Boisjoly v. Morton Thiokol, Inc., 706 F. Supp. 795, 810 (N.D. Utah 1988) ("[The certification] reflects an engineering judgment.... It is clearly not a statement of fact that can be said to be either true or false, and thus cannot form the basis of a FCA claim.").

[79]31 U.S.C. §3729(b).
[80]*Id.*

Consistent with the terms "reckless disregard" and "deliberate ignorance," the legislative history indicates that Congress was generally concerned about two types of conduct that some courts had concluded were not actionable under the pre-1986 FCA. The first type involved instances in which a provider submitted claims in a sloppy, unsupervised fashion without due care regarding the accuracy of the claim (i.e., reckless disregard).[81] The second type concerned instances in which a provider deliberately refused to learn additional facts that, if learned, would disclose that the claim was inaccurate (i.e., deliberate ignorance).[82]

Below are descriptions of cases in which courts have applied the deliberate ignorance and reckless disregard elements of the FCA. Also addressed are cases in which courts have concluded that the provider did not act knowingly because, for example, the conduct was merely negligent and did not rise to the level of knowledge required by the FCA, the relevant regulatory guidance was ambiguous, the government knew and approved of the potential overpayment, or the defendant relied upon a sound legal theory in submitting the claim. These cases also help health care providers confronting a possible billing discrepancy assess whether to disclose the wrongdoing to the OIG pursuant to its Voluntary Disclosure Program or whether they are simply liable for an overpayment and need only reimburse the government's fiscal agent. Furthermore, a review of the FCA intent standard gives health care providers guidance as to what specific steps they may take to minimize the risk that a government enforcement action or a viable *qui tam* action will be filed.

## 1. Reckless Disregard

In *United States v. Krizek,*[83] a psychiatrist with a small practice delegated the task of billing services to his wife and a billing clerk. The wife and clerk assumed the doctor furnished a 50-minute psychotherapy session unless they were told otherwise. The wife believed that "it was fair and appropriate

---

[81]*See, e.g.,* 132 Cong. Rec. 20,535–36 (Aug. 11, 1986). Specifically, Sen. Grassley pointed out:

> While the committee expressed in its report accompanying S. 1562 that mistake, inadvertence or mere negligence in the submission of a false claim would not be actionable under the bill, concerns stemming mainly from the Government contracting community, were raised that such examples of mere negligence might be construed as grossly negligent acts.
>
> To address those concerns, I, along, with the other sponsors of this bill, have agreed to return to a "reckless disregard" standard, but only with the express qualification that "no proof of specific intent is required." Our intent in returning to the reckless disregard standard is only to assure that mere negligence, mistake, and inadvertence are not actionable under the False Claims Act. In doing so, we reconfirm our belief that reckless disregard and gross negligence define essentially the same conduct and that under this act, reckless disregard does not require any proof of an intentional, deliberate, or willful act.

[82]*See, e.g.,* S. Rep. No. 99-345 at 6–7, *reprinted in* 1986 U.S.C.C.A.N. 5271–72 ("the Government is unable to hold responsible those corporate officers who insulate themselves from knowledge of false claims submitted by lower-level subordinates. The 'ostrich-like' conduct which can occur in large corporations poses insurmountable difficulties for civil false claims recoveries.... [T]he Committee does believe the civil False Claims Act should recognize that those doing business with the Government have an obligation to make a limited inquiry to ensure the claims they submit are accurate.").

[83]859 F. Supp. 5 (D.D.C. 1994), *aff'd in part, rev'd in part,* 111 F.3d 934 (D.C. Cir. 1997).

to use the [50-minute] code as a rough approximation of the time spent, because on some days, an examination would last up to two hours and [she] would still bill [the 50-minute code]." The court noted that the "net result of this system, or more accurately 'nonsystem,' of billing was that on a number of occasions, [staff] submitted bills for . . . psychotherapy sessions"[84] but the psychiatrist "could not have spent the requisite time providing services." The court held that the submitted claims exceeding a set hourly threshold per day were false and had been submitted in reckless disregard of their truth or falsity.[85]

In *United States ex rel. Trim v. McKean*,[86] a national billing company submitted claims on behalf of emergency department physicians. The company required its coders to code 40 charts per hour and instructed them to bill based upon the services provided rather than the documentation provided in the charts. The company's billing manual stated that lower-level acuity codes rarely were appropriate because the services involved the emergency department. Comparison with national statistics revealed that the company billed at levels consistently higher than the average. The company instructed coders not to use certain International Classification of Diseases (9th Revision) (ICD-9) codes that would result in lower reimbursements and to use a CPT 52-modifier to notify its physician-clients that documentation was insufficient to support the level of service the coder actually assigned, which resulted in a higher charge being passed on to the government. As in *Krizek*, the court found that the company had submitted claims with knowledge of their falsity or in reckless disregard of their falsity.

---

[84] *Id.* at 11.

[85] Although the defendant psychiatrist claimed that he was at worst merely "negligent" and emphasized the "ma and pa" nature of his small practice, the court nonetheless imposed liability, ruling that the psychiatrist

> failed utterly in supervising [his] agents in their submissions of claims on his behalf. As a result of his failure to supervise, [the physician] received reimbursement for services which he did not provide. These were not "mistakes" nor merely negligent conduct. Under the statutory definition of "knowing" conduct, the Court is compelled to conclude that the defendants acted with reckless disregard as to the truth or falsity of the submissions. As such, they will be deemed to have violated the False Claims Act.

In affirming the district court's ruling, the D.C. Circuit stated that "the best reading of the Act defines reckless disregard as an extension of gross negligence." The court ruled that the defendants' conduct had reached that standard:

> We are also unpersuaded by the Krizeks' argument that their conduct did not rise to the level of reckless disregard. The District Court cited a number of factors supporting its conclusion: Mrs. Krizek completed the submissions with little or no factual basis; she made no effort to establish how much time Dr. Krizek spent with any particular patient; and Dr. Krizek "failed utterly" to review bills submitted on his behalf. *Krizek*, 859 F. Supp. at 13. Most tellingly, there were a number of days within the seven-patient sample when even the shoddiest recordkeeping would have revealed that false submissions were being made—those days on which the Krizeks' billing approached twenty-four hours in a single day. On August 31, 1985, for instance, the Krizeks requested reimbursement for patient treatment using the 90844 code thirty times and the 90843 code once, indicating patient treatment of over 22 hours. *Id.* at 12. Outside the seven-patient sample the Krizeks billed for *more* than twenty-four hours in a single day on three separate occasions. *Krizek*, 909 F. Supp. at 34. These factors amply support the District Court's determination that the Krizeks acted with reckless disregard.

111 F.3d at 942.

[86] 31 F. Supp. 2d 1308 (W.D. Okla. 1998).

In *United States v. Mackby*,[87] defendant, a nonphysician owner of a physical therapy clinic, used the provider identification number of his father, a physician who did not perform services at the clinic, when presenting health care claims to the government. The defendant claimed that he did not knowingly submit false claims to the government because he had asked his office manager to contact Medicare to find out about the appropriate payment rules and had also, on two occasions, requested that the clinic's billing number be changed to a physical therapist who worked at the clinic but that the request was denied. The court ruled that the defendant submitted claims in reckless disregard or in deliberate ignorance of the law. Specifically, the court reasoned: defendant

> was the managing director of the clinic. He was responsible for day-to-day operations, long-term planning, lease and build-out negotiations, personnel, and legal and accounting oversight. It was his obligation to be familiar with the legal requirements for obtaining reimbursement from Medicare for physical therapy services, and to ensure that the clinic was run in accordance with all laws. His claim that he did not know of the Medicare requirements does not shield him from liability. By failing to inform himself of those requirements, particularly when twenty percent of [the] Clinic's patients were Medicare beneficiaries, he acted in reckless disregard or in deliberate ignorance of those requirements, either of which was sufficient to charge him with knowledge of the falsity of the claims in question.[88]

A significant development in the 1986 FCA amendments was Congress's clarification that specific intent to defraud the government is not an essential element for liability under the FCA. Prior to the 1986 amendments, a defendant could escape liability by demonstrating that although the claims were erroneous (i.e., false), there was no liability because the provider did not consciously intend to cheat the government.[89] As *Krizek*, *Trim*, and *Mackby* illustrate, the government or relator can now prevail in a claim by pointing to the defendant's practices that perhaps were not tailored toward the submission of truthful claims even if the defect resulted from a lack of supervision or due care rather than an express desire to cheat the government. Therefore, given these judicial decisions, those who delegate responsibility for billing and claims processing without providing any controls aimed toward ascertaining the truthfulness of the claims being submitted may be at risk under the reckless disregard portion of the FCA's standard for acting knowingly.[90]

---

[87]261 F.3d 821 (9th Cir. 2001).

[88]*Id.* at 828 (citation omitted).

[89]*See, e.g.*, United States v. Davis, 809 F.2d 1509 (11th Cir. 1987); United States v. Mead, 426 F.2d 118 (9th Cir. 1970).

[90]*See also* United States *ex rel.* Hays v. Hoffman, 325 F.3d 982 (8th Cir. 2003); United States v. Cabrera-Diaz, 106 F. Supp. 2d 234 (D.P.R. 2000). In *Hays,* the Eighth Circuit, while acknowledging that the "knowing violation in this case is very close," still found that when viewing the evidence most favorable to the jury's verdict, that the evidence that some

## 2. Deliberate Ignorance

If the defendant is aware of the government's interpretation or policy, and submits claims in violation of that interpretation or policy—even if she genuinely believes her interpretation is superior—the defendant is likely to be found liable under the FCA.

The leading case is *Visiting Nurse Ass'n of Brooklyn v. Thompson.*[91] In that case, CMS, in a *Provider Reimbursement Manual* (PRM) provision, interpreted a cost reporting regulation to require home health service providers to include only "Medicare-type" services in reporting the costs of services rendered to non-Medicare patients for the purpose of securing reimbursement for home health services rendered to Medicare beneficiaries.[92]

The providers contended that their claims were not knowingly false because they reasonably believed that the PRM provision was invalid be-

---

costs claimed on the cost report resulted from a "haphazard, unsupervised process" supported a finding that defendants submitted claims with reckless disregard of the truth or falsity of the claims:

> [the defendants'] internal accountants knew employee gifts were not reimbursable under the applicable Medicaid rules; (ii) gift apple invoices for a number of years were entered on [defendants'] general ledger accounts as "resident food"; and (iii) [the relator] and at least one other employee asked whether these purchases should instead be entered as employee gifts and were told by [the chief executive officer ("CEO")] to continue entering them as food. Defendants countered this showing with evidence that employees who prepared the Medicaid cost reports . . . were expected to exclude any non-reimbursable items entered in multi-purpose general ledger accounts such as the food account. But there was also evidence this was a haphazard, unsupervised process, permitting the jury to infer that, when [the CEO] told employees to enter gift apples in the general ledger as resident food, he knew this would result in Medicaid cost reports that improperly included this item as a reimbursable food expense.

325 F.3d at 991 (footnote omitted). In *Cabrera-Diaz*, the United States filed a motion for a judgment of default. The district court concluded that the defendants were liable under the FCA because an audit conducted by the fiscal agent demonstrated that 455 of the 461 sampled claims "had been overstated, falsely reported, unsupported or undocumented." 106 F. Supp. 2d at 238. As a result of this error rate, the district court concluded that the defendants either had actual knowledge or acted in reckless disregard or deliberate ignorance of the truth or falsity of the information in submitting claims to the United States:

> Th[e audit] demonstrates that Dr. Cabrera, the anesthesiologist that billed Medicare for this [sic] services, and Arbona, his billing secretary, had either actual knowledge or constructive knowledge of the falsity, in that they acted in reckless disregard of the truth, or certified information (anesthesia time) in support of the claims with neither personal knowledge of its accuracy nor reasonable investigative efforts. It appears that either they acted with actual knowledge that the information was false, or hided [sic] behind a shield of self-imposed ignorance. Dr. Cabrera cannot escape liability on the basis of lack of knowledge of the fraud when he has purposefully turn the blind eye of [sic] the conduct of Arbona, his subordinate.

*Id. Cf.* United States *ex rel.* Norbeck v. Basin Elec. Power Coop., 2001 WL 432211, at \*7 (8th Cir. Apr. 30, 2001). In *Norbeck* the court refused to aggregate various overcharges into an FCA violation. Specifically, the court noted that "the district court's reliance on the 'small edges' taken by [the defendant] in the various areas of cost computation cannot support its decision. The district court found that all of [the defendant's] other overcharges were just 'simple contract breaches'. . . . But . . . the mere misinterpretation of a contract cannot be the basis of a False Claims Act violation. All of these other 'simple contract breaches,' therefore, cannot provide evidence of a knowing violation of the Act." (citation omitted).

[91]378 F. Supp. 2d 75 (E.D.N.Y. 2004).

[92]*Id.* at 77.

cause it was a substantive rule that should have been promulgated in accordance with the notice-and-comment provisions of the Administrative Procedures Act (APA).[93] Hence, they contended that because they reasonably believed that the PRM provision was invalid, their conduct was at most an innocent mistake and that the government's claim simply concerned a "dispute[] about the meaning of legal provisions or regulation," which could not create FCA liability.[94]

The court disagreed with the providers. As an initial matter, the court acknowledged that it "is true that FCA liability cannot attach where an incorrect submission results simply from a misunderstanding concerning what the applicable regulations require of a claimant."[95] However, the court found that this is not what occurred because, while "confusion apparently existed on the margins concerning the precise requirements of the new cost-reporting instructions . . . the Providers [did] not point[] to any evidence that they tried to comply with the new regulations, and somehow blundered in the attempt."[96] Instead, according to the court, the providers attempted "to hide behind the general 'abundance of confusion and misdirection' that they contend surrounded the issuance" of the PRM provision to argue that it "created blanket immunity for everyone ordered to comply with the new interpretation."[97] As a result, the court ruled that the providers had actual knowledge that their claims were false. Specifically, the court ruled that the providers gambled that:

> they could comply with the "regulatory directives in *effect at the time of the cost reports'* submission" while ignoring an interpretative directive that they viewed as invalid because it "was not promulgated pursuant to the APA" without incurring liability for certifying that they had complied with all applicable instructions . . . Astonishingly, the Providers now seek to employ that very gamble as a defense. Their argument is as follows: The Providers thought [the PRM provision] was invalid. As such, even though they were aware that they had been instructed to comply with [the PRM provision], they came to believe that that instruction was not applicable. As a result, when they certified that they had complied with all applicable instructions in preparing their 1995 and 1996 cost reports, they did not act with "actual knowledge" that their certification was false because the Providers were certifying only, albeit without making anyone aware of this neat distinction, that they had complied with all portions of the regulations that they felt were "correct and binding." . . . This constitutes chutzpah of the highest order. It is not, however, a valid defense to the charge that the Providers knowingly filed false statements. See *United States v. Weiss*, 914 F.2d 1514, 1522 (2d Cir. 1990) (holding that a person charged with filing false statements may not interpose a defense that the requirement to which he failed to conform was not validly issued); United States v. Calhoon, 97 F.3d 518, 529 (11th Cir. 1996) (holding that "while a provider may submit claims for costs that it knows to be presumptively nonreimbursable, it must do so openly and honestly, describing

---

[93]*Id.*
[94]*Id.* at 95.
[95]*Id.*
[96]*Id.*
[97]*Id.*

them accurately while challenging the presumption and seeking reimbursement").

This court finds that the Providers knew that [the PRM] was part of the governing standard for the submission of [home health agency] cost reports, and nonetheless, in an attempt to game the system, knowingly certified that they had complied with all applicable instructions in compiling their cost reports without attempting to conform their submissions for 1995 and 1996 to that standard. In doing so, the Providers had actual knowledge of the falsity of their certification, or, at best, acted in deliberate ignorance of the truth or falsity of their certification in hewing to the belief that [the PRM provision] was not an applicable instruction. In either case, as the [Magistrate] correctly concluded, they acted "knowingly" within the meaning of the FCA in submitting their 1995 and 1996 cost reports.

The Providers also argue that even if they "knew" that they had falsely certified that their submissions were compliant, FCA liability is still inappropriate because "disagreement about the interpretation of legal language . . . cannot be the basis for a FCA action." . . . This court agrees that, as a general rule, unresolved disputes about the proper interpretation of a statute or regulation should not lead to suits under the FCA, at least where a claimant's interpretation of the governing law is reasonable. *See, e.g., Hagood v. Sonoma County Water Agency,* 81 F.3d 1465, 1477–78 (9th Cir. 1996). This court cannot agree, however, that the safe harbor created for those who rely on a reasonable interpretation of an ambiguous provision also should provide protection where the agency responsible for administering the applicable law or regulation has publicly issued a definitive interpretation intended to resolve that ambiguity. The FCA would be rendered toothless overnight if parties claiming federal funds were permitted to rely on any reasonable interpretation of a regulation they might prefer, even it if directly conflicted with an agency's official interpretation of the same law. This court will not countenance such a result. Rather, I believe that FCA liability is inappropriate only where a claimant has reasonably relied on its interpretation of the law, and that such reliance becomes presumptively unreasonable once the government has formally declared that it has adopted a different interpretation.[98]

---

[98] *Id.* at 95–96 (citations omitted) (emphasis in original). Other courts have similarly ruled that where the defendant knows of the government's interpretation of a rule, regulation, or standard and does not adhere to it, the defendant may have acted in deliberate ignorance or reckless disregard of the truth or falsity of the claim. *See, e.g.,* United States *ex rel.* Plumbers & Steam. v. C.W. Roen Const., 183 F.3d 1088 (9th Cir. 1999), *cert. denied,* 530 U.S. 1203 (2000). There, the relator, a union, alleged that the defendants violated the FCA by falsely certifying that the company paid the applicable prevailing wage, as required by the Davis Bacon Act and related federal laws, when in fact the defendant company had paid its employees at a lower rate. *Id.* at 1090. Specifically, the relator alleged that the defendants had falsely represented that the workers performing piping work were "Laborers" rather than "Plumbers." As support for their contention, the relator pointed out that two unions, the Plumbers union and the Laborers union, had entered into a jurisdictional agreement, which provided that those performing pipe work would be classified as Plumbers—Steamfitters. *Id.* Subsequently, representatives of the Department of Labor had concurred in that agreement. *Id.* at 1090–91. The letter manifesting the government's concurrence was sent to the union, which then transmitted the letter to the defendant company, thereby furnishing the company with notice of the government's position. *Id.* at 1091. Prior to the

Congress inserted a deliberate ignorance standard into the FCA in 1986 when it amended the statute's intent standard. Congress's apparent goal was to capture within the scope of the statute those instances in which providers, when confronted with potential "red flags," avoided obtaining additional information that would reveal whether the claim was in fact truthful.[99] Unlike the recklessly disregardful conduct standard, which does not require willful conduct, the deliberate ignorance standard, by its plain meaning, requires at a minimum that the person intentionally—"deliberate[ly]"—refrained from obtaining additional information. As *Visiting Nurse Ass'n of Brooklyn* illustrates, on becoming cognizant of a potential issue involving a significant amount of money, it is important for the provider to conform its practices to the government's rules and regulations even if thought to be mistaken, because failing to do so may increase the chances of being accused of deliberately ignoring those circumstances. In the current fraud enforcement environment, ignorance is no longer bliss.

## 3. Defenses Demonstrating Lack of Knowledge

The government has a heavy burden in demonstrating that claims are false or fraudulent and that a provider knowingly submitted such claims. As the U.S.

---

time in which the company had submitted any certification, however, one of the unions had withdrawn its concurrence in the agreement. *Id.* However, the government, in a subsequent letter, reconfirmed that the relevant wage classifications were those set forth in the two unions' agreement. *Id.* Finally, shortly after the time charged in the complaint, the government wrote that it would not enforce the initial jurisdictional agreement because there were "indications that the written agreement was not followed." *Id.*

The defendants contended that they could not have knowingly submitted false information to the United States because one union had rescinded its concurrence in the agreement and the government subsequently acknowledged that the written agreement had not been followed. These facts demonstrated the uncertainty regarding what the prevailing wage in the first instance should be. The Ninth Circuit rejected defendants' contention and reversed the district court's grant of summary judgment in defendants' favor. The Ninth Circuit believed that the government's letter, which had established a higher wage and which was transmitted to defendants, suggested that the company's "certification may well have risen at least to the level of 'deliberate ignorance' or 'reckless disregard,' " rendering summary judgment inappropriate. *Id.* at 1094–95. Specifically, in light of the clarity of the government's position, the court found that the defendants, based upon the record before the district court when it granted their summary judgment motion, had failed to establish that they did not know that the underlying certification was false:

> If [the company] believed that the [union's] attempted recission of the Agreement affected the [government's] classifications during the period covered by the complaint, it could have sought clarification. Yet [the company], without making any effort to obtain such clarification, certified that the Laborer's rate was the prevailing wage and that it had paid that wage. [The company] does not explain the theory under which it certified that the Laborer's rate constituted the prevailing wage rate— even [the company] acknowledges that the Department of Labor is the sole authority responsible for determining prevailing wages . . . and the DOL's letter had adopted a different and higher rate. This suggests that [the company's] certification may well have risen at least to the level of "deliberate ignorance" or "reckless disregard."

*Id.*

[99] *See generally* H.R. REP. NO. 99-660, at 2, 20–21 (1986); 132 CONG. REC. 22,339 (Sept. 9, 1986) (providers are liable when they ignore "red flags" and "play 'ostrich' " by burying "their heads in the sand to insulate themselves from the knowledge a prudent person should have before submitting a claim to the Government") (statement of Rep. Berman).

Supreme Court has cautioned, the FCA is "not designed to reach every kind of fraud practiced on the Government."[100] This is because the statute, which the Senate Judiciary Committee characterized at the time of the 1986 legislative amendments as being remedial in nature, could conceivably be applied in a penal fashion.[101] Thus, some courts have strictly construed the statute's false or fraudulent and knowing elements.[102]

---

[100]United States v. McNinch, 356 U.S. 595, 599 (1958).

[101]In amending the Act's knowledge standard, the Senate Judiciary Committee pointed out the following:

> As a civil remedy designed to make the Government whole for fraud *losses*, the civil False Claims Act currently provides that the Government need only prove that the defendant knowingly submitted a false claim. However, this standard has been construed by some courts to require that the Government prove the defendant had actual knowledge of fraud, and even to establish that the defendant had specific intent to submit a false claim.... The Committee believes this standard is inappropriate in a civil remedy....
>
>      The Committee's interest is not only to adopt a more uniform standard, but a more appropriate standard for *remedial* actions.

S. REP. NO. 99-345 at 6–7, *reprinted in* 1986 U.S.C.C.A.N. at 5271–72 (emphasis added).

[102]*See* United States *ex rel.* Weinberger v. Equifax, 557 F.2d 456, 460 (5th Cir. 1977) ("The penal nature of the statute requires careful scrutiny to see if the alleged misconduct violates the statute."); United States v. Bottini, 19 F. Supp. 2d 632, 640 (W.D. La. 1997) ("The statute is penal in nature and must be strictly construed."), *aff'd without op.*, 159 F.3d 1357 (5th Cir. 1998); United States *ex. rel.* Pogue v. American Healthcorp, Inc., 914 F. Supp. at 1511 (M.D. Tenn. 1996) (Because of possible penal application of statute, "a number of courts have denied application of the False Claims Act in particular situations, although a claimant has engaged in fraudulent conduct.") Further, the Supreme Court emphasized that merely an application of the treble damage and civil penalty provision of the FCA could result in a penal application of the statute. *See* Vermont Agency of Natural Res. v. United States, 529 U.S. 765, 785–86 (2000) ("[T]he current version of the FCA imposes damages that are essentially punitive in nature.... Although this Court suggested that damages under an earlier version of the FCA were remedial rather than punitive...that version of the statute imposed only double damages and a civil penalty of $2,000 per claim...the current version, by contrast, generally imposes treble damages and a civil penalty of up to $10,000 per claim.... The very idea of treble damages reveals an intent to punish past, and to deter future, unlawful conduct, not to ameliorate the liability of wrongdoers.") (citations, footnotes, and internal quotation omitted). Besides the effect on the construction of the FCA's knowledge standard, the characterization of the FCA as a penal statute will have a number of other effects in interpreting the provisions of the FCA. For example, courts will apply Rule 9(b) more literally and strictly in FCA jurisprudence, *see generally* United States v. Cheng, 184 F.R.D. 399, 401 (D.N.M. 1998) (pointing out that courts "must be particularly attentive to the heightened pleading requirement in a case brought under the False Claims Act since the Act carries heavy penal consequences"); *see also* SALCIDO, FALSE CLAIMS ACT COUNSELING: OCT. 2003 SUPP., at §3:09 (discussing application of Rule 9(b) to the FCA); courts will be less inclined to apply vicarious liability, *see* United States v. Southern Md. Home Health Servs., 95 F. Supp. 2d 465, 468–69 (D. Md. 2000) (when the recovery sought by the Government is substantially higher than its actual losses, an employer is not vicariously liable under the FCA for wrongful acts undertaken by a non-*managerial* employee unless the employer had knowledge of her acts, ratified them, or was reckless in its hiring or supervision of the employee); finally, courts will be less inclined to apply the FCA's treble damages and civil penalty provisions because the penal application of these provisions could run afoul of the Excessive Fines Clause, *see* United States v. Mackby, 261 F.3d 821, 830–31 (9th Cir. 2001) ("We conclude the civil sanctions provided by the False Claims Act are subject to analysis under the Excessive Fines Clause because sanctions represent a payment to the government, at least in part, as punishment. Inquiry must be made, therefore, to determine whether the payment required by the district court is so grossly disproportionate to the gravity of [the defendant's] violation as to violate the Eighth Amendment.... [And] [w]e conclude that the FCA's treble damages provision is, like the

Following are a number of defenses that parties have used to disprove an FCA plaintiff's theory that a provider knowingly submitted a false claim.[103] Specifically, defendants may demonstrate that they were no more than negligent in confirming entitlement to government funds; that the government knew and approved of the questioned transactions; that the regulatory guidance underlying payment was ambiguous; or that the defendants reasonably relied upon legal opinions in claiming reimbursements.

### a. Merely Negligent Conduct Does Not Result in Liability Under the FCA

In *Hindo v. University of Health Sciences/The Chicago Medical School*,[104] a medical school was informed by the Department of Veterans Affairs (VA) that although there were no guarantees, funding for radiology residents would likely be approved. On the basis of this representation, the medical school included two radiology residencies in its submissions to the national resident matching program. During the academic year, the radiology residents worked at a VA-funded hospital that did not protest their presence. The medical school requested funding for the residents and received payment from the VA-funded hospital. Subsequently, when the VA-funded hospital learned that it had mistakenly made payment for the radiology residents because it had not received authorization from the VA, it demanded—and received—reimbursement from the medical school for the overpayment. The court held that although the medical school may have been negligent in not ascertaining whether funding had been approved before it invoiced the VA-funded hospital, the medical school did not commit fraud against the government because it believed, based on the VA's prior assurances and the fact that the residents were permitted to work full time during the academic year, that funding had in fact been authorized.

There are occasions on which a provider may mistakenly fail to confirm entitlement to federal funds. However, Congress expressly provided that mere negligence is not actionable under the FCA.[105] Thus, in instances in which the plaintiff's contention is simply that the defendant's business practices could or should have been more efficient or effective, the plaintiff cannot state a cause of action under the FCA.[106]

---

statutory penalty provision, not solely remedial and therefore subject to an Excessive Fines Clause analysis under the Eighth Amendment. Accordingly, we remand to the district court for its consideration of the question whether a treble damage award in this case would be unconstitutionally excessive.") (citation omitted); *see also* SALCIDO, FALSE CLAIMS ACT COUNSELING, at §3:05; SALCIDO, FALSE CLAIMS ACT COUNSELING: OCT. 2003 SUPP., at §3:05.

[103] Of course, some of these defenses may also be used to disprove the falsity element of the FCA.

[104] 65 F.3d 608 (7th Cir. 1995).

[105] 132 CONG. REC. 20,536 (Aug. 11, 1986) (Congress settled upon the "reckless disregard" standard "to assure that mere negligence, mistake, and inadvertence are not actionable under the False Claims Act.") (statement of Sen. Grassley).

[106] *See, e.g.*, United States *ex rel.* Hochman v. Nackman, 145 F.3d 1069, 1074 (9th Cir. 1998); Luckey v. Baxter Healthcare Corp., 2 F. Supp. 2d 1034, 1049 (N.D. Ill. 1998) (even if defendant's certifications were false because its testing procedures did not ensure pure plasma, its certifications did not result in FCA liability because they were the product of "defendant's good faith professional opinion or judgment" and the FCA "prevents [the] Court from converting what at best can be called [defendant's] negligence into a lie"), *aff'd*, 183 F.3d 730 (7th Cir.

In *United States ex rel.* Mikes v. Straus,[107] the Second Circuit considered the issue of whether the defendants' submission of "worthless" spirometry services could constitute a violation of the FCA. As an initial matter, the court concurred with the relator that if the defendants' spirometry was so deficient as to be "worthless," the defendants' claims would be false. However, the court found no liability because the relator "makes no showing that defendants knowingly—as the Act defines that term—submitted a claim for the reimbursement of worthless services" and "adopted the Ninth Circuit's standard that the 'requisite intent is the knowing presentation of what is known to be false' as opposed to negligence or innocent mistake."[108]

Specifically, the court noted that "[t]he notion of presenting a claim known to be false does not mean the claim is incorrect as a matter of proper accounting, but rather means it is a lie."[109] The court concluded that the relator could not satisfy that test because the defendants tendered evidence of their "genuine belief that their use of spirometry had medical value," such as the fact that a spirometers' instruction manual, which—contrary to the ATS guidelines—indicated that daily calibration is not required and that individual spirometers had been sent out for periodic servicing. Because of this "good faith belief that their spirometry tests were of medical value," the court concluded that the relator's

---

1999). Other, nonhealth care cases similarly demonstrate that the government may not predicate FCA liability on the submission of mistaken claims. *See, e.g.*, United States *ex rel.* Norbeck v. Basin Elec. Power Coop., 2001 WL 432211, at *7 (8th Cir. Apr. 30, 2001) (even if an accounting error were committed, that does not necessarily result in FCA liability because even "if the district court was correct that the $99.5 million should have somehow been applied directly to debt charged to [the governmental entity], it provides no evidence that the audit team knew or acted in reckless disregard of the possibility that its assumption was incorrect. The audit team's deliberate choice of this assumption cannot be fraud if they honestly believed it was a correct assumption, and the district court does not point to any evidence suggesting that was the case"); *see also* United States *ex rel.* Rueter v. Sparks, 939 F. Supp. 636 (C.D. Ill. 1996), *aff'd mem.*, 111 F.3d 133 (7th Cir. 1997). In *Rueter*, the relator alleged that the defendants had misreported his time and wages on certified payroll records because the defendants reported that he received $18 per hour to perform his work operating heavy equipment when, for approximately one half hour per day, he received a rate of only $8 per hour because for that half hour he performed maintenance work on that equipment. The district court concluded that, at most, the defendants were merely negligent in reporting the time and wages as required by the Davis-Bacon Act and related statutes. The court noted that the government, during previous audits, had never informed the defendants that their method of reporting time and wages was erroneous and that the company did not receive guidance from the government on the proper method of reporting maintenance hours until several years after it had performed work on the government contract that was the subject of the lawsuit. *See generally* Haynes v. United States *ex rel.* Food & Nutrition Serv., 956 F. Supp. 1487 (E.D. Ark. 1995), *aff'd*, 106 F.3d 405 (8th Cir. 1997). In *Haynes*, the district court ruled that the owner of a general store could not be held responsible for the acts of managers of the store, the owner's mother and aunt, who improperly purchased food stamps, because he had no knowledge that they had illegally acquired, possessed, or redeemed food stamps. The court rejected the government's contention that the owner had "turned his back" to avoid learning of the misdeeds, ruling that at most the owner "could be said to have been negligent in failing to more closely monitor the store's compliance with the Food Stamp Act since his name remained on the license despite his lack of further involvement in running the store. Nonetheless, any negligence on his part would not rise to the level of 'reckless disregard.' Given that the store is run by his mother and aunt, it is conceivable that [he] would not have felt the need to monitor the business as closely as he might otherwise have done."

[107] 274 F.3d 687 (2d Cir. 2001).

[108] *Id.* at 703 (citing Hagood v. Sonoma County Water Agency, 81 F.3d 1465, 1478 (9th Cir. 1996)).

[109] *Id.* (citation omitted).

"unsupported allegations to the contrary [did] not raise a triable issue of fact sufficient to bar summary judgment."[110]

### b. The Government Cannot Predicate an FCA Action on Ambiguous Regulatory Guidance

*United States v. Krizek*[111] provides an example of when regulatory ambiguity eliminates FCA exposure. There the government contended that CPT code 90844 required 45 to 50 minutes of face-to-face patient contact. A psychiatrist, who admitted that he did not code according to the amount of face-to-face time he spent with patients, contended that the code only required that he work on cases for that period of time and could include time spent reviewing charts, speaking with relatives, and similar activities without direct patient contact. The court held that because the CPT itself, during the relevant time frame, did not use the term "face to face," and the CPT itself was "ambiguous," the government could not state a FCA cause of action.[112]

---

[110]*Id.* at 704 (citation omitted). *See also* United States *ex rel.* Perales v. St. Margaret's Hosp., 243 F. Supp. 2d 843, 866 (C.D. Ill. 2003) (defendant hospital did not bury "its head in the sand and willfully ignore[ ] the law" when "there is evidence that [it] received and considered relevant publications in this area of the law, established a corporate compliance committee, and routinely consulted counsel in drafting the contracts and agreements, which is suggestive of an intent to abide by the law"); United States *ex rel.* Watson v. Connecticut Gen. Life Ins. Co., No. 98-6698, 2003 U.S. Dist. LEXIS 2054, at *55 (E.D. Pa. Feb. 11, 2003) (rejecting the relator's contention that the defendant submitted false claims when 98.6% of the claims were correctly processed because the "high rate of accuracy undermines any contention that [the defendant] knowingly engaged in a pattern of failing" to adhere to the governing standard regarding claims submission), *aff'd,* 87 Fed. Appx. 257 (3d Cir. Jan. 16, 2004). However, a court may find that a defendant was more than negligent or did not act in good faith if the defendant receives notice that a practice is potentially improper and, notwithstanding that notice, fails to act. *See, e.g.,* United States v. NHC Health Care Corp., 163 F. Supp. 2d 1051, 1058 (W.D. Mo. 2001) (ruling that based "upon complaints from staff, residents, surveyors and family members the Defendants knew or should have known that they had a staffing shortage that impinged upon their ability to properly care for their patients. Defendants also knew or should have known that if they did not have sufficient staff to properly care for their residents, then they should not have submitted bills to Medicare and Medicaid which represented that they provided such care") (footnote omitted). Significantly, the court seemingly imposed an affirmative duty on the defendants, once they received complaints, to investigate those complaints or otherwise to be charged with knowingly submitting false claims. *See id.* ("If Defendants had knowledge that they had severe staffing shortages at their facility, then they had a duty to investigate to see whether all their residents, including Residents 1 and 2, were getting the minimum standard of care to which they were entitled. A reasonable jury could conclude from the record before this Court that Defendants knew that the claims for reimbursement which they submitted were false because [the defendant long term care facility] acted in reckless indifference as to whether Residents 1 and 2 were receiving all the care they were entitled to under Medicare and Medicaid. Finally, the Court holds that an entity who is charging the Government for a minimum amount of care provided to its residents should question whether understaffing might lead to undercare. The knowledge of the answer to that question is charged to the Defendants when they submitted their Medicare and Medicaid claim forms.").

[111]859 F. Supp. 5, 9–10 (D.D.C. 1994), *aff'd in part, rev'd in part,* 111 F.3d 934 (D.C. Cir. 1997).

[112]The court further pointed out:

The Court will not impose False Claims Act liability based on such a strained interpretation of the CPT codes. The government's theory of liability is plainly unfair and unjustified. Medical doctors should be appropriately reimbursed for services legitimately provided. They should be given clear guidance as to what services are reimbursable. The system should be fair. The system cannot be so arbitrary,

The myriad, cumbersome rules governing state and federal health care programs are not a model of clarity. At times prudent health care providers will attempt in good faith to comply fully with the rules, but because of the inherent ambiguity in the rules, will act in accordance with an incorrect interpretation of the law. Under these circumstances, as *Krizek* illustrates, the provider will have a viable defense under the FCA if, notwithstanding the ambiguity of the rules, the actions in question are consistent with a plausible interpretation of the law.[113]

### c. Government Knowledge May Provide a Defense

In *United States ex rel. Bennett v. Genetics & IVF Institute*,[114] the defendant's contract with the state mandated that the defendant conduct two tests

---

so perverse, as to subject a doctor whose annual income during the relevant period averaged between $100,000 and $120,000 dollars, to potential liability in excess of 80 million dollars.

*Id.* at 9–10. However, although the court did not find the defendants guilty on this claim, the court did nonetheless find that the defendants had violated the FCA as a result of submitting an excessive—erroneous—number of claims to the government (i.e., because of inadequate office procedures the defendant psychiatrist had billed, on occasion, for more than 20 hours of services within a 24-hour period). *Id.* at 12.

[113]*Id.* at 10–11 (footnote omitted). *See also* Hagood v. Sonoma County Water Agency, 81 F.3d 1465, 1477 (9th Cir. 1996) (when statute grants government discretion to allocate costs, contractor's reliance on the government's exercise of discretion in allocating costs does not render claim false because all that existed was proof of "a disputed legal issue," which is not enough "to support a reasonable inference" that the claim "was *false* within the meaning of the False Claims Act") (emphasis added); United States v. Data Translation, Inc., 984 F.2d 1256 (1st Cir. 1992) (when supplier's actions conformed with industry practice and were otherwise reasonable, the government could not state a cause of action under the FCA); United States *ex rel.* Swafford v. Borgess Med. Ctr., 98 F. Supp. 2d 822, 831–32 (W.D. Mich. 2000) (where the relator had contended that to bill for an "interpretation or reading" of the "results of the test" of ultrasound studies, the defendant physicians must do more than merely rely upon the findings of the technician and independently review the supporting data from which the technician arrived at her conclusions, the court rejected the relator's claim because it found that those terms were undefined and ambiguous and that the relator's position "devolves to a dispute over the meaning of the terms governing the delivery of the professional component of physicians services" and that such a "legal dispute is . . . insufficient" to establish FCA liability); United States v. Napco Int'l, Inc., 835 F. Supp. 493, 498 (D. Minn. 1993) (because underlying regulation was ambiguous, the court would not permit the government to apply "an interpretative afterthought by the agency" against the contractor in an FCA action); *In re* Genesis Health Ventures, Inc., 272 B.R. 558, 570 (Bankr. D. Del. 2002) ("In this murky area in which no specificity exists in the statutory, regulatory or contractual scheme regarding the provision of credits, with no request by either the state or federal government for unpaid credit, either by way of the filing of proofs of claim or otherwise, there is insufficient basis to charge the debtors with the requisite scienter required to establish a factually false certification."). In asserting the FCA defense of legal ambiguity, the defendants initially have the burden to establish that the pertinent legal standards are ambiguous. If established, then the burden switches to the government (or the relator) to demonstrate that the defendant knew that the statement was false notwithstanding the ambiguity. *See, e.g.,* United States *ex rel.* Minnesota Ass'n of Nurse Anesthetists v. Allina Health Sys., 276 F.3d 1032, 1053 (8th Cir. 2002) ("If a statement alleged to be false is ambiguous, the government (or here, the relator) must establish the defendant's knowledge of the falsity of the statement, which it can do by introducing evidence of how the statement would have been understood in context. . . . If the [relator] shows the defendants certified compliance with the regulation knowing that the HCFA interpreted the regulations in a certain way and that their actions did not satisfy the requirements of the regulations as the HCFA interpreted it, any possible ambiguity of the regulations is water under the bridge.") (citations omitted).

[114]No. 98-2119, 1999 U.S. App. LEXIS 27911 (4th Cir. Oct. 28, 1999).

in providing paternity testing. However, the defendant only conducted one test because the DNA test it used, unlike the type of test originally contemplated, did not scientifically require a second test to ensure accuracy. Because the defendant had openly disclosed to the government what its practice would be (i.e., that it would only conduct one test), the court ruled that the government's knowledge undermined the relator's claim that the defendant acted with the requisite intent to violate the FCA.

At times a provider's conduct may not be entirely consistent with the government's rules and regulations. If the provider discloses the discrepancy to the government and attempts to resolve the issue, it is less likely that the provider will be accused of attempting to deceive the government because those who actually attempt to defraud or deceive the government typically do not inform the government in advance of their actions. For example, it is difficult to contend that a provider acted recklessly or in deliberate ignorance when it informed the government of its actions and attempted to create a dialogue regarding the matter. Thus, although the government-knowledge defense is not a dispositive defense to FCA liability because it is the provider's knowledge— and not necessarily the government's—that matters, proof of government knowledge tends to demonstrate that the provider did not act with the requisite intent to violate the FCA.[115]

In 2002, the Tenth Circuit, in *United States ex rel. Stone v. Rockwell International Corp.,*[116] considered the government knowledge defense in the context of the defendant's challenge to the district court's jury instruction. Specifically, after informing the jury that in order for the defendant to be liable for an FCA violation, the plaintiffs must establish that "Rockwell knew that the statements it made or used or caused to be made or used were false," the judge instructed the jury that:

> Defendant claims that the government, through various employees of the Department of Energy, had prior knowledge of facts relating to the false statements that defendant allegedly made ... at [its facility]. The government denies the existence of such prior knowledge. In considering whether Rockwell knowingly made any false statements, you must consider all direct and circumstantial evidence, if any, concerning whether one or more government employees with authority to act under the Rockwell contracts with DOE knew the relevant facts ... and the costs incurred relating to those activities.

---

[115]*See also* United States *ex rel.* Durcholz v. FKW, Inc., 189 F.3d 542, 545 (7th Cir. 1999) ("If the government knows and approves of the particulars of a claim for payment before that claim is presented, the presenter cannot be said to have knowingly presented a fraudulent or false claim. In such a case, the government's knowledge effectively negates the fraud or falsity required by the FCA."); United States *ex rel.* Butler v. Hughes Helicopters, Inc., 71 F.3d 321 (9th Cir. 1995) (where the contractor disclosed to the Army various nonconforming tests and the Army officials on site had approved of the tests, the government's knowledge defeated any inference that the defendant "knowingly" presented false claims to the government); Wang *ex rel.* United States v. FMC Corp., 975 F.2d 1412, 1421 (9th Cir. 1992) (that the government knew of the defendant's "mistakes and limitations, and that [defendant] was open with the Government about them, suggests that while [defendant] might have been groping for solutions, it was not cheating the Government in its effort").

[116]282 F.3d 787 (10th Cir. 2002), *rev'd other grounds*, 127 S. Ct. 1397 (2007).

Government knowledge may negate the intent by defendant required to establish a violation of the False Claims Act. If you find that government employees with authority to act under the contracts knew the relevant facts, then you may consider it in determining whether Rockwell knowingly presented a false statement to those facts.[117]

The defendant claimed that the instruction was faulty because it seemingly only applied to knowledge of those who had "authority to act" and thus precluded the jury from considering any knowledge obtained by mid- and lower-level government employees.[118] The district court disagreed with the defendant's contention, ruling that "there is nothing in the instructions indicating that the jury was under the impression that they were prohibited from considering [the defendant's] evidence that mid and lower-level [government] employees knew of the environmental, health and safety violations at [the defendant's facility]."[119]

---

[117]*Id.* at 811–12 n.10.

[118]*Id.*

[119]*Id.* at 812. *See generally* United States *ex rel.* Stebner v. Stewart & Stephenson Servs., 144 Fed. Appx. 389, 394 (5th Cir. 2005) (no false claim submitted when "the Government was involved in the design, production, testing, and modification of the [product]; and [the company] and the Government negotiated contract modifications in response to the well-documented ... problem. The Government retained, and exercised, its discretion to conditionally accept or refuse to accept [the product] that did not meet contractual standards; and the [government form] was not signed by the Government until it was ready to accept [the product]") (citation omitted); United States *ex rel.* Costner v. URS Consultants, 317 F.3d 883, 888 (8th Cir. 2003) ("The record shows that the EPA discussed these problems with the defendants and referred the matter to OSHA for investigation and possible sanctions. Although the record indicates that the defendants' performance under the contract was not perfect, the extent of the government's knowledge through its on-site personnel and other sources shows that ... the government knew what it wanted, and it got what it paid for.... Thus, the district court did not err in finding that the defendants' openness with the EPA about their problems and their close working relationship in solving the problems negated the required scienter regarding these issues.") (citation and internal quotation omitted); United States *ex rel.* Becker v. Westinghouse Savannah River, 305 F.3d 284, 289 (4th Cir. 2002) ("we join with our sister circuits and hold that the government's knowledge of the facts underlying an allegedly false record or statement can negate the scienter required for an FCA violation" and hence the government's "full knowledge of the material facts underlying any representations implicit in [the defendant's] conduct negates any knowledge that [the defendant] had regarding the truth or falsity of those representations"); United States *ex rel.* Burlbaw v. Orenduff, 400 F. Supp. 2d 1276, 1285 (D.N.M. 2005) ("Neither negligent misstatements nor innocent mistakes are sufficient to establish liability under the FCA.... Where the government has assured a contracting party that a certain fact is true, and the contracting party has no reason to doubt the government's assurances, it is not a reckless or deliberate falsehood to rely on those assurances in making a claim to the government.") (citations omitted); United States *ex rel.* Grynberg v. Praxair, Inc., 207 F. Supp. 2d 1163, 1181 (D. Colo. 2001) (the relator's "allegations all relate to conduct or concerns that the government has known about and approved. [Governmental payment] based on these disclosed and approved practices cannot reasonably be treated as 'knowingly false' statements meant to reduce [payment] obligations to the government"), *aff'd in part and rev'd on other grounds*, 389 F.3d 1038 (10th Cir. 2004). *See also* United States v. Medica-Rents Co., 285 F. Supp. 2d 742 (N.D. Tex. 2003). In *Medica-Rents,* the district court concluded that in light of the defendants' inquiries of governmental agents and willingness to follow the government's instructions, there was no issue of material fact regarding whether the defendants knowingly submitted false claims to the government:

> Having concluded that the defendants did not have actual knowledge that they could not bill for the ROHO Mattress Overlay under code E0277, the next issue is whether the defendants acted in deliberate ignorance that the ROHO Mattress Overlay could not be billed under code E0277. The plaintiffs claim that suppliers have a duty to familiarize themselves with the legal requirements for

### d. The Defendants' Reliance on Sound Legal Theory Negates an Inference of Fraud

*United States ex rel. Hochman v. Nackman*[120] provides an example of this defense. There the VA had permitted scarce-specialty pay for physicians who practice in high-demand fields. According to the applicable VA guidelines, the physician must work in the specialty area to obtain such pay. However, according to the applicable VA policy handbook, the physician must use the specialty in direct patient care to obtain the pay. The defendants argued that the physician earned the pay because he worked the requisite time within his specialty area by creating preoperative and postoperative procedures and supervising other physicians, although he did not work in direct patient care. The court held that the relators did not state a cause of action under the FCA. "Absent evidence that the defendants knew that the [guidelines] on which they relied did not apply, or that the defendants were deliberately indifferent to or recklessly disregardful of the alleged inapplicability of those provisions, no False Claims Act liability can be found" because to "take advantage of a disputed legal question, as may have happened here, is to be neither deliberately ignorant nor recklessly disregardful."[121]

---

Medicare reimbursement, and to clarify any ambiguous or doubtful guidance they receive from Medicare carrier representatives. The plaintiffs further state that a supplier that fails to inform itself of the reimbursement requirements acts in reckless disregard of the truth of its claims. The plaintiffs claim that the evidence shows that Medica-Rents and Walsh knew that code E0277 did not apply to the ROHO Mattress Overlay and that E1399 was the correct code. By not clarifying the ambiguous or doubtful guidance they received from Medicare carrier representatives to bill under code E0277, the plaintiffs assert that the defendants were acting with deliberate ignorance or reckless disregard.

As stated before, the evidence indicates that there was considerable confusion over what products could be billed under code E0277. Furthermore, the evidence clearly establishes that the defendants repeatedly sought advice on how to code the ROHO Mattress Overlay, and that they always followed the most current advice that they received. In addition, the evidence shows that the defendants, on many occasions, did seek clarification and did double-check coding advice that they received. The Court does not see what more can be expected of the defendants, except that they should be allowed to rely on advice they received from the government officials. There is no evidence that the defendants intentionally withheld information from the plaintiffs or purposely turned a blind eye to certain information in an attempt to file a false or fraudulent claim. Consequently, the Court concludes that there is no genuine issue of material fact as to whether the defendants acted with deliberate indifference or reckless disregard of the truth. They did not.

*Id.* at 775 (footnote omitted). Moreover, the court pointed out that "[a]lthough there is evidence that the defendants may not have explained the whole convoluted history relating to which carriers had allowed them to bill for the ROHO Mattress Overlay under which code, this evidence, without more, does not indicate that the defendants knowingly submitted, caused to be submitted, or conspired to submit false or fraudulent claims. It merely indicates that the defendants were actively trying to obtain permission to bill under a code that allowed them to make the most profit, which is not illegal." *Id.* at 773 n.67.

[120] 145 F.3d 1069 (9th Cir. 1998).

[121] *Id.* at 1073–74 (internal quotation and citation omitted). *See* United States *ex rel.* Siewick v. Jamieson Science & Eng'g, 214 F.3d 1372 (D.C. Cir. 2000). In *Siewick*, the relator asserted that the defendants' claims were implicitly false, because the defendant company had hired a former government employee who assisted the company to obtain government contracts in violation of 18 U.S.C. §207, a criminal statute aimed at "revolving door" abuses by former government employees. *Id.* at 1374–75. The court ruled that even if the relator's contention that a violation of §207 nullified the parties' contract, rendering each claim submitted under the contract to be false, the relator could not prove that the defendant "knowingly" breached the FCA because

In *United States ex rel. Bidani v. Lewis*,[122] the defendant doctor owned a dialysis facility that provided outpatient home dialysis services commonly known as "Method I" and a dialysis supply company that would contract with dialysis patients to provide necessary dialysis equipment and related supplies for self-administered home dialysis under a program commonly known as "Method II." The defendant doctor and his dialysis facility would refer patients to his dialysis supply company for participation in the Method II program. The defendant doctor and his companies had fully apprised their lawyers of the structure of the arrangement and had never been informed that the arrangement was unlawful until the Stark law became operational, at which time the arrangement ceased. The relator contended that the defendant doctor and his companies breached the FCA because the referrals breached the anti-kickback statute and that they breached the FCA because the dialysis supply company did not qualify as a proper supplier because of the doctor's common ownership of both companies. The court ruled that the relator could not prove that the defendants acted with the requisite intent to violate the FCA because, based on advice of counsel, they had a good faith belief that the arrangement complied with the applicable laws and regulations.[123]

---

the legal effect of a breach of §207 to the parties' contract was one of "only legal argumentation and possibility" and "opinion" and hence could not result in a violation of the FCA. *Id.* at 1378. *See also* United States *ex rel.* Hagood v. Sonoma County Water Agency, 929 F.2d 1416, 1421 (9th Cir. 1991). In that case, the court pointed out that although the defendant may have relied on a legal theory that a statute did not govern its contract with the government (and thus, contrary to the relator's claim, it had properly allocated costs on its contract with the government), the Ninth Circuit found that the defendant's defense, if proven, would be dispositive:

> What is crucial—and what must be proven at trial—is that the [defendant] knew that the information was false. . . . Innocent mistake is a defense to the criminal charge or civil complaint. So is mere negligence. The statutory definition of "knowingly" requires at least "deliberate ignorance" or "reckless disregard." To take advantage of a disputed legal question, as may have happened here, is to be neither deliberately ignorant nor recklessly disregardful.

*See generally* United States *ex rel.* Will v. A Plus Benefits, Inc., 139 Fed. Appx. 980, 984 (10th Cir. 2005) ("Expression of a legal opinion, in this case depending, as it does, on the resolution of two sets of inherently ambiguous determinations by defendants, cannot form the basis for an FCA claim."); United States *ex rel.* Burlbaw v. Orenduff, 400 F. Supp. 2d 1276, 1288 (D.N.M. 2005) ("Where disputed legal issues arise from vague provisions or regulations, a contractor's decision to take advantage of a position can not result in his filing a knowingly false claim.") (internal quotations and citations omitted). *Cf.* Harrison v. Westinghouse Savannah River Co., 176 F.3d 776, 792 (4th Cir. 1999).

[122]No. 97 C 6502, 2001 U.S. Dist. LEXIS 260 (N.D. Ill. Jan. 11, 2001), *reh'g granted in part, denied in part,* 2001 U.S. Dist. LEXIS 9204 (N.D. Ill. June 29, 2001).

[123]Specifically, in granting summary judgment to the defendants, the court reasoned that because of the level of communications flowing from the defendants to their attorneys regarding Medicare rules and regulations, the relator could not prove that the defendants "knowingly presented or knowingly caused to be presented any false Medicare claims":

> The undisputed evidence establishes that [the defendant doctor] sought the advice of attorneys in purchasing [the hospital's] dialysis facility, incorporating [the dialysis supply company] and [the facility company], and regarding the operations of [the supply company] as a dialysis supplier. The attorneys, who also did the incorporation work for [the supply company and the facility], were fully aware of the ownership relationship between the two entities and that one functioned as a Method I dialysis facility and one as a Method II dialysis supplier. There is no indication that [the defendant

At times, the law underlying a claim for reimbursement will be subject to dispute. As *Hochman* illustrates, when a provider acts in accordance with one interpretation of the law, even if the government or whistleblower may tenably point to some other equally applicable provision of law, the FCA plaintiff is unlikely to succeed. Similarly, as *Bidani* illustrates, if a provider's actions are based on a legal opinion, it is unlikely that the provider's conduct could be actionable under the FCA. A similar application of these principles was applied in *Tyger Construction Co. v. United States.*[124] There the court rejected the government's contention that the FCA reached "false" legal opinions. In that case, the plaintiff had submitted a number of claims to the government, some of which were based on legal theories, specifically that its construction work complied with the contract specifications and that the project was substantially complete.[125] The government filed a counterclaim alleging violations of the FCA. The court struck those paragraphs of the government's counterclaim that did not allege misrepresentations of fact but misrepresentations of law:

> The principle is fundamental that fraud cannot be predicated upon the mere expression of an opinion. . . . Attaching FCA liability to expressions of legal opinion would have an impermissibly stifling effect on the legitimate presentation of claims. Indication is absent that Congress intended to penalize disputes over contract liability.[126]

---

doctor] hid from the attorneys any pertinent facts regarding the ownership relationship. [The defendant doctor] was continually advised that his operations were lawful and, when advised of changes in applicable statutes and regulations, [he] accordingly revised his conduct. When finally advised that the ownership relationship would be unlawful under a new statute [i.e., the Stark law], [the supply company] ceased operations before the new statute went into effect. The only reasonable inference that can be drawn from the undisputed evidence is that [the defendant doctor] (and the entities he controlled) had no actual knowledge during the pertinent time period that the common ownership either prohibited [the defendant doctor] from referring patients to [the supply company] or that [the supply company] failed to qualify as a dialysis supplier because of the common ownership. Neither can it be inferred that [the defendant doctor] deliberately ignored or acted in reckless disregard of the truth. Therefore, it cannot be found that [the defendant doctor] knowingly presented or knowingly caused to be presented any false Medicare claims and defendants are entitled to summary judgment on the remaining FCA claims.

2001 U.S. Dist. LEXIS 260, at *35–36.

[124]28 Fed. Cl. 35 (1993).

[125]*Id.* at 56.

[126]*Id.* (internal quotation, footnote, and citation omitted). The court, however, did note that the legal opinion must be grounded in fact. For example, one could not assert based on a legal theory that the project was substantially completed when ground had not been broken. *Id.* at 56 n.29. *Cf.* United States v. Medco Physicians Unlimited, No. 98 C 1622, 2001 WL 293110 (N.D. Ill. Mar. 26, 2001). There the person signing the cost report had affixed an addendum to the cost report stating that the disputed meal and transportation costs had been included in the cost report because he believed that such inclusion was consistent "with regulations issued in February, 1994." *Id.* at *3. The court found that the person's statement was knowingly false because, when challenged, he could not "cite to any regulations in 1994" that supported his contention. *See also* United States v. Estate of Rogers, No. 1:97CV461, 2001 WL 818160, at *5 (E.D. Tenn. June 28, 2001) (rejecting defendants' contention that the government's complaint should be dismissed because when they certified that the home health agencies were not related to the management company they relied upon their legal opinion based upon their reasonable interpretation of Medicare regulations "because a statement or certification to HCFA [CMS] and the [fiscal intermediary] that the [home health agencies] and [the management company] were not

Accordingly, as these cases demonstrate, in formulating a defense to an FCA action, the defendant should focus on the precise basis of the government's claim to determine whether the government can discharge its burden of proving a knowing violation of the FCA. In the health care context, if the relator or the government is contending that the defendant knowingly submitted a false claim because another code better fits the service, as occurred in *Krizek*,[127] the defendant should probe into the underlying regulatory basis supporting use of the code. If it can show that its use of the code was reasonable, or at least subject to good-faith disagreement, then the defendant likely will prevail. Moreover, even if the government can show that the claim is in fact false, the defendant may prevail if it can demonstrate that it did not knowingly submit a false claim by retracing each of its steps and proving that it had a reasonable—albeit mistaken—basis to believe that it was entitled to payment.[128]

A person does not act in deliberate ignorance or reckless disregard merely by failing to ask the government for its opinion or seeking advice of counsel when the practice is standard in the industry and the defendant has no basis to suspect wrongdoing.[129] In *United States ex rel. Quirk v. Madonna Towers, Inc.*,[130] the defendant, which operated a combined residential and skilled nursing facility, entered into agreements with residents under which in exchange for the residents paying an up-front fee and monthly rent for the residential apartment, the residents, if they were subsequently transferred to the skilled nursing facility, would only be required to pay the residential fee for the first 90 days of occupancy, instead of the higher skilled-nursing facility fee.[131] Because the defendant would submit Medicare claims during the relevant 90-day period, the relator contended that the defendant's practice breached 42 U.S.C. Section 1395y(a)(2)'s mandate that no payment may be made for services provided if the person receiving the services "has no legal obligation to pay."[132] Further, the relator contended that the defendant "knowingly" submitted false claims because the defendant's administrators testified that they did not seek legal

---

related is a statement of fact and not purely the expression of legal opinions. . . . When the [home health agencies] stated they were unrelated to [the management company] for purposes of applying HCFA's [CMS's] regulations, they in effect said that the [home health agencies] were not to a significant extent associated or affiliated with [the management company], and that [the management company] did not control the [home health agencies]. These are essentially statements of fact. In determining whether the [home health agencies] and [the management company] were related under 42 C.F.R. §413.17, factual issues concerning associations, affiliations, common ownership and control must be resolved").

[127] *See, e.g.*, United States v. Krizek, 859 F. Supp. 5 (D.D.C. 1994), *aff'd in part, rev'd in part*, 111 F.3d 934 (D.C. Cir. 1997), *on remand*, 7 F. Supp. 2d 56 (D.D.C. 1998), *remanded*, 192 F.3d 1024 (D.C. Cir. 1999); *see also* United States *ex rel.* Glass v. Medtronic, Inc., 957 F.2d 605, 608 (8th Cir. 1992) (a statement cannot be false or fraudulent under FCA when the statement is consistent with Medicare rules).

[128] *See, e.g.*, Hindo v. University of Health Scis./The Chicago Med. Sch., 65 F.3d 608 (7th Cir. 1995), *and* United States *ex rel.* Hagood v. Sonoma County Water Agency, 929 F.2d 1416 (9th Cir. 1991); *see generally* SALCIDO, FALSE CLAIMS ACT COUNSELING: OCT. 2003 SUPP., at §§2:03, 2:05.

[129] *See* United States *ex rel.* Quirk v. Madonna Towers, Inc., 278 F.3d 765 (8th Cir. 2002).
[130] *Id.*
[131] *Id.* at 766.
[132] *Id.* at 767.

advice or an opinion from Medicare regarding the practice of billing Medicare for the first 90 days of a patient's stay in a skilled nursing facility and that this failure to seek guidance demonstrated the defendant's deliberate ignorance of the truth or falsity of the claims it submitted to the government.[133]

The Eighth Circuit rejected the relator's contention, holding that "failing to secure a legal opinion, without more, is not the type of deliberate ignorance that can form the basis for a FCA lawsuit."[134] The court concluded that the administrators refrained from obtaining guidance regarding the questioned practice because they considered the billing practice to be an "acceptable standard procedure."[135] Accordingly, because the relator did not produce any evidence "suggesting anyone was lying to the government" or "suspected something wrong," the court affirmed the district court's dismissal of the action.[136]

## III. Defending Against *Qui Tam* Actions

### A. The Public Disclosure Jurisdictional Bar to *Qui Tam* Actions

When the DOJ prosecutes an FCA action on its own, a person generally receives notice that an FCA action may be looming. For example, before instituting an action against a person, the DOJ usually will inform the person that the government believes that the person may have violated the FCA and invites the person to respond. *Qui tam* actions are different in that a defendant may be brought into court without advance notice and may be subjected to legal action by a private individual rather than the federal government.

As noted earlier, after the informer files a *qui tam* action, the DOJ investigates to determine whether to intervene. In such actions, much turns on whether the government chooses to intervene. When the government declines to intervene, which occurs in the vast majority of *qui tam* cases, the FCA action generally does not result in any governmental recovery. Historically, as of November 1999, the DOJ had intervened in approximately 21 percent of all cases.[137] Yet in those 21 percent of cases in which the government had intervened, the government recovered $2.9 billion, whereas in the 79 percent of cases in which the government had declined to intervene,[138] recovery amounted to only $410 million. Thus, the 79 percent of cases in which the government did not intervene contributed only about 13 percent to the government's total recoveries.

The strategies used to handle *qui tam* actions will vary substantially depending on whether the government has intervened. If the government intervenes after conducting an extended investigation, it has done so because it

---

[133] *Id.* at 768.

[134] *Id.*

[135] *Id.*

[136] *Id.* at 768–69.

[137] According to statistics issued in November 1999, the DOJ had investigated or otherwise pursued 462 cases and declined in 1,673. (The remainder were under investigation.) *See Qui Tam* Statistics (*available at* http://www.taf.org).

[138] *Id.*

believes that it has uncovered evidence that establishes a violation of the FCA. These actions typically result in a settlement. When the government declines to intervene, the parties usually engage in protracted discovery before the action is tried, settled, or dismissed. As noted, relators' recoveries in cases in which the government did not intervene have been relatively small.

Whether or not the government intervenes, litigation under the FCA generally proceeds as in any other civil case. However, one defense merits discussion because it has resulted in the dismissal of a substantial number of actions. This defense is based on the FCA's public disclosure jurisdictional bar, which proscribes lawsuits "based upon" public information unless the relator is the "original source" of that information.[139] This defense is a procedural one directed solely at the relator. Thus, it is especially useful in those actions in which the government does not intervene because by eliminating the relator, the defendant eliminates the lawsuit.[140]

The public disclosure jurisdictional bar is examined in detail below. A study of the case law informs a relator's counsel of when an action should not be undertaken because it would be barred and instructs defense counsel on the circumstances under which the relator may successfully be ousted from the action.

## B. History of the *Qui Tam* Public Disclosure Jurisdictional Bar

Understanding the proper application of the public disclosure jurisdictional bar requires a detailed study of its history. Initially, when Congress enacted the FCA in 1863, the statute contained no jurisdictional bar.[141] In 1943, after a series of abuses in which private persons filed *qui tam* actions based expressly on public information, Congress revamped the statute to preclude such lawsuits.[142] Specifically, Congress provided that no action could be filed

---

[139] 31 U.S.C. §3730(e)(4). There are three other lesser-known jurisdictional bars in §3730(e). Subsection (e)(1), in pertinent part, bars suits "brought by a former or present member of the armed forces . . . arising out of such person's service in the armed forces." Subsection (e)(2) bars actions "against a Member of Congress, a member of the judiciary, or a senior executive branch official if the action is based on evidence or information known to the government when the action was brought." Subsection (e)(3), in pertinent part, bars all persons from bringing an action if the government had already brought a civil suit or administrative action involving monetary penalties. Another jurisdictional bar, in §3730(b)(5), prohibits relators from intervening in or bringing a related action that is based on the facts underlying a pending action.

[140] However, where this defense is available, it should be asserted even in those actions in which the government intervenes. Under the statute, if the government obtains a recovery, the relator is entitled to reasonable attorneys' fees and costs. 31 U.S.C. §3730(d)(1). In some actions, relators have incurred more than $1 million dollars in attorneys' fees. *See, e.g.*, United States *ex rel.* Taxpayers Against Fraud v. General Electric Co., 41 F.3d 1032 (6th Cir. 1994) (the district court awarded the relator more than $2.3 million in attorneys' fees; the Sixth Circuit remanded the action so the district court could find additional facts to determine whether the award was reasonable). Thus, although in those cases in which the government is a party the successful assertion of the public disclosure jurisdictional bar defense will result merely in the relator's dismissal, and not the government's, the relator's dismissal, nonetheless, will save the defendant the substantial expense of compensating the relator's counsel.

[141] Act of March 2, 1863, ch. 67, §4, 12 Stat. 698 (1863). *See also* SALCIDO, FALSE CLAIMS ACT COUNSELING, at §1:01.

[142] Act of December 23, 1943, 57 Stat. 608, *recodified in* 31 U.S.C. §3730; SALCIDO, FALSE CLAIMS ACT COUNSELING, at §1:02.

based on information in the government's possession.[143] This jurisdictional bar applied even if the relator was the original source of the information in the government's "possession."[144]

When the Senate and House Judiciary Committees initially considered amending the jurisdictional bar in 1986, both proposed language that would have expressly permitted persons to bring lawsuits based on public information.[145] As initially proposed, the jurisdictional bar would have permitted actions based on public information if the federal government failed to act on that information within six months of its disclosure.[146] The committees believed that such modification was necessary because DOJ files were stuffed with referrals it had received from other governmental agencies, but had failed to process.[147]

This provision, however, was not enacted. Instead, rather than permitting persons to file actions based on public information, Congress opted to prohibit such actions unless the whistleblower was the original source of the publicly disclosed information.[148] If the information is not in the public domain, there is no assurance that the government is aware of the information and is acting as needed to further the public interest. Hence, *qui tam* actions are permitted. But, if the information is in the public domain, *qui tam* actions are barred unless the relator was the government's source of the information. The basis for using a public disclosure as a trigger in activating the bar is that when the allegations or transactions of fraud have been publicly disclosed, the whistleblower's action does not advance the public interest, but hinders it, because the government is compelled to share a portion of its recovery with a whistleblower who merely republishes public allegations.[149] Once allegations are public, citizens rely on

---

[143]*Id.* (no *qui tam* action can be brought "based upon evidence or information in the possession of the United States . . . at the time such suit was brought").

[144]*See, e.g.,* United States *ex rel.* State of Wisconsin v. Dean, 729 F.2d 1100, 1103 (7th Cir. 1984); Pettis *ex rel.* United States v. Morrison-Knudsen Co., 577 F.2d 668, 669 (9th Cir. 1978) ("[W]e conclude that jurisdiction is lacking even when an informer prior to bringing suit supplies the government with the information which under [the *qui tam* provisions] invokes the bar."); Safir v. Blackwell, 579 F.2d 742 (2d Cir. 1978); United States v. Aster, 176 F. Supp. 208 (E.D. Pa. 1959), *aff'd,* 275 F.2d 281 (3d Cir. 1960).

[145]*See* S. Rep. No. 99-345, at 43 (proposed §3730(e)(4)); H.R. Rep. 99-660, at 2–3 (1986) (proposed §3730(b)(5)).

[146]*Id.*

[147]S. Rep. No. 99-345, at 4, 8, *reprinted in* 1986 U.S.C.C.A.N. 5269, 5273 (the Senate report noted that "available Department of Justice records show most fraud referrals remain unprosecuted and lost public funds, therefore remain uncollected" and that a "resource mismatch" exists between the federal government and large contractors who may marshal the efforts of large legal teams).

[148]31 U.S.C. §3730(e)(4).

[149]*See, e.g.,* United States *ex rel.* Feingold v. Adminastar Federal, Inc., 324 F.3d 492, 495 (7th Cir. 2003) ("[T]he function of a public disclosure is to bring to the attention of the relevant authority that there has been a false claim against the government. . . . Where a public disclosure has occurred, that authority is already in a position to vindicate society's interests, and a *qui tam* action would serve no purpose. . . . Where, on the other hand, a transaction or an allegation of fraud has not been publicly disclosed, society benefits by creating a monetary incentive for a knowledgeable person, called a relator, to identify the problem, present his information to the government, and, where the government declines to prosecute, proceed with a *qui tam* action under the FCA") (citations omitted); Findley v. FPC-Boron Employees' Club, 105 F.3d 675, 685 (D.C. Cir.) ("Once the information is in the public domain, there is less need for a financial incentive to spur individuals into exposing frauds. Allowing *qui tam* suits after that point may either pressure

the government to proceed with the action, and if the government does not do so, they have the power to hold the government accountable through the political process. By drawing the line here, Congress ensured that *qui tam* actions would augment the government's recoveries in FCA actions and, at the same time, eliminate *qui tam* actions when such actions were not needed to protect the federal fisc.[150]

A comparison of three of the FCA's jurisdictional bars—subsections 3730(b)(5), (e)(3), and (e)(4)—further illuminates Congress's purpose in creating the public disclosure jurisdictional bar. Under subsection 3730(e)(4), Congress forces would-be whistleblowers to report fraud before it is publicized. If a relator fails to report the information before publication, the suit would be barred unless the relator was the government's informant; that is, the original source of the information. Under subsection 3730(e)(3), Congress, in addition to other procedures, forces relators to race the government to the courthouse by prohibiting any *qui tam* action after the government files a civil lawsuit or administrative civil money penalty proceeding based on the allegations or transactions underlying the government's action. If the government files first, the relator is barred even if the underlying facts were not publicly disclosed and even if the relator was an original source. Under subsection 3730(b)(5), Congress pits relators against each other in a race to the courthouse by prohibiting all actions based on facts underlying a pending action. As in subsection 3730(e)(3), subsection 3730(b)(5) applies even if the pending action is not public (e.g., the action is under court seal) and even if the relator in the subsequent action would otherwise qualify as an original source. The reason that subsections 3730(b)(5) and 3730(e)(3) are broader than subsection 3730(e)(4)—that is, applying even if the underlying allegations or transactions are not public and even if the relator was the original source of the information—is that once a *qui tam* lawsuit has been filed (subsection 3730(b)(5)) or once the government is a party to a proceeding (subsection 3730(e)(3)), no *qui tam* action is necessary for the government to enforce its rights effectively.

---

the government to prosecute cases when it has good reasons not to or reduce the government's ultimate recovery."), *cert. denied*, 522 U.S. 865 (1997); United States *ex rel.* Dhawan v. New York City Health & Hosp. Corp., No. 95 Civ. 7649 (LMM), 2000 U.S. Dist. LEXIS 15677, at *11 (S.D.N.Y. Oct. 24, 2000) ("In cases where the information that forms an FCA action is public, the opportunity for abuse of process is maximized. Section 3730(e)(4) is intended to bar parasitic lawsuits based upon publicly disclosed information in which would be relators seek remuneration although they contributed nothing to the exposure of the fraud.") (citation and internal quotation omitted), *aff'd*, 252 F.3d 118 (2d Cir. 2001); United States v. CAC Ramsay, 744 F. Supp. 1158, 1159 (S.D. Fla. 1990) ("Congress intended to bar parasitic *qui tam* suits, that is, lawsuits based on public information" because "it will usually serve no purpose to reward a relator for bringing a *qui tam* action if the incident of fraud is already a matter of public knowledge by virtue of 'public disclosure.' "), *aff'd mem.*, 963 F.2d 384 (11th Cir. 1992); *see also* Seal 1 v. Seal A, 255 F.3d 1154, 1158 (9th Cir. 2001) ("The compensation available to relators . . . encourages parasitic lawsuits in which those with no independent knowledge of fraud use information already available to the government to reap rewards for themselves without exposing any previously unknown fraud.).

[150] *See, e.g., Findley*, 105 F.3d at 680–81 ("After ricocheting between the extreme permissiveness that preceded the 1943 amendments and the extreme restrictiveness that followed, Congress again sought to achieve the golden mean between adequate incentives for whistle-blowing insiders with genuinely valuable information and discouragement of opportunistic plaintiffs who have no significant information to contribute on their own.") (internal quotations and citations omitted).

The primary purpose underlying the creation of each of these various "races" in the FCA is to compel whistleblowers to disclose perceived wrongdoing to the government at the earliest possible moment.[151] Accordingly, in construing the scope of subsection (e)(4), courts should be mindful that *qui tam* actions are designed only to provide a mechanism by which the government may obtain useful information so that it may protect its interests; they should not be viewed as a means to enrich private individuals and their counsel.[152] Thus, whenever the information underlying the complaint is publicly available and the relator did not furnish the information to the government before that disclosure, the relator should be barred from proceeding. Although, as noted in detail below, some courts have reached this conclusion,[153] other courts have taken an unduly expansive view of the statute, such that if whistleblowers merely demonstrate that they were unaware of the public information, they may proceed with the action.[154] This interpretation serves to enrich relators (and their counsel) but does not appropriately enrich the government, whose recovery is reduced by the relator's share.

## C. Case Law Construing the Public Disclosure Jurisdictional Bar

As enacted, the public disclosure jurisdictional bar provides in part:

(4)(A) No court shall have jurisdiction over an action under this section based upon the public disclosure of allegations or transactions in a criminal, civil, or

---

[151]*See, e.g.*, H.R. REP. NO. 660, at 23 ("[t]he purpose of the *qui tam* provisions of the False Claims Act is to encourage private individuals who are aware of fraud being perpetrated against the Government to bring such information forward"); S. REP. No. 99-345, at 14, *reprinted in* 1986 U.S.C.C.A.N. at 5279 (amendments intended to reward those who "bring . . . wrongdoing to light"); *see also* United States *ex rel.* Jones v. Horizon Healthcare Corp., 160 F.3d 326, 335 (6th Cir. 1998) ("the *qui tam* provisions were intended not only to block freeloading relators, but also to inspire whistleblowers to come forward as soon as possible") (citation omitted); *Findley*, 105 F.3d at 685 ("the *qui tam* provisions of the FCA were designed to inspire whistle-blowers to come forward promptly with information concerning fraud so that the government can stop it and recover ill-gotten gains"); United States *ex rel.* Devlin v. California, 84 F.3d 358, 362 (9th Cir. 1996) ("the purpose of the FCA . . . aims at ferreting out fraud by encouraging persons with first-hand knowledge of alleged wrongdoing to come forward"); United States *ex rel.* Barth v. Ridgedale Elec. & Eng'g, 44 F.3d 699, 704 (8th Cir. 1995) ("the clear intent of the Act . . . is to encourage private individuals who are aware of fraud against the government to bring such information forward at the earliest possible time and to discourage persons with relevant information from remaining silent") (citations omitted); United States *ex rel.* Wang v. FMC Corp., 975 F.2d 1412, 1419–20 (9th Cir. 1992); United States *ex rel.* Dick v. Long Island Lighting Co., 912 F.2d 13, 18 (2d Cir. 1990); *cf.* United States *ex rel.* LaCorte v. SmithKline Beecham Clinical Labs., 149 F.3d 227, 234 (3d Cir. 1998) ("[I]nterpreting section 3730(b)(5) as imposing a broader bar furthers the Act's purpose by encouraging *qui tam* plaintiffs to report fraud promptly. . . . In addition, . . . duplicative claims do not help reduce fraud or return funds to the federal fisc, since once the government knows the essential facts of the fraudulent scheme, it has enough information to discover related frauds.") (citation omitted).

[152]*See, e.g.*, United States v. Health Possibilities, P.S.C., 207 F.3d 335, 340 (6th Cir. 2000) ("The FCA is not designed to serve the parochial interests of relators, but to vindicate civic interests in avoiding fraud against public monies.") (citations omitted); United States v. Northrop Corp., 59 F.3d 953, 968 (9th Cir. 1995) ("The private right of recovery created by the provisions of the FCA exists not to compensate the *qui tam* relator, but the United States. The relator's right to recovery exists solely as a mechanism for deterring fraud and returning funds to the federal treasury.").

[153]*See, e.g.*, *Findley*, 105 F.3d at 685.

[154]*See, e.g.*, United States *ex rel.* Siller v. Becton Dickinson & Co., 21 F.3d 1339 (4th Cir. 1994).

administrative hearing, in a congressional, administrative, or Government Accounting Office [sic] report, hearing, audit, or investigation, or from the news media, unless the action is brought by the Attorney General or the person bringing the action is an original source of the information.[155]

Almost all circuit courts have now construed the bar's various provisions. As the Ninth Circuit explained in *United States ex rel. Lindenthal v. General Dynamics Corp.*, to invoke the public disclosure jurisdictional bar successfully, the defendant must establish four elements:

1. that there has been a "public disclosure"
2. of "allegations or transactions"
3. in a "criminal, civil, or administrative hearing, in a congressional, administrative, or Government [General] Accounting Office report, hearing, audit, or investigation, or from the news media," and
4. that the relator's action is "based upon" that public disclosure.[156]

If these four elements are satisfied, then relators may proceed only if they are an original source. To be an original source, relators must have direct and independent knowledge of the allegations and must have voluntarily provided to the government before publication the information underlying the action. Counsel defending *qui tam* actions should become fully familiar with the body of case law summarized below to determine whether the public disclosure defense is applicable and, if so, which facts should be probed during discovery to maximize the likelihood of a successful defense.

### 1. Meaning of "Public Disclosure"

Courts have disagreed in their construction of the term "public disclosure." The Third and Second Circuits have formulated the broadest interpretation of the word "public," finding that information is public when it is communicated to a stranger to the fraud. The Ninth Circuit has restricted that interpretation, finding that information is not public, even if revealed to a stranger to the fraud, if that stranger has no incentive to disseminate the information to others. The Seventh Circuit has ruled that disclosures to the federal government, if made to appropriate individuals, can be considered public disclosures.

### a. The Majority Rule: Information Is Public if It Is Disclosed to a Stranger to the Fraud

Two cases illustrate the majority rule. In *United States ex rel. Stinson, Lyons, Gerlin & Bustamante, P.A. v. Prudential Ins. Co.*,[157] a person learned by reviewing a document during discovery in an unrelated state court litigation that a company allegedly had defrauded the federal government. Although the document was not filed with the state court, the court found the document to have been publicly disclosed. Similarly, in *United States ex rel. Fine v. Ad-*

---

[155]31 U.S.C. §3730(e)(4)(A).
[156]61 F.3d 1402, 1409 (9th Cir. 1995).
[157]944 F.2d 1149, 1155 (3d Cir. 1991).

*vanced Sciences, Inc.,*[158] a person became aware of a federal government audit, which had not been publicly disclosed, indicating that a company had defrauded the government. That person informed another person of that information and thus the court ruled that the information had been publicly disclosed.

Congress did not define the term "public." Instead, it chose to effectuate the term by reference to specific types of information revealed during hearings, contained in government reports, audits, or investigations, or disseminated through the news media. If the allegations or transactions are divulged through any of these means, the information is public. Congress did not place any restriction on the term and did not, for example, mandate that the information must reach a mass audience or be read by specific individuals. Instead, Congress adopted a general rule that any allegation or transaction revealed through any of the statutorily approved mechanisms is sufficient to put the government on notice of the fraud and hold it accountable should it fail to act.

Consistent with this purpose, the majority of courts have broadly defined the word "public" to encompass any information that is disclosed to a person who is a "stranger to the fraud."[159] Thus, the Third Circuit in *Stinson* held that a "public disclosure" in a "hearing" had occurred when the relevant information was disclosed to one person, the relator, who had received the information pursuant to his discovery request in a state court proceeding.[160] Similarly, the Second Circuit, in *United States ex rel. John Doe v. John Doe Corp.,*[161] held that a "public disclosure" of a government "investigation" had occurred when government investigators had merely interviewed "innocent" employees of the target company regarding allegations of fraud.

After *John Doe*, the Second Circuit took this rule a step further in *United States ex rel. Kreindler v. United Technologies*[162] by holding that not only is information public if it reaches a single individual (i.e., a stranger to the fraud), but that it is also public if it is simply accessible to the public.[163] Accordingly, in that case, the court found that although the relator was prohibited under a confidentiality agreement from disclosing information it had obtained in discovery,

---

[158] 99 F.3d 1000 (10th Cir. 1996).

[159] *See, e.g.,* United States *ex rel.* John Doe v. John Doe Corp., 960 F.2d 318 (2d Cir. 1992); United States *ex rel.* Stinson, Lyons, Gerlin & Bustamante, P.A. v. Prudential Ins. Co., 944 F.2d 1149, 1155 (3d Cir. 1991); *cf.* United States *ex rel.* Springfield Terminal Ry. v. Quinn, 14 F.3d 645, 652–53 (D.C. Cir. 1994) (no public disclosure results from "the discovery process conducted between two private litigants" when that information is not filed with the court) (dictum); United States *ex rel.* Hagood v. Sonoma County Water Agency, 929 F.2d 1416, 1419 (9th Cir. 1991) (no public disclosure occurs merely as a result of internal government debate regarding defendant's acts); United States *ex rel.* Williams v. NEC Corp., 931 F.2d 1493 (11th Cir. 1991) (same).

[160] 944 F.2d at 1155.

[161] 960 F.2d at 323. The basis for the court's ruling was that once innocent employees have learned of the allegations, the government could not defer taking action on the claim by throwing a "cloak of secrecy" over the fraud and thus no whistleblower action was needed. *Id.*

[162] 985 F.2d 1148, 1159 (2d Cir. 1993).

[163] *See also* United States *ex rel.* Branhan v. Mercy Health Sys. of Southwest Ohio, No. 98-3127, 1999 U.S. App. LEXIS 18509, at *5 (6th Cir. Aug. 5, 1999) (HCFA (CMS) report was publicly disclosed because it would be "available to anyone who requested it"); United States *ex rel.* Phipps v. Comprehensive Community Dev. Corp., 152 F. Supp. 2d 443, 453 (S.D.N.Y. 2001) ("If information is equally available to the relator as it is to strangers to the fraud transaction had they chosen to look for it, then there is public disclosure.").

the information nonetheless was public because it was on file with the court and thus "it was available to anyone who wished to consult the court file."[164]

Under this expansive reading of the word, "public" means not just information released to the public, but also information merely available to the public. The implication is that the public disclosure jurisdictional bar possibly reaches all documents or information in any repository from which it may be obtained by the general public.[165]

### b. Ninth and Tenth Circuits' Limitations on the Stranger-to-the-Fraud Rule: Requiring an Incentive to Reveal the Information or an Affirmative Disclosure

In *United States ex rel. Schumer v. Hughes Aircraft*,[166] the government issued an audit report critical of the defendant's accounting practices and released the report to the defendant's and the prime contractor's employees. The defendant contended that the disclosure of the audit report to innocent employees and other strangers to the fraud constituted a public disclosure and that the audit report was a "public" document because it could be obtained under the Freedom of Information Act. The U.S. Court of Appeals for the Ninth Circuit held that the disclosure was not a public disclosure. Rather, any disclosures to the company and its prime contractor were merely disclosures within a "private sphere" because those companies had no economic incentive to further publicize the results of the audit report.

The Ninth Circuit specifically rejected the Second and Third Circuits' broad interpretation of the word "public," holding that even if a stranger to the fraud receives the information, there are pockets of "private spheres" within the public domain in which individuals have no incentive to disseminate the information further and hence the information is not public. This interpretation of "public" is not supported by the plain meaning of the word and would result in a tedious, cumbersome process in every case because courts would have to inquire into how a particular recipient of information would handle that information on its receipt. Limiting the inquiry to whether a stranger to the fraud has received the information will more likely produce uniform results and will furnish courts with an objective test for determining whether they have jurisdiction over the action. Thus, the Third Circuit's formulation in *Stinson* and the Second Circuit's holding in *John Doe* offer better interpretations of the term "public" than *Schumer*.[167]

---

[164]*Id.*

[165]For example, under this broad reading of the public disclosure jurisdictional bar, all repositories of public information that may contain information relating to fraud against the government, such as cost reports submitted to fiscal intermediaries to verify hospital Medicare costs or documents on file with contracting officers regarding government construction or manufacturing projects, could be deemed to be public disclosures. As noted below, however, although this type of information may qualify as public, it may not contain information specific enough to qualify as allegations or transactions under the Court of Appeals for the District of Columbia's test in United States *ex rel.* Springfield Terminal Ry. v. Quinn, 14 F.3d 645 (D.C. Cir. 1994). In that instance, the public disclosure jurisdictional bar would not apply.

[166]63 F.3d 1512 (9th Cir. 1995), *rev'd on other grounds*, 520 U.S. 939 (1997).

[167]*Id.* at 1518. The court believed that its ruling was consistent with the statutory purpose because Congress specifically intended that the relators be able to bring lawsuits when the government possessed identical information. *Id.* at 1519. The court relied, in part, on statements

Additionally, in *Schumer*, the Ninth Circuit, criticizing the Third Circuit's holding in *Stinson*, reasoned that the public disclosure jurisdictional bar applied only to actual disclosures, not theoretical disclosures, and thus the fact that the audit report theoretically was obtainable under the Freedom of Information Act was inconsequential under the FCA.[168] The Tenth Circuit, in *United States ex rel. Ramseyer v. Century Healthcare Corp.*,[169] later similarly interpreted the term "public disclosure" narrowly to require an "affirmative" act of disclosure to a third party.

The relator in *Ramseyer*[170] alleged that she became aware of the defendants' submission of false claims for Medicaid reimbursement while she was employed at the defendants' mental health facility. The state, independent of the relator's efforts, had conducted an inspection and audit of the defendants' facilities and, in a subsequent report, detailed the same Medicaid compliance problems that the relator had discovered in the scope of her employment.[171] Three copies of the audit report were made; two remained within the agency's files, and the third was sent to the defendants. The defendants contended that because the relator's lawsuit was similar to the information contained in the state's audit, which had not been publicly disseminated to anyone but the defendants, the action was based on an audit and therefore barred under the statute.[172]

The Tenth Circuit rejected this contention, ruling that the agency's knowledge of the fraud and the internal circulation of the report did not con-

---

in the Senate Judiciary Committee's report. *Id.* However, the court's reliance on the Senate report undermines the reliability of its holding because the draft jurisdictional bar the Senate Judiciary Committee referenced in its report was substantially narrower than the one that Congress ultimately passed. *Compare* S. REP. NO. 99–345, at 43 (setting forth draft §3730(e)(4)), *with* 31 U.S.C. §3730(e)(4) (the provision as passed); *see generally* Robert Salcido, *Screening Out Unworthy Whistleblower Actions: An Historical Analysis of the Jurisdictional Bar to* Qui Tam *Actions Under the False Claims Act*, 24 PUB. CONT. L.J. 237, 250–60 (1995). As the Third Circuit pointed out in another context, extreme care must be exercised when relying on the FCA's legislative history because "[t]he bill that eventuated in the 1986 amendments underwent substantial revisions during its legislative path. This provides ample opportunity to search the legislative history and find some support somewhere for almost any construction of the many ambiguous terms in the final version." United States *ex. rel.* Stinson v. Prudential Ins. Co., 944 F.2d at 1154. Indeed, to the extent that the audit report was released to the prime contractor (a stranger to the fraud), under the plain language of the statute, which requires only that the information be public, the Ninth Circuit should have found that there had been a public disclosure of the audit report. The statute, unlike the court's ruling, contains no exception for public disclosures within private spheres. Indeed, in 2001, the Ninth Circuit limited its application of *Schumer* in Seal 1 v. Seal A, 255 F.3d 1154 (9th Cir. 2001), where the court ruled that U.S. Attorneys' Office disclosure of information to a single person (the relator) qualified as a "public" disclosure of a governmental investigation. The court reasoned: "Disclosure of information to one member of the public, when that person seeks to take advantage of that information by filing an FCA action, is public disclosure. It may not be public disclosure as to some other member of the public who independently comes upon information already possessed by the government and disclosed to a single person ... and who then files an FCA action based on the information independently obtained. But it is public, as to [the relator], in the sense necessary to the sensible operation of §3730(e)(4)(A). Because it was disclosed to an outsider to the investigation who now seeks to profit from it as an FCA relator, it was publicly disclosed to that person." *Id.* at 1162.

[168] 63 F.3d at 1520.

[169] 90 F.3d 1514, 1516–17 (10th Cir. 1996).

[170] *Id.* at 1519.

[171] *Id.*

[172] *Id.*

stitute public disclosures because "mere possession" of information by an individual or an entity without additional "affirmative" disclosure "does not amount to 'public disclosure.' "[173] Furthermore, the court concluded that although the information was potentially available to the public on request, the public disclosure requirement "signifies more than the mere theoretical or potential availability of information."[174] Instead, to be publicly disclosed, "the allegations or transactions on which a *qui tam* suit is based must have been made known to the public through some affirmative act of disclosure."[175]

The Tenth Circuit thus concurred with the Ninth Circuit, and disagreed with the Second and Third Circuits, holding that the mere availability of the information to the public is not sufficient to trigger application of the public disclosure jurisdictional bar, but that the information must have actually been obtained by an innocent member of the public.[176] However, these cases can be reconciled by reference to the specific mechanism of disclosure. In both *Stinson* and *Kriendler*, the public disclosure occurred in connection with court proceedings, whereas the material in *Schumer* and *Ramseyer* concerned government reports. By their very nature, court proceedings (unless restricted) are public, and anyone may freely witness proceedings or copy court records. Government reports, however, unless specifically requested by the general public, are merely maintained in files and cannot be easily accessed by the public or the news media unless they have some prior knowledge of the information.[177]

---

[173]*Id.* at 1521.

[174]*Id.* at 1519 (citation omitted).

[175]*Id.*

[176]*Id.* at 1519. Although the Tenth Circuit has required that an affirmative act of disclosure to the public occur, it has also ruled that disclosure to a single individual is sufficient to trigger the bar. *See* United States *ex rel.* Fine v. MK-Ferguson Co., 99 F.3d 1538, 1545 (10th Cir. 1996) (court dismissed action by former OIG auditor because government's audit report had been sent to the state of Oregon); United States *ex rel.* Fine v. Advanced Scis., Inc., 99 F.3d 1000, 1005 (10th Cir. 1996) (court dismissed action by former OIG auditor because the auditor had discussed the underlying allegations with another person (i.e., a stranger to the fraud) before filing his action); *cf.* United States *ex rel.* Fallon v. Accudyne Corp., 921 F. Supp. 611, 624–25 (W.D. Wis. 1995) (court rejected the defendants' contention that notices of deficiency transmitted by state agency to one defendant constituted a public disclosure because there was "no evidence that the non-compliance notices sent as a result of routine inspections were received, viewed or disclosed by or to anyone other than [defendant]" and the "mere creation of such a document by a state agency does not constitute [a] public disclosure within the intended meaning of §3730(e)(4)(A)").

[177]*See, e.g.,* United States *ex rel.* Dunleavy v. County of Delaware, 123 F.3d 734 (3d Cir. 1997). In *Dunleavy*, the court had to consider whether a report a county submitted to the federal government had been publicly disclosed because citizens could possibly obtain the report. The court pointed out that it had held previously in United States *ex rel.* Stinson, Lyons, Gerlin & Bustamante, P.A. v. Prudential Ins., 944 F.2d 1149 (3d Cir. 1991), that a document's potential availability was sufficient to trigger the bar and that in the instant action, the state administrative report was potentially available to others under the Freedom of Information Act. However, the court distinguished the two cases by pointing out that *Stinson* "dealt with information produced on the public record in connection with litigation while here we are concerned with reports that may be filed away without the receiving agency being put on notice that there is any reason to give them close attention." *Id.* at 746 (footnote omitted).

### c. Disclosures to Federal Government Are Public

In *United States v. Bank of Farmington*,[178] a government official received a subpoena related to state court litigation. He then called one party, a bank, to inquire into the basis for the subpoena and the bank informed the official that it failed to disclose a guarantee on a federal guaranteed loan. The Seventh Circuit held that the bank's disclosure to the government official of its failure to disclose the guarantee on the loan constituted a public disclosure of that information.

The *Bank of Farmington* case involves a slight variation on the public disclosure test in that it involved a disclosure to the government. In construing the public disclosure jurisdictional bar, the court ruled that the bank's disclosure to the government employee qualified as a public disclosure because the information was "disclosed . . . to a competent public official."[179] The court found that the disclosure of information to a competent public official about an alleged false claim submitted to the government qualifies as a public disclosure "when the disclosure is made to one who has managerial responsibility for the very claims being made."[180] The court pointed out that this construction accords "with a standard meaning of 'public,' which can also be defined as 'authorized by, acting for, or representing the community.' 12 OED, at 779. Disclosure to an official authorized to act for or represent the community on behalf of government can be understood as public disclosure."[181]

The court pointed out that this interpretation also effectuated the purpose of the provision:

> The point of public disclosure of a false claim against the government is to bring it to the attention of the authorities, not merely to educate and enlighten the public at large about the dangers of misappropriation of their tax money. Disclosure to the public at large is a step in lowering the jurisdictional bar precisely because it is likely to alert the authorities about the alleged fraud. After investigation, they can take the proper steps to deal with it—prosecution, settlements involving repayment of funds, or whatever may be called for in the particular case. Since a public official in his official capacity is authorized to act for and to represent the community, and since disclosure to the public official responsible for the claim effectuates the purpose of disclosure to the public at large, disclosure to a public official with direct responsibility for the claim in question of allegations or transactions upon which a *qui tam* claim is based constitutes public disclosure within the meaning of §3730(e)(4).[182]

---

[178] 166 F.3d 853 (7th Cir. 1999).

[179] *Id.* at 861.

[180] *Id.*

[181] *Id.*

[182] *Id.* In essence, the court established a sliding scale regarding the type of disclosures that would be deemed "public." For example, the court noted that disclosures "to officials with less direct responsibility might still be public disclosure if the disclosure is public in the common-sense meaning of the term as 'open' or 'manifest' to all." *Id.* (citation omitted). Further, the "more open a disclosure is, the less any public official need be specifically informed. If it is sufficiently open, no official need be specifically informed. The more likely the competent official is to be apprised of the relevant facts by a disclosure, the less 'public,' in the sense of open or manifest to all, it need be. If the disclosure is made, as here, to precisely the public official responsible for the claim, it need not be disclosed to anyone else to be public disclosure within the meaning of the Act." *Id.* (footnote omitted). *Accord* United States *ex rel.* Cherry v.

On the one hand, the test in *Bank of Farmington* appears to be too broad in that one could contend that one purpose of the 1986 amendments was to eliminate the 1943 government knowledge bar and that the *Farmington* decision resuscitated that bar.[183] Such a contention, however, is faulty on two grounds. First, the primary purpose of the amendments, as noted above, was not merely to repeal the government knowledge bar but to create a means by which the federal government would receive pertinent information at the earliest possible time and reward the informant. The government's receipt of the information puts it on the trail of fraud, and under those circumstances it should not have to share its recovery with a so-called whistleblower who merely repeats to the government what it already knows.[184] Second, a major reform of the 1986 amendments in correcting and amending the 1943 government knowledge jurisdictional bar was to permit actions by relators who were an original source to go forward. Relators who are original sources—those, for example, who would have disclosed their information to the government before the bank in *Bank of Farmington*—could still bring an action even if the government subsequently learned of the information from another source. Thus, *Bank of Farmington* strikes a balance between eliminating those actions that do not advance the government's interest because the information repeats what it has already learned, while not precluding those actions in which persons divulge new, significant information to the government and thus further the government's interest.

## 2. *"Allegations" or "Transactions" of Fraud*

Courts have ruled not only that the information underlying the complaint must be in the public domain but also that the information must be of a specific type: it must set forth either the "transactions" or the "allegations" underlying the complaint. Courts have attempted to simplify the analysis into a basic formula, known as the "$X + Y = Z$" test. This section first discusses the case that formu-

---

Rush-Presbyterian/ St. Luke's Med. Ctr., No. 99 C 06313, 2001 WL 40807, at *3 (N.D. Ill. Jan. 16, 2001) (hospital's voluntary disclosure of inappropriate billing practices to the U.S. Attorney's Office, the FBI, and HCFA (now CMS) "constitutes 'public disclosure' for FCA purposes"); *see also* United States *ex rel.* O'Keeffe v. Sverdup Corp., 131 F. Supp. 2d 87, 92 (D. Mass. 2001) (because the Environmental Impact Statements/Reports were "co-authored by the United States Department of Transportation, any transactions or allegations contained therein would also implicate the jurisdictional bar of §3730(e)(4)(A)") (citation omitted); United States *ex rel.* Coleman v. Indiana, No. 96-714-C-T/G, 2000 U.S. Dist. LEXIS 13666, at *30–33 (S.D. Ind. Sept. 19, 2000) (Indiana's submission of state plans qualified as public disclosures to the federal government and the government's "letters approving the State Plans constitute administrative reports"). *But see* United States *ex rel.* Rost v. Pfizer Inc., 446 F. Supp. 2d 6, 16–17 (D. Mass. 2006) ("The court . . . rejects the holding and rationale of the Seventh Circuit in *Mathews* . . . [and] holds that disclosure to a competent government official, alone, does not, and in fact cannot, constitute a public disclosure under the FCA's public disclosure bar") (footnote omitted).

[183] *See, e.g.,* United States *ex rel.* Dunleavy v. County of Delaware, 123 F.3d 734, 745–46 (3d Cir. 1997).

[184] Some district courts had similarly ruled that information transmitted from state agencies or private persons to the federal government constitute public disclosures because the information is sufficient to put the government on the trail of alleged wrongdoing. *See, e.g.,* United States *ex rel.* Long v. SCS Bus. & Tech. Inst., 999 F. Supp. 78, 87–88 (D.D.C. 1998), *rev'd on other grounds,* 173 F.3d 870 (D.C. Cir. 1999); United States *ex rel.* Alexander v. Dyncorp, Inc., 924 F. Supp. 292, 299 (D.D.C. 1996).

lated the $X + Y = Z$ test, *United States ex rel. Springfield Terminal Railway v. Quinn*,[185] and then considers the application of the test in cases in which the information in the public domain does not specifically identify any individual defendant.

### a. Overview of the $X + Y = Z$ Test

The relator in *Springfield Terminal Railway* alleged that an arbitrator appointed by the National Mediation Board had billed the government for services not actually rendered. The relator first learned of the underlying evidence during discovery in a previous lawsuit. Because of its own involvement in the arbitration, the relator recognized that the arbitrator had no arbitral function to perform on several of the days for which he sought payment. The relator later confirmed its suspicions by conducting its own investigation (e.g., calling numbers listed on the arbitrator's telephone records, which it had obtained during discovery in the previous litigation). On these facts, the appellate court for the District of Columbia held that the information disclosed did not constitute " 'allegations or transactions' within the meaning of the FCA jurisdictional bar." In "order to disclose the fraudulent *transaction* publicly, the combination of $X$ and $Y$ must be revealed, from which readers or listeners may infer $Z$, i.e., the conclusion that fraud has been committed."[186] The information in the public domain did not concern allegations or transactions because all that was in the public domain was the untrue set of facts (i.e., the alleged misrepresentations submitted by the arbitrator), whereas the relator supplied the missing pieces (i.e., the true set of facts). Thus, because both $X$ and $Y$ were not in the public domain, there were not sufficient allegations or transactions in the public arena to bar the *qui tam* action.

Other courts have followed this $X + Y = Z$ formulation.[187] The $X + Y = Z$ test has set the standard for determining whether a lawsuit is based on allegations or transactions in a hearing, report, audit, investigation, or the news media. The *Springfield* court believed that this reading was consistent with the FCA's purpose because otherwise "[m]any potentially valuable *qui tam* suits would be aborted prematurely by a reading of the jurisdictional provision that barred suits when the only publicly disclosed information was itself innocuous."[188]

---

[185] 14 F.3d 645 (D.C. Cir. 1994).

[186] *Id.* (emphasis added).

[187] *See, e.g.*, United States *ex rel.* Foundation Aiding the Elderly v. Horizon West Inc., 265 F.3d 1011, 1015 (9th Cir. 2001); United States *ex rel.* Jones v. Horizon Healthcare Corp., 160 F.3d 326, 331 (6th Cir. 1998); United States *ex rel.* Dunleavy v. County of Delaware, 123 F.3d 734, 741 (3d Cir. 1997); United States *ex rel.* Findley v. FPC-Boron Employees' Club, 105 F.3d 675, 687 (D.C. Cir.), *cert. denied*, 522 U.S. 865 (1997); United States *ex rel.* Rabushka v. Crane Co., 40 F.3d 1509, 1512 (8th Cir. 1994); United States *ex rel.* O'Keeffe v. Sverdup Corp., 131 F. Supp. 2d 87, 94 (D. Mass. 2001); United States *ex rel.* Downy v. Corning, Inc., 118 F. Supp. 2d 1160 (D.N.M. 2000); United States *ex rel.* Pogue v. American Healthcorp., Inc., 977 F. Supp. 1329, 1337–38 (M.D. Tenn. 1997).

[188] 14 F.3d at 654. The court concluded that one may determine whether the information is specific enough to trigger the bar by whether the material was sufficient to enable the DOJ "to investigate the case and to make a decision whether to prosecute"; that is, "whether the

### b. Application of the $X + Y = Z$ Test When Information in the Public Domain Does Not Identify the Defendant

In *United States ex rel. Cooper v. Blue Cross and Blue Shield of Florida, Inc.*,[189] the relator was a Medicare beneficiary who noticed that Medicare paid a claim for which his employer's health plan was responsible. Believing this practice was improper, the relator informed the government of the practice, including the identity of the party, Blue Cross and Blue Shield of Florida (BCBSF), that allegedly engaged in the fraudulent conduct. Subsequently, the General Accounting Office (GAO) issued a report stating that Medicare intermediaries failed to monitor payments to hospitals under Medicare secondary payment (MSP) laws. Further, the report stated that insurers serving as Medicare intermediaries had a conflict of interest when they also served as primary insurers because their financial interest would dictate that the Medicare program pay claims that they could pay as primary insurers. The pertinent GAO report did not identify BCBSF and did not trigger the public disclosure jurisdictional bar, the court held, because "the report [did] not allege that BCBSF in its capacity as a primary insurer actually engaged in wrongdoing." Accordingly, the "report does not constitute a 'public disclosure of allegations or transactions' that BCBSF knowingly violated MSP laws."[190]

In *United States ex rel. Findley v. FPC-Boron Employees' Club*,[191] the relators attempted to obtain a contract to service certain vending machines at a Bureau of Prisons facility. By attending a preproposal conference, the relators learned that an employees' club operated some machines at the facility. The relators questioned the legality of this practice and filed a lawsuit against all employees' clubs of the Bureau of Prisons and DOJ. However, a 1952 Comptroller General opinion, a 1974 Senate report, and a 1986 Federal Circuit opinion had all questioned the legality of retention of such funds by employees' clubs. Therefore, it was held that the allegations underlying the lawsuit had been publicly disclosed although the publicly disclosed material did not identify the specific defendants. The court pointed out that given the information in the public domain, one would only need to identify employees' clubs that provide vending services on federal property to question the appropriateness of the arrangement. The court ruled that the relators' complaint was barred because all it

---

information conveyed [to the government] could have formed the basis for a government decision on prosecution, or could at least have alerted law-enforcement authorities to the likelihood of wrongdoing . . . ." *Id.* (quoting United States ex rel. Joseph v. Cannon, 642 F.2d 1373 (D.C. Cir. 1981)). For a general description of the application of the $X + Y = Z$ test, see SALCIDO, FALSE CLAIMS ACT COUNSELING §3:05.

[189] 19 F.3d 562 (11th Cir. 1994) (per curiam).

[190] *Cooper*, 19 F.3d at 567; *see also Downy*, 118 F. Supp. 2d at 1166 ("It is apparent that in the Tenth Circuit cases, a particular alleged wrongdoer had been identified in the public disclosures or would be readily identifiable given the information in those disclosures, and a specific explanation of the alleged wrongdoing had been provided."); United States ex rel. Butler v. Magellan Health Servs., 74 F. Supp. 2d 1201, 1210–11 (M.D. Fla. 1999) (refusing to apply the public disclosure jurisdictional bar to defendants that were not named in the publicly disclosed state court action but who were named in the *qui tam* action); United States ex rel. Stinson, Lyon, Gerlin & Bustamante, P.A. v. Provident Life, 721 F. Supp. 1247 (S.D. Fla. 1989).

[191] 105 F.3d 675 (D.C. Cir. 1997), *cert. denied*, 522 U.S. 865 (1997).

added was "the identity of particular employees' clubs engaged in the questionable and previously documented generic practice" and that their "conclusory allegations offer at best collateral information; they do not introduce elements of new wrongful transactions or material elements to the publicly disclosed transaction."[192]

The $X + Y = Z$ formulation does not yield mathematical certainty. As the above examples illustrate, one difficult issue is defining the specific degree of match that must exist between the allegations or transactions in the public domain and those in the complaint—or, at an even more basic level, determining whether the information in the public domain must identify the particular defendant. On the one hand, if generic allegations in the public domain suffice to trigger the public disclosure jurisdictional bar, then given the multitude of government investigatory reports and hearings, a number of *qui tam* suits would be barred even under circumstances in which the government could not be expected to have at least constructive notice of the particular practices of a specific party. On the other hand, if generic allegations do not trigger the bar, nothing prevents opportunistic whistleblowers from usurping public information for private gain (and thereby depriving the government of its rightful recovery) by naming a specific party not mentioned in the public information. For example, if the government issued a report pointing out that several providers within an industry breached a regulatory provision and the report did not name the specific parties because they were still under investigation, it would not take much for an enterprising relator (or even a purported "insider") to file a lawsuit claiming that a particular provider committed that specific regulatory breach. If the court were to find that the relator's allegations differed from those in the public domain simply because the relator named the defendant while the public information did not, then the relator would never have to prove that he or she was the original source because the information was not publicly disclosed. Such a result would subvert the purposes underlying the public disclosure jurisdictional bar by substantially minimizing the government's

---

[192] *See also* United States v. Alcan Elec. & Eng'g, Inc., 197 F.3d 1014, 1019 (9th Cir. 1999) (where publicly disclosed document alleged that union had conspired "with local contractors" by deducting set amount from workers' paychecks and remitting that amount back to the union in violation of federal law, the relator's subsequent *qui tam* action was based on the public document although the defendants were not expressly mentioned in the public document because the public document "alleged a narrow class of suspected wrongdoers—local electrical contractors who worked on federally funded projects over a four-year period," and who were required "by statute to file certified payrolls with the government on a weekly basis"—and hence "the government, as regulator and owner, presumably would have ready access to documents identifying those contractors" and this "makes it highly likely that the government could easily identify the contractors at issue") (footnote omitted); United States *ex rel*. Fine v. Sandia Corp., 70 F.3d 568, 572 (10th Cir. 1995). In *Sandia*, a GAO report and a congressional hearing reported that at least two of the nine national laboratories had used funds that were allocated for research involving the storage and disposal of radioactive waste for discretionary research. In his *qui tam* complaint, the relator alleged that one, Sandia National Laboratory, had specifically engaged in this practice. *Id.* at 571. The court ruled that the relator's action was barred by virtue of the information in the public domain. The court distinguished *Sandia* from *Cooper* by pointing out the ease with which the government and the public could identify the responsible individuals: "When attempting to identify individual actors, little similarity exists between combing through the private insurance industry in search of fraud and examining the operating procedures of nine, easily identifiable, DOE-controlled, and government-owned laboratories. *Cooper* is inapplicable to this case." *Id.* at 572.

recovery while adding nothing to the government's knowledge regarding the conduct.

In close cases, the proper response to this issue inevitably turns on whether the public information is sufficient to permit the government to identify the "individual actors engaged in the fraudulent activity."[193] A close analysis of both *Cooper* and *Findley* is useful because these courts, although they arrived at opposite conclusions, both were correct given the factual situation each confronted.

In *Cooper*, as is noted above, the D.C. Circuit ruled that because the publicly disclosed material did not identify the specific defendant, the publicly disclosed information did not trigger the public disclosure jurisdictional bar.[194] There, the relator identified specific information that he believed demonstrated that a particular defendant violated the FCA and named the precise intermediary that he thought was responsible for the misconduct. Accordingly, the court ruled that the information in the public domain, which did not identify the specific defendant, did not bar the relator's action, which named the specific defendant and tied the defendant to the allegedly fraudulent conduct and was reported to the government before any disclosure of the information. In short, the relator's action was based on particular facts, not a legal theory, and the relator contributed specific facts that were not fairly ascertainable from the public material.

Conversely, in *Findley*, the D.C. Circuit ruled that although the information in the public domain did not identify the specific defendant, the relators' action was barred because the information in the public domain was specific enough that the government could have easily identified the individual actors engaging in the alleged misconduct. In *Findley*, the relators relied on a theory regarding the appropriateness of employees' clubs sharing in the profits from vending machines on government premises. From this public material, the court concluded, the government and the public could identify all entities engaged in misconduct by simply inquiring into whether an employees' club operated vending machines and retained the profits. Thus, in *Findley*, unlike *Cooper*, the suit was based on the theory, not the particular defendant-specific facts, and given that the theory was already in the public domain, the relators' action was properly barred since the relators were not the original source of that information.

Finally, in applying the statutory language regarding allegations or transactions of fraud, care must be taken to effectuate the statutory intent of eliminating opportunistic lawsuits. As the Tenth Circuit pointed out in *United States ex rel. Precision Co. v. Koch Industries*,[195] a relator's action is barred even if the relator identified additional facts after the essential allegations or transactions were disclosed. Otherwise, relators (and their counsel) could "with a little artful pleading" circumvent the public disclosure jurisdictional bar by adding one or more new facts that are different from the material in the public domain and assert that their action is therefore somehow different from the

---

[193] *See, e.g., Sandia*, 70 F.3d at 572; *Cooper*, 19 F.3d at 566.

[194] 19 F.3d at 566.

[195] 971 F.2d 548, 552 (10th Cir. 1992).

information in the public domain. Once the essential allegations or transactions are in the public domain, the government could easily undertake the same type of factual investigation.[196] Therefore, the relator's action does not add information of value. Unless the relator is an original source of the information, the action should be dismissed.

### 3. Hearing, Audit, Report, or Investigation

It is not enough that information be publicly disclosed. Rather, the defendant must also show that the disclosure arose from "a criminal, civil, or administrative hearing, in a congressional, administrative, or Government [General] Accounting Office report, hearing, audit or investigation, or from the news media."[197] As the Ninth Circuit pointed out, under this provision, "public disclosure can occur in one of three categories of fora: (1) in a 'criminal, civil, or administrative hearing,' (2) in a 'congressional, administrative, or Government Accounting Office report, hearing, audit, or investigation,' or (3) in the 'news media.' "[198]

The vast majority of courts have ruled that Congress did not intend the words "hearing," "audit," "report," "investigation," or "news media" to be mere examples but intended that these terms comprise the exclusive means through which the underlying information may be publicized. If the publicly disclosed material did not arise from a hearing, audit, investigation, or report or from the news media, the court is unlikely to invoke the public disclosure jurisdictional bar.[199]

---

[196]*Cf.* United States *ex rel.* Devlin v. California, 84 F.3d 358 (9th Cir. 1996) (relators' efforts to confirm the allegations did not provide relators with direct knowledge of the allegations and hence permit relators to qualify as original sources because any federal investigator could have performed the same work based upon the information in the public domain).

[197]31 U.S.C. §3730(e)(4).

[198]A-1 Ambulance Serv. v. California, 202 F.3d 1238, 1243 (9th Cir. 2000) (citation omitted).

[199]*See, e.g.*, United States *ex rel.* Dunleavy v. County of Delaware, 123 F.3d 734, 744 (3d Cir. 1997) ("The prevailing view is that this list constitutes an exhaustive rendition of the possible sources. We agree . . . ."); United States *ex rel.* John Doe v. John Doe Corp., 960 F.2d 318, 323 (2d Cir. 1992) ("Section 3730(e)(4)(A) furnishes an exclusive list of the ways in which a public disclosure must occur for the jurisdictional bar to apply.") (citation omitted); United States *ex rel.* Williams v. NEC Corp., 931 F.2d 1493, 1499–500 (11th Cir. 1991) ("The list of methods of 'public disclosure' is specific and is not qualified by words that would indicate that they are only examples of the types of 'public disclosure' to which the jurisdictional bar would apply. Congress could easily have used 'such as' or 'for example' to indicate that its list was not exhaustive. Because it did not, however, we will not give the statute a broader effect than that which appears in its plain language."); United States *ex rel.* LeBlanc v. Raytheon Co., 913 F.2d 17, 20 (1st Cir. 1990) (the public disclosure bar "does not deny jurisdiction over actions based on disclosures other than those specified, contrary to what the district court seemed to maintain"); United States *ex rel.* Stinson, Lyons, Gerlin & Bustamante, P.A. v. Blue Cross, 755 F. Supp. 1040, 1050 (S.D. Ga. 1990) ("The plain meaning of the statute compels the conclusion that the language following the term 'public disclosure' *does* limit that phrase.") (emphasis added) (citation omitted); *but see* United States *ex rel.* Stinson, Lyons, Gerlin & Bustamante, P.A. v. Prudential Ins., 736 F. Supp. 614, 621 (D.N.J. 1990) ("After careful consideration of the above precepts, the Court finds it reasonable to read 'public disclosure' as a general phrase not specifically limited by the enumerated examples in the remainder of the statute, and thus, it easily encompasses allegations such as those in issue in this case, public disclosures during civil discovery."), *aff'd on other grounds*, 944 F.2d 1149 (3d Cir. 1991). However, as the Tenth Circuit ruled, although the statute establishes an exclusive list of the sources for the disclosure (i.e.,

However, courts have defined what constitutes a hearing, audit, report, or investigation in different ways. The courts have split on two significant issues. The first is whether the audit, report, or investigation must be federal or whether such publicized state material qualifies. The second is whether the pertinent audit, report, or investigation must be completed and issued to trigger the jurisdictional bar.

### a. State Reports, Audits, or Investigations

Federal circuit courts have taken different approaches regarding the extent to which state investigations, audits, or reports can trigger the public disclosure bar.

The Eighth Circuit, in *United States ex rel. Hays v. Hoffman*,[200] determined that a state report can qualify as an administrative report under the public disclosure bar when the federal government funds, at least in part, the state program. Specifically, in *Hays*, the court ruled that "Medicaid compliance audits and audit reports conducted and prepared by the state agency authorized to administer this cooperative federal/state program are public disclosures within the meaning of §3730(e)(4)(A)."[201] The court based its ruling upon the statute's definition of "claim" to include money paid to grantees of the federal government.[202] The court concluded that it "would be inconsistent interpretation of the 1986 amendments to conclude that a fraudulent payment request submitted to [Medicaid] is a false claim against the United States . . . but a [Medicaid] audit is not an 'administrative audit' for purposes of §3730(e)(4)(A) because [the state Medicaid agency] is not a federal agency."[203]

However, prior to the Eighth Circuit's ruling in *Hays*, the Third Circuit had ruled that a state administrative report did not qualify as an administrative report under the FCA. In *United States ex rel. Dunleavy v. County of Delaware*, the purported publicly disclosed document—a Grantee Performance Report—disclosed that the defendant County had breached its duty to report the sale of property and to remit funds to HUD that the County had prepared and submitted

---

hearings, report, investigation, audit, or news media), these sources are not the only means by which a public disclosure can occur. *See* United States *ex rel.* Fine v. Advanced Scis., Inc., 99 F.3d 1000 (10th Cir. 1996). Thus, where a person repeats to a stranger the fraud information contained in a nonpublicly disseminated audit report, a public disclosure of the report has occurred. *Id.* at 1004 (the statute "defines the sources of allegations and transactions which trigger the bar but it does not define the only means by which [a] public disclosure can occur"); *cf.* Seal 1 v. Seal A, 255 F.3d 1154, 1160 (9th Cir. 2001) (noting the Tenth Circuit's ruling in *Advanced Sciences* and declining to decide whether the list of types of disclosures set forth in §3730(e)(4)(A) "is exhaustive").

[200] 325 F.3d 982 (8th Cir. 2003).

[201] *Id.* at 988.

[202] *Id.*

[203] *Id. Accord, In re* Natural Gas Royalties Qui Tam Litig., 467 F. Supp. 2d 1117, 1143–44 (D. Wyo. 2006); United States *ex rel.* Devlin v. County of Merced, No. 95-15285, 1996 U.S. App. LEXIS 17681, at *7 (9th Cir. July 11, 1996) (court applied public disclosure bar to state audit report that had been disseminated "to individuals, community and advocacy groups, and to various other interested parties throughout California").

to the federal government.[204] The court, relying upon the language and purpose of the statute, ruled that the document was not an administrative report.

As to the statutory language, the Third Circuit noted that the words "congressional, administrative, or Government Accounting Office" modified the words "report, hearing, audit, or investigation."[205] Because the term "administrative" otherwise would be susceptible to many meanings, the court concluded that it would apply the doctrine of *noscitur a sociis*—a word "gathers its meaning from the words around it."[206] Applying this doctrine, the court reasoned that an "administrative report" must only include federal administrative reports, not state administrative reports, because the surrounding words "Congress" and "Government Accounting Office" are "entities of our federal government."[207] The court concluded that it was difficult to "believe that the drafters of this provision intended the word 'administrative' to refer to both state and federal reports when it lies sandwiched between modifiers which are unquestionably federal in character."[208]

The Third Circuit believed that the Act's policies supported this interpretation. First, the court noted that those who prepare reports typically control the underlying information. Accordingly, where the state or local government actually prepared the report, there would be no assurance that the federal government had access to the information it needed to detect the fraud.[209] Second, the court pointed out that a substantial purpose of the 1986 legislative amendments was to eliminate the FCA's preexisting jurisdictional bar (known as the "government knowledge" bar), which prohibited *qui tam* actions based upon information in the government's possession.[210] If the bar attached to information state or local governments supplied to the federal government without any additional disclosure, the government-knowledge bar would, contrary to congressional design, be resuscitated because the action would be barred merely upon information in the federal government's possession.[211]

However, if the holding of the case were that all state reports (and presumably, under the court's logic, "audits" or "investigations") are not subject to the bar because they are not "federal" reports, a primary purpose of the statute would be undermined in that relators would be empowered to parrot the results of widely disseminated state reports or investigations regarding fraud (for example, Medicaid fraud, as the Eighth Circuit addressed in *Hays*) and

---

[204] 123 F.3d 734 (3d Cir. 1997).

[205] *Id.* at 745.

[206] *Id.*

[207] *Id.*

[208] *Id.*

[209] *Id.*

[210] *Id.* at 745–46.

[211] *Id.* The court noted that previously, in United States *ex rel.* Stinson v. Prudential Ins. Co., 944 F.2d 1149 (3d Cir. 1991), it had held that a document's "potential availability" was sufficient to trigger the bar and that in *Dunleavy* the state administrative report was "potentially available" to others under the Freedom of Information Act. However, the court distinguished the two cases by pointing out that *Prudential* "dealt with information produced on the public record in connection with litigation while here we are concerned with reports that may be filed away without the receiving agency being put on notice that there is any reason to give them close attention." *Dunleavy*, 123 F.3d at 746 (footnote omitted).

nonetheless be permitted to proceed with their parasitic *qui tam* action merely because the federal government had not issued the pertinent material and the information was not reported in the news media.[212]

### b. Final Issuance or Completion of Report, Audit, or Investigation

The relator in *United States ex rel. Williams v. NEC Corp.* was a government attorney who prepared a report analyzing bidding on telecommunications contracts, which he then submitted to his supervising officer, the Office of the Staff Judge Advocate, and the Office of General Counsel. The court commented that the report was not an administrative report under the FCA because the relator's "report on bidding practices was *not issued* by Congress, an administrative agency, or out of the Government [General] Accounting Office," and hence "is not a 'public disclosure' within the meaning of section 3730(e)(4)(A)."[213]

In *United States ex rel. Foust v. Group Hospitalization & Medical Services,* the Office of Personnel Management (OPM) was investigating whether participating plans (including nondefendants) were properly crediting discounts they received from providers when reporting costs incurred in covering persons under the Federal Employees Health Benefits Program. In conjunction with this review, the government issued an audit inquiry—a formal notice sent pursuant to an existing audit regarding the defendants' handling of provider discounts. The relators contended that there was no audit because there was no final or draft audit report. The court held that because an "audit is a 'formal or official examination and verification of books of account'[], Webster's Third New International Dictionary 143 (1993)," and because it "is clear from the government's declarations and exhibits that OPM was in fact undertaking *an audit* of certain . . . activities by . . . the participating plans . . . , the procedure undertaken by OPM to look into the defendants' handling of provider discounts constituted an administrative audit."[214]

---

[212]*Cf.* A-1 Ambulance Serv., Inc. v. California, 202 F.3d 1238, 1244–45 (9th Cir. 2000). As the Ninth Circuit noted in *A-1 Ambulance,* as to the three categories of fora that trigger the public disclosure bar, the term "hearing" is both in the first fora—"criminal, civil, or administrative *hearing*" (emphasis supplied)—and in the second—"congressional, administrative, or Government Accounting Office *report, hearing,* audit, or investigation (emphasis supplied)"—while the term "*report*" is only in the second fora. 202 F.3d at 1243. The court reasoned that this is one explanation for the court's ruling in *Dunleavy* that "report" only applies to federal reports, because the first fora covered public disclosures by states while the second fora covered public disclosures by the federal government. *Id. See also* United States *ex rel.* Hansen v. Cargill, Inc., 107 F. Supp. 2d 1172, 1180 (N.D. Cal. 2000) ("the Court concludes that the phrase 'administrative . . . report, hearing, audit or investigation' in the second category of FCA fora does not include non-federal agency actions. To hold otherwise would lead to the anomalous result that disclosure of a state administrative report implicates the FCA jurisdictional bar while disclosure of a state legislative report—a report which is neither congressional, administrative or from the General Accounting Office—does not raise the jurisdictional bar. The Court declines to read the statute to compel such a nonsensical result"), *aff'd,* 26 Fed. Appx. 736 (9th Cir. 2002), *cert. denied,* 537 U.S. 1147 (2003). *Cf.* United States *ex rel.* Atkinson v. Pennsylvania Shipbuilding, 255 F. Supp. 2d 351, 380 n.32 (E.D. Pa. 2002) (Coast Guard title abstract is a federal administrative report because "the Coast Guard unquestionably is a federal entity, and an abstract of title certainly is an official Coast Guard document").

[213]931 F.2d 1493 (11th Cir. 1991) (emphasis added).

[214]26 F. Supp. 2d 60, 70 (D.D.C. 1998) (emphasis added).

The question posed above is whether there is a tacit requirement that the audit, report, or investigation be completed and/or formally issued by an administrative agency to trigger the public disclosure jurisdictional bar. The clear response must be that no such finality is required. A relator can usurp a draft report or audit as easily as a completed report or audit. Moreover, the fact that the government is preparing such material is proof that the government is aware of the fraud and no *qui tam* action is needed. Rather, a *qui tam* action at that point would likely only reduce the government's potential recovery as it would have to share a substantial percentage of the recovery with the relator. Therefore, any draft or otherwise incomplete but public report, audit, or investigation that reveals allegations or transactions of misconduct should be sufficient to trigger the public disclosure jurisdictional bar.

### 4. *"Based Upon" a Public Disclosure*

In *United States ex rel. Jones v. Horizon Healthcare Corp.*,[215] the relator learned of possibly fraudulent conduct of her employer during the course of her employment. After she was terminated, she filed an action under the state whistleblower protection law (which publicly disclosed the underlying allegations) before filing her *qui tam* suit. The Sixth Circuit held that the relator's lawsuit was based upon the earlier state court action, although the basis for her *qui tam* lawsuit was her personal knowledge, because all that is required to trigger the bar is that the allegations or transactions in a complaint mirror the information in the public domain and not that relators actually derive their information from the public information.

In *United States ex rel. Siller v. Becton Dickinson & Co.*,[216] the relator, who was employed by Scientific Supply Inc. (SSI), a distributor of the defendant's supplies, filed a *qui tam* action after SSI brought a lawsuit alleging that the defendant had wrongfully terminated its distributorship agreement because SSI was prepared to disclose to the government that the defendant was overcharging the government. The relator contended that the allegations underlying his *qui tam* complaint were based upon personal experience and independent investigation, and that he had not read SSI's complaint until the defendant brought the action to his attention in its motion to dismiss the complaint. The defendant contended that the relator's action was based upon SSI's complaint, and that the relator was not an original source. The Fourth Circuit held that the relator's action would not be based upon allegations of fraud in the public domain if the relator could prove that he learned of the allegations independent of the public disclosure.[217]

---

[215] 160 F.3d 326, 335 (6th Cir. 1998).

[216] 21 F.3d 1339 (4th Cir. 1994).

[217] Specifically, the court concluded:

Section 3730(e)(4)(A)'s use of the phrase "based upon" is, we believe, susceptible of a straightforward textual exegesis. To "base upon" means to "use as a basis for." *Webster's Third New International Dictionary 180* (1986) (definition No. 2 of verb "base"). Rather plainly, therefore, a relator's action is "based upon" a public disclosure of allegations only where the relator has actually derived from that disclosure the allegations upon which his *qui tam* action is based. Such an understanding of the term "based upon," apart from giving effect to the language chosen by Congress, is fully consistent with

As illustrated by the contrast between *Jones* and *Siller*, there is a split in the circuits regarding the meaning of the term "based upon" in the public disclosure jurisdictional bar. The issue arises when there has been a public disclosure of allegations or transactions of fraud contained in or resulting from a hearing, audit, report, investigation, or news media account, but the relator claims ignorance of the public information or claims that the information was obtained from another source. Under these circumstances, the issue is whether the relator's action can be "based upon" the public information if the relator in fact did not know of that information.

Initially, it appeared that this issue would be significant in FCA jurisprudence, requiring resolution by the Supreme Court. However, since *Siller* was decided, substantially all other circuits have disagreed with its reasoning.[218]

---

section 3730(e)(4)'s undisputed objective of preventing "parasitic" actions, *see, e.g., Stinson,* [944 F.2d], at 1154, for it is self-evident that a suit that includes allegations that happen to be similar (even identical) to those already publicly disclosed, but were not actually derived from those public disclosures, simply is not, in any sense, parasitic.

*Id.* at 1348.

[218] *See, e.g.,* United States *ex rel.* Grynberg v. Praxair, Inc., 389 F.3d 1038, 1051 (10th Cir. 2004) (" 'Based upon' means 'supported by' and the threshold analysis is 'intended to be a quick trigger for the more exacting original source analysis.'. . . Even *qui tam* actions only partially based upon publicly disclosed allegations or transactions may be barred. The test is whether 'substantial identity' exists between the publicly disclosed allegations or transactions and the *qui tam* complaint.") (citations omitted); United States *ex rel.* Minnesota Ass'n of Nurse Anesthetists v. Allina Health Sys., 276 F.3d 1032, 1047 (8th Cir. 2002); United States *ex rel.* Mistick PBT v. Housing Auth., 186 F.3d 376, 385–88 (3d Cir. 1999), *cert. denied,* 529 U.S. 1018 (2000); United States *ex rel.* Jones v. Horizon Healthcare Corp., 160 F.3d 326, 335 (6th Cir. 1998) (adopting broad interpretation of "based upon" and holding that the relator's lawsuit was based upon an earlier state court action, although the basis for her *qui tam* lawsuit was her personal knowledge, because all that is required to trigger the bar is that the allegations or transactions in a complaint mirror the information in the public domain and not that the relator actually derive her information from the public information); United States *ex rel.* Biddle v. Board of Trustees of Stanford Univ., 161 F.3d 533 (9th Cir. 1998), *cert. denied,* 526 U.S. 1066 (1999); United States *ex rel.* McKenzie v. BellSouth Telecomms., Inc., 123 F.3d 935, 940 (6th Cir. 1997), *cert. denied,* 522 U.S. 1077 (1998); United States *ex rel.* Findley v. FPC-Boron Employees' Club, 105 F.3d 675 (D.C. Cir.), *cert. denied,* 522 U.S. 865 (1997); *cf.* United States *ex rel.* Feingold v. Adminastar Fed., Inc., 324 F.3d 492, 497 (7th Cir. 2003) ("a lawsuit is based upon public disclosures when it both depends essentially upon publicly disclosed information and is actually derived from such information") (internal quotation and citation omitted); United States v. Bank of Farmington, 166 F.3d 853, 863 (7th Cir. 1999) (noting in dicta that the "Fourth Circuit's interpretation of 'based upon' is the better on the grounds of plain meaning and public policy"); United States *ex rel.* Rost v. Pfizer Inc., 446 F. Supp. 2d 6, 20, 22 (D. Mass. 2006) (ruling that the "minority view's interpretation . . . is more consistent with the plain language of the statute and the plain and ordinary words therein" and therefore where the relator's complaint "is not derived from Defendants' disclosures to the government" but "derives from his own independent investigation of Defendants' off-label marketing scheme, and from his personal knowledge of Defendants' activities," relator's *qui tam* complaint is not 'based upon' that disclosure"); United States *ex rel.* Fowler v. Caremark RX, Inc., No. 03 C 8714, 2006 U.S. Dist. LEXIS 58992, at *16–17 (N.D. Ill. Aug. 21, 2006) (relators' action was not based upon public disclosures, although they attached to their amended complaint several of defendant's documents that defendant had previously produced to the government, because they had filed their *qui tam* action three years before defendant's disclosure to government, aided the government in its investigation, and had information sources independent of the public disclosure); United States *ex rel.* Olson v. ITT Educational Servs., Inc., No. 1:04-cv-647, 2006 U.S. Dist. LEXIS 1668, at *21–22 (S.D. Ind. Jan. 9, 2006) (ruling that as long as relator did not rely upon publicly disclosed material, the public disclosure bar does not prohibit his action); *see generally* United States *ex rel.* Dingle v. Bioport Corp., 388 F.3d 209, 214–15 (6th Cir. 2004) ("The words fraud or allegations need not appear in the disclosure for it

These subsequent decisions better accord with the FCA's structure, history, and policy.

First, a narrow construction of "based upon"—requiring that a relator actually derive his or her information from public information—would eliminate the original source exception.[219] The FCA's original source exception permits relators to bring actions based upon public information if they have direct and independent knowledge of the alleged fraud. If "based upon" were construed to mean "derived from" as *Siller* contends, then the relator could still pass the public disclosure jurisdictional bar by obtaining direct and independent knowledge of the allegations after having already learned of the information from a public source.[220] Courts have noted that Congress's imposition of such a requirement would make little sense because once information is in the public domain, anyone, including the government, could conduct the same investigation.[221] As the circuit court pointed out in *Findley*, a better reading of "based upon" is that the term is used as a "proxy for whether the relator's complaint merely parrots what is already in the public domain" which, if it does, would "lead[] logically to a subsidiary inquiry into whether the relator had obtained the information in his complaint independently *prior to* the disclosure."[222] Relators who learn of information before public disclosure and deliver that information to the government constitute the class of whistleblowers that Congress intended to benefit from the FCA.

---

to qualify. Nor does the allegation have to be exactly what Relators' allege. So long as the government is put on notice to the potential presence of fraud, even if the fraud is slightly different than the one alleged in the complaint, the *qui tam* action is not needed."); United States *ex rel.* Bledsoe v. Community Health Sys., Inc., 342 F.3d 634, 646 (6th Cir. 2003) (where previously filed state court action had alleged some discrete acts of fraud in hospital's psychiatric unit and relator's complaint had alleged those and additional acts of alleged fraud in the psychiatric unit, relator's action was "based upon" the state court action even though relator's "complaint contains more detailed allegations about the fraudulent billing practices in [the hospital's] psychiatric unit" because the state court action "already effectively alerted the public to the fraud occurring therein"); United States *ex rel.* Heath v. Dallas/Fort Worth Int'l Airport Bd., No. 3:99-CV-0100-M, 2004 U.S. Dist. LEXIS 11301, at *16–17 (N.D. Tex. May 28, 2004) (public disclosures did not raise an inference of fraud because "read alone, the disclosures indicate that Defendant was working with state and federal agencies to reduce the likelihood that small amounts of pollutants would escape the [industrial waste] System. It is Relator's Complaint that provides the allegations from which fraud may be inferred. Specifically, the Complaint alleges that Defendant was at all times aware that large amounts of pollutants were actually escaping the [industrial waste] System, that Defendant routinely failed to adhere to the precautionary procedures it had developed in order to be compliant with applicable state and federal law, that Defendant routinely submitted false information to federal agencies during the preparation of its environmental assessments, and that Defendant nonetheless certified to the [government] that it was in full compliance with state and federal law"). Further, courts have adopted this broad interpretation of the meaning of "based upon" even when the relator was the source of the information that is publicly disclosed. *See* United States *ex rel.* Laird v. Lockheed Martin Eng'g, 336 F.3d 346, 352 n.2 (5th Cir. 2003) (relator "does generally argue that the jurisdictional bar is inapplicable here because he is the one who made the public disclosure in the first place. . . . To the extent [the relator] . . . argues that relators involved in the initial public disclosure of information are not subject to the 'public disclosure' bar, we reject that argument).

[219] *See Stanford Univ.*, 161 F.3d at 538 (citing Salcido, *Screening out Unworthy Whistleblower Actions*, at 272–73); *Findley*, 105 F.3d at 683 (citing Salcido, *Screening Out Unworthy Whistleblower Actions*, at 272–73).

[220] *Findley*, 105 F.3d at 683.

[221] *See, e.g., id.*

[222] *Id.* (emphasis added).

Second, the courts have pointed out that "based upon" had an established meaning under the FCA that was not repealed *sub silincio* when Congress amended the statute in 1986. Specifically, courts have noted that the jurisdictional bar prior to 1986 had prohibited actions "*based upon* evidence or information in the possession of the United States" and that in applying this test, courts had implicitly rejected any interpretation of the phrase "based upon" that required relators to have obtained their information from governmental files, but instead construed the provision more broadly to apply whenever information from relators mirrored the information in the possession of the government.[223] As the D.C. Circuit pointed out in *Findley*, no evidence existed in either the language of the FCA or the legislative history of the 1986 amendments that in amending the jurisdictional bar Congress intended to change the established meaning of "based upon."[224]

Third, as mentioned previously, the purpose of the public disclosure jurisdictional bar is not merely to ferret out truly parasitic lawsuits. Rather, Congress intended to create incentives to encourage individuals to come forward at the earliest opportunity with information regarding possible fraud. "Once the information is in the public domain, there is less need for a financial incentive to spur individuals into exposing fraud."[225] Furthermore, rewarding relators for merely republishing public information only serves to reduce the government's ultimate recovery because relators are entitled to a portion of any recovery.

In *Siller*, the Fourth Circuit based its reading on a dictionary definition of the term.[226] However, such a definition does not account for the historical meaning attributed to the term as used in the jurisdictional bar and, more significantly, the Fourth Circuit did not explain how its interpretation makes sense in light of the structure of the statute. Furthermore, the Fourth Circuit unduly confined the purpose of the statute to preventing parasitic lawsuits. An interpretation requiring only that the complaint mirror the allegations or transactions in the public domain to potentially trigger the bar best effectuates Congress's purpose and maximizes the government's recovery while minimizing the social costs occasioned by the filing of unnecessary *qui tam* actions.[227]

---

[223] *See, e.g., id.* at 684 (emphasis added).

[224] *Id.* at 684–85.

[225] *Id.* at 685.

[226] 21 F.3d at 1349.

[227] Finally, no matter which "based upon" test a court ultimately adopts, it is important to note that *each* separate cause of action in the complaint must be evaluated under that test. Thus, for example, if one separate cause of action is not based in any part upon publicly disclosed material, then that cause of action is not subject to dismissal—even if other causes of action are dismissed under the public disclosure jurisdictional bar. *See, e.g.,* United States *ex rel.* Merena v. SmithKline Beecham Corp., 205 F.3d 97, 102 (3d Cir. 2000) ("What happens under these provisions if a relator files a multi-claim suit and some, but not all, of the claims fall into one of [the jurisdictional bars]? The plaintiff's decision to join all of his or her claims in a single lawsuit should not rescue claims that would have been doomed by section (e)(4) if they had been asserted in a separate action. And likewise, this joinder should not result in the dismissal of claims that would have otherwise survived. Thus, in applying section (e)(4), it seems clear that each claim in a multi-claim complaint must be treated as if it stood alone."); United States *ex rel.* Settlemire v. District of Columbia, 198 F.3d 913 (D.C. Cir. 1999) (The relator "correctly points out that each

## 5. The Original Source Provisions

If each of the four elements of the public disclosure jurisdictional bar is satisfied, then relators must prove that they are an original source or the action will be barred. In defining "original source," the statute provides as follows:

> (4)(A) No court shall have jurisdiction . . . based upon the public disclosure of *allegations or transactions* . . . unless the action is brought by the Attorney General *or the person bringing the action is an original source of the information.*
>
> (B) For purposes of this paragraph, "original source" means an individual who has direct and independent knowledge of *the information* on which the allegations are based and has *voluntarily* provided *the information* to the Government before filing an action under this section which is based *on the information.*[228]

Thus, to qualify as an original source, relators must satisfy three conditions: they must possess direct knowledge of the information on which the allegations are based; possess independent knowledge of the information on which the allegations are based; and provide the information voluntarily to the government before the information has been publicly disclosed.

Courts have offered various interpretations of these provisions. However, largely as a result of Judge Wald's analysis in *United States ex rel. Findley v. FPC-Boron Employees' Club*,[229] there is a possibility that future court interpretations will be more uniform, making it less likely that relators will be able to forum shop by filing in circuits that broadly construe the original source provision.[230] Specifically, *Findley* defined, for the first time, when precisely the informer must obtain direct and independent knowledge and provide the information to the government. On the basis of the statutory language, the court concluded that a relator must obtain his or her knowledge and provide the information to the government before its public disclosure.

---

count of fraud alleged in a *qui tam* action is considered separately under the jurisdictional bar provision.") (citation omitted); United States *ex rel.* Koch v. Koch Indus., No. 91-CV-763-K(J), 1999 U.S. Dist. LEXIS 16637 (N.D. Okla. Sept. 27, 1999) ("Nothing in . . . §3730(e)(4) suggests that a relator must qualify as an original source with regard to an allegation in a *qui tam* complaint that is not based upon a publicly disclosed allegation."); United States *ex rel.* Aflatooni v. Kitsap Physicians Servs., 163 F.3d 516 (9th Cir. 1999); Wang v. FMC Corp., 975 F.2d 1412 (9th Cir. 1992).

[228]The statutory references to "information" are italicized here because, as noted below, the word plays an important role in some courts' construction of the original source provision.

[229]105 F.3d 675 (D.C. Cir.), *cert. denied*, 522 U.S. 865 (1997).

[230]The statute provides that the plaintiff may file the action "in any judicial district in which the defendant or, in the case of multiple defendants, any one defendant can be found, resides, transacts business, or in which any act proscribed by section 3729 occurred." 31 U.S.C. §3732(a). Thus, a relator has great discretion as to where to file. He or she can file in any district in which a defendant can be found, resides, or transacts business or where the alleged proscribed act occurred (which could be interpreted to mean where the claim was made or where the claim was processed and paid by the United States). Furthermore, when there are multiple defendants, this discretion is substantially magnified because a number of unrelated defendants could be brought into one judicial district in which one person happens to transact business. *Cf.* United States *ex rel.* Merena v. SmithKline Beecham Corp., 114 F. Supp. 2d 352, 372 (E.D. Pa. 2000) (noting that "because of inter-circuit conflicts as to [the] interpretation" of the original source provision, "litigants and litigants' attorneys [are forced], wherever possible, to attempt to choose the most favorable jurisdiction; i.e., 'forum shop'. This should not have to occur when actions are filed under a federal statute that should be applied and interpreted uniformly throughout the land.")

### a. Timing of the Relator's Knowledge and Disclosure of Information

There are three schools of thought regarding the necessary elements to being an original source. One approach provides that the relator must be a true "whistleblower" to qualify—that is, provide the information to the government before the information is publicly disclosed. A second approach, which is closely akin to the true whistleblower approach, dictates that the relator must be the source to the entity that made the public disclosure (i.e., not necessarily a whistleblower to the government because under this formulation the person could blow the whistle by filing a non-*qui tam* action, which publicly discloses the allegations or by disclosing the facts to the news media, which later results in a public disclosure). The third approach provides that the relator need not be an informer to qualify as an original source, but only must have direct and independent knowledge of the alleged misconduct and voluntarily provide that information to the government (even minutes before filing) to qualify as an original source.

### i. The D.C. and Sixth Circuits' Rule That the Relator Must Be a True Whistleblower to Qualify as an Original Source

Of the three approaches, the D.C. and Sixth Circuit rule[231]— requiring the relator to disclose the information underlying the lawsuit *before* it is publicly disclosed—provides a better interpretation of the statutory language, legislative history, and statutory purpose of the original source provision than the other two approaches.

The statutory language supports the conclusion that the relator must be the person who "blew the whistle" to the government in order to qualify. First, that construction comports with the usual meaning of the term "original source"; second, any other construction would lead to an absurd result.

First, as to the statutory language, any fair characterization of who is an "original source" includes the notion that the person must be the first to report the information. As the Sixth Circuit, in *United States ex rel. McKenzie v. BellSouth Telecomms., Inc.,* concluded, the term "original source" necessarily includes the notion that the relator must be the person who alerted the government to the alleged misconduct:

> We find it difficult to understand how one can be a "true whistleblower" unless she is responsible for alerting the government to the alleged fraud before such information is in the public domain. Therefore, we adopt the approach of the District of Columbia Circuit and conclude that, to be an original source, a relator must inform the government of the alleged fraud before the information has been publicly disclosed.[232]

---

[231] *See* United States *ex rel.* Walburn v. Lockheed Martin Corp., 431 F.3d 966, 975–76 (6th Cir. 2005); United States *ex rel.* Jones v. Horizon Healthcare Corp., 160 F.3d 326, 335 (6th Cir. 1998); United States *ex rel.* McKenzie v. BellSouth Telecomms., Inc., 123 F.3d 935, 942 (6th Cir. 1997); United States *ex rel.* Findley v. FPC-Boron Employees' Club, 105 F.3d 675 (D.C. Cir. 1997).

[232] 123 F.3d 935 (6th Cir. 1997).

Further, the interpretation of the Eighth Circuit in *United States ex rel. Minnesota Ass'n of Nurse Anesthetists v. Allina Health Systems*,[233]—that the relator need not be a whistleblower—interprets the last clause of subparagraph (B) (which mandates that the relator "voluntarily provide[] the information to the Government before filing an action . . . ") in a manner that would lead to an absurd result. Courts adhering to this rule point out that under this provision the relator must only provide her information before "filing the action," and not before the public disclosure.

However, inasmuch as the relator must submit the material to the government at the time of filing under subsection (b)(2), it would make no sense to require that the relator also submit this same information to the government prior to filing the action (such as five minutes prior to filing).[234] It does make sense, however, to require the relator to provide this information to the government prior to the publication of the information. This allows the government to use the information for investigative purposes *prior* to the time in which the defendant is tipped off, by virtue of the public disclosure of the information, and can promptly undertake any remedial actions that are needed to minimize its losses.

Indeed, the more likely purpose of the clause in Subparagraph (B) is to indicate the time period in which a relator must voluntarily provide information to the government. Any relator will, of course, provide information to and cooperate with the government *after* the action is filed because it is in her interest to do so. The apparent purpose of the language in Subparagraph (B) is to underscore the fact that the relator must also *voluntarily*

---

[233]276 F.3d 1032 (8th Cir. 2002). *Allina* is discussed in Section III.C.5.iii., below.

[234]*See, e.g., Findley*, 105 F.3d at 690–91. As the court pointed out:

We previously noted that the government notice part of the "original source" exception may appear extraneous in light of the statute's filing provisions, which require cases to be filed under seal for a period of at least sixty days and served only on the government. The "original source" government notification provision is not superfluous, however, for it serves an entirely different purpose from the statute's filing and government notice provisions. By protecting a party who initially exposes fraud to the government, Congress "corrected" the holding of United States *ex rel.* Wis. v. Dean. Once the information has been publicly disclosed, however, there is little need for the incentive provided by a *qui tam* action. Thus, the only reading of the statute that accounts for the requirement that an "original source" voluntarily provided information to the government before filing suit, and Congress' decision to use the term "original source" rather than simply incorporating subparagraph (B)'s description into subparagraph (A), is one that requires an original source to provide the information to the government prior to any public disclosure.

*See also* United States *ex rel.* King v. Hillcrest Health Ctr., 264 F.3d 1271, 1280 (10th Cir. 2001) ("It is also clear from the statute that compliance with the disclosure requirements of §3730(b)(2) at the time of filing does not satisfy the pre-filing disclosure requirement of §3730(e)(4). . . . More must be done to qualify as an original source than file the action. The government must be voluntarily notified beforehand.") (citation and internal quotation omitted); United States *ex rel.* Ackley v. International Bus. Machs., 76 F. Supp. 2d 654, 667 (D. Md. 1999) (holding that the relator's assertion that he could satisfy the original source provision by disclosing his information to the government seconds before filing "leads to an obviously absurd result since, at the time of the filing of the complaint, a formal written disclosure statement must also be filed. It makes no sense at all to require what might be a disclosure, oral or written, to be made a few seconds before a written one is required to be filed").

provide information to and cooperate with the government *before* filing the action.

The legislative history also supports this reading. Both the primary Senate sponsor and the primary House sponsor stated that, to qualify as an original source, the person must be the source of the subsequent disclosure of the information. For example, Senator Grassley stated that "a *qui tam* action based solely on public disclosures cannot be brought by an individual . . . who had not been an *original source to the entity that disclosed the allegations.*"[235] Representative Berman stated that "[o]nce the public disclosure of the information occurs through one of the methods referred to above, then only a person who qualifies as an 'original source' may bring the action. A person is an original source if he had some of the information related to the claim *which he made available to the government or the news media in advance of the false claims being publicly disclosed.*"[236] Thus, the legislative history is consistent with the statutory language mandating that the original source must be the person that supplies the pertinent information to the government prior to its public disclosure.

Finally, the policy underlying the FCA supports the position that the relator must disclose the information to the government prior to the time in which the information is publicly disclosed. Both the legislative history and several cases make clear that the purpose of the *qui tam* provisions is to ensure that the United States learns of the misconduct at the earliest possible time.[237] Indeed, it is

---

[235] 132 CONG. REC. 20,536 (1986) (emphasis supplied). Presumably, the reason Senator Grassley used the word "entity" rather than "government" is that, at the time he made these statements, a person could qualify as an original source if the person had "voluntarily informed the Government or the news media prior to an action filed by the Government." *Id.* at 20,351. The words "news media" were subsequently struck; instead, relators were required to supply their information solely to the government.

[236] *Id.* at 29,322 (emphasis supplied).

[237] *See* H.R. REP. No. 99-660, at 23 ("The purpose of the *qui tam* provisions of the False Claims Act is to encourage private individuals who are aware of fraud being perpetrated against the Government to bring such information forward."); S. REP. No. 99-345, at 14, *reprinted in* 1986 U.S.C.C.A.N. at 5279 (noting that the amendments were intended to reward those who "bring . . . wrongdoing to light"); *cf.* United States *ex rel.* King v. Hillcrest Health Ctr., 264 F.3d 1271, 1281 (10th Cir. 2001) (holding that in cases in which there has been a public disclosure the relator must voluntarily provide the government with the essential elements or information on which the *qui tam* allegations are based before filing the *qui tam* action because this interpretation of the jurisdictional bar "encourages private individuals to come forward quickly with their information, to not dawdle when there has been a public disclosure, and to discourage persons from withholding or remaining silent about their relevant information") (citation omitted); United States v. Bank of Farmington, 166 F.3d 853, 866 (7th Cir. 1999) ("The intent of the Act . . . is to encourage private individuals who are aware of fraud against the government to bring such information forward at the *earliest possible time* and to discourage persons with relevant information from remaining silent.") (quoting United States *ex rel.* Barth v. Ridgedale Elec., Inc., 44 F.3d 699, 704 (8th Cir. 1995)) (emphasis added); United States *ex rel.* Biddle v. Board of Trs. of Stanford Univ., 161 F.3d 533, 538–39 (9th Cir. 1998) (stating that the FCA's two primary purposes are "to alert the government as early as possible to fraud that is being committed against it and to encourage insiders to come forward with such information where they would otherwise have little incentive to do so") (citations omitted); United States *ex rel.* Jones v. Horizon Healthcare Corp., 160 F.3d 326, 335 (6th Cir. 1998) ("[T]he *qui tam* provisions were intended not only to block freeloading relators, but also to inspire whistleblowers to come forward as soon as possible."); United States *ex rel.* LaCorte v. SmithKline Beecham Clinical Labs., Inc., 149 F.3d 227, 234 (3d Cir. 1998); United States *ex rel.* Findley v. FPC-Boron Employees' Club, 105 F.3d

illogical, on the one hand, to believe that Congress required that lawsuits be placed under seal, as it did, so that the United States' interest could be protected by not prematurely disclosing an investigation to defendants,[238] but, on the other hand, that Congress, in the original source provision, would reward relators who publicly disclosed the allegations underlying the lawsuit before informing the government of that conduct. Once the United States learns of this information, it may undertake remedial action and minimize its potential losses. Contrary to this purpose, the minority rule will encourage alleged "whistle-blowers" to "sit on their hands" and fail to disclose their information in the hope that damages will mount and thus their bounty will increase.

### ii.   The Second and Ninth Circuits' Rule That the Relator Must Be the Source to the Entity That Made the Public Disclosure

Before the D.C. Circuit's ruling in *Findley* and the Sixth Circuit's decision in *McKenzie*, the Second and Ninth Circuit had previously ruled that the information must be disclosed prior to the public disclosure, but reached this result on slightly different grounds.[239]

The Second Circuit, in *United States ex rel. Dick v. Long Island Lighting Co.*, was the first court to impose the "source" requirement—i.e., that the relator must be the whistleblower, the source to the entity making the public disclosure.[240] The court reasoned that the statute required the relator to be the source because, according to the court, "information" means something different in 31 U.S.C. §3730(e)(4)(A)—that the relator must be the "original source of the information" publicly disclosed—than it does in §3730(e)(4)(B)—that relator must have "direct and independent knowledge of the information on which the allegations are based." According to the Second Circuit, the word "information"

---

675, 685 (D.C. Cir. 1997) ("[T]he *qui tam* provisions of the FCA were designed to inspire whistleblowers to come forward promptly with information concerning fraud so that the government can stop it and recover ill-gotten gains."); United States *ex rel.* Wang v. FMC Corp., 975 F.2d 1412, 1419–20 (9th Cir. 1992); United States *ex rel.* Dick v. Long Island Lighting Co., 912 F.2d 13, 18 (2d Cir. 1990); United States *ex rel.* Ackley v. International Bus. Machs., 76 F. Supp. 2d 654, 668 (D. Md. 1999); *Koch Indus.*, 188 F.R.D. 617, 635–36 ("Despite its lack of clarity on other issues, there is at least one point on which the legislative history of the 1986 amendments to the FCA is clear. The main purpose behind the *qui tam* provisions of the FCA is to encourage private individuals, who are aware of fraud being perpetrated against the Government, to bring their information forward. . . . Thus, nothing in the FCA should be construed in such a way as to create any incentive for *qui tam* relators to hold on to information evidencing fraud rather than promptly disclosing that information to the government."). As the Sixth Circuit pointed out in *McKenzie*, permitting the relator to obtain a substantial bounty for repeating public knowledge also undermines the statutory goal that the relator's bounty be proportionate to the amount of her contribution in exposing the alleged misconduct:

> Anyone who alerts the government and is a "true whistleblower" deserves any *reward* that may be obtained by pursuing a qui tam action under the FCA. However, the individual who sits on the sidelines while others disclose the allegations that form the basis of her complaint should not be able to participate in any award. This would be contrary to the purpose of the statute.

123 F.3d at 942–43.

[238] *See* 31 U.S.C. §3730(b)(2).

[239] *See* United States *ex rel.* Wang v. FMC Corp., 975 F.2d 1412, 1419–20 (9th Cir. 1992); United States *ex rel.* Dick v. Long Island Lighting Co., 912 F.2d 13, 18 (2d Cir. 1990).

[240] 912 F.2d 13 (2d Cir. 1990).

must have a different meaning in (e)(4)(A) than in (e)(4)(B) because (1) otherwise Congress would have placed a period after original source in (e)(4)(A) and the meaning of the statute would have remained the same; (2) the use of "information" in (e)(4)(A) is without modification, while "information" in (e)(4)(B) is modified; therefore, the modification was intended to have some application; and (3) "information" in (e)(4)(A) refers to the publicly disclosed information, while "information" in (e)(4)(B) refers to that "which supplies the basis for the qui tam action itself," which the court believed "is a slightly more expansive definition."[241]

The Ninth Circuit concurred with the Second Circuit's ruling in *Long Island Lighting Co.* In *United States ex rel. Wang v. FMC Corp.*, the court ruled that the best application of the Act's purpose required that after a public disclosure occurred, the relator must prove that he was the source to the entity that made the disclosure:

> The paradigm qui tam plaintiff is the "whistleblowing" insider. . . . Qui tam suits are meant to encourage insiders privy to a fraud on the government to blow the whistle on the crime. In such a scheme, there is little point in rewarding a second toot.
>
> . . . If, however, someone *republishes* an allegation that already has been publicly disclosed, he cannot bring a qui tam suit, even if he had "direct and independent knowledge" of the fraud. He is no "whistleblower." A "whistleblower" sounds the alarm; he does not echo it. The Act rewards those brave enough to speak in the face of a "conspiracy of silence," and not their mimics. . . .
>
> . . . Because he had no hand in the original public disclosure of the Bradley's troubles, [relator's] claim regarding the [Bradley] is blocked by the jurisdictional bar of section 3730(e)(4)(A).[242]

---

[241] *Id.* at 16–17. The court also asserted that its reading of the statute was supported by the Act's history and purpose. As to the legislative history, the court noted that sponsors of the legislation in the House and Senate stated that the original source must be a source to the entity that made the disclosure. For example, Rep. Berman stated that the original source must have "some of the information related to the claim which he made available to the government or the news media *in advance of the false claims being publicly disclosed*," and Sen. Grassley stated that the public disclosure bar prohibited persons "who had not been an original source *to the entity that disclosed the allegations*" from bringing a *qui tam* claim based on publicly disclosed information. *See* 132 CONG. REC. 29,322 (statement of Rep. Berman) (emphasis supplied); 132 CONG. REC. 20,536 (1986) (statement of Sen. Grassley) (emphasis supplied).

As to the statutory purpose, the court stated that its interpretation was consistent with the Act because it required the relator to blow the whistle at the earliest possible time:

> Our interpretation is in accord with this purpose and is most likely to bring "wrongdoing to light" since, by barring those who come forward only *after* public disclosure of possible False Claims Act violations from acting as qui tam plaintiffs, it discourages person[s] with relevant information from remaining silent and encourages them to report such information at the earliest possible time.

Thus, "if the information on which a *qui tam* suit is based is in the public domain, and the *qui tam* plaintiff was not a source of that information, then the suit is barred." *Long Island Lighting Co.*, 912 F.2d at 18 (citation omitted).

[242] 975 F.2d 1412, 1419–20 (9th Cir. 1992) (citations omitted). *See also* United States *ex rel.* Campbell v. Redding Med. Ctr., 421 F.3d 817, 822 (9th Cir. 2005); Hagood v. Sonoma County Water Agency, 81 F.3d 1465, 1474 (9th Cir. 1996); United States *ex rel.* Kreindler & Kreindler v. United Techs. Corp., 985 F.2d 1148, 1158–59 (2d Cir. 1993). However, the Ninth Circuit expressly disagreed with the D.C. and Sixth Circuit rulings that the relator must disclose the information to the government prior to filing. *See* United States *ex rel.* Zaretsky v. Johnson Controls, Inc., 457 F.3d 1009, 1014 (9th Cir. 2006) ("The only dispute regarding the FCA claim

The Fourth Circuit, however, disagreed with the Second and Ninth Circuits in *United States ex rel. Siller v. Becton Dickinson & Co.*[243] The court rejected the Second Circuit's holding that the relator must be the "source" of the information that was publicly disclosed.[244] As to the Second Circuit's contention that "information" in (e)(4)(A) would be superfluous if it did not have a separate meaning than the use of "information" in (e)(4)(B), the court answered that "the phrase is not superfluous in a way or to a degree that warrants ascribing different meanings to the same word used in two successive clauses." In fact, the court concluded that "information" as used in (e)(4)(A) has the same meaning as "information" in (e)(4)(B) in that on both occasions the "information" that is referred to is the information "on which the allegations are based" that was publicly disclosed, and, thus, contrary to the Second Circuit's contention, "information" in (e)(4)(B) does not refer to information underlying the allegations in the *qui tam* complaint.[245] Given this analysis of the statutory language, the Fourth Circuit rejected the Second Circuit's rule "as imposing an additional, extra-textual requirement that was not intended by Congress."[246]

---

is thus over a single question of law: Does the FCA require . . . that prospective relators provide relevant information to the government prior to the public disclosure at issue? The Eighth Circuit has held that the FCA does not so require, and the Sixth and D.C. Circuits have held that it does. . . . In concert with the Eighth Circuit and in light of our related FCA case law . . . we hold that there is no such requirement.").

[243]21 F.3d 1339, 1351–54 (4th Cir. 1994).

[244]*Id.* at 1351.

[245]*Id.* at 1352–53. The Fourth Circuit also rejected the Second Circuit's conclusion that a primary purpose of the Act was to penalize whistleblowers who did not promptly report the allegations of fraud. Instead, the court found that the predominant purposes of the jurisdictional bar are to prohibit "parasitic" lawsuits while, at the same time, encouraging citizens to report fraud. *Id.* at 1355. The court ruled that actions that are not "based upon" public information are not in any way "parasitic"—because the relator is relying upon her own information. *Id.* at 1348. The Fourth Circuit, however, construes the jurisdictional bar too narrowly in reading it as simply a bar on parasitic lawsuits. The bar is much broader than that. By focusing on public information, Congress intended to root out all *qui tam* actions—not just parasitic actions—that do not provide the government with new information and to compel the person to report that information to the government prior to the time in which the information is publicly known. As the Sixth Circuit pointed out, in barring the relator from proceeding in an action in which the person relied upon her personal knowledge as an employee of the company but filed a state court action under a state whistleblower protection law (which publicly disclosed the underlying allegations) prior to filing her *qui tam* action, the "*qui tam* provisions of the Federal False Claims Act are intended to encourage private individuals who are aware of fraud being perpetrated against the government to bring such information forward and to prevent parasitic *qui tam* actions in which relators simply feed off of previous disclosures of government fraud . . . Although [relator's] lawsuit in this case was neither parasitic nor opportunistic, the *qui tam* provisions were intended not only to block freeloading relators, but also to inspire whistleblowers to come forward as soon as possible." United States *ex rel.* Jones v. Horizon Healthcare Corp., 160 F.3d 326, 335 (6th Cir. 1998) (citations omitted). Once the information is public, the government does not need any "whistleblower" and thus there is no need to permit such an action, which only reduces the government's recovery, unless the relator actually furnished the government with the underlying information prior to its disclosure. Reporting the information before it is publicized is advantageous to the government because it can then investigate the alleged misconduct prior to the time in which the target is necessarily tipped off by virtue of the public disclosure.

[246]21 F.3d at 1352–53. Three days after the Fourth Circuit's decision in United States *ex rel.* Siller v. Becton Dickinson & Co., the Eleventh Circuit, in Cooper v. Blue Cross and Blue Shield of Fla., 19 F.3d 562 (11th Cir. 1994), similarly ruled that the original source provisions of the Act did not contain a separate "source" requirement. *Id.* at 568 n.13 ("We are unable to agree with the Second Circuit's opinion that the relator must also prove he was the original source of the

The end result of the Second and Ninth Circuits' rule is that when those decisions are coupled with the D.C. Circuit's reading of the statute in *Findley* and the Sixth Circuit's in *McKenzie*, four circuits require that relators possess information regarding the fraud and have either provided that information to the news media or government prior to the time in which the information becomes public. These circuits, unlike the Fourth Circuit in *Siller*, properly conclude that those who remain silent after learning of fraud and only appear after another has broken the conspiracy of silence are simply not entitled to any reward for merely republishing public information in the form of a *qui tam* complaint.

### iii. The Eighth Circuit's Rule That the Relator Need Not Be a Whistleblower to Qualify as an Original Source

The Eighth Circuit in *United States ex rel. Minnesota Ass'n of Nurse Anesthetists v. Allina Health Systems*,[247] and several district courts,[248] have ruled that the relator did not need to disclose the information underlying the action to the United States prior to its public disclosure. In *Allina*, the court held that the rule that the relator must have revealed the allegations to the government before the public disclosure to qualify as an original source "has no textual basis in the statute."[249] Set forth below is an analysis of the Eighth Circuit's decision in *Allina* and a discussion of why that opinion is not consistent with the statutory language and policy.

In *Allina*, the relator, the Minnesota Association of Nurse Anesthetists (MANA), filed a *qui tam* action on December 28, 1994, alleging that the de-

---

information *to the entity that disclosed it.* . . . This rule does not appear in the plain language of the statute, and we find no support for it in the legislative history.") (citation omitted). *See also* United States *ex rel.* Findley v. FPC-Boron Employees' Club, 105 F.3d at 690 (concurring with the Fourth Circuit that "there is no additional requirement that the 'original source' be responsible for providing the information to the entity that publicly disclosed the allegations of fraud").

[247] 276 F.3d 1032 (8th Cir. 2002).

[248] United States *ex rel.* Rost v. Pfizer Inc., 446 F. Supp. 2d 6, 24 (D. Mass. 2006) ("In the face of unambiguous statutory language, it is inappropriate to look beyond the text of the FCA's original source provision. That text requires that an original source: (1) have independent knowledge of the fraud alleged in this complaint; (2) have direct knowledge of that fraud; and (3) have disclosed his information to the government before filing suit. No other requirements are even suggested by the statutory text.") (footnotes omitted); United States *ex rel.* Coleman v. Indiana, No. 96-714-C-T/G, 2000 U.S. Dist. LEXIS 13666, at *45 (S.D. Ind. Sept. 19, 2000); United States *ex rel.* Merena v. SmithKline Beecham Corp., 114 F. Supp. 2d 352, 358 (E.D. Pa. 2000) ("The statute merely requires that a relator, in order to qualify as an 'original source,' have direct and independent knowledge of the information on which the allegations are based and have 'voluntarily provided the information to the Government before filing an action under this section.' 31 U.S.C. §3730(e)(4)(B). The statute by its express wording, at least, makes no other temporal requirement as to when the information must be provided to the government. Had the statute intended an additional requirement that the voluntary disclosure occur before there is any public disclosure, the statute could easily have so stated quite plainly and simply.") (footnote omitted); United States *ex rel.* Butler v. Magellan Health Servs., 74 F. Supp. 2d 1201, 1211–12 (M.D. Fla. 1999); United States *ex rel.* Johnson v. Shell Oil Co., 33 F. Supp. 2d 528, 542 (E.D. Tex. 1999) ("adding a temporal requirement . . . could discourage citizen involvement, even when the citizen has direct and independent knowledge of fraud"); United States *ex rel.* Bidani v. Edmund J. Lewis, No. 97 C 6502, 1998 U.S. Dist. LEXIS 20647, at *16–18 (N.D. Ill. Jan. 3, 1999) (ruling that the court would apply the "plain language of the statute," and require only that the relator voluntarily provide the information to the government prior to filing the action, not requiring that the information be provided to the government prior to the time in which the information is publicized).

[249] 276 F.3d at 1050.

fendant hospitals and anesthesiologists had knowingly made false claims on the United States by mischaracterizing services they had provided to Medicare patients.[250] Specifically, the relator claimed that the defendant anesthesiologists and hospitals made the following types of misrepresentations: billing on a reasonable charge basis when the services the anesthesiologists provided did not meet the criteria for reasonable charge reimbursement; billing services as personally performed by the anesthesiologist when the services did not meet the criteria for personal performance; billing as if the anesthesiologist involved were directing fewer concurrent cases than he or she actually did direct; and certifying that it was medically necessary for both an anesthesiologist and anesthetist to personally perform cases that in fact an anesthetist alone personally performed.[251] The relator asserted that the defendants violated the FCA by overcharging the government for their services, and that they had conspired among each other to do so. The United States declined to intervene.[252]

Significantly, however, for purposes of the FCA's public disclosure bar, on November 8, 1994, approximately seven weeks before filing its *qui tam* case, the relator and several individual anesthetists sued many of the same defendants alleging various federal antitrust and state law violations, again in connection with their anesthesia billing practices.[253] The antitrust complaint alleged:

> The defendant anesthesiology groups and their co-conspirators have engaged in a wide-spread practice of fraudulent billing of anesthesia services in violation of . . . Federal statutes, including §1128(a)(1)(A). Such violations include, but are not limited to, billing for operations at which they were not present and inaccurately designating operations as one-on-one for Medicare purposes.[254]

These allegations in MANA's antitrust case were immediately reported in the local newspapers in St. Paul and St. Cloud on November 10 and 11.[255] MANA also provided a copy of the antitrust case to the United States government.[256] Only after this publicity did MANA file its *qui tam* action in which it republished these same allegations.[257]

After concluding that the relator's action was "based upon" the publicly disclosed antitrust action and resulting newspaper articles, the court evaluated whether the relator could qualify as an original source. A focal point in the court's analysis was the Seventh Circuit's decision in *United States ex rel. Wisconsin v. Dean*,[258] which the court believed was the catalyst to Congress' 1986 amendments to the public disclosure bar.[259] Specifically, the court noted: "Since we know from the history of the False Claims Act that the original

---

[250] *Id.* at 1036.

[251] *Id.* at 1037.

[252] *Id.* at 1040.

[253] *Id.*

[254] *Id.*

[255] *Id.*

[256] *Id.*

[257] *Id.*

[258] 729 F.2d 1100 (7th Cir. 1984).

[259] 276 F.3d at 1046, 1047. In *Dean*, the State of Wisconsin had investigated Medicaid fraud and, consistent with its duty under the Social Security Act to report various fraud and abuse information

source provision was added in 1986 to permit claims like the one in *Dean,* in which a claimant investigated the fraud and then revealed it to the government before filing suit, we would expect that the effect of the original source provision is to protect from the public disclosure bar those who first bring a claim to light."[260]

With that in mind, the court turned to the issue of whether the relator must provide the information underlying its lawsuit to the government prior to the time in which the information is publicly disclosed to satisfy the statutory test that the relator must be "an original source of the information" and have "voluntarily provided the information to the Government before filing an action under this section which is based on the information."[261] The defendants contended that the relator could not satisfy this standard because it filed its *qui tam* complaint *after* it had publicly filed its antitrust action. Although the court recognized that the District of Columbia and Sixth Circuits had adopted this rule,[262] it found that "[t]his additional requirement has no textual basis in the statute." Moreover, in balancing utility versus fairness, the court reasoned that the D.C. and Sixth Circuit rule should be rejected because it undermines the purpose of the original source provision to extend "fairness" to the relator:

> [T]he courts adopting this requirement have justified it by arguing that after public disclosure, the relator has no utility to the government. *FPC-Boron Employees' Club,* 105 F.3d at 691 ("Once the information has been publicly disclosed, however, there is little need for the incentive provided by a qui tam action."). However, as we have seen, through the original source provisions Congress chose to reward persons who discovered and revealed fraud, rather than confiscating their claims. At the same time, Congress limited that beneficence by denying the bounty even to those who uncovered the fraud unless they had revealed it to the government before filing suit. Sec. 3730(e)(4)(B). We would change the balance Congress struck if we were to further restrict the class of those whose discoveries had been made public but who were nevertheless permitted to proceed as relators. We decline to adopt the proposed additional requirement.[263]

The two policy grounds the *Allina* court identified in support of its construction—the purported need to adhere to the *Dean* ruling and to balance utility and fairness—has no basis in the statutory language or legislative history.

In *Allina,* the court believed that it was critical that it construe the original source provision in a manner consistent with the *Dean* decision.[264] However, if

---

to the government, disclosed its findings to the HHS. *See* 729 F.2d at 1106. Although the lower court acknowledged that the government possessed the information, it concluded that public policy compelled it to allow the suit. The Seventh Circuit reversed, concluding that the relator's action was barred because the suit was based on information in the government's possession, which triggered the pre-1986 FCA jurisdictional bar.

[260]276 F.3d at 1047–48.

[261]31 U.S.C. §3730(e)(4).

[262]276 F.3d at 1049 (citing United States *ex rel.* Findley v. FPC-Boron Employees' Club, 105 F.3d 675 (D.C. Cir. 1997); United States *ex rel.* McKenzie v. BellSouth Telecomms., Inc., 123 F.3d 935 (6th Cir. 1997)).

[263]*Id.* at 1050–51.

[264]*Id.* at 1047–48.

the court had compared the facts in *Dean* to those in *Allina*, it would have found that an application of the *Dean* rule would result in the dismissal of the relator in *Allina*. In *Dean*, the following events occurred: the relator investigated the fraud; the relator reported the fraud to the United States, and then the allegations of the fraud were publicly disclosed (in the form of criminal proceedings and news media accounts).[265] Under any interpretation of the public disclosure bar, the relator under the facts in *Dean* should be protected: the relator broke the conspiracy of silence and divulged critical information to the government so that the government could conduct its own investigation before the same material was publicly disseminated.

That, however, is not what occurred in the *Allina* case. There, the sequence was quite different. In *Allina,* the relator apparently investigated the alleged misconduct; the relator publicly disclosed the misconduct (in the form of a civil complaint and newspaper accounts); and only then did the relator disclose the allegations to the government. Hence, in making its disclosure to the government, the relator did not break any conspiracy of silence, but merely handed over to the government public material.

If the *Allina* court had literally adhered to the teaching of the *Dean* case and the language of the public disclosure bar, it would have dismissed the relator. By publicizing the allegations before making any disclosure to the federal government, the relator in *Allina* deprived the government of the very important opportunity to control and conduct its investigation in secrecy without prematurely tipping off the target of the investigation. In *Dean,* conversely, the government was afforded this opportunity. Because the original source provision is intended to benefit relators like the relator in *Dean,* who disclosed the information before it became public knowledge, and not relators like the relator in *Allina, who divulged* information to the government that had already been publicized, the relator in *Allina* should have been dismissed.

Further, the court, without statutory basis, believed that it had to balance utility and fairness in interpreting the public disclosure bar. However, the court, in its opinion, did not point to any specific language in the statute or the legislative history to support its construction. Moreover, from the structure of the statutory language, it appears that Congress' predominant concern was with utility. It, for example, prohibited a relator, under 31 U.S.C. §§3730(b)(5) and 3730(e)(3), from bringing an action even if there had been no public disclosure and even if the relator otherwise qualified as an original source, because such

---

[265] Although in *Dean,* neither the appellate nor the district court set forth the precise dates of the disclosures to the government and the subsequent dates of the publicly disclosed criminal proceedings and news accounts, it seems clear from the state's statutory duty to report misconduct regarding federal grant funds and the court's factual rendition of the disclosures that the state made disclosures to the federal government before any public disclosure of the defendant's misconduct. *See* 729 F.2d at 1106 ("Under Title XIX of the Social Security Act, 42 U.S.C. §§1396–1396p, states that receive grants from the federal government under the Act must report various fraud and abuse information to the Health Care Financing Administration of the Department of Health and Human Services. 42 C.F.R. §455.17 (1980)."); *see also* 729 F.2d at 1104 ("First, the Wisconsin Medicaid Fraud Control Unit provided the United States Department of Health and Human Services with many reports about the allegedly fraudulent Medicaid claims during the State's investigation and prosecution of the appellant on state criminal grounds. . . . Second, the state criminal proceedings were reported extensively in two Milwaukee newspapers.").

actions served no utility to the government. There is no basis to believe that it made a different policy choice in the public disclosure bar.

Moreover, the court's conception of "fairness" is elusive and subjective. When the relator does not break the conspiracy of silence by reporting misdeeds to the government before the information is publicized, is it "fair" that the whistleblower should obtain up to 30 percent of the government's recovery for republishing public information? Or, under these circumstances, is it fairer that the federal government (and ultimately taxpayers) should receive the full 100 percent? Most courts have ruled that the *qui tam* provisions are a mechanism to supply the government with information to prosecute fraud and not merely a mechanism to enrich relators and their counsel.[266] Under this construction of the public disclosure bar, it would be fairer to have dismissed the relator from the action.[267]

### b. The Nature of the Relator's Knowledge: The "Direct" and "Independent" Requirements

Below is the definition of "direct" that courts have used and an analysis of court decisions requiring relators to possess a certain threshold of direct knowledge before filing actions. This is followed by a discussion of the second qualification on the nature of information a relator must possess to be an original source—the "independent" requirement.

#### i. When Knowledge Is "Direct"

In *United States ex rel. Stinson, Lyons, Gerlin & Bustamante, P.A. v. Prudential Insurance Co.*,[268] the relator, a law firm, obtained in a prior state court lawsuit two documents that the relator believed demonstrated that the defendant had violated federal law. The court held that the relator did not have direct knowledge, pointing out that a dictionary defined "direct" as "marked by absence of an intervening agency, instrumentality, or influence; immediate." The court ruled that the relator's knowledge was not direct because it was dependent on two intermediaries—the employee who drafted the questioned documents and the discovery procedure by which the documents were produced.

---

[266] *See, e.g.,* United States v. Health Possibilities, P.S.C., 207 F.3d 335, 340 (6th Cir. 2000) ("The FCA is not designed to serve the parochial interests of relators, but to vindicate civic interests in avoiding fraud against public monies.") (citations omitted); United States v. Northrop Corp., 59 F.3d 953, 968 (9th Cir. 1995) ("The private right of recovery created by the provisions of the FCA exists not to compensate the *qui tam* relator, but the United States. The relator's right to recovery exists solely as a mechanism for deterring fraud and returning funds to the federal treasury.").

[267] The court in *Allina* had stated that the fairness point that Congress had sought to address in the original source provision was that of the government "not biting the hand that fed the government the information." 276 F.3d at 1047. However, when the relator only discloses the information *after* the public disclosure, this is simply not a concern. In *Allina,* for example, the United States could have obtained the same information by simply reading the newspaper. Under these circumstances the relator's information is not necessary, and permitting the relator to proceed only diminishes the government's ultimate potential recovery in the lawsuit.

[268] 944 F.2d 1149 (3d Cir. 1991).

Although it did not cite to *Stinson*, the U.S. Supreme Court in 2007 arrived at a similar conclusion in *Rockwell International v. United States*.[269] In *Rockwell*, the relator was an insider, an engineer at defendant's plant.[270] As part of his duties, he evaluated the defendant's manufacturing process to create "pondcrete" (a mixture of toxic pond sludge and cement).[271] He concluded that the proposed manufacturing process was faulty and would result in defective pondcrete that would release toxic waste into the environment and he communicated that finding to management in writing.[272] He later produced that document to the government.[273] His notification to the government resulted in the execution of a search warrant.[274] Ultimately, the defendant pleaded guilty to criminal charges and paid $18.5 million in fines.[275]

Notwithstanding his insider status and direct internal communications regarding the defective product, the Court ruled that the relator lacked "direct and independent" knowledge. In reaching this conclusion, the Court pointed out that by the time the pondcrete became defective, the relator had left the company. Thus, he did not know that the product became defective;[276] he did not know that the product was subject to governmental regulations; he did not know whether the defendant had failed to remedy the defect; and he did not know that the defendant had submitted false statements regarding the product.[277] Significantly, the Court ruled that the relator "did not *know* that the pondcrete failed; he *predicted* it."[278]

In light of the Supreme Court's decision in *Rockwell*, courts will continue to rule that a relator must have firsthand information to satisfy the direct knowledge requirement. Indeed, one essentially must be the employee on the shop floor.[279] The Third Circuit supported its construction of "direct" by noting

---

[269] 127 S. Ct. 1397 (2007).

[270] *Id.* at 1401.

[271] *Id.*

[272] *Id.* at 1401–1402.

[273] *Id.* at 1402.

[274] *Id.*

[275] *Id.* at 1403.

[276] The relator had predicted that the product would fail because of a flaw in the piping system. He was wrong in his prediction. The reason it failed, according to the final pretrial order, was because a new foreman reduced the cement-to-sludge ratio, which occurred only after the relator had left his employment. *Id.* at 1410.

[277] *Id.*

[278] *Id.* (emphasis in original).

[279] *See also* Grayson v. Advanced Management Tech., 221 F.3d 580, 583 (4th Cir. 2000) (relators, who were lawyers who had represented their client in an administrative proceeding when they learned of the alleged misconduct by reading a complaint filed by another party, did not have direct knowledge because they "at best verified" the other party's information and such "conduct is insufficient to render [them] original sources," nor did they "become 'original sources' due to their 'specialized' experience as government contract lawyers"); United States *ex rel.* Fine v. MK-Ferguson Co., 99 F.3d 1538, 1548 (10th Cir. 1996) (relator's allegations are not based on direct knowledge when they "are derivative of the facts uncovered" by others); United States *ex rel.* Fine v. Advanced Scis., Inc., 99 F.3d 1000, 1007 (10th Cir. 1996) (same); United States *ex rel.* Devlin v. State of Cal., 84 F.3d 358 (9th Cir. 1996) (the relators did not have direct knowledge because they had received information underlying action from an insider although they had conducted some independent investigation after learning of the allegations from the insider); United States *ex rel.* Barth v. Ridgedale Elec. & Eng'g, Inc., 44 F.3d 699, 703 (8th Cir.

that the legislative history indicated that the only persons qualified to be original sources are those "individuals who are close observers or otherwise involved in the fraudulent activity."[280]

## ii. The Level of Direct Knowledge Relators Must Possess

The relators in *United States ex rel. Springfield Terminal Railway v. Quinn*[281] through an unrelated civil lawsuit obtained payment vouchers and telephone records a federal arbitrator had submitted to the government to obtain reimbursement. The relators, who were participants in the arbitration proceeding, investigated by calling the numbers on telephone records and learned that the arbitrator had billed the government for activities unrelated to the arbitration proceedings. The relators then publicly disclosed this allegation by adding a claim to the lawsuit that the arbitrator had inaccurately billed the government and later filed a *qui tam* action based upon the same allegation. The court held that the relators had direct knowledge of the allegation of fraud because they learned of the fraud through their "own efforts and experience, which in this case included personal knowledge of the arbitration proceedings and interviews with individuals and businesses identified in the telephone records."[282]

In *United States ex rel. Hafter v. Spectrum Emergency Care, Inc.*,[283] a lawyer handling a medical malpractice action contacted a physician regarding the practices of the defendants, companies that managed emergency departments. The physician was the medical director of a company that contracted with a hospital for the provision of emergency department services. The physician stated that the companies providing the management services directed

---

1995) ("a person who obtains secondhand information from an individual who has direct knowledge of the alleged fraud does not himself possess direct knowledge and therefore is not an original source under the Act") (citation omitted); United States *ex rel.* Kreindler & Kreindler v. United Techs. Corp., 985 F.2d 1148, 1159 (2d Cir. 1993) (the relator did not have direct knowledge because he received the core facts from the defendant); United States *ex rel.* Dhawan v. New York City Health & Hosp. Corp., No. 95 Civ. 7649 (LMM), 2000 U.S. Dist. LEXIS 15677, at *13–17 (S.D.N.Y. Oct. 24, 2000) (the relators, who were hospital officials who alleged that their hospital had paid inflated rates to other hospitals for staffing services and that their concerns resulted in an internal audit being conducted that confirmed their suspicions, lacked direct and independent knowledge because the "original source" to the fraud would be "the auditor that investigated, reported and uncovered the alleged fraudulent claims submitted for reimbursement" and not the relators, who did not discover any information upon which the fraud allegations are based or make any first-hand observations of such fraud during the course of their employment), *aff'd*, 252 F.3d 118 (2d Cir. 2001); United States *ex rel.* Hansen v. Cargill, Inc., 107 F. Supp. 2d 1172, 1182–85 (N.D. Cal. 2000); *cf.* United States *ex rel.* Cooper v. Blue Cross & Blue Shield of Fla., 19 F.3d 562, 568 (11th Cir. 1994) (per curiam) (the relator possessed direct knowledge when his investigation triggered the government's investigation); United States *ex rel.* Springfield Terminal Ry. v. Quinn, 14 F.3d 645, 656–57 (D.C. Cir. 1994) (the relator possessed direct knowledge when it made the public disclosure itself after conducting its own investigation); United States *ex rel.* Wang v. FMC Corp., 975 F.2d 1412, 1417 (9th Cir. 1992) (the relator had direct knowledge because he saw the transactions with "his own eyes" and his knowledge was "unmediated by anything but [his] own labor"). For a detailed analysis of the cases, see SALCIDO, FALSE CLAIMS ACT COUNSELING, at §3:05; *see also* SALCIDO, FALSE CLAIMS ACT COUNSELING: OCT. 2003 SUPP., at §3:05.

[280]944 F.2d at 1154, 1160.

[281]14 F.3d 645 (D.C. Cir. 1994).

[282]*Id.* at 658.

[283]9 F. Supp. 2d 1273 (D. Kan. 1998), *aff'd*, 190 F.3d 1156 (10th Cir. 1999).

physicians in their practice of medicine and engaged in improper billing practices. His latter contention was based on information he had heard from another physician. On the basis of this information, the lawyer amended the malpractice claim to assert that the defendants also had violated the Texas Medical Practices Act. The physician then filed a *qui tam* action. The defendants asserted that the physician's action was barred under the public disclosure jurisdictional bar and the court agreed, ruling that it was based on the allegations in the malpractice action (a public disclosure). Further, the physician-relator did not qualify as an original source because his knowledge was indirect in that he had no firsthand knowledge of how the management company prepared its claims.

The relator in *United States v. Daniel F. Young, Inc.*[284] was an owner of a company who learned through an investigation that a former customer and another individual had defrauded the government. The government criminally prosecuted those contractors. Through that investigation, the relator suspected that another company and two of its employees had similarly defrauded the government. The relator then filed a *qui tam* action in which he named as John Doe defendants the additional contractors he suspected of misconduct. A grand jury then returned an indictment against some of these John Doe defendants. The relator amended his *qui tam* complaint to name these persons directly as defendants. The court found that the relator did not have sufficient direct knowledge regarding the allegations because, in part, his initial allegations regarding that scheme could not survive a challenge under Rules 9(b) and 11 of the Federal Rules of Civil Procedure.

The more difficult issue regarding the direct element is how much direct knowledge relators must have, or, stated another way, what is the minimum threshold of direct knowledge relators must possess? For example, if some information is traceable to public information, but the relator also witnessed directly other facts that are material to the claim, does he or she have sufficient direct knowledge to proceed with the action?

The most liberal construction of this requirement is set forth by the D.C. Circuit in *Springfield*. There, the court ruled that the original source provision did not require that the relator have direct knowledge of all the vital ingredients of the fraudulent transaction. Instead, the relator could proceed if she had direct knowledge of one element of the transaction. Applying the same $X + Y = Z$ test it used in determining whether the allegations or transactions were in the public domain (i.e., $X$ is the misrepresented facts, $Y$ is the true state of facts, and $Z$ is the allegation of fraud), the court concluded that the relator needed to have direct knowledge of only one element of the transaction, either the $X$ or the $Y$, to have direct knowledge under the original source provision. Thus, in that case, where the relator lacked direct knowledge of the $X$ element (the untrue state of facts—the payment vouchers and telephone logs produced in discovery) but had direct knowledge of the $Y$ element (the true state of facts—that, based on the relator's interviews and personal knowledge, the arbitrator did not perform the functions for which he billed), the court ruled that the relator qualified as an

---

[284]909 F. Supp. 1010 (E.D. Va. 1995).

original source.[285] The court concluded that the relator's knowledge was direct because it would be "[r]are" for the relator to have direct knowledge of the $X$ element because that "would almost always have been disclosed to the government independently by the alleged defrauder."[286] Thus, "in light of the aims of the statute, . . . 'direct and independent knowledge of information on which the allegations are based' refers to direct and independent knowledge of *any* essential element of the underlying fraud transaction (e.g., $Y$)."[287]

Two district courts, however, have developed more restrictive tests. *Hafter* requires that relators have direct knowledge of both the $X$ and the $Y$ transactions of fraud, and *Young* mandates that based on their personal knowledge, relators have enough direct knowledge to satisfy Rules 9(b) and 11 of the Federal Rules of Civil Procedure. The *Hafter* ruling makes the best use of the statutory language and, together with *Young*, best effectuates the statutory purpose of the public disclosure jurisdictional bar by limiting *qui tam* actions to those instances when there has been a public disclosure in which the relator brings significant, useful information to the government's attention.

Specifically, in *Hafter*, the district court pointed out that the D.C. Circuit in *Springfield* simply ignored the statutory language. In *Hafter*, the relator, like the relator in *Springfield*, knew the $Y$ element—the true state of affairs (i.e., that billing problems existed)—but did not know the $X$ element—the misrepresented state of affairs (i.e., the actual claims the defendants submitted to the government). Applying the plain language, the court ruled that the relator "must demonstrate that he had some direct and independent knowledge as to all the essential elements of the claim."[288] The court pointed out that the statute "does not provide that all that is necessary is that the relator have 'direct and independent knowledge of *some of* the information on which the allegations are based'. . . . [T]here is no indication in the language of the statute that the supporting information need only provide a fraction of the necessary elements of the allegations."[289]

Furthermore, the district court in *Young* required that the relator not only have firsthand (i.e., "direct") knowledge, but also that "the nature and quantum of knowledge" be sufficient to withstand a challenge under Rules 9(b) and 11 of the Federal Rules of Civil Procedure. If the relator's action is based on a public disclosure and his or her knowledge of the underlying information is not specific enough to withstand such a challenge, but is based upon additional investigation the government conducted (even if the relator initially tipped off the government regarding the wrongdoing), the relator's action will be dismissed.[290] The district court pointed out that to permit the relator to proceed absent sufficient knowledge

---

[285] 14 F.3d at 656–57.

[286] *Id.* at 657.

[287] *Id.* (emphasis added).

[288] 9 F. Supp. 2d at 1278.

[289] *Id.* at 1277 (citation omitted).

[290] 909 F. Supp. at 1022–23. The relator did not proceed against the defendants named initially because the government had waived civil prosecution against some of the defendants who were criminally prosecuted and another defendant did not participate in any federally funded contracts. *Id.* at 1015.

would be tantamount to encouraging citizens to initiate parasitic lawsuits feeding entirely off government information, or to run to the government with only a suspicion of fraud in the hope that they might later be able to win the relator status by riding piggyback on information subsequently developed by a government investigation. Although the *qui tam* provisions of §3730 are designed to encourage citizens with actual knowledge of fraud to come forward, they are plainly not designed to result in government agencies pursuing fishing expeditions at the behest of suspicious citizens. Moreover, the FCA is not designed to have the government function as a sort of free private investigator to help persons achieve *qui tam* relator status and the resulting opportunity of financial gain.[291]

### c. When Knowledge is "Independent"

The Department of Energy OIG in *United States ex rel. Fine v. MK-Ferguson Co.*[292] conducted an audit of a contractor's charges for a construction project. The relator did not work directly on the audit, but he did help draft the final report. The audit was circulated to the state of Oregon, which had a cooperative agreement with the Department of Energy regarding the project. Hence, the government report was publicly disclosed. The relator contended, however, that he was an original source, but the court disagreed, ruling that the relator did not have direct and independent knowledge. Independent knowledge is knowledge that is not secondhand. Because the relator's knowledge regarding the underlying conduct was derivative of the facts uncovered by others, the relator's knowledge was not independent and he did not qualify as an original source.

Numerous courts have ruled that the independent knowledge requirement is separate from the direct knowledge requirement.[293] If direct knowledge means knowledge gained by the relator's own efforts and not acquired from the labors of others,[294] then what could "independent" mean? Initially, courts ruled that "independent" meant that the relator must have knowledge independent of the public information.[295] Although that certainly is true, that definition is

---

[291] *Id.* at 1022 (emphasis added). The United States similarly takes this position in litigation, asserting that if the relator's initial complaint and statement of material evidence, unaided by any information in the public domain, cannot satisfy Rule 9(b) or 11, then the relator is not entitled to any statutory recovery. *See, e.g.*, Brief of the United States in Response to Motion of Relators for Determination of Relators' Share and Motion to Dismiss Relators as to "Automated Chemistry" Allegations (filed Dec. 22, 1997), *in* United States *ex rel.* Merena v. SmithKline Beecham Corp., No. 93-5974 (E.D. Pa. July 21, 1997); *see generally* Robert Salcido, *The Government Declares War on* Qui Tam *Plaintiffs Who Lack Inside Information: The Government's New Policy To Dismiss These Parties In False Claims Act Litigation*, 13 HEALTH LAW. 1 (A.B.A., Oct. 2000) (describing the government's position that non-insider relators should be dismissed when the statement of material evidence they supply to the government could not satisfy FED. R. CIV. P. 9(b)). In light of the Supreme Court's rationale in *Rockwell*, 127 S. Ct. at 1409–11, it appears that courts, in the future, are much more likely to follow the literal approach to defining "direct" knowledge reflected in *Hafter* and *Young* and not the expansive approach reflected in *Springfield*.

[292] 99 F.3d 1538 (10th Cir. 1996).

[293] *See* United States *ex rel.* Springfield Terminal Ry. v. Quinn, 14 F.3d 645, 656 (D.C. Cir. 1994) (citing cases).

[294] *See, e.g.*, United States *ex rel.* Fine v. Advanced Scis., Inc., 99 F.3d 1000, 1006–07 (10th Cir. 1996); United States *ex rel.* Hafter v. Spectrum Emergency Care, Inc., 9 F. Supp. 2d at 1276.

[295] *See, e.g.*, *Springfield Terminal Ry.*, 14 F.3d at 656 (" 'Independent knowledge' is knowledge that is not itself dependent on public disclosure.") (citation omitted).

inconsistent with the structure of the statute. If a relator is required to have direct knowledge of the information before its public disclosure—as the better reading of the statute requires—the relator's knowledge will always be independent of the public disclosure.

The best interpretation of the term—and the one that fits most neatly within the structure of the statute—requires that the relator's information not be independent of the publicly disclosed information but that the relator's knowledge be independent of any other person or source. For example, there may be instances in which a person has direct knowledge (e.g., he or she witnessed the misconduct on the shop floor), but he or she may not appreciate the extent of the misconduct or may not understand that the conduct resulted in the submission of false or fraudulent claims, but is given the remaining pieces of the puzzle by another person. Under those circumstances, the person's knowledge would be direct, but not independent, because it is dependent on another source. Thus, the formulation of the rule the Tenth Circuit applied in *MK-Ferguson* is correct.[296] Furthermore, this reading effectuates the statutory purpose of limiting *qui tam* actions after information is publicly disclosed to true informers (i.e., those who witnessed or participated in the conduct and understand its significance). Limiting actions to this narrow category of true whistleblowers is appropriate because, as numerous courts have found, once information is in the public domain "no incentive for a private *qui tam* suit is needed."[297]

### d. The "Voluntary" Requirement

One relator in *United States ex rel. Barth v. Ridgedale Electric & Engineering*[298] was an electrician who claimed that his employer had failed to pay the prevailing wages required under the Davis Bacon Act. The relator did not

---

[296] *See also Advanced Scis.*, 99 F.3d at 1007 ("to be independent, the relator's knowledge must not be derivative of the information of others, even if those others may qualify as original sources") (citation omitted); *Hafter*, 9 F. Supp. 2d at 1276–77 (same); *cf.* United States *ex rel.* Mistick PBT v. Housing Auth., 186 F.3d 376, 388–89 (3d Cir. 1999) (relator's knowledge could not qualify as "direct and independent" knowledge when it could not identify the defendant's alleged misrepresentation without obtaining information under FOIA); United States v. Bank of Farmington, 166 F.3d 853, 864–65 (7th Cir. 1999) (relator's knowledge could not qualify as "direct and independent" when it was dependent upon a disclosure the defendant had made to a government employee); *but see* United States v. Lamers, 168 F.3d 1013, 1018 (7th Cir. 1999) (the relator's knowledge qualified as independent although it had learned of defendant's alleged misrepresentations by virtue of a FOIA request because the relator's investigation of the defendant assisted the government). Other courts have dismissed relators' claims when they have obtained essential information regarding the alleged misconduct from public sources after the lawsuit is filed. *See, e.g.*, United States *ex rel.* Waris v. Staff Builders, Inc., No. 96-1969, 1999 U.S. Dist. LEXIS 15247 (E.D. Pa. Oct. 4, 1999). In *Waris*, the relator's initial complaint was dismissed under Fed. R. Civ. P. 9(b) for failure to plead fraud with particularity. *Id.* at *5. The relator then used public information (such as information he obtained under FOIA) to amend his complaint. *Id.* at *10–11. The court ruled that when the relator's initial complaint was deficient and the relator could only correct the deficiency by reference to public information, the relator could not qualify as an original source. *Id.* at *21–22; *see also* United States *ex rel.* Branhan v. Mercy Health Sys., No. 98-3127, 1999 U.S. App. LEXIS 18509, at *4–7 (6th Cir. Aug. 5, 1999) (same).

[297] *MK-Ferguson Co.*, 99 F.3d at 1546 (citation omitted).

[298] 44 F.3d 699 (8th Cir. 1995).

report the fraud himself; instead, a business representative of the union reported the allegations to a government investigator. The investigator then interviewed the relator, who subsequently filed a *qui tam* action. The news media had reported the allegations before the relators filed their *qui tam* action. The relator contended that he voluntarily provided information to the government because he cooperated with the government once he was contacted, but the court disagreed, finding that the relator did not voluntarily provide the information to the government because the government, not the relator, initiated the contact. The court ruled that to permit such an action would undermine "the clear intent of the Act which is to encourage private individuals who are aware of fraud against the government to bring such information forward at the earliest possible time and to discourage persons with relevant information from remaining silent."[299]

The relator in *United States ex rel. Fine v. Chevron, U.S.A.,*[300] was a Department of Energy OIG auditor who claimed that he had uncovered evidence of contractor fraud in the course of his duties as an OIG agent. The court ruled that the information underlying the action had been publicly disclosed and that the relator did not qualify as an original source where he did not voluntarily provide the information to the government because he had a legal duty as an OIG agent to disclose the information to the government.[301]

Only a few courts have construed the "voluntary" provision of the statute. These courts have interpreted the word broadly and found that when the government initiated contact with the relator or the relator had a legal obligation to disclose the information, the information was not voluntarily furnished to the government. These rulings effectuate the statutory purpose of the FCA. If the government compels a person to speak or even initiates contact with a person (with the option that if the person does not cooperate it can compel that person's testimony), no incentive is needed to lure the person to provide information. The person has come to the government's attention. Any bounty would only nullify the taxpayer's right to obtain a full recovery. The only person who should obtain the bounty is the whistleblower who goes to the government.

## D. Developing Evidence That Supports Application of the Public Disclosure Jurisdictional Bar

The public disclosure jurisdictional bar is not, of course, the only nonsubstantive defense that defendants have raised to dismiss *qui tam* actions—but

---

[299]*Barth,* 44 F.3d at 704; *cf.* United States *ex rel.* Stone v. AmWest Sav. Ass'n, 999 F. Supp. 852, 857 (N.D. Tex. 1997) (relator who received immunity from prosecution and brought information during the government's criminal fraud investigation, did not "voluntarily" provide the information to the government because the term is interpreted to mean "uncompensated" or "unsolicited," not "uncompelled") (citations omitted).

[300]72 F.3d 740 (9th Cir. 1995) (en banc).

[301]*See also* United States v. Board of Trustees of Stanford Univ., 161 F.3d 533 (9th Cir. 1998) (same); United States *ex rel.* Schwedt v. Planning Research Corp., 39 F. Supp. 2d 28, 36 (D.D.C. 1999) (relator "performed a management role that obligated him to alert superiors to any suspicions of contractor wrongdoing that threatened to impede development of the [product]"); *cf.* United States v. A.D. Roe Co., Inc., 186 F.3d 717 (6th Cir. 1999), *vacating* United States *ex rel.* Burns v. Roe Co., 919 F. Supp. 255 (W.D. Ky. 1996).

it has been the most successful.[302] As outlined in the discussion above, the relator contemplating filing an action and the attorney defending one should quickly ascertain what information underlying the action is in the public domain. As the case law instructs, this can be accomplished by:

- reviewing all news media reports involving the affected company or industry that may have raised similar allegations;
- examining all government reports, such as OIG or GAO reports, that have been issued and may have covered the same transactions raised in the complaint;
- determining whether the government has previously investigated allegations similar to those identified in the complaint and whether the government has publicly disclosed its findings; and

---

[302] Among other procedural defenses that have been tried with mainly negative results are the following:
- *Dismissal based on relator's failure to file the action under seal or breach of the seal.* Compare United States *ex rel.* Lujan v. Hughes Aircraft Co., 67 F.3d 242 (9th Cir. 1995) (failure to abide by statute's mandatory seal provision does not per se require dismissal of action), *with* United States *ex rel.* Pilon v. Marietta Corp., 60 F.3d 995, 1000 (2d Cir. 1995) (dismissing action because relator did not file complaint under seal); Erickson *ex rel.* United States v. American Inst. of Bio. Scis., 716 F. Supp. 908 (E.D. Va. 1989) (same).
- *Dismissal because action is brought by government employee.* There is no automatic bar to a government employee filing a *qui tam* action. However, courts, at times, have read the public disclosure jurisdictional bar broadly to eliminate such actions. *See* United States *ex rel.* Fine v. MK-Ferguson Co., 99 F.3d 1538 (10th Cir. 1996); United States *ex rel.* Fine v. Advanced Scis., Inc., 99 F.3d 1000 (10th Cir. 1996); United States *ex rel.* Fine v. Chevron, U.S.A., 72 F.3d 740 (9th Cir. 1995) (dismissing former government employee under original source provision) (en banc); United States *ex rel.* LeBlanc v. Raytheon Co., 913 F.2d 17, 20 (1st Cir. 1990); *cf.* United States v. A.D. Roe Co., Inc., 186 F.3d 717 (6th Cir. 1999), *vacating* United States *ex rel.* Burns v. Roe Co., 919 F. Supp. 255 (W.D. Ky. 1996); United States *ex rel.* Tipton v. Niles Chem. Paint, No. C98-5177RJB, 1999 U.S. Dist. LEXIS 21604 (W.D. Wash. May 6, 1999); *but see* United States *ex rel.* Williams v. NEC Corp., 931 F.2d 1493 (11th Cir. 1991) (no jurisdictional bar on government employees filing a *qui tam* action based on facts obtained through their government employment).
- *Dismissal because relator signed a broad release prior to filing the action.* United States v. Northrop Corp., 59 F.3d 953 (9th Cir. 1995) (prefiling release of *qui tam* claim could not be enforced to bar subsequent *qui tam* action); United States *ex rel.* DeCarlo v. Kiewit, 937 F. Supp. 1039 (S.D.N.Y. 1996) (same); United States v. American Healthcorp, Inc., 1995 Medicare & Medicaid Guide (CCH) ¶43,681 (M.D. Tenn. Sept. 14, 1995) (same), *reh'g granted and order vacated on other grounds,* 914 F. Supp. 1507 (M.D. Tenn. 1996). *But see* United States *ex rel.* Hall v. Teledyne Wah Chang Albany, 104 F.3d 230 (9th Cir. 1997) (release enforced when government had full knowledge of relator's charges and had investigated them before relator and defendant had executed their release).
- *Dismissal because* qui tam *statute is unconstitutional.* The Supreme Court ruled that relators have constitutional standing to file *qui tam* actions. *See* Vermont Agency of Natural Res. v. United States, 529 U.S. 765 (2000). Moreover, several circuits have ruled that the relator's ability to institute litigation on behalf of the United States does not unconstitutionally infringe upon the Executive Branch's duties under Article II's Take Care Clause, which commands that the Executive "take Care that the Laws be faithfully executed." *See* United States *ex rel.* Riley v. St. Luke's Episcopal Hosp., 252 F.3d 749 (5th Cir. 2001); United States *ex rel.* Kelly v. Boeing Co., 9 F.3d 743, 747–59 (9th Cir. 1993); United States *ex rel.* Kreindler & Kreindler v. United Techs. Corp., 985 F.2d 1148, 1153–55 (2d Cir. 1993); United States *ex rel.* Taxpayers Against Fraud v. General Electric Co., 41 F.3d 1032 (6th Cir. 1994).

- inquiring of the relator whether he, she, or any person he or she knows has been involved in other litigation that covered the same subject matter.

Of course, by unearthing publicly disclosed allegations and transactions of fraud, the defendant has no guarantee of success. For example, counsel must still grapple with whether the action in question is "based upon" those disclosures and whether the relator is an "original source" of the information. However, such information may provide the defendant with a viable, proven defense.

## IV. Preempting FCA Actions: The Office of Inspector General's Voluntary Disclosure Program

If providers become aware of conduct that they believe may subject them to liability under the FCA, and they are interested in possibly preempting any *qui tam* action that may be filed, the OIG's voluntary disclosure program may be the most attractive option.

### A. The Voluntary Disclosure Process

The preliminary issue for a provider in determining whether to submit a voluntary disclosure is to first determine whether there is a potential violation of the FCA. If, as described earlier in this chapter,[303] a strong defense exists, such as that the provider acted within a good-faith interpretation of ambiguous regulatory guidance or at most was merely mistaken, then, as the OIG pointed out in its recent Voluntary Disclosure Protocol, the provider need not submit a voluntary disclosure.[304] However, if reasonable, responsible government officials could deem the conduct to be unlawful, then the conservative approach would be to report the conduct. Indeed, if such conduct did occur, the OIG believes that the provider has an affirmative duty to disclose the misconduct. Specifically, the OIG has stated:

---

[303]See Sections II.B.2. to II.B.3.a., above.

[304]Specifically, the OIG pointed out that its program "is intended to facilitate the resolution of only matters that, in the provider's reasonable assessment, are potentially violative of Federal criminal, civil or administrative laws." 63 Fed. Reg. 58,399–58,400 (Oct. 30, 1998). The OIG further provided:

> Matters exclusively involving overpayment or errors that do not suggest that violations of law have occurred should be brought directly to the attention of the entity (e.g., a contractor such as a carrier or an intermediary) that processes claims and issues payment of behalf of the Government agency responsible for the particular Federal health care program (e.g., HCFA [(CMS)] for matters involving Medicare). The program contractors are responsible for processing the refund and will review the circumstances surrounding the initial overpayment. If the contractor concludes that the overpayment raises concerns about the integrity of the provider, the matter may be referred to the OIG. Accordingly, the provider's initial decision of where to refer a matter involving non-compliance with program requirements should be made carefully.

*Id.* at 58,400–401.

[A]s participants in the Federal health care programs, health care providers have an ethical and legal duty to ensure the integrity of their dealings with these programs. This duty includes an obligation to take measures, such as instituting a compliance program, to detect and prevent fraudulent, abusive and wasteful activities. It also encompasses the need to implement specific procedures and mechanisms to examine and resolve instances of non-compliance with program requirements. Whether as a result of voluntary self-assessment or in response to external forces, health care providers must be prepared to investigate such instances, assess the potential losses suffered by the Federal health care programs, and make full disclosure to the appropriate authorities.[305]

If, after discovering the misconduct, providers determine that they must submit a voluntary disclosure, they will first make initial disclosures to the OIG's Assistant Inspector General for Investigative Operations. Under the OIG guidelines, providers must, in addition to other procedures, identify who is making the disclosure, describe the matter being disclosed, explain why they believe that their conduct may have violated the law, describe whether there are any governmental inquiries pending against the company, and certify that their submissions contain truthful information.[306]

After submitting the initial disclosure, it is anticipated that the provider will conduct an internal review regarding the matter and submit the results of the investigation to the OIG. The OIG generally will agree, "for a reasonable period of time, to forego an investigation of the matter if the provider agrees that it will conduct the review in accordance with the Internal Investigation Guidelines and the Self-Assessment Guidelines...."[307] On completing an internal review, the provider submits a final report. The report should additionally contain a written narrative that identifies the questioned conduct in detail; describe how the practice was identified; describe remedial efforts the provider undertook to stop the inappropriate conduct and to prevent its recurrence, including any disciplinary action taken against corporate officials and employees;

---

[305]*Id.* at 58,400. *See also* the OIG's Compliance Program Guidance for Hospitals, 63 Fed. Reg. 8987, 8998 (Feb. 23, 1998) (pointing out that if the hospital learns of "misconduct [that] may violate criminal, civil or administrative law, then the hospital promptly should report the existence of misconduct to the appropriate governmental authority") (footnote omitted).

[306]63 Fed. Reg. at 58,401. Failure to disclose this precise information is not fatal to the submission of a voluntary disclosure but will likely delay resolution of the matter. *Id.* at 58,400 ("Failure to conform to each element of the Protocol is not necessarily fatal to the provider's disclosure, but will likely delay the resolution of the matter.").

[307]*Id.* at 58,401. The OIG also noted, however, that a provider should not conduct its internal review when it learns of an "ongoing fraud scheme within its organization." *Id.* at 58,400 ("[A] provider that uncovers an ongoing fraud scheme within its organization immediately should contact the OIG, but should not follow the Protocol's suggested steps to investigate or quantify the scope of the problem. If the provider follows the Protocol in this type of situation without prior consultation with the OIG, there is a substantial risk that the Government's subsequent investigation will be compromised."). Presumably, when whether the matter in fact concerns "an ongoing fraud scheme within the organization" is not clear, the OIG will give the provider guidance on the issue after the provider submits an initial disclosure and at that time advise the provider whether to refrain from conducting an internal review.

estimate the monetary impact of the incident or practice upon federal health care programs; and certify that the report is truthful.[308]

After the provider submits its report, the government performs a verification investigation of the disclosed matter. "The extent of the OIG's verification effort will depend, in large part, upon the quality and thoroughness of the internal investigative and self-assessment reports."[309] The OIG noted that it "will use the validated provider self-assessment report in preparing a recommendation to DOJ for resolution of the provider's False Claims Act or other liability."[310]

## B. Benefits and Risks of Submitting a Voluntary Disclosure

Any provider that submits a voluntary disclosure ventures into uncharted terrain. Indeed, the OIG expressly refuses to give any advance assurance regarding how the provider will be treated once it submits the disclosure.[311] Because of this uncertainty, providers have been reluctant to submit voluntary disclosures.[312] Set forth below are some of the specific risks a provider incurs

---

[308]*Id.* at 58,401–403.

[309]*Id.* at 58,403.

[310]*Id.* at 58,402.

[311]*See, e.g.*, 63 Fed. Reg. 58,399–58,400 (Oct. 30, 1998). Specifically, the OIG noted:

> Because a provider's disclosure can involve anything from a simple error to outright fraud, the OIG cannot reasonably make firm commitments as to how a particular disclosure will be resolved or the specific benefit that will enure to the disclosing entity. In our experience, however, opening lines of communication with, and making full disclosure to, the investigative agency at an early stage generally benefits the individual or company. In short, the Protocol can help a health care provider initiate with the OIG a dialogue directed at resolving its potential liabilities.

[312]For example, according to a recent press release from the OIG, from May 1995 to October 1998, "[f]ew providers took advantage" of the OIG's pilot Voluntary Disclosure Program—which applied to health care providers in the home health and nursing home industries, and medical suppliers to these providers, in the five states with the highest Medicare expenditures (California, Florida, New York, Texas, and Illinois)—with 20 providers making self-disclosures and 4 being accepted. *See* http://www.hhs.gov/oig/modcomp/disclosenews.htm. Since the OIG has issued its "new, more flexible self-disclosure protocol" that is open to all health care providers that obtain federal funds, "55 providers have self-disclosed with 50 being accepted into the program." *Id.* Furthermore, to make the existing program more attractive, HHS's Inspector General, in an open letter to the health care community, offered additional reforms such as reversing its previous policy that all self-disclosing entities must agree to enter into a Corporate Integrity Agreement (CIA) and agree to exclusion if they breach the terms of the CIA. *See* http://www.hhs.gov/oig/modcomp/openletter.htm. Specifically, the Inspector General stated that "[i]f the self-disclosing provider has demonstrated that its compliance program is effective and agrees to maintain its compliance program as part of the False Claims Act settlement, we may not even require a CIA." *Id.* Factors the Inspector General will use in determining whether to impose a CIA include: "the scope and seriousness of the misconduct, the risk of recurrence, whether the disclosed matter was identified and reported as a result of the provider's compliance measures and the degree of the provider's cooperation during the disclosure verification process." *Id.* Moreover, the Inspector General stated that even in those cases where a CIA must be imposed, the OIG may determine that "the provider may need to make only limited changes to its existing policies and procedures to meet most of the requirements of the CIA." Finally, the OIG stated that "a provider that has made an appropriate self-disclosure and has demonstrated sufficient trustworthiness may lead [the OIG] to conclude that [it] can sufficiently safeguard the programs through a CIA without the exclusion remedy for a material

when submitting a disclosure and some of the incentives the government furnishes those that submit disclosures.

### 1. Risks of Disclosure

The submission of a voluntary disclosure is not without risk. Of greatest concern is that the government itself, a friendly adversary at the start of a voluntary disclosure proceeding, may turn hostile and threaten to file an action based on the conduct underlying the disclosure and/or accuse the provider of submitting a false disclosure statement because the provider did not fully disclose the entire scope of the misconduct.[313] A provider can reduce the likelihood of government prosecution by ensuring that its disclosure report does in fact disclose, not conceal, the misconduct in question. The disclosure should include all material facts underlying the provider's internal investigation. If witnesses or documents reveal that the provider withheld material facts, the government will accuse the provider of submitting a false report and, at a minimum, become more aggressive in its negotiations.

A secondary concern is that an employee will file a *qui tam* action based on the provider's internal review or, if an employee is disciplined as a result of misconduct that contributed to the need to submit a voluntary disclosure, the disciplined or discharged employee may challenge the employer's actions.[314] Because of recent developments in the interpretation of the public disclosure jurisdictional bar, it is less likely that an employee can appropriate the results of an internal investigation to file a *qui tam* action.[315] However, a provider should use only highly trusted employees to assist in an internal investigation and should ensure that the voice of each, to the extent possible, is incorporated into the final product. Another risk of making a disclosure to the government is that the disclosing party may potentially waive the attorney-client privilege or work

---

breach. Therefore, [the OIG] will forego the exclusion remedy in appropriate self-disclosure cases." Moreover, the OIG has issued additional guidance setting forth specific examples of when an entity has made a voluntary disclosure and, as a result of the disclosure, the OIG has declined to impose any CIA on the provider. *See* Self-Disclosure of Provider Misconduct: Assessment of CIA Modifications, *available at* http://www.hhs.gov/oig/cia/assessment.htm.

[313]In this regard, the OIG in its guidelines points out that "the intentional submission of false or otherwise untruthful information, as well as the intentional omission of relevant information, will be referred to DOJ or other Federal agencies and could, in itself, result in criminal and/or civil sanctions, as well as exclusion from participation in the Federal health care programs." 63 Fed. Reg. at 58,403.

[314]Once a provider discovers that its employees have engaged in wrongdoing, it often will initiate specific disciplinary measures against those who participated in the misconduct. Indeed, as part of its report to the government, the provider must "[d]escribe any disciplinary action taken against corporate officials, employees and agents as a result of the disclosed matter." *See id.* at 58,402.

[315]*See* Salcido, *The Use of Voluntary Disclosures to Pre-Empt* Qui Tam *Actions Under the False Claims Act: An Analysis of the* Bank of Farmington *Case and the OIG's Voluntary Disclosure Program*, 27 HEALTH L. DIG. 3 (American Health Lawyers Ass'n Apr. 1999). Indeed, in one case, a district court dismissed the relator's allegations in a *qui tam* action that stemmed from a hospital's voluntary disclosure to the government pursuant to the FCA's public disclosure bar. *See* United States *ex rel.* Cherry v. Rush-Presbyterian/St. Luke's Med. Ctr., No. 99 C 06313, 2001 WL 40807 (N.D. Ill. Jan. 16, 2001).

product protection associated with the disclosed material.[316] The Sixth Circuit's opinion in *In re Columbia/HCA Healthcare Corp. Billing Practices Litigation*[317] illustrates precisely how a disclosure to the government of privileged information may later undermine a company's interest because the confidential information must later be produced to private parties in related litigation.

In *Columbia/HCA Healthcare Corp.*, the Sixth Circuit had to consider whether HCA had waived the attorney-client privilege and work product immunity when it had disclosed the results of an internal investigation to the government. Specifically, beginning in the mid-1990s, HCA, either in response to a government investigation or in anticipation of it, conducted several internal audits of its Medicare patient records.[318] The audits examined the various billing codes HCA assigned to the patients in order to receive reimbursement from the Medicare program and any potential miscoding of the Medicare patients. When the DOJ attempted to obtain the audits, HCA rebuffed the request based on attorney-client privilege and the work product doctrine.[319]

Subsequently, HCA determined to engage in negotiations with the DOJ to settle the fraud investigation.[320] In coordination with this effort, HCA agreed to produce some of the coding audits and related documents to the government. In exchange for this cooperation, the DOJ consented to certain stringent confidentiality provisions governing the disclosure of the documents. Specifically, HCA's agreement with the DOJ provided that

> [t]he disclosure of any report, document, or information by one party to the other does not constitute a waiver of any applicable privilege or claim under the work product doctrine. Both parties to the agreement reserve the right to contest the assertion of any privilege by the other party to the agreement, but will not argue that the disclosing party, by virtue of the disclosures it makes pursuant to this agreement, has waived any applicable privilege or work product doctrine claim.[321]

As a result of the parties' negotiations, they ultimately reached a settlement, resulting in HCA paying an $840 million fine to the government.[322] Once the results of the DOJ's investigation were publicized, private insurance companies and private individuals undertook to evaluate the billing they

---

[316]Regarding confidentiality, the OIG provides the following in its guidelines:

In the normal course of verification, the OIG will not request production of written communications subject to the attorney-client privilege. There may be documents or other materials, however, that may be covered by the work product doctrine, but which the OIG believes are critical to resolving the disclosure. The OIG is prepared to discuss with provider's counsel ways to gain access to the underlying information without the need to waive the protections provided by an appropriately asserted claim of privilege.

63 Fed. Reg. at 58,403.

[317]293 F.3d 289 (6th Cir. 2002).

[318]*Id.* at 291–92.

[319]*Id.*

[320]*Id.*

[321]*Id.*

[322]*Id.*

received from HCA. This review culminated in the filing of numerous lawsuits around the country in which various plaintiffs contended that HCA overbilled them for various services, as it had the government.[323] Significantly, in these lawsuits, the private plaintiffs alleged that, notwithstanding whatever privilege HCA's coding audits may have held, HCA waived the protections of those privileges by disclosing the materials to the government.[324]

As it had initially with the DOJ, HCA refused to produce the coding audits based on the work product doctrine and attorney-client privilege. Furthermore, HCA pointed out that in disclosing the information to the government, it had expressly reserved the right to assert the attorney-client privilege and the work product doctrine pursuant to the confidentiality agreement it had negotiated with the DOJ.[325]

Notwithstanding that agreement, the district court granted the plaintiffs' motion to compel the production of the coding audit.[326] Specifically, it found that the "voluntary disclosure of privileged materials to the government constitutes a waiver of the attorney-client privilege to all other adversaries."[327] Further, the court found that by disclosing the documents to the DOJ, HCA waived any protections afforded under the work product doctrine as well.[328]

The Sixth Circuit affirmed the district court's ruling. In evaluating the district court's opinion, the Sixth Circuit noted that the general rule is that the "attorney-client privilege is waived by voluntary disclosure of private communications by an individual or corporation to third parties."[329] Notwithstanding the general rule, the court pointed out that various courts have adopted one of three separate positions regarding whether "selective waiver" is possible: (1) some have held that selective waiver is possible; (2) others have found that selective waiver is not permissible under any circumstances; and (3) some have ruled that selective waiver is possible when the government agrees to a confidentiality order.[330]

As the court noted, the leading case espousing the view that selective waiver is possible is the Eighth Circuit's opinion in *Diversified Industries v. Meredith*.[331] In *Diversified,* an independent audit committee retained outside counsel to review allegations that the company had paid bribes to purchasing agents of other companies to obtain business.[332] Counsel prepared an internal report that was circulated to the company's board of directors and later to the Securities and Exchange Commission (SEC) pursuant to a subpoena.[333]

---

[323] *Id.*

[324] *Id.* at 293.

[325] *Id.*

[326] *See In re* Columbia/HCA Healthcare Corp. Billing Practices Litig., 192 F.R.D. 575 (M.D. Tenn. 2000).

[327] *Id.* at 579.

[328] *Id.* at 579–80.

[329] *In re* Columbia/HCA Healthcare Corp. Billing Practices Litig., 293 F.3d 289, 294 (6th Cir. 2002) (internal quotation and citation omitted).

[330] *Id.* at 295.

[331] 572 F.2d 596 (8th Cir. 1978) (en banc).

[332] *Id.* at 607.

[333] *Id.* at 611.

Another company then filed an antitrust action against Diversified and sought the internal report on the grounds that Diversified had waived the privilege by voluntarily surrendering it to the SEC pursuant to its subpoena. The Eighth Circuit rejected the company's request for the document, holding that because "Diversified disclosed these documents in a separate and nonpublic SEC investigation, . . . only a limited waiver of the privilege occurred" and to "hold otherwise may have the effect of thwarting the developing procedure of corporations to employ independent outside counsel to investigate and advise them in order to protect stockholders, potential stockholders and customers."[334]

The Sixth Circuit noted that several courts have rejected the *Diversified* court's "selective waiver" theory and instead have ruled that any waiver of the privilege to some parties necessarily waives the privilege to all parties.[335] The rationale underlying this viewpoint is that the client should not "be permitted to pick and choose among his opponents, waiving the privilege as to some and resurrecting the claim of confidentiality to obstruct others, or to invoke the privilege as to communications whose confidentiality he has already compromised for his own benefit"[336] because such a selective waiver does nothing to "serve the purpose of encouraging full disclosure to one's attorney in order to obtain informed legal assistance,"[337] which is the purpose underlying the attorney-client privilege.

Finally, the Sixth Circuit pointed out that some courts have held that a disclosure to the government would constitute a waiver unless the right to assert the privilege in subsequent proceedings was specifically reserved at the time the disclosure was made.[338] By asserting this right, the party makes clear that it "had made some effort to preserve the privacy of the privileged communication, rather than having engaged in abuse of the privilege by first making a knowing decision to waive the rule's protection and then seeking to retract that decision in subsequent litigation."[339]

Ultimately, the Sixth Circuit adopted the most stringent test, ruling that although the selective waiver approach of *Diversified* had "considerable appeal," policy considerations militated against adopting that rule:

> There is considerable appeal, and justification, for permitting selective waiver when the initial disclosure is to an investigating arm of the Government. Undoubtedly, by waiving privilege as to the Government, a client furthers the "truth-finding process." *Permian* [*Corp. v. United States*, 665 F.2d 1214,] 1221 [(D.C. Cir. 1981)]. Considerable savings are realized to the Government, and through it to the public, in time and fiscal expenditure related to the investigation of crimes

---

[334]*Id.* (citations omitted).

[335]*See, e.g., In re* Columbia/HCA Healthcare Corp. Billing Practices Litig., 293 F.3d 289, 295–98 (6th Cir. 2002).

[336]*Id.* at 296 (quoting Permian Corp. v. United States, 665 F.2d 1214, 1221 (D.C. Cir. 1981)) (footnote omitted).

[337]*Id.* at 297 (quoting Westinghouse Elec. Corp. v. Republic of Philippines, 951 F.2d 1414, 1425 (3d Cir. 1991)).

[338]*See, e.g., id.* at 299–303.

[339]*Id.* at 300 (quoting Teachers Ins. & Annuity Ass'n of Am. v. Shamrock Broadcasting Co., 521 F. Supp. 638, 646 (S.D.N.Y. 1981)).

and civil fraud. Such a policy might also ... increase the likelihood that corporations would engage in the type of self-policing represented by [HCA's] Coding Audits. Without a doubt, disclosure of information to the Government in a cooperative manner encourages settlement of disputes and by encouraging cooperative exchange of information, selective waiver would improve the ability of the Government and private parties to settle certain actions.

However, this argument has several flaws. As noted by the First Circuit, it "has no logical terminus." [United States v. Massachusetts Inst. of Tech., 129 F.3d 681, 686 (1st Cir. 1997)]. Insofar as the "truth-finding process" is concerned, a private litigant stands in nearly the same stead as the Government. This argument holds considerable weight in the numerous circumstances whereby litigants act as private attorneys general, and through their actions vindicate the public interest. A plaintiff in a shareholder derivative action or a qui tam action who exposes accounting and tax fraud provides as much service to the "truth finding process" as an SEC investigator. Recognizing this, a difficult and fretful line-drawing process begins, consuming immeasurable private and judicial resources in a vain attempt to distinguish one private litigant from the next.[340]

The Sixth Circuit went on to state that

[a] countervailing policy concern, heretofore not discussed, is whether the Government should assist in obfuscating the "truth-finding process" by entering into such confidentiality agreements at all. The investigatory agencies of the Government should act to bring to light illegal activities, not to assist wrongdoers in concealing the information from the public domain. Governmental agencies "have means to secure the information they need" other than through voluntary cooperation achieved via selective waiver (albeit at a higher cost in time and money). *MIT,* 129 F.3d at 685. It is not necessary for the courts to create a new method, one which effectively prevents further litigants from obtaining the same

---

[340]293 F.3d at 303. However, as Judge Boggs noted in his dissenting opinion, the majority's view appears to be mistaken. Specifically, as he pointed out, government representatives' interest (the public good) is vastly different from that of private litigants (private financial gain):

> The government's investigations are generally more important. Government officials, with finite litigative resources and no individual monetary stake in the outcome of litigation, generally are more selective regarding the matters they choose to pursue than are private parties. Because of these incentives, government investigations are more likely to be in the public interest. Private litigants, often encouraged by large potential liability, on balance will have a greater incentive to press the legal envelope and to pursue legal actions less certainly within the public interest.

*Id.* at 312. Indeed, in FCA *qui tam* actions, which the Sixth Circuit panel referenced, relators file actions alleging that a defendant submitted a false or fraudulent claim to the United States and, if their action is successful, obtain a substantial bounty. The Supreme Court has underscored the vastly different footing on which relators stand as opposed to governmental officials. Specifically, the court noted that "as a class of plaintiffs, qui tam relators are different in kind than the Government. They are motivated primarily by prospects of monetary reward rather than the public good." Hughes Aircraft Co. v. United States *ex rel.* Schumer, 520 U.S. 939, 949 (1997); *see also* United States *ex rel.* Foulds v. Texas Tech. Univ., 171 F.3d 279, 293 (5th Cir. 1999). Further, the Court pointed out that just because "a qui tam suit is brought by a private party 'on behalf of the United States' ... does not alter the fact that a relator's interests and the Government's do not necessarily coincide." 520 U.S. at 949 n.5 (citation omitted).

information, when other means (means which will not result in the information being concealed from the public) are available to the Government.[341]

Finally, the Sixth Circuit determined that it would not grant work product protection to the requested documents:

> Other than the fact that the initial waiver must be to an "adversary," there is no compelling reason for differentiating waiver of work product from waiver of attorney-client privilege. Many of the reasons for disallowing selective waiver in the attorney-client privilege context also apply to the work product doctrine. The ability to prepare one's case in confidence, which is the chief reason articulated in *Hickman* [*v. Taylor*, 329 U.S. 495 (1947)], for the work product protections, has little to do with talking to the Government. Even more than attorney-client privilege waiver, waiver of the protections afforded by the work product doctrine is a tactical litigation decision. Attorney and client both know the material in question was prepared in anticipation of litigation; the subsequent decision on whether or not to "show your hand" is quintessential litigation strategy. Like attorney-client privilege, there is no reason to transform the work product into another "brush on the attorney's palette," used as a sword rather than a shield. [*In re* Steinhardt Partners, L.P., 9 F.3d 230, 235 (2d Cir. 1993).][342]

The teaching of the Sixth Circuit's opinion is that "[r]elatively narrow cooperation with the government in the form of a disclosure of privileged information can expose an individual or firm to massive liability and reveal privileged documents far afield from the disclosure itself."[343] However, one issue not fully addressed in the *Columbia/HCA Healthcare Corp.* opinion is the precise scope of the waiver when a party submits a disclosure to the government. That is, for example, if a company submits a disclosure report to the

---

[341]293 F.3d at 303. *See also In re* Lupron Mktg. & Sales Practices Litig., 313 F. Supp. 2d 8, 14 (D. Mass. 2004). However, as Judge Boggs pointed out in his dissenting opinion in *Columbia/ HCA Healthcare Corp. Billing Practices Litigation,* the majority's view is based on a flawed premise that there is an equal nonprivileged analogue to privileged material that the government is able to obtain, albeit at a higher cost. Specifically, he noted:

> Contrary to the court's argument, increased access to privileged information increases the absolute efficacy of government investigations, regardless of increased investigatory costs to the government. There is some evidence provided by privileged information for which there is no non-privileged substitute or to which there is no path without privileged evidence. The court . . . argues that the government has "other means" to secure the information that they need, while conceding that those other means may consume more government time and money. . . . Presumably, the court is referring to search warrants or civil discovery. It should be emphasized, however, that the government has no other means to secure otherwise privileged information. That the documents or other evidence sought is privileged permits the target of an investigation to refuse production through civil discovery, to quash any subpoena *duces tecum,* or to prevent the admission of the privileged information even by the government. The only way that the government can obtain privileged information is for the holder of the privilege voluntarily to disclose it. The court's argument about the adequacy of other means, suggesting that the only difference between them and voluntary disclosure is cost, requires the premise that all privileged information has a non-privileged analogue that is discoverable with enough effort. That premise, however, does not hold.

*Id.* at 311.

[342]293 F.3d at 306–07 (footnote omitted).

[343]*Id.* at 311 (Boggs, J., dissenting).

government, is any privilege that is waived limited to the report itself? Does it include all attorney-client communications and attorney work product related to preparing the report, such as notes of interviews and client correspondence? Or does it include the attorney-client communications and work product regarding the facts discussed in the report, but not attorney opinion work product? Discussed below are the general rules regarding waiver and some tips for making a report to the government that potentially limits the scope of any waiver.[344]

The "attorney-client privilege is waived if the holder of the privilege voluntarily discloses or consents to disclosure of any significant part of the matter of communication."[345] A waiver may further be subcategorized into various types. For example, cases under "the 'waiver' heading include situations as divergent as an express and voluntary surrender of a privilege, partial disclosure of a privileged document, selective disclosure to some outsiders but not all, and inadvertent overhearings or disclosures."[346] A waiver may include both the entirety of communications that a party has disclosed only in part and all other privileged communications insofar as they touch on subjects voluntarily disclosed by the privilege holder.[347]

Especially relevant to FCA voluntary disclosures are "partial" and "selective" disclosures or waivers. A partial waiver occurs when a party reveals only segments of privileged communication.[348] This situation may occur, for example, when a company submits a disclosure report to the government but does not produce the underlying attorney-client correspondence regarding the scope of the investigation to be conducted and the notes underlying witness interviews. A selective waiver occurs when a party discloses privileged communications to one party but not another.[349] This situation occurs, for example, when, as in the *Columbia/HCA Healthcare Corp.* case,[350] a company takes the position that although it divulged confidential information to the United States, it need not disclose the material to any other third party in related litigation.

A court's treatment of waiver may vary depending on whether it is a partial or selective waiver. In the case of a partial waiver, a court will apply the

---

[344]For a more detailed discussion of the application of the attorney-client privilege when submitting disclosures to the government, see David Orbuch & Robert Salcido, *Preserving and Protecting Attorney-Client Information When Operating a Compliance Department,* AM. HEALTH LAW. (Sept. 2002).

[345]*In re* Kidder Peabody Secs. Litig., 168 F.R.D. 459, 468 (S.D.N.Y. 1996) (internal quotation and citations omitted).

[346]United States v. Massachusetts Inst. of Tech., 129 F.3d 681, 684 (1st Cir. 1997).

[347]*Kidder Peabody,* 168 F.R.D. at 469.

[348]Harding v. Dana Transp., Inc., 914 F. Supp. 1084, 1092 (D.N.J. 1996).

[349]*Id.; see also* Westinghouse Elec. Corp. v. Republic of Philippines, 951 F.2d 1414, 1423 n.7 (3d Cir. 1991) ("Selective waiver permits the client who has disclosed privileged communications to one party to continue asserting the privilege against other parties. Partial waiver permits a client who has disclosed a portion of privileged communications to continue asserting the privilege as to the remaining portions of the same communications.").

[350]*In re* Columbia/HCA Healthcare Corp. Billing Practices Litig., 293 F.3d 289 (6th Cir. 2002).

"fairness doctrine," which aims to prevent prejudice to a party and distortion of the judicial process that may be caused by the privilege holder's partial disclosure to an adversary.[351] Hence, in *In re Kidder Peabody Securities Litigation,*[352] in which a company that was under investigation submitted a report to the SEC to obtain favorable treatment, the court found that the company had waived the privilege both for the report and the underlying documents, such as witness interviews, that would be needed to evaluate the reliability and accuracy of the report.[353] The court reasoned that it would be unfair to find that no waiver occurred, because then the company would be able to use the privilege as a sword (by using partial disclosure to obtain lenient treatment from the SEC) and as a shield (by refusing to produce less flattering findings to a private party).[354]

In the case of selective waiver, a court may decline to apply the fairness doctrine and simply rule that a waiver encompassing the entire subject matter exists.[355] The reason for this approach is the view that when there is a disclosure to one adverse party, there is no unfairness to any other adverse party and hence there is no concern of proportionality that exists in cases of partial disclosure.[356] Hence, in *In re Martin Marietta Corp.,*[357] the Fourth Circuit ruled that a position paper the company submitted to the government, which asserted that all consulted by the company would testify that they had no concerns regarding

---

[351] *See Westinghouse,* 951 F.2d at 1426 n.12 ("When a party discloses a portion of otherwise privileged materials while withholding the rest, the privilege is waived only as to those communications actually disclosed, unless a partial waiver would be unfair to the party's adversary.... If partial waiver does disadvantage the disclosing party's adversary by, for example, allowing the disclosing party to present a one-sided story to the court, the privilege will be waived as to all communications on the same subject."); *Kidder Peabody,* 168 F.R.D. at 469. *See generally In re* Grand Jury Proceedings, 219 F.3d 175 (2d Cir. 2000) ("as the animating principle behind waiver is fairness to the parties, if the court finds that the privilege was waived, then the waiver should be tailored to remedy the prejudice to the [adverse party]").

[352] 168 F.R.D. 459, 468 (S.D.N.Y. 1996).

[353] *Id.* at 472; *see also* Harding v. Dana Transp., Inc., 914 F. Supp. 1084, 1093, 1096 (D.N.J. 1996) (when attorney investigated allegations that defendant company had engaged in sex discrimination and the company represented in its defense in an administrative proceeding that it had "fully investigated the complaints raised in the Verified Complaint and has found that there is no supporting evidence that the same occurred," the company had waived the privilege as to the full scope of the lawyer's investigation (such as interview notes of witnesses, billing sheets or records that reflect the amount of time expended on the investigation, and correspondence between the company and lawyer regarding scope of investigation to be conducted) because "[c]onsistent with the doctrine of fairness, the plaintiffs must be permitted to probe the substance of [the company's] alleged investigation to determine its sufficiency").

[354] *Kidder Peabody,* 168 F.R.D. at 472–73.

[355] *See Westinghouse,* 951 F.2d at 1426 ("Generally, the 'fairness doctrine' is invoked in partial (as opposed to selective) disclosure cases.") (footnote omitted); *Harding,* 914 F. Supp. at 1092 ("While the Third Circuit does not apply the fairness doctrine to situations of selective waiver, it has recognized the validity of the District of Columbia Circuit's fairness rationale in partial disclosure cases."); *but see* Dellwood Farms, Inc. v. Cargill, Inc., 128 F.3d 1122, 1127–28 (7th Cir. 1997) (in selective waiver case, refusing to find waiver because the party making the disclosure—the government—was not "using coy disclosure to gain litigation leverage" over other parties).

[356] *See Westinghouse,* 951 F.2d at 1426 n.13; *see also id.* at 1430 ("We decline to extend the fairness doctrine to cases involving selective disclosures because... we do not see how disclosing protected materials to one adversary disadvantages another.").

[357] 856 F.2d 619 (4th Cir. 1988).

fraudulent conduct, was sufficient to waive the privilege regarding the position paper and underlying details such as witness statements when the company received a subpoena from a former employee.[358]

Finally, consistent with the approach the Sixth Circuit adopted in the *Columbia/HCA Healthcare Corp.* case, most courts have taken a similarly strict view regarding waiver of attorney work product when a company tenders a disclosure to the government.[359] The basis for this viewpoint is that the work product doctrine serves to protect the attorney work product from adversaries, and if an attorney waives the protection as to one party, he or she must be willing to waive it as to all others.[360] However, a court may limit the waiver to non-opinion work product.[361] Hence, for example, attorney notes regarding the credibility of certain witnesses or employees or the strength of particular legal theories may remain protected.[362]

---

[358] *Id.* at 623. *Cf.* Picard Chem. Inc. Profit Sharing v. Perrigo Co., 951 F. Supp. 679, 688–89 (W.D. Mich. 1996) (no waiver when company did not reveal a significant part of its report and did not summarize evidence found in the report in its motion to dismiss).

[359] *See, e.g.,* United States v. Massachusetts Inst. of Tech., 129 F.3d 681, 687 (1st Cir. 1997); *In re* Steinhardt Partners, L.P., 9 F.3d 230, 235 (2d Cir. 1993); *Martin Marietta,* 856 F.2d at 625 ("The disclosure [report] of [the company] was made broad by its express assurance of completeness of its disclosure to the United States Attorney, so that the subject matter of the disclosure and the waiver is comprehensive, and includes all of the company's non-opinion work product relating to the investigation that it conducted."); United States v. Bergonzi, 216 F.R.D. 487, 498 (N.D. Cal. 2003).

[360] *See, e.g., Steinhardt Partners,* 9 F.3d at 235 (refusing to apply work product doctrine to memorandum attorney furnished to the SEC when the same document was later requested in class action lawsuit, pointing out that "[o]nce a party allows an adversary to share the otherwise privileged thought processes of counsel, the need for the privilege disappears. Courts therefore accept the waiver doctrine as a limitation on work product protection. The waiver doctrine provides that voluntary disclosure of work product to an adversary waives the privilege as to other parties.") (citations omitted).

[361] *See, e.g., Martin Marietta,* 856 F.2d at 626 ("We think that when there is subject matter waiver, it should not extend to opinion work product for two reasons. First . . . opinion work product is to be accorded great protection by the courts. . . . Secondly, the underlying rationale for the doctrine of subject matter waiver has little application in the context of a pure expression of legal theory or legal opinion. . . . There is relatively little danger that a litigant will attempt to use a pure mental impression or legal theory as a sword and as a shield in the trial of a case so as to distort the fact finding process. Thus, the protection of lawyers from the broad repercussions of subject matter waiver in this context strengthens the adversary process, and, unlike the selective disclosure of evidence, may ultimately and ideally further the search for the truth."); *see also Kidder Peabody,* 168 F.R.D. at 473 ("in the exercise of our discretion, . . . we limit the piercing of the privilege to purely factual summaries of witness statements, and thus avoid any danger that the waiver might encompass core attorney mental processes, for which we are required to demonstrate particular solicitude") (citations omitted).

[362] *See, e.g., Martin Marietta,* 856 F.2d at 626 n.2 ("in the instant case, [the company] having quoted from some audit interviews, the transcript of these interviews has been waived under the broad doctrine of subject matter waiver. Similarly, work product protection has been waived as to most of the internal notes and memoranda on these interviews which, by way of summarizing in substance and format the interview results, [the company] used as the basis of its disclosure to the government on its audit results. These are evidentiary materials from which [the third party former employee] hopes to adduce evidence supporting his scapegoat theory. However, in disclosing such results, [the company] apparently would not disclose nor would intend to disclose, hypothetically, marginal notations on such documents such as: 'This person does not appear credible; let's not call him as a witness if we have to go to trial on this one.' Such an expression of legal opinion, thus detached from the data which [the company] did disclose, would not be subject to subject matter waiver.").

The most important lesson in this area is to be immersed in the case law of the applicable circuit when contemplating any disclosure to the government. Unfortunately, however, because a company can typically be sued under the FCA in more than one circuit, a party should be aware of the law of other circuits as well.[363] Moreover, besides knowledge of the case law, some of the following guidelines may be used to reduce the risk of needless waiver of the attorney-client privilege or work product protection:

- *Obtain a Confidentiality Agreement.* Only two circuits have ruled that obtaining another party's consent is irrelevant to determining whether the party sought to waive either the attorney-client privilege or work product protection.[364] Several courts have implied that obtaining such an agreement may result in a court ruling that there was no waiver.[365] Hence, such an agreement should be requested before any disclosure to the United States of potentially damaging admissions.

- *Carefully Document the Basis for the Waiver of the Privilege.* For example, if the basis for the waiver is to cooperate with government officials, state that plainly in the document. Courts are more likely to find waiver when it appears that the waiver was purely self-interested rather than for the public good.

- *Limit the Scope of the Privileged Material That Is Disclosed.* If the government requests additional privileged material, resist its request to the greatest possible extent and document the basis for assertion of the privilege. A corporation that so documents and raises its concern for privilege establishes a reliance on a continued existence of confidentiality even after disclosure.

- *Avoid Testimonial Use of the Results of the Investigation.* Broad statements vouching for the credibility of corporate employees or the

---

[363]*See, e.g.,* 31 U.S.C. §3732(a) ("Any action under section 3730 may be brought in any judicial district in which the defendant or, in the case of multiple defendants, any one defendant can be found, resides, transacts business, or in which any act proscribed by section 3729 occurred.").

[364]*See In re* Columbia/HCA Healthcare Corp. Billing Practices Litig., 293 F.3d 289, 303 (6th Cir. 2002) (although confidentiality agreement protects "the expectations of the parties," it "does little to serve the 'public ends' of adequate legal representation that the attorney-client privilege is designed to protect") (citation omitted); Westinghouse Elec. Corp. v. Republic of Philippines, 951 F.2d 1414, 1427, 1430 (3d Cir. 1991) (ruling, as to the attorney-client privilege, that "[e]ven though the DOJ apparently agreed not to disclose the information, under traditional waiver doctrine a voluntary disclosure to a third party waives the attorney-client privilege even if the third party agrees not to disclose the communications to anyone else" and, as to the work product doctrine, rejecting the company's "argument that it did not waive the work-product protection because it reasonably expected the agencies to keep the documents it disclosed to them confidential") (citations omitted).

[365]*See, e.g., In re* Steinhardt Partners, L.P., 9 F.3d 230 (2d Cir. 1993) (refusing to adopt a per se rule that all voluntary disclosures to the government waive the work product rule because establishing "a rigid rule would fail to anticipate situations in which the disclosing party and the government may share a common interest in developing legal theories and analyzing information, or situations in which the SEC and the disclosing party have entered into an explicit agreement that the SEC will maintain the confidentiality of the disclosed materials"); *Kidder Peabody,* 168 F.R.D. at 471–72 (disclosure of draft report to SEC would waive privilege "unless [the company] has assurances from the [SEC] that no further inquiry will be made" regarding the disclosed documents).

completeness of the review are open invitations to subsequent litigants to state that they have a right to probe into whether such broad representations have merit.[366] Instead, in drafting a disclosure to the government, attempt to address the pertinent issues at a more general level without quoting or paraphrasing (for example, specific witness statements or specific communications with the client).

• *Develop a Disclosure Strategy.* At the start of the investigation, develop a strategy for determining what information needs to be protected under the privilege and what information, because of an eventual release to the government, should not be protected.

Notwithstanding these general guidelines, however, an entity should be aware that any disclosure is fraught with risk and that by submitting a disclosure to the government, a party at some point in the future may have to produce not only the disclosed documents but all related documents underlying the disclosure as well.

### 2. Incentives for Disclosure

Although the risks mentioned above are tangible and must be seriously evaluated any time a provider submits a voluntary disclosure, the government's enforcement history of the FCA's voluntary disclosure provision demonstrates that the disclosing provider substantially minimizes its criminal, civil, and administrative liability. By submitting a disclosure, a provider may effectively eliminate any risk of being criminally prosecuted as a result of the misconduct that forms the basis of the voluntary disclosure. The government has not had a practice of instituting criminal proceedings against providers as a result of voluntary disclosures.[367]

Furthermore, a provider substantially minimizes potential civil exposure if the government accepts a voluntary disclosure. As noted previously, the FCA empowers the court to reduce a party's liability to double, rather than treble, damages when the party submits a valid disclosure and to limit civil penalties to $5,000 per claim rather than the statutory maximum of $10,000 per claim.[368] Additionally, the DOJ in many cases has exercised its discretion to refrain from recovering any civil penalties under the statute (i.e., it has unilaterally capped its recovery at double damages and has not applied the civil penalty provision of

---

[366] *Compare* Picard Chem. Inc. Profit Sharing Plan v. Perrigo Co., 951 F. Supp. 679, 688–89 (W.D. Mich. 1996) (no waiver because report did not summarize evidence), *with Martin Marietta,* 856 F.2d at 623 (waiver found when company reported what it had learned from those interviewed).

[367] For example, under the DOD Voluntary Disclosure Program, as of Feb. 18, 1992, of the 249 contractors who had made Voluntary Disclosures, the DOJ had criminally prosecuted only 4, and in each of those cases the government claimed that it was investigating the company before the disclosure. *See* William F. Pendergast & Marc S. Gold, *Surviving Self-Governance: Common Interests Approach to Protecting Privileges under the DOD Voluntary Disclosure Program,* 22 Pub. Cont. L.J. 195, 201–03 (1993) [hereinafter Pendergast & Gold, *Surviving Self-Governance*].

[368] *See* 31 U.S.C. §3729(a). *See also* 132 Cong. Rec. 28,581 (1986) (The False Claims Act provides a procedure "for corporations to come forward when they discover fraud within their midst. When corporations follow these procedures in cooperating with the Government, the court may impose not only the lesser level of damages, but also a lesser level of penalty.") (statement of Sen. Grassley).

$5,000 to $10,000 per claim) against providers to encourage the submission of additional disclosures. If this practice is continued under the OIG's voluntary disclosure program, providers will have considerable incentive to submit disclosures because it is the civil monetary penalty provision of the statute that often imposes the larger element of liability.

Finally, a provider substantially reduces the likelihood that the OIG will institute any exclusion action against it as a result of the misconduct that formed the basis of the voluntary disclosure.[369] Even in the unlikely event that the government undertakes an administrative action against the provider, submission of the disclosure will likely result in the government's limiting the duration of the exclusion because of the provider's demonstrated willingness to institute corrective action and exercise self-governance.

## V. Conclusion

The 1986 amendments to the FCA transformed the rules for all health care providers. By deputizing all employees as bounty hunters and offering them huge financial incentives to disclose misconduct, the statute almost ensures that any large-scale questionable or fraudulent practice will be reported to the government.

However, health care providers can easily modify their practices as needed to meet this challenge. They can—and should—develop internal compliance programs that will assist them in identifying fraud before they become embroiled in costly litigation. Providers should familiarize themselves with court interpretations of the FCA to ensure that their practices conform to its standards. They should also develop procedures to disclose questionable practices to the government to preempt the government or private persons from instituting actions against them. By taking these steps, a health care provider can substantially reduce the likelihood that it will confront allegations that it has defrauded the government under the FCA.

---

[369] *See* Pendergast & Gold, *Surviving Self-Governance*, at 201–03. In nonbinding guidelines regarding the circumstances under which the OIG will exercise its discretion to impose a permissive exclusion on a provider, one factor the OIG considers is whether the provider brought "the activity in question to the attention of the appropriate Government officials prior to any Government action, e.g., was there any Voluntary Disclosure regarding the alleged wrongful conduct?" 62 Fed. Reg. 67,392–93 (Dec. 24, 1997).

# 4

# Practical Considerations for Defending Health Care Fraud and Abuse Cases*

---

*Patric Hooper & Amanda S. Abbott, Hooper, Lundy & Bookman, Inc., Los Angeles, California.

# I. The Evolving Nature of Health Care Fraud and Abuse Enforcement

To understand the current realities of defending parties accused of health care fraud or abuse, it is important to be aware of how enforcement activities have evolved. That evolution provides a critical context for understanding current enforcement practices.

## A. The Early Days

Fraudulent and abusive practices in health care are as old as the practice of health care itself. Historic purveyors of snake-oil remedies were not tolerated in the towns of the Old West any more than fraudulent and abusive practitioners are tolerated throughout the country today. The sheriffs and marshals of the Old West were in many ways as vigilant as government enforcement agencies are now in regulating health care. However, rather than exercising government health care program exclusionary authority, the town marshal simply ran the snake-oil salesman out of town with a stern warning never to return. Today, such action would be construed as a permanent exclusion implemented by an executive agency officer without due process—a scenario many perceive as not dissimilar to some current enforcement initiatives.

More recently, however, as the practice of health care became more regulated, state licensing authorities assumed the bulk of the responsibility for protecting consumers from questionable health care practitioners. Through such licensing authority, states were able to safeguard the public against fraudulent, abusive, and unprofessional conduct by licensees, including physicians, hospitals, and other health care providers.

In addition to state licensing regulation, health care professional and trade organizations established codes of conduct and ethics to govern their members. Private accreditation agencies also policed the health care industry. Government agencies often incorporated the credentialing processes of the private associations and accreditation agencies to help regulate the health care industry. Of course, general criminal and civil law sanctions against fraudulent and abusive business and professional practices, such as criminal actions for theft, have been available to federal and state prosecutors for years.[1] Until relatively recently, however, those sanctions typically were reserved for the most egregious cases of fraud and abuse.

## B. Medicare and Medicaid

Health care fraud and abuse did not receive national attention until the establishment of the Medicare and Medicaid programs in 1965.[2] Because the creation of these programs caused the federal and state governments to become major purchasers of health care services, and because of ever-increasing federal and state expenditures for Medicare and Medicaid services, it is not surprising that Congress established specific Medicare and Medicaid fraud and abuse laws in 1972.[3] The 1972 laws were aimed at preventing unlawful kickbacks, bribes, and rebates as well as other types of fraudulent and abusive practices affecting the federal Medicare and Medicaid programs.

To appreciate Congress's original intent, the 1972 laws must be considered in the context in which they were enacted. Although the Medicare and Medicaid programs were then, as now, substantial in their scope, Congress mandated that the programs not interfere with the practice of medicine.[4] Additionally, the Secretary of the Department of Health and Human Services (HHS), then the Secretary of Health, Education, and Welfare, was instructed to consider existing third-party payor principles and practices in determining Medicare and Medicaid payment principles and practices.[5] However, unlike other third-party payors that often paid providers based on the providers' customary charges, Congress intended to impose limits on the amounts Medicare and Medicaid would pay providers.[6] For example, Congress established across-the-board limits on Medicare and Medicaid reimbursement for inpatient hospital services.[7]

---

[1] *See, e.g.,* CAL. PENAL CODE §487. *See* People v. Brown, 61 Cal. App. 3d 476, 478 (1976) (physician prosecuted for grand theft for filing false claims with Medi-Cal).

[2] Title XVIII and Title XIX of Social Security Act, as added July 30, 1965, *codified at* 42 U.S.C. §§1395 *et seq.,* 1396 *et seq.*

[3] Social Security Act Amendments of 1972, *codified as amended at* 42 U.S.C. §§1395nn(b), 1396h.

[4] 42 U.S.C. §1395.

[5] 42 U.S.C. §1395x(v)(1)(A).

[6] *See, e.g.,* SENATE FIN. COMM., S. REP. NO. 92-1230 (1972).

[7] *See, e.g.,* 42 U.S.C. §1396b(i)(3) (imposing limit based on provider's customary charges).

In 1972, Congress also had an early opportunity to review the breadth and complexity of the Medicare and Medicaid payment rules. Upon review, Congress realized that there were likely to be payment disputes regarding the interpretation of the Medicare statutes and regulations. Therefore, it created a specialized administrative agency tribunal, the Provider Reimbursement Review Board (PRRB), as the first step in adjudicating such disputes.[8] State Medicaid agencies also developed specialized administrative appeal processes for state Medicaid programs.[9]

The contemporaneous enactment of the law establishing the PRRB and the Medicare and Medicaid fraud and abuse statutes is a significant historical development that should not be overlooked. As emphasized later, complex Medicare and Medicaid payment disputes, although originally intended to be resolved through administrative agency adjudicatory processes because of the intricacy and enormous volume of the governing rules, have now become the regular source of health care fraud and abuse enforcement actions.[10]

## C. The Late 1970s and 1980s

Because of a perceived need for stronger antifraud weapons, Congress enacted substantial amendments to the Medicare and Medicaid fraud and abuse statutes in 1977.[11] The 1977 amendments were intended not only to strengthen the government's enforcement abilities but also to alleviate concerns about the vagueness of the 1972 laws. Violations of the Medicare and Medicaid fraud and abuse statutes also were upgraded from misdemeanors to felonies, demonstrating congressional seriousness regarding the issue.[12]

Although early enforcement actions under the Medicare and Medicaid fraud and abuse statutes were prosecuted by U.S. Department of Justice (DOJ) criminal attorneys—thus helping to ensure that prosecutions were limited to circumstances involving genuine fraud and abuse—it quickly became obvious that the concept of fraud and abuse in health care could be subject to considerable definitional debate. It is important to note that in response to this possibility of overly broad definitions of health care fraud, the courts emphasized in early cases that they were not interested in "refereeing" ethical conflicts within the health care industry. Instead, they would decide only whether specific conduct violated specific criminal laws. Thus, for example, the U.S. Court of Appeals for the Fifth Circuit articulated in *United States v. Porter*[13] a clear distinction between issues of ethics and issues of fraud and abuse in health care

---

[8]42 U.S.C. §1395oo(1)(B) (1993).

[9]*See, e.g.,* CAL. WELF. & INST. CODE §14171.

[10]The courts have described the Medicare and Medicaid payment process and rules as "among the most completely impenetrable texts within human experience" and as "baffling." *See* Rehabilitation Ass'n of Va., Inc. v. Kozlowski, 42 F.3d 1444, 1450 (4th Cir. 1994); Beverly Community Hosp. Ass'n v. Belshe, 132 F.3d 1259, 1266 (9th Cir. 1977).

[11]Medicare-Medicaid Anti-Fraud and Abuse Amendments, Pub. L. No. 95-142, 91 Stat. 1175, 1182 (1977), *codified as amended at* 42 U.S.C. §1320a-7.

[12]*See* 42 U.S.C. §1320a-7b.

[13]591 F.2d 1048, 1058 (5th Cir. 1979).

and confirmed that the court's function was not to evaluate medical ethics but to decide legal issues.

Shortly after *Porter* was decided by the Fifth Circuit, Congress again amended the Medicare and Medicaid fraud and abuse laws to incorporate an express scienter (i.e., state of mind) requirement to ensure that criminal penalties were not imposed for acts undertaken without criminal intent.[14] The scienter or intent requirement was, and continues to be, critical in the defense of health care fraud and abuse cases, whether criminal, civil, or administrative agency actions. Simply put, under most laws a provider cannot be guilty of fraud or abuse in any forum without some proof of wrongful intent.

## D. Deregulation

In the late 1970s and early 1980s, primary responsibility for federal agency enforcement of Medicare and Medicaid fraud and abuse laws rested with the U.S. Health Care Financing Administration (HCFA)[15]—now the Centers for Medicare and Medicaid Services (CMS)—the agency within HHS responsible for the day-to-day operation of the Medicare and Medicaid programs. CMS attorneys drafted several important opinion letters in the late 1970s and early 1980s interpreting some of the more vague concepts of the Medicare and Medicaid fraud and abuse laws (e.g., the Medicare/Medicaid anti-kickback provisions).[16] These opinion letters, which were circulated widely within the health care industry, constituted realistic, practical analyses that coincided with the government's movement toward deregulating the health care industry. For example, CMS opined that health care joint ventures in which physicians had ownership in ancillary service providers such as clinical laboratories did not violate the Medicare/Medicaid anti-kickback statute per se, even though physician owners could benefit financially by referring business to such providers.[17]

In the early 1980s, as a means of curbing costs, the Reagan administration insisted that the health care industry operate more like a business than it had. For example, certificate of need laws, which were thought by some to be anticompetitive, were abolished in various states, allowing the forces of free enterprise to determine the best and the most efficient use of health care resources. In 1983, Congress established the Medicare Prospective Payment System (PPS) to encourage hospitals to control their own expenditures, which no longer would be generally subsidized by the Medicare program.[18]

---

[14]Omnibus Budget Reconciliation Act of 1980, Pub. L. No. 96-499, 94 Stat. 2599.

[15]As of July 1, 2001, the former Health Care Financing Administration (HCFA) was renamed the Centers for Medicare and Medicaid Services (CMS). For the purposes of this discussion, references typically will be to CMS.

[16]*See* 42 U.S.C. §1320a-7b(b). For text of the anti-kickback statute, see Appendix A-1 on the disk accompanying this volume.

[17]*See* Bradley Tully, *Federal Anti-Kickback Law*, BNA's HEALTH L. & BUS. SERIES §1500:0607 (2001). Although a large number of informal interpretive opinions were written, no official or unofficial compendium of these letters exists.

[18]42 U.S.C. §1395ww(d) (Pub. L. No. 98-21, §601(e), 97 Stat. 65, 152–62 (1983)).

In the laissez-faire atmosphere of the 1980s, most health care providers furnished services on a fee-for-service basis, under which their revenues depended primarily on the volume of services provided. In the health care industry, unlike manufacturing industries, financial efficiency and productivity are measured in terms of "patient days" and "patient visits" rather than number of products manufactured. Medicare and Medicaid cost accounting uses patient days and charges as the means for identifying Medicare and Medicaid activity in hospitals and other patient-care settings. Therefore, providers' internal and external financial analyses projected health care revenues in terms of patient days, patient visits, or patient charges. Health care businesses relied on such projections to perform feasibility studies and other financial analyses. In future years, however, these data would come to be viewed suspiciously by enforcement agencies. The agencies often consider these data to be evidence of wrongful intent to encourage the referral of health care business.

Competition was not welcomed by all members of the health care industry. Many health care providers had been successful, in large part, because of the absence of traditional competitive forces. The continued viability of some providers was threatened by increased competition. In instances in which a new, competing provider would affect the patient days, patient visits, or patient charges of another provider, the affected provider had every reason to view such competition negatively. This was especially true of business practices designed to encourage changes in patient referral patterns.

## E. Office of Inspector General

In the mid-1980s, CMS (then HCFA) stopped issuing interpretations of health care fraud and abuse laws, including the Medicare/Medicaid anti-kickback statute. Primary responsibility for enforcement of the Medicare and Medicaid fraud and abuse laws shifted to the HHS Office of Inspector General (OIG).[19] In 1987, the OIG's authority was boosted significantly by Congress, which gave the OIG the authority to enforce health care fraud and abuse laws (including the anti-kickback statute) by excluding guilty providers from the Medicare and Medicaid programs through an administrative agency process.[20] Until that time, the remedy for violations of the anti-kickback statute was exclusively judicial, and it was enforced at the discretion of the DOJ. After enactment of the 1987 legislation, however, the OIG no longer had to convince a busy prosecutor from the U.S. Attorney's Office to prosecute a case of suspected wrongdoing. Instead, the OIG could unilaterally seek to impose substantial penalties through the HHS administrative process.

Congress also recognized in the 1987 amendments that the breadth of the statutory language in the Medicare and Medicaid fraud and abuse laws had created uncertainty among health care providers as to which commercial arrangements were legitimate and which were not. Thus, Congress authorized the Secretary of HHS to develop "safe harbor" regulations specifying those

---

[19]5 U.S.C. Appendix 3.
[20]42 U.S.C. §1320a-7(b)(7) (the 1987 Amendments).

practices that, regardless of underlying intent, would not be prosecuted.[21] The Secretary, in turn, delegated the development of these safe harbors to the OIG.[22]

Significantly, neither Congress nor the Secretary of HHS expressly delegated any authority to the OIG to establish regulations or other policy defining acts prohibited by the Medicare and Medicaid fraud and abuse statutes. Although the OIG was thus empowered by the safe harbor legislation to identify practices that would *not* be prosecuted under the anti-kickback statute, regardless of their legality or illegality, the OIG was not authorized to make laws announcing or defining what it perceived to be illegal practices under the Medicare and Medicaid fraud and abuse statutes.

The OIG has, nevertheless, undertaken continuing responsibility for determining what is illegal and what is not illegal under the Medicare and Medicaid fraud and abuse laws. To do so, it has issued "fraud alerts," "management advisories," and other general pronouncements that purport to interpret and construe the fraud and abuse laws.[23] Because the OIG is an enforcement agency, it is not surprising that its pronouncements often are skewed toward an expansive interpretation of prohibited acts.

Understanding the role of the OIG's pronouncements is important in defending health care fraud and abuse cases. Since the late 1980s, the OIG has occupied an extremely important position in the hierarchy of both federal and state enforcement agencies. Additionally, the OIG has led a number of investigatory initiatives focusing on health care practices that previously had been considered benign by many members of the health care industry. Moreover, the OIG is maintaining a constant vigil to ensure that CMS and other administrative agencies are not allowing any unnecessary health care dollars to be left available for providers. For example, the OIG routinely suggests ways that CMS could reduce payments to providers.[24]

## F. The *Hanlester* Case

The *Hanlester* case, which culminated in a 1995 decision by the U.S. Court of Appeals for the Ninth Circuit in *Hanlester Network v. Shalala*,[25] illustrates how the rules of acceptable conduct in health care are changing dramatically as a result of enforcement activities.

Because of the *Hanlester* case's notoriety and the fact that the OIG considered it to be an important test case for its enforcement of the Medicare and Medicaid fraud and abuse laws, specifically the anti-kickback statute, the facts and circumstances of the *Hanlester* case are used for illustration throughout this

---

[21] 42 U.S.C. §1320a-7b(b)(3).

[22] 59 Fed. Reg. 37,202 (July 21, 1994).

[23] *See, e.g.,* Special Fraud Alert: Joint Venture Arrangements (Aug. 1989), 59 Fed. Reg. 65,372 (Dec. 19, 1994); Financial Arrangements Between Hospitals and Hospital-Based Physicians, OIG Mgmt. Advisory Rep. No. OEI-09-89-00330 (Oct. 1991). For text of these documents, see Appendix F on the disk accompanying this volume.

[24] See, for example, Memorandum from Office of Inspector Gen. to Health Care Financing Admin. (Nov. 16, 1998), recommending "corrective audits" regarding testing by hospital outpatient department laboratories.

[25] 51 F.3d 1390 (9th Cir. 1995).

chapter. Additionally, the case's history parallels the increase in enforcement activities in health care.

The Hanlester Network, a partnership, was established in the mid-1980s to create freestanding independent clinical laboratories to compete for clinical laboratory testing business referred from physicians' offices and clinics. The Hanlester Network principals hoped to ensure the laboratories' success by offering laboratory ownership to physicians who were in a position to refer specimens to the Hanlester Network laboratories.

Although this type of joint venture arrangement had been generally determined to be lawful in the past, as evidenced by earlier CMS opinion letters, the OIG believed that many joint ventures possessed "suspect" criteria that caused them to violate the anti-kickback statute. The OIG also believed that the proliferation of health care joint ventures was bad public policy. Thus, in 1989, in addition to issuing a special health care fraud alert announcing the criteria of suspect joint ventures, the OIG issued a barrage of investigative subpoenas to obtain information about other potentially suspect joint ventures and continued addressing Congress and others about the evils of physician self-referral, as epitomized by joint ventures such as the Hanlester Network.[26]

## II. Sources of Health Care Fraud and Abuse Investigations

By the late 1980s, fear had beset the health care industry, particularly those providers that had heeded the government's earlier messages about the need for competition in the industry and had set out to compete using common business practices. This fear was fueled by three federal appellate court cases, *United States v. Greber*, *United States v. Kats*, and *United States v. Bay State Ambulance & Hospital Rental Service,* that were interpreted by the OIG and many health care attorneys as stating that if any purpose of a health care transaction was to encourage patient referrals, the transaction was unlawful if it was motivated by any form of remuneration.[27] This overly expansive interpretation of the holdings in *Greber, Kats*, and *Bay State Ambulance* ignored the well-established distinction in criminal law between a defendant's motive for doing an act and the defendant's intent in doing the act. In short, motive is not controlling if the defendant lacked the requisite wrongful intent. Thus, for example, when *Hanlester* reached the Ninth Circuit, the court concluded that the *Hanlester* defendants lacked wrongful intent even though they structured their business transactions so that physician owners were actively encouraged to refer Medicare and Medicaid patient specimens to Hanlester Network laboratories.

By the late 1980s, the subject of health care fraud and abuse had become central to the health care industry. Although the topic previously was only a minor part of health care law seminars, by the late 1980s it was dominant. The

---

[26]59 Fed. Reg. 65,372, 65,373 (Dec. 19, 1994).

[27]United States v. Greber, 760 F.2d 68 (3d Cir.), *cert. denied,* 474 U.S. 988 (1985); United States v. Kats, 871 F.2d 105 (9th Cir. 1989); United States v. Bay State Ambulance & Hosp. Rental Serv., 874 F.2d 20 (1st Cir. 1989).

health care media also gave priority to the issue, which made the problem well known throughout the health care industry. Indeed, almost anyone in the industry knew of either someone being investigated or someone about to be investigated. This created an environment fertile for producing many new fraud and abuse investigations in the years to come.

## A. Internal Sources

Although there are no precise statistics on the subject, many experienced health care fraud practitioners believe that a substantial percentage of health care fraud and abuse investigations start with disgruntled current or former employees. Almost every confrontation between a health care employer and employee has the potential to develop into an allegation of fraud or abuse. Employer–employee issues, which used to be the exclusive province of human resources officers and labor lawyers, now require the involvement of a health care lawyer. Wrongful discharge complaints in health care commonly involve contentions of fraud and abuse. Employees and others are encouraged to become whistleblowers by the prospect of substantial bounties offered under federal and state false claim laws and the special protections afforded to employee whistleblowers.[28]

The OIG and other enforcement agencies are well aware of the value of disgruntled current and former employees as sources of information regarding health care fraud and abuse allegations. Investigative agencies seek the identities of former employees early in health care investigations, hoping to find cooperative witnesses.

In addition to disgruntled employees, internal sources of fraud allegations include medical staff physicians and other professionals affiliated with providers. Disputes over treatment practices and policies may easily expand into charges of fraud and abuse. Medical staff members also are becoming false claims *qui tam* relators more now than they have been in the past. Allegations of wrongdoing often develop out of business disputes between professionals.

Other sources of fraud and abuse reporting, which may not be wholly internal, are friends, lovers, and relatives. Not only may an office romance turned sour become the subject of a charge of sexual harassment, it also may give rise to a health care fraud and abuse investigation. One important early health care fraud and abuse case arose between two physician brothers associated with a prestigious medical clinic. Whether that action was motivated by longstanding sibling rivalry, actual good-faith concern about the clinic's billing practices, or some combination of the two is not known. However, the consequence of the resulting investigation was significant to the clinic involved.

More recently, a potentially important federal health care fraud and abuse investigation relied heavily on the testimony of the father in a longstanding and very personal father-son dispute. The government relied heavily on the father's testimony during the trial of the case.[29] This example also illustrates the tactics

---

[28] *See* Federal Civil False Claims Act, 31 U.S.C. §§3729 *et seq.*; Cal. Gov't Code §12652.

[29] United States v. Mackby, 261 F.3d 821 (9th Cir. 2001), *cert. denied,* 541 U.S. 936 (2001), *aff'd,* 68 Fed. Appx. 776 (9th Cir. 2003).

used by some health care fraud and abuse investigators who, according to the father, requested that he not contact his son to discuss the charges being investigated.

## B. External Sources

The *Hanlester* case began when a marketing representative mistook a competing laboratory owner for a prospective physician investor. The competing laboratory owner deceived the Hanlester marketing representative by telling her he was a physician interested in investing in the Hanlester laboratories rather than disclosing the truth (i.e., that he was the owner of a competing laboratory with no interest in investing). The competing laboratory owner provided a congressional staff member with a copy of his surreptitiously tape-recorded conversation with the Hanlester Network employee, which eventually made its way to the OIG. The OIG considered the tape-recorded conversation to be critical evidence of wrongdoing in the Hanlester Network investigation.

Medicare fiscal intermediaries and carriers are also important external sources of information in health care fraud and abuse investigations. These organizations employ fraud and abuse specialists who scrutinize transactions to identify fraud and abuse. Carrier and intermediary auditors also may serve that purpose. Because CMS has defined abusive practices as including inappropriate billings caused by a provider's misunderstanding of Medicare policy,[30] it can be expected that Medicare fiscal intermediaries and carriers will be even more active in searching out fraud and abuse than they have already been.

Beginning in the late 1990s federal and state health care facility surveyors were "deputized" to report fraud and abuse to government enforcement agencies.[31] Although the regulatory surveyors traditionally have limited their role to monitoring a provider's compliance with licensing and certification (i.e., health and safety) requirements, survey teams, such as the multidisciplinary teams involved in the so-called "wedge audits" of Operation Restore Trust,[32] increased their focus on fraud and abuse.[33]

Additionally, patients themselves may complain of perceived fraud and abuse. The government has undertaken substantial efforts to educate Medicare beneficiaries about fraud and abuse. The government's hope is that patients will become knowledgeable about and comfortable with reporting incidents of alleged fraud and abuse.

Finally, under the Health Insurance Portability and Accountability Act of 1996 (HIPAA), HHS is required to implement the Medicare Integrity Program,[34]

---

[30] *See, e.g.*, 42 C.F.R. §455.2.

[31] Testimony on Efforts to Control Medicare/Medicaid Waste, Fraud and Abuse by Bruce Merlin Fried before the House Committee on Commerce, Subcommittee on Oversight and Investigations (Sept. 29, 1997), summary available at www.hhs.gov/asl/testify/t970929a.html.

[32] Operation Restore Trust was a two-year demonstration project started in 1995 by President Clinton. The initiative was concentrated in California, Florida, Illinois, New York, and Texas and was designed to test innovations in fighting Medicare and Medicaid fraud and abuse.

[33] *See* Press Release, U.S. Dep't of Health & Human Servs., *Secretary Shalala Launches New "Operation Restore Trust"* (May 20, 1997).

[34] 42 U.S.C. §1395ddd.

which expands HHS's authority to contract with private parties to perform so-called "integrity activities." These private contractors perform medical fraud and utilization review, cost report audits, and other investigatory activities to fight fraud and abuse.

## C. Importance of Determining the Source of Disclosed Information

Obviously, those who report health care fraud and abuse perform a very important role in the investigation and prosecution of health care fraud and abuse cases. Such persons are entitled to protection so that they and others are not deterred from reporting instances of fraud and abuse. However, because of the possibility of hidden agendas, it is important for a party under investigation to identify the source of the government's information as early as possible.

Competitors may be motivated to exaggerate anecdotal information. Patients may not be reliable because they may lack the competence necessary to evaluate instances of fraud or abuse. On more than one occasion, patients have complained to government authorities about a lack of medical testing when the testing in question actually had been performed on them. Patients simply did not realize that the test or tests had been performed.

The government often will not know a critical fact about the trustworthiness or motives of a person providing information. Such a fact could affect the reporting person's credibility and the accuracy of that person's information. For example, in the Spectra Laboratories investigation (involving a San Francisco-area clinical laboratory), the person who reported the alleged fraud and abuse was a "professional" whistleblower who regularly pursued actions against his employers shortly after being employed. Information about the frequent "problems" with each of his many employers discovered by this whistleblower was relevant not only to the reliability of the information being supplied by him to the government, but also to the issue of whether he simply was repeating something already known to the government.

The identity of the reporting person might eventually be disclosed or become obvious. For example, if a reporting party has filed a false claims action, his or her identity will be revealed when the *qui tam* complaint is unsealed. The *qui tam* plaintiff is then subject to the same discovery obligations as any other plaintiff. However, where the reporting party does not become a plaintiff, his or her identity may remain unknown.

## III. Enforcement and Investigative Agencies

Now that health care fraud and abuse has become a priority for federal and state law enforcement agencies, myriad public and private enforcers are getting involved. Advocating the prevention and prosecution of fraud and abuse in health care is a particularly popular political cause. Cracking down on health care fraud and abuse is not only popular, but the subject gives federal and state policy makers a way to divert attention from other, more difficult problems facing the health care system, such as health care services or resources rationing. In fact, major cost savings are routinely projected in both federal and state health care budgets as a result of anticipated recoveries from fraud and abuse investigations.[35]

Because so many different government agencies are involved in health care fraud and abuse investigations, identifying precisely which agency is conducting an investigation is important but often difficult. Identifying the agency is important for a number of reasons, including, for example, determining the fundamental question of whether the investigating agency actually has the authority to regulate the conduct under review. A simple illustration is a case in which a local enforcement agency of limited jurisdiction (e.g., a county attorney) attempts to enforce a state law against a party located outside of the enforcement agency's geographic jurisdiction. It should not be assumed that anyone with a badge has the authority to investigate allegations of health care fraud and abuse. To the contrary, there may be substantial limitations on the authority of a particular investigating agency.

## A. Federal Enforcement Agencies

As noted above, since establishing the Medicare and Medicaid programs, the federal government has been increasingly active in health care fraud and abuse investigation and law enforcement. One of the most important federal enforcement and investigation agencies is the HHS OIG. The OIG has assumed primary responsibility for enforcing Medicare and Medicaid fraud and abuse laws throughout the United States. Although the OIG may act as an investigatory agency for another federal agency (e.g., the DOJ) in a particular matter, the OIG has its own authority to enforce the Medicare and Medicaid fraud and abuse laws through various administrative agency proceedings, including exclusion proceedings and civil monetary penalty proceedings.

Other federal agencies, such as the U.S. Department of Defense (DOD), also have enforcement and investigatory units. The DOD's Criminal Investigative Services is an important investigatory agency in the health care industry because of Tricare, formerly the Civilian Health and Military Program of the Uniformed Services (CHAMPUS). Tricare uses civilian health care providers to furnish services to the dependents of active and retired military personnel. The Tricare program is an especially important payor of mental health services, which have been a frequent target of health care fraud and abuse enforcement activities.

The Federal Employees Health Benefits Program, which insures approximately 9 million federal employees, also has become active in health care fraud and abuse investigations. The Office of Program Management, the agency responsible for administering the program, has independent authority to debar fraudulent and abusive providers without waiting for Medicare or some other government payor to do so. The Railroad Retirement Board exercises similar authority on behalf of the beneficiaries of the Railroad Retirement Insurance Program.

---

[35]*See* U.S. GEN. ACCOUNTING OFFICE, MEDICARE: HEALTH CARE FRAUD AND ABUSE CONTROL PROGRAM FINANCIAL REPORT FOR FISCAL YEAR 1997, at 5 (1998) (tracing contributions made to Medicare trust fund for fiscal year 1997).

The Federal Bureau of Investigation (FBI) is also extremely active in health care fraud and abuse investigations now that health care fraud and abuse has become a high priority to the federal government. FBI agents have been newly hired or reassigned throughout the country to investigate health care fraud and abuse allegations. Significantly, the FBI may be involved in both criminal and civil investigations and also may be used to investigate health care fraud in programs other than government health care programs.[36] For example, if it is suspected that health care fraud or abuse may have been accomplished by the use of the U.S. Postal Service (USPS), the FBI is authorized to investigate for mail fraud, even if only private health care payors are allegedly damaged.

Similarly, when mail fraud is suspected, USPS inspectors have been assigned to investigate health care fraud and abuse. Although USPS inspectors typically do not take lead roles in such investigations, they provide additional resources to the federal government.

The DOJ maintains criminal and civil health care fraud and abuse units. The Washington, D.C., office often coordinates with local offices in investigating (and often ultimately prosecuting) health care fraud and abuse. And, when the government suspects the presence of organized crime, the Organized Crime Sections of the DOJ are also investigating health care fraud and abuse.

Additionally, health care fraud and abuse has become of great interest to the Internal Revenue Service, with respect to nonprofit providers of health care services, and to the Federal Trade Commission, with respect to the enforcement of federal antitrust laws.

## B. State Enforcement and Investigative Agencies

Whereas Medicare, Tricare, and other public programs are wholly federal programs, Medicaid is a combined federal/state program that is administered at the state level by a single state Medicaid agency in each state. In most states, the single state agency is the state's health or social services department, which is required to be the exclusive authority under federal law to administer the state Medicaid program in that state.[37]

In addition to the single state Medicaid agency, Medicaid-participating states typically have Medicaid Fraud Control Units. Such units often are located in the state prosecuting attorney's office, which in many states is the state attorney general. Although most Medicaid Fraud Control Units are authorized to prosecute criminal health care fraud and abuse cases, they also have the right to pursue civil actions against providers suspected of fraud and abuse. Medicaid Fraud Control Units employ their own investigators, who may work jointly with other state or federal investigators.

Because of the widespread interest in the enforcement of health care fraud and abuse laws, other state agencies are also becoming involved in investigation and enforcement activities. Thus, a state controller or a state insurance commissioner might initiate his or her own independent health care fraud and abuse

---

[36]For discussion of the increasing role of the FBI in health care fraud enforcement, see Chapter 1, at Section I.C. (Baumann, An Introduction to Health Care Fraud and Abuse).

[37]42 C.F.R. §431.10.

investigations. Similarly, state professional licensing agencies, such as state medical boards, also are investigating and enforcing laws against health care fraud and abuse. For example, such licensing agencies are construing acts of alleged excessive billing to constitute unprofessional conduct, which could give rise to disciplinary action against the licensee.[38]

At the local level, district attorneys and other local government prosecutors, such as city attorneys, are enforcing state health care fraud and abuse laws. Special health care fraud sections have been and are continuing to be established for the local investigation and enforcement of health care fraud and abuse.

## C. Private Enforcers

Private insurance companies are no longer content to let government enforcement agencies investigate and enforce allegations of health care fraud and abuse. Instead, they now are aggressively conducting their own independent investigations. Of course, private investigators do not have the authority or the breadth of enforcement weapons available to them that the public agencies have. However, it can be expected that such private enforcers will be even less mindful of due process and fairness than their public agency counterparts.

Another private force that may be significant is the shareholders of health care companies. They may initiate shareholder derivative actions when stock values fall as a result of government investigations, arguing that the company failed to deal with incidents of fraud and abuse appropriately, thus damaging the value of the company's stock and causing them considerable financial harm.[39]

The Medicare Integrity Program permits HHS to contract with private parties to perform investigatory activities.[40] This may present problems of fairness and due process similar to those encountered with private insurance investigations.

Regarding private enforcers, it must be emphasized that *qui tam* relators are acting on behalf of the government, not as private citizens, when they file false claims actions. At least one court[41] initially concluded that Congress lacked the constitutional authority to provide such private relators with the requisite standing to enforce the False Claims Act[42] and thus declared the *qui*

---

[38]For example, California licensing authorities have relied on §§2227 and 2261 of the California Business and Professional Code to argue that improper billing practices constitute "unprofessional conduct."

[39]For further discussion of such shareholder derivative lawsuits, see Chapter 8, at Sections II.B. and III. (Walton, Humphreys, and Jacobs, Potential Liabilities for Directors and Officers of Health Care Organizations).

[40]*See* Medicare Program Integrity Manual, Ch. 1, §1.1 (Nov. 17, 2006), *available at* http://www.cms.hhs.gov/manuals/downloads/pim83c01.pdf.

[41]*See* United States *ex rel.* Riley v. St. Luke's Episcopal Hosp., 196 F.3d 514 (5th Cir. 1999), *reh'g en banc granted, opinion vacated by* 196 F.3d 561 (5th Cir. 1999), *rev'd,* 252 F.3d 749 (5th Cir. 2001). *Qui tam* relators may not maintain false claims actions against public entities. *See* United States *ex rel.* Garibaldi v. Orleans Parish Bd., 244 F.3d 486 (5th Cir. 2001), *cert. denied,* 534 U.S. 1078 (2002), *reh'g denied,* 534 U.S. 1172 (2002), *appeal after remand,* 397 F.3d 334 (5th Cir. 2005), *cert. denied,* 546 U.S. 813 (2005).

[42]31 U.S.C. §§3729 *et seq.*

*tam* relator provisions of the federal False Claims Act to be unconstitutional. However, that decision was reversed on rehearing.

## IV. Enforcement Weapons

As identified above, there are various federal, state, local, and private enforcement agencies affecting the health care industry. The identity of the enforcement agency may have a significant effect on the agency's jurisdiction and ability to search for and obtain evidence. Equally important as identifying the agency conducting an investigation is identifying the particular laws and regulations that the agency may enforce against the target of an investigation.

### A. Federal Criminal Laws

#### 1. General Criminal Laws

Federal criminal law prohibits a variety of acts that are not unique to the health care industry. Such general criminal laws as mail fraud and money laundering may be applied to participants in health care fraud schemes just as they may be applied in other industries. For example, a false entry in a Medicare patient's chart can violate the criminal prohibition against making false statements to the federal government.[43]

#### 2. Health Care–Specific Criminal Statutes

However, there are also specific federal criminal statutes uniquely governing health care activities. The Medicare/Medicaid anti-kickback statute is a special health care criminal statute that has been used in a variety of federal criminal actions to prevent offering, paying, soliciting, or receiving kickbacks for the referral of health care business.[44]

#### 3. Health Insurance Portability and Accountability Act of 1996 (HIPAA)

HIPAA implemented the most sweeping amendments to the federal health care fraud laws to date. The Act created five new federal health care fraud crimes. First, HIPAA prohibits executing or attempting to execute a scheme or artifice to defraud or to fraudulently obtain money or property of any health care benefit program.[45] Second, HIPAA prohibits embezzling, stealing, misapplying, or converting money, property, premiums, or other assets of a health care benefit program.[46] Third, HIPAA prohibits making false statements or con-

---

[43] 18 U.S.C. §1001.

[44] *See* 42 U.S.C. §1320a-7b.

[45] 18 U.S.C. §1347. For text of §1347, see Appendix E-2 on the disk accompanying this volume.

[46] 18 U.S.C. §669.

cealing material facts in connection with the delivery of or payment for health care benefits, items, or services.[47] Fourth, HIPAA prohibits willfully obstructing, preventing, misleading, or delaying, or attempting to do so, the communication of information or records relating to a federal health care fraud offense to a criminal investigator.[48] Finally, HIPAA also prohibits disposing of assets to enable a person to become eligible for Medicaid.[49]

In addition to adding the new health care fraud crimes listed, HIPAA expanded existing money laundering, asset forfeiture, and fraud injunction statutes to cover federal health care offenses. The 1996 act also expanded the scope of the "specified unlawful activity," which forms the predicate for a money-laundering violation under 18 U.S.C. §1956, to include any act or activity constituting an offense involving the federal health care laws.[50] In addition, the 1996 amendments expanded the anti-kickback statute to other federal health care programs such as Tricare.[51]

Most important, however, is that four of the five new criminal statutes created by the 1996 Act apply to any health care benefit program, including any private health care plan or contract that affects commerce, thus bringing private insurance plans and contracts within the provisions of the new health care criminal statutes.[52]

## B. State Criminal Laws

As with the federal laws, general state criminal laws may be used to prosecute health care fraud and abuse. For example, in California, the state Medicaid Fraud Control Unit routinely charges the owners of independent clinical laboratories with grand theft in connection with alleged overbilling of the Medi-Cal program.

Additionally, there are specific state health care criminal laws. Various states have enacted their own versions of the Medicare/Medicaid anti-kickback laws, which may be applicable to certain specific payors, such as state Medicaid payors or workers' compensation programs, or to all payors in general.[53]

Many of the state health care criminal laws are modeled after specific federal health care criminal laws. However, it should not be assumed that a state law is consistent with the related federal law. For example, Section 14107.2 of the California Welfare and Institutions Code, which purports to be modeled after the federal Medicare/Medicaid anti-kickback statute, does not contain the specific scienter requirements or the "inducement" factor required by the federal law. These omissions could arguably raise constitutional issues. However, one court has rejected this argument.[54]

---

[47]18 U.S.C. §1035. For text of §1035, see Appendix E-1 on the disk accompanying this volume.

[48]18 U.S.C. §1518.

[49]42 U.S.C. §1320a-7b(a)(6).

[50]Pub. L. No. 104-191, §§246, 247, 249.

[51]42 U.S.C. §1320a-7b.

[52]18 U.S.C. §24(b) (amending the definition of "health care benefit program").

[53]*See, e.g.,* CAL. BUS. & PROF. CODE §650; CAL. WELF. & INST. CODE §14107.2.

[54]California v. Duz-Mor Diagnostic Lab., 68 Cal. App. 4th 654 (1998).

Similarly, although states have expressly adopted the Medicare/Medicaid anti-kickback statute as a model, many have not expressly incorporated the federal regulatory safe harbors,[55] which are intended to alleviate the uncertainty and over-breadth of the federal law. It has yet to be determined whether the federal safe harbors would protect a defendant in a state court prosecution under a state anti-kickback law that does not expressly incorporate the federal safe harbors.

## C. Federal Civil Laws

Once again, although there are various generic statutes that may be applied in a federal civil health care fraud and abuse case, the most important and widely used civil statute is the federal False Claims Act.[56] Indeed, most major civil enforcement actions and health care settlements have been brought under that act.

Although the elements of a civil False Claims Act action are dealt with extensively elsewhere in this volume,[57] two aspects of such actions are mentioned briefly here because of their practical implications. The first is the attempt by the federal government and private *qui tam* relators to expand the breadth of the False Claims Act by trying to redefine "false claims" to include any violation of any law or regulation governing a health care provider. A common example is the allegation that a purported violation of the Medicare/Medicaid anti-kickback statute necessarily gives rise to false claims with respect to all services provided by the payor of the kickback. The courts generally have not supported this position. Instead, they have held that more must be proven than simply a violation of the anti-kickback law.[58]

The second practical element pertains exclusively to false claims actions initiated by private *qui tam* relators. The government is well aware of various generic allegations of health care fraud and abuse in the health care industry, as various agencies have published fraud alerts and other documents describing fraudulent activities. Indeed, at most health care seminars, speakers routinely identify areas of suspected fraud and abuse. It is unlikely that Congress intended such publicly disclosed and generally known allegations to constitute the type of whistleblowing that is to be encouraged and rewarded by the provisions of the False Claims Act.

When a *qui tam* relator's false claims action appears to repeat common fraud and abuse themes, defense counsel will want to consider pursuing the issue of public disclosure because the relator's suit will have to be dismissed if the allegations are shown to be so generally well known that the relator must be doing nothing more than repeating previous allegations.[59]

---

[55] *See, e.g.,* CAL. WELF. & INST. CODE §14107.2.

[56] 31 U.S.C. §§3729 *et seq.*

[57] For in-depth discussion of the False Claims Act, see Chapter 3 (Salcido, The False Claims Act in Health Care Fraud Prosecutions: Application of the Substantive, *Qui Tam*, and Voluntary Disclosure Provisions). For text of the Act, see Appendix C-1 on the disk accompanying this volume.

[58] *See, e.g.,* United States *ex rel.* Thompson v. Columbia/HCA Healthcare Corp., 125 F.3d 899 (5th Cir. 1997).

[59] *See* United States *ex rel.* Findley v. FPC-Boron Employees' Club, 105 F.3d 675 (D.C. Cir. 1997), *cert. denied,* 522 U.S. 865 (1997).

In addition to seeking relief under the federal False Claims Act, federal enforcement agencies typically add causes of action for common law fraud and unjust enrichment to supplement false claims allegations. However, false claims allegations generally remain the primary focus of federal civil actions.[60]

## D. State Civil Remedies

Many states have their own false claims acts. For example, the California False Claims Act[61] is modeled after the federal False Claims Act. Note again, however, that when a state statute is modeled after a federal statute, it is arguable whether interpretations of the federal statute, such as federal court cases and agency interpretations, should be persuasive in interpreting the state law.

In addition to using false claims statutes, state health care enforcement agencies also are actively using state unfair competition laws to remedy and enjoin health care fraud and abuse.[62] Because unfair competition statutes are broadly written and traditionally interpreted expansively by the courts, such statutes provide state and local enforcement agencies with potentially wide authority. However, as a practical matter, if the enforcement agency is not able to prove the wrongfulness of the underlying conduct, it is unlikely that a court or jury will be persuaded to characterize the conduct as constituting unfair competition.

Additionally, it is questionable whether a court or jury would find a party liable for unfair competition if the party is able to establish that the practice engaged in was common for the industry. Although the plea of "everybody's doing it" generally is not an effective defense, the fact that a major segment of the industry engages in the practice could have a significant effect on the determination of whether the competition is unfair.

The state courts also have been the forum of choice when private health care parties become enmeshed in disputes over the legality of their financial arrangements. For example, a hospital that owns a medical office building may refuse to continue to honor its lease obligations to its physician tenants because it fears that the favorable rental terms may be construed as disguised kickbacks. Such action has given rise to civil lawsuits over the issue of whether the contract is unenforceable because it is illegal. Indeed, substantial case law is being developed from such controversies.[63]

## E. Federal Administrative Agency Remedies

As discussed in Section I.E., above, one of the most significant aspects of the 1987 amendments to the Medicare and Medicaid Act was the provision

---

[60]For discussion of the civil Stark law restrictions, see Chapter 2 (Crane, Federal Physician Self-Referral Restrictions). For text of the Stark law, see Appendix B-1 on the disk accompanying this volume.

[61]CAL. GOV'T CODE §12650.

[62]CAL. BUS. & PROF. CODE §§17200 *et seq.*

[63]*See, e.g.,* Vana v. Vista Hosp. Sys., No. 233623, 1993 WL 597402 (Cal. Super. Ct. Oct. 25, 1993).

authorizing the HHS OIG to bring administrative actions against health care providers as a remedy to curb health care fraud and abuse. Thus, in *Hanlester*, the OIG did not have to convince the U.S. Attorney's Office to bring criminal proceedings against the Hanlester Network principals. Rather, after the local U.S. Attorney declined to prosecute, the OIG was able to initiate its own proceedings in the form of an administrative exclusion proceeding.

The administrative remedy of exclusion is extremely significant because most health care providers rely heavily on Medicare, Medicaid, and other government payors for their revenues. Without such revenues, most providers would not be able to continue to provide services. In addition to the far-reaching impact of such exclusion actions, the OIG is able to maintain an action in HHS's own quasi-adjudicative forum, which places respondents at substantial risk of an adverse result.

The OIG also has the authority to assess and impose civil monetary penalties against a health care provider in an administrative proceeding to enforce the fraud and abuse laws. Although the civil monetary penalty provisions are very similar to those of the federal False Claims Act, the fact that they can be implemented through an administrative proceeding, which ultimately is subject only to somewhat limited judicial review, is very important.[64]

## 1. Limited Judicial Review

Indeed, the OIG has assumed that because Congress authorized it to enforce the health care fraud and abuse laws through exclusion and civil monetary penalties, it may determine the rules governing the administrative proceedings.[65] For example, the OIG takes the position in such cases that its initial determinations are presumed to be valid and are subject to somewhat limited review by the administrative law judges and the appellate board charged with presiding over exclusion and civil monetary penalty proceedings. The OIG's attempt to limit the authority of the HHS administrative law judges is especially troublesome because the HHS administrative law judges typically are the only adjudicators who actually view the witnesses and evidence and function as de novo decision makers.

Another extremely important practical consequence of the OIG's authority to remedy fraud and abuse through administrative proceedings is that the final agency decision is subject to a limited standard of judicial review.[66] Adverse factual findings must be upheld by a reviewing court if they are supported by any competent evidence in the record. Although the courts are the final arbiters of the correct interpretation of the law, the OIG typically will argue that a reviewing court must give substantial deference to the agency's interpretation of the governing statutory and regulatory provisions.

Because of the limited nature of judicial review, it is very important that a defendant prevail at the administrative hearing level regarding civil exclu-

---

[64]*See* 42 C.F.R. §§1003.100–.128.

[65]*See* 42 C.F.R. §1005.21(h).

[66]*See, e.g.,* 42 U.S.C. §1320a-7(f).

sion and monetary penalty remedies. However, as was the case in *Hanlester*, it is possible to prevail on judicial review under the appropriate circumstances when the terms of a statute are at issue and factual findings are not being challenged.

In addition to the exclusion and civil monetary penalty provisions of the federal law, the Secretary of HHS and the heads of other government programs (e.g., the director of the Tricare program) may impose other administrative remedies. For example, a provider's Medicare or Tricare certification may be removed through an administrative proceeding.[67]

## 2. Suspension of Payments

Often, a more troubling result is the temporary suspension of payment by government payors in cases of suspected fraud or abuse. The federal government, through the Medicare fiscal intermediary or carrier, has the authority to suspend payments to a provider temporarily.[68] The temporary suspension of payments can, and often does, have devastating cash flow consequences to a provider. And, as a practical matter, it is difficult to challenge a temporary suspension of payments because of the temporary nature of the action and the lack of a formal administrative review process or the availability of judicial review of the suspension action.

Similarly, a Medicare fiscal intermediary or carrier may subject a provider's claims to "special review" for issues such as medical necessity. Although payment technically is not suspended under these prepayment reviews, the reviews can cause payments to be slowed to a point at which a provider eventually may be unable to operate because of cash flow problems. Once again, such prepayment review is considered a temporary remedy, and thus it is difficult to prevent such action through administrative or legal proceedings. Rather, informal methods of resolution may be the most efficient way to stop or lessen the duration of such action. The key is to satisfy the Medicare fiscal intermediary or carrier that no recoupment of an overpayment is necessary because of corrective actions taken by the provider.

A Medicare fiscal intermediary or Medicare carrier does not have the authority to delay the administrative hearing process during the pendency of a criminal or civil investigation. Thus, for example, if a Medicare carrier has temporarily suspended a supplier's Medicare payments due to suspicion of fraud or abuse, the carrier must nevertheless continue to proceed through the administrative process, including issuing an overpayment determination, which should trigger administrative appeal rights for the affected supplier.[69] Nowhere do the Medicare statutes or regulations authorize the Secretary of HHS to postpone an overpayment determination pending the outcome of judicial inquiry into the presence of fraud.

---

[67]*See, e.g.,* 42 C.F.R. §489.53.

[68]42 C.F.R. §405.371.

[69]*See* United States *ex rel.* Rahman v. Oncology Assocs., P.C., 198 F.3d 502, 514 (4th Cir. 1999).

## F. State Administrative Agency Remedies

Once again, it is important to note that state Medicaid agencies and other state agencies possess their own authority, similar to that of federal administrative agencies, to impose civil monetary penalties and suspend a provider from the state's Medicaid program. As with federal administrative agency actions, such state action generally is subject to full administrative review and limited judicial review.

Similarly, state agencies have the authority to suspend payments, such as Medicaid payments, temporarily.[70] However, it is important to emphasize that because the Medicaid program is a federal/state program, any action undertaken by any state agency ultimately is subject to compliance with federal Medicaid laws and regulations. Thus, for example, if, as in the case of *Doctor's Medical Laboratory, Inc. v. Connell,*[71] a state controller, who is not part of the single state Medicaid agency, decides to suspend Medicaid payments to a provider, the action arguably must comply with the provisions of the governing federal Medicaid law as well as any independent state law.

Although state licensing boards, such as state medical boards, traditionally have restricted their activities to monitoring the quality of services furnished by professionals and other licensees, there is a growing trend to broaden the authority of these professional licensing boards to include taking action against professionals and others involved in excessive billing or other abusive financial practices. For example, the California Medical Board considers such practices to be "unprofessional conduct," which purportedly authorizes it to take disciplinary action against a licensee.[72]

Such action by licensing boards provides private payors with a dangerous weapon for alleged payment errors by physicians and other health care professionals with respect to private-pay patients. For example, private insurers may report examples of suspected fraud and abuse to state licensing agencies, which are not limited to policing the provision of services to public sector patients.

In *Doctor's Medical Laboratory, Inc. v. Connell,* the California state controller was prohibited from unilaterally withholding Medicaid payments from a provider and from auditing the Medicaid payments of the provider because the court held that only the single state Medicaid agency, the state Department of Health Services, had such authority under the controlling federal Medicaid laws and regulations. However, in a subsequent decision, the same court of appeal concluded that a state Medicaid plan approved by HHS and authorizing the state controller to conduct Medicaid audits constituted an interpretation of the federal Medicaid regulations, which allowed the single state Medicaid agency to delegate audit authority to another state agency—here, the

---

[70]42 C.F.R. §455.23.

[71]69 Cal. App. 4th 891 (1999), *abrogated on other grounds by* RCJ Medical Servs. v. Bonta, 91 Cal. App. 4th 986, 1002, 1004 (2001), *cert. denied,* 535 U.S. 1096 (2002).

[72]CAL. BUS. & PROF. CODE §§2227, 2261.

state controller's office—as long as the delegating state agency retained final authority to review the audit results.[73]

Because the controlling federal Medicaid regulation prohibiting the delegation of discretionary authority from the single state Medicaid agency to another state agency[74] did not change between the two California Court of Appeal decisions, it is difficult to reconcile the decisions. However, from a practical standpoint, it is quite obvious that the federal government's approval of a state plan amendment, which expressly permitted the delegation of audit authority from the single state Medicaid agency to the state controller, was considered to be the equivalent of a change in the governing provisions of the Medicaid regulations by the court.

The reasoning of the California Court of Appeal in *RCJ Medical Services*[75] was cited with approval by the U.S. Court of Appeals for the Ninth Circuit in *San Lazaro Ass'n v. Connell.*[76] In reversing the district court decision, which had prohibited the delegation of authority from the single state Medicaid agency to the state controller, the Ninth Circuit concluded that Medicaid providers could not maintain a right of action under the controlling federal Medicaid statute or Medicaid regulation regarding the single state agency provision.

## G. Identifying the Remedy Threatened by the Enforcement Agency

Federal and state enforcement agencies, as well as private parties, have a variety of remedies available to them to prevent and punish health care fraud and abuse. Unfortunately, especially at the early stages of an investigation, it is not always easy to determine the particular remedy being threatened. In fact, many times parallel proceedings are being considered. For example, the government may be reviewing the facts for both False Claims Act purposes and a potential exclusion proceeding. Therefore, it is not unusual for the Civil and Criminal Divisions of the DOJ to be investigating the very same conduct and threatening both a civil False Claims Act action and a criminal indictment.

The subject of defending potentially parallel proceedings is complicated and beyond the scope of this chapter. Perhaps it is sufficient to say, however, that a potential defendant may have different rights with respect to the investigation or prosecution of different agencies and remedies. Obviously, for example, the target of a criminal prosecution has constitutional rights that might be unavailable to a defendant in an administrative proceeding involving the termination of the defendant's provider agreement.

Moreover, as a practical matter, the government usually is not especially helpful in identifying the types of remedies threatened. To the contrary, as a matter of strategy, the government often prefers to be vague about the breadth and nature of an investigation and the remedies that ultimately might be sought.

---

[73]*See* RCJ Medical Servs. v. Bonta, 91 Cal. App. 4th 986 (2001), *review denied*, No. S100878 (Cal. Dec. 12, 2001), *cert. denied*, 535 U.S. 1096 (2002).

[74]42 C.F.R. §431.10(e).

[75]91 Cal. App. 4th 986.

[76]286 F.3d 1088 (9th Cir. 2002), *cert. denied*, 537 U.S. 878 (2002).

Although there obviously is good reason for such vagueness at the onset of an investigation, there is little justification for the government's continued lack of clarity about its purposes as the investigation progresses.

## V. Health Care Principles Being Enforced

### A. Hierarchy

At the risk of being elementary, it is worth emphasizing that not every written statement of health care payment or coverage is binding on the public, nor does every rule or guideline cited by a government investigator as a basis for taking action constitute a proper interpretation of the law. Health care lawyers must be vigilant to ensure that they are advising their clients correctly. In a field in which the statutes are amended annually, and the governing regulations are changed even more often, every analysis of every health care dispute should begin with a review of the statutes and regulations. In fact, even a periodic review of the U.S. Constitution is helpful to remind lawyers that the OIG is *not* a constitutional office.

As is the case with many complex regulatory areas, Congress established the general statutory principles governing the Medicare and Medicaid programs and left most of the responsibility for the details to the Secretary of HHS. This is true of the Tricare program as well. However, surprisingly, in some areas of Medicare and Medicaid law, Congress has spoken very specifically and has delegated no discretion to the Secretary of HHS or to any other administrative agency to establish alternative interpretations of the governing statutes.

Government health care investigators seldom are aware of the actual provisions of the governing statutes. They, like the industry, tend to focus on the "rules" that provide the day-to-day interpretations of the "law." Those rules typically are found in the many CMS manuals, Medicare fiscal intermediary and carrier bulletins, and other informal guidelines, such as the American Medical Association's (AMA's) *Current Procedural Terminology* (CPT) *Code Manual*. These informal guidelines often are vague and inconsistent.

As a result, for example, although an enforcement agency may be convinced that an independent clinical laboratory billing Medicare for a laboratory test ordered by an end-stage renal disease (ESRD) dialysis unit constitutes unlawful billing (because the laboratory test presumably is subject to the confusing and esoteric Medicare "50–50" rule), it is questionable whether the governing Medicare statute allows HHS to establish such a rule in the first place because the statute compels an independent clinical laboratory to bill for all laboratory testing it performs, subject to certain exceptions that do not include ESRD laboratory testing.

### B. Importance of Reviewing All the Rules

It simply is not possible to discuss or even list in this chapter all of the rules that might be applicable to a health care dispute involving, for example, the Medicare program. However, unless substantial effort is made to identify and reconcile all of the potentially applicable rules to a given set of facts, it is not possible to be certain that all the rules are being considered.

Fortunately, Congress publishes its policies through statutes. However, when a statute is vague, or even when it appears to be clear, considerable assistance in interpreting Congress's intent may be gathered from the statute's legislative history. Although the Secretary of HHS publishes formal regulations in the *Code of Federal Regulations*, their sheer volume can be overwhelming. Yet, this volume must be mastered because of the surprisingly specific details set forth within the regulations.

Once one extends his or her research and information gathering beyond the statutes and regulations, the task becomes more complex. Researching Medicare, Medicaid, and Tricare policies is a triple-tiered process. The statutes form the first layer, the regulations form the second, and the other guidelines and rules form the third layer.

### 1. Informal Guidelines

CMS publishes many manuals containing thousands of very important rules interpreting the hundreds of Medicare statutes and regulations. These include, for example, the *Medicare Coverage Issues Manual* (CMS Publication 6); *State Operations Manual* (now part of CMS Internet Only Manual (IOM) No. 100-07); *Hospital Manual* (CMS Publication 10); *Home Health Agency Manual* (CMS Publication 11); *Skilled Nursing Facility Manual* (CMS Publication 12); *Medicare Intermediary Manual* (CMS Publication 13); *Carriers Manual* (CMS Publication 14); *Provider Reimbursement Manual* (CMS Publication 15); and *Medicare Peer Review Organization Manual* (CMS Publication 19). CMS also issues Medicare intermediary letters and other program memoranda. Medicare intermediaries and carriers, in turn, issue bulletins and local medical review policies.

These informal interpretations and guidelines are not promulgated according to applicable federal rulemaking requirements. Thus, they may be established on an ad hoc basis without consideration of public input. Yet, such guidelines are commonly relied on by government enforcement agents as the basis for health care false claims and other allegations.

That these principles have not been promulgated as formal regulations raises the important question of whether they even can be relied on by government enforcement agents.[77] However, regardless of the outcome of that issue, such guidelines also may be of questionable substantive validity because they often contain requirements not set forth in the statutes and regulations they purport to interpret.

In addition to relying heavily on interpretations developed by the government, enforcement agencies also rely on so-called rules established by private organizations, such as the AMA's CPT codes, noted above, which are

---

[77]In *Cedars-Sinai Med. Ctr. v. Shalala*, 125 F.3d 765, 766 (9th Cir. 1997), the court suggested that violation of such a rule could give rise to a false claim. However, in *United States ex rel. Swafford v. Borgess Med. Ctr.*, 98 F. Supp. 2d 822, 828 (W.D. Mich. 2000), *aff'd*, 24 Fed. Appx. 491 (6th Cir. 2001), *cert. denied*, 535 U.S. 1096 (2002), the court refused to base liability on a provision of the *Medicare Carriers' Manual*.

incorporated as rules for billing Medicare.[78] In fact, noncompliance with the CPT codes often is alleged as the basis for False Claims Act actions.

### 2. Agency Adjudicative Decisions

Although enforcement agencies rely heavily on informal rules and guidelines to judge the conduct of health care providers for purposes of determining whether fraud or abuse has occurred, they may be unaware of the interpretations given these provisions by agency adjudicators such as the Medicare PRRB and HHS's administrative law judges. For example, enforcement agencies began aggressively challenging certain items claimed by providers on Medicare cost reports, such as advertising and marketing costs. Enforcement agencies often consider claiming such costs to be abusive or even fraudulent. However, there is a well-established history of debate over the allowability of these advertising-type costs. Significantly, the federal courts, reviewing PRRB and CMS decisions several years ago, allowed such costs, using the reasoning that the costs were incurred for the purpose of alerting patients who suffer from alcoholism to the need and availability of treatment, an activity related to patient care.[79]

Similarly, for many years, a provision of the Medicare *Provider Reimbursement Manual* (PRM) was interpreted by Medicare fiscal intermediaries as prohibiting psychiatric hospitals from claiming the direct and indirect costs of providing education services to children and adolescent patients as allowable Medicare costs.[80] CMS and its fiscal intermediaries considered these costs to be particularly nonallowable given that there are few, if any, child and adolescent Medicare patients in psychiatric hospitals.

There is little doubt that if issues such as these, which have been the subject of disputes before the PRRB since its inception, were viewed by enforcement agencies today, the agencies would be inclined to characterize the claiming of such costs as fraudulent or abusive.

However, notwithstanding CMS and its fiscal intermediaries' positions and their reliance on a provision of the Medicare *Provider Reimbursement Manual*, the PRRB and reviewing federal courts, applying the governing Medicare statutory and regulatory provisions, concluded that Medicare was, in fact, required to share in such costs notwithstanding the fact that education services were seldom, if ever, furnished to Medicare patients.[81]

The point to be emphasized is that the government's reliance on informal rules must be scrutinized very closely for both consistency with the actual law (the Medicare statutes and regulations) and internal consistency. Moreover, health care lawyers cannot ignore the considerable body of quasi-judicial determinations that have dealt with many of the rules relied on by government enforcement agencies.

---

[78] See the discussion at 65 Fed. Reg. 13,082, 13,087 (Mar. 10, 2000).

[79] *See* Advanced Health Sys. v. Schweiker, 510 F. Supp. 965 (D. Colo. 1981).

[80] *See* PRM-I §2104.5.

[81] Vista Hill Found. v. Heckler, 767 F.2d 556 (9th Cir. 1985).

### 3. Other Pronouncements

In addition to official government guidelines and quasi-judicial decisions, additional government pronouncements are being relied on by government and private parties in connection with health care fraud and abuse enforcement and compliance issues. For example, fraud alerts issued by the OIG are considered by many to be the equivalent of binding regulations. However, these fraud alerts are nothing more than the viewpoints of government enforcement agencies, specifically the OIG, as to how they would like to see the fraud and abuse laws interpreted. As such, they are no different from the opinions of a police officer or investigator on how the law should be interpreted.

Similarly, model compliance programs issued by the OIG are not binding laws or regulations.[82] Indeed, they have no legal effect. However, government and even some industry spokespersons are seemingly affording the terms of such documents the dignity of formal regulations. Such a reaction, especially among lawyers, is especially confounding, because they are trained during the early days of law school to give little effect to nonbinding pronouncements. It is indeed strange when health care lawyers give more weight to the musings of OIG officials than to dicta in a Supreme Court decision.

### C. Impact of the Rules

The importance to be attached to fraud alerts, model compliance plans, and even the terms of out-of-court settlement agreements depends on the role of the health care lawyer in a particular situation. If the lawyer is advising a client about structuring a particular transaction or engaging in other future activities, the lawyer naturally will give substantial deference to these informal government pronouncements because they are helpful to the client that wishes to structure its activities as much as possible in accordance with the pronouncements even though they may not be legally binding. A client can hardly be accused of possessing wrongful intent if it has attempted to adhere not only to formal, legally binding government policies, such as formal regulations, but also to nonbinding pronouncements and interpretations. However, for the lawyer defending a client in a fraud and abuse investigation or action, the informal pronouncements should be challenged to the extent the enforcement agency is relying on an informal pronouncement in its investigation and potential prosecution.

A final comment on informal pronouncements and interpretations: arguably, although informal pronouncements and interpretations are not binding on the public, including members of the health care industry, such interpretations and pronouncements should be binding on a government agency. Thus, for example, when an enforcement agency is pursuing a False Claims Act investigation against a provider because a physician has used the Medicare billing

---

[82]*See, e.g.,* OIG Compliance Program Guidance for Hospitals, 63 Fed. Reg. 8987 (Feb. 23, 1998); OIG Supplemental Compliance Program Guidance for Hospitals, 70 Fed. Reg. 4858 (Jan. 27, 2005); OIG Compliance Program Guidance for Clinical Laboratories, 62 Fed. Reg. 9435 (Mar. 3, 1997), *as revised in* 63 Fed. Reg. 45,076 (Aug. 24, 1998); OIG Compliance Program Guidance for Home Health Agencies, 63 Fed. Reg. 42,410 (Aug. 7, 1998); OIG Compliance Program Guidance for Pharmaceutical Manufacturers, 68 Fed. Reg. 23,731 (May 5, 2003). OIG compliance program guidances are available at http://oig.hhs.gov/fraud/complianceguidance.html.

number of another affiliated physician to bill for services, the issue may involve nothing more than a technical violation of the Medicare provisions prohibiting reassignment of Medicare claims. Under a provision of a CMS manual, the violation of the reassignment rules in such a situation may not even give rise to an overpayment. Thus, such an act can hardly be said to constitute a false claim.

## D. Private Party Interpretations, Practices, and Codes of Conduct

As enforcement agencies have become more aggressive and have publicized their successful investigations and prosecutions, health care lawyers and consultants have grown increasingly more conservative in interpreting the governing law. For example, a scenario that is somewhat common in health care shows how health care policy making is evolving. A government lawyer from the OIG responds to a question from the audience at a seminar by relying on a recently issued OIG fraud alert to opine that a particular practice could constitute fraudulent or abusive activity. Health care lawyers and media representatives attending this seminar publish the OIG lawyer's opinion in subsequent newsletters and articles. When repeated often enough, the OIG lawyer's opinion becomes virtually a new standard of conduct.

This characterization of health care fraud and abuse policy making is not merely anecdotal. Indeed, during the *Hanlester* administrative hearings, to try to support its position, the OIG relied on articles written by private health care lawyers who quoted informal pronouncements and statements made by the OIG. Fortunately for the *Hanlester* defendants, the HHS administrative law judge who heard the case was aware of the authorities of law he was obligated to follow, which did not include the OIG's "wish list" of prohibited activities.

Advice and opinions by private lawyers obviously are not the law. However, as with reliance on informal government pronouncements and interpretations, a client's reliance on a private lawyer's advice and opinion regarding a particular activity may be very important in determining the intent element of an allegedly wrongful act.

The related issue of the relevance of widespread industry practice is questionable. It is likely that every health care lawyer has heard that a client undertook a particular action because everyone in the industry, or perhaps more important, all of the client's competitors, are engaging in the same practice. Although industry practices may be some evidence of a standard of care, if the industry practice is illegal, the practice is still illegal. However, as with reliance on informal government pronouncements and interpretations and reliance on the advice and opinions of private counsel, reliance on industry practice may be relevant to the intent issue for a party involved in a health care fraud and abuse investigation or proceeding. This is particularly true when the defendant can demonstrate that he or she relied not only on the industry practice itself but also on the government's knowledge of and acquiescence to the practice. For example, when a laboratory is able to show that its billing practices were known to and approved by the government's fiscal intermediary, the practices can hardly be characterized as false.[83]

---

[83]*See* California v. Duz-Mor Diagnostic Lab., 68 Cal. App. 4th 654, 672–73 (1998).

Formalized industry standards, including ethical and other standards established by professional organizations and trade associations, also may be evidence of a standard of conduct. Most certainly, if a particular practice is considered to be ethical or consistent with the standards established by a professional organization or a trade association, such evidence is, at the very least, relevant to the intent element of a defense in a fraud and abuse case.

The *Hanlester* proceedings provide an example of the relevance of such standards.[84] The *Hanlester* defendants were able to establish that, during the period involved in that case, the AMA did not consider physician ownership in clinical laboratories to be unethical. They also pointed out that the legislative history supporting the Medicare/Medicaid anti-kickback statute indicated that the statute was intended to prohibit wrongful acts of the type considered to be unethical by professional organizations. Thus, although the determination of whether a particular act is fraudulent or abusive should not depend on questions of ethics, the fact that the act being scrutinized is consistent with the ethical standards of the profession may be important.

## VI. GOVERNMENT INVESTIGATORY STRATEGIES

### A. Overview

Health care fraud and abuse enforcement agencies typically conduct investigations using a variety of tools to obtain information. Although some tactics are common, other tools available vary according to the severity of the suspected fraud and abuse. For example, if criminal conduct is suspected, the government may seek a search warrant to inspect and seize records and other documents (or even an arrest warrant).

To obtain a search warrant, the enforcement agency seeking the warrant must involve either a court or grand jury. However, under Section 248 of HIPAA, DOJ attorneys may now issue investigative demands, in the form of subpoenas duces tecum, to obtain information without convening a grand jury or requesting permission from a judge.[85] Although this process does not have the force and effect of a search warrant, federal attorneys are now using it to conduct preliminary investigations in cases in which there is no need for a search warrant.

In addition to the criminal processes described above, government enforcement agencies have available a variety of other mechanisms to obtain information for an investigation. For example, the HHS OIG often issues subpoenas for information. In False Claims Act investigations, in addition to having subpoena authority, U.S. Attorneys have the ability to issue civil investigatory demands, which enable them to depose potential witnesses in an investigation in which a *qui tam* complaint has not yet been unsealed.[86]

---

[84]Hanlester Network v. Shalala, 51 F.3d 1390 (9th Cir. 1995).

[85]18 U.S.C. §3486.

[86]31 U.S.C. §3733.

Moreover, because health care is a regulated business, government regulators generally are permitted to inspect health care facilities and the offices of health care practitioners during reasonable business hours without obtaining any special permission or using any special investigatory instrument. Generally, Medicare, Medicaid, and other government and private third-party payors require providers to agree to make records and other information available as a condition of program participation.[87] Government payors, including Medicare, may impose substantial penalties on a provider that refuses to cooperate with a request for an inspection or review of records.

The California Attorney General's Office in 2004 requested and obtained authority from the state legislature to perform searches of provider's records without warrants or subpoenas.[88] However, not every health care provider's office or workplace should be considered part of a highly regulated business. For example, in *Tucson Women's Clinic v. Eden*,[89] the court concluded that physicians and patients have high expectations of privacy at physicians' offices and clinics, which could require regulatory agencies to secure warrants in certain circumstances.[90]

## B. Enforcement Agency Interviews

Generally, most government interviews in health care fraud and abuse investigations are conducted informally. Although the government has procedures available to compel the testimony of a particular person under particular circumstances, the government seldom is required to resort to those procedures. Thus, persons generally are free to choose not to be interviewed by enforcement agents. However, in the health care field, persons are reluctant to refuse to be interviewed by government officials and, thus, often willingly agree to talk with investigating agents. Health care personnel are accustomed to assisting government regulators and might not wish to appear defensive. Of course, potential targets of possible criminal investigations cannot be compelled to testify because of the privilege against self-incrimination under the Fifth Amendment.

The informal interview process can be filled with risk and potential negative consequences. Just as compliance programs have become standard in the health care industry, regularly advising employees of the possibility of government investigations should also be a standard business practice. Employees should be advised that they might be contacted during nonworking hours by government enforcement agents and investigators who will ask them questions about their jobs and their employer's business practices. Employees should be informed that they may request identification from the investigator and that although they have the right to speak to an investigator, they also have the right not to speak or to speak with the investigator at a different time. Moreover, they have the right to have counsel or other persons present during the interview.

---

[87] 42 C.F.R. §489.53.

[88] *See* S.B. 1358 (2004), *codified at* CAL. GOV'T CODE §12528.1.

[89] 371 F.3d 1173, 1192 (9th Cir. 2004), *rev'd on other grounds*, 379 F.3d 531 (9th Cir. 2004).

[90] *See also* De La Cruz v. Quackenbush, 80 Cal. App. 4th 775 (2000).

Experience shows that the presence of counsel at interviews helps to ensure the accuracy of the subsequently developed investigative report. Thus, to the extent possible, defense counsel should attempt to be present at all interviews conducted during an investigation. Additionally, it is good practice to conduct such interviews at a neutral location. Interviews at a person's place of employment can be disruptive and embarrassing, whereas interviews at government agents' offices can be intimidating.

Interviews generally are not tape recorded by investigators, although interviews may be recorded with the permission of the agent. Instead, the investigator takes notes of the interview and ultimately prepares investigatory reports including information from the interview. The investigatory reports contain the impressions of the investigator rather than a verbatim record of the discussion that actually occurred. Because interview reports typically are not shown to interviewees immediately after their interviews, they may not be a reliable means of refreshing the memories of those persons interviewed. However, these reports often are used for that purpose by the government. Thus, it is important that the interviewee and other persons present during an interview take notes of the discussion or be debriefed regarding the details of the interview if no one other than the interviewee and the investigator were present at the interview.

Without such record, contemporaneous notes, or a debriefing, an interviewee who becomes a witness may rely inappropriately on the possibly unfounded impressions of the investigator. As a result, an interviewee's subsequent testimony based on the investigator's written interview report may be very different from the actual discussion that occurred during the original interview itself.

Enforcement agencies conduct extensive interviews with disgruntled employees and competitors and other persons who may have reason to be hostile toward a provider under investigation. Under those circumstances, it is unusual for defense counsel to be present during such interviews. As a result, a party under investigation may not know the substance of such interviews until actual proceedings begin.

In addition to being excluded from interviews of disgruntled employees and competitors, a party under investigation also will probably not be present during government interviews of patients and their families, who enforcement agencies are now actively interviewing in connection with investigations. This absence from interviews of patients, especially very elderly, confused, or incompetent patients, may be extremely prejudicial to a provider. Counsel must explore the circumstances surrounding such interviews if an enforcement agency intends to rely heavily on them in making investigatory findings. For example, it is not unusual for a patient to believe that a particular procedure, such as one of several laboratory tests, was not performed when, in fact, the procedure actually was performed.

Unfortunately, government investigators are not always fair or truthful. Indeed, when examined about investigatory techniques during the *Hanlester* proceedings, the OIG investigator who had conducted various interviews in that case admitted during the administrative hearing that she had made statements during interviews that were not completely accurate. She indicated that she was trained to use misstatements as an investigatory technique "to obtain the truth."

For example, the OIG investigator began some interviews by asking the interviewee whether he or she would be "surprised" if the investigator had a tape recording of the interviewee's previous unspecified conversations. The investigator admitted that she asked this question even though she did not have such tape recordings because she had been taught that this technique helps to ensure the truthfulness of the content of the interview.

Investigators might also respond to a proposed interviewee's inquiry about the need for an attorney to be present during an interview by indicating that an attorney is only necessary if the interviewee has something "to worry about." Investigators might also inform interviewees that they are not the focus of the government's investigation when, in fact, an interviewee later becomes the target of an enforcement action.

It appears that aggressive investigators will use virtually any tactic short of physical intimidation to further their investigation. And, when they have a preconceived notion of the results of the investigation, those methods can border on coercion. For example, in the false claims action of *United States v. Mackby*,[91] the target of a fraud and abuse investigation reported that his own father was told not to talk to him about the father's interview with the investigator.

In some cases, interviews also may be used as the bases for seeking search warrants. When an investigator's impressions of an interview are biased or clearly inconsistent with the truth of the interview, improper consequences may follow. For example, in a state Medicaid fraud investigation, a state police officer relied almost exclusively on a misstatement of a state surveyor to obtain a search warrant to conduct an unjustified search of a laboratory owner's home.

These types of abuses will continue so long as health care enforcement agencies reward overzealous investigators and take no adverse actions against investigators who act inappropriately or dishonestly. The safeguards embodied in the system, such as the requirement that a magistrate issue a search warrant only if there is probable cause to believe a crime has occurred, are effective only if government enforcement agents act in good faith.

## C. Document Production

Most health care fraud and abuse investigations depend heavily on documentary evidence. As discussed in Section VI.A., above, enforcement agencies have a variety of procedures available to compel the production of documents, including computerized information and data. Given the broad enforcement authority delegated to agencies such as the OIG, challenging such authority may not be the best use of legal resources. With rare exceptions, courts will confirm the authority of enforcement agencies to compel the production of documents.

However, because the government has such general authority does not mean that there can be no limits on document requests. For example, if documents are seized pursuant to a valid search warrant, the warrant must define

---

[91]261 F.3d 821 (9th Cir. 2001), *aff'd,* 68 Fed. Appx. 776 (9th Cir. 2003), *cert. denied,* 541 U.S. 936 (2004).

with some precision the scope of the documents that may be seized. Additionally, statutory and common law protections, such as attorney–client privilege, protect many documents from being produced. Yet, it is not uncommon for privileged documents to be seized during a search. Therefore, as a standard business practice, privileged documents should be maintained separately from nonprivileged documents if possible.

A practical comment regarding the seizure of documents, including computer information: The seizure of such documents can devastate a health care provider's continuing operations. Thus, a provider is not being overly cautious if it retains duplicates of important documents at an off-site location. Although enforcement agencies typically allow a party eventual access to documents seized pursuant to a search warrant, it is often difficult to obtain copies of such documents in a timely and convenient manner.

When search warrants are not used to obtain documents, there typically is more flexibility. For example, absent unusual circumstances (such as when the government suspects potential altering of documents), copies of documents ordinarily are acceptable to an investigating agency. The attorneys for most government enforcement agencies also are willing to discuss reasonable requests to narrow the scope of documents requested. Furthermore, although subpoenas typically provide for a relatively short return period, extensions are routine. Staggered production of documents often is permitted.

Defense counsel should exercise the same degree of care regarding document production that would be used in responding to any investigation by a government enforcement agency. For example, because the information requested and produced may contain trade secrets, it is appropriate to identify and label such documents as "trade secrets" so the documents are not inadvertently released inappropriately.

## VII. Responding to an Investigation

### A. Understanding the Government's Interests

Government agencies at all levels are convinced that fraud and abuse are widespread in the health care industry.[92] Presently, little can be done to convince them otherwise. However, counsel's knowing and responding to the goals and interests of the various enforcement agencies may assist clients.

Government investigations are undertaken with cost–benefit goals in mind. For example, HHS has indicated that the Operation Restore Trust antifraud program collected $23 for every $1 spent.[93] Not surprisingly, the government wants to get the most for its money. Thus, the more expensive an investigation,

---

[92] According to government statistics, 10% of every health care dollar spent is wasted on fraud and abuse. *See* Pamela H. Bucy, *Health Care Reform and Fraud by Health Care Providers*, 38 Vill. L. Rev. 1003 (1993) (citing Prospective Payment Assessment Comm'n, Report and Recommendation to the Congress 15 (1993)).

[93] *See* Office of Inspector Gen., U.S. Dep't of Health & Human Servs., Semiannual Report, Oct. 1, 1994–Mar. 21, 1995, at 23 (1995).

the greater the return the government expects. Therefore, if after assessing the facts and the law applicable to a particular situation, defense counsel believes that liability exists, it may be unwise to require the government to incur substantial additional costs that may be avoided through cooperative fact-finding.

Other factors motivating government enforcement agencies are more political. For example, the OIG may have an interest in demonstrating that CMS or the Medicare fiscal intermediaries or carriers are not adequately enforcing the governing payment principles in a particular area. The OIG has issued numerous reports critical of CMS's administration of the Medicare and Medicaid programs.[94] This criticism has not been overlooked by CMS. The resulting interagency tension may provide positive opportunities to defense counsel under appropriate circumstances. For example, because many fraud and abuse investigations are based on complicated Medicare and Medicaid rules that are being interpreted for the first time by the government enforcement agencies, knowledgeable CMS employees may be an important source of unbiased, independent information that may be important to present to the lawyer for the enforcement agency.

The political issue is also important in state and local matters. For example, a state attorney general or state insurance commissioner may have political reasons to discredit other state officials charged with the administration of Medicaid or another health care program. Thus, if an enforcement agency headed by a political foe of the head of the agency charged with administering the state health care program becomes overly aggressive, the latter agency may have a motive for agreeing with the position being advocated by defense counsel to deter the overly aggressive enforcement agency.[95]

## B. Communicating with Enforcement Agents and Their Attorneys

As with many areas of the law, one of the most important assets of an effective health care defense attorney is his or her credibility with the opposing party. This is particularly true of the health care industry, in which government regulators must continue to interact with clients even after an investigation is over. If the regulators or their attorneys decide that defense counsel's representations cannot be relied on, the negotiation process (and even the litigation process) can be damaged, to the detriment of the client.

Civility is almost as important as credibility. Although a client may obtain temporary satisfaction from an attorney's outburst at the government's lawyer, little is achieved in the long run. Notwithstanding the anxiety and hostility engendered by an investigation, defense counsel does little to advance the client's cause by insulting or attempting to intimidate enforcement agency employees and their attorneys. Indeed, rather than helping the client, inappropriate tactics can injure the client in the long run.

---

[94] *See, e.g.*, Office of Inspector Gen., U.S. Dep't of Health & Human Servs., Audit of HCFA's FY 1997 Financial Statements (1998); *see also* OIG Reports, Office of Audit Services, CMS, *available at* http://oig.hhs.gov/oas/oas/cms.html.

[95] The controller of the state of California, a Democrat, repeatedly criticized the enforcement practices of the former state attorney general, a Republican, in the 1990s.

However, lack of courtesy, consideration, or manners should not be confused with the aggressive representation of a client's case. A favorable settlement or litigation outcome cannot be expected unless the enforcement agency knows the defendant's counsel will use all ethical tactics available to protect his or her client.

## C.  Explaining the Client's Position

An unfortunate consequence of the ongoing crackdown on health care fraud and abuse is that persons unfamiliar with health care laws, regulations, practices, and procedures sometimes are given substantial authority to make critical decisions. Not surprisingly, these persons are not always equipped to make those determinations. For example, many government lawyers, without any health care experience, must rely on investigators who also may have very little, if any, health care experience to assess allegedly suspicious circumstances.

The health care industry is not analogous to the defense industry or the savings and loan industry. Many issues in health care do not lend themselves to clear-cut answers. For example, issues of medical necessity involve subjective judgments for which there might be no "true" answer. However, government enforcement agency lawyers and investigators commonly view the health care industry as being the same as other industries and are predisposed to be skeptical of pleas of good-faith confusion or misunderstanding as possible defenses to alleged acts of fraud or abuse.

Health care lawyers can play an important role in educating government attorneys and investigators about the rules and practicalities governing health care. For example, they can place perceived problems in their proper context for government enforcement agency lawyers and investigators to avoid automatic adverse reactions. Means for doing so include submitting position papers and using outside consultants and even persons within CMS or other health care regulators to help educate the government representatives.

## D.  Position Papers

Preparing position papers during the investigatory stages of a fraud and abuse case serves not only to communicate the client's position to the government but also to prepare the lawyer for further proceedings. Such documents set forth the facts, policies, and laws that might be favorable to the client. Of course, the preparation process works both ways: Not only does it prepare the client's attorneys, it also alerts the government's attorneys and investigators to the strategies that ultimately may be used if the investigation is not settled short of formal proceedings. Nevertheless, on balance, the advantages of submitting position papers generally outweigh the disadvantages. Almost without exception, government attorneys are very receptive to position papers.

As with other communications, credibility is critical in the preparation of position papers. Overstating or misrepresenting the facts or the law may be overlooked temporarily, but ultimately the true facts will surface, and damaged credibility is difficult to repair.

### E. The Context Concept

Using position papers and other communications to place suspect practices in the appropriate context and perspective is imperative. For example, since at least 2005, enforcement agencies have been characterizing some quality-of-care issues as areas of potential fraud and abuse.[96] For example, at seminars, enforcement officials graphically portray, through slide presentations, evidence of nursing home care that appears so poor that billing for the services could arguably constitute a false claim.

Most individuals who have represented providers of skilled nursing facility services have encountered instances in which the delivery of care at a facility is below minimum standards. Existing enforcement mechanisms are in place to remedy these serious problems. However, it is also a very sad fact that elderly patients admitted to nursing facilities often spend the remainder of their lives at those facilities. Sometimes, during the end stage of a disease, symptoms are present that would be distasteful to anyone when viewed outside of the context of the nursing facility. As systems begin to fail before a person's death, the body begins to deteriorate rapidly, and, even with the best of care, the last days of a patient's life may be unpleasant.

In a Los Angeles County coroner's inquest of several years ago, the coroner examined a 102-year-old nursing facility patient who had developed decubitus (bedsores) that rapidly deteriorated in degree, requiring debridement. When a Stage III or Stage IV decubitus is debrided, the resulting open sore is painfully ugly. For a patient with debrided decubitus who is 102 years old and whose life systems are failing, the result can be deadly, as was the case with this patient. Yet, the fact that the patient died with Stage IV decubitus did not automatically reflect poor care. To the contrary, the evidence at the coroner's inquest showed that the care furnished to the patient before death was more than adequate. Thus, the death was deemed to be accidental rather than death at the hands of another. However, if this episode had been taken out of context and if photographs of the patient had been circulated, there is little doubt that one could conclude that subquality care was given.

Another relatively common example of allegedly deficient care at a nursing facility occurs when medications are given to patients without physician orders. When considered in the abstract, this allegation appears to be extremely serious. Indeed, it can evoke visions of ill-intentioned nurses drugging recalcitrant patients to control them. However, when placed in context, this allegation may mean no more than that after a patient's longstanding renewed orders for a certain medication had expired without the facility obtaining a signed order renewing the prescription on a particular date, the medicine was nevertheless given to the patient by the attending nurse. This can happen in the best of facilities, and it may occur because the patient's physician has either

---

[96] *See* OIG Supplemental Compliance Program Guidance for Hospitals, 70 Fed. Reg. 4858, 4870 (Jan. 31, 2005), reprinted as Appendix I-1.1 on the disk accompanying this volume; *see also* Wagonhurst *et al.*, *Compliance and the Quality of Care Revolution: Fitting the Pieces Together in the Government's New Enforcement Landscape,* 11 HEALTH LAW. NEWS No. 9 at 18 (Sept. 2007).

failed to visit the patient on a timely basis or simply overlooked signing a tele-phone order for the medication. Surveyors might cite the facility for "medi-cations being given without orders," which, although literally true, may not accurately describe the situation. When placed in its proper context, the deci-sion to provide the medication without a signed order was probably neither wrongful nor harmful. Although the "letter of the law" might have required the facility to cease giving the medication until a signed order was obtained, the absence of a signed order should not result in the facility being denied payment for the services provided. In fact, *not* administering a medication might have resulted in harm to the patient.

Financial issues also must be placed in their appropriate context. Giving enforcement lawyers and investigators an overview of the background and circumstances surrounding a perceived problem can be very beneficial for a client. For example, as indicated earlier, marketing and advertising costs are now being scrutinized closely by enforcement agencies, which often come to the unfounded conclusion that such costs should not be reimbursed by the government under a cost-based reimbursement system. However, there is a substantial history of such costs being considered necessary indirect costs of patient care.

Another example of an issue pursued by enforcement agencies out of its proper context is a hospital or other health care provider's claims for losses on the sale of depreciable assets under the reasonable-cost reimbursement system. In 1997, government enforcement agencies indicated their skepticism about the validity of Medicare reimbursement for substantial losses that were occurring on the sale of facilities. This investigatory concern clearly was spurred by an increase in Medicare reimbursement for losses claimed by providers following the disposal of health care assets.[97]

Although such sales and the corresponding losses may have increased Medicare expenditures, the Medicare rules allowing losses on the bona fide disposal of hospitals and their assets have existed since the beginning of the Medicare program.[98] Indeed, when it was more typical of assets to be sold for a profit, as was the situation in the majority of cases until the mid-1990's, the government applied those rules to recapture excessive depreciation paid for past years based on the gain on sale. The very same regulations that allowed the government to recapture depreciation for a gain on sale required the govern-ment to share in the additional reimbursement owed a provider when assets were sold at a loss. If such losses are perceived by policy makers to be a problem, the remedy is legislation, not prosecution. Indeed, in 1997 Congress legislated away gains and losses on sales of depreciable health care assets.[99]

Another example of the need to place suspicious facts in the appropriate context so as to enable the government to respond appropriately is the perva-sive misconception that independent clinical laboratories essentially dictate the laboratory tests ordered by physicians for Medicare, Medicaid, and other

---

[97]*See* OIG Report: Medicare Losses on Hospital Sales, OEI-030-96-00170 (June 1997), *available at* http://oig.hhs.gov/oei/reports/oei-03-96-00170.pdf.

[98]See 42 C.F.R. §413.134 and its predecessor, 42 C.F.R. §405.415 (1970).

[99]*See* Balanced Budget Act of 1997, *codified at* 42 U.S.C. §1395x(v)(1)(O).

government patients. According to national investigations, such as the National Health Laboratories investigation, the government believes that laboratory marketing employees, at the direction of the laboratory owners, arbitrarily add unnecessary tests to the menu of laboratory tests on requisition sheets supplied to physicians to "trick" them into ordering excessive laboratory testing for their patients.[100] For example, the government accused National Health Laboratories of surreptitiously adding ferritin testing to the laboratory requisition sheets of their client physicians without informing the physicians that when a laboratory profile containing ferritin was ordered the laboratory would perform the ferritin test and bill separately for it.

Regardless of the merits of the government's position and suspicions in general, it does not necessarily follow that the routine ordering of ferritin testing is always an unlawful ploy by laboratories to increase Medicare and other payor revenues through the delivery of medically unnecessary laboratory testing. For example, patients suffering from ESRD have chronic health care problems that often include anemia. Thus, ferritin testing for these patients on a regular basis is medically necessary under virtually any definition of the term. Therefore, for ESRD patients, the routine ordering of ferritin testing may be very appropriate.

## F. Explaining Industry Terms and Practices

In addition to placing events and actions in context, it also may prove helpful to interpret and explain common terms or jargon used by health care providers that may cause unnecessary suspicion. As in other industries, members of the health care industry often use terms or phrases that, when taken out of context, may sound suspicious.

An example that became known in one FBI investigation was the use of the term "back office." Physicians often refer to the "front office" and the "back office" of their premises to distinguish office administrative activities occurring in or near the waiting room area from bookkeeping and other activities that are performed elsewhere in the facility. However, when an investigating agent obtains an internal memo that refers to adjustments to the physician's financial records to be made in the "back office," suspicion can arise.

Mistaken interpretations of dialects and foreign languages can be made by investigating agents. Wiretapped telephone conversations have been translated incorrectly, causing substantial unjustified harm to persons being investigated. Defendants who are members of ethnic minorities are especially vulnerable to such mistakes in interpretation or translation.

Additionally, just as members of the health care industry are not experts in law enforcement, law enforcement employees are not experts in health care. Enforcement agencies thus may be unnecessarily troubled by the application of common business practices to the delivery of health care, even though the industry has been encouraged by the government to be more businesslike to try to lower costs and increase competition. This fact became obvious in the *Hanlester* proceedings.

---

[100]Press Release, Dep't of Justice, *NHL Will Pay $100 Million to Settle Longest Fraud Case Ever* (Dec. 18, 1992).

Although the Hanlester Network Laboratories were established when the Reagan administration was encouraging competition in the health care industry, the enforcement agency in that case, the HHS OIG, characterized many of the business practices used by the Hanlester Network as improper. An important example was the government's criticism of the Hanlester Network's practice of monitoring the referral patterns of physicians who used the Hanlester Network Laboratories. When laboratory usage decreased for a particular physician, the Hanlester Network's medical director was instructed to contact the physician to discuss why usage had decreased. The OIG concluded that such contacts, in and of themselves, were unlawful attempts to interfere with the referring physicians' medical judgment by forcing them to order more tests than they believed to be medically necessary.

However, at the administrative hearing, it became obvious that there were legitimate reasons why the laboratory medical director contacted physicians when their laboratory usage decreased. For example, if usage had decreased because a physician became dissatisfied with the service he or she was receiving from the laboratory, the contact by the medical director was believed to be a good method for trying to resolve the problem. Ironically, the OIG's model compliance guidelines for independent clinical laboratories now require independent clinical laboratories to monitor the ordering of laboratory services by physicians.[101] Yet, in *Hanlester*, this practice was considered to be suspect, and evidence of illegal kickback activity.

Enforcement agency lawyers and investigators must be made aware that the health care industry is competitive and there is nothing unlawful or immoral about using common business practices to compete effectively. Although there is little case law in the area, one aspect of the decision of the U.S. Court of Appeals for the Ninth Circuit in *Hanlester* that often is overlooked is the court's conclusion that Hanlester Network's practice of encouraging physicians, including physician owners, to use Hanlester Network Laboratories was *not* unlawful.[102]

## VIII. IMPACT OF INVESTIGATIONS

### A. Timing

Members of the health care industry are extremely troubled by the disruption caused by the length and breadth of health care fraud and abuse investigations. Because of the nature of its role in serving the public, the health care industry is particularly sensitive to adverse publicity, and an investigation alone may be enough to destroy a health care provider. For example, in the *Hanlester* case, shortly after the government had begun its investigation of the three Hanlester Network laboratories, there was so much fear and apprehension on the part of referring physicians that the laboratories essentially went out of business.

---

[101]OIG Compliance Program Guidance for Clinical Laboratories, 62 Fed. Reg. 9435 (Mar. 3, 1997), *as revised in* 63 Fed. Reg. 45,076 (Aug. 24, 1998).

[102]Hanlester Network v. Shalala, 51 F.3d 1390, 1398 (9th Cir. 1995).

Fairness requires that internal guidelines or legislation be developed to establish deadlines for the completion of health care fraud and abuse investigations. The statute of limitation periods that exist (e.g., 6 years to initiate a false claims action, which may be extended up to 10 years under certain circumstances[103]) simply do not provide a sufficient safeguard.

## B. Publicity

Health care lawyers disagree regarding the amount of information that should be shared with employees of a health care provider under investigation for fraud and abuse. Some believe that the dissemination of information should be carefully controlled among a very small group of persons within the organization. Others believe that virtually all employees should be made aware of an ongoing investigation so they will not be surprised if they are asked to be interviewed by a government investigator one evening when they return home from work.

The fact is, once a full-fledged investigation is under way, there is very little that can be gained from attempting to limit all information about the investigation to select employees. The rumors and innuendos that will circulate as part of normal office gossip may be much worse than the reality. Thus, the better practice is to inform employees of the existence of the investigation without speculating about the details or disclosing privileged information. Owners and shareholders also must be informed. And, of course, public company disclosure requirements also must be adhered to carefully.

Controlling publicity outside of the organization is difficult. Although the official policy of enforcement agencies generally prohibits comments on an ongoing investigation, word of such investigations often becomes public. The health care media may become aware of an investigation even before the general media.

There is not a great deal that can be done to respond to the publicity generated by a health care fraud and abuse investigation. Typically, statements such as "The company intends to cooperate fully in the investigation" are issued. Some parties prefer to take a more active role with the media. Although such an approach may be therapeutic, it is important to remember that media outlets are in business to sell their products or generate advertising dollars, not necessarily to tell the truth or even to present a balanced story.

One tool that has been used successfully in some cases is the press release. Press releases typically are not edited as much as interviews. However, if a health care provider wishes to avoid the possible negative consequences of editing, the provider should consider purchasing advertising space, as advertisements generally are not subject to editorial changes or comments.

## C. Effect on Business

The publicity from an investigation not only has an effect on the public and the employees of a health care provider but, more important, it also has an effect

---

[103]31 U.S.C. §3731(b).

on the provider's customers. If the provider is an independent clinical labora-tory, for example, its primary customers are referring physicians. Obviously, referring physicians may be reluctant to use a laboratory that is under suspicion of fraudulent or abusive practices. Similarly, patients naturally become wary when their local hospital or physician is under investigation. Potential merger partners and investors are affected as well.

Competitors who learn of an investigation may use that information to attempt to gain a competitive advantage. For example, in the highly competitive laboratory industry, marketers commonly mention the existence of investiga-tions to physicians they are pursuing as customers. If a provider believes that negative statements are being circulated by competitors, efforts should be made to inform customers of the truth and, if necessary, to discourage competitors from making untrue statements. In extreme situations, lawsuits for trade libel, for example, may be an effective remedy.

In short, investigations present a substantial public relations challenge. Inevitably, an investigation will injure a provider. However, an investigation need not destroy a provider's business. Indeed, some companies, such as Tenet Healthcare (formerly known as National Medical Enterprises), have used the investigation process as a tool to create a state-of-the-art compliance program.

## D. Cash Flow Consequences

In addition to the consequences of investigations discussed above, the government has authority to affect payments (e.g., temporary suspension of payments or exclusion) made to a provider being investigated for fraud or abuse. When the government has reliable evidence that fraud or abuse has occurred, Medicare and Medicaid payments may be temporarily withheld pending the outcome of the investigation. This authority is not without limits, however. The government is not allowed to withhold as much money as it likes for as long as it likes. Rather, there are certain minimal procedural requirements that are afforded a provider under investigation.[104] Nevertheless, any with-holding can cause significant disruption to the operations of a provider that is substantially dependent on Medicare and Medicaid revenues.

If the government threatens such withholding, the lawyer for the provider should make certain that the procedural requirements of the regulations are strictly followed. Additionally, there may be ways the provider can satisfy the government's questions and concerns about the potential for recovering any overpayments. Such tactics may affect the government's decision regarding withholding of payments. For example, offering to provide the government with a letter of credit could satisfy the government's concerns in some situations.

## E. Suing Government Officials for Reckless Investigations and Related Actions

As previously noted, government fraud and abuse investigations can se-verely disrupt the operations of a health care provider. Such investigations can

---

[104]*See, e.g.,* 42 C.F.R. §§455.23, 405.371.

result in adverse publicity, which can destroy a provider's business and reputation. Competitors who learn of the investigation may use the information to attempt to gain a competitive advantage. Moreover, during the course of an investigation, government agencies may withhold or suspend payments to the providers.

When government officials ignore the law and act unreasonably in connection with such actions, providers may have the right to pursue equitable and legal remedies against those officials. Under Section 1983 of the Civil Rights Act,[105] when a person acting under color of state law deprives someone of a constitutional or federal right, the aggrieved person may pursue an action for injunctive relief and damages. Such actions have been successful in compelling state officials to lift Medicaid sanctions. For example, in *Labotest, Inc. v. Bonta,*[106] two providers successfully brought an action to compel the director of the California Department of Health Services to lift certain Medi-Cal sanctions, which, in turn, entitled them to an award of attorneys' fees. Providers may also pursue actions under Section 1983 of the Civil Rights Act for damages against state officials and employees.[107]

These civil rights actions, in which state officials and employees are being sued in their individual capacities, might not only result in providers being compensated for damages caused by constitutional torts, but might also serve to restrain overzealous government enforcement agencies.

## IX. Settlement Considerations

Many more health care fraud and abuse investigations are settled than litigated. While published statistics do not appear to exist, trials are relatively rare. The substantial array of remedies available to the government if it is successful in litigation creates a powerful incentive for a provider to settle a dispute short of litigation. Obviously, the decision to settle depends on the unique facts of each case. Moreover, the terms of a settlement vary with the circumstances of the specific case. However, there are some common considerations, which are discussed in more detail below.

### A. Collateral Consequences

The collateral consequences of settling a health care fraud and abuse case can be significant. For example, if a party settles a state health care fraud and abuse investigation by pleading "no contest" to a misdemeanor count of paying a kickback to obtain health care services, the provider may receive a fairly light criminal sentence, such as a minimal fine and a minimal period of probation.

---

[105] 42 U.S.C. §1983.

[106] 297 F.3d 892 (9th Cir. 2002).

[107] Azer v. Connell, 306 F.3d 930 (9th Cir. 2002), *dismissed on subsequent appeal,* 87 Fed. Appx. 684 (9th Cir. Feb. 13, 2004) (unpublished); *see also* Maynard v. Bonta, No. CV 02-06539 MMM (CTx), 2003 U.S. Dist. LEXIS 16201 (C.D. Cal. Aug. 29, 2003) (physician who was suspended from Medi-Cal program because of alleged fraud sued state officials in individual capacities for depriving him of name-clearing hearing required by due process of the law).

However, the consequences of the no contest plea are nevertheless substantial and far-reaching.

First, the no contest plea to a one-count misdemeanor involving health care fraud and abuse will automatically cause the provider to be excluded from the Medicare, Medicaid, and other state and federal health care programs for a minimum of five years.[108] Such program exclusion prevents the provider or any future employer of the provider from billing such government programs for any services delivered by the excluded provider. Because most health care providers are extremely dependent on revenues from government payors, this automatic exclusion is thus a very significant collateral consequence of a plea agreement.

In addition, the provider's professional license likely will be subject to discipline under most state laws.[109] As with Medicare and Medicaid program exclusion, a no contest plea is treated the same as a guilty plea and conviction under most state professional licensing statutes. The relevant licensing authorities can be expected to take action against the provider's professional license some time after the court disposes of the criminal settlement.

There are a variety of other practical consequences that may result from a no contest plea. For example, if the provider is a physician, he or she may be subject to disclosure requirements that could affect his or her medical staff privileges, private third-party payor contracts, independent practice association arrangements, and even his or her malpractice insurance coverage.

## B. Binding the Government

When settlement is contemplated, the attorney for the defendant must try to bind as many government agencies as possible through the terms of the settlement agreement. For example, if the U.S. Attorney's Office is contemplating a federal False Claims Act action based on the facts of an investigation, the attorney for the provider being investigated should attempt to reach agreement with the civil and criminal sections of the U.S. Attorney's Office or DOJ and with the Medicaid Fraud Control Unit of any state in which the provider performs services. The OIG and other federal payors, such as the Tricare program, also should be bound by the terms of the settlement agreement. Unless bound, the OIG could initiate exclusion proceedings or seek civil monetary penalties through the administrative process based on the same facts that gave rise to the settlement with the U.S. Attorney's Office.

It is virtually impossible, as a practical matter, to bind all potential enforcement agencies and regulators when settling a dispute over a particular set of facts. However, the inability to bind every possible future prosecutor or regulator should not stop a party from settling if the major enforcement agencies have agreed to be parties to the settlement. Indeed, the argument can be made that a state attorney general signing a settlement agreement on behalf of the state Medicaid Fraud Control Unit binds a local district attorney in the same state.

In addition to binding as many parties to a settlement as possible, there are other techniques to minimize the collateral consequences of settlements. For

---

[108]42 U.S.C. §1320a-7(a), (c)(3)(B).
[109]*See* CAL. BUS. & PROF. CODE §2236.

example, in the hypothetical situation above, if the corporate entity, rather than the individual owner of the corporate entity, pleaded no contest to a misdemeanor, only the corporate entity would automatically be excluded from the Medicare and Medicaid programs. Although the owner arguably may be subject to a permissive exclusion proceeding, the likelihood of that occurring can be reduced by having the appropriate government agencies provide in the settlement agreement that no permissive exclusion will be pursued.

## C. Settlement Goals

The exact terms of a settlement will vary depending on the bargaining positions of the government and the provider under investigation. Early on in the settlement negotiations, the government should be able to disclose whether one of its goals is to force the provider out of business. If the government does not have as its goal the termination of the business or practice of the provider under investigation, the terms of the settlement can help to ensure the provider's continued viability.

Although most government demand letters threaten staggering financial remedies and penalties, the enforcement agencies are practical enough to know that a provider's ability to pay is a significant factor in determining the ultimate financial terms of a settlement agreement. Thus, not only should the lawyer for the provider focus on rationalizing the client's behavior, but he or she also should address the client's ability to satisfy the government's financial demands. In short, even if the enforcement agency could clearly prove allegations that would give rise to a judgment involving tens of millions of dollars, it would be foolish for the government to reject a settlement proposal that included an admission of wrongdoing simply because the settling party was unable to pay the requested tens of millions of dollars.

In this regard, there are various ways to structure a settlement so that payment of the settlement amount does not force the provider into bankruptcy, such as providing for installment payments over time. However, the government will want to be secure about its ability to collect settlement payments from the settling party if terms other than immediate payment are agreed to. For example, the government may insist on settlement terms that protect it in the event of a provider's subsequent bankruptcy.

The government's primary goal in a particular case may be deterrence. It may want to send a message to the industry. Recognizing this goal, a settling party may be able to minimize other consequences of a settlement by agreeing to stop practices that are the government's targets at the time.

Just as the investigation process is lengthy (investigations can drag on for years), so too is the settlement process. Settling a health care fraud and abuse case may result in a party's actually incurring more time and higher expenses than litigating. However, considerations such as adverse publicity may dictate against litigation.

## D. Life After a Settlement

One of the most important matters that often is not fully appreciated by a party to a settlement agreement is that the party must be able to live with the terms of the settlement agreement long after the anxiety created by the investigation has passed. Thus, although a party to a settlement agreement may be willing to stop engaging in various activities and practices to reach settlement, ceasing such practices and activities may ultimately incapacitate the health care provider. Moreover, typically, the terms of a settlement agreement are required to be binding on the successors and assigns of the party. A settlement agreement with onerous terms may make it extremely difficult to sell a company.

As part of most settlement agreements, the private party is required to implement a corporate integrity agreement containing specific requirements that otherwise might not be binding on the provider. For example, third-party consultants may have to be hired to review billing practices. The terms and conditions of an integrity agreement will typically require substantial expenditures for ongoing monitoring activities and staffing (e.g., a compliance officer must be hired, and compliance policies and procedures established).[110]

On the other hand, the terms of the settlement agreement and any accompanying integrity program may be used to the settling party's advantage by specifically defining those practices that the enforcement agency considers to be appropriate. Therefore, from a public relations standpoint, customers of the settling provider can be assured that the practices engaged in by the settling party are appropriate, because they have been "blessed" by the government. This could give the customers of the settling party comfort that they otherwise might not have when doing business with a competitor.

## X. LITIGATION DEFENSE STRATEGIES

### A. Importance of the Fundamentals

As discussed previously, health care fraud and abuse enforcement agencies have a range of remedies that can apply in a variety of settings against a provider accused of fraud and abuse. For example, numerous criminal acts (e.g., making false statements) can be prosecuted in federal and state courts. Civil actions, such as civil false claims proceedings, also may be pursued in both federal and state courts. Additionally, administrative remedies, such as exclusion proceedings and the imposition of civil monetary penalties, may be sought through administrative proceedings.

Although different substantive and procedural rules are applicable to the various remedies in different settings, health care fraud and abuse cases generally require the government to prove that a wrongful act has been committed by someone with a wrongful intent. Surprisingly, these two fundamental elements are overlooked in many cases.

---

[110] *See* Barbara Frederickson, *Corporate Integrity Agreements Impose Additional Obligations on Providers*, 1 J. HEALTH CARE COMPLIANCE 26–27 (1999). For a detailed discussion of corporate integrity agreements, see Chapter 7, at Section III.A. (Baumann, Corporate Compliance Programs).

## 1. Necessity of Prohibited Act or Omission

Significantly, the law governing the health care industry, like the law governing other industries or areas, is contained in federal and state statutes and duly enacted agency regulations. The law is not made by administrative agencies through the issuance of informal guidelines or by enforcement agencies through the issuance of model compliance programs or fraud alerts. Nor is the law established through the terms and provisions of settlement agreements between health care organizations and the government. And, most definitely, the law is not created by statements made by government enforcement officers at seminars and by health care lawyers repeating those statements. Notwithstanding these facts, it is common for government enforcement agencies to base investigations and potential prosecutions on alleged violations of Medicare intermediary letters, bulletins, and other informal guidelines.

The starting point for any defense strategy must be an analysis of the statutes and regulations governing the activity and practices under investigation. If it is determined that the government is relying on a guideline published in a Medicare manual or bulletin, an initial analysis of the statutory and regulatory authority for the guideline is mandatory. It is possible that the guideline that the government contends has been violated lacks statutory or regulatory support. In such a situation, it is questionable whether the conduct that violates the guideline can be considered to be prohibited by the law.[111]

Of course, not only must a guideline be authorized by an agency's enabling statute and regulations, but it also must be written clearly enough to give adequate notice to members of the health care industry. Ambiguous guidelines, like ambiguous regulations and statutes, cannot be used as the basis for a successful health care fraud or abuse prosecution. Thus, a Medicaid "Bulletin" that is vague about the grouping of laboratory tests for billing purposes may not support a false claims action.[112]

## 2. Necessity of Wrongful Intent

Almost without exception, some form of scienter or wrongful intent must be established before any adverse action can be taken against a defendant. For example, although there is ongoing debate over the nature of the intent required to violate the federal anti-kickback statute, it generally is agreed that some wrongful intent is required. The intent requirement serves the very important purpose of protecting persons from being punished or sanctioned for innocent acts and omissions. Although much emphasis is placed by enforcement agencies on prohibited acts or omissions, little attention is paid to the mental state necessary to constitute a violation of the law for purposes of imposing some form of remedy or penalty.

When an act or omission is not inherently nefarious, which may often be the case in a health care fraud and abuse situation, common law and statutory

---

[111]It is fundamental that an administrative agency guideline must be consistent with the agency's enabling statutes and formal regulations. *See, e.g.*, National Med. Enters. v. Bowen, 851 F.2d 291 (9th Cir. 1988).

[112]*See* California v. Duz-Mor Diagnostic Lab., 68 Cal. App. 4th 654 (1998).

law ordinarily require the government to prove some type of wrongful intent before any substantial penalty or sanction may be imposed. For example, in *Hanlester*, where there was nothing inherently nefarious about the clinical laboratory making profit distributions to the laboratory owners on the basis of their ownership percentages, the government was required to prove wrongful intent before the profit distributions could be said to constitute prohibited kickbacks under the federal Medicare/Medicaid anti-kickback statute. Under the Ninth Circuit's decision in *Hanlester*, the wrongful intent required to be proven was that the defendants knew what they were doing and that their actions violated the anti-kickback statute. Although other cases have not insisted on such a strict definition of scienter, they continue to require that defendants know their acts are unjustifiable or wrongful before the defendants can be deemed to possess the requisite wrongful intent necessary to violate the federal anti-kickback statute and other health care criminal laws.[113]

Similarly, a scienter requirement is necessary under the federal False Claims Act. To constitute an actionable false claim, a party must knowingly present a false or fraudulent claim to the federal government. Although reckless disregard of the truth also satisfies the intent requirement of the False Claims Act, innocent mistakes, good-faith disagreements over the interpretation of the law, and even negligence do not give rise to False Claims Act liability.[114]

Because health care regulatory requirements, especially Medicare regulatory requirements such as coding instructions for payment, often are complex and frequently vague, payment disputes will arise. However, not all alleged overpayments constitute false claims. In fact, not all alleged overpayments constitute genuine overpayments. Where reasonable minds differ regarding the interpretation of a particular requirement and where the party has submitted a bill in good-faith reliance on a reasonable interpretation of the rule, it is questionable whether there will be any False Claims Act liability if it turns out that the interpretation relied on is ultimately deemed to be erroneous.[115]

There are also a variety of examples in health care in which a particular business practice not only is widespread in the industry but also is a practice that the government historically has permitted through acquiescence. For example, the industry-wide practice of clinical laboratories giving discounts to physician customers when performing testing for private-pay patients has been known to the federal and state governments for years. The government also knows that this practice continues because the laboratories seek to encourage physicians to use the laboratories for all of their testing needs, including for Medicare and Medicaid patients. Although there has been considerable debate over the propriety of the practice, the government has not taken the position that the practice is illegal per se. Thus, a clinical laboratory charged by a state attorney general with violating a state Medicaid anti-kickback statute (modeled after the federal

---

[113] *See, e.g.*, United States v. Neufeld, 908 F. Supp. 491 (S.D. Ohio 1995) (rejecting the *Hanlester* analysis); United States v. Jain, 93 F.3d 436 (8th Cir. 1996) (requiring no "heightened mens rea"), *cert. denied*, 520 U.S. 1273 (1997).

[114] *See* United States *ex rel.* Hagood v. Sonoma County Water Agency, 929 F.2d 1416, 1421 (9th Cir. 1991), *cert. denied*, 519 U.S. 865 (1996), *reh'g denied*, 519 U.S. 1001 (1996).

[115] *See* United States *ex rel.* Hochman v. Nackman, 145 F.3d 1069, 1073 (9th Cir. 1998) ("superficially plausible" interpretation may negate wrongful intent).

anti-kickback statute) for giving discounts to physicians was able to defend itself successfully in a state court unfair competition action on the grounds that the laboratory objectively and subjectively believed that the physician discounting practice was lawful.[116]

The intent issue is very fact specific. The same type of act may or may not give rise to some type of liability depending on the unique circumstances of a case and the defendant's thought processes. Although the intent requirement will not, and should not, protect someone who intends to defraud or abuse health insurance programs, it is an important safeguard against overzealous or mistaken enforcement in situations in which someone acting in good faith misinterprets a complex or confusing regulation.

In March 2002, the U.S. Court of Appeals for the Eleventh Circuit issued a very important decision regarding the intent (and act) necessary to sustain a false statement conviction under the criminal false statement laws.[117] In *United States v. Whiteside*,[118] a jury had convicted the defendants of knowingly and willfully filing false statements in certain Medicare and Medicaid cost reports concerning reimbursement for certain capital-related costs claimed in the reports.

The court pointed out that in a criminal case where the truth or falsity of a statement centers on an interpretative question of law, the government bears the burden of proving beyond a reasonable doubt that the defendants' statement is not true under a reasonable interpretation of the law. The court reversed the conviction of the defendants, concluding that as a matter of law the government could not meet its burden of proof in the case because no Medicare regulation, administrative ruling, or judicial decision existed that clearly required interest expense to be reported in accordance with the position advocated by the government. Because the experts in the case disagreed at trial as to the validity of the theory of reimbursement of the capital-related costs adjusted by the government, the court concluded that the defendants' interpretation was not unreasonable. As a result, "the government failed to meet its burden of proving the actus reus of the offense—actual falsity as a matter of law."[119] Ironically, the "ghost" of *Hanlester* has been visiting government prosecutors in several high-profile prosecutions, including *TAP* (discussed in Sections XII.A., XII.B.1., XII.C.1., and XII.C.4., below) and *United States v. Weinbaum (Tenet Alvarado)*.[120] The court's jury instructions in these cases incorporated the *Hanlester* court's intent discussion.[121]

---

[116]California v. Duz-Mor Diagnostic Lab., 68 Cal. App. 4th 654 (1998).

[117]Although the court spoke in terms of actus reus, the reasoning is probably most useful in a discussion of mens rea, i.e., intent.

[118]285 F.3d 1345 (11th Cir. 2002).

[119]*Id.* at 1352.

[120]*See, e.g.,* United States v. Weinbaum, Case No. 03-CR-1587 MLJ (S.D. Cal. Mar. 8, 2005) (Order Denying Weinbaum's Motion for Judgment of Acquittal, Denying in Part and Granting in Part Defendant Tenet Healthsystem Hospitals, Inc.'s Motion for Judgment of Acquittal Under Rule 29 of the Rules of Criminal Procedure, and Entering of Judgment of Acquittal as to Counts 16 and 17 of the Fourth Superceding Indictment).

[121]*Id.*

### 3. Necessity of Agency Authority to Act

In addition to the two fundamental concepts discussed above, a defense lawyer should be certain that the enforcement agency that is threatening to act against his or her client does, in fact, possess the legal authority required to take the action threatened. An agency may not always have the right to initiate a particular action it threatens.

First, local prosecutors, such as district attorneys, county prosecutors, and city prosecutors, have a legitimate interest in ensuring that health care fraud and abuse do not occur within their jurisdictions. However, most state laws do not allow a district attorney from one county to prosecute allegedly wrongful acts committed in another county by a resident of the other county. This limit applies whether the local prosecutor is attempting to apply a state law or a local ordinance.

Second, some agencies that are accustomed to exercising considerable state statutory and constitutional authority in other areas may lack authority over health care programs. For example, under the federal Medicaid law, only the state agency designated as the single state Medicaid agency is authorized to administer the Medicaid program within that state.[122] Administration of the program includes the promulgation of policies and procedures governing such matters as auditing and determining overpayments made to providers. Although a state controller ultimately may have state statutory and even state constitutional authority to audit and determine the correctness of state payments, that authority may be restricted or inapplicable with respect to auditing and determining the correctness of Medicaid payments.

It must be assumed that the limits imposed on the federal and state enforcement agencies and regulators are intended for valid reasons. Thus, when an enforcement agency threatens to exceed those limits, defense counsel is justified in insisting on strict adherence to the limits.

## B. Other Practical Defense Concepts

### 1. Stressing the Facts

The most important defenses to fraud and abuse allegations are generally found within the facts of the case. If there are compelling facts to explain or justify a client's actions, a court will be more likely to interpret the governing law in favor of the client. There is no substitute for good facts.

In health care fraud and abuse prosecutions, special facts may strengthen a client's defense. For example, although it is no defense to argue that other providers are performing the same act, if the reality is that the practice for which a party is being prosecuted is widespread in the industry, that fact is bound to have some practical effect on a judge or jury so long as the act is not inherently nefarious.

In the *Hanlester* proceedings, the fact that physicians throughout the country possessed ownership interests in laboratories and other health care

---

[122]42 C.F.R. §431.10.

providers to which they referred their patients was not lost on the administrative law judge or the Ninth Circuit. It is hard for a decisionmaker to ignore such a fact, especially if it means that tens of thousands of physicians must be considered felons if they have violated the federal anti-kickback law as a result of such self-referral arrangements.

Similarly, the fact that an activity that is being prosecuted was reviewed and "approved" by the defendant's attorney may be beneficial. Most government enforcement agencies will consider this "advice of counsel" evidence to be very problematical to the successful prosecution of the case. Whether considered to be relevant to the intent element or some other element necessary to prove liability, the advice of defense counsel can be very useful.

As discussed earlier in the chapter, because of the sheer volume of regulations, guidelines, and other informal interpretations applicable to health care activities, inconsistent agency interpretations regarding a particular practice are not unusual. Although the interpretations may not have the legal authority to bind the federal or state governments under a theory of equitable estoppel, the existence of contrary interpretations tends to negate any wrongful intent if a party has relied on those interpretations. Contrary agency interpretations also tend to show the arbitrariness of a particular interpretation even if a party has not relied on the interpretation.

Finally, unlike some administrative agency matters in which the complexity of an issue favors the government, complexity favors the defendant in enforcement actions. In short, the more confusing the requirements alleged to have been violated, the more likely the court or jury will sympathize with the defendant.

## 2. Burden of Proof Requirements

Appreciating and applying the appropriate burden of proof and determining the correct quantum of evidence necessary to satisfy the burden of proof are as important in defending health care fraud and abuse cases as they are in any other type of litigation. Although these issues must be resolved differently in different actions depending on the forum, it is accurate to state in general that the enforcement agency typically has the initial burden of producing evidence to establish a prima facie case in most actions. Of course, in a criminal action, the government has not only the burden of going forward with the evidence but also the burden of proving beyond a reasonable doubt each element of a crime.

The importance of requiring the government to satisfy its burden of proof cannot be overemphasized. Enforcement agencies are not used to having to do so in most health care fraud enforcement investigations because of the willingness of health care providers to settle and resolve potential disputes short of litigation. Although no defense attorney can expect to present the defendant's entire case through the prosecution witnesses, it is possible in health care fraud and abuse cases to cast substantial doubt on the viability of the government's case before the defendant's side of the case is even presented. In other words, defense counsel should attempt to use the government's presentation as an opportunity to question the government's case. Issues such as the inconsistency of agency interpretations are particularly effective when presented during the cross-examination of government witnesses.

## 3. Credibility of Defendant

Notwithstanding the above, the most critical evidence in a health care fraud and abuse case can be the testimony of the defendant. Whereas typical criminal defense strategies may caution against calling a defendant to testify at his or her own trial, in health care fraud and abuse cases the judge and jury will likely expect to hear from the defendant. Therefore, if defense counsel doubts the credibility of the defendant or has other reasons for being concerned about the impact of the defendant testifying at trial, this factor alone may encourage settling the case short of trial or attempting to prevail through summary judgment motions.

As with any case, the defendant's credibility is critical. If the defendant is believable and can sincerely persuade the trier of fact that he or she was acting in good faith and without any wrongful intent in performing the allegedly wrongful acts, the government will have a difficult time prevailing in most fraud and abuse cases. On the other hand, if the trier of fact believes the defendant is not trustworthy and not credible about any aspect of his or her testimony, regardless of how relevant or immaterial, the government's case will be strengthened significantly.

## 4. Limited Judicial Review

Unlike most criminal and civil litigation, the defense of health care fraud and abuse cases often originates with administrative hearings within federal or state agencies. In *Hanlester*, the only "trial" at which witnesses actually testified and were observed by the trier of fact occurred before the assigned HHS administrative law judge. As a consequence of the case being tried administratively, the extent of judicial review was limited.

Under well-established principles of administrative law, judicial review of federal and state agency adjudication typically is restricted to a review of the legal determinations made by the agency. Among the legal issues to be resolved is whether the findings made by the agency decision maker are supported by substantial evidence. This is a very deferential level of review, similar to the review an appellate court performs of the factual findings of a trial court.

At the judicial review level of an agency decision, evidence in addition to that presented during the administrative hearing typically is not permitted. The reviewing court ordinarily must limit the scope of its review to the evidence presented during the administrative hearing, which is presented to the court in the form of an administrative record.

In situations in which judicial review of a final agency decision following a hearing must be sought initially from the lower level of the court system, such as the federal district court in OIG exclusion cases, appellate review of the district court's decision is not limited. Because the federal district court is limited to reviewing the administrative record of the agency proceedings and determining questions of law, the appellate court standard and scope of review are the same as the lower court's. For example, no special deference is owed to the lower court's determinations of law. The practical result is that if the final agency decision is adverse to the provider, and if the district court upholds that adverse decision, as was the situation in *Hanlester*, there is still a chance of prevailing before the appellate court if there are compelling legal arguments that can be presented.

Of course, in cases in which an enforcement action is initiated in a federal or state court rather than in an administrative hearing, the trial judge and jury have the same responsibilities as in any typical case. Appellate review of a trial court or jury's verdict is also the same as in other cases.

## XI. CURRENT ENFORCEMENT PRIORITIES

A review of historical trends in False Claims Act cases provides context for the government's current enforcement priorities. For example, the number of new *qui tam* cases has substantially increased over the years. In 1987 just 66 new False Claims Act *qui tam* cases were filed.[123] In 2005, the number was 394. In contrast, the number of non-*qui tam* new False Claims Act cases has generally declined over the years, with 361 filed in 1987 and just 100 filed in 2005.[124] This trend may reflect the increased protection against retaliation that whistleblowers enjoy and more reliance by the government on *qui tam* actions. Indeed, health care cases made up 46 percent of all *qui tam* cases filed between 1987 and 2005.[125] The DOJ also pursued health care fraud cases more than any other type of fraud case, intervening in or settling 32.5 percent of *qui tam* actions.[126] The mean of *qui tam* recoveries from 1987 to 2005 was just over $10 million, whereas the median was $784,597.[127] Eighteen cases have resulted in a recovery of between $100 million and $1 billion.[128]

### A. Focus Areas for OIG Investigation and Enforcement

To deter health care fraud and abuse, the government enforcement agencies periodically publish their enforcement priorities. The annual work plans issued by the OIG, for example, outline that office's priorities, which often dictate federal enforcement priorities in general.

Additionally, the government regularly advises the health care industry of areas of concern in its model compliance programs. The following risk areas are identified in the OIG's original model compliance program for hospitals:

- billing for items or services not actually rendered;
- providing medically unnecessary services;
- upcoding (using a billing code that provides for higher payment than that for the services actually performed);
- diagnosis-related group (DRG) creep (using a DRG code that provides for higher payment than the accurate patient DRG code);
- outpatient services rendered in connection with inpatient stays;
- teaching physician and resident requirements for teaching hospitals;

---

[123]U.S. Government Accountability Office (GAO), *Briefing for Congressional Requesters*, at 25 (Dec. 15, 2005), *available at* http://www.gao.gov/new.items/d06320r.pdf.

[124]*Id.*

[125]*Id.* at 28.

[126]*Id.* at 29.

[127]*Id.* at 31.

[128]*Id.*

- duplicate billing;
- false cost reports;
- unbundling (submitting separate bills for services that should be bundled into one bill);
- billing for discharge in lieu of transfer;
- patients' freedom of choice;
- failure to refund credit balances;
- hospital incentives that violate the anti-kickback statute or other similar federal or state statutes or regulations;
- joint ventures;
- financial arrangements between hospitals and hospital-based physicians;
- Stark physician self-referral laws;
- knowing failure to provide covered services or necessary care to members of a health maintenance organization; and
- patient dumping.[129]

In 2005, the OIG issued a Supplemental Compliance Program Guidance for Hospitals, setting forth additional areas of concern, including:

- submission of accurate claims and information;
- improper claims for clinical trials;
- improper claims for cardiac rehabilitation services;
- physician recruitment arrangements;
- billing for substandard care;
- improper remuneration to federal health care beneficiaries;
- HIPAA privacy and security rules;
- billing Medicare and Medicaid substantially in excess of usual charges; and
- discounts.[130]

Because many of these risk areas apply not only to hospitals but also to other types of providers, the OIG's descriptions and definitions contained in the hospital model compliance plan are instructive. For example, billing for services not actually rendered is defined as submitting a claim that represents that the provider performed a service, all or part of which was not performed. According to the OIG, this form of billing fraud occurs in many health care entities, including hospitals and nursing homes, and represents a significant part of the OIG's investigative caseload.

According to the OIG, a claim requesting payment for medically unnecessary services "intentionally" seeks reimbursement for a service that is not warranted by the patient's current and documented medical condition. The OIG points out that a physician must certify on every CMS claim form that the services provided were medically necessary for the health of the beneficiary.[131]

---

[129]63 Fed. Reg. 8987 (Feb. 23, 1998). Compliance guidance can be found on the OIG's Web site at http://www.oig.hhs.gov/fraud/complianceguidance.html.

[130]OIG Supplemental Compliance Program Guidance for Hospitals, 70 Fed. Reg. 4858 (Jan. 27, 2005). For text of the guidance, see Appendix I-1.2 on the disk accompanying this volume.

[131]63 Fed. Reg. at 8990 n.14.

The practice of upcoding is defined by the OIG as the use of a billing code that provides a higher payment rate than the billing code that actually reflects the services furnished to the patient. The OIG also points out that upcoding has been a major focus of its enforcement efforts.[132] The OIG includes the concept of DRG creep as a type of upcoding. DRG creep is the practice of billing using a DRG code that provides a higher payment rate than the DRG code that accurately reflects the service furnished to the patient.[133]

Hospitals that submit claims for nonphysician outpatient services that were already included in the hospital's inpatient payment under the Medicare Prospective Payment System are considered by the OIG to be submitting duplicate claims. Duplicate billing is also considered to occur when a hospital submits more than one claim for the same service or the bill is submitted to more than one primary payor at the same time. Although the OIG recognizes that such duplicate billing can occur as a result of simple error, it indicates that systematic or repeated double billing may be viewed as a false claim, particularly if any overpayment is not promptly refunded.[134]

The submission of false cost reports usually is limited to certain Medicare Part A providers such as hospitals, skilled nursing facilities, and home health agencies. The OIG refers to one of its audit reports concerning the purported mischaracterization by providers of fringe benefits and general and administrative costs as allowable costs. The OIG also indicates an awareness of practices in which hospitals and other providers inappropriately shift certain costs to cost centers that are below their Medicare reimbursement cap and shift costs not related to Medicare to Medicare-allowable cost centers.[135]

The practice of submitting bills piecemeal or in fragmented fashion to maximize the reimbursement for various tests or procedures that must be billed together is the "unbundling" referred to by the OIG as a risk area for hospitals and other providers. The unbundling issue is most commonly found in billing for laboratory services, but it also may occur in other areas such as fragmenting global billings.[136]

Examples of arrangements that may run afoul of the anti-kickback statute given by the OIG include excessive payment for medical directorships, free or below-market rents or fees for administrative services, interest-free loans, and excessive payment for intangible assets in physician practice acquisitions.[137] Other equally troubling areas to the OIG with respect to the anti-kickback statute include the proliferation of business arrangements that may violate the anti-kickback statute, such as those that generally are established between persons in a position to refer business and those providing items or services for which a federal health care program pays.[138] These are the same joint ventures

---

[132]*Id.* at n.15.
[133]*Id.* at n.16.
[134]*Id.* at nn.17, 18.
[135]*Id.* at n.19.
[136]*Id.* at n.20.
[137]*Id.* at n.23.
[138]*Id.* at n.24.

that the OIG warned about in its 1989 fraud alert, which became the subject of the *Hanlester* proceedings.[139]

The OIG also continues to warn hospitals and other providers about financial arrangements with hospital-based physicians that compensate physicians for less than the fair market value of services they provide to the hospital or require physicians to pay more than fair market value for services provided by the hospital. The OIG issued a management advisory report regarding this topic in October 1991.[140]

In addition to the risk areas described in the model compliance plan for hospitals, other areas of health care have been targeted for special scrutiny. According to 2006 and 2007 OIG work plans, these include the home health care industry in general, ambulance services, partial hospitalization services, physician evaluation and management coding, DME, and pharmaceuticals.[141]

With the increase in managed care programs, the government is shifting considerable resources to investigating managed care companies and arrangements.[142] Managed care companies that structure capitation payments in a way that encourages physicians to withhold treatment or offer incentives to limit services could be subject to investigation.

Managed care plans may be victimized by providers with whom they contract. Providers may submit false financial status reports or falsify quality reports and make misrepresentations about secondary payors. Evidence of providers falsifying patient encounter data to bolster increases in capitation payments and even to disguise underutilization of services also has been discovered.

As with fee-for-service arrangements, substantial fraud and abuse risk arises from the marketing practices of managed care plans. Payments to marketing agents to enroll new members are often commission driven, which may create an incentive for marketers to misrepresent plan services.[143]

By monitoring government enforcement initiatives, providers and other members of the health care industry may keep informed of areas of priority for enforcement agencies. However, it is not enough simply to know about such enforcement priorities. Steps must be taken to avoid future problems and

---

[139]Special Fraud Alert: Joint Venture Arrangements (Aug. 1989), 59 Fed. Reg. 65,372 (Dec. 19, 1994). For text of this document, see Appendix F-11 on the disk accompanying this volume.

[140]Financial Arrangements Between Hospitals and Hospital-Based Physicians, OIG Mgmt. Advisory Rep. No. OEI-09-89-00330 (Oct. 1991). For text of this document, see Appendix F-17 on the disk accompanying this volume.

[141]*See* OFFICE OF INSPECTOR GEN., U.S. DEP'T OF HEALTH & HUMAN SERVS., OIG WORK PLAN, FISCAL YEAR 2006 & 2007, *available at* http://oig.hhs.gov/reading/workplan/2006/WorkPlanFY2006.pdf; http://oig.hhs.gov/reading/workplan/2007/WorkPlanFY2007.pdf.

[142]*See* OIG Compliance Program Guidance for Medicare+Choice Programs, 64 Fed. Reg. 61,893 (Nov. 15, 1999).

[143]For comprehensive coverage of fraud and abuse risks in the managed care context, see Chapter 6 (Rinn and Ryland, Managed Care Fraud and Abuse: Risk Areas for Government Program Participants).

correct past problems in these areas. This is precisely why health care compliance programs are needed.[144]

The OIG's Fiscal Year 2007 Work Plan for CMS[145] contains 81 pages of issues that the OIG is examining. The Work Plan is an excellent source for determining current enforcement priorities.

## B. Settlements Since 2005

A review of OIG settlements since 2005 with providers accused of False Claims Act violations further illustrates the government's current enforcement priorities. For example, Intrepid, U.S.A., a Minnesota-based company with more than 150 home health agencies, paid $8 million dollars in February 2006 to settle a False Claims Act action alleging fraudulent billing of federal health care programs where services had not been provided by a qualified person and necessary documentation had not been completed, among other things. The alleged false claims were submitted between 1997 and 2004.[146]

In June 2006, Tenet Healthcare agreed to pay $900 million plus interest over four years to settle False Claims Act and fraud allegations. The settlement included $788 million to resolve claims arising from Tenet's receipt of excessive outlier payments for inflated patient care charges; $47 million for kickbacks to physicians for Medicare referrals to Tenet facilities and billing Medicare for services ordered and referred by physicians with whom Tenet had an improper relationship; and $46 million for upcoding where Tenet was either unable to support the diagnosis codes or improper codes were used resulting in increased reimbursement. Like most False Claims Act cases, several issues in the government's case against Tenet arose following case filings by *qui tam* relators.[147]

Also in June 2006, Saint Barnabas Corporation of New Jersey settled a False Claims Act action by agreeing to pay the United States $265 million. In two separate federal actions, whistleblowers alleged that between 1995 and August 2003, Saint Barnabas hospitals had inflated charges for patient care, resulting in improper outlier payments by Medicare.[148]

Dallas-based Odyssey HealthCare, a national hospice provider, paid the United Stated $12.9 million in July of 2006 to settle False Claims allegations. Odyssey's former Vice President, JoAnne Russell, filed a *qui tam* action

---

[144]For discussion of effective corporate compliance programs, see Chapter 7 (Baumann, Corporate Compliance Programs).

[145]OFFICE OF INSPECTOR GEN., U.S. DEP'T OF HEALTH & HUMAN SERVS., OIG WORK PLAN, FISCAL YEAR 2007, *available at* http://oig.hhs.gov/publications/workplan.html.

[146]*See* U.S. Dep't of Justice press release, *available at* http://www.usdoj.gov.opa/pr/2006/February/06_civ_072.html.

[147]*See* U.S. Dep't of Justice press release, *available at* http://www.usdoj.gov.opa/pr/2006/June/06_civ_406.html.

[148]*See* U.S. Dep't of Justice press release, *available at* http://www.usdoj.gov.opa/pr/2006/June/06_civ_373.html.

claiming that hospice services were provided to patients who were not terminally ill. Odyssey improperly obtained Medicare hospice benefit reimbursement for these services.[149]

Beverly Enterprises, Inc., agreed in August 2006 to pay the United States more than $14 million and California more than $5 million to settle allegations that its former wholly-owned subsidiary, MK Medical, violated the False Claims Act from 1998 through 2002. MK Medical was a wholesaler of durable medical equipment and allegedly billed federal health care programs for equipment provided without proper claims or medical documentation.[150]

In September 2006, Horizon West, Inc., and its wholly-owned subsidiary Horizon West Healthcare, Inc., settled False Claims allegations for $14.7 million. Horizon West operates a nursing home chain with about 30 facilities in California and Utah. The company allegedly had been falsely inflating the number of nursing hours spent on Medicare patients when reporting costs to Medicare from 1991 to 1998. As is commonly the situation, the case originated in 2000 with a former employee's *qui tam* action. The government intervened in June 2004 and the case was unsealed in July 2005. The government then filed its complaint on October 21, 2005.[151]

In January 2007, Texas long-term acute-care facilities operator SCCI Health Services Corporation and its subsidiary SCCI Hospital Ventures, Inc., paid $7.5 million to settle a False Claims Act and anti-kickback action by the United States. The action involved allegations that SCCI had from 1996 to 1999 either submitted or caused the submission of false claims to the Medicare program as a result of its illegal kickbacks to three physicians in exchange for referrals of Medicare patients. The case began on April 1, 1999, with a *qui tam* action. The government intervened in October 2002 on the kickback claims and filed its complaint on March 10, 2003. Following the settlement, the five whistleblowers shared a $1.7 million recovery.[152]

The DOJ announced on March 1, 2007, that Raritan Bay Medical Center, with headquarters in New Jersey, had settled allegations of Medicare fraud for $7.5 million. The alleged fraud involved improperly increasing charges to obtain enhanced Medicare reimbursement designed to take advantage of the supplemental outlier payment system. The settlement resolves three separate *qui tam* actions filed against Raritan Bay for these alleged False Claims Act violations.[153]

---

[149] *See* U.S. Dep't of Justice press release, *available at* http://www.usdoj.gov.opa/pr/2006/July/06_civ_430.html.

[150] *See* U.S. Dep't of Justice press release, *available at* http://www.usdoj.gov.opa/pr/2006/August/06_civ_560.html.

[151] *See* U.S. Dep't of Justice press release, *available at* http://www.usdoj.gov.opa/pr/2006/September/06_civ_650.html.

[152] *See* U.S. Dep't of Justice press release, *available at* http://www.usdoj.gov.opa/pr/2007/January/07_civ_003.html.

[153] *See* U.S. Dep't of Justice press release, *available at* http://www.usdoj.gov.opa/pr/2007/March/07_civ_150.html.

## XII. Enforcement Actions Involving Pharmaceuticals

### A. Introduction

In recent years, state and federal law enforcement agencies have focused resources on eradicating fraud related to the pricing, marketing, and prescribing of pharmaceuticals. According to CMS, the Medicaid program is the largest single pharmaceutical purchaser in the United States, with an estimated $40 billion spent on drugs in 2005. Starting in the mid-1990s, the OIG placed prescription drug pricing at the top of its watch list.[154] Since that time, nearly every state has participated in litigation against pharmaceutical manufacturers.

Enforcement actions typically involve four common areas: false claims actions based on manufacturers' pricing methodology or the Medicaid Drug Rebate Program, violations of the federal anti-kickback statute in connection with manufacturers' marketing to physicians and discounting practices, and common-law fraud based on illegal sales of counterfeit drugs or improper internet sales. Typically, enforcement actions allege a combination of violations of multiple anti-fraud provisions (e.g., the federal False Claims Act (FCA) and anti-kickback statute) in connection with certain allegedly illegal activities (e.g., inflated pricing and improper marketing schemes). Although pharmaceutical pricing cases eventually may become obsolete pursuant to changes brought about by the Medicare Prescription Drug, Improvement, and Modernization Act of 2003 (MMA) and Deficit Reduction Act of 2005 (DRA), there is no indication that regulators are slowing their enforcement efforts against the pharmaceutical industry at this time.

Two cases against manufacturers in 2001 and 2003 yielded landmark settlements that fueled the enforcement community. In October 2001, TAP Pharmaceutical Products, Inc. (TAP) paid $875 million to resolve massive claims arising out of sales and marketing practices involving its prostate cancer drug, Lupron.[155] In 2003, AstraZeneca paid $355 million to settle similar claims involving its competing drug, Zoladex.[156] In the *TAP* and *AstraZeneca* cases, the government alleged a myriad of fraud allegations in connection with the sale, marketing, and pricing of pharmaceuticals. Specifically, in both cases, initiated by the same *qui tam* relator, the complaint alleged that the companies illegally manipulated the average wholesale price (AWP) of certain drugs, violated the anti-kickback statute in marketing products to physicians, violated the Prescription Drug Marketing Act by encouraging physicians to bill for free samples, and improperly failed to include certain discounts in the Medicaid Best Price calculation. Given these record settlements, powerful enforcement

---

[154]*See* Office of Inspector Gen., U.S. Dep't of Health & Human Servs., OIG Work Plan, Fiscal Year 1999, *available at* http://oig.hhs.gov/reading/workplan/1999/99wkpln.pdf.

[155]Press Release, U.S. Dep't of Justice, *TAP Pharmaceutical Products, Inc. and Seven Others Charged with Health Care Crimes; Company Agrees to Pay $875 Million to Settle Charges* (Oct. 3, 2001), *available at* http://www.usdoj.gov/opa/pr/2001/October/513civ.htm.

[156]Press Release, U.S. Dep't of Justice, *AstraZeneca Pharmaceuticals LP Pleads Guilty to Healthcare Crime; Company Agrees to Pay $355 Million to Settle Charges* (June 20, 2003), *available at* http://www.usdoj.gov/opa/pr/2003/June/03_civ_371.htm.

tools, and the new Medicare drug benefit program, this area will certainly prove to be a hotbed of enforcement activity for years to come.

## B. Enforcement Actions Involving Pricing Methodologies

### 1. Price Inflation Through Average Wholesale Price Data

In the mid-1990s, the government began aggressively pursuing pharmaceutical companies in connection with pricing policies.[157] Over the years, state and federal regulators have argued that manufacturers intentionally overstated the AWP of prescription drugs, which resulted in artificially inflated pricing of drugs provided to Medicare and Medicaid beneficiaries. Until enactment of the MMA, payment for prescription drugs under Part B of the Medicare Act was made at the lower of billed charges or 95 percent of the AWP as reported by pharmaceutical manufacturers to information clearinghouses, such as the Red Book or Medspan.[158] Likewise, many states rely on AWP data to set payment rates for prescription drugs reimbursed by the Medicaid program.

According to the OIG, manufacturers could be subject to FCA liability for reporting inaccurate AWP data to information clearinghouses. Specifically, in guidance to manufacturers published in May 2003, the OIG stated that manufacturers may run afoul of the FCA if "reimbursement of the product depends, in whole or in part, on information generated or reported by the manufacturer, directly or indirectly, and the manufacturer has knowingly . . . failed to generate or report such information completely and accurately."[159] The government has argued that manufacturers know that the AWP data they report in wholesalers' catalogs bears little to no resemblance to the actual wholesale prices of the drugs available to health care providers. By intentionally providing inaccurate information about the costs of their products that will form the basis of government reimbursement, enforcement agencies contend that manufacturers have *caused* the submission of false claims.[160]

In 2000, Bayer Corporation settled the first widely reported AWP FCA case with the government for $14 million.[161] The government alleged that

---

[157]Press Release, U.S. Dep't of Justice, *Bayer Agrees to Settle Allegations That It Caused Providers to Submit Fraudulent Claims to 47 State Medicaid Programs* (Sept. 19, 2000), *available at* http://www.usdoj.gov/opa/pr/2000/September/551civ.htm; *Bayer to Pay $14 Million in FCA Lawsuit Alleging Fraudulent Medicaid Claims*, 5 HEALTH CARE FRAUD REP. (BNA) 125 (No. 3) (Feb. 7, 2001).

[158]42 U.S.C. §1395u(o); 42 C.F.R. §405.517; HCFA Program Memorandum AB-99-63 (Sept. 1999).

[159]OIG Compliance Program Guidelines for Pharmaceutical Manufacturers, 68 Fed. Reg. 23,731, 23,733 (May 5, 2003).

[160]In addition to risking FCA liability in connection with reporting inaccurate AWP data, the OIG has declared, manufacturers risk violating the anti-kickback statute if they knowingly establish or "inappropriately maintain a particular AWP if one purpose is to manipulate the 'spread' to induce customers to purchase its product." *Id.* at 23,737.

[161]Press Release, U.S. Dep't of Justice, *Bayer Agrees to Settle Allegations That It Caused Providers to Submit Fraudulent Claims to 47 State Medicaid Programs* (Sept. 19, 2000), *available at* http://www.usdoj.gov/opa/pr/2000/September/551civ.htm; *Bayer to Pay $14 Million in FCA Lawsuit Alleging Fraudulent Medicaid Claims,* 5 HEALTH CARE FRAUD REP. (BNA) 125 (No. 3) (Feb. 7, 2001). The government also alleged that Bayer violated the "best price" regulations in agreements with states in connection with the Medicaid Drug Rebate Program.

Bayer caused providers to submit fraudulently inflated reimbursement claims to the Medicaid programs of 47 states. Specifically, the government alleged that Bayer falsely inflated reported the AWP of certain hemophilia drugs and illegally marketed the "spread" between the AWP and actual price to prescribers as an inducement to prescribe the Bayer drugs over competing products. The case started as *qui tam* litigation initiated by Florida-based independent pharmacy Ven-A-Care. As part of the settlement, Bayer signed a five-year corporate integrity agreement obligating the company to provide the government with the average sale prices of the drugs at issue. The government has used this information to bolster its case against the AWP.

Following the Bayer settlement in 2000, AWP cases exploded throughout the country and have yielded record settlements for prosecutors. The record $875 million TAP settlement in 2001 and the $355 million settlement with AstraZeneca in 2003 both concerned allegations that the companies violated the FCA in connection with setting the AWP of their respective cancer drugs in addition to other allegations. Based on the perceived success of these settlements, states also brought claims against drug manufacturers based on AWP data in addition to claims arising under the Medicaid Drug Rebate Program.[162] As discussed below, AWP claims may eventually evaporate in light of the new pricing structure established by the MMA.

First DataBank is the most widely-used and established reporter and publisher of AWP for pharmaceuticals. First DataBank does not set drug prices but instead publishes information received from drug manufacturers. In October 2006, First DataBank announced that it would make certain changes to its drug pricing reporting practices as part of a settlement of class action litigation against it, pending approval of the settlement by the court.[163] The lawsuit alleged that First DataBank arbitrarily and artificially raised the spread between wholesale acquisition cost (WAC) and AWP to 25 percent for over 400 brand-name drugs.[164] The spread mark-up benefited providers and pharmacies that enjoyed a profit from the difference between their cost and reimbursement from federal health care programs, including Medicaid.

The changes First DataBank must make to its drug pricing reporting practices include: (1) adjustment of reporting of Blue Book AWP for certain prescription drugs by reducing the mark-up factor used in connection with the calculation of the Blue Book AWP data field (by about five percent), (2) discontinuing publication of the Blue Book AWP data field for all drugs no later than two years after the court-ordered settlement is final, (3) establishing a centralized data repository to facilitate reasonable access to discoverable material from First DataBank concerning its drug reporting practices,

---

[162]*See, e.g.,* Connecticut v. Aventis Pharms., Inc., No. CV03-0824415S (Conn. Super. Ct. Mar. 14, 2003); *In re* Pharmaceutical Industry Average Wholesale Price Litig., 321 F. Supp. 2d 187 (D. Mass. 2004). GlaxoSmithKline, a defendant in the *Average Wholesale Price* litigation, agreed in August 2006 to pay $70 million to cancer patients and health plans that were overcharged for certain medications. This amount includes a $4.5 million payment to certain state attorneys general. *See* http://www.prescriptionaccess.org/press/pressreleases?id=0007.

[163]*See In re* Pharmaceutical Average Wholesale Price Litigation, MDL No. 1456 (D. Mass. Oct. 5, 2006).

[164]This case was deemed related to the *Average Wholesale Price Multi-District Litigation.*

and (4) working with major health care industry participants to facilitate the establishment of a sustainable benchmark for drug reimbursement.[165] The proposed settlement would not affect First DataBank's publication of other drug pricing information, including WAC, direct price, suggested wholesale price, and clinical drug information.[166]

The MMA and DRA,[167] along with the First DataBank case, have almost obliterated the much-criticized AWP model for drug pricing. The MMA replaced the AWP with the average sales price (ASP) for Part B physician-administered drugs. The ASP is based on data submitted by manufacturers and includes all forms of rebates and price reductions.[168] An OIG study found that on average the ASP was 26 percent lower than the AWP for sole source brand drugs, 30 percent lower for multi-source brand drugs, and 68 percent lower for generic drugs.[169] Pharmacy and managed care organizations, as well as other government agencies, have formed task forces to determine a new methodology of pharmacy claims processing and pricing. Still, the AWP will be used by many states until another reliable methodology is developed and implemented.

In May 2006 the government intervened in a False Claims Act case against Abbott Laboratories, Inc., that was initially instituted by Ven-A-Care of the Florida Keys, Inc., and its principals. Ven-A-Care is a home infusion company.[170] The suit alleged that Abbott violated the False Claims Act by engaging in a scheme to report fraudulent and inflated prices for pharmaceuticals knowing that the government used those reported prices to establish reimbursement rates by federal health care programs. The alleged reporting of inflated prices goes all the way back to January 1, 1991, when Abbott's Hospital Products Division allegedly reported prices that were more than 1000 percent of the actual sales price of many drugs it manufactured. The federal government reimbursed more than $175 million for drugs, which was the basis of the complaint. The government argued that Abbott used the inflated prices to market, promote, and sell drugs to existing and potential customers. Abbott's provider customers profited when federal reimbursement exceeded the cost to providers. Abbott allegedly caused the providers to submit false claims to the government because the requested reimbursement was based on Abbott's inflated price reporting.

Similar to the *Abbott Laboratories* case, in January 2007, the DOJ announced that the United States had intervened in a whistleblower False Claims Act suit against Ohio-based pharmaceutical manufacturer Boehringer Ingelheim Roxane, Inc. As in *Abbott Laboratories*, the government began investigating Roxane after Ven-A-Care filed a *qui tam* complaint. The government's

---

[165]*See* First DataBank AWP Communications, *available at* http://65.88.137.196/support/rcs/communications/awp.

[166]*Id.*

[167]See Section XII.A., above.

[168]*See* 42 U.S.C. §1395w-3a(c)(3).

[169]DEP'T HEALTH & HUMAN SERVS., OFFICE OF INSPECTOR GENERAL, MEDICAID DRUG PRICE COMPARISON: AVERAGE SALES PRICE TO AVERAGE WHOLESALE PRICE, OEI-03 05 00200 (June 2005), *available at* http://oig.hhs.gov/oei/reports/oei-03-05-0200.pdf.

[170]*See* U.S. Dep't of Justice press release, *available at* http://www.usdoj.gov.opa/pr/2006/May/06_civ_309.html.

theory was identical to the *Abbott Laboratories* case: allegedly since at least January 1, 1996, Roxane reported inflated prices on certain generic drugs it manufactures. The Medicare and Medicaid programs claimed to have reimbursed Roxane customers in excess of $500 million for these drugs. The government further alleged that Roxane used artificially inflated spreads (the difference between government reimbursement rates and the actual price paid by providers for the drug) to market, promote, and sell the drugs. Because Medicare and Medicaid reimbursements were allegedly based on the inflated prices, Roxane was alleged to have caused false and fraudulent claims to be submitted to federal health care programs.[171]

Ongoing pharmaceutical pricing enforcement actions should be closely monitored over the next few years as the effects of the MMA and DRA take hold in the industry.

## 2. Medicaid Drug Rebate Program

Under the federal Medicaid law, state Medicaid agencies must pay the lowest price possible for prescription drugs.[172] Accordingly, manufacturers that participate in the Medicaid program enter into agreements with states that include a provision that requires manufacturers to report to CMS the best price they offer to any commercial, for-profit customer and pay a quarterly rebate to Medicaid based upon the best price for each drug sold.[173] OIG guidance issued in 2003 suggests that manufacturers must report all "discounts" in the "best price" calculation, including price reductions, cash discounts, free goods, rebates, coupons, grants, and other price concessions.[174] The OIG has opined that the Medicaid Drug Rebate Program encourages manufacturers to conceal discounts because "manufacturers have a strong financial incentive to hide de facto pricing concessions to other purchasers to avoid passing on the same discounts to the states."[175] The government has aggressively prosecuted fraud claims against manufacturers for violation of the Medicaid "best price" regulations. Furthermore, since the 1990s, nearly every state has participated in "best price" litigation based on discounts, rebates, or other financial incentives offered by manufacturers.[176]

---

[171]*See* U.S. Dep't of Justice press release, *available at* http://www.usdoj.gov.opa/pr/2007/January/07_civ_052.html.

[172]42 U.S.C. §1396r-8.

[173]"Best price" is defined as "the lowest price available from the manufacturer during the rebate period to any wholesaler, retailer, provider, health maintenance organization, nonprofit entity, or governmental entity within the United States." 42 U.S.C. §1396r-8(c)(1)(C)(i). "Best price" calculations include discounts and are "without regard to special packaging, labeling, or identifiers on the dosage form or product or package." 42 U.S.C. §1396r-8(c)(1)(C)(ii)(I) and (II). The lower the best price on the drugs, the higher the rebate payment to the states.

[174]OIG Compliance Program Guidance for Pharmaceutical Manufacturers, 68 Fed. Reg. 23,731, 23,733–34 (May 5, 2003), reprinted as Appendix I-3.1 on the disk accompanying this volume.

[175]68 Fed. Reg. at 23,735.

[176]*See, e.g.,* Connecticut v. Aventis Pharms., Inc., CV03-0824415S (Conn. Super. Ct. Mar. 14, 2003); *In re* Pharmaceutical Industry Average Wholesale Price Litigation, 321 F. Supp. 2d 187 (D. Mass. 2004); California *ex rel.* Ven-A-Care v. Abbott Labs., Inc. Case No. BC 287198A (Cal. Super. Ct. Jan. 7, 2003).

For example, in 2002, Pfizer paid $49 million to settle allegations that it failed to include discounts and rebates provided to physicians in its "best price" for the cholesterol drug Lipitor.[177] Parke-Davis Labs, then a subsidiary of Warner-Lambert, which was subsequently acquired by Pfizer in 2000, allegedly overstated the Lipitor best price in the first and second quarters of 1999 by concealing $250,000 of discounts as "educational grants" that were given to a large managed care organization in Louisiana in exchange for favorable status on the organization's drug formulary. The government alleged that Parke-Davis/Warner-Lambert improperly retained more than $20 million in Medicaid rebates owed to the Medicaid program in connection with the discounts.

Similarly, in 2003, the Bayer Corporation made headlines again with a settlement involving allegations that the company improperly concealed the "best price" of certain drugs through "private labeling" of sales to Kaiser Permanente (Kaiser). This time, Bayer agreed to pay $257 million to settle allegations that Bayer (and its subsidiary GlaxoSmithKline) gave Kaiser a 40 percent discount on the antibiotic Cipro but reported only a 15 percent discount to the government.[178] Bayer allegedly concealed the true discount by changing labels on products delivered to Kaiser by including Kaiser's National Drug Code (NDC) on the label instead of its own. By so doing, the government alleged that the companies circumvented the reporting requirement, thereby lowering rebates to the Medicaid program.

## C. Illegal Marketing

### 1. Kickbacks

Many of the headline-making cases against pharmaceutical manufacturers allege that the companies' marketing programs include illegal kickbacks to physicians in exchange for prescriptions.[179] Under the federal anti-kickback law, payments, gifts, or other remuneration by manufacturers to physicians or other health care providers made with the intention to generate referrals constitute improper kickbacks.[180] In cases involving pharmaceutical fraud, the government has alleged that companies disguise illegal kickbacks to physicians and others in the form of discounts, educational grants, consultation fees,

---

[177]Press Release, U.S. Dep't of Justice, *Drug Giant and Two Subsidiaries to Pay $49 Million for Defrauding Medicaid Drug Rebate Program* (Oct. 28, 2002), *available at* http://www.usdoj.gov/opa/pr/2002/October/02_civ_622.htm.

[178]The 2001 suit also alleged that Bayer failed to report discounts provided to physicians and home health agencies in its "best price."

[179]*See, e.g.,* Press Release, U.S. Dep't of Justice, *TAP Pharmaceutical Products, Inc. and Seven Others Charged with Health Care Crimes; Company Agrees to Pay $875 Million to Settle Charges* (Oct. 3, 2001), *available at* http://www.usdoj.gov/opa/pr/2001/October/513civ.htm; United States *ex rel.* Durand v. AstraZeneca Pharms. LP, Case No. 03-122-JJF (D. Del. 2003); Press Release, U.S. Dep't of Justice, *AstraZeneca Pharmaceuticals LP Pleads Guilty to Healthcare Crime; Company Agrees to Pay $355 Million to Settle Charges* (June 20, 2003), *available at* http://www.usdoj.gov/opa/pr/2003/June/03_civ_371.htm; United States *ex rel.* Franklin v. Parke-Davis, Div. of Warner-Lambert Co., Case No. 96-11651-PBS, 2003 WL 22048255 (D. Mass. 2003); *see also* United States *ex rel.* Franklin v. Parke-Davis, Div. of Warner-Lambert Co., 147 F. Supp. 2d 39 (D. Mass. 2001).

[180]42 U.S.C. §1320a–7b(b).

entertainment, and free goods. The OIG has also opined that a manufacturer's "manipulation" of AWP data to purposely increase a customer's profits by increasing federal reimbursement also implicates the anti-kickback statute.[181]

The OIG first targeted marketing programs in a 1994 fraud alert that detailed several marketing programs that were potentially violative of the anti-kickback law.[182] The suspect scenarios included cash awards to pharmacies for drug switching, frequent flier miles provided to physicians for completing questionnaires after prescribing a company's drug to a new patient, and "research grants" where physicians were paid for de minimis record keeping. In the 1994 fraud alert, the OIG stated that these incentives would violate the anti-kickback statute if even one purpose was to induce the physician to prescribe a drug item reimbursable by Medicaid.[183] The OIG further stated that such conduct would not benefit from safe harbor protection. Since the issuance of this fraud alert, the government, and *qui tam* relators, have aggressively attacked manufacturers' marketing tactics under the anti-kickback statute.

For example, in both the *TAP* and *AstraZeneca* cases discussed above, the government and *qui tam* relators alleged that the companies paid physicians and others improper kickbacks in the form of "educational" grants to encourage use of their products. In *TAP,* the *qui tam* relator, an HMO-employed urologist, alleged that the company offered him educational grants if he reversed the HMO's decision to include a competing drug on the formulary.[184] Seven TAP employees were indicted for allegedly paying kickbacks and bribes including free consulting services, trips to golf and ski resorts, and funding office Christmas parties and bar tabs, in addition to the improper "educational grants."[185] And in January of 2004, Joanne Richardson, a TAP regional account manager, was found guilty of perjury in connection with statements she made to a federal grand jury. Federal prosecutors presented evidence that Richardson and others at TAP offered to give a clinic off-contract hidden price reductions in the form of free samples and education and research grants to prescribe Lupron over a competing drug.[186] Similar allegations were made against AstraZeneca.

Similarly, in the Pfizer (Parke-Davis) case settled in 2002, the *qui tam* relator, a former "medical liaison" for Parke-Davis, alleged that the company violated the anti-kickback statute by paying physicians for inconsequential drug

---

[181]The OIG states that "it is illegal for a manufacturer knowingly to establish or inappropriately maintain a particular AWP if one purpose is to manipulate the 'spread' to induce customers to purchase its product." OIG Compliance Program Guidance for Pharmaceutical Manufacturers, 68 Fed. Reg. 23,731, 23,737 (May 5, 2003).

[182]OIG Special Fraud Alert: Prescription Drug Marketing Schemes, 59 Fed. Reg. 65,376 (Dec. 19, 1994).

[183]*Id.*

[184]Press Release, U.S. Dep't of Justice, *TAP Pharmaceutical Products, Inc. and Seven Others Charged with Health Care Crimes; Company Agrees to Pay $875 Million to Settle Charges* (Oct. 3, 2001), *available at* http://www.usdoj.gov/opa/pr/2001/October/513civ.htm.

[185]*Id.* On July 14, 2004, a jury acquitted the TAP employees of charges that they provided illegal incentives to physicians, including free samples, in exchange for prescriptions. *Drug Company Employees Acquitted in Kickback Trial,* USA Today, *available at* http://www.usatoday.com/money/industries/health/2004-07-14-pharmaceutical-freebies_x.htm.

[186]*Former TAP Pharma Account Manager Found Guilty of Lying to Grand Jury, Health Care Fraud Report,* 8 Health Care Fraud Rep. (BNA) 109–10 (Feb. 4, 2004).

studies, minimal participation in speakers' bureaus, and cash payments for small record-keeping tasks in addition to direct "gifts" of travel and tickets to the Olympics in exchange for prescribing the anti-seizure drug Neurontin.[187]

On the heels of the swell of AWP litigation, the OIG has targeted manufacturers' marketing programs that "actively" market the "spread" to customers. Specifically, in the 2003 Pharmaceutical Compliance Guidance, the OIG stated that active marketing of the spread includes statements by sales representatives "promoting the spread as a reason to purchase the product or guaranteeing a certain profit or spread in exchange for the purchase of a product."[188] Such promotions, according to the OIG, may violate the anti-kickback statute, i.e., "[t]he conjunction of manipulation of the AWP to induce customers to purchase a product with active marketing of the spread is strong evidence of the unlawful intent necessary to trigger the anti-kickback statute."[189] The *AstraZeneca* case provides a poignant example of government claims of marketing the spread.

In the *AstraZeneca* case, documents from the company's marketing department revealed that AstraZeneca engaged in a full-scale marketing campaign to physicians detailing the profitability of the "spread" between AWP and the cost to physicians.[190] The program, called a "Return-to-Practice," consisted of inflating the AWP of the cancer drug Zoladex, heavily discounting the price paid by physicians, and marketing the spread between the AWP and the discounted price as an additional profit to be "returned" to the physician's practice.[191] The government used this powerful evidence to elicit the hefty settlement.

In February 2005, a subsidiary of Novartis pleaded guilty to criminal charges of endeavoring to obstruct a federal audit and was fined $4.5 million in connection with those charges.[192] The plea was obtained due to the efforts of a massive federal sting operation, "Operation Headwaters." Investigators established a sham entity called Southern Medical Distributors (SMD) that attempted to do business with various suppliers. In the Novartis case, the target companies were accused of offering improper inducements such as conversion bonuses to encourage SMD to order enteral products that would be billed to the Medicare program in violation of the anti-kickback statute. The government also alleged that the company encouraged purchasers to bill Medicare for enteral pumps that had been provided free of charge. As of February 2005, Operation Headwaters had assisted in procuring 11 criminal convictions for health care fraud.[193] In September 2005, GlaxoSmithKline agreed to pay $150 million and enter into an addendum to its existing corporate integrity agreement to

---

[187]United States *ex rel.* Franklin v. Parke-Davis, 147 F. Supp. 2d 39, 54 (D. Mass. 2001).

[188]OIG Compliance Program Guidance for Pharmaceutical Manufacturers, 68 Fed. Reg. 23,731, 23,737 (May 5, 2003).

[189]*Id.*

[190]Press Release, U.S. Dep't of Justice, *AstraZeneca Pharmaceuticals LP Pleads Guilty to Healthcare Crime; Company Agrees to Pay $355 Million to Settle Charges* (June 20, 2003), *available at* http://www.usdoj.gov/opa/pr/2003/June/03_civ_371.htm.

[191]*Id.*

[192]News Release, U.S. Dep't of Justice, *Subsidiary of Novartis Pleads Guilty to Nine Felony Audit Obstruction Charges and Is Sentenced with $4.5 Million Fine; Company Also Reaches Civil Settlement Requiring Separate Payment of $44,656,229* (Feb. 11, 2005), *available at* http://www.usdoj.gov:80/usao/ils/newsreleases/05%20February/02.11.05Novartis%20plea%20pr.pdf.

[193]Thom Wilder, *Novartis, Affiliate Pay More Than $40 Million to Settle Investigation of Product Marketing*, 9 HEALTH CARE FRAUD REP. (BNA) 185 (Mar. 2, 2005).

resolve allegations that it violated the FCA by undertaking marketing campaigns that marketed "the spread" and engaged in fraudulent pricing of two anti-emetic drugs, Zofran and Kytril, used primarily in conjunction with oncology and radiation treatment.[194]

Similarly, Schering Sales Corporation and its parent company Schering-Plough agreed in August 2006 to plead guilty to criminal charges, pay a $180 million criminal fine, and settle False Claims Act liabilities in the amount of $255 million.[195] Of the civil settlement amount $91 million plus interest was apportioned among the states to cover Medicaid program losses. The charges and allegations against Schering Sales related to multiple drugs (Temodar, Intron A, Claritin Redi-Tabs, and K-Dur) and included improper Medicaid best price reporting, illegal remuneration in the form of improper preceptorships, sham advisory boards, lavish entertainment, improper clinical trials, and encouragement of improper billing for free samples and overfilled vials, among other things.

One of the larger recent False Claims Act settlements resulted from allegations that the nation's second largest pharmacy benefit management company, Medco Health Solutions, accepted kickbacks from pharmaceutical manufacturers to favor particular drugs and paid kickbacks to obtain business. In October 2006, Medco Health Solutions agreed to pay the United States $155 million to settle these allegations.[196] The case began with two separate *qui tam* actions in 1999 and 2000, which were consolidated. The United States intervened and filed a complaint alleging that in addition to the above, Medco submitted false claims for mail order prescription drug services it was required by contract to provide to federal health care program beneficiaries. The government also alleged that Medco cancelled valid prescriptions it could not timely fill in order to avoid contract penalties, shorted pills from filled prescriptions, failed to conduct necessary utilization review, and used drugs other than those prescribed by physicians to earn undisclosed rebates from drug manufacturers (as discussed below). The *qui tam* relators reportedly received $23 million of the recovery. Medco was required to enter into a corporate integrity agreement to continue participating in federal health care programs.

## 2. Drug Switching

In a December 1994 fraud alert, the OIG identified a trend of suspicious activity it then termed "product conversion."[197] Product conversion, or drug

---

[194]Press Release, U.S. Dep't of Justice, *GlaxoSmithKline Pays $150 Million to Settle Drug Pricing Fraud Case* (Sept. 20, 2005), *available at* http://www.usdoj.gov/opa/pr/2005/September/ 05_civ_489.html. In its own press release on the settlement, GSK argued that the government was well aware of the inaccuracy of AWP data as a benchmark for setting prices of pharmaceuticals to be reimbursed by federal programs. Press Release, GlaxoSmithKline, *GlaxoSmithKline, Government Reach Civil Settlement* (Sept. 20, 2005), *available at* http://www.gsk.com/media/archive.htm#nolink.

[195]*See* http://www.secinfo.com/dsvr4.vcPc.htm#eeje.

[196]*See* U.S. Dep't of Justice press release, *available at* http://www.usdoj.gov.opa/pr/2006/ October/06_civ_722.html.

[197]OIG Special Fraud Alert: Prescription Drug Marketing Schemes, 59 Fed. Reg. 65,376 (Dec. 19, 1994).

switching, as it is now known, occurs when a manufacturer or pharmacy benefit manager (PBM) offers cash awards or other incentives to physicians or pharmacies to prescribe its product over a competing product without regard to medical efficacy.[198] The OIG stated that while switching arrangements between manufacturers and physicians or pharmacies "clearly" trigger the anti-kickback statute, drug switching "may be permissible in certain managed care arrangements."[199] States began to take an increased interest in drug switching cases, arguing that the practice violated the Medicaid Drug Rebate Program as well as state anticompetition laws.

In March 2004, the State of Louisiana intervened in a *qui tam* case brought by a physician against Merck & Co. (Merck), the manufacturer of Pepcid.[200] The state's complaint alleged that the company paid hospitals and physicians to prescribe Pepcid over its competitor Zantac without regard to the medical efficacy and failed to appreciate side effects associated with the switched drug. The complaint further alleged that Merck offered hospitals significant discounts that were not provided to the state. Specifically, Merck allegedly charged hospitals $0.10 per tablet, while charging the state's Medicaid program $1.65 per tablet.[201] The state argued that by paying incentives for drug switching, the company failed to comply with the "best price" regulations. Furthermore, the state alleged that Merck's actions violated state anticompetition laws.

Similarly, in April 2004, 20 states settled cases against Medco Health Solutions, Inc. (Medco), the world's largest PBM, resolving claims that the company violated state unfair trade practices laws.[202] The states argued that Medco encouraged prescribers to switch patients to prescription drugs based on rebates paid to the company by pharmaceutical manufacturers but failed to pass on savings to patients or health plans. The states further alleged that Medco failed to inform the prescribers and patients of additional rebates that were paid by pharmaceutical manufacturers for using the drugs. Medco paid more than $29 million to states to resolve the case and agreed to make certain disclosures about its pricing policies to physicians and patients, including information about any financial incentives the company receives in connection with prescription drugs.[203]

---

[198]OIG Compliance Program Guidance for Pharmaceutical Manufacturers, 68 Fed. Reg. 23,731, 23,737 (May 5, 2003).

[199]*Id.* at 23,738.

[200]United States *ex rel.* LaCorte v. Merck & Co., No. 99-3807, 2004 WL 595074 (E.D. La. Mar. 23, 2004). Claims that the company violated the anti-kickback statute and best price requirements were dismissed in June 2004. The relator was also ordered to amend the complaint to allege more facts showing how the company violated the False Claims Act through drug switching. United States *ex rel.* LaCorte v. Merck & Co., No. 99-3807, 2004 WL 1373276 (E.D. La. June 16, 2004) (unpublished).

[201]*Id.*

[202]*See* Press Release, National Ass'n of Attorneys General, *Settlement: 20 Attorneys General Settle Unfair Practices Claims Against Medco Health Solutions* (Apr. 26, 2004), *available at* http://www.naag.org/issues/20040426-settlement-medco.php.

[203]*Id.*

### 3. *Marketing of Off-Label Uses*

The federal Food, Drug, and Cosmetic Act (FDCA) prohibits manufacturers and retailers from promoting any use of a drug that the FDA has not approved.[204] Once the FDA approves a drug for a particular use, the FDCA does not prevent physicians from *prescribing* the drug for another purpose (an "off-label use"); however, the FDCA prohibits manufacturers from *marketing* or *promoting* a drug for that unapproved use.[205] The government often prosecutes off-label marketing cases under the FCA where the government-sponsored health care program at issue limits reimbursement to only those FDA-approved drugs/uses.[206]

In May 2004, Pfizer agreed to pay $430 million to settle allegations brought against the recently-acquired Parke-Davis company that Parke-Davis marketed off-label uses of certain drugs to physicians, who then submitted claims for reimbursement to state Medicaid programs.[207] Although Pfizer settled the *Parke-Davis* case, many of the company's arguments were well received by the court.

For example, in August 2003, the court denied the company's motion for summary judgment based on the existence of factual disputes, but entertained an argument that no false claims were submitted in states where off-label uses are permitted based on a federal law that allows states to reimburse off-label uses, and where such uses were permitted in at least 42 states.[208] The court requested amicus briefs from government officials regarding the legislative intent behind the Medicaid statute and off-label prescription prohibitions, stating, "[i]f the Medicaid statute gives states the discretion to cover off-label, non-compendium prescriptions, and a state exercised its discretion to cover such prescriptions, then an off-label Neurontin prescription in that state would not be a false claim."[209] Earlier, the court partially granted the company's motion to dismiss, forcing the relator to drop certain anti-kickback claims.[210]

In October 2005, Merck Serono International S.A. and EMD Serono, Inc. (Serono) agreed to pay the United States $704 million to settle civil liabilities

---

[204]21 U.S.C. §331 (2000).

[205]*See* 21 U.S.C. §331(a)–(d), which prohibit distribution of drugs for non-approved uses and "misbranded" drugs.

[206]*See, e.g.,* definition of "covered outpatient drugs," which does not include drugs that are used for a medical indication which is not a medically accepted indication. 42 U.S.C. §1396r–8(k)(3). The Medicaid Act defines "medically accepted indication" as a use "which is approved under the Federal Food Drug and Cosmetic Act" or which is included in specified drug compendia. 42 U.S.C. §1396r–8(k)(6). Off-label marketing is discussed in detail in Chapter 4, Paul W. Radensky *et al., Potential Liability for Drug Companies, Health Care Providers, and Insurers: Off-Label Prescribing and Internet Advertising, in* PHARMACEUTICAL LAW: REGULATION OF RESEARCH, DEVELOPMENT, AND MARKETING (BNA 2007).

[207]*See* U.S. Dep't of Justice press release, *available at* http://www.usdoj.gov/opa/pr/2004/May/04_civ_322.htm.

[208]The company cited 42 U.S.C. §1396r-8(d)(1)(B), which states in pertinent part: "[a] state *may exclude* or otherwise restrict coverage of a covered outpatient drug if—(i) the prescribed use is not for a medically accepted indication" (emphasis added). United States *ex rel.* Franklin v. Parke-Davis, Div. of Warner-Lambert Co., Case No. 96-11651-PBS, at 5–6 (D. Mass. Aug. 22, 2003).

[209]*Id.* at 7.

[210]United States *ex rel.* Franklin v. Parke-Davis, Div. of Warner-Lambert Co., 147 F. Supp. 2d 39 (D. Mass. 2001).

and pleaded guilty to criminal charges for unlawful promotion of its AIDS drug Serostim.[211] Of this amount, $262 million was paid to state Medicaid programs. Serono allegedly wrongfully encouraged physicians to prescribe Serostim to patients for whom it was not medically necessary. Serono was also excluded from participation in federal health care programs for five years. The case began with a *qui tam* action filed by five relators alleging that, as early as 1996, Serono undertook a sales and marketing campaign to create a market for Serostim by redefining the medical condition of AIDS wasting, which had recently declined in prevalence. The relators also alleged that Serono had offered physicians trips to Europe in exchange for writing new Serostim prescriptions.[212]

In the Schering-Plough case,[213] Schering was also accused of making false statements to the FDA regarding its off-label marketing of Intron A and Temodar. The government estimated that Schering Sales had profited $124,179,000 from improper promotion of these drugs. Schering Sales has been permanently barred from participating in federal health care programs.[214]

One of the most widely publicized settlements resulting from alleged improper off-label use marketing occurred in October 2006 when California biopharmaceutical company InterMune, Inc., agreed to pay more than $36 million ($30 million to federal program, $6 million to state Medicaid programs) to resolve criminal charges and civil liabilities related to the marketing and promotion of Actimmune, a drug approved by the FDA to treat chronic gran-ulomatous disease and severe osteoporosis.[215] From August 2002 through January 2003, the majority of Actimmune sales were for treatment of idiopathic pulmonary fibrosis, for which it is not an FDA-approved treatment. The criminal investigation against InterMune was resolved by the filing of an in-formation and the company's entry into a deferred prosecution agreement. The criminal charges included a violation of the Food, Drug, and Cosmetic Act for promoting, with the intent to defraud, the drug Actimmune for treatment of idiopathic pulmonary fibrosis. According to the deferred prosecution agree-ment, from 2000 to 2002 InterMune conducted clinical trials of Actimmune for idiopathic pulmonary fibrosis. The trials failed to demonstrate statistically significant evidence of a benefit from the drug. However, in August 2002 InterMune issued a press release stating that Actimmune may extend the lives of patients with the disease and was the only available treatment demonstrated to have clinical benefit in idiopathic pulmonary fibrosis "with improved sur-vival data in two controlled clinical trials." InterMune also entered into a five-year corporate integrity agreement as part of the settlement.[216]

---

[211]*See* http://www.dc37.net/news/newsreleases/2007/2_20drug.pdf.

[212]The Serono Corporate Integrity Agreement is available at http://oig.hhs.gov/fraud/cia/agreements/SeronoHoldings_101405.pdf.

[213]*Schering-Plough* is also discussed in Section XII.C.1., above.

[214]*See* http://www.usdoj.gov/usao/ma/Press%20Office%20-%20Press%20Release%20Files/Schering-Plough/press%20release.pdf.

[215]*See* U.S. Dep't of Justice press release, *available at* http://www.usdoj.gov/opa/pr/2006/October/06_civ_728.html.

[216]*See* http://oig.hhs.gov/fraud/cia/docs/InterMuneCIA.pdf.

### 4. Free Samples

Some of the most publicized claims in the *TAP* and *AstraZeneca* cases were allegations that the companies improperly encouraged prescribers to bill Medicare and Medicaid for free samples provided by the manufacturer in violation of the Prescription Drug Marketing Act (PDMA). The PDMA regulates the distribution and receipt of drug samples, as well as record keeping of manufacturers and distributors.[217] The PDMA prohibits resale of samples and requires recipients to request samples in writing and provide manufacturers and distributors with a written receipt. Violators may be subject to criminal penalties, including up to 10 years' imprisonment.[218]

In the criminal prosecution of one of the individual physicians in the *TAP* case in connection with the illegal sale of Lupron samples, the physician defendant moved to dismiss the case on the grounds that the samples provided by the company were not illegally dispensed under the PDMA.[219] Specifically, Dr. Romano argued that because the Lupron samples were given directly by TAP to him and were then injected by him into the patient, there was no "prescription" for them and therefore, the drugs were not dispensed in violation of the PDMA.[220] Despite these defense strategies, Romano pleaded guilty to one count of fraudulent billing in March 2005.[221]

In 2005, the United States Attorney in Connecticut teamed up with the Connecticut Attorney General to pursue pediatricians who were billing the state's Medicaid program for vaccines that were received free of charge from a joint federal-state immunization program.[222] Under the program, providers agreed not to bill third-party payors (including Medicaid) for free vaccines, although they were permitted to recover minimal administrative fees for the costs of inoculating children. "Operation Free-Shot" uncovered two pediatric practices that were billing for the free vaccines.

### D. Defense Strategies

#### 1. Federal False Claims Act

The FCA imposes liability on any person who "(1) knowingly presents, or causes to be presented, to an officer or employee of the United States Government . . . a false or fraudulent claim for payment or approval; [or] (2) knowingly makes, uses, or causes to be made or used, a false record or

---

[217]21 U.S.C. §353.

[218]21 U.S.C. §333(b)(1).

[219]United States v. MacKenzie, No. 01-CR-10350-DPW (D. Mass. June 13, 2003).

[220]Romano argued that the PDMA, 21 U.S.C. §353 *et seq.*, applies to drug samples that are part of a unit of a drug subject to §353(b). Section 353(b) states that it applies to drugs that are dispensed by prescription or refill. Based on this rationale, Romano argued that the drugs provided by TAP were not "samples" because they were not provided by prescription.

[221]United States v. MacKenzie, No. 01-CR-10350 DPW (D. Mass. Mar. 9, 2005).

[222]Press Release, U.S. Dep't of Justice, *Operation Free Shot: Two Pediatric Practices Settle Civil Allegations Under False Claims Act* (Jan. 3, 2005), *available at* http://www.usdoj. gov:80/ usao/ct/Press2005/20050103.html.

statement to get a false or fraudulent claim paid or approved by the Government. . . . "[223] In order to assert a valid claim under the FCA, the government must prove three key elements: (1) that the defendant presented or caused another person to present a claim for payment to the government; (2) that the claim was false or fraudulent; and (3) that the defendant knew the claim was false or fraudulent. Defendants in FCA cases such as those discussed above have attacked these elements with varying degrees of success.

### a. Government Knowledge of Pricing Scheme

In FCA cases based on AWP data, defendants often challenge the action on the ground that the government knows that the AWP does not represent the actual price of drugs, and thus cannot prove that a claim is "false." This strategy has had a mixed track record, with results hinging on the extent of the government's knowledge. Furthermore, the weight given to the government's knowledge is determined by the courts on a case-by-case basis,[224] but the government's knowledge that AWP may not accurately reflect the actual drug price has not been an automatic bar to an FCA claim.

*Boisjoly v. Morton Thiokol, Inc.,*[225] is the seminal case that applied the government knowledge defense to rebut FCA claims. In *Boisjoly,* a *qui tam* relator claimed that the defendant, a manufacturer of space shuttle rocket motors, submitted false claims because it knew that the rocket motor seals and joints were defective and did not meet specifications. The court dismissed the complaint on the grounds that the responsible government officials were aware of the alleged defects in the products when the claims for payment were made. The *Boisjoly* court held that "if the complaint itself alleges that the government knew of those very facts or characteristics which allegedly make the claim false, no claim has been stated."[226]

Similarly, in *Woodbury v. United States,*[227] the court rejected the government's FCA allegations regarding a construction contract for Naval housing. Specifically, the government alleged that the contractor had concealed an additional subcontract for appliances provided in connection with pre-fabricated housing packages. The court found that there was no FCA liability because the government knew of the additional contract prior to payment of any claims. The *Woodbury* court explained, "[w]hen a person has knowledge . . . and no effort is made to prevent that person from making a full, adequate and complete inquiry into the exact terms of the transaction, such person will not be heard to say that he has been deceived to his injury by the misrepresentation of the person originally furnished the knowledge."[228]

---

[223]31 U.S.C. §3729(a).

[224]United States *ex rel.* Durcholz v. FKW, Inc., 997 F. Supp. 1159, 1157 (S.D. Ind. 1998), *aff'd,* 189 F.3d 542 (7th Cir. 1999).

[225]706 F. Supp. 795 (D. Utah 1988).

[226]*Id.* at 810.

[227]232 F. Supp. 49 (D. Or. 1964), *aff'd in part, rev'd in part,* 359 F.2d 370 (9th Cir. 1966).

[228]*Id.* at 55.

In the case of pharmaceutical pricing, there are numerous reports detailing the government's knowledge of the character of the AWP data.[229] But the weight of government knowledge has not carried the day in other courts.[230] In *United States v. Southland Management Corp.*,[231] the court rejected the defendant's argument that the government's knowledge of certain housing conditions negated the falsity of the claim for payment. The *Southland* court stated pointedly, "we find it difficult to comprehend how the government's awareness that a claimant's submission was false would in any way affect the truth or falsity of the claim. A lie does not become the truth simply because the person hearing it knows that it is a lie."[232]

Relatedly, in a 2003 civil Racketeer-Influenced and Corrupt Organizations Act (RICO) suit by cancer patients and health care plans against manufacturers, a federal court dismissed the manufacturers' argument that Congress understood that the AWP would be inflated. The court wrote, "[a]s defendants portray the Congressional purpose in setting the reimbursement rate at 95 percent of AWP, Congress meant to turn a blind eye to the inflated AWPs as a means of enticing physicians to treat Medicare patients. In other words, Congress deliberately invited the very fraud of which defendants are accused.... The suggestion that Congress would deliberately condone a bribery scheme using public funds to enrich drug manufacturers and physicians is, to say the least, unusual."[233]

### b. Challenging Scienter

The existence of government knowledge is also used to defeat the FCA's scienter requirement with varying degrees of success. To show violation of the FCA, the government must prove that the party making the claim for payment knew at the time the claim was submitted that it was false or fraudulent.[234] "Knowingly," as defined under the FCA, means that the person (1) has actual knowledge of the information; (2) acts in deliberate ignorance of the truth or falsity of the information; or (3) acts in reckless disregard of the truth or falsity of the information, and no proof of specific intent to defraud is required.[235] Dispelling accusations that a defendant acted "knowingly" is often an effective means of quashing a False Claims Act case.

In *United States ex rel. Durcholz v. FKW, Inc.*,[236] the court found that a contractor did not intentionally submit false claims by submitting certain

---

[229]For example, in the OIG WORK PLAN FY 1999, the OIG acknowledged that the average wholesale price is "generally inflated over actual acquisition costs." *See* http://www.oig.hhs.gov/reading/workplan/1999/99wkpln.pdf.

[230]*See* United States *ex rel.* Lamers v. City of Green Bay, 998 F. Supp. 971 (E.D. Wis. 1998), *aff'd*, 168 F.3d 1013 (7th Cir. 1999).

[231]288 F.3d 665 (5th Cir. 2002), *rev'd on other grounds en banc,* 326 F.3d 669 (5th Cir. 2003).

[232]288 F.3d at 681.

[233]*In re* Lupron, 295 F. Supp. 2d 148, 163 (D. Mass. 2003).

[234]31 U.S.C. §3729(a).

[235]31 U.S.C. §3729(b).

[236]997 F. Supp. 1159, 1171 (S.D. Ind. 1998), *aff'd,* 189 F.3d 542 (7th Cir. 1999).

documents related to a contract to clear sedimentation from ponds where the government knew of the methods to be used by the contractor although the documents submitted by the contractor listed a different removal method. In granting summary judgment in favor of the defendants, the *Durcholz* court emphasized the relative value of government knowledge in negating scienter: "[t]he extent and nature of government knowledge may show that the defendant did not 'knowingly' submit a false claim. . . . Conversely, the government's knowledge may be too incomplete or come too late in the process to defeat the 'knowingly' requirement."[237] This position has not been widely adopted.

For example, in *United States ex rel. Hagood v. Sonoma County Water Agency,* the Ninth Circuit rejected the government-knowledge defense.[238] In *Hagood,* the court explained that while government knowledge may show that the defendant had no intent to deceive, "the requisite intent [under the FCA] is the knowing presentation of what is known to be false. That the relevant government officials know of the falsity is not in itself a defense."[239] Accordingly, the *Hagood* court left open the viability of the government-knowledge defense for factual situations where the defendant is not acting on what it knows is false information.[240]

Similarly, in *Shaw v. AAA Engineering & Drafting, Inc.,*[241] the court stated that "government knowledge of a contractor's wrongdoing is no longer an automatic defense to an FCA action." The *Shaw* court found that the government's knowledge was not extensive enough to overcome FCA liability because the *qui tam* relator (and not the defendant) provided the information in question to the government, and also because it was shown that the defendant had evaded inquiries from the government regarding the practices that were the basis of the false claims. But the court did not foreclose the government-knowledge defense; rather, the *Shaw* court explained that, "there may still be occasions when the government's knowledge of or cooperation with a contractor's actions is so extensive that the contractor could not as a matter of law possess the requisite state of mind to be liable under the FCA."[242]

In *Southland Management Corp.* discussed below,[243] the court rejected the argument that the government's knowledge negated the defendant's intent. In *Southland Management,* the government alleged that owners of a federally subsidized low-income apartment complex violated the FCA in submitting claims for housing assistance where the apartments were in deplorable condi-

---

[237]997 F. Supp. at 1167.

[238]929 F.2d 1416, 1421 (9th Cir. 1991), *cert. denied,* 519 U.S. 865 (1996), *reh'g denied,* 519 U.S. 1001 (1996).

[239]*Id.*

[240]*Id.*

[241]213 F.3d 519 (10th Cir. 2000).

[242]213 F.3d at 534 (*citing* United States *ex rel.* Butler v. Hughes Helicopters, Inc., 71 F.3d 321, 327 (9th Cir. 1995), *and* Wang *ex rel.* United States v. FMC Corp., 975 F.2d 1412, 1421 (9th Cir. 1992)). *See also* United States *ex rel.* Becker v. Westinghouse Savannah River Co., 305 F.3d 284, 289 (4th Cir. 2002), *cert. denied,* 538 U.S. 1012 (2003) (noting that there are instances where "[the government's] full knowledge of material facts underlying any representation implicit in [defendant's] conduct" negate scienter for FCA purposes).

[243]288 F.3d 665, 686 (5th Cir. 2002), *rev'd on other grounds,* 326 F.3d 669 (5th Cir. 2003) (en banc).

tion. In order to qualify for payments, the property owner was required to submit an application to the Department of Housing and Urban Development certifying that the property was in a "decent, safe, and sanitary condition." Although the *Southland Management* Court rejected the government-knowledge defense, the court stated that the defense would remain viable in government-initiated FCA cases, "in the rare situation where the falsity of the claim is unclear and the evidence suggests that the defendant actually believed his claim was not false because the government approved and paid the claim with full knowledge of the relevant facts."[244]

The dissenting opinion disagreed with the majority's attempt to "cabin" the government-knowledge defense. Specifically, the dissent argued that only two scenarios would justify FCA liability in the face of government knowledge: "either the person making the statement did not know that the government knew it was false, or the person making the statement was colluding with a government employee who also knew the claim was false."[245] Apart from these situations, according to the dissent, the government's knowledge of the particulars of a claim and acceptance of what would otherwise have been fraudulent "effectively negates the fraud or falsity required by the FCA."[246] Thus, the divided court in *Southland Management* emphasizes the sharp discord about the weight of the government-knowledge defense among the circuits.

### c. *Challenging Causation*

To make a claim under the FCA, the government is required to prove that the defendant *caused* a false claim to be presented.[247] Some pharmaceutical manufacturers have challenged the causation element on the ground that they themselves do not submit any claim for payment and merely make their products available to prescribers. This strategy has not been well received by the courts.

As discussed in Section XII.C.3., above, in the off-label case filed against Parke-Davis, the relator had alleged that the company marketed off-label uses of certain drugs to physicians, who then submitted claims for reimbursement to state Medicaid programs.[248] In a motion to dismiss, Parke-Davis argued that the relator failed to state a claim in part because the acts of the prescribing physicians who wrote the off-label prescriptions, and the pharmacies who sought reimbursement, were the intervening causes of the false claim. The court rejected this argument, stating that "the participation of doctors and pharmacists in the submission of false Medicaid claims was not only foreseeable, it was an intended consequence of the alleged scheme of fraud." The court further explained that the FCA reaches beyond claims made directly by the defen-

---

[244]*Id.*

[245]*Id.* at 698.

[246]*Id.*

[247]31 U.S.C. §3729(a).

[248]United States *ex rel.* Franklin v. Parke-Davis, Div. of Warner-Lambert Co., 147 F. Supp. 2d 39 (D. Mass. 2001).

dants, "to all fraudulent attempts to cause the Government to pay out sums of money."[249] Although acknowledging that the relator's claims were in "territory that is not well charted by the existing decisional law," the court found that the claims fit squarely within the FCA's remedial purpose.[250]

## 2. Anti-Kickback Statute

To make a prima facie case of liability under the anti-kickback statute, the government must show that a defendant (1) knowingly and willfully (2) offered or paid remuneration to another person (3) to induce that person to purchase, order, or arrange for the ordering of any good or item for which payment may be made by a federal health care program.[251] As discussed above, numerous cases have included allegations that manufacturers' marketing and discounting practices violate the anti-kickback statute. Alternatively, and in addition, government enforcement agencies and *qui tam* relators have argued that violations of the anti-kickback statute trigger FCA liability in connection with the sale of pharmaceuticals.

### a. Kickbacks as False Claims: Lack of Certification

In most circuits, regulatory violations render a claim legally false under the FCA only where compliance with the regulation at issue is a condition of payment. In the case of discounts or other financial incentives provided to physicians by manufacturers, who do not make any certification to the government in connection with receiving a payment, manufacturers have argued that the FCA does not apply. The *Parke-Davis* court agreed and dismissed the relator's claim that the company violated the FCA in allegedly paying kickbacks to physicians.[252] The court held that violation of the anti-kickback statute was not a per se violation of the FCA.[253] The court further held that the relator failed to plead any facts showing that the company ever caused or induced a false certification of compliance with the anti-kickback statute.[254]

---

[249] *Id.* at 53 (citing United States v. Neifert-White Co., 390 U.S. 228, 233, (1968)). Similarly, in a 2005 False Claims Act case arising in the higher education context, a district court emphasized the role of the false statement in the government's decision to make a payment. United States *ex rel.* Main v. Oakland City Univ., 426 F.3d 914, 916 (7th Cir. 2005), *cert. denied,* 126 S. Ct. 1786 (2006). Specifically, the Seventh Circuit observed that, "[i]f a false statement is integral to a causal chain leading to payment, it is irrelevant how the federal bureaucracy has apportioned the statements among layers of paperwork." *Id.*

[250] 147 F. Supp. 2d at 53. Although the *Parke-Davis* court upheld the relator's allegations regarding the company's marketing of off-label uses, the court dismissed claims (with leave to amend) that the company's payment of alleged kickbacks violated the FCA where there was no evidence that the government's payment was conditioned upon any certification of compliance with the anti-kickback statute. *Id.* at 54.

[251] 42 U.S.C. §1320a–7b(b).

[252] 147 F. Supp. 2d 39 (D. Mass. 2001).

[253] *Id.* at 54–55.

[254] *Id.*

### b. Statutory Exception and Safe Harbor Protection: Discounts and Educational Grants

By its terms, the anti-kickback statute excepts from improper remuneration "a discount or other reduction in price obtained by a provider of services or other entity under a Federal health care program if the reduction in price is properly disclosed and appropriately reflected in the costs claimed or charges made by the provider or entity under a Federal health care program."[255]

Similarly, discounts provided to prescribers may be eligible for safe harbor protection, but such protection requires strict compliance with all applicable conditions set out in the applicable safe harbor. Various different discount safe harbor criteria apply to buyers, offerors, and sellers. Generally speaking, however, under the discount safe harbor, a discount does not violate the anti-kickback statute if: (1) the discount is in the form of a reduction in the price of the good or services based on an arms'-length transaction; (2) the discount is given at the time of sale; and (3) the manufacturer informs the customer of the discount and the customer's reporting obligations with respect to the discount.[256] Therefore, practices that fit the discount exception and/or safe harbor would not violate the anti-kickback statute and thus could not form the basis for an FCA claim.[257]

The OIG has also issued guidance on appropriate educational grants provided to health care providers.[258] The OIG acknowledges that funding of educational activities can provide valuable information to the health care community, but that these activities can run afoul of the anti-kickback law if not provided appropriately. Specifically, the OIG has stated that funding that is in any way contingent on the purchase of the product implicates the statute, even if the educational or research purpose is legitimate.[259] The OIG further cautions that educational activities may be used as inappropriate marketing purposes if the manufacturer has any influence over the substance of the program or presenter.[260] To remove the specter of suspicion, the OIG recommends that manufacturers separate grant-making functions from sales and marketing. Accordingly, strict compliance with the regulatory safe harbor and OIG guidance may help sanitize discounts or educational grants from classification as illegal kickbacks.[261]

### E. Class Action Lawsuits on Behalf of Private Payors and Patients

Following the avalanche of government and *qui tam* litigation against pharmaceutical companies, citizen groups and private payors have initiated broad-scale litigation against manufacturers on a variety of legal theories.

---

[255]42 U.S.C. §1320a–7b(b)(3)(A).

[256]42 C.F.R. §1001.952(h).

[257]Note, however, that the OIG has taken the position that the discount exception and discount safe harbor protect identical conduct, although at least one court has disagreed.

[258]OIG Compliance Program Guidance for Pharmaceutical Manufacturers, 68 Fed. Reg. 23,731, 23,735 (May 5, 2003).

[259]*Id.*

[260]*Id.*

[261]Compliance with informal agency guidance does not afford the same protections as compliance with statutory or regulatory exceptions.

For example, a group of cancer patients and health care plans brought a class action lawsuit against three major pharmaceutical manufacturers, including TAP, alleging that the companies conspired to artificially inflate the price of Lupron in violation of the civil provisions of RICO.[262] The suit also alleged that the companies violated state anti-competition laws for conduct similar to that targeted in the government's case against TAP. The court dismissed some of the RICO claims on the grounds that the plaintiffs were unable to establish the existence of an "enterprise" among the manufacturer defendants.[263]

Similarly, in December 2001, a class of consumer groups and senior citizens brought antitrust and civil RICO claims against Abbott Laboratories and more than 20 other manufacturers, challenging the companies' AWP data, alleging illegal discounts that were not passed on to consumers, and alleging that the companies improperly encouraged providers to bill for free samples.[264]

## F. Counterfeit Drugs, Illegal Wholesaling, and Internet Pharmacies

In addition to the sophisticated enforcement landscape governing drug pricing and marketing, the enforcement community is taking an active role in prosecuting various types of fraudulent prescription schemes. At the federal level, there is increased interest in developing new strategies to monitor Web-based pharmacies. Specifically, the White House has established a work group including members of the FDA, the Drug Enforcement Administration (DEA), the White House Office of Drug Control Policy, and various states to develop policies aimed at eradicating fraud by Internet pharmacies.[265] Likewise, a subcommittee of the House Committee on Energy and Commerce issued document requests to physicians and drug manufacturers seeking information regarding efforts taken to curb illegal prescriptions.

## G. New Laws Empowering Enforcement Agencies

Since the late 1990s, the OIG has expanded its presence in the pharmaceutical industry. The Medicare Prescription Drug, Improvement, and Modernization Act of 2003 (MMA) vested the OIG with explicit oversight of pharmaceutical pricing.[266] The MMA scraps the AWP pricing methodology for a new system that relies on average sales price (ASP).[267] The ASP system went into effect on January 1, 2005.[268] Under the new system, manufacturers have to

---

[262]*In re* Lupron Marketing & Sales Practices Litig., MDL No. 1430, Master File No. 01-CV-10861-RGS (D. Mass. May 28, 2001).

[263]*In re* Lupron, 295 F. Supp. 2d 148, 163 (D. Mass. 2003).

[264]Citizens for Consumer Justice v. Abbott Labs., Inc., Case No. 01-12257-PBS (D. Mass. Dec. 19, 2001).

[265]*See* http://www.whitehousedrugpolicy.gov/publications/pdf/interim_rpt.pdf.

[266]Medicare Prescription Drug, Improvement, and Modernization Act of 2003 (MMA), Pub. L. No. 108-173, 117 Stat. 2066 (codified as amended in scattered sections of 42 U.S.C.).

[267]Pub. L. No. 108-173, §303, *adding* §1874A *and amending* §§1842(o) and 1927(a) of the Social Security Act; the AWP system remained in force until December 31, 2004.

[268]42 U.S.C. §1395w-a3(a)(1).

report their ASPs to CMS on a quarterly basis. Also, the ASP pricing is now publicly accessible.[269]

Specifically, the MMA requires a senior officer of a pharmaceutical company to certify to the truth, completeness, and accuracy of pricing data reported by the company, which will be subject to audits by the OIG. This requirement could pave the way for new litigation against manufacturers. The MMA further authorizes the OIG to conduct periodic studies to determine the widely available market price (WAMP). If the WAMP is lower than the reported ASP, then the Secretary of Health and Human Services (HHS) may disregard the reported ASP and substitute the lesser of the WAMP or 103 percent of the average manufacturers' price.[270] Through the MMA, which authorizes civil monetary penalties of up to $10,000 for each price misrepresentation in reporting ASP, Congress affirmed the OIG's position that liability may result from inaccurate reporting of pharmaceutical pricing data.[271]

Furthermore, CMS established new record-keeping rules that require manufacturers to retain pricing data for at least 10 years.[272] Specifically, manufacturers must maintain data and any other materials from which the calculations of the average manufacturer price and best price are derived. If the manufacturer is aware of an audit or government investigation related to the data, records must be kept beyond 10 years.[273]

The 2005 Deficit Reduction Act (DRA) primarily affected Part D pricing of pharmaceuticals by increasing Medicaid rebates, decreasing Medicaid reimbursement to pharmacies, and changing pricing methodology by eliminating AWP in favor of Average Manufacturers' Price (AMP).[274] The DRA also made the AMP available to the public on the CMS Web site.[275] CMS proposed rules for implementing DRA pricing, including changes for AMP and best price calculations, and a final rule was issued on July 17, 2007.[276]

The DRA also provided a financial incentive for states to enact false claims statutes that establish liability to the state for false claims submitted to the state's Medicaid program.[277] Specifically, if the OIG determines that a state's false claims act meets the requirements of the DRA,[278] the state will obtain an increase in the amount it recovers under a state false claims act case. The OIG must determine in conjunction with the state attorney general whether a state has a false claims act that meets these requirements.[279] Additionally, the OIG published a notice setting forth its guidelines for reviewing state false claims acts.[280]

---

[269]*See* http://www.cms.hhs.gov/McrPartBDrugAvgSalesPrice/02_aspfiles.asp.

[270]MMA, §303(c)(1) (codified at 42 U.S.C. §1395w-3).

[271]H.R. Conf. Rep. No. 108-391, at 392 (2003).

[272]42 C.F.R. §447.534(h) & (i) (2007); 69 Fed. Reg. 68,815 (Nov. 26, 2004).

[273]42 C.F.R. §447.534(h)-(i).

[274]42 U.S.C. §1396r-8(e)(5).

[275]42 U.S.C. §1396r-8(b)(3)(A).

[276]72 Fed. Reg. 39142 (July 17, 2007).

[277]42 U.S.C. §1396d.

[278]*See* 42 U.S.C. §1396d(b).

[279]42 U.S.C. §1396h(b).

[280]*See* 71 Fed. Reg. 48,552 (Aug. 21, 2006).

In 2006, the OIG reviewed the following states' laws and determined each did not meet the requirements of the DRA: California, Florida, Indiana, Louisiana, Michigan, Nevada, and Texas.[281] The False Claims Act statutes of Illinois, Massachusetts, and Tennessee were deemed to meet the requirements.[282]

States have stepped up enforcement capabilities in other ways as well. For example, in 2004 Florida enacted a law targeting Medicaid prescription drug fraud.[283] Specifically, the proposal created criminal penalties for buying, selling, or trafficking Medicaid prescriptions and authorized the state attorney general's Office of Statewide Prosecution to investigate and prosecute Medicaid prescription fraud. Florida also enacted a law in 2006 requiring manufacturers to post the AWP for the 200 most frequently prescribed drugs for the elderly on a government-sponsored Web site.[284] The legislation further provided that seniors shall not pay more than a stated percentage of AWP for certain drugs. Similarly, in March 2004, New Mexico enacted a Medicaid False Claims Act that mirrors the federal False Claims Act and that will be used to address Medicaid prescription drug fraud.[285] And in California, although ultimately unsuccessful, the attorney general backed legislation that would have forced drug manufacturers to report accurate pricing data to "end what is arguably the largest, single-source of Medi-Cal fraud and abuse."[286] California also codified the OIG and PhRMA compliance guidelines with a mandate that requires pharmaceutical companies to adopt Comprehensive Compliance Programs (CCPs) to be posted on company Web sites.[287] CCPs must include specific annual limits on the amount of gifts, promotional materials, or other items that companies offer health care professionals.[288] The law is silent as to penalties for noncompliance.

The DRA also required that the OIG review the requirements for and the manner in which calculations of the AMP for prescription drugs are determined. The OIG performed this review in 2006 and determined that some AMP requirements were unclear and that the manufacturers' calculation methods were inconsistent.[289] The OIG reported to Congress that Medicare could have saved between $64 million and $164 million a year had correctly calculated prices been used to set reimbursement.[290] Further, while conducting price comparisons,

---

[281]*Available at* http://oig.hhs.gov/fraud/falseclaimsact.html.

[282]*Id.*

[283]FLA. STAT. ch. 2004–344 (2004).

[284]FLA. STAT. ch. 409.9066 (2006).

[285]2004 N.M. Adv. Legis. Serv. 49.

[286]S.B. 1170 (Cal. 2003); Press Release, Office of Attorney Gen., California Dep't of Justice, *Attorney General Lockyer and Legislators Unveil Bi-Partisan, 10-Point Plan to Fight Medi-Cal Fraud* (Apr. 21, 2004), *available at* http://www.caag.state.ca.us/newsalerts/2004/04-047.htm; *see also* http://ag.ca.gov/publications/agRprtSpnsrdLeg99-06_ada.pdf.

[287]S.B. 1765 (Cal. 2004), *codified* at CAL. HEALTH & SAFETY CODE §119402.

[288]The law excludes from the annual limit: drug samples, financial support for continuing education, and health educational scholarships, as well as payments for legitimate professional services (e.g., consulting services) provided by health care professionals.

[289]U.S. DEP'T OF HEALTH & HUMAN SERVS., OFFICE OF INSPECTOR GEN., SEMIANNUAL REPORT TO CONGRESS, APR. 1, 2006–SEPT. 30, 2006 [hereinafter OIG SEMIANNUAL REPORT, APR. 1, 2006–SEPT. 30, 2006], at i.

[290]*Id.* at ii.

the OIG determined that CMS' method for calculating a volume-weighted ASP was mathematically flawed.[291] Based on its review, the OIG recommended that the Secretary of HHS direct CMS to (1) clarify requirements for determining certain aspects of AMP, and (2) issue guidance on the implementation of AMP-related reimbursement provisions of the DRA.[292]

The 2007 OIG Work Plan highlighted several areas on which the OIG intended to focus its investigation and enforcement efforts. In the realm of Medicare Part B drug reimbursement, the OIG announced an intent to evaluate drug manufacturers' methodologies for computing ASP. Similarly, the OIG would carry out the MMA mandate that it conduct studies to determine widely available market prices for Part B drugs. The OIG intended to compare the widely available market price to the ASP.[293] Likewise, the OIG would be gathering data and information on the AMP for certain drugs and comparing these to ASP.[294] The OIG also intended to look for duplicate payments to physicians for Part B drugs purchased from vendors selected through a competitive bidding process and those directly reimbursed under the ASP system. The OIG also said it would evaluate whether independent dialysis facilities are billing Medicare for administering Epogen, an anemia drug, beyond medical necessity and physician orders. For Part D drugs, the OIG's 2007 Work Plan included examining various dual eligibility and duplicate claims concerns. It also intended to determine whether marketing materials for Medicare prescription drug plans are in compliance with CMS regulation and guidelines.[295]

The OIG also focused in its 2007 Work Plan on the following Medicaid prescription drug issues: review of the AMP for consistency with statute, rebate agreements, and CMS Releases; review of CMS' oversight of the Medicaid drug rebate program; pharmacies' ability to purchase drugs at AMP; computation of AMP and best price for Medicaid drug rebates, indexing generic drug rebates; examining fluctuations in average manufacturer prices; state use of CMS' AMP and retail sales price data (sharing of this data was mandated by the DRA); and reimbursement of drugs under the federal upper limit program, among other things.[296]

## H. Conclusion

Based on the fury of massive settlements, enactment of the MMA, and broad reach of the FCA and other anti-fraud provisions, litigation against

---

[291] *Id.* For summaries of OIG studies comparing ASP to AMP and WAMP, *see* OIG SEMIANNUAL REPORT, APR. 1, 2006–SEPT. 30, 2006, at 5.

[292] *Id.*

[293] U.S. DEP'T OF HEALTH & HUMAN SERVS., OFFICE OF INSPECTOR GEN., OIG WORK PLAN, FISCAL YEAR 2007, *available at* http://oig.hhs.gov/reading/workplan/2007/07wkpln.pdf.

[294] If the ASP for a particular drug exceeds 5% of the AMP, the OIG is charged with notifying the Secretary of HHS. Effective the next quarter, CMS must substitute the ASP for the widely available market price or 103% of the AMP. The widely available market price is the price that a prudent physician or supplier would pay for the drug or biological. 42 U.S.C. §1395w-3a(d).

[295] OIG WORK PLAN, FISCAL YEAR 2007, *available at* http://oig.hhs.gov/reading/workplan/2007/07wkpln.pdf.

[296] *Id.*

manufacturers and others in connection with prescription drugs will likely continue to be on the radar screens of *qui tam* relators, government regulators, and private plaintiffs.

## XIII. THE INTERSECTION OF THE STARK LAW AND THE FALSE CLAIMS ACT

### A. Introduction

Since the late 1990's, the government has expanded its enforcement efforts by trying to use the FCA to prosecute violations of the Stark law.[297] The Stark law prohibits physician "self-referral," which generally means referring Medicare and/or Medicaid patients for certain health care services to entities in which the physician or an immediate family member has a financial relationship.[298] The statute creates exceptions that permit physician compensation or ownership under certain circumstances.[299]

Unlike the anti-kickback statute, the Stark law is a "strict liability" civil statute that has no specific intent requirement. In other words, the government is not required to show that an organization acted "knowingly or willfully" to prove a violation of the prohibition. Furthermore, there was relatively little litigation in the past because the interpretative regulations were not finalized until 2004 and the full scope of the law had not been defined. With the publication of the Stark II/Phase II final regulations in 2004,[300] and Stark III in 2007,[301] enforcement efforts relating to Stark/FCA violations were expected to increase.[302]

### B. Basis for Liability

In FCA cases involving allegations of regulatory noncompliance, the government typically alleges that the organization made false statements to obtain payment through signed certification statements accompanying a cost report, CMS Form 1500, or other claim form.[303] The certifications on these forms often state that the person signing certifies that he or she has complied

---

[297] *See, e.g.,* United States *ex rel.* Thompson v. Columbia/HCA Healthcare Corp., 20 F. Supp. 2d 1017 (S.D. Tex. 1998); United States *ex rel.* Barbera v. Tenet, No. 97-CV-6590 (S.D. Fla. May 13, 1997), *notice of election to intervene in part and to decline to intervene in part* (Feb. 16, 2001); United States *ex rel.* Pogue v. Diabetes Treatment Ctrs. of Am., Inc., 238 F. Supp. 2d 258 (D.D.C. 2002).

[298] 42 U.S.C. §1395nn.

[299] 42 U.S.C. §1395nn(b)–(e).

[300] 69 Fed. Reg. 16,053 (Mar. 26, 2004).

[301] 72 Fed. Reg. 51,012 (Sept. 5, 2007). The *Federal Register* notice announcing the Stark III regulations is available as Appendix B-4 on the disk accompanying this volume.

[302] For detailed discussion of the Stark law and the Stark II/Phase II regulations, and a first look at the Phase III final rule, see Chapter 2 (Crane, Federal Physician Self-Referral Restrictions), and the Addendum to Chapter 2.

[303] *See, e.g.,* Gublo v. Novacare, Inc., 62 F. Supp. 2d 347 (D. Mass. 1999); *Pogue,* 238 F. Supp. 2d 258.

with all applicable laws and regulations.[304] These certifications form the basis for an "implied certification" theory, under which FCA liability may lie "where the government pays funds to a party, and would not have paid those funds had it known of a violation of a law or regulation, [thus,] the claim submitted for those funds contained an implied certification of compliance with the law or regulation and was fraudulent."[305]

According to certain courts, liability under the implied certification theory requires analysis of whether the government actually conditions payment upon compliance with the statute or regulation at issue.[306] Thus, under this analysis, certification of compliance with the statute or regulation must be so material to the claim for payment that the government would not have honored the claim if it were aware of the violation.[307] Some courts have held that noncompliance with the Stark law is "material" in this way.[308]

## C. Litigation Involving the Stark Law and the FCA

The government has achieved some successful settlements using the Stark law and the FCA in tandem. In March 2004, Tenet Health Systems paid a record $22.5 million to resolve allegations that a Florida hospital owned by the chain billed Medicare for referrals by physicians with whom it had prohibited financial arrangements.[309] The government intervened in a *qui tam* action alleging that Tenet violated the FCA by submitting claims for reimbursement to the Medicare program for designated health services provided in violation of the Stark law based on Tenet's purchase of certain physician practices.[310]

---

[304]For example, the certification statement in the Medicare Health Care Provider/Supplier Application provides in pertinent part: "I understand that payment of a claim by Medicare or other federal health care programs is conditioned on the claim and the underlying transaction complying with such laws, regulations and program instructions." OMB Approval No. 0938-0685. *See also* CMS Form 2552 (cost report) that is certified as follows: "I further certify that I am familiar with the laws and regulations regarding the provision of health care services and that the services identified in this cost report were provided in compliance with such laws and regulations."

[305]*Pogue,* 238 F. Supp. 2d at 264 (citing Ab-Tech Constr., Inc. v. United States, 31 Fed. Cl. 429, 434 (1994), *aff'd,* 57 F.3d 1084 (Fed. Cir. 1995)).

[306]*Id.* at 265–66. *See also* United States *ex rel.* Mikes v. Straus, 274 F.3d 687, 699 (2d Cir. 2001) (although the *Mikes* court stated in dicta that the implied certification theory did not apply in the health care context "because the False Claims Act was not designed for use as a blunt instrument to enforce compliance with all medical regulations—but rather only those regulations that are a precondition to payment"). *Id.*

[307]*Pogue,* 238 F. Supp. 2d at 264.

[308]*See, e.g.,* United States *ex rel.* Thompson v. Columbia/HCA Healthcare Corp., 20 F. Supp. 2d 1017, 1047 (S.D. Tex. 1998); *Pogue,* 238 F. Supp. 2d 258 (citing 42 U.S.C. §1395nn(a)(1)(B), which provides "the entity may not present or cause to be presented a claim under this subchapter or bill to any individual, third-party payor, or other entity for designated health services furnished pursuant to a referral prohibited under subparagraph (A)").

[309]Press Release, U.S. Dep't of Justice, *Tenet Healthcare to Pay $22.5 Million for Improperly Billing Medicare* (Mar. 24, 2004), *available at* http://www.usdoj.gov/usao/fls/Tenet. html.

[310]United States *ex rel.* Barbera v. Tenet, No. 97-CV-6590 (S.D. Fla. May 13, 1997), *notice of election to intervene in part and to decline to intervene in part* (Feb. 16, 2001).

The government claimed that Tenet paid physicians amounts that exceeded payments to virtually all similarly situated health care professionals across the country.[311]

In December 2003, a Michigan hospital paid $6.25 million to settle allegations that the hospital violated the FCA. The government alleged that the hospital violated the Stark law by paying compensation to certain vascular surgeons, which the government contended exceeded fair market value. In that case, the government alleged that the hospital leased office space to two primary care physicians below fair market value and at terms that were not commercially reasonable.[312]

Also in December 2003, a hospital in Rapid City, South Dakota, paid $6.5 million to resolve allegations that it had improperly billed Medicare for referrals from a group of oncologists with which the hospital had a prohibited financial relationship.[313]

Additional settlements are likely given the 2007 activities of a multi-agency strike force of federal, state, and local investigators investigating providers for alleged false claims, violations of anti-kickback statutes, and conspiracy to defraud Medicare. The strike force uses real time analysis of Medicare billing data and has so far focused on infusion therapy and DME suppliers.[314] The work of the strike force led to 38 arrests in Florida by May 2007.[315] Between March and August 2007, efforts of the strike force had led to four convictions of providers, at least one of which was related to kickbacks paid to physicians by a DME provider.[316]

### D. Defense Strategies

Courts have been reluctant to uphold defense challenges to the Stark/FCA enforcement scheme, concluding that compliance with the Stark law is material for Medicare payment purposes.[317] But defendants have been successful in disputing the underlying allegations of noncompliance with the Stark law. Specifically, several health care providers have successfully defended Stark/

---

[311]*Id.*

[312]Press Release, U.S. Dep't of Justice, *Grand Rapids' Metropolitan Hospital & Related Entities to Pay U.S. $6.25 Million to Resolve False Claims Allegations* (Dec. 10, 2003), *available at* http://www.usdoj.gov/opa/pr/2003/December/03_civ_679.htm.

[313]United States *ex rel.* Johnson-Porchardt v. Rapid City Reg'l Hosp., 01-CV-0519-KES (D.S.D. Jan. 21, 2003); Press Release, U.S. Dep't of Justice, *Justice Department Announces Settlements with South Dakota Hospital and Physicians for $6,525,000* (Dec. 20, 2002), *available at* http://www.usdoj.gov/opa/pr/2002/December/02_civ_739.htm.

[314]Press Release, U.S. Dep't of Justice, *Strike Force Formed to Target Fraudulent Billing of Medicare Program by Health Care Companies* (May 9, 2007), *available at* http://ww.usdoj.gov/opa/pr/2007/May/07_ag-339.html.

[315]*Id.*

[316]Press Release, U.S. Dep't of Justice, *Owner and Operator of Durable Medical Equipment Company Convicted of Medicare Fraud* (Aug. 31, 2007), *available at* http://www.usdoj.gov/opa/pr/2007/August07_crm_678.html.

[317]United States *ex rel.* Thompson v. Columbia/HCA Healthcare Corp., 20 F. Supp. 2d 1017, 1047 (S.D. Tex. 1998); United States *ex rel.* Pogue v. Diabetes Treatment Ctr. of Am., Inc., 238 F. Supp. 2d 258 (D.D.C. 2002).

FCA cases by presenting evidence that the suspect transactions complied with the Stark law or its exceptions.[318]

For example, in 2003, a federal district court in Illinois dismissed allegations that a hospital violated the Stark law in connection with purchases of physician practices.[319] The court found that the government failed to present evidence demonstrating that the hospital's purchases were above fair market value.[320] The case was initiated by a physician whistleblower who was previously in a contractual relationship with the defendant hospital. The court found a lack of consensus among the circuits over whether a *qui tam* relator could use the FCA as a vehicle for pursuing violations of the Stark and anti-kickback laws, but dismissed the case on summary judgment based on evidence that the suspect transactions did not violate the Stark law.[321]

Similarly, in 2002, the federal district court in Illinois had dismissed allegations that Advocate Health Care violated the Stark law in connection with the purchase of physician practices and certain employment agreements.[322] The court found that the relator had presented no evidence that the transaction did not fall within the Stark law's "isolated transactions" exception.[323] The court also held that a percentage compensation arrangement between the hospital and its physician employees did not run afoul of the Stark law, because the compensation depended on the work performed by the physician and not the value of any referrals.[324]

Also in 2002, a Michigan hospital defeated allegations that it violated the Stark law and the FCA in connection with medical office building leases entered into with referring physicians.[325] Following trial on the issue of whether the leases were at fair market value, the court held that the hospital did not violate the Stark law. The court wrote, "the Government has failed to present any evidence to establish that because of potential patient referrals, McLaren [the hospital] paid a higher rental rate than it otherwise would have paid, or that FOR [realty company] and the Defendant physicians received a higher rental rate than they would have otherwise received because of any patient referrals that McLaren might receive from the FOA [medical group] physicians."[326]

---

[318]*See, e.g.,* United States *ex rel.* Obert-Hong v. Advocate Health Care, 211 F. Supp. 2d 1045 (N.D. Ill. 2002); United States *ex rel.* Goodstein v. McLaren Reg'l Med. Ctr., 202 F. Supp. 2d 671 (E.D. Mich. 2002); United States *ex rel.* Perales v. Saint Margaret's Hosp., 243 F. Supp. 2d 843 (C.D. Ill. 2003).

[319]*Perales,* 243 F. Supp. 2d 843.

[320]*Id.*

[321]*Id.*

[322]*Obert-Hong,* 211 F. Supp. 2d 1045.

[323]*Id.* at 1050.

[324]*Id.* at 1050–51.

[325]United States *ex rel.* Goodstein v. McLaren Reg'l Med. Ctr., 202 F. Supp. 2d 671 (E.D. Mich. 2002).

[326]*Id.* at 686.

Additionally, some providers have been successful in attacking the pleadings of FCA cases based on Stark law violations, either for failure to state a claim or failure to plead facts with sufficient particularity.[327]

## E. Conclusion

Given the courts' expanded view of the applicability of the FCA and the issuance of the final Stark II and III regulations, health care organizations can expect increased enforcement efforts aimed at their relationships with physicians. As demonstrated by these settlements and court decisions, health care organizations are best advised to structure such relationships in strict compliance with the Stark law.

## XIV. EMERGING ISSUES: SARBANES-OXLEY AND THE NEW ERA OF CORPORATE RESPONSIBILITY

### A. Relevant Provisions of the Sarbanes-Oxley Act

The Sarbanes-Oxley Act[328] was enacted in 2002 following the highly publicized demise of the Enron, Global Crossing, and WorldCom corporations. The accounting scandals plaguing these companies resulted in an erosion of public confidence in corporate integrity. Thus, Congress set out to create a regulatory scheme that would infuse a new era of responsibility among publicly traded corporations and their executives.

The three main areas of new regulation under Sarbanes-Oxley include increased responsibility for corporate executives and boards of directors, increased corporate disclosure requirements, and independence of auditors. Sarbanes-Oxley also created new criminal penalties for corporate finance-related crimes.[329] Specifically, the Act requires certain officers to certify that the company's financial statements contain no misstatements and that the

---

[327]*See* United States *ex rel.* Woods v. North Arkansas Reg'l Med. Ctr., No. 03-3086, 2006 WL 2583662 (W.D. Ark. Sept. 7, 2006); United States *ex rel.* Grandeau v. Cancer Treatment Ctrs. of Am., No. 99 C 8287, WL 2035567 (N.D. Ill. Aug. 19, 2005); United States *ex rel.* Schmidt v. Zimmer, Inc., No. 00-1044, WL 1806502 (E.D. Pa. July 29, 2005).

[328]15 U.S.C. §7201 *et seq.*

[329]Based on mandates in Sarbanes-Oxley, the United States Sentencing Commission (the Commission) made permanent emergency amendments to the white-collar fraud provisions of the federal sentencing guidelines to include increased penalties. Press Release, U.S. Sentencing Comm'n, *Sentencing Commission Toughens Penalties for White Collar Fraudsters* (Apr. 18, 2003), *available at* http://www.ussc.gov/PRESS/rel0403.htm. For example, an officer of a publicly traded corporation who defrauds more than 250 employees or investors of more than $1 million will receive a sentence of more than 10 years in prison (121–51 months) under the emergency amendment, almost double the term of imprisonment previously provided by the guidelines. The amendment also increases penalties significantly for offenders who obstruct justice by destroying documents or records. Defendants who substantially interfere with the administration of justice by shredding a substantial number of documents or especially probative documents will receive a guideline sentencing range of approximately 3 years' imprisonment (30–37 months). Likewise, in April 2004, the Commission adopted more stringent requirements for corporate compliance programs under the guidelines. Press Release, U.S. Sentencing Comm'n, *Sentencing Commission Toughens Requirements for Corporate Compliance and Ethics Programs* (Apr. 13, 2004), *available at* http://www.ussc.gov/PRESS/rel0404.htm.

financial information provided fairly represents the financial condition of the company. Corporate officers who knowingly sign false financial statements can face fines up to $5 million and up to 20 years in prison.[330]

While there are relatively few publicly traded health care corporations that fall directly within the reach of Sarbanes-Oxley, several of Sarbanes-Oxley's provisions may extend to nonprofits. For example, the Act imposes criminal penalties on anyone who destroys documents "for use in an official proceeding."[331] Additionally, Sarbanes-Oxley creates new protections for whistleblowers and criminalizes whistleblower retaliation that applies in both for-profit and nonprofit settings alike.[332] Furthermore, commentators expect that states will amend existing nonprofit corporate laws to more closely mirror Sarbanes-Oxley.[333]

## B. Recent Litigation

In 2003, executives of the giant rehabilitation company, HealthSouth Corporation, faced criminal charges in connection with allegedly filing false financial statements with the Securities and Exchange Commission (SEC).[334] Thereafter, the SEC launched an investigation of HealthSouth and its executives alleging accounting fraud against the company and two of its executives.[335]

The SEC complaint filed against HealthSouth CEO Richard Scrushy alleged that Scrushy caused the company to overstate its earnings by at least $1.4 billion.[336] The SEC alleged that Scrushy directed HealthSouth's accountants to artificially inflate the company's earnings to match earnings projected by Wall Street analysts. The complaint further alleges that by the third quarter of 2002, the company's assets were overstated by at least $800 million, or approximately 10 percent of total assets. Scrushy certified the company's annual financial statements submitted to the SEC, the Form 10-K, stating that the statements contained "no untrue statement of a material fact." In June 2005, HealthSouth paid $100 million to settle the suit.

---

[330] 18 U.S.C. §1350.

[331] 18 U.S.C. §1512(c).

[332] 18 U.S.C. §1513(e).

[333] *See* Cynthia Reaves, *Corporate Responsibility Issues for Board Members and Senior Executives of Nonprofit Corporations in a Post-Sarbanes-Oxley Act Environment,* CCH Healthcare Compliance Ltr. (Jan. 12, 2004); BoardSource, *The Sarbanes-Oxley Act and Implications for Nonprofit Organizations* (2003). California passed the "Nonprofit Integrity Act" (NIA), which took effect January 1, 2005. Under the NIA, nonprofit organizations with gross revenues over $2 million must comply with certain auditing and disclosure requirements. S.B. 1262 (Cal. 2004). For further discussion of the Sarbanes-Oxley Act, see Chapter 1, at Section I.B., and Chapter 8, at Sections II.C. and V.

[334] *See, e.g.,* United States v. Harris, No. CR-03-3-0157-S (N.D. Ala. Mar. 31, 2003) (charging Emory Harris, Vice President of Finance and Assistant Controller of HealthSouth, with conspiracy to commit wire fraud and securities fraud and falsifying financial information filed with the SEC).

[335] SEC v. HealthSouth Corp., No. CV-03-J-06150S (N.D. Ala. Mar. 19, 2003), *available at* http://www.sec.gov/litigation/complaints/comphealths.htm. HealthSouth CEO Richard Scrushy was later acquitted of all charges in the accounting scandal. Greg Farrell, *Scrushy Acquitted of All 36 Charges,* USA TODAY (June 28, 2005).

[336] *Health South,* No. CV-03-J-061505.

In a 2003 settlement of a shareholder derivative suit with HCA, Inc., the New York State Comptroller touted provisions of the agreement that forced the company to implement new corporate governance standards that were perceived as "tougher" than Sarbanes-Oxley.[337] In 1997, the comptroller sued HCA in his capacity as sole trustee of the state's public pension fund, valued at about $100 billion, alleging that the fund was damaged by health care fraud at HCA. Under the terms of the settlement, HCA is required to assemble an independent board of directors under a stringent definition of "independence."[338] Additionally, the board's audit committee, comprised solely of independent directors, will have more power than under the pre-Sarbanes-Oxley law, and the board is mandated to maintain an ethics and compliance committee to monitor corporate ethics and oversee compliance with applicable standards.[339]

At this time, private or nonprofit health care organizations appear to be shielded from the reach of Sarbanes-Oxley. In the future, however, it is likely that both the courts and states will use Sarbanes-Oxley as a guideline for examining corporate governance in these organizations.

## XV. Conclusion

Although the government enforcement agencies perceive that health care fraud and abuse have increased significantly in terms of the dollars paid out because of fraud and abuse, there is at least anecdotal evidence that fraudulent and abusive practices have not actually increased, but rather, the ever-changing definition of fraud and abuse is creating the perception of increasing fraudulent and abusive practices.[340] Payment practices that previously would have generated an overpayment assessment at most are now being subjected to investigation by enforcement agencies for fraud and abuse.

Concern on the part of some members of the health care industry about continued changes in the definition of fraud and abuse is not unwarranted. Indeed, in a December 1997 Clarification issued by CMS to Section 7500 of the *Medicare Carriers Manual*, Medicare carriers are instructed that their medical review programs must ensure that all payments made by the Medicare program are appropriate, accurate, and consistent with Medicare policy. Obviously, this is a perfectly appropriate goal of any medical review program. However, the 1997 amendment also states as follows:

> Problem areas identified will represent a continuum of intent for those providers involved. For example, some inappropriate billing will be the result of provider

---

[337]Press Release, New York State Comptroller, *Precedent-Setting Corporate Governance Plan Established in Settlement of HCA Shareholder Suit* (Feb. 4, 2003), *available at* http://www.osc.state.ny.us/press/releases/feb03/20403.htm.

[338]*Id.*

[339]*Id.*

[340]In fact, the OIG has conceded that its estimate of approximately $20.3 billion in overpayments during fiscal year 1997 could be the result of problems ranging from inadvertent mistakes to outright fraud and abuse. *See* Office of Inspector Gen., U.S. Dep't of Health & Human Servs., Audit of HCFA's 1997 FY Financial Statements, n.12 (1998).

misunderstandings or failure to pay adequate attention to Medicare policy. Other incidents of inappropriate billing will represent calculated plans to knowingly acquire unwarranted payment. *Either case* results in abusive billing practices.

Before the December 1997 amendment, inappropriate billings that were the result of a provider misunderstanding or a failure to pay adequate attention to Medicare policy were not considered to be examples of abuse. Indeed, under the governing Medicare statutes, regulations, and manual provisions, in situations in which there was a provider misunderstanding of a billing requirement, the liability for overpayments resulting from the misunderstanding could be waived under appropriate circumstances.[341] The December 1997 verification not only made such waiver unlikely, it also suggested that a misunderstanding may be construed as billing abuse by enforcement agencies.

In the resulting enforcement environment, in which virtually any mistake can be construed by an enforcement agency as fraudulent or abusive conduct, it is absolutely critical that lawyers defending health care clients accused of fraud and abuse be mindful of the importance of fundamental principles of law, such as the supremacy of statutes and regulations over guidelines, and be certain that they are able to apply the appropriate historical and factual context to allegations of possible fraud and abuse.

---

[341]42 U.S.C. §§1395gg, 1395pp.

# 5

# Legal Issues Surrounding Hospital and Physician Relationships*

*Dennis M. Barry, Vinson & Elkins L.L.P., Washington, D.C. The author gratefully acknowledges the substantial assistance provided by his colleagues, Douglas Grimm, Lori Mihalich, and Melissa Waugh.

## I. Background on the Nature of Relationships Between Hospitals and Physicians and the Factors Affecting Those Relationships

In these early years of the twenty-first century, relationships between hospitals and physicians are often complex but are founded in mutual dependence. In the first half of the twentieth century, many hospitals were established, owned, and operated by physicians. These facilities often operated as an extension of physician practices. If any such hospitals continue to exist now, they are rare. Hospitals require too much capital and too much management time for an individual physician to want to undertake the responsibilities of operating a hospital facility. Just as hospital ownership is no longer commonly held by physicians (other than small interests as limited partners), hospital management is generally entrusted to professionals whose training concentrates on facility and personnel management rather than the clinical management of patients.

Hospitals need physicians. Under state law, only a physician can order hospital services;[1] literally no services can be furnished by a hospital without the order of a physician (or in limited instances, the order of certain other "mid-level" health professionals).[2] Physicians are not ignorant of their importance to a hospital's financial viability. Commonly, physicians will remind hospital administrators that millions of dollars in hospital charges arise from patients the physicians have admitted. But hospital dependence on physicians is not limited to reliance on referrals and orders made by physicians. The accreditation standards of the Joint Commission, as well as the Medicare conditions of participation, require hospitals to have physicians on their governing boards, a medical director who is a physician, an organized medical staff, and physician control of many medical functions.[3]

Hospital dependence on physicians is not one-sided; many physicians cannot function without hospitals. Notwithstanding occasional unflattering portraits of physicians as being interested solely in their wealth or their egos, what motivates most physicians more than anything else is seeing that their patients are treated as effectively as possible. In this era, that level of care requires a hospital. A hospital is necessary not just for the availability of 24-hour nursing service but also because only a large institution can afford the immense capital expenditures for services that are accepted as necessary. For example, magnetic resonance imaging (MRI) is now routinely ordered, but the machines and their sites require capital expenditures well in excess of $1 million. While the price tag for an MRI is a dramatic illustration of the cost of

---

[1]*See, e.g.*, Tex. Health & Safety Code Ann. §162, Subch. D; Md. Code Regs. 10.07.01.24.

[2]The categories of various "physician extenders" such as nurse practitioners and physician assistants who have been afforded increased stature and power in recent years, including the power to order certain services, do not, at least yet, have any material effect on the virtually exclusive control physicians have in determining what health care services shall be furnished.

[3]Joint Comm'n on Accreditation of Healthcare Orgs., Hospital Accreditation Standards, LD.1.10, MS.1.10, and MS.2.10 (2006).

capital equipment, it is not unique. Mid-size community hospitals routinely spend $10 million or more a year on new capital equipment.

A physician's dependence on a hospital varies greatly, depending on the physician's specialty. Indeed, there is an increasing trend for some family practice physicians to avoid treating their patients in hospitals. When their patients require admission, family practitioners may refer patients to a "hospitalist." Other physician specialties rely heavily on the availability of hospital services. For example, surgeons conduct most surgeries in hospitals, particularly the more complicated or dangerous procedures that cannot be done on an outpatient basis. A cardiac surgeon relies on the skills of the operating room team, including specialty nurses, perfusionists, and anesthesiologists (including certified registered nurse anesthetists supervised by anesthesiologists) to furnish a very high level of service expertly. Thus, surgeons and other physicians will lobby hospitals to purchase certain types of equipment and hire qualified personnel so that the physician can furnish services using that equipment and personnel—services they otherwise would be unable to perform. Some physician specialties, such as pathologists, anesthesiologists, and radiologists, work almost exclusively in hospitals. Unlike their counterparts in private practice, hospital-based physician specialists are dependent on hospitals to practice their specialties.

The growth of managed care has also affected relationships between hospitals and physicians. Managed care payors often seek to contract with an existing network for the obvious reason that it is much easier to have a single contract than to try to assemble a network of multiple individual contracts with separate physician practices. Thus, it is advantageous for physicians to join a larger group, and one way to do so is to become affiliated with a network. Sometimes a hospital controls the network. One reason that physicians may affiliate with a network that has hospital involvement is the need for capital. Managed care payors often try to shift risk to contracting physicians and providers. Bearing that risk requires access to capital, and even physicians with handsome incomes often have very little capital, or at least insufficient capital compared to the amount needed to bear risk in the world of managed care. Managed care also reduces a physician's discretion in ordering services in terms of both the volume and nature of services ordered, as well as the choice of service providers. Thus, in some markets, it is more important for a hospital to have contracts with managed care payors than good relationships with referring physicians, because the payor controls where the services will be furnished.

Relationships between hospitals and physicians are obviously affected by the relative balance of power between the parties. This relationship is subject to the rules of supply and demand, with physicians in overbedded urban areas with multiple hospitals having much more power than physicians practicing in areas with a single hospital. Moreover, there simply are cultural differences among various parts of the country, so that physicians are treated with more deference in some areas than in others.

Physician and hospital relationships can run the gamut from the physician's having no direct economic connection to the hospital to the hospital's being the sole source of the physician's income. For example, there is often no direct economic or contractual relationship between hospitals and physicians. Physicians, as members of the hospital's "voluntary" medical staff, admit patients and order services in their sole discretion, and may serve on more than one voluntary medical staff at a time. As voluntary medical staff members, physicians may also serve on various hospital medical staff committees and on hospital boards of directors.[4] It is also common for hospitals to have limited contractual relationships with physicians. For example, a hospital may lease to a physician space in an adjacent medical office building. Hospitals also commonly pay physicians to assume medical director responsibilities in various departments, but these physicians continue to spend the bulk of their time and derive the bulk of their income from their private practices. Finally, there are situations in which physicians are employed by, or contract with, a hospital on a full-time basis, and are solely dependent on the hospital for their incomes.

## II. Legal Issues

A host of legal issues can come into play in the relationships between physicians and hospitals, including:

- Medical staff bylaw rights and responsibilities;
- Contractual duties, obligations, and remedies;
- Malpractice liability and vicarious liability;
- EMTALA[5] compliance;
- Antitrust laws as they affect exclusive contracts;
- State laws on the corporate practice of medicine and fee splitting;
- Federal and state laws barring illegal remuneration or kickbacks;[6]
- Limitations applicable to federally tax-exempt organizations, including the bars on inurement and private benefit;[7]
- Federal Stark law and state laws barring certain financial relationships between physicians and entities from which they order services;[8] and
- Medicare reimbursement requirements.

The purpose of this chapter is not to explore these areas in depth, but rather to illustrate the practical impact these laws have on relationships between hospitals and physicians, so that lawyers can try at the outset to structure relationships to comply with the law and, in the event of an unfortunate occurrence, minimize the resulting costs and disruptions.

Several key legal developments in this area are worthy of note at the outset of this discussion—the continuing evolution of the Stark II regulations and final regulations relating to health information technology. First, in March 2004, the Department of Health and Human Services (HHS) Centers for Medicare and Medicaid Services (CMS) issued the anxiously-awaited interim final rule on

---

[4]In nonprofit corporations, the board of directors may often be called the board of trustees. Regardless of name, it is the governing board of the hospital.

[5]Emergency Medical Treatment and Active Labor Act, 42 U.S.C. §1395dd; implementing regulations at 42 C.F.R. §489.24.

[6]42 U.S.C. §1320a-7b(b); *e.g.*, Ala. Code §22-1-11(b) & (c); N.J. Stat. Ann. §30:4D-17(c); Va. Code §32.1-315(A) & (B). (See Appendix A-1 on the disk accompanying this volume for full text of the anti-kickback statute.)

[7]26 U.S.C. §501(c)(3).

[8]42 U.S.C. §1395nn; *e.g.*, Fla. Stat. Ann. §483.245(1).

Phase II of the Stark II regulations; correcting amendments were published on September 24, 2004.[9] These regulations became effective on July 26, 2004. The Stark II/Phase II rule created more Stark law exceptions and provided clarification of certain existing Stark law exceptions. In 2007, CMS then published a Stark proposed rule (what has been referred to as Stark 2.5)[10] as well as its Stark Phase III Final Regulations.[11] The final rule includes clarifications and relatively minor modifications to the Phase II Interim Final Regulations.[12]

It is quite important for hospitals and physicians to monitor their relationships and ensure that they are Stark compliant, because if a physician in a financial relationship with an entity refers patients for certain "designated health services" (DHS) to that entity, and does not fully satisfy the criteria of an appropriate Stark law exception, it can be very costly. The penalty for failing to comply with an exception when the Stark law is implicated, even if there is no improper intent, is the denial of payment to the entity for almost all DHS[13] furnished to Medicare and Medicaid beneficiaries that were provided pursuant to referrals made by the physician who had the financial relationship with the entity (or whose family member did). Further, if the entity knew or should have known that the referrals were prohibited, the entity could be subject to a civil monetary penalty of up to $15,000 per occurrence.[14] Both unwitting and knowing violations of the Stark law and regulations could result in many thousands, if not millions, of dollars in losses to affected entities.[15]

Second, in August 2006, the HHS Office of Inspector General (OIG) and CMS published anti-kickback safe harbors and exceptions to the Stark law as a response to rapid growth in electronic health information technology (HIT). The regulations, which address both electronic prescribing and electronic health records arrangements,[16] came both as a result of President Bush's Health Information Technology Plan announced in 2004,[17] and as a result of requirements contained in Section 101 of the Medicare Prescription Drug, Improvement, and Modernization Act of 2003[18] (MMA) to offer protection for hospitals, group

---

[9]69 Fed. Reg. 16,054 (Mar. 26, 2004); 69 Fed. Reg. 57,226 (Sept. 24, 2004) (correcting amendment).

[10]72 Fed. Reg. 38,122, 38,179–87 (July 12, 2007).

[11]72 Fed. Reg. 51,012 (Sept. 5, 2007). The *Federal Register* document is provided as Appendix B-4 on the disk accompanying this volume.

[12]For additional discussion of the Phase III regulations, see the Addendum to Chapter 2 (Crane, Federal Physician Self-Referral Restrictions). Further changes to the Stark regulations are also expected when the 2008 Physician Fee Schedule regulations are finalized.

[13]DHS are defined at 42 U.S.C. §1395nn(h)(6) and include inpatient and outpatient hospital services. The scope of these services is further defined in regulations at 42 C.F.R. §411.351.

[14]42 U.S.C. §1395nn(g)(3).

[15]The Stark law and Phase II regulations are discussed in detail in Chapter 2 (Crane, Federal Physician Self-Referral Restrictions) of this volume.

[16]71 Fed. Reg. 45,110 (Aug. 8, 2006) (anti-kickback regulations), Appendix A-3 on the disk accompanying this volume; 71 Fed. Reg. 45,140 (Aug. 8, 2006) (Stark regulations), Appendix B-6 on the disk accompanying this volume.

[17]Fact Sheet: Improving Care and Saving Lives Through Health IT, *available at* http://www.whitehouse.gov/news/release/2005/01/20050127-2.html.

[18]Pub. L. No. 108-173.

practices, prescription drug plan sponsors, and Medicare Advantage organizations that seek to provide physicians with the technology for electronic pre-scribing.[19] The Stark HIT regulations will be discussed in greater detail in Section III.H., below.

## III. RELATIONSHIPS WITH PHYSICIANS WHO ARE MEMBERS OF THE VOLUNTARY MEDICAL STAFF

### A. Medical Staff Membership

#### 1. Open Staff

Medical staff bylaws are created by the medical staff, but must be approved by the hospital board of directors.[20] Statutory, regulatory, and accreditation standards govern how the medical staff is organized and the way its bylaws and related documents are drafted.[21] Although the medical staff may resist admitting particular individuals or classes of individuals to the medical staff, the hospital bears the responsibility and liability for any illegal or wrongful conduct.

A threshold issue in regard to medical staff bylaws is who is entitled to admission to the medical staff. In some states, provisions of the medical staff bylaws are deemed to be contractual, and provisions concerning who may join the staff are viewed as open offers.[22] Thus, physicians or other practitioners who meet the requirements set forth in the medical staff bylaws must be admitted to membership. Medicare conditions of participation also require hospitals to open their medical staffs to qualified physicians,[23] although many teaching hospitals condition membership on a willingness to assume teaching responsibilities, and hospitals may enter "exclusive" contractual arrangements that limit other physicians' opportunities for admission to the medical staff.

---

[19]*Id.* at 59,185.

[20]JOINT COMM'N ON ACCREDITATION OF HEALTHCARE ORGS., HOSPITAL ACCREDITATION STANDARDS, MS.1.10, MS.1.20, and MS.1.30 (2006).

[21]*See* Health Care Quality Improvement Act of 1986, 42 U.S.C. §§11101 *et seq.*; Americans with Disabilities Act of 1990, 42 U.S.C. §§12101 *et seq.*; Hospital Survey and Construction Act of 1946 (Hill-Burton Act), 42 U.S.C. §§291 *et seq.*; Fair Credit Reporting Act, 15 U.S.C. §§1681 *et seq.*; 42 C.F.R. §§482.12, 482.22; JOINT COMM'N ON ACCREDITATION OF HEALTHCARE ORGS., HOSPITAL ACCREDITATION STANDARDS (2006).

[22]*See, e.g.,* Strauss v. Peninsula Reg'l Med. Ctr., 916 F. Supp. 528, 536 (D. Md. 1996) (stating that Maryland law is well settled that hospital bylaws are enforceable contracts); Islami v. Covenant Med. Ctr., 822 F. Supp. 1361, 1370–71 (N.D. Iowa 1992) (recognizing a split of authority in the states on this issue, the court found that the majority view that a hospital's medical staff bylaws constitute a contract between the hospital and the medical staff is in accord with Iowa law); Gonzalez v. San Jacinto Methodist Hosp., 880 S.W.2d 436 (Tex. App.-Tex-arkana 1994) (writ denied); *contra* Zipper v. Health Midwest, 978 S.W.2d 398, 416 (Mo. Ct. App. 1998) (holding that hospital bylaws are not contracts under Missouri law due to lack of consideration); Robles v. Humana Hosp. Cartersville, 785 F. Supp. 989, 1000-01 (N.D. Ga. 1992).

[23]42 C.F.R. §482.22.

## 2. *Open Staff and Exclusive Contracts*

Sometimes one or more physicians already on the medical staff may oppose the admission of a new member to the medical staff who may interfere with their "exclusive" contract to furnish services at the hospital in a particular specialty. On occasion, there is no exclusive contract, but physicians already on staff want to protect themselves from competition. In either case, the physician seeking medical staff membership may complain that denial of such membership violates antitrust laws. Exclusive contracts are, by definition, a restraint of trade, but in virtually all cases they have been upheld by the courts.[24] The courts have found that legitimate needs for 24-hour coverage and quality assurance, as well as other hospital and patient concerns, override the limited restraint on trade caused by the exclusivity provisions.[25]

If a hospital has exclusive arrangements, it is preferable for those arrangements to be reflected in contracts, even if no monetary consideration flows from the hospital to the physicians. Exclusive contracts, with appropriate recitations of the legitimate need for exclusivity, facilitate exclusion of practitioners who seek to join the staff. In addition, medical staff bylaw provisions allowing for an open staff should be qualified to avoid the appearance of a conflict between the bylaws and the terms of an exclusive contract. Similarly, exclusive contracts should be drafted so that termination or non-renewal of the contract terminates medical staff appointments and clinical privileges and cannot be contested by physicians or physician groups through the medical staff appeal procedures. Exclusive contracts should also make clear that when contracts and medical staff bylaws conflict, contracts prevail. All of these provisions should also be a part of the medical staff bylaws.

With the increase in hospital use of economic credentialing criteria in approving members of their medical staff, there has been a rise in legal conflicts between hospitals and physicians who challenge their exclusions from admission to the medical staff. Courts will not usually substitute their own judgment for that of the hospital in conflicts related to medical staff privileges. Indeed, two courts found that the exclusion of a physician from practicing in a private hospital is a discretionary matter to be decided by hospital management.[26] When a credentialing decision is based solely on economic interests, however, it is unclear whether courts will be as willing to acquiesce to the judgment of the hospital. In 2003, one court acknowledged that hospital implementation of an economic credentialing policy is an appropriate method through which to

---

[24]*See, e.g.*, Beard v. Parkview Hosp., 912 F.2d 138 (6th Cir. 1990) (holding that exclusive contract for provision of radiological services did not violate antitrust law); Dos Santos v. Columbus-Cuneo-Cabrini Med. Ctr., 684 F.2d 1346, 1352 (7th Cir. 1982) (finding that a plaintiff can only prevail on an exclusive dealing arrangement "by showing that the agreement in question results in a substantial foreclosure of competition in an area of effective competition, that is, in a relevant market"); Nilavar v. Mercy Health Sys. W. Ohio, 142 F. Supp. 2d 859 (S.D. Ohio 2000) (dismissing plaintiff's tying claims based on an exclusive contract); Gonzalez v. San Jacinto Methodist Hosp., 880 S.W.2d at 443 (holding that a hospital is entitled to enter into an exclusive services contract).

[25]Jefferson Parish Hosp. Dist. No. 2 v. Hyde, 466 U.S. 2, 104 S. Ct. 1551 (1984).

[26]Madsen v. Audrain Health Care, Inc., 297 F.3d 694, 698 (8th Cir. 2002); Sadler v. Dimensions Healthcare Corp., 836 A.2d 655, 663 (Md. 2003).

protect a hospital's financial viability; the court found that health care is a competitive market, and physicians who have employment or contractual arrangements with competing health systems can draw significant business away from the credentialing hospital or medical center.[27]

The HHS OIG issued a supplement to its Hospital Compliance Program Guidance in 2004[28] that addressed the issue of economic credentialing for medical staff.[29] The guidelines state that staff privileges based on a particular number of referrals or requiring the performance of a particular number of procedures beyond volumes necessary to demonstrate clinical proficiency implicate the federal anti-kickback statute.[30] At the same time, the OIG indicated a willingness to permit credentialing policies that categorically refuse privileges to physicians with significant conflicts of interest.[31] The OIG also solicited comments regarding economic credentialing to better understand the potential for fraud and abuse in this setting through a separate notice issued in 2002.[32]

State licensing statutes are also implicated in economic credentialing conflicts. Some states permit more leeway to hospitals in their credentialing policies than others. For example, a Texas licensing statute states: "A hospital, by contract or otherwise, may not refuse or fail to grant or renew staff privileges, or condition staff privileges, based in whole or in part on the fact that the physician, or a partner, associate, or employee of the physician is providing medical or health care services at a different hospital or health system."[33] Conversely, Idaho "recognizes the general rule that hospitals have the authority 'to make such rules, standards or qualifications for medical staff members as they, in their discretion, may deem necessary or advisable.' "[34]

### 3. Osteopaths and Podiatrists

In some parts of the country, the medical community itself holds strong prejudices against certain types of practitioners. For example, allopathic-trained physicians (MDs) may hold great disdain for osteopathic-trained physicians (DOs). Similarly, some physicians hold podiatrists in low regard. Some states, however, have laws requiring hospitals to accept osteopathic physicians or podiatrists on their medical staffs.[35]

---

[27]Walborn v. UHHS/CSAHS-Cuyahoga, Inc., No. CV-02-479572 (Ohio C.P., Cuyahoga Cty. June 16, 2003) (unpublished).

[28]70 Fed. Reg. 4858 (Jan. 31, 2005).

[29]*Id.* at 4869.

[30]*Id.*

[31]*Id.*

[32]67 Fed. Reg. 72,894 (Dec. 9, 2002). The OIG had not issued any final guidelines regarding economic credentialing as of August 2007.

[33]TEX. HEALTH & SAFETY CODE §241.1015(b) (Vernon 2004).

[34]Miller v. St. Alphonsus Reg. Med. Ctr., Inc., 87 P.3d 934, 943 (Idaho 2004) (quoting IDAHO CODE §39-1395).

[35]*See, e.g.,* 225 ILL. COMP. STAT. 62/5 (osteopaths); CAL. HEALTH & SAFETY CODE §1316 (1998) (podiatrists).

## B. Credential Review and Corrective Action

### 1. Verification of Credentials and Checking Available Databases

Hospitals absolutely must verify that any physician seeking medical staff membership has the required credentials for membership, including a degree from an accredited medical school, satisfactory completion of a residency program, and a currently valid license to practice in the state in which the hospital is located (and in the state(s) where the physician has an office). In addition, hospitals must check the National Practitioner Data Bank (NPDB) to determine if there have been adverse actions with respect to the physician. [36] The hospital should also verify that the physician has not been excluded from any government health care program.

In fiscal year 2006, approximately 3,425 persons and entities, or an average of more than nine people per day, were excluded from participation in federal health care programs.[37] Hence, screening and detection of excluded individuals are as important as ever to hospitals in ensuring their reimbursement under Medicare and other federal health care programs. Unfortunately, difficulties with the two principal resources for providers—the Office of Inspector General List of Excluded Individuals/Entities (OIG LEIE) and the General Services Administration Excluded Parties List System (GSA EPLS)—have caused problems for users. In a 2001 survey of practitioners operating under a corporate integrity agreement, the OIG found many discrepancies and inaccuracies in the information provided through these Web sites, as well as difficulty in accessing them, a lack of identifiers for common names, and incomplete data.[38] Despite problems arising because of incomplete information, most providers feel that they can, after inquiry, assure that no members of their medical staffs are on either list of excluded persons. Although CMS has implemented two screening databases, the Provider Enrollment, Chain, and Ownership System (PECOS),[39] and the Medicare Exclusion Database (MED),[40] neither database is available to providers to meet their own screening needs.

---

[36] 42 U.S.C. §11135. The information in this data bank is considered confidential and is not available to the public. The information from the NPDB is available only to state licensing boards, hospitals, and other health care entities, professional societies, certain federal agencies, and others as specified by law. *See* Health Resources and Servs. Admin., U.S. Dep't of Health & Human Servs., National Practitioner Data Bank/Healthcare Integrity and Protection Data Bank, *available at* http://www.npdb-hipdb.hrsa.gov.

[37] OFFICE OF INSPECTOR GENERAL, U.S. DEP'T OF HEALTH & HUMAN SERVS., SEMI-ANNUAL REPORT TO CONGRESS, 2006, at i, *available at* http://oig.hhs.gov/publications/docs/semiannual/2006/Semiannual%20Final%20FY%202006.pdf.

[38] U.S. DEP'T OF HEALTH & HUMAN SERVS., OFFICE OF INSPECTOR GENERAL, RESULTS OF CORPORATE INTEGRITY AGREEMENT SURVEY (Aug. 2001), *available at* http://oig.hhs.gov/fraud/docs/complianceguidance/ciasurvey.pdf.

[39] PECOS was implemented in the spring of 2002 to assist CMS in determining whether a provider applicant will be permitted to enroll in federal health care plans as well as to combat fraud and abuse. *See* Notice of New System Records, Provider Enrollment, Chain and Ownership System, 66 Fed. Reg. 51,961 (Oct. 11, 2001).

[40] The MED system is used to aid CMS and contractors in ensuring that no Medicare payments are made to any excluded entity or person that has provided any item or service that was not an emergency item or service. *See* Medicare Program Integrity Manual, CMS Pub. 100-08, §4.19.4.1; *see also* Medicare and Medicaid System of Records; Medicare Exclusion Database, 67 Fed. Reg. 8810 (Feb. 26, 2002).

## 2. Physician Malpractice Insurance

Many hospitals require physicians to carry adequate malpractice insurance as a condition of medical staff membership, which offers some limited assurance of quality as a demonstration of a physician's insurability. Physician malpractice insurance also offers protection for the hospital. If a physician is uninsured, it is much more likely that an injured patient will sue the hospital as a "deep pocket" and assert that the hospital had been negligent in permitting the physician to practice at the facility.

## 3. Hospital Duty to Deal With Problem Practitioners

A hospital's obligations do not lapse upon credentialing a new member of the medical staff. Should a hospital become aware of incidents or conduct that reflect on a physician's ability to treat patients with an acceptable level of skill and in accordance with community and hospital standards of care, the hospital must take corrective action. If a hospital negligently admits a physician to its medical staff or fails to take appropriate corrective action with respect to a physician who the hospital knew or should have known was not practicing appropriately, the hospital can be held liable for the damage caused by the physician's negligence.[41]

On the flip side, physicians who are denied privileges or have their privileges revoked often initiate antitrust litigation against the hospital. Although some circuit courts have ruled that a hospital cannot conspire (as prohibited under the Sherman Act §1[42]) with its medical staff,[43] other circuit courts have held otherwise.[44] For this reason, it is important that medical staff bylaws, as well as bylaws of the health care entity, clearly state that the medical staff is a constituent part of the hospital and not a separate entity. This tension between a hospital's duty to deal with problem practitioners and the threat of antitrust litigation was one of the reasons the Health Care Quality Improvement Act (HCQIA) was enacted. This law provides antitrust immunity for peer review activities that meet specific standards.[45]

In 2002, the Fifth Circuit found that a hospital peer review committee did not conspire to monopolize a cardiology market by suspending the privileges of one of its competitors.[46] The court noted that it was inevitable in any peer

---

[41] Advincula v. United Blood Servs., 176 Ill. 2d 1, 28 (Ill. 1996), *citing* Darling v. Charleston Cmty. Mem'l Hosp., 33 Ill. 2d 326 (Ill. 1965), *cert. denied*, 86 S. Ct. 1204 (1966); *see also* Johnson v. Misericordia Cmty. Hosp., 99 Wis. 2d 708 (Wis. 1981) (holding hospital liable for failing to establish procedures to determine a physician's competence when granting privileges; in particular, for failing to check the National Practitioner Data Bank).

[42] 15 U.S.C. §1.

[43] *See* Balaklaw v. Lovell, 14 F.3d 793 (2d Cir. 1994); Oksanen v. Page Mem'l Hosp., 945 F.2d 696 (4th Cir. 1991), *cert. denied*, 11 S. Ct. 973 (1992); Nurse Midwifery Ass'n v. Hibbert, 918 F.2d 605, 614 (6th Cir. 1990), *opinion modified on reh'g*, 927 F.2d 904, *cert. denied*, 112 S. Ct. 407 (1991); Nanavati v. Burdette Tomlin Mem'l Hosp., 857 F.2d 96, 118 (3d Cir. 1988).

[44] *See* Bolt v. Halifax Hosp. Med. Ctr., 851 F.2d 1273 (11th Cir. 1988), *aff'd*, 980 F.2d 1381 (11th Cir. 1993); Oltz v. St. Peter's Cmty. Hosp., 861 F.2d 1440 (9th Cir. 1988), *rev'd on other grounds*, 19 F.3d 1312 (9th Cir. 1994).

[45] 42 U.S.C. §11111(a).

[46] Patel v. Midland Mem'l Hosp. & Med. Ctr., 298 F.3d 333 (5th Cir. 2002).

review process that a physician's competitors would be involved in the process.[47] However, in this case, the hospital obtained an outside evaluation to confirm the findings of the internal reviewers, which further refuted any idea of conspiring against a competitor.[48] Indeed, the court was impressed by the hospital's effort in getting an outside assessment to obtain a different perspective and avoid bias before it made its final decision.[49] Thus, independent review participation in addressing a perceived practitioner problem offers some protection from claims that practitioners involved in the review improperly recommended exclusion of another practitioner for competitive reasons.

## C. Corrective Action Under the Medical Staff Bylaws

At such time as a hospital learns that a physician may not be practicing in a manner consistent with hospital[50] or community standards, the hospital must take corrective action to protect itself pursuant to its medical staff bylaws. The corrective action need not necessarily be termination of medical staff privileges. In many instances, medical staff bylaws permit a lesser sanction, such as additional training, monitoring on a case-by-case basis by a respected member of the medical staff, or some other appropriate measure tailored to meet the observed problem.

If there is a dispute with the physician whose conduct is in question, JCAHO requires the hospital to have an appeal mechanism in the medical staff bylaws affording the physician an opportunity to present his or her side of a case.[51]

Government health care programs such as Medicare and Medicaid can exclude practitioners.[52] As a general rule, if practitioners are excluded from one governmental health care program, they will be excluded from all of them.[53] If practitioners are excluded, no services ordered by those practitioners are covered.[54] Hence, if a physician who is a member of a hospital's voluntary medical staff is excluded from Medicare, but retains medical staff membership and privileges, the physician may order services for which the hospital will not be paid. This is an unacceptable position for a hospital for two reasons.

---

[47]*Id.* at 345.

[48]*Id.* at 345–46.

[49]*Id.* at 346.

[50]If it is not careful in its advertising or other public statements, a hospital can be held to a standard of care above that of the community standard of care. For example, if a hospital holds itself out as furnishing only "the highest quality of patient care," a plaintiff's attorney may try to rely on that puffery as creating a warranty or otherwise setting a standard above the community standard of care. Denton Reg'l Med. Ctr. v. LaCroix, 947 S.W.2d 941, 946 (Tex. App.–Ft. Worth 1997), *review denied* (Tex. Feb. 13, 1998) (alleging that hospital was negligent for "representing to the public that it provided the highest quality anesthesia care when, in fact, it only provided unsupervised CRNAs").

[51]Joint Comm'n on Accreditation of Healthcare Orgs., Hospital Accreditation Standards, MS.4.50 (2006).

[52]42 U.S.C. §1320a-7.

[53]42 C.F.R. §1001.601.

[54]42 C.F.R. §1001.1901; *see also* U.S. Dep't of Health & Human Servs., Office of Inspector General, Special Advisory Bulletin, The Effect of Exclusion from Participation in Federal Health Care Programs (Sept. 1999), *available at* http://oig.hhs.gov/fraud/docs/alertsandbulletins/effected.htm, and as Appendix F-14 on the disk accompanying this volume.

First, whatever conduct the physician engaged in to merit exclusion may very well be conduct that is relevant to the physician's fitness to remain on the medical staff. Second, regardless of the merits of the physician's exclusion from government health care programs, a hospital should not place itself in the position of being barred from billing for services ordered by that practitioner. Therefore, it is preferable for a hospital to have a procedure in its medical staff bylaws permitting summary suspension of privileges when a practitioner is excluded or suspended from one or more governmental health care programs.

If adverse action is taken against a physician by a hospital, or if the physician resigns from the medical staff under threat of such action, the hospital is legally obligated to report the matter to the NPDB.[55] Failure to report can result in sanctions against the hospital.[56]

The OIG has provided guidance on how, in unusual circumstances, an excluded individual may still be employed by a health care entity without subjecting the entity to administrative sanctions. In OIG Advisory Opinion No. 01-16,[57] a health plan requested advice on whether it could employ a physician who had been excluded from participation in federal health care programs. In its analysis of the situation, the OIG explained that

> [a] provider or entity that receives Federal health care program funding may only employ an excluded individual in limited situations. Those situations would include instances where the provider pays the individual's salary, expenses, and benefits exclusively from private funds or from other non-Federal funding sources, and where the services furnished by the excluded individual relate solely to non-Federal programs or patients.[58]

The OIG also notes in the advisory opinion that an excluded employee's work responsibilities must not relate to any medical or administrative skills. The duties of an excluded individual need to be far removed from the provision of items and services to program beneficiaries and should also be unassociated with any federal funding or regulatory mandates in order to avoid administrative sanctions. Although there may be good reasons for a hospital to want to employ an excluded individual, the measures that it would have to take in order to avoid Medicare liability in separating the excluded person from any Medicare-related activity may be so arduous as not to be worth the expense and administrative complications.

## D. Physician Attestation of Accuracy of Medicare Diagnoses

Under the Medicare prospective payment system for hospital inpatient services, the level of payment is determined by the diagnosis-related group (DRG) to which the patient's case is assigned. The DRG assignment is determined by the patient's principal and secondary diagnoses, as well as procedures

---

[55]45 C.F.R. §60.9.

[56]42 C.F.R. §1003.102(b)(5).

[57]OIG Advisory Op. No. 01-16 (Sept. 28, 2001), *available at* http://oig.hhs.gov/fraud/docs/advisoryopinions/2001/ao01-16.pdf.

[58]*Id.*

performed. Medicare payment regulations previously required physicians to acknowledge in writing that diagnosis information had been entered correctly for each Medicare discharge. That requirement was eliminated in 1995 and replaced by the requirement that every physician, on entering into medical staff membership or before admitting patients, must sign a single acknowledgment that the hospital keeps on file for as long as the physician is on the medical staff. By signing the acknowledgment, a physician attests to the diagnoses and procedures in the medical record and recognizes that he or she is liable for the misrepresentation or falsification of that information.[59]

In many situations, it is quite difficult for a physician to evaluate whether a patient needs inpatient services or outpatient observation services at the time the services are ordered. Thus, it may be necessary for the physician to reevaluate medical diagnoses and change or modify the original orders he or she has given. Unfortunately, there is very little guidance from CMS on what changes may be made and how they can be made. In February 2004, CMS announced the new billing code for form CMS-1450. The code permits hospitals to bill, as an outpatient service, an inpatient service ordered by a physician.[60]

In October 2004, CMS provided guidance on when it is appropriate to use this code. *Condition Code 44—Inpatient Admission Changed to Outpatient,* became effective April 1, 2004, and is used when the physician ordered inpatient services, but upon internal utilization review performed before the claim was originally submitted, the hospital determined that the services did not meet its inpatient criteria. The code is applicable provided all of the following conditions are met:

1. The change in patient status from inpatient to outpatient is made prior to discharge or release, while the beneficiary is still a patient of the hospital;
2. The hospital has not submitted a claim to Medicare for the inpatient admission;
3. A physician concurs with the utilization review committee's decision; and
4. The physician's concurrence with the utilization review committee's decision is documented in the patient's medical record.[61]

## E. Physician Coverage of the Emergency Room

Historically, many hospitals arranged for emergency room coverage by rotating the obligation through members of the medical staff. Now such an arrangement for basic coverage of the emergency room is the exception. In

---

[59]42 C.F.R. §412.46.

[60]Medicare Claims Processing Manual, Pub. No. 100-04, Transmittal No. 81 (Feb. 6, 2004) (including Condition Code 44 where inpatient admission changed to outpatient); Clarification of Medicare Payment Policy When Inpatient Admission Is Determined Not to Be Medically Necessary, Including the Use of Condition Code 44: "Inpatient Admission Changed to Outpatient," MLN Matters No. SE0622, *available at* http://www.cms.hhs.gov/MLNMattersArticles/downloads/SE0622.pdf.

[61]*Id.*

most cases, hospitals employ or contract with specialists experienced in emergency medicine to staff emergency rooms. However, hospitals still often rely on members of the voluntary medical staff for specialist services required by emergency room patients. For example, a hospital that holds itself out as handling major trauma will need to have available the services of a neurologist, orthopedist, and similar specialists. Under the obligations created by EMTALA, a hospital must accept certain referrals of emergency patients from other hospitals, and failure to accept such patients can subject the refusing hospital to termination of its participation in Medicare and fines up to $50,000.[62] One problem that arises is that a hospital may violate its EMTALA obligations because a member of its voluntary medical staff refuses to honor his or her agreement to be on-call.[63] A hospital needs a mechanism, through its medical staff bylaws, or otherwise, to deal with this potential problem.

Reimbursement for on-call physicians at critical access hospitals was addressed in the August 1, 2001, *Federal Register*.[64] Effective October 1, 2001, reasonable costs of outpatient services for critical access hospitals can include compensation and related costs for a physician who is on call, but who is not present on the premises of the critical access hospital, as long as the on-call physician is not otherwise furnishing physician services, and is not on call at any other provider or facility.[65] In addition, physicians who qualify for on-call status must actually come to the facility when summoned in order to be reimbursable. Further, CMS only reimburses for costs when the requirement to come to the facility when summoned during on-call hours is included in the written contract with physicians.[66]

CMS recently expanded reimbursable emergency on-call services to include various providers rather than solely physicians. Effective January 1, 2005, the payment amount of 101 percent of the reasonable costs of outpatient critical access hospital services may also include amounts for reasonable compensation and related costs for the following emergency room providers who are on call but are not present on the premises of the critical access hospital involved, are not otherwise furnishing physicians' services, and are not on call at any other provider or facility: physician assistants, nurse practitioners, and clinical nurse specialists.[67]

---

[62]42 U.S.C. §1395dd(d)(1)(A); 42 C.F.R. §1003.102(c); *see also* U.S. Dep't of Health & Human Servs., Office of Inspector General, Special Advisory Bulletin on the Patient Anti-Dumping Statute, 64 Fed. Reg. 61,353–59 (Nov. 10, 1999) (see Appendix F-13 on the disk accompanying this volume).

[63]*See* St. Anthony Hosp. v. Office of Inspector General, Doc. No. A-2000-12, Dec. No. 1728 (HHS Departmental Appeals Bd., Appellate Div.), Medicare & Medicaid Guide (CCH) ¶120,147 (June 5, 2000), *aff'd,* Office of Inspector General v. St. Anthony Hosp., Doc. No. C-98-460, CR 620 (HHS Departmental Appeals Bd., Civil Remedies Div.), Medicare & Medicaid Guide (CCH) ¶120,101 (Oct. 5, 1999), *aff'd,* 309 F.3d 680 (10th Cir. 2002) (holding that a hospital violated EMTALA when its on-call surgeon told a community hospital emergency room physician seeking to transfer a critical patient that he was "not interested" in taking the case).

[64]66 Fed. Reg. 39,828, 39,922–23 (Aug. 1, 2001).

[65]42 C.F.R. §413.70(b)(4)(i).

[66]*Id.* at §413.70(b)(4)(ii).

[67]69 Fed. Reg. 48,916, 49,253 (Aug. 11, 2004) (codified at 42 C.F.R. §413.70(b)(4)(ii)(B)).

### 1. Emergency Room Physicians' Interpretations of Diagnostic Images

Medicare policy does not resolve who should interpret images and issue reports that become part of a patient's medical record. However, Medicare does have rules[68] that address whether and to whom Medicare will pay for an interpretation of X-rays and electrocardiograms (EKGs). Emergency room physicians can bill for interpretations of X-rays and EKGs that they read as long as they create a written narrative report of the interpretation that becomes a part of the patient's medical record. A hospital can insist that all images be interpreted by a radiologist when it has an exclusive contract with a radiology group. However, if this interpretation does not occur contemporaneously with treatment, then there is an issue as to whether the radiologists can properly bill Medicare. It seems, however, that the real policy goal of the "contemporaneous"[69] requirement for reimbursement is to ensure that no double billing occurs when both the emergency room physician and the radiologist interpret an X-ray. If CMS receives two claims for the same diagnostic interpretation, it will determine which interpretation contributed to the treatment of the patient-beneficiary and reimburse that one. To the extent that a non-contemporaneous interpretation by a radiologist does not affect the patient's treatment, Medicare will deem it to be a quality control measure provided by the hospital, and thus will deny reimbursement for the radiologist's claim.

### F. Perquisites for Members of the Medical Staff

At most hospitals, physicians enjoy modest perquisites by reason of their medical staff membership. For example, hospitals have routinely offered professional courtesy to physicians on the medical staff and members of their immediate families. Hospitals have also routinely furnished to physicians on the medical staff free parking in a lot convenient to the hospital entrance, cafeteria discounts, coffee and donuts in the physician lounge, and occasional entertainment. Even items that seem innocuous raise potential problems under various fraud and abuse laws including the Stark law.[70] Under the Stark law, a hospital may not bill Medicare or Medicaid for services ordered by a physician with a financial relationship with the hospital. Unwitting violations subject a hospital to nonpayment for the services; violations when the hospital knew or should have known of the prohibited financial relationship can also result in a civil monetary penalty (CMP) of up to $15,000 per occurrence.[71] "Financial relationship" is defined with sufficient breadth to encompass any remuneration given by a hospital to a physician.[72] Thus, it is necessary to fit within an exception to the law to avoid the risk of draconian penalties.

---

[68] 60 Fed. Reg. 63,124, 63,132 (Dec. 8, 1995).

[69] *Id.* at 63,130–31. Although CMS would seem to require that the interpretation occur "contemporaneously" with treatment, the preamble language would indicate that an interpretation by a radiologist would be reimbursed as long as there is no bill from another physician.

[70] 42 U.S.C. §1395nn. See generally Chapter 2 (Crane, Federal Physician Self-Referral Restrictions), and Appendix B-1 on the disk accompanying this volume for full text of the Stark law.

[71] 42 U.S.C. §1395nn(g)(3).

[72] 42 U.S.C. §1395nn(a)(2), (h)(1).

Phase I of the Stark II final rules issued by the Health Care Financing Administration (HCFA), now the Centers for Medicare and Medicaid Services (CMS),[73] on January 4, 2001, created two new exceptions for perquisites to physicians. The first is a non-monetary compensation exception that exempts from the Stark II ban non-cash or cash equivalent items or services up to an aggregate yearly amount of $300.[74] This compensation cannot take into consideration the volume or value of referrals or other business generated by the referring physician, cannot be solicited by the physician, and cannot violate the anti-kickback statute. Unlike the proposed Stark II rule for de minimis compensation, there is no per gift limit or requirement that such compensation be made available to all similarly situated individuals.[75] The second is a new exception for medical staff incidental benefits. This provision exempts non-cash or cash equivalent items or services given to a member of the medical staff when used on the hospital campus if they are:

- Offered to all members of the medical staff practicing in the same specialty and do not consider the volume or value of referrals or other business generated between the parties;
- Offered only when staff are making rounds or performing other duties for the hospital;
- Reasonably related to or facilitate the provision of medical services at the hospital;
- Consistent with what other hospitals offer;
- Less than $25 value for each occurrence (e.g., each meal); and
- Not in violation of the anti-kickback statute.[76]

The Stark II/Phase II rule[77] modifies and clarifies the nonmonetary compensation exception of up to $300 per year and the medical staff incidental benefits exceptions,[78] providing a mechanism to increase the cost limits in these exceptions to account for inflation.[79] Both the $300 limit in the nonmonetary annual compensation exception and the $25 limit under the incidental benefits exception will be updated annually for inflation based on the Consumer Price Index update, and the updates for these exceptions will be displayed on the CMS self-referral Web site as soon as possible after September 30 of each year.[80]

---

[73] As of July 1, 2001, the former Health Care Financing Administration (HCFA) was renamed the Centers for Medicare and Medicaid Services (CMS). For the purposes of this discussion, however, references typically will be to CMS.

[74] 66 Fed. Reg. 856, 961 (Jan. 4, 2001) (codified at 42 C.F.R. §411.357(k)).

[75] 63 Fed. Reg. 1646, 1725 (Jan. 9, 1998).

[76] 66 Fed. Reg. at 962 (codified at 42 C.F.R. §411.357(m)) (for text of regulations under Stark I and II, see generally Appendix B on the disk accompanying this volume). The anti-kickback statute is codified at 42 U.S.C. §1320a-7b(b) (for text of the anti-kickback statute, see Appendix A-1 on the disk accompanying this volume).

[77] 69 Fed. Reg. 16,054 (Mar. 26, 2004); 69 Fed. Reg. 57,226 (Oct. 24, 2004) (correcting amendment).

[78] 42 C.F.R. §411.357(k) and (m).

[79] 69 Fed Reg. at 16,112.

[80] 42 C.F.R. §411.357(k)(2) and (m)(5).

Additionally, the Phase II rule clarifies that the exception for medical staff incidental benefits can cover the provision of pagers, two-way radios, and Internet access to physicians, if such items and services are used during times when medical staff members are engaged in hospital or patient activities. For example, it is permissible under the exception to provide pagers and two-way radios to physicians to ensure that they can be contacted in an emergency and other urgent patient-care situations when the physicians are away from the hospital campus.[81] According to the Phase II preamble, the incidental benefits exception also covers including a simple listing for a physician or practice on a hospital Web site (however, inclusion of any advertising or promotion for a physician's private practice on a hospital Web site would have to qualify under another Stark II exception such as the $300 nonmonetary compensation exception).[82] Finally, the Stark III final rule expands the nonmonetary compensation exception to address circumstances of noncompliance, and to allow an entity with a formal medical staff to provide one local medical staff appreciation event each year.

In addition to evaluating perquisites under the Stark law, hospitals and physicians must also evaluate these benefits from a tax perspective. The IRS views perquisites as "compensation" under the excess benefit transaction section of the Internal Revenue Code and has stated that a "reasonable compensation" defense is unavailable if the perquisite was not reported as compensation.[83]

## 1. Professional Courtesy

Many hospitals commonly engage in "insurance only" billing for members of the medical staff and their immediate families. The Phase II rule provides a Stark exception for professional courtesy.[84] Professional courtesy may be extended to a physician, a physician's immediate family member, or a member of the physician's office staff as long as the following conditions are met:

(1) The professional courtesy is offered to all physicians on the entity's bona fide medical staff or in the entity's local community or service area without regard to the volume or value of referrals or other business generated between the parties;

(2) The health care items and services provided are of a type routinely provided by the entity;

---

[81] 69 Fed. Reg. at 16,112–13. The provision of two-way radios and pagers is compliant with 42 C.F.R. §411.357(m) even though these are not incidental benefits provided "on campus." The "on campus" requirement was intended to apply to benefits such as parking, cafeteria meals, etc., which are incidental to services being provided by physicians at the hospital. This way, the provision of tangential, off-site benefits such as restaurant dinners and theater tickets must comply with the exception for nonmonetary compensation up to $300.

[82] *Id.* at 16,113.

[83] IRC §4958 (2006); *see also* Brauer, Lawrence M. and Leonard J. Henzke, Jr., " 'Automatic' Excess Benefit Transactions Under IRC 4958," *available at* http://www.irs.gov/pub/irs-tege/eotopice04.pdf, for a detailed explanation of the type of "written contemporaneous substantiation" the IRS requires in reporting economic benefits as compensation for services.

[84] 69 Fed. Reg. at 16,115; 42 C.F.R. §411.357(s). Phase II defines professional courtesy as "the provision of free or discounted health care items or services to a physician or his or her immediate family members or office staff." 69 Fed. Reg. at 16,116; 42 C.F.R. §411.351.

(3) The entity's professional courtesy policy is set out in writing and approved in advance by the entity's governing body;

(4) The professional courtesy is not offered to a physician (or immediate family member) who is a federal health care program beneficiary, unless there has been a good faith showing of financial need;

(5) If the professional courtesy involves any whole or partial reduction of any coinsurance obligation, the insurer is informed in writing of the reduction;[85] and

(6) The arrangement does not violate the anti-kickback statute[86] or any federal or state law or regulation governing billing or claims submission.[87]

In the Phase II rule, CMS strongly cautioned that many professional courtesy arrangements may violate the federal anti-kickback statute[88] or may violate the civil monetary penalties law's prohibition against giving inducements to Medicare and Medicaid beneficiaries.[89] Also, CMS noted that many private insurers may have concerns about the use of coinsurance waivers as a form of professional courtesy.[90]

The Phase III final rule deleted the requirement that an entity notify an insurer when the professional courtesy involves the whole or partial reduction of any coinsurance obligation. The Phase III rule also clarified CMS's intent that the professional courtesy exception apply only to hospitals and other providers with formal medical staffs.[91]

## 2. Entertainment

It is also common for hospital management to entertain members of the medical staff at lunches, dinners, or golf outings. If total charges for meals, green fees, tips, and similar fees for physicians (and their spouses, if present) exceed $300 per year, the Stark exception for nonmonetary compensation would not apply.

## 3. Parking

In its discussion of the new medical staff incidental benefits exception[92] in the preamble to the Phase I final rule, CMS distinguished between furnishing

---

[85]This requirement was eliminated by the Phase III rule. *See* 72 Fed. Reg. 51,012, 51,064. (Sept. 5, 2007).

[86]42 U.S.C. §1320a-7(b).

[87]42 C.F.R. §411.357(s)(1)–(6).

[88]*See also* U.S. Dep't of Health & Human Servs., Office of Inspector General, Draft Supplemental Compliance Program Guidance for Hospitals, 69 Fed. Reg. 32,012, 32,027–28 (June 8, 2004), which discusses professional courtesy in the context of hospital compliance with the federal anti-kickback statute, the civil monetary penalty law, and the Stark law.

[89]69 Fed. Reg. at 16,116.

[90]*Id.*

[91]72 Fed. Reg. 51,012, 51,064, 51,096 (Sept. 5, 2007). The *Federal Register* notice announcing the Stark III regulations is available as Appendix B-4 on the disk accompanying this volume.

[92]42 C.F.R. §411.357(m).

parking to physicians while they are seeing patients at the hospital and furnishing spaces to physicians regardless of whether they are seeing patients in the hospital at the time:

> It is our [CMS'] view that, while a physician is making rounds, the parking benefits both the hospital and its patients, rather than providing the physician with any personal benefit. Thus, we do not intend to regard parking for this purpose as remuneration furnished by the hospital to the physician, but instead as part of the physician's privileges. However, if a hospital provides parking to a physician for periods of time that do not coincide with his or her rounds, that parking could constitute remuneration.[93]

Parking provided to all members of the medical staff for times they are making rounds or performing other duties at the hospital would, therefore, fall under this exception.[94]

### 4. Compliance Training

Another new exception in the Phase I final rule was created for compliance training. CMS believes that these programs are beneficial and pose little risk of fraud or abuse.[95] These programs will be exempt as long as they are provided to physicians who practice in the local community and are conducted in the local community.[96]

### G. Physician-Hospital Organizations

Physician-hospital organizations (PHOs) are joint ventures between hospitals and members of their medical staffs.[97] The principal purpose is to have a ready-made network to contract with managed care payors. Often, physicians in a PHO with a hospital have no other financial relationship with the hospital. In ideal circumstances, PHOs offer hospitals and members of their medical staffs the opportunity to work together to support each other and provide their communities with cost-effective medical services. On behalf of all of its members, the PHO contracts with managed care payors, handles utilization review, and may bear some risk under capitation arrangements. Unfortunately, these goals are often difficult to achieve because of legal or practical limitations. Several fundamental legal problems arise with PHOs under (1) tax law limitations on tax-exempt organizations; (2) antitrust laws barring monopolies; (3) antitrust laws barring price setting and agreements to act in concert; and (4) state laws defining the business of insurance.

---

[93] 66 Fed. Reg. at 921.

[94] *Id.*

[95] *Id.*

[96] *Id.* at 962 (codified at 42 C.F.R. §411.357(o)).

[97] *See generally* AMERICAN HEALTH LAWYERS ASS'N, 3 HEALTH LAW PRACTICE GUIDE §34:2, at 34-3 (West 1998).

## 1. Capital Requirements and the Need to Avoid Hospital Subsidization of Physician Members

PHOs do not require immense amounts of capital because they own no medical equipment, can rent the premises they need, do not need to employ medical personnel, and do not furnish services directly. What they do is negotiate and contract with third-party payors, engage in utilization review including case management, and may bear some risk under capitation arrangements. In addition, PHOs are not established with the expectation of making a profit, but instead the intent is to provide members greater revenues through greater volume and cost savings or to preserve existing market shares. For a start-up period of three years or more, PHOs often lose money. Thus, although capital needs are not great, there is a need for a capital contribution of several hundred thousand dollars at the outset and during the start-up period.

In the ideal model, physicians in the aggregate hold equal ownership, make equal capital contributions, and have a vote equal to that of the hospital. In the real world, however, physicians are often reluctant to invest sufficient capital to fund half of the capital needs of the PHO. Serious inurement and private benefit issues arise if a tax-exempt hospital subsidizes physician capital contributions by making larger investments for equal ownership and power.[98] Sometimes this problem can be solved by having the hospital hold more than half ownership, with minority physician shareholder protections such as super majority requirements when certain actions are taken.

As the PHO matures, particularly if it has been successful, the issue of its capital needs may continue to arise. For example, some joint ventures between hospitals and physicians have gone beyond contracting with managed care payors and have obtained licenses as HMOs or insurance companies. To ensure sufficient reserves to satisfy state insurance commissioners requires immense amounts of capital. In such instances, success in enrolling patients is a mixed blessing, because it will raise the reserve requirements. In several such ventures, the hospital has bought out all or a portion of physician interests. Of course, such buyouts have to be at fair market value and satisfy an appropriate Stark exception, such as the exception for isolated transactions.[99]

## 2. Antitrust Issues

In a large, highly competitive market, there is not much concern that a relatively small percentage of physicians joining together in a network is monopolization. But in smaller markets with only one or two hospitals, there is a risk of being accused of monopolization if too many physicians become involved in a PHO and will only contract with managed care payors through a PHO. This issue needs to be considered not only in regard to all physicians generally, but also on a specialty-by-specialty basis. Some PHOs provide that physician members are free to contract with a managed care payor separately

---

[98]There also are Stark law and anti-kickback issues.

[99]42 C.F.R. §411.357(f). This exception was addressed in the Phase II final rule. *See* 69 Fed. Reg. 16,054, 16,098–99. The buyout would also have to be structured so as not to violate the anti-kickback statute.

from the PHO, but only after presenting the opportunity to the PHO. The extent to which this ameliorates potential monopolization issues depends on the facts and circumstances of each PHO and the market.

An antitrust issue inherent in virtually all PHOs is the extent to which they may negotiate on behalf of otherwise independent members. If members have bound themselves not to deal with payors other than through the PHO, there is a risk that the arrangement will be treated as an impermissible boycott. Moreover, virtually any delegation to the PHO by independent physician members to negotiate prices on their behalf can raise risks of illegal price fixing. The safest structure is one in which the PHO acts solely as a messenger between the managed care payor and independent physicians.[100]

The extent to which PHOs can negotiate on behalf of their independent physician members has always been an important aspect of health care antitrust enforcement. Both the Federal Trade Commission (FTC) and the Department of Justice (DOJ) have made it clear that a hospital cannot become a vehicle to encourage, facilitate, and thus conspire with otherwise independent physician competitors in what will amount to *per se* illegal price-fixing, boycott of payor, or unlawful division of markets. Such actions may expose a hospital to potential liability as a consequence of federal antitrust agency enforcement, private party litigation brought by aggrieved payors or patients, or even litigation initiated by state antitrust enforcement officials. Therefore, hospitals must ensure that they do not act as facilitators of *per se* unlawful conduct by physician competitors in the network.

PHOs cannot establish or negotiate fees for physicians who have not clinically integrated their practices or do not share financial risk. How PHOs are structured and the way that they operate in practice are therefore very significant questions. The issue of the extent to which PHOs or physician organizations can negotiate on behalf of their independent physician members has recently come to the forefront in FTC consent decrees. For example, the FTC complaint for *In re South Georgia Health Partners*[101] described an arrangement where four PHOs consisting of 15 hospitals and 500 physicians (the physicians comprising 90 percent of all physicians practicing in the region) joined together to form one large PHO, South Georgia Health Partners (SGHP). The FTC alleged that the PHO, hospital, and physician members of SGHP canceled current contracts with payors, and from that point, all physicians and hospitals would only deal with the payors through SGHP. It was also alleged that payors had to accept the SGHP fixed fee schedule and could obtain a fixed discount of no more than 10 percent. The prices demanded by SGHP were found to be higher than the

---

[100] *See generally* U.S. Dep't of Justice & Federal Trade Comm'n, Statements of Antitrust Enforcement Policy in Health Care (Aug. 28, 1996), *reprinted in* 4 Trade Reg. Rep. (CCH) ¶ 13,153, *available at* http://www.ftc.gov/reports/hlth3s.pdf; James H. Sneed & David Marx, Jr., Antitrust: Challenge of the Health Care Field 75–92 (National Health Lawyers Ass'n, 1990). *See* Memorandum from Kenney Shipley, Chair, Health Plan Accountability Working Group, National Ass'n of Insurance Commissioners, to All Commissioners, Directors, and Superintendents (Aug. 10, 1995), *available at* http://www.netreach.net/~wmanning/naicrsk.htm.

[101] *In re* South Georgia Health Partners, L.L.C. (F.T.C. Sept. 9, 2003), *available at* http://www.ftc.gov/os/2003/09/sgeorgiado.pdf.

physicians and hospitals would have obtained by negotiating unilaterally. In order to remedy the alleged problematic behavior and artificially increased costs, the consent decree prohibited SGHP from becoming involved in any way with physician negotiations with payors.[102]

In a separate case, the FTC found that a PHO in North Carolina was engaging in price fixing and anticompetitive behavior. Piedmont Health Alliance (PHA) and ten individual physicians allegedly fixed prices for the services of PHA physician members. Frye Regional Medical Center (Frye) and its parent company, Tenet Healthcare Corporation (Tenet), were involved in the activities of PHA,[103] and this is the first case where the FTC has named a hospital as a participant in an alleged price fixing conspiracy. PHA used a "modified messenger model" to enter into payor contracts. The FTC alleged that instead of correctly using the messenger model to facilitate individual contract negotiations with physicians, PHA coordinated physician responses and set fee schedules on predetermined price levels. Additionally, it was alleged that Frye funds were used in developing PHA and that Frye's chief operating officer initially directed the PHO. Frye and Tenet settled with the FTC and agreed to refrain from interaction with payors in any way on behalf of any physician. Frye and Tenet were also required to cease receiving any payments from fee schedules set under the alleged unlawful fee schedules.[104]

PHOs composed of substantial numbers of physicians in a particular geographic area that act in an exclusive or *de facto* exclusive capacity can clearly open themselves up to claims of monopolization or attempted monopolization of physician services. Therefore, it is important to take away from both these cases that the safest structure for either a physician-only or hospital-physician organization is one where the group functions solely as a messenger between the physicians and any managed care payor and the physicians negotiate individually with all payors.

### 3. *Business of Insurance*

To engage in the business of insurance, an entity must be licensed as an insurance company under state law. Hospitals and PHOs do not normally pursue this avenue because as many as several million dollars must be set aside in reserves. Thus, engaging in the business of insurance is not a practical option for most PHOs. The business of insurance generally assumes the entity is accepting risk. In many states, insurance commissioners find the types of risks that PHOs think they want to accept fit within the definition of the "business of insurance."

### H. Donations of Health Information Technology

Several recently-adopted Stark exceptions and anti-kickback safe harbors recognize the growing importance of health information technology. The

---

[102]*In re* South Georgia Health Partners, L.L.C., Agreement Containing Consent Order to Cease and Desist, *available at* http://www.ftc.gov/os/2003/09/sgeorgiaagree.pdf.

[103]Tenet Healthcare Corporation and Frye Regional Medical Center Consent Decree, *available at* http://www.ftc.gov/os/caselist/0210119/040203dotenet0210119.pdf.

[104]*Id.*

following three Stark exceptions encourage the growth of hospital-physician electronic connectivity by permitting hospitals (and other entities that furnish designated health services) to donate certain types of software, hardware, and network access to physicians.

### 1. Community-Wide Health Information Systems Exception

A number of hospitals now give physicians on the voluntary medical staff access to their wide-area computer network. By connecting physician offices to the hospital's network, the physician is able to schedule patients for procedures more easily, approve orders sooner and more efficiently, communicate with the hospital and other physicians by e-mail, gain access to clinical databases to assist in determining the best treatment of a patient, obtain demographic information for his or her own billing, and otherwise interface more efficiently and effectively with the hospital. To provide these benefits, a hospital may find it easier to furnish the physician with a computer, modem, and other hardware and software. The obvious issue is whether doing so constitutes remuneration to the physician and presents a problem under the triple threat of the Stark law, the anti-kickback statute, and the limitations applicable to tax-exempt organizations.

The answer to these questions requires an analysis of precisely what hardware, software, or other items or services the hospital furnishes to physicians. In virtually all instances, the benefits to the hospital itself, or to hospital care for its patients, are apparent. For example, if a physician reviews test results by computer, enabling the patient to be discharged sooner, the hospital avoids increased costs from a longer stay, and the patient can return home or proceed sooner to the next level of care. But there are ancillary benefits of such arrangements as well. To the extent that the physician can use the equipment for purposes unrelated to the hospital or hospital patients, there is not much question that the physician has received a benefit. In some instances, that benefit may be incidental and immaterial; but in other instances, it could be substantial. To avoid legal problems, the hospital may either install in physician offices dummy terminals that are only capable of interfacing with the hospital mainframe or charge the physician fair market value for the non-hospital-related use of the equipment. The charge need relate only to the value to the physician apart from the benefit to the hospital or the hospital's patients. This risk area has been discussed in the preambles to both the anti-kickback safe harbors and the Stark regulations,[105] and more generally in other guidance materials, including a Special Fraud Alert.[106]

The Stark II/Phase II rule created a new regulatory exception for the provision of information technology items and services (including both hardware and software) by an entity to a physician to enable the physician to participate in a community-wide health information system designed to enhance the overall health of the community.[107] This community-wide health information system exception allows a hospital to provide physicians with use

---

[105] 56 Fed. Reg. 35,952, 35,978 (1991) (distinguishing between a computer that only prints out laboratory test results and a regular personal computer that can be used for other purposes); 63 Fed. Reg. 1646, 1693–94 (Jan. 9, 1998).

[106] 59 Fed. Reg. 65,372, 65,377 (Dec. 19, 1994).

[107] 69 Fed. Reg. at 16,113; 42 C.F.R. §411.357(u).

of technology that is dedicated to the service of the hospital and the provision of health care for hospital patients.[108]

Under this exception, the hospital or health care system providing the technology must provide access to the technology to all community providers and practitioners who desire to participate and share electronic health care records.[109] Also, this exception only allows hospitals or health systems to provide information technology items that are necessary to enable a physician to participate in the entity's health information system. Thus, if a physician already owns a computer, a hospital could not provide the physician with a new computer.[110] However, the hospital could provide the physician with software or other materials required to allow a physician's existing computer to interface with the hospital's health information system.[111] Among other criteria, this exception requires that any community-wide health system arrangement not be provided to a physician in any manner that takes into account the volume or value of referrals or other business generated by the physician, and the arrangement cannot violate the federal anti-kickback statute or any other federal or state law or regulation governing claims submission or billing.[112]

## 2. Electronic Prescribing Exception

A 2006 Stark exception published as a final rule on August 8, 2006, permits a hospital, under certain conditions, to donate items and services that are "necessary and used solely to transmit and receive electronic prescription information."[113] To meet the requirement that the items and services be "necessary," the hospital's donations must not replicate any technology the physician currently possesses.[114] To meet the requirement that the items and services be used "solely" to transmit and receive electronic prescription information, the donated technology can *only* be used for that purpose.[115] Under this exception, hospitals may provide to members of their medical staffs such nonmonetary remuneration as hardware, software, information technology, and training services as long as these items and services are provided as part of, or are used to access, an electronic prescription drug program that meets the standards of Medicare Part D at the time the items and services are provided.[116] Licenses, rights of use, intellectual property, upgrades, education and support services (for example, help

---

[108] 69 Fed. Reg. at 16,113.

[109] *Id.*; 42 C.F.R. §411.357(u)(2).

[110] 69 Fed. Reg. at 16,113.

[111] *Id.*

[112] 42 C.F.R. §411.357(u)(1)–(3). Note that in 2006 the OIG declined to adopt an anti-kickback safe harbor that would mirror the Stark law's community-wide health information systems exception. 71 Fed. Reg. 45,110, 45,134 (Aug. 8, 2006); Appendix B-6 on the disk accompanying this volume.

[113] 71 Fed. Reg. 45,140, 45,169 (Aug. 8, 2006) (codified at 42 C.F.R. §411.357(v)). The same day, the OIG also published an anti-kickback safe harbor that mirrors this electronic prescribing exception to the Stark law. 71 Fed. Reg. 45,110 (Aug. 8, 2006); Appendix A-3 on the disk accompanying this volume.

[114] 71 Fed. Reg. at 45,144 and 45,170 (codified at 42 C.F.R. §411.357(v)(8)).

[115] 71 Fed. Reg. at 45,145–46.

[116] 71 Fed. Reg. at 45,170 (codified at 42 C.F.R. §411.357(v)(2)).

desk and maintenance services), operating software necessary for the hardware to function, and interfaces designed to link the hospital's existing electronic prescribing system to the physician's existing electronic prescribing system are all included in the types of items covered by this exception; billing, scheduling, administrative and general office software, however, are not covered.[117]

In selecting the recipient(s) of its electronic prescribing donation, a hospital may not take into account either directly or indirectly the volume or value of referrals from the physician or any other business generated between the parties.[118] To promote interoperability,[119] the hospital may not take any action to limit or restrict the use or compatibility of the donated items or services with other electronic prescribing or electronic health records systems.[120] Further, neither the physician nor the physician's practice (including employees and staff members) may condition doing business with the hospital on the receipt of these items or services.[121] Finally, the donation arrangements must be set forth in writing.[122]

Despite its liberal donation parameters that extend from software to hardware and beyond, this exception will likely assume little importance, given its "used solely" requirement. Hospitals and physicians will likely look more frequently to the electronic health records exception described below, as it permits the donation of technology for much broader purposes than merely electronic prescribing.

### 3. Electronic Health Records Exception

The other Stark exception published as a final rule on August 8, 2006, permits a hospital to donate to *any* physician (i.e., not just to a member of its medical staff) certain software that is necessary and used predominantly to create, maintain, transmit, or receive electronic health records.[123] Unlike the electronic prescribing exception, this exception is limited to items and services in the form of software or information technology and training services and excludes the provision of hardware.[124] Also unlike the electronic prescribing exception, this technology need not be "used solely" for electronic health records, but rather can also be used for other software directly related to the care and treatment of individual patients (for example, patient administration,

---

[117]71 Fed. Reg. at 45,144–45.

[118]71 Fed. Reg. at 45,170 (codified at 42 C.F.R. §411.357(v)(6)).

[119]For purposes of this regulation, "interoperable" means that at the time of the donation, the software is "able to (1) communicate and exchange data accurately, effectively, securely, and consistently with different information technology systems, software applications, and networks, in various settings, and (2) exchange data such that the clinical or operational purpose and meaning of the data are preserved and unaltered." 71 Fed. Reg. at 45,155.

[120]71 Fed. Reg. at 45,170 (codified at 42 C.F.R. §411.357(v)(3)).

[121]*Id.* (codified at 42 C.F.R. §411.357(v)(5)).

[122]*Id.* (codified at 42 C.F.R. §411.357(v)(7)).

[123]*Id.* (codified at 42 C.F.R. §411.357(w)). In this final rule, CMS adopted a broad definition of "electronic health record" as "a repository of consumer health status information in computer processable form used for clinical diagnosis and treatment for a broad array of clinical conditions." The same day, the OIG also published an anti-kickback safe harbor that mirrors this electronic health records exception to the Stark law. 71 Fed. Reg. 45,110 (Aug. 8, 2006).

[124]*Id.*

scheduling functions, billing, clinical support software, etc.), as long as the *predominant* use of the software is for health records.[125] The regulation does exclude from its protection, however, the staffing of physician offices as well as any item or service used to conduct personal business or business unrelated to the physician's medical practice.[126]

To qualify for this exception, several conditions must be met. First, the software must be interoperable at the time it is donated.[127] The software may be deemed interoperable if a certifying body recognized by the Secretary has certified the software no more than twelve months prior to the date it is provided to the physician.[128] Also regarding interoperability, the regulations bar the donor (or anyone taking action on the donor's behalf) from taking any actions to disable or limit interoperability.[129] This condition is designed to protect against donors that improperly attempt to create closed or limited electronic health records systems by offering technology that locks in business for the donor.[130]

Second, the physician is required to share the costs of all of the technology and services covered by this exception by paying 15 percent of the donor's costs for the items and services. The donor is forbidden from financing this amount or providing the physician with a loan to make this payment.[131] CMS believes that the 15 percent requirement "is high enough to encourage prudent and robust electronic health records arrangements without imposing a prohibitive financial burden on physicians" and that it will "increase the likelihood that the physician will actually use the technology."[132] Costs and payments must be documented *before* this Stark exception will protect the arrangement.[133]

Next, the requirements of necessity (i.e., that the physician not already have comparable software) and that the donation of items not be a condition of doing business are identical to those requirements in the electronic prescribing exception.[134] The donated software must also contain electronic prescribing capability that meets the Medicare Part D standards at the time it is provided.[135] Finally, a hospital-donor's selection of a physician-recipient may not take into account the volume or value of referrals or other business generated between the parties.[136] If the hospital's selection of its donor(s) is based on any of the following, this requirement is deemed to be met:

- The total number of prescriptions written by the physician (but not the volume or value of prescriptions dispensed or paid by the donor or billed to the program);

---

[125]71 Fed. Reg. at 45,151 and 45,170 (codified at 42 C.F.R. §411.357(w)).
[126]71 Fed. Reg. at 45,170 (codified at 42 C.F.R. §411.357(w)(11)).
[127]*Id.* (codified at 42 C.F.R. §411.357(w)(2)).
[128]*Id.*
[129]71 Fed. Reg. at 45,170 (codified at 42 C.F.R. §411.357(w)(3)).
[130]*Id.* at 45,150.
[131]71 Fed. Reg. at 45,170 (codified at 42 C.F.R. §411.357(w)(4)).
[132]71 Fed. Reg. at 45,161.
[133]*Id.*; 42 C.F.R. §411.357(w)(7).
[134]71 Fed. Reg. at 45,170 (codified at 42 C.F.R. §§411.357(w)(8), (5)).
[135]*Id.* (codified at 42 C.F.R. §411.357(w)(11)).
[136]*Id.* (codified at 42 C.F.R. §411.357(w)(6)).

- The size of the physician's medical practice (for example, total patients, total patient encounters, or total relative value units);
- The total number of hours that the physician practices medicine;
- The physician's overall use of automated technology in her or his medical practice (without specific reference to the use of technology in connection with referrals made to the donor);
- Whether the physician is a member of the donor's medical staff;
- The level of uncompensated care provided by the physician (including a consideration of the total number of Medicaid patients served by a physician's practice, as long as there is no direct correlation with the number of Medicaid patients referred to the donor);[137] or
- A determination made in any reasonable and verifiable manner that does not directly take into account the volume or value of referrals or other business generated between the parties.[138]

Consistent with the President's goal of the swift adoption of electronic health records technology, this particular Stark exception will sunset on December 31, 2013.[139]

## I. Medicare Prohibition on Unbundling

When Congress enacted the prospective payment system for hospitals, one of its concerns was that while full DRG payment could be made to hospitals, entities other than hospitals could submit additional charges for the hospitalized patient. Hence, Congress amended the law to bar anyone, except hospitals and physicians (and now certain other allied health professionals such as certified nurse anesthetists), from billing for services furnished to Medicare hospital patients. The exception for professional billing is solely for services personally furnished by physicians or mid-level professionals.[140] This is called the "prohibition against unbundling." Some physicians use their own equipment or personnel in treating hospital patients. Nothing in the law prohibits this practice. However, physicians may not charge Medicare for their equipment or personnel services. For example, a physician directing a staff nurse to take equipment to a hospital and administer a diagnostic test to a patient may not bill for any service other than interpretation of that test. If Medicare is billed for services other than test interpretation, in this case, the physician and the hospital are subject to CMPs, and the hospital is also at risk of termination of its provider agreement.

Accordingly, hospitals must ensure that neither physicians nor anyone else bill Medicare for services furnished to hospital patients, other than services personally performed by a physician or other mid-level professional falling

---

[137]71 Fed. Reg. at 45,160.

[138]71 Fed. Reg. at 45,170 (codified at 42 C.F.R. §411.357(w)(6)).

[139]71 Fed. Reg. at 45,171 (codified at 42 C.F.R. §411.357(w)(13)).

[140]42 U.S.C. §1395cc(a)(1)(H); 42 C.F.R. §489.20(d); *see also* 53 Fed. Reg. 29,486 (Aug. 5, 1988); 63 Fed. Reg. 47,552, 47,555–59 (Sept. 8, 1998).

within an exception to the prohibition on unbundling. If outside suppliers furnish other than separately billable professional services to hospital patients, the hospital may pay for such services and bill Medicare.[141]

Because Stark II treats all inpatient and outpatient hospital services for Medicare and Medicaid patients as designated health services subject to Stark II referral and billing prohibitions, when a physician orders these services, the financial arrangements between the physician and the hospital must qualify for an exception under Stark II. It is possible to structure a permissible compensation arrangement under Stark II whereby the hospital pays the physician on a per service or per unit of time basis for performing these services, provided that the per service or per unit of time payment is agreed to in advance and constitutes the fair market value of the services actually provided by the physician, not taking into account the volume or value of any of the physician's referrals to the hospital or other business generated by the physician for the hospital.[142]

The Stark II Phase II final rule clarified and modified the different exceptions that may apply where a physician provides services to the hospital that may not be unbundled. The modifications to these exceptions, including the revised definitions of "fair market value" and "set in advance," are addressed below in Sections IV.B., C., D., and I.

## J. Physician Use of Hospital Clinic Space

Some hospitals operate their own clinics. Those clinics may qualify as hospital outpatient departments or may simply operate as physician offices. Medicare payment differs depending on whether the site is a hospital-based outpatient department. Many other payors do not make that distinction and will pay for the services as if they were furnished in a physician office. When a hospital operates a clinic, the hospital must ordinarily collect payments to cover its costs from either third-party payors or from the physicians practicing at that site. The failure to do so raises issues under the Stark law, the limitations applicable to tax-exempt hospitals, and the anti-kickback statute.

When a hospital-operated clinic operates as a hospital outpatient department,[143] there are two charges: one for physician services and another for hospital technical component services. The hospital's charge is recorded regardless of whether the patient received any ancillary tests; this technical component charge covers all costs except services personally furnished by the physician or other mid-level professional who may bill independently. Medicare honors the hospital's bill, but because it is paying the hospital for overhead costs ordinarily deemed to be included in the physician's fee, Medicare will reduce the physician payment for services furnished in a hospital outpatient department.[144] This reduction is referred to as the "site of service" differential and its

---

[141] Although the service will be included on the hospital's bill to Medicare, under the DRG system, there will not be any additional payment to the hospital unless the patient is a cost outlier.

[142] 42 C.F.R. §411.354(d).

[143] 65 Fed. Reg. 18,434, 18,538 (Apr. 7, 2000) (codified at 42 C.F.R. §413.65).

[144] 42 C.F.R. §414.22(b)(5)(i)(A).

application is triggered when the physician indicates on the face of the bill that the site of service was a hospital outpatient setting.

Medicare is almost unique among third-party payors in honoring a hospital facility charge for clinic services. Most other payors will not pay the hospital bill, but will pay the physician bill without any reduction for a site of service differential. In such instances, the hospital must obtain payment from the physician for the use of its facilities for which payment is included as an undifferentiated part of the payment to the physician from non-Medicare payors. If the hospital fails to do so, it is furnishing value in-kind to the physician, which constitutes a "financial relationship" within the meaning of the Stark law, and the transaction will not ordinarily fit within an exception. For the same reason, the transaction poses risks under tax laws applicable to tax-exempt hospitals. Finally, the transaction could be viewed as a kickback to the extent that there is evidence of intent to induce or reward the physician for referring patients to the hospital.

When a hospital-operated clinic is not treated for Medicare purposes as a hospital outpatient department, the same issue exists, except it pertains to all payors, not just Medicare. For the reasons discussed above, it is critical for a hospital to obtain fair market value payment from physicians for the space, personnel, and other items or services furnished to them. Such payments should be able to fit within the Stark exception for payment of fair market value compensation by physicians for items or services.[145]

There may be one circumstance in which a hospital could furnish clinic space to physicians at no charge. In some remote parts of the country or in inner city areas, it is difficult to persuade physicians to maintain offices or even visit. If there is demonstrated difficulty in obtaining physician services, a hospital may furnish clinic space at no charge to a physician as fair compensation for physician availability and travel time in coming to the site. Assuming that the facts are consistent with the claim of physician shortage and there is no evidence of any improper intent to motivate referrals, both anti-kickback and tax-exempt organization problems should be eliminated. However, it remains unclear whether there might still be Stark law problems in such a case.

## IV. CONTRACTUAL RELATIONSHIPS WITH PHYSICIANS

### A. Generally Applicable Limitations Arising From Tax-Exempt Status Can Be the Basis for Intermediate Sanctions Under the Internal Revenue Code

The Internal Revenue Service (IRS) perceives that hospitals are prone to furnish benefits to physicians for admitting patients who bring in revenues beyond payment of fair market value for necessary services. However, the only weapon that the IRS had historically to deal with violations of the limitations on tax-exempt hospitals was revocation of the hospital's tax-exempt status. The severity of the penalty meant that it was rarely used. To make the threat of enforcement of

---

[145]42 U.S.C. §1395nn(e)(8); 42 C.F.R. §411.357(i).

the prohibitions on tax-exempt organizations engaging in transactions resulting in inurement or private benefit more credible, Congress amended the law to permit the imposition of intermediate sanctions for violations of these prohibitions.[146]

The intermediate sanctions provisions impose an excise tax whenever a Section 501(c)(3) public charity or a Section 501(c)(4) organization provides an excess benefit (e.g., unreasonable compensation, a bargain sale or lease, or other non-fair market value transaction) to or for the benefit of a "disqualified person." The amount of the tax is initially 25 percent of the excess benefit provided to the disqualified person, but if the transaction is not timely corrected, a second-tier tax of 200 percent of the excess benefit is imposed.[147] In addition, a 10 percent excise tax (up to a per-transaction maximum of $10,000) is imposed on any individual organization manager for the tax-exempt organization who approves or participates in the transaction knowing it to be an excess benefit transaction.[148] In each case, the excise tax is imposed on the individuals involved and not on the organization itself. The IRS published final regulations in January 2002 to address an array of interpretational issues related to the intermediate sanctions statute, some of which are summarized below.[149]

## 1. Definition of "Disqualified Persons"

One of the major uncertainties regarding intermediate sanctions has been precisely who would be a "disqualified person" subject to the rules. The statute provides simply that a disqualified person is a person who is in a position to exercise substantial influence over the affairs of the applicable tax-exempt organization at any time during a five-year look-back period, as well as family members of a disqualified person and certain 35 percent controlled entities.[150] The regulations add considerable meat to these statutory bones. In this regard, the regulations specifically identify certain persons who hold the following powers, responsibilities, or interests as having substantial influence over the affairs of a tax-exempt organization. These include:

- Any individual who serves as a voting member of the governing body of the organization;
- Any individual or individuals who have the power or responsibilities of the president, chief executive officer, chief operating officer, treasurer, or chief financial officer of an organization, regardless of title; and
- Any person who has material financial interest in certain provider-sponsored organizations in which a tax-exempt hospital participates.[151]

The regulations also identify categories of persons deemed not to have substantial influence over the affairs of a tax-exempt organization.[152] These

---

[146]Taxpayers Bill of Rights 2, Pub. L. No. 104-168, §1311, 110 Stat. 1452 (1996) (codified at 26 U.S.C. §4958).

[147]26 U.S.C. §§4958(a)(1), (b).

[148]26 U.S.C. §§4958(a)(2), (d)(2).

[149]67 Fed. Reg. 3076 (Jan. 23, 2002) (codified at 26 C.F.R. §53.4958–0 et *seq.*).

[150]26 U.S.C. §4958(f)(1).

[151]26 C.F.R. §53.4958-3(c).

[152]*Id.* at §53.4958-3(d).

categories include any employee who receives economic benefits from the organization that are less than what a highly compensated employee earns,[153] who is not otherwise defined in the proposed regulations as a disqualified person or identified as having substantial influence, and who is not a substantial contributor to the organization.[154]

Apart from these more specific rules, the regulations provide that the determination of whether a person has substantial influence over the affairs of an organization is based on all relevant facts and circumstances.[155] Some of the facts and circumstances tending to show that a person has substantial influence over the affairs of an organization include that the person:

- Is the founder of the organization;
- Is a substantial contributor to the organization;
- Receives compensation based on revenues derived from activities of the organization that the person controls;
- Has authority to control or determine a significant portion of the organization's capital expenditures, operating budget, or compensation for employees;
- Has managerial authority;
- Owns a controlling interest in a corporation, partnership, or trust that is defined as a disqualified person; or
- Is in legal terms a non-stock entity controlled by a disqualified person.[156]

There are also several factors that tend to show no substantial influence over the organization:

- The person has taken a bona fide vow of poverty as an employee, agent, or on behalf of a religious organization;
- The person is an independent contractor who merely provides professional advice and does not have decisionmaking authority;
- The direct supervisor of the person is not a disqualified person;
- The person participates in no management decisions affecting the whole or discrete parts of the organization; or
- Any preferential treatment offered to a person based on a contribution is offered to all other donors making a similar donation.[157]

Any physician on a hospital's board of directors, or who has been on the board in the last five years, is a disqualified person. Other physicians may also be disqualified persons, as illustrated by the following IRS examples:

- A cardiologist employed by a tax-exempt hospital is a disqualified person when the cardiologist is managerial head of the department and has authority to allocate the budget for that department, including authority to determine employee compensation.

---

[153] As defined under 26 U.S.C. §414(q)(1)(B)(i).

[154] 26 C.F.R. §53.4958-3(d).

[155] *Id.* at §53.4958-3(e)(2).

[156] *Id.*

[157] *Id.* at §53.4958-3(e)(3).

- A radiologist employed by a tax-exempt hospital in a non-managerial capacity is *not* a disqualified person when the radiologist does not receive revenue-based compensation from activities he controlled and has no authority to control or determine any significant portion of the hospital's capital expenditures, operating budget, or employee compensation.
- A management company of a whole hospital joint venture with a tax-exempt hospital participant is a disqualified person when the management company is given broad discretion to manage the joint venture's day-to-day operations.[158]

## 2. Definition of "Reasonable Compensation"

Under the regulations, compensation for the performance of services is reasonable, and thus does not confer an excess benefit, only if it is an "amount that would ordinarily be paid for like services by like enterprises (whether taxable or tax-exempt) under like circumstances."[159] Generally, the circumstances to be considered are those existing on the date the contract for services was made, with special rules taking into account any material modification and certain termination rights with respect to the contract. However, when reasonableness of compensation cannot be determined based on circumstances existing on the date the contract for services was made, then the determination of whether the compensation is reasonable is made based on all facts and circumstances, up to and including circumstances as of the date of payment.[160] Compensation under the regulations includes all items provided by a tax-exempt organization in exchange for the performance of services by a disqualified person, regardless of whether cash or non-cash compensation and (subject to some exceptions) whether taxable or nontaxable compensation.[161]

## 3. Rebuttable Presumption That a Transaction Is Not an Excess Benefit

The regulations state that a compensation arrangement between a tax-exempt organization and a disqualified person is presumed to be reasonable—and a transfer of property, a right to use property, or any other transaction with a disqualified person is presumed to be at fair market value—if three conditions are satisfied: (1) the compensation arrangement or terms of transfer are approved by an authorized body of the organization or by a committee of the governing body composed entirely of individuals who do not have a conflict of interest with respect to the arrangement or transaction; (2) the authorized body obtained and relied on appropriate comparability data prior to making its determination; and (3) the governing body or committee adequately documented the basis for its determination concurrently with making that determination.[162]

---

[158]*Id.* at §53.4958-3(g).
[159]26 C.F.R §53.4958-4(b)(1)(ii)(A).
[160]*Id.* at §53.4958-4(b)(2).
[161]*Id.* at §53.4958-4(a)(4)(iv)(B).
[162]26 C.F.R. §53.4958-6(a).

The IRS may rebut this presumption "only if it develops sufficient contrary evidence to rebut the probative value of the comparability data relied upon by the authorized body."[163] It is highly advisable for hospitals to take the steps to fit within this safe harbor whenever entering into transactions with physicians who may be disqualified persons.

## 4. Rules for Revenue-Sharing Transactions

Under the intermediate sanctions statute, the IRS has authority to promulgate regulations that address whether certain revenue-sharing transactions with disqualified persons (e.g., compensation based in whole or in part on the revenues of one or more activities of the tax-exempt organization) result in inurement, and therefore constitute an excess benefit transaction.[164] The IRS proposed rules in 1998 to govern these transactions, but due to the overwhelming number of conflicting comments on this issue, it did not publish rules governing these transactions in the temporary regulations. The IRS indicated that it may issue proposed rules on this topic in the future, but in the meantime, revenue-sharing transactions will be evaluated under the general rules for excess benefit transactions.[165]

## B. Hospitals Often Lease Space to Physicians

Physicians often prefer office space in or near a hospital for the convenience of seeing and treating hospitalized patients. Hospitals also benefit from this close proximity because physicians who are nearby are readily available to patients if needed. In addition, a hospital may believe that a physician is more likely to admit patients to it instead of a competitor if it is more convenient for the physician to do so. For all of these reasons, most hospitals have at least one professional office building, if not more, on or near campuses owned by the hospital or a hospital affiliate.

Again, the trinity of legal issues—limitations on tax-exempt organizations, the Stark law, and the anti-kickback statute—is of concern. For all of these issues, there is a simple solution: the hospital must lease space at fair market value.

The HHS OIG created a safe harbor under the anti-kickback statute for leases of space. The requirements of the safe harbor are:

(1) The lease agreement must be set out in writing and signed by the parties;

(2) The lease must specify the premises it covers;

(3) If the lease is intended to provide the lessee with access to the premises for periodic intervals of time, rather than on a full-time basis, it must specify exactly the schedule of such intervals, their precise length, and the exact rent for such intervals;

(4) The term of the lease must be for not less than one year;

---

[163] *Id.* at §53.4958-6(b).

[164] 26 U.S.C. §4958(c)(2).

[165] 66 Fed. Reg. 2144, 2152–53 (Jan. 10, 2007).

(5) The aggregate rental charge must be set in advance, be consistent with fair market value in arm's length transactions, and not be determined in a manner that takes into account the volume or value of any referrals or business otherwise generated between the parties for which payment may be made in whole or in part under Medicare, Medicaid, or other federal health care programs; and

(6) The amount of space rented must not exceed that reasonably necessary to accomplish a commercially reasonable business purpose.[166]

A transaction that does not fit within a safe harbor does not necessarily violate the anti-kickback statute; failure to fit within a safe harbor simply means that the parties do not have absolute assurance that the transaction will not be challenged. Depending on the nature of the transaction, the parties often can have a very high level of comfort without precisely fitting within a safe harbor. However, the safe harbor for leases of space is so easily met, there is usually no reason not to do so.

Because a lease is a financial relationship under the Stark law, physician leases of hospital-owned space must necessarily meet an exception to Stark. Unlike the safe harbor for leases under the anti-kickback statute, the need to meet a Stark exception when there is a financial relationship between a hospital and a referring physician is not optional. The requirements for the Stark exception for leases of space (as supplemented by the Phase II rule) are:

(1) The agreement must be set out in writing, signed by the parties, and specify the premises covered by the lease;

(2) The term of the agreement must be for at least one year, and if the lease is terminated during the term with or without cause, the parties may not enter into a new agreement during the first year of the original term of the agreement;

(3) The space rented or leased must not exceed that which is reasonable and necessary for the legitimate business purposes of the lease or rental and must be used exclusively by the lessee when being used by the lessee, except that the lessee may pay for the use of space consisting of common areas if those payments do not exceed the lessee's pro rata share of expenses based on the ratio of the space used exclusively by the lessee to the total amount of space (other than common areas) occupied by all persons using the common areas;

(4) The rental charges over the term of the lease must be determined in advance and be consistent with fair market value;

(5) The charges must not be determined in a manner that takes into account the volume or value of any referrals or other business generated between the parties;

(6) The agreement would be commercially reasonable even if no referrals were made between the lessee and the lessor; and

(7) A holdover month-to-month rental for up to six months immediately following an agreement of at least one year that meets the above

---

[166]42 C.F.R. §1001.952(b). (For text of the safe harbor, see Appendix A-2 on the disk accompanying this volume.)

requirements is permitted as long as the holdover rental is on the same terms and conditions as the immediately preceding agreement.[167]

The provision allowing for termination of the lease with or without cause prior to the end of the first year of the agreement was added by the Phase II rule. CMS determined that without-cause terminations do not pose a high risk of anti-kickback abuse and, in fact, allow parties to get out of an agreement without the expense of litigation that may arise from leases that can be terminated "for cause" only.[168] The Phase II rule also eased the "exclusive use" criterion to allow subleases. The "exclusive use" test is considered met as long as the lessee or sublessee does not share the rental space with the lessor or any entity related to the lessor[169] during the time it is rented or used by the lessee or sublessee.[170] It is important to note, however, that certain subleases may create indirect compensation arrangements that would have to fit within the indirect compensation arrangement exception.[171]

There is no specific IRS regulation for leases between tax-exempt hospitals and physicians, but the general principles of the prohibition against inurement and private benefit require that the lease be at fair market value. The IRS does consider the leasing of office space to a physician as a related activity and a tax-exempt hospital is not subject to the tax on unrelated business taxable income (UBTI) for lease payments.[172]

For Medicare cost-reporting purposes, costs associated with hospital space leased to physicians are not allowable.[173] This is of virtually no significance for most acute care hospitals, because such cost reimbursement accounts for a small percentage of total payments to hospitals. However, this remains a relevant consideration for some hospitals.[174]

## 1. Clarification of "Fair Rental Value"

The key determinant of compliance under the three statutes of greatest concern is whether rent was determined and collected at fair market value. In the abstract, fair market value (or fair rental value) is the amount negotiated between a willing landlord and a willing tenant when neither is coping with exigent circumstances.[175] In almost all instances, fair market value can be expressed in a

---

[167]42 U.S.C. §1395nn(e)(1); 42 C.F.R. §§411.357(a)(1)–(7).

[168]69 Fed. Reg. 16,054, 16,086 (Mar. 26, 2004).

[169]*Id.*

[170]42 C.F.R. §411.357(a)(3).

[171]42 C.F.R. §411.357(p). Note that the Phase III final rule modifies the definition of indirect compensation to consider a physician to "stand in the shoes" of a physician organization of which the physician is a member. *See* 72 Fed. Reg. 51,012, 51,061–63 (Sept. 5, 2007).

[172]*See* Rev. Rul. 69-463, 1969-2 C.B. 131; Rev. Rul. 69-464, 1969-2 C.B. 132; Priv. Ltr. Rul. 84-52-099.

[173]PROVIDER REIMBURSEMENT MANUAL, Pt. I §2108.5.

[174]*E.g.*, critical access hospitals in rural areas, which continue to be cost-reimbursed. In addition, there are a few Blue Cross plans that continue to pay cost reimbursement using the Medicare principles of reimbursement.

[175]63 Fed. Reg. 1659, 1686, 1721 (Jan. 9, 1998); 56 Fed. Reg. 35,942, 35,972 (July 29, 1991). But see the Stark Phase I regulations for a somewhat different definition. 42 C.F.R. §411.351. (For text of the Stark Phase I regulations, see Appendix B-3 on the disk accompanying this volume.)

range, not a single amount. A hospital is well advised to obtain contemporaneous documentation for its files showing that the amounts at which it is leasing to physicians are within the range of fair market value. Usually, a real estate broker in the community with access to market information can explain in writing the basis for arriving at an estimate of fair market value. Fair market value is not necessarily related to cost. It is quite possible that cost may be greater than fair market value. Thus, the recovery of cost is not necessarily the measure of fair market value.

In some instances when hospitals examine their compliance with Stark and other applicable laws, they discover that leases entered into years ago or by prior management do not satisfy requirements of the law because the rent is too low. If a significant portion of time remains in the lease term, this presents a problem to the hospital. Physicians have often been more sympathetic than one might expect to renegotiating an increased rent in the middle of a lease term. In other instances, however, physicians refuse to renegotiate the rent and rely on what they believe to be a binding obligation under state law. In such a case, the hospital could seek a declaratory judgment that the lease is not enforceable because it violates the anti-kickback statute, in that the low rent had been offered to the physician in exchange for referrals.[176] This is a risky strategy because voiding the contract involves admitting a violation of a federal criminal statute.

If rent is too low, but the intent was not to reward or induce the physician to refer patients to the hospital, there is no violation of the anti-kickback statute. However, there remains a problem under the Stark law. The only cure, apart from renegotiating fair market rental, is for the physician not to refer or admit Medicare or Medicaid patients to the hospital.

Issued in February 2002, *United States ex rel. Goodstein v. McLaren Regional Medical Center*[177] addressed how to determine fair market value in a space lease.[178] A *qui tam* relator alleged that McLaren Medical Center (McLaren) induced referrals of Medicare patients to its facility by providing remuneration to physician-owned Family Orthopedic Realty (FOR) by leasing space from FOR. In determining whether McLaren's payment was meant to induce referrals, the court focused on whether the payment made by McLaren to referring FOR physicians for the leased space was at or above fair market value, as evaluated under the Stark II statute and the anti-kickback statute.[179] The court found that the lease agreement was an arm's-length transaction and that the agreed-upon rental amount was fair market value.

Much of the court's determination hinged on the fact that the defendant's witnesses engaged in an in-depth, thorough review of types of leases and lease costs for the relevant geographic area.[180] Additionally, the lengthy negotiations engaged in by the parties and the terms of the lease demonstrated that their transaction was indeed set at fair market value. For example, McLaren and the FOR physicians negotiated for nine months before reaching an agreement on

---

[176] *See* Polk County v. Peters, 800 F. Supp. 1451 (E.D. Tex. 1992) (physician defended against hospital claim by asserting illegality of contract under anti-kickback statute).

[177] 202 F. Supp. 2d 671 (E.D. Mich. 2002).

[178] *Id.*

[179] *Id.* at 674–75.

[180] *Id.* at 685.

the terms of the lease.[181] Also, McLaren leased space based on measurements from the interior walls rather than the exterior (which would have included a great deal of unusable space), and McLaren did not pay for use of common areas.[182] Thus, McLaren was indeed only paying to lease the space that it was actually using. Further, McLaren did not pay rent while its space was being renovated, it had the option of paying the $35,000 security deposit via promissory note, and it was permitted to self-insure.[183] An analysis of the factors considered by the *McLaren* court can be extremely helpful in determining whether the terms of a space lease are indeed at fair market value.

## C. Leases of Equipment

On occasion, a hospital leases equipment from a physician. It is not uncommon for physicians to lobby hospitals to purchase certain pieces of equipment. If hospitals fail to do so, physicians may make the purchase themselves and be able to perform procedures that they otherwise would have to refer to other physicians at other facilities. However, physicians may not recover equipment costs from Medicare or most other payors. As explained in Section III.I., above, under the Medicare prohibition against unbundling, physicians may charge Medicare only for services furnished personally to hospitalized patients. Thus, physicians may not charge Medicare for use of equipment when patients are hospitalized.

While most other payors do not have a similar rule, the cost of equipment used by physicians in hospitals is not usually reflected in "usual and customary" fee schedules or in other fee schedules negotiated by payors. Thus, for physicians to recover the cost of equipment purchased and used for hospital patients, physicians must look to hospitals for payment. One avenue for equipment cost recovery is through lease transactions in which hospitals pay physicians on a per procedure basis for the use of the equipment.

Because an owner/lessor physician is also the physician most often using the equipment covered by the lease, the amount of rent paid on a per procedure basis may be closely tied to the volume of the physician's referrals.

The Phase II rule permits equipment and space leases to be structured such that lease payments are based on a per-use amount (a "click" fee). This type of arrangement is now permitted because CMS revised the definition of "set in advance,"[184] which is incorporated in the equipment-lease exception[185] and the space-lease exception.[186] The definition states that compensation will be considered "set in advance" if

---

[181]*Id.* at 676.

[182]*Id.*

[183]*Id.* The *McLaren* court subsequently declined to award costs and fees to the hospital, because it found the Government's position to have been "substantially justified." United States *ex rel.* Goodstein v. McLaren Reg'l Med. Ctr., No. 97-CV-72992-DT, 2003 U.S. Dist. LEXIS 27313, at *9–10 (E.D. Mich. Feb. 28, 2003).

[184]42 C.F.R. §411.354(d)(1).

[185]42 C.F.R. §411.357(b)(4).

[186]42 C.F.R. §411.357(a)(4).

the aggregate compensation, a time-based or per unit of service based (whether per use or per service) amount, or a specific formula for calculating the compensation is set in an agreement between the parties before the furnishing of the items or services for which the compensation is to be paid. The formula for determining the compensation to be paid must be set forth in sufficient detail so that it can be objectively verified, and the formula may not be changed or modified during the course of the agreement in any manner that reflects the volume or value of referrals or other business generated by the referring physician.[187]

The revised definition of "set in advance" specifically permits payments to be structured as time-based and per unit of service. Furthermore, the regulations explain that unit-based—including time-based—compensation will be deemed not to take into account the "volume or value of referrals" or "other business generated between the parties" if the compensation is fair market value for services or items actually provided, and the compensation formula does not vary during the course of the agreement in any manner that takes into account referrals of designated health services or referrals or other business generated by the referring physician—including private-pay health care business. Equipment leases may also fit under the fair market value exception,[188] whereas space leases are not eligible for this exception.

A lease based on volume, however, still will not meet the equipment rental safe harbor to the anti-kickback statute because of the problems with setting a per procedure lease aggregate contract price in advance.[189] This issue was raised by commenters and was addressed in the final safe harbor rules. Although the OIG recognized that this requirement would be a problem for as-needed arrangements, it found the requirement necessary to prevent abusive arrangements and reminded commenters "that safe harbors do not define the scope of legal activities under the anti-kickback statute."[190] These arrangements can still be lawful as long as payments are not made to induce referrals.

## D. Medical Director Agreements

Hospitals commonly compensate medical directors for services provided not only to the hospital as a whole, but also to individual departments. Indeed, Medicare requires a hospital to have medical directors for psychiatric units and rehabilitation units.[191] Thus, there is nothing wrong with compensating physicians for services as medical directors. Yet in some situations, compensation to medical directors has been characterized as payment for referrals, not for medical

---

[187]42 C.F.R. §411.354(d)(1).

[188]42 C.F.R. §411.357(*l*).

[189]42 C.F.R. §1001.952(c)(5).

[190]64 Fed. Reg. 63,518, 63,526 (Nov. 19, 1999). The anti-kickback statute is codified at 42 U.S.C. §1320a-7b(b) (see Appendix A-1 on the disk accompanying this volume for full text of the anti-kickback statute).

[191]42 C.F.R. §§412.27(d)(2), 412.29(f).

director duties.[192] Thus, there necessarily must be a demonstrable need for the physician's medical director services, and compensation paid for those services must be at fair market value.

Two Stark exceptions cover medical directors. First, under the "bona fide employment relationships" exception, a hospital can employ a medical director, full-time or part-time, as long as the amount paid is fair market value, does not relate to the volume or value of referrals made by that physician, and is paid pursuant to a commercially reasonable agreement that specifically identifies the services rendered.[193]

As a practical matter, however, most medical directors serve as independent contractors and not as employees. The Stark exception for personal services arrangements, therefore, can also come into play. This exception requires:

(1) The arrangement must be set out in writing, signed by the parties, and specify the services covered by the arrangement;

(2) The arrangement must cover all of the services to be furnished by the physician (or an immediate family member of the physician) to the entity;

(3) The aggregate services contracted for must not exceed those that are reasonable and necessary for the legitimate business purposes of the arrangement;

(4) The term of the arrangement must be for at least one year;

(5) The compensation to be paid over the term of the arrangement must be set in advance, must not exceed fair market value, and, except in the case of a physician incentive plan, must not be determined in a manner that takes into account the volume or value of any referrals or other business generated between the parties; and

(6) The services to be furnished under the arrangement must not involve counseling or promotion of a business arrangement or other activity that violates any state or federal law.[194]

The Phase II rule modifies the original exception to make clear that independent contractor physicians can receive compensation that takes into account the volume or value of personally performed services and can be compensated using a percentage-based methodology that is set in advance as defined under the Stark II regulations.[195]

---

[192]Indeed, suspect medical director contracts were a component of two Stark and anti-kickback enforcement actions that led to multi-million dollar settlements. Both Erlanger Medical Center in Chattanooga, Tennessee, and Northside Hospital in Atlanta, Georgia, have settled claims relating to, among other things, improper directorship agreements. *See Erlanger Agrees to Pay $40 Million on "Ongoing" Federal Investigation: Payments to Be Stretched Out Through 2007*, THE CHATTANOOGAN (Oct. 24, 2005), *available at* http://www.chattanoogan.com/articles/article_74681.asp; *Northside Hospital Settles Medicare Lawsuit for $5.7M*, ATLANTA BUSINESS CHRONICLE (Oct. 20, 2006), *available at* http://www.bizjournals.com/atlanta/stories/2006/10/16/daily48.html (prosecution alleging that medical directorship fees paid to transplant physicians exceeded fair market value).

[193]42 U.S.C. §1395nn(e)(2).

[194]42 U.S.C. §1395nn(e)(3).

[195]69 Fed. Reg. 16,054, 16,090 (Mar. 26, 2004).

The Phase II rule also establishes two new safe harbors for assuring that compensation will be deemed to meet the Stark law's fair market value requirement. These safe harbors are set forth in the fair market value definition[196] and are for hourly payments to physicians for personal services. These safe harbors are not limited to medical director services but may be used for any hourly physician compensation for personal services furnished to any designated health services (DHS) entity.[197]

The first new Phase II safe harbor requires that the hourly rate be equal to or less than the average hourly rate for emergency room physician services in the relevant physician market, provided that there are at least three hospitals providing emergency room services in the market.[198] The second new safe harbor requires averaging the fiftieth percentile salary for the physician's specialty of four national salary surveys and dividing the resulting figure by 2,000 hours to establish an hourly rate.[199] This option in the safe harbor provides a choice of six nationally recognized surveys from which to obtain salary data.[200]

Another clarification in Phase II regarding the personal services arrangement exception concerns the requirement that the parties' written arrangement specify all of the services to be furnished by the physician (or an immediate family member) to the entity.[201] CMS has clarified that this requirement can be met by cross-referencing all the agreements between the parties or by cross-referencing a master list of agreements that is updated centrally.[202] This master list must be made available to the Secretary upon request.[203]

The Phase II rule also revised the personal services arrangement exception such that an agreement may be terminated with or without cause during the first year of the agreement as long as the parties do not enter a substantially similar new agreement during the first year of the original term of the agreement.[204]

The anti-kickback statute also contains a relevant safe harbor provision: the "personal services and management contracts" safe harbor.[205] One difference between this safe harbor and the Stark exception is that the anti-kickback safe harbor requires the specific times for part-time service to be stated. That constraint is impractical for medical director arrangements. Although there is no legal guarantee that an arrangement meeting the Stark exception would not be viewed as violating the anti-kickback statute, in most situations compliance with the Stark exception should give the parties a high level of comfort that there is not a material anti-kickback risk.

---

[196]42 C.F.R. §411.351.

[197]69 Fed. Reg. at 16,092. Note, however, that these safe harbors were eliminated by the Stark Phase III regulations.

[198]42 C.F.R. §411.351.

[199]*Id.*

[200]*Id.*

[201]69 Fed. Reg. at 16,091.

[202]*Id.*; 42 C.F.R. §411.357(d)(1)(ii).

[203]42 C.F.R. §411.357(d)(1)(ii).

[204]42 C.F.R. §411.357(d)(1)(iv).

[205]42 C.F.R. §1001.952(d).

Three elements must be satisfied to demonstrate that a medical director's compensation is set at fair market value: the amount per hour (or however the unit of service is defined) must be reasonable, the amount of time used must be necessary, and that the time paid is the amount of time actually spent must be documented. Fortunately, a reasonable amount of data is available on physician compensation. At the low end of the scale are the Medicare reasonable compensation equivalents (RCEs). The RCEs are used to evaluate the allowability of physician compensation. The original RCEs were set at the median, have been updated only to 1997, and even then use a methodology yielding a low percentage increase.[206] Compensation above the RCEs is common and RCEs do not define fair market value.

Justifying the need for the medical director services goes hand-in-hand with showing that the services are actually furnished. Any situation with more than one medical director for a single department is likely to be viewed with suspicion. If such arrangements exist, hospitals should be especially thorough in demonstrating the necessity for the arrangements.

Documentation of medical director services is also important. For Medicare cost reporting purposes, a provider may not claim costs for physician compensation unless the provider has time records or other verifiable documentation showing that the physician actually worked the time for which compensation has been claimed.[207] With the declining importance of cost reimbursement, many hospitals do not insist that compensated physicians maintain the time records required to claim reimbursement. However, those records could be very useful if the government ever challenged, for purposes of the Stark exception or otherwise, whether the amount paid to a physician was fair market value.

## E. Employing and Contracting With Physicians for the Provision of Patient Care Services

Many hospitals seek to employ or contract with physicians to furnish not just medical director services, but to provide direct patient care. Hospitals do this for a number of reasons. One is to provide physician services in an underserved geographic area. For a charitable hospital to meet its mission to furnish health care services to the community it serves, it sometimes must retain physicians directly. Hospitals may also place physicians in outlying communities to expand the hospital's service area. Some hospitals seek control over physicians to facilitate the negotiation of managed care contracts. Directly controlling a network of physicians is much easier to manage, both legally and practically, than dealing through a PHO for managed care contracts.

### 1. Federal Compliance Issues

From a federal compliance perspective, employing physicians is the simplest way to avoid risk. The anti-kickback statute has an express exception for employees.[208] Similarly, the Stark exception for employees is very simple and

---

[206]62 Fed. Reg. 24,483 (May 5, 1997).

[207]42 C.F.R. §415.60(g)(1).

[208]42 U.S.C. §1320a-7b(b)(3)(B); *see also* 42 C.F.R. §1001.952(i).

requires only that the employment be bona fide and compensation be at fair market value and not tied to the volume or value of referrals (but it can be tied to personal productivity).[209] The Stark exception for personal services contracts is also fairly easy to comply with although it is more formal, as discussed in Section IV.D., above. The personal services exception is sometimes limiting in that it requires that the term of the agreement be a minimum of one year. But even that is not a problem if the arrangement can fit within the general fair-market-value exception appearing in the Stark II, Phase I final rule allowing arrangements for less than one year if they are renewed with the same terms.[210]

The difficulty with most situations in which hospitals employ or contract with physicians for the provision of medical services in hospital-operated clinics is that the vast majority of such clinics lose money. Losing money can raise the inference that physicians are being paid too much, i.e., that they are making more money than they would make in their own private practices. If physicians are paid more than they would make in private practice, there is a serious problem under the Stark law, a problem of inurement or private benefit under the applicable IRS law for tax-exempt hospitals, and a potential risk of being accused of violating the anti-kickback statute. Accordingly, it is necessary to determine why the practice is losing money and whether the physician is being paid too much in comparison with market data or if other factors are causing the loss.

Hospital-owned clinics have higher costs than physician offices for several reasons. First, many hospitals have greater expectations for what the space should look like, where it should be located, and how it should be furnished. While physicians often tolerate a cramped, poorly decorated space, most hospitals avoid that type of cost savings for image reasons. Second, clinic personnel are often paid at a level comparable to hospital scales for comparably qualified personnel. Those compensation levels usually are substantially in excess of what physician offices normally pay. Similarly, the Employee Retirement Income Security Act (ERISA) usually requires that hospitals offer the same benefit packages to clinic and hospital employees, and those benefits are almost always more generous than those typically offered by physicians. Thus, the costs of hospital operation of physician practices are greater than costs that physicians typically incur on their own.

In addition, revenue may suffer in hospital-operated practices. Hospital clinics are more likely to accept indigent and Medicaid patients. Usually, fewer ancillary services will be furnished in practices operated by hospitals because of the greater efficiency of sending patients to the hospital rather than duplicating those services in clinics. Thus, revenue for such ancillary services that is often captured in physician practices, and that under Stark may properly be distributed to physicians as long as the basis for distribution is not the volume or value of referrals from any individual physician, is not captured in hospital-operated clinics. Prevailing compensation levels for physicians reflect profits on ancillary services. Although hospitals may not pay physicians for referrals for ancillary

---

[209]42 U.S.C. §1395nn(e)(2); 42 C.F.R. §411.357(c).
[210]66 Fed. Reg. 856, 917–19, 961–62 (Jan. 4, 2001) (codified at 42 C.F.R. §411.357(*l*)).

services, there is no requirement to pay less than fair market value compensation for physician services furnished in a hospital-owned practice.

An issue related to hospital operation of physician practices is hospital acquisition of physician practices. In the 1990s, hospitals commonly acquired physician practices and the amounts paid often included payments for goodwill and other intangible assets. "Goodwill" is the value of a business based on future profitability. The problem that some hospitals encountered in acquiring physician practices was that they paid considerable amounts for the goodwill of practices that did not produce any net income. This left open the question of whether the amount paid was in excess of fair market value, which posed problems under the Stark law, the tax-exempt hospital restrictions, and the anti-kickback statute.

Physician practice acquisitions by hospitals can fit within the isolated transaction exception to the Stark law provided that the amount paid is fair market value, it does not directly or indirectly take into account the volume or value of referrals, the agreement would be commercially reasonable, and "there are no additional transactions between the parties for 6 months after the [sale of the practice]."[211] Goodwill is not the only intangible asset acquired in most transactions; hospitals also acquire the value of an ongoing business that includes an assembled workforce, telephone listing, arrangements for space and with vendors, and similar business assets. Hospitals establishing practices on their own would have to duplicate all of these items, and therefore, reasonable value should be attributed to these items. In addition, hospitals should be certain to obtain written valuations of acquired practices prepared by experts familiar with physician practice value. The nature of the appraisal is discussed below in connection with IRS treatment of physician practice acquisitions.

The OIG has created an anti-kickback safe harbor for physician acquisition of other physician practices, but it specifically refrained from extending that safe harbor to hospital acquisition of physician practices in most cases.[212]

The IRS has also expressed concern that hospitals may pay too much to acquire physician practices, but it does not otherwise object to such transactions. In determining the appropriate valuation for physician practice acquisitions, the IRS wants to see appraisals based on the future expected income stream from the practice after physician compensation has been paid.[213] This discounted cash flow methodology, of course, presumes that there will be profit from acquired practices. There are at least two crucial elements in the valuation process, the first of which concerns assumptions used to estimate expected future income such as payor rates, patient volume, the impact of managed care, and physician compensation and other costs. The second element is the imputed interest rate applied to discount future expected income, which will be driven by prevailing interest rates and the risk associated with physician practices.

---

[211]42 C.F.R. §411.357(f).

[212]42 C.F.R. §1001.952(e); 56 Fed. Reg. 35,952, 35,975 (July 29, 1991). In 1999, the safe harbor was extended to cover hospital acquisition of physician practices located in a health professional shortage area (HPSA) under certain circumstances. 64 Fed. Reg. 63,518, 63,553 (codified at 42 C.F.R. §1001.952(e)(2)).

[213]Internal Revenue Serv., U.S. Dep't of Treasury, *Exempt Organizations Continuing Professional Education Technical Instruction Program Textbook 2001.*

In 2003, the OIG issued an advisory opinion on payment to physicians at a county-owned women's health clinic where it allowed the provision of physician services at below fair market value fees.[214] In that opinion, a medical center was seeking to provide physician services to the clinic and to provide inpatient hospital services, including inpatient services at no charge for the county's primarily indigent and low-income self-paying patients. While the arrangement raised potential issues under the federal anti-kickback statute, the OIG concluded that it would not impose sanctions on the arrangement, because the requisite intent to induce or reward referrals of federal health care business was not present.[215]

The OIG specifically stated that the annual fee for physician services, while less than fair market value, was not unreasonable, because it covered the medical center's additional costs and gave the medical center an opportunity to strengthen its residency program by allowing its residents to explore a broader range of medical conditions. Also, any benefit of deriving referrals for federal health care programs for inpatient care was offset by the medical center's commitment to provide free care to county clinic patients who were unable to pay for the services, and the arrangement was unlikely to result in overutilization or increased costs to federal health programs, since the primary inpatient business generated by the clinic was labor and delivery services. Those admissions would be reimbursed on a prospective fixed fee basis. Additionally, since it was a county clinic, the public derived the benefits of getting the best possible price for the clinic's physician services.[216]

There also may be antitrust concerns when a hospital employs or contracts with physicians for the provision of patient care. Physician practices can be accused of collusion when they negotiate for payment with a hospital. In 2003, two San Diego anesthesiologist groups settled with the FTC based on the allegation that they jointly agreed on certain fees and other relevant competitive terms that they demanded from a San Diego hospital in order to provide on-call services.[217] These two groups made up three-quarters of the anesthesiologists with medical staff privileges at a San Diego hospital and worked on approximately 70 percent of the hospital's cases requiring anesthesiology services. Usually, anesthesiologists are reimbursed for their services by health insurance companies and other third-party payors. In addition to these payments, the anesthesiology groups attempted to obtain stipends from the hospital as payment for obstetric calls and for rendering services to uninsured emergency room patients. The hospital had never paid its anesthesiologists a stipend for taking calls. The FTC viewed the conduct of these two groups in attempting to obtain stipend payments as collusive and anticompetitive. The groups entered consent decrees with the FTC whereby they will refrain from engaging in future anticompetitive practices.[218]

---

[214]OIG Advisory Op. No. 03-06 (Mar. 26, 2003), *available at* http://oig.hhs.gov/fraud/docs/advisoryopinions/2003/ao0306.pdf.

[215]*Id.*

[216]*Id.*

[217]*In re* Grossmont Anesthesia Services Medical Group Inc. and *In re* Anesthesia Service Medical Group Inc., *available at* http://www.ftc.gov/opa/2003/05/asmg.htm.

[218]*Id.*

## 2. State Corporate Practice of Medicine Prohibitions

The greater problem for either employment or independent contractor arrangements arises under state statutes barring the corporate practice of medicine.[219] The underlying purpose of these statutes is to bar nonlicensed laypersons from interfering in the medical judgment of licensed physicians. In an era when managed care personnel freely make clinical judgments (but "only" on what is covered and not what should be done clinically), this doctrine may seem quaint, but it is a very serious legal issue in some states. In so-called "corporate practice states," physicians may be barred in any way from sharing income from professional services with any non-physician. Thus, even an arrangement in which the hospital contractually states that it will not interfere with a physician's medical judgment may be illegal in some states if the physician's revenue is assigned or shared with the hospital or any other non-physician.

There are several ways to deal with the corporate practice issue. Some hospitals and physicians choose to ignore the problem. In some states, the employment of physicians is a common practice that has continued for many years without challenge. In these instances, the principal risk of ignoring the doctrine may be that the contract between the hospital and physician is found to be void as a matter of public policy. This occurred initially in *Holden v. Rockford Memorial Hospital*,[220] where a court barred enforcement of the non-competition clause in a physician's contract with the hospital by invoking the corporate practice doctrine to void the contract. Although that particular case was reversed on appeal, the nonenforceability of an agreement with a physician is a potential risk in a number of states.

Ignoring the corporate practice doctrine in some states would be foolhardy. In Texas, for instance, violation of the bar on the corporate practice of medicine is a criminal offense and physicians can also lose their licenses. Even if the only sanction is the physician's loss of license, one can imagine that the physician might seek damages from both the hospital and the hospital's lawyer who drafted the agreement.

Some states have created exceptions to the corporate practice doctrine for separate entities controlled by nonprofit hospitals. For example, under the Texas Occupations Code, a corporation may employ physicians, provided that the organization is a nonprofit corporation, organized for a specific medical purpose, and organized and incorporated by persons licensed by the Texas State Board of Medical Examiners. [221]

---

[219] *See, e.g.,* TEX. OCC. CODE ANN. §§164.052(a)(13), 164.052(a)(17), 165.156. A summary of corporate practice limitations, by state, can be obtained from Cameron Dobbins of Dobbins, Fraker, Tennant Joy & Perlstein ("Survey of State Laws Relating to the Corporate Practice of Medicine"), *available at* http://www.dobbinslaw.com/cpmarticle.html.

[220] 678 N.E.2d 342 (Ill. App. Ct. 1997), *vacated by* 688 N.E.2d 309 (Ill. 1997), *on remand,* 692 N.E.2d 374 (Ill. App. Ct. 1998). *See also* Berlin v. Sarah Bush Lincoln Health Ctr., 688 N.E.2d 106 (Ill. 1997) (initially finding entire agreement unenforceable under corporate practice of medicine doctrine, but ultimately finding that a licensed hospital, whether for-profit or nonprofit, is exempt from prohibition of corporate practice of medicine).

[221] TEX. OCC. CODE ANN. §162.001 (Vernon Supp. 2004) (exception to the corporate practice of medicine prohibition). This exception was formerly contained in TEX. REV. CIV. STAT. ANN. art. 4495b, §5.01(a).

Another tool to deal with the corporate practice problem is a management agreement with an independent physician practice, through which the hospital manager controls the space and other aspects of the practice to achieve management goals without employing physicians or contracting for physician services. Even these arrangements could possibly be viewed as violating the corporate practice prohibition, though, if the management fee is closely tied to physician revenue.

### 3. Medicare and Medicaid Prohibitions on the Reassignment of Revenue

Both Medicare and Medicaid statutes bar the reassignment of revenue by a physician, supplier, or provider unless an exception to that prohibition is satisfied.[222] (The first assignment of revenue is deemed to be from the patient to the provider, physician, or supplier although that assignment may be required by law.) Thus, absent an exception, physicians may not arrange for reimbursements for treating Medicare patients to be paid to any other entity.

The first question in analyzing a potential reassignment issue is whether there actually is a "reassignment" of revenue as defined by Medicare and Medicaid. The definition of "reassignment" is not a limited legal definition but covers powers of attorney, and any situation in which someone other than the physician has control over payment.[223] Reassignment occurs in any instance in which a hospital directly receives and controls Medicare and Medicaid payments.

When reassignments occur, the next question is whether they fit within an exception[224] to the general prohibition. Hospitals may qualify for several exceptions. One broadly applicable exception exists when physicians are in an employment relationship with the entity receiving the reassignment; physicians may always reassign their payments to employers. A second exception applies when physicians reassign payments to hospitals for services furnished at the hospital. By its terms, however, that exception is limited to services furnished on certified hospital premises. Usually, a physician will have an office outside the hospital and will see patients there as well. Services in off-premises offices can also fit within the exception for services furnished in clinics. Again, however, the exception is limited to services furnished on-site. If physicians provide services to patients elsewhere, such as in nursing facilities, and are not employed by hospitals, payments for those services provided in neither hospital-owned clinics nor on hospital premises do not technically fit within an existing exception to the prohibition against reassignment.

An issue that emerged in the late 1990s involved hospital contracts with commercial companies to furnish emergency room physician coverage to the hospital. Typically, those commercial companies required their contractor physicians to assign revenue to them. These arrangements did not fit within any existing exception.

---

[222] 42 U.S.C. §§1395g(c), 1396a(a)(32).

[223] MEDICARE CLAIMS PROCESSING MANUAL (CMS Pub. 100-4), Ch. 1, §§30.2, 30.2.2. The definition of "reassignment" does not include those situations in which someone other than the physician is authorized simply to endorse a government check "for deposit only" and deposit it in an account controlled solely by the physician.

[224] The exceptions are set forth at *id.* at §30.21.

Although the prohibition against reassignment has existed for many years, it has not been enforced vigorously. Indeed, the Medicare Carriers Manual suggests that the proper enforcement is to inform the physician that the assignment is not proper and if the arrangement is not changed within a reasonable period of time, to withhold payments.[225] Nothing in the Manual suggests that a violation of the prohibition against reassignment is a false claim or otherwise sanctionable with any of the multiple CMPs in the law. However, the OIG has alleged that violations of the prohibition against reassignment are actionable as false claims.[226]

The Medicare Prescription Drug, Improvement, and Modernization Act of 2003 (MMA)[227] remedied certain problems related to the furnishing of physician emergency room coverage. Prior to January 1, 2004, hospitals experienced difficulties in obtaining physician coverage of emergency rooms because they were not able to use certain staffing methods. Many hospitals hoped to obtain physician coverage through outside contractors; however, most commercial contractors would require their physicians to assign their revenue from emergency room services to the contractor. Such assignments did not fit within any then-existing Medicare exception to the "prohibition against reassignment." Congress remedied this problem in Section 952 of the MMA by expanding the exception for reassignment of revenue to allow payment to be made to an entity enrolled in the Medicare program that submits a claim for services provided by a physician or other person under a contractual arrangement with that entity, regardless of where the service was furnished.[228] Now, a carrier may make payment to an entity enrolled in the Medicare program that submits a claim for services provided by a physician under a contractual arrangement (such as where the services are furnished in an emergency room) as long as: (1) joint and several liability is shared between the entity submitting the claim and the person actually furnishing the service for any Medicare overpayment relating to such claim, and (2) the person furnishing the service has unrestricted access to claims submitted by the entity for the services provided by that person.[229]

## F. Hospital-Based Physicians

Hospitals routinely employ or contract with physicians for pathology and radiology services, as well as anesthesiology and the reading of electrocardio-

---

[225]*Id.* at §30.2.15 A, C.

[226]United States *ex rel.* Schwartz v. Coastal Healthcare Group, 232 F.3d 902 (10th Cir. 2000) (affirming dismissal of a physician's *qui tam* suit alleging Coastal violated the anti-assignment provisions of 42 U.S.C. §1395u(b)(6), which constitutes the making of false or fraudulent claims); U.S. Dep't of Health & Human Servs., Office of Inspector General, Health Care Fraud Report Fiscal Year 1997, *available at* http://www.usdoj.gov/dag/pubdoc/health97.htm (addressing false claims submitted through billing firms generally, and Coastal Healthcare Group specifically); U.S. Dep't of Health & Human Servs., Office of Inspector General, Statement of Lewis Morris, Assistant Inspector General for Legal Affairs, Medicare: Third-Party Billing Companies, Testimony Before the House Committee on Commerce, Subcommittee on Oversight and Investigations (Apr. 6, 2000), *available at* http://oig.hhs.gov/reading/testimony/2000/00406fin.htm.

[227]Pub. L. No. 108-173, 117 Stat. 2066 (2003).

[228]*Id.* at §952 (codified at 42 U.S.C. §1395u(b)(6)).

[229]Medicare Claims Processing Manual, CMS Pub. 100-4, Chapter 1, §30.2.7.

grams (EKGs). Contractual arrangements may extend to other departments, such as nuclear medicine and various subsets of radiology, such as radiation therapy if separate from the radiology department. The terms of such contracts typically ensure the hospital of coverage at all times when coverage is needed (e.g., during normal business hours with on-call availability for emergencies); define what the hospital will make available to physicians, such as office space and certain equipment; define physician services for patients (e.g., interpretation of all diagnostic images within certain performance parameters); define physician duties within the hospital, such as the development of departmental policies, training of hospital personnel, and performance of quality assurance functions within the department; address who is entitled to revenue from the physicians' services for patients; provide for exclusivity with the physician group; and set forth monetary compensation, if any, that one party will pay to the other.

## 1. Exclusivity

As noted in Section III.A.2., above, exclusivity provisions of many hospital-based physician contracts may be challenged by physicians outside the group trying to obtain work. The overwhelming weight of authority has upheld exclusivity provisions in hospital contracts,[230] although it is still wise to recite in the contract the reasons exclusivity is appropriate, such as to ensure 24-hour coverage and consistent quality. Because both radiology and pathology are viewed as hospital functions, albeit with a physician element, the hospital needs accountability in those departments more than elsewhere, and accountability is more easily obtained when a single person or entity is responsible.

Challenges to exclusivity arise not just from outsiders trying to get in, but also from a physician or physician group who had an exclusive contract that has been terminated. Notwithstanding that they benefited from exclusivity for many years, some groups view the benefits of such arrangements quite differently when they are on the outside looking in. Physicians in such instances may attempt to challenge termination of their exclusive contract as tantamount to termination of medical staff privileges and appeal through the medical staff bylaw appeal process. It is unseemly that physicians should be able to enjoy the benefits of an exclusive contract and then subsequently challenge a hospital's determination to award an exclusive arrangement for the same department to another group. To prevent this scenario, many hospitals use what is referred to as a "go quietly" clause in their contracts with hospital-based physicians. As the name implies, these provisions bind contracting physicians not to use the medical staff bylaw appeal process to contest the termination of the contract.

## 2. Kickbacks

An exclusive contract for a hospital department can be a valuable franchise. Virtually every hospital patient undergoes diagnostic imaging, and most

---

[230] *See, e.g.,* Jefferson Parish Hosp. Dist. No. 2 v. Hyde, 466 U.S. 2 (1984); Korshin v. Benedictine Hosp., 34 F. Supp. 2d 133 (N.D.N.Y. 1999); Ezekwo v. American Bd. of Internal Med., 18 F. Supp. 2d. 271, 278 (S.D.N.Y. 1998); Finkelstein v. Aetna Health Plans of N.Y., 1997 WL 419211, at *4–5 (S.D.N.Y. July 25, 1997), *aff'd,* 152 F.3d 917 (2d Cir. 1998); Collins v. Associated Pathologists, Ltd., 676 F. Supp. 1388 (C.D. Ill. 1987).

surgical patients require anatomic pathology services. Physician fees for interpreting the diagnostic images or reading slides of tissue removed surgically can be lucrative. Some hospitals have sought to extract value for the franchise for physician services in these departments. Some rumored schemes have not been subtle at all and include required "donations" from the physician group to the hospital, or a rebate of a stated percentage of the physician's collected revenue. Other schemes are a bit more refined and may include a requirement that physicians use the hospital billing service at a fee that is well above prevailing market rates for similar services. The OIG views such arrangements as illegal kickbacks from physicians to hospitals in exchange for all of the hospital radiology or pathology physician work.[231]

The OIG has also criticized arrangements in which hospital-based physicians are not required to give anything to the hospital but are required to furnish certain services without compensation. For example, pathologists are expected to train clinical laboratory personnel, calibrate equipment, and engage in other quality assurance activities in the laboratory. To the extent that such services have value and the hospital provides no consideration for these services, the anti-kickback statute may be implicated. However, hospitals often furnish physicians a place to work, equipment, demographic information for their billing, and other support services. Thus, the absence of cash compensation is not necessarily evidence that the hospital is obtaining kickbacks through free services in exchange for exclusive contracts.

## G. Discounts on Reference Laboratory Services

Standard hospital charges for laboratory tests usually exceed the customary charges of competing reference laboratories. Thus, to compete successfully in the reference testing market, hospitals must discount their laboratory charges significantly.

Some Medicare reimbursement specialists have concluded that a hospital may not discount its charges under Medicare's cost reimbursement principles. This is a myth. In fact, CMS has stated expressly that "the Medicare program cannot dictate to a provider what its charges or charge structure may be."[232]

At one time, CMS had suggested that laboratory discounts to physicians would violate the Stark law. However, Congress amended the law to create an exception for physician payments to laboratories (including hospitals acting as reference laboratories) "in exchange for the provision of clinical laboratory services."[233]

Deep discounts to physicians in certain circumstances can still present problems. The law requires laboratories to bill Medicare and Medicaid directly for all laboratory tests, but physicians often purchase laboratory services for

---

[231]U.S. DEP'T OF HEALTH & HUMAN SERVS., OFFICE OF INSPECTOR GENERAL, FINANCIAL ARRANGEMENTS BETWEEN HOSPITALS AND HOSPITAL-BASED PHYSICIANS, OEI-09-89-00330 (Oct. 1991), *available at* http://oig.hhs.gov/oei/reports/oei-09-89-00330.pdf. This report predated the general applicability of the Stark law to hospital services and does not discuss Stark issues.

[232]PROVIDER REIMBURSEMENT MANUAL, CMS Pub. 15-1, Pt. I, §2203.

[233]42 U.S.C. §1395nn(e)(8).

nongovernmental patients. Physicians presumably mark up the charges for those tests when they bill the patient or the third-party payor. If laboratories discount physician-purchased tests with the intent of inducing physicians to refer tests for governmental patients, a concern is created under the anti-kickback statute. Thus, the issue becomes at what point discounts to physicians are so deep as to be "remuneration" and not the offering of services at fair market value. Naturally, this question must be answered on the basis of the facts of each situation. Unless the market is acting irrationally (or everyone is violating the anti-kickback statute), meeting prevailing market prices for laboratory services should not ordinarily expose hospital laboratories to charges relating to the anti-kickback statute.

Discounts below the Medicare allowable fee schedule for laboratory tests can also raise the possibility that the hospital will be accused of charging Medicare an amount "substantially in excess of [its] usual charges."[234] This is a complex area, but as a general rule, most hospital reference laboratory pricing should not raise a serious risk of being viewed as violating this law.[235]

## H. Practice Management Services Furnished by Hospitals to Physicians

Some hospitals have entered into physician practice management businesses to make money and to try to make themselves indispensable to physicians. As long as hospitals charge fair market value for their services, these arrangements should not create legal problems. The Stark statute creates a broad exception for physician payments to hospitals or other entities for "items or services . . . at a price consistent with fair market value."[236] Similarly, for purposes of the anti-kickback statute and the limitations applicable to a tax-exempt organization, the permissibility of furnishing services to a physician turns on whether fair value is received in return.

## I. Academic Medical Centers

Generally, teaching hospitals as a group generate positive operating margins. In contrast, faculty practice plans often experience difficulty paying competitive compensation and operating in the black. Thus, at many sites, there is a perceived need to supplement the income of faculty practice plans and affiliated teaching hospitals are the logical source of these funds.

---

[234] 42 U.S.C. §1320a-7(b)(6); 42 C.F.R. §1001.701(a)(1). The OIG issued a proposed rule on payment "substantially in excess" in 2003. *See* 68 Fed. Reg. 53,939 (Sept. 15, 2003). In 2007, the OIG withdrew this rule. 72 Fed. Reg. 33,430 (June 18, 2007).

[235] At one time, the OIG proposed to interpret this law as requiring providers to offer "most favored nation" status to Medicare; however, in the final rule, OIG did not take that position. 62 Fed. Reg. 47,182, 47,186, 47,192 (Sept. 8, 1997), 63 Fed. Reg. 46,676, 46,681 (Sept. 2, 1998). In a letter from Kevin McAnaney, Chief, Industry Guidance Branch, Office of Inspector General (Apr. 26, 2000), *available at* http://oig.hhs.gov/fraud/docs/safeharborregulations/lab.htm, the OIG interpreted "usual" charges to mean median charges. "Substantially in excess" has not been defined in statute or regulation. *See* U.S. Dep't of Health & Human Servs., OIG Advisory Op. 99-2 (Mar. 4, 1999), *available at* http://oig.hhs.gov/fraud/docs/safeharborregulations/laboratory.htm; OIG Advisory Op. 98-8 (July 6, 1998), *available at* http://www.hhs.gov/fraud/docs/advisoryopinions/1998/ ao98_8.pdf.

[236] 42 U.S.C. §1395nn(e)(8).

Donative or equity transfers from tax-exempt teaching hospitals to faculty practice plans will be barred unless the faculty practice plans are also tax exempt. If faculty practice plans in these cases are tax exempt, such transfers without consideration from hospitals are not likely to be challenged by the IRS, if the plans are designed to include performance targets related to the hospital's charitable mission, i.e., the promotion of health, indigent care, medical education, and research.

The Stark II, Phase I final rule created, and the Phase II final rule supplemented and clarified, a new compensation exception for payments made to faculty of academic medical centers (AMCs).[237] This exception is in addition to other exceptions that may apply, such as the personal service arrangements or employment exceptions. An arrangement only needs to meet the requirements of one of these exceptions to comply with the law.

The requirements of the academic medical center exception include:

- The referring physician must:
  —Be a bona fide, full- or substantial part-time employee of a component[238] of the AMC;
  —Be state-licensed;
  —Have a bona fide faculty appointment at the affiliated medical school or at one or more of the educational programs at the accredited academic hospital; and
  —Provide and be compensated for substantial academic or clinical teaching services.
- The total compensation paid by all components of the AMC must:
  —Be set in advance;[239]
  —Not exceed fair market value; and
  —Not be determined in a way that accounts for the value or volume of referrals or other business generated.
- The AMC must:
  —Only transfer money among its components that directly or indirectly support its missions of teaching, indigent care, research, or community service, which includes patient care;
  —Set out the relationship of the components in an agreement adopted by the governing bodies of each component; and
  —Assure research money paid to a referring physician solely supports bona fide research.
- The arrangement cannot violate the anti-kickback statute.[240]

---

[237] 66 Fed. Reg. 856, 915–17, 960–61 (Jan. 4, 2001); 69 Fed. Reg. 16,054, 16,136–37 (Mar. 26, 2004) (codified at 42 C.F.R. §411.355(e)).

[238] A "component" means an affiliated medical school, faculty practice plan, hospital, teaching facility, institution of higher education, departmental professional corporation, or nonprofit support organization whose primary purpose is supporting the teaching mission of the academic medical center. The components need not be separate legal entities. 42 C.F.R. §411.355(e)(1)(i)(A).

[239] 42 C.F.R. §411.354(d)(1). The revision of the "set in advance" standard in Phase II changed the exception to permit a physician's compensation for academic services or clinical teaching services to be calculated using a percentage-based methodology. CMS continues to be concerned, however, about percentage-based arrangements in the context of equipment and office space rentals. *See* 72 Fed. Reg. 38,122, 38,184 (July 12, 2007).

[240] 42 C.F.R. §411.355(e)(1).

To be deemed an academic medical center under the Stark exception, an entity must be one of the following:

(1) An accredited medical school or an accredited academic hospital;
(2) One or more faculty practice plans that are affiliated with the medical school or academic hospital; and
(3) One or more affiliated hospitals in which a majority of the physicians on the medical staff are faculty members, and a majority of admissions to the hospital are made by physicians who are faculty members.[241]

In order to be considered an accredited academic hospital, the hospital or health system must sponsor four or more approved medical education programs.[242] Also, the accredited academic hospital and the affiliated hospital may be the same entity.[243] Hospitals may aggregate multiple faculty practice plans to satisfy the requirement in 42 C.F.R. Section 411.355(e)(iii) (listed in item (3), above) that the majority of the medical staff be on the faculty and that the majority of admissions to the hospital be made by faculty members.[244] However, primary care physicians without substantial academic or clinical teaching responsibilities do not qualify for protection under this exception.[245]

In clarifying "substantial" academic services and clinical teaching service, the Phase II rule notes that parties should use a reasonable and consistent method of calculating a physician's academic services and clinical teaching services.[246] The rule also instructs that any referring physician who spends at least 20 percent of his or her professional time or eight hours per week providing academic services or clinical teaching services (or a combination of both) will fulfill the requirement.[247] Because this is a safe harbor and not an absolute requirement, there may be referring physicians who do not fit these time parameters but who still provide sufficient academic services or clinical teaching services, depending on the individual physician's circumstances.[248]

One practical problem common at many AMCs is the sheer number of arrangements among the hospital, the medical school, and the faculty practice plan. These arrangements are so numerous that there is no single source of information or recordkeeping. Another problem arises when arrangements are not in writing; these impromptu arrangements must be formalized, the parties must identify financial relationships, and then each arrangement must be analyzed.

The Phase II rule also clarifies the requirement for a written agreement, specifying that all relationships between the different components of the academic medical center may be met through one agreement or multiple agreements.[249] Additionally, where all components of an academic medical center

[241] *Id.* at §411.355(e)(2).
[242] *Id.* at §411.355(e)(3).
[243] *Id.* at §411.355(e)(2)(iii).
[244] 69 Fed. Reg. at 16,109.
[245] *Id.*
[246] 42 C.F.R. §411.355(e)(1)(i)(A).
[247] 42 C.F.R. §411.355(e)(1)(i)(D).
[248] 69 Fed. Reg. at 16,110.
[249] 69 Fed. Reg. at 16,110; 42 C.F.R. §411.355(e)(1)(iii)(B).

are owned by a single legal entity, the financial reports of the entity, which document the transfer of funds between the components, including the medical center, may be sufficient evidence to verify an academic medical center's compliance with the written agreement requirement.[250]

Finally, while relationships in the aggregate may be set at fair market value, individual arrangements standing by themselves may not be defended as easily. To the extent that the parties desire to move funds from the hospital to the faculty practice plan or the medical school, the easiest way to do so is to pay full fair market value for the services furnished by the physicians to the hospital. For example, at the same time that some teaching hospitals are agonizing about how they may legally transfer funds to a medical school, they are paying far less than fair market value for teaching services furnished by physicians employed by the medical school.

In a 2002 advisory opinion, the OIG declined to impose administrative sanctions under the anti-kickback statute against components of an AMC where a teaching hospital proposed to make certain contributions to a state university endowment organization to be used by the medical school of the state university to support education and research.[251] In its opinion, the OIG specifically recognized that relationships among components of academic medical centers are often organizationally and financially complex and declined to impose sanctions for the following reasons: (1) the hospital and medical school, in this case, shared a common heritage as public institutions and had a common mission in training physicians, (2) when the state legislature established the hospital as a public body apart from the state university, which had previously owned and operated the hospital, the state legislature required the hospital to continue to support the education, research, and public service activities of the medical school; and (3) the medical school certified that it would take steps to insulate faculty physician judgment and income from pressure to refer to the hospital. Such steps included an agreement that the medical school would not require, encourage, or track referrals from faculty physicians to the hospital, that compensation paid to the faculty physicians, including income derived from contributions, would not be based on the volume or value of the physicians' referrals to any component of the AMC, including the hospital, and that the overall compensation would not exceed fair market value.[252]

## J. Gainsharing

Some hospitals have expressed interest in gainsharing, which is generally understood to refer to incentive plans for physicians to reduce hospital costs and enhance productivity. Gainsharing raises significant legal issues un-

---

[250]*Id.*

[251]OIG Advisory Op. No. 02-11 (Aug. 12, 2002), *available at* http://www.oig.hhs.gov/fraud/docs/advisoryopinions/2002/ao0211.pdf.

[252]*Id.*

der the Medicare program, with implications under the civil monetary penalty statute,[253] physician incentive plan regulations,[254] the Stark law,[255] the anti-kickback statute,[256] and tax-exemption issues. The tax issues, however, appear to be more manageable since a favorable ruling has been issued on gainsharing.[257]

## 1. Civil Monetary Penalties for Improper Incentive Plans

The Social Security Act prohibits hospitals from knowingly making "a payment, directly or indirectly, to a physician as an inducement to reduce or limit services provided *with respect* to individuals" entitled to Medicare and Medicaid.[258] The sanction for hospitals that pay or physicians who receive such a prohibited payment is a CMP in the amount of not more than $2,000 for each individual for whom such a payment is made. In addition, violators will be subject to a $50,000 penalty for each act and "not more than 3 times the total amount of remuneration offered, paid, solicited, or received."[259] Congress enacted this provision in response to Medicare's conversion from cost-based reimbursement to the prospective payment system (PPS). In other words, because the PPS allows a single payment for an inpatient stay, Congress and CMS worried that hospitals would attempt to discharge patients prematurely or not furnish appropriate services. Therefore, the law was amended to prohibit the inappropriate limitation or reduction of services for Medicare and Medicaid beneficiaries.[260]

The literal wording of the prohibition suggests that it refers to reduction or limitation of services to individual patients and not, specifically, to a group or class of individuals. A payment by a hospital to a physician for each Medicare patient discharged a day under the expected length of stay for the patient's DRG clearly would be improper under this law. However, it is not nearly so clear that payments to a group of physicians for the reduction in the length of stay for a large group of Medicare patients over a period of time (e.g., all discharges for the year) would violate the law. The latter example arguably does not reward the reduction of services to "individuals." The wording of the amount of the penalty supports the conclusion that the statute is directed only toward payments with respect to individual patients, because the sanction is "not more

---

[253] A general provision barring incentive payments to physicians relating to reducing care to individual patients. 42 U.S.C. §1320a-7a.

[254] 59 Fed. Reg. 61,571 (Dec. 1, 1994).

[255] 42 U.S.C. §1395nn. See generally Chapter 2 (Crane, Federal Physician Self-Referral Restrictions), and Appendix B-1 on the disk accompanying this volume for full text of the Stark law.

[256] 42 U.S.C. §1320a-7b(b). See Appendix A-1 on the disk accompanying this volume for full text of the anti-kickback statute.

[257] *IRS Approves Gainsharing Programs in Unreleased Private Letter Rulings*, 33 Daily Tax Rep. (BNA) G-1 (1999) (describing two private letter rulings approving gainsharing arrangements between tax-exempt hospitals and physician groups).

[258] 42 U.S.C. §1320a-7a(b)(1) (emphasis added). See Appendix D-1 on the disk accompanying this volume for full text of the CMP statute.

[259] 42 U.S.C. §§1320a-7a(a)(7).

[260] Omnibus Budget Reconciliation Act of 1986, Pub. L. No. 99-509, §9313(c), 100 Stat. 1874, 2003–04 (1986).

than $2,000 for each such individual with respect to whom the payment is made." If incentives were paid in the aggregate, the penalty provision would be much more difficult to apply, because the incentives do not relate directly to individuals.

Similarly, the General Accounting Office's (GAO) report of July 1986 on physician incentive plans[261] provides some insight into the government's concern about gainsharing programs. Although this report preceded the enactment of the CMP provision, it was issued after the inception of the PPS and reflects continuing concerns regarding decreased services to Medicare and Medicaid beneficiaries. In this report, the GAO provides specific recommendations to reduce the risk of abuse under physician incentive plans:

- Plan payments should be based on the cost performance of a group of physicians rather than individual physicians;
- Payments should be based on physician performance over a long period of time (at least one year);
- Incentive payments should not be based on hospital profits resulting from the treatment of any individual patient; and
- Incentive plans should include strong utilization review and quality assurance programs.

Again, although this GAO report is not a rule or regulation promulgated by CMS or OIG, it may be instructive in determining how to implement a physician incentive or gainsharing plan.

In a December 1994 proposed rule,[262] the OIG referred to the GAO report, acknowledging the existence of physician incentive plans. However, the proposed rule is virtually useless in offering guidance on which incentive plans are allowable. The proposed rule states that "it is impossible and impractical for the OIG to specifically indicate in regulations what specific criteria may make up an acceptable hospital physician incentive plan."[263] The latter statement clearly implies an acceptable incentive plan is possible. The proposed rule further indicates that each incentive plan will be evaluated on a case-by-case basis. So, although these rules have never been finalized, the OIG has stated in the preamble to the proposed rule and in the context of other laws that these arrangements *may* be acceptable with certain safeguards. As discussed below, this idea was later dispelled by the OIG in an advisory bulletin but was subsequently revived through a series of advisory opinions approving certain gainsharing arrangements.

---

[261] *See* U.S. GENERAL ACCOUNTING OFFICE, PHYSICIAN INCENTIVE PAYMENTS BY PREPAID HEALTH PLANS COULD LOWER QUALITY OF CARE, GAO/HRD-89-29, at 26 (Dec. 12, 1988); U.S. GENERAL ACCOUNTING OFFICE, REPORT TO THE CHAIRMAN, SUBCOMMITTEE ON HEALTH, COMMITTEE ON WAYS AND MEANS, HOUSE OF REPRESENTATIVES, GAO/HRD-86-103, 99TH CONG. 2D SESS. 3, MEDICARE-PHYSICIAN INCENTIVE PAYMENTS BY HOSPITALS COULD LEAD TO ABUSE (July 1986).

[262] 59 Fed. Reg. 61,571 (Dec. 1, 1994).

[263] *Id.* at 61,573 (generally approving incentive plans that do not impact direct patient care such as rewards for "timely review and completion of medical records").

On July 8, 1999, the OIG issued a special advisory bulletin that addressed gainsharing arrangements between hospitals and physicians.[264] While recognizing that gainsharing arrangements offered significant benefits, the OIG concluded that the CMP provision clearly prohibited them and called for the expeditious termination of such arrangements. Although the OIG agreed that reducing health care costs without adversely affecting patient care would be in the nation's best interest, it nonetheless believed that the plain language of the law prohibited tying reductions in items or services to payments made to physicians.

The OIG based its conclusions on the fact that when Congress wanted CMS to regulate managed care physician incentive plans it did so explicitly, but in the case of hospital-physician incentive plans, a lack of statutory authorization meant Congress considered such plans to be flatly prohibited. The bulletin went on to say that the law did not require that "the prohibited payment be tied to a specific patient or to a reduction in medically necessary care."[265] Although the preamble to the 1994 proposed rules indicated CMS would engage in a case-by-case analysis of these plans, the bulletin concluded that a case-by-case analysis would be inadequate and inequitable. A little over a month after the bulletin was published, the then Assistant Inspector General for Legal Affairs, Lewis Morris,[266] published a letter affirming that hospital-physician incentive plans in managed care plans, including Medicare+Choice, were not subject to the CMP prohibition.[267]

This letter was later followed by a response from the OIG to commentary in the trade press that the Department felt distorted the gainsharing bulletin.[268] In this response, the OIG restated its position that the law prohibits "any physician incentive plan that conditions hospital payments to physicians or physician groups on savings attributable to reductions in hospital costs for treatment of fee-for-service Medicare or Medicaid patients under the physicians' clinical care."[269] It also maintained that case-by-case determinations that were mentioned in the 1994 proposed rules were only for physician incentive plans that did not involve direct patient care and that were irrelevant to the arrangements discussed in the bulletin. A warning was issued to hospitals and physicians to heed the bulletin and unwind any existing gainsharing arrangements as expeditiously as possible.

---

[264]U.S. Dep't of Health & Human Servs., Office of the Inspector General, Gainsharing Arrangements and CMPs for Hospital Payments to Physicians to Reduce or Limit Services to Beneficiaries, 64 Fed. Reg. 37,985 (July 14, 1999), *available at* http://www.oig.hhs.gov/fraud/docs/alertsandbulletins/gainsh.htm.

[265]*Id.*

[266]Lewis Morris was, at the time of this printing, the Chief Counsel to the Inspector General.

[267]Lewis Morris, U.S. Dep't of Health & Human Servs., Office of Inspector General, Letter Regarding Social Security Act §1128A(b)(1) and (2) and Hospital-Physician Incentive Plans for Medicare or Medicaid Beneficiaries Enrolled in Managed Care Plans (Aug. 19, 1999), *available at* http://www.oig.hhs.gov/fraud/docs/alertsandbulletins/gsletter.htm.

[268]D. McCarty Thornton & Kevin G. McAnaney, U.S. Dep't of Health & Human Servs., Office of Inspector General, *Recent Commentary Distorts HHS IG's Gainsharing Bulletin*, *available at* http://oig.hhs.gov/fraud/docs/alertsandbulletins/bnagain.htm.

[269]*Id.*

Then, in a surprising turn of events, the OIG issued an advisory opinion on January 18, 2001, declining to impose sanctions on a gainsharing arrangement, even though it implicated both the CMP and anti-kickback statutes.[270] The proposed arrangement was for a hospital to pay a group of cardiac surgeons a percentage of hospital savings directly attributable to cost reduction measures implemented by the surgeons. The arrangement contained several safeguards to protect beneficiaries:

- The transparency of identifying the specific cost-saving actions and resulting savings will allow for public scrutiny;
- Credible medical support that the cost reduction measures will not adversely affect patient care was provided;
- Payments will be based on surgeries performed on all patients regardless of insurance;
- Objective historical and clinical measures were used to establish a baseline threshold below which no savings would accrue to the physicians;
- Written disclosures will be provided to patients;
- Financial incentives will be limited in duration and amount; and
- Profits will be distributed to physicians on a per capita basis mitigating any incentive for one physician to generate disproportionate cost savings.[271]

The advisory opinion also listed several features of a gainsharing plan that would heighten the risk of payments for improper reductions or limitations on services:

- Lack of a direct connection between physician actions and hospital cost-savings;
- Failure to identify individual cost-saving actions with specificity;
- Insufficient safeguards against other actions actually accounting for any "savings";
- Quality-of-care indicators of questionable validity and statistical significance; and
- No independent review of cost savings, quality of care, or other aspects of the arrangement.[272]

In contrast to the 2001 favorable OIG advisory opinion, a New Jersey federal district court held on April 15, 2004, that CMS' proposed gainsharing Demonstration Project violated the civil monetary penalties statute, and therefore enjoined the project.[273] The Demonstration Project, entitled "Hospital Performance-Based Incentives Demonstration," involved allowing hospitals to "make incentive payments to physicians that reward a combination of 'high

---

[270]U.S. Dep't of Health & Human Servs., OIG Advisory Op. No. 01-1 (Jan. 11, 2001), *available at* http://www.oig.hhs.gov/docs/advisoryopinions/2001/ao01_01.pdf.

[271]*Id.*

[272]*Id.*

[273]Robert Wood Johnson Univ. Hosp., Inc. v. Thompson, No. 04-142 (JWB), 2004 WL 3210732, at *10 (D.N.J. Apr. 15, 2004).

quality and efficient utilization of care' . . . 'much like those paid by managed care organizations.' "[274] The court stated that "the CMP . . . takes aim at curtailing the diminution of patient care and services for the sake of increased profits or reduced losses—the very goal and/or inevitable result of the Demonstration Project. Therefore the Demonstration Project violates the CMP. . . ."[275] The court also held that the project did *not* violate the anti-kickback statute, since the requisite intent to induce referrals was not present.[276] The court concluded that the goals of the Demonstration Project did not constitute the type of "fraudulent and abusive practices" prohibited by the anti-kickback statute.[277] In making its decision, the court relied heavily on the 1999 OIG Bulletin on Gainsharing, and also stated that the Secretary should have sought an advisory opinion from the OIG before proceeding with the demonstration project.[278]

Then, in early 2005, the OIG issued six advisory opinions on various gainsharing arrangements, evidencing a more favorable view of gainsharing than it had shown in the past.[279] The arrangements were similar to one another, in that all involved cardiology groups, cardiac surgeons, or cardiologists, and the details for each proposed arrangement were more or less the same. The proposed arrangements generally involved the hospital's sharing 50 percent of the cost savings arising from the implementation of certain cost-reduction measures with the given group of doctors. The cost-reduction measures included only opening disposable items as needed, performing blood cross-matching as needed, substituting less costly items for items currently in use, and standardizing certain cardiac devices when medically appropriate.[280]

In all six cases, the OIG stated that while the proposed arrangements would constitute improper payment to induce reduction or limitation of services under Sections 1128A(b)(1)–(2) of the Social Security Act (Act), and would potentially generate prohibited remuneration under the anti-kickback statute (Section 1128B(b) of the Act), the OIG would not impose sanctions.[281]

---

[274] *Id.* at *5–6.

[275] *Id.* at *13.

[276] *Id.* at *7.

[277] *Id* at *8.

[278] *Id.* at *10–13.

[279] OIG Advisory Op. Nos. 05-01 (Jan. 28, 2005), 05-02 (Feb. 10, 2005), 05-03 (Feb. 10, 2005), 05-04 (Feb. 10, 2005), 05-05 (Feb. 18, 2005), 05-06 (Feb. 18, 2005), *available at* http://oig.hhs.gov/fraud/advisoryopinions.html. These opinions indicate a departure from the wariness the OIG showed toward gainsharing arrangements in its 1999 Special Advisory Bulletin.

[280] *Id. See also* OIG Advisory Op. No. 06-22 (Nov. 9, 2006), *available at* http://oig.hhs.gov/fraud/docs/advisoryopinions/2006/AdvOpn06-22NewA.pdf. Like the plans approved the year before, the OIG found that this similar program also contained sufficient safeguards to protect against patient or program abuse.

[281] Potentially, the OIG could have imposed sanctions pursuant to the Social Security Act under the civil monetary penalty provision at §1128A(b)(1)–(2), the exclusion authority at §1128A(b)(7), and the civil monetary penalty provision at §1128A(a)(7) of the Act. The OIG stated further that the arrangements could also potentially implicate the physician self-referral law, §1877 of the Act, but because that law is outside of the scope of the OIG's advisory opinion authority, it did not express an opinion as to the application of §1877 of the Act to the proposed arrangement.

With respect to the anti-kickback statute, the OIG stated that it would not impose sanctions due to the presence of the following safeguards in the proposed arrangement:

- Participation in the proposed arrangement would be limited to doctors already on staff;
- The savings would be capped based on the prior year's admissions of federal health care beneficiaries;
- The contract term would be limited to one year, and admissions would be monitored for changes in severity, age, or payor;
- The distributions would be shared among only the same type of doctors on a per-capita basis, thus reducing the incentive for an individual doctor to generate disproportionate cost savings; and
- The actions that would generate cost savings would be set out with specificity, and the payments, which would not be unreasonable, would be limited in amount, duration, and scope.

The OIG also cited the following safeguards in the proposed arrangements as key factors in their decision that sanctions would not be imposed under Sections 1128A(b)(1)–(2), the civil monetary penalties provision of the Act:

- The proposed arrangements would utilize objective historical and clinical measures to establish a "floor" beyond which no savings would accrue to the doctors;
- With respect to product standardization measures, the doctors would still make a patient-by-patient determination of the most appropriate device from a full range of devices, and the devices they used before would still be available to them if they requested them;
- The savings would be paid out to the doctors as a group, and then distributed on a per-capita basis, thus removing the incentive for any one doctor to underutilize certain items or services;
- To minimize doctors' incentives to steer more costly patients to other hospitals, the case severity, ages, and payors of the patient population would be monitored by a committee and if significant changes occurred in the population, the doctor at issue would not be allowed to participate in the arrangement;
- The financial incentives of 50 percent of savings for a certain period of time would be reasonably limited in duration and amount;
- The arrangement would be disclosed in writing to patients;
- The cost-saving actions would be clearly and separately identified, and the transparency of the arrangement would allow for public scrutiny;
- The requestors offered credible medical support for the position that implementation of the recommendations would not adversely affect patient care; and
- The payments would be based on all procedures, regardless of the patient's insurance coverage.

The OIG also pointed out that the proposed arrangements in question did not have the types of features that would heighten the risk that payments would lead to inappropriate reductions or limitations of services, such as a lack of demonstrable direct connection between individual actions and any reduction in the hospital's out-of-pocket costs, a lack of specificity in identifying individual actions giving rise to savings, insufficient safeguards against the risk that other unidentified actions might account for savings, quality of care indicators of questionable validity and statistical significance, or a lack of independent verification of cost savings, quality of care indicators, or other essential aspects of the arrangement.[282] A gainsharing plan with these characteristics would be more likely to merit the imposition of sanctions from the OIG. The OIG has also cautioned that it would be very concerned with a gainsharing arrangement involving length of stay decisions.[283]

Also in 2005, the Medicare Payment Advisory Commission (MedPAC) issued a report to Congress that is evidence of a potentially more permissive approach toward gainsharing arrangements in the future.[284] The report was required by Congress in the Medicare Prescription Drug, Improvement, and Modernization Act of 2003. In the report, MedPAC supports gainsharing as a way to align physician and hospital incentives and further recommends that Congress amend the law to allow gainsharing arrangements and regulation by the Secretary.[285] The MedPAC report notes the *Robert Wood Johnson University Hospital v. Thompson* decision and recommends that Congress change the law to allow for gainsharing arrangements meeting certain specifications to be exempt from the civil monetary penalties provision and anti-kickback statute.[286]

In 2006, Congress, CMS, and the OIG continued to take a favorable approach toward gainsharing arrangements. Through the Deficit Reduction Act of 2005[287] Congress gave CMS the authority to approve up to six demonstration projects related to hospital and physician gainsharing. Of these six projects, at least two must be rural sites, and all proposals must include at least three types of safeguards:

- Measures that promote accountability, transparency, and full disclosure to the patient;
- Adequate quality controls that include independent review, establishing baseline thresholds, and ongoing monitoring and compliance; and
- Controls on payments that may change referral patterns, calculating savings based on hospitals' actual acquisition costs, limiting participating to physicians already on the hospitals' medical staffs, and limiting the amount, duration, and scope of the payments.

Each of the six sites selected for "demonstration" would receive protection from challenge. CMS set an application deadline of November 17, 2006 for the program[288] but, despite Congress' instruction that the demonstration projects

---

[282]*Id.*

[283]American Health Lawyers Ass'n Teleconference, "The State of Gainsharing— Implications of the OIG's Recent Advisory Opinions," Apr. 6, 2005.

[284]The MedPAC report is available at http://www.medpac.gov/publications/congressional_reports/Mar05_SpecHospitals.pdf.

[285]*Id.* at 44–47.

[286]*Id.* at 46.

[287]Pub. L. No. 109-171, §5007 (Feb. 8, 2006).

[288]71 Fed. Reg. 54,664 (Sept. 18, 2006).

be operational by January 1, 2007, CMS had not yet selected participants as of the current-through date for this volume.[289]

In September 2006, CMS also announced its Physician-Hospital Collaboration Demonstration (PHCD), which examines gainsharing programs in no more than 72 hospitals over a three-year period.[290] Gainsharing incentives under this program are limited to 25 percent of what physicians would ordinarily be paid for the types of cases in the demonstration. Through this project, CMS announced its intent to focus on longer-term effects of physician-hospital partnerships in "preventing short- and longer-term complications, duplication of services, coordination of care across settings, and other quality improvements that hold great promise for eliminating preventable complications and unnecessary costs."[291]

### 2. Physician Incentive Plan Regulations

When the CMP statute was originally enacted, Congress prohibited physician incentive plans by both hospitals and Medicare managed care plans that encouraged physicians to reduce or limit services.[292] In 1990, Congress deleted the reference to Medicare managed care plans and created a new section of the law that allowed these plans to implement incentive plans that did not induce reduction of medically necessary care to individual patients and did not place the physician at substantial risk for the costs of services not provided by that physician.[293] CMS issued a final rule implementing these amendments on December 31, 1996.[294] In addition to prohibiting reduction of medically necessary services and placing physicians at substantial financial risk, the rules also require managed care plans to file a disclosure of all incentive plans to CMS annually.[295]

### 3. Stark Limitations on Gainsharing

In the typical hospital-physician gainsharing arrangement the hospital and participating physicians have a financial arrangement under Stark II, because the hospital shares with physicians a portion of the hospital's cost savings attributable to various cost saving measures implemented by the physicians. Because the participating physicians make referrals to the hospital for inpatient

---

[289]In July 2007, CMS reissued its solicitation for proposals from rural hospitals, stating that it had received only a "limited response from rural hospitals" to its initial application request. The new deadline for rural hospital applications for the program was September 4, 2007. *See* 72 Fed. Reg. 36,710, 36,711 (July 5, 2007).

[290]71 Fed. Reg. 53,455 (Sept. 11, 2006).

[291]*Id.* As of the current-through date for this volume, the participants in this program had not yet been selected.

[292]Omnibus Budget Reconciliation Act of 1986, Pub. L. No. 99-509, §9313(c) (codified at 42 U.S.C. §1320a-7a).

[293]Omnibus Budget Reconciliation Act of 1990, Pub. L. No. 101-508, §§4204(a), 4731, 104 Stat. 1388, 1388-108-09, 1388-195 (1990) (codified at 42 U.S.C. §1876(i)(8)).

[294]61 Fed. Reg. 69,034 (Dec. 31, 1996) (following the publication of a final rule with comment period, 60 Fed. Reg. 13,430 (Mar. 27, 1996), and a final rule correction, 61 Fed. Reg. 46,384 (Sept. 3, 1996)) (codified at 42 C.F.R. §417.479).

[295]42 C.F.R. §417.479(h).

and outpatient hospital services (both of which are "designated health services" covered by Stark II), the typical gainsharing arrangement will violate the Stark II referral and billing prohibitions unless a Stark II exception applies.[296]

The Stark II exceptions that potentially could apply to a typical gain-sharing arrangement include exceptions for academic medical centers, personal services arrangements, fair market value arrangements, and indirect compensation arrangements.[297] If the gainsharing arrangement were between a hospital and its physician employees, the Stark II exception for employment arrangements might also be applicable.[298] All of these potentially applicable Stark II exceptions provide that the compensation involved in the arrangement cannot vary with the volume or value of referrals by the physician to the entity providing designated health services (i.e., the hospital in the case of a gainsharing arrangement), and the compensation cannot take into account any other business generated by the physician for the entity providing designated health services. Unfortunately, in the typical gainsharing arrangement the hospital cost savings that produce the funds for distribution to the participating physicians do vary with the volume or value of referrals by the participating physicians. As a result, none of the potentially applicable Stark II exceptions would cover a typical gainsharing arrangement.[299]

## 4. Anti-Kickback Limitations on Gainsharing Arrangements

The anti-kickback statute prohibits offers, payments, solicitations, or receipt of any remuneration to induce referrals of items or services paid by the federal government.[300] A gainsharing arrangement could disguise remuneration from the hospital to physicians for making referrals to the hospital. The more procedures a physician refers to a hospital with a gainsharing arrangement, the more that physician stands to gain from the hospital.

The OIG has promulgated safe harbor regulations to define practices that pose little risk of fraud or abuse. For complete assurance that a gainsharing arrangement will not invoke prosecution or sanction, it must meet the personal

---

[296]It may be possible to establish a gainsharing arrangement that does not involve a financial arrangement between the hospital and the participating physicians. For example, if an academic medical center enters into a gainsharing arrangement whereby a portion of the academic medical center's cost savings is used to fund research activities, it is possible that the gainsharing arrangement itself would not create any financial arrangement involving the participating physicians. If no financial arrangement exists, the Stark II prohibitions do not apply. However, given the broad definition of "indirect compensation arrangements" in the Stark II regulations, 66 Fed. Reg. 856, 958–59 (Jan. 4, 2001) (codified at 42 C.F.R. §§411.354(b)(5), (c)(2)), it is likely that most gainsharing arrangements will be deemed to establish a financial arrangement within the meaning of Stark II.

[297]42 C.F.R. §§411.355(e), 411.357(d), (*l*), (p).

[298]42 C.F.R. §411.357(c).

[299]Although the "physician incentive plan" provisions of the Stark II personal services exception do permit payments to a physician to reduce or limit services subject to certain limitations, those provisions would not cover the typical gainsharing arrangement, because the physician incentive plan provisions only apply to payments by an HMO or similar managed care entity with respect to reductions or limitations of services for the entity's enrollees. 42 U.S.C. §1395nn(e)(3)(B); 42 C.F.R. §411.357(d)(2).

[300]42 U.S.C. §1320a-7b(b). (For text of the anti-kickback statute, see Appendix A-1 on the disk accompanying this volume.)

services and management contracts safe harbor.[301] The arrangement must meet all of the following conditions to qualify:

- A term of one year;
- Compensation must be determined in advance and paid over the term of the arrangement;
- Compensation must be consistent with fair market value; and
- Compensation cannot take into account the volume or value of referrals.

Any incentive plan paid on a percentage basis would not meet the requirements for this safe harbor, because the amount of compensation would not be set in advance. In the absence of safe harbor protection, hospitals and physicians must rely on case-by-case evaluations.

The OIG stated in its January 2001 advisory opinion that the proposed agreement could violate the anti-kickback statute, but that the OIG would not impose sanctions for several reasons.[302] First, the arrangement is limited to surgeons who are already on the medical staff, the contract term is limited to one year, the potential savings are capped based on the prior year's admissions, and changes in admissions based on severity, age, or payor will be monitored. Second, any incentive for an individual surgeon to generate a disproportionate cost saving is minimized because profits are distributed on a per capita basis. Finally, the particular actions that will generate cost savings are set out with specificity; payments will be limited in amount, duration, and scope; and the payments themselves seem reasonable.

### 5. Tax-Exemption Issues for Gainsharing Arrangements

In February 1999, the IRS approved a gainsharing program through an unreleased private letter ruling.[303] Specifically, the proposed program was for a limited twelve-month period; the physicians would have to meet a threshold of quality care and patient satisfaction before being eligible for an award; awards would be reasonable and fair market value for the physician's efforts; reasonableness of the awards would be reviewed by an independent appraiser at the end of each year; and the hospital would continually monitor the physician's adherence to program integrity requirements.

Using existing factors for analyzing compensation plans and benefits provided to medical staff physicians, the IRS indicated that these programs must abide by the following principles:

- There can be no private inurement. Payments must be consistent with tax-exempt status and serve a real business purpose; parties must be engaged in arm's length bargaining; and payments must result in reasonable compensation; and

---

[301]42 C.F.R. §1001.952(d).

[302]U.S. Dep't of Health & Human Servs., OIG Advisory Op. No. 01-1 (Jan. 11, 2001), *available at* http://www.oig.hhs.gov/fraud/docs/advisoryopinions/2001/ao01-01.pdf.

[303]*IRS Approves Gainsharing Programs in Unreleased Private Letter Rulings*, 33 DAILY TAX REP. (BNA) G-1 (1999); *see also* Internal Revenue Serv., *Full Text Letter Rulings: IRS OKs Gainsharing Arrangement in Unreleased Letter Ruling*, 25 EXEMPT ORG. TAX REV. 252 (1999) (containing the full text of the unreleased letter).

- Payments must further a charitable purpose. Payments must bear a reasonable relationship to the charitable purpose; there must be no inurement; payments may not cause the hospital to operate for the benefit of a private interest; and payment transactions may not constitute a substantial unlawful activity.

Despite this favorable ruling from the IRS, after the release of the OIG advisory bulletin, the IRS said it would issue no further rulings without talking to HHS first to see if it had a problem with the arrangement.[304] Presumably, even with the favorable OIG advisory opinion, it is likely the IRS will continue to work closely with HHS to make these determinations.

The IRS has issued further information on gainsharing programs since the January 1999 unreleased private letter ruling. A January 9, 2002, information letter provides informal guidance to a Medicare demonstration program for certain cardiovascular and orthopedic services.[305] This program provides incentive-based compensation for doctors when they assist the hospital in achieving the goal of improving efficiency in inpatient care for Medicare beneficiaries while maintaining a certain quality of care standard. In addressing the program, the information letter explained that there is no *per se* rule that would prevent health care organizations from making incentive payments to physicians. Rather, certain incentive compensation factors should be analyzed to determine whether the utilization of an incentive compensation arrangement results in private inurement or impermissible private benefit. The list below is a noninclusive set of factors that, according to the information letter, the IRS will consider in analyzing a gainsharing arrangement for private inurement or impermissible private benefit:

- Was the compensation arrangement established by an independent board of directors or by an independent compensation committee? Was the board of directors/compensation committee subject to a conflicts-of-interest policy?
- Does the compensation arrangement result in total compensation that is reasonable?
- Is there an arm's-length relationship between the health care organization and the physician?
- Is there a ceiling or maximum on the amount of the incentive?
- Does the compensation arrangement have the potential for reducing charitable services or benefits that the organization would otherwise provide?
- Does the compensation arrangement take into account quality of care and patient satisfaction data?
- When the compensation arrangement depends on net revenues, does the arrangement accomplish the organization's charitable purposes?

---

[304]Barbara Yuill, *Government Officials Discuss Gainsharing; IRS "Reluctant" to Issue Favorable Rulings,* 149 DAILY TAX REP. (BNA) G-3 (1999); *see also* 66 Fed. Reg. 2144, 2155–56 (Jan. 10, 2001) (stating in rules published one day before the release of the OIG Advisory Opinion on gainsharing that the IRS would not issue private letter rulings on these arrangements).

[305]IRS Info. Ltr. No. 2002-0021 (Jan. 9, 2002), *available at* http://www.irs.gov/pub/irs-wd/02-0021.pdf.

- Does the compensation arrangement transform the principal activity of the organization into a joint venture between it and a group of physicians?
- Is the compensation arrangement merely a device to distribute all or a portion of the health care organization's profits to persons in control of the organization?
- Does the compensation arrangement serve a real and discernible business purpose of the exempt organization?
- Does the compensation result in any abuse or unwarranted benefits?
- Does the compensation arrangement reward the services that the physician actually performs?

Although this letter offers helpful guideposts for structuring a gainsharing arrangement so as to mitigate tax-exemption risks, it is important to remember that these are not the only factors that may be analyzed by the IRS and that this is only a nonbinding, nonprecedential information letter.[306]

## K. Physician Recruitment

### 1. Tax-Exemption Issues

Hospitals have historically offered a wide range of incentives to attract and retain physicians, such as signing bonuses and guaranteed minimum collections. In recent years, there have been two major developments affecting the physician recruitment activities of tax-exempt hospitals. The first development was the release of physician recruitment guidelines on October 17, 1994, which were attached to a closing agreement for Hermann Hospital.[307] Unlike conventional IRS guidance, these guidelines were released as an attachment to a closing agreement entered into between the IRS and a tax-exempt hospital. As one of the conditions of the closing agreement, the hospital agreed to abide by the guidelines attached to the agreement and publish them in certain tax publications. Although the guidelines have no precedential value, given their narrowness, it is relatively safe to say that a hospital recruitment program that complies with their terms is not likely to be challenged by the IRS.

In April 1997 the IRS released Revenue Ruling 97-21,[308] which was the culmination of its long-awaited physician recruitment guidance project. This document varied significantly from the guidelines and threw additional light on the IRS position on physician recruitment by tax-exempt hospitals. The primary significance of the revenue ruling is that it establishes for the first time direct legal precedent that physician recruitment by tax-exempt hospitals is a perfectly appropriate charitable activity. Thus, unlike the IRS's prior informal pro-

---

[306]Potential risks remain in connection with gainsharing arrangements. The IRS standards do not necessarily satisfy the OIG's anti-kickback standards. For a discussion of the new Deficit Reduction Act gainsharing developments see Chapter 1 (Baumann, An Introduction to Health Care Fraud and Abuse), at Section II.D.4.

[307]*See Closing Agreement Demonstrates How IRS Will Apply Physician Recruitment Rulings*, Daily Tax Rep. (BNA) No. 200, at d8 (Oct. 19, 1994).

[308]Rev. Rul. 97-21, 1997-1 C.B. 121 (Apr. 21, 1997), *available at* http://www.taxlinks.com/rulings/1997/revrul97-21.htm.

nouncements, including the guidelines, Revenue Ruling 97-21 can be cited by tax-exempt hospitals as authority in support of properly structured recruitment transactions.

Highlights of this important revenue ruling include the following:

- The ruling focuses on nonemployee physicians.
- The ruling maintains three longstanding IRS physician recruitment requirements: (1) there must be a demonstrable community need for a physician; (2) all incentives must be "reasonable"; and (3) the recruitment agreement must be in writing.
- The ruling makes it clear that the IRS places substantial emphasis on a tax-exempt hospital's board of directors becoming involved in and assuming responsibility for the hospital's physician recruitment activities, and requires that each physician recruitment arrangement be approved either (1) by the hospital's full board of directors, or (2) by a designated committee or officer in accordance with recruitment guidelines established, monitored, and reviewed by the board of directors.

Revenue Ruling 97-21 does not list permissible and impermissible physician recruitment incentives, but describes five factually detailed recruitment situations and determines that four of them would not jeopardize tax exemption and one would. These examples throw light on the IRS's thought process concerning differing recruitment situations.

In the first situation described, the IRS is obviously sympathetic to the plight of rural hospitals and communities and gives them considerable latitude in physician recruitment. According to Revenue Ruling 97-21, the hospital can offer a wide range of recruitment incentives such as a signing bonus, malpractice insurance for a limited period, office space for a limited number of years at below market rent, a mortgage guarantee on the physician's home, and financial practice start-up assistance. Although signing bonuses, malpractice insurance payments, and below market rent were three recruitment incentives called into question by the IRS in the guidelines, they are permitted for a rural hospital in a health professional shortage area (HPSA). HPSAs are designed to designate geographic regions within which an inadequate number of practitioners in certain specialties practice.[309] However, that a rural hospital is not in an HPSA does not preclude it from offering a wide range of recruitment incentives, as long as it can demonstrate community need for a physician in other ways.

In the second situation, the IRS determined that given an arm's length written agreement approved by the hospital's board, a hospital in an economically depressed inner-city area with a demonstrated need for a pediatrician could offer reimbursement of moving expenses, malpractice coverage, and a private practice income guarantee for a limited number of years. However, income guarantees must be reasonable based on "national surveys regarding income earned by physicians in the same specialty."[310] Once again, the IRS

---

[309]The database to determine if a particular geographic area is a designated HPSA for each specialty is *available at* http://hpsafind.hrsa.gov/.

[310]Rev. Rul. 97-21, 1997-1 C.B. 121.

makes clear that those areas with a demonstrable need for a physician will be able to offer a liberal range of physician recruitment incentives.

The third and fourth situations demonstrate that the IRS will allow incentives to physicians already in a hospital's community or on its staff (sometimes referred to as "cross-town recruiting"). In the third situation, a hospital can reimburse the physician for the cost of one year's malpractice insurance in return for an agreement by the physician to treat a "reasonable number of Medicaid and charity care patients for that year."[311] The IRS expressly approves of the hospital's carrying out its mission to treat Medicaid and charity patients by ensuring that a physician already in the area will commit to serve these patients. In the fourth situation, the IRS approves of recruiting a diagnostic radiologist who already practices in the community and is on the staff of another hospital to replace diagnostic radiologists who are relocating to another community. If there is an arm's length agreement approved by the board and an income amount that is reasonable, the hospital can offer a net income guarantee for the first few years that the physician works in the hospital's radiology department.

In the fifth and final situation, the IRS determined that a hospital that has knowingly and willfully paid physicians for referrals through the provision of physician recruitment incentives, in violation of the fraud and abuse statute, will lose its tax-exempt status. It is significant to note that under this scenario the hospital losing its tax-exempt status had engaged in "substantial" illegal physician recruitment activities. This suggests that the IRS is principally interested in punishing knowing, substantial violators of the law, not those who have made a good faith effort to comply with regulations.

Although it would be preferable for the IRS to provide additional recruitment scenarios, the message from the five situations discussed is quite clear. Tax-exempt hospitals will not have to fear the loss of their tax-exempt status as long as there is a demonstrable community need for recruiting a physician, the incentives offered are reasonable, the recruitment agreement is negotiated at arm's length and is in writing, and their boards and legal counsel are involved in the process.

## 2. Anti-Kickback Issues

The OIG first communicated its views concerning the anti-kickback implications of recruitment activities in a special fraud alert published in 1994 that addressed incentives offered to physicians by hospitals and listed the following examples of practices that the OIG considered suspect under the anti-kickback statute:

- Payment of any sort of incentive by the hospital each time a physician refers a patient to the hospital;
- Use of free or significantly discounted office space or equipment in facilities usually located close to the hospital;

---

[311] *Id.*

- Provision of free or significantly discounted billing, nursing, or other staff services;
- Free training for a physician's office staff in such areas as management techniques, CPT coding, and laboratory techniques;
- Guarantees which provide that, if the physician's income fails to reach a predetermined level, the hospital will supplement the remainder up to a certain amount;
- Low-interest or interest-free loans, or loans that may be forgiven if a physician refers patients (or some number of patients) to the hospital;
- Payment of the cost of a physician's travel and expenses for conferences;
- Payment for a physician's continuing education courses;
- Coverage on hospital's group health insurance plans at an inappropriately low cost to the physician; and
- Payment for services (that may include consultations at the hospital) that require few, if any, substantive duties by the physician, or payment for services in excess of the fair market value of services rendered.[312]

It was brought to the attention of the OIG,[313] however, that some hospitals in rural and urban underserved areas were having great difficulty attracting physicians to their communities. The OIG was concerned that beneficiaries were being denied access to quality health care in these areas. A final rule for a practitioner recruitment safe harbor was published in the *Federal Register* on November 19, 1999.[314] The intent of the safe harbor was to protect certain entities that offer inducements to entice a physician to practice in their communities from running afoul of the anti-kickback statute.[315] It was not meant to protect all physician recruitment arrangements, but only those in rural and urban underserved areas where it is difficult to recruit practitioners.

Protection under this safe harbor is limited to arrangements with new (within one year of completing a residency) or relocating practitioners practicing in an HPSA. HPSAs currently recognize only three types of specialties (primary care, which includes general and family practice, general internal medicine, pediatrics, and obstetrics and gynecology; dentistry; and mental health); thus, the practitioner recruitment safe harbor appears to be limited to practitioners in those specialties.

Physician recruitment agreements will be afforded safe harbor protection as long as the following nine standards are met:

(1) The arrangement is set forth in a written document signed by the parties that specifies the benefits provided by the entity, the terms under which the benefits are to be provided, and the obligations of each party;

---

[312]U.S. Dep't of Health & Human Servs., Office of Inspector General, Special Fraud Alert issued Aug. 1994, reprinted at 59 Fed. Reg. 65,373, 65,375–76 (Dec. 19, 1994).

[313]64 Fed. Reg. 63,518, 63,541 (Nov. 19, 1999).

[314]64 Fed. Reg. at 63,554; 42 C.F.R. §1001.952(n).

[315]64 Fed. Reg. at 63,541.

(2) If a practitioner is leaving an established practice, at least 75 percent of the revenues of the new practice must be generated from new patients;

(3) Benefits are paid for no more than three years, and the terms of the agreement are not renegotiated during this three-year period in any substantial way; however, if the HPSA ceases to be an HPSA during the term of the agreement, payments made under the agreement will continue to satisfy this paragraph as long as that agreement is in effect;

(4) There is no requirement that the practitioner refer to or generate business for the entity as a condition for receiving the benefits, although the entity may require that the practitioner maintain staff privileges at the entity;

(5) The practitioner is not restricted from establishing staff privileges at, referring any service to, or otherwise generating any business for any other entity of his or her choosing;

(6) The amount or value of the benefits provided by the entity do not vary based on the volume or value of referrals or other business generated for the entity;

(7) The practitioner agrees to treat patients receiving medical benefits or assistance under the Medicare and Medicaid programs;

(8) At least 75 percent of the revenues of the new practice are generated from patients residing in an HPSA or a medically underserved area (MUA) or who are part of a medically underserved population (MUP); and

(9) The payment may not directly or indirectly benefit any person (other than the practitioner being recruited) or entity in a position to make or influence referrals.[316]

Thus, in the limited situations described in the safe harbor, physician recruitment arrangements would be exempt from liability under the anti-kickback statute. Worth noting is that, in the preamble to the final regulations, the OIG stated that the safe harbor does not protect payments to a group or solo practitioner to assist in recruiting a new physician.[317] While the OIG conceded that these types of joint recruitment arrangements could be efficient and cost-effective, there remains a concern that the recruitment benefits could be used to disguise payments for referrals. It may be possible to remain within the protection provided by the practitioner recruitment safe harbor, if a hospital makes certain recruitment payments directly to the recruited physician who then may assign such payments to a group that employs the physician.

One of the primary factors in considering the risks associated with a potential physician recruitment arrangement is the status of the physician with respect to the community. Although the new practitioner recruitment safe harbor is only available for arrangements involving practice in an HPSA, the failure to qualify for safe harbor protection does not necessarily render an arrangement illegal. Compliance with the safe harbor standards above should reduce the risks associated with a physician recruitment arrangement, even if

---

[316]42 C.F.R. §1001.952(n).
[317]64 Fed. Reg. at 63,544.

safe harbor protection would not be available because the physician would not be recruited to practice in an HPSA. It is also a good idea to include a provision in the agreement that specifically disclaims an intent to require referrals, and the hospital should not engage in any activities that could be construed as indicia of an intent to induce the physician to refer patients to the hospital.

OIG's supplement to its hospital compliance guidance outlines factors that a hospital should consider when attempting to recruit physicians.[318] Specifically, hospitals should look at the size and value of the recruitment benefit and whether it is reasonably necessary to attract a qualified physician to the community.[319] Another factor to examine is the duration of the payout of the recruitment benefit.[320] The OIG notes in the proposed guidance that a benefits period extending more than three years would trigger heightened scrutiny of the arrangement.[321] Furthermore, the hospital should look at the existing practice of the physician and whether the physician is a new physician with few or no patients, a physician who has an established practice with potential for referrals, or a physician who will be relocating the practice from a substantial distance so that current patients will be unlikely to follow the physician or to be an established patient base for the relocated practice.[322] Last, the draft supplement encourages hospitals to analyze whether there is a need for the recruitment and whether the recruited physician's specialty is necessary to provide adequate care to patients in the community.[323]

OIG Advisory Opinion No. 01-04[324] presents an example of the type of physician recruitment the OIG does not believe should be subject to penalties, even though it does not fit in the safe harbor for physician recruitment.[325] The proposed relationship at issue involved a tax-exempt hospital in a rural, medically underserved area (MUA) and its proposed recruiting arrangement with a medical school resident who was training in otolaryngology—an underrepresented specialty in the hospital's service area. This relationship did not fit in the safe harbor, because the hospital was not located in an HPSA and the term of the relationship would exceed the three-year limit imposed in the safe harbor. HPSA determinations are only made when a geographic location is lacking in one of seven types of health professionals: primary medical care, dental care, mental health care, vision care, podiatric care, pharmacy services, and veterinary services. Thus, an area lacking in otolaryngologists would not be considered an HPSA.

When the OIG evaluates recruitment arrangements that do not fit within the safe harbor, it typically focuses on whether:

---

[318]70 Fed. Reg. 4858, 4868 (Jan. 31, 2005).

[319]*Id.*

[320]*Id.*

[321]*Id.*

[322]*Id.*

[323]*Id.*

[324]OIG Advisory Op. No. 01-04 (May 3, 2001), *available at* http://oig.hhs.gov/fraud/docs/advisoryopinions/2001/ao01-04.pdf.

[325]42 C.F.R. §1001.952(n).

(1) There is documented objective evidence of a need for the practitioner's services;

(2) The practitioner has an existing stream of referrals within the recruiting entity's service area;

(3) The benefit is narrowly tailored so that it does not exceed that which is reasonably necessary to recruit a practitioner; and

(4) The remuneration directly or indirectly benefits other referral sources.

In the opinion, the OIG elaborated on these factors for analysis.[326] For example, when a physician in one of the seven HPSA-designated specialties listed above is recruited in an HPSA for that specialty, the OIG considers that recruitment prima facie evidence of the need for the physician. However, the OIG will require more evidence for any alleged need for a non-HPSA specialist. Also, the OIG will look more favorably on the recruitment of a practitioner who does not have an established referral base, because there would be less likelihood that the hospital and the practitioner would have suspect incentives and loyalties. Additionally, the OIG will look at whether an incentive or benefit lasts longer than three years or is broader than the scope of the recruitment.[327]

In *United States v. LaHue/United States v. Anderson,*[328] practitioners and hospital administrators alike were sent a clear message about the types of physician compensation practices that will constitute criminal illegal remuneration under the anti-kickback statute. Indeed, this was the first case where a hospital executive was convicted on criminal charges for violations of the federal anti-kickback statute. The alleged conduct at issue was the type that had been identified as suspect under the 1994 Special Fraud Alert relating to hospital incentives to referring physicians[329]—payment for services that require few, if any, substantive duties by the physician, or payment for services in excess of the fair market value of services rendered.

This case involved a transaction between Baptist Hospital, arranged by Dan Anderson, the chief executive officer (CEO), and Drs. Ronald and Robert LaHue. The contract made the LaHues "Co-directors of Gerontology Services" for Baptist Hospital. As compensation for their roles as co-directors, the LaHues each received $75,000 annually, as well as additional compensation that, when combined, totaled more than $1.8 million between 1985 and 1995. After the payments began, Blue Valley, the LaHues' own medical practice and clinic, began to refer many patients who were Medicare beneficiaries to Baptist Hospital. As a result, Blue Valley patients constituted 8 to 10 percent of Baptist hospital admissions and over 90 percent of Baptist's volume in its outpatient clinic.[330] Overall, Baptist received over $39 million in Medicare payments for patients referred to the hospital by the LaHues. The government convinced the jury that neither LaHue ever really operated the gerontology services program

---

[326] OIG Advisory Op. No. 01-04.

[327] *Id.*

[328] 261 F.3d 993 (10th Cir. 2001).

[329] U.S. Dep't of Health & Human Servs., Office of Inspector General, Special Fraud Alerts, 59 Fed. Reg. 65,372 (Dec. 19, 1994), *available at* http://www.oig.hhs.gov/fraud/docs/alertsandbulletins/121994.html.

[330] 261 F.3d at 998.

at Baptist and that they were only receiving their medical director fees to refer patients from Blue Valley to the hospital. In addition, the jury found that Anderson knew that the hospital's payments to the LaHues were more than fair market value for their actual services. All three defendants were convicted. Anderson was sentenced to 51 months in prison and was fined $75,000; Robert LaHue was sentenced to 70 months in prison and was fined $75,000; and Ronald LaHue was sentenced to 37 months in prison and was fined $25,000.[331]

On appeal to the Tenth Circuit, the defendants argued that the convictions should be overturned because the court instructed jurors to find a defendant guilty if "one purpose" of the payments was to induce referrals, and that conviction is appropriate only when the motivation to solicit or receive remuneration is the person's primary purpose. The Tenth Circuit joined numerous other circuits in rejecting the primary purpose test,[332] stating that, "as a practical matter, if we held otherwise, we could illogically be faced with a case in which the offeror/payor is deemed to violate the statute, but the offeree/payee is not."[333]

In 2004, Alvarado Hospital Medical Center, its administrator, and Tenet Healthcare were charged with violating the anti-kickback law based on their use of physician relocation agreements, which the prosecution alleged were merely disguises for bribes intended to induce more referrals to the hospital.[334] The relocation agreements included approximately $10 million in guaranteed salaries and payment for equipment and overhead to roughly 100 physicians. While the anti-kickback law allows hospitals to pay some expenses to attract doctors with specialties that are not well represented in a given geographic area, the prosecution alleged that the area in question had no shortage of doctors, and that some of the "recruited" doctors already worked in the area. On February 17, 2005, the court declared a mistrial due to the jury's inability to reach a verdict, and on April 4, 2006, a second mistrial was declared after the jury was again unable to reach a verdict.[335] While the defendants were acquitted of two counts of violating the anti-kickback law, the judge allowed 17 counts of anti-kickback violations to remain, in addition to one count of conspiracy. On May 8, 2006, the OIG announced its intent to exclude Alvarado from participation in all federal health care programs.[336] Nine days later the OIG announced a

---

[331]*Id.* at 1001–02.

[332]*See* United States v. Greber, 760 F.2d 68 (3d Cir. 1985); United States v. Kats, 871 F.2d 105, 108 (9th Cir. 1989). *See contra* United States v. Bay State Ambulance & Hosp. Rental Serv., 874 F.2d 20 (1st Cir. 1989). *See also* Chapter 1 (Baumann, An Introduction to Health Care Fraud and Abuse), at Section II.A.1., for further discussion of this issue.

[333]261 F.3d at 1004.

[334]Lisa Girion, *Tenet Trial Ends with Hung Jury*, Los Angeles Times, Feb. 18, 2005, at C-1; Sarah Skidmore, *Alvarado Defendants Win 2 Acquittals*, San Diego Union-Tribune, Mar. 11, 2005, at C-3; *Defense Attacks Government's Case in Tenet Healthcare Kickback Trial*, 9 Health Care Fraud Rep. (BNA) 151 (Feb. 16, 2005).

[335]Rachel Laing, *2nd Mistrial Declared in* Alvarado *Case*, San Diego Union-Tribune, April 5, 2006, *available at* http://www.signonsandiego.com/news/business/20060405-9999-1n5mistrial.html.

[336]U.S. Dep't of Health & Human Servs., Office of Inspector General, *OIG Notifies Tenet of Potential Exclusion of Alvarado Hospital*, OIG News (May 8, 2006), *available at* http://oig.hhs.gov/publications/docs/press/2006/Alvarado%20MW%20Press%20Release%205.8.061.pdf.

settlement agreement with Tenet Healthcare Corporation requiring the company to sell or close the hospital and pay a $21 million fine.[337] Tenet completed the sale of Alvarado to Plymouth Health of Sherman Oaks, California, in early 2007,[338] thereby protecting Alvarado from exclusion from federal health care programs.

### 3. Stark Issues

A physician recruitment agreement establishes a financial relationship between the hospital and the recruited physician that implicates the Stark law.[339] However, the statute contains an exception for remuneration provided by a hospital to recruit a physician to relocate to the geographic area and become a member of the hospital's medical staff as long as:

- The arrangement and its terms are in writing and signed by both parties;
- The physician is not required to refer patients to the hospital;
- The amount of the remuneration under the arrangement is not based on the volume or value of any referrals; and
- The physician can have staff privileges at another hospital or refer business to another entity.[340]

The Phase II rule significantly revised the Stark law recruitment exception.[341] The amended exception focused on the relocation of a physician's practice rather than the relocation of a physician's residence.[342] Under the revised exception, a recruited physician may either move his or her practice at least 25 miles to relocate to the hospital's geographic area, or establish a new practice where at least 75 percent of the revenues from the new practice are derived from new patients (i.e., patients who have not been seen by the physician for at least three years).[343] A hospital's geographic area is defined as the lowest number of contiguous zip codes from which the hospital draws 75 percent of its patients.[344] Residents and physicians who have been in practice for less than one year may be recruited without meeting either the relocation or

---

[337]Office of Inspector General, *Tenet Agrees to Divest Alvarado Hospital,* OIG News (May 17, 2006), *available at* http://oig.hhs.gov/publications/docs/press/2006/051706Tenet.pdf; *see also Tenet Settles Suit Over Physician Relocation Agreements at Alvarado Hospital, Agrees to Sell or Close Facility,* DAILY HEALTH POLICY REP. (May 18, 2006), Kaiser Family Foundation, *available at* http://www.kaisernetwork.org/daily_reports/rep_index.cfm?DR_ID=37344.

[338]*Regional News,* MODERN HEALTHCARE at 17, Jan. 8, 2007.

[339]The Stark law is discussed at length in Chapter 2 (Crane, Federal Physician Self-Referral Restrictions).

[340]42 U.S.C. §1395nn(e)(5); 42 C.F.R. §411.357(e).

[341]42 C.F.R. §411.357(e).

[342]69 Fed. Reg. 16,054, 16,094–95 (Mar. 26, 2004).

[343]42 C.F.R. §411.357(e)(2) and (3). In the Phase III final regulations, CMS clarified that a recruited physician must relocate his or her practice from outside the geographic area served by the hospital into such geographic area, and must either (1) move at least 25 miles or (2) meet the 75 percent new patient test. *See* 72 Fed. Reg. 51,012, 51,048 (Sept. 5, 2007). The Phase III final rule also provides for greater flexibility in physician recruitment and retention for rural hospitals.

[344]42 C.F.R. §411.357(e)(2).

"new practice" requirement, because they are deemed not to have established a practice in their limited career experience.[345]

In an advisory opinion issued in November 2006, CMS addressed the issue of whether a physician had adequately relocated his medical practice to the geographic area served by a hospital for purposes of the Phase II rule, if the physician was spending a portion of his time practicing outside of the hospital's service area.[346] Under the proposed arrangement at issue in the opinion, 80 to 90 percent of the physician's practice was within the hospital's geographically served area, while 10 to 20 percent was outside that area. CMS found that the arrangement did in fact meet the requirements of the recruitment exception, noting that there is "no explicit requirement . . . that the recruited Physician spend 100 percent of his or her medical practice time in the geographic area served by the hospital."[347] CMS warned, however, that "more substantial" time spent outside the geographic area served by the hospital may have led to a different conclusion.[348]

In a significant development, the recruitment exception has also been expanded to allow a hospital to make payments to an existing group practice in order to recruit a new physician to join the group.[349] However, recruitment arrangements involving a group or other physicians in addition to the recruited physician (collectively referred to as "the group") must meet all the following requirements:

- The arrangement between the hospital and the group is set out in writing and signed by the parties;
- Except for actual costs incurred by the group in recruiting the new physician, the remuneration is passed directly through to or remains with the recruited physician; records of the actual costs and the passed-through amounts must be maintained for a period of at least five years and made available to the Secretary of HHS upon request;
- In the case of an income guarantee made by the hospital to a physician who joins a local physician practice, costs allocated by the group to the recruited physician may not exceed the actual additional incremental costs to the group attributable to the recruited physician;
- The new physician must establish a group in the hospital's geographic service area and join the hospital's medical staff;
- The group's arrangement with the recruited physician is set out in writing and signed by the parties;
- The new physician is not required to refer patients to the hospital and is allowed to establish staff privileges at any other hospital(s) and to refer

---

[345]42 C.F.R. §411.357(e)(3); 69 Fed. Reg. at 16,094.

[346]Advisory Opinion No. CMS-AO-2006-01, *available at* http://www.cms.hhs.gov/ PhysicianSelfReferral/Downloads/CMS-AO-2006-01.pdf.

[347]*Id.* at 5.

[348]*Id.*

[349]42 C.F.R. §411.357(e)(4). Prior to Phase II, the hospital had to pay the benefits directly to the recruited individual physician (who might have, in turn, assigned the benefits to the employer) for the physician recruitment exception to apply.

business to other entities (except insofar as required referrals are permitted under Section 411.354(d)(4));

- The remuneration from the hospital under the arrangement is not determined in any manner that takes into account (directly or indirectly) the volume or value of any referrals (actual or anticipated) by the recruited physician or by the group receiving the direct payments from the hospital (or any physician affiliated with that group); and
- The group receiving the hospital payments may not impose additional practice restrictions on the recruited physician (for example, a noncompete agreement), but may impose conditions related solely to quality considerations.[350]

## L. Physician Retention

### 1. Stark Exception

The Phase II rule also includes a retention exception for physicians to assist hospitals in rural and underserved areas in preventing physicians from moving to other locations.[351] The only hospitals eligible for this exception are those located in an HPSA or those deemed to be in need of the physician's practice as supported by a Stark advisory opinion. In order for the hospital to make such a retention payment, the physician must have a firm, written recruitment offer from an unrelated hospital or federally qualified health center (FQHC) that specifies the remuneration being offered, and the offer must require the physician to move his or her practice at least 25 miles and be located outside the geographic area served by the hospital.[352]

Any retention payment to the physician cannot exceed the lower of (a) any amount obtained by subtracting the physician's current income from physician and related services from the income the physician would receive from performing comparable services under the recruitment offer (for no more than 24 months) or (b) the reasonable costs of the hospital's recruiting a new physician to the geographic area served by the hospital to replace the physician it would like to retain.[353] The parties must use a reasonable methodology (and the same methodology) to determine the physician's income from both his or her current job and the anticipated income from the recruitment offer.[354] The physician may not enter into a retention agreement with a hospital more than once every five years, and the terms of the agreement may not be altered during the lifetime of the arrangement to take into account the volume or value of referrals or other business generated by the physician.[355] It is also important to note that the retention exception does not protect payments made indirectly to a retained physician via another person or entity, including a physician group practice.

---

[350]69 Fed. Reg. at 16,096–97; 42 C.F.R. §411.357(e)(1), (4).

[351]42 C.F.R. §411.357(t).

[352]69 Fed. Reg. at 16,097; 42 C.F.R. §411.357(t)(1)(iii).

[353]42 C.F.R. §411.357(t)(1)(iv).

[354]*Id.*

[355]42 C.F.R. §411.357(t)(1)(vi).

Alternatively, a retention arrangement may be structured to fit within the employee exception.[356]

## 2. Provision of Malpractice Insurance Assistance

With the rising costs of malpractice insurance for physicians, there is an increased possibility that physicians will curtail or cease practicing in order to avoid these expenses. Many hospitals are looking into the option of assisting physicians with their malpractice insurance costs in order to keep them from terminating their practice. Although CMS and the OIG have not issued clear guidance on this issue, they have been concerned with the potential fraud and abuse implications of malpractice subsidies to potential referral sources, including hospital medical staff. There is a limited malpractice premium subsidy safe harbor under the anti-kickback statute for physicians providing obstetrical care in primary health care shortage areas.[357] Additionally, the OIG acknowledged that it is possible that malpractice premium subsidies may fit into the employee or physician recruitment safe harbors for the federal anti-kickback statute.[358]

Indeed, in a letter addressing malpractice insurance assistance, Chief Counsel to the Inspector General, Lewis Morris, observed that one proposed malpractice insurance subsidy arrangement contained a number of safeguards.[359] While this letter was unable to offer an opinion on the viability of the proposed arrangement because it was not submitted in accordance with the advisory opinion process set forth at 42 C.F.R. Part 1008, the letter does offer some insight into what policies and procedures may help protect a malpractice insurance subsidy from violating the anti-kickback statute. Additionally, the safeguards cited in this letter have been included in the OIG's proposed supplement to its hospital compliance guidance.[360] Some of the relevant factors include:

- Whether the subsidy is being provided on an interim basis for a fixed period;
- In states where assistance is offered, whether it is only offered to current active medical staff or physicians joining the staff who are new to the locality or have been in practice for less than a year;
- Whether the receipt of the subsidy is related to the volume or value of referrals or other business generated;
- Whether each physician should pay as much as he or she currently pays now for medical malpractice insurance;
- Whether participating physicians are required to perform services for the subsidizing hospital and give up certain litigation rights;

---

[356] 42 C.F.R. §411.357(c).

[357] 42 C.F.R. §1001.952(o).

[358] *See* Letter from Lewis Morris, Chief Counsel to the Inspector General, on Malpractice Insurance Assistance, *available at* http://oig.hhs.gov/fraud/docs/alertsandbulletins/MalpracticeProgram.pdf.

[359] *Id.*

[360] 69 Fed. Reg. 32,012, 32,023 (June 8, 2004).

- Whether the value of such services and litigation rights is equal to the fair market value of the malpractice insurance assistance; and
- Whether the insurance is available regardless of the locations at which the physician provides services, including, but not limited to, other hospitals.[361]

The OIG explained in the draft guidance that no individual factor is determinative of whether a hospital has a valid malpractice insurance subsidy program, and the list of considerations is not exhaustive. The OIG further noted that the provision of a subsidy implicates the Stark law.[362]

In 2004, the OIG issued two opinions relating to hospital subsidization of physician malpractice insurance premiums.[363] In Advisory Opinion No. 04-11, the OIG examined an arrangement in which a hospital subsidized malpractice insurance premiums for four obstetricians in a health professional shortage area with a high population of low-income, migrant farm worker, and homeless people.[364] The arrangement did not meet the safe harbor for obstetrical malpractice subsidies, found at 42 C.F.R. §1001.952, because the area was not a primary care HPSA, as required for the safe harbor. The OIG stated that although the arrangement could potentially generate prohibited remuneration under the anti-kickback statute, the OIG would not impose sanctions. Key factors in the OIG's analysis included: the arrangement's similarity to the safe harbor requirements; the temporary and fixed period in which the subsidies would be provided; the fact that the obstetricians did not receive a windfall from the subsidy; the fact that the insurance covered the doctors regardless of the site where they performed services; and the arrangement's substantial benefit to the community.[365]

The second advisory opinion concerned malpractice insurance subsidies for two neurosurgeons who would have retired due to high insurance costs, had the hospital not provided subsidization.[366] The OIG again held that although the arrangement could potentially generate prohibited remuneration under the anti-kickback statute, it would not impose sanctions on the hospital. The neurosurgeons were the only ones in the community, and the next closest hospital providing neurosurgical services was located 45 miles away. The surgeons were not required to refer patients to the hospital, were permitted to furnish services at sites other than the hospital, and the amount of the subsidy did not take into account the volume or value of any business generated by the doctors for the hospital. These factors, combined with the following, were persuasive to the OIG: the arrangement was an urgent and temporary measure to prevent a gap in availability of local neurosurgical services; the physicians did not receive a

---

[361] *Id.*

[362] 69 Fed. Reg. at 32,023–24.

[363] OIG Advisory Op. No. 04-11 (Sept. 2, 2004), *available at* http://www.oig.hhs.gov/fraud/docs/advisoryopinions/2004/ao0411.pdf; OIG Advisory Op. No. 04-19 (Dec. 30, 2004), *available at* http://www.oig.hhs.gov/fraud/docs/advisoryopinions/2004/ao0419.pdf.

[364] OIG Advisory Op. No. 04-11 (Sept. 2, 2004).

[365] *Id.*

[366] OIG Advisory Op. No. 04-19 (Dec. 30, 2004).

windfall from the arrangement and were still paying more for insurance than they had in the previous year; the physicians performed various services as consideration for the subsidy, such as providing call coverage and furnishing indigent care services; and the insurance covered services furnished at sites other than the hospital.[367]

---

[367]*Id.*

# 6

# Managed Care Fraud and Abuse: Risk Areas for Government Program Participants*

*Christine C. Rinn and Barbara H. Ryland, Crowell & Moring LLP, Washington, D.C.

# I. Introduction

## A. Managed Care Fraud and Abuse Enforcement as Outgrowth of Fee-for-Service Model

Governmental anti-fraud efforts historically have focused primarily on the fee-for-service (FFS) delivery model. Under the FFS model, the more services a provider bills, the more payment it receives. However, as more people have become enrolled in managed care organizations (MCOs), both voluntarily (e.g., Medicare) and involuntarily (e.g., Medicaid), the government has increased its scrutiny of managed care activities at both the state and federal levels. In doing so, the government has had to appreciate that managed care differs dramatically from FFS, both operationally and economically. Most fundamentally, whereas FFS payment policies can provide an incentive for providers to overtreat patients, capitated payment for a bundle of services under managed care can create an incentive for undertreatment.

Despite its appreciation of the differences in the FFS and managed care payment systems, the government has historically had difficulty translating its managed care concerns into a coherent enforcement policy. However, with an increasing portion of health care expenditures funded by government and an increasing portion of those government funds flowing through MCOs, the government now has in place the requisite enforcement tools and capability to focus on fraud and abuse issues in the managed care industry.

Government oversight and enforcement activity go far beyond the historical concern regarding underutilization. Areas of this expanded monitoring and enforcement activity include

- "cherry-picking" or recruiting healthier-than-average enrollees through improper screening (enrollment fraud);
- systemic efforts to move high-risk managed care patients out of managed care plans (disenrollment fraud);
- improper beneficiary inducements to enrollment;
- failure to provide advertised or mandated benefits;
- systemic delays in providing treatment or benefit information;
- unreasonable times and distances for appointments to prevent beneficiaries from obtaining services;
- misrepresentations in "encounter data" or other data submitted to the government and utilized to determine payment rates;
- submission of falsely elevated cost data to government to justify higher payments;
- failure to assign revenues and expenses to appropriate "claims cost" or "administrative" buckets, resulting in inaccurate bid submissions or subsidy calculations; and
- misrepresentations to the government or to federal program beneficiaries in marketing or other materials.

## B. Medicare Modernization Act

In 2003, Congress enacted the Medicare Prescription Drug, Improvement, and Modernization Act (MMA).[1] The MMA established Part D of the Medicare Program to provide a "voluntary" prescription drug benefit plan for individuals who are entitled to Part A or enrolled in Part B of the Medicare Program (via newly created Sections 1860D-1 through 1860D-42 of the Social Security Act). Under Part D, drug coverage is available as an "add-on" to fee-for-service Medicare coverage, through a stand-alone prescription drug plan (PDP). In

---

[1]Pub. L. No. 108-73 (Dec. 8, 2003); 42 U.S.C. §1395w-101 *et seq.*

addition, a beneficiary who enrolls in a Medicare Advantage (MA) plan (the successors to Medicare+Choice Part C plans) that provides Part D qualified prescription drug coverage (MA-PD plans) will obtain coverage through the MA-PD plan. The MMA also provides for the payment of a subsidy to employer-sponsored retiree benefit plans that provide a prescription drug benefit that is at least actuarially equivalent in value to the Part D prescription benefit.[2]

The MMA imposes both substantive and financial obligations on entities that offer a Part D prescription drug benefit. And although the most significant difference between the Medicare Advantage program and its predecessor program, Medicare+Choice, is the new program's pricing structure, there are other significant differences that translate to greater obligations for Medicare Advantage organizations. The historic changes to Medicare brought about by the MMA have caused a level of government scrutiny never before seen in the managed care industry. This heightened scrutiny is not only by the various federal agencies charged with administering and overseeing these programs, but also by Congress.

This chapter reviews many of the more significant substantive issues concerning managed care fraud and abuse, primarily focusing on Medicare, but also addressing other government programs, including the Federal Employees Health Benefits Program (FEHBP). Specifically, this chapter considers the following issues that are being scrutinized by federal and state agencies:

- mandatory compliance program and disclosure requirements that apply to organizations that participate in the Medicare Advantage and Medicare Part D programs;
- the OIG's model compliance program guidance for Medicare+Choice organizations and its continued applicability to Medicare Advantage organizations;
- Centers for Medicare and Medicaid Services' (CMS) guidance for preventing, detecting, and reporting fraud, waste, and abuse under the Medicare Part D program;
- marketing by and on behalf of Medicare Advantage and Part D Plan Sponsors;
- applicability of the federal False Claims Act (FCA) and other federal enforcement provisions to federal managed care programs; and
- adverse actions in which denial of care has been alleged and "prompt payment" statutes allegedly have been violated.

## II. Compliance Programs in Managed Care Organizations

In an effort to reduce both the likelihood of adverse actions and the severity of any action taken, many MCOs have adopted compliance programs voluntarily. Compliance programs are designed to ensure that an MCO is meeting all legal requirements. In addition to such voluntary actions, both Medicare Advantage organizations and Part D Plan Sponsors are required to

---

[2]42 U.S.C. §1395w-132; 42 C.F.R. part 423, subpart R.

have compliance programs as a condition of participation.[3] This requirement represents a turning point in the history of compliance. Previously, merely having a compliance program was seen as indicating organizational sensitivity to legal obligations. Now, the absence of an effective compliance program is, by itself, grounds for suspicion and, at the very least, a technical violation of regulations that can lead to termination of the organization's contract by CMS.

## A. Medicare Advantage Organizations

CMS carried over to the Medicare Advantage program many of the regulatory requirements that existed under the predecessor Medicare+Choice program, including the requirement that the Medicare Advantage organization have a compliance program. However, in issuing the proposed rule for the Medicare Advantage program, CMS included as part of the compliance program requirement an affirmative obligation to self-report offenses. In response to comments that the proposed mandatory reporting obligation was vague and overbroad and had no basis in statute, CMS did not include the reporting requirement in the final rule.[4] It is important to keep in mind that the OIG has taken the position that 42 U.S.C. §1320a-7b(a)(3) requires disclosure in that it exposes to criminal penalty a person who has knowledge "of the occurrence of any event affecting [a person's] initial or continued right to any [government] benefit or payment . . . [and] conceals or *fails to disclose* such event with an intent fraudulently to secure such benefit or payment either in a greater amount or quantity than is due or when no such benefit or payment is authorized."[5]

As of August 2007, CMS had not issued formal guidance to Medicare Advantage organizations regarding the agency's expectations or requirements for compliance programs.[6] The Medicare Managed Care Manual[7] provides that the organization must demonstrate a commitment to compliance, integrity, and ethical values as demonstrated by the following:

- Written policies, procedures, and standards of conduct that articulate the organization's commitment to comply with all applicable federal and state standards;
- The designation of a compliance officer and compliance committee that are accountable to senior management;

---

[3]42 C.F.R. §§422.503(b)(4)(vi); 423.504(b)(4)(vi).

[4]70 Fed. Reg. 4588, 4673 (Jan. 28, 2005). "While we are not requiring MA organizations to engage in mandatory self-reporting, we continue to believe that self-reporting of fraud and abuse is a critical element to an effective compliance plan; and we strongly encourage MA organizations to alert CMS, the OIG, or law enforcement of any potential fraud or misconduct relating to the Part D program."

[5](Emphasis added.) *See also* 18 U.S.C. §§669, 1035.

[6]In May 2007, CMS issued a notice of proposed rulemaking that among other changes would require Medicare Advantage Organizations and PDPs to self-report potential fraud or misconduct. *See* 72 Fed. Reg. 29,368 (May 25, 2007). According to the preamble, CMS believes "it is important for the government to have information on possible fraud or misconduct as soon as possible in order to determine whether any actions would be appropriate." *Id.* at 29,373.

[7]Medicare Managed Care Manual, Ch. 11, at §20.1. The Medicare Managed Care Manual is available at http://www.cms.hhs.gov/Manuals/IOM/itemdetail.asp?filterType=none&filterBy DID=-99&sortByDID=1&sortOrder=ascending&itemID=CMS019326&intNumPerPage=10.

- Effective training and education between the compliance officer and organization employees;
- Effective lines of communication among the compliance officer, the organization's employees, and MA-related contractors that, at a minimum, includes a mechanism for employees or contractors to ask questions, seek clarification, and report potential or actual noncompliance without fear of retaliation;
- Enforcement of standards through well-publicized disciplinary guidelines;
- Provision for internal monitoring and auditing that includes a risk assessment process to identify and analyze risks associated with failure to comply with all applicable Medicare Advantage compliance standards; and
- Procedures for ensuring prompt response to detected offenses and development of corrective action initiatives relating to the organization's MA contract.

In the absence of more specific guidance from CMS, the only guidance for Medicare Advantage organizations is that issued by the Department of Health and Human Services (HHS) Office of Inspector General (OIG) for Medicare+Choice organizations (the OIG Guidance).[8] However, the OIG Guidance is relatively old. It predates the bid process and other changes under the Medicare Advantage program, and does not address Medicare Advantage private fee-for-service plans, which have grown in number and enrollment during the last few years. Nevertheless, many of the risk areas identified in the OIG Guidance remain relevant today.

### 1. The OIG Guidance

The OIG Guidance expanded on the seven required elements of a compliance program for a Medicare MCO.

### a. Standards, Policies, and Procedures

The OIG stressed the need for Medicare MCOs to address in their policies, standards, and practices specific areas that are vulnerable to abuse, including issues of particular concern within the HMO industry (e.g., marketing, quality of care, and illegal enrollment inducements) and any areas with which the MCO has had a history of compliance problems. Before developing written policies, each MCO should identify the minimum standards of conduct it expects from its employees. These standards of conduct establish the MCO's principal values and framework and its commitment to prevent fraud and abuse and comply with all federal and state standards. The standards of conduct are the equivalent of the MCO's fundamental values and goals.

Written policies are the mechanism by which an MCO implements its standards of conduct and creates procedures and processes to provide day-to-day guidance to its employees. The OIG Guidance states that a Medicare MCO

---

[8]64 Fed. Reg. 61,893 (Nov. 15, 1999).

"should establish a comprehensive set of written policies addressing all applicable statutes, rules and program instructions that apply to each function or department of [the] organization"[9] and through a comprehensive risk analysis (either self-administered or performed by an independent contractor) identify and rank the various compliance and business risks the MCO may experience in its daily operations. This risk analysis and subsequent identification and ranking of risk areas should be based on applicable state and federal health care program requirements (i.e., statutes, regulations, and other agency guidance documents) and should include a review of the MCO's history of noncompliance, if any.

The OIG Guidance identifies seven areas of particular concern to the OIG: (a) marketing materials and personnel; (b) selective marketing and enrollment; (c) disenrollment; (d) underutilization and quality of care; (e) data collection and submission processes; (f) anti-kickback statute and other inducements; and (g) emergency services. These areas of concern are equally applicable to Medicare Advantage organizations.

### i. *Marketing Materials and Personnel*

In addition to meeting CMS's marketing requirements, the OIG wants Medicare MCOs to have policies regarding the completeness and accuracy of their marketing materials and marketing personnel. A Medicare MCO *should not* rely on CMS approval as the basis for claiming that its marketing materials are complete and accurate. Instead, it should conduct its own thorough review of its marketing materials. In addition to meeting CMS requirements, a Medicare MCO's marketing materials should contain an adequate description of its rules, procedures, and basic benefits and services and an explanation of the grievance and appeals process. These materials should also especially address the concept and role of a primary care physician and how managed care limits health care provider choices.

Because a Medicare MCO must have control over its marketing personnel to ensure that they are presenting clear, complete, and accurate information to potential enrollees and the OIG believes that control is much more likely when marketing personnel are employees of the Medicare MCO, the OIG has strongly recommended that Medicare MCOs employ their own marketing personnel rather than contract for those services. However, in its *Medicare Marketing Guidelines*,[10] CMS acknowledges the use of contracted agents and establishes certain minimum requirements for the organization with respect to both its employed and contracted marketing force. Organizations must:

- Use compensation structures that avoid incentives to mislead beneficiaries, cherry-pick beneficiaries, or churn beneficiaries between plans.
- Provide reasonable compensation in line with industry standards.

---

[9] *Id.* at 61,896.

[10] The Medicare Marketing Guidelines are available at http://www.cms.hhs.gov/ ManagedCareMarketing/. The guidelines apply to Medicare Advantage organizations, Part D Plan Sponsors (including MA-PDs), and 1876 cost contractors.

- Withhold or withdraw payments if an enrollee disenrolls in an un-reasonably short time frame (known as rapid disenrollment).
- Monitor marketing activities to ensure compliance with applicable law, regulations, and CMS guidance.
- Use state licensed individuals to perform marketing.

The OIG Guidance reiterates the OIG's and CMS's longstanding position of discouraging Medicare MCOs from using providers as marketing agents. The *Medicare Marketing Guidelines* contain detailed guidance on the activities in which providers may and may not engage. For example, providers contracted with plans (and their subcontractors) can:

- Provide the names of plans with which they contract and/or participate;
- Provide information and assistance in applying for the low income subsidy;
- Provide objective information on specific plan formularies, based on a particular patient's medications and health care needs;
- Provide objective information regarding specific plans, such as covered benefits, cost sharing, and utilization management tools;
- Distribute PDP marketing materials, including enrollment application forms; and
- Distribute MA and/or MA-PD marketing materials, excluding enrollment application forms.

Providers contracted with plans (and their contractors) cannot:

- Direct, urge, or attempt to persuade any prospective enrollee to enroll in a particular plan or to insure with a particular company based on financial or any other interest of the provider (or subcontractor);
- Collect enrollment applications;
- Offer inducements to persuade beneficiaries to enroll in a particular plan or organization;
- Health screen when distributing information to patients, as health screening is a prohibited marketing activity;
- Offer anything of value to induce plan enrollees to select them as their provider;
- Expect compensation in consideration for the enrollment of a beneficiary; or
- Expect compensation directly or indirectly from the plan for beneficiary enrollment activities.

### ii. Selective Marketing and Enrollment

The OIG Guidance states that each Medicare MCO should implement policies to prevent selective enrollment practices known as "cherry picking" that are intended to attract healthier and therefore less costly Medicare beneficiaries. Although it remains true that Medicare Advantage organizations (and their agents) are prohibited from selectively marketing their plans, it is arguable that the implementation of the risk-adjusted payment methodology under the

Medicare Advantage program significantly changes the financial incentive to engage in such practices.[11]

### iii. Disenrollment

Similar to the concerns with selective marketing and enrollment, the OIG fears that MCOs may encourage members to disenroll to obtain more costly services under FFS Medicare. Consequently, the OIG Guidance recommends that Medicare MCOs implement policies to ensure against inappropriate disenrollment and that disenrollment policies identify those rare circumstances in which medical personnel may initiate a discussion of disenrollment (e.g., when the Medicare MCO cannot provide the covered medical items or services needed by the patient). Although encouraging disenrollment remains a valid concern, the risk-adjustment payment methodology rewards Medicare MCOs that are able to manage the health care of sick Medicare beneficiaries in less costly treatment settings (e.g., at home).

### iv. Underutilization and Quality of Care

Although not reflective of all of the types of policies that a Medicare MCO should implement to ensure quality care, the OIG has highlighted three types of policies that Medicare MCOs should develop to help address underutilization and quality of care:[12]

(1) policies against physician "gag" rules;[13]
(2) policies to ensure that if a Medicare MCO uses a physician incentive plan (PIP), the PIP provides no payments to physicians to reduce or limit medically necessary services. The MMA specifically requires that MA organizations provide assurances to CMS that they are in compliance with the PIP requirements. The final MA rule reduced the administrative burden on MA organizations with respect to PIPs by eliminating the requirements for enrollee surveys and disclosures to CMS.[14] However, the requirement remains that, if a PIP puts a physician or physician group at "substantial financial risk" for referral services, the MA organization ensure that there is adequate and appropriate stop-loss protection; and
(3) policies and procedures for selection of providers, including credentialing criteria such as valid license, clinical privileges in good standing, and appropriate educational requirements.[15]

### v. Data Collection and Submission Processes

There are numerous reporting and submission requirements under the Medicare Advantage program.[16] Therefore, Medicare Advantage organizations

---

[11]42 C.F.R. §§422.308 and 422.310.
[12]64 Fed. Reg. at 61,899–900.
[13]42 C.F.R. §422.206.
[14]*See* 42 C.F.R. §§422.208 and 422.210.
[15]42 C.F.R. §422.204.
[16]42 C.F.R. §§422.504(f) and (l).

should have policies that all required submissions to CMS be accurate, timely, and complete and that all appropriate reporting requirements be met. However, the OIG Guidance particularly emphasizes the need for Medicare MCOs to submit accurate information when the data determine the amount of payment the Medicare MCO receives from CMS.[17] Although the adjusted community rate process of the Medicare+Choice program has been replaced by the bid process under the Medicare Advantage program,[18] the OIG's recommendations that Medicare MCOs have the following two types of policies and procedures in place remain true:

- policies and procedures to ensure that the administrative component of the bid is calculated accurately; and
- adequate internal controls to ensure that the status of beneficiaries is reported accurately.

### vi. Anti-Kickback Statute and Other Inducements

The basis of the contractual relationship between an MCO and a provider is the understanding that the MCO will funnel a stream of patients to the provider in exchange for the provider accepting the MCO's payment terms. This can implicate the federal anti-kickback statute[19] because the primary purpose of that statute is to curtail improper payment for referrals to government-funded programs. In this regard, the OIG Guidance refers to the 1999 interim final rule on the risk-sharing safe harbor[20] of the anti-kickback statute, which provides protections for certain financial arrangements between MCOs (including Medicare MCOs) and entities with which they contract for health care services under which a federal health care program pays the MCO a capitated amount. However, as indicated in the rule, there are three significant limitations.

First, there is no protection from the anti-kickback statute if the payments made under the managed care agreement are part of a broader agreement to steer federal FFS business to the entity giving the discount. Second, there is no safe harbor protection for remuneration for items and services not reasonably related to the provision of health care (e.g., marketing services or services provided before a beneficiary's enrollment in a federal health plan). Third, the safe harbor applies only to MCOs that do not claim any payment from the federal government other than the capitated payment.

In addition to the safe harbor limitations described above, the OIG has recommended that Medicare MCOs have policies in place to ensure that any incentives offered to beneficiaries and potential beneficiaries do not violate the anti-kickback statute or the civil monetary penalty (CMP) law prohibiting beneficiary inducements, which was added by the Health Insurance Portability and Accountability Act of 1996 (HIPAA).[21] The OIG stated its belief that it is

---

[17] 64 Fed. Reg. at 61,900.

[18] *See* 42 C.F.R. §422 Subpart F.

[19] 42 U.S.C. §1320a-7b(b).

[20] 64 Fed. Reg. 63,504 (Nov. 19, 1999) (codified at 42 C.F.R. §1001.952(u)).

[21] 42 U.S.C. §1320a-7a(a)(5).

not a violation of the CMP law for Medicare MCOs to offer limited incentives[22] to federal health care program beneficiaries to enroll in a plan. However, the OIG believes it would be a violation of the CMP law if the Medicare MCO or any other entity were to offer a beneficiary remuneration to use a particular provider, practitioner, or supplier once he or she was enrolled in the plan. The OIG formalized its belief when it published the final CMP rule.[23] CMS has reflected this position in its *Medicare Marketing Guidelines.*

### vii. Emergency Services

All Medicare MCOs should have policies in place to ensure that beneficiaries have appropriate access to emergency services and hospitals within the MCO's network and that the contracts with such hospitals ensure that the hospitals provide the services required under the federal anti-dumping statute[24] without regard to the patient's insurance status or any prior authorization of such insurance. These policies are even more important if a Medicare MCO, through an agreement with the hospital, places its own physician in the hospital's emergency room for the purpose of screening and treating the Medicare MCO's managed care enrollees.[25]

### b. Record Retention

A Medicare MCO should have a record retention system that includes policies and procedures regarding the creation, distribution, retention, storage, retrieval, and destruction of documents. In addition, there are three types of documents a Medicare MCO should ensure that it creates as a part of its compliance program:

(1) all records and documentation required by federal or state law and federal or state health care programs;
(2) records listing the persons responsible for implementing each part of the compliance program; and
(3) all records necessary to protect the integrity of the Medicare MCO's compliance process and confirm the effectiveness of the program.

The third category listed above includes items such as evidence of adequate employee training, reports from the Medicare MCO's fraud and abuse hotline, results of any investigation conducted as a consequence of a hotline call, modifications to the MCO's compliance program, all written notifications to providers regarding compliance activities, and results of the Medicare MCO's auditing and monitoring efforts. Record retention policies and procedures also should specifically address electronic data and regular backup requirements.

---

[22]The anti-kickback statute prohibits the provision of cash or other monetary rebates as an inducement for enrollment in a plan. However, CMS allows Medicare MA organizations to give Medicare beneficiaries gifts valued at less than $15.

[23]65 Fed. Reg. 24,400, 24,407 (Apr. 26, 2000).

[24]Emergency Medical Treatment and Labor Act (EMTALA), *codified at* 42 U.S.C. §1395dd.

[25]*See* Office of Inspector Gen., U.S. Dep't of Health & Human Servs., Special Advisory Bulletin on the Patient Anti-Dumping Statute, 64 Fed. Reg. 61,353 (Nov. 10, 1999).

It should be noted that one of the changes that CMS made in the Medicare Advantage final rule was to increase the record retention period to 10 years.[26] This was done to coincide with the statute of limitations under the federal False Claims Act.[27]

### c. Compliance as Part of Employee Evaluation

The OIG Guidance also provides that a relevant employee's promotion of and adherence to applicable elements of the organization's compliance program be a factor in evaluating his or her performance. Furthermore, employees should be trained periodically in new compliance policies and procedures, and managers should be required to educate employees regarding applicable policies and legal requirements and the disciplinary actions that may be taken if an employee does not adhere to the compliance program.

### d. Subcontractor Compliance

The OIG has strongly recommended that Medicare MCOs coordinate with both first-tier and downstream providers[28] to establish compliance responsibilities in addition to the contractual responsibilities required by CMS.

### e. Compliance Officer

According to the OIG, each Medicare MCO should appoint a compliance officer responsible for the following functions:

- overseeing and monitoring the implementation of the MCO's compliance program;
- reporting on a regular basis to the MCO's chief executive officer (CEO) and compliance committee on the progress of program implementation and also providing input on ways to improve the organization's efficiency and quality of services and reduce its vulnerability to fraud, abuse, and waste;
- revising the compliance program as necessary to meet the MCO's needs and comply with any changes in applicable laws, regulations, or government policies;
- reviewing employee certifications that state that an employee has received, read, and understood the MCO's standards of conduct;
- developing, coordinating, and participating in compliance program training and education;
- ensuring through coordination with the MCO's human resources department that the MCO does not employ or contract with excluded persons or entities;

---

[26] *See* 70 Fed. Reg. 4588, 4674 (Jan. 28, 2005) *codified at* 42 C.F.R. §422.504(d).

[27] 31 U.S.C. §3731(b).

[28] "First tier" providers are those with which the MCO contracts directly. "Downstream" providers are those with which the first-tier providers contract, but with which the MCO does not have a direct contractual relationship. *See* 42 C.F.R. §422.500.

- assisting with internal compliance review and monitoring activities;[29]
- investigating and acting on compliance matters;
- developing policies and programs that encourage employees to report suspected fraud and abuse; and
- ensuring that the compliance program remains effective after its implementation.

The compliance officer should have direct access to the CEO and members of senior management and the governing body of the MCO, but the OIG does not advise having the compliance officer report to the general counsel or any type of financial officer. In addition, the compliance officer should have appropriate authority to perform all of the functions of his or her job. In addition, a compliance committee managed by the compliance officer should be established.

### f. The Compliance Committee

The compliance committee should include individuals with a variety of skills and significant professional experience in working with quality assurance, enrollment, marketing, clinical records, and auditing. The committee's responsibilities should include such tasks as assessing existing policies and procedures to ensure that they fit with the organization's regulatory environment, working with the MCO's departments as well as affiliated providers to develop standards of conduct and policies and procedures to further the organization's compliance program, recommending improvements or additions to internal systems to further the organization's compliance goals, and developing and evaluating a system or systems to detect and respond to potential violations.

### g. Compliance Training

The OIG Guidance recommends both formal and informal training regarding the MCO's compliance program. Formal training should include both general sessions (i.e., designed for all employees) and specialized sessions (i.e., designed for individuals involved in the risk area addressed in a particular policy). Employee attendance at the formal training sessions should be mandatory, and employees should be required to sign a certification stating that they have read the compliance program policies and standards, understand them, and will adhere to and support the program.

Informal training and education methods suggested by the OIG include a monthly compliance newsletter and maintaining a Web site devoted to compliance issues.[30] The OIG also has encouraged Medicare MCOs to permit contractors to participate in the organization's compliance training and to encourage contractors to develop compliance programs that complement the MCO's program.

---

[29]However, see U.S. Dep't of Health & Human Servs., Office of Inspector Gen., Advisory Op. No. 01-16 (Oct. 5, 2001) (permitting Medicare+Choice organization to hire excluded provider for employee development purposes).

[30]64 Fed. Reg. 61,893, 61,905 (Nov. 15, 1999).

### h. Effective Lines of Communication

The OIG has stressed that a good compliance program must have an effective system through which employees, enrollees, or other parties can report potential violations without fear of retaliation. This can be accomplished through (1) a hotline or some other mechanism that encourages persons to report suspected fraud or abuse and (2) developing confidentiality and non-retaliation policies. In addition, the compliance officer or an authorized designee should maintain a log of reports of compliance program violations and any resulting investigation and conclusions. The compliance officer also should be available to respond to any questions regarding the application or interpretation of the compliance program and its policies and procedures.

### i. Auditing and Monitoring

A primary function of the compliance officer and compliance committee is to monitor the effectiveness of the Medicare MCO's compliance program. One of the most effective ways to monitor compliance is through audits by internal or external auditors who have expertise in federal and state health care statutes and regulations and federal health care program requirements. Audits should focus on identified risk areas. Other monitoring techniques include sampling protocols that permit the compliance officer to identify and review variations from an established baseline, on-site visits, questionnaires (e.g., for providers, enrollees, and employees), and trend analyses. Monitoring should not only review compliance with all applicable federal and state laws, regulations, and policies, but it also should ensure the effectiveness of the compliance program itself. Reports created as a result of auditing and monitoring activities should be maintained by the compliance officer and reviewed with members of the compliance committee and senior management.[31]

### j. Discipline

The OIG recommended that a Medicare MCO's compliance program include policies that (1) provide for appropriate disciplinary policies that are applied consistently when an employee violates the compliance program, and (2) ensure that a Medicare MCO does not employ or contract with excluded persons or entities or with persons or entities convicted of a criminal offense related to health care.

### k. Corrective Action

The OIG recommends that an effective compliance program should include steps to correct any identified violation of the compliance program. Such steps may include an immediate referral to criminal and/or civil law enforcement authorities, a corrective action plan, a report to the government, and/or notification to the provider of any discrepancies or overpayments, if applicable.

---

[31] In performing such audits, organizations should refer to the Medicare Advantage Monitoring Guide and the 2006 MA Audit Guide to identify risk areas and conduct self-audits. Both documents are available at http://www.cms.hhs.gov/HealthPlansGenInfo/.

A Medicare MCO should document clearly all of its attempts to comply with all federal and state requirements. Policies that address responses to compliance program violations should include (1) an internal investigation, (2) identification of the proper persons or entities to whom or which the violation should be reported, (3) the procedure for reporting violations, and (4) corrective actions to be taken to ensure compliance. At a minimum, the internal investigation should include interviews with appropriate personnel and a review of relevant documents. The Medicare MCO should consider hiring outside counsel, auditors, or health care experts to assist in the investigation. The investigation as well as any subsequent reports and corrective actions should be well documented.

## B. Medicare Part D

Pursuant to 42 C.F.R. §423.504(b)(4)(vi), Plan Sponsors approved to provide Part D benefits are required to have compliance plans in place. In June 2005, CMS issued an eight-page summary document, "Review of Sponsors' Fraud, Waste, and Abuse Responsibilities," that contained compliance plan guidance for applicants to use during the bidding process. CMS issued final guidance to Part D Plans on April 25, 2006, on program requirements to control fraud, waste, and abuse.[32] All Part D Plan Sponsors[33] are required to have a comprehensive plan to detect, correct, and prevent fraud, waste, and abuse. PDBM Chapter 9 provides recommendations for implementing the Plan Sponsor's compliance program for controlling fraud, waste, and abuse.[34] CMS notes that Part D compliance programs for detecting and controlling fraud and abuse should be aimed not only at the conduct of third parties submitting claims to the plan, but that Plan Sponsors must have policies and procedures in place to identify and address fraud, waste, and abuse at the Plan Sponsor level as well as in the delivery of prescription drugs through the Medicare benefit.

CMS has grouped specific requirements for Part D compliance programs into the following categories:

(1) Written Policies and Procedures and Standards of Conduct,[35]
(2) Compliance Officer and Compliance Committee,[36]
(3) Training and Education,[37]
(4) Effective Lines of Communication,[38]
(5) Enforcement of Standards through well publicized disciplinary guidelines,[39]

---

[32]CMS, Chapter 9–Part D Program to Control Fraud, Waste and Abuse, Prescription Drug Benefit Manual (Apr. 25, 2006), *available at* http://www.cms.hhs.gov/PrescriptionDrugCov Contra/Downloads/PDBManual_Chapter9_FWA.pdf [hereinafter PDBM Chapter 9].

[33]MA organizations offering a prescription drug benefit under Part D must also follow the fraud, waste, and abuse requirements.

[34]PDBM Chapter 9, §10.

[35]*Id.* §50.2.1.

[36]*Id.* §50.2.2.

[37]*Id.* §50.2.3.

[38]*Id.* §50.2.4.

[39]*Id.,* §50.2.5.

(6) Monitoring and Auditing,[40]

(7) Corrective Action Procedures,[41] and

(8) Comprehensive Fraud and Abuse Plans—Procedures to voluntarily self-report potential fraud or misconduct.[42]

CMS provides a detailed explanation of the basic compliance parameters in each of these categories. With respect to the last requirement, procedures for self-reporting, CMS strongly encourages plans to refer evidence of fraudulent practices to CMS for further investigation and follow-up; nonetheless, CMS affirms that self-reporting of potential fraud is voluntary.[43]

CMS has contracted with private organizations, called Medicare Drug Integrity Contractors (MEDICs), to assist in the management of CMS's audit, oversight, and anti-fraud and abuse efforts in the Part D benefit. CMS indicated in its guidance that it will release future information on CMS's expectations and responsibilities for Plan Sponsors' interactions with MEDICs as CMS specifically authorizes MEDICs to undertake oversight functions related to uncovering and eradicating fraud and abuse on behalf of CMS.

PDBM Chapter 9 specifies 17 requirements relating to the eight compliance plan elements. With respect to the eighth element, a comprehensive fraud and abuse plan to detect, correct, and prevent fraud, waste, and abuse, PDBM Chapter 9 contains 11 specific recommendations:[44]

(1) Plan Sponsor has procedures for the identification of fraud, waste, and abuse in its network.

(2) Plan Sponsor has a process to identify overpayments at any level within its network and to properly repay such overpayments in accordance with CMS policy.

(3) Plan Sponsor has policies and procedures for coordinating and cooperating with MEDICs, CMS, and law enforcement, including policies that fully cooperate with any audits conducted by the above-mentioned entities or their designees.

(4) Plan Sponsor's compliance officer's duties include responding to reports of potential and actual instances of Part D fraud, waste, or abuse, including the coordination of internal investigations and the development of appropriate corrective or disciplinary actions.

(5) Plan Sponsor's compliance officer's duties include maintaining documentation for each report of potential fraud, waste, or abuse received through any of the reporting methods (i.e., hotline, mail, in person) which summarizes the initial report of noncompliance, the investigation, the results of the investigation, and all corrective and/or disciplinary action(s) taken as a result of the investigation.

---

[40]*Id.* §50.2.6.

[41]*Id.* §50.2.7.

[42]*Id.* §50.2.8.

[43]*Id.* §50.2.8.2.

[44]DEP'T HEALTH & HUMAN SERVS., OFFICE OF INSPECTOR GEN., PRESCRIPTION DRUG PLAN SPONSORS' COMPLIANCE PLANS, OEI-03-06-00100 (Dec. 2006), *available at* http://oig.hhs.gov/oei/reports/oei-03-06-00100.pdf.

(6) Plan Sponsor's compliance training addresses pertinent laws related to fraud and abuse.

(7) Plan Sponsor has various methods to educate enrollees on prescription drug fraud, waste, and abuse.

(8) Plan Sponsor has procedures for internal monitoring and auditing to test and confirm compliance with the Part D benefit regulations, subregulatory guidance, contractual agreements, and all applicable state and federal laws, as well as internal policies and procedures to protect against potential fraud, waste, or abuse.

(9) Plan Sponsor receives and reviews at least one of the following data reports: payment reports, drug utilization reports, prescribing patterns by physician reports, geographic ZIP reports.

(10) Plan Sponsor conducts data analysis that includes the comparison of claim information against other data (e.g., provider, drug provided, diagnoses, or beneficiaries) to identify potential errors and/or potential fraud.

(11) Plan Sponsor has procedures in place to voluntarily self-report potential fraud or misconduct to government authorities such as OIG (through OIG's Provider Self-Disclosure Protocol)[45] or the Department of Justice (DOJ).

CMS included in PDBM Chapter 9 examples of fraud, waste, and abuse at various levels in delivery of the drug benefit including the Plan Sponsor, PBM, pharmacy, prescriber, and manufacturer levels. Plan Sponsors can use these examples when identifying potential risk areas for their own operations and targeting areas for oversight. The examples provided include the following activities:

(1) Part D sponsor fraud, waste, and abuse.[46]

- Failure to provide medically necessary services, and
- Marketing schemes that violate federal law or CMS guidance, including:
  - Offering beneficiaries a cash payment as an inducement to enroll in Part D,
  - Unsolicited door-to-door marketing,
  - Use of unlicensed agents,
  - Enrollment of beneficiaries without their knowledge or consent,
  - Stating that a marketing agent/broker works for or is contracted with the Social Security Administration or CMS,
  - Misrepresents the product being marketed as an approved Part D Plan when it actually is a Medigap policy or non-Medicare drug plan,
  - Misrepresents the Medicare Advantage or Prescription Drug Plan being marketed (i.e., enrolling Medicare beneficiaries in a MA-PD when they wanted a PDP),

---

[45] 63 Fed. Reg. 58,399 (Oct. 30, 1998).
[46] PDBM Chapter 9 at §70.01.1.

- ○ Requests financial beneficiary information or check numbers (i.e., potential identity theft by a Part D Plan's marketing agents), and
  - ○ Requires beneficiaries to pay up front premiums.
- Improper bid submissions. The Plan Sponsor inappropriately over-estimates or underestimates the bid to manipulate risk corridors and/or payments, including miscalculations of administrative ratio costs within the bids (wrong service lines).
- Inappropriate formulary decisions. Where Plan Sponsors or PBMs engage in formulary decision processes in which costs take priority over criteria such as clinical efficacy and appropriateness.
- Inappropriate enrollment/disenrollment. The Plan Sponsor improperly reports enrollment and disenrollment data to CMS to inflate prospective payments. For example, the Plan Sponsor fails to effect timely disenrollment of beneficiary from CMS systems upon beneficiary's request.
- Appeals process handled incorrectly. The Medicare beneficiary is denied his or her right to appeal or is denied a timely appeal.
- Adverse selection.
- False information to CMS.
- Inaccuracies in eligibility or coordination of benefits. Inaccurate or incomplete information on eligibility or benefits can lead to wasteful expenditure on drugs. D Plan Sponsors and/or PBMs can mitigate waste associated with inaccurate information through the use of real-time systems to verify eligibility, available benefits, and payor status.
- Incorrect calculation of true out-of-pocket (TrOOP) costs. Miscalculation of a beneficiary's TrOOP to manipulate beneficiary status in coverage (e.g., falsifying TrOOP calculations to keep beneficiaries in the coverage gap, or falsifying TrOOP calculations to push beneficiaries through the coverage gap into catastrophic coverage), or other incorrect calculation of TrOOP that may result in improper payments by CMS or beneficiaries.
- Inaccurate data submission. Plan Sponsor submits inaccurate or incomplete prescription drug event (PDE) data or Part D plan quarterly data.
- Failure to disclose or misrepresentation of rebates, discounts, or price concessions. Plan Sponsor fails to disclose or misrepresents rebates, discounts, price concessions, or other value added gifts, including concessions offered by pharmaceutical manufacturers.

(2) PBM fraud, waste, and abuse.[47]

- Prescription drug switching. The PBM receives a payment to switch a beneficiary from one drug to another or influence the prescriber to switch the patient to a different drug.
- Unlawful remuneration. PBM receives unlawful remuneration in order to steer a beneficiary toward a certain plan or drug, or for

---

[47]PDBM Chapter 9 at §70.01.2.

formulary placement. Includes unlawful remuneration from vendors beyond switching fees.

- Inappropriate formulary decisions. PBMs or their Pharmacy & Therapeutics (P&T) Committees make formulary decisions where cost takes precedence over clinical efficacy and appropriateness of formulary drugs.
- Prescription drug shorting. PBM mail order pharmacy intentionally provides less than the prescribed quantity and does not inform the patient or make arrangements to provide the balance but bills for the fully prescribed amount. Splits prescription to receive additional dispensing fees.
- Failure to offer negotiated prices. Occurs when a PBM does not offer a beneficiary the negotiated price of a Part D drug.

(3) Pharmacy fraud, waste, and abuse.[48]

- Inappropriate billing practices, including the following types of billing practices:
  - Incorrectly billing for secondary payors to receive increased reimbursement.
  - Billing for nonexistent prescriptions.
  - Billing multiple payors for the same prescriptions, except as required for coordination of benefit transactions.
  - Billing for brand when generics are dispensed.
  - Billing for noncovered prescriptions as covered items.
  - Billing for prescriptions that are never picked up (i.e., not reversing claims that are processed when prescriptions are filled but never picked up).
  - Billing based on "gang visits," e.g., a pharmacist visits a nursing home and bills for numerous pharmaceutical prescriptions without furnishing any specific service to individual patients.
  - Inappropriate use of dispense as written (DAW) codes.
  - Prescription splitting to receive additional dispensing fees.
  - Drug diversion.
- Illegal remuneration schemes. Pharmacy is offered, paid, solicits, or receives unlawful remuneration to induce or reward the pharmacy to switch patients to different drugs, influence prescribers to prescribe different drugs, or steer patients to plans.
- TrOOP manipulation.
- Failure to offer negotiated prices.

(4) Prescriber fraud, waste, and abuse.[49]

- Illegal remuneration schemes. Prescriber is offered, paid, solicits, or receives unlawful remuneration to induce or reward the prescriber to write prescriptions for drugs or products.

---

[48]PDBM Chapter 9 at §70.01.3.
[49]PDBM Chapter 9 at §70.01.4.

- Prescription drug switching. Drug switching involves offers of cash payments or other benefits to a prescriber to induce the prescriber to prescribe certain medications rather than others.
- Script mills. Provider writes prescriptions (scripts) for drugs that are not medically necessary, often in mass quantities, and often for patients who are not theirs. These scripts are usually written, but not always, for controlled drugs for sale on the black market, and might include improper payments to the provider.
- Provision of false information. Prescriber falsifies information (not consistent with medical record) submitted through a prior authorization or other formulary oversight mechanism in order to justify coverage. Prescriber misrepresents the dates, descriptions of prescriptions or other services furnished, or the identity of the individual who furnished the services.
- Illegal remuneration schemes. Prescriber is offered, paid, solicits, or receives unlawful remuneration to induce or reward prescriber to write prescriptions.

(5) Manufacturer fraud, waste, and abuse.[50]

- Lack of integrity of data to establish payment and/or determine reimbursement. Pharmaceutical manufacturers may be liable under the False Claims Act, CMPs, and/or the federal anti-kickback statute if government reimbursement for the manufacturer's product depends, in whole or in part, on information generated or reported by the manufacturer, including rebates, directly or indirectly, and the manufacturer has knowingly failed to generate or report such information completely and accurately.
- Kickbacks, inducements, and other illegal remuneration. The anti-kickback statute may be implicated by the following types of activities: inappropriate marketing and/or promotion of products (sales, marketing, discounting, etc.) reimbursable by federal health care programs.
  - ○ Inducements offered if the purchased products are reimbursable by any of the federal health care programs. Examples of potentially improper inducements include inappropriate discounts, inappropriate product support services, inappropriate educational grants, inappropriate research funding, or other inappropriate remuneration.

The OIG conducted an audit of Plans Sponsors' compliance programs.[51] The stated objectives were to (1) determine whether Plan Sponsors had developed compliance plans as required by the MMA, and (2) determine whether Plan Sponsors' compliance plans, as of January 2006, addressed all of the

---

[50]PDBM Chapter 9 at §70.01.6.

[51]Dep't Health & Human Servs., Office of Inspector Gen., Prescription Drug Plan Sponsors' Compliance Plans, OEI-03-06-00100 (Dec. 2006). The OIG review focused on sponsors of stand-alone prescription drug plans and did not include Part D plans offered by Medicare Advantage organizations.

requirements and selected recommendations regarding the eight compliance elements presented in federal regulations.

The OIG found that all 79 Plan Sponsors had compliance plans. However, 72 of the 79 plans did not address all of the CMS requirements regarding the eight compliance plan elements. Moreover, while all compliance plans addressed the fraud and abuse element in some way, only 15 of 79 plans addressed all 11 recommendations listed above regarding fraud detection, correction, and prevention. The compliance plans most often did not address CMS recommendations relating to Plan Sponsors' fraud detection procedures, fraud awareness training, and efforts to coordinate and cooperate with CMS and law enforcement entities regarding potential fraud.

## C. The Deficit Reduction Act

Section 6031 of the Deficit Reduction Act of 2005 (DRA),[52] which was signed into law on February 1, 2006, signals Congress's intent to increase private, individual, and state-level enforcement efforts specifically for entities that participate in the Medicaid program. Under this provision, any entity that receives or makes annual payments of at least $5 million under a state Medicaid plan must have written policies applicable to all its employees (including management), contractors, and agents that include "detailed" information about the False Claims Act, about federal administrative remedies for false claims and false statements, about state laws pertaining to civil and criminal penalties for false claims and false statements, and about the whistleblower protections in these laws and their role in preventing and detecting fraud, waste, and abuse. The written policies must also include detailed provisions about the entity's own policies and procedures for detecting and preventing fraud, waste, and abuse. Any employee handbook maintained by the entity must include a specific discussion of the laws described above, the rights of the employees to be protected as whistleblowers, and the entity's policies and procedures for detecting and preventing fraud, waste, and abuse.

The DRA provides a financial incentive for states to enact false claims acts that establish liability to the state for the submission of false or fraudulent claims to the state's Medicaid program. A state whose false claims act meets the applicable requirements is entitled to a ten percent increase in its share of any amounts recovered under a state action brought under such a law. Specifically, the state false claims act must:

(1) Establish liability to the state for false or fraudulent claims described in the False Claims Act (FCA) with respect to any expenditures related to state Medicaid plans described in section 1903(a) of the Act;

(2) Contain provisions that are at least as effective in rewarding and facilitating *qui tam* actions for false or fraudulent claims as those described in the FCA;

(3) Contain a requirement for filing an action under seal for 60 days with review by the State Attorney General;

---

[52]Pub. L. No. 109-171, Title VI, §6031, *codified at* 42 U.S.C. §1396h.

(4) Contain a civil penalty that is not less than the amount of the civil penalty authorized under the FCA.[53]

In August 2006, the OIG published a notice setting forth its guidelines for reviewing state false claims acts.[54] A list of those states that the OIG has determined satisfy the DRA requirements is on the OIG's Web site.[55]

## III. AREAS OF GOVERNMENT REVIEW, MONITORING, AND AUDIT

### A. Centers for Medicare and Medicaid Services

#### 1. Audits

MA organizations and Plan Sponsors can expect to be audited by CMS in a number of areas. These audits will likely be multiple, overlapping, and frequent. CMS audits will consist of regular program audits, the statutory "1/3 payment audits,"[56] and focused/targeted audits. These audits are exclusive of OIG audits, which are discussed below.

Program audits of MA organizations will focus on the following:[57]

- Enrollment and Disenrollment
- Marketing
- Benefits and Beneficiary Protections
- Quality Improvement
- Provider Relations
- Contracts
- Organizational Determinations, Grievances, and Appeals

With respect to the Part D program, CMS has identified 14 areas for program audits:[58]

- Provider/Communications
- Enrollment/Disenrollment
- Marketing
- Privacy and Confidentiality
- Drug Utilization Management and Quality Assurance
- Pharmacy Access
- Formulary, Transition, and P&T Committee
- Medication Therapy Management
- Coordination of Benefits and TrOOP

---

[53]42 U.S.C. §1396h(b).

[54]71 Fed. Reg. 48,552 (Oct. 21, 2006).

[55]*See* http://www.oig.hhs.gov/fraud/falseclaimsact.html.

[56]42 U.S.C. §1395w-27(d).

[57]The MA Audit Guide is available at http://www.cms.hhs.gov/HealthPlansGenInfo/28_MAGuide.asp#TopOfPage.

[58]The Part D Audit Guide is available at http://www.cms.hhs.gov/PrescriptionDrugCovContra/Downloads/PDPAuditGuide.pdf.

- Compliance Plan
- Downstream Contracts and Record Retention
- Claims Processing and Payment
- Grievances, Coverage Determinations, and Appeals
- Licensure and Solvency

MA-PDs will also be audited for compliance with Part D requirements. These audits will focus on

- Enrollment and Disenrollment
- Provider Communication
- Marketing and Beneficiary Information
- Privacy and Confidentiality
- Drug Utilization Management, Quality Assurance, and Electronic Prescribing
- Pharmacy Access
- Formulary, Transition Process, and P&T Committee
- Medication Therapy Management
- Coordination of Benefits/TrOOP Costs
- Compliance Plan
- First-Tier and Downstream Contracts/Maintenance of Records
- Claims Processing and Payment
- Grievances, Coverage Determinations, and Appeals
- Licensure and Financial Solvency

CMS contracted with Advanced Pharmacy Concepts/Booz Allen Hamilton (APC/BAH) to assist it with its audit work. The contractor coordinates comprehensive audits, conducts focused audits, and provides staff assistance to CMS audits teams.[59]

For the statutory 1/3 payment audits of Plan Sponsors, CMS identified 16 areas of review:

- Bids
- Utilization
- Reinsurance
- Risk corridors
- Low income subsidies
- Direct subsidy payments
- Reinsurance subsidies
- Risk corridor payments
- Other subsidized coverage
- Administrative cost and allocations
- Rebates
- Formulary
- Claims data
- TrOOP data

---

[59]*See* CMS Memorandum, Final MA-PD and PDP Part D Audit Guides for Part D Program Audits (Nov. 13, 2006).

- Allocations between MAs and PDPs
- Co-pays.

## 2. Marketing

The marketing activities of MA organizations, Plan Sponsors, and their contracted agents will be an area of particular scrutiny by CMS due to complaints regarding false and misleading marketing activities and congressional attention. CMS has the authority to impose intermediate sanctions and penalties including freezing all marketing and enrollment, CMPs, and other enforcement actions against organizations violating Medicare program requirements.[60] CMS has indicated that it is closely monitoring beneficiary complaints and other marketplace-based information to determine whether compliance and/or enforcement actions are warranted. Of particular note is the focus placed on MA private fee-for-service (PFFS) plans. In May 2007, CMS issued a memorandum to PFFS plans that outlined marketing processes that all PFFS plans must have in place before marketing their 2008 PFFS plans.[61]

The required marketing processes include those described below.

(1) Sales presentation schedules. Organizations must provide their CMS Regional Office Plan Manager with listings of planned PFFS marketing and sales events. Data for events conducted by both employed and contracted sales representatives is required. Each submitted spreadsheet must be accompanied by a signed and dated attestation from the organization's Medicare program vice president or director, attesting to best knowledge, information, and belief that the information provided to CMS is accurate as of the date submitted.

(2) Prohibition against implying PFFS plans function as Medicare supplements. Organizations are prohibited from using any materials or making any presentations that imply PFFS plans function as Medicare supplement plans or use terms such as "Medicare Supplement replacement."

(3) PFFS marketing material disclaimer. Organizations must prominently display the following disclaimer in all advertisements and enrollment related materials as well as in sales presentations in public venues and private meetings with beneficiaries:

> *A Medicare Advantage Private Fee-for-Service plan works differently than a Medicare supplement plan. Your doctor or hospital must agree to accept the plan's terms and conditions prior to providing healthcare services to you, with the exception of emergencies. If your doctor or hospital does not agree to accept our payment terms and conditions, they may not provide healthcare services to you, except in emergencies. Providers can find the plan's terms and conditions on our website at: [insert link to PFFS terms and conditions].[62]*

---

[60] *See* 42 C.F.R. Part 422 Subparts K and O.

[61] *See* CMS Memorandum, Ensuring Beneficiary Understanding of Private Fee-for-Service Plans, Actions and Best Practices (May 25, 2007), *available at* http://www.cms.hhs.gov/PrivateFeeforServicePlans/.

[62] *Id.* at 2.

(4) Beneficiary and provider leaflet. Organizations must provide enrollees with a complete description of plan rules, including detailed information on a provider's choice whether to accept plan terms and conditions of payment.

(5) Outbound education and verification calls. Organizations must conduct outbound education and verification calls to ensure that beneficiaries requesting enrollment understand the plan rules.

PFFS plans also will be required to have staff available to assist providers with questions concerning plan payment and payment accuracy.

Subsequent to issuing the memorandum, CMS announced that in response to concerns about marketing practices, seven MA organizations have signed an agreement to suspend voluntarily the marketing of their PFFS plans. This suspension for a given plan will be lifted when CMS certifies that the plan has the systems and management controls in place to meet all of the conditions specified in the 2008 Call Letter and the May 25, 2007 memorandum.[63] The voluntary suspension triggered a request for additional information from Senate Finance Committee Chairman Max Baucus (D-Mont.).[64]

The OIG audited MA organizations' compliance with CMS marketing requirements.[65] The OIG found that some MA marketing materials lacked CMS-required information "essential for beneficiaries to make information choices."[66] Missing information included prescription drug benefit limitations and details on how beneficiaries can access plan information. The OIG also found that some marketing materials used unclear and technical language.

## B. The OIG Work Plans

The OIG's work plans for 2006 and 2007[67] identify numerous areas of scrutiny that focus on the operations Medicare Advantage organizations and Part D Drug Sponsors, and the potential for fraud, waste, and abuse in these programs. According to the 2007 Work Plan, the OIG has invested in efforts to understand thoroughly the various aspects of the laws and regulations that are related to the Medicare drug benefit. The OIG indicated that it will "conduct investigations related to drug benefit fraud, and assist CMS in identifying program vulnerabilities."[68]

The areas identified for OIG review are discussed below.

---

[63]The June 15, 2007, press release is available at http://www.cms.hhs.gov/apps/media/press_releases.asp. The call letter is discussed in Chapter 10, Section II.A.1.b.

[64]The June 26, 2007, press release is located at http://finance.senate.gov/sitepages/baucus.htm.

[65]DEP'T HEALTH & HUMAN SERVS., OFFICE OF INSPECTOR GENERAL, MEDICARE ADVANTAGE MARKETING MATERIALS FOR CALENDAR YEAR 2005, OEI-01-05-00130 (Aug. 2006), *available at* http://oig.hhs.gov/oei/reports/oei-01-05-00130.pdf.

[66]*Id.* at iii.

[67]The OIG Work Plans are available at http://www.oig.hhs.gov/publications.html.

[68]DEP'T HEALTH & HUMAN SERVS., OFFICE OF INSPECTOR GENERAL, FISCAL YEAR 2007 WORK PLAN, at 51, *available at* http://oig.hhs.gov/publications/docs/workplan/2007/Work%20Plan%202007.pdf.

*1. Medicare Advantage*

- Enrollee Access to Negotiated Prices for Covered Part D Drugs. The OIG is investigating whether Medicare Advantage and Part D enrollees are being given access to negotiated prices for covered drugs, including all discounts, direct or indirect subsidies, rebates, and direct or indirect remunerations, regardless of whether the drug was paid for under the benefit.

- Regional Plan Stabilization Fund. The OIG is assessing compliance with MMA requirements and CMS guidance pertaining to the establishment and management of the "Regional Plan Stabilization Fund," including the adequacy, propriety, and timeliness of CMS's review processes for evaluating MCO proposals and awarding stabilization funds.

- Administrative Costs. Using the Federal Employees Health Benefits Program guidelines, the OIG is examining the administrative accounts currently claimed by MCOs. This is, in part, in response to Congress's expressed interest in how MCOs determine funding amounts to meet administrative costs, which must be allocable, reasonable, and limited under the program.

- Managed Care Encounter Data. The OIG is assessing the accuracy of Part A encounter data on Medicare beneficiaries. MCOs are required to submit this data for CMS's use in developing each organization's monthly capitation rate. As a result, incorrect encounter data could have a significant impact on future Medicare reimbursement.

- Duplicate Medicare Fee-for-Service Payments. The OIG is investigating whether duplicate Medicare fee-for-service payments were made to providers for beneficiaries enrolled in MCOs operating under a risk-based contract, including whether CMS or its intermediaries have sufficient controls in place to prevent such duplicate payments.

- Marketing Practices by Managed Care Organizations. The OIG is examining whether Medicare MCOs market their plans pursuant to CMS guidelines and how CMS monitors compliance. CMS prohibits discriminatory marketing activities that include selectively enrolling beneficiaries through monetary inducements, soliciting enrollment door-to-door, and using providers to distribute or accept plan materials. The OIG is concerned about this issue because a prior study found that 43 percent of beneficiaries were asked about health problems when applying with an MCO.

- Medicare Capitation Payments to Managed Care Plans After a Beneficiary's Death. The OIG is examining to what extent payments are made to MA plans for deceased beneficiaries, the CMS processes that identify MA overpayments due to beneficiary deaths, and what portion of those payments are subsequently recovered by CMS.

- Medicare Advantage Regional Plans: Availability, Physician Participation, and Beneficiary Enrollment in Rural Areas. The OIG is examining the availability of regional MA plans to rural beneficiaries, the extent to which rural beneficiaries enroll in MA plans, and whether physician practices in rural areas participate in regional MA plans.

- Dissemination of Beneficiary Information Materials by Medicare Advantage Prescription Drug Plans. The OIG is examining the extent to which MA-PD plans meet statutory and regulatory requirements regarding the content of materials distributed to beneficiaries, and whether MA-PD marketing materials comply with CMS guidelines.
- Medicare Advantage Lock-In Provisions. This review will examine CMS and MA plan communications and beneficiary understanding of lock-in provisions. The MMA limits the number of times and the time of year that beneficiaries may change health plans. To assist beneficiaries, CMS or MCOs provide written descriptions of rules, procedure, benefits, fees, and other charges, services, and other information necessary to make an informed decision about enrollment. This study will assess how effectively CMS and MA plans are fulfilling this requirement.

## 2. Medicare Part D

- CMS Program Integrity Safeguards for Medicare Drug Plan Applicants. The OIG is assessing the safeguards that CMS uses to confirm that drug plan applicants qualify to provide Part D benefits and whether CMS sufficiently addresses program integrity concerns associated with the sponsors who apply to offer drug plan benefits. The OIG also is reviewing the regulations and guidance associated with the application process with an eye to business integrity and compliance.
- Beneficiary Awareness of the Medicare Part D Low-income Subsidy. The OIG is evaluating whether beneficiaries are aware of the Part D low-income subsidy and analyzing the methods used to educate beneficiaries about the subsidy.
- Tracking Beneficiaries' TrOOP Costs for Part D Prescription Drug Coverage. The OIG is examining CMS's oversight of the calculation of TrOOP expenses that qualify toward catastrophic coverage and the accuracy of tracking these expenses in the Coordination of Benefits system.
- Prescription Drug Plan and Marketing Materials for Prescription Drug Benefits. The OIG is examining prescription drug plan marketing materials to ensure that they are clear and understandable to Medicare beneficiaries and in compliance with regulations and guidance.
- Auto-enrollment of Dual Eligibles into Medicare Part D Plans. The OIG is studying CMS's auto-enrollment of dualy eligibles, the proportion of dual eligibles that selected their own plan, and those who are not enrolled in any Part D plan.
- Enrollee Access to Negotiated Prices for Covered Part D Drugs. The OIG is investigating whether Medicare Advantage and Part D enrollees are being given access to negotiated prices for covered drugs, including all discounts, direct or indirect subsidies, rebates, and direct or indirect remunerations, regardless of whether the drug was paid for under the benefit.
- Prescription Drug Plans' Use of Formularies. The OIG is investigating whether (1) the Pharmacy and Therapeutics committees that construct the formularies, (2) the breadth and depth of drugs in the formularies, and (3) the beneficiary management tools (including exception and appeal rights) conform to rules and regulations.

- Coordination Between State Pharmaceutical Assistance Programs and Medicare Part D. The OIG is examining the coordination between State Pharmaceutical Assistance Programs and Part D to identify whether beneficiaries are able to obtain needed assistance and appropriate drug coverage.
- Prescription Drug Plans' and Medicare Advantage Plans' Implementation of Required Programs to Deter Fraud, Waste, and Abuse. Following an OIG inspection to assess program integrity safeguards in the PDP and MA-PD application process, the OIG will evaluate PDPs' and MA-PDs' implementation of required programs to deter fraud, waste, and abuse, and CMS programs' integrity systems to oversee the PDP and MA-PD programs.
- Medicare Part D Drug Benefit Payments. The OIG is sampling Part D beneficiaries' claim files to determine whether controls have been implemented and is working to ensure that (1) benefits are paid on behalf of eligible beneficiaries and (2) Medicare, as well as the beneficiaries, paid appropriate amounts for drug coverage.
- Medicare Part D Risk-sharing Payments and Recoveries. The OIG is determining whether CMS and the prescription drug plans have established adequate controls over Part D risk-sharing payments and recoveries to ensure that (1) the plans submit accurate and timely information to CMS, (2) CMS calculations are performed in accordance with applicable laws and regulations, and (3) payments and recoveries are made in accordance with applicable laws and regulations.
- Third Party Liability Safeguards. The MMA requires coordination between CMS, state programs, insurers, employers, and all other payors of prescription drug coverage. The OIG is reviewing safeguards in place to ensure that Medicare Part D does not inappropriately pay for prescription drug claims for which a third party is liable.
- Comparisons of Part D Drug Pricing. The OIG is conducting pricing comparisons for Medicare Part D prescription drugs and contrasting prescription drug prices under Part D with the same drug prices covered under Medicare Part B. The OIG will also compare prices of selected Part D prescription drugs to Medicaid reimbursement amounts.
- Medicare Part D. Drug Access Through Prior Authorization and Exceptions: The OIG is investigating controls that CMS has instituted to ensure that Plan Sponsors implement appropriate prior authorization and formulary exceptions processes. The study will also explore how policies and processes compare across PDPs.
- Monitoring Drug Prices of Medicare Part D Drug Plans. The OIG is examining changes and trends in Medicare Part D prescription drug prices, and will explore to what extent drug plans' prices fluctuated over time to include price variations during the open enrollment period compared with patterns after enrollment closed.
- Part D Dual-Eligible Demonstration Project. As part of the transition of beneficiaries into the Part D program, CMS has initiated a demonstration project to reimburse states for their efforts in assisting their dual eligible and low-income subsidy entitled populations in obtaining Medicare Part D coverage and paying for prescriptions for beneficiaries lacking cov-

erage. Medicare will reimburse states for the difference between the drug plan reimbursement and Medicaid costs, as well as certain state administrative costs. The OIG is investigating CMS's system to reimburse states participating in the Part D Dual-Eligible Demonstration Project and will also review the states' submission of data to determine accuracy of payments.

- Dually Eligible Hospice Patients. The OIG is determining the propriety of drug claims for individuals that are receiving hospice benefits under Medicare Part A and drug coverage under Medicare Part D. CMS established daily per diem rates to pay for hospice benefits, which include prescription drugs (used for pain relief and symptom control) related to the beneficiary's terminal illness. Hospice providers are paid daily per diem amounts, which include drugs related to a hospice beneficiary's terminal illness. Medicare Part D covers prescription drugs for Medicare beneficiaries enrolled in this voluntary benefit. Because the hospice program continues to cover prescription drugs related to a hospice beneficiary's terminal illness, Medicare Part D drug plans may unknowingly duplicate payments for prescription drugs related to a hospice beneficiary's terminal illness. The OIG will identify whether this is a widespread problem and, if so, the controls needed to prevent duplicate drug payments.

- Medicare Part D Duplicate Claims. The OIG is reviewing CMS's controls to prevent duplicate Part D claims for the same beneficiary, particularly when a beneficiary changes plans, tries to enroll in more than one plan, or tries to enroll in a plan and a retiree-subsidy covered plan. These beneficiaries are allowed to change their enrollment in a prescription drug plan monthly.

- Coordination and Oversight of Medicare Parts B and D to Avoid Duplicate Payments. The OIG is determining whether there is sufficient coordination and oversight of Medicare Parts B and D to prevent duplicate payments for drugs. Drugs for which payment is available under Medicare Part B will continue to be covered by Part B and should not also be reimbursed under Medicare Part D drug coverage. Proper coordination will be needed to prevent duplicate payments for the same prescription under Part D.

- State Contribution to Drug Benefit Costs Assumed by Medicare. Under the MMA, full benefit, dual eligible individuals receive drug coverage under Medicare Part D rather than Medicaid. Each state and the District of Columbia are responsible for making monthly payments to the federal government to defray a portion of the Medicare drug expenditures for these individuals. The OIG is determining states' compliance with laws and regulations related to states' contribution payments toward Medicare Part D. The review will include reviews of data used to calculate states' contribution payments, calculation of the states' contribution payments and the states' payment amounts, and CMS and states' controls related to contribution payments.

## IV. Enforcement Actions

### A. Medicare

In July 2003, CMS ordered CarePlus Health Plans, Inc., of South Florida to pay $75,000 for marketing violations by two of its Medicare Plans. The violations arose in part from a misstatement made by a sales representative on a radio talk show.[69] Earlier that same month CMS ordered another Florida HMO, Vista Healthplan, Inc., to stop marketing of and enrolling members in its Medicare HMO. The order was to be lifted once CMS approved a corrective action plan for the HMO's marketing plan.[70]

In June 2005, AmeriChoice of Pennsylvania, Inc., agreed to pay $1.6 million to the government and enter into a corporate integrity agreement with the U.S. Attorney's Office for the Eastern District of Pennsylvania to settle allegations relating to claims processing and coverage determinations from September 1995 through June 1998.[71] During the time period covered by the settlement, AmeriChoice participated in the Medicare and/or Medicaid programs. The government alleged that AmeriChoice violated the federal civil False Claims Act by

- failing to process and pay claims in a timely manner;
- inaccurately reporting claims processing data to the Commonwealth of Pennsylvania, including failing to meet self-reporting requirements and impose penalties on itself in accordance with its contract with the Commonwealth of Pennsylvania; and
- failing to provide coverage of home health services to qualified beneficiaries.

Pursuant to the settlement, AmeriChoice will, among other things, give providers access to information systems so that providers can check the status of claims, communicate claim status information to providers, modify its claims processing systems with respect to processing multiple procedure codes, and not automatically down code certain types of services.[72]

### B. Medicaid

In *United States ex rel. Tyson v. Amerigroup Ill., Inc.*, the Illinois Attorney General intervened in a whistleblower suit accusing an Illinois HMO of defrauding Medicaid by submitting false claims by cherry-picking certain Med-

---

[69] *CMS Fines South Florida Health Plan for Medicare+Choice Marketing Violations,* 9 Health Plan & Provider Rep. (BNA) 832 (Aug. 6, 2003).

[70] *CMS Orders Florida Health Plan to Halt Marketing, Enrolling Medicare Members,* 9 Health Plan & Provider Rep. (BNA) 808 (July 30, 2003).

[71] *See* Press Release, U.S. Dep't of Justice, *Philadelphia-Based Managed Care Company to Pay Government $1.6 Million to Resolve False Claims Allegations* (June 30, 2005), *available at* http://www.usdoj.gov/usao/pae/News/Pr/2005/jun/ACPA.html; and Settlement Agreement Between the U.S. and AmeriChoice of Pennsylvania, Inc., *available at* http://www.usdoj.gov/usao/pae/News/Pr/2005/jun/ACPA%20settlement%20FINAL.pdf.

[72] *Id.*

icaid patients and avoiding pregnant women and other seriously ill persons as a way to improve profits. In March 2007, a jury found Amerigroup Illinois and its parent liable for knowingly submitting or causing to be submitted false claims to state and federal governments for payment. The $48 million verdict was trebled, resulting in a $144 verdict.[73]

## C. Federal Employees Health Benefits Program

### 1. Overview

The Office of Personnel Management Office of Inspector General (IG-OPM) has aggressively pursued the recoupment from health plans participating in the FEHBP of overpayments made on the basis of defective certificates of accurate pricing. These overpayments typically stem from the following activities:

- Similarly sized subscriber group (SSSG) designation. An FEHBP community-rated MCO must offer the FEHBP the same rating methodology that it uses to rate its two SSSGs. The IG-OPM's audits often include a review of the MCO's SSSG designations, and the IG-OPM has aggressively pursued repayment of funds paid on the basis of incorrect SSSG designations.
- Discounted market rates. Because the OPM is entitled to the same pricing methodology (including discounts) as the two SSSGs closest to a federal account, FEHBP contractors must pass on to the FEHBP any discount provided to an SSSG. Consequently, IG-OPM audits often include a review of discounts offered to SSSGs, and the IG-OPM has aggressively pursued repayment of funds paid because such discounts were not extended to the FEHBP.
- Rating factors. The IG-OPM also routinely reviews the rating factors used by FEHBP MCOs to calculate rates charged to OPM to ensure that such rates are consistent with those charged to the applicable SSSGs and that the FEHBP's rates are properly credited or discounted for benefit variances.

### 2. Enforcement Actions Against Managed Care Organizations in the Federal Employees Health Benefits Program

In January 2007, the DOJ announced a settlement with RightChoice Managed Care Inc., a subsidiary of Wellpoint, whereby the HMO agreed to pay $975,000 to resolve allegations that it overcharged the FEHBP in violation of the False Claims Act. The government alleged that RightCHOICE, which participates in the FEHB Program as part of the Blue Cross and Blue Shield Service Benefit Plan (SBP), passed on excessive costs to the FEHBP in connection with compensating a preferred provider network of physicians known as Alliance. The government contended that RightCHOICE paid higher fees to

---

[73]No. 02 C 6074 (N.D. Ill. Mar 13, 2007). A copy of the court's memorandum opinion and order is available at http://www.crowell.com/pdf/managedcare/Tyson_v_Amerigroup-IL_opinion.pdf.

Alliance physicians for serving patients insured through the SBP than these same physicians were reimbursed for providing the same types of services to patients insured through various other health plans. The government also alleged the physicians passed on these higher rates to the OPM as purportedly "reasonable" costs to the FEHBP.[74]

Anthem Insurance Companies agreed to pay the United States $1.5 million to settle allegations that, from 1992 through 2002, it improperly calculated drug rebates due to OPM and overcharged the FEHBP by including impermissible profits in the cost of billed services. The settlement resolves a *qui tam* action brought by a former Anthem employee under the federal False Claims Act.[75]

In April 2002, after a former employee brought a *qui tam* action, PacifiCare Health Systems agreed to pay $87 million to settle alleged False Claims Act violations.[76] The government had alleged that many PacifiCare-owned MCOs had overcharged for health benefits under FEHBP contracts by failing to follow applicable OPM rules regarding premium rates. Specifically, PacifiCare allegedly "submitted inflated claims for insurance payments based on rates that were not developed in accordance with OPM regulations and rating instructions."[77]

In December 2003, HealthAmerica Pennsylvania, Inc. agreed to pay more than $29 million to settle a False Claims Act investigation. The investigation stemmed from an audit conducted by the IG-OPM wherein the auditors had identified alleged overcharges by the company in its FEHBP operations during contract years from 1993 through 1999, as well as potential False Claims Act violations. Allegedly, HealthAmerica failed to apply a price reduction to the FEHBP that was comparable to the pricing it provided to commercial groups used as a contract price benchmark. The government also expressed concern about demographic information HealthAmerica used in developing its rates.[78]

## V. POTENTIAL FALSE CLAIMS ACT AND FALSE STATEMENT LIABILITY UNDER MEDICARE ADVANTAGE AND MEDICARE PART D

The civil False Claims Act[79] presents the most severe threat of liability for MCOs. Increased government resources and consumer awareness have led to escalated federal enforcement activities and significant monetary recoveries for

---

[74]Press Release, U.S. Dep't of Justice, *RightCHOICE Managed Care to Pay United States $975,000 to Resolve False Claims Act Allegations* (Jan. 31, 2007), *available at* http://www.usdoj.gov/opa/pr/2007/January/07_civ_062.html.

[75]United States *ex rel.* Garner v. Anthem Ins. Cos., No. 00-00463-SAS (S.D. Ohio settlement announced Aug. 8, 2005), *available at* http://www.usdoj.gov/opa/pr/2005/August/05_civ_412.htm.

[76]*See* Press Release, U.S. Dep't of Justice, *PacifiCare Health Systems to Pay U.S. More Than $87 Million to Resolve False Claims Act Allegations* (Apr. 12, 2002), *available at* http://www.usdoj.gov/opa/pr/2002/April/02_civ_217.htm.

[77]*Id.*

[78]*See* OFFICE OF PERSONNEL MANAGEMENT, OFFICE OF THE INSPECTOR GENERAL, OCT. 1, 2003–MARCH 31, 2004 SEMI-ANNUAL REPORT TO CONGRESS (Apr. 30, 2004), *available at* http://www.opm.gov/about_opm/reports/InspectorGeneral/pdf/SAR30.pdf.

[79]31 U.S.C. §3729 *et seq.*

fraudulent activity, some of which have been shared with private citizens. Since the mid-1980s, the federal government has recovered more than $4 billion under the FCA—more than half was collected in the last few years alone, with more than $500 million going to private citizens. Although the government has applied the FCA to managed care, the nature of managed care presents unique FCA issues, as discussed below.

## A. Culpable Parties

The FCA imposes civil liability on persons or entities who (1) knowingly present or cause to be presented to the federal government a false or fraudulent claim for payment or approval,[80] (2) knowingly use a false record or statement to get a false or fraudulent claim paid or approved[81] or to avoid or decrease an obligation to the government,[82] or (3) conspire to defraud the government by getting a false or fraudulent claim allowed or paid.[83]

In May 2000, the U.S. Supreme Court resolved conflicting circuit court holdings in deciding that states are not "persons" under the FCA.[84] The Court expressed no view on the question of whether the Eleventh Amendment to the U.S. Constitution barred FCA suits by private citizens against state entities, a moot issue given the holding, but it stated its "serious doubt" regarding that question.[85]

## B. Levels of Knowledge

The FCA definition of "knowing" does not require the government to prove that the defendant had specific intent to defraud. Rather, the government must show that the defendant (1) had actual knowledge of the falsity of the information supporting the claim or claims, (2) acted in deliberate ignorance of the truth or falsity of the information, or (3) acted in reckless disregard of the truth or falsity of the information.[86] Under this standard, communication difficulties that often occur within large MCOs in which massive exchanges of data occur daily are potential liability risks. For example, a "disconnect" that leads to an inaccurate government payment may be characterized as "reckless" even if the "disconnect" resulted from "one hand" not knowing what the "other hand" was doing.

## C. Definition of "Claim"

Under the FCA, a "claim" is any request or demand for money or property if the U.S. government provides any portion of that money or property,

---

[80]31 U.S.C. §3729(a)(1).
[81]31 U.S.C. §3729(a)(2).
[82]31 U.S.C. §3729(a)(7).
[83]31 U.S.C. §3729(a)(3).
[84]Vermont Agency of Natural Res. v. United States *ex rel.* Stevens, 529 U.S. 765 (2000).
[85]529 U.S. at 787.
[86]31 U.S.C. §3729(b).

including reimbursement. The concept of a "claim" is fairly straightforward in the FFS system where a provider furnishes a service or supply and submits a claim for payment. However, under managed care, payment is not based on submission of a claim. Rather, the government and MCO engage in massive data exchanges and the amount paid to the MCO will depend on information generated by both the MCO and the government. In an effort to "claim-ify" this process, the Medicare Advantage and Medicare Part D programs require the MCO's CEO or chief financial officer (CFO) to "request payment under the contract based on a document that certifies the accuracy, completeness, and truthfulness of relevant data that CMS requests."[87]

In addition, unlike the FFS system where the "per claim" penalty gives the government tremendous leverage over providers that submit high volume–low dollar value claims, even if one were to accept that the payment to an MCO is based on a "claim," these "claims" are paid only once per month. Given the relatively large dollar value of the monthly managed care claim payments, the FCA "per claim" penalty probably does not offer the government the same leverage it enjoys over high volume–low dollar value claims. This might increase the potential that an MCO could try to litigate an FCA action.

## D. Damages

Liability for violating the FCA includes penalties of between $5,500 and $11,000 for each violation, plus treble damages.[88] In addition, a violation may result in exclusion from federal health care programs.[89]

The U.S. government or a private person (referred to as a *qui tam* relator), or both, may sue under the FCA.[90] A relator who chooses to invoke the statute files an action on the government's behalf [91] and can receive from 15 percent to 30 percent of the proceeds of the action or settlement of the claim.[92] In *Vermont Agency of Natural Resources v. United States ex rel. Stevens*,[93] the U.S. Supreme Court rejected a constitutional challenge to the ability of *qui tam* relators to bring suits on behalf of the government. The petitioner had alleged that *qui tam* relators do not satisfy the judicially created "injury in fact" prong of Article III's "case or controversy" requirement for federal court jurisdiction. Although the Court refused to grant relators standing either as agents[94] or on "representational" grounds,[95] it found nevertheless that relators have standing as partial assignees of the government's claim by statutory designation under the FCA.[96]

---

[87]42 C.F.R. §422.504(l).
[88]31 U.S.C. §3729(a). See 18 C.F.R. §85.3 for inflation adjustment to CMPs.
[89]42 U.S.C. §1320a-7(a) & (b).
[90]31 U.S.C. §3730(b) & (c).
[91]31 U.S.C. §3730(b)(1).
[92]31 U.S.C. §3730(d).
[93]529 U.S. 765 (2000).
[94]529 U.S. at 773.
[95]*Id.*
[96]*Id.*

An MCO that furnishes to CMS or a state agency an attestation or other information that it knows is false also faces substantial risk of liability under federal false statement and false claim statutes, including the "health care benefits" false statement provision adopted as Section 244 of HIPAA. Section 244 makes it a felony, punishable by fines or imprisonment, to knowingly or willfully falsify or conceal a material fact; to knowingly or willfully make a materially false, fictitious, or fraudulent statement or representation; or to make or use any materially false writing or document knowing that it contains a materially false, fictitious, or fraudulent statement or entry in connection with the delivery of or payment for health care benefits, items, or services.[97]

In addition, the Secretary of HHS is authorized to (1) impose CMPs of $15,000 to $100,000 (plus, in some circumstances, double damages) and (2) suspend enrollment or payment for specified conduct, including

(1) failing to substantially to provide medically necessary items and services that are required (under law or under the contract) to be provided to an individual covered under the contract, if the failure has adversely affected (or has substantial likelihood of adversely affecting) the individual;

(2) imposing premiums in excess of those permitted under 42 U.S.C. §1395w-24;

(3) expelling or refusing to enroll a person in violation of Part C;

(4) engaging in any practice that reasonably would be expected to have the effect of denying or discouraging enrollment (except as permitted under Part C) on the basis of a person's health condition or history;

(5) misrepresenting or falsifying information provided to a person, CMS, or any other entity under Part C;

(6) failing to comply with the prompt payment or PIP provisions of 42 U.S.C. §§1395w-22(j)(3) or 1395w-22(k)(2)(A)(ii); or

(7) employing or contracting with any individual or entity that is excluded from participation in a federal health care program for the provision of health care, utilization review, medical social work, or administrative services or employs or contracts with any entity for the provision (directly or indirectly) through such an excluded individual or entity of such services.[98]

The Secretary is also authorized to impose CMPs of $10,000 to $50,000 per violation for a number of specified acts, including the following:

(1) improperly filing claims (e.g., for services not provided, for false or fraudulent claims, or for services rendered by unqualified or excluded providers);

(2) paying inducements to reduce or limit services;

---

[97] *See* 18 U.S.C. §1035. This provision is notable because it applies to statements submitted to private payors as well as to federal health care programs.

[98] 42 U.S.C. §1395w-27(g) (Medicare Advantage plans).

(3) offering inducements to Medicare or Medicaid beneficiaries if the offeror knows or should know that the inducements are likely to influence the recipient to select a particular provider of items or services;

(4) contracting with an excluded person or entity; and

(5) violating the anti-kickback provisions of the Social Security Act.[99]

Another provision of the Social Security Act[100] requires the exclusion from participation in federal health care programs of persons or entities convicted of specified criminal offenses related to the delivery of an item or service under the Medicare or Medicaid programs, including those who have pled guilty or entered a "no contest" plea to such charges. It also authorizes exclusion, inter alia, of persons or entities convicted of federal program fraud and abuse or other specified violations, persons determined to have engaged in certain prohibited activities, and entities controlled by sanctioned individuals.

## E. Liability for Submission of Certified Rate, Enrollment, and Encounter Data

Participation in the Medicare Advantage and/or Medicare Part D programs increases an organization's potential for FCA liability. One area of particular vulnerability for MCO false claims liability is the submission of certified rate, enrollment, and encounter data to the government. These data affect the level of reimbursement paid. Errors relating to bid, enrollment, and encounter data, all of which must be submitted to CMS and certified by an MCO, could lead to significant false claims exposure.

### 1. Medicare Advantage Bid Submission

As a result of the MMA, MCOs that wish to participate in the Medicare Advantage program must submit a bid for each Medicare Advantage benefit plan the MCO intends to offer. The bid is intended to represent the average monthly estimated required revenue to provide coverage in the service area of the plan for a Medicare Advantage member. The bid includes three components: (1) the amount to provide original Medicare benefits (i.e., Medicare Parts A and B benefits), (2) the amount to provide basic prescription drug coverage as required by the MMA, and (3) the amount to provide supplemental coverage, if any.[101] After submission of bids, CMS will then review, conduct negotiations with Medicare Advantage organizations, and, if final bids are acceptable, approve the bids.[102] The information provided by the Medicare Advantage programs will likely continue to be an area of focus by the OIG and others, as it had been with the Medicare+Choice program.

---

[99] 42 U.S.C. §§1320a-7a, 1320a-7b(b).

[100] 42 U.S.C. §1320a-7(a)–(b).

[101] 42 C.F.R. §422.250 *et seq.*

[102] *Id.* at §422.256.

## 2. Part D

There is little program guidance and no experience regarding specific fraud and abuse risks pertaining to the Part D benefit.[103] Risks that arise under Medicare Advantage plans would likely also arise with respect to Part D plans. However, offering a Part D plan could also raise particular risks for health plans under the False Claims Act because its use of risk corridors and reinsurance features (discussed below) involves government sharing of the excess risk assumed by the health plan on a basis that is related to the health plan's costs.[104] Inaccurate reporting of plan claims costs, for example, could lead to False Claims Act allegations. Therefore, accurate accounting for rebates or other payments received from drug manufacturers will be critical.

Section 1860D-15 provides for the payment of subsidies to certain entities that offer PDP and MA-PD plans; however, unlike Medicare+Choice and Medicare risk plans, the subsidy is subject to subsequent adjustment based on the plan's actual costs, both with respect to individual enrollees and in the aggregate. Reinsurance payments, equal to 80 percent of allowable costs, would also be provided to the plan with respect to an enrollee whose costs exceeded the annual out-of-pocket threshold ($3,600 in 2006). Section 1860D-15 also provides a mechanism that can result in adjustments to the amount of payment due to the PDP plan through the use of risk corridors, which are defined as specified percentages above and below a target amount.

During 2006 and 2007, plans would be at full risk for adjusted allowable risk corridor costs within 2.5 percent above or below the target. Plans with adjusted allowable costs above this level would receive increased payments. If their costs were between 2.5 percent of the target and 5 percent of the target, they would be at risk for 25 percent of the increased amount; that is, their payments would equal 75 percent of adjusted allowable costs for spending in this range. If their costs were above 5 percent of the target, they would be at risk for 25 percent of the costs between the first and second threshold upper limits and 20 percent of the costs above that amount. Conversely, if plans fell below the target, they would share the savings with the government.

Although the process that was in place for determining the premium payments for Medicare+Choice and Medicare risk plans also required cost reporting to some degree, the relationship between the estimating of costs prior to a contract year and the plan's ultimate premium was much less direct than it will be under the MMA. This makes issues of accurate reporting of actual costs extremely important.

With respect specifically to rebates, any rebate (or any payment that can be considered as a discount) must be factored into a Part D plan's overall costs for purposes of sharing discounts with enrollees, and reinsurance and risk corridor reconciliation.[105] An open issue is the treatment of administrative expenses and

---

[103]Medicare Part D is also discussed in Chapter 10 (Short and Liner, Controlling Fraud, Waste, and Abuse in the Medicare Part D Program).

[104]*See* 42 C.F.R. §423.301 *et seq.* (Part G of the final Part D plan regulations).

[105]*See, e.g.,* 42 C.F.R. §423.308, defining "actually paid" costs to be costs that are net of discounts, rebates, or other adjustments for purposes of reinsurance and reconciliation with the

the allocation of "administrative service fees" that are provided for in a rebate arrangement.

Relationships with manufacturers that would have the effect of subsidizing a Part D benefit can raise complex actuarial issues for Part D plans that have yet to be addressed, let alone resolved, by CMS. Actuarial valuation affecting the reinsurance and risk sharing aspects of the Part D program may be raised by benefit design decisions as well as by special programs, such as coupon programs or other copayment waiver, or programs that fill the "donut hole" for beneficiaries.[106]

Finally, in order to claim the retiree plan subsidy, the plan sponsor must submit documentation of the value of the plan (in advance of the plan year for which the subsidy is to be claimed) and the costs incurred under the plan (after the plan year for which the subsidy is to be claimed). Where any party (whether the plan sponsor, the plan administrator or underwriter, or a third-party actuary) provides the certification of actuarial equivalence of a prescription drug benefit on behalf of employers claiming the employer subsidy for coverage provided to retirees, such certification clearly raises potential false claim issues if it is materially incorrect.[107] Reporting of costs to employer plan sponsors, for purposes of calculating the subsidy, will also need to be accurate.

## F. Medicare Secondary Payer Provisions

During the first 15 years of the program, Medicare was primary payor for all services to Medicare beneficiaries, with the sole exception of services covered under workers' compensation. Beginning in 1980, Congress enacted a series of amendments to 42 U.S.C. §1395y(b) requiring automobile, liability, no-fault insurance, and, finally, employer-group health plans to pay primary to Medicare. These are known as the Medicare Secondary Payer (MSP) provisions.

Under the MSP provisions, the primary payment responsibility of employer-sponsored group health plans (EGHPs) hinges on the number of employees that work for the employer. In *United States ex rel. Drescher v. Highmark, Inc.*,[108] the United States joined a *qui tam* action against Highmark, sued as a Medicare fiscal intermediary and as a private health insurance company, for alleged violations of the FCA, as well as to recover overpayments made by Medicare pursuant to the MSP statute,[109] and for unjust enrichment

---

government. *See also* 42 C.F.R. §423.100, which defines "negotiated prices" to be prices for covered Part D drugs that
    (1) Are available to beneficiaries at the point of sale at network pharmacies;
    (2) Are reduced by those discounts, direct or indirect subsidies, rebates, other price concessions, and direct or indirect remunerations that the Part D sponsor has elected to pass through to Part D enrollees at the point of sale; and
    (3) Includes any dispensing fees.
[106]The "donut hole" is a gap in prescription drug coverage that goes into effect after the initial coverage limit ($2,250 for 2006) is reached. Beneficiaries with total drug costs exceeding the initial benefit limit, but not yet at the point where catastrophic coverage begins, are responsible for paying all prescription drug costs out-of-pocket. 70 Fed. Reg. 4237 (Jan. 28, 2005). See the CMS Web site for additional details at http://www.medicare.gov/Publications/Pubs/pdf/11102.pdf.
[107]*See* 42 C.F.R. §423.884(d).
[108]305 F. Supp. 2d 451 (E.D. Pa. 2004).
[109]42 U.S.C. §1395y(b)(2)(B)(ii).

and breach of contract. The *qui tam* relator had been a Highmark employee responsible for implementing a 1995 settlement agreement entered into by the government and Highmark's predecessors. Highmark allegedly violated the FCA as a private insurer by improperly paying MSP claims on a secondary basis that it should have paid on a primary basis, thereby causing providers and beneficiaries to submit false claims to the Medicare program for primary payment. Highmark allegedly obtained information to assist with submission of claims and then failed to integrate such steps into its internal systems. The court denied Highmark's motion to dismiss, and deferred ruling on separate claims that Highmark submitted false claims as a Medicare administrative contractor.

## G. Reporting of Commissions and Fees Paid to Insurance Brokers and Agents

In February 2005, the Department of Labor issued an advisory opinion regarding the reporting of commissions, fees, and other compensation paid by insurers to brokers and agents for ERISA-covered plans.[110] The guidance follows a series of lawsuits brought by state enforcement authorities alleging under-reporting of commissions and fees by insurers, and failures to disclose to customers the compensation received from insurers by brokers and agents.[111] State officials have claimed that the acceptance by brokers of contingent compensation that is not disclosed to the customer may involve false representations or concealment of material facts. In addition, state enforcement authorities have alleged that certain brokerage firms and insurers have illegally steered insurance business, or have participated in anti-competitive fictitious bidding schemes.[112]

## H. PBM Fraud and Abuse Issues

In August 2004, the State of New York filed a complaint in state trial court[113] alleging that Express Scripts Inc., the pharmacy benefits manager (PBM) for the state's largest employees' and retirees' health plan, engaged in "self-dealing" with regard to the plan, including that it

---

[110]Dep't of Labor, Advisory Op. No. 2005-02A (Feb. 24, 2005).

[111]*See* State v. Marsh & McLennan Co. (N.Y. Sup. Ct. filed Oct. 14, 2004); State v. Universal Life Resources (N.Y. Sup. Ct. filed Nov. 12, 2004); State v. Marsh & McLennan Co., No. CV-05-4007742-S (Conn. Super. Ct. filed Jan. 21, 2005); State v. Universal Life Res. (Cal. Super. Ct. filed Nov. 17, 2004).

[112]*See* State v. Marsh & McLennan Co. (N.Y. Sup. Ct. filed Oct. 14, 2004); Blumenthal v. Aon Corp. (Conn. Super. Ct. filed Mar. 4, 2005); People v. Aon Corp. (N.Y. Sup. Ct. filed Mar. 4, 2005); State v. Aon Corp. (Ill. Cir. Ct., Cook County, filed Mar. 4, 2005). New York Attorney General Spitzer's case against Marsh & McLennan was settled in early 2005; *see* State *ex rel.* Spitzer v. Marsh & McLennan Cos., Index No. 04/403342 (Agreement Between the Attorney General of the State of New York and the Superintendent of Insurance of the State of New York, and Marsh & McLennan Companies, Inc., Marsh Inc. and their subsidiaries and affiliates) (N.Y. Ins. Dep't Jan. 30, 2005), *available at* http://www.oag.state.ny.us/press/2005/feb/marsh_settlement.pdf.

[113]State v. Express Scripts, Inc., No. 4669-04 (N.Y. Sup. Ct., Albany County, filed Aug. 4, 2004); complaint *available at* http://www.oag.state.ny.us/press/2004/aug/aug4a_04_attach.pdf.

- retained manufacturer rebates it was obligated to pay to the plan by "disguising" them as service fees;
- generated revenue by selling or licensing data that belonged to the customer plan;
- negotiated and paid inflated pharmacy prices for plans that paid the entire fee negotiated with the pharmacy, which enabled it to obtain much lower prices for the same drugs dispensed to the members of "spread" plans, i.e., those plans for which the PBM had guaranteed a certain price to the plan and earned the difference or spread if the PBM was able to negotiate a lower fee with the pharmacy; and
- manipulated the pricing of generic drugs.

In another suit regarding a PBM, *Chicago District Council of Carpenters Welfare Fund v. Caremark Rx, Inc.,*[114] a federal court dismissed claims alleging breach of ERISA fiduciary status based on the PBM's failure to pass through rebates. The court reasoned that because the agreement between Caremark Rx, Inc., and the plan clearly stated that the PBM would keep rebates, the PBM did not exercise discretion over plan funds that would have made it an ERISA fiduciary for that purpose. However, the court refused to dismiss claims alleging that the PBM committed state consumer fraud by

- negotiating secret rebates and discounts with drug manufacturers without passing on those savings to the plan;
- placing more expensive drugs on the formulary so that the PBM could receive secret rebates, discounts, and other savings;
- keeping the difference between the PBM's agreed price with retail pharmacies and the higher price the PBM defendants charged the plan;
- charging the plan the higher average wholesale price (AWP) for smaller lot sizes while the PBM purchased the drugs in larger lot sizes with a lower AWP; and
- charging the plan a higher maximum allowable charge for generic drugs than was permitted under the agreement.

The U.S. Attorney for the Eastern District of Pennsylvania filed an amended complaint against Merck-Medco Managed Care, LLC, on December 9, 2003. The complaint alleged that Medco Health Solutions, Inc., violated the federal False Claims Act, the fraud injunction statute, and the federal Anti-Kickback Act.[115] During the time period at issue, according to the complaint, the company provided mail-order prescription drug benefits for federal health programs, including the Federal Employees Health Benefits Program, the Civilian Health and Medical Program of the Uniformed Services (CHAMPUS), and TRICARE. The complaint alleged that in the eight years preceding the filing, the pharmacy benefits manager (PBM) caused its employees to falsify prescription orders to meet performance guarantees under the FEHBP contract

---

[114]No. 04 C 5868, 2005 U.S. Dist. LEXIS 7891 (N.D. Ill. Apr. 14, 2005).

[115]*See* United States v. Merck-Medco Managed Care, LLC, No. 00-CV-737 (E.D. Pa.; amended complaint filed Dec. 9, 2003). The amended complaint is available at http://www.usdoj.gov/usao/pae/News/Pr/2003/dec/Medcoamendedcomplaint.pdf.

and make false records of physician contacts about drug risks and interactions. The complaint alleged that the PBM improperly delivered fewer pills than reported and then created false records about the quantity of drugs that were delivered and dispensed. The complaint also alleged that the PBM violated the federal Anti-Kickback Act by paying a federal health plan more than $87 million allegedly to influence the awarding of a PBM subcontract to Medco. In April 2004, one count in the case was resolved through a consent order requiring Medco to be more transparent in its business practices, including pricing.[116] The company also settled unfair trade practices claims brought by 20 state attorneys general.[117] In September 2004, count four of the government's complaint, relating to active and constructive fraud, was dismissed,[118] but other counts alleging anti-kickback violations were not dismissed.[119] Medco announced a final settlement with the government in October 2006, agreeing to pay $155 million.[120]

A similar action against AdvancePCS[121] was settled in 2005 for $137.5 million to resolve False Claims Act and Anti-Kickback Act allegations concerning FEHBP and Medicare plans. AdvancePCS allegedly received improper and excessive payments from pharmaceutical manufacturers for services and products as a reward for favorable treatment of the manufacturers' drugs in connection FEHBP and Medicare plans, and allegedly made payments to its own customers in order to be chosen as the PBM for federally funded health plans.

## I. Other Statutes

Other statutes potentially applicable to fraud and abuse by MCOs with criminal penalties include, but are not limited to, the following:

- the federal Health Care Program Anti-Kickback Act,[122]
- the Health Care Fraud Act,[123]

---

[116]United States v. Merck-Medco Managed Care, LLC, No. 00-CV-737 (E.D. Pa. order filed Apr. 26, 2004). The consent order is available at http://www.usdoj.gov/usao/pae/News/Pr/2004/apr/consentordermedco.pdf.

[117]*See* U.S. Dep't of Justice, Press Release, *The United States Settles Its Anti-Fraud Claims for Injunctive Relief and 20 State Attorneys General Settle Unfair Trade Practices Claims Against Medco Health Solutions, available at* http://www.usdoj.gov/usao/pae/News/Pr/2004/apr/medcoinjunctivereliefrelease.pdf.

[118]United States *ex rel.* Hunt v. Merck-Medco Managed Care, LLC, 336 F. Supp. 2d 430 (E.D. Pa. 2004).

[119]*Id.*

[120]United States *ex rel.* Piacentile v. Merck & Co. Inc., No. 00-cv-00737 (E.D. Pa. final settlement announced Oct. 23, 2006); *Medco Announces Settlement Agreement to Resolve False Claims Kickback Charges*, 10 Health Care Fraud Rep. (BNA) 770 (Oct. 25, 2006).

[121]United States v. AdvancePCS, Civ. A. Nos. 02-CV-9236, 03-CV-5425 (E.D. Pa. Sept. 8, 2005).

[122]42 U.S.C. §1320a-7b(b). For text of the statute, see Appendix A-1 on the disk accompanying this volume.

[123]18 U.S.C. §1347. For text of §1347, see Appendix E-2 on the disk accompanying this volume.

- the Obstruction of Health Care Investigations statute,[124]
- the Theft or Embezzlement in Relation to a Health Care Benefit Program statute,[125] and
- the Racketeer Influenced and Corrupt Organizations Act (RICO).[126]

## VI. MANAGED CARE EXCEPTIONS TO THE ANTI-KICKBACK STATUTE

Section 216 of HIPAA created a new managed care exception to the Medicare and Medicaid anti-kickback provisions.[127] This exception allows (1) remuneration between a Medicare MCO and an individual or entity providing items or services pursuant to a written agreement between the parties, and (2) remuneration between an organization and an individual provider or a provider entity if the provider is at "substantial financial risk"[128] for the cost of utilization of items or services that the provider is obligated to provide, whether through a withhold, capitation, incentive pool, or per-diem payment, or any other similar risk arrangement.

### A. Negotiated Rulemaking

Section 216(b) of HIPAA provided that the Secretary of HHS, through an expedited negotiated rulemaking process, set standards for the new managed care exception to the Medicare and Medicaid anti-kickback provisions. Consequently, the OIG engaged in a negotiated rulemaking process to develop a safe harbor regulation, and that process was completed in January 1998. The negotiation process was conducted by the OIG over a six-month period, with approximately 20 participants from the private sector (e.g., managed care and health care provider trade associations), as well as government agencies such as the DOJ. The OIG promulgated an interim final rule on November 19, 1999, that established two new safe harbors to satisfy the exception set forth in 42 U.S.C. §1320a-7b(b)(3)(F). The resulting safe harbors are relatively narrow and clearly reflect areas of concern to the OIG and other anti-fraud enforcement authorities. Despite the regulation's limited scope, the preamble includes a statement that arrangements falling outside of the safe harbors are not presumed to be illegal, but must be judged on a case-by-case basis.[129] This language clearly is aimed at the anxieties expressed by private participants to the rulemaking regarding the potential stigma for any arrangement that does not fall within the safe harbors. It should be noted that prior to the issuance of these new safe harbors, the OIG, in an advisory opinion, approved an arrangement

---

[124] 18 U.S.C. §1518.

[125] *Id.* §669.

[126] *Id.* §1961.

[127] 42 U.S.C. §1320a-7b(b)(3)(F).

[128] *Id.*

[129] Statutory Exception to the Anti-Kickback Statute for Shared Risk Arrangements, 64 Fed. Reg. 63,504 (Nov. 19, 1999) (interim final rule codified at 42 C.F.R. pt. 1001).

whereby an independent physician association acquired an equity interest of less than 15 percent in an MCO.[130]

As noted above, the rule established two separate safe harbors, and each of these safe harbors is further broken down into two components: the first component covers arrangements directly between the managed care entity and a contractor; the second component addresses arrangements between a managed care contractor and its subcontractors.

## B. Capitated Managed Care Entity Safe Harbor

The safe harbor set forth in 42 C.F.R. §1001.952(t) extends protection from the anti-kickback statute to most managed health care program arrangements in which the federal health care programs pay on a capitated or fixed aggregate basis (e.g., certain Medicare Part C plans). Furthermore, it extends safe harbor protection to cover subcontracts with other providers and entities to provide items and services in accordance with a protected managed care arrangement. As long as the federal health care program's aggregate financial exposure is fixed in accordance with its contract with the MCO, such subcontracting arrangements are protected regardless of the payment methodology, subject to the following requirements: the agreement (1) is set out in writing and signed by both parties; (2) specifies the items and services covered under the agreement; (3) is for a period of at least one year; and (4) with the exception of certain types of MCOs and first-tier contractors, provides that the contractors and subcontractors cannot make a claim to the federal government for services covered under the agreement.

## C. Risk-Sharing Safe Harbor

The safe harbor set forth in 42 C.F.R. §1001.952(u) extends protection from the anti-kickback statute to those managed care arrangements that encompass substantial risk-sharing between the qualified managed care plan and its first-tier or downstream contractors. There are several requirements that have to be met for an MCO and a provider to avail themselves of this safe harbor. However, there are two major limitations. First, to qualify for this safe harbor, a provider must be at substantial financial risk for items or services provided to *federal health care program beneficiaries.* However, as the preamble candidly notes, risk-sharing arrangements that cover federal health care program beneficiaries may be covered under the other new managed care safe harbor, 42 C.F.R §1001.952(t), as discussed above. Second, providers must be at risk for the cost or utilization of items or services that they are personally "obligated to provide," which may have the effect of excluding arrangements under which a physician's compensation may be at risk for services provided by other providers. For example, risk-sharing arrangements with primary care physicians (PCPs) often base the PCP's bonus, in part, on the volume or value

---

[130]*See* U.S. Dep't of Health & Human Servs., Office of Inspector Gen., Advisory Op. No. 98-19 (Dec. 14, 1998).

of referral services, such as diagnostic and lab tests ordered by the PCP, or hospital admissions authorized by the PCP. Those types of risk-sharing arrangements are not protected under this new safe harbor.

In addition to the above-listed restrictions, the arrangement between the MCO and the first-tier contractor must

(1) be in writing and signed by the parties;

(2) specify the items and services covered by the arrangement;

(3) be for a period of at least one year;

(4) require that the contractor participate in the MCO's quality assurance program;

(5) set a payment formula that results in periodic payments that are commercially reasonable and consistent with fair market value;

(6) use one of the following payment methodologies:

- a periodic fixed payment per patient that does not take into account the dates services are provided, the frequency of services, or the extent or kind of services provided;
- percentage of premium;
- inpatient federal health care program diagnosis related groups (other than those for psychiatric services); and
- bonus and withhold arrangements, provided that certain specified percentage thresholds and risk proportions are met and payments are reasonable given the MCO's population and utilization;

(7) if there are services or items not covered under the capitated payment made by the government to the MCO, the MCO (not the contractor or provider) must submit the claims to the federal government for reimbursement, pursuant to a valid reassignment agreement;

(8) payments to contractors (first-tier and downstream) for providing or arranging for items and services for federal health plan enrollees must be identical (allowing adjustments related to utilization patterns or costs of providing services to the relevant population) for payments to contractors for providing or arranging for items and services for commercial enrollees with similar health status; and

(9) if a first-tier contractor has an investment interest in the MCO, the investment interest must meet the requirements set forth in 42 C.F.R §1001.952(a)(1). The preamble notes that this requirement is intended to eliminate any concern that the contractor's substantial financial risk may be offset by returns on its ownership interest in the organization and therefore undermine protections against overutilization.

Many of the above requirements also apply to contracts between the first-tier contractor and the downstream entity (i.e., provider).

### D. Some Common Elements of Both Safe Harbors

In addition to the requirements particular to each safe harbor set forth above, the safe harbors share several common definitions and requirements.

## 1. Health Care Items and Services

The safe harbors apply only to remuneration for health care items or services (as do the previously promulgated managed care safe harbors), but for these two new safe harbors, HHS has added a definition of "items and services" that appears to broaden the term in comparison to how it is used in the rest of the regulation. "Items and services" is defined to include "items, . . . or services reasonably related to the provision of health care items, devices, supplies, or services," such as "non-emergency transportation, patient education, attendant services, social services (e.g., case management), utilization review and quality assurance."[131] Marketing and other preenrollment activities are not considered to be "items or services" that fall within this definition.[132]

## 2. No Swapping or Shifting of Financial Burden

In addition to the requirements listed above for the new safe harbors, arrangements under either 42 C.F.R §1001.952(t) or (u) (both between MCOs and first-tier contractors and first-tier contractors and downstream entities) cannot provide for "swapping" or allow a shifting of the financial burden of the arrangement to a federal health care program.

Arrangements are excluded from the protection of both new safe harbors if the contracting parties give or receive remuneration in return "for or to induce the provision or acceptance of business (other than business covered by the arrangement) for which payment may be made in whole or in part by a federal health care program on a fee-for-service or cost basis."[133] This exclusion reflects the OIG's concern about swapping arrangements. Swapping occurs when the risk arrangement is agreed to in exchange for the right to participate in a program that provides greater compensation to the provider (e.g., a commercial preferred provider organization) but that could result in greater utilization in the FFS Medicare program.[134]

Furthermore, the parties also cannot shift the financial burden of such arrangement to the extent that increased payments are claimed from a federal health care program to cover the cost of this arrangement. As in previous regulatory issuances in which this or similar language has been used,[135] it is unclear exactly what this standard entails. At a minimum, an entity may not seek additional compensation from a federal health care program for services that were provided under the arrangement. For example, in the case of permitted Medicare copayment waivers by hospitals (in the older safe harbor regulations), the hospital would not be able to include the waived copayment as a bad debt and thus seek additional financial benefits from the Medicare program.

---

[131]64 Fed. Reg. 63,504, 63,513–14 (Nov. 19, 1999) (codified at 42 C.F.R. §1001.952(t)(2)(iv) and (u)(2)(iv)).

[132]*Id.*

[133]64 Fed. Reg. 63,504, 63,513–14 (Nov. 19, 1999) (codified at 42 C.F.R. §1001.952(t)(1)(i)(B) and (u)(1)(i)(E)(1)).

[134]*See* U.S. Dep't of Health & Human Servs., Office of Inspector Gen., Advisory Op. No. 99-2 (Feb. 26, 1999).

[135]*See* 57 Fed. Reg. 43,906 (Sept. 23, 1992); 54 Fed. Reg. 3448 (Jan. 24, 1989); and 52 Fed Reg. 35,044 (Sept. 16, 1987).

## VII. Prompt Payment and Denial of Care Compliance Issues

### A. Prompt Payment

There are several respects in which MCOs resemble indemnity insurers in that they simply pay claims for services provided by others. When doing so, Medicare requires its MCO contractors to pay 95 percent of "clean" claims submitted by noncontract providers within 30 days after receipt.[136] "Clean claims" are claims that (1) are not defective or lacking necessary substantiating documentation, and (2) conform to the Medicare fee-for-service definition of clean claim.[137] Failure to comply with the prompt payment requirement can result in adverse action, including the imposition of intermediate sanctions or CMPs.[138] In addition, under 42 U.S.C. §1395w-27(f)(2), if prompt payment is not made by a Medicare Advantage organization, the Secretary can choose to pay these claims directly and reduce the amounts paid from the amounts due to the Medicare Advantage contractor.[139]

The issue of prompt payment also can arise under state law, and many states have enacted prompt payment statutes. For example, New York State engaged in a highly visible confrontation under the state's consumer protection laws with an MCO concerning a claims backlog that exceeded $230 million. This backlog, which included claims to contracted providers, was resolved by an agreement with the New York State Attorney General to make the payments with interest within a specific time frame.[140] Soon after this settlement, the New York legislature enacted a statute requiring insurers and MCOs to make payment within 45 days of receipt of a claim and imposing a substantial interest penalty for late payments.[141] It imposes a $100 per violation fine on companies that have generated multiple complaints.[142] In January 1999, the New York State Insurance Department fined 12 insurers and MCOs a total of $72,200 for violating the state's prompt payment law. The largest fine of $40,900 was levied against Oxford Health Plans; smaller fines ranged from $1,000 to $2,900.[143] Actions of this sort have become common throughout the United States.

Some states have recognized that a prompt payment statute that is applied to all MCOs can run afoul of ERISA. In response, Maryland's prompt payment statute, for example, states that it "applies to an insurer or nonprofit health service plan that acts as a third-party administrator" only "[t]o the extent consistent with [ERISA]."[144]

---

[136] *See* 42 U.S.C. §1395w-27(f).

[137] 42 C.F.R. §422.500.

[138] *See* 42 C.F.R. §§417.50, 422.752(b).

[139] *See also* 42 C.F.R. §522.520(c).

[140] *See* 6 Health Law Rep. (BNA) 32 (Aug. 7, 1997).

[141] *See* 6 Health Law Rep. (BNA) 39 (Oct. 2, 1997).

[142] *See* 3 Health Care Fraud Rep. (BNA) 77–78 (Jan. 27, 1999).

[143] *See id.*

[144] *See* Md. Code Ann., Ins. §15-1005.

States continue to assess penalties against MCOs for violations of state prompt payment laws.[145]

## B. Denial of Care

As discussed above, the managed care system brings to the health care industry a reversal of FFS incentives. Under FFS, providers receive financial incentives to deliver more care (e.g., extra office visits, tests, and procedures). Hence, there is concern about overutilization. In contrast, underutilization is the source of many disputes in the managed care industry. Although negotiated capitated rates may create incentives for MCOs to deny services, the managed care system is based on the understanding that payments are received by MCOs for enrollees to whom no services were provided during the applicable payment period.

The DOJ has stated that it will consider several factors in determining whether the denial or unavailability of services by an MCO could constitute fraud and abuse. These factors include the following:

- representations made to beneficiaries by the plan, physicians, sales representatives, customer service employees, contractors, and plan documents;
- internal records maintained by an MCO, specifically its system of tracking utilization by practice, demographics, subscriber, and outcome;
- accounting and actuarial records systems that reveal where the MCO makes its profits;
- incentives and bonuses;
- quality measurement;
- complaints made by subscribers, providers, regulators, accreditation agencies, and competitors;
- failure to follow state, federal, or professional or trade association guidelines;
- use of a system that discourages access to reviewers, such as complex voice mail systems, broken fax machines, or long delays in returning telephone calls;
- measurement systems for provider referrals that penalize those who appeal, reward those below the median in utilization, or reward a group for reduced utilization;

---

[145]*See, e.g., Health Plans Fined by Regulators for Prompt Payment Law Violations,* 10 Health Plan & Provider Rep. (BNA) 475 (May 5, 2004); *Thirty New York Health Plans Fined for Violating Prompt Pay Law,* 10 Health Plan & Provider Rep. (BNA) 138 (Feb. 4, 2004); *CIGNA Will Pay More than $2 Million to Settle Claims Handling Allegations,* 9 Health Plan & Provider Rep. (BNA) 1288 (Dec. 17, 2003); *Insurance Department Fines Horizon $200,000 for Claims-Handling Violations,* 9 Health Plan & Provider Rep. (BNA) 1076 (Oct. 15, 2003); *Anthem Health Plan Agrees to Pay $1.75 Million for Late, Underpaid Claims,* 9 Health Plan & Provider Rep. (BNA) 882 (Aug. 20, 2003); *Attorney General Announces Settlement of Prompt-Pay Case Against PacifiCare,* 9 Health Plan & Provider Rep. (BNA) 355 (Apr. 2, 2003); *New Jersey Fines CIGNA Under Prompt-Pay Law,* 10 Health Care Pol'y Rep. (BNA) 1520 (Nov. 18, 2002); *Pacific Life Fined for Prompt Pay Violations,* 8 Health Plan & Provider Rep. (BNA) 777 (July 3, 2002); *Oxendine Fines Humana $400,000 for Prompt Pay Law Violations,* Atlanta Bus. Chron., Jan. 24, 2002.

- testimony by trained professional reviewers or case managers about training instructions or tapes of conversations indicating that the review process is designed to deny needed care;
- lack of articulated standards;
- decisions to allow coverage regardless of the criteria when the patient has a powerful patron;
- personal benefit to individual reviewers (e.g., bonuses and promotions);
- evidence that patients did not receive promised benefits; and
- institution and practice comparative records showing that statistically similar patients are treated differently by the physician, hospital, or clinic.[146]

Policyholders have challenged the denial of medically necessary care under state deceptive business practices laws. For example, policyholders of the Prudential Insurance Company of America filed a class action lawsuit claiming that Prudential's alleged denials of medically necessary care violated New York business laws relating to deceptive acts and practices. A New York state court upheld a trial court's decision to permit the class action to proceed.[147]

The State of California has also levied large penalties against health plans for their alleged denials of care.[148]

## VIII. INCREASED STATE ENFORCEMENT EFFORTS

In addition to these federal actions, states have been increasing their focus on the delivery of managed care services, operational issues (including "prompt payments" statute), and fraud and abuse issues. Most states have taken steps to require insurers to implement anti-fraud measures, such as reporting suspicious claims to state officials and developing training, detection, and procedures manuals. For example, a California law requires insurers doing business in the state to establish and maintain a "special investigative unit (SIU)" to investigate possible claims of fraud and abuse. SIUs must refer fraud and abuse allegations to the state insurance department.

States continue to look at the delivery of managed care services, operational issues, and fraud and abuse issues in connection with managed care organizations. In April 2004, the New York State Insurance Department imposed a fine of $500,000 on Health Net of New York and required Health Net to (i) reprocess emergency room claims that were improperly denied based on the "prudent layperson standard," (ii) reprocess claims from July 1999 through December 2002 for which Health Net used an outdated schedule of reasonable and customary charges to determine payment rates, and (iii) establish a new appeals process for claims that were denied and for which Health Net issued an

---

[146]*See* 3 HEALTH CARE FRAUD REP. (BNA) 561 (June 30, 1999); 2 HEALTH CARE FRAUD REP. (BNA) 319 (May 6, 1998).

[147]Batas v. Prudential Ins. Co. of Am., 724 N.Y.S.2d 3 (N.Y. App. Div. 2001).

[148]*See Kaiser Plan Will Pay $100,000 Fine for Failing to Provide Home Health Care,* 8 HEALTH PLAN & PROVIDER REP. (BNA) 1015 (Sept. 11, 2002); *Kaiser Health Plan to Pay $1,000,000 to Settle Case Involving Patient Death,* 8 HEALTH PLAN & PROVIDER REP. (BNA) 1297 (Nov. 20, 2002).

incorrect explanation of benefit form. The reprocessing of claims resulted in an estimated $5 million in additional claim payments.[149] In January 2004, Anthem agreed to pay a $50,000 fine to the Indiana Department of Insurance relating to errors in Anthem's claims processing systems.[150] Finally, in November 2004, HealthGuard of Lancaster, Inc., agreed to pay $1.6 million to the Pennsylvania Department of Insurance for overcharging and undercharging group health policies. HealthGuard was also ordered to pay $195,000 in restitution to affected customers.[151]

The Kentucky Office of Insurance (KOI) in 2005 ordered Anthem Health Plans of Kentucky, Inc. to refund approximately $23.7 million to more than 81,000 individuals enrolled in Anthem's Medicare supplement plans.[152] The refunds were ordered because Anthem's Medicare supplement premiums for 2005 were allegedly "unreasonable in relation to the benefits provided." KOI also fined Anthem $2 million for overstating medical cost projections, which at that time was reported to be the largest insurer fine ever issued by the agency.

KOI alleged that in 2004 Anthem realized that it had overpaid providers for medical claims and began recouping extra payments. According to KOI, Anthem did not notify the agency when it learned of these errors; rather, KOI claims that Anthem requested a 17 percent increase in premiums for Medicare supplement plans, partially based on higher payments to providers made in 2004.

## IX. Conclusion and Practical Pointers

The managed care fraud environment has been dynamic over the past few years as the government continues to develop new theories for civil and criminal liability and program requirements become more complex. In the face of this threat, MCOs should be proactive in their approach to potential fraud and abuse issues in three basic ways. First, MCOs must be resolute about reviewing all available government sources for identification of "new" potential fraud issues, including HHS OIG work plans, fraud alerts, compliance guidance, and advisory opinions. Second, MCOs must monitor changes in government program requirements vigilantly by tracking government issuances, including the *Medicare Managed Care Manual.* Finally, MCOs must be attentive to deviations from normal practices.

Indeed, the government has come to expect this kind of vigilance from Medicare MCOs because of the requirement that they have compliance plans. Because of this requirement, the government has been particularly harsh when

---

[149]*See Health Net Agrees to Pay Fine, Refund $5 Million to Policyholders,* 10 Health Plan & Provider Rep. (BNA) 414 (Apr. 21, 2004).

[150]*See Indiana Plan Agrees to Improve Claims Processing, Pay $50,000 Fine,* 10 Health Plan & Provider Rep. (BNA) 8 (Jan. 7, 2004).

[151]*See State Levies Record $1.6 Million Fine Against Health Plan for Pricing Violations,* 10 Health Plan & Provider Rep. (BNA) 1126 (Nov. 10, 2004).

[152]*Kentucky Regulator Orders Anthem to Repay $23M in Premium Overcharges,* 9 Health Care Fraud Rep. (BNA) 906 (Dec. 7, 2005).

addressing alleged fraud and abuse violations by these MCOs, apparently because such violations show that the compliance plans may not be effective. For example, the government has imposed corporate integrity agreements on Medicare MCOs that are broad in both scope and duration even where the underlying regulatory violation was discreet and has been corrected. By keeping current on government requirements and being sensitive to deviations from "normal" practices, attorneys can help protect their MCO clients from the risk of adverse government action.

# 7

# Corporate Compliance Programs*

* Linda A. Baumann, Arent Fox LLP, Washington, D.C. The author gratefully acknowledges the assistance of Anthony Choe, Arent Fox LLP, in preparing this chapter.

## I. Introduction

As recently as the early 1990s, few health care organizations had any official or organized fraud and abuse compliance program, and the designation of an employee as corporate compliance officer with the sole function of overseeing and enforcing compliance with health care fraud and abuse laws was almost unheard of. By 2007, however, compliance programs are a standard feature of corporate life in health care.

A well-planned compliance program is vital for health care organizations for several reasons. Increased government scrutiny and enforcement is one. For example, the Health Insurance Portability and Accountability Act of 1996 (HIPAA),[1] the Balanced Budget Act of 1997 (BBA),[2] and the Medicare Prescription Drug,

---

[1]Pub. L. No. 104-191, 110 Stat. 1936 (1996).
[2]Pub. L. No. 105-33, 111 Stat. 251 (1997).

Improvement, and Modernization Act of 2003 (MMA)[3] each added significant new laws and enforcement programs to the government's health care compliance enforcement arsenal.[4] The BBA revised sanctions available for fraud and abuse violations (e.g., exclusion provisions).[5] The MMA increased the Centers for Medicare and Medicaid Services (CMS) oversight over a greater range of programs, including the Medicare-approved drug discount card program, Medicare managed care plans, and ultimately the prescription drug benefit.[6] Most notably, Section 6032 of the Deficit Reduction Act of 2005 (DRA)[7] made certain compliance policies a requirement, effective January 1, 2007, for certain health care providers that receive or pay $5 million or more in annual Medicaid funds.

In addition, several high-profile cases have heightened providers' sensitivity to and awareness of enforcement issues and demonstrated the government's willingness to invest significant time and resources in uncovering and prosecuting health care fraud and abuse.[8] Another reason is the growing number of whistleblower or *qui tam* lawsuits. Employees, competitors, and even patients have become increasingly sophisticated about health care fraud and abuse and the potentially lucrative rewards that can come from whistleblower suits.[9] As a

---

[3]Pub. L. No. 108-173, 117 Stat. 2066 (2003).

[4]HIPAA, for example, added four new health care crimes relating to "health benefit programs," which are defined as including any "public or private plan or contract." 18 U.S.C. §24(b). A new health care fraud statute (18 U.S.C. §1347) prohibits knowingly defrauding any health care benefit program and includes penalties of fines and up to 10 years imprisonment (20 years if the violation results in bodily harm and life imprisonment if the violation results in death). In addition to the new health care fraud statute, there are new statutes criminalizing theft and embezzlement in connection with health care fraud (18 U.S.C. §669), false statements relating to health care matters (18 U.S.C. §1035), and obstruction of justice relating to health care matters or investigations (18 U.S.C. §1518).

[5]*See* Subtitle D-Anti-Fraud and Abuse Provisions, Legislative Summary: Balanced Budget Act of 1997 Medicare and Medicaid Provisions, *available at* http://www.cms.hhs.gov/Demo ProjectsEvalRpts/downloads/CC_Section4016_BBA_1997.pdf.

[6]Press Release, CMS, *CMS Strengthens Efforts to Reduce Fraud and Abuse in Medicare, Medicaid* (Aug. 27, 2004), *available at* http://www.cms.hhs.gov/apps/media/press/release.asp? Counter=1178.

[7]Pub. L. No. 109-171, 120 Stat. 4 (2006).

[8]*See, e.g.*, News Release, *Bristol-Myers Squibb Announces Agreement in Principle to Settle Federal Investigation into Pricing, Sales and Marketing Practices* (Dec. 21, 2006), *available at* http://newsroom.bms.com/index.php?s=press_releases&item=226; Press Release, U.S. Dep't of Justice, *Tenet Healthcare Corporation to Pay U.S. more than $900 Million to Resolve False Claims Act Allegations* (June 29, 2006), *available at* http://www.usdoj.gov/opa/pr/2006/June/ 06_civ_406.html; Press Release, U.S. Dep't of Justice, *Largest Health Care Fraud Case in U.S. History Settled HCA Investigation Nets Record Total of $1.7 Billion* (June 26, 2003), *available at* http://www.usdoj.gov/opa/pr/2003/June/03_civ_386.htm.

[9]In addition to the *qui tam* provision of the civil False Claims Act (FCA) (31 U.S.C. §§3729–33), under which a successful *qui tam* relator can collect up to 25% of the civil monetary penalties paid by a provider, Congress, through §203 of HIPAA, mandated the creation of new reward programs to encourage the reporting of suspected fraud or abuse. If reported information leads to the government's collection of at least $100, HHS may pay a reward to the reporting person. *See also* 42 U.S.C. §1320a-7c. To further encourage private whistleblowing efforts, §203 also requires the issuance of Explanation of Medicare Benefits forms to beneficiaries for every item or service furnished. Each form includes a toll-free number for the beneficiary to report suspected fraud or abuse. Finally, Section 6032 of the DRA requires that health care employers that receive or pay at least $5 million in annual Medicaid funds establish written policies to educate their employees, contractors, and agents regarding applicable False Claims Act whistleblower laws.

For in-depth discussion of the FCA, see Chapter 3 (Salcido, The False Claims Act in Health Care Prosecutions: Application of the Substantive, *Qui Tam*, and Voluntary Disclosure Provisions).

result, corporate compliance programs designed to prevent fraud and abuse and to provide employees with a mechanism for reporting suspected fraud or abuse internally are important for reducing the number of such suits.

This chapter discusses the benefits of adopting a corporate compliance program and describes the elements of an effective program. The chapter also focuses on the major operational issues associated with both the implementation and ongoing operation of a health care corporate compliance program.

## II. Benefits of a Corporate Compliance Program

There are many benefits for a health care provider in adopting a corporate compliance program. Most importantly, of course, a compliance program can help to detect and prevent improper conduct. Further, the federal government expects most, if not all, health care providers to have a compliance program in place although only a few types of providers are legally required to have them.[10]

Many providers have already adopted a corporate compliance program, or are considering enhancing their existing program. Given such peer pressure, a provider that fails to adopt and implement an effective compliance program could be argued to be "below the standard of care in the industry." In the context of a government investigation and settlement, the failure to voluntarily adopt a compliance program could lead the Department of Health and Human Services (HHS) Office of Inspector General (OIG) to mandate an onerous Corporate Integrity Agreement (CIA).

In contrast, having an effective program can be a mitigating factor in the event of a government investigation, e.g., making it more likely that government officials will exercise their discretion in your favor in deciding whether to institute enforcement litigation, and when making decisions about the magnitude of potential civil monetary penalties (CMPs) or whether to impose exclusion. Further, case law suggests that the failure of a corporate director to attempt in good faith to institute a compliance program may, in certain situations, be a breach of the director's fiduciary duty.[11]

Finally, a compliance program also can be an invaluable tool in helping an organization comply with the numerous new compliance responsibilities it faces under the Sarbanes-Oxley Act of 2002[12] and other federal and state legal requirements. Moreover, some laws are beginning to require organizations to implement compliance programs.[13]

### A. Federal Sentencing Guidelines

While the Sentencing Guidelines are no longer mandatory, as discussed in more detail in Section II.A.4. below, they are often followed by the courts. The

---

[10]*See, e.g.,* 42 C.F.R. §§422.503(b)(4)(vi) & 423.504(b)(4)(vi).

[11]*See, e.g., In re* Caremark Int'l Inc. Derivative Litig., 698 A.2d 959 (Del. Ch. 1996), and its progeny. For an in-depth discussion of director and officer liability, see Chapter 8 (Walton, Humphreys, and Jacobs, Potential Liabilities for Directors and Officers of Health Care Organizations).

[12]Pub. L. No. 107-204, 116 Stat. 745 (2002).

[13]See the discussion in Section IV.H., below, concerning the California Drug Marketing Practices Law.

Sentencing Guidelines contain several incentives for a provider to adopt a corporate compliance program. First, if a provider has an effective compliance program in place, a court is not required to impose a period of probation or any of the special conditions of probation, including the regular reporting and unannounced examinations of the organization's books and records provided for in Section 8D1.4(b) of the Sentencing Guidelines.[14] Although the financial impact of these special conditions is not easy to quantify, it is obvious that having to pay a public accounting firm to conduct periodic financial audits is costly. Second, if a provider has in place at the time of sentencing a compliance program that the court determines is "effective," the provider's culpability score (as determined under the Sentencing Guidelines) will be reduced significantly, resulting in a smaller range of fines.

## 1. Probation

Obviously, a business organization[15] convicted of a federal crime cannot be sentenced to confinement in a correctional institution. An entity can, however, be sentenced to a period of probation under the Sentencing Guidelines.[16] After either a plea of guilty on behalf of the organization by an appropriate official or a verdict of guilty following a trial, the Sentencing Guidelines direct a court to impose a period of probation if the organization has 50 or more employees and does not have an "effective compliance and ethics program."[17] The term of probation should be at least one year but not more than five years.[18]

As conditions of probation, the sentencing court may impose a restitution order[19] and any other conditions[20] reasonably related to the "nature and circumstances of the offense or the history and characteristics of the organization."[21] If the court imposes a fine or orders the organization to make restitution, it can

---

[14]The standard duration of a CIA required by the OIG for health care organizations entering into plea agreements to resolve criminal investigations is five years. This is the maximum period of probation the court can impose under U.S.S.G. §8D1.2(a)(1). A CIA generally also incorporates the conditions of probation found in U.S.S.G. §8D1.4(b)(1)–(4).

[15]The term "organization" is defined as "corporations, partnerships, associations, joint-stock companies, unions, trusts, pension funds, unincorporated organizations, governments and political subdivisions thereof, and non-profit organizations." U.S.S.G. §8A1.1, App. n.1. For purposes of this discussion, it is assumed that the defendant organization has 50 or more employees; is a solvent, ongoing concern at the time of sentencing; and has been convicted of an offense for which the restitution owed to the government is more than $1 million. Organizations are sentenced under the probation guideline for felony and Class A misdemeanor offenses. U.S.S.G. §8A1.1.

[16]Section 8D1.1 prescribes the conditions under which the sentencing court must order a period of probation.

[17]U.S.S.G. §8D1.1(a)(3). An "effective program to prevent and detect violations of law" is one that has been "reasonably designed, implemented, and enforced so that the program is generally effective in preventing and detecting criminal conduct." U.S.S.G. §8B2.1(a)(2). Significantly, the failure of the program to prevent or detect the offense of conviction, by itself, does not mean that the program is not "effective." *Id.*

[18]U.S.S.G. §8D1.2(a)(1). The guidelines for sentencing organizations became effective in November 1991. *See* U.S.S.G. §8C1.1, historical note (amended 1995).

[19]U.S.S.G. §8D1.3(b).

[20]Section 8D1.4 sets out various other recommended conditions of probation, including publicizing the nature of the offense, the fact of the conviction, the nature of the punishment imposed, and the steps taken to prevent the occurrence of similar offenses. U.S.S.G. §8D1.4(a).

[21]U.S.S.G. §8D1.3(c).

require the organization to make periodic reports to its probation officer concerning its financial condition, including an accounting of all funds disbursed.[22] The court also can require the organization to submit to periodic unannounced examinations of its books and records by experts selected by the court and paid for by the organization.[23] The organization can be required to notify the court "immediately" on its learning of a material adverse change in its business or financial condition or on the filing of a bankruptcy proceeding, major civil litigation, administrative proceeding, or any type of investigation against it.[24]

As a further condition of probation, the court can impose a requirement that the organization develop and submit a plan for a corporate compliance program, along with a schedule for its implementation.[25] In determining whether the proposed program is appropriate, the Sentencing Guidelines suggest that the court consider the views of any governmental regulatory body that oversees the conduct involved in the offense.[26] The Sentencing Guidelines direct a court to approve a proposed program that "appears reasonably calculated to prevent and detect violations of law" and is consistent with applicable statutory and regulatory requirements.[27]

Once the court approves the corporate compliance program, the organization must then notify all employees and shareholders of both its criminal behavior and its program to prevent and detect future violations.[28] The organization must make periodic reports to its probation officer concerning its progress in implementing the corporate compliance program.[29] To monitor whether the organization is in fact implementing its program, the court may select experts to conduct periodic unannounced examinations of the organization's books and records as well as to interview knowledgeable individuals within the organization and to report back to the court.[30] The court can require that the organization pay for these expert services.[31]

## 2. Reduced Fines

Having a corporate compliance program in effect at the time of sentencing can significantly reduce the amount of the fine imposed by the court. To calculate the appropriate fine,[32] the court determines the base offense level for the count of conviction by applying the criteria in Chapter 2 of the Sentencing Guidelines.[33] The base offense level determines the base fine.[34] The court then

---

[22]U.S.S.G. §8D1.4(b)(1).

[23]U.S.S.G. §8D1.4(b)(2).

[24]U.S.S.G. §8D1.4(b)(3).

[25]U.S.S.G. §8D1.4(c)(1).

[26]U.S.S.G. §8D1.4, App. n.1.

[27]*Id.*

[28]U.S.S.G. §8D1.4(c)(2).

[29]U.S.S.G. §8D1.4(c)(3).

[30]U.S.S.G. §8D1.4(c)(4).

[31]*Id.*

[32]The hypothetical scenario assumes that the court has made a finding pursuant to U.S.S.G. §8C2.2 that the organization has the financial ability to pay restitution and a fine.

[33]U.S.S.G. §8C2.3(a).

[34]U.S.S.G. §8C2.4.

calculates the entity's culpability score pursuant to Section 8C2.5 of the Sentencing Guidelines.

The culpability score determines the minimum and maximum multipliers the court uses to calculate the fine range for an entity.[35] If the court determines that the organization had an effective corporate compliance program in effect at the time of the offense, three points are subtracted from the culpability score.[36] A reduction in the culpability score directly reduces the multiplier used and lowers the range of the fine to which the organization is subject.[37]

The following hypothetical example of a calculation in a fairly common health care prosecution scenario illustrates the financial impact of having in place a corporate compliance program that the court determines is effective:

> Example: A hospital with more than 200 employees is convicted of submitting false claims to Medicaid based on the billing department supervisor's intentional miscoding of certain services. The billing fraud spanned nearly two years and resulted in the hospital receiving $1.8 million to which it was not entitled.

If the court decides to follow the Sentencing Guidelines, in addition to imposing a restitution order for the $1.8 million in accordance with Section 8B1.1, the court would determine the appropriate fine. The fine is determined by first calculating the offense level for conviction of a false claims violation, applying the provisions of Section 2B1.1 as follows: 6 points for the base offense level[38] plus 16 points for the amount of the loss.[39] The resulting total offense level is 22 points, which sets the base fine at $1.2 million.[40]

Without an effective corporate compliance program, the culpability score is 8, with resulting minimum and maximum multipliers of 1.60 and 3.20, respectively.[41] With a compliance program, the minimum and maximum multipliers are 1.00 and 2.00, respectively. The calculation of the fine range under these alternative scenarios would be as follows:

- Without a compliance program          $1.2 million base fine
  - Minimum multiplier (1.60)          $1.92 million
  - Maximum multiplier (3.20)          $3.84 million
- With a compliance program          $1.2 million base fine
  - Minimum multiplier (1.00)          $1.2 million
  - Maximum multiplier (2.00)          $2.4 million

---

[35] U.S.S.G. §8C2.6.

[36] U.S.S.G. §8C2.5(f). The reduction is not available, however, in certain situations in which high-level personnel are involved or the organization unreasonably delayed reporting the offense. U.S.S.G. §8C2.5(f)(2)–(3).

[37] Self-reporting and cooperation also may lead to reductions of the culpability score. U.S.S.G. §8C2.5(g)(1)–(3).

[38] U.S.S.G. §2B1.1(a).

[39] U.S.S.G. §2B1.1(b)(I).

[40] U.S.S.G. §8C2.4(d).

[41] Pursuant to U.S.S.G. §8C2.5(a), the culpability score calculation starts with 5 points. In this hypothetical scenario, 3 points would be added under §8C2.5(b)(3)(A)(i) because the hospital has more than 200 employees and the director of billing, an individual whose position falls within the definition of "high-level personnel" found in §8A1.2, App. n.3, was personally involved in the commission of the offense. Multipliers are available at U.S.S.G. §8C26.

As these calculations illustrate, an organization with an effective corporate compliance program would realize a savings of $720,000 if sentenced to a fine at the low end of the range or $1.44 million if sentenced at the high end.

### 3. Elements of an "Effective" Compliance Program

On December 30, 2003, the United States Sentencing Commission issued proposed amendments to the organizational sentencing guidelines, currently contained in Chapter 8 of the Federal Sentencing Guidelines Manual.[42] After the notice and review period, the final amendments (the Amendments) were formally submitted to Congress on May 19, 2004,[43] and took effect on November 1, 2004. The Amendments expanded and codified the requirements of an effective compliance program in a guideline to Chapter 8 at Section 8B2.1, which provides that organizations must: "(1) exercise due diligence to prevent and detect criminal conduct; and (2) otherwise promote an organizational culture that encourages ethical conduct and a commitment to compliance with the law."[44]

Subsection (b) to Guideline Section 8B2.1 sets forth the following minimum requirements for an effective compliance program:

(1) *Standards and Procedures.* Under the revised Sentencing Guidelines, "[t]he organization shall establish standards and procedures to prevent and detect criminal conduct,"[45] which are defined as "standards of conduct and internal controls that are reasonably capable of reducing the likelihood of criminal conduct."[46] Accordingly, organizations cannot achieve effective compliance by simply relying on the existence of a compliance policy, without taking steps to implement that policy through a system of internal controls.

(2) *Responsibility of High-Level Personnel.* The organization's governing authority should "be knowledgeable about the content and operation of the compliance and ethics program,"[47] and "exercise reasonable oversight with respect to the implementation and effectiveness of the compliance and ethics program."[48] "Governing authority" is defined as "(A) the Board of Directors; or (B) if the organization does not have a Board of Directors, the highest-level governing body of the organization."[49] In addition, the organization should assign high-level personnel with "overall responsibility for the compliance and ethics program," as well as specific individual(s) with "day-to-day operational responsibility for the compliance and ethics program."[50] The Sen-

---

[42] 68 Fed. Reg. 75,340 (Dec. 30, 2003).

[43] 69 Fed. Reg. 28,994 (May 19, 2004).

[44] *Id.* The Amendments (which deleted the previous criteria set forth in the commentary to §8A1.2.) were a significant departure from the previous Sentencing Guidelines in emphasizing disincentives for unethical and/or illegal behavior as well as incentives for ethical behavior and compliance with the law.

[45] U.S.S.G. §8B2.1(b)(1).

[46] U.S.S.G. §8B2.1, n.1.

[47] U.S.S.G. §8B2.1, n.3.

[48] U.S.S.G. §8B2.1(b)(2)(A).

[49] U.S.S.G. §8B2.1, n.1.

[50] U.S.S.G. §8B2.1(b)(2)(C).

tencing Guidelines further stipulate that "to carry out such operational responsibility, such individual(s) shall be given adequate resources, appropriate authority, and direct access to the governing authority or an appropriate subgroup of the governing authority."[51]

(3) *Screening of High-Level Personnel.* Organizations should "use reasonable efforts not to include within the substantial authority personnel of the organization any individual whom the organization knew, or should have known through the exercise of due diligence, has engaged in illegal activities or other conduct inconsistent with an effective compliance and ethics program."[52] Toward this objective, when screening high-level personnel, "an organization shall consider the relatedness of the individual's illegal activities and other misconduct (i.e., other conduct inconsistent with an effective compliance and ethics program) to the specific responsibilities the individual is anticipated to be assigned and other factors such as: (i) the recency of the individual's illegal activities and other misconduct; and (ii) whether the individual has engaged in other such illegal activities and other such misconduct."[53]

(4) *Training and Communication.* Organizations also should "take reasonable steps to communicate periodically and in a practical manner its standards and procedures, and other aspects of the compliance and ethics program" to members of the organization's governing authority, high-level personnel, substantial authority personnel, employees, and, as appropriate, the organization's agents, "by conducting effective training programs and otherwise disseminating information appropriate to such individuals' respective roles and responsibilities."[54] Moreover, in addition to training employees, the organization should provide compliance training and information to high-level personnel and its governing authority, as well as to its agents.[55]

(5) *Auditing and Monitoring.* The fifth factor in achieving an effective compliance program is the requirement that an organization use monitoring and auditing systems to detect criminal conduct and to "evaluate periodically the effectiveness of the organization's compliance and ethics program."[56] Further, the organization should provide and publicize internal reporting systems free from the risk of retaliation, which may include confidential or anonymous reporting mechanisms.[57]

(6) *Performance Incentives and Discipline.* An organization should promote and enforce its compliance program through "(A) appropriate incentives to perform in accordance with the compliance and ethics program; and (B) appropriate disciplinary measures for engaging in

---

[51]*Id.*

[52]U.S.S.G. §8B2.1(b)(3) (this includes persons whose offenses were not sufficient to warrant exclusion).

[53]U.S.S.G. §8B2.1, n.4(B).

[54]U.S.S.G. §8B2.1(b)(4)(A).

[55]*Id.*

[56]U.S.S.G. §8B2.1(b)(5)(B).

[57]U.S.S.G. §8B2.1(b)(5)(C).

criminal conduct and for failing to take reasonable steps to prevent or detect criminal conduct."[58]

(7) *Remedial Action.* Further, if criminal conduct has been detected, the organization should take appropriate remedial action to respond to the criminal conduct and prevent further similar violations.[59] Such remedial action may include "making any necessary modifications to the organization's compliance and ethics program."[60]

In implementing these seven requirements for an effective compliance program, subsection (c) to Guideline Section 8B2.1 requires that the organization conduct periodic risk assessments.[61] Moreover, the organization must continually evaluate the adequacy of its compliance and ethics program in light of its own history, practices, and legal issues. In addition to the seven requirements for an effective compliance program, the commentary to Guideline Section 8B2.1 emphasizes the need for the organization's compliance program to incorporate any standards required by applicable government regulations.[62] Failure to incorporate such standards weighs against any finding that the organization's compliance program was effective.

Guideline Section 8C2.5(f) allows for a three-point reduction in an organization's culpability score if the organization had an effective compliance and ethics program as defined in Guideline Section 8B2.1.[63] However, an organization is not eligible for the three-point reduction if "the organization unreasonably delayed in reporting the offense to appropriate governmental authorities."[64] Further, if substantial authority or high-level personnel in the organization participated in, condoned, or were willfully ignorant of the offense, there is a rebuttable presumption that the organization did not have an effective compliance program.[65] Finally, Guideline Section 8C4.10 has been modified to provide for an upward departure from the organization's base offense level if the organization was required by law to have an effective compliance and ethics program but did not have such a program.[66]

## 4. Implication of the Supreme Court's Booker Decision on Corporate Compliance Programs

In *United States v. Booker*,[67] the U.S. Supreme Court held that use of the Sentencing Guidelines will no longer be mandatory in federal sentencing

---

[58]U.S.S.G. §8B2.1(b)(6).
[59]U.S.S.G. §8B2.1(b)(7).
[60]*Id.*
[61]U.S.S.G. §8B2.1(c).
[62]U.S.S.G. §8B2.1, n.2(B).
[63]U.S.S.G. §8C2.5(f)(1).
[64]U.S.S.G. §8C2.5(f)(2).
[65]U.S.S.G. §8C2.5(f)(3)(A).
[66]U.S.S.G. §8C4.10.

[67]543 U.S. 220 (2005). In *Booker*, the sentence authorized by the jury verdict, pursuant to the Sentencing Guidelines, was 210 to 260 months in prison. At the sentencing hearing, the judge found additional facts by a preponderance of the evidence. Because these findings mandated a sentence of between 360 months and life, the judge gave Booker a 30-year sentence instead of

proceedings. The *Booker* Court also held that certain sentencing enhancements under the Sentencing Guidelines violated a defendant's right to a jury trial under the Sixth Amendment. This ruling came on the heels of the Supreme Court's 2004 decision in *Blakely v. Washington*,[68] in which the Court held that similar mandatory sentencing enhancements under the State of Washington's guidelines were unconstitutional.

Nevertheless, the Sentencing Guidelines are likely to remain an important factor in the future. The Supreme Court emphasized in *Booker* that federal trial courts should still consult the Guidelines and take them into account when sentencing. Further, one post-*Booker* decision stated that the Guidelines are still entitled to "heavy weight" and should only be departed from "in unusual cases for clearly identified and persuasive reasons."[69] In addition, the United States Department of Justice (DOJ) announced on January 28, 2005, that it will continue to follow the Sentencing Guidelines in making charging decisions and sentencing recommendations. In a memorandum to all federal prosecutors, the DOJ deputy attorney general instructed prosecutors to adhere to the Sentencing Guidelines in charging defendants and negotiating plea agreements and to "actively seek sentences within the range established by the Sentencing Guidelines in all but extraordinary cases."[70] The memorandum further stated that "departures are reserved for rare cases involving circumstances that were not contemplated by the Sentencing Commission." As a result, corporations and other organizations should expect that charging decisions or sentencing proceedings will, at least to some degree, continue to be governed by the Sentencing Guidelines.

In March 2006, the Sentencing Commission issued its final report on the impact of *United States v. Booker* on federal sentencing.[71] The report noted that

---

the 21-year, 10-month sentence he could have imposed based on the facts proven to the jury beyond a reasonable doubt. Booker appealed, and the Supreme Court held that imposition of a sentence under the Sentencing Guidelines based on facts not found by a jury or admitted by the defendant violates the Sixth Amendment, and that the Sentencing Guidelines are not mandatory but rather merely advisory provisions that recommend a particular sentencing range, rather than require it. The Supreme Court emphasized that a judge must tailor the sentence in light of other statutory concerns as well as the Sentencing Guidelines.

[68]542 U.S. 296 (2004). In *Blakely*, the defendant pleaded guilty to kidnapping his wife. Under Washington state law, the defendant's crime was subject to a statutory maximum of 10 years and a "standard range" of 49 to 53 months (under Washington's sentencing guidelines), based on the facts admitted in Blakely's plea agreement. After hearing Blakely's wife describe the kidnapping, however, the sentencing judge imposed an enhanced sentence of 90 months based on his conclusion that the kidnapping involved "deliberate cruelty." The issue on appeal was whether Washington's sentencing scheme violated the Sixth Amendment by permitting the judge to impose a sentence in excess of the maximum authorized under the guidelines based on facts not admitted by the defendant or submitted to a jury. The Court's five-member majority said: "[W]hen a judge inflicts punishment that the jury's verdict does not allow, the jury has not found all the facts which the law makes essential to the punishment, and the judge exceeds his authority." *Id.* at 302. By striking down Washington's Sentence Reform Act, the *Blakely* Court cast grave doubt on the vitality of mandatory guidelines schemes nationwide, including the federal Sentencing Guidelines.

[69]United States v. Wilson, 350 F. Supp. 2d 910 (D. Utah 2005).

[70]*See* Letter from James Comey, Deputy Attorney General, to all Federal Prosecutors (Jan. 28, 2005).

[71]UNITED STATES SENTENCING COMM'N, FINAL REPORT ON THE IMPACT OF UNITED STATES V. BOOKER ON FEDERAL SENTENCING (Mar. 2006), *available at* http://www.ussc.gov/booker_report/Booker_Report.pdf.

all federal circuit courts now begin with the calculation within the guideline range and that six circuits hold that a sentence within the guideline range is presumptively reasonable. Only one circuit court has found that a sentence within the guideline range is unreasonable. The report also indicates that a majority of federal cases continue to be sentenced in conformity with the sentencing guidelines.[72]

Therefore, the implementation of an effective corporate compliance program likely will remain an important mitigating factor for consideration by government officials and courts in investigations, prosecutions, and sentencing proceedings.

## B. HHS Guidelines on Permissive Exclusion

In addition to the U.S. Sentencing Guidelines, which provide for reduced fines and penalties for a provider that can show evidence of an effective corporate compliance program, HHS guidelines on permissive exclusion (permissive exclusion guidelines) provide yet another reason for a provider to adopt a corporate compliance program. These guidelines indicate that the existence of an effective corporate compliance program can favorably affect the OIG's decision whether to exclude a sanctioned provider from further participation in federal health care programs.

The permissive exclusion guidelines, which were published December 24, 1997, are nonbinding guidance to be used by the Secretary of HHS in deciding permissive exclusion cases.[73] The guidelines define several criteria to be used in determining whether to exercise the permissive exclusion authority, including:[74]

(1) *The circumstances of the misconduct and the seriousness of the offense.* This first category considers the seriousness of the misconduct. The provider's history of past misconduct is considered an indicator of its likelihood of abusing federal programs in the future.

(2) *The provider's response to the allegations and determinations of unlawful conduct.* This second category indicates whether the provider is willing to affirmatively modify its conduct, make injured parties whole, and otherwise acknowledge and remedy past wrongdoing.

(3) *The likelihood that the same offense will recur or some similar offense will occur.* The guidelines indicate that the existence of an effective corporate compliance program is a key factor in the Secretary's determination whether it is likely that the organization will commit the same or a similar offense in the future.

---

[72]*Id.* at vi.

[73]62 Fed. Reg. 67,392 (Dec. 24, 1997).

[74]*Id.* at 67,393–94. The Secretary's permissive exclusion authority, which is found in 42 U.S.C. §1320a-7(b)(7), allows the Secretary of HHS to use his or her discretion to exclude individuals or entities from further participation in federal or state health care programs. This statute was substantially amended by HIPAA to include, as grounds for permissive exclusion, among other things, misdemeanor convictions relating to fraud, theft, embezzlement, breach of fiduciary duty, or other financial misconduct in connection with the delivery of health care services or items or resulting from any act or omission in connection with any state or federal health care program. In addition, HIPAA further amended the statute to allow the Secretary to permissively exclude individuals who *control* (through ownership or management) a sanctioned entity.

As noted, the guidelines' third criterion emphasizes the importance of an effective corporate compliance program in influencing the determination of whether the provider is likely to engage in misconduct in the future. In making that determination, HHS asks the following questions, many of which relate to the provider's compliance program:

(1) Was the misconduct the result of a unique circumstance that is not likely to recur? Is there minimal risk of repeat conduct?

(2) What previous measures were taken to ensure compliance with the law? Can the organization demonstrate that it had an effective compliance program in place when the activities that constitute cause for exclusion occurred?

   (a) Did the organization make any efforts to contact the OIG, CMS, or its contractors to determine whether its conduct complied with the law and applicable program requirements? Were such contacts documented?

   (b) Did the organization bring the activity in question to the attention of appropriate government officials before any government action (e.g., was there any voluntary disclosure of the alleged wrongful conduct?)?

   (c) Did the organization have effective standards of conduct and internal control systems in place at the time of the wrongful activity (e.g., was there a corporate compliance program in place?)? If there was an existing corporate compliance program,

      (i) How long had it been in effect?

      (ii) What problems had been identified?

      (iii) Were any overpayments refunded or system changes made if problems were identified?

      (iv) Were appropriate staff members sufficiently trained in applicable policies and procedures pertaining to Medicare and other federal and state health care programs?

      (v) Were a corporate compliance officer and an effective corporate compliance committee (if appropriate for the size of the organization) in place?

   (d) What measures have been taken, or will be taken, to ensure compliance with the law? Has the organization agreed to implement adequate compliance measures, including institution of a CIA?

As is evident by the permissive exclusion guidelines, the government places great emphasis on the existence of an effective corporate compliance program. The adoption and appropriate implementation of such a program can favorably influence the OIG in its determination of whether a particular unlawful activity is likely to recur and thus whether the provider should be excluded from further participation in federal health care programs.

## III. ELEMENTS OF AN EFFECTIVE COMPLIANCE PROGRAM

Given the existing regulatory climate, most providers readily acknowledge that they should adopt a compliance program, but they are less certain about exactly what constitutes an "effective compliance program."

It is important to note that the government does not expect a provider's compliance program to be foolproof, merely effective. According to the Sentencing Guidelines, an "effective program" is one that has been "*reasonably* designed, implemented and enforced so that it *generally* will be effective in preventing and detecting criminal conduct."[75] Accordingly, a provider's failure to prevent a particular offense, by itself, does not mean that its program is ineffective.[76]

Further detailed indications of what elements the government expects to see as part of an effective corporate compliance program can be found in the OIG's model compliance programs. Although each model program is specific to a particular industry segment, the OIG has indicated that at least seven elements are essential to a compliance program:

- Implementing written policies and procedures,
- Designating a compliance officer and compliance committee,
- Conducting effective training and education,
- Developing effective lines of communication,
- Conducting internal monitoring and auditing,
- Enforcing standards through well-publicized disciplinary guides, and
- Responding promptly to detected problems and undertaking corrective action.[77]

Other key characteristics of effective compliance programs include the following:

- High-level involvement in and support for the compliance program from members of senior management and the organization's board of directors,
- Policies not to hire persons excluded from participation in any federal program,
- Customizing that compliance program to reflect the size and resources of the organization, and
- Prompt implementation of corrective action, including disciplinary sanctions, when necessary.[78]

It is becoming increasingly important to incorporate contractors into elements of the compliance program, e.g., providing them with information/education on the compliance program, and checking them against the OIG and General Services Administration (GSA) exclusion lists to ensure they are not excluded from participating in federal health programs.

The OIG elaborates, often extensively, on these issues in its model compliance program guidance documents. Some of the more significant additional details are noted in the discussions of each of the compliance program guidance

---

[75]U.S.S.G. §8B2.1 (emphasis added).

[76]*Id.*

[77]*See, e.g.,* OIG Compliance Program Guidance for Pharmaceutical Manufacturers, 68 Fed. Reg. 23,731 (May 5, 2003), *available at* http://www.oig.hhs.gov/authorities/docs/03/050503FRCPGPharmac.pdf.

[78]*See, e.g.,* OIG Supplemental Compliance Program Guidance for Hospitals, 70 Fed. Reg. 4858 (Jan. 31, 2005), *available at* http://www.oig.hhs.gov/fraud/docs/complianceguidance/012705HospSupplementalGuidance.pdf, and included as AppendixI-1.2 on the disk accompanying this volume.

documents that follow. Most of this additional information is relevant to compliance program operation regardless of the type of organization at issue.

## A. Corporate Integrity Agreements

A Corporate Integrity Agreement (CIA) has often been referred to as a compliance program on steroids. A CIA is a three- to eight-year agreement (five years is the most typical term) entered into between a health care provider and the government in conjunction with the settlement of fraud and abuse allegations. These OIG-imposed agreements typically contain specific rules of conduct designed to address the issues that were the subject of the government's investigation, as well as specific monitoring and reporting requirements. While corporate compliance programs are voluntarily adopted, CIAs are imposed by the government and generally are more stringent and expensive to implement than a corporate compliance program, particularly if the CIA requires engaging an independent review organization (IRO).

A CIA has become a standard feature in all significant Medicare and Medicaid fraud and abuse settlements approved by the OIG. Although each CIA is tailored to the specific health care provider involved, the CIAs entered into by the OIG have similar characteristics. A material violation of a CIA can result in significant monetary penalties and exclusion from federal and state health care programs. Copies of corporate integrity agreements can be found on the OIG's Web site.[79]

## B. Model Corporate Compliance Programs

The OIG has published compliance program guidance[80] for 11 segments of the health care industry:

(1) Hospitals;[81]
(2) Clinical laboratories;[82]
(3) Durable medical equipment (DME), prosthetics, orthotics, and supplies providers;[83]
(4) Third-party medical billing companies;[84]
(5) Hospices;[85]
(6) Nursing facilities;[86]
(7) Medicare+Choice (now Medicare Advantage) organizations;[87]

---

[79] *See* http://www.oig.hhs.gov/fraud/cia/index.html.

[80] With the publication of the final guidance for hospitals, the government began calling these instructions "compliance program guidance" instead of "model plans."

[81] *See* 63 Fed. Reg. 8987 (Feb. 23, 1998) and 70 Fed. Reg. 4858 (Jan. 31, 2005), available in Appendix I-1 on the disk accompanying this volume.

[82] *See* 63 Fed. Reg. 45,076 (Aug. 24, 1998).

[83] *See* 64 Fed. Reg. 36,368 (July 6, 1999).

[84] *See* 63 Fed. Reg. 70,138 (Dec. 18, 1998).

[85] *See* 64 Fed. Reg. 54,031 (Oct. 5, 1999).

[86] *See* 65 Fed. Reg. 14,289 (Mar. 16, 2000).

[87] *See* 64 Fed. Reg. 61,893 (Nov. 15, 1999).

(8) Individual and small group physician practices;[88]
(9) Home health agencies;[89]
(10) Ambulance suppliers;[90] and
(11) Pharmaceutical manufacturers.[91]

It is essential to remember that the vast majority of these guidance materials are not mandatory. However, as a practical matter, these model programs serve as benchmarks against which the government likely will judge the effectiveness of a provider's compliance program. Each model contains similar elements and gives providers valuable insight into what features the government is looking for in a corporate compliance program, as well as the "high risk" areas applicable to each industry segment.

Each model program contains the seven basic elements described above.[92] Moreover, the OIG has indicated that providers should consult all potentially applicable compliance documents, not just those specific to the provider's particular industry. For example, the Supplemental Compliance Program Guidance for Hospitals contains extensive detail on auditing that the OIG thinks is necessary for an effective compliance program.[93] All types of providers would be well advised to review these auditing recommendations.

In addition to the 11 industry segments listed above, the government has published a draft compliance program guidance for recipients of research grants from the Public Health Service.[94] Also, in February 2006, CMS issued an updated Chapter 9 of its Prescription Drug Benefit Manual (PDBM) entitled "Part D Program to Control Fraud, Waste and Abuse."[95] Chapter 9 is analogous to the OIG's compliance program guidance, but is even more important to Medicare Part D plan sponsors and others as it addresses both mandatory and voluntary compliance standards for these participants in the Medicare Part D program.

## 1. Compliance Program Guidance for Hospitals

The OIG's Compliance Program Guidance for Hospitals (the original Hospital CPG), one of the earliest of the OIG's series of health care industry

---

[88]See 65 Fed. Reg. 59,434 (Oct. 5, 2000); included as Appendix I-2 on the disk accompanying this volume.

[89]See 63 Fed. Reg. 42,410 (Aug. 7, 1998). All of the OIG compliance program guidance documents can be accessed at http://oig.hhs.gov/fraud/complianceguidance.html.

[90]OIG Compliance Program Guidance for Ambulance Suppliers, 68 Fed. Reg. 14,245 (Mar. 24, 2003).

[91]See 68 Fed. Reg. 23,731 (May 5, 2003); included as Appendix I.3.1 on the disk accompanying this volume.

[92]The Draft Compliance Program Guidance for Recipients of Public Health Service Research Awards included an eighth element: Defining roles and responsibilities and assigning oversight responsibility. See 70 Fed. Reg. 71,312–13 (Nov. 28, 2005). This document is also available at Appendix I-5 on the disk accompanying this volume.

[93]See 70 Fed. Reg. 4858, 4875–76 (Jan. 31, 2005).

[94]70 Fed. Reg. 71,312 (Nov. 25, 2005).

[95]CMS, Chapter 9—Part D Program to Control Fraud, Waste and Abuse, Prescription Drug Benefit Manual (Apr. 25, 2006), available at http://www.cms.hhs.gov/PrescriptionDrugCovContra/Downloads/PDBManual_Chapter9_FWA.pdf; PDBM Chapter 9 is discussed in more detail in Section III.B.13., below.

guidances, was issued in February 1998.[96] While acknowledging that the document provided voluntary guidelines, and was not legally binding, the OIG sought to encourage hospitals to implement a compliance program by noting the following potential benefits:

- Preventing the submission of false or inaccurate claims to the government and other payors;
- Demonstrating the hospital's strong commitment to ethical corporate conduct to employees and to the community at large;
- Identifying and preventing criminal and unethical conduct;
- Providing an accurate view of employee and contractor behavior related to fraud and abuse;
- Tailoring the compliance program to the needs of the specific hospital/ health system;
- Establishing a centralized source for the distribution of information on health care laws, regulations, and other guidance;
- Creating a methodology to encourage employees to report potential problems;
- Developing procedures to facilitate prompt and complete investigation of alleged misconduct;
- Initiating immediate, appropriate corrective action; and
- Minimizing the loss to the government from false claims (thereby reducing the hospital's exposure to civil and criminal penalties and other sanctions).

The guidance refined the seven essential elements of a compliance program for hospitals into the following recommendations, noting that each hospital could tailor its compliance program to meet its needs and financial realities:

(1) *Written policies and procedures.* The government placed great emphasis on the establishment of written compliance standards, policies, and procedures, suggesting that there be high-level involvement in the development of the standards (e.g., by members of the hospital's senior management and board of directors). Written policies and procedures should reflect current regulations, procedures, and problem areas within hospitals, and should be distributed to all affected individuals, including hospital agents and contractors.[97] The policies should be easily comprehensible by all employees and thus should be written in easily comprehensible language, and translated into other languages when appropriate.

The government stressed that a provider's list of high risk issues likely will evolve over time, and a hospital may need additional policies or procedures as time passes to address new areas of concern. At a minimum, the guidance indicates that the written policies and procedures should address the major operational aspects of the hospital. At the time of publication of the original

---

[96]63 Fed. Reg. 8987 (Feb. 23, 1998) and included as Appendix I-1.1 on the disk accompanying this volume.

[97]*Id.* at 8989.

Hospital CPG, some of the key high risk areas affecting hospitals identified by the government included

- billing for services not rendered;
- providing medically unnecessary services;
- outpatient services provided in connection with inpatient stays;[98]
- requirements related to teaching physicians and residents in teaching hospitals;
- false cost reports;
- billing for discharge instead of transfer;[99]
- patient freedom of choice;
- joint ventures;
- violations of the anti-kickback statute, the Stark Law, and similar statutes;
- patient dumping;
- relationships with hospital-based physicians;
- failure to provide necessary care to HMO members;
- double billing;
- unbundling;[100]
- upcoding/DRG (diagnosis related group) creep;[101]
- credit balances;
- admission and discharge policies and procedures; and
- proper documentation.

Each of the issues listed above, as well as various additional risk areas, are discussed in some detail in the original Hospital CPG.

(2) *Designation of compliance officer.* The original Hospital CPG also stresses the importance of assigning oversight responsibility for compliance to an employee high in the hospital's organization, with direct access to the hospital's chief executive officer (CEO) and board of directors. The compliance officer should not be subordinate to the hospital's general counsel or chief financial officer, and should have sufficient resources (including personnel and funding) to fully perform his or her compliance functions. Further, in describing a compliance officer's primary responsibilities, the government indicates that he or she should ensure that independent contractors and other hospital agents are aware of the hospital's compliance program. This raises an

---

[98]This OIG concern refers to a hospital submitting claims for nonphysician outpatient services that, under the prospective payment system, are already reimbursed through the hospital's inpatient payment.

[99]Medicare regulations with regard to transferred hospital patients provide that only the hospital to which the patient was transferred may charge Medicare the full DRG rate. The transferring hospital receives only a per diem amount.

[100]"Unbundling" refers to a hospital's practice of submitting piecemeal bills for different services that should be "bundled" into one bill (i.e., paid together in one global payment). The purpose of the piecemeal billing is to obtain greater total reimbursement than would be paid in the global payment.

[101]"DRG creep" refers to the practice of using a DRG code that provides a higher payment rate than the DRG code that accurately reflects the actual service provided to the patient.

important issue for many hospitals seeking to determine to what extent their compliance responsibilities can be limited to employees. In the original Hospital CPG (and other compliance guidance), the OIG takes a more expansive view, and indicates that many, if not all, compliance functions should apply to independent contractors as well as to employees. For hospital systems with multiple locations, the compliance program guidance suggests a chief compliance officer located at the corporate office and local compliance officers located at each hospital. The original Hospital CPG suggests that a compliance committee be established and include individuals with diverse responsibilities at the hospital, e.g., operations, finance, coding, legal, human resources, audit, and utilization review.

(3) *Education and training.* The original Hospital CPG recommends that hospitals conduct effective educational and training programs. At a minimum, the guidance indicates that all employees should receive basic training in the following:

- reimbursement principles applicable to federal health care programs as well as private payors;
- general anti-kickback law principles;
- proper diagnosis confirmation;
- accurately submitting billing for physicians' services only when services actually are rendered by a physician;
- ensuring that all documentation requiring physician authorization is properly executed;
- preventing the alteration of medical records;
- accurate documentation of services furnished; and
- duty to report misconduct.

Additionally, targeted employees, such as those who work in the hospital's billing and coding department, should receive more extensive training on topics specific to their job functions. The OIG recommends that a hospital use a variety of teaching methods, and that all formal training should be documented.

(4) *Communication.* The guidance suggests that a hospital should develop and maintain meaningful lines of communication for clarifying policies and procedures and reporting violations. An anonymous hotline can be one component of this communication system, and communications suggesting substantial violations of laws, regulations, or compliance policies should be documented and promptly investigated. Written confidentiality and nonretaliation policies also are strongly recommended.

(5) *Auditing and monitoring.* As part of an effective compliance program, a hospital should conduct periodic audits and continually monitor its operations to detect noncompliance and improve quality according to the original Hospital CPG. Such audits may be conducted by internal or external auditors as long as they have the appropriate expertise. The guidance suggests a number of auditing techniques, including on-site visits, interviews, review of written materials, and trend analysis studies. It also details certain minimum issues to be audited, such as compliance with the anti-kickback statute and the Stark law, coding, claim

development and submission, cost reporting, marketing, and other high risk issues. The OIG recommends that when a compliance program is established, providers take a "snapshot" of the current compliance situation, which can then be used as part of benchmarking analyses.

(6) *Discipline and enforcement.* According to the original Hospital CPG, a hospital should have well-publicized disciplinary guidelines and procedures related to compliance violations. Intentional or reckless noncompliance should result in significant sanctions, ranging from oral warnings to suspension, termination, or financial penalties. Discipline should be consistent, regardless of the level of employee involved. The OIG takes the position that officers and supervisors should be held accountable for the foreseeable failure of their subordinates to comply with applicable law, standards, and procedures.

(7) *Corrective action.* As an integral part of its compliance program, the guidance indicates that a hospital should have mechanisms in place to respond appropriately and immediately to detected offenses through corrective action to prevent further offenses. In one of the more controversial provisions, the OIG recommended that a hospital promptly report (within 60 days) to the appropriate government authority if, after a reasonable inquiry, there is credible evidence of misconduct that may violate criminal, civil, or administrative law. Nevertheless, the guidance acknowledged that normal repayment channels are the appropriate way to repay identified overpayments.[102]

The OIG issued Supplemental Compliance Guidance for Hospitals (Supplemental Hospital CPG)[103] in 2005. The Supplemental Hospital CPG was intended to emphasize risk areas that emerged after the original 1998 Compliance Program Guidance for Hospitals.[104] In addition, the Supplemental Hospital CPG provides guidance on other topics of general interest to hospitals, contains extensive references to other materials that provide guidance and clarification on various compliance issues, and delineates the requirements for an "effective" compliance program. As a result, the Supplemental Hospital CPG is a "must read" for hospitals and for those who work closely with hospitals. Moreover, while the OIG has always encouraged providers to take advantage of the various compliance guidance documents, as appropriate, the Supplemental Hospital CPG is notable because the criteria it describes for an "effective compliance program" are generally applicable to all types of health care organizations. Although the recommendations provided in this document are not legally binding, the OIG's position on these issues will likely serve as the government's benchmark in evaluating hospital arrangements and procedures for compliance when making decisions on potential investigations and/or prosecution.

The Supplemental Hospital CPG highlights outpatient procedure coding, admissions and discharges, supplemental payment considerations, and the ef-

---

[102]*See* 63 Fed. Reg. 8987, 8998 (Feb. 23, 1998).

[103]70 Fed. Reg. 4858 (Jan. 31, 2005). This document is also available at Appendix I-1.2 on the disk accompanying this volume.

[104]63 Fed. Reg. 8987 (Feb. 23, 1998).

ficient use of information technology as potentially high-risk areas. There is also a detailed discussion of various fraud and abuse topics, including joint ventures, compensation arrangements with physicians, malpractice insurance subsidies, recruitment practices, gainsharing, cost-sharing waivers, gifts and gratuities, and the offer of free transportation to federal health care program beneficiaries. In addition, the Supplemental Hospital CPG provides advice regarding areas of recent concern to hospitals, including discounts to uninsured patients, preventative care services, and professional courtesy activities. Finally, one of the most important sections of the Supplemental Hospital CPG discusses detailed benchmarks to use in evaluating a compliance program's efficacy.

### a. Hospital Risk Areas

The Supplemental Hospital CPG identifies new fraud and abuse risk areas that are relevant to the hospital industry, offers specific recommendations for assessing and improving existing compliance programs to better address the identified risk areas and ensure that the compliance program is effective, and sets forth actions hospitals should take to self-report possible violations.[105] The identified risk areas are submission of accurate claims and information, the fraud and abuse statutes (e.g., the Stark law and anti-kickback statute), payments to reduce or limit services (gainsharing), the Emergency Medical Treatment and Active Labor Act (EMTALA), substandard care, relationships with federal health care beneficiaries, HIPAA privacy and security rules, billing of Medicare or Medicaid substantially in excess of usual charges, and areas of general interest.

#### i. Submission of Accurate Claims and Information

According to the OIG, the "single biggest risk area" for hospitals continues to be the preparation and submission of accurate claims. The Supplemental Hospital CPG reiterates the general rule that claims for reimbursement "must be complete and accurate and must reflect reasonable and necessary services ordered by an appropriately licensed medical professional who is a participating provider in the health care program from which the individual or entity is seeking reimbursement."[106] Rather than discuss familiar risk areas such as upcoding, duplicate billing, and unbundling of services, the Supplemental Hospital CPG focuses on risk areas the OIG considers "under-appreciated by the industry."[107] These "under-appreciated" risk areas include outpatient procedure coding, admissions and discharges, supplemental payment considerations, and use of information technology.[108]

#### (a) Outpatient Procedure Coding

The Supplemental Hospital CPG places particular emphasis on risks that have emerged since the implementation of Medicare's hospital outpatient prospective payment system (HOPPS) in 2001. In particular, the OIG cautions

---

[105] 70 Fed. Reg. at 4859.
[106] *Id.*
[107] *Id.* at 4860.
[108] *Id.* at 4860–62.

that the improper use of procedure codes and modifiers for outpatient coding may lead to overpayment and subject the hospital to liability for the submission of false claims. Consequently, the OIG strongly advises hospitals to pay close attention to coder qualifications and training. Hospitals are urged to review outpatient documentation practices on a regular basis and to make sure that the underlying medical record is complete and supports the level of service claimed.

The OIG identifies the following other specific risk areas associated with outpatient procedure coding:

- Using billing procedures identified as "inpatient-only" on an outpatient basis,
- Submitting claims for medically unnecessary services by failing to follow the fiscal intermediary's local medical review policies,
- Circumventing the multiple procedure discounting rules,
- Submitting incorrect claims for ancillary services due to a failure to incorporate updates to the Healthcare Common Procedure Coding System (HCPCS) and Ambulatory Payment Classification (APC) into Charge Description Masters (CDM),[109]
- Failing to select proper evaluation and management codes, and
- Improperly billing for observation services.

The OIG appears to be especially concerned that duplicate billing may result from the failure to adhere to the National Correct Coding Initiative (NCCI) guidelines in billing for multiple codes. In some of the strongest language in the Supplemental Hospital CPG, the OIG warns that the intentional manipulation of code assignments in order to avoid NCCI edits constitutes an act of fraud.

### (b) Admissions and Discharges

Particular risk areas highlighted by the OIG in the Supplemental Hospital CPG regarding the admission and discharge process include the following:

- Failure to follow the "same-day rule,"[110]
- Same-day discharges and readmissions,
- Violation of Medicare's post-acute care transfer policy in order to receive full DRG payment instead of a per diem transfer payment,
- Abuse of partial hospitalization payments for services rendered to behavioral and mental health patients, and
- "Churning" of patients from acute care hospitals to co-located long-term care hospitals in order to take advantage of the PPS-exempt status of the latter.

### (c) Supplemental Payment Considerations

In limited circumstances, hospitals may claim payments in addition to, or in lieu of, normal reimbursement. Noting that hospitals that make improper

---

[109] *See also* http://www.cms.hhs.gov/medhcpcsgeninfo/01_overview.asp? (HCPCS updates); http://www.cms.hhs.gov/hospitaloutpatientpps/01_overview.asp? (APC updates).

[110] HOPPS rules generally require all outpatient services provided to a particular patient at the same hospital and on the same date be included on the same claim.

claims for supplemental payments are liable for fines and penalties under federal law, the OIG focuses on seven risk areas with regard to supplemental payments:

- Reporting the costs of "pass-through" items,[111]
- Claims related to clinical trials,
- Abuse of DRG outlier payments,
- Claims for incorrectly designated "provider-based" entities,[112]
- Failure to follow Medicare rules regarding reimbursement for educational activities, such as dental or other programs,
- Claims for cardiac rehabilitation services,[113] and
- Claims related to organ acquisition costs.

### (d)  Use of Information Technology

The OIG concludes that hospitals will be increasingly reliant on information technology due to the expanding use of electronic claims submission, medical error-tracking systems, electronic prescribing, and the implementation of the HIPAA privacy and security rules. Consequently, the supplemental guidance urges hospitals to be thorough when assessing new computer systems and software that impact the billing, coding, and transfer of information for federal health care programs. While acknowledging the difficulties in selecting, implementing, and understanding new information systems, the OIG suggests that the failure to do so adequately will not excuse hospitals from liability for duplicate or false claims.

### ii.  The Physician Self-Referral Law (Stark Law) and Federal Anti-Kickback Statute

### (a)  Stark Law Compliance

The Supplemental Hospital CPG places great emphasis on compliance with the Stark law and the anti-kickback statute warning that "hospitals face significant financial exposure unless their financial relationships with referring physicians fit squarely in statutory or regulatory exceptions to the [Stark law]."[114] To analyze Stark law compliance, the Supplemental Hospital CPG suggests the following three questions:

(1) Is there a referral from a physician for a designated health service? If so:

(2) Does the physician (or an immediate family member) have a financial relationship with the entity furnishing the designated health service? If so, the final inquiry is:

---

[111]"Pass-through" items are certain new devices and drugs for which Medicare will reimburse the hospital an additional amount during a limited transitional period.

[112]Designating certain hospital-affiliated entities as "provider-based" can result in higher reimbursement for certain services.

[113]The OIG cautions against both unnecessary services and services not supervised directly by a physician.

[114]70 Fed. Reg. at 4863.

(3) Does the financial relationship fit an exception? If not, the Stark law has been violated.[115]

To ensure Stark compliance, the Supplemental Hospital CPG recommends that hospitals undertake "frequent and thorough review of their contracting and leasing processes" and "have appropriate processes for making and documenting reasonable, consistent, and objective determinations of fair market value and for ensuring that needed items and services are furnished or rendered."[116]

The OIG also identifies operational problems that can cause a hospital to violate the Stark law and exceptions inadvertently, e.g., by failing to obtain a signed written agreement (for example, in the case of a short-term project) or failing to obtain appropriate amendments or renewals (for example, in the case of a holdover lease). The OIG notes that such common business practices can trigger significant financial exposure and emphasizes that the new Stark law exception for temporary noncompliance may only be used on an occasional basis, and is not a substitute for "vigilant" oversight of a hospital's contracting and leasing functions.

Other areas identified by the OIG as implicating Stark compliance include the following:

- Reviewing the new reporting requirements that require hospitals to retain records that hospitals know or should know of in the course of prudently conducting business;[117]
- Maintaining appropriate procedures for making and documenting "reasonable, consistent, and objective" fair market value determinations;
- Tracking the total value of nonmonetary compensation provided annually to referring physicians, including tracking the provision and value of medical staff incidental benefits, and monitoring the provision of professional courtesy; and
- Recruiting efforts, especially what are characterized as "high risk" joint recruiting efforts by hospitals and group practices, which involve mechanisms that transfer remuneration from the hospital to the group practice.

Finally, the Supplemental Hospital CPG notes that Stark law compliance is only a "minimum standard." Even if a hospital-physician relationship qualifies for a Stark law exception, compliance with the anti-kickback statute is a separate requirement.

### (b) Anti-Kickback Compliance

The Supplemental Hospital CPG also emphasizes the need for compliance programs to address compliance with the anti-kickback statute, using the following two questions:

(1) Does the hospital have any remunerative relationship between itself (or its affiliates or representatives) and persons or entities in a position

---

[115]*Id.*
[116]*Id.*
[117]*See* 42 C.F.R. §411.361.

to generate federal health care program business for the hospital (or its affiliates) directly or indirectly?

(2) With respect to any remunerative relationship so identified, could one purpose of the remuneration be to induce or reward the referral or recommendation of business payable in whole or in part by a federal health care program?[118]

If an arrangement implicates the statute, the supplemental guidance lists four aggravating circumstances that are likely to place the hospital at greater risk of prosecution. An arrangement should be closely scrutinized if it (i) has the potential to interfere with clinical decisionmaking; (ii) includes the potential to increase costs to the government, beneficiaries, or enrollees; (iii) contains the potential for overutilization or inappropriate utilization; or (iv) presents increased risks to patient safety or quality of care.

The OIG notes that multiple "safe harbors" exist to allow a number of common business arrangements.[119] Although failure to comply with a safe harbor does not mean an arrangement is necessarily illegal, not surprisingly, the Supplemental Hospital CPG recommends structuring arrangements to slip into a safe harbor whenever possible. Further, the Supplemental Hospital CPG indicates that both the written and actual arrangement between the parties will be examined in assessing whether specific arrangements comply with a safe harbor.

Areas highlighted by the OIG as vulnerable to attack under the anti-kickback statute include the following:

- The manner in which joint ventures are structured, participants are selected and retained, investments are financed, and profits are distributed;
- Compensation arrangements with physicians;[120]
- Relationships with other health care entities (including those with managed care organizations);
- The use of physician recruitment arrangements;
- Disclosure and amount of discounts (with a warning against "swapping" by accepting an unreasonably low price on Part A services for which the hospital pays out of its own pocket, in exchange for referring Part B services billable to federal health care programs);
- Medical staff credentialing; and
- Malpractice insurance subsidies.

The OIG's discussion of joint ventures is sobering, with the OIG reaffirming its position, previously described in a Special Advisory Bulletin, on the risks of so-called contractual joint ventures. The OIG is particularly skeptical of turnkey arrangements where the hospital is expanding into a new line of

---

[118]*Id.* at 4864.

[119]*See* 42 C.F.R. §§1001.952(a)–(v) (enumerating the currently available safe harbors).

[120]According to the Supplemental Hospital CPG, hospitals should monitor various aspects of physician services covered by a contract between them, including the site-of-service modifier physicians use when billing for their services in staffing outpatient departments. 70 Fed. Reg. at 4867. Many hospitals will likely be surprised to learn of this new "responsibility." The Supplemental Hospital CPG also confirms that an arrangement requiring a hospital-based physician to perform certain reasonable administrative or clinical duties, at no charge to the hospital or patients, would not violate the anti-kickback statute. *Id.*

business to serve its existing patient base, a would-be competitor supplies the services, and the hospital assumes little or no risk. Similarly, with respect to ambulatory surgery centers (ASCs), the OIG reaffirms that the safe harbor protects only investments in Medicare-certified ASCs owned by hospitals and certain qualifying doctors, but does not protect hospital and physician investments in vascular laboratories, oncology centers, and dialysis facilities.

To reduce the amount of risk involved in embarking on a joint venture with physicians, the OIG suggests the following:

- Barring physicians employed by the hospital or its affiliates from referring to the joint venture;
- Taking steps to ensure that medical staff and other affiliated physicians are not encouraged in any manner to refer to the joint venture;
- Notifying affected physicians, in writing, of the above policies on an annual basis;
- Not tracking, in any manner, the volume of referrals from any referral source;
- Not tying physician compensation, in any manner, to the volume or value of referrals or other business generated for the venture;
- Disclosing all financial interests to patients; and
- Requiring that other participants in the venture adopt similar steps.

The OIG further indicates that hospitals that have multiple arrangements with different physicians should assess the totality of the arrangements "so that in the aggregate the items or services provided by all physicians" do not exceed the hospital's actual needs. Thus, while the personal services and management contracts safe harbor requires that a specific arrangement must be "commercially reasonable," hospitals cannot make this assessment in isolation but should consider all the circumstances, including the hospital's arrangements with other physicians.

The OIG also lists factors that can be used to evaluate whether there is potential fraud and abuse risk in a compensation arrangement. Such factors include (i) whether the service can be obtained from a nonreferral source at a cheaper rate, (ii) whether the compensation paid is commensurate with the skill level necessary to perform the contracted services, and (iii) whether physicians were selected in whole or in part because of their past or anticipated referrals.

The OIG devotes a substantial portion of the Supplemental Hospital CPG to recruitment agreements, noting that they pose substantial fraud and abuse risks. Observing that the scope of the existing recruitment safe harbor is very limited, the OIG emphasizes that this safe harbor (unlike the Stark exception) does not protect joint recruitment with an existing physician group(s) and that such arrangements, particularly when there is any payment to the group, present a high level of risk. Suspect payments include income guarantees or other payments that provide remuneration to existing referral sources by allowing them to use payments to the recruited physician to cover the existing groups' expenses.

### iii. Gainsharing Arrangements

The supplemental guidance strongly cautions hospitals about the use of "gainsharing" arrangements, e.g., arrangements where a hospital provides a physician with a percentage share of any reduction in the hospital's costs for patient care attributable to the physician's efforts. Although recognizing that such agreements may legitimately increase efficiency and reduce waste, the OIG advises that gainsharing may violate a CMP provision that prohibits payments made as inducements to limit care to federal health care program beneficiaries, the anti-kickback statute, and the Stark law.[121] Because of these concerns, the OIG strongly advises hospitals to avoid such arrangements whenever possible. This discussion is surprising, however, in light of several advisory opinions approving certain gainsharing arrangements.[122]

### iv. EMTALA

The Supplemental Hospital CPG recommends that hospitals review their obligations under EMTALA and ensure that all staff understand those obligations.[123] In particular, hospitals need to educate on-call physicians as to their responsibilities to emergency patients and periodically train and remind all emergency room staff regarding the hospital's EMTALA obligations.

### v. Substandard Care

The Supplemental Hospital CPG places strong emphasis on compliance with quality of care standards and reminds hospitals of the OIG's authority to exclude individuals or entities from participation in federal health care programs if they provide unnecessary or substandard items or services to *any* patient, not just Medicare or Medicaid beneficiaries. Hospitals are encouraged to "develop their own quality of care protocols and implement mechanisms for evaluating compliance with those protocols" in addition to complying with Medicare's conditions of participation and Joint Commission on Accreditation of Healthcare Organizations (JCAHO) accreditation standards.[124] Finally, the Supplemental Hospital CPG recommends that hospitals take an active part in monitoring the quality of medical services provided at the hospital by overseeing the credentialing and peer review process, not just nursing and ancillary services.[125]

### vi. Relationships With Federal Health Care Beneficiaries

The Supplemental Hospital CPG also discusses the following risk areas: gifts and gratuities, cost-sharing waivers, and free transportation to federal health care program beneficiaries.[126] These practices should be addressed by compliance programs to avoid potential violations of the CMP statute that prohibits inducements to Medicare and Medicaid beneficiaries that the hospitals know or should know are likely to influence the beneficiary's selection of a particular provider.[127]

---

[121] 70 Fed. Reg. 4869–70.

[122] *See, e.g.*, Advisory Op. Nos. 05–01, 05–02, 05–03, 05–04, 05–05, and 05–06.

[123] 70 Fed. Reg. at 4870.

[124] *Id.*

[125] *Id.* at 4870–71.

[126] *Id.* at 4871–72.

[127] *Id.* at 4871; *see* 42 U.S.C. §1320a–7a(a)(5).

- Gifts and Gratuities—With regard to gifts and gratuities, the Supplemental Hospital CPG emphasizes that hospitals generally are prohibited from offering gifts and gratuities valued at more than $10 per item and $50 annually per patient.
- Cost-Sharing Waivers—The OIG advises hospitals that any cost-sharing waivers provided in conjunction with inpatient services should be structured to fit the applicable safe harbor to the anti-kickback statute.[128] If a hospital chooses to waive cost-sharing amounts on the basis of a beneficiary's financial need, the waiver should be based on objective criteria, should be appropriate for the applicable locality, and may also take into account other factors as discussed in more detail in the Supplemental Hospital CPG. A patient's eligibility should also be rechecked periodically.
- Free Transportation—A hospital's provision of free transportation to federal program beneficiaries is generally prohibited because, according to the OIG, it often results in the selection of the transporting hospital for covered services. While a regulatory exception for some complimentary local transportation to beneficiaries residing in the hospital's primary service area remains under consideration,[129] the OIG states in the Supplemental Hospital CPG that it will not impose administrative sanctions on transportation programs provided for a hospital's (or hospital-based ASCs) primary service area that meet certain criteria specified in the Supplemental Hospital CPG.

### vii. HIPAA Privacy and Security Rules

Hospitals should ensure compliance with the HIPAA Privacy Rule,[130] including provisions pertaining to required disclosures, e.g., those disclosures to the HHS that are required when the hospital is undertaking a Privacy Rule investigation or compliance review. Hospitals are also encouraged to comply with the final HIPAA Security Rule,[131] which specifies a series of administrative, technical, and physical safeguards for the protection of protected health information (PHI).

### viii. Topics of General Interest to Hospitals

During the formulation of the Supplemental Hospital CPG, the OIG received numerous inquiries regarding topics that are of general interest to the hospital industry but do not necessarily pose significant risks of fraud and abuse. In response, the OIG uses the Supplemental Hospital CPG to provide clarification to hospitals regarding the provision of discounts to uninsured patients, the performance of preventive care services, and the use of "professional courtesy." The Supplemental Hospital CPG provides some reassurance that these activities generally will not pose a significant risk of liability as long as

---

[128]42 C.F.R §1001.952(k) (permitting certain waivers of beneficiary inpatient coinsurance and deductible amounts).

[129]*See* 65 Fed. Reg. 24,400, 24,411 (Apr. 26, 2000).

[130]Pub. L. No. 104-191, 110 Stat. 1936 (1996).

[131]The final HIPAA Security Rule is available on the CMS Web site at http://www.cms.hhs.gov/hipaageninfo/01_overview.asp?.

hospitals adhere to current regulations and other guidance materials. However, they also describe certain factors that may be "problematic" and lead to abuse in connection with the provision of professional courtesy.[132]

### b. Ensuring Compliance Program Effectiveness

According to the OIG, a successful compliance program should serve several important goals, including (i) reducing fraud and abuse, (ii) improving the quality of care, and (iii) reducing the overall cost of services. One of the most novel aspects of the Supplemental Hospital CPG is the listing of specific factors that hospitals should consider in evaluating the effectiveness of their compliance programs. In several cases, the breadth of these factors may surprise some hospitals that did not previously realize the OIG took such an expansive view of the extent of their compliance obligations.

### i. Developing a General Code of Conduct

A significant aspect of the OIG's ongoing initiative to promote voluntary compliance efforts is its emphasis on the need for high-level management and board involvement in the compliance program and process. For example, the OIG strongly advises that hospital codes of conduct be developed with the participation and encouragement of the board of directors, officers, and senior management personnel. Moreover, the OIG advocates a strong and explicit commitment by management to foster compliance with the code of conduct and all applicable federal program requirements and policies.[133] In particular, the Supplemental Hospital CPG suggests that company leadership ensure that compensation structures do not create undue pressure to pursue profit over compliance.[134]

### ii. Regularly Reviewing Compliance Program Elements

The Supplemental Hospital CPG refers to the seven basic elements the OIG has consistently specified as the basis for a compliance program, but strongly recommends that hospitals also assess the overall program at least annually, including the underlying structure and process related to each compliance program element, rather than simply focusing on numerical audit results of individual issues. To assist hospitals in undertaking this much more extensive review, the OIG provides the following criteria for evaluating each of the seven key compliance elements.

### (a) Designating a Compliance Officer and Compliance Committee

The Supplemental Hospital CPG recommends that a member of senior management lead the compliance department with the regular assistance of a

---

[132]70 Fed. Reg. 4874–75.

[133]*See, e.g.*, ABA Coordinating Committee on Nonprofit Governance, "Guide to Nonprofit Corporate Governance in the Wake of Sarbanes-Oxley" (2005); and "An Integrated Approach to Corporate Compliance: A Resource for Health Care Boards of Directors." The latter, developed by the American Health Lawyers Association and the OIG, is available at http://oig.hhs.gov/fraud/docs/complianceguidance/Tab%204E%20Appendx-Final.pdf.

[134]70 Fed. Reg. 4874.

compliance committee. The OIG urges that hospitals, in performing an annual review of the compliance department itself, assess the following factors (although it is not clear whether the OIG would find it acceptable for the compliance office to self-audit or if some other entity must perform this review):[135]

- Does the compliance department have a clear, well-crafted mission and is it properly organized?
- Does the department have sufficient resources, training, authority, and autonomy?
- Is the relationship between the compliance function and the general counsel function appropriate?
- Does the compliance officer have direct access to the governing body, president or CEO, all senior management, and legal counsel?
- Does the compliance officer have a good working relationship with key operational areas such as the billing, internal audit, coding, and clinical departments?
- Does the compliance officer make regular reports to the board of directors and other hospital management?
- Are *ad hoc* groups or task forces created to carry out special investigations or evaluations?
- Is there an active compliance committee with trained representatives from relevant departments and senior management?

### (b) Developing Compliance Policies and Procedures

The Supplemental Hospital CPG also suggests that the compliance department reassess written policies and procedures to ensure that they comport with applicable statutes and regulations concerning federal health care programs as well as the objectives of the hospital itself, in light of the following factors:[136]

- Are the policies and procedures clearly written, readily available, and relevant to daily responsibilities?
- Does the hospital monitor staff compliance with internal policies and procedures?
- Has the hospital developed a risk-assessment tool to identify and assess operational risks that it reviews on a regular basis?
- Are federal program requirements and publications reviewed regularly?
- Have all standards of conduct been distributed to all staff and employees, the board of directors, all officers, managers, hospital contractors, and medical staff?

Like the OIG's earlier compliance program guidance documents, the Supplemental Hospital CPG suggests including contractors in various aspects of a compliance program. In this regard, hospitals that have limited their compliance efforts to employees thus far should consider expanding certain compliance program elements to contractors as well.

---

[135] 70 Fed. Reg. 4874–75.
[136] 70 Fed. Reg. 4875.

### (c) Developing Open Lines of Communication

The Supplemental Hospital CPG explains that open lines of communication stem from the organizational culture of a hospital and its internal mechanisms for reporting fraud and abuse, and suggests considering whether:[137]

- The hospital has fostered an organizational culture that encourages open dialogues without fear of reprisal;
- The hospital has an anonymous hotline or similar mechanism so that potential compliance issues may be reported by hospital employees, contractors, patients, visitors, and medical staff;
- The hotline is well advertised, with calls logged and addressed in a timely manner, and reviewed for possible patterns;
- All instances of potential fraud and abuse are investigated;
- The hospital's governing body and relevant departments regularly receive the results of internal investigations;
- The hospital uses alternative communication methods such as a periodic newsletter or Intranet site (it is not clear whether or why an alternative method is necessary in cases where the hotline appears to be working); and
- The governing body actively pursues appropriate remedies to institutional or recurring problems.

Placing the obligation to address certain institutional or recurring problems on the governing body (presumably in addition to senior management) may well expand the scope of responsibilities boards previously thought they were required to undertake.

### (d) Appropriate Training and Education

The OIG asserts that the failure to adequately train and educate hospital staff and other agents may lead to hospital liability for violating the health care fraud and abuse laws. To reduce this risk, the Supplemental Hospital CPG suggests evaluating the compliance program in light of the following:[138]

- Does the hospital provide qualified trainers to conduct annual general and specialized compliance training?
- Are the contents of educational programs reviewed annually to determine whether they are sufficient in scope and depth for the range of issues faced by employees?
- Do training and education programs incorporate the latest changes to federal rules and regulations?
- Does the training reflect audit and investigation results, hotline trends, and federal agency guidance and advisories?
- Has the format of training sessions been evaluated in terms of frequency, length of sessions, and method of information delivery (e.g., live or via computer)?

---

[137] *Id.*
[138] *Id.*

- Is post-training evaluation and testing provided to determine the efficacy of such programs; i.e., to ensure that the training is understood and retained?
- Are the training and education programs performed regularly and with appropriate technological resources?
- Is the hospital governing body trained regularly with regard to fraud and abuse laws?
- Does the hospital document who has completed training?
- Has the hospital considered whether to impose sanctions for failure to attend training or whether to provide appropriate incentives for training session attendance?

### (e) Internal Monitoring and Auditing

The OIG emphasizes that effective monitoring and auditing plans will enable hospitals to avoid submitting incorrect claims to the federal health care programs. Hospitals are advised to develop detailed annual audit programs with consideration of the following standards:[139]

- Does the audit plan address identified risk areas, high volume services, and findings from previous years' audits?
- Is the audit department available to conduct unscheduled reviews and capable of responding in a timely fashion to compliance department requests for further review?
- Does the audit plan assess both billing systems and claims accuracy in order to identify the source of common billing errors?
- Are coding and audit personnel independent and are their roles clearly established? Do they have the requisite certifications for their positions?
- If error rates are not decreasing, has the hospital conducted further investigations?
- Does the audit consider all billing documentation, including clinical documentation, in support of claims?

### (f) Responding to Detected Deficiencies

The Supplemental Hospital CPG recommends that a hospital consider the following when evaluating its own plan for addressing recognized deficiencies:[140]

- Has the hospital identified a team of personnel from the compliance, audit, and other applicable departments to quickly evaluate any detected deficiencies?
- Does the hospital promptly and thoroughly investigate?
- Are corrective action plans developed to address the root causes of violations, and are they periodically reviewed to verify elimination of the deficiency?
- Are detected overpayments promptly repaid and probable violations of law promptly reported to the appropriate law enforcement agencies?

---

[139]70 Fed. Reg. 4875–76.
[140]70 Fed. Reg. 4876.

### (g)  Enforcing Disciplinary Standards

The OIG has consistently placed special emphasis on a hospital's duty to enforce disciplinary standards. When assessing internal disciplinary efforts, hospitals are advised to take into account the following:[141]

- Are disciplinary standards well publicized and readily available to all hospital personnel?
- Does the hospital uniformly and consistently enforce disciplinary standards?
- Are employees, contractors, and medical staff checked, at least annually, against government sanctions lists, including the OIG's List of Excluded Individuals/Entities (LEIE)[142] and the GSA's Excluded Parties Listing System?[143]

The supplemental guidance concludes with a discussion of self-reporting, noting that prompt voluntary reporting will be considered a mitigating factor by the OIG when considering administrative sanctions. The OIG continues to promote use of the Provider Self-Disclosure Protocol, which has not been used frequently in the past due to its inherent limitations.[144]

### 2.  Compliance Program Guidance for Clinical Laboratories

The compliance program guidance for clinical laboratories (Clinical Lab CPG)[145] provides nonbinding guidance regarding the elements of an effective corporate compliance program for clinical laboratories. The Clinical Lab CPG emphasizes several key compliance features specifically applicable to clinical laboratories, including the following:

- Although physicians can order any tests they believe to be appropriate, Medicare will only pay for tests that are covered, reasonable, and necessary;
- Individuals other than physicians may order tests in some states;
- Physicians are required to submit diagnostic information to the laboratory when they order most laboratory tests;
- Tests performed pursuant to standing orders must be both reasonable and necessary; and
- Laboratories should not charge physicians less than fair market value (FMV) for nonfederal health care program tests in order to obtain the physician's federal business.[146]

---

[141] *Id.*

[142] *Available at* http://oig.hhs.gov/fraud/exclusions.html.

[143] *Available at* http://epls.arnet.gov.

[144] See the additional discussion on the Provider Self-Disclosure Protocol in section II.A.6. of Chapter 1 (Baumann, An Introduction to Health Care Fraud and Abuse).

[145] 63 Fed. Reg. 45,076 (Aug. 24, 1998), *available at* http://www.oig.hhs.gov/authorities/docs/cpglab.pdf.

[146] *Id.* at 45,077.

### a. Clinical Laboratory Risk Areas

In addition, the following risk areas for clinical laboratories are among those highlighted.

#### i. Medical Necessity

The OIG recommends that laboratory compliance programs make sure that physicians understand that a service will only be paid for if the service is covered, reasonable, and necessary given the beneficiary's clinical condition. Further, the laboratory should be able to produce the requisite documentation from the physician or other person, authorized by law, who ordered the test. In addition, clinical laboratories are directed to notify clients that tests submitted for Medicare reimbursement must meet program requirements or the claim may be denied. Toward this end, the OIG offers a number of recommendations.[147]

##### (a) Requisition Form

Laboratories are directed to develop a requisition form that encourages the "conscious" ordering of tests by physicians (or other authorized individuals), and to ensure that the ordering individual has made an independent medical decision. The form should also contain language stating that Medicare generally does not provide reimbursement for routine screening tests.[148]

##### (b) Notices

While acknowledging that laboratories do not have educational requirements under the law, the OIG recommends that laboratories provide all physician clients with annual written notices that (i) describe Medicare national policy and local medical review policy for laboratory tests, (ii) state that organ or disease related panels will only be billed if all components are medically necessary, (iii) provide the Medicare laboratory fees schedule and state that Medicaid will reimburse for the same or a lesser amount, and (iv) furnish the phone number of the clinical consultant as required under the Clinical Laboratory Improvement Amendment certification.[149] This CPG also strongly recommends that any laboratory giving clients the opportunity to order customized profiles should provide an annual written notice about the fraud and abuse potential of such profiles.[150]

##### (c) Physician Acknowledgements

The OIG recommends that clinical laboratories exceed legal requirements by having a physician sign an acknowledgement that he or she understands the implications of ordering a customized profile.[151]

---

[147]*Id.* at 45,079.
[148]*Id.*
[149]*See* 42 C.F.R. §493.1452.
[150]63 Fed. Reg. at 45,079–80.
[151]*Id.* at 45,080.

### (d) Advanced Beneficiary Notices

Noting the difficulty for clinical laboratories in obtaining an advance beneficiary notice (ABN) directly from a beneficiary, the Clinical Lab CPG recommends educating physicians about the appropriate use of ABNs. The OIG emphasizes that routine notices that simply state that denial is possible are insufficient, but that notices should not be provided to beneficiaries unless there is genuine doubt about the likelihood of payment.[152]

### (e) Test Utilization Monitoring

The Clinical Lab CPG implicitly tries to impose a duty on laboratories to monitor for excessive test utilization by indicating that a laboratory has a duty to modify its practices and notify the applicable physician if it discovers that it has "in some way contributed to the ordering of unnecessary tests."[153] Toward this end, the OIG recommends hiring an outside consultant to monitor utilization patterns. Alternatively, the OIG provides detailed guidance on various methods to analyze test utilization data, e.g., by CPT or HCPCS code for the top 30 tests performed each year, and recommends that the laboratory investigate further if it finds a 10 percent or greater increase in a test's utilization from one year to the next.[154]

### ii. Billing

To ensure accurate billing the Clinical Lab CPG recommends various measures including those described below.

### (a) Selecting CPT or HCPCS Codes

Noting that laboratories are not permitted to alter the physician's order in any way without the express consent of the physician (or other ordering individual), the Clinical Lab CPG recommends that an expert in laboratory testing review the codes before they are submitted.[155]

### (b) Selecting ICD-9-CM Codes

Emphasizing the importance of documentation, the OIG provides a list of dos and don'ts, including a warning that laboratories should not use information from earlier dates of service (except in certain limited cases related to standing orders) or use computer programs that automatically insert diagnosis codes without the receipt of appropriate authorizing information.[156]

### (c) Tests Covered by Claims for Reimbursement

Clinical laboratories should verify tests with missing or ambiguous orders before submitting them to Medicare for reimbursement, and similarly should not bill Medicare unless the test was actually performed.[157]

---

[152]*Id.*
[153]*Id.*
[154]*Id.*
[155]*Id.*
[156]*Id.*
[157]*Id.* at 45,080–81.

### (d) Calculations

Laboratories are warned not to bill both for calculations, such as calculated LDLs, T7s, and indices, as well as for the tests performed to derive these calculations.[158]

### (e) Reflex Testing

The OIG suggests that a laboratory design its requisition form so that the condition under which a reflex test will be performed is clearly indicated. A similar policy is recommended for confirmation testing.[159]

### (f) Reliance on Standing Orders

The Clinical Lab CPG discusses how frequently standing orders have led to abuses. As a result, laboratories are directed to periodically monitor the use of standing orders, which should have a fixed term of validity, and require renewal when they expire. The OIG further recommends that, consistent with state laws, clinical laboratories contact nursing homes to request verification of current standing orders, verify standing orders relied upon at draw stations, and contact each end stage renal disease (ESRD) facility or unit to request confirmation in writing of the continued validity of existing standing orders, at least once a year[160]

### iii. Marketing

The Clinical Lab CPG emphasizes the need for fully informative and nondeceptive marketing.[161]

### iv. Prices Charged to Physicians

Laboratory policies are directed to address the prices that physicians are charged. The OIG is particularly concerned that laboratories not charge physicians prices that are below FMV for nonfederal health care program business in order to induce the physician to refer federal health care program business (for which the laboratory would presumably charge higher fees).[162]

### b. Ensuring Compliance Program Effectiveness

The Clinical Lab CPG contains numerous OIG recommendations, some of which are extremely detailed, on the appropriate operation of a compliance program. A number of these "suggestions" are particularly important because they generally are applicable to other types of providers. Some of the more important recommendations are summarized below.

---

[158]*Id.* at 45,081.
[159]*Id.*
[160]*Id.*
[161]*Id.*
[162]*Id.*

### i. Dealing with Employees and Contractors

Contractors, i.e., physicians, using the laboratory should be informed of the applicable compliance program standards related to coding, billing, marketing, and other key issues.[163]

Employee attendance and participation in compliance training programs should be a condition of continued employment, and adherence to the precepts of the compliance program should be a factor in the employee's annual evaluation.[164]

A compliance program should include a written policy setting forth the degrees of disciplinary sanctions that may be imposed on employees, managers, and corporate officers.

All new employees should be subject to a reasonable and prudent background investigation, including a check of references. Further, the prospective employee should be required to disclose any criminal conviction or exclusion action. The laboratory should terminate its contract or other relationship with any existing employee or physician (or other individual) authorized to order tests, if that individual is convicted, disbarred, or excluded from participation in federal health care programs.[165]

### ii. Audits

Audits should be designed to address the following issues:

- Kickbacks;
- The Stark Law's self-referral prohibitions;
- CPT/HCPCS coding and billing;
- ICD-9 coding;
- Claim development/submission;
- Reimbursement;
- Marketing;
- Reporting and record keeping; and
- Issues highlighted in OIG guidance documents, such as Special Fraud Alerts and audit reports, as well as issues of recent concern to Medicare contractors and law enforcement authorities.[166]

When conducting an audit, the compliance officer or other reviewer should consider techniques such as the following:

- On-site visits;
- Interviews;
- Questionnaires;
- Review of written materials, requisition forms, and other documentation supporting claims; and
- Trend analyses.[167]

---

[163]*Id.* at 45,082.
[164]*Id.* at 45,083.
[165]*Id.* at 45,084.
[166]*Id.* at 45,084–85.
[167]*Id.* at 45,085.

### iii. Investigations

Investigations may need to be conducted by outside counsel, auditors, or health care experts in certain cases.[168]

According to the OIG, records of an investigation should include the following:

- Documentation of the alleged violation,
- Description of the investigative process,
- Copies of interview notes and key documents,
- A log of the witnesses interviewed and the documents reviewed,
- Results of the investigation, and
- Disciplinary sanctions and/or corrective action taken.[169]

Finally, with regard to reporting suspected misconduct, the OIG enunciates the following standards (which have largely remained the same over the years since the issuance of the Clinical Lab CPG). After a reasonable investigation, if there is credible evidence of misconduct that may violate criminal, civil, or administrative law, the clinical laboratory should report the matter to the appropriate government authority within 60 days. Such reporting demonstrates the provider's good faith and will be considered a mitigating factor by the OIG in determining sanctions, such as exclusion. According to the OIG, when reporting to the government, a provider should provide all relevant evidence concerning the potential violation and the potential cost impact. The provider may be asked to investigate further with guidance from government authorities. If an investigation ultimately determines that a criminal or civil violation may have occurred, appropriate state and federal government officials should be notified immediately. The provider should take corrective action, impose disciplinary sanctions, and identify and return any overpayments promptly. (Overpayments that are not promptly returned may be viewed by the government as an independent criminal violation.)[170]

### 3. Compliance Program Guidance for Durable Medical Equipment, Prosthetics, Orthotics, and Supplies Providers

The OIG issued compliance program guidance for DME, prosthetics, orthotics, and supplies providers (DME CPG) in June 1999.[171] According to the OIG, the DME CPG is relevant to all DME, prosthetics, orthotics, and supplies (DMEPOS) suppliers, regardless of size. However, the applicability of certain recommendations and guidelines may vary based on the company's size and structure.

---

[168] *Id.* at 45,086.

[169] *Id.* at 45,086. Although the Clinical Lab CPG does not discuss this point, a laboratory (or any other company) conducting an investigation should consider having an attorney direct the investigation in order to establish attorney-client privilege for such documents, as appropriate.

[170] *Id.*

[171] 64 Fed. Reg. 36,368 (July 6, 1999). The OIG released this guidance on June 22, 1999, before its publication in the *Federal Register*.

### a. DME Risk Areas

In general, the requirements outlined in this guidance are similar to those in other compliance guidance documents. However, the OIG identified a large number of risk areas for DMEPOS suppliers, many of which are highlighted below:

- Billing for items or services not provided;
- Billing for services that the DMEPOS supplier believes may be denied;
- Billing patients for denied charges without a signed written notice;
- Duplicate billing;
- Billing for items or services not ordered;
- Using a billing agent whose compensation arrangement violates the reassignment rule;
- Upcoding;
- Unbundling items or supplies;
- Billing for new equipment and providing used equipment;
- Continuing to bill for rental items when they are no longer medically necessary;
- Resubmission of denied claims with different information;
- Refusing to submit a claim to Medicare for which payment is made on a reasonable charge or fee schedule basis;
- Inadequate management/oversight of contracted services, resulting in improper billing;
- Charge limitations;
- Providing and/or billing for substantially excessive amounts of DMEPOS;
- Providing and/or billing for an item or service that does not meet the quality/standard of the DMEPOS item claimed;
- Capped rentals;
- Failure to monitor medical necessity on an ongoing basis;
- Delivering or billing for certain items or supplies prior to receiving a physician's order and/or appropriate certificate of medical necessity (CMN);
- Falsifying information on the claim form/CMN/accompanying documentation;
- Inappropriately completing portions of CMNs;
- Altering medical records;
- Manipulating the patient's diagnosis;
- Failing to maintain medical necessity documentation;
- Inappropriate use of place of service codes;
- Cover letters encouraging physicians to order medically unnecessary items or services;
- Improper use of the ZX modifier;
- Routine waiver of deductibles and coinsurance;
- Providing incentives to actual or potential referral sources that may violate the fraud and abuse laws;
- Improper telemarketing;
- Co-locating DMEPOS items with a referral source;
- Compensation programs that offer incentives for items or services ordered and revenue generated;

- Joint ventures including a referral source,
- Improper patient solicitation activities and high-pressure marketing;
- Noncompliance with the federal, state, and private payor supplier standards;
- Providing false information on the Medicare DMEPOS supplier enrollment form;
- Improperly updating the DMEPOS supplier enrollment form;
- Misrepresenting status as an agent or representative of Medicare;
- Knowing misuse of a supplier number;
- Failure to meet individual payor requirements;
- Performing tests on a beneficiary to establish medical necessity;
- Failure to refund overpayments;
- Improper billing; and
- Employing individuals excluded from participation in federal health care programs.[172]

The OIG recommends that suppliers develop written policies on the various high risk areas described above.

With regard to claims development procedures, the DME CPG places special emphasis on medical necessity (and certification), physician orders, CMNs, proper billing, correct selection of HCPCS codes, supplier numbers, mail-order issues, assignment, liability, routine waivers of deductibles and coinsurance, capped rental prices, use of the ZX modifier, cover letters, and oxygen policies and procedures.[173]

The DME CPG also emphasizes anti-kickback and self-referral issues, marketing, and retention of records.

### b. Ensuring Compliance Program Effectiveness

The DME CPG contains a number of recommendations, which generally are applicable to all providers, on ways to increase the effectiveness of a compliance program.

#### i. Compliance Officer Responsibilities

A compliance officer should:

- manage the compliance committee,
- be copied on the results of all internal audit reports,
- look for aberrant trends and patterns that require a change in policy, and
- have full authority to stop claims processing when necessary.[174]

Further, a compliance officer can be staffed on a part-time basis if the provider is small and/or does not have the resources to hire a full-time compliance officer. Similarly, providers that do not have the resources or need for a

---

[172]64 Fed. Reg. 36,373–75.

[173]*Id.* at 36,375–79.

[174]*Id.* at 36,382.

full-time compliance committee should consider using a compliance task force as the need arises.[175]

### ii. Education and Training

DMEPOS suppliers (and other types of providers and suppliers) may wish to make their compliance training sessions open to interested contractors and physicians. Employees should be required to have a minimum number of training hours each year. Employees also should sign and date a certification that reflects their knowledge of, and commitment to adhere to, the company's standards of conduct. Further, the standards of conduct set forth in employee handbooks should be regularly updated.

In addition, training should emphasize employees' duty to report misconduct. A variety of teaching formats and methods are recommended, such as offering the training in several different languages where the workforce is diverse. All training should be documented, and attendance logs, as well as any materials distributed, should be maintained in the compliance files.

### (a) Claim Development and Billing Training

The content of specialized training on these issues should cover the following:[176]

- Specific government and private payor reimbursement principles,
- Providing and billing DMEPOS items without proper authorization, and
- Improper documentation alteration.

### (b) Sales and Marketing Training

Specialized education provided to sales and marketing personnel should include topics such as the following:[177]

- Kickbacks,
- Routine waiver of coinsurance and deductibles,
- Disguising referral fees as salaries,
- Offering free goods or services to induce referrals,
- High pressure marketing of unnecessary items, and
- Improper patient solicitation.

### (c) Ongoing Education Responsibilities

The OIG recommends using a monthly compliance newsletter to address areas of ambiguity, and informing employees about the risk areas identified by the OIG in Special Fraud Alerts and other guidance materials. Like all other compliance-related materials, these newsletters should be retained in the compliance files.[178]

---

[175]*Id.* at 36,382–83.
[176]*Id.* at 36,383.
[177]*Id.*
[178]*Id.* at 36,383–84.

### iii. Hotline

The OIG notes that when employees use the hotline and want to remain anonymous, DMEPOS suppliers should strive to maintain confidentiality but also should explicitly inform the employee that his or her identity may become known or have to be revealed at a certain point in the investigation.[179]

### iv. Auditing and Monitoring

When returning overpayments, the DME CPG recommends that the following information be sent along with the overpayment:[180]

- Statement that the refund is being made in accordance with a voluntary compliance program,
- Complete description of the causes and circumstances surrounding the overpayment,
- Methodology used to determine the overpayment,
- Amount of the overpayment, and
- Claim-specific information used to determine the overpayment.

The DME CPG also describes numerous additional auditing techniques to be considered, such as the following:[181]

- Testing billing staff on their knowledge of reimbursement coverage criteria and official coding guidelines (preferably through use of hypotheticals),
- On-site visits to all facilities and locations,
- Assessment of all existing relationships with physicians and other referral sources,
- Unannounced audits and mock surveys,
- Examination of complaint logs,
- Interviews with physicians and others who order services from the DMEPOS supplier and interviews with contractors who provide services to the DMEPOS supplier,
- Validating the qualifications of physicians and others who order items and services,
- Review of medical necessity documentation, and
- Utilization/trend analyses.

### v. Corrective Action

In the DME CPG, the OIG emphasizes that when potential fraud, including a violation of the False Claims Act, is involved, any repayment should be made following a report to law enforcement authorities. Otherwise, the overpayment simply should be promptly refunded to the appropriate payor.[182]

---

[179] *Id.* at 36,384–85.
[180] *Id.* at 36,385.
[181] *Id.* at 36,385–86.
[182] *Id.* at 36,389.

### 4. Compliance Program Guidance for Third-Party Medical Billing Companies

A fourth compliance program guidance covers third-party medical billing companies (Billing Company CPG).[183] This program guidance represents the government's first compliance program guidance targeted to nonproviders. Program guidelines apply to physician practice management companies that provide billing services, as well as to traditional third-party billing companies. These guidelines were developed in part in response to the government's concerns about possible overbilling and overutilization resulting from promises made by billing companies and reimbursement consultants to maximize revenues from government-funded health care programs. Such arrangements may lead to abusive billing practices, especially if the billing agent or consultant receives a percentage of the provider's revenues.

Much of the compliance program guidance for third-party medical billing companies is the same as that of other programs (i.e., the seven essential elements). The medical billing company guidelines differ significantly, however, in that they seem to impose a duty on billing agents and managers to monitor their clients' conduct and encourage, but do not require, the reporting of any misconduct to the government. Consequently, as a result of these guidelines, third-party billing companies and managers for hospitals, physician practices, and other providers may wish to review their relationships with their clients. Managers may consider adding a provision to their client contracts clearly specifying each party's compliance responsibilities and requiring clients to implement and maintain an effective compliance program.

#### a. Billing Company Risk Areas

Within the guidance framework, the OIG identified the following special concerns for billing companies, among others:

- Billing for services or items that are undocumented,
- Unbundling,
- Upcoding and DRG creep,
- Inappropriate balance billing,
- Duplicate billing,
- Inadequate resolution of overpayments,
- Lack of integrity of computer systems,
- Software programs that encourage billing staff to enter data indicating that services were performed though not actually performed or documented,
- Failure to maintain the confidentiality of information and records,
- Knowing misuse of provider identification numbers resulting in improper billing,
- Outpatient services rendered in connection with inpatient stays,
- Billing for discharge in lieu of transfer,
- Improper use of billing modifiers,

---

[183]63 Fed. Reg. 70,138 (Dec. 18, 1998).

- Billing company incentives that violate the anti-kickback statute or other similar federal or state law,
- Joint ventures,
- Routine waiver of copayments, and
- Improper discounts on professional services.[184]

The government is particularly concerned with abusive coding procedures. The guidelines suggest that billing companies that provide coding services should implement safeguards that ensure that coding is based on complete and accurate documentation. If a billing company does not provide coding services, but instead relies on coding provided by a provider, the billing agent should obtain the provider's written agreement to abide by safeguards. For example, the billing company or provider should have written policies and procedures that

- Ensure that proper and timely documentation of professional services is obtained before billing,
- Emphasize that a claim should be submitted only when proper documentation supports the claim and is maintained in a form available for audit,
- Require that information contained on a claim be based on chart documentation and make such documentation available to coding staff at the time of coding,
- Avoid providing financial incentives to billing and coding staff members to upcode claims,
- Establish and maintain processes for pre- and postsubmission review of claims to ensure that they are accurate and supported by proper documentation, and
- Obtain clarification from the provider or from the billing agent's medical director when documentation is confusing or lacks adequate justification. [185]

### b. Reporting Provider Misconduct

One of the more significant sections in the Billing Company CPG is the section addressing corrective action. If a billing agent believes a provider is engaging in improper coding or billing activities, the billing company must refrain from submitting questionable claims. Further, the billing company must notify the provider, in writing, within 30 days of discovering the problem, why the activity appears to be improper. If the provider continues to engage in conduct that appears to be fraudulent or abusive, the Billing Company CPG states that the billing agent should

- Refrain from submitting the claim,
- Terminate the contract with the provider, and/or

---

[184]63 Fed. Reg. 70,142–43.
[185]*Id.* at 70,144.

- Report the misconduct to the appropriate federal and state authorities within 60 days of determining that there is credible evidence of a violation. [186]

## 5. Compliance Program Guidance for Hospices

In September 1999, the OIG issued compliance program guidance for hospices.[187] As with the program guidance previously discussed, the OIG emphasized that all seven basic elements must be included in a hospice's compliance program, and the hospice guidance generally is very similar to that described for other industry segments.

### a. Hospice Risk Areas

Through its investigative and audit functions, the OIG identified 28 risk areas for hospices, including (i) inadequate management and oversight of subcontracted services, (ii) knowingly billing for inadequate or substandard care, (iii) incentives to referral sources, and (iv) pressure on an eligible patient to revoke the hospice benefit when the patient's care becomes too expensive for the hospice to deliver.[188]

Additional risk areas include the following:

- Uninformed consent to elect the Medicare hospice benefit;
- Admitting patients to hospice care who are not terminally ill;
- Arrangement with another health care provider who a hospice knows is submitting claims for services already covered by the Medicare hospice benefit;
- Underutilization;
- Falsified medical records or plans of care;
- Untimely and/or forged physician certifications on plans of care;
- Inadequate or incomplete services rendered by the Interdisciplinary Group;
- Insufficient oversight of patients, particularly those patients receiving more than six consecutive months of hospice care;
- Overlap in the services that a nursing home provides, resulting in insufficient care provided by a hospice to a nursing home resident;
- Improper relinquishment of core services and professional management responsibilities to nursing homes, volunteers, and privately paid professionals;
- Providing hospice services in a nursing home before a written agreement has been finalized, if required;
- Billing for a higher level of care than was necessary;
- Billing for hospice care provided by unqualified or unlicensed clinical personnel;

---

[186]*Id.* at 70,151.

[187]64 Fed. Reg. 54,031 (Oct. 5, 1999). The OIG released this guidance on September 30, 1999, before its publication in the *Federal Register*.

[188]*Id.* at 54,035–37.

- False dating of amendments to medical records;
- High-pressure marketing of hospice care to ineligible beneficiaries;
- Improper patient solicitation activities, such as "patient charting," sales commissions based upon length of stay in hospice, deficient coordination of volunteers, and improper indication of the location where hospice services were delivered;
- Failure to comply with verbal orders requirements for hospice services;
- Nonresponse to late hospice referrals by physicians;
- Knowing misuse of provider certification numbers;
- Failure to adhere to hospice licensing requirements and Medicare conditions of participation; and
- Knowing failure to return overpayments.[189]

However, the OIG seems most concerned that hospices establish and follow policies and procedures to ensure that all eligibility requirements for the hospice benefit are satisfied. The OIG noted particular concerns regarding the terminal illness eligibility requirement, the plan of care, utilization of services, appropriate levels of care, and services provided to patients in nursing homes.[190]

The OIG also outlined risks in contracting with or providing services to actual or potential referral sources, in particular, nursing homes. A hospice's policies and procedures should reflect the safe harbor for such contracts. In addition, counsel should review all such contracts.[191]

### 6. Compliance Program Guidance for Nursing Facilities

The OIG published compliance program guidance for nursing facilities in March 2000 (SNF CPG).[192] The guidance emphasizes the seven essential elements and states that all seven elements must be contained in an effective compliance program for a nursing facility, regardless of size.

#### a. Nursing Facility Risk Areas

The OIG identified the following specific risk areas to be addressed by policies and procedures for nursing facilities.

##### i. Quality of Care

The OIG noted in particular that nursing facility compliance plans should include a commitment to providing quality care, including the development of quality of care protocols as well as the implementation of a mechanism to evaluate compliance with the protocols. Special areas of concern in this context include the following:

- Absence of a comprehensive, accurate assessment of each resident's functional capacity and a comprehensive care plan that includes mea-

---

[189]*Id.*

[190]*Id.* at 54,037–40.

[191]*Id.* at 54,040.

[192]65 Fed. Reg. 14,289 (Mar. 16, 2000).

surable objectives and timetables to meet the resident's medical, nursing, mental, and psychosocial needs;

- Inappropriate or insufficient treatment and services to address residents' clinical conditions, including pressure ulcers, dehydration, malnutrition, incontinence, and mental/psychosocial problems;
- Failure to accommodate individual resident needs and preferences;
- Failure to properly prescribe, administer, and monitor prescription drug usage;
- Inadequate staffing levels or insufficiently trained or supervised staff;
- Failure to provide appropriate therapy services;
- Failure to appropriately assist residents with activities of daily living (e.g., feeding, dressing, bathing, etc.);
- Failure to provide an ongoing activities program to meet individual resident needs; and
- Failure to report incidents of mistreatment, neglect, or abuse to the administrator of the facility and other officials as required by law.[193]

### ii. Residents' Rights

The OIG recommends that providers address risk areas including discrimination in admission policies; verbal, mental, or physical abuse, corporal punishment and involuntary seclusion, and the inappropriate use of physical or chemical restraints; failure to ensure that residents have personal privacy and access to their personal records upon request and that the privacy and confidentiality of those records are protected; denial of a resident's right to participate in care and treatment decisions; and the failure to safeguard residents' financial affairs.[194]

### iii. Billing and Cost Reporting

Special areas of concern in this context include the following:

- Billing for items or services not rendered or provided as claimed;
- Submitting claims for equipment, medical supplies, and services that are medically unnecessary;
- Submitting claims to Medicare Part A for residents who are not eligible for Part A coverage;
- Duplicate billing;
- Failing to identify and refund credit balances;
- Submitting claims for items or services not ordered;
- Knowingly billing for inadequate or substandard care;
- Providing misleading information about a resident's medical condition on the MDS or otherwise providing inaccurate information used to determine the Resource Utilization Group assigned to the resident;
- Upcoding the level of service provided;

---

[193]*Id.* at 14,293–94.
[194]*Id.* at 14,294.

- Billing for individual items or services when they are included in the facility's per diem rate or must be billed as a unit and may not be unbundled;
- Billing residents for items or services that are included in the per diem rate or otherwise covered by a third-party payor;
- Altering documentation or forging a physician signature on documents used to verify that services were ordered and/or provided;
- Failing to maintain sufficient documentation; and
- False cost reports.[195]

### iv. Employee Screening

In this context, the OIG suggests that providers

- Investigate the background of employees by checking with all applicable licensing and certification authorities;
- Require all potential employees to certify (e.g., on the employment application) that they have not been convicted of an offense that would preclude employment in a nursing facility and that they are not excluded from participation in federal health care programs;
- Require temporary employment agencies to ensure that temporary staff assigned to the facility have undergone appropriate background checks;
- Check the OIG's List of Excluded Individuals/Entities and the GSA's list of debarred contractors to verify that employees are not excluded from participation in federal programs;
- Require current employees to report to the nursing facility if, subsequent to their employment, they are convicted of an offense that would preclude employment in a nursing facility or are excluded from participation; and
- Periodically check the OIG and GSA web sites to verify the participation/ exclusion status of independent contractors, and retain the results of that query on file.[196]

### v. Kickbacks, Inducements, and Self-Referrals

Special areas of concern in this context include the following:

- Routinely waiving coinsurance or deductible amounts without a good faith determination that the resident is in financial need, or absent reasonable collection efforts;
- Arrangements with a hospital, home health agency, or hospice that involve the referral or transfer of any resident to or by the nursing home;
- Soliciting, accepting, or offering any gift or gratuity of more than nominal value to or from residents, potential referral sources, and other individuals and entities with which the nursing facility has a business relationship;
- Conditioning admission or continued stay at a facility on a third-party guarantee of payment, or soliciting payment for services covered by

---

[195]*Id.* at 14,295–96.
[196]*Id.* at 14,295–97.

Medicaid, in addition to any amount required to be paid under the State Medicaid plan;

- Arrangements between a nursing facility and a hospital under which the facility will only accept a Medicare beneficiary on the condition that the hospital pays the facility an amount over and above what the facility would receive through PPS;
- Arrangements with physicians, including the facility's medical director;
- Arrangements with vendors under which the nursing facility, which orders Medicare-reimbursed products, receives noncovered items (such as disposable adult diapers) at below market prices or no charge;
- Soliciting or receiving items of value in exchange for providing the supplier access to residents' medical records and other information needed to bill Medicare;
- Joint ventures with entities supplying goods or services; and
- Swapping.[197]

#### b. Ensuring Compliance Program Effectiveness

##### i. Auditing and Monitoring

In addition to evaluating a facility's compliance with program rules, the OIG emphasizes that an effective compliance program should also include at least annual assessments as to whether the program's compliance elements have been satisfied, such as ongoing education and training, dissemination of program standards, and appropriate investigations of reported misconduct.[198]

The OIG recommends consulting several CIAs to help design an organization's self-audit protocol. In addition, the OIG warns that audit plans should reflect both identified risk areas (including areas of past deficiencies) and the organization's resources. Compliance plans that fail to do so are less likely to receive favorable treatment under the Sentencing Guidelines.[199]

##### ii. Disciplinary Guidelines

The SNF CPG states that intentional noncompliance should lead to significant sanctions ranging from oral warnings to suspension, financial penalties, or termination. Policies should describe the procedures for handling disciplinary problems and those responsible for implementing these sanctions. The OIG emphasizes that sanctions should be applied consistently, whether the transgressor is an employee, manager, or corporate officer.[200]

##### iii. Corrective Action

In response to ongoing provider confusion about when and whether it is necessary to report on overpayment to law enforcement authorities, the SNF CPG states that "where potential fraud is not involved, the OIG recommends

---

[197]*Id.* at 14,297–98.
[198]*Id.* at 14,302.
[199]*Id.*
[200]*Id.* at 14,303.

that the nursing facility use normal repayment channels to return overpayments as they are discovered."[201]

### 7. Compliance Program Guidance for Medicare+Choice Organizations

The OIG published compliance program guidance for Medicare+ Choice organizations in November 1999 (Managed Care CPG).[202] The OIG acknowledged that the elements of the optional guidance are the same as elements required by CMS in the Medicare+Choice regulations.[203] In light of the extensive regulation of these organizations, the OIG recommended that each organization "determine the extent to which [its] activities need to be modified or supplemented to create an effective compliance program."[204]

#### a. Risk Areas

In the guidance, the OIG noted that the Medicare program requirements for Medicare+Choice organizations constituted de facto risk areas, including (1) the election process; (2) benefits and beneficiary protections; (3) quality assessment and performance improvement; (4) cost sharing; (5) solvency, licensure, and other state regulatory issues; (6) claims processing; and (7) appeals and grievance procedures.[205] CMS also indicated its concerns regarding

- Marketing materials and personnel,[206]
- Selective marketing and enrollment,[207]
- Disenrollment,[208]

---

[201] *Id.*

[202] 64 Fed. Reg. 61,893 (Nov. 15, 1999). Although the Medicare + Choice program has been renamed Advantage, the Managed Care CPG remains relevant. For a more complete discussion of the compliance program guidance for Medicare+Choice entities, see Chapter 6 (Rinn and Ryland, Managed Care Fraud and Abuse: Risk Areas for Government Program Participants).

[203] 42 C.F.R. part 22.

[204] 64 Fed. Reg. at 61,895.

[205] *Id.* at 61,897.

[206] Organizations that submit misrepresentations or false information are subject to civil monetary penalties and other intermediate sanctions. Consequently, all marketing materials should be scrutinized for completeness, accuracy, and compliance with Medicare program rules. *Id.* at 61,897–98. Of particular concern is that Medicare+Choice organizations clearly explain to beneficiaries the concept of "lock-in" (limitations on the enrollee's choice of provider) and the potential for their enrollment to terminate if the Medicare+Choice organization or CMS does not renew its contract. The guidance also discourages the use of physicians as marketing agents. *Id.* at 61,898.

[207] The guidance cautions against the cherry-picking of enrollees based on health status. For example, holding pre-enrollment medical screenings or marketing primarily in places where healthy enrollees are more likely to be present (e.g., exercise clubs) may represent a problem. *Id.* at 61,898, 61,899.

[208] Medicare+Choice organizations are generally barred from disenrolling or encouraging an individual to disenroll unless the organization cannot furnish the items or services needed by the patient. The OIG is concerned that Medicare+Choice organizations may disenroll sicker patients to reduce their expenditures. *Id.* at 61,899.

- Underutilization and quality of care,[209]
- Data collection and submission processes,[210]
- Anti-kickback statute and other inducements,[211] and
- Emergency services.[212]

The OIG further discussed its concerns regarding inappropriate withholding or delaying of services for enrollees.[213] Medicare+Choice organizations should have policies and procedures ensuring (1) that there is no interference between health care professionals and the enrollees they advise, and (2) that incentive plans are fully disclosed to CMS and do not inappropriately encourage underutilization.[214] Additionally, organizations should establish policies and procedures to ensure that all data submissions to CMS are accurate, timely, and complete.[215]

### 8. Compliance Program Guidance for Individual and Small-Group Physician Practices

The OIG released final compliance program guidance for individual and small-group physician practices in September 2000 (Physician CPG).[216] Unlike in the guidance for other types of programs and entities, in the physician

---

[209]Medicare+Choice enrollees must have access to all covered services. The guidance cautions Medicare+Choice organizations against the practice of stinting (e.g., the inappropriate withholding or delay of services). The guidance recommends that Medicare+Choice organizations adopt policies that prohibit gag rules, which limit the ability of health care professionals to advise enrollees on treatment options, ensure that physician incentive plans are appropriately disclosed and comply with Medicare requirements, and verify that providers are appropriately credentialed. *Id.* at 61,899, 61,900.

[210]The guidance focuses on data submissions that determine the amount of Medicare payment. The OIG notes that when the officers of a Medicare+Choice organization certify its encounter data, it is submitting a "claim" for capitated payment. As a result, Medicare+Choice organizations should develop policies to ensure that these data submissions are accurate, complete and truthful. In particular, the guidance recommends that Medicare+Choice organizations ensure that the administrative component of the adjusted community rate (ACR) proposal is accurately calculated and ensure that the institutional status of beneficiaries is reported accurately. *Id.* at 61,900, 61,901.

[211]The guidance cautions that despite the protection of the safe harbor for capitated managed care organizations, there are three important limitations. First, swapping arrangements that direct fee-for-service federal health care program business to the entity giving the discount in exchange for managed care business referrals is not protected. Second, the safe harbor does not apply to remuneration for marketing services or for services furnished before the beneficiary enrolled in the plan. Finally, the safe harbor is limited to risk-based managed care plans that are only paid by a federal health care program through capitation. *Id.* at 61,901, 61,903.

[212]Medicare+Choice organizations may not require prior authorization for emergency services and must cover such services without regard to the provider's contractual relationship with the Medicare+Choice organization. Coverage for emergency services must be determined from the perspective of a reasonable patient at the time symptoms presented. Medicare+Choice organizations must also comply with EMTALA. The guidance warns Medicare+Choice organizations against dual staffing situations where the managed care organization places its own physicians in the emergency room and employs different policies and procedures. *Id.* at 61,901, 61,903.

[213]64 Fed. Reg. at 61,899.

[214]*Id.*

[215]*Id.* at 61,900.

[216]65 Fed. Reg. 59,434 (Oct. 5, 2000). The OIG released this final guidance on September 25, 2000, before its publication in the *Federal Register*.

practice guidance, the OIG acknowledges that a small physician practice may not need to satisfy all seven elements to have an effective compliance program. Assuming that some of the basic elements will not be fully implemented, the Physician CPG suggests that small physician practices start with (i) auditing and monitoring to identify any problem or risk areas requiring further change; and then (ii) develop written policies and procedures to address particular concerns uncovered during an audit, useful practice procedures and standards, and risk areas.

### a. Risk Areas for Physicians

The OIG identified the following risk areas in the Physician CPG:

(i)   coding and billing;[217]
(ii)  determination of reasonable and necessary services;[218]
(iii) documentation;[219] and
(iv)  improper inducements, kickbacks, and self-referrals.[220]

In Appendix A of the Physician CPG, the OIG makes the following recommendations to address certain additional risk areas for physician practices, including among others:

(1)   Physicians should apply the appropriate local medical review policies (LMRP), now local coverage determinations,[221] despite the policy variations among carriers;[222]

---

[217]Coding and billing risk areas include billing for items or services not rendered or not furnished as claimed; submitting claims for equipment, medical supplies, and services that are unreasonable and unnecessary; double billing; billing for noncovered services; knowing misuse of provider identification numbers; unbundling (billing for each component of the service instead of billing or using an all-inclusive code); failure to properly use coding modifiers; clustering; and upcoding the level of service provided. *Id.* at 59,439.

[218]Although a physician should only bill for services that meet Medicare's standard for reasonableness and necessity, a physician may bill to receive a denial for services if the denial is necessary for payment by a secondary payor. *Id.*

[219]Documentation of a patient's care should be timely, accurate, and complete. Documentation guidelines should ensure that the medical record is complete and legible, that each patient encounter is documented, that the rationale for services is documented or can be inferred, that the documentation supports the billing codes used, and that appropriate health risk factors are identified. Guidelines also should ensure that physicians properly complete claim submission forms to ensure that the diagnosis code is appropriately linked with the reason for the visit, that modifier codes are appropriately used, and that Medicare is given information regarding the beneficiary's other payors. *Id.* at 59,440.

[220]The OIG notes that "arrangements with hospitals, hospices, nursing facilities, home health agencies, DME suppliers, pharmaceutical manufacturers and vendors are areas of particular concern." The guidance recommends that physician practices develop guidelines to avoid inducements such as the routine waiver of coinsurance or deductibles without a good faith determination of patient need or reasonable collection efforts. *Id.* The OIG also cautions against financial arrangements with outside entities to which the physician could refer federal health care program business, joint ventures with entities that supply goods/services to the practice or its patients, consulting contracts or medical directorships, office and equipment leases with referral entities, and soliciting or accepting gifts to or from referral sources. *Id.* at 59,440–41.

[221]*See* Local Coverage Determinations, *available at* http://www.cms.hhs.gov/Determination Process/04_LCDs.asp.

[222]65 Fed. Reg. at 59,445.

(2) Physician practices should educate physicians and office staff on the proper use of Advance Beneficiary Notices (ABNs);[223]

(3) Physicians should carefully review CMNs before signing them;[224]

(4) Teaching physicians should comply with Medicare's billing requirements, which may require the teaching physician to be present during the provision of the service;[225]

(5) Physicians should avoid gainsharing arrangements with hospitals that induce a reduction or limitation in services to Medicare and Medicaid beneficiaries;[226]

(6) Physicians should avoid questionable incentive arrangements with hospitals, such as the hospital's provision of free nursing staff or the hospital's payment for a physician's travel and expenses for conferences;[227]

(7) Physicians should be familiar with the practices of their third-party billing services because the physicians are ultimately responsible for their claims;[228]

(8) Physicians who do not participate in Medicare must abide by the requirements on limiting charges and the refund of payments in excess of the limiting charge;[229]

(9) Physicians should ensure that any professional courtesy they provide does not take into account referrals generated by physicians receiving the courtesy and does not otherwise violate the prohibition on waiving copayments for federal health care program beneficiaries;[230] and

(10) Physicians should comply with the space rental safe harbor provisions.

### b. Other Helpful Resources for All Health Care Organizations

The Physician CPG contains several very useful appendices, including Appendix B describing various potentially applicable criminal statutes in easy to understand language (with examples); Appendix C on Civil and Administrative Statutes (with examples) including the Stark law, CMPs, and exclusion authorities; Appendix D on OIG/HHS Contact Information including the Provider Self-Disclosure Protocol; Appendix E with information on contacting Medicare and Medicaid contractors; and Appendix F on Internet Resources.[231] While some of the information may be dated since the Physician CPG was published in 2000, it can still provide a useful starting point in many cases.

---

[223] *Id.*

[224] *Id.*

[225] *Id.*

[226] *Id.*

[227] *Id.* at 59,447.

[228] *Id.*

[229] *Id.*

[230] *Id.* at 59,447–48.

[231] *Id.* at 59,448–52.

### 9. Compliance Program Guidance for Home Health Agencies

The compliance program guidance for home health agencies[232] acknowledges that home health agencies often are small businesses and therefore may not be of sufficient size or have adequate resources to fully implement all aspects of the compliance guidance. Nevertheless, the government expects that each home health agency, no matter what its size, will implement some type of compliance program that contains as many elements of the model as possible. The government considers this necessary to both (1) show good faith, and (2) help create "a culture that promotes prevention, detection and resolution of non-compliant activities."[233] The guidance suggests implementation of the seven basic elements as follows:

#### a. Home Health Agency Risk Areas

Specific risk areas highlighted in the guidance include the following:[234]

##### i. Improper Joint Ventures

The home health agency should have policies and procedures in place that establish parameters for joint ventures and that prohibit improper joint ventures between home health agencies and referral sources.[235]

##### ii. Billing for Unallowable Costs of Home Health Coordination

The home health agency should not bill for patient solicitation or other activities that duplicate services furnished as part of a hospital's or a skilled nursing facility's discharge planning responsibilities.[236]

---

[232] 63 Fed. Reg. 42,410 (Aug. 7, 1998).

[233] *Id.* at 42,411.

[234] Additional risk areas identified for home health agencies include billing for items or services not actually rendered; billing for medically unnecessary services; duplicate billing; false cost reports; credit balances—failure to refund; home health agency incentives to actual or potential referral sources (e.g., physicians, hospitals, patients, etc.) that may violate the anti-kickback statute or other similar federal or state statute or regulation; Stark physician self-referral law; over-utilization and underutilization; knowing billing for inadequate or substandard care; insufficient documentation to evidence that services were performed and to support reimbursement; billing for unallowable costs of home health coordination; false dating of amendments to nursing notes; untimely and/or forged physician certifications on plans of care; forged beneficiary signatures on visit slips/logs that verify services were performed; inadequate management and oversight of subcontracted services, which results in improper billing; discriminatory admission and discharge of patients; billing for unallowable costs associated with the acquisition and sale of home health agencies; compensation programs that offer incentives for number of visits performed and revenue generated; improper influence over referrals by hospitals that own home health agencies; patient abandonment in violation of applicable statutes, regulations, and federal health care program requirements; knowing misuse of provider certification numbers, which results in improper billing; duplication of services provided by assisted living facilities, hospitals, clinics, physicians, and other home health agencies; knowing or reckless disregard of willing and able caregivers when providing home health services; failure to adhere to home health agency licensing requirements and Medicare conditions of participation; and knowing failure to return overpayments made by federal health care programs. *Id.* at 42,414–15.

[235] 63 Fed. Reg. at 42,414.

[236] *Id.*

### iii.  Unqualified or Unlicensed Personnel

The home health agency's policies and procedures should indicate clearly that bills will be submitted only for the services of individuals who are properly qualified or licensed to provide the type of services billed.[237]

### iv.  Falsified Plans of Care

The home health agency should have policies and procedures to ensure that it provides only medically necessary services that are appropriately certified by a physician. A plan for furnishing home health services must be certified by a physician who is a doctor of medicine, osteopathy, or podiatry medicine and who does not have a significant ownership interest in or a significant financial or contractual relationship with the home health agency.[238]

### v.  Improper Patient Solicitation Activities and High-Pressure Marketing

The government has noted that home health agencies sometimes offer free gifts or services to patients. Because they may be intended to improperly maximize business growth and patient retention, such gifts are highly suspect. Moreover, the guidance indicates that any marketing materials should be clear, correct, nondeceptive, and fully informative.[239]

### vi.  Billing for Services to Patients Who Are Not Truly Homebound

For a home health agency to receive reimbursement for home health services under either Medicare Part A or Part B, the beneficiary must be "confined to the home."[240] Therefore, home health agencies should develop oversight mechanisms to ensure that the homebound status of a Medicare beneficiary is verified and properly documented. The program guidance suggests the use of written "prompts" on nursing note forms as a safeguard. Such prompts would direct the home health agency's nurses and other clinicians to properly assess and document the homebound status of the Medicare beneficiary. Another safeguard suggested is the distribution of written notices to the home health agency's Medicare beneficiaries reminding them that they must satisfy the regulatory requirements for homebound status to be eligible for Medicare coverage.[241]

### vii.  Billing for Visits to Patients Who Do Not Require a Qualifying Service

To receive Medicare reimbursement for home health services, a beneficiary must require skilled nursing care on an intermittent basis, physical therapy

---

[237] *Id.*

[238] *See* 63 Fed. Reg. at 42,416. Note that the Stark II regulations amend this provision to track Stark II's "financial relationship" definition and the applicable exceptions. 66 Fed. Reg. 856, 962 (Jan. 4, 2001). The Stark law is discussed at length in Chapter 2 (Crane, Federal Physician Self-Referral Restrictions).

[239] 63 Fed. Reg. at 42,414.

[240] *See* CMS Home Health Agency Manual (CMS Pub. 11) §204.1; *see also* 63 Fed. Reg. at 42,416.

[241] 63 Fed. Reg. at 42,414.

services, or speech-language pathology services or have a continuing need for occupational therapy. If services can be safely and effectively performed (or self-administered) by the average nonmedical person without the direct supervision of a licensed nurse, the service does not qualify as a skilled service even if a registered nurse actually performs the service.[242] The government considers it critical that the home health agency's written policies and procedures contain mechanisms to prevent billing for services after any qualifying service has ceased.

### viii. Duplication of Services

There should be safeguards in place to prevent the home health agency from providing or billing for services that are being provided to the patient by assisted living facilities, hospitals, clinics, physicians, or other home health agencies.[243]

### ix. Willing Caregivers

Policies and procedures should ensure that the home health agency does not provide services when the home health agency is aware of willing and able caregivers who can provide the same services.[244]

## 10. Compliance Program Guidance for Ambulance Suppliers

The compliance program guidance for ambulance suppliers (Ambulance CPG)[245] acknowledges that the ambulance industry has experienced several cases of fraud and abuse, and has received guidance from the OIG in the form of several advisory opinions[246] and a safe harbor for certain ambulance restocking programs.[247]

### a. Ambulance Risk Areas

The Ambulance CPG describes the risk areas associated with Medicare coverage and reimbursement requirements for ambulance suppliers.

### i. Medical Necessity and Upcoding

Medically unnecessary transport and charging for a higher level of service than was provided (upcoding) have been a focus of prosecution. Nonemergency transports are subject to significant precoverage requirements.[248]

---

[242] *See* HOME HEALTH AGENCY MANUAL §205.1(A)(2).

[243] *Id.* at 42,415.

[244] 63 Fed. Reg. at 42,415; *see* HOME HEALTH AGENCY MANUAL §203.2.

[245] 68 Fed. Reg. 14,245 (Mar. 24, 2003).

[246] *See, e.g.,* OIG Advisory Op. Nos. 97–6, 98–7, 98–13, 98–14, 00–9, 01–10, 01–11, 01–12, 01–18, 02–2, 02–3, 02–08, 02–15, 03–09, 3–11, 03–14, 04–02, 04–06, 04–10, 04–12, 04–13, 04–14, 05–07, 05–09, 05–10, 06–06, 06–07, 06–11, and 06–12, *available at* http://oig.hhs.gov/fraud/advisoryopinions/opinions.html. OIG advisory opinions are indexed by topic and summarized in Appendix G-2 on the disk accompanying this volume.

[247] *See* 66 Fed. Reg. 62,979 (Dec. 4, 2001).

[248] 68 Fed. Reg. at 14,250.

### ii. Documentation, Billing, and Reporting

Faulty documentation is a key risk area. When documenting services provided, "ambulance personnel should not make assumptions or inferences to compensate for a lack of information or contradictory information on a tip sheet, ACR, or other medical source documents."[249] To ensure that adequate and appropriate information is documented, the OIG recommends that ambulance suppliers gather and record the following items: dispatch instructions, if any; reasons why transportation by other means was contraindicated; reasons for selecting the level of service; information on the status of the individual; who ordered the trip; time spent on the trip; dispatch, arrival at scene, and destination times; mileage traveled; pickup and destination codes; appropriate zip codes; and services provided including drugs or supplies. Suppliers should also take care to determine which payors are primarily and secondarily liable.[250]

### iii. Medicare Part A Payment for Services "Under Arrangements"

Ambulance suppliers should not bill Medicare when a facility is responsible for payment.[251]

### iv. Medicaid Requirements

Medicaid covers many transportation services not covered by Medicare. Suppliers should be careful to comply with Medicaid requirements for service provided to Medicaid beneficiaries.[252]

### v. Arrangements With Patients and Other Providers

Ambulance suppliers should not offer remuneration to cities or counties in order to secure emergency medical services (EMS) contracts. Similarly, the provision of EMS should not be conditioned on referrals of non-EMS services. Ambulance suppliers are prohibited from making inflated payments to first responders to generate business. Arrangements with hospitals and nursing homes are subject to particular scrutiny because such facilities are key sources of nonemergency business. Additionally, giving patients items of value or waiving co-payments to induce them to select a particular supplier are generally prohibited under both the anti-kickback statute and the CMP statute.[253]

### vi. Additional Risk Areas

In Appendix A to the guidance, the OIG identifies four additional areas of concern: "no transport" calls and pronouncement of death; multiple-patient transports; multiple ambulances responding to and assisting with a single transport; and billing Medicare substantially in excess of usual charges [254]

---

[249]*Id.*

[250]68 Fed. Reg. at 14,251.

[251]*Id.*

[252]*Id.*

[253]*See id.* at 14,252–53.

[254]*Id.* at 14,254.

### b. Making a Compliance Program Effective

#### i. Auditing and Monitoring

The OIG noted several areas key to effective auditing and monitoring compliance programs for ambulance suppliers.

- *The claims submission process.* Ambulance suppliers should conduct pre-billing review of claims, paid claims, and claims denials. Suppliers should consider using the results of benchmarking audits along with external information to set benchmarks for measuring future performance.
- *System reviews and safeguards.* Coding and billing systems should be periodically reviewed for system weaknesses.
- *Sanctioned individuals and entities.* Ambulance suppliers should periodically (not less than annually) check the OIG[255] and GSA[256] exclusion and debarment lists before they employ or contract with new employees or new contractors.

### 11. Compliance Program Guidance for Pharmaceutical Manufacturers

In May 2003, the OIG issued its final compliance program guidance for pharmaceutical manufacturers (Drug Manufacturer CPG).[257]

Although the OIG's original solicitation of comments indicated that the guidelines would address the pharmaceutical industry as a whole, specifically including retail pharmacies,[258] the final Drug Manufacturer CPG addresses only pharmaceutical manufacturers.[259] Nevertheless, the OIG notes that the compliance program elements and potential risk areas identified in the Drug Manufacturer CPG "may have application to manufacturers of other products that may be reimbursed by federal health care programs, such as medical devices and infant nutritional products."[260] The most significant portions of the Drug Manufacturer CPG are its discussion of specific pharmaceutical risk areas and the OIG's view of how existing law applies.

---

[255] *See* http://oig.hhs.gov/fraud/exclusions.html.

[256] *See* http://epls.arnet.gov.

[257] 68 Fed. Reg. 23,731 (May 5, 2003). This document is also available in Appendix I-3.1 on the disk accompanying this volume.

[258] 67 Fed. Reg. 62,057 (Oct. 3, 2002).

[259] 68 Fed. Reg. 23,731 (May 5, 2003).

[260] *Id.* At the same time, there are important differences between the drug and device industries, such as the ongoing need for many device manufacturers to provide hands-on training in device safety. Hence, as appropriate, manufacturers should consider both the PhRMA Code on Interactions with Health Care Professionals (PhRMA Code) contained in Appendix I-3.2 on the disk accompanying this volume and the AdvaMed Code of Ethics on Interactions with Health Care Professionals (AdvaMed Code), *available at* http://www.advamed.org/publicdocs/coe_with_faqs_4–15–05.pdf.

### a. Compliance Program Elements

As in the prior compliance program guidance documents,[261] the OIG identifies seven compliance program elements in the Drug Manufacturer CPG: (1) distribution of written standards of conduct addressing areas of compliance risk; (2) designation of a compliance officer and compliance committee; (3) implementation of regular training programs; (4) creation of a hotline or other reporting system; (5) use of audits or risk evaluation techniques; (6) policies and procedures addressing the nonemployment or retention of excluded individuals or entities; and (7) investigation procedures for identified instances of noncompliance.

Moreover, certain aspects of these seven core elements are emphasized or tailored to the pharmaceutical industry in the Drug Manufacturer CPG as described below.

- *Designation of a compliance officer and compliance committee.*[262] According to the Drug Manufacturer CPG, every pharmaceutical manufacturer should designate a compliance officer to oversee compliance activities. The individual may have other responsibilities, provided that the manufacturer ensures that the compliance officer devotes adequate time and substantive attention to compliance. The compliance officer should report regularly to the board of directors, compliance committee, and CEO or president. The Drug Manufacturer CPG recommends establishing a compliance committee to assist in implementation of the compliance program and to advise the compliance officer. If a small manufacturer chooses not to establish a full compliance committee, it should create a task force to address particular compliance issues when they arise.[263]
- *Conducting effective training and education.*[264] The Drug Manufacturer CPG recommends that participation in training programs should be a condition of continued employment and adherence to compliance requirements should be a factor in employee evaluations.
- *Developing effective lines of communication.*[265] Employees must have access to supervisors and the compliance officer in order to ask questions and report problems. Confidentiality and nonretaliation policies should be implemented. The OIG also encourages the use of hotlines and other forms of communication, including exit interview programs. Such

---

[261]The OIG has issued compliance program guidance for a number of segments of the health care industry. These documents are available on the OIG Web site at http://oig.hhs.gov/fraud/complianceguidance.html. Although each compliance program guidance document is specific to a particular industry segment, all contain the same basic elements, and the OIG has frequently encouraged providers to consult various compliance documents, as appropriate, in order to get the most recent guidance available on a particular topic. In addition, there is often considerable overlap in risk areas; e.g., physicians may find it helpful to review the risk areas described in the Supplemental Hospital CPG as well as the risks identified in other compliance documents.

[262]68 Fed. Reg. 23,739.

[263]*Id.* at 23,740.

[264]*Id.*

[265]*Id.* at 23,741.

mechanisms should be available to all employees and independent contractors.

### b. Risk Areas for Drug (and Device) Companies

The Drug Manufacturer CPG identifies the following three risk areas to be of significant concern for pharmaceutical manufacturers:

- The integrity of data used by state and federal governments to establish payments under federal health care programs;
- Kickbacks and other illegal remuneration; and
- Compliance with laws regulating drug samples.

The Drug Manufacturer CPG is not legally binding and acknowledges that it does not create any new law or legal obligation. However, on certain issues, it advances positions taken in litigation by various parties that have been challenged by many other segments of the industry.

### i. Integrity of Data Used to Establish Reimbursement

The government has, for the last several years, investigated manufacturer practices relating to the reported pricing of pharmaceuticals. The Drug Manufacturer CPG notes that a pharmaceutical manufacturer may be liable under the federal False Claims Act (FCA) if government reimbursement for the manufacturer's product depends, in whole or in part, on information generated or reported by the manufacturer, directly or indirectly, and the manufacturer has knowingly failed to generate or report such information completely and accurately. Such manufacturers also may be liable for civil money penalties under various authorities. Further, according to the Drug Manufacturer CPG, in some circumstances, inaccurate or incomplete reporting also may be probative of liability under the anti-kickback statute.[266]

The Drug Manufacturer CPG states that manufacturers' reported prices should, as appropriate, accurately account for price reductions, cash discounts, free goods contingent on a purchase agreement, rebates, up-front payments (prebates), coupons, goods in kind, free or reduced price services, grants, or other price concessions or similar benefits offered to some or all purchasers. If a discount, price concession, or similar benefit is offered on purchases of multiple products, that benefit should be apportioned fairly among the products. Moreover, underlying assumptions for reported prices should be reasoned, consistent, and appropriately documented. Pharmaceutical manufacturers are urged to retain all relevant records reflecting reported prices and efforts to comply with federal health care program requirements.

Finally, the OIG highlights the importance of Medicaid rebate program price reporting requirements. The guidance encourages manufacturers to pay particular attention to ensuring that they accurately calculate prices as specified in the Medicaid program and that they pay appropriate rebate amounts for their drugs.

---

[266]*Id.* at 23,733.

## ii. Kickbacks and Other Illegal Remuneration

The Drug Manufacturer CPG emphasizes that the anti-kickback statute extends equally to the solicitation or acceptance of remuneration for referrals, and it notes that the statute prohibits some practices in the health care industry that are common in other business sectors. The OIG recommends that pharmaceutical manufacturers structure arrangements whenever possible within the terms of a safe harbor, noting that safe harbor protection requires "strict compliance with all applicable conditions" of the safe harbor in question. Interested parties also can seek an OIG opinion for guidance on the potential applicability of the anti-kickback statute to a particular business arrangement.[267]

The Drug Manufacturer CPG also recommends that manufacturers identify any remunerative relationship between themselves (or their representatives) and persons or entities in a position to directly or indirectly generate federal health care business for the manufacturer. According to the OIG, these types of persons or entities include purchasers, benefits managers, formulary committee members, group purchasing organizations (GPOs), physicians and certain allied health care professionals, and pharmacists.

The OIG reiterates the "one purpose test" in determining whether remuneration is intended to induce or reward a referral or recommendation of business payable by a federal health care program, noting that "a lawful purpose will not legitimize a payment that also has an unlawful purpose." The guidance goes on to list "aggravating considerations" identified by courts, which present the "greatest risk of prosecution," including the following:

- Does the arrangement or practice have a potential to interfere with, or skew, clinical decisionmaking? Could it undermine the clinical integrity of a formulary process? If the arrangement or practice involves providing information to decision makers, prescribers, or patients, is the information complete, accurate, and not misleading?
- Does the arrangement or practice have the potential to increase costs to federal health care programs, beneficiaries, or enrollees? Does the arrangement or practice have the potential to be a disguised discount to circumvent the Medicaid Rebate Program Best Price calculation?
- Does the arrangement or practice have the potential to increase the risk of overutilization or inappropriate utilization?
- Does the arrangement or practice raise patient safety or quality of care concerns?

### iii. Risks Related to Purchasers

#### (a) Discounts and Remuneration to Purchasers

Generally, pharmaceutical manufacturers offer purchasers price concessions and similar benefits to induce the purchase of their products. Purchasers include direct purchasers (e.g., hospitals, nursing homes, pharmacies, and some

---

[267]*Id.* at 23,734.

physicians), as well as indirect purchasers (e.g., health plans). The Drug Manufacturer CPG recommends review of any remuneration (including grants) from a manufacturer provided to a purchaser that is related to a sale that may implicate the anti-kickback statute. According to the OIG, discounting arrangements in the pharmaceutical industry require "special scrutiny" because of their potential to implicate the Best Price requirements of the Medicaid Rebate Program. (The Medicaid Rebate Program requires that states receive rebates based on the best price offered by a pharmaceutical manufacturer to other purchasers.)

- *Discount Safe Harbor Provisions.* The guidance asserts that manufacturers offering discounts should thoroughly familiarize themselves with the discount safe harbor provisions.[268] In particular, manufacturers should pay attention to safe harbor requirements applicable to "sellers" and "offerors" of discounts, particularly those requiring sellers/offerors to (i) inform customers of any discount and of the customer's reporting obligations with respect to that discount, and (ii) refrain from any action that would impede a customer's ability to comply with the safe harbor. To fulfill the safe harbor requirements, the Drug Manufacturer CPG points out that manufacturers need to know how their customers submit claims to federal health care programs (i.e., whether the customer is a managed care, cost-based, or charge-based biller), because the applicable standards vary based on the type of customer.

- *Product Support Services.* The guidance also raises the issue of product support services in connection with the sale of a manufacturer's products.[269] If a manufacturer provides a service with no independent value (such as limited reimbursement support services in connection with its own products) together with another service providing a benefit to a referring provider (such as a reimbursement guarantee that eliminates normal financial risks), the arrangement could raise kickback concerns.

- *Educational Grants.* The Drug Manufacturer CPG addresses grant funding for a wide range of educational activities. Even if the educational or research purpose is legitimate, funding that is conditioned, in whole or in part, on the purchase of product implicates the statute. Furthermore, there is a risk that the educational program may be used for inappropriate marketing purposes to the extent the manufacturer has any influence over the substance of an educational program or the presenter.

- *Grant-Making Functions.* The OIG urges that manufacturers separate their grant-making functions from their sales and marketing functions, in order to reduce the risks that a grant program would be used improperly to induce or reward product purchases. According to the OIG, effective

---

[268] 42 C.F.R. §1001.952(h). The safe harbors for price reductions in the managed care context, 42 C.F.R. §§1001.952(m), (t), and (u), also may offer protection for some arrangements.

[269] Examples given by the OIG include "billing assistance tailored to the purchased products, reimbursement consultation, and other programs specifically tied to support of the purchased product." These types of services are referenced as appropriate in the AdvaMed Code developed by the Advanced Medical Technology Association for its device company members. *See* AdvaMed Code §§II, VII.

separation of these functions will help ensure that grant funding is not inappropriately influenced by sales or marketing motivations and that the educational purposes of the grant are legitimate. The OIG also encourages manufacturers to establish objective criteria for making grants that do not take into account the volume or value of purchases made by, or anticipated from, the grant recipient and that serve to ensure that the funded activities are *bona fide*. Additionally, the manufacturer should have no control over the speaker or content of the educational presentation. Compliance with such procedures should be documented and regularly monitored.

- *Research Funding.* The Drug Manufacturer CPG recommends that contracts between manufacturers and purchasers of their products to conduct research whenever possible to fit within the personal services safe harbor, with payments for research services reflecting fair market value for legitimate, reasonable, and necessary services. The OIG cautions that post-marketing research activities should be reviewed carefully to ensure that they are legitimate and "not simply a pretext to generate prescriptions of a drug." Further, manufacturers are directed to develop contracting procedures that clearly separate the awarding of research contracts from marketing. Research contracts that originate through the sales or marketing functions—or that are offered to purchasers in connection with sales contacts—are particularly suspect, according to the OIG.

- The OIG also notes that pharmaceutical manufacturers sometimes provide funding to their purchasers for use in the purchasers' own research. Although such research has a public health benefit, research grants can be misused to induce the purchase of business without triggering Medicaid Best Price obligations, if linked directly or indirectly to the purchase of product.

- *Other Remuneration to Purchasers.* Examples of potentially problematic remuneration in connection with a sale include, but are not limited to, "prebates" and "upfront payments," other free or reduced-price goods or services, and payments to cover the costs of "converting" from a competitor's product. According to the Drug Manufacturer CPG, selective offers of remuneration (i.e., offers made to some but not all purchasers) may increase the potential risk if the selection criteria relate directly or indirectly to the volume or value of business generated. In cases where manufacturers contract with purchasers to provide services to the manufacturer, such as data collection services, these contracts should be structured to fit in the personal services safe harbor. In all cases, the remuneration should be fair market value for legitimate, reasonable, and necessary services.

### (b)  Formularies and Formulary Support Services

The Drug Manufacturer CPG notes that, to date, Medicare and Medicaid involvement with outpatient drug formularies has been limited primarily to Medicaid and Medicare managed care plans, and they have received relatively little scrutiny under the anti-kickback statute. However, as federal program expenditures for, and coverage of, outpatient pharmaceuticals increase, scrutiny under the anti-kickback statute also increases. Accordingly, the Drug Manufacturer CPG lists several practices with "the potential for abuse."

- *Relationships with formulary committee members*—Any remuneration from a manufacturer or its agents directly or indirectly to person in a position to influence formulary decisions related to the manufacturer's products will be "suspect."[270]
- *Payments to PBMs*—The OIG states that rebate or other payments by drug manufacturers directly to PBMs that are based on, or otherwise related to, the PBM's customers' purchases potentially implicate the anti-kickback statute.[271] However, the Drug Manufacturer CPG suggests that such payments may be protected if structured to fit the GPO safe harbor.[272]
- *Formulary placement and support payments*—The OIG specifically states that lump sum payments for inclusion in a formulary or for exclusive or restricted formulary status are problematic. It further questions manufacturer payments to PBMs for formulary support activities that are linked directly or indirectly to drug purchases. The OIG recommends that manufacturers, in assessing the appropriateness of payments for formulary support activities, determine whether they receive a benefit from the payments, or whether the formulary sponsor is benefiting. In this regard, the OIG recommends that manufacturers consider a series of questions in evaluating payments to PBMs: Is the funding tied to specific drugs or categories? If so, are the categories especially competitive? Is the formulary sponsor funding similar activities for other drug categories? Has funding of PBM activities increased as rebates are increasingly passed back to PBM customers?"

#### (c) Average Wholesale Price

The OIG asserts that "the conjunction of manipulation of the AWP to induce customers to purchase a product with active marketing of the spread is strong evidence of the unlawful intent necessary to trigger the anti-kickback statute."[273] Such active marketing of the spread would include, for example, sales representatives promoting the spread as a reason to purchase the product or guaranteeing a certain profit or spread in exchange for the purchase of a product.

### iv. Relationships With Physicians and Other Referral Sources

The Drug Manufacturer CPG notes that pharmaceutical manufacturers have a variety of remunerative relationships with persons or entities in a position to refer, order, or prescribe—or influence the referral, ordering, or pre-

---

[270]Such arrangements also might implicate state commercial bribery laws.

[271]While the draft guidance specifically listed "market share rebates" as a potentially suspect practice, the final guidance appears to have backed away from that comment.

[272]42 C.F.R. §1001.952(j).

[273]68 Fed. Reg. at 23,737.

scribing of—the manufacturers' products. These remunerative relationships potentially implicate the anti-kickback statute, and include not only physicians, but pharmacists and other health care professionals as well. According to the OIG, any time a manufacturer provides something of value to a physician (or other health care professional), it should consider whether it is providing a valuable tangible benefit with the intent to induce or reward referrals. The OIG specifically questions a manufacturer's providing goods or services that eliminate an expense the physician would have otherwise incurred (i.e., that has independent value to the physician), or providing items or services at less than their fair market value.

Arrangements that do not fit squarely in a safe harbor should be reviewed in light of the totality of all facts and circumstances. According to the Drug Manufacturer CPG, appropriate considerations include the nature of the relationship between the parties, the manner in which the remuneration is determined, the value of the remuneration, the potential federal program impact of the remuneration, and potential conflicts of interest. Within the guidance, each of these considerations is accompanied by a series of questions to be used in reviewing arrangements between manufacturers and physicians or other health care professionals.

The Drug Manufacturer CPG references the PhRMA Code on Interactions with Healthcare Professionals (PhRMA Code) as providing useful and practical advice for reviewing and structuring these relationships.[274] In some parts of the Drug Manufacturer CPG, compliance with the PhRMA Code is viewed as a favorable evidentiary or risk management factor. However, other sections indicate the PhRMA Code may be viewed by the OIG as closer to a minimum standard.

The guidance also lists several common or problematic relationships between manufacturers and physicians, including "switching" arrangements, consulting and advisory payments, payments for detailing, business courtesies and other gratuities, and educational and research activities, described more fully below.

- *"Switching" arrangements.* In the Drug Manufacturer CPG, the OIG focuses on questionable switching arrangements (sometimes called "product conversion arrangements") involving pharmaceutical manufacturers offering pharmacies, physicians, or other prescribers cash payments or other benefits *each time* a patient's prescription is changed to the manufacturer's product from a competing product. The OIG acknowledges that "such programs may be permissible in certain managed care arrangements," presumably in the context of market share rebates or therapeutic intervention, but cautions that manufacturers should carefully review such arrangements.
- *Consulting and advisory payments.* The OIG continues to urge caution for pharmaceutical manufacturers engaging physicians as consultants.

---

[274] Adopted on April 18, 2002, the PhRMA Code had an effective date of July 1, 2002. It is available in Appendix I-3.2 on the disk accompanying this volume. For additional information, see PhRMA's Web site at http://www.phrma.org.

The guidance states that fair market value payments to small numbers of physicians for bona fide consulting or advisory services are generally unlikely to raise any significant concern. However, compensation arrangements in which the physician "consultants" are expected to attend meetings or conferences primarily in a passive capacity are suspect, as are certain speaking, research, and preceptor or "shadowing agreements." The OIG further questions the use of health care professionals for marketing, through ghost-written papers or speeches. According to the OIG, full disclosure by physicians of any potential conflicts of interest and of industry sponsorship or affiliation may reduce, but will not necessarily eliminate, the risk of fraud and abuse.

- *Payments for detailing.* The Drug Manufacturer CPG addresses recent practices by some manufacturers to pay physicians for the time the physicians spend listening to sales representatives market pharmaceutical products, including both live presentations and e-detailing arrangements. The OIG identifies such practices as "highly suspect" and "highly susceptible to fraud and abuse," along with compensating physicians to complete minimal paperwork, to access Web sites, to view or listen to marketing information, or to perform "research." The OIG asserts that such activities should be strongly discouraged.

- *Business courtesies and other gratuities.* The final guidance reiterates the OIG's general concerns regarding other forms of remuneration, including gifts and entertainment, which potentially implicate the anti-kickback statute if any one purpose of the arrangement is to generate business for the pharmaceutical company. Stating that each case will depend upon individual facts and circumstances, the OIG recommends that manufacturers comply with the PhRMA Code with respect to these arrangements to substantially reduce a manufacturer's risk of violation of the anti-kickback statute.[275]

- *Educational and research funding.* The Drug Manufacturer CPG lists indicia of questionable research that include the following:
  ○ Research initiated or directed by marketers or sales agents;
  ○ Research that is not transmitted to, or reviewed by, a manufacturer's science component;
  ○ Research that is unnecessarily duplicative or is not needed by the manufacturer for any purpose other than the generation of business; and
  ○ Post-marketing research used as a pretense to promote product.

The OIG recommends that manufacturers develop contracting procedures that clearly separate the awarding of research contracts from marketing or promotion of their products. It acknowledges that, generally, grants or support for educational activities sponsored and organized by medical professional organizations raise little risk of fraud or abuse, provided that the grant or support is not restricted or conditioned with respect to content or faculty.

---

[275]68 Fed. Reg. 23,738. (The Drug Manufacturer CPG does not comment on the differences between the PhRMA code and the AdvaMed code developed for device manufacturers.)

The guidance also notes that manufacturers that act as sponsors of continuing medical education (CME) programs should take steps to ensure that neither they nor their representatives are using CME to generate business for the manufacturer or to influence or control the content of the program.[276] In addition, the Drug Manufacturer CPG reminds manufacturers and sponsors of educational programs to pay attention to the relevant rules and regulations of the Food and Drug Administration. The OIG also recommends that the CME industry's codes of conduct may provide a useful starting point for manufacturers when reviewing their CME agreements.

### v. Relationships With Sales Agents

The Drug Manufacturer CPG notes that the OIG will measure a pharmaceutical manufacturer's commitment to an effective fraud and abuse compliance program by its training and monitoring of its sales force. Moreover, according to the OIG, a compensation arrangement with a sales agent that fits in a safe harbor can still be evidence of a manufacturer's improper intent when evaluating the legality of the manufacturer's relationships with persons in a position to influence business for the manufacturer. Thus, the Drug Manufacturer CPG concludes, the payment of "extraordinary incentive bonuses and expense accounts" for sales agents could lead to an inference that the manufacturer "intentionally motivated the sales force to induce sales through lavish entertainment or other remuneration."[277]

The OIG states that the following should be evaluated for sales agent relationships:

- The amount of compensation;
- The identity of the sales agent engaged in the marketing or promotional activity (e.g., is the agent a "white coat" (health care professional) marketer or otherwise in a position of exceptional influence);
- The sales agent's relationship with his or her audience;
- The nature of the marketing or promotional activity;
- The item or service being promoted or marketed; and
- The composition of the target audience.

### vi. Drug Samples

Generally, providing drug samples can pose a potential risk area for pharmaceutical manufacturers. Manufacturers must comply with the Prescription Drug Marketing Act of 1987 (PDMA), which governs the distribution of drug samples and forbids their sale. In particular, the Drug Manufacturer CPG recommends (i) training the sales force to inform sample recipients that samples may not be sold or billed, (ii) conspicuously labeling individual samples as not

---

[276]The guidance states that CME programs with no industry sponsorship, financing, or affiliation should not raise anti-kickback concerns, although tuition payments by manufacturers (or their representatives) for persons in a position to influence referrals (e.g., physicians or medical students) may raise concerns. 68 Fed. Reg. at 23,742.

[277]*Id.* at 23,739.

for sale, and (iii) including a notice on packing stating that the sample is subject to the PDMA and not for sale.[278]

### 12. Draft Compliance Program Guidance for NIH Grant Recipients

In September 2003, the OIG issued a notice seeking information and recommendations regarding proposed compliance program guidance for recipients of NIH research grants.[279] It issued Draft OIG Compliance Program Guidance for Recipients of PHS Research Awards (draft NIH Grant Recipient CPG) in November 2005.[280] In the draft NIH Grant Recipient CPG, the OIG added a new element to the traditional seven components of a comprehensive compliance program for NIH recipients, i.e., defining the roles and responsibilities within the institution and ensuring the effective assignment of oversight.

In June 2006, the Committee on Science, National Science and Technology Council (NSTC), offered to further the goals of the OIG's draft compliance program "by providing voluntary guidance to all recipients of Federal research funding as they address the prudent management and stewardship of research funds."[281] Specifically, the NSTC "will establish an inter-agency initiative to develop voluntary compliance guidance for recipients of Federal research funding from all agencies across the Federal Government."[282] The draft NIH Grant Recipient CPG was not finalized as of August 2007.

#### a. High Risk Areas for NIH Grant Recipients

The OIG identified three risk areas of particular interest: (1) "time and effort" reporting, including accurate reporting of the commitment of effort by researchers; (2) proper allocation of charges to grant projects; and (3) use of program income.[283]

##### i. Time and Effort Reporting

Because the compensation for the researchers' personal services constitutes a major portion of a project's cost, the OIG cautions that these costs must be accurately apportioned to the appropriate project, particularly for researchers with multiple responsibilities. Otherwise, the recipients of research awards run the risk of overcharging the payor, leading to civil and criminal fraud liability. For example, it would be improper for a researcher to claim that he/she spent 50 percent of his/her time on each of three projects. Similarly, it would be improper to report that a researcher spent 70 percent of his/her time on one project and 50 percent on another. As a result, the OIG recommends the imple-

---

[278]*Id.*

[279]68 Fed. Reg. 52,783 (Sept. 5, 2003).

[280]70 Fed. Reg. 71,312 (Nov. 28, 2005). This document is also available at Appendix I-5 on the disk accompanying this volume.

[281]*NSTC Launches Government-wide Initiative Based on OIG Draft Guidance for HHS Research Grants,* OIG News (June 7, 2006), *available at* http://www.oig.hhs.gov/publications/docs/press/2006/ResearchCPG-finalrelease06072006.pdf.

[282]*Id.*

[283]*Id.*

mentation of effective timekeeping systems to accurately capture the time spent on a particular project.[284]

The OIG further cautions that institutions must accurately and consistently report researchers' "institutional base salary" so that salary costs are properly allocated. Specifically, the institution should report both the clinical and non-clinical work activities of the researchers.[285]

### ii. Proper Allocation of Charges

Because a research institution usually manages many research awards, its accounting systems must be able to distinguish the funding by its source. Further, institutions must monitor for fraudulent practices, such as the banking or trading of award funds among research investigators. For example, the OIG cited the practice of transferring research costs from overspent accounts to underspent accounts to maximize federal reimbursement and avoid refunding unspent funds. The policy rationale for this position is founded not only on OMB Circular A-21 for colleges and universities, but also on the premise that improper allocation draws funds away from other research worthy of federal funding.[286]

### iii. Reporting Financial Support from Other Sources

If an institution fails to report other funding support, the Public Health Service (PHS) cannot determine whether it should fund a particular project. As a result, for the PHS to direct funds to the most worthy projects, it must have a complete assessment of available funding sources. Because an institution is required to report other financial support on its award application, the failure to disclose these sources could lead to a criminal or civil fraud investigation of the institution. Further, because the principal investigator/program director and the application organization both attest to the veracity of the application, a fraudulent claim also brings these parties within the reach of criminal, civil, or administrative penalties.[287]

### 13. Part D Program to Control Fraud, Waste, and Abuse

In February 2006, CMS (not the OIG) issued an updated Chapter 9 of its Prescription Drug Benefit Manual entitled "Part D Program to Control Fraud, Waste and Abuse" (PDBM Chapter 9).[288] Unlike the lengthy voluntary CPGs issued by the OIG described previously in this chapter, PDBM Chapter 9 implements the law and regulations[289] that require Part D plan sponsors (Sponsors) to implement a comprehensive program to control, correct, and prevent fraud, waste, and abuse. PDBM Chapter 9 emphasizes that while Sponsors must

---

[284]70 Fed. Reg. at 71,315.

[285]*Id.*

[286]*Id.* at 71,316.

[287]*Id.*

[288]CMS, Chapter 9—Part D Program to Control Fraud, Waste and Abuse, Prescription Drug Benefit Manual (Apr. 25, 2006), *available at* http://www.cms.hhs.gov/PrescriptionDrugCovContra/Downloads/PDBManual_Chapter9_FWA.pdf [hereinafter PDBM Chapter 9].

[289]42 U.S.C. §1395w-104 and 42 C.F.R. §423.504(b)4)(vi)(H).

implement a comprehensive fraud and abuse program, many of the methods suggested in PDBM Chapter 9 are discretionary. Toward this end, in PDBM Chapter 9, recommendations are denoted by the term "should" and requirements are denoted by "shall" or "must," a distinction reflected in the discussion below. PDBM Chapter 9 also notes its limited applicability to Medicare Advantage (MA) programs and directs MA organizations to consult the Medicare Managed Care Manual concerning Part C benefit issues.[290] While PDBM Chapter 9 is qualitatively different in various ways from the OIG's voluntary compliance guidance documents, its identification of high risk issues and discussion of compliance program criteria nevertheless may be helpful to other health care companies.

### a. *Description of Compliance Program Elements*

After defining numerous terms, PDBM Chapter 9 contains a list of eight elements required for a Part D compliance program, which generally mirror those of other compliance program guidance documents:

(1) Written policies, procedures, and standards of conduct that articulate the Sponsor's commitment to comply with all applicable federal and state standards;

(2) Designation of a compliance officer and compliance committee accountable to senior management;

(3) Effective training and education between the compliance officer and Sponsor employees, subcontractors, agents, and directors involved with the Part D benefit;

(4) Effective means of communication between the compliance officer, employees, contractors, other agents, directors, and the compliance committee;

(5) Enforcement of standards through publicized disciplinary guidelines;

(6) Effective internal monitoring and auditing;

(7) Prompt responses when offenses are detected; and

(8) Execution of corrective actions to resolve underlying problems and prevent future misconduct.[291]

PDBM Chapter 9 contains detailed guidelines on implementing these eight elements. However, certain aspects of these guidelines are particularly notable because they are tailored to Medicare Part D Sponsors or contain standards that differ from those in other compliance program guidance documents. For example:

- *Written policies and procedures and standards of conduct that articulate the Sponsor's commitment to comply with all applicable federal and state standards.*[292] In addition to the numerous other detailed policies and procedures recommended in this area, PDBM Chapter 9 indicates that a Sponsor should have a process to disclose all pricing decisions for

---

[290] *See* http://www.cms.hhs.gov/manuals.

[291] *See* PDBM Chapter 9, §20 at 8.

[292] *Id.* §50.2.1 at 18.

Part D items and services, including all rebates and negotiated price discounts. Further, policies should address the conduct of Pharmacy & Therapeutic (P&T) Committee decisionmaking, e.g., clinical efficacy and the appropriateness of formulary drugs should take precedence over cost considerations.[293]

- *Designation of a compliance officer and compliance committee accountable to senior management.*[294] The Part D compliance officer may be the same individual as the corporate compliance officer, but CMS strongly recommends that the two positions be staffed independently. The Part D compliance officer should report at least quarterly to the corporate compliance officer (if separate), the board of directors and the president/CEO of the Sponsor. Further, the Part D compliance officer should ensure that first tier, downstream, and related entities (collectively, Related Entities)[295] comply with the Medicare Part D sales and marketing requirements.[296] In addition, the Part D compliance officer should ensure that the OIG and GSA exclusion lists have been checked in connection with all Sponsor employees, officers, directors, and managers, in addition to Related Entities.[297]

- *Implementation of training and education between the compliance officer and Sponsor employees, subcontractors, agents, and directors involved with the Part D benefit.*[298] In addition to general compliance training, CMS recommends that Sponsors require Related Entities to have their own specialized compliance training available or participate in Sponsor-organized programs. Areas for specialized training include prescription drug benefit marketing; calculating true out of pocket cost (TrOOP); administration of the exceptions and appeals process; making negotiated prices available to beneficiaries; negotiating pharmacy network agreements; negotiating rebate agreements with drug manufacturers, wholesalers, and other suppliers; and security and authorization instructions for health information technology.[299]

- *Enforcement of standards through publicized disciplinary guidelines.*[300] CMS recommends that Sponsor contracts with Related Entities contain a

---

[293] *Id.* §50.2.1.2 at 21–23.

[294] *Id.* §50.2.2.1 at 25.

[295] A "first tier entity" is a party that has a CMS acceptable written agreement with a Sponsor to provide administrative or health care services (e.g., pharmacy benefit managers (PBMs)). A "downstream entity" is a contracted party below the level of arrangement between the Sponsor and a first tier entity and includes arrangements down to the ultimate provider of health and administrative services (e.g., pharmacies). "Related Entity" means any party related to the Sponsor by common ownership or control that (a) performs some of the sponsor's management functions, (b) provides services to Medicare enrollees, or (c) leases real property or sells materials to the Sponsor at a cost of more than $2,500 during a contract period.

[296] *See* Part D Plan Marketing Guidelines, *available at* http://www.cms.hhs.gov/PrescriptionDrugCovContra/Downloads/FinalMarketingGuidelines.pdf.

[297] PDBM Chapter 9, §50.2.2.1 at 25–26.

[298] *Id.* §50.2.3 at 29.

[299] *Id.* §50.2.3.2 at 30–31.

[300] *Id.* §50.2.5 at 35.

provision stating that violating the Sponsor's standards of conduct may result in termination of the contractual relationship.[301]

- *Implementation of internal monitoring and auditing procedures.*[302] CMS recommends that Sponsors monitor and audit certain activities of their Related Entities. Sponsors are encouraged to use both routine and random auditing and to interview Related Entity staff to assess whether Part D requirements are being satisfied.[303] If the Sponsor allows its Related Entities to perform the auditing, the Sponsor should obtain written assurance that an adequate audit work plan is in effect and that correction action is taken, as appropriate. In addition, the Sponsor should regularly receive these audit reports. Further, the Sponsor should review reports on (i) payment; (ii) drug utilization; (iii) prescribing patterns by physician; and (iv) geographic zip reports.[304]

- *Execution of corrective actions to resolve underlying problems.*[305] Although recognizing that self-reporting potential fraud is voluntary under applicable law, PDBM Chapter 9 notes CMS's belief that such self-reporting is a "critical element" of an effective compliance program.[306] CMS recommends that Sponsors self-report potential fraud that is discovered at the plan level as well as at the Related Entity level to its MEDIC.

### b. Medicare Drug Integrity Contractors (MEDICs)

PDBM Chapter 9 discusses the responsibilities of private contractors, called Medicare Drug Integrity Contractors (MEDICs), to help CMS curb Part D fraud, waste, and abuse. The primary role of a MEDIC is to identify and investigate potential Part D fraud and abuse, develop such cases for referral to law enforcement agencies, coordinate with these agencies, and audit Part D Sponsors and subcontractor operations.[307] Although CMS notes that it may include additional MEDIC requirements later, PDBM Chapter 9 describes numerous potential MEDIC activities drawn from the MEDICs Umbrella Statement of Work.[308]

MEDIC duties regarding prevention include the following:

- Reviewing bids for Part D participation;
- Reviewing the fraud and abuse components of compliance plans;
- Helping CMS develop a list of historically problematic entities that require future monitoring;
- Using data systems to evaluate inappropriate activity;

---

[301] *Id.* §50.2.6 at 37.

[302] *Id.* §50.2.6.1.3 at 41.

[303] *Id.* §50.2.6 at 37.

[304] *Id.* §50.2.6.1.3 at 41.

[305] *Id.* §50.2.8.2 at 50.

[306] *Id.* §50.2.8.2 at 50.

[307] *Id.* §30 at 10.

[308] *Id.* n.8, citing CMS RFP CMS-2006–0017, Medicare Prescription Drug Benefit (Part D), Medicare Drug Integrity Contractor (May 25, 2005).

- Educating entities about potential fraud, waste, and abuse; and
- Facilitating intermediate sanctions when appropriate.

Some MEDIC duties regarding detection include the following:

- Conducting audits and complaint investigations;
- Investigating aberrant behavior and referring cases to law enforcement or to CMS for administrative action;
- Conducting data analysis to identify outliers indicating potential fraud, waste, and abuse;
- Identifying potential overpayments; and
- Supporting enforcement efforts to investigate potential fraud and abuse.

Further, among other audit topics, the MEDIC also may perform one-third audits of various types of data (e.g., reinsurance and risk corridor costs; low-income, direct, and risk corridor subsidy payments; administrative costs and allocation; rebates; formulary; data related to claims and TrOOP; and copayments) as well as audits of fraud and abuse compliance plans, the P&T Committee, actuarial equivalence attestation, and Sponsor oversight of its contractors.[309]

### c. Part D Sponsor Accountability and Oversight

Although various compliance functions may be delegated by a Sponsor to others, the Sponsor may not delegate the compliance functions of a Part D compliance officer and the compliance committee.[310] Moreover, even when a Sponsor appropriately delegates some of its responsibilities to Related Entities, CMS will hold the Sponsor ultimately responsible.[311]

In addition, where a contract requires a Related Entity to generate data for submission to CMS, the entity must certify that the data is complete, accurate, and truthful.[312] One provision in this section of PDBM Chapter 9 also cautions Sponsors about preemption of certain state laws by those federal laws and regulations related to Part D.[313]

### d. Risk Factors for Part D Plans

Section 70 of PDBM Chapter 9 identifies numerous potential risk areas based on the type of entity involved. As summarized below, these risk factors include, but are not limited to, those listed below.

---

[309]*Id.* at 11–12.

[310]*Id.* §40.1 at 15.

[311]CMS regulations require that contracts with Related Entities include specific provisions relating to inspections, Medicare enrollee protection, Sponsor accountability, delegation, and the retention of records. For example, a contract must allow the Sponsor to either revoke the delegated functions or specify other remedies in the event that CMS or a Sponsor determines a Related Entity's contracted work to be unsatisfactory. §40 at 14; *see also* 42 C.F.R. §§423.505(e)(2); (i); (j).

[312]PDBM Chapter 9, §40.2 at 15–16.

[313]*Id.* §40 at 14.

### i. Part D Plan Sponsors

Risk factors for Part D plan sponsors[314] include the following:

- Failure to provide medically necessary services;
- Marketing schemes (e.g., offering beneficiaries a cash inducement to enroll, unsolicited door-to-door marketing, requiring up-front premiums, misrepresenting the product being marketed, use of unlicensed agents, and improper beneficiary enrollment);
- Improper bid submissions (e.g., over- or underestimating the bid to manipulate risk corridors or payments);
- Payments for excluded drugs (e.g., payment for a noncovered item);
- Multiple billing of a single item;
- Noncompendium payments (e.g., payments for drugs that are not for a "medically accepted indication");
- Inappropriate formulary decisions (e.g., when costs take priority over clinical efficacy and appropriateness);
- Improper enrollment/disenrollment;
- Incorrectly handling the appeals process;
- Adverse selection (e.g., improperly using illness profiles or other discriminating factors to select or deny beneficiaries);
- False information;
- Delinquent reimbursement (following retroactive low income subsidy determination);
- Excessive premiums;
- Inaccuracies in eligibility or coordination of benefits;
- Incorrect calculation of TrOOP;
- Inaccurate data submission (e.g., inaccurate prescription drug event or quarterly data);
- Catastrophic coverage manipulation;
- Failure to disclose or misrepresentation of rebates, discounts, or price concessions;
- Bait and switch pricing (e.g., inducing a patient to sign up for a drug that is later removed from the formulary); and
- Manipulation of low-income subsidy enrollees.

### ii. PBMs

Risk factors for PBMs[315] include the following:

- Prescription drug switching (e.g., improperly switching a beneficiary from one drug to another or influencing the prescriber);
- Unlawful remuneration (e.g., the PBM receives unlawful payment to steer beneficiaries or for formulary placement);
- Inappropriate formulary decisions;

---

[314] *Id.* §70.1.1 at 54–57.

[315] *Id.* §70.1.2 at 57. If a Sponsor operates its own PBM, as is often the case, these risk factors will apply to the Sponsor as well.

- Prescription drug splitting or shorting (e.g., providing less than the prescribed quantity or splitting a prescription to receive additional dispensing fees); and
- Failure to offer negotiated prices.

### *iii. Pharmacies*

Risk factors for pharmacies[316] include the following:

- Inappropriate billing practices (e.g., billing for nonexistent prescriptions, billing multiple payors inappropriately, billing for a proprietary drug when dispensing a generic drug, billing for noncovered items, billing when prescriptions are not picked up, billing based on gang visits, inappropriate use of the "dispense as written" code, diversion, prescription splitting);
- Prescription drug shorting;
- Bait and switch pricing;
- Prescription forging or altering;
- Dispensing expired or adulterated drugs;
- Prescription refill errors;
- Illegal remuneration schemes (e.g., whether paid to induce a patient to switch drugs, to influence a prescriber, or to steer a patient to a particular Plan);
- TrOOP manipulation (e.g., to push a beneficiary through the donut hole, or keep a beneficiary within the donut hole); and
- Failure to offer negotiated prices.

### *iv. Prescribers*

Risk factors for prescribers[317] include the following:

- Illegal remuneration schemes;
- Prescription drug switching;
- Script mills (*e.g.*, when a prescriber writes a high volume of prescriptions for drugs that are not medically necessary, often for beneficiaries who are not the prescriber's own patients);
- Provision of false information (in order to justify coverage);
- Theft of prescriber's DEA number or prescription pad (including the theft of login/authentication information related to e-prescribing).

### *v. Wholesalers*

Risk factors for wholesalers[318] include the following:

- Dealing in counterfeit and adulterated drugs through black and gray market purchases (e.g., fake, diluted, expired, or illegally imported drugs);

---

[316]*Id.* §70.1.3 at 58–59.
[317]*Id.* §70.1.4 at 59.
[318]*Id.* §70.1.5 at 60.

- Diverters (e.g., brokers who take control of discounted drugs and sell them at a mark up); and
- Inappropriate documentation of pricing information.

### vi. Manufacturers

Risk factors for manufacturers[319] include the following:

- Lack of integrity of data to establish payment and/or determine reimbursement (e.g., manufacturer fails to maintain accurate and complete pricing information documentation);
- Kickbacks, inducements, and other illegal remuneration (e.g., inappropriate marketing, discounts, product support services, education grants, or research funding);
- Formulary and formulary support activities (e.g., improper relationships with formulary committee members, payments to PBMs);
- Inappropriate relationships with physicians (e.g., switching arrangements, incentives to promote prescription of medically unnecessary drugs, and improper inducements such as (i) entertainment or other incentives; (ii) consulting and detailing payments; (iii) business courtesies; and (iv) educational or research funding);
- Illegal off-label promotion (through marketing, financial incentives, or other types of promotion); and
- Illegal use of free samples (e.g., providing free samples to physicians expecting them to bill federal health care programs).

### vii. Medicare Beneficiaries

Risk factors for Medicare beneficiaries[320] include the following:

- Misrepresentation of status (in order to obtain Part D coverage);
- Identity theft;
- TrOOP manipulation (e.g., beneficiary tries to push through the donut hole to prematurely obtain catastrophic coverage);
- Forging or altering prescriptions;
- Prescription diversion and inappropriate use;
- Resale of drugs on the black market;
- Prescription stockpiling;
- Doctor shopping;
- Improper coordination of benefits; and
- Marketing schemes.

In addition to these risk areas, PDBM Chapter 9 outlines four additional areas of concern that CMS has taken steps to address: (1) the coordination of benefits with other prescription drug benefit programs, including state pharmacy assistance programs; (2) drugs and devices that are vulnerable to counterfeiting; (3) preventing payment for drugs not covered under Part D; and (4)

---

[319]*Id.* §70.1.6 at 60–61.
[320]*Id.* §70.1.7 at 61–62.

coordinating the potential for duplicate coverage for drugs under Medicare Parts A, B, and D.[321]

There is a lengthy discussion of Part B and Part D coverage issues in PDBM Chapter 9. Because of the potential for inappropriate overlapping coverage under several parts of Medicare, CMS suggests that Sponsors have procedures to properly process drug claims to the appropriate Medicare payor. Determining whether a drug is covered under Part B or Part D will generally depend on the context. CMS believes there should be little difficulty in making these determinations under most circumstances because drugs that are provided in the context of a service or procedure will usually be covered under Part B, not Part D. However, in some situations pharmacists or infusion providers will have to determine whether to bill Part B or Part D, and Sponsors should confirm that the billing is done correctly. The high risk issues identified by CMS in this area include home infusion, duplicate billing, crossover drugs, and differential copayments.[322]

PDBM Chapter 9 concludes with an Appendix that contains a list of resources that may be useful in developing and implementing a Part D compliance program.[323]

## IV. Practical Issues in Developing and Implementing a Compliance Program

There are many practical issues involved in a provider's decision to develop and implement a corporate compliance program. The first step in developing a program should be the selection of a corporate compliance officer. The compliance officer then can oversee the development and implementation of the full program, including the adoption of written policies, procedures, and ethical standards. The compliance officer also should oversee the selection of a compliance committee and other compliance personnel, as needed; education and training of the organization's employees; the establishment of a compliance hotline; and the implementation of periodic internal audits and monitoring systems.

### A. Selecting a Compliance Officer

The selection of a competent compliance officer is vital for several reasons. A compliance officer will oversee the development, implementation, operation, and appropriate modification of the program. Further, employees will identify the compliance officer with the compliance program. For this reason, it is important to choose a compliance officer who already is widely respected by the organization's employees or who can engender their respect. In addition, a compliance officer should have sound judgment and be able to work well with others throughout the organization. It is also very helpful if the

---

[321]*Id.* §70.2 at 63–64.

[322]*Id.* §70.2.4 at 64–66.

[323]*Id.* Appendix A: Resources at 69–70.

compliance officer has substantive knowledge about the company's operations as well as the applicable legal standards.

If possible, depending on the size and resources of the organization, the position of compliance officer should be full time. If an employee has compliance-officer responsibilities added to his or her existing duties, the organization faces the risk that the compliance program could become a low priority. In addition, such dual responsibilities could send the message to the organization's employees, as well as to the government, that the provider is not serious about its compliance program.

The compliance officer should have direct access to members of the organization's senior management and board of directors. It is best if the compliance officer reports directly to the CEO rather than to the general counsel or the chief financial officer. The compliance officer should be someone with knowledge of the industry and the organization's operations, because compliance is, at its core, about operations. The compliance officer does not have to be an attorney. In fact, unless he or she has substantial experience with health care operations matters, an attorney may not be the most effective compliance officer.

The OIG has recommended in various compliance program documents that the compliance officer should *not* be the organization's general counsel or chief financial officer. However, this recommendation is not a legally binding requirement. The American Bar Association has taken an opposing position and has supported having the general counsel serve as the compliance officer.

Depending on the size of the organization, the compliance officer also may head a "compliance team." Such a compliance team often consists of employees in affiliated entities who supervise the operation of the compliance program in those entities and report back to the chief compliance officer.

## B. Developing a Corporate Compliance Program

It is particularly important for a compliance program to be well written and understandable by all employees. It should contain both substance and structure. Accordingly, the program should include policies and procedures on the basic issues central or problematic to the provider and its particular industry segment. The OIG's compliance program guidance documents provide detailed descriptions of risk areas that the government expects to be controlled through the use of written policies and procedures. At a minimum, a health care compliance program should include policies and procedures on proper billing; the anti-kickback statute, the Stark law (where applicable) and other fraud and abuse laws; Medicare and Medicaid (and private payor) reimbursement issues; and conflicts of interest. However, because new regulations are frequently issued, and new problem areas may be identified by the government or within the company at issue, the compliance program cannot be static and should evolve to meet the provider's changing needs. The compliance officer should play a key role in overseeing periodic amendments and revisions to the written program. Many companies integrate health care along with other issues such as Sarbanes-Oxley, employment, antitrust, environmental and/or OSHA into a comprehensive compliance program for the company.

Because compliance at its core involves operations, the preparation of the compliance program should include input from key employees from across the provider's entire operations. Soliciting input from all areas of operations also has the added benefit of helping to ensure that the final compliance program will have broad support from within the organization, which is essential for its success.

Trade associations often have developed model compliance programs for their particular industries. In addition, there are various compliance consultants available who will, for a fee, help a provider design and implement a compliance program. Other consultants provide draft programs to providers. The use of such form programs can be very helpful, so long as the provider realizes that the simple adoption of a form program, without more, would not be considered to constitute an "effective compliance program" by the government. It can be useful to start the process with a form program, but it is necessary to individualize as much as possible to the concerns and issues of the particular provider. It is also critical that senior management and the Board be actively involved in the development and operation of a company's compliance program. Such high level involvement is essential to create a "culture of compliance" that employees will take seriously.

## C. Education and Training

Once the compliance officer has been appointed and a written compliance program drafted and adopted, the next step is presenting the compliance program to the organization's employees, to affiliated physicians (and possibly to contractors as well). The initial presentation and training should be conducted on site at the provider's facility or facilities. To ensure that training sessions are small enough to allow participants the opportunity to ask questions and make comments, several sessions may need to be scheduled. In addition, to reach "graveyard shift" employees, some training sessions may have to be conducted at odd hours or on weekends.

Despite a company's best efforts, it may be impossible to reach all employees and consultants (e.g., per-diem employees and independent contractors). In such cases, the best (or possibly only) way of presenting the compliance program to those persons may be mailing (or e-mailing) a copy of the written compliance program to their home address and requiring that they sign and return a certification stating that they have received a copy of the written program, that they have read it, and that they agree to comply with the compliance program and to report any suspected fraud or abuse to the compliance officer or to the organization's compliance hotline.

It is crucial to stress the importance of the compliance program to all employees. Many employees may be jaded, having lived through many other corporate initiatives. It is important to impress on them that this is a serious commitment, not just the fad of the moment. A company's serious commitment to the program can be demonstrated by the active involvement of upper management and by selecting a compliance officer who is well respected by other employees. The education and training process is not over once the program is presented to an organization's employees. Follow-up sessions at least annually should reinforce the original message and address any new questions or concerns.

Part of the training should, of course, include a requirement that each employee sign a certification stating that he or she (1) has received training,

(2) will comply with the organization's compliance program, (3) is not aware of any compliance problems at the current time, except as described on the form, and (4) will report any suspected misconduct to the hotline or to a member of the compliance team. In addition, the provider may wish to consider adopting a policy of conducting exit interviews with departing employees, so as to give those employees a final opportunity to report any compliance or ethical problems. These steps will go a long way toward discouraging *qui tam* lawsuits and, in the event of an investigation, can be cited to the government as evidence that the organization took compliance issues seriously and gave its employees many opportunities to report fraud and abuse.

## D. Budgeting

One practical issue that often arises is how much a provider should budget for the implementation and operation of an effective compliance program. The government's position is that adequate resources must be devoted to compliance, no matter the cost. The Health Care Compliance Association frequently surveys organizations on various aspects of their compliance budgets and this data may provide helpful benchmarks.[324]

The OIG has stated consistently that compliance programs can be tailored to fit an organization's resources. Therefore, smaller organizations may find that a less formal compliance program may be more appropriate from a financial perspective. Nevertheless, sufficient resources of time, personnel, and funds should be devoted to ensure that the compliance program will be effective. Generally, this will require, at a minimum, budgeting for the compliance officer's salary (full or part time), general and specialized training for employees,[325] and several annual audits of high-risk areas.[326] It is also advisable to establish a compliance fund that can be used to pay for investigations, updating policies as necessary, or other compliance-related needs that may arise each year.[327]

## E. Compliance Hotline

A key component of most compliance programs is the establishment of a hotline or other means of communication that employees can use to report anonymously suspected fraud or abuse. Hotlines are important for several reasons. First, the government views hotlines or similar means of communication as an essential element of an effective compliance program. Second, hotlines provide a clear mechanism for reporting fraud or abuse. If there is no internal hotline, employees' frustration with the organization and lack of re-

---

[324]*Available at* http://www.hcca-info.org/Content/NavigationMenu/ComplianceResources/Surveys/default.htm.

[325]Computer training may be a viable and less expensive option, particularly if it includes follow-up testing to ensure that it is successful.

[326]Internal audits will likely be less expensive although they may have less credibility than external audits if questions arise.

[327]Larger organizations will be expected to have more comprehensive compliance budgets.

sponsiveness to their concerns may lead them to call the OIG's hotline or file a *qui tam* lawsuit instead.

To be meaningful and useful, the hotline should be accessible 24 hours per day. No effort should be made to track callers (unless they ask to be kept informed). Employees should be reassured that the hotline does not have any type of caller identification feature or other mechanism for identifying callers, and that the company enforces its nonretaliation policy. The existence of the hotline should be publicized within the organization regularly, perhaps through the organization's newsletter or on its bulletin board.

The compliance officer or other employees who monitor the hotline should log each call carefully and assign each call a tracking number so that the caller can call back, refer to the tracking number, and obtain information on what follow-up steps were taken while remaining anonymous. The compliance officer or another member of the compliance team also should immediately refer information on incoming calls to the proper person within the organization for follow-up. Of course, the compliance officer also should ensure that any needed follow-up is actually taken and that all actions taken in response to a call, as well as information on the final resolution of the call, are properly documented.

Companies should expect most calls to be of a human resources nature (e.g., discrimination or sexual harassment). To minimize the possibility of hotline abuse, the compliance team should educate employees as to what types of calls are—and are not—appropriate. In addition, the provider must achieve a workable balance between its need to encourage use of the hotline to report suspected fraud or abuse, no matter how minor, and its desire to discourage frivolous calls.

## F. Compliance Helpline

The compliance team also may consider adopting a compliance "helpline." In this context, a helpline is a toll-free number, separate from the compliance hotline, that employees can call for assistance regarding particular compliance concerns (e.g., billing issues). The helpline could have a recorded message instead of a live monitor, but any inquiries should be referred immediately to the compliance officer or another member of the compliance team and then assigned to the appropriate person or persons within the organization for resolution. Because of the nature of the questions and the need for follow-up information, the compliance officer probably would want to encourage employees making helpline calls to reveal their identities. However, the organization should also be willing to accept anonymous calls, because some employees may be reluctant to ask questions if they have to reveal their identities. Some employees may be afraid that too many calls to the helpline would make them appear ignorant or would otherwise reflect poorly on them in their performance evaluations.

## G. Auditing and Monitoring

Any discussion of the practicalities of implementing a corporate compliance program would not be complete without mention of the problems associated with auditing and monitoring. Periodic internal audits are an integral component of the government's compliance guidances. Practically speaking, in the area of Medicare billing regulations, there is tremendous value in getting claims right when they are first filed. Providers therefore should consider auditing claims *before* they are submitted. Problematic claims can be corrected, and there will be no violations to report.

Many audits and reviews, however, will uncover *past* illegal activity or billing errors. Although the government's compliance guidances encourage such audits, notably absent from the government's discussions is any mention of how a provider is expected to conduct internal audits and maintain privilege or confidentiality for the audit results. The answer is that routine self-reviews probably should be part of an organization's standard business operations and do not need the protection of the attorney-client privilege. More serious internal investigations or external reviews of a particular problem, on the other hand, should be structured so as to preserve the attorney-client privilege where possible.

### 1. Attorney-Client Privilege

In conducting any internal audit or review, a provider should consider whether, and to what extent, it wants the attorney-client privilege to apply.[328] If an internal review is conducted by an attorney, or under the direction of an attorney, then the attorney-client privilege and work-product doctrine generally will apply to all conversations and correspondence produced by the review, assuming that dissemination of these materials is limited to those with a need to know.[329] Disclosure of confidential information constitutes a waiver of the privilege, and the waiver extends to all materials on the same subject matter. Agreeing to allow the government to review an audit report may also waive the privilege with respect to all aspects of that review.[330] This issue can become particularly sensitive during a government investigation if the government asks a company to demonstrate its "good faith" by sharing investigation findings

---

[328] A brief reminder of what constitutes attorney-client privilege and attorney work-product doctrine is in order. The attorney-client privilege applies to confidential communications between lawyer and client, made for the purpose of obtaining legal advice of any kind. Fausek v. White, 965 F.2d 126 (6th Cir. 1992). Its purpose is to encourage full and frank communications between attorneys and their clients and thereby promote broader public interests. Upjohn Co. v. United States, 449 U.S. 383 (1981). The attorney-client privilege protects confidential communications both to and from counsel. *In re* Grand Jury Subpoena, 765 F.2d 1014 (11th Cir. 1985); Colton v. United States, 306 F.2d 633 (2d Cir. 1962).

In contrast, the attorney work-product doctrine protects from disclosure an attorney's notes, materials, and mental process prepared in anticipation of litigation. It is separate and distinct from the attorney-client privilege. United States v. Nobles, 422 U.S. 225 (1975). The Supreme Court has distinguished between two types of work product. "Fact" work product is the evidence or materials gathered by an attorney. It is afforded less protection than the second type of work product, "opinion" work product, which consists of an attorney's mental impressions, opinions, and conclusions. Hickman v. Taylor, 329 U.S. 495 (1947).

[329] It is also important that the attorney involved in the investigation be acting in his or her legal capacity. The courts have sometimes withheld privilege from investigations conducted by in-house counsel who may be perceived as acting as a business advisor, rather than as a lawyer, in certain contexts.

[330] *In re* Martin Marietta Corp., 856 F.2d 619 (4th Cir. 1988); Weil v. Investment Indicators Research Mgmt., 647 F.2d 18 (9th Cir. 1981).

and other potentially privileged materials. Fortunately, the Department of Justice McNulty memorandum has restricted government efforts to require waiver of attorney-client privilege.[331]

The protection of attorney-client privilege should not necessarily be used for all reviews. Routine compliance reviews do not need attorney-client privilege protection and should be part of the ongoing monitoring of business operations. Nonprivileged routine reviews can be conducted as part of an organization's financial audit or part of its periodic internal review program. In conducting routine internal audits, it is important that the organization avoid reaching unfounded legal conclusions. It is equally important to know when to stop an internal review and seek counsel. It also is important to avoid having reviews conducted by the same persons responsible for the operations being reviewed.

### 2. External/Expert Reviews

In some cases, a provider will want to retain an expert to conduct a more extensive review than it may be able to do on its own. Outside consultants may also be used because their independence and/or experience can lend the audit more credibility. In such cases, the expert should be retained through legal counsel so as to have all communications with the expert subject to the attorney-client privilege. The terms of the engagement of the expert also should be structured so that the expert's work product will be privileged. The scope of the work should be defined clearly before the expert begins his or her review. These parameters should include such features as time frame, type of error or activity, personnel, type of program (e.g., Medicaid, Medicare, private insurer), and geographic (i.e., if more than one location is owned or managed by the provider).

### 3. Expert Findings

If an outside consultant or expert discovers errors, it is important that the organization immediately create a work plan to implement corrective action. All corrective actions taken should be documented, and, if the review uncovered billing errors, the amount of repayments and methods for restitution should be established.

### 4. Types of Reviews

There are two major types of reviews: (1) current audits, and (2) forensic audits. Current audits are exactly what they sound like: audits covering the provider's current practices and billing policies and procedures. Current reviews help ensure that billing processes are effective and that submitted bills are accurate. Forensic audits, on the other hand, cover past activities and practices.

---

[331]Memorandum from Deputy Attorney General Paul McNulty to U.S. Attorneys *re* Principles of Federal Prosecution of Business Organizations (Dec. 13, 2006), *available at* http://www.usdoj.gov/dag/speeches/2006/mcnulty_memo.pdf and included as Appendix C-4 on the disk accompanying this volume. See additional discussion of the McNulty Memorandum in Chapter 1 (Baumann, An Introduction to Health Care Fraud and Abuse), at Section I.C.

Forensic audits can determine if there have been overpayments or underpayments. Forensic audits typically are not part of the annual audit schedule absent some indication of a problem. These types of reviews can take place in response to a government investigation, in response to the announcement of a national enforcement program, or in response to a hotline "tip" or other suggestion of potential compliance problems.

## 5. Disclosure Obligations and Repayments

If an audit uncovers significant problems or fraud, the provider is faced with making a decision about what to do with that information. The provider may wonder if it is under an obligation to disclose the fraud or mistakes, and whether it would be better to keep silent.[332] These are extremely complex issues and the following discussion can only briefly summarize some of the relevant issues.

If a provider becomes aware that it has received an overpayment, the government takes the position that the company is legally obligated to refund or at least disclose the overpayment.[333] In addition, the *Provider Reimbursement Manual* requires a provider to amend its cost report to correct "material" errors.[334] Finally, the OIG's model compliance program guidance suggests that a company report suspected misconduct within 60 days after determining there is credible evidence of a potential violation of law.

As indicated above in the discussion of various compliance program documents, an overpayment generally should be returned to the appropriate payor through normal channels, absent evidence of fraud. If illegal conduct is to be reported, the OIG or the local office of the U.S. Attorney may be the best place to disclose the activity. However, the provider also should consider promptly refunding any overpayment to the appropriate payor rather than waiting for discussions with law enforcement authorities to conclude. Deciding which (and how many) government agencies to contact if there is a potential violation can be a key part of a company's defense strategy. This decision may impact the company's ability to obtain a global settlement, and thus should be carefully evaluated.

If a provider decides to make a disclosure, it should report the information in such a way as to minimize the risk that the report will waive the attorney-client privilege. It is important to keep in mind that the attorney-client privilege is applicable only to communications made to an attorney, not to the underlying

---

[332]The Joint Commission on Accreditation of Healthcare Organizations (JCAHO) also encourages certain disclosures. JCAHO's "sentinel event" policy is designed to promote self-reporting and examination of the root causes of medical errors. Accredited health care organizations that report sentinel events to JCAHO within five business days and submit a thorough root-cause analysis and action plan within an additional 30 days will not be placed on JCAHO's publicly disclosed Accreditation Watch. For more information on the JCAHO's sentinel event policy, see the JCAHO Web site *at* http://www.jointcommission.org/SentinelEvents/.

[333]*See* 42 U.S.C. §1320a-7b(a)(3), which prohibits the knowing failure to disclose the occurrence of any event affecting the provider's "initial or continued right to any such benefit or payment . . . with an intent fraudulently to secure such benefit or payment either in greater amount than is due or when no such benefit or payment is authorized." Several legal commentators have taken issue with the government's interpretation of this provision.

[334]*See* PROVIDER REIMBURSEMENT MANUAL §2931.1.

facts. Similarly, the attorney work-product privilege applies only to conclusions drawn by an attorney from the underlying facts, not to the facts themselves. Therefore, a provider should be careful to disclose only the relevant facts, not the process or conclusions of an internal investigation. When making a report, a provider also should refund any overpayment and report what corrective action was taken.

The OIG's Provider Self-Disclosure Protocol (the Protocol)[335] provides another means to disclose serious compliance violations to the government. The OIG specifically recommends that the Protocol only be used for matters that potentially violate criminal, civil, or administrative laws. According to the OIG, overpayments or errors that do not suggest violations of law should be brought to the attention of the appropriate government program contractor instead.[336] Use of the Protocol is not mandatory, and it has not been used extensively because many providers do not think its benefits outweigh the potential disadvantages. Nevertheless, disclosing through the Protocol may be an important option to consider in certain cases, particularly in light of the OIG's April 2006 Open Letter,[337] which offered providers incentives to disclose certain potential Stark and anti-kickback violations.

## H. Recent Compliance Developments at the State Level

California enacted a drug marketing practices law in 2004.[338] The statute applies to pharmaceutical companies that are engaged in the production, preparation, propagation, compounding, conversion, or processing of dangerous drugs. However, the law goes on to broadly define "dangerous drug" as follows: "any drug or device that may be dispensed only by prescription."[339] The legislation mandates that manufacturers adopt comprehensive compliance programs (compliance plans) governing marketing practices, to be made publicly available via the Internet and other means. Moreover, the law specifies that the mandated compliance plans must conform to the PhRMA Code and the OIG's Drug Manufacturer CPG. Specifically, the California law requires a pharmaceutical company to adopt and update a compliance plan that includes policies on interactions with health care professionals and sets limits on gifts and incentives to medical or health professionals. The program must include a specific annual dollar limit on gifts, promotional materials, or items or activities that the pharmaceutical company may give or otherwise provide. The manufacturer may exclude from the limits drug samples intended for free distribution to patients, financial support for continuing medical education forums, financial support for certain scholarships, and payment for legitimate professional services (e.g.,

---

[335] *See* 63 Fed. Reg. 58,399 *et seq.* (Oct. 30, 1998).

[336] *Id.* at 58,400.

[337] Open Letter to Health Care Providers (Apr. 24, 2006), *available at* http://www.oig.hhs.gov/Fraud/openletters.html. The Open Letter is also discussed in Chapter 1 (Baumann, An Introduction to Health Care Fraud and Abuse), at Section II.A.6.

[338] CAL. HEALTH & SAFETY CODE §§119400 *et seq.*

[339] The impact of the reference to "devices" in a law that generally refers to drugs and pharmaceuticals is unclear at this point.

consulting) if such services reflect fair market value and are provided in a manner that conforms to the PhRMA Code and the Drug Manufacturer CPG. Compliance plans are to be updated within six months of changes being made to either the PhRMA Code or the OIG guidance. The manufacturer must annually declare, in writing, that it is in compliance with both its compliance plan and the California law; must make its compliance plan and written declaration of compliance available to the public on the company's Web site; and must provide a toll-free telephone number which can be called to obtain copies of the program and declaration. The law became operative on July 1, 2005.

# V. Conclusion

Providers must recognize that the adoption of a corporate compliance program is not without risk. There is no guarantee that a compliance program will prevent compliance problems, whistleblowers, or government investigations and enforcement. The very operation of the compliance program, especially the auditing and monitoring functions, may result in the identification and disclosure of problems that would not otherwise have been discovered. While compliance programs can discourage *qui tam* lawsuits by providing conscientious, ethical employees with an internal means of reporting fraud or abuse, on the other hand, a compliance program could, through its training sessions and internal investigations, actually be educating potential *qui tam* plaintiffs.

Furthermore, because it will uncover and likely result in punishment for certain employees for violations of the organization's policies, procedures, and ethical standards, an effective compliance program undoubtedly will result in increased litigation for the organization. Some employees may even be terminated, and discharged employees tend to sue. Similarly, the compliance-monitoring program may uncover contracts that do not fit within applicable exceptions to the Stark law or that otherwise present an unacceptable level of risk. The organization's decision to terminate or modify such contracts may, in some instances, lead to litigation.

Nevertheless, in light of the government's clear expectation that every health care company have an effective corporate compliance program, the risks of *not* adopting a compliance program appear to far outweigh the risks of adopting one. As with most areas of corporate life, the keys to minimizing risk and obtaining maximum benefits from a compliance program are in thorough preparation and detailed execution of the program.

It is a fact of modern health care that no provider likely is in total compliance in all aspects of its operations throughout each day. This state of affairs arises from several factors, including the tremendous increase in the number and complexity of federal regulations affecting the health care industry over the past decade. This complex regulatory structure presents significant challenges for any organization in both its operations and claims submission functions. As the size of an organization grows, compliance issues arise simply from the number of people receiving services each day and the number of employees delivering those services or submitting claims related to such services.

An effective corporate compliance program acknowledges this fact and strives to prevent problems in the first instance, and then detects and appropriately deals with problems when they do occur. Moreover, even when government agencies become involved in an investigation or prosecution, where an effective corporate compliance program is in place, the likelihood that severe sanctions will be sought, e.g., through criminal prosecution or the exclusion process, generally is reduced significantly.

# 8

# Potential Liabilities for Directors and Officers of Health Care Organizations*

*Leigh Walton, Angela Humphreys, and Clevonne Jacobs, Bass, Berry & Sims PLC, Nashville, Tennessee.

# I. Introduction

The health care industry has witnessed exponential growth in the number of government investigations and enforcement actions since the late 1990s. For fiscal year 1999, the U.S. Department of Health and Human Services (HHS) reported the following:

- HHS's Office of Inspector General (OIG) participated in 942 prosecutions or settlements related to health care fraud,

- 396 defendants were convicted of health care fraud-related crimes,
- federal prosecutors filed criminal charges in 371 new health care fraud cases and initiated 91 new civil health care fraud cases,
- HHS excluded 2,976 individuals and entities from participation in federal health care programs for fraud or abuse, and
- the federal government won or negotiated approximately $524 million in judgments, settlements, and administrative penalties in health care cases and proceedings.[1]

Seven years later, the statistics reported by HHS demonstrate the government's continued focus on health care fraud and abuse. For fiscal year 2006,

- HHS excluded 3,425 individuals and entities from participation in health care programs for fraud or abuse involving federal health care programs and/or their beneficiaries,
- the OIG participated in 472 criminal actions against individuals or entities that engaged in crimes against departmental programs, and 272 civil actions, including False Claims Act and unjust enrichment suits filed in federal district court, Civil Monetary Penalties Law settlements, and administrative recoveries related to provider self-disclosure matters, and
- the OIG reported expected recoveries of nearly $2.4 billion, with $789.4 million in audit receivables, and $1.6 billion in investigative receivables.[2]

The amount of fines and penalties imposed for health care fraud or abuse can be staggering, and liability is being imposed on individuals, as well as on corporations. For example, in October 2001, TAP Pharmaceutical Products, Inc. (TAP) agreed to pay a record $875 million in criminal and civil penalties to resolve allegations of health care fraud, including a $290 million criminal fine, one of the highest criminal fines ever imposed on any health care company.[3] In 2003, the government recovered $1.7 billion in criminal and civil penalties from HCA, Inc. (formerly known as Columbia/HCA and HCA–The Healthcare Company) as a result of a series of settlement agreements entered into between December 2000 and June 2003 related to allegations of cost report fraud and payment of kickbacks to physicians, together representing by far the largest

---

[1] *See* U.S. Dep't of Health & Human Servs. & U.S. Dep't of Justice, HHS/DOJ Health Care Fraud and Abuse Control Program Annual Report for Fiscal Year 1999 (Jan. 2000), *available at* http://www.oig.hhs.gov/reading/hcfac/HCFAC%20Annual%20Report%20FY%201999.htm; U.S. Dep't of Health & Human Servs., Office of Inspector General, Semiannual Report to Congress Apr. 1, 1999–Sept. 30, 1999, *available at* http://www.oig.hhs.gov/reading/semiannual/1999/99semif.pdf.

[2] *See* U.S. Dep't of Health & Human Servs. Office of Inspector Gen., Semiannual Report to Congress Apr. 1, 2006–Sept. 30, 2006, *available at* http://www.oig.hhs.gov/publications/docs/semiannual/2006/semiannual%20final%20FY%202006.pdf.

[3] *See* U.S. Department of Justice, Press Release, *TAP Pharmaceutical Products, Inc. and Seven Others Charged with Health Care Crimes; Company Agrees to Pay $875 Million to Settle Claims* (Oct. 3, 2001), *available at* http://www.usdoj.gov/opa/pr/2001/October/513civ.htm. Six TAP managers, including the former Vice President of Sales, were indicted on conspiracy charges and four physicians pleaded guilty to health care fraud. Massachusetts U.S. Attorney Michael J. Sullivan was quoted as stating that the criminal fines and indictments in the TAP case send "a very strong signal" that companies best police their employees' conduct and deal strongly with those who would gain sales at the expense of federal health care programs for the poor and elderly. Jurors acquitted all of the TAP managers in July 2004.

recovery ever by the government in a health care fraud investigation.[4] In May 2006, Lincare Holding, Inc. and its subsidiary Lincare, Inc. (collectively, Lincare) agreed to pay $10 million to settle allegations relating to violations of the federal anti-kickback statute and the Physician Self-Referral (Stark) law, the largest settlement to date under the Civil Monetary Penalties Law.[5] In June 2006, Tenet Healthcare Corporation (Tenet) agreed to pay $725 million (plus interest) and to forgo its right to receive an additional $175 million in certain Medicare payments to resolve multiple investigations relating to Medicare outlier payments, physician financial arrangements, and Medicare coding issues.[6] In April 2007, the U.S. Securities and Exchange Commission (SEC) filed civil fraud charges in federal district court against Tenet and its former chief financial officer and co-president, its former chief operating officer and co-president, its former general counsel and chief compliance officer, and its

---

[4]*See* U.S. Department of Justice, Press Release, *Largest Health Care Fraud Case in U.S. History Settled—HCA Investigation Nets Record Total of $1.7 Billion* (June 26, 2003), *available at* http://www.usdoj.gov/opa/pr/2003/June/03_civ_386.htm. HCA was the subject of the most comprehensive health care fraud investigation ever undertaken by the U.S. Department of Justice (DOJ), working with HHS, the U.S. Department of Defense, the U.S. Office of Personnel Management, and several states. *See id.*

[5]*See OIG Settles Largest Ever Civil Monetary Penalty Case,* OIG NEWS (May 15, 2006), *available at* http://oig.hhs.gov/publications/docs/press/2006/Lincare051506.pdf. As a part of the settlement, Lincare also agreed to sign a five-year corporate integrity agreement (Lincare CIA). The Lincare CIA set forth several requirements specific to the officers and directors of Lincare: officers and directors must report suspected violations of federal health care program requirements or of Lincare's policies and procedures as set forth in the company's code of conduct, which all full-time employees of Lincare are required to sign; each full-time employee, including officers and directors, must receive one hour per year of general training with regard to the Lincare CIA requirements and the related company compliance program, and each officer of Lincare must receive two hours per year of "Arrangements Training," which must cover the implications of the federal anti-kickback statute and the Stark law, legal sanctions under those acts, and examples of violations of each, and within 30 days after an officer discovers an investigation or proceeding by a governmental entity against Lincare, Lincare must notify the OIG of the proceeding and any subsequent resolution. *See* Corporate Integrity Agreement Between the Office of Inspector General of the U.S. Department of Health and Human Services and Lincare Holdings, Inc. and Lincare, Inc. (May 15, 2006), *available at* http://oig.hhs.gov/fraud/cia/agreements/Lincare%20EXECUTED%20CIA.pdf.

[6]*See* Tenet Healthcare Corporation, Press Release, *Tenet, U.S. Department of Justice Reach Broad Settlement* (June 29, 2006), *available at* http://www.tenethealth.com/NR/rdonlyres/BE8B8557-A94B-4CDD-9B16-0E4ABE9EF525/97564/DOJSettlement.pdf. Tenet is one of the largest hospital chains in the United States, with 57 hospitals in 12 states. The cash settlement will be paid according to the following schedule: $450 million, plus interest of approximately $20 million on the full amount of $725 million from November 1, 2005, through June 30, 2006; and $275 million, plus interest accruing on that amount at a simple rate of 4.125%, to be paid in 12 quarterly installments beginning November 1, 2007, and ending August 1, 2010. As a part of the settlement, Tenet also entered into a five-year corporate integrity agreement (Tenet CIA) in which the company agreed to (a) maintain its existing company-wide compliance program and code of conduct; (b) formalize in writing its policies and procedures in the areas of billing and reimbursement, compliance with the federal anti-kickback and Stark laws, and clinical quality; and (c) provide a variety of general and specialized compliance training to its employees, contractors, and the physicians it employs or who serve as medical directors and/or serve on a Tenet hospital governing board. *See* Corporate Integrity Agreement Between the Office of Inspector General of the Dep't of Health & Human Servs. and Tenet Healthcare Corp. (Sept. 27, 2006), *available at* http://oig.hhs.gov/fraud/cia/agreements/TenetCIAFinal.pdf. Tenet also announced a strategic plan to divest a total of 11 hospitals in order to help fund the settlement. *See* Tenet Healthcare Corporation, *Tenet, U.S. Department of Justice Reach Broad Settlement* (June 29, 2006), *available at* http://www.tenethealth.com/NR/rdonlyres/BE8B8557-A94B-4CDD-9B16-0E4ABE9EF525/97564/DOJSettlement.pdf.

former chief accounting officer for failing to disclose to investors that Tenet's strong earnings growth from 1999 to 2002 was driven largely by its use of a loophole in the Medicare reimbursement system related to outlier payments.[7] To settle the charges, Tenet agreed to pay a civil penalty of $10 million to be distributed to harmed investors pursuant to the Sarbanes-Oxley Act.[8]

In addition, courts continue to expand the potential liabilities that directors and officers may face for failing to adequately monitor corporate activities. In 1996, the Delaware Chancery Court's decision in *In re Caremark International*[9] held that a corporation's directors may be subject to liability for breach of their duty of care for failing to adequately control the corporation's employees where due attention would, arguably, have prevented the corporation's loss. As stated by one commenter, *Caremark* "allows the prosecutor to consider whether the board of directors of a corporation can be held criminally liable for actions of the corporation's employees."[10] Class action and/or derivative lawsuits under various legal theories have been filed against the directors and officers of several major health care organizations, including Columbia/HCA Healthcare Corporation, now HCA, Inc. (discussed at length in Section III.D., below) and Allegheny Health Education Research Foundation (discussed at length in Section III.F., below).[11] Meanwhile, the number and complexity of the laws and regulations businesses must observe in the health care industry are steadily increasing. Under these circumstances, it is hardly surprising that directors and officers of health care organizations are becoming increasingly concerned about their potential liabilities as overseers and managers of companies in such a closely scrutinized industry.

---

[7]U.S. Securities and Exchange Commission, Press Release, *SEC Charges Tenet Healthcare Corporation and Four Former Senior Executives with Concealing Scheme to Meet Earnings Targets by Exploiting Medicare System: Tenet Healthcare Corporation Agrees to Pay $10 Million Penalty to Settle Charges* (Apr. 2, 2007), *available at* http://www.sec.gov/news/press/2007/2007-60.htm. In addition to Tenet, the SEC's complaint named Thomas B. Mackey, Tenet's former chief operating officer and co-president; Christi R. Sulzbach, the former general counsel and chief compliance officer; David L. Dennis, the former chief financial officer and co-president; and Raymond L. Mathiasen, the former chief accounting officer. Dennis and Mathiasen have agreed to settle the SEC's charges. Mathiasen agreed to be permanently enjoined from violating the antifraud, reporting, and recordkeeping provisions of the federal securities laws, to pay a civil penalty of $240,000, and to be barred from serving as an officer or director of a public company for five years. Mathiasen, a certified public accountant, also agreed to be permanently denied the privilege of appearing or practicing before the SEC as an accountant. Dennis agreed to be permanently enjoined from future violations of the antifraud and reporting provisions of the federal securities laws and to pay a $150,000 civil penalty. The SEC's complaints against Mackey and Sulzbach sought permanent injunctions against future violations of the antifraud and reporting provisions of the federal securities laws, orders barring each of them from serving as an officer or director of a public company, disgorgement of ill-gotten gains, with prejudgment interest, and civil penalties. *Id.*

[8]*Id.* Without admitting or denying the allegations in the SEC's complaint, Tenet also agreed to be permanently enjoined from violating the antifraud, reporting, and recordkeeping provisions of the federal securities laws.

[9]698 A.2d 959 (Del. Ch. 1996).

[10]Mathias H. Heck, Jr. & Rhonda R. Mims, *The Corporate Officer: To Pay or Not to Pay?*, PROSECUTOR, July–Aug. 1998, at 24.

[11]Lawsuits alleging securities fraud also have been filed against directors and officers of health care companies; however, such cases are outside the purview of this chapter. *See, e.g.*, Helwig v. Vencor, Inc., 251 F.3d 540 (6th Cir. 2001).

This chapter provides an overview of the general principles and major issues relating to director and officer liability, with particular focus on those topics and new developments of special interest to corporate board members and officers in the health care industry. The duties and responsibilities corporate officers and directors owe to an organization is a complex subject that has been discussed in numerous articles and books, including several multivolume sets.[12] Therefore, this chapter can offer only an introduction to the subject. Because many companies are incorporated under the laws of Delaware, these issues frequently arise and are resolved under Delaware law. As a result, this discussion focuses primarily on the applicable laws of Delaware, while noting some of the important variations in other jurisdictions.

The chapter is divided into four substantive sections, in addition to this introductory discussion. After briefly describing the basic duties and responsibilities of corporate directors and officers, and the potential for criminal and civil liability, Section II of this chapter discusses the various doctrines, statutes, and other measures that potentially limit liability. Section III analyzes the types of litigation that often are directed at directors and officers and focuses on several recent health care cases. Section IV provides information on corporate compliance programs (*e.g.*, what they require and how they can help reduce liability for corporate directors and officers) and examines some of the limitations of corporate compliance programs. The chapter concludes with recommendations for further minimizing exposure (Section V).

## II. RESPONSIBILITIES OF DIRECTORS AND OFFICERS

### A. Criminal Liability

#### 1. General Rule

The issue of criminal liability typically is paramount in any legal analysis. The desire to avoid the criminal process and its attendant sanctions is a primary concern for all corporate officers and directors. The general rule is that a corporation's officers and directors cannot be criminally liable unless they personally participate in misconduct. Officers must be active and knowing participants in the criminal behavior to be held culpable.[13]

The level of participation required to make a person individually culpable for a crime does not necessarily rise to direct commission of an element of the proscribed act. Rather, a person may be held culpable if he or she commands, procures, or induces the performance of the act, or if he or she aids or abets its commission.[14] Thus, some affirmative act or conduct designed to aid the criminal scheme is required of the individual. Corporate officers and directors be-

---

[12]For more extensive discussion of directors' and officers' liability generally, see WILLIAM E. KNEPPER & DAN A. BAILEY, LIABILITY OF CORPORATE OFFICERS AND DIRECTORS (7th ed. 2002); JON F. ELLIOT, DIRECTORS' AND OFFICERS' LIABILITY (2003).

[13]*See, e.g.,* United States v. Gibson, 690 F.2d 697, 701 (9th Cir. 1982). For discussion of the responsible-corporate-officer doctrine, see Section II.A.2., below.

[14]*See* 18 U.S.C. §2.

come culpable when they expressly, or by implication, authorize criminal acts, which are then carried out by employees or agents of the corporation.[15] Likewise, the express or implied ratification of criminal conduct may also create culpability in this context.[16]

However, the law does not hold that an officer's simple knowledge or awareness of the criminal conduct of an employee is sufficient to establish the officer's culpability. Where an officer's awareness of the criminal conduct of others is coupled with his or her active concealment of the offense, culpability can attach.[17] Questions of a corporate officer's awareness of criminal conduct and his or her ratification, authorization, or active concealment of that conduct are all subject to an after-the-fact analysis of the facts and circumstances surrounding the events and a corporate officer's guilty state of mind may be inferred from these circumstances. The corporate officer may face a prosecutor's argument that under the facts of the situation, his or her awareness of the misconduct and failure to act to halt it constitutes an implied authorization for the act to continue, which in turn establishes criminal culpability on the officer's part.

In November 2003, the ousted chief executive of one of the nation's largest health care chains was indicted on charges that he directed a $2.7 billion fraud designed to boost the company's stock price and to bankroll an extravagant lifestyle.[18] Richard M. Scrushy, founder and former CEO of HealthSouth Corp., was indicted on 85 criminal counts, including charges of conspiracy, money laundering, securities fraud, and mail fraud.[19] The charges detailed what prosecutors labeled "a code of silence" that Scrushy allegedly imposed on the company—a combination of electronic and personal surveillance, threats, intimidation, and payoffs meant to prevent employees and board members from challenging his control.[20] The indictment also sought forfeiture of more than $278.8 million in property that Scrushy derived from the proceeds of the alleged offenses, including several residences, boats, aircraft, and luxury automobiles.[21] Scrushy's was the first criminal indictment under the Sarbanes-Oxley Act.[22]

---

[15]*See, e.g.,* United States v. Cattle King Packing Co., 793 F.2d 232, 240–41 (10th Cir.), *cert. denied sub nom.* Stanko v. United States, 479 U.S. 985 (1986); *Gibson,* 690 F.2d at 701.

[16]*See Gibson,* 690 F.2d at 701 (citation omitted).

[17]*See* 18 U.S.C. §4.

[18]Carrie Johnson, *HealthSouth Founder Is Charged with Fraud,* WASH. POST, Nov. 5, 2003, at A01.

[19]*Id.* Scrushy served as chairman of the board of HealthSouth from 1984 through early 2002; he also served as the company's CEO during that time, except for periods in late 2002 and early 2003.

[20]*Id.*

[21]Steven Taub, *Scrushy Indicted on 85 Counts,* CFO.COM (Nov. 5, 2003), *available at* http://www.cfo.com/article.cfm/3010823.

[22]*Id.* Other former HealthSouth executives pleaded guilty to Sarbanes-Oxley Act violations pursuant to plea agreements requiring them to testify as government witnesses against Scrushy. In May 2006, the U.S. Court of Appeals for the Eleventh Circuit granted the appeal of the United States and vacated the sentence imposed on Malcolm E. McVay, a former CFO, Senior Vice President, and Treasurer of HealthSouth. United States v. McVay, 447 F.3d 1348 (11th Cir. 2006). The *McVay* decision marks the fourth time the Eleventh Circuit has vacated a sentence of a cooperating witness in the Scrushy investigation, each time citing the sentencing court's failure to properly apply the substantial assistance guideline provisions. *See also* United States v. Botts,

During the trial, U.S. District Court Judge Karen Bowdre dismissed two of the three Sarbanes-Oxley charges from the superseding indictment (leaving only the charge for false certification of financial results in August 2002 for the jury to consider), as well as an obstruction of justice charge and eight other charges related to money laundering and fraud.[23] After 21 days of deliberation, the Birmingham, Alabama, jury found Scrushy not guilty on all of the remaining counts. In July 2006, prosecutors dropped their appeal from the dismissal of three perjury counts against Scrushy and announced that they would not seek a second trial. Their actions effectively resolved the criminal case against Scrushy.[24] Meanwhile, HealthSouth paid

---

135 Fed. Appx. 416 (11th Cir. 2005); United States v. Martin, 135 Fed. Appx. 411 (11th Cir. 2005); United States v. Livesay, 146 Fed. Appx. 403 (11th Cir. 2005). McVay pleaded guilty to an Information charging him with conspiracy to commit wire and securities fraud and with filing a false certification of financial information with the SEC. With no prior criminal history his sentencing range was 87 to 108 months imprisonment. As a part of its substantial assistance motion under Guideline §5K1.1, the government recommended incarceration for 65 months. The sentencing court found that the loss to investors as a result of the defendant's fraudulent conduct was $400 million, but without explanation departed to a level eight and sentenced McVay to 60 months probation, with the first six months in home detention. The Eleventh Circuit reviewed the sentence for "reasonableness" under *United States v. Booker*, 543 U.S. 220 (2005), and vacated the sentence, holding that, in the face of the multibillion dollar securities fraud, a term of probation could not be reconciled with the need under the law for a sentence to reflect the seriousness of the offense, to promote respect for the law, and to provide just punishment. *McVay*, 447 F.3d 1348, 1356–1357. In May 2006, the case was remanded to the U.S. District Court for the Northern District of Alabama for resentencing. *Id.* In February 2007, McVay was sentenced to five years probation, with credit given for the two years of probation he had already served. *See* Dave Cook, *HealthSouth CFO Avoids Prison, Again*, CFO.com (Feb. 23, 2007), *available at* http://www.cfo.com/printable/article.cfm/8758655/c_8757373?f=options.

[23] Associated Press, *Judge Throws out Charges in Scrushy Trial*, MSNBC (May 12, 2005), *available at* http://msnbc.msn.com/id/7828444.

[24] *See* Associated Press & Bloomberg News, *U.S. drops appeal against Scrushy*, TENNESSEAN (July 14, 2005). Scrushy also faced several civil lawsuits, including a securities fraud case filed by the SEC. *See* SEC v. HealthSouth Corp., Civil Action No. CV-03-J-0615-S (N.D. Ala. 2003). The SEC's civil case was stayed in May 2003 pending the resolution of Scrushy's criminal trial. In November 2005, United States District Judge Inge Johnson dismissed, without prejudice, two of the SEC's fraud charges against Scrushy, citing the vagueness of the factual allegations underlying the charges. *See* Michael Tomberlin, *Fraud Counts Dropped*, BIRMINGHAM NEWS (Nov. 30, 2005). Judge Johnson's decision left four other nonfraud charges in place and granted leave for the SEC to amend its complaint. The SEC filed a third amended complaint in December 2005. In April 2007, the SEC announced that the United States District Court for the Northern District of Alabama entered a final judgment against Scrushy that permanently bars him from serving as an officer or director of a public company, permanently enjoins him from committing future violations of the antifraud and other provisions of the federal securities laws, and requires him to pay $81 million in disgorgement and civil penalties. *See* U.S. Securities and Exchange Commission Litigation Release Number 20084, *HealthSouth Founder Settles SEC Fraud Action for $81 Million* (Apr. 23, 2007), *available at* http://www.sec.gov/litigation/litreleases/2007/lr20084.htm. Scrushy consented to the entry of the final judgment without admitting or denying any of the allegations in the SEC's complaint. In his consent to the settlement, which is incorporated into the final judgment, Scrushy agreed to refrain from seeking indemnification or reimbursement from any third party for any part of the $81 million.

In January 2006, Scrushy was ordered to repay nearly $48 million in bonuses to HealthSouth in a shareholder suit that alleged that Scrushy was unjustly enriched through the bonuses he received while CEO of HealthSouth from 1997 to 2002. *See* Stephen Taub, *Scrushy Ordered to Repay Bonuses*, CFO.com (Jan. 4, 2006), *available at* http://www.cfo.com/article.cfm/5354197/c_5353602?f+TodayInFinance_Inside. Judge Allwin E. Horn, III, of Jefferson County Circuit Court in Birmingham, Alabama, determined that knowledge was immaterial under the law of unjust enrichment and ruled that Scrushy was not entitled to the bonus payments he received, whether or not he participated in the fraud at the company or knew about the scheme. *Id.* Scrushy appealed

hundreds of millions of dollars to settle civil lawsuits relating to Scrushy's conduct.[25]

In March 2005, Bernard Ebbers, the former chief executive of WorldCom, was found guilty of one count of securities fraud, one count of conspiracy, and seven counts of filing false documents with regulators as a part of the biggest accounting fraud in corporate history.[26] Ebbers was sentenced to 25 years in prison for the $11 billion securities fraud, which drove WorldCom into the nation's largest corporate bankruptcy.[27]

---

the order granting partial summary judgment. In August 2006, the Alabama Supreme Court unanimously upheld the lower court ruling and ordered Scrushy to pay back the bonuses he received during the years HealthSouth overstated its earnings, plus interest. *See Scrushy v. Tucker*, No. 1050564, 2006 Ala. LEXIS 230 (Ala. Aug. 25, 2006). *See also Court: Scrushy Must Repay HealthSouth $47.82M*, BIRMINGHAM BUS. J. (Aug. 25, 2006), *available at* http://www.bizjournals.com/birmingham/stories/2006/08/21/daily22.html?t=printable.

[25] In June 2005, HealthSouth agreed to pay $100 million to settle a SEC lawsuit accusing the company of accounting fraud while under Scrushy's leadership. The money was scheduled to be paid in five installments over two years, starting October 15, 2005. HealthSouth neither admitted nor denied wrongdoing. As a part of the settlement, the company also agreed to create an inspector-general position with a staff of at least five people. Moreover, HealthSouth committed to retaining a consultant to review corporate governance practices, and to either have a consultant review internal controls or give the SEC all communications between the company and its auditors after filing its financial statements for 2005. HealthSouth also agreed to pay $325 million to settle Justice Department civil charges that the company overbilled Medicare. *See* Geraldine Ryerson-Cruz and Otis Bilodeau, *HealthSouth Settles with SEC, Will Pay $100 Million*, TENNESSEAN (June 9, 2005).

In September 2006, HealthSouth entered into definitive settlements with investors to end the federal securities class action and the derivative actions investors brought against the company and its officers and directors in 2003. Under the agreements, HealthSouth agreed to pay $215 million in HealthSouth common stock and warrants, and HealthSouth's insurance carriers agreed to pay $230 million in cash, for total aggregate compensation of $445 million. In addition, the plaintiffs in the federal securities class action would receive 25% of any net recoveries from future judgments obtained by or on behalf of HealthSouth with respect to certain claims against Scrushy, Ernst & Young (the company's former auditors), and UBS (the company's former primary investment bank), each of whom remained a defendant in the derivative actions as well as the federal securities class actions. *See* HealthSouth, *HealthSouth Enters Into Definitive Settlement Agreement in Class Action and Derivative Litigation* (Sept. 27, 2006), *available at* http://ww2.healthsouth.com/healthsouth/PressRelease.jsp?oid=536970518. *See also* Associated Press, *HealthSouth Investors Settle Suits*, LOS ANGELES TIMES (Sept. 28, 2006), *available at* http://www.latimes.com. The settlement was approved by the court in January 2007. *See* HealthSouth, Press Release, *HealthSouth Receives Final Court Approval of Settlements in Class Action and Derivative Litigation* (Jan. 11, 2007), *available at* http://www.healthsouth.com/who_we_are/press_releases.asp. At that time, the company indicated that it would continue to pursue its claims against Scrushy, Ernst & Young, and UBS. *See id.*

Also in September 2006, an arbitrator determined that HealthSouth must pay a portion of Scrushy's attorney's fees incurred in the criminal trial in which he was acquitted. *See* Associated Press, *HealthSouth on Hook for Scrushy Defense*, YAHOO! FINANCE (Sept. 12, 2006). The $17 million award is only slightly more than half of the $32 million Scrushy sought from HealthSouth, and will be used to partially offset millions of dollars that courts have said Scrushy must repay to HealthSouth (see note 24 above).

[26] MSNBC Staff & News Service Reports, *Jury Convicts Ebbers on All Counts in Fraud Case*, MSNBC NEWS (Mar. 15, 2005), *available at* http://msnbc.msn.com/id/7139448. Ebbers was one of the founders of WorldCom, and was its CEO from 1985 until 2000. *See* Dan Ackman, *Bernie Ebbers Guilty*, FORBES (Mar. 15, 2005), *available at* http://www.forbes.com/home/management/2005/03/15/cx_da_0315ebbersguilty.html.

[27] Krysten Crawford, *Ebbers Gets 25 Years*, CNN MONEY (July 13, 2005), *available at* http://money.cnn.com/2005/07/13/news/newsmakers/ebbers_sentence/index.htm. Judge Barbara Jones ordered Ebbers to begin serving his sentence by October 12, 2005. Ebbers reported to federal prison in Yazoo City, Mississippi on September 27, 2006. At that time, he planned to

In July 2004, Kenneth L. Lay, former chairman and CEO of Enron Corp., was indicted on one count of conspiracy to commit securities and wire fraud, two counts of wire fraud, and three counts of securities fraud related to an accounting scandal that resulted in the company's 2001 bankruptcy.[28] Jeffrey K. Skilling, another former CEO of Enron, was also indicted on 35 counts in this same indictment: one count of conspiracy to commit securities and wire fraud, 14 counts of securities fraud, four counts of wire fraud, six counts of false statements to auditors, and 10 counts of insider trading.[29] In May 2006, Lay and Skilling were convicted. Lay was convicted of all six counts against him. Skilling was convicted of 19 of the 28 counts against him, and acquitted on the remaining 9 counts. Lay died on July 5, 2006, prior to his sentencing. As a result, his conviction was vacated.[30] In October 2006, Skilling was sentenced to

---

appeal his conviction. In June 2006, Ebbers agreed to forfeit the bulk of his assets to injured WorldCom investors and MCI, including a Mississippi mansion and other holdings estimated to be worth as much as $45 million.

In September 2005, United States District Judge Denise Cote approved a settlement in the civil suit brought against Ebbers by investors who lost billions of dollars in the collapse of WorldCom in 2002. *See* Judgment Approving Settlement and Dismissing Action Against Bernard Ebbers, *In re* WorldCom, Inc. Securities Litigation, Civil Action No. 02 Civ. 3288 (filed Sept. 21, 2005). Under the settlement, Ebbers will pay $5 million in cash and will turn over nearly everything he owns, including his Mississippi mansion, to a trust that will eventually sell the assets for an expected $25 million to $40 million. *Id. See also* New York—AP, *Judge Okays Settlement in Ebbers Civil Trial*, 7online.com WABC-TV/WABC-DT New York (July 11, 2005), *available at* http://www.abclocal.go.com/wabc/story?section=business_week&id= 3239959. The settlement also resulted in the dismissal of the company's separate civil suit against Ebbers. *See* MCI, Inc. v. Ebbers, Adv. Pro. No. 04-03389 (AJG) (Bankr. S.D.N.Y. May 18, 2006).

[28] Enron succumbed to an accounting scandal that surfaced in 2001. Enron and 78 of its subsidiaries filed for bankruptcy in December 2001 after the Houston-based energy corporation disclosed billions of dollars in debt previously hidden from investors and securities regulators through Enron-controlled off-books limited partnerships. *See* Catherine Tomasko, *Judge Oks Enron Directors' $168 Million Settlement*, FINDLAW LEGAL NEWS & COMMENTARY (Mar. 8, 2005). Lay also was indicted on four counts in a separate case involving allegations of bank fraud (one count of bank fraud and three counts of false statements to banks) and was convicted on all counts.

[29] *See* Superceding Indictment Cr. No. H-04-25 (S-2) (S.D. Tex. July 7, 2004). At trial, Lay faced six counts (as one count had been dropped) and Skilling faced 28 counts (as seven counts had been dropped, including four counts of wire fraud related to charges against Enron's chief accounting officer, Richard Causey, all 36 of which had been dropped when Causey pleaded guilty to one count of securities fraud on December 28, 2005). *See* The Associated Press, *Count By Count The Charges Against Skilling and Lay*, CHICAGO TRIBUNE (May 25, 2006); Tom Fowler and John C. Roper, *Causey Pleads Guilty, Leaving Just Skilling, Lay*, HOUSTON CHRONICLE (Dec. 28, 2005).

[30] In light of Lay's death, his estate filed a motion with the U.S. District Court for the Southern District of Texas requesting that the conviction be vacated and the indictment against Lay be dismissed, citing the inability to pursue a planned appeal. Prior to his death, Lay faced a maximum of 45 years in prison for the corporate trial and 120 years for the bank fraud case. The government filed a motion in opposition. In a related move, the DOJ proposed legislation that would essentially prevent judges from vacating criminal convictions if a defendant dies before going through the entire appeals process. In November 2006, Senator Diane Feinstein (D–Cal.) and Senator Jeff Sessions (R–Ala.) came forward to sponsor the legislation proposed by the DOJ. The Senate proposal passed without amendment by unanimous consent and was referred to the Senate Committee on the Judiciary in December 2006. An identical proposal was introduced in the House by Representative Adam Schiff (D–Cal.) and was referred to the House Committee on the Judiciary in December 2006. Meanwhile, the government withdrew its opposition to the motion from Lay's estate in light of the pending legislation. Lay's conviction was vacated in October 2006. *See* Motion of Estate of Kenneth H. Lay to Vacate His Conviction and Dismiss the Indictment, Cr. No. H-04-25 (S2) (S.D. Tex. Aug. 16, 2006); United States' Opposition to the

24 years, 4 months in prison.[31] In addition, Lay, Skilling, and several other officers and directors were held liable for significant civil penalties in lawsuits brought by former shareholders and other government agencies.[32]

---

Motion of the Estate of Lay to Vacate His Conviction and Dismiss the Indictment, Cr. No. H-04-25 (S2) (Lake, J.) (S.D. Tex. Sept. 6, 2006); Memorandum Opinion and Order, Cr. No. H-04-25 (S2) (S.D. Tex. Oct. 17, 2006). *See also* MSNBC, *The Enron Trial* (May 25, 2006); Associated Press, *Lay's Death Likely to Erase His Convictions*, MSNBC (July 6, 2006); Tom Fowler, *Prosecutors Seek a New Law to Keep His Conviction Alive, Despite His Death*, HOUSTON CHRONICLE (Sept. 7, 2006).

[31] *See* Carrie Johnson, *Skilling Gets 24 Years for Fraud at Enron*, WASHINGTON POST (Oct. 24, 2006).

[32] The bankruptcy led to numerous shareholder suits. In 2004, a dozen former Enron board members agreed to pay $1.5 million out of their own pockets, in addition to turning over $85 million in insurance proceeds, to settle their liability in a lawsuit filed by employee pension funds of the former energy trader. *See Ex-Enron Directors Settle Investor Suit for $168 Mln (Update 3)*, BLOOMBERG.COM (Jan. 7, 2005), *available at* http://www.bloomberg.com/apps/news?pid=10000103&refer=us&sid=avNqBEZE6klw. In March 2005, a U.S. District Judge approved a $168 million settlement between a group of outside directors and investor plaintiffs. *See* Tomasko, *Judge Oks Enron Directors' $168 Million Settlement*. The settlement was funded by $155 million in insurance policy proceeds and more than $13 million in personal contributions by some of the outside director defendants. *Id.* In addition to the $168 million settlement amount, the directors agreed to pay $32 million to Enron creditors, which will be paid out of the insurance proceeds. *See Ex-Enron Directors Settle Investor Suit for $168 Mln (Update 3)*, BLOOMBERG. COM. This settlement was the fourth such deal negotiated in the 2002 class action. Other Enron settlements include Lehman Brothers Holdings, Inc., for $222.5 million; Bank of America Corp. for $69 million; Andersen Worldwide (an arm of Arthur Andersen LLP) for $40 million; and Citigroup for $2 billion. *Id.*

    In June 2003, the United States Department of Labor (in conjunction with current and former Enron workers and retirees) filed suit against Enron, former CEOs Kenneth L. Lay and Jeffrey K. Skilling, the former board of directors, and the former administrative committee for Enron's retirement plans for failing to prudently protect Enron workers' retirement assets invested in the stock of Enron. *See* U.S. Department of Labor, News Release, *U.S. Labor Department Sues Enron Executives and Plan Officials for Failing to Protect Workers* (June 26, 2003), *available at* http://www.dol.gov/_sec/media/announcements/release.pdf. In February 2006, U.S. Secretary of Labor Elaine L. Chao announced a settlement in which Enron workers and retirees received $133.95 million in cash distributed through the company's retirement plans. *See* U.S. Department of Labor, News Release, *Secretary of Labor Elaine L. Chao Announces $134 Million to Be Distributed to Enron Workers and Retirees* (Feb. 16, 2006), *available at* http://www.dol.gov/opa/media/press/ebsa/EBSA20060232.htm. The major portion of the cash total, $124.6 million, represented proceeds from the sale of the Enron Corp. bankruptcy claim to Bear Stearns Investment Products, Inc.; the remaining $9.33 million was paid separately by Enron earlier in the month as a distribution for part of the bankruptcy claim. *Id.* The Labor Department previously announced an $85 million settlement with Enron officers and fiduciaries who served on the plans' administrative committee, which returned $66.5 million to the Enron 401(k) and employee stock ownership plans and barred the former outside directors of Enron's board of directors from knowingly assuming fiduciary responsibility with respect to ERISA-covered plans for five years unless agreed to by the Labor Department. The sale of the bankruptcy claim increases the total amount paid in this case for the Enron retirement plans to more than $220.8 million, subject to attorneys' fees and expenses. *Id.* The agreement resolved the Labor Department's lawsuit and private class action suit brought on behalf of the plans' participants. The agreement did not resolve the Department's claims against former Chairman Kenneth Lay or former CEO Jeffrey Skilling. *Id.* In September 2006, the Labor Department announced an agreement with Lay's estate granting a $12 million claim against the estate on behalf of participants covered by Enron's pension plans. *See* U.S. Department of Labor, News Release, *U.S. Department of Labor Announces $12 Million Settlement With the Estate of Kenneth L. Lay* (Sept. 7, 2006), *available at* http://www.dol.gov/opa/media/press/ebsa/EBSA20061514.htm. *See also Lay Estate, Labor Dept. Reach Pension Agreement*, HOUSTON CHRONICLE (Sept. 7, 2006), *available at* http://www.chron.com/disp/story.mpl/special/enron/4170278.html. In November 2006, the Labor Department announced a settlement agreement with Skilling under which Skilling agreed to drop his opposition to the previous $85 million settlement, waive his right to benefits from Enron's

In June 2003, Barry Weinbaum, the former chief executive of Tenet Healthcare Corporation's Alvarado Hospital Medical Center, was indicted on one count of conspiracy and seven counts of paying illegal remuneration in violation of the anti-kickback statute for allegedly using physician relocation agreements to funnel money to existing physician practices in the San Diego area.[33] The case went to trial twice, each ending in a mistrial. On May 17, 2006, Tenet entered into a settlement with the government pursuant to which the government agreed not to re-try the criminal case against Weinbaum[34] and the criminal charges against him were dismissed on May 31, 2006 (although numerous sanctions were imposed against Tenet).[35]

Other enforcement actions demonstrate that the scope of activities for which the government may allege criminal liability against corporate officers

---

pension plans, and be permanently barred from serving in a fiduciary capacity to any employee benefit plan governed by ERISA. *See* U.S. Department of Labor, News Release, *U.S. Department of Labor Announces Settlement With Former Enron Executive Jeffrey Skilling* (Nov. 16, 2006), *available at http://www.dol.gov/opa/media/press/ebsa/ebsa20061976.htm. The settlement acknowledged that Skilling was already subject to an order of forfeiture obtained by the DOJ requiring the establishment of a $45 million restitution fund for victims of Enron-related fraud, including plan participants and securities investors. The Skilling and Lay settlements were consolidated and approved by the court on February 23, 2007.*

[33]Tenet Healthcare Corporation (Tenet) is the second-largest hospital chain in the United States, with 71 hospitals in 13 states. Alvarado opened in San Diego, California, in 1972 and became a part of Tenet in 1995. Federal regulators began investigating an alleged kickback scheme at Alvarado in December 2002. The 2003 indictment alleged that the defendants recruited new doctors with lucrative relocation packages into host practices in San Diego, while disguising payments to the host physicians as tenant improvements and overhead. The indictment also alleged that the defendants made the payments to the host physicians with the intent to induce patient referrals to the hospital. *See* Office of the U.S. Attorney for the Southern District of California, News Release (May 17, 2006), *available at* http://www.usdoj.gov/usao/cas/press/cas60517-1.pdf.

[34]In May 2006, the OIG notified Alvarado that it intended to exclude the hospital from participating in Medicare, Medicaid, and all other federal health care programs. Later that month, Tenet reached a settlement with the OIG to resolve civil allegations of kickback violations by Alvarado, agreeing to pay $21 million to the government and to sell (or otherwise divest) its interest in Alvarado. As a part of the civil settlement, the government agreed to dismiss the pending criminal charges against the hospital and its officers, including Weinbaum. *See* Office of the U.S. Attorney for the Southern District of California, News Release (May 17, 2006), *available at* http://www.usdoj.gov/usao/cas/press/cas60517-1.pdf. In June 2006, Tenet agreed to pay more than $900 million to the United States to resolve its liability under the False Claims Act and related federal statutes. In September 2006, Tenet entered into a five-year Corporate Integrity Agreement (CIA) with the OIG, pursuant to which Tenet has agreed to implement a comprehensive compliance program that includes corporate, regional, and hospital compliance officers; compliance policies and training; an employee hotline and reporting mechanism; and mandatory reporting and repayment of overpayments. In addition, Tenet is required to engage independent review organizations to review Tenet's DRG claims, outlier payments, physician relationships, and clinical quality management. The agreement also includes "unprecedented" provisions requiring the Quality, Compliance, and Ethics Committee of Tenet's Board of Directors to annually review the effectiveness of Tenet's compliance program; adopt resolutions with respect to this review stating that the committee has concluded that the company has implemented an effective compliance program that meets the requirements of the federal health care programs and the CIA, or stating why the committee is unable to make such a representation; and submit annual reports to the OIG that include certifications by Tenet's officers that the company is in compliance with the requirements of the federal health care programs. *See OIG Executes Tenet Corporate Integrity Agreement: Unprecedented Provisions Include Board of Directors Review,* OIG NEWS (Sept. 28, 2006), *available at* http://oig.hhs.gov/fraud/docs/press/Tenet%20CIA%20press%20release.pdf.

[35]*See* Order of Dismissal, Criminal Case No. 03cr1587 (S.D. Cal. May 30, 2006).

and directors continues to expand. In February 2007, Robert Wachter, the former director and CEO of American Healthcare Management (AHM), pleaded guilty to charges of conspiracy to defraud the United States for making false statements and representations to the government regarding the quality of care provided to patients of the company's nursing homes.[36] The allegations underlying the indictment involved instances of neglect and abuse caused by staff shortages.[37] The staff shortages were alleged to have been the result of a mandated 40 percent formula for staffing imposed by Wachter, i.e., that staff payroll could not exceed 40 percent of the Medicare patient per diem. The government contended that Wachter should be held criminally responsible because he determined the budget and staffing levels for the company's nursing homes, which resulted in insufficient nursing staff to meet the needs of the facilities' residents. Wachter was sentenced to 18 months in prison, plus two years of supervised release, and ordered to pay a $29,000 fine.[38] Wachter and AHM also faced civil liability for their conduct.[39]

---

[36] *See* United States v. Wachter, Criminal Case No. 4:05-cr-00667-SNL-1 (E.D. Mo. Feb. 28, 2007). Wachter was originally indicted on one count of conspiracy to defraud the United States and five counts of making false statements to a federal health care benefits program. During the time period at issue, Wachter owned 50% of AHM and was a director of AHM. Wachter had also served as the President of AHM for a portion of the relevant time period.

[37] *See id.* The government claimed that from January 1998 until July 2001 inadequate staffing at the company's affiliated nursing homes resulted in numerous residents suffering from dehydration and malnutrition. According to the allegation, staff were often unavailable to assist residents who could not feed themselves or drink liquids without help. Residents went without cleaning or bathing for extended periods of time and developed life-threatening bed sores that would have been preventable with proper care. During the same time, the government claimed, Wachter and AHM billed Medicare and Medicaid for services they knew were inadequate or not performed at all. The government further asserted that the purpose of the conspiracy was for the defendants to enrich themselves by means of such reimbursement and to conceal from federal and state governments the actual conditions and the nature of the care provided. *See* Office of the U.S. Attorney for the Eastern District of Missouri, Press Release, *American Healthcare Management, Its CEO & Three Local Nursing Homes Are Sentenced on Conspiracy Charges Involving Failure of Care at Nursing Facilities* (Feb. 28, 2007), *available at* http://www.usdoj.gov/usao/moe/press%20releases/archived%20press%20releases/2007_press_releases/february/american_healthcare.html.

[38] *See* Office of the U.S. Attorney for the Eastern District of Missouri, Press Release, *American Healthcare Management, Its CEO & Three Local Nursing Homes Are Sentenced on Conspiracy Charges Involving Failure of Care at Nursing Facilities* (Feb. 28, 2007), *available at* http://www.usdoj.gov/usao/moe/press%20releases/archived%20press%20releases/2007_press_releases/february/american_healthcare.html. If convicted, Wachter would have faced up to five years in prison and a fine of up to $250,000 on each count, and the company (along with each of its affiliated nursing homes) would have faced criminal fines of up to $500,000 on each count. AHM and the affiliated nursing homes pleaded guilty to conspiracy to defraud the United States and each was fined $180,250 and placed on two years probation. *See id.*

[39] In fall 2005, AHM, Wachter, and the company's affiliated nursing homes agreed to settle a related False Claims Act civil suit. As a part of the civil settlement, the parties agreed to pay the government $1.25 million to settle the allegations of submitting false and fraudulent nursing home billings to Medicare and Medicaid. AHM and the affiliated nursing homes agreed to permanent exclusion from participation in any federal health care program. Wachter was also barred from participation in the federal health care programs for 20 years. None of the parties admitted any wrongdoing and denied any civil, criminal, or administrative liability in the settlement. *See* U.S. DEP'T OF HEALTH & HUMAN SERVS., OFFICE OF INSPECTOR GEN., SEMIANNUAL REPORT TO CONGRESS APR. 1, 2006–SEPT. 30, 2006, at 25, *available at* http://www.oig.hhs.gov/publications/docs/semiannual/2006/semiannual%20final%20FY%202006.pdf.

### 2. Responsible-Corporate-Officer Doctrine

At common law, a criminal offense required mens rea, or a guilty state of mind. This requirement served to punish only those who committed knowing or deliberate violations. The state-of-mind requirement largely has been preserved in modern criminal statutes. However, there are some instances in which certain corporate officers have been held criminally liable where they did not know of, or personally participate in, the proscribed conduct.

The primary application of the responsible-corporate-officer doctrine is found in the prosecution of officers for violations of the various statutes designed to promote, protect, and ensure public health and safety. Courts have held that Congress intended to impose a form of criminal strict liability on corporate officers for corporate violations of certain of these statutes.

For example, the federal Food, Drug, and Cosmetic Act (FDCA) prohibits the sale (or introduction into interstate commerce) of misbranded or adulterated materials.[40] In the famous case of *United States v. Dotterweich*,[41] the U.S. Supreme Court interpreted the FDCA and placed criminal liability squarely on the shoulders of corporate officers based solely on their position of responsibility in the business. The FDCA imposes this culpability by setting the "burden of acting at hazard upon a person otherwise innocent but standing in responsible relation to a public danger."[42] By dispensing with "the conventional requirement for criminal conduct—awareness of some wrongdoing," the FDCA effectively establishes strict criminal liability.[43] The FDCA makes criminally accountable those "responsible corporate agents" who deal with products that may affect the health of the public at large.[44] For the Court, the imposition of strict liability in this context is consistent with the officers' "voluntarily assume[d] positions of authority in business enterprises whose services and products affect the health and well-being of the public."[45] Moreover, in a 2001 decision, a federal district court held that the potential criminal liability for corporate officers under the FDCA may justify the imposition of civil liability on these corporate agents as well.[46]

Consistent with the Court's rationale in FDCA cases, the responsible-corporate-officer doctrine has been applied to impose strict liability in the food industry for violations of the Federal Meat Inspection Act.[47] The reach of the responsible-corporate-officer doctrine is not altogether clear, however. Prosecutors have sought to apply it in criminal prosecutions for violations of federal environmental statutes as well, with mixed results. In prosecutions for alleged

---

[40]21 U.S.C. §§331, 352.

[41]320 U.S. 277 (1943).

[42]*Id.* at 281 (citation omitted).

[43]*Id.*

[44]United States v. Park, 421 U.S. 658, 673 (1975).

[45]*Id.*

[46]United States v. Undetermined Quantities of Articles of Drug, 145 F. Supp. 2d 692, 705 (S.D. Md. 2001) (holding that the FDCA rationale for imposing criminal liability on corporate officers was even more persuasive for holding a corporate officer responsible for acts of the corporation where only civil liability was involved).

[47]*See* United States v. Cattle King Packing Co., 793 F.2d 232, 240 (10th Cir.), *cert. denied sub nom.* Stanko v. United States, 479 U.S. 985 (1986).

violations of the Resource Conservation and Recovery Act (RCRA), courts have refused to apply the strict liability encompassed in the responsible-corporate-officer theory. Instead, these courts have ruled that a defendant's status as a responsible official is not sufficient to overcome his or her lack of actual guilty knowledge.[48]

Unlike the FDCA, the Clean Water Act explicitly brings within the scope of its criminal sanctions "any responsible corporate officer."[49] Courts have debated the precise meaning of this language. One court concluded that culpability attaches where the officer is aware of the criminal conduct and has authority to halt it, yet fails to exercise that authority.[50]

However, in the environmental context, another court explicitly refused to follow *United States v. Park*.[51] In *Kaites v. Commonwealth of Pennsylvania Department of Environmental Resources*, the president and chief executive officer (CEO) was the corporate officer responsible for all management decisions concerning the particular environmental nuisance in question.[52] The state sought an abatement order directed to the CEO, rendering him personally responsible for terminating the nuisance. Despite the CEO's control and the strict liability standard in the statute, the court refused to permit the abatement order. The court considered and rejected *Park* and declined to impose liability on the CEO merely because of his status.[53]

## B. Civil Liability

As in most contexts, the civil liability of a corporate director or officer arises from the breach of some duty and a loss or injury to another as a proximate result of the breach. Suits against directors and officers complain that the defendant violated a fiduciary duty owed to the corporation or its shareholders. Such a breach of obligation can result in at least two categories of suit: shareholder suits and class action suits.

Fiduciary responsibilities are recognized broadly as the duty of loyalty and the duty of care. General doctrines or defenses, such as the business judgment rule, limit the liability that these duties can place on directors and officers.

### 1. Fiduciary Responsibilities and Duties

Corporate directors generally are expected to oversee the corporation, set the policies of the business, and select the corporate officers who will, in turn,

---

[48] *See, e.g.,* United States v. MacDonald & Watson Waste Oil Co., 933 F.2d 35, 51–52 (1st Cir. 1991); United States v. White, 766 F. Supp. 873, 894–95 (E.D. Wash. 1991).

[49] 33 U.S.C. §1319(c)(6).

[50] *See, e.g.,* United States v. Iverson, 162 F.3d 1015, 1024–25 (9th Cir. 1998). Various law review articles provide a general discussion of corporate officer liability in the environmental context. Noel Wise, *Personal Liability Promotes Responsible Conduct: Extending the Responsible Corporate Officer Doctrine to Federal Civil Environmental Enforcement Cases*, 21 Stan. Envtl. L.J. 283 (June 2002); Jonathan Snyder, Comment, *Back to Reality: What "Knowingly" Really Means and the Inherently Subjective Nature of the Mental State Requirement in Environmental Criminal Law*, 8 Mo. Envtl. L. & Pol'y Rev. 1 (2002).

[51] 421 U.S. 658 (1975).

[52] 529 A.2d 1148 (Pa. Commw. Ct. 1987).

[53] *See id.* at 1150.

run the business on a day-to-day basis and implement the policies set by the directors.

The board of directors' responsibilities fall into several broad areas:

- authorizing major corporate actions;
- overseeing management, including selecting the chief executive officer, establishing objectives for the senior management, providing advice and counsel to the corporation's senior management, and developing and implementing succession plans for members of senior management;
- overseeing and monitoring functions to keep abreast of the corporation's performance in light of its strategic objectives;
- selecting, instituting, and monitoring procedures and internal controls to ensure that the board will be adequately informed of the corporation's financial status (this function typically encompasses selection of the audit procedures and auditors as well as establishment of a formal board committee charged with oversight of the audit function); and
- developing and monitoring effective compliance programs, policies, and systems to promote ethical conduct and conducting annual (or more frequent) reviews of the corporation's investments for compliance with law and regulations.

Directors are expected to devote a meaningful amount of time to their role. They must be aware of developments within the corporation, address any material adverse developments that are brought to their attention, and follow through with exploration and analysis when their own knowledge and expertise advises them of facts that require further scrutiny. Directors also must take care to observe their fiduciary duties to the corporation.[54] As noted above, these fiduciary duties fall into two broad categories: the duty of loyalty and the duty of care.

### a. Duty of Loyalty

Directors and officers are fiduciaries in positions of trust, and others necessarily rely on them. Accordingly, directors and officers must defend and protect the interests entrusted to them. The duty of loyalty is a broad and encompassing duty that imposes on directors and officers an affirmative obligation to protect the interests of the corporation, and mandates that they absolutely refrain from any conduct that would harm the corporation, thereby demanding the most scrupulous observance.[55] This duty is derived from the self-dealing prohibition found in every fiduciary relationship and prohibits tak-

---

[54]Directors of wholly owned solvent subsidiaries only owe fiduciary duties to the parent corporation and its stockholders. *See* Trenwick America Litigation Trust v. Ernst & Young, 906 A.2d 168, 200 (Del. Ch. 2006).

[55]*See, e.g., In re* Walt Disney Co. Derivative Litig. Consol., C.A. No. 15452, 2004 Del. Ch. LEXIS 132, at *24 n.49 (Del. Ch. Sept. 10, 2004), *aff'd,* Brehm v. Eisner, 906 A.2d 27 (Del. 2006) (holding that directors who consciously and intentionally disregard their duties in relation to executive compensation matters could be held personally liable) (*quoting* BelCom, Inc. v. Robb, C.A. No. 14663, 1998 Del. Ch. LEXIS 58, 1998 WL 229527, at *3 (Del. Ch. Apr. 28, 1998)). *See also* Official Comm. of Unsecured Creditors of Integrated Health Servs. v. Elkins, C.A. No. 20228-NC, 2004 Del. Ch. LEXIS 122, 2004 WL 1949290 (Del. Ch. Aug. 24, 2004) (holding that once an employee becomes a fiduciary of an entity, he or she has a duty to negotiate

ing for oneself a business opportunity that properly belongs to the corporation. The duty of loyalty requires that a director act in good faith in decisionmaking, practice fairness to the corporation and, in certain instances, refrain from pursuing corporate opportunities.

### i. Good Faith

A key aspect of the duty of loyalty is the overarching obligation of directors and officers to exercise good faith in their decisionmaking role. Directors and officers must act in good faith when making decisions regarding the corporation, always seeking to act in a way that will serve the best interests of the corporation. Liability for failure to exercise good faith is not limited to intentional acts against the corporation's interests; a director or officer may also be held liable for unintentional failures to act to promote the corporation's interests. The obligation to exercise good faith also requires a director to avoid conflicts of interest.[56]

For some time, Delaware law was neither clear nor consistent with respect to whether officers or directors owe a distinct duty of good faith to the corporation. Although the Delaware General Corporation Law does not explicitly state that officers or directors have an independent duty to act in good faith with respect to corporate matters, some Delaware courts appeared to recognize that officers and directors owe a discrete duty of good faith to the corporation, separate and apart from their duties of loyalty and care.[57] Other courts have held that there is no independent duty of good faith under Delaware law; rather, good faith is a requirement of the duty of loyalty.[58] In 2006, the Delaware Supreme Court in *Stone v. Ritter* silenced the debate by affirmatively stating that the good faith obligation is not an independent fiduciary duty of directors, but rather is a

---

further compensation agreements honestly and in good faith so as not to advantage him- or herself at the expense of the entity's shareholders; this duty does not prevent fiduciaries from negotiating their own employment agreements so long as the negotiations are performed in an adversarial and arms'-length manner). In April 2005, Abercrombie & Fitch Co. settled a similar lawsuit with regard to the compensation of its CEO, Michael Jeffries. *See* Form 8-K for Abercrombie & Fitch Co., Item 1.01 (Apr. 13, 2005).

[56]See Section II.B.1.a.ii., below.

[57]*See* Cede & Co. v. Technicolor, Inc., 634 A.2d 345, 361 (Del. 1993) (to overcome the presumptions of the business judgment rule, a "plaintiff assumes the burden of providing evidence that directors, in reaching their challenged decision, breached any of the *triads* [sic] of their fiduciary duty—*good faith*, loyalty or due care") (emphasis added). *See also* Emerald Partners v. Berlin, 787 A.2d 85, 90 (Del. 2001) (Delaware Supreme Court stated "[t]he directors of Delaware corporations have a *triad of primary fiduciary duties*: due care, loyalty, *and good faith*. These fiduciary responsibilities do not operate intermittently. Accordingly, the shareholders of a Delaware corporation are entitled to rely upon their board of directors to discharge *each* of their *three* primary fiduciary duties at all time[s].") (emphasis added). *But see* Roselink Investors, LLC v. Shenkman, 386 F. Supp. 2d 209 (S.D.N.Y. 2004); Emerald Partners v. Berlin, No. 9700, 2003 Del. Ch. LEXIS 42, 139 (Del. Ch. Apr. 28, 2003).

[58]*See* Roselink Investors, LLC v. Shenkman, 386 F. Supp. 2d 209 (S.D.N.Y. 2004) (specifically refuting plaintiff's claim that Delaware law recognizes an independent duty of good faith, saying instead that a duty of good faith is merely a part of the duty of loyalty). *See also* Emerald Partners v. Berlin, No. 9700, 2003 Del. Ch. LEXIS 42, 139 (Del. Ch. Apr. 28, 2003) (Delaware Chancery Court dicta in subsequent proceeding states that there is no independent duty of good faith: "Good faith is a fundamental component of the duty of loyalty. . . . Confusion about the relationship between the fiduciary duty of loyalty and its good faith component is attributable in part . . . to the way that the [Delaware General Corporation Law] is drafted").

condition of the duty of loyalty.[59] A director's or officer's failure to exercise good faith may only *indirectly* result in liability if such failure causes the director or officer to breach the duty of loyalty.[60] The Delaware Supreme Court did not clearly define the scope of the obligation to exercise good faith in *Stone v. Ritter*; however, the supreme court stated that when a director or officer consciously disregards his or her responsibilities by failing to act when there is a clear duty to act, the failure to act in good faith results in a breach of the duty of loyalty.[61] A director's or officer's failure to act in good faith may also serve to prohibit a director or officer from obtaining indemnification from the corporation under some state laws.[62] Despite the Delaware Supreme Court's clarification of the nature of the obligation to exercise good faith in *Stone v. Ritter*, some courts continue to refer to the "duty of good faith."[63]

### ii. Fairness (No Conflicts)

Conflicts may arise during a director's service to the corporation. A director may have a direct or indirect, financial, or nonfinancial interest in a transaction involving the corporation. Generally, directors should refrain from benefiting personally from their position within the corporation. In those situations where a director or officer does have an interest in a transaction involving the corporation, the director is an "interested" director and should disclose the interest to the other board members. The directors taking the matter under consideration should promptly screen the interested director from further discussion of the matter and prohibit the interested director from voting on the matter. The disinterested directors' evaluation should include careful deliberation of the interested director's conflict. An interested director generally will not be deemed to be liable for any harm to the corporation resulting from a conflict of interest transaction if the interested director provides full disclosure of all material information to the disinterested directors. Similarly, disinterested directors generally will not be held liable for harm to the corporation resulting from their approval of a conflict of interest transaction provided that they have considered the fairness of the transaction to the corporation in light of the conflict. In the event the transaction is later challenged, courts will look to

---

[59] 911 A.2d 362, 369–370 (Del. 2006) (upholding the *Caremark* standard for director oversight liability and explaining that "[w]here directors fail to act in the face of a known duty to act . . . they breach their duty of loyalty by failing to discharge that fiduciary obligation in good faith"; the Delaware Supreme Court explained that "the failure to act in good faith may result in liability because the requirement to act in good faith is a subsidiary element, i.e., a condition, of the fundamental duty of loyalty. . . . [A]lthough good faith may be described colloquially as part of the 'triad' of fiduciary duties that includes the duties of care and loyalty, the obligation to act in good faith does not establish an independent duty that stands on the same footing as the duties of care and loyalty"). *But see* Buckley v. O'Hanlon, No. 04-955 (GMS), 2007 U.S. Dist. LEXIS 22211 (D. Del. Mar. 28, 2007).

[60] 911 A.2d at 370.

[61] *Id.*

[62] *See, e.g.*, DEL. STAT. ANN. TIT. 8, §145(a)–(b) (2007); N.Y. BUS. CORP. LAW §722(a) (2007).

[63] *See* Buckley v. O'Hanlon, No. 04-955 (GMS), 2007 U.S. Dist. LEXIS 22211, at *9 (D. Del. Mar. 28, 2007) (stating that corporate officers and directors owe the corporation a *triad* of fiduciary duties—the duty of loyalty, the duty of due care, and the *duty of good faith*) (emphasis added).

determine if (a) the terms of the transaction were at least as fair to the corporation as they would have been to other third parties, (b) the transaction was reasonably likely to further the corporation's business activities, and (c) the decisionmaking process was fair.[64]

### iii.  Usurping Corporate Opportunity

In certain circumstances, the duty of loyalty further requires directors and officers to first offer to the corporation an opportunity related to the business of the corporation before pursuing such opportunity for their own benefit—failure to do so may be deemed to be a breach of the director's or officer's duty of loyalty.[65] The determination of whether a director or officer has violated the fiduciary duty of loyalty by pursuing a particular opportunity is fact-intensive.[66] In evaluating whether a director is obligated to first offer the opportunity to the corporation, courts will consider (a) the degree of similarity between the proposed transaction and the corporation's existing or contemplated business (i.e., whether the opportunity is, by its nature, in the line of the corporation's business and is of practical advantage to the corporation); (b) the origin of the director's knowledge of the opportunity (i.e., was the opportunity presented to the officer or director in his or her individual capacity or in his or her capacity as a director or officer of the corporation); (c) the corporation's interest or expectancy in the proposed transaction; and (d) whether the corporation is financially able to exploit the opportunity.[67]

### b.  Duty of Care

The duty of care obligates the officer or director to perform his or her duties in good faith, relying on adequate information, and in the best interests of the corporation as the actor reasonably believes. The care required is that which a reasonably prudent director would use in similar circumstances. Obviously, this duty requires regular attendance at board meetings, obtaining and using adequate information to arrive at decisions, overseeing corporate management, requesting information from management as needed to stay informed of corporate activities, and carrying out other board functions.

### c.  Duty of Candor

In addition to the duties of care and loyalty, courts have held that directors owe shareholders a fiduciary duty of candor (also referred to as the duty of

---

[64]*See, e.g.*, Stroud v. Grace, 606 A.2d 73 (Del. 1992); Rabkin v. Philip A. Hunt Chem. Corp., 498 A. 2d 1099 (Del. 1985); Aronson v. Lewis, 473 A.2d 805 (1984); Lynch v. Vickers Energy Corp., 383 A.2d 278 (Del. 1977).

[65]*See* Broz v. Cellular Info. Sys., 673 A.2d 148, 151 (Del. 1996) (holding that a corporate director did not usurp a corporate opportunity belonging to the corporation). Although presentation of a purported corporate opportunity to the board of directors and the board's refusal to pursue the opportunity may serve to shield the interested officer or director from liability for breach of the duty of loyalty, there is no per se rule requiring a director or officer to present the opportunity to the board prior to accepting the opportunity. *Id.* Similarly, presentation of the opportunity to the board is not required where the opportunity is one that the corporation is incapable of exercising. *Id.*

[66]*Id.*

[67]*Id.*

complete candor or the duty of disclosure), pursuant to which directors must disclose all information in their possession germane to the matter at issue (i.e., any and all information that a reasonable shareholder would consider important in making a decision about the matter).[68] Specifically, the duty of candor encompasses an obligation to provide information, a duty to be materially accurate and complete with respect to the information provided, and the duty to be entirely fair by fully disclosing material information.[69] The duty is strict: directors may be held liable without regard to whether they were negligent in their failure to make a disclosure, and shareholders are afforded a remedy without regard to whether they relied on a statement (or lack thereof) made (or not made) in violation of the duty.[70] Moreover, shareholders are not required to establish actual loss as a result of a breach of the duty of candor in order to receive money damages.[71]

### d. Duties of Nondirector Officers

Nondirector officers generally are held to conform to the same obligations as directors.[72] However, officers and directors have different roles within an organization. Corporate officers are personally responsible for their actionable torts or breach of duty. A director's liability for an officer's conduct depends on whether the director breached his or her own duty of care to the corporation. Moreover, nondirector officers and directors operate with different sets of information. An officer may, as day-to-day manager, have greater knowledge about a particular business issue than one could expect a director to have. On other matters, directors may have superior or broader knowledge. In determining whether a duty of care was satisfied, one must make a case-by-case analysis of the information available to a specific decision maker. Clearly, different information may lead to different results.

---

[68] *See* Lynch v. Vickers Energy Corp., 383 A.2d 278 (Del. 1977) (describing a fiduciary duty of complete candor and complete frankness under which completeness, not adequacy, is both the norm and the mandate); Smith v. Van Gorkom, 488 A.2d 858 (Del. 1985) (directors have an obligation to know, share, and disclose information that is material and reasonably available for discovery); Stroud v. Grace, 606 A.2d 75 (Del. 1992) (it is now well recognized that fiduciary duty requires directors to disclose all material information within their control when they seek stockholder action). *See also* Ciro, Inc. v. Gold, 816 F. Supp. 253, 266 (D. Del. 1993) (directors are obligated under the duty of complete candor to disclose all material facts, even when the disclosure being made is voluntary and shareholders are not requested or expected to act in reliance on the disclosure); Johnson v. Shapiro, No. 17651, 2002 Del. Ch. LEXIS 122 (Del. Ch. Oct. 18, 2002) (Delaware law clearly establishes that directors owe a corporation's stockholders a fiduciary duty to disclose all facts germane to a transaction involving stockholder action, in an atmosphere of complete candor).

[69] *See* Feldman v. Cutaia, No. 1656-N, 2006 Del. Ch. LEXIS 70, at *31–32 (Del. Ch. Apr. 5, 2006) (denying a defendant's motion to dismiss a claim for breach of fiduciary duty of candor where the plaintiff adequately alleged that defendant failed to disclose all material information relating to a tender offer).

[70] *See, e.g.*, Arnold v. Society for Savings Bancorp, Inc., 678 A.2d 533 (Del. Ch. 1996); *In re* Anderson, 519 A.2d 669, 675 (Del. Ch. 1986); Zirn v. VLI Corp., 621 A.2d 773, 779 (Del. 1993); *In re* Tri-Star Pictures, Inc., 634 A.2d 319, 327 n.10 (Del. 1993) (*citing Van Gorkom*, 488 A.2d at 858; Weinberger v. UPO, Inc., 457 A.2d 701 (Del. 1983)).

[71] *Tri-Star Pictures*, 634 A.2d at 333.

[72] *See* MODEL BUS. CORP. ACT §8.42 (1998).

The question of whether the business judgment rule applies to nondirector officers is unsettled.[73] Several Delaware cases have determined that the rule does apply to such officers.[74] However, other courts, even those purporting to apply Delaware law, have determined that it does not.[75]

Even when an individual has knowledge that he is soon to become an officer, his fiduciary duty does not begin until the date he actually becomes an officer.[76]

### e. Other Types of Exposure

Under several statutes, corporate officers (and managing employees) may be personally excluded from participation in federal health care programs[77] if the entity that employed them has been convicted of certain offenses or excluded from participation in federal health care programs, even if the individuals themselves did not participate in the wrongdoing.[78] In addition, in certain cases, any individual, including a director or officer, convicted of a criminal offense involving the breach of fiduciary responsibility is subject to exclusion.[79] Once an individual is excluded, the employer is subject to civil monetary penalties[80] and possible exclusion for hiring him or her, and reinstatement is discretionary.[81]

## 2. Limitations on the Liability of Directors and Officers

### a. Business Judgment Rule

Not every decision made by a director is the correct one. Some decisions, viewed retrospectively, may appear less than judicious. However, the law does not permit directors' decisions to be contested as long as the directors followed appropriate procedures in arriving at the decision.[82] The business judgment rule is an important tool that often serves to limit liability for claims of director mismanagement and breach of the duty of care.[83] Please note, however, that the

---

[73]*See* WILLIAM E. KNEPPER & DAN A. BAILEY, LIABILITY OF CORPORATE OFFICERS AND DIRECTORS (7th ed. 2002), at 39.

[74]*See, e.g.,* Ella M. Kelly & Wyndham, Inc. v. Bell, 266 A.2d 878 (Del. 1970).

[75]*See, e.g.,* Platt v. Richardson, Civ. No. 88-0144, Fed. Sec. L. Rep. (CCH) ¶94,786, 1989 WL 159584, at *2 (M.D. Pa. June 6, 1989). For a more in-depth discussion of this issue, see KNEPPER & BAILEY, LIABILITY OF CORPORATE OFFICERS AND DIRECTORS, at 39.

[76]*In re* Walt Disney, 2004 Del. Ch. LEXIS 132, at *18–19.

[77]The federal health care programs include Medicare, Medicaid, Federal Employees Health Benefits Program, etc.

[78]42 U.S.C. §1320a-7(b)(15).

[79]42 U.S.C. §1320a-7(b)(1).

[80]42 U.S.C. §1320a-7a(a)(6); 42 C.F.R. §1003.102(a)(2).

[81]42 U.S.C. §1320a-7(g); 42 C.F.R. §1001.3002.

[82]Note that although the business judgment rule is a defense to claims of breach of fiduciary duty owed to a corporation, it has no applicability to defense of claims against directors for violation of state or federal statutes or regulations.

[83]By its focus and scope, the business judgment rule addresses claims of breach of the duty of care. Claims of self-dealing, conflict of interest, and the like involve the duty of loyalty. The business judgment rule does not insulate against claims of breach of the duty of loyalty. *See, e.g.,* Cuker v. Mikalauskas, 692 A.2d 1042 (Pa. 1997).

protections generally afforded to a director or officer under the business judgment rule are not available when the director or officer is deemed to have
breached the duty of loyalty.[84]

The business judgment rule "is a presumption that in making a business
decision the directors of a corporation acted on an informed basis, in good faith
and in the honest belief that the action taken was in the best interests of the
company."[85] Unless an abuse of discretion is established, the courts will respect
the business decision. The rule places the burden of rebutting the presumption
on the challenger.[86]

The business judgment rule is composed of the following elements, each
of which must generally be present to shield directors from liability:

- a business decision,
- disinterestedness: a lack of personal interest or self-dealing,
- due care: an informed decision based on a reasonable effort to become
  aware of important facts and circumstances, and
- good faith: a reasonable belief that the best interests of the corporation
  and its shareholders are being served.

The requirement that a director actually make a business decision requires
action within the scope of corporate authority.[87] Questions arise concerning the
applicability of the rule to inaction or failure to act. The rule provides no
protection where a director has eschewed his or her role and failed to perform
the function to decide. Where, however, the failure to act is a result of a conscious decision to refrain from acting, the rule applies.[88]

Disinterestedness requires that the director not be permitted to use the trust
and confidence accompanying the office to expand his or her personal interests.[89] The element of disinterestedness makes the business judgment rule
available only to those who are without conflict of interest. Appearing on both
sides of a transaction is a paradigm example of lack of disinterestedness. Under
Delaware law, directors are "interested" not solely where they are on both sides
of a transaction, but also where they expect personally to receive gain from the
transaction in addition to the gain they receive as shareholders.[90]

Directors can establish the exercise of due care sufficient to invoke the
business judgment rule where they have informed themselves, before the decision, of all material information reasonably available to them and acted
with requisite care in assessing the information and reaching the decision. The
rule will not protect directors who acted "so far without information that

---

[84]*See* Continuing Creditors' Comm. of Star Telecomm. v. Edgecomb, 385 F. Supp. 2d 449,
462 (D. Del. 2004) (*citing* Emerald v. Berlin, 787 A.2d 85, 90 (Del. 2001).

[85]Aronson v. Lewis, 473 A.2d 805, 812 (Del. 1984) (citations omitted), *overruled on other
grounds by* Brehm v. Eisner, 746 A.2d 244 (Del. 2000). *See also* Resolution Trust Corp. v. Acton,
844 F. Supp. 307 (N.D. Tex. 1994).

[86]*See, e.g., Aronson*, 473 A.2d at 812.

[87]*See, e.g.,* Crouse-Hinds Co. v. InterNorth, Inc., 634 F.2d 690, 702 (2d Cir. 1980).

[88]*See, e.g., Aronson*, 473 A.2d at 813; Rales v. Blasband, 634 A.2d 927, 933–34 (Del.
1993).

[89]*See, e.g., Aronson*, 473 A.2d at 812.

[90]*See, e.g., id.*

they . . . passed an unintelligent and unadvised judgment."[91] In *Smith v. Van Gorkum*, the Delaware Supreme Court rejected the directors' attempts to invoke the rule's protection in response to claims surrounding a merger.[92] The directors' lack of awareness of the CEO's role in championing the transaction and setting the per-share compensation and the intrinsic value of the corporation rendered their approval of the transaction with only two hours' consideration grossly negligent.[93] The *Van Gorkum* analysis was reiterated in *Cede & Co. v. Technicolor*, again in the context of a failure to reach an informed decision in approving the sale of the company.[94]

The general standard for determining whether a director has exercised appropriate due care is gross negligence.[95] Courts will assume that a director has made an informed decision unless the evidence demonstrates gross negligence in the director's investigation and inquiry. Gross negligence is a high standard. It includes the concepts of reckless indifference, gross abuse, and, in some instances, conscious indifference.[96] Note, however, that a magistrate judge in a 1998 case held that directors and officers would not be held liable for gross negligence; rather, liability would attach if they acted intentionally to harm the corporation.[97]

Good faith sufficient to obtain the protection of the business judgment rule generally means that the director's actions were taken in the good faith belief that the decision was in the corporation's best interests.[98] To overcome the presumption of good faith, a challenger "must show some sort of bad faith on the part of the defendant."[99] A challenger's hurdle is high. A court may infer bad faith only where the challenged business decision is "so far beyond the bounds of reasonable judgment that it seems essentially inexplicable on any ground other than bad faith."[100] If the decision can be attributed to "any rational business purpose," it will be considered to have been made in good faith.[101]

Courts continue to follow the business judgment rule[102] as set forth in *Aronson v. Lewis,*[103] and continue to rely on the *Aronson* standard of gross

---

[91]Smith v. Van Gorkum, 488 A.2d 858, 873 n.13 (Del. 1985) (quoting Mitchell v. Highland-Western Glass, 167 A. 831, 833 (Del. Ch. 1933)).

[92]488 A.2d 858, 874–81 (Del. 1985).

[93]*See id.*

[94]634 A.2d 345, 368–71 (Del. 1993).

[95]*See Van Gorkum*, 488 A.2d at 873 (*citing Aronson*, 473 A.2d at 812).

[96]*See, e.g.,* Briggs v. Spaulding, 141 U.S. 132 (1891), *implicitly overruled on other grounds by* Erie R.R. Co. v. Tompkins, 304 U.S. 64, 78 (1938).

[97]*See* Magistrate Judge's Report and Recommendation, at 56, McCall v. Scott, No. 3:97-0838 (M.D. Tenn. July 1, 1998). See also the discussions in Sections III.D.4.b.ii. and III.D.5., below.

[98]*See Van Gorkum*, 488 A.2d at 872; *Aronson*, 473 A.2d at 812.

[99]Johnson v. Trueblood, 629 F.2d 287, 293 (3d Cir. 1980) (citation omitted), *cert. denied*, 450 U.S. 999 (1981).

[100]*In re* J.P. Stevens & Co. Shareholders Litig., 542 A.2d 770, 780–81 (Del. Ch. 1988).

[101]Unocal Corp. v. Mesa Petroleum Co., 493 A.2d 946, 954 (Del. 1985) (*citing* Sinclair Oil Corp. v. Levien, 280 A.2d 717, 720 (Del. 1971)).

[102]*See, e.g.,* Emerald Partners v. Berlin, 787 A.2d 85, 90 (Del. 2001); Telxon Corp. v. Meyerson, 802 A.2d 257, 264 (Del. 2002).

[103]473 A.2d 805 (Del. 1984), *overruled on other grounds by* Brehm v. Eisner, 746 A.2d 244 (Del. 2000).

negligence to determine whether a director has exercised due care.[104] Courts also have maintained that "bad faith" will be inferred only in those rare circumstances where the decision under attack is far beyond the bounds of reasonable judgment.[105] If, however, a director has acted with either intentional or conscious disregard of his or her duties, the director will be found to have violated the duty of good faith.[106]

### b. Statutory and Corporate Measures to Reduce Directors' and Officers' Liability

Most state legislatures have taken steps permitting corporations to limit the personal liability of directors. The most common type of "shield" statute is the Delaware model.[107] Delaware permits corporations to enact provisions relieving directors of personal liability for damages resulting from breach of the duty of care. The law has no effect unless the corporation adopts the relief in its original charter or validly approved changes to its articles of incorporation. Accordingly, the measure adopted may be broad, as most are, or more narrow. The law provides relief for directors only—not officers. The law does not permit corporations to eliminate or restrict liability in certain areas, including the following:

- Liability for breach of the duty of loyalty remains unaffected.
- Liability is preserved for acts not undertaken in good faith.
- Directors remain liable for violation of federal statutes (e.g., the Racketeer Influenced and Corrupt Organizations Act (RICO) and securities laws).
- Attempts to obtain equitable relief (e.g., injunctions) remain unaffected.[108]

### c. Indemnification and Insurance

In addition to including liability limitations pursuant to statute, corporations can provide statutorily authorized indemnification to officers and directors, further protecting them from personal liability exposure. Most states have passed statutes that permit corporations to indemnify directors and officers under specified circumstances. Again, the Delaware statute is instructive, both be-

---

[104]*See, e.g.,* McCall v. Scott, 250 F.3d 997, 999 (6th Cir. 2001); Roselink Investors, L.L.C. v. Shenkman, 386 F. Supp. 2d 209 (S.D.N.Y. 2004).

[105]Orman v. Cullman, 794 A.2d 5, 20 (Del. Ch. 2002); McMichael v. United States Filter Corp., 2001 U.S. Dist. LEXIS 3918, at *31 (C.D. Cal. Feb. 22, 2001).

[106]*See In re* Emerging Communications, Inc. Litig., 2004 Del. Ch. LEXIS 70, at *153 (Del. Ch. 2004) (explaining that three directors did not violate their duty of good faith where no evidence was presented that they acted with conscious and intentional disregard of their responsibilities or that their decisions were made without obtaining necessary material information). *See also* Gesoff v. IIC Indus., Inc., 902 A.2d 1130, 1167 (Del. Ch. 2006) (in finding that a director did not intentionally prevent an arm's length bargaining process within the context of a merger, the Delaware Chancery Court quoted the following language from its opinion in *In re Emerging Communications, Inc. Litigation*: "[N]egligent or even gross negligent conduct does not equate to disloyalty or bad faith").

[107]*See* DEL. CODE ANN. tit. 8, §102(b)(7).

[108]*See id. See also* Melvin A. Eisenberg, *Corporate Law and Social Norms,* 99 COLUM. L. REV. 1253, 1267 (June 1999).

cause it serves as a model for other statutes and because of the breadth of its coverage.[109] The Delaware statute states as follows:

> A corporation shall have power to indemnify any person [sued or threatened to be sued] . . . by reason of the fact that the person is or was a director, officer, employee or agent of the corporation . . . [provided that] the person acted in good faith and in a manner the person reasonably believed to be in or not opposed to the best interests of the corporation, and, with respect to any criminal action or proceeding, had no reasonable cause to believe the person's conduct was unlawful.[110]

Most statutes permit, but do not require, indemnification. Some states require indemnification if the person is successful in defense of the claim. In such cases, indemnification is limited to expenses actually incurred in the defense (e.g., attorneys' fees).[111] Where indemnification is permissive, the statute generally requires a finding that the person seeking indemnification has met the applicable standards of conduct (e.g., good faith; reasonable belief that the conduct was in the corporation's best interests; and, with respect to criminal actions, no reasonable cause to believe the conduct was not lawful).[112] This determination must be made by (a) the board by a majority vote of those not a party to the proceedings, (b) independent legal counsel, or (c) the shareholders by majority vote. These statutes also frequently contain clauses that suggest that directors may have additional rights beyond those enumerated in the law, and some director compensation contracts provide benefits that exceed those available under the statute. However, some laws have categories of expenses that cannot be indemnified, including adverse final judgments or derivative suit settlements.[113]

Indemnification or other statutes also may authorize corporations to purchase insurance coverage protecting directors and officers (D&O) against liability exposure (i.e., D&O policies). The Delaware provision is typical:

> A corporation shall have power to purchase and maintain insurance on behalf of any person who is or was a director, officer, employee or agent of the corporation, . . . against any liability asserted against such person and incurred by such person in any such capacity, or arising out of such person's status as such, whether or not the corporation would have the power to indemnify such person against such liability under this section.[114]

Thus, a corporation is empowered to purchase D&O policies providing broader protection than the corporation itself may provide through corporate indemnification.[115] D&O policies are available with a wide variety of terms and

---

[109]Indemnification is an internal corporate matter; as such, it generally is governed by the law of the state of incorporation. *See, e.g.,* McDermott, Inc. v. Lewis, 531 A.2d 206, 215 (Del. 1987). Delaware is the state of incorporation for many corporations.

[110]DEL. STAT. ANN. tit 8, §145(a).

[111]*See, e.g.,* N.Y. BUS. CORP. LAW §723 (McKinney 2007).

[112]DEL. CODE ANN. tit. 8, §§145(d), (a).

[113]*See* Mae Kuykendall, *Assessment and Evaluation: Retheorizing the Evolving Rules of Director Liability,* 8 J.L. & POL'Y 1, 6 (1999).

[114]DEL. CODE ANN. tit. 8, §145(g).

[115]In 1996, the Second Circuit clarified that Delaware law explicitly allows a corporation to circumvent the requirement that an individual seeking indemnification have acted in good faith

conditions. The exclusions limiting coverage differ widely, as do the circumstances required for an insured to qualify for the protections offered by the policy.

D&O policies often offer two types of coverage within the same policy. The first type of coverage indemnifies directors and officers for losses for which they are not indemnified by the corporation (personal coverage). The second type of coverage reimburses the corporation for monies that it lawfully expends in indemnifying its directors and officers for their losses (reimbursement coverage).

## C. The Sarbanes-Oxley Act and Related Developments

In July 2002, President George W. Bush signed into law the Sarbanes-Oxley Act of 2002,[116] which was, in large part, a response to public outrage over the corporate scandals at Enron[117] and WorldCom.[118] The Sarbanes-Oxley Act mandated numerous corporate governance changes for publicly traded companies, increased the type and frequency of disclosure required for such companies, and dramatically revised the oversight of the public accountacy industry.

The Sarbanes-Oxley Act applies generally to each "issuer" (as defined in Section 3 of the Securities Exchange Act of 1934),[119] the securities of which are registered under Section 12 of that Act[120] or that is required to file reports under Section 15(d),[121] or "that files or has filed a registration statement that has not yet become effective under the Securities Act of 1933,"[122] "and that it has not withdrawn."[123] The Sarbanes-Oxley Act directed the SEC to direct,

---

by purchasing a D&O policy. *See* Waltuch v. Conticommodity Services, Inc., 88 F.3d 87, 93 (2d Cir. 1996) ("[s]ubsection (g) explicitly allows a corporation to circumvent the 'good faith' clause of subsection (a) by purchasing a directors and officers liability insurance policy").

[116]Pub. L. No. 107-204, 116 Stat. 745 (2002) [hereinafter Sarbanes-Oxley Act].

[117]Enron succumbed to an accounting scandal that surfaced in 2001. Enron and 78 of its subsidiaries filed for bankruptcy in December 2001 after the Houston-based energy corporation disclosed billions of dollars in debt previously hidden from investors and securities regulators through Enron-controlled off-books limited partnerships. *See* Catherine Tomasko, *Judge OKs Enron Directors' $168 Million Settlement*, FINDLAW LEGAL NEWS & COMMENTARY (Mar. 8, 2005). The bankruptcy led to numerous shareholder suits and the criminal convictions of several top executives, including former chairman Kenneth Lay and former CEO Jeffrey Skilling. *Id.*

[118]The collapse of WorldCom began in 2002 when the company disclosed that employees falsified records to inflate revenues reported on financial statements from 1999 through 2002. An investigation uncovered an $11 billion fraud, which drove WorldCom into the largest corporate bankruptcy in the nation's history. WorldCom's shareholders filed suit against the company, its directors and officers, the investment banks that underwrote WorldCom Securities, as well as the company's auditor, Arthur Andersen LLP, alleging, among other things, fraud and breach of fiduciary duty. The SEC also filed a civil action against WorldCom. *See* SEC v. WorldCom, Civil Action No. 02-CV-4963 (S.D.N.Y. filed June 26, 2002). The company's collapse led to numerous shareholder suits (resulting in the payment of more than $6 billion in settlements with shareholders) and the criminal conviction of former CEO Bernard Ebbers. *See* Steven Taub, *WorldCom Director's Settlement Back On*, CFO.COM (Mar. 22, 2005), *available at* http://www.cfo .com/article.cfm/3784902?f=related.

[119]15 U.S.C. §78c.

[120]15 U.S.C. §78e.

[121]15 U.S.C. §78d.

[122]15 U.S.C. §§77a *et seq.*

[123]Sarbanes-Oxley Act §2(a)(7) (codified at 15 U.S.C. §7201).

by rule, the national securities exchanges and national securities associations to prohibit the listing of any security of an issuer that is not in compliance with several enumerated standards regarding issuer audit committees.[124] In April 2003, as required by the Sarbanes-Oxley Act, the SEC adopted Rule 10A-3.[125]

In response to Rule 10A-3, the New York Stock Exchange (NYSE), the National Association of Securities Dealers, Inc. (NASD), and the American Stock Exchange (Amex) have each adopted changes to their self-regulatory organization (SRO) listing standards—i.e., alterations to their respective corporate governance rules—and these changes have been approved by the SEC.[126] In general, registered companies were required to be in compliance with the SRO rules changes by the earlier of their first annual meeting of shareholders after January 15, 2004, or by October 31, 2004.[127]

A detailed discussion of the Sarbanes-Oxley Act and the SRO rules changes is beyond the scope of this chapter, but the following discussion outlines some of the more significant provisions. Neither the Sarbanes-Oxley Act nor the SRO rules changes alter a director's duties of care and loyalty under state corporate law. Rather, the corporate governance changes mandated by Sarbanes-Oxley and the SRO rules are largely process-oriented and increase the influence and involvement of a registered company's independent directors by, among other things, mandating that certain decisions be delegated to the independent directors, including decisions relating to the company's audit, the compensation of its executive officers, the nomination of individuals to the company's board of directors, and the overarching governance principles of each registered company.[128]

More specifically, under the Sarbanes-Oxley Act and the SRO rules:

- a majority of the board of directors of each registered company must be independent; [129]
- a registered company's outside auditor must report to the audit committee of the board of directors (which must consist solely of independent directors);[130]

---

[124]Sarbanes-Oxley Act §301.

[125]Standards Relating to Listed Company Audit Committees, 68 Fed. Reg. 18,788 (Apr. 16, 2003) (final rule codified at 17 C.F.R. pts. 228, 229, 240, 249, and 274).

[126]NYSE Corporate Governance Rules, as approved by the SEC November 4, 2003, and amended on November 3, 2004, are contained in Section 303A of the NYSE's Listed Company Manual (the NYSE Rules), *available at* http://www.nyse.com; NASDAQ Corporate Governance Rules, as approved by the SEC on November 4, 2003, are contained in NASDAQ Rules, Rule 4000 Series (the NASDAQ Rules), *available at* http://www.nasdaqnews.com; and Amex Corporate Governance Rules, as approved by the SEC on December 1, 2003, are contained in Amex Company Guide Part 1 and Part 8 (the Amex Company Guide), *available at* http://www.amex.com.

[127]68 Fed. Reg. 18,788 (Apr. 16, 2003).

[128]Sarbanes-Oxley Act §§202, 204, 301; NYSE Rules ¶¶303A.04, 303A.05, 303A.07, and 303A.09; NASDAQ Rules 4350(c) and 4350(d); and Amex Company Guide Part 8 §§804(a) and ¶807.

[129]NYSE Rules ¶303A.01; NASDAQ Rules 4350(c)(1); and Amex Company Guide Part 1 ¶121(A).

[130]Sarbanes-Oxley Act §301.

- the audit committee has the mandate to hire, fire, and perform oversight of the outside auditor,[131] and must pre-approve nonaudit services provided by the outside auditor;[132]
- a board committee consisting solely of independent directors (or a majority of all independent directors) must make certain determinations relating to executive compensation;[133]
- a board committee consisting solely of independent directors (or a majority of all independent directors) must make certain determinations relating to board nominations and corporate governance;[134]
- the nonmanagement directors (i.e., those directors not employed by the company) must meet regularly without the executive officers of the company;[135] and
- the definition of "independence" has been tightened.[136]

Under the SRO rules, registered companies are required to maintain a code of business conduct and ethics applicable to all employees and directors covering matters such as compliance with laws and avoidance of conflicts of interest.[137] Moreover, the Sarbanes-Oxley Act mandates that each registered company have a code of ethics applicable to the CEO and senior financial officer that is reasonably designed to deter wrongdoing and promote, among other things, full, fair, accurate, timely, and understandable disclosure in the reports and documents the company files with the SEC and prompt internal reporting to an appropriate person in the event of a violation of the code.[138]

The disclosure obligations under the Securities Exchange Act of 1934, as amended, and the Securities Act of 1933, as amended, were also revised under the Sarbanes-Oxley Act to require more rapid disclosure of material adverse changes and more detailed disclosure of off-balance-sheet transactions and pro forma financial disclosure.[139] The SEC has issued detailed final rules implementing these additional disclosure requirements.[140]

---

[131]*Id.*

[132]Sarbanes-Oxley Act §201.

[133]NYSE Rules ¶303A.05; NASDAQ Rules 4350(c)(3); and Amex Company Guide Part 8 ¶805.

[134]NYSE Rules ¶303A.04; NASDAQ Rules 4350(c)(4); and Amex Company Guide Part 8 ¶804.

[135]NYSE Rules ¶303A.03; NASDAQ Rules 4350(c)(2); and Amex Company Guide Part 8 ¶802 (b).

[136]NYSE Rules ¶303A.02; NASDAQ Rules 4200; and Amex Company Guide Part 1 ¶121A.

[137]NYSE Rules ¶303A.010; NASDAQ Rules 4350 (n); and Amex Company Guide Part 8 ¶807A.

[138]Sarbanes-Oxley Act §406; Disclosure Required by §§404, 406, and 407 of the Sarbanes-Oxley Act of 2002, 67 Fed. Reg. 66,208 (SEC Release Nos. 33-8138; 34-46701; IC-25775: File No. S7-40-02) (proposed Oct. 30, 2002).

[139]Sarbanes-Oxley Act §§401, 409.

[140]Additional Form 8-K Disclosure Requirements and Acceleration of Filing Date, 69 Fed. Reg. 15,594 (SEC Release Nos. 33-8400; 34-49562; File No. S7-22-02) (Mar. 16, 2004); Disclosure in Management's Discussion and Analysis About Off-Balance Sheet Arrangements and Aggregate Contractual Obligations (SEC Release Nos. 33-8182; 34-47264; File No. S7-42-02) (Jan. 28, 2003); Conditions for Use of Non-GAAP Financial Measures (SEC Release Nos. 33-8176; 34-47226, File No. S7-43-02) (Jan. 22, 2003).

Two critical and controversial provisions of the Sarbanes-Oxley Act, Sections 302 and 906, place CEOs and chief financial officers (CFOs) of registered companies under the public magnifying glass by requiring personal certifications to the effect that, in pertinent part, the information filed with the SEC complies with all legal requirements and does not omit any fact necessary to make the information not misleadingly incomplete. In addition, the Section 302 certification requires the CEO and CFO to certify, among other things, that the financial statements in the report fairly present in all material respects the financial condition, results of operations, and cash flows of the company, that the company has disclosure controls and procedures and internal controls over financial reporting, and that the CEO and CFO have evaluated the effectiveness of these controls as of the end of the period covered by the report. The Section 906 certification exposes a CEO and a CFO to criminal penalties and fines of up to $5 million, imprisonment of up to 20 years, or both. The Section 302 certification and the annual internal control report mandated under Section 404 of the Sarbanes-Oxley Act require each CEO and CFO of a registered company to accept responsibility for, and periodically assess the effectiveness of, the company's internal disclosure controls and procedures, and internal controls over financial reporting.[141]

In addition, Section 304 of the Sarbanes-Oxley Act mandates the forfeiture by the CEO and the CFO of certain bonuses and other compensation and profits from the sale of certain company securities if a registered company is required to prepare an accounting restatement due to the company's material noncompliance with any financial reporting requirement under the securities laws, due to misconduct (the misconduct that triggers the forfeiture does not have to be the misconduct of the CEO or CFO).

Section 303 of the Sarbanes-Oxley Act makes it unlawful for a director or officer (or person acting under their direction) to fraudulently influence, coerce, manipulate, or mislead a registered company's auditor for purposes of rendering financial statements materially misleading. Conduct that could violate Section 303 includes offering bribes or financial incentives, threatening to cancel the auditor's engagement, and attempting to have the audit partner removed from the engagement. Section 806 of the Sarbanes-Oxley Act strengthens protections intended to protect "whistleblowers" and witnesses from discrimination and retaliation, including fines or imprisonment for knowing violations against witnesses.

In January 2006, following months of discussion, the SEC proposed the most sweeping set of changes to executive and director compensation disclosure since 1992.[142] The rules became final in August 2006. The rules amended the disclosure requirements for executive and director compensation, related

---

[141] "Accelerated filers" (generally, U.S. issuers with an equity capitalization of more than $75 million that have filed an annual report with the SEC) must comply with the requirements of §404 for fiscal years ending on or after November 15, 2004. Nonaccelerated filers must comply with the requirements of §404 for fiscal years ending on or after July 15, 2006.

[142] *See* U.S. Securities and Exchange Commission, *SEC Votes to Propose Changes to Disclosure Requirements Concerning Executive Compensation and Related Matters* (Jan. 17, 2006), *available at* http://www.sec.gov/news/press/2006-10.htm. The proposed rule is available at 71 Fed. Reg. 6542 (Feb. 8, 2006).

party transactions, security ownership of officers and directors, and director independence and other corporate governance matters. In December 2006, the SEC further amended the executive and director compensation disclosure rules to make them more consistent with the standards of the Financial Accounting Standards Board.[143] The purpose of the new rules is to provide investors with complete disclosure regarding director and executive compensation.[144]

Although the duties of care and loyalty were not directly altered by the Sarbanes-Oxley Act and the SRO rules changes, courts have more closely scrutinized the decisionmaking process used by corporate boards. In other words, although the business judgment rule has continued to be respected by courts, appropriate "business judgment" is largely a reflection of the Sarbanes-Oxley standards, e.g., boards should exercise a heightened level of diligence prior to relying on reports of outside experts or officers of the company. Further, many of the disclosure requirements imposed on registered companies have been, and likely will continue to be, used by the securities plaintiffs' bar as additional bases for attack and litigation. In addition, although these standards are only legally binding on publicly traded companies, some have attempted to use them against all other companies as well.

## III. Litigation Against Officers and Directors

Directors and officers face the risk of civil lawsuits when shareholders suspect fraud or mismanagement, when the price of the company's stock falls, and under a wide variety of other circumstances. The vehicles for bringing such complaints to court most commonly are shareholder derivative actions and class action suits.

### A. Shareholder Derivative Actions

#### 1. Shareholder Derivative Actions in General

A shareholder derivative action is a case brought by a shareholder or a group of shareholders against directors and/or officers of the company. The claim is brought on behalf of the corporation, and it is one that the corporation is unwilling to assert itself.[145] As such, the claim (or loss) is not the shareholders' but the corporation's, and the recovery, if any, belongs not to the complaining shareholders but to the corporation. The derivative suit is an equitable creation designed to provide a remedy for a breach of the fiduciary duty a director or officer owes to the corporation where the corporation will not act to address the breach.[146]

---

[143] 17 C.F.R. §228.402 (2006).

[144] *See* U.S. Securities and Exchange Commission, *SEC Amends Executive Compensation Disclosure to More Closely Align with FAS 123R* (Dec. 22, 2006), *available at* http://www.sec. gov/news/press/2006/2006-219.htm. In the release, SEC Chairman Christopher Cox explains that "[t]he new disclosure requirements will make it easier for companies to prepare and for investors to understand."

[145] *See, e.g.,* Ross v. Bernhard, 396 U.S. 531, 534 (1970).

[146] *See, e.g.,* Koster v. (American) Lumbermens Mut. Cas. Co., 330 U.S. 518, 522 (1947).

Several important preconditions or requirements attach to derivative actions and serve to limit them:

- The corporation must have failed to enforce a right after demand on its managers to do so.
- The corporation may properly assert that right.
- The plaintiff must have been a shareholder at the time of the transaction complained of.
- The action must not be collusive.
- The plaintiff must fairly and adequately represent the interests of similarly situated shareholders.[147]

### 2. Presuit Demand Requirements

The first condition for a shareholder derivative action—that the corporation must have failed to enforce a right—establishes that the plaintiff is suing to enforce a corporate right. Claim of injury to a group of shareholders, for instance, is not a corporate claim enforceable by derivative action in the name of the corporation. Suing to enforce a corporate right is not itself sufficient: The plaintiff must "allege with particularity the efforts . . . made by the plaintiff to obtain the [desired] action . . . from the directors or comparable authority and, if necessary, from the stockholders or members, and the reasons for . . . fail[ing] to obtain the action or for not making the effort."[148]

The purpose of this demand requirement is to

> insure that a stockholder exhausts his intracorporate remedies, and then to provide a safeguard against strike suits. Thus, by promoting this form of alternative dispute resolution, rather than immediate recourse to litigation, the demand requirement is a recognition of the fundamental precept that directors manage the business and affairs of the corporations.[149]

The demand requirement merely obliges shareholders to communicate to the directors the identity of the alleged wrongdoer(s), describe the facts and the legal theories available, identify the shareholder(s), describe the injury to the corporation, and specifically request the action.[150] No particular form of written communication or level of formality is required.

Plaintiffs frequently assert that demand on the corporation would be futile and should be excused. Delaware excuses the demand requirement only if facts are alleged with particularity that create a reasonable doubt that the directors' action was entitled to the business judgment rule. According to the Delaware Supreme Court in *Aronson v. Lewis*, a plaintiff must show either that a majority of the directors were not independent and disinterested or that because of the substance of the transaction or the manner in which they reached

---

[147]*See* FED. R. CIV. P. 23.1; *see also* DEL. CODE ANN. tit. 8, §327.

[148]FED. R. CIV. P. 23.1.

[149]Aronson v. Lewis, 473 A.2d 805, 811–12 (Del. 1984), *overruled on other grounds by* Brehm v. Eisner, 746 A.2d 244 (Del. 2000).

[150]*See, e.g.,* Allison v. General Motors Corp., 604 F. Supp. 1106, 1117 (D. Del. 1986), *aff'd*, 782 F.2d 1026 (3d Cir. 1985).

their decision, the directors could not have validly exercised business judgment.[151] However, the *Aronson* test is inapplicable in cases where the board is accused of inaction:

> [T]he absence of board action, therefore, makes it impossible to perform the essential inquiry contemplated by *Aronson*—whether the directors have acted in conformity with the business judgment rule in approving the challenged transaction....
>
> [A] court should not apply the *Aronson* test for demand futility where the board that would be considering the demand did not make a business decision which is being challenged in the derivative suit....
>
> [Demand is necessary] where directors are sued derivatively because they have failed to do something (such as a failure to oversee subordinates).[152]

In such circumstances "Delaware courts will excuse a failure to make...a demand if a majority of the board was interested or lacked independence to review the derivative claim."[153] Various courts continue to uphold the *Aronson* rule to determine whether to excuse a plaintiff's failure to make a demand on the board.[154]

In 1994, the American Law Institute (ALI) proposed a "universal demand" requirement under which the *Aronson* demand-futility exemption would be abolished. The proposed rule would excuse demand *only* "if the plaintiff makes a specific showing that irreparable injury to the corporation would otherwise result," and even then it would require demand promptly after commencement of the action.[155] Pennsylvania adopted the ALI universal-demand rule in an opinion critical of Delaware's more liberal rule.[156] Moreover, the Model Business Corporation Act's strict-demand rule had been adopted by 19 states as of September 2007.[157] The Model Act prohibits suit until 90 days after a written demand is made, unless the demand is rejected earlier or unless waiting for the 90-day

---

[151]*See Aronson*, 473 A.2d at 812–13; *Brehm*, 746 A.2d at 254–56 (reaffirming the *Aronson* standard but rejecting *Aronson*'s deference to the Chancery Court's demand-futility analysis in favor of de novo review of the issue).

[152]Rales v. Blasband, 634 A.2d 927, 933–34 & n.9 (Del. 1993).

[153]Katz v. Halpen, No. 13,811, 1996 WL 66006, at *7 (Del. Ch. Feb. 5, 1996), *reprinted in* 21 DEL. J. CORP. L. 690 (1996).

[154]*See, e.g.,* White v. Panic, 783 A.2d 543, 551 (Del. 2001); Werbowsky v. Collomb, 766 A.2d 123, 138–44 (Md. 2001) (also contains an extended discussion of the demand futility rule); Salsitz v. Nasser, 208 F.R.D. 589, 591 (E.D. Mich. 2002); *In re* Walt Disney Co. Derivative Litig., 825 A.2d 275 (Del. Ch. 2003); Beam v. Stewart, 845 A.2d 1040, 1057 (Del. 2004) (holding that the demand requirement was not excused).

[155]1 ALI PRINCIPLES OF CORPORATE GOVERNANCE: ANALYSIS AND RECOMMENDATIONS §7.03(b) (1994).

[156]*See, e.g.,* Cuker v. Mikalauskas, 692 A.2d 1042, 1048–49 (Pa. 1997). *See also* Audio Visual Xperts, Inc. v. Walker, No. 17261-NC, 2000 WL 222152, at *2 (Del. Ch. Feb. 18, 2000) (recognizing Pennsylvania's adoption of the ALI demand requirement).

[157]*See, e.g.,* ARIZ. REV. STAT. ANN. §10-742; CONN. GEN. STAT. ANN. §33-722; FLA. STAT. ANN. §607.07401; GA. CODE ANN. §14-2-742; HAW. REV. STAT. ANN. §414-173 (2004); IDAHO CODE §30-1-742; ME. REV. STAT. ANN. TIT. 13C, §53; MICH. COMP. LAW. ANN. §450.1493a; MISS. CODE ANN. §79-4-7.42; MONT. CODE ANN. §35-1-543; NEB. REV. STAT. §21-2072; N.H. REV. STAT. ANN. §293-A:7.42; N.C. GEN. STAT. §55-7-42; R.I. GEN. LAWS §7-1.2-711(C) (effective July 1, 2005); TEX. BUS. ORG. CODE ANN. §21.553 (effective Jan. 1, 2006); UTAH CODE ANN. §16-10a-740(3)(2); VA. CODE ANN. §13.1-672.1(B); WIS. STAT. ANN. §180.0742; WYO. STAT. ANN. §17-16-742.

period to expire would result in irreparable injury to the corporation.[158] A minority of jurisdictions also require that if the board of directors rejects the demand, shareholders must present the demand to all other shareholders before they can file a derivative suit.[159] This requirement has been adopted to allow the majority of shareholders to determine whether the suit is in the corporation's best interest.

### 3. Other Requirements for Derivative Actions

The remaining requirements for derivative actions collectively constitute standing requirements. The plaintiff must be a stockholder of the corporation whose interests he or she seeks to enforce. He or she must have been a stockholder at the time of the alleged injury or a successor to the shares by operation of law.[160] One cannot buy the right to bring a derivative action by purchasing shares after the conduct complained of has occurred.[161] Furthermore, a merger eliminates a plaintiff's standing to bring a derivative claim when the plaintiff ceases to be a stockholder as a result of the merger.[162]

As individuals seeking to vindicate the rights of others, derivative plaintiffs must be prepared to demonstrate their adequacy to fill that role. This question of adequate representation usually requires a showing that plaintiffs' counsel is qualified and experienced in these matters and generally able to thoroughly and diligently prosecute the case.[163] The courts also will look to plaintiffs' interests and require a demonstration that those interests are not antagonistic to interests of similarly situated shareholders.[164]

Derivative actions may not be dismissed or settled without court approval. The parties must provide notice to shareholders in a form and manner approved by the court.[165] Part of the court's responsibility is to ensure that the proposed settlement is fair to the parties, reasonable, and adequate.[166]

### B. Class Actions

Class actions, like shareholder derivative actions, face substantial procedural hurdles. Class actions, however, do not seek to assert claims of injury to the corporation. Rather, class actions seek compensation for harm done directly

---

[158] *See* MODEL BUS. CORP. ACT §7–42.

[159] *See* Wolgin v. Simon, 722 F.2d 389, 392 (8th Cir. 1993) (Missouri); Allright Missouri, Inc. v. Billeter, 829 F.2d 631, 639 (8th Cir. 1987) (Missouri); Strougo on behalf of Brazil Fund, Inc. v. Scudder, Stevens & Clark, Inc., 964 F. Supp. 783, 795 (S.D.N.Y. 1997) (Maryland); Grill v. Hoblitzell, 771 F. Supp. 709, 713 n.5 (D. Md. 1991) (Maryland); Bell v. Arnold, 487 P.2d 545, 547–48 (Colo. 1997) (Colorado); Harhen v. Brown, 730 N.E.2d 859, 868 (Mass. 2000) (Massachusetts); Skolnik v. Rose, 55 N.Y.2d 964, 965, 434 N.E.2d 251, 252, 449 N.Y.S.2d 182, 183 (1982) (Massachusetts); McLeese v. J.C. Nichols Co., 842 S.W.2d 115, 119 (Mo. Ct. App. 1992) (Missouri); Burdon v. Erskine, 401 A.2d 369, 370–71 (Pa. Super. Ct. 1979) (Pennsylvania).

[160] *See* FED. R. CIV. P. 23.1; DEL. CODE ANN. tit. 8, §327.

[161] *See, e.g.,* Blasband v. Rales, 971 F.2d 1034, 1041 (3d Cir. 1992).

[162] Lewis v. Ward, 852 A.2d 896, 900–02 (Del. 2004).

[163] *See, e.g.,* Wetzel v. Liberty Mut. Ins. Co., 508 F.2d 239, 247 (3d Cir.), *cert. denied*, 421 U.S. 1011 (1975).

[164] *See id.*

[165] *See* FED. R. CIV. P. 23.1.

[166] *See, e.g.,* Prince v. Bensinger, 244 A.2d 89, 93 (Del. Ch. 1968).

to the class members, often shareholders. Class actions are predicated on the theory that a few representative individuals effectively can become advocates in litigation for others in a similar situation. The class action device makes it economically feasible for a group of plaintiffs with relatively small claims to aggregate them, pursue them, and obtain relief.

## 1. Class Action Requirements

Rule 23 of the *Federal Rules of Civil Procedure* sets forth the requirements for maintenance of a class action:

- *Commonality.* There must be questions of law or fact common to the class of plaintiffs.
- *Typicality.* The claims of the representative plaintiffs must be typical of the claims of the class.
- *Numerosity.* The class must be so numerous that actual joinder in the action of all class members is not practicable.
- *Adequacy of representation.* The representative plaintiffs must be able to adequately represent the class.

Additionally, Rule 23 requires a showing of one of the following: (a) separate, non-class actions would create a risk of incompatible standards of conduct being established or would be dispositive as to nonparties; (b) the class as a whole may be entitled to injunctive or declaratory relief; or (c) the common questions of law or fact "predominate" over questions affecting only individual class members, and a class action is the superior method for the fair and efficient adjudication of the controversy.

Much litigation has surrounded the implementation of these standards.[167] With respect to commonality, courts look to whether class members are "united by a common interest"[168] or have the same case to prove.[169] While minor differences in facts will not prohibit maintenance of the class, claims that contain characteristics unique to each class member do not meet the commonality requirement.[170]

Numerosity is satisfied when the aggregate number of potential class members is so large that joinder of each as individual plaintiffs is impracticable. Class members typically exceed 100 in number; however, the numbers may vary. Class actions have been permitted to proceed with as few as 18 members,[171] while 95 has been deemed too few.[172]

Typicality requires that the named representatives' claims be sufficiently like the claims of others that one can assume that the interests of those others will not be neglected. Typicality does not exist where the conflict between such

---

[167]*See, e.g.,* HERBERT B. NEWBERG & ALBA CONTE, NEWBERG ON CLASS ACTIONS (4th ed. 2002).

[168]Blackie v. Barrack, 524 F.2d 891, 902 (9th Cir. 1975), *cert. denied*, 429 U.S. 816 (1976).

[169]*See, e.g.,* Castro v. Becker, 459 F.2d 725, 732 (1st Cir. 1972).

[170]*See, e.g., In re* Fibreboard Corp., 893 F.2d 706, 712 (5th Cir. 1990).

[171]*See* Gaspar v. Linvatec Corp., 167 F.R.D. 51, 56 (N.D. Ill. 1996).

[172]*See, e.g.,* Joshlin v. Gannett River States Publ'g Corp., 152 F.R.D. 577, 579 (E.D. Ark. 1993).

sets of interests is material, at the core of the controversy, and directly related to the subject matter.[173]

Adequacy of representation seeks to ensure that the named plaintiff will discharge his or her fiduciary duties to the class as its representative in the litigation.[174] The named plaintiff's interests must be sufficiently aligned with class members' to establish that his or her incentive to prosecute the matter is consistent with his or her obligation as a fiduciary. In addition, courts will consider the experience of plaintiff's counsel in class action litigation to arrive at a determination that counsel representing the class will themselves properly pursue the litigation.[175] When plaintiffs' counsel are involved in multiple lawsuits against the same defendant, conflicts of interest—or the appearance of conflict—may arise that render counsel inadequate. In *Krim v. pcOrder.Com, Inc.*,[176] the U.S. District Court for the Western District of Texas found that the plaintiffs failed to show the adequacy of counsel. In this case, lead counsel were involved in multiple lawsuits against pcOrder.com, in which counsel sought to represent different classes of pcOrder.com shareholders.[177] Lead counsel had failed to timely disclose to their clients their participation in multiple class representations against the same defendant.[178] According to the court, the multiple representation raised actual and potential conflicts between different classes. This risk of conflict intensified when class counsel participated in negotiations with the defendant for settlement of all the class action cases because the various classes' interests might well not coincide.[179]

Settlement or dismissal of class action matters requires court approval and notice to the class members. Approval by the court will be dependent on a finding that the settlement is fair to the various class members.[180] Settlement of a class action requires a court determination that the requirements for maintaining a class action have been met. Parties may not agree to a "settlement class" unless that class meets the class requirements set forth in Rule 23.[181] Since 1997, courts have continued to apply the *Amchem Products, Inc. v. Windsor*[182] approach to determine the appropriateness of settlement in class action matters.[183]

## 2. Class Not Limited to Shareholders

Although commonly brought to vindicate the rights of a group of shareholders against officers and directors, class actions are in no sense limited to claims of shareholders. For instance, class actions are a particularly common

---

[173]*See, e.g.*, Redmond v. Commerce Trust Co., 144 F.2d 140, 151–52 (8th Cir. 1944).

[174]*See, e.g.*, Koenig v. Benson, 117 F.R.D. 330, 333–34 (E.D.N.Y. 1987).

[175]*See, e.g.*, *In re* Northern Dist. of Cal., Dalkon Shield IUD Prods. Liab. Litig., 693 F.2d 847, 855 (9th Cir. 1982).

[176]210 F.R.D. 581 (W.D. Tex. 2002), *aff'd*, 402 F.3d 489 (5th Cir. 2005).

[177]*Id.* at 589.

[178]*Id.* at 590.

[179]*Id.*

[180]*See, e.g.*, Amchem Prods., Inc. v. Windsor, 521 U.S. 591, 619–22 (1997).

[181]*See id.*

[182]521 U.S. 591 (1997).

[183]Uhl v. Thoroughbred Tech. & Telecomms., Inc., 309 F.3d 978 (7th Cir. 2002).

device for maintaining securities fraud claims. The class can be quite large, including trading plaintiffs in its number. Such claims frequently are based on alleged material misrepresentations or omissions of directors and officers.

Similarly, any aggrieved group can assert direct class actions against directors and officers. For example, in *Spitzer v. Abdelhak*,[184] the plaintiffs were physicians who sold their practices to a large health care organization. The plaintiffs claimed that they were defrauded in the sale of their practices; they brought a class action suit on behalf of similarly situated physicians against the purchaser and certain of its officers and directors. The plaintiffs alleged violations of RICO[185] and state common law claims.

### 3. The Private Securities Litigation Reform Act and the Securities Litigation Uniform Standards Act

Intending to provide national, uniform standards for the securities market and nationally marketed securities,[186] Congress enacted the Private Securities Litigation Reform Act of 1995 (PSLRA).[187] In order to eliminate frivolous securities litigation,[188] the PSLRA heightens the pleading requirements in private securities fraud litigation by requiring that both falsity and scienter be pleaded with particularity.[189] To allege securities fraud, a complaint must now specify

- each statement alleged to have been misleading;
- the reason or reasons why the statement is misleading; and
- if an allegation regarding the statement or omission is made on information and belief, all facts on which that belief is formed.[190]

In April 2005, the U.S. Supreme Court held that the PSLRA requires plaintiffs to adequately allege and prove both the causation and loss elements to successfully bring a securities fraud action.[191] The PSLRA also provides guidelines for the appointment of the lead plaintiff in class actions, specifying that the lead plaintiff should be the plaintiff "most capable of adequately representing the interests of class members (. . . the 'most adequate plaintiff')."[192] The PSLRA creates a rebuttable presumption that the plaintiff who (1) has filed the complaint or made a motion to serve as lead plaintiff, (2) has the largest financial interest sought by the class, and (3) otherwise satisfies the requirements of Rule 23 of the Federal Rules of Civil Procedure is the "most adequate plaintiff."[193] After court

---

[184]No. 98-6475, 1999 WL 1204352 (E.D. Pa. Dec. 15, 1999). *Spitzer* is discussed at length in Section III.F., below.

[185]*See* Racketeer Influenced and Corrupt Organizations Act, 18 U.S.C. §§1951–60.

[186]*See* Patenaude v. Equitable Assurance Soc'y of U.S., 290 F.3d 1020, 1026 (9th Cir. 2002).

[187]Pub. L. No. 104-67, 109 Stat. 737 (1995) (codified in scattered sections of U.S.C. Title 15).

[188]*See* Falkowski v. Imation Corp., 309 F.3d 1123 (9th Cir. 2002), *reprinted as amended*, 320 F.3d 905 (9th Cir. 2003).

[189]*Id.*

[190]15 U.S.C. §78u-4(b)(1).

[191]*See* Dura Pharm. v. Broudo, 544 U.S. 336, 346 (2005).

[192]15 U.S.C. §78u-4(a)(3)(B)(i).

[193]15 U.S.C. §78u-4(a)(3)(B)(iii).

approval of the lead plaintiff, the lead plaintiff then selects counsel to represent the class.[194] The selection of class counsel is also subject to court approval.[195]

To avoid the PSLRA's strictures, plaintiffs began filing securities fraud litigation actions in state courts under state statutory or common law theories. Congress responded by passing the Securities Litigation Uniform Standards Act of 1998 (SLUSA).[196] This Act establishes a defendant's right to remove "covered securities" litigation actions to federal court.[197] A party seeking to establish that an action falls within the SLUSA's preemptive scope must show that (1) the action is a covered class action under the SLUSA; (2) the action purports to be based on state law; (3) the defendant is alleged to have misrepresented or omitted a material fact (or to have used or employed any manipulative or deceptive device or contrivance); and (4) the defendant is alleged to have engaged in conduct described by criterion (3) in connection with the purchase or sale of a covered security.[198] Generally, a covered security is a security listed on a national stock exchange such as the NYSE or an exchange with equivalent listing standards.[199] Notwithstanding the SLUSA's broad restriction on state securities class actions, it contains a savings clause that permits a narrow range of class actions to remain in state court.[200]

In March 2006, the U.S. Supreme Court held that the SLUSA applies broadly to preempt state law class action claims brought by holders of securities, as well as by purchasers and sellers of securities, alleging the fraudulent manipulations of stock prices.[201] The named plaintiff in *Merrill Lynch v. Dabit*, Shadi Dabit, was a broker at the financial services firm of petitioner Merrill Lynch. Dabit brought a class action suit in federal court alleging that Merrill Lynch had violated Oklahoma law by willfully distorting its stock recommendations and breaching both the covenant of good faith and fair dealing implied in the brokers' employment contracts and its fiduciary duties to its brokers. Dabit's original complaint, which was amended (in accordance with the district court's ruling) to exclude individuals who had "purchased" stocks, defined the class as including those brokers who "suffered damages as a result of owning and holding . . . [Merrill Lynch] Stocks" during the relevant time period. The class was also defined to include those brokers who suffered damages as a consequence of loss of clients due to Merrill Lynch's wrongful actions.[202] Citing Congress's intent in enacting the SLUSA to stem the shift in private securities class action litigation from federal to state courts and to prevent certain private

---

[194]*See* 15 U.S.C. §77z-1(a)(3)(B)(v).

[195]*Id.*

[196]Pub. L. No. 105-353, 112 Stat. 3227 (1998) (codified in scattered sections of U.S.C. Title 15).

[197]15 U.S.C. §77p(c).

[198]Green v. Ameritrade, Inc., 279 F.3d 590, 597 (8th Cir. 2002). *See* 15 U.S.C. §78bb(f)(1)–(2).

[199]*Green,* 279 F.3d at 596. *See* 15 U.S.C. §78bb(f)(1)–(2). *See also* 15 U.S.C. §78bb(f)(5)(E).

[200]15 U.S.C. §78bb(f)(3).

[201]*See* Merrill Lynch, Pierce, Fenner & Smith, Inc. v. Dabit, 547 U.S. 71 (2006).

[202]*See* Michah Smith, *Today's Argument in Merrill Lynch v. Dabit,* SCOTUSblog.com, *available at* http://www.scotusblog.com/movabletype/archives/2006/01/todays_argument_6.html.

securities class action lawsuits alleging fraud from being used to frustrate the objectives of the PSLRA, the Supreme Court determined that the distinction between holders and purchasers or sellers is irrelevant for purposes of SLUSA preemption—the identity of the plaintiffs does not determine whether the complaint alleges fraud "in connection with the purchase or sale" of securities.[203] The Supreme Court held that the misconduct alleged in the complaint—fraudulent manipulation of stock prices—unquestionably qualifies as fraud "in connection with the purchase or sale" of securities as the phrase is defined in the statute and the relevant case law.[204]

## C. The *Caremark* Decision

*In re Caremark International Derivative Litigation,*[205] a case that coincidentally involved a health care provider, has become a focal point for those concerned with potential liability for corporate directors and officers. During the relevant period, Caremark's primary lines of business involved alternative-site health care services, including infusion therapy, growth hormone therapy, and certain managed care services such as prescription drug programs.[206] Beginning in 1994, Caremark's shareholders filed a number of derivative lawsuits[207] claiming that the members of Caremark's board of directors breached their fiduciary duty of care to the corporation in connection with alleged violations by Caremark employees of federal and state laws applicable to health care providers, including the federal anti-kickback statute.[208]

### 1. Background of the Case

A brief review of the underlying facts in this case, including Caremark's compliance activities and the government's investigation, is instructive. Beginning in 1989, Caremark began issuing a *Guide to Contractual Relationships* to help its employees comply with certain laws, including the federal anti-kickback statute.[209] The *Guide* generally was reviewed annually by legal counsel and updated.[210] In July 1991, when the safe harbors to the anti-kickback statute were published, many of Caremark's standard contract forms were amended to comply with the safe harbors.[211]

---

[203] *See* 547 U.S. at 89.

[204] *Id.*

[205] 698 A.2d 959 (Del. Ch. 1996).

[206] *See id.* at 961.

[207] Five stockholder derivative actions alleging breach of the directors' duty of care were filed (and consolidated) in the Delaware Chancery Court. The complaint was amended three times in response to additional indictments and allegations concerning kickbacks, improper referrals, and overbilling resulting from an ongoing investigation by the government. The final, amended complaint added allegations that the federal indictments had caused Caremark to incur significant legal fees and forced it to sell its home infusion business at a loss. Several shareholder derivative suits were also filed in other jurisdictions. *See id.* at 964.

[208] 42 U.S.C. §1320a-7b(b).

[209] *See Caremark*, 698 A.2d at 962.

[210] *See id.*

[211] *See id.*

Beginning in August 1991, the HHS OIG began an investigation of Caremark's predecessor organization.[212] The investigation was joined by the DOJ and several additional state and federal agencies, and focused on potentially improper patient referrals, billing practices, medically unnecessary treatments, waivers of patient copayments, and the adequacy of records kept by Caremark pharmacies.[213] In response to these investigations, Caremark implemented an internal audit plan and instituted new compliance policies (e.g., requiring regional officers to approve each contract between Caremark and a physician and requiring local branch managers to certify compliance with the corporation's ethics program).[214] Further, Caremark retained an outside auditor (Price Waterhouse) to prepare a report, which concluded that there were no material weaknesses in Caremark's control structure.[215] In addition, Caremark initiated a comprehensive review of its compliance policies and the compilation of an employee ethics handbook.[216]

The Caremark board apparently was advised of these and other compliance initiatives, which included training sessions provided to Caremark's sales force and a letter sent by Caremark's president to all senior, district, and branch managers specifically stating that (1) physicians were not to be paid for referrals, (2) the standard contract forms in the *Guide* were not to be modified, and (3) deviation from these policies would result in immediate termination.[217] In addition, the chief financial officer was appointed as Caremark's chief compliance officer.

The Caremark board was informed when a grand jury indictment was issued in August 1994 against the corporation, two of its officers, an employee, and a physician for anti-kickback violations.[218] Caremark's management advised the board at this time of the basis for its view that the challenged contracts were in compliance with the law.[219]

In June 1995, the Caremark board approved a settlement agreement with numerous government agencies[220] for more than $160 million[221] and agreed to enter into a compliance agreement with HHS. (Notably, neither the settlement agreement nor any of the prior indictments charged any senior officers or directors of Caremark with direct participation in any wrongdoing.)[222] In March

---

[212]*See id.*

[213]*See id.* at 962 n.2.

[214]*See id.* at 963.

[215]*See id.*

[216]*See id.*

[217]*See id.* at 963 and n.5.

[218]*See id.* at 963–64.

[219]*See id.* at 966.

[220]These agencies included the DOJ, the OIG, the Veterans Administration, the Federal Employee Health Benefits Program, the Civilian Health and Medical Program of the Uniformed Services (CHAMPUS; now Tricare), and related state agencies in all 50 states and the District of Columbia. *See Caremark,* 698 A.2d at 965.

[221]This included $29 million in criminal fines, $129.9 million for civil claims relating to payment practices, and $5.5 million in additional penalties. *See id.* at 965 n.10.

[222]As part of the sentencing process in an Ohio action, the United States stipulated that no senior executive of Caremark had participated in, condoned, or was willfully ignorant of wrongdoing in connection with the home infusion business.

1996, the Caremark board also approved a $98 million settlement agreement with certain private payors.[223]

With regard to the shareholder derivative suit, the defendants filed a motion to dismiss, contending that the complaint failed to allege particularized facts to excuse the demand requirement under Delaware law and that Caremark's charter eliminated director personal liability for money damages to the extent permitted by law.[224] The parties began settlement negotiations and presented the proposed terms of a settlement to the court to determine whether it was fair and reasonable to protect the best interests of the corporation and its absent shareholders. In this context, the court approved the settlement agreement as reasonable given the weakness of the plaintiffs' claims.[225]

### 2. The Court's Decision

The court began its analysis by stating that a claim for director duty of care violations based on inadequate director monitoring of corporate performance is "possibly the most difficult theory in corporation law upon which a plaintiff might hope to win a judgment."[226] According to the court, director liability for a breach of the duty to exercise appropriate attention theoretically may arise in two different contexts: (a) when a board decision results in loss because the decision was ill advised or negligent or (b) when the board fails to act under circumstances in which due attention would have prevented the loss.[227]

#### a. Board's Duty of Care Responsibilities

Citing *Aronson v. Lewis*[228] to the effect that the first type of case should be analyzed under the business judgment rule, the *Caremark* court stated that "compliance with a director's duty of care can never appropriately be judicially determined by reference to *the content of a board decision* ... apart from consideration of the good faith or rationality of the *process* employed."[229] In other words,

> [W]hether a magistrate judge or jury considering the matter after the fact, believes a decision substantively wrong, or degrees of wrong extending through "stupid" to "egregious" or "irrational," provides no ground for director liability, so long as the court determines that the process employed was either rational or employed in a *good faith* effort to advance corporate interests.[230]

The court concluded that the business judgment rule is "process oriented" and that the concept of negligence is not appropriately used for judicial review of board attentiveness, particularly if looking at the substance of the board's

---

[223] *See Caremark,* 698 A.2d at 966.

[224] *See id.* at 964–65.

[225] *See id.* at 960–61.

[226] *Id.* at 967.

[227] *See id.*

[228] 473 A.2d 805 (Del. 1984).

[229] *See Caremark,* 698 A.2d at 967 (second emphasis added).

[230] *Id.* at 967 (emphasis in original).

decision for evidence of such negligence.[231] Referring to Learned Hand's opinion in *Barnes v. Andrews*,[232] the *Caremark* court stated that the core element of any corporate law duty of care is whether there has been a good faith effort to be informed and exercise judgment.[233]

There is considerable discussion in the *Caremark* opinion of *Graham v. Allis-Chalmers Manufacturing Co.*,[234] which involved the liability of board members for losses experienced by a corporation resulting from antitrust violations.[235] The plaintiffs in *Graham* did not allege that the board members knew about improper employee behavior, but rather that the directors should have known so that they could have brought the corporation into compliance.[236] The *Graham* court concluded that "absent cause for suspicion there is no duty upon the directors to install and operate a corporate system of espionage to ferret out wrongdoing which they have no reason to suspect exists."[237] Using this standard, the *Graham* court held that the directors did not have grounds for suspicion and thus were not liable.[238] As explained by the *Caremark* court, absent grounds to suspect deception, corporate boards and senior officers cannot be "charged with wrongdoing simply for assuming the integrity of employees and the honesty of their dealings on the company's behalf."[239]

Some other courts have reiterated the proposition in *Caremark*[240] that in determining whether a director is liable (under the second prong of *Aronson*) a court may not consider "the content of the board decision that leads to corporate loss, apart from consideration of the good faith or rationality of the process employed."[241] However, a few cases have begun considering whether an arrangement can be so egregious on its face that board approval cannot meet the business judgment test.[242]

One of the more recent cases implementing the standard set in *Caremark* is *Saito v. McCall*.[243] In *Saito,* HBO & Company (HBO) merged with McKesson Corporation (McKesson) to form McKesson HBOC, Inc. (NewCo). The plaintiff shareholders brought a derivative suit to recover damages from the directors, officers, and advisors of all three companies, alleging that (1) HBO's

---

[231] *See id.* at 967–68.

[232] 298 F. 614, 618 (E.D.N.Y. 1924).

[233] *See* 698 A.2d at 968.

[234] 188 A.2d 125 (Del. 1963).

[235] *See* 698 A.2d at 969.

[236] *See id.*

[237] *Id.* at 969 (quoting Graham v. Allis-Chalmers Mfg. Co., 188 A.2d 125, 130 (Del. 1963)).

[238] *See* 698 A.2d at 969.

[239] *Id.* (citation omitted).

[240] *In re* Caremark Int'l Derivative Litig., 698 A.2d 959 (Del. Ch. 1996) [hereinafter *Caremark*].

[241] Salsitz v. Nasser, 208 F.R.D. 589, 591 (E.D. Mich. 2002) (*citing Caremark,* 698 A.2d at 967); *see also* United Artists Theater Co. v. Walton, 315 F.3d 217, 232 (3d Cir. 2003).

[242] *See, e.g., In re* Abbott Laboratories Derivative Shareholders Litig., 325 F.3d 795 (7th Cir. 2003) [hereinafter *Abbott Laboratories*]. This case is discussed in more detail in Section III.D., below.

[243] C.A. No. 17132-NC, 2004 WL 3029876 (Del. Ch. Dec. 20, 2004).

directors and officers presided over a fraudulent accounting scheme prior to the merger; (2) McKesson's directors, officers, and advisors uncovered the fraudulent accounting scheme at HBO during their due diligence for the merger, but nonetheless proceeded with the merger; and (3) NewCo's directors did not act quickly enough to rectify the accounting fraud following the merger.[244] The court noted that, under *Caremark,* "a derivative plaintiff must allege facts constituting 'a sustained or systematic failure of the board to exercise oversight—such as an utter failure to attempt to assure a reasonable information reporting system exists.' "[245] In order to state a claim under *Caremark,* the court determined that the plaintiffs must show that the NewCo board should have known that unlawful accounting improprieties were occurring or had occurred and that no good faith effort to remedy the unlawful accounting improprieties was made.[246] Giving plaintiffs the benefit of all reasonable inferences that may be drawn from the facts, the court found that the plaintiffs had alleged sufficient facts to infer that the boards of HBO and McKesson—members of which made up the board of NewCo—knew, or should have known, of HBO's accounting irregularities and that HBO's accounting practices were unlawful. Moreover, the court found that despite this knowledge, the NewCo board failed to take any remedial action for several months.[247] Although noting that facts later adduced at trial could prove that the directors did not violate their duties under *Caremark,* the court allowed the plaintiffs' claim to survive a motion to dismiss.[248]

### b. Appropriate Information Gathering and Reporting Systems

Nevertheless, the *Caremark* court refused to accept a broad reading of the *Graham* decision, stating that in light of more recent legal developments, including the effect of the U.S. Sentencing Guidelines, the Delaware Supreme Court would be unlikely to accept the proposition that corporate boards have no responsibility to ensure that management implements appropriate information gathering and reporting systems that are reasonably designed to provide senior management and the board with timely, accurate information to allow each to reach informed judgments concerning compliance with the law and business performance.[249] The *Caremark* court acknowledged that the level of detail that such information gathering systems must have is a question of business judgment, and ultimately it held that the board must exercise a good faith judgment that the corporation's information gathering and reporting system is, in concept and design, adequate to ensure the board that appropriate information will come to its attention in a timely manner as a matter of ordinary operations.[250]

On facts before it, the *Caremark* court found that there was no knowing violation of law, particularly because experts had informed the Caremark board

---

[244] *Id.* at *1.
[245] *Id.* at *6.
[246] *Id.* at *6.
[247] *Id.* at *7.
[248] *Id.* at *7.
[249] *See* 698 A.2d at 969–70.
[250] *See id.*

that the company's practices, although subject to some question, were lawful.[251] Moreover, the duty to act in good faith to be informed does not require that the directors have detailed information about all aspects of a company's operations.[252] With regard to the "failure to monitor" claim, the court held that "only a sustained or systematic failure of the board to exercise oversight—such as an utter failure to attempt to assure a reasonable information and reporting system exists—will establish the lack of good faith that is a necessary condition to liability."[253]

It is important to remember the procedural posture of the case. The court was assessing the adequacy of the oversight exercised by the Caremark board only in the context of evaluating the fairness and reasonableness of the proposed settlement. Nevertheless, the court found that there was no evidence that the directors were guilty of a sustained failure to exercise their oversight function and could not be faulted if they did not know the specifics of the activities that led to the indictments.[254] Although the Caremark settlement agreement required that the corporation adopt certain additional compliance measures, the court characterized these measures as "modest" but adequate given the underlying weakness of the plaintiffs' claims.[255]

Therefore, although raising the possibility that corporate boards could face liability for failing to implement a reasonable information gathering and reporting system, the *Caremark* decision ostensibly set a fairly high standard that plaintiffs must meet to demonstrate that a board has breached its duty of care. A close examination of the facts in *Caremark,* however, indicates that this standard is not as high as it may first appear because the Caremark corporation was, in fact, unusually active in the compliance area from an early stage. Although the OIG did not begin publishing documents providing compliance guidance for various types of health care organizations until the late 1990s,[256] Caremark started to implement certain compliance activities beginning almost a decade earlier, in 1989. From that time forward, the Caremark board oversaw a range of compliance initiatives, including the development of certain standards, education and training, auditing, and monitoring. There was clear involvement in these compliance efforts by the highest levels of corporate personnel (e.g., in 1993 the president of the corporation sent a letter to branch managers providing further guidance on certain compliance policies). Although Caremark's compliance efforts initially did not have a comprehensive, formal structure, it is not surprising that a court would have suggested the board's compliance oversight was reasonable under the circumstances. The question remains as to what level of board oversight a court would find reasonable and adequate today given the

---

[251] *See id.* at 971.

[252] *See id.*

[253] *Id.*

[254] *See id.* at 971–72.

[255] *Id.* at 972.

[256] The first such guidance—for clinical laboratories—was not published in proposed form until 1997, and it was not finalized until 1998. *See* Publication of OIG Compliance Program Guidance for Clinical Laboratories, 63 Fed. Reg. 45,076 (1998).

detailed prescriptions for compliance programs provided in the OIG's Compliance Program Guidance documents.

## D. The Columbia/HCA Litigation

Because the *Caremark* opinion was handed down in the context of court approval of a settlement, the issue of the necessity for presuit demand was never decided. However, this issue has taken on a great deal of importance in other cases, notably including the Columbia/HCA litigation.

### 1. Columbia/HCA Operations and Government Investigations

The numerous government investigations and lawsuits surrounding Columbia/HCA have been extensively publicized.[257] To briefly summarize, in 1997, Columbia Corporation (Columbia or Columbia/HCA), now HCA–The Healthcare Company, was one of the largest hospital companies in the world, owning 348 hospitals and treating 125,000 people per day. The company and its affiliates had operations in 37 states, including a comprehensive health care network with home health agencies and surgery centers. As part of an ongoing federal investigation, 200 federal agents from four federal agencies[258] raided two Columbia hospitals in El Paso, Texas, in March 1997. *The New York Times* had been conducting its own investigation and published an article describing improper practices at Columbia, including upcoding, improper referrals for home health care, possible violations of the Stark statute prohibiting physician self-referrals, and suspicious Medicare charges for respiratory patients. The newspaper also reported a seven percent drop in the company's stock price two days after the government raid,[259] and the shareholders filed the first class action and derivative complaint against Columbia in April 1997.[260]

Allegations against Columbia continued to surface in the media, including quotes from several former Columbia administrators about illegal activities going on within the company. The government expanded its investigation in July 1997 by serving 35 sealed search warrants on Columbia facilities in seven states related to their Medicare cost reports. With heavy media coverage of these events, stock prices dropped another 12.2 percent. Meanwhile, several other government agencies joined the investigation.

---

[257]For a detailed description, see DENNIS KLEIN, PROTECTING DIRECTORS AND OFFICERS OF HOSPITALS AND HEALTHCARE ORGANIZATIONS FROM CIVIL LIABILITY 12–23 (American Health Lawyers Ass'n 1999). In addition, 12 pages of HCA's September 2000 quarterly report were devoted to summarizing each of the many state and federal legal proceedings that the company faced. See THE HEALTHCARE CO., SEPTEMBER 2000 QUARTERLY REP. 31–42 (Nov. 8, 2000).

[258]The agencies were the Federal Bureau of Investigation (FBI), the Internal Revenue Service, HHS, and the Department of Defense Criminal Investigations Service.

[259]Martin Gottlieb & Kurt Eichenwald, *For Biggest Hospital Operation a Debate Over Ties That Bind*, N.Y. TIMES, Apr. 6, 1997, at A4.

[260]See Morse Complaint, Morse v. McWhorter, No. 97-CV-370, 1998 U.S. Dist. LEXIS 19053 (M.D. Tenn. July 1, 1998). The *Morse* court dismissed the shareholders' complaint with prejudice on July 28, 2000.

Three Columbia executives from Florida were indicted in July 1997 and charged with conspiring to defraud the government by submitting false cost reports to the Medicare and CHAMPUS programs for reimbursement.[261] The government alleged a scheme in which hospital debt was submitted in a category that led to Columbia improperly receiving 100 percent reimbursement from federal government programs. In addition, the government charged that these executives had failed to notify authorities of an accounting error that had resulted in additional unjustified reimbursement. Two of the executives were convicted, sentenced to prison, and ordered to pay restitution and fines totaling more than $1 million; however, their convictions were ultimately overturned.[262]

At this point, the value of the company's stock had fallen 19 percent since March 1997, and Richard Scott was removed as chairman of the board of directors and replaced by Thomas Frist, who initiated an internal investigation.

In December 2000, Columbia, by then known as HCA/The Healthcare Company (HCA), signed a plea agreement with the DOJ that resolved all then-pending federal criminal claims against the company arising out of the investigation initiated more than three years earlier.[263] On the same day, the company signed a civil settlement agreement and a corporate integrity agreement with the DOJ, as previously announced in May 2000.[264] Under the criminal and civil agreements, HCA must pay a combined total of approximately $840 million in restitution and fines.

DOJ officials emphasize that "even though the Government and HCA ... have reached a settlement, the Government will continue to investigate and prosecute any individuals [presumably including any directors and officers] who committed illegal acts in relation to this case."[265] In addition, the civil settlement resolved only those issues relating to outpatient laboratory billing, home

---

[261] *See* Keith Snyder, *Two Columbia/HCA Executives Found Guilty of Fraud, Conspiracy,* TENNESSEAN, July 3, 1999.

[262] *See Hospital Official Gets 33 Months in Prison,* APBNEWS.COM, Dec. 22, 1999. *See also* THE HEALTHCARE CO., SEPTEMBER 2000 QUARTERLY REP. 31–42 (Nov. 8, 2000), at 31. The U.S. Court of Appeals for the Eleventh Circuit overturned the convictions of Jay Jarrell and Robert Whiteside in March 2002. *See* United States v. Whiteside, 285 F.3d 1345 (11th Cir. 2002). In this case, the government alleged that the hospital's classification of interest expense in its 1981 cost report was fraudulent because the hospital classified the interest expense based on how the debt was being used at the time of the filing of the cost report rather than on how the funds were used at the time of the loan origination. The court determined that the government could not prove that the defendants "knowingly and willfully" made false statements because no Medicare regulation, administrative ruling, or judicial decision existed at the time that clearly required interest expense to be reported in accordance with the original use of the loan. Since neither the statute, regulations, nor administrative authority clearly addressed the issue and the expert testimony demonstrated that reasonable people could disagree as to how such amounts should be reported, the court found that the government failed to meet is burden of proof with respect to the actual falsity of the statements in the cost report and reversed the defendants' convictions.

[263] *See HCA Signs Agreements in Columbia Investigation: Columbia Management Companies, Inc. and Columbia Homecare Group, Inc. Agree to Pleas,* PRNEWSWIRE, Dec. 14, 2000.

[264] *See id. See also* U.S. Dep't of Justice, Press Release, *Attorney General Announces Largest Department of Justice Fraud Settlement in History* (Dec. 14, 2000), *available at* http://www.usdoj.gov:80/opa/pr/2000/December/697ag.htm.

[265] *See* Press Release, *HCA—The Health Care Company to Pay over $30 Million in El Paso; $840 Million Nationwide in Settlement for Fraudulent Billing Practices* (Dec. 14, 2000), *available at* http://www.usdoj.gov:80/usao/txw/columbia.htm. *See also* William Borden, *Hospitals to Get Less Scrutiny Under Bush Analysts,* REUTERS, Dec. 15, 2000.

health issues, and diagnosis related group (DRG) upcoding, leaving cost reporting and other issues open. In fact, the United States has intervened in eight existing *qui tam* cases, and *qui tam* relators are currently pursuing 12 others without the participation of the United States.[266] Furthermore, HCA and those who served as officers and directors during the times of the alleged improprieties still face numerous unresolved private actions, including federal and state shareholder derivative actions, class actions, and patient/payor suits.[267] The text that follows covers the most notable of the HCA shareholder derivative actions.

In May 2002, the U.S. Court of Appeals for the Sixth Circuit vacated the court's order dismissing the complaint in *Morse v. McWhorter*[268] and remanded the case.[269] In February 2004, the district court issued an order and final judgment approving a $51 million settlement and dismissed the case.[270] The settlement was expected to result in an average shareholder recovery of $0.21 per share before the deduction of court-awarded attorneys' fees and expenses.[271]

### 2. Shareholders' Allegations in McCall v. Scott

The second major shareholder derivative action, *McCall v. Scott*,[272] was filed in August 1997. At this time, the judge consolidated all class actions under the *Morse v. McWhorter* suit,[273] while all derivative actions were consolidated under *McCall*. Both actions contained allegations that HCA's ineffective compliance program led to the government investigation, which had resulted in a 40 percent drop in stock prices, and that the illegal acts occurred because of the knowledge or reckless disregard of the HCA board. The *McCall* suit named as defendants the corporation and certain HCA directors or officers[274] and specifically alleged that they had intentionally and negligently breached their fiduciary duties and engaged in illegal insider trading.

---

[266] *See HCA Signs Agreements in Columbia Investigation.*

[267] *See* THE HEALTHCARE CO., SEPTEMBER 2000 QUARTERLY REP. 31–42 (Nov. 8, 2000), at 35–41.

[268] 200 F. Supp. 2d 853 (M.D. Tenn. 2000), *vacated by* 290 F.3d 795 (6th Cir. 2002).

[269] *Morse,* 290 F.3d 795 (6th Cir. 2002).

[270] Morse v. McWhorter, No. 97-CV-370 (M.D. Tenn. Feb. 2, 2004).

[271] Morse v. McWhorter, No. 97-CV-370 (M.D. Tenn. Oct. 27, 2003) (Notice of Pendency of Class Action, Hearing on Proposed Settlement and Attorneys' Fee Petition and Rights to Share in Settlement Fund). The final order directing the distribution of the net settlement funds was issued in February 2005. Morse v. McWhorter, No. 97-CV-370 (M.D. Tenn. Feb. 8, 2005) (Order).

[272] Complaint, McCall v. Scott, No. 3:97-0838 (M.D. Tenn. Aug. 13, 1997).

[273] 200 F. Supp. 2d 853 (M.D. Tenn. 1998). The court dismissed the shareholders' complaint, with prejudice. Morse v. McWhorter, No. 3-97-0370 (M.D. Tenn. July 28, 2000). The Sixth Circuit vacated the dismissal and remanded the case in 2002, Morse v. McWhorter, 290 F.3d 795, and as noted above in Section III.D.1., in 2004 the district court approved a $51 million settlement and dismissed the case. Morse v. McWhorter, No. 97-CV-370 (M.D. Tenn. Feb. 2, 2004).

[274] The named defendants were Thomas Frist, Richard Scott, David Vandewater, R. Clayton McWhorter, Magdalena Averhoff, Frank S. Royal, T. Michael Long, William R. Young, Donald MacNaughton, Carl Reichart, and Sister Judith Ann Karam.

The specific allegations included charges of upcoding and that senior management, with the HCA board's knowledge, had adopted a management policy that gave its employees "strong incentive" to commit fraud.[275] In addition, the complaint alleged numerous improper cost-reporting practices, e.g., disguising nonreimbursable facility-acquisition costs as reimbursable management fees; "grossing up" outpatient revenues that affected the cost-to-charge ratio leading to improper reimbursement; seeking unjustified reimbursement for advertising and marketing expenses and for funds expended to recruit physicians; and improperly shifting costs on cost reports to obtain unwarranted reimbursement.[276] There also were allegations that HCA offered improper inducements to physicians to induce referrals[277] and overbilled (e.g., without regard to medical necessity), and billed for inpatient services that should have been billed as outpatient services.[278]

The plaintiffs also noted that HCA was a defendant in numerous *qui tam* False Claims Act cases, including more than 12 in which the government intervened, and was a defendant in two whistleblower actions involving former employees. The corporation also was a defendant in a federal antitrust lawsuit and a private RICO class action. Private payors also were allegedly investigating HCA's billing practices.[279]

The plaintiffs alleged that the individual defendants committed various securities violations by signing 10-K forms that misrepresented or omitted material facts about HCA's financial position and its compliance with federal law. The plaintiffs alleged that these acts and omissions created personal liability for the directors, which created a conflict of interest that prevented them from acting in the corporation's best interest.

The plaintiffs also alleged various types of corporate damage resulting from the defendants' actions, including (1) the securities class actions for damages, (2) possible exclusion from Medicare and other federal health care programs, (3) payments of higher amounts to acquire certain facilities, (4) $64 million paid for severance packages, (5) legal and accounting fees incurred in the internal investigation and defense of individual defendants, and (6) the significant decline in the price of the company's common stock. Furthermore, HCA's credit rating was adversely affected, and the HCA board allegedly repurchased corporate stock at artificially inflated prices. Moreover, HCA acknowledged that the ongoing investigations would have a negative effect on its profits.[280]

---

[275]This policy involved setting targets of 15–20% growth; allegedly three to four times the industry average. *McCall,* No. 3:97-0838, ¶17. HCA purportedly paid cash bonuses up to 50% of base salary to encourage managers to meet these growth targets. *See id.* ¶18c.

[276]HCA allegedly assigned square footage to its comprehensive outpatient rehabilitation facilities (CORFs) when the space actually was used for services unrelated to CORFs. Nonreimbursable items, such as gift shops, were shifted from a hospital to the home health operations where they could be reimbursed, and interest expenses were shifted from one facility to another. *See id.* ¶19.

[277]Physicians allegedly were provided inducements such as loans, guaranteed income, expense allowances, reduced rent, free or reduced-cost training, vacations and other recreational activities, equity interests in HCA operations, and directorship and consulting fees. *See id.* ¶20.

[278]*See id.* ¶22.

[279]*See id.* ¶29.

[280]*See id.* ¶¶24–28.

The specific references in the complaint to the corporation's directors and officers included numerous detailed allegations against individual directors, as well as allegations against the board as a whole, including that management devised schemes to improperly increase HCA's revenues and profits and provided strong incentive for employee fraud "with the Board's knowledge."[281] The board also was allegedly implicated in the improper acquisition of other health care companies and knew of the growth rate targets set by senior management.[282] The complaint also referred to an affidavit by a government special agent that alleged that there was a systemic corporate scheme perpetrated by corporate officers and managers of HCA hospitals, and to statements by former executives and employees that violations of the law were "the inevitable product" of corporate policies coming from headquarters that were designed to improperly maximize government reimbursement.[283]

The plaintiffs alleged illegal insider trading and intentional and negligent breaches of the directors' fiduciary duties, including failure to monitor the reports of internal and external auditors to ensure that the corporation was not violating applicable federal and state laws and regulations.[284] The plaintiffs further alleged that the monitoring function required appropriate information gathering and reporting systems to detect and report to the board on a timely basis any employee or corporate misconduct that may have resulted in loss to the company.[285] There also were allegations that the board failed to exercise proper business judgment in managing the corporation.[286] Finally, there were claims that certain directors had engaged in insider trading on terms not equally available to other stockholders because of these directors' awareness of HCA's alleged illegal acts, which precluded these directors from impartially considering a presuit demand.[287]

The Sixth Circuit vacated the district court's order dismissing the complaint in *Morse v. McWhorter*[288] in May 2002, and the case was remanded.[289] The shareholders' remaining claims in *McCall v. Scott*[290] for breach of the duty of care were settled in June 2003. Under the settlement, HCA was required to adopt a corporate governance plan that goes beyond the requirements of both the Sarbanes-Oxley Act and the rules proposed to the SEC by the New York Stock Exchange.[291] The new governance plan includes a substantially inde-

---

[281] *See id.* ¶17.

[282] *See id.* ¶¶4, 33.

[283] *See id.* ¶¶34–35.

[284] *See id.* ¶40.

[285] *See id.* ¶¶45–46.

[286] *See id.* ¶¶56, 59.

[287] *See id.* ¶62.

[288] 200 F. Supp. 2d 853 (M.D. Tenn. 2000).

[289] *Morse*, 290 F.3d 795.

[290] No. 97-CV-838 (M.D. Tenn. June 3, 2003).

[291] Office of the New York State Comptroller Alan G. Hevesi, Press Release, *Precedent-Setting Corporate Governance Plan Established in Settlement of HCA Shareholder Suit* (Feb. 4, 2003), *available at* http://www.osc.state.ny.us/press/releases/feb03/20403.htm. In accordance with the terms of the settlement, HCA adopted new corporate governance guidelines on July 24, 2003. The new guidelines are available on the HCA Web site at http://www.hcahealthcare.com.

pendent board of directors by mandating a higher percentage of independent directors and providing for a stronger definition of director independence.[292] The board's audit committee, comprised solely of independent directors, will have more power than required under existing laws and regulations. Moreover, the board is required to maintain an ethics and compliance committee to monitor corporate ethics and oversee compliance with applicable standards.[293] In addition to the governance plan, the settlement provides that the insurance carriers for HCA's directors and officers will pay the company $14 million.[294] Unlike the settlements in the Enron and WorldCom cases, the HCA directors and officers did not have to contribute their own funds to settlement of the suit; however, there is no indication whether the insurance carriers will seek to recover the settlement payment from the personal assets of HCA's directors and officers.

### 3. Defendants' Response

The defendants (except Scott and Vandewater) filed a motion to dismiss, claiming that the plaintiffs had (1) failed to make a presuit demand on the corporation as required under applicable Delaware law; (2) failed to allege "particularized facts" to demonstrate that a demand would have been futile; (3) failed to set forth specific facts that a majority of the board was disqualified from acting independently in HCA's interest; (4) failed to allege specific facts to state a claim for intentional breach of fiduciary duties, claiming that under Delaware law and HCA's corporate charter, corporate directors cannot be liable for any negligent breach of their fiduciary duties; and (5) failed to allege facts demonstrating any illegal insider trading. Scott and Vandewater adopted these contentions, and Vandewater further stated that the derivative claims against him had no merit because of his status as a former corporate officer, not a director.[295]

### 4. The Magistrate's Report and District Court Decision

Applying Delaware law, the magistrate judge granted the defendants' motions to dismiss because the plaintiffs did not establish that the presuit demand normally required under Delaware law would have been futile.[296] The *McCall* Magistrate Judge's Report contains a lengthy analysis of the presuit demand rule, noting that it is designed to prevent abuses of a derivative action and that it (1) gives corporate management the opportunity to seek alternative options, thereby avoiding expensive litigation; (2) provides an opportunity for the early

---

[292]Office of the New York State Comptroller Alan G. Hevesi, Press Release, *Precedent-Setting Corporate Governance Plan Established in Settlement of HCA Shareholder Suit* (Feb. 4, 2003), *available at* http://www.osc.state.ny.us/press/releases/feb03/20403.htm.

[293]*Id.*

[294]*Id.*

[295]*See* Magistrate Judge's Report and Recommendation at 4, McCall v. Scott, No. 3:97-0838 (M.D. Tenn. July 1, 1998) [hereinafter *McCall* Magistrate Judge's Report].

[296]*See id.* The *McCall* Magistrate Judge's Report was approved by and adopted as the opinion of the court on September 1, 1999, and the plaintiffs' action was dismissed with prejudice. *See* McCall v. Scott, No 3:97-0838 (M.D. Tenn. Sept. 1, 1999) (mem. op.).

termination of meritless claims; and (3) prevents strike suits. The demand rule arises from the business judgment rule (i.e., the directors of a corporation are presumed to act in its best interests unless facts demonstrate otherwise).[297] Quoting *Rales v. Blasband*,[298] the *McCall* Magistrate Judge's Report stated as follows:

> A plaintiff, therefore, who chooses not to make a demand prior to suit is faced with the responsibility of demonstrating with particularity why his demand on the Board of Directors would have been futile and if he fails in meeting this burden, he will find that his suit will be dismissed, even if he has an otherwise meritorious claim.[299]

As a threshold matter, the magistrate judge concluded that Delaware, rather than federal, law should apply and that demand futility should be analyzed as of the date that the original complaint was filed in the *Morse* case (i.e., April 8, 1997).[300]

### a. The Test Under Delaware Law

The magistrate judge found that the only relevant claims involving actions taken by the HCA board (rather than inaction) related to the acquisition of other hospital companies and their facilities. There were no allegations that the directors were involved in other actions, such as the recruitment of physicians or upcoding. The magistrate judge noted that this is common practice and cited *Caremark* for the proposition that most corporate decisions are not the subject of director attention, as ordinary business decisions are made by lower-level managers and employees.[301] Other allegations against the directors were deemed irrelevant by the magistrate judge because they occurred after the operative date for demand-futility purposes (April 8, 1997).[302] The magistrate judge concluded that because this was a "failure to monitor" case involving the absence of a conscious board decision, the *Rales* test for presuit demand controlled (i.e., whether there is a reasonable doubt that a majority of directors is disinterested or lacks the independence to act in the corporation's best interest). The magistrate judge rejected the two-part test described in *Aronson* (involving the dual factors of disinterested directors and whether the board exercised valid business judgment), noting *Aronson's* statement that the "business judgment rule operates only in the context of director action. Technically speaking, it has no role where directors have either abdicated their functions, or absent a conscious decision, failed to act."[303]

As a result, the magistrate judge used the following test, drawn from language in *Rales,* to assess whether the HCA board was disinterested:

---

[297] *See Aronson*, 466 A.2d 375, 380.

[298] 634 A.2d 927, 933 (Del. 1993).

[299] *McCall* Magistrate Judge's Report at 33.

[300] *See id.* at 35–37.

[301] *See id.* at 40.

[302] *See id.* at 41.

[303] *Id.* at 38 (quoting *Aronson*, 473 A.2d at 813).

[W]hether or not the particularized factual allegations of a derivative stockholder complaint create a reasonable doubt that, as of the time the complaint is filed, the board of directors could have properly exercised its independent and disinterested business judgment in responding to a demand.[304]

Again quoting *Rales*, the *McCall* magistrate judge defined "interest" in this context to mean whether a director

has received, or is entitled to receive, a personal financial benefit from the challenged transaction which is not equally shared by the stockholders....

Directorial interest also exists where a corporate decision will have a materially detrimental impact on a director, but not on the corporation and the stockholders.... Independence means that a director's decision is based on the corporate merits of the subject rather than on extraneous considerations or influences. To establish lack of independence, [the plaintiff] must show that the directors are "beholden to [others] or so under their influence that their discretion would be sterilized."[305]

Under Delaware law, the mere threat of personal liability for approving a questioned transaction, standing alone, is insufficient to challenge the independence or disinterestedness of directors, and the potential for liability must not be a "mere threat" but rather a "substantial likelihood." The magistrate judge cited several cases for the proposition that allegations that directors participated in or approved the alleged wrongs have been rejected consistently by Delaware courts as the basis for disqualifying a director.[306]

### b. Applying the Test to the Facts in McCall

#### i. Improper Actions by Defendants

With regard to the specific factual allegations in *McCall* and whether the directors knew or should have known of the alleged improper acts, the magistrate judge found no allegations that any of the board members, as a group or individually, were personally involved in improper conduct. Moreover, Delaware law recognizes that

directors of a corporation do not run the day-to-day affairs of a corporation, and ... to put such an informational burden on the directors of a huge multinational corporation ... to know everything that's going on at every plant is unrealistic and no legal liability can attach.[307]

Furthermore, merely signing a 10-K form does not give rise to liability under the federal securities laws, because a director must be shown to have substantially assisted the violation or to have been a substantial participant in fraud perpetrated by others.[308] In any event, the magistrate judge found that

---

[304] *McCall* Magistrate Judge's Report at 39 (quoting Rales v. Blasband, 634 A.2d 927, 934 (Del. 1993)).

[305] *McCall* Magistrate Judge's Report at 39–40 (alterations in original) (citations omitted).

[306] *See id.* at 42 (*citing* Decker v. Clausen, 1989 WL 133617, at *2 (Del. Ch. Nov. 6, 1989), and Lewis v. Curtis, 671 F.2d 779, 785 (3d Cir. 1982), *cert. denied*, 459 U.S. 880 (1982)).

[307] *McCall* Magistrate Judge's Report at 43 (citations omitted).

[308] *See id.* at 43–44 (citations omitted).

HCA's Securities and Exchange Commission (SEC) filings were appropriate because they disclosed that there had been inquiries by the government about HCA's operations. Moreover, HCA's statements about billing practices and/or compliance with federal laws were matters of opinion or soft information and thus were not actionable under the securities laws.[309]

The insider trading allegations were dismissed because the allegations focused simply on the sale of certain directors' stock at the same prices as any other stockholder's shares were sold during the same time period. Thus, according to the magistrate judge, the alleged insider trading did not create substantial liability for those directors.[310]

Finally, the magistrate judge found that although two of the directors who conducted business with HCA were "interested," they did not constitute a majority of the board, and thus filing a presuit demand was required.

### ii. The "Red Flag" Theory

The magistrate judge next analyzed what he called the "red flag" theory, based on the unconsidered failure of the board to act under circumstances in which due attention would arguably have prevented the loss. Quoting extensively from *Graham v. Allis Chalmers*, the magistrate judge stated that "no rule of law . . . requires a corporate director to assume . . . that all corporate employees are incipient law violators who, but for a tight checkrein will give free vent to their unlawful propensities."[311] He further emphasized the language in *Caremark* indicating that this theory of director liability is "possibly the most difficult theory" on which to prevail. Noting that HCA had an audit committee, and internal as well as independent auditors preparing reports on HCA's business, the magistrate judge cited *Caremark* for the proposition that the appropriate level of detail for such a system is a matter of business judgment, and no system can remove all possibility that the corporation will violate laws or regulations or that senior officers or directors may be misled at times or otherwise fail to detect acts material to the corporation's compliance. However, the board can satisfy its responsibility by exercising a good faith determination that the corporation's information gathering and reporting system is adequate to ensure that appropriate information will come to its attention in a timely manner.[312]

The magistrate judge found that HCA had an internal system to detect compliance. Although the plaintiffs alleged that the system did not work, there were no red flags that should have made the board suspicious before the operative date for filing the presuit demand. For example, the FBI agent's affidavit was made after the operative date for demand futility. The magistrate judge

---

[309]*See id.* at 44 (*citing In re* Sofamor Danek Group, 123 F.3d 394, 400–404 (6th Cir. 1997)).

[310]Although acknowledging that filing an SEC Form S-4 that did not reflect the searches of the Texas hospitals two days earlier was a securities violation, the magistrate judge found that the extensive publicity about these searches cured any omission. *See McCall* Magistrate Judge's Report at 46.

[311]*Id.* at 49 (quoting Graham v. Allis-Chalmers, 188 A.2d 125, 130 (Del. 1963)).

[312]*See McCall* Magistrate Judge's Report at 50 (quoting *In re* Caremark, 698 A.2d 959, 970 (Del. Ch. 1996)).

added, in dicta, that even if the affidavit were considered, there were no facts demonstrating that any of the directors on the board as of the operative date had committed any illegal acts. Moreover, the fact that unlawful activities occurred in one office out of 300 facilities worldwide would not support an inference of corporatewide criminal conduct that should have alerted the directors.[313] In addition, the fact that HCA's DRG codings and case mix index were above the industry average was not alarming due to HCA's position in the hospital industry and its corporate strategy to pursue acute-care patients in good-sized facilities.[314] The serious allegations in the *New York Times* article would not necessarily raise a red flag because the article was published within two weeks of the operative date for demand futility and a board might reasonably need more than two weeks to evaluate such a report. Various other red flags identified by the plaintiffs were dismissed by the magistrate judge as occurring after the operative date or as being insufficient to suggest corporatewide fraud in such a large corporation.[315]

Finally, the magistrate judge found that a director cannot be held liable for gross negligence in the performance of his or her directorial duties, citing *Caremark* for the proposition that the business judgment rule is "process oriented" and does not depend on a substantive assessment of a decision as long as the process used was "rational or employed in a good-faith effort to advance corporate interests."[316] The magistrate judge concluded that "this language requires a complaint to allege facts that the director intentionally acted to harm the corporation."[317] He bolstered this position by citing the Delaware Code,[318] which allows a corporation to amend its certificate of incorporation to eliminate any claims against its directors for gross negligence, and noted that Delaware courts deem any claim for gross negligence to be barred as a matter of law when a corporation has so amended its certificate.[319] Therefore, the magistrate judge concluded that *Caremark* stands for the position that plaintiffs cannot prevail on the red-flags or failure-to-monitor theories unless they allege particularized facts that the board "*intentionally* failed to 'assure a reasonable information and reporting system.'"[320] The magistrate judge failed to address the holding in *Smith v. Van Gorkum*[321] that despite the business judgment rule, a board must make informed decisions after first informing itself "of all material information reasonably available to [it]."[322] Because the HCA board had an audit com-

---

[313] *See McCall* Magistrate Judge's Report at 52.

[314] According to the magistrate judge, the court in United States *ex rel.* Thompson v. Columbia/HCA Healthcare Corp., 125 F.3d 899, 903 (5th Cir. 1997), would not accept similar statistical allegations to establish fraud. *See McCall* Magistrate Judge's Report at 52–53.

[315] A $475,000 settlement and the $1.1 million repaid by HCA were contrasted with the over $8 billion HCA received from the federal government in 1996 alone. *See id.* at 55.

[316] *Id.* at 55–56.

[317] *Id.* at 56.

[318] *See id.* (*citing* DEL. CODE ANN. tit. 8, §102(b)(7)).

[319] *See McCall* Magistrate Judge's Report at 56–57.

[320] *Id.* at 57 (*citing In re* Caremark Int'l Derivative Litig., 698 A.2d 959, 971 (Del. Ch. 1996)).

[321] Smith v. Van Gorkum, 488 A.2d 858 (Del. 1985).

[322] *Id.* at 872.

mittee consisting of board members, an internal audit staff, and an independent auditor, there was an appropriate structure. According to the magistrate judge, in the absence of specific allegations that the board members intentionally failed to monitor the corporation's affairs to prevent violations of the law, the plaintiffs failed to state the facts necessary to disqualify the entire board and thus excuse the need for a presuit demand.[323]

Because the plaintiffs did not excuse their failure to make a presuit demand, the magistrate judge recommended that the case be dismissed. The federal district court adopted and approved the magistrate judge's findings and dismissed the plaintiffs' action with prejudice in September 1999.[324]

## 5. The Appellate Court Decisions

In February 2001, the Sixth Circuit issued an opinion that affirmed the district court's dismissal of the duty of loyalty claim for failure to make a presuit demand, but reversed the dismissal of the claim for intentional or reckless breach of the duty of care, and remanded the case for further proceedings (*McCall* Appeal 1).[325] Two months later, in April 2001, the Sixth Circuit denied the petitions for rehearing but amended one portion of its earlier opinion with regard to the intentional or reckless breach of the duty of care (*McCall* Appeal 2).[326]

### a. The Legal Standards Used

The Sixth Circuit court reviewed the district court's decision to dismiss de novo, noting that motions to dismiss under *Federal Rules of Civil Procedure* 12(b)(6) should not be granted "unless it appears beyond doubt that the plaintiff can prove no set of facts in support of his claim which would entitle him to relief."[327] The appellate court held that the plaintiffs had sufficiently alleged demand futility with regard to their claims for intentional or reckless breach of the duty of care.[328]

The appellate court concurred with the district court that the *Rales* test, rather than the *Aronson* test, should be used since plaintiff's claims did not "allege a conscious Board decision to refrain from acting."[329] The Sixth Circuit reiterated that the *Rales* test requires that the court determine whether the specific factual allegations "create a reasonable doubt that, as of the time the complaint is filed, [a majority of] the board of directors could have properly exercised its independent and disinterested business judgment in responding to a demand."[330] Although the mere threat of personal liability is not sufficient, reasonable doubt is created when particularized allegations present "a sub-

---

[323] *See McCall* Magistrate Judge's Report at 58.

[324] *See* McCall v. Scott, No. 3:97-0838 (M.D. Tenn. Sept. 1, 1999).

[325] McCall v. Scott, 239 F.3d 808 (6th Cir. 2001) [hereinafter *McCall* App. 1].

[326] McCall v. Scott, 250 F.3d 997 (6th Cir. 2001) [hereinafter *McCall* App. 2].

[327] *McCall* App. 1 at 815.

[328] *Id.* at 814.

[329] *Id.* at 816.

[330] *Id., citing Rales*, 634 A. 2d at 934.

stantial likelihood" of liability on the part of a director.[331] However, in applying the *Rales* test, the Sixth Circuit held that the district court had erred by viewing the factual allegations separately, and by refusing to draw reasonable inferences in plaintiffs' favor.[332]

Although both *McCall* appellate decisions reverse the district court's dismissal of the claim for intentional or reckless breach of the duty of care, the rationale of the *McCall* Appeal 1 opinion is modified somewhat in *McCall* Appeal 2. Both decisions struggled to apply the concept of intentional or reckless conduct to a director's duty of care in the context of traditional Delaware corporate legal norms, particularly in light of a provision of Title 8 of the Delaware Code, which allows a corporation to amend its certificate of incorporation to protect its directors against liability for certain acts. Section 102(b)(7) states that a corporation's certificate of incorporation may contain:

> A provision eliminating or limiting the personal liability of a director to the corporation or its stockholders for monetary damages for breach of fiduciary duty as a director, provided that such provision shall not eliminate or limit the liability of a director: (i) for any breach of the director's duty of loyalty to the corporation or its stockholders; (ii) for acts or omissions not in good faith or which involve intentional misconduct or a knowing violation of law; (iii) under § 174 of this title; or (iv) for any transaction from which the director derived an improper personal benefit.[333]

The magistrate judge (and the district court) had concluded that under this provision and Delaware case law, a director could not be held liable for gross negligence in the performance of his or her directorial duties, and thus liability could only be predicated on an intentional failure to act.[334] The Sixth Circuit acknowledged that Delaware law, specifically Section 102(b)(7), allows a corporation to amend its certificate of incorporation to protect its directors against allegations of gross negligence.[335] Nevertheless, the Sixth Circuit refuted the lower court's opinion, in part, stating that under Delaware law, "unconsidered inaction can be the basis for director liability."[336]

Columbia had adopted a waiver provision in its Restated Certificate of Incorporation, very similar to the Delaware provision, that stated:

> TWELFTH: A director of the Corporation shall not be personally liable to the Corporation or its stockholders for monetary damages for breach of fiduciary duty as a director; *provided, however*, that the foregoing shall not eliminate or limit the liability of a director (i) for any breach of the director's duty of loyalty to the Corporation, or its stockholders, (ii) *for acts or omissions not in good faith* or which involve intentional misconduct or a knowing violation of law, (iii) under Section 174 of the General Corporation Law of Delaware, or (iv) for any transaction from which the director derived an improper personal benefit.[337]

---

[331] *McCall* App. 1 at 817 (*citing Rales* at 936).
[332] *Id.*
[333] 8 DEL. CODE ANN. §102(b)(7).
[334] *See McCall* Magistrate Judge's Report at 55–58.
[335] *McCall* App. 2 at 1000.
[336] *Id.* at 999.
[337] *Id.* (emphasis added).

To avoid the waiver of director liability created by this provision, *McCall* plaintiffs alleged that their duty of care claims were not based on gross negligence, but rather on reckless and intentional acts or omissions. Citing a treatise on Delaware corporate law, the *McCall* Appeal 2 court found that "while it is true that duty of care claims alleging only grossly negligent conduct are precluded by a [Section] 102(b)(7) waiver provision, it appears that duty of care claims based on reckless or intentional misconduct are not."[338] The *McCall* Appeal 2 opinion notes that such claims do not easily fit the terminology of Delaware corporate law where courts do not discuss a breach of the duty of care in terms of a mental state. Such allegations are more usually analyzed as either a breach of the duty of loyalty or a breach of the duty of good faith. Therefore, the Sixth Circuit construed plaintiffs' complaint as alleging a breach of the directors' duty of good faith, and found that this duty may be violated "where a director *consciously* disregards his duties to the corporation, thereby causing its stockholders to suffer."[339] Because plaintiffs had not merely alleged "sustained inattention" to their management duties, but rather had alleged "intentional ignorance" of and "willful blindness" to red flags indicating fraudulent practices throughout the company, the plaintiffs had, in effect, alleged a conscious disregard of known risks, "which conduct, if proven, cannot have been undertaken in good faith."[340] Therefore, the court concluded that plaintiffs' claims were not precluded by the waiver of director liability provision in Columbia's corporate charter.[341]

The Delaware Supreme Court vacated the prior decision in *Emerald Partners v. Berlin*[342] on November 28, 2001, and remanded the case to the Delaware Court of Chancery.[343] The lower court had rendered judgment in favor of the corporation's directors, ruling that a provision in the defendant corporation's certificate of incorporation, enacted pursuant to Section 102(b)(7) of Title 8 of the Delaware Code, exculpated the corporation's directors from personal liability for payment of monetary damages.[344] The high court held that the business judgment rule did not apply in the *Emerald Partners* case.[345] There-

---

[338] *Id.*, *citing* BALOTTI & FINKELSTEIN, DELAWARE LAW OF CORPORATIONS AND BUSINESS ORGANIZATIONS (3d ed. Supp. 2000).

[339] *Id.* at 1000 (emphasis added). In support of this statement, the court cites Nagy v. Bistricer, 770 A.2d 43, 2000 WL 1759860 at *3 n.2 (Del. Ch. 2000). Note that *Bistricer* discusses good faith in the context of the duty of loyalty.

[340] *McCall* App. 2 at 1001.

[341] The *McCall* App. 2 court distinguishes its decision from that of the Delaware Court of Chancery in Emerald Partners v. Berlin, No. Civ. A 9700 (Mem. Op. Feb. 7, 2001), stating that while the claims in both cases appeared to be similar on a superficial level, the plaintiff in *Emerald Partners* had offered no evidence that the directors had acted with intentional or reckless indifference, while the plaintiffs in *McCall* had proffered particularized factual statements, which would establish a breach of the duty of good faith, if proven. *McCall* App. 2 at 1001. (*Emerald Partners* was not a demand-futility case but did involve a waiver of liability provision, which, in that case, was held to preclude plaintiffs from prevailing on claims that the directors had breached their duty of loyalty/good faith or duty of care.)

[342] No. 9700, 2001 Del. Ch. LEXIS 20 (Del. Ch. Feb. 7, 2001), *vacated by* 787 A.2d 85 (Del. 2001).

[343] *Emerald Partners,* 787 A.2d 85 (Del. 2001).

[344] *Id.* at 88.

[345] *Id.* at 97.

fore, the chancery court had to evaluate the board members' actions in light of the "entire fairness" standard of review, and the application of Section 102(b)(7) was premature because the lower court was first required to make a finding of "unfairness" and determine the basis of liability for monetary damages before examining the exculpatory nature of the Section 102(b)(7) provision.[346] On remand, the chancery court found the actions in question were in fact fair, and the shareholder appealed. The Delaware Supreme Court held that the finding of fairness was valid despite serious questions as to the independent directors' good faith.[347] In particular, the supreme court noted that "many process flaws in this case raise serious questions as to the independent directors' good faith," particularly the directors' "we don't care" attitude about risks to the corporation. However, the supreme court upheld the chancery court's finding that the price ultimately paid was fair. As a result, even if the exculpatory clause in the company's certificate of incorporation would not have protected the directors because of their bad faith, they would not be liable for any monetary damages. Thus, the Delaware Supreme Court's decision in *Emerald Partners* implicitly confirms the conclusion in *McCall v. Scott*[348] that the two cases are distinguishable, although for different reasons.

### b. Analysis of the Facts

Using this analytical approach, the Sixth Circuit held that the facts alleged were sufficient to create a substantial likelihood of liability for at least five of Columbia's directors, thereby creating a reasonable doubt as to whether a majority of the board was disinterested.[349] The appellate court's analysis of plaintiffs' specific allegations is particularly interesting because the Sixth Circuit judges often draw very different inferences from the facts than did the magistrate and district court judges.[350]

The Sixth Circuit begins by emphasizing the prior experience of many of Columbia's directors, particularly as directors or managers of the health care companies that had been acquired by Columbia.[351] The opinion further examines several specific issues including those relating to Columbia's audit committee and acquisition practices; the *qui tam* action; the federal investigations; the *New York Times'* investigation; and certain Columbia board inaction. First, the appellate court agrees with the district court that there was no substantial likelihood of liability based on a failure to establish and implement reasonable reporting systems, despite the fact that the audit procedures in place apparently did not prevent the alleged fraud. However, while the district court had found "no sinister motives" when director Frist circulated a *Business Week*

---

[346]*Id.*

[347]*See* 840 A.2d 641 (Del. 2003) (unpublished opinion).

[348]250 F.3d 997, 1001 (6th Cir. 2001).

[349]The court emphasized that this determination applies only to the sufficiency of the pleadings with regard to demand futility, and does not determine the truth of the allegations or outcome on the merits.

[350]The remaining description of the *McCall* appellate opinion applies to both *McCall* App. 1 and *McCall* App. 2.

[351]*McCall* App. 1 at 819.

article on another company's high-pressure tactics to meet aggressive growth targets, the appellate court found that no such motives were necessary. According to the Sixth Circuit, the incident suggested an inference that Frist may have been aware of the danger that aggressive growth targets could lead to questionable billing practices.[352]

Similarly, the district court had found that Columbia's repayment of $475,000 plus $1.1 million for questionable expenditures did not suggest corporate-wide fraud at a company receiving hundreds of millions of dollars in reimbursement. The appellate court indicated that such facts could reasonably lead to the inference that directors, with prior experience managing the company, "would be sensitive to the circumstances that prompted the investigation of Columbia's practices."[353] Likewise, the district court had stated that one could reasonably expect that Columbia's DRGs and Case Mix Indices (CMIs) would be higher than the norm for most hospitals in the same markets due to Columbia's size and corporate strategy. However, the Sixth Circuit found that "it would be just as reasonable to infer that the consistently high CMIs and DRGs were a sign of possible improper billing activities."[354]

With regard to Columbia's acquisition practices, the appellate court found that the allegations against five of the directors based on the fact that they were former directors or officers of companies acquired by Columbia were too speculative because the complaint did not allege any particularized impropriety in these transactions. However, directors Scott and Frist attended meetings of Columbia's Acquisition Development Group and their participation implied knowledge of the arrangements that allegedly violated health care laws and regulations.

Plaintiffs had also alleged that Columbia interfered with physician relationships, citing a lawsuit awarding a physician $6.2 million dollars including $5 million in punitive damages against Columbia. The appellate court agreed with the district court that the verdict alone did not suggest corporate-wide wrongdoing. However, the Sixth Circuit stated that the lawsuit and the verdict should be considered, along with all of the facts.

The appellate court came to very different conclusions than had the district court with regard to several other issues. The *qui tam* complaint filed by Dr. James Thompson was unsealed in September 1995, when the government declined to intervene. Moreover, the action was dismissed in July 1996 and was not reversed until October 1997 (several months after the operative date for determining demand futility, i.e., April 8, 1997). Nevertheless, the Sixth Circuit determined that despite its dismissal, the complaint clearly presented claims of improper physician inducements and illegal billing practices, indicating possible federal intervention, all of which were relevant to determining whether the board's failure to take action or investigate was in good faith.[355]

Similarly, the district court had found that the FBI agent's affidavit in support of the July 1997 search warrants used by federal agents to raid 35

---

[352] *Id.* at 820.
[353] *Id.* at 821.
[354] *Id.*
[355] *Id.* at 822.

Columbia facilities could not be considered because it was attested to after the April 8, 1997, demand-futility date. However, the appellate court declares that facts in existence before derivative claims are filed may be considered in determining demand futility even if these facts were not discovered until later.[356] The Sixth Circuit also criticizes the district court for viewing the search of the El Paso offices in isolation, stating:

> When the particularized allegations are taken together, there are sufficient facts from which one could infer that the Board knew of or recklessly disregarded the allegedly improper policies and practices being systematically followed in Columbia's facilities nationwide. In fact, the magnitude and duration of the alleged wrongdoing is relevant in determining whether the failure of the directors to act constitutes a lack of good faith. See *In re Oxford Health Plans, Inc.*, 192 F.R.D. 111 (S.D.N.Y. 2000) (Del. law).[357]

The Sixth Circuit seems to agree with the district court that the *New York Times* articles did not necessarily put the Columbia board on notice of irregularities. Nor did the failure of the board to remove Scott before July 26, 1997, indicate that a presuit demand in April 1997 would have been futile since the fundamental goal of the demand requirement is the opportunity to prod the board into action.

Nevertheless, the Sixth Circuit concluded that there were sufficient facts alleged to create a reasonable doubt as to the disinterestedness of at least five of Columbia's directors by alleging facts that presented a substantial likelihood of director liability for intentional or reckless breach of the duty of care. However, the Sixth Circuit agreed with the lower court that there were insufficient facts alleged to create doubt as to the disinterestedness of a majority of the board to consider a demand with respect to the duty of loyalty claim which related to insider trading.[358]

### c. McCall *and the* Abbott Laboratories *Case*

Although the Sixth Circuit does not directly address this case, it is interesting to note that the *McCall* Appeal 1 analysis was criticized in *In re Abbott Laboratories Derivative Shareholder Litigation*.[359] The *Abbott Laboratories* case involved allegations that the defendant directors were liable for harm resulting from a consent decree between the company and the Food and Drug Administration (FDA). The plaintiffs' derivative suit was dismissed for failure to plead demand futility with particularity by the federal district court in the Northern District of Illinois.

The *Abbott Laboratories* case involved the diagnostic division of the company (Abbott), which had continuing problems with the FDA over certain regulatory procedures for the past several years. The FDA had conducted numerous inspections and reported violations. Abbott received warning letters from the FDA four times, and copies of these letters had been given to the

---

[356] *Id.* at 823.

[357] *Id.*

[358] *Id.* at 825–26.

[359] 141 F. Supp. 2d 946 (N.D. Ill. 2001).

chairman of the board. These letters outlined the potential consequences of failure to remedy the violations, and ultimately resulted in a consent decree that required Abbott to pay a $100 million fine, withdraw 125 types of medical diagnostic test kits from the market, destroy certain inventory, and make various changes in its manufacturing procedures.[360]

The *Abbott Laboratories* court emphasizes that Abbott had 13 directors, of which only two were "insider directors," i.e., Abbott employees. The applicable Illinois statute was very similar to the Delaware law allowing corporations to exempt certain director behavior from liability. Abbott had incorporated a waiver of liability in its certificate of incorporation, and the district court in Illinois had to determine whether, notwithstanding that waiver, Abbott directors could be liable for reckless conduct. The *Abbott Laboratories* court cites a portion of the *McCall* App. 1 opinion on this issue but finds that labeling defendants' behavior "reckless" is not a useful standard. Rather, the court suggests that the facts should be analyzed in light of the operative language of the statute, i.e., was the directors' behavior "not in good faith"?[361]

Distinguishing the facts in *McCall*, where "the complaint detailed many facts about the directors, their backgrounds, their roles within the company and extraordinary events of which they were undoubtedly aware,"[362] the *Abbott Laboratories* court found that "even drawing inferences favorable to plaintiffs, we cannot find a substantial likelihood of liability on these facts."[363] First, the court found it "far from clear" that a majority of the Abbott board had knowledge of the various FDA inspections, violation notices, and warning letters. Unlike *McCall* where there had been detailed allegations about each of the directors, detailed information had only been presented with regard to two of the 13 directors in *Abbott Laboratories*. Second, according to the court, the warning letters contained boilerplate language and thus did not necessarily mean any regulatory action was imminent.[364] Therefore, the court found that while it was possible the directors had knowledge about FDA compliance issues, there was no suggestion they knew the details of the FDA's actions. Nor were the problems so widespread and egregious (as in *McCall*) that the court was willing to presume the directors' knowledge.

Moreover, the court found the ongoing pattern of inspections, negotiations, and re-inspections between Abbott and the FDA appeared to be routine, with the violations affecting only a small percentage of Abbott's products. The fact that some problems persisted while new ones arose would not, by itself, indicate bad faith.[365] There had been a clear give and take between the company and the FDA, with the government continually allowing Abbott to address the reported violations. Thus, according to the court, a director would not have reasonably believed Abbott's management was not making a good faith effort

---

[360] *Id.* at 947–48.

[361] *Id.* at 949.

[362] *Id.* at 950.

[363] *Id.* at 951.

[364] *Id.* at 950.

[365] The court seems to take further comfort from the fact that each successive FDA letter addressed a different violation. *Id.* at 951.

to address the violations. The *Abbott Laboratories* court concludes that "perhaps" the directors might have been more aggressive in their investigations of the FDA violations, but such inaction was negligent, at most, falling far short of a showing of bad faith or a knowing violation of the law.[366]

The district court's decision in *In re Abbott Laboratories Derivative Shareholder Litigation*[367] was reversed and remanded by the Seventh Circuit Court of Appeals after some unusual proceedings.[368] The 2003 decision in *Abbott Laboratories* (*Abbott Laboratories-2003*) found that under applicable Delaware law, the more stringent *Rales* test,[369] which is generally used rather than the *Aronson*[370] test when board omissions or inaction are alleged, did not apply in this case. Looking back to *Caremark,* the Seventh Circuit found that director liability for breach of the duty to monitor corporate actions could result from an ill-advised or negligent board decision or from "an unconsidered failure of the board to act" in circumstances where due attention might have prevented loss.[371] The Seventh Circuit distinguished the situation in *Caremark* where the directors were "blamelessly unaware of the conduct leading to corporate liability"[372] with no grounds for suspicion, from the *Abbott Laboratories* case where directors were made aware of potential liability in several ways, including (i) numerous FDA warning letters (some of which were sent or copied directly to board members), (ii) board members annually signed SEC disclosure forms acknowledging noncompliance with certain government requirements, and (iii) several articles were published in the national press discussing the FDA findings that regulatory violations had occurred. Although the Seventh Circuit did not cite definitive evidence demonstrating that all board members were aware of these facts, the court found that "where there is a corporate governance structure in place, we must then assume the corporate governance procedures were followed and that the board knew of the problems and decided no action was required."[373] Accordingly, the *Abbott Laboratories-2003* court says the facts are clearly distinguishable from the "unconsidered inaction" in *Caremark,* and the more stringent *Rales* test for demand futility does not apply.[374]

---

[366]*Id.*

[367]*In re* Abbott Labs. Derivative Shareholder Litig., 141 F. Supp. 2d 946 (N.D. Ill. 2001).

[368]The case was initially reversed by the Seventh Circuit in an opinion at 293 F.3d 378 (7th Cir. 2002), which was subsequently withdrawn without explanation at 299 F.3d 898 (7th Cir. 2002). A new opinion by the Seventh Circuit, reversing and remanding the district court decision (and superseding 293 F.3d 378), was issued at 325 F.3d 795 (7th Cir. 2003).

[369]Rales v. Blasband, 634 A.2d 927 (Del. 1993).

[370]Aronson v. Lewis, 473 A.2d 805 (Del. 1984), *overruled on other grounds by* Brehm v. Eisner, 746 A.2d 244 (Del. 2000).

[371]*In re* Abbott Labs. Derivative Shareholder Litig., 325 F.3d 795, 805 (7th Cir. 2003), *citing Caremark,* 698 A.2d 959, 967 (Del. Ch. 1996).

[372]325 F.3d at 805, citing 698 A.2d at 969.

[373]325 F.3d at 806. Thus board members may be at risk even if the appropriate compliance structure and procedures are in place, if they do not actively implement and take advantage of them.

[374]*Id.*

Using the second standard in the *Aronson* test, indicating that demand futility may be established if there is reasonable doubt that the challenged transaction resulted from a valid exercise of the directors' business judgment, the Seventh Circuit cites a 1989 case[375] as requiring it to examine both the substance of the transaction and the procedures used by the directors.[376] Then, citing *Emerald Partners*[377] for the proposition that Delaware law imposes three fiduciary duties on directors, i.e., care, loyalty, and good faith, the Seventh Circuit holds that the *Abbott Laboratories* allegations support a finding that the directors breached their duty of good faith, thereby taking their conduct outside the protection of the business judgment rule.

Although implicitly acknowledging that the lower court had come to the opposite conclusion based on the same set of facts, the appellate court cites six years of noncompliance, FDA inspections and Warning Letters, articles in the press, the largest civil fine ever imposed by the FDA, and the destruction and suspension of products worth approximately $250 million in corporate assets as evidence that the directors' decision to not act was not made in good faith. The appellate court refutes the lower court's finding that the facts in *McCall v. Scott* involved more serious board misconduct, acknowledging that there may have been more specific allegations against certain individual directors in *McCall*, but that the magnitude and duration of the FDA violations by Abbott, which led to the highest fine ever imposed by the FDA, were of an equally serious magnitude and duration to justify a finding of lack of good faith. The Seventh Circuit further emphasizes that the violations in *Abbott Laboratories* continued over a six-year period, while the Columbia Board's failure to act occurred only during a more limited two-year period.[378] The Seventh Circuit also relies heavily on the Sixth Circuit's opinion in *McCall* to find that the Section 102(b)(7) waiver provision similarly would not protect the *Abbott Laboratories* directors if the plaintiffs were able to prove "omissions not in good faith." Further, to the extent the directors' conduct constituted reckless disregard of a known risk, this could well be found to be the "bad faith" that would not be protected by a Section 102(b)(7) waiver provision.[379]

The parties in *Abbott Laboratories* reached a $35 million settlement in December 2004. The district court entered an order and final judgment approving the settlement and dismissing the case in March 2005.[380]

---

[375] Starrels v. First Nat'l Bank of Chicago, 870 F.2d 1168, 1171 (7th Cir. 1989) (*citing* Grobow v. Perot, 539 A.2d 180, 189 (Del. 1988), *overruled on other grounds by* Brehm v. Eisner, 746 A.2d 244 (Del. 2000)).

[376] *Abbott Labs.,* 325 F.3d at 807–08.

[377] Emerald Partners v. Berlin, 787 A.2d 85 (Del. 2001).

[378] 325 F.3d at 808–09.

[379] *Id.* at 810.

[380] *In re* Abbott Labs. Derivative Shareholder Litig., No. 99-CV-7246 (N.D. Ill. Mar. 1, 2005). *See also In re* Abbott Labs. Derivative Shareholder Litig., No. 99-CV-7246 (N.D. Ill. Dec. 29, 2004) (Stipulation and Agreement of Settlement) (Abbott will fund regulatory/compliance activities in an amount not less than $27 million. The directors have agreed to pay from insurance proceeds an award of attorneys' fees and expenses, provided the award does not exceed $9 million.).

## 6. *Implications of the* Columbia/HCA *and* Abbott Laboratories *Decisions*

### a. *The Sixth Circuit Decision in McCall*

The Sixth Circuit opinion in *McCall* indicates the court's belief that the demand-futility rule, along with the Delaware law allowing the waiver of certain director liability, should not become a means for corporate boards to escape almost all liability if they fail to take appropriate actions. The lower court decision provided considerable comfort to corporate boards because the *Caremark* failure-to-monitor theory had been substantially narrowed so that it created liability only where there had been an *intentional* failure to act, at least in those instances where a corporate charter included a provision modeled on Section 102(b)(7) of Title 8 of the Delaware Code.[381] Moreover, the district court had applied presuit demand requirements so stringently to the facts that few cases involving a board's failure to monitor would seem likely to qualify for an exception to the rule. The Sixth Circuit decision acknowledges that Delaware law precludes claims against directors for gross negligence if the corporation has amended its certificate of incorporation in accordance with Section 102(b)(7). However, the court finds a narrow window where failure to act can create exposure for the board, despite Section 102(b)(7) and the demand-futility rule, i.e., where a director *consciously* disregards his or her duties to the corporation, causing its stockholders to suffer.[382] This type of behavior is also characterized as a breach of a director's duty of good faith.[383]

As compared to the lower court's opinion, the circuit court's analysis is more consistent with Delaware case law, particularly the *Caremark* decision. Despite the magistrate judge's statements, it is open to some question whether *Caremark* held that liability in the failure-to-monitor context could arise only if there was an intentional failure. The *Caremark* opinion refers to "a *sustained* or *systematic failure* of the board to exercise oversight."[384] This formulation is different from *intentional* failure.

Although the appellate court was careful to note that it was not issuing an opinion on the underlying merits of plaintiffs' claims, the lengthy discussion in the opinion indicates that court's view that most of the allegations would support at least an inference of improper conduct by the board. The appellate court seemed to reject the lower court's implication that a number of the allegations might be considered "de minimis" in light of the size of the corporation as a whole. For example, the magistrate judge (and district court) had found that a $1.1 million repayment and a $475,000 settlement were not suggestive of corporate-wide fraud in light of Columbia's receipt of $8 billion from the federal government in a single year. Similarly, the magistrate judge found that a widely reported investigation involving over 200 federal agents raiding two hospitals and serving a dozen physicians' offices with search warrants was not of sufficient magnitude, given Columbia's size, to support an inference of

---

[381] *See McCall* Magistrate Judge's Report at 57.

[382] *See McCall* App. 2 at 1001.

[383] *E.g., id.* at 1000; *Abbott Labs.,* 141 F. Supp. 2d at 949.

[384] *In re* Caremark, 698 A.2d 959, 971 (Del. Ch. 1996).

corporate-wide fraud.[385] The Sixth Circuit's analysis also seemed to rely heavily on the fact that most of Columbia's directors had substantial prior experience as directors or managers of health care companies.

In this evolving area of the law, clear standards are difficult to identify and thus, outcomes are difficult to predict. Theoretically, plaintiff shareholders are more likely to prevail if the board's inaction results in very extensive and serious consequences. For example, the *Abbott Laboratories* court distinguished that case (where defendant directors prevailed) from *McCall*, in part, by characterizing the *McCall* violations as far more widespread and egregious. However, the violations in the *Abbott Laboratories* case were substantial: The FDA had issued four warning letters, and, as part of the consent settlement, ultimately imposed a $100 million fine, required the company to withdraw 125 types of medical diagnostic test kits from the market, required the destruction of certain inventory, and further insisted on various changes in the company's manufacturing processes.[386]

However, several additional factors may have contributed to the result in the *Abbott Laboratories* case. First, the court emphasized that the *Abbott Laboratories* plaintiffs had not made sufficiently detailed allegations concerning the directors' backgrounds, roles, and knowledge. Moreover, the *Abbott Laboratories* court also seemed inclined to view the facts in a light more favorable to the defendants, perhaps because most of the directors were "outside directors" and not Abbott employees. Thus, the court implied that these outside directors would assume that the pattern of inspections, negotiations, and reinspections were "routine," and that the discussion of potential consequences in the FDA warning letters, including a potential freeze on sales, was mere "boilerplate."[387] The fact that the continuing violations involved various different issues was viewed in a surprisingly positive perspective, i.e., Abbott was not attempting to "stonewall" the FDA.[388] The court also emphasized that the violations only affected "a small percentage" of Abbott's products.[389] In any event, the case clearly indicates that plaintiffs attempting to demonstrate director "bad faith," in cases involving a waiver of director liability provision in the corporation's charter, may have a particularly high hurdle to overcome.

The standards required for director and officer oversight of corporate affairs continue to evolve. In *Dellastatious v. Williams,*[390] the Fourth Circuit did not cite the district court's decision in *Abbott Laboratories.* However, both courts seemed to accept the premise that "outside" directors should not be held to as high a

---

[385] *McCall* Magistrate Judge's Report at 59.

[386] *See* 141 F. Supp. 2d 946 (N.D. Ill. 2001).

[387] *Abbott Labs.*, 141 F. Supp. 2d at 950.

[388] *Id.* at 951.

[389] Plaintiffs alleged that the affected products accounted for 20% of Abbott's revenues, but the court dismissed this allegation in fairly summary fashion by finding no facts suggesting Abbott's management had reason to believe the Diagnostic Division's revenues were in any serious jeopardy. *Id.* at 950.

[390] 242 F.3d 191 (4th Cir. 2001).

standard as inside directors and could reasonably rely on legal counsel, accountants, and other experts (unless the outside director had knowledge that such reliance was unwarranted).[391] Stating that "service as director of a corporation should not be a journey through liability land mines,"[392] the *Dellastatious* court cited *Caremark* to support the proposition that directors can avoid liability for insufficiently supervising corporate affairs by showing that they attempted, in good faith, to ensure that an adequate information-gathering and reporting system was in place.[393]

Subsequently, the district court's decision in *Abbott Laboratories* was reversed and remanded by the U.S. Court of Appeals for the Seventh Circuit in an opinion, described in more detail above, that brought the standards used by the Sixth and Seventh Circuits in evaluating demand futility and Section 102(b)(7) claims into much closer alignment.[394] Nevertheless, the federal district court in Delaware, in a 2004 opinion, indirectly disputed part of the holding in the *Abbott Laboratories–2003* opinion. In *Stanziale v. Nachtomi*,[395] the court referred to the "theoretical exception" to the business judgment rule that some decisions may be so egregious that liability may be imposed even without proof of conflict of interest or improper motivation. Nevertheless, the *Stanziale* court did use the "egregious" standard as part of its analysis of the board's actions in that case. In addition, another federal district court, in *Roselink Investors, LLC v. Shenkman*,[396] specifically refuted the plaintiff's contention that Delaware law recognizes an independent duty of good faith. Nevertheless, the court conceded that such an obligation was subsumed within the duty of loyalty.

### b. Other Developments Relating to Presuit Demand

In contrast, several other cases, applying Delaware law, have indicated certain courts' reluctance to let the presuit demand rule prevent a resolution of the issues on the merits, even in shareholder derivative litigation where director inaction is at issue. In a March 2000 decision, *In re Oxford Health Plans, Inc., Securities Litigation*,[397] the U.S. District Court for the Southern District of New York excused the need for demand by the plaintiffs in a derivative suit because

---

[391] *Id.* at 196.

[392] *Id.*

[393] *Id.* (*citing Caremark*, 698 A.2d at 969–70). Both *McCall* and the *Abbott Labs.* district court cases were distinguished by a federal district court in Michigan in *Salsitz v. Nasser*, 208 F.R.D. 589 (E.D. Mich. 2002), which found that *Salsitz*, unlike the other two cases, did not involve clear violations of federal law or allegations of criminal or civil investigations that would have put the board on notice of illegal behavior. *Salsitz* at 598–99.

[394] *See In re* Abbott Labs., 325 F.3d 795 (7th Cir. 2003).

[395] No. 01-403 KAJ, 2004 WL 878469 (D. Del. Apr. 20, 2004).

[396] 386 F. Supp. 2d 209 (S.D.N.Y. 2004).

[397] 192 F.R.D. 111 (S.D.N.Y. 2000). The *Oxford Health Plans* presuit demand rule was followed in 2002 in *Dollens v. Zionts*, No. 01 C 2826, 2002 U.S. Dist. LEXIS 13511, 19–20 (N.D. Ill. July 22, 2002) (excusing presuit demand because plaintiffs adequately pleaded that five of eight directors faced a substantial likelihood of personal liability that would prevent them from exercising impartiality in considering a shareholder demand).

of defendant directors' nonfeasance and generalized failure to properly monitor the activities of management. These failures included (1) not having sufficient financial controls and procedures to monitor the planned conversion to a new computer system; (2) not implementing and enforcing procedures to prevent appropriation of company information and assets by certain directors; (3) knowingly or recklessly disseminating misleading information to shareholders; and (4) allowing the company to engage in improper billing practices and to violate numerous insurance regulations, thereby subjecting the company to fines, penalties, and further investigations. The court applied Delaware law and the *Rales v. Blasband*[398] test to find that "[i]n numerous cases where liability is based upon a failure to supervise and monitor, and to keep adequate supervisory controls in place, demand futility is ordinarily found, especially where the failure involves a scheme of significant magnitude and duration which went undiscovered by the directors."[399] The district court in *Oxford Health Plans* cited *Miller v. Schreyer*,[400] which excused demand in a derivative suit by stating the following:

> It does not appear that the Delaware Supreme Court, in deciding *Rales*, intended to suggest that a board of directors is absolved of all responsibility to prevent the repeated misuse of corporate resources for illegal purposes.[401]

The *Miller* case involved allegations that, according to the court, created "obvious danger signs."[402] In light of the magnitude, duration, timing, and illegality of certain transactions and the identity of the parties, the court held that it was hardly unreasonable to require directors to implement basic financial oversight procedures sufficient to disclose a patently improper scheme extending over a five-year period.[403]

It is also important to remember that these cases generally deal with precedents under Delaware law (or under other state laws similar to Delaware's). However, as previously discussed, some states follow other types of demand-futility laws or precedents, including states such as Pennsylvania that follow the demand rule set forth in the ALI *Principles of Corporate Governance*, which is more deferential to corporate boards.

---

[398] 634 A.2d 927 (Del.1993).

[399] *Oxford Health Plans*, 192 F.R.D. at 117. The court acknowledged that plaintiffs had alleged both affirmative misconduct and nonfeasance but noted that claims based on board inaction appeared to predominate.

[400] 683 N.Y.S.2d 51 (N.Y. Sup. Ct. App. Div. 1999).

[401] *Id.* at 55.

[402] *Id.* (citation omitted).

[403] The first *Miller* decision, Miller v. Schreyer, 606 N.Y.S.2d 642 (N.Y. Sup. Ct. App. Div. 1994), was criticized by Marx v. Akers, 88 N.Y.2d 189, 200 (N.Y. 1996), and *In re* Baxter Int'l, Inc. Shareholders Litig., 654 A.2d 1268, 1271 (Del. Ch. 1995). However, the subsequent *Miller* decision (cited with approval in *Oxford Health Plans*) reaffirmed the original holding, partly relying on the "law of the case doctrine." *Miller*, 683 N.Y.S.2d at 54.

### E.  *Stone v. Ritter*—Upholding the *Caremark* Standard for Director Liability

In June 2006, the Delaware Supreme Court in *Stone v. Ritter* stated that the *Caremark* decision accurately states the elements plaintiffs must prove to establish the basis for director liability.[404] Specifically, the court held that whether or not a director will be held liable is dependent on the plaintiff's ability to demonstrate that the directors knew that they were not discharging their fiduciary obligations.[405] The supreme court's holding in *Stone v. Ritter* makes it clear that a showing of bad faith is a condition for director liability under the *Caremark* standard.

Quoting *Caremark*, the Delaware Supreme Court stated that a derivative plaintiff must plead that "the directors utterly failed to implement any reporting or information system or controls." Alternatively, the derivative plaintiff must plead that "having implemented such a system or controls, [the directors] consciously failed to monitor or oversee its operations thus disabling themselves from being informed of risks or problems requiring their attention."

As a practical matter, the court's affirmation of the standard outlined in *Caremark* demonstrates that corporations must ensure that they have effective mechanisms in place to aid directors' ability to obtain information. Directors, in turn, must actively use such internal control systems to adequately monitor the corporation's operations.

### F.  *Spitzer v. Abdelhak*

RICO[406] has established itself as a worrisome source of potential liability for officers and directors. RICO created a private cause of action through which a person injured by a RICO violation may recover both attorneys' fees and treble damages.

### 1.  Background of the Case

*Spitzer v. Abdelhak*[407] was filed following the financial difficulties and bankruptcy of the Allegheny Health Education and Research Foundation (AHERF). This class action was brought by a group of physicians who sold their medical practices to AHERF prior to its demise. The plaintiffs brought the suit against AHERF's directors and officers, alleging that they were injured by the defendants' RICO violations.[408]

---

[404]911 A.2d at 370. The *Stone* plaintiffs were shareholders of AmSouth Bancorporation who filed a derivative complaint without making a presuit demand on the board of directors of the corporation. *Id.* at 364. The *Stone* plaintiff-appellants argued that the lower court erred in dismissing their complaint asserting that the defendant directors failed to implement any form of monitoring or internal controls to apprise them of the problems occurring at the corporation. *Id.* at 365. The Delaware Supreme Court held that the lower court properly applied *Caremark*. *Id.* at 373.

[405]*Id.*

[406]18 U.S.C. §§1951–60.

[407]No. 98-6475, 1999 WL 1204352 (E.D. Pa. Dec. 15, 1999).

[408]*See id.* at *1–3.

The plaintiffs claimed that the defendants engaged in a scheme to defraud them through the use of false statements about the financial viability of AHERF. The plaintiffs alleged both financial damage and damage to their professional reputations. They also asserted common law claims for conspiracy and intentional interference with contractual relations. In response to the defendants' motion to dismiss for failure to state a claim, the district court analyzed the plaintiffs' allegations and declined to dismiss the RICO claims.[409]

Among the major factors leading to AHERF's demise were a series of acquisitions of heavily indebted hospitals and medical schools.[410] That "path to bankruptcy" began in 1988 under the guidance of Sherif Abdelhak, AHERF's CEO during the time period relevant to the plaintiffs' suit.[411] AHERF's acquisitions made it Pennsylvania's largest statewide integrated delivery system. By the time AHERF filed for bankruptcy in 1998, it was losing up to $1 million per day.[412]

Observers also pointed to AHERF's weak management structure and lack of oversight as causes for AHERF's failure. AHERF's weak structure was exemplified by (1) an "enormous parent board" of up to 35 directors and (2) a network of boards for each of its operations, which "reportedly were never sure what was happening elsewhere in the AHERF empire."[413] Of importance to potential director and officer liability are allegations that Abdelhak dominated all board decisions and discouraged board members from "asking tough questions."[414] Abdelhak and his senior management allegedly made many decisions without formal board approval; some decisions were relayed to the board only after the fact, if at all.[415]

Particularly related to the *Spitzer* plaintiffs' RICO claim was the allegation that AHERF's directors and officers depicted AHERF's subsidiary, Allegheny East, as a "viable health care system" to increase their salaries and their prestige in the community.[416] The plaintiffs specifically alleged that the defendants voted themselves salary increases when AHERF's bankruptcy was imminent. In addition, the plaintiffs alleged that the defendants caused large

---

[409] *See id.* at *10. The federal district court also declined to dismiss the state law conspiracy claim. A discussion of that aspect of the opinion is beyond the scope of this chapter.

[410] For a detailed history of AHERF and its failure, see Lawton Burns et al., *The Fall of the House of AHERF: The Allegheny System Debacle*, 19 HEALTH AFF. 7 (2000).

[411] *Spitzer*, 1999 WL 1204352 at *1.

[412] *See id.*; Lawton Burns et al., *The Fall of the House of AHERF: The Allegheny System Debacle*, 19 HEALTH AFF. 7 (2000).

[413] Lawton Burns et al., *The Fall of the House of AHERF: The Allegheny System Debacle*, 19 HEALTH AFF. 7 (2000).

[414] *Id.*

[415] *See id.*

[416] *Spitzer*, 1999 WL 1204352, at *6. For example, commentators observed that in a January 1998 speech—just six months before AHERF and Allegheny East filed for bankruptcy—Abdelhak discussed AHERF's "phenomenal growth" and "productivity improvements," but failed to mention either the internal cash transfers and other mechanisms used to finance the growth or AHERF's financial deterioration. Lawton Burns et al., *The Fall of the House of AHERF: The Allegheny System Debacle*, 19 HEALTH AFF. 7 (2000).

sums of money to be transferred from restricted accounts "to cover Allegheny East's pitiful financial state."[417] The plaintiffs also claimed that every defendant officer signed a fraudulent annual report.

## 2. *The Court's Decision*

As noted above,[418] the district court denied the defendants' motion to dismiss the plaintiffs' RICO claims. Generally, to establish a RICO claim, a plaintiff must show (1) the existence of an enterprise that affects interstate commerce; (2) that the defendant (separate from the enterprise) engaged in a pattern of racketeering activity; (3) that through that pattern the defendant conducted the enterprise, acquired an interest in it, or controlled it; and (4) that the plaintiff suffered an injury as a result of the RICO violation.[419]

The defendants unsuccessfully challenged each element of the plaintiffs' RICO claim. An enterprise is a group of persons or entities associated together for the purpose of engaging in a course of conduct. It is proven by an ongoing organization, formal or not, together with evidence that the various associates function together as a continuing unit.[420] The court found that plaintiffs' allegation that the enterprise consisted of the corporation and one of its subsidiaries adequately described a RICO enterprise.[421]

The directors and officers also challenged the adequacy of plaintiffs' claims that the directors and officers controlled the enterprise.[422] The court held that control was established when the defendants participated in the operation or management of the enterprise; liability is not limited to those with primary responsibility, and the degree of participation need not be substantial.[423] Accordingly, the officer-defendants' roles as senior managers of the business were sufficient to establish control for RICO purposes. Similarly, the director-defendants' votes on crucial issues, such as officer and employee compensation, established their control under RICO.

Having determined that plaintiffs satisfied the enterprise and control elements, the court looked to the pattern of racketeering activity.[424] RICO identifies numerous state and federal crimes, the occurrence of which is a precondition to a RICO violation.[425] RICO does not require a criminal con-

---

[417] *Spitzer*, 1999 WL 1204352, at *7.

[418] See Section III.F.1., above.

[419] *See* 18 U.S.C. §1962(c). Regarding the injury element, which applies to standing to bring a RICO claim, the court distinguished the case before it from others in which the plaintiffs' injuries were caused solely by the organization's insolvency. *See Spitzer*, 1999 WL 1204352, at *3. In other words, unless a plaintiff adequately alleges that his or her losses would have occurred even without the insolvency, he or she may be faced with a successful motion to dismiss. The *Spitzer* court found for the plaintiffs on that issue.

[420] *See* United States v. Turkette, 452 U.S. 576, 580–81 (1981); 18 U.S.C. §§1961(4), 1962(c).

[421] *See Spitzer,* 1999 WL 1204352, at *4.

[422] *See id.*

[423] *See id. (citing* Reves v. Ernst & Young, 507 U.S. 170, 179, 183 (1993)).

[424] *See Spitzer*, 1999 WL 1204352, at *7.

[425] 18 U.S.C. §1961(1).

viction before a plaintiff can bring a civil RICO claim based on that predicate act.[426] Plaintiff's complaint satisfied the racketeering activity requirement by alleging violations of federal statutes prohibiting mail fraud,[427] wire fraud,[428] money laundering,[429] and interstate transportation of fraudulently obtained money.[430] These predicate acts were based on plaintiffs' claim that money was fraudulently obtained and distributed.[431]

To show a pattern of racketeering activity, plaintiffs "must show that the racketeering predicates are related, and that they amount to or pose a threat of continued criminal activity."[432] The plaintiffs alleged that the defendants' scheme was operating for over four years, during which time the predicate acts occurred.[433] The court found that this four-year period satisfied the continuity requirement and established a pattern of racketeering activity.

The court's refusal to dismiss the RICO counts of the *Spitzer* complaint merely means that plaintiffs had adequately pled it. The procedural posture of a motion to dismiss means that the court must accept the truth of all plaintiffs' allegations and draw from them all inferences favorable to plaintiffs. Dismissal is appropriate only if it is clear that "beyond a doubt . . . the plaintiff can prove no set of facts in support of his claim which would entitle him to relief."[434]

Litigation between the plaintiffs' class and the directors and officers of AHERF continued following the district court's denial of the defendants' motion to dismiss the RICO claims.[435] The parties reached a settlement, and the case was dismissed on May 6, 2002.[436] The court order approving the settlement awarded over $1.4 million in attorneys' fees to plaintiffs' counsel,[437] but details concerning the size of the settlement fund and the nonmonetary obligations of AHERF officers and directors were not made public.

Chief Financial Officer David McConnell settled a criminal charge that he had misused AHERF funds by allegedly obtaining $25,000 and keeping the balance for personal use after using $7,300 to renovate a box at Pittsburgh's Three Rivers Stadium. He was sentenced to 12 months of probation, and was required to perform 150 hours of community service and to pay $16,700 in restitution. Charges against AHERF's general counsel, including theft, conspiracy, and misapplication of entrusted property, were dropped in May 2001. The court found no evidence that the general counsel knew about the chief executive officer's policy of using AHERF endowment funds for general

---

[426] *See, e.g.,* Sedima, S.P.R.L. v. Imrex Co., 473 U.S. 479 (1985).

[427] *See* 18 U.S.C. §1341.

[428] *See* 18 U.S.C. §1343.

[429] *See* 18 U.S.C. §1957.

[430] *See* 18 U.S.C. §2314.

[431] *See Spitzer,* 1999 WL 1204352, at *5–7.

[432] *See id.* at *7 (quoting H.J., Inc. v. Northwestern Bell Tel. Co., 492 U.S. 229, 241 (1989)).

[433] *See Spitzer,* 1999 WL 1204352, at *7

[434] *Id.* (quoting Conley v. Gibson, 355 U.S. 41, 45–46 (1957)).

[435] Civil Docket at entries 68–111, Spitzer v. Abdelhak, No. 98-6475, 1999 U.S. Dist. LEXIS 19110 (E.D. Pa. Dec. 15, 1999).

[436] *Id.* at entry 111.

[437] *Id.*

operating purposes.[438] Finally, Sherif Abdelhak, the AHERF CEO, was sentenced by a Pennsylvania state court for his role in raiding AHERF's charitable endowments in 1998 to postpone its financial collapse, despite the reported finding that the money was used to prop up the failing health care system rather than for personal gain.[439] Abdelhak pleaded no contest to one count of misapplication of entrusted property and was sentenced to a prison term of 11-1/2 to 23 months.[440]

## IV. Corporate Compliance

The principles of criminal and civil liability described above, as well as the *Caremark* case and its progeny, indicate that directors and officers of health care organizations may face a significant risk of exposure. Implementing a corporate compliance program is one mechanism directors and officers can use to minimize that risk. An effective compliance program is particularly important because it can create corporate information gathering and reporting systems sufficient to withstand scrutiny under a *Caremark* analysis, and may help demonstrate the board's "good faith," a critical part of the *McCall* court's analyses. Corporate compliance programs are discussed in detail elsewhere in this volume, including compliance programs' benefits for an organization and their requirements,[441] but the discussion that follows focuses on their implications for director and officer liability.

Corporate compliance programs also may form the basis for registered (publicly traded) companies to fulfill certain requirements of the Sarbanes-Oxley Act and the SRO rules changes, such as the required code of ethics.[442]

### A. U.S. Sentencing Guidelines

Chapter 8 of the U.S. Sentencing Guidelines on the sentencing of organizations (the Sentencing Guidelines) became effective in November 1991. The Sentencing Guidelines encourage, although they do not require, organizations to implement a corporate compliance program.[443] The Sentencing Guidelines were developed under the Sentencing Reform Act,[444] which was enacted to provide greater fairness, certainty, and effectiveness in federal sentencing and to eliminate much of the discretion formerly vested in trial

---

[438] *Former Nonprofit Health System Executive Sentenced for Misusing Charitable Funds*, 7 Health Care Daily Rep. (BNA) (Sept. 6, 2002).

[439] *Id.*

[440] *Id.* Abdelhak was paroled after serving three months in prison. *See* Cindy Becker, *Early Release: Abdelhak Wins Parole After Serving Three Months*, Modern Healthcare (Feb. 3, 2003).

[441] See Chapter 7 (Baumann, Corporate Compliance Programs).

[442] See Section II.C., above.

[443] U.S. Sentencing Guidelines (U.S.S.G.) Manual ch. 8, introductory cmt. (2000).

[444] Sentencing Reform Act of 1984, 28 U.S.C. §991.

judges. The Sentencing Reform Act also established the U.S. Sentencing Commission,[445] which was charged with drafting guidelines to control sentencing in federal courts. The resulting guidelines use a mechanistic approach to achieve uniformity and certainty, and a series of very complicated calculations are used to determine the penalty imposed. As a result, there has been a sharp increase in penalties, particularly for white-collar offenders and organizations.

First, a base fine calculation ranges from $5,000 to $72.5 million. This fine generally is based on the applicable offense level or the pecuniary gain or loss, whichever is higher.[446] Next, a multiplier is developed based on the "culpability score." This multiplier can range from 0.05 to 4; thus, a fine can reach $290 million or higher, depending on the pecuniary gain or loss involved.[447] Although a court's discretion is narrowly limited, certain specified considerations can be factored into the culpability score. For example, points can be added to the calculation if there was involvement in or tolerance of the offense by high-level personnel.[448] Alternatively, points may be deducted if the company reported the violation or cooperated in the investigation.[449] Points also may be deducted if the organization had an effective compliance program.[450]

## 1. Advantages of Compliance Programs

There are specific advantages under the Sentencing Guidelines to the development of a compliance program. Although most of the benefits accrue more directly to the corporation, directors and officers benefit at least indirectly because shareholders are less likely to file suit against them if the corporation is not facing any serious financial problems or legal liabilities. For example, under the Sentencing Guidelines, the existence of an effective corporate compliance program can reduce the corporate fine by as much as 80 percent. In an environment of multimillion-dollar fines, the magnitude of this reduction can create substantial financial benefits for the corporation. Moreover, an organization with a compliance program may be able to avoid the imposition of a probationary period, which could create a significant burden on the company's subsequent operations.[451] Government officials also may be persuaded not to seek the company's exclusion from participation in federal health care programs, at least in those cases where such exclusion is permissive. Exclusion, if imposed, can be a financial death sentence for such companies.

More directly, providing evidence of an effective compliance program can help to persuade the government to use its discretion in favor of the corporation and its executives. For example, if a compliance plan has been implemented,

---

[445]28 U.S.C. §991(a).

[446]*See* U.S.S.G. §8C2.4 (1998).

[447]*See id.* §§8C2.5, 8C2.6.

[448]*See id.* §8C2.5(b).

[449]*See id.* §8C2.5(g).

[450]*See id.* §8C2.5(f). This reduction does not apply in certain cases in which one or more high-level employees within the organization were involved in the offense.

[451]In the absence of a compliance program, the court is required by the Sentencing Guidelines to impose a period of probation if the company has more than 50 employees. *See id.* §8D1.1(a)(3). For the conditions of probation, see U.S.S.G. §§8D1.3–1.4.

the CIA imposed by the government as part of a settlement agreement is likely to be less onerous.[452] In addition, if a compliance program has been implemented, the government may agree not to file criminal charges against senior officers for the misdeeds of lower-level employees. Finally, a compliance program also can assist in the defense of *qui tam* actions, shareholder suits, and civil damage actions by demonstrating that management has acted appropriately, thus countering claims for punitive damages.

### 2. Compliance Programs Must Be "Effective"

There are numerous intrinsic advantages to compliance programs, such as (1) making it more likely that improper conduct will be detected sooner, thus reducing the damage caused; (2) allowing the company and its directors to better assess their options (e.g., to consider participating in a voluntary disclosure program);[453] and (3) most important, increasing the likelihood that a culture of compliance will prevent many violations from ever occurring.

As a result of these factors and the great increase over recent years in the number of investigations and enforcement actions the government has initiated in the industry, numerous health care organizations have begun implementing corporate compliance programs, and many others are considering doing so. Moreover, as stated by two authorities on director and officer liability,

> [a]n effective corporate compliance program is an undertaking so comprehensive [that it] is probably more elaborate than what many organizations have attempted to date, but its benefits may be so substantial that it should receive serious consideration without further delay. It is reasonable to suggest that boards of directors will be derelict in their duties if they neglect to do so.[454]

However, directors and officers should be aware of additional concerns they must address in connection with compliance programs. First, to obtain benefits, it is essential that the program be "effective." The Sentencing Guidelines have established minimum requirements that must be met before a program will be deemed "effective."[455] In summary, these requirements are as follows:

- Compliance standards and procedures must be established "that are reasonably capable of reducing the prospect of criminal conduct."
- Specific high-level personnel must be assigned responsibility for overseeing compliance.
- Due care must be exercised not to delegate discretionary authority to those who are known or should have been known to have a propensity to engage in illegal conduct.

---

[452] In certain situations, the government may not impose a CIA if an effective compliance program is in place.

[453] For a discussion of the voluntary disclosure program, see Chapter 3 (Salcido, The False Claims Act in Health Care Prosecutions: Application of the Substantive, *Qui Tam*, and Voluntary Disclosure Provisions).

[454] WILLIAM E. KNEPPER & DAN A. BAILEY, LIABILITY OF CORPORATE OFFICERS AND DIRECTORS (7th ed. 2002), at 47.

[455] U.S.S.G. §8B2.1.

- Standards and procedures must be communicated effectively to all employees and agents (e.g., by requiring participation in training programs or by dissemination of practical compliance information).
- Reasonable steps must be taken to achieve compliance with these standards, including the use of auditing and monitoring systems, and by implementing and publicizing a system that allows criminal conduct to be reported without fear of retaliation.
- Standards must be consistently enforced through appropriate disciplinary mechanisms.
- After detection, all reasonable steps must be taken to respond appropriately and to prevent further similar offenses.

The Sentencing Guidelines specifically state, however, that failure to prevent or detect an offense does not, in and of itself, mean that the program was not effective.[456] According to the Sentencing Guidelines, some of the factors to be used in determining the actions necessary for an effective program are as follows:

- *Size of the organization.* The requisite degree of formality of a compliance program will vary with the size of the organization: the larger the organization, the more formal the program typically should be. A larger organization generally should have established written policies defining the standards and procedures to be followed by its employees and other agents.
- *Likelihood that certain offenses may occur because of the nature of the business.* If, because of the nature of an organization's business, there is a substantial risk that certain types of offenses may occur, management must have taken steps to prevent and detect those types of offenses. For example, if an organization handles toxic substances, it must have established standards and procedures designed to ensure that those substances are properly handled at all times.
- *Prior history of the organization.* An organization's prior history may indicate types of offenses that it should have taken actions to prevent. Recurrence of misconduct similar to that which an organization has previously committed casts doubt on whether it took all reasonable steps to prevent such misconduct. An organization's failure to incorporate and follow applicable industry practice or the standards called for by any applicable governmental regulation weighs against a finding of an effective program to prevent and detect violations of law.[457]

The U.S. Sentencing Commission established an Advisory Group on Organizational Guidelines to review the general effectiveness of Chapter 8 of the U.S. Sentencing Guidelines. The Advisory Group focused on the application of the criteria for an effective compliance program and requested public comment on a variety of issues, including:

---

[456] *See id.*
[457] *See id.*

- whether the Sentencing Guidelines should articulate the responsibilities of the CEO, CFO, and/or others responsible for high-level oversight of compliance programs;
- to what extent the responsibilities of boards of directors, board committees, or comparable governance bodies in overseeing compliance programs should be described in the Sentencing Guidelines;
- whether the Sentencing Guidelines should be more specific with regard to required compliance training methodologies;
- whether the Sentencing Guidelines comments should more specifically encourage whistleblower protections, a privilege for good faith self-assessment and corrective action, or other means to encourage reporting without fear of retribution;
- whether auditing and monitoring activities should be given greater emphasis and importance in the Sentencing Guidelines;
- whether the Sentencing Guidelines should give organizations credit for evaluating employee performance using compliance criteria and increase an organization's culpability score for failure to implement a compliance program;
- whether different considerations apply when implementing and enforcing effective compliance programs depending on the size of the organization; and
- what incentives would encourage greater self-reporting—for example, whether the Sentencing Guidelines should state that the waiver of existing legal privileges will not be required to qualify for a reduction in culpability score.[458]

In addition, Section 1104 of the Sarbanes-Oxley Act called for the U.S. Sentencing Commission to issue new or amended guidelines to enhance penalties for officers or directors of publicly traded corporations who commit fraud and related offenses.[459] The Sarbanes-Oxley Act specifies numerous factors to be considered in carrying out this mandate, including the requirement that guideline offense levels and enhancements for an obstruction of justice offense be adequate when documents or other physical evidence are destroyed or fabricated.

In April 2004, the Sentencing Commission voted to adopt many of the recommendations of the Advisory Group and amended the Organizational Sentencing Guidelines to make the criteria for effective compliance programs more stringent and to place greater responsibility on directors and officers for oversight and management of corporate compliance programs. The amended Sentencing Guidelines were submitted to Congress on May 1, 2004, and became effective November 1, 2004.[460]

---

[458] Advisory Group on Organizational Guidelines to the U.S. Sentencing Comm'n, Request for Additional Public Comment Regarding the U.S. Sentencing Guidelines for Organizations (Aug. 21, 2002), *available at* http://www.ussc.gov/corp/pubcom8_02.pdf.

[459] Sarbanes-Oxley Act §1104. Several other sections in the Sarbanes-Oxley Act also call for various other changes to the Sentencing Guidelines. *See, e.g., id.* §§805, 905.

[460] The full text of the amended Sentencing Guidelines is available at http://www.ussc.gov/2004guid/tabcon04.htm.

At the time the amended Sentencing Guidelines became effective, cases pending before the U.S. Supreme Court were granted emergency consideration based upon certiorari petitions filed by DOJ. In January 2005, in *United States v. Booker,*[461] the Supreme Court held that "any fact (other than a prior conviction) which is necessary to support a sentence exceeding the maximum authorized by the facts established by a plea of guilty or a jury verdict must be admitted by the defendant or proved to a jury beyond a reasonable doubt." As a result, Section 3553(b)(1), which makes the U.S. Sentencing Guidelines mandatory, violates the Sixth Amendment right to a jury trial and had to be severed from the Sentencing Reform Act of 1984. Thus, the Sentencing Guidelines remain in effect as an advisory matter (i.e., providing a judge with guidance as to the appropriate sentence). The Supreme Court's decision in *Booker* has not had a *major practical* impact on the Guidelines that provide that an effective compliance program may mitigate an organizational defendant's penalty in certain circumstances, since reductions in sentences for cooperation are necessarily the result of very fact-intensive inquiries.[462]

The amended Sentencing Guidelines indicate that corporate compliance programs should be focused on detecting and preventing criminal conduct (which is somewhat narrower than the earlier reference to criminal and civil violations of law). However, in most respects the amended Sentencing Guidelines raise the bar for an "effective" compliance program in various ways. For example, the requirement for "compliance standards and procedures" is defined to include internal controls, thereby imposing an additional requirement for compliance program implementation through auditing and monitoring. In addition, under the amended Sentencing Guidelines, compliance programs should meet the following standards to be considered "effective":[463]

---

[461]543 U.S. 220 (2005). *Booker* followed Blakely v. Washington, 542 U.S. 296 (2004), in which the Supreme Court invalidated a portion of a criminal sentence imposed by a state court judge under the state of Washington's sentencing guidelines that was based upon facts not admitted by the defendant, finding that the use of conduct not charged in the indictment or offered in evidence at trial constituted a violation of the defendant's Sixth Amendment right to trial by jury.

[462]In the aftermath of the Supreme Court's ruling in *United States v. Booker,* 543 U.S. 220 (2005), the Sentencing Commission undertook a study of the impact of the decision on federal sentences. The results of the study were published in March 2006. *See* FINAL REPORT ON THE IMPACT OF *UNITED STATES V. BOOKER* ON FEDERAL SENTENCING (Mar. 2006) [hereinafter BOOKER REPORT]. The Commission's review of sentencing data following *Booker* demonstrated that the majority of federal crimes continued to be sentenced in conformance with the Sentencing Guidelines. *Id.* at vi. The BOOKER REPORT noted that the federal circuit courts have uniformly agreed that post-*Booker* sentences must begin with a sentencing guideline calculation and that six of those courts had determined that a sentence imposed within the guideline range is presumptively reasonable. *Id.* at v. The Commission's review of sentencing data from around the country revealed that the severity of sentences had not changed substantially and, in fact, the average length of the period of incarceration imposed actually increased post-*Booker*. *Id.* at vii. In connection with sentences for fraud offenses, including health care fraud and securities laws violations, the imprisonment rates for individual defendants rose from 53.4% on April 30, 2003, to 61.6% in the post-*Booker* period. *Id.* at 74. In addition to the trend of sentences of incarceration increasing across the board, the Commission attributed the rise in sentences of incarceration in fraud offenses to a number of additional factors, including the Economic Crime Package of 2001 and the Sarbanes-Oxley Act. *Id.*

[463]These amendments are generally found in §8B2.1 of the amended Sentencing Guidelines (which would replace the earlier commentary to §8A1.2 which would be largely deleted).

- High-level personnel of the organization[464] must ensure the organization has an effective compliance program with overall responsibility for the program assigned to specified high-level individuals;
- Specified individual(s) within the organization must have daily operational responsibility for the compliance program and periodically report to high-level personnel or the board (or a subgroup of the board). These individuals should have adequate resources, authority, and direct access to the governing authority (or an appropriate subgroup);
- The organization should use reasonable efforts and due diligence not to include any individual within its "substantial authority personnel"[465] whom the organization knew/should have known has a history of engaging in violations of law or other conduct inconsistent with an effective compliance program;
- Compliance training should be provided to board members, upper level management, employees, and agents, as appropriate;
- Auditing and monitoring systems designed to detect violations of law (that are periodically evaluated), and anonymous reporting systems should be in place;
- Compliance incentives, as well as penalties for compliance violations, should be used to encourage compliance; and
- The organization's governing authority[466] must be knowledgeable about the content and operation of the compliance program and exercise reasonable oversight of its implementation and effectiveness.

In terms of the organization's culpability score, the amended Sentencing Guidelines would allow a three-point deduction for an effective compliance and ethics program. However, the deduction would not be available if the organization unreasonably delayed reporting to the appropriate authorities after becoming aware of an offense.[467] The deduction also would not apply if certain

---

[464]This term is defined as individuals who have substantial control over the organization or who have a substantial role in the making of policy within the organization. The term includes a director; an executive officer; an individual in charge of a major business or functional unit of the organization, such as sales, administration, or finance; and an individual with a substantial ownership interest. Application Note 3(b) to §8A1.2 of the amended Sentencing Guidelines.

[465]This term includes individuals who within the scope of their authority exercise a substantial measure of discretion in acting on behalf of an organization. The term includes high-level personnel of the organization, individuals who exercise substantial supervisory authority (e.g., a plant manager, a sales manager), and any other individuals who, although not a part of an organization's management, nevertheless exercise substantial discretion when acting within the scope of their authority (e.g., an individual with authority to negotiate or set price levels or to negotiate or approve significant contracts). Application Note 3(c) to §8A1.2 of the amended Sentencing Guidelines.

[466]This term is defined as the Board of Directors, or if the organization does not have a Board of Directors, the highest-level governing body of the organization. Application Note 1 to §8B2.1 of the amended Sentencing Guidelines.

[467]Amended Sentencing Guidelines §8C2.5(f). However, the commentary to this section indicates that organizations will be allowed a reasonable period to conduct an internal investigation and no report is required if, based on the information available at that time, the organization reasonably concludes that no offense was committed.

high-level personnel participated in, condoned, or were willfully ignorant of the offense.[468] Further, an organization that implemented its compliance program in response to a court or administrative order may lose all or part of the deduction.[469]

However, one of the more controversial provisions in the amended Sentencing Guidelines relates to Section 8C2.5(g), which authorizes a reduction in an organization's culpability score if it fully cooperated in the investigation of its wrongdoing. To mitigate some of the concerns that this provision would increase the pressure on organizations to waive their rights to the protection of attorney-client privilege and/or work product doctrine, the amended Sentencing Guidelines indicate that such waivers are not a prerequisite to a culpability score reduction under Section 8C2.5(g) "unless such waiver is necessary in order to provide timely and thorough disclosure of all pertinent information known to the organization."[470] The American Bar Association, defense lawyers, and in-house counsel, in conjunction with industry groups, were vocal in their opposition to this 2004 amendment. Less than a year after its effective date in November 2004, the U.S. Sentencing Commission solicited public comment and held public hearings on the advisability of the Section 8C2.5(g) application note. Ultimately, the Commission reversed its position and in early 2006 sent Congress a proposed amendment that would repeal in its entirety the 2004 amendment to this Application Note.[471] In addition, in 2006 the DOJ revised its position regarding corporate attorney-client privilege waivers and other issues related to the evaluation of the level of a corporation's cooperation in federal investigations.

In January 2003, then-Deputy Attorney General Larry Thompson issued a memorandum (Thompson Memo) that had the effect of discouraging companies from asserting the attorney-client privilege in federal investigations or advancing legal fees to employees.[472] The Thompson Memo set forth nine factors that federal prosecutors were required to consider in determining whether to charge a corporation or other business organization and indicated that a corporation's refusal to waive the attorney-client privilege or its advancement of legal fees to employees facing investigation would negatively affect the corporation's ability to gain credit for cooperation under the Sentencing Guide-

---

[468]There is a further presumption that an organization did not have an effective compliance program if certain specified personnel participated, condoned, or were willfully ignorant of the offense. *Id.*

[469]Amended Sentencing Guidelines §8C4.10.

[470]Application Note 12 to §8C2.5 of the amended Sentencing Guidelines.

[471]Pursuant to Section 994(p) of Title 28, the proposed amendment became effective November 1, 2006.

[472]*See* Memorandum from Larry D. Thompson, Deputy Attorney General, to Heads of Department Components, United States Attorneys (Jan. 20, 2003), *available at* http://www.usdoj.gov/dag/cftf/corporate_guidelines.htm, and Appendix C-3 on the disk accompanying this volume. The Thompson Memo was issued after the DOJ had indicted Arthur Andersen for its participation in the Enron accounting fraud (March 2002) and after President George W. Bush had established the Corporate Fraud Task Force by Executive Order 13271 (July 9, 2002). Federal prosecutors were bound by the guidelines set forth in the Thompson Memo when prosecuting business organizations.

lines.[473] In light of the Thompson Memo, corporations were increasingly reluctant to assert the attorney-client privilege when responding to federal investigations. There was also great concern among business organizations that federal prosecutors would view a corporation's advancement of legal fees to employees facing investigation as uncooperative behavior that could subject the corporation to additional penalties under the Sentencing Guidelines.

In the summer of 2006, Judge Lewis A. Kaplan of the Southern District of New York held in *United States v. Stein* that the Thompson Memo's provisions on advancing legal fees to company employees, and the actions of federal prosecutors in implementing those provisions, violated the Fifth and Sixth Amendments of the United States Constitution.[474] In December 2006, then-Deputy Attorney General Paul J. McNulty issued a follow-up memorandum (McNulty Memo) that reversed the positions previously taken by the DOJ in the Thompson Memo.[475] Most notably, the McNulty Memo makes it clear that a corporation's waiver of attorney-client privilege is not a prerequisite to a determination that a corporation is being cooperative in a federal investigation for purposes of calculations performed under the Sentencing Guidelines. Further, the McNulty Memo adopts the view of the court in *Stein* and expressly instructs prosecutors to refrain from considering a corporation's advancement of legal fees to employees or agents under investigation or indictment when determining the level of a corporation's cooperation with legal authorities.

### 3. Concerns Raised by Compliance Programs

Despite their advantages, compliance programs, particularly effective ones, can reveal troublesome issues that demand resolution. Auditing and monitoring may reveal violations and substantial amounts of money that may have to be repaid. Having identified an overpayment or other compliance issue, the corporation and board cannot ignore it. In addition, the documentation created can provide a roadmap for the government and other adverse parties to use in suits against corporate officials. Internal investigations conducted as part of compliance efforts can be discoverable and may lead to employee claims of discrimination, defamation, or violation of constitutional or civil rights. Working

---

[473] *Id.*

[474] *See* United States v. Stein, 440 F. Supp. 2d 315 (S.D.N.Y. 2006). *Stein* was a case against former partners and employees of KPMG, one of the country's largest accounting firms, in which the government alleged that the defendants defrauded the Internal Revenue Service by tax shelter sales that allegedly generated false tax losses for their firm's clients. Under threat of indictment and in light of the guidelines under the Thompson Memo regarding corporate cooperation with federal investigations, KPMG advised its partners and employees that the company would stop paying their legal expenses if the individuals refused to talk to the government, invoked the Fifth Amendment, or were indicted. The court found that the government was responsible for the pressure KPMG exerted on the individual defendants, and that such actions by the government violated the defendants' constitutional rights.

[475] *See* Memorandum from Deputy Attorney General Paul McNulty to U.S. Attorneys *re* Principles of Federal Prosecution of Business Organizations (Dec. 13, 2006), *available at* http://www.usdoj.gov/dag/speeches/2006/mcnulty_memo.pdf, and Appendix C-4 on the disk accompanying this volume. *See also* U.S. Department of Justice, Press Release, *U.S. Deputy Attorney General Paul J. McNulty Revises Charging Guidelines for Prosecuting Corporate Fraud: New Guidance Further Encourages Corporate Compliance* (Dec. 12, 2006), *available at* http://www.usdoj.gov/opa/pr/2006/December/06_odag_828.html.

with legal counsel can help protect some documents from discovery under certain circumstances through the application of attorney-client and other privileges. (The parameters of such privileges are beyond the scope of this chapter.) As a practical matter, however, it is important to recognize that corporations and boards may be forced to disclose materials traditionally screened by privilege.[476]

## B. The Office of Inspector General Compliance Program Guidance

Beginning in 1997, the OIG published a series of compliance program guidance (Compliance Guidance) documents for various entities in the health care industry. There are compliance guidance materials specifically designed for hospitals;[477] clinical laboratories;[478] durable medical equipment (DME), prosthetics, orthotics, and supplies providers;[479] third-party medical billing companies;[480] hospices;[481] nursing facilities;[482] Medicare+Choice organizations;[483] individual and small group physician practices;[484] home health agencies;[485] ambulance suppliers;[486] and pharmaceutical manufacturers.[487] In addition, the OIG and the American Health Lawyers Association (AHLA) have published

---

[476]Privileges have complex requirements, and courts do not always uphold claims of privilege. Moreover, organizations are increasingly being asked to waive privileges that might otherwise protect documents to demonstrate their willingness to cooperate during government investigations.

[477]*See* 63 Fed. Reg. 8987 (Feb. 23, 1998). In January 2005, the OIG published a Supplemental Compliance Program Guidance for Hospitals, revising the previously issued guidance to reflect the significant changes in the way hospitals deliver, and are reimbursed for, health care services. *See* 70 Fed. Reg. 4858 (Jan. 31, 2005). The supplemental guidance identifies fraud and abuse risk areas for hospitals and outlines practical measures hospitals can use to gauge the effectiveness of their compliance programs. For the text of this guidance, see Appendix I-1.2 on the disk accompanying this volume. Also see the discussion in Section III.B.1 of Chapter 7 (Baumann, Corporate Compliance Programs).

[478]*See* 63 Fed. Reg. 45,076 (Aug. 24, 1998).

[479]*See* 64 Fed. Reg. 36,368 (July 6, 1999).

[480]*See* 63 Fed. Reg. 70,138 (Dec. 18, 1998).

[481]*See* 64 Fed. Reg. 54,031 (Oct. 5, 1999).

[482]*See* 65 Fed. Reg. 14,289 (Mar. 16, 2000).

[483]*See* 64 Fed. Reg. 61,893 (Nov. 15, 1999).

[484]*See* 65 Fed. Reg. 59,434 (Oct. 5, 2000).

[485]*See* 63 Fed. Reg. 42,410 (Aug. 7, 1998).

[486]*See* 68 Fed. Reg. 14,245 (Mar. 24, 2003).

[487]*See* 68 Fed. Reg. 23,731 (May 5, 2003) and Appendix I-3.1 on the disk accompanying this volume. All of these documents are located in the *Federal Register* and on the OIG's Web site at http://www.oig.hhs.gov/fraud/complianceguidance.html.

additional resource materials for health care organization boards of directors to assist them in developing and implementing compliance programs.[488] The OIG has indicated that all types of health care organizations should adopt compliance programs as expeditiously as possible, and to the extent that there is no Compliance Guidance specifically designed for a particular type of provider, that provider should look to the other available documents to help establish an effective compliance program.

Because they are not legally binding and often contain a great deal of detail about how the OIG thinks an organization should operate, the various Compliance Guidance documents often have been characterized as the OIG's "wish list." Nevertheless, it generally is advisable to adhere to these standards when possible. For example, the OIG specifically states in the Compliance Guidance documents that it "will consider the existence of an effective compliance program that pre-dated a [g]overnmental investigation" when considering the imposition of administrative penalties.[489] Presumably, a compliance program that covers many of the topics recommended by the OIG would more likely be considered effective than one that does not. It is important to note that the OIG has recognized the need for some flexibility in compliance programs, emphasizing that corporate compliance programs should be tailored to meet the specific needs of the organization and indicating that an organization with limited resources may not be able to adopt as comprehensive a compliance program as another entity with more extensive resources.

## 1. Seven Basic Elements

The OIG's recognition of the need for individualized programs notwithstanding, the OIG generally expects each organization to establish a program that implements the following seven basic elements:

(1)  written standards of conduct, including written policies and procedures to promote compliance;

(2)  designation of a chief compliance officer and other appropriate bodies such as a compliance committee;

(3)  establishment of regular, effective education and training programs;

(4)  development of a system to respond to allegations of improper or illegal activities and enforce appropriate disciplinary action;

(5)  maintenance of a system, such as a hotline, to receive complaints anonymously and protect whistleblowers from retaliation;

(6)  use of auditing and monitoring to evaluate compliance; and

---

[488]U.S. Dep't of Health & Human Servs. Office of Inspector General & American Health Lawyers Ass'n, *Corporate Responsibility & Corporate Compliance: A Resource for Health Care Boards of Directors* (Apr. 2, 2003); U.S. Dep't Health & Human Servs. Office of the Inspector General & American Health Lawyers Ass'n, *An Integrated Approach to Corporate Compliance: A Resource for Health Care Organization Boards of Directors* (July 1, 2004); U.S. Dep't of Health & Human Servs. Office of Inspector General & American Health Lawyers Ass'n, *Corporate Responsibility & Corporate Compliance: A Resource for Health Care Boards of Directors* (Sept. 10, 2007). These resources are designed to help health care organization directors ask informed questions related to health care corporate compliance and help them affirmatively demonstrate that they have followed a reasonable compliance oversight process. The pamphlets are available at http://www.oig.hhs.gov/fraud/complianceguidance.html.

[489]Compliance Program Guidance for Hospitals, 63 Fed. Reg. 8987, 8988 (Feb. 23, 1998).

(7)  investigation and remediation of identified systemic problems and the development of policies to prevent employment or retention of sanctioned individuals.[490]

## 2. Specific References to Caremark

Significantly, there is a specific reference to the *Caremark* decision in most of the Compliance Guidance documents, along with the statement that "recent case law suggests that the failure of a corporate Director to attempt in good faith to institute a compliance program in certain situations may be a breach of a Director's fiduciary obligation."[491] Furthermore, there are numerous statements throughout these documents stressing the need for a high level of organizational commitment to a compliance program. For example, the OIG emphasizes that "[i]t is incumbent upon a hospital's corporate officers and managers to provide ethical leadership to the organization and to assure that adequate systems are in place to facilitate ethical and legal conduct."[492] In addition, the OIG calls on senior management and the company's *governing body* to provide substantial commitments of time, energy, and resources to implement an effective compliance program, warning that "[p]rograms hastily constructed and implemented without appropriate ongoing monitoring will likely be ineffective and could result in greater harm or liability to the hospital than no program at all."[493]

## 3. Director and Officer Responsibilities for Compliance

By virtue of their differing roles and responsibilities within an organization, the compliance responsibilities of officers and directors will necessarily vary. Consistent with their areas of corporate responsibility, board members are unlikely to directly participate in many of the organization's compliance activities, while officers will be actively involved. However, there are various measures that both directors and officers should take to ensure that the compliance program is developed, implemented, and effective, and thus meets the corporate goal of minimizing exposure for the organization and its agents.

### a. Establishing a Compliance Program

As part of its efforts to demonstrate high-level commitment to compliance within the organization, the board should adopt a resolution authorizing the establishment of a corporate compliance program for the company. This same resolution also could be used to appoint a chief compliance officer and compliance committee. It also is important that the board ensure that adequate resources, in terms of both finances and staff time, are available for the corporate compliance program. The organization's mission statement also should

---

[490]*See id.* at 8989.

[491]This statement was quoted in the following Compliance Guidance documents: 63 Fed. Reg. 8987, 8988 (Feb. 23, 1998) (hospitals); 63 Fed. Reg. 42,410, 42,411 (Aug. 7, 1998) (home health agencies); 63 Fed. Reg. 45,076, 45,077 (Aug. 24, 1998) (clinical laboratories); 64 Fed. Reg. 36,368, 36,369 (July 6, 1999) (DME suppliers); 64 Fed. Reg. 54,031, 54,032 (Oct. 5, 1999) (hospices); 65 Fed. Reg. 14,289, 14,290 (Mar. 16, 2000) (nursing facilities).

[492]Compliance Program Guidance for Hospitals, 63 Fed. Reg. 8987, 8988 (Feb. 23, 1998).

[493]*Id.*

be reviewed to ensure that it includes a commitment to compliance. Once the compliance program is developed, senior management should send a "roll out" letter to all employees announcing the program, encouraging all to participate, and noting that failure to comply may result in disciplinary sanctions.

### b. Continuing Compliance Responsibilities

Many companies do a good job at the introductory phase of compliance but fail to follow through and continue the compliance process. If the compliance program reveals issues that are not addressed, this discontinuity can subject the organization to heightened rather than lowered risks of liability. Therefore, directors and officers should be prepared to continue participating in the compliance process on an ongoing basis. As a preliminary matter, the board should assess whether the seven basic elements of a compliance program are in place. In addition, as described in the *Corporate Director's Guidebook,*[494]

> [a] significant aspect of the board's responsibility, often referred to the Audit Committee, is oversight of the corporation's policies and procedures regarding compliance with the law and with significant corporate policies. Most large, publicly owned corporations have adopted codes of conduct expressing principles of business ethics, legal compliance, and other matters relating to business conduct. Subjects commonly addressed by such codes are legal compliance . . . conconflicts of interest, corporate opportunities, gifts from business associates, misuse of confidential information and political contributions. The board of directors should assure itself that the corporation has such a code of conduct, that the code is widely circulated to appropriate employees, that adherence to the code is enforced, that the corporation maintains procedures for monitoring and enforcing compliance and that the support of the CEO and the board is clearly evidenced.[495]

Senior management should be required to participate in compliance training. Even board members should participate in initial compliance education to better understand the operation of the compliance program and demonstrate high-level commitment to it.

The *Caremark* decision clearly indicates that board members should institute a system to collect appropriate information on the company's business performance and compliance with applicable laws and regulations. To this end, most compliance programs require the chief compliance officer or the compliance committee to present a report on the organization's compliance to the board at least once a year.[496] Certain "hands on" boards may want to directly review all or some of the underlying audit reports generated as part of the compliance process. In any event, board members should be prepared to engage in more than a cursory review of the compliance materials they receive. In this connection, note *In re W.R. Grace & Co.,*[497] in which the SEC found that

---

[494] A.B.A. COMM. ON CORPORATE LAWS, CORPORATE DIRECTOR'S GUIDEBOOK (4th ed. 2004).

[495] *Id.* at 31.

[496] In some organizations, the compliance report is presented to a board subcommittee.

[497] FED. SEC. L. REP. (CCH) ¶85,963 (1998).

directors and officers cannot necessarily rely on the information generated by the company's programs and procedures:

> If an officer or director knows or should know that his or her company's statements concerning particular issues are inadequate or incomplete, he or she has an obligation to correct that failure. An officer or director may rely upon the company's procedures for determining what disclosure is required only if he or she has a reasonable basis for believing that those procedures have resulted in full consideration of those issues.[498]

In *W.R. Grace*, the SEC found that the directors' reliance on the corporation's legal counsel to determine the adequacy of disclosure of certain information was not justified.[499] Certainly, if patterns or systemic problems appear in the compliance officer's or committee's report, the board would be well advised to require follow-up action. In addition, the scope of audits should be assessed to ensure that they are adequate and conducted by appropriate personnel (e.g., in some cases, outside auditors may be necessary).

The board should ensure that the compliance reports it receives include information on the "high risk" areas that have been identified by the government in the Compliance Guidance documents and other relevant materials, including Special Fraud Alerts, OIG Work Plans, and advisory opinions.[500] Similarly, compliance reports should include information on compliance at any subsidiary organizations because the parent may be held responsible for activities there.[501]

In addition, many compliance programs require that the board be notified immediately of any serious compliance violations. Each organization will need to decide at what point it wants the board to become involved. Under some programs, the board (or a subcommittee) is notified if the situation is sufficiently serious to warrant the retention of outside counsel. Alternatively, the compliance program may require that the board be notified if a certain level of financial exposure is involved or if there is evidence of fraud. If sufficiently senior members of management may be involved in compliance violations, the board should be notified and/or involved in the investigation, and it may be called on to participate in the disciplinary process. Finally, to the extent that they are involved in performance assessments, both directors and officers should include compliance as one of the factors used to evaluate and reward subordinates.

## V. RECOMMENDATIONS TO REDUCE EXPOSURE

Although no measures can eliminate all risk of liability for corporate directors and officers, there are a number of steps that can be taken to reduce

---

[498] *Id.*

[499] The context of the finding is somewhat unusual because it involves an administrative cease-and-desist order imposed as part of a settlement for alleged violations of the securities laws. Nevertheless, the breadth of the obligation imposed on the company's directors is noteworthy.

[500] *See* Compliance Program Guidance for Hospitals, 63 Fed. Reg. 8987, 8989 (1998), and Appendix I-1.1 on the disk accompanying this volume.

[501] Typically, a parent organization and its subsidiaries will, to a certain extent, coordinate their compliance activities.

such exposure. Board members are well served by corporations that take advantage of the statutes limiting director liability. The statutes are not self-executing, and corporations wishing to offer these liability limitations need to review the applicable statute (e.g., Delaware Code, Title 8, Section 102(b)(7)) and make the appropriate amendments to their articles of incorporation. When forming a new corporation, the framers should remember to enact the necessary language in the original articles.

Similarly, corporations can provide indemnification for a good faith breach of a director's or officer's duty of care. These statutes are generally permissive and not self-executing. Accordingly, director and officer contracts should contain appropriate indemnification provisions, tracking any relevant statutory language and setting forth the circumstances under which the corporation is providing the indemnification. When possible, these contracts should take advantage of those state laws that allow the provision of expanded protection beyond that which is specified under the statute.

Corporations may provide insurance coverage in addition to indemnification. For example, Delaware permits corporations to purchase policies for directors and officers providing coverage for "any liability asserted against" them by virtue of their status.[502] Moreover, such policies can provide coverage to the director or officer for his or her acts as well as reimburse the corporation for monies it spends directly indemnifying the director or officer. Thus, corporations should consider purchasing broad coverage policies. A multitude of policy provisions, coverages, and exclusions are available, and various legal issues also should be considered.[503] Accordingly, an insurance professional or experienced lawyer can provide valuable assistance in selecting an appropriate policy.

Finally, directors and officers should take an active role in establishing and promoting a corporate compliance program. A compliance program can (1) prevent many problems from occurring, (2) help reduce the risk of exposure to the corporation and its directors and officers if compliance violations do occur, and (3) reduce the magnitude of the problem and penalties encountered if compliance violations are uncovered. However, to attain these objectives, it is essential that the compliance program be designed and implemented so as to be "effective." Directors and officers should be involved in the compliance efforts to help demonstrate good faith and high-level commitment to the program, to provide the necessary resources, and to ensure that the information gathering and reporting systems called for in the *Caremark* decision are in place and functioning properly.

It is important to remember that compliance plans are not "effective," and thus do not provide protection, unless they are actively implemented. To this end, they should be individually designed to meet the specific needs of the corporation. In addition, although directors oversee, rather than manage, the business of a corporation, they should carefully monitor compliance activities.

---

[502]DEL. CODE. ANN. tit. 8, §145(g).

[503]*See, e.g.,* JOHN OLSON, ET AL., DIRECTOR AND OFFICER LIABILITY: INDEMNIFICATION AND INSURANCE §§10.01–.12 (1999).

Collecting information alone is not sufficient. Audits and other reports should be carefully scrutinized and questions pursued when necessary.

Board members might consult the applicable Compliance Guidance documents issued by the OIG. Although these documents are not legally binding, they provide guidance helpful in evaluating the corporation's compliance program and identify some of the high-risk issues that, in the OIG's view, the compliance program should address.

If, despite all these efforts, there is a compliance violation that leads to a government investigation, directors and officers should consider retaining their own counsel who can best protect their individual interests. Obviously, this admonition is particularly important in the event of subsequent litigation or settlement negotiations.

In light of developments over the past decade, including the scandals relating to Enron, WorldCom, ImClone, and various other corporations, directors and officers should recognize that their actions are likely to be much more carefully examined by government regulators and the public (some of whom may be potential whistleblowers or plaintiffs in class action and shareholder derivative lawsuits). Restrictive laws and regulations relating to directors and officers of public companies, such as the Sarbanes-Oxley Act and SRO rules, have been promulgated. However, although privately held companies may not be legally obligated to comply, government officials and plaintiffs may well attempt to hold all companies to the criteria set forth in the Sarbanes-Oxley Act, perhaps by describing these criteria as the "industry standard." Some of the Sarbanes-Oxley types of standards will likely be made indirectly applicable to private companies under the application of the Sentencing Guidelines. Moreover, the heightened scrutiny, which is the Enron legacy, will likely be applied to all actions of all directors and officers, not just those actions related to federal health care program reimbursement.[504] Directors should also be aware that the nature and extent of their fiduciary duties can change depending on whether the corporation is solvent.[505]

Various organizations have begun developing "best practice" guidelines to assist nonprofit organizations and their boards in reducing the risk of liability.[506] Among various suggestions for nonprofit governance, these guidelines often emphasize

---

[504]For example, companies that are not "public" and therefore not subject to the Sarbanes-Oxley Act, particularly those that are operated as not-for-profits, are often subject to other specialized legal requirements, such as the IRS rules relating to board member conflict of interest statements and so-called excess benefit transactions, and state laws that regulate the use of charitable assets. Failure to strictly comply with any such legal requirements can create a risk of exposure for the directors and officers of these companies.

[505]*See* Richard Epling et al., *Selected Bankruptcy Problems for Non-Profit Entities,* Hospital Workouts & Restructurings Summit Materials (Dec. 2000) (noting that in light of the growing number of bankruptcies in the health care industry, change in director duties may be increasingly important).

[506]*See, e.g.,* BoardSource, *The Sarbanes-Oxley Act and Implications for Nonprofit Organizations* (BoardSource and Independent Sector 2003); AMERICAN HEALTH LAWYERS ASS'N, LESSONS FOR HEALTHCARE FROM ENRON: A BEST PRACTICES HANDBOOK, *available at* http://www.healthlawyers.org. *Also see* ABA SECTION ON BUSINESS LAW, CORPORATE DIRECTOR'S GUIDEBOOK (4th ed. 2004), *available at* http://www.abanet.org/buslaw/catalog/pubindex.html.

- The importance of independent directors, particularly on the audit committee;
- Providing financial "literacy" training for those directors who need it;
- Developing (and enforcing) a strong conflict of interest policy;
- Changing auditors every five years and not having these same firms provide nonaudit services;
- Having the board, CEO, and CFO review and approve Forms 990 and/or 990-PF, and ensure timely filing;
- Prohibiting the provision of private loans to company directors or executives;[507]
- Implementing formal procedures to address compliance complaints and prevent retaliation (any decision not to take further action should be justified and documented); and
- Adopting a mandatory document retention (and periodic destruction) policy that includes guidelines for electronic files and voicemail, back-up procedures, and prevents any document destruction if an investigation is underway or suspected.[508]

In addition to the other measures described above to reduce the risk of liability, directors and officers of all organizations should be sure they are actively involved in oversight of the corporation, develop a working knowledge of accounting and financial reporting rules, and work closely with the Audit Committee. Toward this end, board members should consider using the following checklist as a guide:

**Figure 8-1. Checklist: Recommendations Following Sarbanes-Oxley**

☐ Stay abreast of current legal requirements and new developments in the corporate governance area.

☐ Ensure that a corporate information and reporting system exists that is adequate to assure that compliance information will come to the board's attention in a timely manner as a matter of ordinary operations, and at least annually.

☐ As a part of the corporate information and reporting system, develop a compliance program that proactively promotes compliance.

☐ Ensure that the compliance program is monitored so that if any information that arouses suspicion comes to the company's attention (and, in particular, to the attention of a Board member), it is acted upon and not ignored.

☐ Supplement the existing compliance program code of ethics as necessary to satisfy other applicable legal requirements, including those contained in the Sarbanes-Oxley Act.[509]

---

[507] If such loans are to be provided, they should be formally approved by the board pursuant to a documented process, including disclosure of the value and terms of the loan.

[508] *See* BoardSource, *The Sarbanes-Oxley Act and Implications for Nonprofit Organizations,* at 2–10.

[509] In some cases, it may be possible to expand the existing code of ethics. However, some organizations may decide to develop a separate code of ethics specific to the CEO and management members, as applicable, to satisfy the Sarbanes-Oxley standards.

☐ Closely monitor the organization's financial situation, including investment management and off-balance-sheet arrangements.

☐ Assess "independence" of directors under the new SRO rules and ensure that all members of the Audit Committee and other applicable committees are independent.[510] Independence is a contextual issue. Although a director may as a general matter be independent, he or she may have relationships affecting particular transactions.

☐ Require complete, accurate, and timely disclosure of financial information from the CFO and other corporate managers and employees; for example:

  ☐ Require regular reports on internal processes to test and assure compliance with laws;

  ☐ Require reports and statements to be based on detailed, documented representations about the substance of the transaction as well as the reporting methodology used; and

  ☐ Focus on high-risk issues, such as arrangements between affiliated organizations, off-balance-sheet transactions, and any public disclosure requirements.

☐ Ask questions about the way arrangements have been structured and reported. For example:

  ☐ Which accounting policies were used and why?

  ☐ Are any transactions (or the ways in which they were reported) open to question or likely to create a significant degree of risk?

  ☐ Did audits identify any irregularities, and if so, what is the explanation for them?

  ☐ Were auditors subjected to pressure from management?

  ☐ What, if any, corrective action has been taken?

☐ Bring in outside experts when necessary, such as independent auditors and lawyers, and make sure they have appropriate expertise—for example, experts in health care, tax, or corporate law.

☐ Scrutinize the contractual and other arrangements between the corporation and its auditors.

☐ Ensure that all reports and the judgments they contain are supported by reliable documentation.

☐ Develop a working familiarity, through director education programs or other means, with the major substantive legal requirements relevant to the company's operations, including

  ☐ health care laws, particularly Medicare requirements;

  ☐ IRS regulations;

  ☐ SEC requirements; and

  ☐ other applicable federal and state laws.

☐ Review, update if necessary, and implement conflict of interest policies applicable to the board and management, including policies relating to required pre-approval of "related party" transactions (e.g., contracts between the company and directors or officers (or entities they control)).

---

[510] *See* Sarbanes-Oxley Act §301; see Section II.C., above.

☐ Examine executive compensation to be sure it is reasonable in amount and appropriately structured,[511] documented, and approved, as required under applicable law. Because executive compensation is a complex and sensitive issue, consider getting advice from an independent advisor before approving the compensation packages for senior executives.

☐ Ensure a direct line of communication to the compliance officer.

☐ Ask questions, and be sure to follow up promptly and thoroughly when issues arise. Be alert to news stories as well as allegedly "routine" government investigations. Demand to be informed of whistleblower complaints and calls to the company compliance hotline. In this environment, board members ignore "red flags" at their peril.

☐ Create a leadership structure for the board. Consider a nonexecutive chair, lead director, or committee chairs.

☐ Outside directors should meet regularly in executive session outside the presence of management.

---

[511]Compensation should avoid incentives that encourage management to adopt a short-term focus or emphasize a particular aspect of the organization's business.

# 9

# The Disclosure Dilemma: How, When, and What to Tell Stockholders and Stakeholders About Your *Qui Tam* Suit or Investigation*

*William W. Horton, Haskell Slaughter Young & Rediker, LLC, Birmingham, Alabama, and Monty G. Humble, Vinson & Elkins LLP, Dallas, Texas.

# I. Introduction

## A. A Brief Vignette

Mary Jones, general counsel of Megalithic Healthcare, Inc. (NYSE: BIG), completed Megalithic's annual report on Form 10-K, which would be filed with the Securities and Exchange Commission (SEC) the next day. As soon as the filing was confirmed, Megalithic would go effective with the registration statement for its latest public offering: ten million shares of common stock being sold by the company, and a million being sold by her CEO as he finalized his vacation plans. By Friday, Mary would be finished with her comments on Megalithic's new bank credit agreement, under which a syndicate of financial institutions led by First Second Bank, N.A., would provide the company with a billion-dollar line of credit. When she left her law firm partnership to become Megalithic's general counsel, she had never dreamed how fast the company would grow and how quickly she would be working with the biggest players in the capital markets.

Before leaving the office, she reviewed the day's mail. At the bottom of the pile was an envelope bearing the return address of the U.S. Attorney for the Southern District of North Dakota. Upon opening the letter, she read with growing disbelief:

Dear Ms. Jones:

The United States Attorney's Office for the Southern District of North Dakota, together with the Department of Justice in Washington, D.C., is conducting an investigation to determine whether to intervene in a lawsuit filed under the *qui tam* provisions of the civil False Claims Act, 31 U.S.C. §§3729–3732. This lawsuit has been filed under seal. However, we have obtained a partial lifting of the seal from the Court for the purpose of informing you of our investigation.

While we are not able to provide you with a copy of the complaint at this time, under the partial lifting of the seal we are able to advise you that our investigation concerns the possibility that a large number of Megalithic hospitals have routinely overbilled the Medicare program and have entered into contracts with physicians that violate the Anti-Kickback Statute, 42 U.S.C. §1320a-7b(b). Please call me to arrange a meeting to discuss these matters and certain information that we will be requesting that your company provide us.

You are reminded that this matter is under seal. While we have obtained a partial lifting of the seal for the purposes described in this letter, you are not to disclose the existence of this matter without further order of the Court.

Very truly yours,
Dudley D. Wright
United States Attorney
By M. Gruff Crimedog
Assistant United States Attorney

The following questions quickly came to Mary's mind:—What do I do? My 10-K doesn't say there's any problem.—Do I have to talk about this in my prospectus?—What do I tell my banks?—How do I say anything when the case is under seal?—How can I even figure out what's going on when they won't even tell me who filed the complaint or what the specific claims are?—Will the SEC send me to jail if I don't say something?—Will the judge send me to jail if

I break the seal?—What will my CEO do if I make some announcement and our stock price tanks?

## B. The Problem

Health care providers, like other business organizations, face numerous circumstances where legal or contractual obligations require them to make various disclosures about their business operations and the material risks, events, and uncertainties that affect them. For a publicly traded health care company, those obligations arise whenever the company seeks to sell equity or debt securities in the market and whenever it files the periodic reports required under the securities laws. For a tax-exempt provider, those obligations arise when it seeks to raise capital in the municipal bond markets and may arise when it has existing bonds outstanding for which it is obligated to provide periodic reports. For any provider, those obligations may arise by way of contractual representations when it is obtaining bank loans, seeking funding from venture capitalists, or entering into acquisition or merger agreements with other companies.

Where a business organization operates in a heavily regulated environment, such as health care, a key issue for disclosure recipients—in any context—is understanding the exposure that the organization may have to civil or criminal regulatory sanctions. Thus, if the organization has publicly traded securities, investors, research analysts, prospective underwriters, and other market participants will ask questions and seek information concerning the organization's compliance status and its exposure to regulatory litigation. Similarly, with regard to all providers, lenders, potential merger partners, and others entering into contractual relationships with the organization may well seek representations and warranties concerning these issues.

The disclosure of regulatory problems or enforcement litigation can have a severe impact in any setting. In the world of publicly traded securities, expansive disclosure concerning such matters can cause a company's stock price to plummet and make it impossible to complete transactions, while untimely or inadequate disclosure will likely lead to stockholder suits and investigations by the SEC. For tax-exempt issuers, some types of violations may call into question the validity of the issuer's exempt status and may make its bonds taxable, as well as triggering bondholder suits and SEC investigations. Bad news may also kill a merger or put a credit facility into default.

The current regulatory and enforcement environment in health care (coupled with the intense interest in corporate disclosure, in the post-Enron/Sarbanes-Oxley environment), however, can make it particularly difficult to respond effectively and appropriately to the various disclosure imperatives an organization may face. There are several reasons for this:

- Health care providers are subject to a complex web of state and federal laws and regulations, with key statutes often being subjective, ambiguous, or incompletely implemented by regulation. Not uncommonly, this body of law is interpreted by hindsight, with stricter current standards being applied to the review of past events.
- Even purely technical violations of health care regulations can, at least theoretically, lead to punitive per-claim penalties, exclusion from par-

ticipation in Medicare and other federal and state reimbursement programs, loss of tax-exempt status, and other extreme sanctions.[1]

- Increasingly, health care violations can involve a sort of "cross default" impact. For example, acts that allegedly violate the federal anti-kickback statute,[2] which carries its own penalties, may also expose a provider to sanctions under numerous other health care statutes and under the tax laws.[3] Further, a provider that incurs sanctions under federal health care programs may find that those sanctions raise problems under managed care contracts, credit agreements, and other private arrangements. Thus, quantifying the potential risk of a regulatory violation may require applying a multiplier effect to the exposure from the basic violation.

- The range of penalties theoretically available for regulatory violations may substantially exceed the amounts actually likely to be obtained through litigation or settlement. Thus, quantifying the materiality of alleged violations may be difficult. Further, disclosure of the organization's best estimate of the exposure may compromise its ability to defend against the claims.

- Perhaps most significantly, the government has increasingly relied on *qui tam* cases filed under the civil False Claims Act (FCA)[4] as its chief vehicle for enforcement.[5] The government and the *qui tam* bar have become very aggressive in asserting that alleged violations of the anti-kickback statute, the Stark law,[6] the Medicare conditions of participation, and even quality-of-care standards give rise to false claims.[7] In a scenario that has become

---

[1]For illustrative lists of relevant federal statutes and regulations and their associated sanctions, see Chapter 1 (Baumann, An Introduction to Health Care Fraud and Abuse); Thomas C. Fox, Carol Colborn Loepere, & Joseph W. Metro, Health Care Financial Transactions Manual §§7.2–7.9 (West rev. ed. 2007); American Health Lawyers Ass'n, Health Law Practice Guide §§24:2–24:12; 24:34–24:62 (West rev. ed. 2007). As to the interaction with the tax exemption statutes, see Practice Guide §31:10–31:10.1.

[2]42 U.S.C. §1320a–7b(b).

[3]Claimed violations of the anti-kickback statute may, for example, be alleged, in certain circumstances, to give rise to sanctions under the criminal False Claims Act, 42 U.S.C. §1320a–7b(a); the civil False Claims Act, 31 U.S.C. §§3729–3733; the Program Fraud Civil Remedies Act, 31 U.S.C. §§3801–3812; the Health Insurance Portability and Accountability Act (HIPAA) health care fraud criminal statute, 18 U.S.C. §1347; the Civil Monetary Penalties provisions, 42 U.S.C. §1320a–7a; and the exclusion law, 42 U.S.C. §1320a–7, among others. As a practical matter it is unlikely that the government would seek (or obtain) duplicative relief under *all* these statutes, but there is nothing on the face of the statutes that prevents cumulating sanctions. In addition, payments or transactions that violate the anti-kickback statute may also constitute private inurement, potentially jeopardizing the tax-exempt status of a tax-exempt violator. *See, e.g.,* Rev. Rul. 97-21, 1997-1 C.B. 121.

[4]31 U.S.C. §§3729–3733. The Civil False Claims Act is discussed in more detail in Chapter 3 (Salcido, The False Claims Act in Health Care Prosecutions: Application of the Substantive, *Qui Tam,* and Voluntary Disclosure Provisions).

[5]For a succinct discussion of why this is so, see Timothy S. Jost & Sharon L. Davies, *The Empire Strikes Back: A Critique of the Backlash Against Fraud and Abuse Enforcement,* 51 Ala. L. Rev. 239, 247–48 (1999).

[6]The Ethics in Patient Referrals Act, 42 U.S.C. §1395nn. The Stark law is described in more detail in Chapter 2 (Crane, Federal Physician Self-Referral Restrictions).

[7]*See, e.g.,* Pamela H. Bucy, *Growing Pains: Using the False Claims Act to Combat Health Care Fraud,* 51 Ala. L. Rev. 57, 77–86 (1999); Robert Fabrikant & Glenn E. Solomon, *Application of the Federal False Claims Act to Regulatory Compliance Issues in the Health Care Industry,* 41 Ala. L. Rev. 105, 124–56 (1999).

quite familiar, a private relator files a sealed complaint under the FCA, and the government uses the period allowed for its intervention decision to obtain substantial and far-reaching unilateral discovery while the case is under seal—even where the underlying complaint makes only vague and general allegations that would not survive a motion to dismiss. In that circumstance, the putative defendant frequently lacks adequate information to assess the strength of the potential case and the materiality of the potential exposure, and must weigh its legal and contractual disclosure obligations against the FCA's sealing provisions. In some cases, the government may use its broad investigatory powers to obtain information from the provider without even disclosing the nature or scope of its investigation or the fact that a sealed *qui tam* suit is pending, further clouding the provider's ability to accurately assess the situation.

In this environment, providers face the challenge of reconciling conflicting obligations and prohibitions concerning disclosure, often without the quality and quantity of data that they may be accustomed to using to evaluate loss contingencies. Not infrequently, the advice of securities or corporate counsel and the advice of regulatory or defense counsel on the disclosure issues may conflict. The risk of an erroneous judgment may have enormous consequences, both for the defense of the underlying claims and for the ongoing business interests of the organization. This chapter attempts to provide a brief overview of the substantive law affecting these types of disclosure decisions, combined with practical suggestions as to how to analyze and respond to the issues, with a particular focus on securities law issues affecting publicly traded and tax-exempt provider organizations.

## II. SOURCES OF DISCLOSURE OBLIGATIONS UNDER THE FEDERAL SECURITIES LAWS

### A. Publicly Traded Issuers

Health care organizations seeking to sell stock to the public,[8] or which have already done so, are subject to myriad affirmative disclosure duties under the Securities Act of 1933[9] and the Securities Exchange Act of 1934.[10] The 1933 Act and the regulations thereunder prescribe the disclosures that must be

---

[8]For simplicity, the discussion of securities law issues in this section assumes that the issuer is, or is seeking to become, publicly traded. However, the offer or sale of securities in "private placement" transactions not registered under the federal securities laws is still subject to many of the same disclosure obligations as are public offerings, either directly through the requirements of the registration exemption being relied on or through the application of the antifraud provisions of the securities laws.

[9]15 U.S.C. §§77a–77aa.

[10]15 U.S.C. §§78a–78mm. Disclosure obligations may also arise under state securities laws, or "blue sky" laws, particularly with respect to the offering and sale of securities in private placement transactions and initial public offerings (IPOs). To the extent those obligations differ from the federal statutes, however, they are not addressed in this chapter.

made in connection with the offer or sale of securities, while the 1934 Act and its regulations establish the duties of issuers to provide ongoing disclosure to the market. In addition, case law, administrative interpretations, and established practice in the securities industry impose additional disclosure standards on publicly traded issuers, both with regard to the disclosures mandated under the 1933 and 1934 Acts and the more informal disclosures issuers may make to current and prospective investors, securities analysts, and others.[11]

In reviewing the particular disclosure obligations imposed by the federal securities laws, as amplified through regulation and interpreted through case law and administrative pronouncements, issuers must always bear in mind the polestar of Section 10(b) of the 1934 Act and Rule 10b-5 thereunder.[12] Rule 10b-5 provides that it is unlawful, in connection with the purchase or sale of securities, to make an untrue statement of a material fact or to fail to state a material fact necessary to make the statements made not misleading. This regulation provides the principal private right of action against an issuer or its affiliates for fraud in connection with the purchase or sale of securities.

The next few sections of this chapter outline some of the statutory, regulatory, and case law requirements with which health care issuers must grapple in determining how to handle disclosure issues regarding government investigations and related litigation.[13] Later sections will discuss the particular application of those requirements in the health care industry and suggest practical approaches for responding to those requirements.

---

[11]Note that, in addition to legally mandated disclosures, the rules of the stock exchanges and the NASDAQ Stock Market impose disclosure obligations on issuers that, read literally, may be broader in some circumstances than those imposed by the securities laws. Discussion of these obligations is pretermitted in this chapter, in part for considerations of brevity, and in part because, as a practical matter, it is unlikely that those entities will impose disciplinary action in circumstances where there is no associated liability under the securities laws and it is generally held that there is no private right of action under general stock exchange disclosure rules. *See, e.g.,* State Teachers Retirement Bd. v. Fluor Corp., 654 F.2d 843, 851–53 (2d Cir. 1981). However, in litigation or other proceedings relating to an issuer's alleged wrongful failure to disclose material information, any violation of exchange or NASDAQ standards may well be asserted as additional evidence of the issuer's breach of its disclosure duties.

[12]15 U.S.C. §78j(b) and 17 C.F.R. §240.10b–5, respectively. *See also* §11(a) of the 1933 Act, 15 U.S.C. §77k(a) (liability of persons for material misrepresentations or omissions in registration statement); §12(a)(2) of the 1933 Act, 15 U.S.C. §77*l*(a)(2) (liability of persons for material misrepresentations or omissions in prospectus or oral communication relating to offers or sales of securities); §15 of the 1933 Act, 15 U.S.C. §77o (liability of "control persons" for violations of §§11 and 12); §17(a) of the 1933 Act, 15 U.S.C. §77q(a) (liability of persons who obtain money or property in connection with the offer or sale of securities by means of material misrepresentations or omissions or otherwise through fraud or deceit); and the respective regulations promulgated thereunder.

[13]For a broad, if somewhat dated, overview of securities disclosure requirements and practice as applied to the health care industry, see William W. Horton & F. Hampton McFadden, Jr., *Disclosure Obligations of the Newly Public Healthcare Company: Practical Strategies for the Company and Its Counsel,* 32 J. HEALTH L. 1 (1999). For a more specific discussion of the federal securities disclosure regime as applied to disclosure of unpleasant corporate events, including government investigations, see Linda C. Quinn & Ottilie L. Jarmel, *Disclosing Bad News: An Overview for Securities Counsel,* in COUNSELING CLIENTS IN TURBULENT MARKETS & UNCERTAIN TIMES: DISCLOSURE & FINANCING ISSUES 7 (Practising Law Institute 2001).

## 1. The 1934 Act

Although disclosure issues may have the greatest immediacy in the context of a pending offering of securities, they are perhaps most easily understood in the context of the ongoing integrated disclosure system established under the 1934 Act, which sets forth detailed requirements for periodic and current reports for issuers with a class of securities registered under the federal securities laws. Under the 1934 Act, an issuer is required to file reports designed to ensure that the market has detailed current information concerning the issuer and its business and financial condition on which investors can rely when buying or selling its securities in everyday trading. These reports comprise the annual report on Form 10-K, which must be filed within 60 to 90 days (depending on the market capitalization of the issuer) after the end of the issuer's fiscal year; quarterly reports on Form 10-Q, which must be filed within 40 to 45 days (likewise depending on the market capitalization of the issuer) after the end of each fiscal quarter; and current reports on Form 8-K, which must be filed on a relatively immediate basis when certain specified events occur and which may also be filed when the issuer elects to report information not otherwise required to be disclosed in an 8-K but that it "deems of importance to security holders."[14]

### a. The 10-K and General Principles of 1934 Act Disclosure

The 10-K is intended to provide a comprehensive overview of the issuer's business, its financial condition, and its results of operations. The 10-K requires disclosure under enumerated "Items," which in turn refer to information required under the SEC's Regulation S-K[15] (covering information other than financial statements) and Regulation S-X[16] (covering the form and content of financial statements). Three specific items under Regulation S-K may, depending on the circumstances, require disclosure of potential civil or criminal exposure relating to violation of health care laws and regulations:[17]

- Item 103 of Regulation S-K requires disclosure regarding "any material pending legal proceedings, other than ordinary routine litigation" to which the issuer is a party. Item 103 also requires similar disclosure

---

[14]*See generally* Horton & McFadden, *Disclosure Obligations,* 32 J. HEALTH L. at 4–13. Since the publication of that article, both the scope of information required by Form 8-K and the time in which reports on the form must be filed have changed substantially. For the current requirements, see Form 8-K, *available at* http://www.sec.gov/about/forms/form8-k.pdf.

[15]17 C.F.R. Subparts 229.1–229.900.

[16]17 C.F.R. §§210.1–01 through 210.12–29.

[17]In addition, note that Item 101(c)(1)(vii) of Regulation S-K requires the issuer to discuss, "[t]o the extent material to an understanding of the [issuer's] business as a whole," the "dependence of [a business segment of the issuer] upon a single customer, or a few customers, the loss of any one or more of which would have a material adverse effect on the [issuer]," and to provide a "description of any material portion of the business that may be subject to renegotiation of profits or termination of contracts or subcontracts at the election of the Government ...." Does, for example, the risk of exclusion from federal reimbursement programs fit within those types of disclosure requirements? Note also that Item 101(c)(1)(xii) specifically requires "[a]ppropriate disclosure as to the material effects that compliance with Federal, State and local" environmental protection laws "may have upon the capital expenditures, earnings and competitive position" of the issuer.

regarding "any such proceedings *known to be contemplated* by governmental authorities."[18]

- Item 303 of Regulation S-K requires various disclosures concerning the issuer's financial condition, changes in its financial condition, and its results of operations. Such disclosures are required in the 10-K under Item 7, "Management's Discussion and Analysis of Financial Condition and Results of Operations," commonly referred to as "MD&A." Included in the MD&A requirements are requirements that the issuer "[i]dentify any known demands, commitments, events or uncertainties that will result in or that are reasonably likely to result in [its] liquidity increasing or decreasing in any material way";[19] "[d]escribe any known trends or uncertainties that have had or that [the issuer] reasonably expects will have a material favorable or unfavorable impact on net sales or revenues or income from continuing operations";[20] and focus its discussion and analysis "on material events and uncertainties known to management that would cause reported financial information not to be necessarily indicative of future operating results or of future financial condition."[21]

- Finally, Item 401(f)(2) requires certain disclosure relating to a director, nominee for director, or executive officer of the issuer if, during the previous five years, "[s]uch person was convicted in a criminal proceeding or is a named subject of a pending criminal proceeding" if the information is "material to an evaluation of the ability or integrity of such person."[22]

The requirements of Item 103 and Item 401(f) are, with some wrinkles imposed by the case law, relatively straightforward.[23] Aside from the threshold question of materiality, which is discussed later,[24] the first issue in the

---

[18] 17 C.F.R. Subparts 229.1–229.900 (emphasis added).

[19] Item 303(a)(1).

[20] Item 303(a)(3)(ii).

[21] Item 303(a), Instruction 3.

[22] Item 401(f)(2). Item 401(g) imposes the same requirements with respect to "promoters" and "control persons" for certain types of issuers. In addition, note that Item 401(f)(3)(ii) requires disclosure if any of the foregoing persons has been the subject of any order, judgment, or decree "enjoining him from, or otherwise limiting . . . [e]ngaging in any type of business practice." That language is sandwiched between two subsections that relate solely to securities, banking, and other financial and insurance activities; however, the "business practice" language stands curiously distinct and nonlimited between those subsections, suggesting that it could have broader application. Note that Item 401(f)(2) requires disclosure only with respect to a person who is a "named subject" of a pending criminal proceeding, while Item 401(f)(3) speaks only of someone who is a "subject" of the types of orders, judgments, or decrees enumerated therein. At least one court has read this distinction to mean that Item 401(f)(3) imposes a duty of disclosure under that item where a director, nominee for director, or executive officer knows himself or herself to be the subject of such an order, even if such person is not expressly named therein. *See* United States v. Yeaman, 987 F. Supp. 373, 381–82 (E.D. Pa. 1997).

[23] Note that most cases discussing Item 401 arise in claims alleging fraud in proxy solicitations governed by Section 14(a) of the 1934 Act and the regulations thereunder. Item 401 disclosure is required in proxy statements relating to the election of directors, and, indeed, many issuers satisfy the Item 401 10-K disclosure requirements by incorporating information by reference to their proxy statements, as permitted under rules of the Securities and Exchange Commission (SEC). Because, however, Item 401 information must be disclosed in the 10-K, either at length or through incorporation by reference, Item 401 issues are discussed here in the 10-K context.

[24] See Section II.A.4., below.

application of each of these provisions is whether there is a "proceeding." In the context of Item 103, it has been said that,

> [w]hile there is little guidance, either in the Commission's regulations or elsewhere, as to what constitutes a "proceeding" for purposes of Item 103, the plain meaning of the term "proceeding" as stated in Item 103 suggests that it refers to administrative or adjudicatory proceedings rather than law enforcement investigations.[25]

Assuming that to be the case, Item 103 still requires disclosure of material proceedings "known to be contemplated" by government authorities, even if they are not yet pending. However, as a former director of the SEC's Division of Enforcement has pointed out, it is frequently difficult to determine exactly when an issuer *knows* that a proceeding is contemplated, given the protracted investigatory process that government agencies tend to engage in before filing civil, criminal, or administrative proceedings and the multiple layers of authority that often must approve the decision to institute formal proceedings.[26] Item 401(f) does not require disclosure with respect to contemplated proceedings, but only with respect to past convictions or proceedings that are actually pending (and note that Item 401(f) only applies where the proceedings involve the individual in question, and not where they only involve the issuer as an entity or other persons related to the issuer who are not directors, director nominees, or executive officers).

Although the cases are not uniform, a number of them affirmatively hold that neither Item 103 nor Item 401(f) requires disclosure of uncharged criminal conduct, at least in the context of actions alleging that such nondisclosure itself constituted a criminal violation of the federal securities laws.[27] In the leading case of *United States v. Matthews,*[28] which involved a claim of an alleged

---

[25]Karl A. Groskaufmanis, Matt T. Morley, & Michael J. Rivera, *To Tell or Not to Tell: Reassessing Disclosure of Uncharged Misconduct,* 1 33RD ANNUAL INSTITUTE ON SECURITIES REGULATION 457, 459 (internal page 3) (Practising Law Institute 2001) (republished from INSIGHTS, June 1999).

[26]*See* Gary G. Lynch & Eric F. Grossman, *Disclosure of Corporate Wrongdoing,* in RESPONDING TO BAD NEWS: HOW TO DEAL WITH THE BOARD OF DIRECTORS, STOCKHOLDERS, THE PRESS, ANALYSTS, REGULATORS AND THE PLAINTIFFS' BAR 207, 220–21 (internal pages 10–11) (Practising Law Institute 1999) (questioning whether such things as subpoenas for documents, employee subpoenas, requests for "Wells submissions," and receipt of "target" and "subject" letters from prosecutors give rise to knowledge of a threatened proceeding, where the ultimate decision to initiate a proceeding must still be approved at higher levels).

[27]For useful surveys and discussion of the case law, see Groskaufmanis, Morley & Rivera at 458–63 (internal pages 2–5) and Lynch & Grossman at 217–19 (internal pages 7–19).

[28]787 F.2d 38 (2d Cir. 1986). The facts in *Matthews* are, in themselves, quite interesting. Matthews, who had begun his career as an SEC staff attorney, was the general counsel of the issuer. He was approached about being nominated for the issuer's board of directors. At the time of the nomination, he and the issuer were aware that he was one of the "subjects" of a grand jury investigation involving an alleged conspiracy to bribe certain state tax officials for the benefit of the issuer. After consulting counsel, Matthews and the issuer determined not to disclose this fact in the proxy statement relating to the election of directors. Two years later, the issuer and two individuals were indicted for conspiracy to commit bribery and tax fraud. One year after that, Matthews was indicted as a co-conspirator and was also indicted for an alleged criminal violation of the 1934 Act for failure to disclose, in the proxy statement relating to his original election as a director, his knowledge that he was a subject of the grand jury investigation. The U.S. Attorney's Office prosecuted the indictment without involvement by the SEC, and both SEC Regional

criminal violation of the proxy rules under the 1934 Act, the Second Circuit held that Item 401(f) (as applied in that case to proxy statements under Section 14(a) of the 1934 Act) did not require the disclosure of uncharged criminal conduct[29] and that, in the absence of a lawfully promulgated regulation requiring such disclosure, "nondisclosure of such conduct cannot be the basis of a criminal prosecution."[30]

*Matthews* was extensively analyzed, approved, and expanded by the U.S. District Court for the District of Columbia in *United States v. Crop Growers Corp.*[31] In *Crop Growers* (a case brought by the independent counsel investigating former U.S. Secretary of Agriculture Mike Espy), the defendants, including both the issuer and individual officers of the issuer, were accused of criminally violating the securities laws by failing to disclose alleged violations of the Federal Election Campaign Act in the issuer's SEC filings, which violations were first charged in the same indictment as the securities fraud counts.[32] The defendants relied on *Matthews* for the proposition that there was no duty to disclose uncharged criminal conduct. After reviewing *Matthews* and cases interpreting it in both the civil and criminal contexts, the court concluded that there was no duty to disclose uncharged criminal conduct under Items 103, 303, and 401, at least in the context of a criminal prosecution for such nondisclosure.[33] In reaching that conclusion, the court noted that

> [t]he specific forms at issue [both 1933 Act and 1934 Act forms] do not specify that criminal liability can be imposed if the forms are not completed in compliance with law. Further, the terms of the regulations do not set forth required disclosures in precise terms. Qualitative terms such as "risk," "trend," and "uncertainty" do not provide sufficient notice that a particular disclosure is required to allow criminal liability to attach for alleged non-disclosure.... Such terms are, quite simply, too vague and amorphous to give fair notice, required by the Due Process clause, of what disclosure is required. ... Thus, neither regulation [i.e., items 303 and 503 of Regulation S-K], even when read in conjunction with [Rule 12b-20 under the 1934 Act], will support criminal liability for failing to disclose uncharged, uninvestigated criminal conduct.[34]

---

Director Ira Sorkin and former SEC General Counsel Harvey Pitt (who later served as chairman of the SEC) publicly questioned the validity of the securities fraud prosecution. At trial, Matthews was acquitted on the conspiracy count but was convicted on the securities fraud count—that is, he was convicted for concealing an uncharged criminal offense of which he was subsequently acquitted, and the conviction, remarkably, occurred in the same trial as the acquittal. The Second Circuit reversed the conviction and remanded the case with instructions to dismiss the indictment.

[29] *See id.* at 46–48.

[30] *Id.* at 49.

[31] 954 F. Supp. 335 (D.D.C. 1997).

[32] *See id.* at 339–40.

[33] *See id.* at 345–48. The court also held that disclosure was not required under Item 503 of Regulation S-K, which relates to the disclosure of material risk factors in a 1933 Act registration statement.

[34] *Id.* at 348. Rule 12b-20, 17 C.F.R. §240.12b–20, requires that, "[i]n addition to the information expressly required to be included in a statement or report, there shall be added such further material information, if any, as may be necessary to make the required statements, in light of the circumstances under which they are made[,] not misleading."

Although there appears to be some consensus, if not necessarily a universal one, that the securities laws should not be read to impose criminal liability for failure to disclose uncharged criminal conduct, the case law arising from civil proceedings is more mixed. For example, in *Roeder v. Alpha Industries*,[35] a class action suit seeking damages and declaratory relief, the First Circuit found that information concerning alleged bribery by officers of the issuer in order to obtain defense subcontracts could be "material information" under the 1934 Act, even at a time before the indictment of one of the officers.[36] In its analysis, the court distinguished *Matthews* on the basis that *Matthews* was an appeal from a criminal conviction involving Fifth Amendment issues.[37] However, the court affirmed the district court's dismissal of the class action, finding that there was no liability under Rule 10b-5 for failure to disclose material information absent an affirmative duty to disclose it:

> [The plaintiff] claims that a corporation has an affirmative duty to disclose all material information even if there is no insider trading, no statute or regulation requiring disclosure, and no inaccurate, incomplete, or misleading prior disclosures. The prevailing view, however, is that there is no such affirmative duty of disclosure.[38]

In *Ballan v. Wilfred American Educational Corp.*,[39] the plaintiff claimed that the defendants had violated Rule 10b-5 by failing to disclose in the issuer's 1934 Act filings (1) that they had failed to comply with certain government regulations (for which indictments subsequently issued) and (2) "the potential consequences of government investigations into that failure."[40] The court noted that the issuer had no obligation "to disclose information of which it had no knowledge or about which it could only speculate" and that "it would be misleading for it to do so."[41] However, the court went on to suggest that disclosure of facts relating to specific acts and specific practices could be material, even if those acts might be alleged to be crimes: "Such acts or practices are not speculations or confessions but 'facts' relevant to a person's decision to invest in [the issuer]."[42] Without analyzing the existence of any duty to disclose such facts, the court denied the defendants' motion to dismiss the securities fraud claims.

Further, in *In re Par Pharmaceutical, Inc. Securities Litigation*,[43] the court reaffirmed the principle that, in order for liability to attach under Rule 10b-5,

---

[35] 814 F.2d 22 (1st Cir. 1987).

[36] *See id.* at 24–26.

[37] *Id.* at 26.

[38] *Id.* at 26–27. *See also* Gallagher v. Abbott Labs., 269 F.3d 806, 808 (7th Cir. 2001) ("Much of plaintiffs' argument [relating to defendants' "deferred" disclosure of $100 million FDA fine] reads as if firms have an absolute duty to disclose all information material to stock prices as soon as news comes into their possession. Yet that is not the way the securities laws work. We do not have a system of continuous disclosure. Instead firms are entitled to keep silent (about good news as well as bad news) unless positive law creates a duty to disclose."). However, see Section IV.A.3., below, for observations concerning the expanding requirements of "positive law."

[39] 720 F. Supp. 241 (E.D.N.Y. 1989).

[40] *Id.* at 243.

[41] *Id.* at 248.

[42] *Id.* at 249.

[43] 733 F. Supp. 668 (S.D.N.Y. 1990).

the defendant must have failed to disclose material information in the face of a duty to disclose it.[44] The court also held that the issuer "was not obligated to speculate as to the myriad of consequences, ranging from minor setbacks to complete ruin, that might have befallen the company if the [scheme to bribe Food and Drug Administration (FDA) officials to obtain expedited drug manufacturing approvals] was discovered, disclosed or terminated."[45] However, the court denied the defendants' motion to dismiss with respect to claims that the failure to disclose the bribery scheme (for which the issuer and some of the individual defendants entered guilty pleas) rendered statements made by the issuer in its 1934 Act filings and press releases, which concerned the issuer's success and expertise in obtaining FDA approvals, misleading.[46]

Carried through to a logical conclusion, these cases arising in the civil context suggest that, for purposes of the 10-K, the most important consideration may not be the relatively narrowly defined disclosure required by Items 103 and 401. Instead, the greater potential exposure under the securities laws may arise from the more intrinsically subjective requirements for MD&A disclosure contained in Item 303. As noted earlier, Item 303 requires the disclosure of known trends, events, and uncertainties that could materially affect the issuer's future financial position, liquidity, or results of operations or cause future results to differ materially from historic results.[47] In interpreting those

---

[44] *See id.* at 674.

[45] *Id.* at 678.

[46] *See id.* at 675–79. In contrast to *Matthews,* where the facts were almost unreasonably favorable to the defendant, the *Par Pharmaceutical* case presents a particularly unappealing case for the defense. Based on the facts alleged, throughout the period that the bribery scheme was in effect, the issuer went out of its way to tout its success in obtaining rapid FDA approvals in its SEC filings and press releases. Even after publicly disclosing the existence of a congressional investigation into FDA generic drug approvals and after disclosing that it was a target of the investigation, the issuer continued to affirmatively disclaim any knowledge of wrongdoing or any reason to think there would be a material impact on its business. *See id.* at 672–74, 675–77. Consider whether the result would have been different if the issuer's disclosures had been more subdued and temperate.

Later cases more explicitly articulate the nexus between an issuer's other disclosures and a duty to disclose illegal acts. For example, in *In re* Sotheby's Holdings, Inc. Sec. Litig., No. 00 Civ. 1041 (DLC), 2000 WL 1234601 (S.D.N.Y. Aug. 31, 2000), the court declined to dismiss a claim that the issuer had breached its duty to disclose an illegal price-fixing arrangement with its major competitor where its public filings indicated that price competition was a major factor in a customer's decision to engage the services of the issuer rather than one of its competitors. *See id.* at *4. *See also In re* Axis Capital Holdings Ltd. Sec. Litig., 456 F. Supp. 2d 576, 588–590 (S.D.N.Y. 2006) (no duty to disclose participation in allegedly illegal scheme where plaintiffs did not establish that there was a "direct nexus" between allegedly illegal conduct and specific statements by issuer that made such statements materially misleading); *In re* Marsh & McLennan Cos., Inc., Sec. Litig., No. MDL No. 1744, 04 Civ. 8144 (SWK), 2006 WL 2057194, at *12 (S.D.N.Y. July 20, 2006) (no duty to disclose that revenues were derived from illegal activity where revenues were accurately reported and were not accompanied by misleading statements concerning source of revenues). *Cf.* Steiner v. Medquist, Inc., Civil No. 04-5487, 2006 WL 2827740 (D.N.J. Sept. 29, 2006) (denying motion to dismiss where plaintiffs had adequately pleaded that defendants' participation in an illegal billing scheme rendered statements attributing issuer's revenues to legitimate business practices misleading). *Id. at* *13–16.

[47] For general discussion of the SEC's view of MD&A requirements, see Management's Discussion and Analysis of Financial Conditions and Results of Operations; Certain Investment Company Disclosures, Securities Act Release No. 6835, Fed. Sec. L. Rep. (CCH) ¶72,436 (May 18, 1989); *In re* Caterpillar, Inc., Exchange Act Release No. 30,532, Fed. Sec. L. Rep. (CCH) ¶73,830 (Mar. 31, 1992); Securities & Exchange Comm'n v. Sony Corp., Exchange Act Release

requirements in the context of governmental investigations and litigation, it is instructive to review the SEC's 1988 interpretive release relating to a nation-wide investigation into misconduct in defense contract procurement, also known as the Defense Contractors Release.[48]

In the Defense Contractors Release, the SEC advised defense companies to "review on an ongoing basis the need for appropriate disclosure" in the context of a national investigation into "illegal or unethical activity in the procurement of defense contracts," while acknowledging that "the exact subjects and scope" of the investigation were "still unknown."[49] The SEC noted that the consid-erations suggested in the release

> equally apply to companies that are subject to the inquiry and to companies that, although not targeted in the investigation, otherwise may be materially affected by the investigation as a result of additional expenditures incurred or policies and practices altered in connection with defense contract procurement. For example, disclosure of a change in practice may be required where a company, through its consultants, agents or otherwise, has been engaged in questionable conduct and thereafter alters its policies for obtaining defense contracts, or if general industry procedures change as a result of issues highlighted by the inquiry.[50]

The Defense Contractors Release noted that Items 103, 401(f), and 303 were potentially implicated by the government's investigation, and went on to sug-gest that disclosure should be provided "when, *in light of the uncertainty re-garding the government's inquiry,* reported financial information would not necessarily be indicative of the company's future operating results or financial condition"[51]—a somewhat unusual suggestion in light of the admitted lack of clarity as to the scope of the investigation, and one that would seem to carry the concept of known trends or uncertainties to its extreme. The release focused on the need to disclose "additional material information, beyond information specifically required to be disclosed, that is necessary to make the required statements not misleading,"[52] and indicated that issuers must consider the fi-nancial and business impact of various possible events, such as the likelihood that, as a result of illegal acts, their rights to receive payment under government contracts might be suspended, their government contracts might be terminated, they might have to alter business practices, or their competitive position might be harmed. The Defense Contractors Release is somewhat unique in suggesting

---

No. 40,305, 1998 SEC LEXIS 1650 (Aug. 5, 1998); Interpretation: Commission Guidance Re-garding Management's Discussion and Analysis of Financial Condition and Results of Opera-tions, Securities Act Release No. 8350 (Dec. 19, 2003), *available at* http://www.sec.gov/rules/interp/33-8350.htm. Note that in *Gallagher,* the court assumed the correctness of the plaintiffs' claim that Item 303 required disclosure of a letter to the issuer from the FDA threatening "severe consequences" for noncompliance with regulatory requirements and subsequent negotiating demands from the FDA, but held that the issuer did not have a duty to disclose the information at the specific time in question. *See* Gallagher v. Abbott Labs., 269 F.3d 806, 810 (7th Cir. 2001).

[48] Statement of the Commission Regarding Disclosure Obligations of Companies Affected by the Government's Defense Contract Procurement Inquiry and Related Issues, Securities Act Release No. 6791, 1988 SEC LEXIS 1580 (Aug. 3, 1988).

[49] *Id.,* 1988 SEC LEXIS 1580, at *1–2.

[50] *Id.* at *2–3.

[51] *Id.* at *6 (emphasis added).

[52] *Id.* at *7.

that disclosure might be required not only if the issuer itself were under investigation, indicted, or convicted, but also if it were likely to be affected by the general industry impact of the investigation.

The Defense Contractors Release suggests a very expansive view of disclosure obligations, particularly as it construes the already broad MD&A requirements concerning disclosure of known trends, events, and uncertainties. Although, as described earlier, there is significant case law authority questioning and contradicting the notion that issuers must disclose uncharged criminal conduct involving themselves and their officers and directors,[53] the Defense Contractors Release seems to indicate that an issuer might be required to disclose facts and potential facts that could have the effect of implicating it in criminal activity, even where the issuer has no notice that it (or any of its officers, directors or agents) is the specific subject or target of an investigation.

The approach suggested by the Defense Contractors Release takes on renewed force in light of more recent pronouncements by the SEC's Division of Enforcement. In 2004, the Division's then-Director announced that the Division intended to pursue "investigations where, at the outset, it is not clear that a securities violation has occurred . . . to probe industries or practices about which [the Division has] concerns or suspicions, but no clear roadmap to wrongdoing."[54] This practice, known to the Division staff as "wildcatting," has already been reflected in a number of wide-ranging investigations, and it has been suggested that issuers in a targeted industry should consider the need to make public disclosure of industry-wide investigations, at least in some circumstances.[55] While issuers will want to be cautious about premature disclosures where it does not appear that they themselves are particular targets of an investigation, if it becomes publicly known that practices of a type engaged in by an issuer are the focus of such a general investigation, that issuer should consider whether the principles enunciated in the Defense Contractors Release might apply.[56]

### b. Quarterly Reports on Form 10-Q

In addition to the 10-K, the 1934 Act requires issuers to file quarterly reports on Form 10-Q within forty to forty-five days after the end of each fiscal

---

[53]For additional discussion of director and officer liability generally, see Chapter 8 (Walton, Humphreys, and Jacobs, Potential Liabilities for Directors and Officers of Health Care Organizations).

[54]*See* Speech by SEC Staff: *Remarks Before the District of Columbia Bar Ass'n* (Feb. 11, 2004), *available at* http://www.sec.gov/news/speech/spch021104smc.htm (remarks of Stephen M. Cutler, Director, Division of Enforcement).

[55]*See generally* Latham & Watkins Client Alert No. 380, " 'Wildcatting' for Fraud: A New Investigative Approach by SEC Enforcement?" (Apr. 12, 2004), *available at* http://www.lw.com/upload/pubContent/_pdf/pub970_1.pdf.

[56]For example, in the wake of widely publicized 2006 investigations concerning stock option "backdating," a number of issuers announced internal investigations of their stock option granting practices, changes in such practices, and financial restatements even where those issuers had not previously publicly announced governmental investigations or otherwise been identified as the subject of such investigations. *See, e.g.,* the "Options Scorecard" maintained by The Wall Street Journal at http://online.wsj.com/public/resources/documents/info-optionsscore06-full.html; Joann S. Lublin, *Untainted Firms Alter How They Offer Options*, Wall St. J., Dec. 11, 2006, at B1.

quarter. The 10-Q is primarily a financial document, and the bulk of the typical 10-Q consists of comparative financial statements for the quarter then ended and the fiscal year to date. However, while there is no requirement for a detailed business description, Part I, Item 2 of Form 10-Q requires the issuer to include an MD&A section covering the interim periods and meeting the relevant requirements of Item 303, and Part II, Item 1 requires disclosure under Item 103 of legal proceedings in the quarter in which they first become reportable and in subsequent quarters in which there are material developments. Thus, the considerations discussed earlier with respect to Items 103 and 303 remain relevant, as applicable in particular quarters, to the issuer's 10-Q disclosure obligations.[57]

### c. Current Reports on Form 8-K

In general, the provisions of Form 8-K that require a report to be filed in a specific time frame would not pick up alleged criminal conduct, charged or uncharged, or regulatory violations. However, Item 8.01 of Form 8-K provides for discretionary disclosure of events that the issuer deems material, and an issuer that has determined that disclosure is appropriate or necessary may elect to file an Item 8.01 Form 8-K as a means of disseminating that information.[58] Current reports on Form 8-K are not subject to the specific requirements of Regulation S-K, but the disclosures, once made, would be subject to the same 10b-5 standards as those described earlier. In addition, an issuer may use an 8-K to satisfy its obligations under Regulation FD, as discussed later.[59]

---

[57]In *Securities & Exchange Comm'n v. Fehn*, 97 F.2d 1276 (9th Cir. 1996), the court upheld a permanent injunction obtained by the SEC against an outside securities lawyer for his role in aiding and abetting an issuer's 10b-5 violations in its 10-Qs. In that case, the issuer had committed various 1933 Act violations (as well as violations of state blue sky laws) in connection with its IPO and had failed, in its IPO registration statement, to disclose that the FDA had banned sales of its primary product. The issuer had also failed to file required 10-Qs. Fehn, the lawyer, advised the issuer that it must file the 10-Qs and disclose in them the adverse FDA action. He also advised the issuer that it was unnecessary to disclose in the 10-Qs the apparent 1933 Act violations. The issuer disclosed the FDA action in the 10-Qs but did not correct the other misstatements in its registration statement or disclose the potential civil liability associated with the 1933 Act and blue sky violations. Fehn assisted the issuer in preparing and filing the 10-Qs, although the extent of that assistance was disputed. *See id.* at 1279–81. In determining whether there was a primary violation of Section 10(b) and Rule 10b-5 that would support the aiding and abetting charge, the court held that disclosure of the potential exposure arising from the earlier violations of the securities laws was required in order to make the disclosures contained within the 10-Qs "not misleading," even where such disclosure was not expressly required by Form 10-Q. The court stated that the potential liabilities faced by the issuer were "not inevitable, but . . . contingent, [disclosure was required because] they represented a potentially large financial loss to [the issuer]." *See id.* at 1289–91. The court, in particular, focused on the presence in the 10-Qs of misleading affirmative disclosure concerning the facts underlying the 1933 Act violations. *See id.* at 1290 n.12. *Cf.* Gallagher v. Abbott Labs., 269 F.3d 806, 809 (7th Cir. 2001) (10-Q only requires disclosure as to items specified therein; no duty to update 10-K disclosure in 10-Q unless a specific 10-Q item so requires).

[58]In addition, Item 2.04 requires the disclosure of a "triggering event" that accelerates or increases a direct (or indirect) financial obligation of an issuer. *See* Form 8-K, Item 2.04. If, for example, a government investigation or FCA suit were an event of default giving rise to acceleration of indebtedness under a credit facility, the issuer might be required to disclose the event under Item 2.04 whether or not the issuer had otherwise determined that it had a disclosure obligation.

[59]See Section II.A.3., below.

## 2. The 1933 Act

While the 1934 Act regulates the disclosures that must be made by an issuer with a class of securities registered under the federal securities laws, the 1933 Act regulates the disclosures that must be made by an issuer seeking to sell securities in a registered public offering. Under the 1933 Act, an issuer seeking to offer securities to the public must file with the SEC a registration statement that must include a prospectus containing (or, where permitted, incorporating by reference from the issuer's 1934 Act filings) extensive information concerning the issuer's business and financial condition.

The disclosures described earlier under Items 101, 103, 303, and 401 of Regulation S-K must be included or incorporated by reference in a 1933 Act registration statement. In addition, Item 503(c) of Regulation S-K requires that a 1933 Act prospectus include a "Risk Factors" section that "[discusses] the most significant factors that make the offering speculative or risky," as specifically relevant to the particular issuer and offering.[60] Many health care issuers include general descriptions of the regulatory and enforcement environment in their risk factors. Where an issuer knows that it is the subject of an investigation, an FCA suit, or other enforcement action, the issuer must consider whether the potential impact of such an investigation or proceeding must, because of its materiality, be identified as a risk that investors in the offering should take into account.

Note that, although an issuer that treads carefully may avoid encountering a duty to disclose information until its next relevant 1934 Act report, even where that information is material and adverse, the circumstance is different when the issuer is engaged in a securities offering. It is a well-settled principle that "[a]n issuer has a duty to disclose material information prior to trading in its own securities."[61] Thus, an issuer engaged in a 1933 Act registration undertakes a heightened duty to evaluate the need for early disclosure of investigations and similar events.[62] It has been held that "[t]he failure of an offering document to disclose a company's violations of law provides a valid basis for asserting

---

[60]While risk factor disclosure was historically not required in 1934 Act documents, many issuers developed a practice of including it in 10-Ks and sometimes even in 10-Qs. Form 10-K was amended in 2005 to require the inclusion of risk factors pursuant to the requirements of S-K Item 503(c). *See* Form 10-K, Item 1A.

[61]Meredith B. Cross, Denise Manning-Cabrol, & Deborah M. Wiggin, *Overview of Disclosure Obligations of Public Companies: Mandatory Disclosure, Voluntary Disclosure and Duties of Officers and Directors,* in THE ART OF COUNSELING DIRECTORS, OFFICERS & INSIDERS: HOW, WHEN & WHAT TO DISCLOSE 7, 16 (internal page 8) (Practising Law Institute 1998) (citing LOUIS LOSS & JOEL SELIGMAN, FUNDAMENTALS OF SECURITIES REGULATION 789–90 (1995)).

[62]Note that corporate insiders proposing to trade for their own account in the issuer's securities also have a duty to disclose material information in their possession or abstain from trading. *See, e.g.,* Chiarella v. United States, 445 U.S. 222, 228–29 (1980). *See also* Securities & Exchange Comm'n v. Brenner, Civil Action No. 1:97-CV-0607-GET (N.D. Ga.), Litigation Release No. 15301, 1997 SEC LEXIS 626 (Mar. 19, 1997) (Medaphis general counsel advised her mother and a co-defendant that FBI had executed two search warrants on Medaphis offices before issuer's public announcement of the investigation; mother, co-defendant, and co-defendant's father and brother sold stock before announcement; general counsel forced to pay disgorgement and civil penalties and was permanently enjoined from further violations). In some situations, then, the trading desires of a corporate insider may conflict with the issuer's own perceived disclosure obligations, to the potential detriment of all concerned.

claims under the [1933] Act if the violations were material."[63] Where an issuer's knowledge of a pending investigation puts it on notice that it may have committed such violations, it may be alleged that the issuer has a responsibility to make appropriate disclosure in a 1933 Act registration statement.[64]

### 3. *Informal Disclosures: Analysts, Investor Relations, the Press, and Regulation FD*

Although the 1934 Act and the 1933 Act prescribe standards for formal, required disclosures in statutorily mandated contexts, issuers must be aware that in many ways the market's perception of them is shaped more, and more immediately, by informal, frequently unstructured disclosures: discussions with securities analysts who "follow" the issuer's securities for brokerage firms;[65] presentations at investor conferences; conference calls with investors and analysts; press releases and interviews; and the daily interaction between the issuer's investor relations personnel and securityholders, whether institutional money managers or "widow and orphan" retail investors.[66]

There are no substantive regulatory requirements as to what an issuer communicates through these avenues, as there are required disclosures in 1933 Act and 1934 Act forms, but an issuer is no less subject to liability under the antifraud provisions for false or misleading disclosures made through informal channels such as these.[67] Thus, if an issuer undertakes a duty to disclose information in such contexts—for example, by voluntarily choosing to comment on particular matters that it otherwise has no duty to talk about—the issuer will

---

[63] *In re* MobileMedia Sec. Litig., 28 F. Supp. 2d 901, 932 (D.N.J. 1998).

[64] *See id.* at 932–33. *See also* Greenfield v. Professional Care, Inc., 677 F. Supp. 110 (E.D.N.Y. 1987) (failure to disclose a pending criminal investigation in both 1934 Act filings and a 1933 Act registration statement; discussed in Section II.A.4.a., below). *But see* United States v. Crop Growers Corp., 954 F. Supp. 335, 348 (D.D.C. 1997) (passage quoted in Section II.A.1.a., above). In addition, where an issuer has filed a registration statement relating to a current offering or distribution, the issuer has a duty to amend or supplement it to disclose material changes that have occurred since the original filing of the registration statement, so long as the registration statement remains "live." *See, e.g.,* Gallagher v. Abbott Labs., 269 F.3d 806, 810–11 (7th Cir. 2001).

[65] The term "analysts" can be used to refer both to "sell-side" analysts, who are employed by brokerage firms to provide research and analysis to customers of the brokerage, generally through reports that are widely available in the market, and to "buy-side" analysts, who work for money managers and institutional investors and who perform research solely for their employers or clients. Communications with buy-side analysts are, thus, equivalent to communications with specific securityholders, and not to the market in general. As used in this chapter, the term is intended to refer to sell-side analysts.

[66] For an overview of certain general considerations in these types of informal disclosures, see William W. Horton & F. Hampton McFadden, Jr., *Disclosure Obligations of the Newly Public Healthcare Company: Practical Strategies for the Company and Its Counsel*, 32 J. HEALTH L. 1, 16–25 (1999).

[67] *See, e.g.,* Basic, Inc. v. Levinson, 485 U.S. 224, 227 n.4 (1988) (describing allegedly misleading statements in interview and press release); *In re* Par Pharm., Inc. Sec. Litig., 733 F. Supp. 668, 673 (S.D.N.Y. 1990) (describing press release with misleading information); Simon v. American Power Conversion Corp., 945 F. Supp. 416, 430 (D.R.I. 1996) (issuer could be responsible for misrepresentations in analyst reports if it provided false or misleading information to the analyst). In the municipal securities market, there may also be a blurry line dividing information that "speaks to the markets," which must conform to the requirements of Rule 10b-5, and "political speech," which is permitted to be less than candid. See Section II.B., below.

be deemed to have undertaken a duty to disclose such information as is necessary to make the voluntary disclosures not false or misleading.[68]

This duty was made more complex and compelling with the SEC's adoption in October 2000 of Regulation FD,[69] which was designed to eliminate the practice of "selective disclosure." Regulation FD requires that, when an issuer or a person acting on behalf of an issuer selectively discloses any material, nonpublic information regarding the issuer or its securities to, essentially, any investment professional (a broker, an analyst, a money manager, a mutual fund or hedge fund, etc.) or to any securityholder of the issuer, in circumstances where it is reasonably foreseeable that the securityholder will purchase or sell the issuer's securities on the basis of the information, the issuer must simultaneously make public disclosure of that information (if the selective disclosure was intentional) or promptly make public disclosure of that information (if the selective disclosure was unintentional; "promptly" means within 24 hours or before the opening of the market on the next trading day, whichever is later).[70] Such public disclosure must be made through an 8-K filing[71] or through a broadly disseminated press release or similar method designed to get the information out broadly to the market as a whole.[72]

The Regulation FD Adopting Release identifies a number of specific types of information that could be considered material under Regulation FD.[73] Nothing in this illustrative, nonexclusive list specifically addresses government investigations or uncharged criminal conduct. However, it is clear that Regulation FD can pose particular challenges for the issuer and its investor relations personnel in that context. First, in an industry such as health care where such investigations are ever more common (and rumors of investigations even more

---

[68]*See, e.g., In re* Presstek, Inc., Exchange Act Release No. 39,472, 1997 SEC LEXIS 2645 (Dec. 22, 1997) (issuer found liable where it edited some projections in draft of analyst's report, but failed to correct other projections that were misleading).

[69]Final Rule: Selective Disclosure and Insider Trading, Securities Act Release No. 33-7881, 65 Fed. Reg. 51,716 (Aug. 24, 2000), *available at* http://www.sec.gov/rules/final/33-7881.htm [hereinafter FD Adopting Release].

[70]*See id.* §II.B.

[71]Regulation FD added a new Item 9 to Form 8-K (renumbered as Item 7.01 in 2004), pursuant to which an issuer may "furnish" information that it wishes to disclose in compliance with Regulation FD, but that information will not be deemed "filed" (and thus automatically incorporated by reference into those 1933 Act registration statements that require 8-Ks to be so incorporated and subject to liability under §11 of the 1933 Act and §18 of the 1934 Act). *See id.* §II.B.4.a.

[72]*See id.* §II.B.4.b. There has been much discussion and writing about Regulation FD, both before and after its adoption. For general overviews and commentary, see, e.g., John J. Huber & Thomas J. Kim, *The SEC's Regulation FD—Fair Disclosure,* in COUNSELING CLIENTS IN TURBULENT MARKETS & UNCERTAIN TIMES: DISCLOSURE & FINANCING ISSUES 113 (Practising Law Institute 2001); Karl A. Groskaufmanis & Daniel H. Anixt, *The Twilight Zone of Disclosure: A Perspective on the SEC's Selective Disclosure Rules,* in 1 33d ANNUAL INSTITUTE ON SECURITIES REGULATION 435 (Practising Law Institute 2001) (reprinted from INSIGHTS); *see also* NATIONAL INVESTOR RELATIONS INST., STANDARDS OF PRACTICE FOR INVESTOR RELATIONS, App. B (2d ed. Jan. 2001); Letter from the Committee on Federal Regulation of Securities, Business Law Section, American Bar Association, to Jonathan G. Katz, Secretary, Securities & Exchange Comm'n, Selective Disclosure (May 8, 2000) (File No. S7-31-99), *available at* http://www.sec.gov/rules/proposed/s73199/keller2.htm [hereinafter ABA FD Comment Letter] (commenting on originally proposed form of Regulation FD).

[73]*See* FD Adopting Release, at text accompanying n.47.

so), it is likely that analysts and institutional investors may from time to time question the issuer about whether it is the subject of an investigation or *qui tam* suit, based on publicly disclosed investigations of similar issuers, issuer-specific rumors, or blind poking around based on the industry environment. Assuming that the issuer wishes to retain some discretion over how and when it makes such disclosures, it is critical that the issuer maintain a consistent policy over how it is going to answer such questions—whether that answer is something general and noncommittal, or simply "no comment." An issuer that, on nine occasions, says "We don't have any problems" and, on the tenth occasion, says "We can't comment on that" has probably effectively disclosed a problem.[74] This analysis holds true even in the absence of Regulation FD, but the new rule puts even more pressure on an issuer and its investor relations personnel to handle such issues with great care and consistency.

Further, although the practice may have been questionable in the pre-FD era, Regulation FD essentially eliminates the ability of an issuer to filter bad news out to the market through analysts before making a formal public disclosure. Under the conventions prevailing before Regulation FD, an issuer that communicated information simultaneously to all analysts who regularly followed its stock was ordinarily not regarded as engaging in selective disclosure, but was instead using a means generally accepted as providing broad disclosure to the market, even if that means was not expressly sanctioned by the law.[75] Thus, an issuer who felt that it was necessary or desirable to disclose the existence of a government investigation, an actual or pending indictment, or a similar event might, before putting out a press release or filing an 8-K, disclose the matter to its analyst group in a way that allowed the issuer to put its desired spin on the matter before a sophisticated, industry-familiar audience. The issuer would, presumably, hope and expect that at least some of the analysts would interpret and report on the disclosure in a manner relatively favorable to the issuer, thus ameliorating some of the potential adverse market reaction.

Under Regulation FD, however, this type of practice is expressly proscribed. If the information to be communicated is material, the issuer must communicate it in a way that provides broad dissemination to the public. Further, if the issuer inadvertently communicates the information, as when an investor relations officer is caught off-guard by an unexpected question, the issuer must promptly correct that error through broad dissemination. The split-second nature of the materiality decisions that must be made in the world of Regulation FD puts

---

[74]*Cf.* Basic, Inc. v. Levinson, 485 U.S. 224, 239 n.17 (1988) ("It has been suggested that given current market practices, a 'no comment' statement [in response to questions about a possible merger] is tantamount to an admission that merger discussions are underway.... That may well hold true to the extent that issuers adopt a policy of truthfully denying merger rumors when no discussions are underway, and of issuing 'no comment' statements when they are in the midst of negotiations.").

[75]*See generally* William W. Horton & F. Hampton McFadden, Jr., *Disclosure Obligations of the Newly Public Healthcare Company: Practical Strategies for the Company and Its Counsel,* 32 J. HEALTH L. 1, 19 (1999). Thus, issuers would commonly discuss material developments in conference calls that were open to all analysts following their stock, but were closed to the general public and the press. On the other hand, communications to one analyst (or a few favored analysts), without general simultaneous disclosure to all analysts following the issuer's stock, have always been regarded as troublesome.

a great premium on having a management and investor relations team that pays attention to every question and every answer and has a plan in place for dealing with questions about investigations and regulatory litigation at all times.

### 4. The Elusive Concept of "Materiality"

Although almost all disclosure requirements in the federal securities laws—including those under Regulation FD[76]—are predicated on the threshold standard that the information must be "material" in order for disclosure to be required, the concept of materiality is not defined in the 1933 or 1934 Act or the regulations thereunder. Instead, the concept has historically been developed and articulated through case law and through the evolution of accepted practices among securities professionals. However, recent interpretive guidance from the SEC adds new dimensions to materiality analysis.

#### a. Common Law and Lore

The seminal case in defining materiality is the U.S. Supreme Court's decision in *TSC Industries, Inc. v. Northway, Inc.*,[77] which held that, in the context of a proxy solicitation, "an omitted fact is material if there is a substantial likelihood that a reasonable shareholder would consider it important in deciding how to vote."[78] The *TSC Industries* Court went on to state that in order for an omitted fact to be material, "there must be a substantial likelihood that [its] disclosure . . . would have been viewed by the reasonable investor as having significantly altered the 'total mix' of information made available."[79] In *Basic, Inc. v. Levinson*,[80] the Supreme Court "expressly adopt[ed]" the standard of materiality in *TSC Industries* for application in the Section 10(b)/Rule 10b-5 context.[81] The *Basic* Court went on to state:

> Where the impact of [a] corporate development is certain and clear, the *TSC Industries* materiality definition admits straightforward application. Where, on the other hand, the event is contingent or speculative in nature, it is difficult to ascertain whether the "reasonable investor" would have considered the omitted information significant at the time.[82]

In discussing the evaluation of materiality in the context of "contingent or speculative" developments, the Court quoted with approval an earlier Second

---

[76]Indeed, one of the concerns expressed by the securities bar and others when Regulation FD was proposed was that, if an issuer expressly disclosed information pursuant to Regulation FD, the issuer might be deemed to have conceded that such information was "material" and would thus be estopped from arguing that point. *See* ABA FD Comment Letter, at 10. As finally adopted, Regulation FD provided that filing or furnishing information on Form 8-K would not, in and of itself, constitute an admission of materiality. *See* FD Adopting Release; Form 8-K, General Instruction B.6.

[77]426 U.S. 438 (1976).

[78]*Id.* at 449.

[79]*Id.*

[80]485 U.S. 224 (1988).

[81]*Id.* at 232. The SEC incorporated this standard in the definitional provisions of Rule 12b-2 under the 1934 Act and Rule 405 under the 1933 Act.

[82]485 U.S. at 232.

Circuit decision: "Under such circumstances, materiality 'will depend at any given time upon a balancing of both the indicated probability that the event will occur and the anticipated magnitude of the event in light of the totality of the company activity.' "[83]

Numerous cases involving the disclosure of uncharged criminal conduct have considered the application of this standard in that context, with varying results. In *United States v. Matthews*,[84] the court implicitly concluded that the lack of a specific requirement in SEC proxy regulations to disclose such conduct amounted to a determination by the SEC that such disclosure was not material in that setting, at least in the context of a criminal prosecution for nondisclosure.[85] In contrast, in *Roeder v. Alpha Industries*,[86] the court "[did] not think it is necessarily true that information about bribery is not material until it becomes the subject of an indictment" and noted that "otherwise material information does not become any less material because someone may be indicted if it is discovered by the authorities."[87] In language that has some resonance in the health care arena, the *Roeder* court said:

> Illegal payments that are so small as to be relatively insignificant to the corporation's bottom line can still have vast economic implications. See *SEC v. Jos. Schlitz Brewing Co.*, 452 F. Supp. 824, 830 (E.D. Wis. 1978) (it may be material that brewery risked losing its license to sell beer by engaging in illegal practices). Even small illegal payments can seriously endanger a corporation's business, especially when it relies heavily on government contracts, because such activity can result in the corporation being barred from obtaining future government contracts or subcontracts. . . . Such a bar would be devastating to Alpha [the issuer]; it relied on defense-related contracts for sixty to sixty-five percent of its sales.[88]

In a case directly involving health care fraud, *Greenfield v. Professional Care, Inc.*,[89] the court articulated a distinction between "qualitative" information concerning alleged misconduct and information that directly related to the financial condition and results of the issuer. In that case, the issuer, two of its officers, and another employee had been indicted for various offenses relating to Medicaid fraud. The plaintiff brought a class action complaint, alleging that numerous 10-Ks and 10-Qs and a 1933 Act registration statement filed by the issuer before the indictment were "materially misleading for failing to disclose that certain portions of [the issuer's] earnings reflected payments that were illegally obtained and subject to forfeiture," as well as for failing to disclose that the issuer had engaged in various practices that could (and eventually did) result in its being excluded from Medicaid participation. The plaintiff also

---

[83]*Id.* at 238 (quoting Securities & Exchange Comm'n v. Texas Gulf Sulphur Co., 401 F.2d 833, 849 (2d Cir. 1968)).

[84]787 F.2d 38 (2d Cir. 1986) (discussed in Section II.A.1.a., above).

[85]*Id.* at 46–49.

[86]814 F.2d 22 (1st Cir. 1987) (discussed in Section II.A.1.a., above).

[87]*Id.* at 25.

[88]*Id.* at 26.

[89]677 F. Supp. 110 (E.D.N.Y. 1987).

alleged that some of the filings were misleading for failing to disclose a pending state investigation into the alleged fraud.[90]

In denying the defendants' motion to dismiss, the court distinguished *Matthews* and various cases discussed therein on the basis that they related to the question of whether disclosure of " 'qualitative' information relating to management ability and integrity" was required.[91] In contrast, the court stated that

> the [*Greenfield*] complaint alleges that defendants made misstatements and omissions that directly related to [the issuer's] earnings. Information going directly to the financial condition of the company falls squarely within the range of information for which there is a "substantial likelihood that a reasonable shareholder would consider... important in deciding [whether to invest]." Thus, unlike the purely "qualitative" information cases, the omitted information here is material,... and, if true, ought to have been disclosed in order to render [the issuer's] public statements concerning its financial condition not misleading.[92]

The court did not distinguish between the failure to disclose the alleged facts that, if true, would have made the issuer's financial information materially misleading and the failure to disclose the issuer's alleged knowledge of the pre-indictment investigation.

What is apparent from these and other precedents is that the question of materiality is highly fact- and context-specific[93] and, in the context of alleged disclosure violations relating to government investigations and uncharged criminal conduct, the courts appear to be greatly influenced by (1) whether the issue arises in the context of a charge of criminal securities fraud or in a private stockholder suit and (2) whether the underlying investigation resulted in indictments or convictions. Further, it is apparent that it is critical to the analysis to remember that the question of materiality is distinct from the question of whether there is, in the particular situation, a duty to disclose, and the defendant in such a case must strive to ensure that the court undertakes those inquiries as separate analyses.[94]

### b. SAB 99

Although, as noted earlier, neither the 1933 nor the 1934 Act, nor the regulations thereunder, establish a definition of materiality, the SEC staff

---

[90]*Id.* at 111–12.

[91]*Id.*

[92]*Id.* at 113 (quoting TSC Indus. v. Northway, Inc., 426 U.S. 438, 449 (1976)) (citations omitted).

[93]*See In re* MobileMedia Sec. Litig., 28 F. Supp. 2d 901, 932 (D.N.J. 1998) ("The issue of materiality is a mixed question of law and fact which ordinarily is decided by the trier of fact.... If the alleged misrepresentations and omissions, however, are so obviously unimportant to an investor that reasonable minds cannot differ on the question of materiality, the allegations are not actionable as a matter of law.... When assessing materiality, not only the statement or omission itself but, as well, the context in which it occurs must be considered.") (citations omitted).

[94]*See* Basic, Inc. v. Levinson, 485 U.S. 224, 239 n.17 (1988) ("Silence, absent a duty to disclose, is not misleading under Rule 10b-5."). Note, however, that silence is easily distinguishable from false, incomplete, or otherwise misleading affirmative statements, which then give rise to an obligation to make disclosure sufficient to correct the statements or make them not misleading. See Section IV.A.3.b., below.

undertook to articulate a more specific analytical approach to materiality in the context of financial statements in Staff Accounting Bulletin (SAB) 99, released on August 12, 1999.[95] While this chapter does not attempt to address the accounting issues associated with contingencies relating to regulatory violations and investigations relating thereto, it is useful to look at some of the staff's analytical approach to materiality issues in the financial statement context.

In SAB 99, the staff cautioned issuers and their auditors about using numerical "rules of thumb" to conclude that an item is not material.[96] The staff stressed that the issuer and its auditor must take into account "*all* the relevant circumstances," including "[q]ualitative factors [that] may cause misstatements of quantitatively small amounts to be material."[97] Included in a list of qualitative factors to be considered in assessing the materiality of misstatements in financial information is "whether the misstatement involves concealment of an unlawful transaction."[98] SAB 99 also suggested that the issuer and its auditors should take into account any expectation of "a significant positive or negative market reaction" resulting from a "known misstatement."[99]

Although SAB 99 purports to relate only to materiality in the context of financial information, it has been suggested that its "qualitative factors" analysis may well be extended to other contexts.[100] Thus, the analytical

---

[95] SEC Staff Accounting Bulletin No. 99—Materiality (Aug. 12, 1999), *available at* http://www.sec.gov/interps/account/sab99.htm [hereinafter SAB 99]. For an extensive critical discussion of SAB 99 in the context of historical materiality analysis, see John J. Huber & Thomas J. Kim, *SAB 99: Materiality as We Know It or Brave New World for Securities Law,* in Counseling Clients in Turbulent Markets & Uncertain Times: Disclosure & Financing Issues 213 (Practising Law Institute 2001) [hereinafter Huber & Kim—SAB 99].

[96] In particular, the staff criticized "exclusive reliance" on a particular rule of thumb that "suggests that the misstatement or omission [in an issuer's financial statements] of an item that falls under a 5% threshold is not material in the absence of particularly egregious circumstances, such as self-dealing or misappropriation by senior management." *See* SAB 99, text accompanying n.2.

[97] SAB 99, text preceding n.13 (emphasis in original).

[98] *Id.,* text preceding n.15.

[99] *Id.,* text accompanying n.17. This suggestion is sharply criticized in Huber & Kim—SAB 99, at 225–26 (internal pages 11–12) ("Following SAB 99 would mean that any potential impact, real or believed, has to be included in the materiality analysis, but the absence of any market impact does not alone provide a basis for a conclusion that the fact or event is not material."). *But see* Helwig v. Vencor, Inc., 251 F.3d 540, 563 (6th Cir. 2001) (en banc) ("Materiality is about marketplace effects, not just mathematics.").

[100] *See* Huber & Kim—SAB 99, at 233–35 (internal pages 19–21) (predicting expansive application of SAB 99 and quoting news reports suggesting that SEC officials expect SAB 99 to influence the materiality analysis in nonfinancial statement contexts). *See also* The Business Roundtable—SEC SAB 99 Conference Call Transcript (Oct. 13, 1999), at 2 (then-SEC General Counsel Harvey Goldschmid (who became an SEC commissioner in July 2002): "[SAB 99's] focus is on financial statements, but we understand that it has implications for other areas. Materiality is a unified concept. The basic law is controlled by the Supreme Court. What happens in one area will have implications in another.") and 4 ("Our focus in drafting the SAB was on financial statements. But [there are] clear implications through other areas. [There] have to be. We used the same words, we used the same concept."), *available at* http://64.203.97.43/pdf/344.pdf; John J. Huber & Thomas J. Kim, *The SEC's Regulation FD—Fair Disclosure,* in Counseling Clients in Turbulent Markets & Uncertain Times: Disclosure & Financing Issues 113, 128 (internal page 14) (Practising Law Institute 2001) (noting that the FD Adopting Release "approvingly references" SAB 99 and suggesting that the SEC "intends by Regulation FD to extend the scope of SAB 99's application beyond materiality in financial statements to all communications").

framework of SAB 99 should, as a matter of prudence, be reviewed in considering the materiality of potential disclosures concerning regulatory violations and related investigations, particularly where (as in the *Greenfield* case), those violations may have a direct effect on reported financial information.

## B. Tax-Exempt Issuers

### 1. Concerns Under the Federal Securities Laws

Unlike corporate issuers, not-for-profit providers do not issue equity securities, and their debt securities are usually issued by special purpose units of government created to permit tax-exempt financing to be available for not-for-profit borrowers. As a result, such tax-exempt securities are exempt from registration under the 1933 Act[101] and from the periodic reporting requirements under the 1934 Act.[102] However, such exemptions do not apply to the antifraud provisions of Sections 12 and 17 of the 1933 Act or Section 10(b) of the 1934 Act and Rule 10b-5 thereunder. This means that, although there is no regulatory scheme that dictates disclosure on a line-item basis for a tax-exempt issuer, the issuer must decide what to disclose and when to disclose it based on common sense and the antifraud provisions.

The general absence of a periodic disclosure regime provides the tax-exempt issuer with substantial luxury to determine the time and manner of disclosure, because there is no general obligation to disclose material events either in the corporate world or the not-for-profit world.[103] Silence is almost always an option, although certain circumstances may force disclosure. For example, a proposed primary offering of municipal securities generally requires thorough disclosure;[104] annual reports filed in response to an undertaking under Rule 15c2-12 under the 1934 Act[105] must contain annual financial statements, so that any information material to the financial position of the issuer is likely to be required to be disclosed; discovery of a misstatement that was erroneous when made in a document that remains "live" probably must be corrected; and voluntary statements by the issuer that are expected to reach the market must be accurate and complete, even if the statements are not compelled in the first instance.[106]

The considerations related to primary offering disclosure in the tax-exempt offering context are similar to those in the corporate context, although there is no registration statement and no specific list of items that must be disclosed. Instead, there is a general understanding of the types of information

---

[101] *See* Securities Act of 1933 §3(a)(2), 15 U.S.C. §77c(a)(2). However, SEC Chairman Christopher Cox has long favored elimination of at least some of the exemptions available to issuers of municipal securities, and in 2007 renewed his call for changes in treatment of municipal securities to harmonize municipal securities disclosure with disclosure in the corporate securities markets. *See* Lynn Hume, *SEC's New Muni Initiative: Commission to Examine Tower Amendment*, THE BOND BUYER, Mar. 7, 2007, at 1, 5.

[102] *See* Securities Exchange Act of 1934 §3(a)(12)(A)(ii), 15 U.S.C. §78c(a)(12)(A)(ii).

[103] *See* Basic, Inc. v. Levinson, 485 U.S. 224 n.17 (1988).

[104] See Section II.A.3., above.

[105] 17 C.F.R. §240.15c2–12.

[106] See Section IV.A.3.b., below.

expected to be disclosed, including financial information, information about the issuer, a description of the securities, relevant risk factors, and so on. There has also long been an understanding that Rule 10b-5 applies to a primary offering of municipal securities by an issuer.[107] Accordingly, as in the corporate context, information that a reasonable investor would consider as altering the "total mix" of available information in assessing whether to purchase the offered securities must be disclosed.[108] In general, the analysis of what is material does not change substantially from the analysis of what is material for a corporate issuer.[109] A bond default or risk of nonpayment is not a prerequisite to an SEC enforcement proceeding, so the standards of materiality for municipal investors are likely to be similar to those applicable to corporate equity investors.[110]

Until July 1995, there was no requirement for a municipal issuer to provide any information to bondholders following the primary offering of the securities. Thus, fixed-rate securities could remain in the market for 30 years without any additional or updated information regarding the issuer being disclosed. In July 1995, however, amendments to Rule 15c2-12 under the 1934 Act became effective, and, with limited exceptions, broker-dealers were barred from entering into underwriting agreements with a municipal issuer unless they had determined that the issuer had entered into a binding agreement to provide, on an annual basis, statistical and financial information of the type provided in the bond offering document.[111] There was some initial uncertainty about the sanctions for supplying inaccurate or misleading information in reports filed pursuant to undertakings under the rule, but that uncertainty was dispelled by the SEC enforcement proceedings brought against the City of Miami[112] and against certain individuals associated with the Allegheny Health, Education and Research Foundation.[113] It is now clear that, despite the "warm and fuzzy" noises coming from the staff of the SEC at the time the 1995 Rule 15c2-12 amendments were being considered ("Just file the material that you have always

---

[107]*See, e.g.,* Securities & Exchange Comm'n v. Whatcom County Water Dist. #13, Case No. C77-103 (W.D. Wash.), Litigation Release No. 7912, 12 SEC Docket 417, 1977 WL 175582 (May 10, 1977) (final settled order); Securities & Exchange Comm'n v. San Antonio Mun. Util. Dist. No. 1, Civil Action No. H-77-1868 (S.D. Tex.), Litigation Release No. 8195, 13 SEC Docket 920, 1977 WL 173871 (Nov. 18, 1977) (final settled order); Municipal Securities Disclosure, Exchange Act Release No. 26,985, 1989 WL 281659, n.84 (July 10, 1989).

[108]See Section II.A.4., above.

[109]*See* Statement of the Commission Regarding Disclosure Obligations of Municipal Securities Issuers and Others, Securities Act Release No. 7049, 1994 WL 73628, nn.46–59 and accompanying text (Mar. 9, 1994) [hereinafter 1994 Interpretive Release].

[110]*See, e.g., In re* Maricopa County, Ariz., Sec. Act Release No. 7345 (Sept. 30, 1996), *available at* http://www.sec.gov/litigation/admin/337345.txt (alleging that municipal issuer violated antifraud provisions by providing misleading or erroneous information in offering documents concerning worsening financial condition and actual use of bond proceeds and by failing to revise or supplement offering documents).

[111]*See* Municipal Securities Disclosure, Exchange Act Release No. 34961, 1994 WL 640013 (Nov. 10, 1994).

[112]*In re* City of Miami, Fla., Cesar Odio and Manohar Surana, Initial Decision Release No. 185 (June 22, 2001), *available at* http://www.sec.gov/litigation/aljdec/id185bpm.htm.

[113]*In re* Albert Adamczak, C.P.A., Exchange Act Release No. 42743 (May 2, 2000), *available at* http://www.sec.gov/litigation/admin/34-42743.htm. *See also In re* Allegheny Health, Educ. & Research Found., Exchange Act Release No. 42992, 72 SEC Docket 1978, 2000 WL 868604 (June 30, 2000).

prepared for internal use."), filings under the rule must meet the same standards of accuracy and completeness that other filings that include full financial statements must meet.

The 1994 Interpretive Release made clear that, even in the absence of continuous reporting obligations under the 1934 Act, when an issuer

> releases information to the public that is reasonably expected to reach investors and the trading markets, those disclosures are subject to the antifraud provisions. The fact that they are not published for purposes of informing the securities markets does not alter the mandate that they not violate antifraud proscriptions. Those statements are a principal source of significant, current information about the issuer of the security, and thus reasonably can be expected to reach investors and the trading market.[114]

As a result, there is a need for tax-exempt issuers to carefully vet other public statements that may be misleading where they have determined not to disclose a threatened investigation.

### 2. *Concerns Under Circular 230 and the* Weiss *Decision*

The decision by the Treasury Department to include tax-exempt bond opinions within the scope of Circular 230[115] has heightened the potential sensitivity of disclosure decisions for tax-exempt health care organizations and their counsel. As discussed below, violations of health care laws may call into question the exempt status of health care organizations under Section 501(c)(3) of the Code. This in turn will raise issues concerning the tax-exempt status under Section 103 of the Code of the organization's tax-exempt borrowings under Section 145(a)(1) of the Code. Circular 230 governs practice before the Internal Revenue Service, and was amended effective June 20, 2005, to require that most opinions concerning the tax effect of transactions comply with those requirements. As a part of the amendments, a longstanding exception for opinions related to tax-exempt bonds was dropped. As a result, opinions related to tax-exempt bonds can now be subject to the Circular 230 requirements. In the face of strong expressions of concern from the municipal bond bar, as well as other market participants,[116] the Treasury included in the final regulations under Circular 230 an exclusion for state and local bond opinions that will be

---

[114] 1994 Interpretive Release at text accompanying nn.88–90.

[115] 31 C.F.R. §§10.33–.37; proposed regulation, 31 C.F.R. §10.39.

[116] *See, e.g.,* Letter of the National Association of Bond Lawyers, dated Feb. 12, 2004; Letter of the Investment Company Institute, dated Mar. 4, 2004; Letter of the American Bar Association Section of Taxation, dated Feb. 12, 2004; Letter of the Healthcare Financial Management Ass'n, dated Feb. 12, 2004; Letter on behalf of the American Public Power Ass'n, Council of Development Finance Agencies, Council of Infrastructure Financing Authorities, Government Finance Officers Ass'n, International City/County Management Ass'n, Large Public Power Council, National Ass'n of Counties, National Ass'n of Higher Educational Facilities Authorities, National Ass'n of State Treasurers, National Council of Health Facilities Finance Authorities, National League of Cities, New York State Economic Development Council, and U.S. Conference of Mayors, dated Feb. 13, 2004; Letter of The Bond Market Ass'n, dated Feb. 13, 2004.

separately covered by a new proposed regulation.[117] Subsequently, apparently based upon anecdotal reports of market disruption and continued expressions of concern from the bar as the effective date drew near,[118] concurrently with the effective date of the main Circular 230 regulations, the Treasury announced that it would broaden the scope of the exclusion that had been granted for state or local bond opinions to include opinions that addressed "one or more other Federal tax issues reasonably related and ancillary to" a state or local bond opinion, including "whether the organization that is borrowing the proceeds of the State or local bond is described in Section 501(c)(3) of the Internal Revenue Code."[119] As a result, opinions relating to Section 501(c)(3) status, which are necessary underpinnings to state and local bond opinions for nonprofit health care providers, are *also* excluded from the scope of the final regulations, at least when given as a part of a tax exempt bond offering.

The future prospects for Circular 230 as it would apply to tax exempt securities are unclear at this time. In 2006, both the Treasury and the Internal Revenue Service personnel responsible for preparing the final version of the regulation that would apply to state or local bond opinions indicated that the final version of Section 10.39 is unlikely to be completed before the final approach to the larger part of Circular 230 is resolved.[120]

The SEC added an additional consideration for the municipal securities practitioner through the position that it took in the *Weiss* case.[121] Ira Weiss served as bond counsel for an issue of municipal securities that was audited by the Internal Revenue Service. Following the audit, the issuer made a payment and entered into a closing agreement. The SEC brought an enforcement action against Weiss, claiming that his opinion to the effect that the interest on the bonds was excludable from gross income for federal income tax purposes constituted a misleading statement made in connection with the offer and sale of the bonds, and that his failure to conduct appropriate due diligence before rendering the opinion was recklessly negligent. The SEC required that Weiss disgorge the fee he had received on the subject transaction and imposed a cease-and-desist order on him, enjoining him from future violations of the securities laws. The D.C. Circuit upheld the SEC's position on appeal, meaning that bond counsel's opinion must now be considered a disclosure document of which the lawyer is the author, and tax opinion practice is subject to review by the SEC under the securities laws. Thus, bond counsel for a provider facing an investigation must consider the not unlikely prospect of being treated as a primary violator of Rule 10b-5 if the investigation develops into the worst case.

---

[117]Proposed Regulation 31 C.F.R. §10.39.

[118]*See* Letter of the National Ass'n of Bond Lawyers, dated March 1, 2005; Letter of the American Bar Ass'n Section of Taxation, dated March 15, 2005.

[119]Notice 2005-47, IRB 2005-26, dated June 27, 2005.

[120]*See* Alison McConnell, *Circular 230: Treasury Official: Too Early to Set Deadlines for Final Rules*, THE BOND BUYER, Jan. 23, 2006; Alison McConnell, *IRS: Circular 230 Re-evaluation to Begin Soon*, THE BOND BUYER, June 6, 2006.

[121]Weiss v. Securities & Exchange Comm'n, 468 F.3d 849 (D.C. Cir. 2006). *See also In re Ira Weiss*, Securities Act Release No. 8641 (Dec. 2, 2005), *available at* http://www.sec.gov/litigation/opinions/33-8641.pdf.

## C. Disclosure as a Matter of Prudence

The foregoing sections discuss some of the specific statutory and regulatory requirements for disclosure of government investigations and related litigation, as well as some of the judicial interpretations of those requirements. It should not be overlooked, however, that the question of whether, how, and when to disclose problems of this nature may be more than simply a question of what the law requires. For any number of reasons, an issuer may elect to disclose the existence of an investigation even when it has a defensible position that disclosure was not, or at least not yet, required.[122] An issuer may, for example, be pummeled by rumors in the market about the potential existence of an investigation and may wish to bring those rumors down to earth by disclosing the specific situation it faces. Likewise, an issuer may believe that its future plans (for example, a merger or a significant financing transaction) make disclosure inevitable and may wish to get the news out in the open before it is under time pressure to do so. The nature of the investigation itself and the associated likelihood of information leaks may make early disclosure seem the wisest course; if, for example, armed FBI agents (or postal inspectors, or what have you) stage a daylight raid on 10 of the issuer's facilities and seize all the computers, the issuer must recognize that there is a good chance that the story will get out, even if no misconduct has yet been charged.

Later portions of this chapter suggest some possible approaches to making these sorts of timing decisions on disclosure.[123] For present purposes, however, two critical points should be noted: (1) the question of when disclosure *is required* does not always answer the question of when disclosure *should be made,* and (2) regardless of whether disclosure is required or voluntary at the time it is made, an issuer that begins disclosure of an investigation or similar problem must be prepared to disclose all material facts necessary to make the disclosure not misleading.[124]

## III. THE PROBLEM, RESTATED AND AMPLIFIED

After the foregoing overview of the general securities law issues surrounding the disclosure of government investigations, uncharged criminal conduct, and the like, it is appropriate to revisit the peculiar nature of the current regulatory and enforcement environment in the health care industry and to attempt to place it in context in light of the securities law principles described earlier.

---

[122]For example, in *Ballan v. Wilfred American Educational Corp.,* 720 F. Supp. 241 (E.D.N.Y. 1989), the issuer disclosed the existence of investigations against the issuer and certain employees before any indictments issued, although the issuer apparently did not argue that no disclosure was necessary at that time. 720 F. Supp. at 244–45, 248.

[123]See Section IV., below.

[124]See Section IV.A.3.b., below.

## A. The Nature of Health Care Investigations and Prosecutions in General

As alluded to in the introduction to this chapter, health care investigations, prosecutions, and civil and administrative proceedings have a somewhat unique nature, and one that may present particular problems in the disclosure context.

### 1. Complexity of the Regulatory Environment

Health care providers are, of course, subject to a plethora of complex laws and regulations arising under federal and state law, relating to facility licensure, clinician licensure, certification for participation in reimbursement programs, business arrangements among providers, sources of patient or business referrals, and so on. The scope and complexity of this regulatory structure, absent any other considerations, would make it difficult for providers to ensure that they are operating in compliance with all material laws and regulations affecting their business and that they do not have material exposure to enforcement actions for noncompliance. In addition, many health care statutes take years to be interpreted and clarified by regulation, during which time providers may have difficulty determining whether they are complying with vague and general statutory provisions.[125]

This situation is, moreover, exacerbated by the fact that the anti-kickback statute and the Stark law, among others, impose liability for business arrangements that, in settings not covered by those statutes, might be regarded as simply good business.[126] Further, liability under some of those statutes requires a (frequently subjective) determination of the intent of the parties, which means that a transaction that may be innocuous if undertaken with a pure heart may result in civil or criminal liability if, with the benefit of hindsight, it is determined to have an improper purpose.[127] Thus, it may be difficult in some circumstances to assess whether a particular set of facts may, at some point, give rise to material exposure or whether it will be possible to raise effective defenses to any claim of liability.

### 2. The Wide Range of Remedial Statutes

Under federal law alone, the enforcement agencies have available to them a multitude of potentially duplicative remedies for violations of health care

---

[125]For example, the original version of the Stark law was passed in 1989. It was amended and expanded in 1992. Proposed regulations under the initial version were promulgated in 1992, but were not issued in final form until 1995. Proposed regulations under the amended version were not issued until January 1998. Partial final regulations under the amended version were then issued in January 2001 (and amended in December 2001), the remaining final regulations were not issued until March 2004, and Phase III regulations were issued in 2007. See Chapter 2 and the Addendum to Chapter 2 (Crane, Federal Physician Self-Referral Restrictions).

[126]In many businesses (for example, the legal profession), providing expensive gifts, lavish trips, and so forth to those persons who provide business is regarded as good marketing and "relationship building." In health care, it can mean five years in prison. *See generally* Daniel R. Roach & Cori MacDonneil, *The Compliance Conundrum,* 32 J. HEALTH L. 565, 577–78 (Fall 1999).

[127]*See, e.g.,* United States v. Greber, 760 F.2d 68 (3d Cir.), *cert. denied,* 474 U.S. 988 (1985) (business arrangement may violate the anti-kickback statute if even one purpose of the arrangement is to induce Medicare referrals).

laws. Some of these statutes, such as the anti-kickback statute, both substantively regulate conduct and provide penalties for violations, while others, such as the Civil Monetary Penalties law,[128] simply establish penalties and sanctions generally available for violations of other statutes. Some of them relate specifically to health care programs and claims, while others relate more broadly to fraud or misconduct in connection with government programs generally. Many of these statutes impose civil or criminal penalties on a "per claim" or "per item" basis, which, in the health care context, can lead to staggering numbers, because the government may assert that each bill, each line item on a bill, or each service encounter constitutes a separate claim or item. Thus, a provider that makes the same error in 1,000 Medicare claims can be subject to 1,000 times the maximum civil penalty or criminal fine applicable under each relevant statute, in addition to being liable for actual damages (which may be doubled or trebled under some statutes). These civil penalties may, in many cases, exceed the available penalties under applicable criminal statutes and lack the procedural protections provided for defendants under criminal statutes. Further, many of these civil statutes provide for enforcement through administrative, rather than judicial, processes, meaning that the first time the provider is able to make a case before a truly independent judge is when the provider is seeking to overturn an administrative sanction that has already been imposed.[129]

In addition to the specific penalties provided for in these statutes, the government also has the hammer of exclusion to hold over a provider's head. Section 1128 of the Social Security Act[130] mandates that individuals convicted of program-related crimes, federal or state crimes relating to patient abuse or neglect, federal or state health care fraud felonies, or federal or state controlled substance–related felonies be excluded from participation in any federal health care program for not less than five years. The statute also gives permissive (i.e., discretionary) exclusion authority to the Secretary of Health and Human Services with respect to persons or entities who have taken (or failed to take) any of a laundry list of specified actions, including violating the anti-kickback statute and other "substantive behavior" statutes.[131] The statute also provides that state Medicaid agencies may impose their own exclusions, the length of which may exceed the federal exclusions.[132] Exclusion may be imposed in administrative proceedings, without the necessity of filing a lawsuit.[133]

---

[128]See the discussion in Chapter 1 (Baumann, An Introduction to Health Care Fraud and Abuse), at Section II.D.

[129]It is beyond the scope of this chapter to enumerate and discuss the specifics of the remedial statutes, but they are extensively described in the sources listed in Section I.B., above.

[130]42 U.S.C. §1320a–7.

[131]See the discussion in Chapter 1 (Baumann, An Introduction to Health Care Fraud and Abuse), at Section II.E.

[132]*See* 42 U.S.C. §1320a–7(d).

[133]Note that the practical effects of exclusion may exceed those specified in the statute. For example, many managed care agreements require that providers be participating or eligible providers under Medicare, and an exclusion may have the effect of foreclosing a provider from such private contracts as well as from federal reimbursement programs.

## 3. The Overarching Impact of the False Claims Act

Increasingly more significant than this veritable smorgasbord of available remedies is the role played by the civil FCA.[134] Originally adopted during the Civil War to combat profiteering by Union Army contractors, the FCA now imposes civil penalties ranging from $5,500 to $11,000 per claim, plus treble damages, on persons or entities who knowingly present, or cause to be presented, to the federal government any false or fraudulent claim for payment. The statute defines "knowingly" to mean that the defendant acted with actual knowledge that information was false or in deliberate ignorance or reckless disregard of the truth or falsity of information, expressly disclaiming any necessity for proof of a specific intent to defraud. Although the government may directly initiate actions under the statute, the FCA also authorizes *qui tam* suits brought by private individuals in the name and on behalf of the government. As described earlier, such suits are initially filed under seal, and the government is given an opportunity to "intervene" and take over prosecution of the action. If the government declines to do so, the *qui tam* plaintiff—the relator—may proceed with the action, subject to certain rights of the government. A relator is entitled to receive 15 to 25 percent of the ultimate recovery (whether by judgment or settlement) if the government intervenes, or 25 to 30 percent if the government declines to intervene, plus reasonable attorneys' fees and expenses incurred.[135]

The FCA has become the vehicle of overwhelming choice for health care fraud investigations, for three major reasons:

- The "per claim" sanctions under the statute quickly aggregate to enormous levels with respect to ordinary health care billing practices, because the typical bill or claim consists of numerous individual items or services, and providers typically are engaged in rendering services or providing items to numerous patients for relatively small amounts (in contrast to, for example, defense contract fraud, which may involve a handful of large claims over a long period). These per-claim penalties, plus treble damages, are mandatory if the defendant litigates the case and loses at trial or on appeal.[136]
- These penalties are potentially hugely punitive, but by proceeding under the FCA the government can avoid the higher burden of proof and other restraints on prosecutors imposed in criminal actions.

---

[134] See Chapter 3 (Salcido, The False Claims Act in Health Care Prosecutions) for detailed discussion of this topic.

[135] *See generally* THOMAS C. FOX, CAROL COLBORN LOEPERE, & JOSEPH W. METRO, HEALTH CARE FINANCIAL TRANSACTIONS MANUAL §7.8 (West rev. ed. 2007); AMERICAN HEALTH LAWYERS ASS'N, HEALTH LAW PRACTICE GUIDE §24.12 (West rev. ed. 2007); JACK E. MEYER & STEPHANIE E. ANTHONY, REDUCING HEALTH CARE FRAUD: AN ASSESSMENT OF THE IMPACT OF THE FALSE CLAIMS ACT 26–31 (New Directions for Policy for Taxpayers Against Fraud, Sept. 2001).

[136] As to the effect of per-claim penalties, see, for example, United States v. Krizek, 111 F.3d 934 (D.C. Cir. 1997), in which the court characterized the $81 million in damages sought by the government on $245,392 in actual damages as "extraordinary" and "astronomical." *Id.* at 936, 940.

- The *qui tam* provisions of the statute, in effect, deputize as bounty hunters disgruntled employees and ex-employees, disappointed business partners, unfaithful consultants, total strangers, and even the occasional "patriot" referred to by government prosecutors. *Qui tam* relators, even those who file flimsy and unsustainable complaints, both bring potential prosecutions to the government's attention and, by virtue of the sealing and intervention provisions of the statute, provide a basis for the government to begin unilateral discovery before the defendant is even served with the action.[137]

Further, because the statute does not describe in detail what makes a claim "false," both the government and the relators' bar have sought to use almost any violation of a substantive health care statute or standard of practice as a basis for alleging that a claim for payment is a false claim, even where there is no question that services were rendered or that they were medically necessary. Thus, alleged violations of the anti-kickback statute and the Stark law have been used to support allegations that claims resulting from associated patient referrals were false claims, without regard to whether the services were necessary, whether they were actually rendered, or whether the amounts billed for them were otherwise appropriate.[138] Other cases have sought to impose liability where the quality of services rendered allegedly fell so far below applicable standards as to render fraudulent the claims for payment with respect to those services.[139]

An early study found that as of the fiscal year ended September 30, 2000, government recoveries in civil fraud cases since 1986, primarily arising under the FCA, totaled nearly $7 billion, with $2.85 billion of that coming from health care–related cases. Some $4 billion of that was generated from *qui tam* cases, with $2.3 billion of that coming from health care–related cases.[140] In fiscal year 2005, the government "won or negotiated approximately $1.47 billion in judgments and settlements . . . in health care fraud cases and proceedings" and

---

[137]*See* Timothy S. Jost & Sharon L. Davies, *The Empire Strikes Back: A Critique of the Backlash Against Fraud and Abuse Enforcement,* 51 ALA. L. REV. 239, 247–48 (1999).

[138]*See, e.g.,* United States *ex rel.* Thompson v. Columbia/HCA Healthcare Corp., 938 F. Supp. 399 (S.D. Tex. 1996), *aff'd in part, vacated in part and remanded in part,* 125 F.3d 899 (5th Cir. 1997), *on remand,* 20 F. Supp. 2d 1017 (S.D. Tex. 1998); United States *ex rel.* Pogue v. American Healthcorp, Inc., 914 F. Supp. 1507 (M.D. Tenn. 1996). *See also* John T. Boese & Beth C. McClain, *Why* Thompson *Is Wrong: Misuse of the False Claims Act to Enforce the Anti-Kickback Act,* 51 ALA. L. REV. 1 (1999). As to the Stark law in the FCA context, see Robert Salcido, *The Government Unleashes the Stark Law to Enforce the False Claims Act: The Implications of the Government's Theory for the Future of False Claims Act Enforcement,* 13 HEALTH LAW. 1 (Aug. 2001).

[139]For cases illustrating these and other theories, see Pamela H. Bucy, *Growing Pains: Using the False Claims Act to Combat Health Care Fraud,* 51 ALA. L. REV. 57, 77–86 (1999); Robert Fabrikant & Glenn E. Solomon, *Application of the Federal False Claims Act to Regulatory Compliance Issues in the Health Care Industry,* 41 ALA. L. REV. 105, 124–56 (1999). See also Chapter 3 (Salcido, The False Claims Act in Health Care Prosecutions), at Section II.A.1.b.

[140]*See* MEYER & ANTHONY, REDUCING HEALTH CARE FRAUD: AN ASSESSMENT OF THE IMPACT OF THE FALSE CLAIMS ACT, at 32–35. An update of that study found that during the five-year period 1997–2001, the government had obtained $4.8 billion in civil fraud recoveries, with $3.1 billion of that related to health care fraud and $4.1 billion attributable to cases brought by *qui tam* relators. *See* JACK MEYER, FIGHTING MEDICARE FRAUD: MORE BANG FOR THE FEDERAL BUCK 6 (New Directions for Policy for Taxpayers Against Fraud Education Fund, Nov. 2003).

provided transfers of "nearly $1.55 billion" to the Medicare Trust Fund and $63.64 million in federal Medicaid recoveries to the Centers for Medicare and Medicaid Services (including some amounts relating to previous years).[141] As these figures make clear, the government's focus on health care fraud continues to intensify, and the dollar amounts involved continue to grow. Much of that focus appears from the statistics to be directed at matters originally arising as *qui tam* cases under the FCA.

### 4. The Curious Nature of Prosecutorial Discretion in Health Care Cases

Even before the substantial influx of new resources devoted to rooting out and punishing health care fraud that began in the late 1990s as a result of the Health Insurance Portability and Accountability Act of 1996 (HIPAA),[142] one commentator memorably summarized the peculiar environment created by the current health care enforcement scheme:

> The modern American medical center has the legal status of a speakeasy because lawless conduct is being ignored. Though illegal, conduct deemed harmless by enforcement authorities is being countenanced. Enforcement authorities refuse to provide legal safeguards because of their perception that such safeguards would insulate abusive as well as appropriate conduct. Prosecutorial discretion—trust us—has replaced the rule of law. Thus, innovative participants in the marketplace can follow the law and be condemned by the realities of the market, or they can participate in the health care speakeasy and hope for the best—a prospect made more risky by the potential availability of private-party (*qui tam*) actions under the [False Claims Act].[143]

Prosecutors in any field enjoy a certain level of discretion, of course. In general, government agencies, as others with prosecutorial authority, have significant flexibility to determine whether or not to pursue potential violations of law based on their assessment of the seriousness of the offense, the presence or absence of any necessary level of scienter or criminal intent, the quality of the evidence that may be offered, and any countervailing public policy considerations, among other things.[144]

---

[141]U.S. Dep't of Health & Human Servs. & U.S. Dep't of Justice, Health Care Fraud & Abuse Control Program Annual Report for FY 2005, *available at* http://www.usdoj.gov/dag/pubdoc/hcfacreport2005.pdf (Aug. 2006) [hereinafter 2005 Fraud Control Report]. The figures cited are not limited to FCA recoveries, but include criminal fines, civil money penalties, etc., under other statutes as well.

[142]Pub. L. No. 104-191, 110 Stat. 1936. HIPAA, among many other things, provided voluminous multi-year appropriations for health care fraud enforcement initiatives, as well as creating a new federal criminal offense of "health care fraud" (§242 of HIPAA, now codified as 18 U.S.C. §1347).

[143]James F. Blumstein, *The Fraud and Abuse Statute in an Evolving Health Care Marketplace: Life in the Health Care Speakeasy*, 22 Am. J.L. & Med. 205, 224–25 (1996).

[144]Indeed, it may be argued that there is an evolving institutionalization of prosecutorial consideration of countervailing public policy considerations in the health care enforcement arena. Under 42 U.S.C. §1320a–7d(b), the Office of Inspector General (OIG) of the Department of Health and Human Services (HHS) must respond to written requests for advisory opinions interpreting the anti-kickback statute in connection with particular fact situations. The OIG has posted a list of recommended preliminary questions and supplementary information to be included in such requests at http://oig.hhs.gov/fraud/docs/advisoryopinions/prequestions.htm. Included

However, the enforcement scheme that has evolved with respect to federal health care offenses has arguably taken prosecutorial discretion to new heights (or depths, depending on one's perspective):

- First, as noted earlier, any given violation of federal health care laws likely involves potential remedies under numerous statutes—ranging from civil money penalties to criminal fines, to program exclusion, to imprisonment—as well as the potential for double or treble damages.
- As also noted, many of the remedies may be obtained through administrative proceedings, without the necessity of filing a lawsuit in court.
- The civil penalties available for many violations exceed, in financial terms, the criminal penalties available, thus allowing the government to obtain punitive financial relief without dealing with the "beyond a reasonable doubt" standard of proof required for a criminal conviction.
- The threat of voluminous per-claim penalties, multiple damages, and program exclusion makes it an enormous gamble for a provider to risk going to trial even on questionable theories of prosecution.

As the government's emphasis on use of the FCA as the dominant vehicle for enforcing all manner of health care regulations has grown, there have been many allegations and much concern over the abuse of prosecutorial discretion and authority under the statute. In July 1998, the U.S. General Accounting Office (GAO) issued a report criticizing some prosecution practices under the statute and acknowledging legitimate concerns raised by providers, who, the GAO noted, were "surprised" by the "relatively recent" "widespread application [of the False Claims Act] to the health care field."[145] The report described in some detail the much-criticized "72-Hour Window Project," in which Department of Justice (DOJ) officials sent demand letters to over 3,000 hospitals, indicating that the government had determined that it was likely that the hospitals had filed false claims and that it would pursue lawsuits, fines, and even program exclusion if the hospitals did not promptly enter into a settlement for a specified amount—an approach undertaken even though the government would have ordinarily had the fiscal intermediary seek repayment of improperly billed amounts.[146] The GAO report also described the similarly criticized "Lab Unbundling Project," in which providers complained that the government's

---

in the suggested topics to be covered are various considerations relating to whether the arrangement in question may result in increased access to health care services, increased quality of services, increased patient freedom of choice among providers, increased competition among providers, increased services to medically underserved areas or populations, and decreased cost to federal health care programs. Although it is not apparent from the statute why these considerations should make an otherwise impermissible remuneration arrangement—indeed, one that violates a criminal prohibition—legal, the OIG has frequently looked at these and other factors in indicating that it would not prosecute an arrangement that, despite potentially violating the anti-kickback statute, was deemed by the OIG not to have a significant potential for program abuse.

[145]U.S. GOVERNMENT ACCOUNTING OFFICE, MEDICARE—APPLICATION OF THE FALSE CLAIMS ACT TO HOSPITAL BILLING PRACTICES, GAO/HEHS-98-195 (July 1998), at 18 [hereinafter GAO JULY 1998 REPORT].

[146]*See id.* at 6–10. *See also* Daniel R. Roach & Cori MacDonneil, *The Compliance Conundrum,* 32 J. HEALTH L. 570–72, 580–81 (Fall 1999).

"overly aggressive" demand letters ignored conflicting guidance from intermediaries and were often unsupported by accurate data.[147] The GAO report stressed that it was important that DOJ officials test the data underlying FCA allegations before threatening action, and "give providers a realistic opportunity to review and analyze the data in question before legal action against providers is either threatened or undertaken."[148]

Even before this report, some DOJ officials had apparently recognized the validity of some of the issues raised. In June 1998, Deputy Attorney General Eric Holder had advised all U.S. Attorneys and a range of other DOJ personnel on a series of steps that must be undertaken and factors that must be considered before proceeding with an FCA action, including giving providers "(i) an adequate opportunity to discuss the matter before a demand for settlement is made, and (ii) an adequate time to respond."[149] However, an August 1999 GAO report concluded that the DOJ's "process for assessing the U.S. Attorneys' Offices' compliance [with the June 1998 guidance] may be superficial."[150] This report described several circumstances in which U.S. Attorneys' offices had alleged FCA violations against hospitals based on insufficient, unverified, or incomplete data and had failed to share necessary data with the hospitals, all in violation of the June 1998 guidance. In one case, the allegations were made without evidence of false claims, but primarily on the basis that the subject hospitals were the largest Medicare billers in the state.[151] Other anecdotal reports abound of government attorneys pursuing heavy-handed threats against providers and failing to give providers information necessary to evaluate and defend the claims.[152]

Government attorneys, perhaps unsurprisingly, protest that they use the discretion and flexibility provided to them firmly but wisely.[153] It would be

---

[147]*See* GAO July 1998 Report at 10–15. *See also* Roach & MacDonneil, 32 J. Health L. at 574–75.

[148]*See* GAO July 1998 Report at 18.

[149]Memorandum from Eric H. Holder, Jr., Deputy Attorney General, to All United States Attorneys, Guidance on the Use of the False Claims Act in Civil Health Care Matters (June 3, 1998), *available at* http://www.ffhsj.com/quitam/chcm.htm.

[150]U.S. Government Accounting Office, Medicare Fraud and Abuse—DOJ's Implementation of False Claims Act Guidance in National Initiatives Varies, GAO/HEHS-99-170 (Aug. 1999), at 4 [hereinafter GAO August 1999 Report].

[151]*See id.* at 11–13.

[152]For examples, *see generally* Roach & MacDonneil, *passim. See also* Siddiqi v. United States, 98 F.3d 1427, 1440 (2d Cir. 1996) (in non-FCA health care fraud case, court was "firmly convinced . . . that the conviction would not have occurred but for the government's shifting of theories that impaired both [the defense of the case and the court's consideration on the first appeal]"). In fairness, however, the GAO later concluded that the DOJ "seems to have made substantive progress in ensuring compliance with the False Claims Act guidance." U.S. Government Accounting Office, Medicare Fraud and Abuse—DOJ Has Improved Oversight of False Claims Act Guidance, GAO-01-506 (Mar. 2001), at 11. In its fifth and final required report on the DOJ's compliance with the FCA guidance, the GAO found that the "DOJ has instituted sufficient monitoring of U.S. Attorneys' Offices participating in the national initiatives and other civil health care fraud matters to help ensure that offices use the [False Claims Act] in a fair and even-handed manner." U.S. Government Accounting Office, Medicare Fraud and Abuse—DOJ Continues to Promote Compliance with False Claims Act Guidance, GAO-02-546 (Apr. 2002), at 13.

[153]*See generally, e.g.,* D. McCarty Thornton, *"Sentinel Effect" Shows Fraud Control Effort Works,* 32 J. Health Law. 493 (Fall 1999). *See also* GAO July 1998 Report at 14 (DOJ officials and a U.S. Attorney in Texas "indicated [to the GAO] that the harsher aspects of the

wrong to suggest that government investigators or attorneys have improper motives in pursuing health care fraud, or to question that, in most cases, they proceed with professionalism and diligence. Even so, it seems indisputable that the growing use of the FCA—with its per-claim penalties and treble damages— to combat financial and nonfinancial health care fraud far beyond what most observers would have thought the statute contemplated, combined with the vast range of other remedies available to investigators and prosecutors, gives a significant advantage to the government and makes the evaluation of exposure difficult for the provider.

The provider who is notified of a government investigation or a *qui tam* suit must try to judge its potential liability and evaluate the prospects for a successful defense in light of the many statutes under which the government may elect to proceed, with their potentially voluminous penalties.[154] Further, the provider is seldom allowed to forget that the government may have available to it the option of proceeding under criminal statutes as well as pursuing civil and administrative remedies.[155] Oftentimes, the provider will not have a complete understanding of the theories under which the government is proceeding, and it may not be given access to the data on which the government is relying in determining the probable existence of a violation. In addition, where the seal of the FCA is in place, the government will likely seek to obtain, voluntarily or otherwise, extensive information from the provider while not being itself subject to discovery requests from the provider.[156] This further disadvantages the provider, which may be

---

[lab unbundling] demand letters do not reflect the reality of the process. For example, they stated that hospitals in Texas have always been granted additional time to analyze their situation if they requested it, *and the threat of legal action if hospitals failed to respond within 14 days has never been carried out.*") (emphasis added). The quality of mercy, it appears, remains unstrained.

[154]*See, e.g.,* Ohio Hosp. Ass'n v. Shalala, 978 F. Supp. 735 (N.D. Ohio 1997), *aff'd in part and rev'd in part,* 201 F.3d 418 (6th Cir. 1999). The district court noted the plaintiffs' argument that "even though they would not be found guilty under the False Claims Act, they cannot risk rejecting the [Secretary of Health and Human Services'] invitation to settle, because the damages available under the False Claims Act are so overwhelming," and stated that, despite the "heavy handed" actions of the Secretary, "the practical barriers of challenging the Secretary leave the hospitals with little choice and no bargaining room . . . ." 978 F. Supp. at 738, 742.

[155]*See, e.g., Ohio Hosp. Ass'n,* 201 F.3d at 421 ("Some of the hospitals were first apprised of the investigation [part of the Lab Unbundling Project mentioned earlier] when agents of the Federal Bureau of Investigation appeared on their premises, unannounced, and began interviewing hospital staffers. The FBI agents said that they were conducting an investigation that might lead to the imposition of civil or criminal sanctions, including imprisonment."). Anecdotally, it is common practice in some U.S. Attorneys' Offices for criminal prosecutors to sit in on meetings involving civil health care fraud claims, and it appears to be the routine practice for the government, in settling civil fraud litigation, to decline to expressly release claims under criminal statutes.

[156]*Cf.* United States *ex rel.* Costa v. Baker & Taylor, Inc., 955 F. Supp. 1188 (N.D. Cal. 1997). In ordering a non-health-care-related *qui tam* FCA case unsealed after 18 months, the court noted that "the government appears to be fully engaged in its discovery, without giving the defendants the opportunity even to answer the complaint," and further found that "[t]his practice of conducting one-sided discovery for months or years while the case is under seal was not contemplated by Congress and is not authorized by the statute." *Id.* at 1190, 1191. The *Costa* court also implicitly criticized the government's apparent use of the seal to exploit an information disequilibrium in settlement negotiations: "[The defendants] are apparently discussing the settlement of a case without knowing with certainty the allegations leveled against them. . . . [O]ne cannot help wondering whether the fact that the defendants must guess about the case filed against them is not the more significant settlement advantage [i.e., more significant than the benefit of keeping the charges confidential if the case is settled] currently enjoyed by the government." *Id.* at 1190–91.

forced to devote significant time and resources to responding to these information requests (or demands) without even being served with a complaint, much less having the opportunity to challenge its legal sufficiency.[157]

The provider's analysis and evaluation can be further complicated by the element of nonprosecutorial discretion vested in private relators under the FCA. As described earlier, the financial data indicate that a growing majority of health care fraud recoveries arise as a result of *qui tam* suits. The dissenting opinion in *Riley v. St. Luke's Episcopal Hospital*[158] eloquently describes the role of the *qui tam* relator:

> The decision to initiate the lawsuit is made by the relator, without input from the Executive [branch of the government]. The Executive has absolutely no control of the relator and therefore no way to ensure that he "takes care that the laws be faithfully executed." The relator does not have to follow [DOJ] policies, has no agency relationship with the government, has no fiduciary or other duties to it, and has no obligation whatsoever to pursue the best interests of the United States. Instead, the relator can negotiate a settlement in his own interest rather than in the public interest. While the government must be consulted in all such settlements, there is no guarantee that it will take an active interest in these cases or that the settlements reached by a relator and approved by the DOJ will be of the same sort that the government would reach on its own for the benefit of the public.
>
> Nor may the Executive [branch] freely dismiss a qui tam action. If the relator objects to the decision to dismiss, the government must notify him of the filing of the motion to dismiss, and the court must grant him a hearing before deciding whether to permit dismissal. Moreover, the Executive may not freely settle a qui tam action. If the relator objects to the government's attempt to settle, the government must obtain court approval, and the court may approve only after it holds a hearing and finds that the settlement is "fair, adequate, and reasonable under all the circumstances.
>
> The Executive may not freely restrict the relator's position in the qui tam action. . . . Nor can the Executive control the breadth of the matter litigated by the relator. . . . Finally, the Executive has no power to remove the relator from the litigation under any circumstances.[159]

---

[157] A graphic example of this is found in the long-running investigation of Apria Healthcare Group, Inc. According to Apria, it began to receive subpoenas and document requests from various U.S. Attorneys' Offices and HHS that sought various documents relating to its billing practices. In January 2001, one U.S. Attorney's Office informed Apria that the investigation conducted by that office related to its determination whether to intervene in pending *qui tam* litigation. As of July 16, 2001, Apria reportedly had not been informed of the "identity of the court or courts where the proceedings are pending, the date or dates instituted, the identity of the [relator] plaintiffs or the factual bases alleged to underlie the proceedings"; however, it was advised by government representatives and relator's counsel that Apria's potential exposure, giving effect to per-claim penalties and treble damages, could (based on an extrapolation from a 300-patient sample to Apria's total billings under government programs) range from $4.8 billion to over $9 billion. *See* Apria Healthcare Group, Inc.'s Form S-3/A, Amendment No. 1 to Form S-3 Registration Statement (Registration No. 333-62556) (filed July 16, 2001), at 31–32; *see also* Press Release, Apria Healthcare Comments on SEC Filing (July 16, 2001), *available at* http://www.prnewswire.com/cgi-bin/stories.pl?ACCT=105&STORY=/www/story/07-16-2001/0001533756. The range of liability described, it should be noted, represented a multiple of several times Apria's then-current market capitalization, and an even larger multiple of its then-current stockholders' equity. The matter was finally resolved in September 2005, with a payment of $17.6 million. *See* Apria's Quarterly Report on Form 10-Q for the quarterly period ended September 30, 2005, at Part II, Item 1, "Legal Proceedings."

[158] 252 F.3d 749 (5th Cir. 2001).

[159] *Id.* at 761–63 (Smith, J., dissenting) (citations and footnotes omitted).

As is apparent from this description, even in a case where the government intervenes, a recalcitrant relator can potentially delay the resolution of a *qui tam* case and affect the amount required to settle it. Further, available data overwhelmingly suggest that the ultimate value of a case is greatly affected by the government's intervention decision. One study noted that, "while the government has intervened in only about 22 percent of *qui tam* cases to date, recoveries in these cases represent about 95 percent of the total recoveries [in *qui tam* cases from 1986 through September 2000]."[160] In addition to the analytical problems for the provider described earlier, this suggests yet another set of highly subjective judgments that the provider must make in evaluating exposure that arises through a *qui tam* case:

- How much is the case worth if the government intervenes?
- How likely is it that the relator will, because of particular knowledge or sheer persistence, be able to drive that amount up?
- How likely is it that the government will intervene, how likely is it that the relator will proceed if the government declines, and how much is the case worth if the relator must go it alone?

Obviously, the provider's opinion with regard to these matters, as well as the others discussed earlier, will not be a constant but will evolve as the investigation progresses, stalls, or shifts direction. Frequently, the provider will not know who the relator is until fairly far along in the process, and the provider may or may not be given the actual *qui tam* complaint to review as part of its early negotiations with the government.[161] Further, the provider's first sign that an investigation is going on may not put it on notice of a pending *qui tam* suit at all. Instead, the government's investigation may take the initial form of letters from DOJ or agency lawyers requesting particular information, the appearance of agency or intermediary auditors, a suspension of payments from the intermediary, or some other more indirect approach that may not give the provider any meaningful basis to assess the potential problem or its associated exposure.

## B. Special Problems for Tax-Exempt Providers

The November 1991 issuance of General Counsel Memorandum (GCM) 39,862[162] by the Internal Revenue Service (IRS), announcing that a provider's failure to comply with governmental health care program regulatory

---

[160]Jack E. Meyer & Stephanie E. Anthony, Reducing Health Care Fraud: An Assessment of the Impact of the False Claims Act 36 (New Directions for Policy for Taxpayers Against Fraud, Sept. 2001). The data include both health care and other FCA cases. More recent data indicate that this 95% figure remained relatively constant through fiscal 2003. *See* Taxpayers Against Fraud, *Qui Tam* Statistics, *available at* http://www.taf.org/statistics. html; *see also Riley,* 252 F.3d at 767 n.37 (Smith, J., dissenting).

[161]The government may suggest that this is necessary to ensure that the relator is not the subject of retaliation, that key documents are not destroyed or altered, and the like, all of which may be true in particular cases. However, a review of unsealed *qui tam* complaints, particularly those in which the government has declined intervention, may suggest a further concern—that it is not desirable for the putative defendant to see how vulnerable the original complaint is to attack for failure to meet applicable pleading standards relating to knowledge, particularity, and so forth.

[162]General Counsel Memorandum No. 39,862, 1991 WL 776308 (Nov. 22, 1991). The holding of GCM 39,862 was reaffirmed in Rev. Rul. 97-21, 1997-1 C.B. 121.

requirements—in that case, the anti-kickback statute—would be viewed as a basis for attacking the provider's tax-exempt status, marked the emergence of a new set of problems for tax-exempt providers.[163] Now, the stakes for regulatory violations not only included potential civil and monetary penalties and exclusion from participation in governmental health care programs, but also the loss of tax-exempt status, potentially resulting in a whole cascade of additional horrors, including loss of tax-exempt status for interest paid on bonds issued to provide capital for the provider;[164] income tax liabilities; loss of tax deductions for donors; and, frequently, loss of state sales, income, franchise, and ad valorem tax exemptions that are commonly conditioned on or linked to federal tax exemption under Section 501(c)(3) of the Internal Revenue Code.

The analysis offered by the GCM was as follows:

> We believe that engaging in conduct or arrangements that violate the anti-kickback statute is inconsistent with continued exemption as a charitable hospital. No matter how economically rewarding, such activities cannot be viewed as furthering exempt purposes.... [A] section 501(c)(3) hospital is a charitable trust. All charitable trusts (and, by implication, all charitable organizations, regardless of their form) are subject to the requirement that their purposes or activities may not be illegal or contrary to public policy. See Restatement (Second) of Trusts, section 377, comment c. (1959) (a charitable trust cannot be created for a purpose which is illegal or contrary to public policy); IVA A. Scott, The Law of Trusts, section 377 (4th ed. 1989) (where a policy is articulated in a statute making certain conduct a criminal offense, a trust is illegal if its performance involves such criminal conduct or tends to encourage such conduct)....
>
> In GCM 36153, I-4036 (Jan. 21, 1975) (considering Rev. Rul. 75-384), this Office stated that "As a matter of general trust law, one of the main sources of the law of charity, it may be said that planned activities that violate laws cannot be in furtherance of a charitable purpose." Of particular relevance to the issue at hand is the finding in Rev. Rul. 75-384 that the generation of illegal acts increases the burdens of government, which is directly inconsistent with charitable ends. If, in the instant cases, the net revenue stream purchase [associated with certain joint ventures between physicians and hospitals] results in illegal remunerations, the arrangements could increase the burdens of government by creating incentives for unnecessary utilization of hospital services at government expense. See also GCM 34631, I-4111 (Oct. 4, 1971) (stating that illegal acts that make up a substantial portion of an organization's activities will disqualify it from exemption and that violations of law are not in furtherance of exempt purposes even where, for example, illegally obtained funds are used to finance a charity).[165]

The GCM indicated that the illegal activity must be "substantial" and, in noting that "the relative amount required to be considered substantial will vary

---

[163] Although states enjoy immunity from FCA liability (*see* Vermont Agency of Natural Resources v. United States *ex rel.* Stevens, 529 U.S. 765 (2000)), cities and counties are subject to such liability. Cook County v. United States *ex rel.* Chandler, 538 U.S. 119 (2003). Nonprofit corporation providers are subject to the FCA.

[164] The stakes are further raised and personalized by the 2004 amendments to Circular 230, now codified at 31 C.F.R. pt. 10, and by the position taken by the SEC in Weiss v. Securities & Exchange Comm'n, 468 F.3d 849 (D.C. Cir. 2006). *Weiss* is also discussed in Section II.B.2., above.

[165] GCM 39,862, at text accompanying nn.14–16 (footnotes omitted).

according to the character and non-exempt quality of the activity," suggested that the following might indicate that the activity engaged in by the exempt hospitals was substantial:

> [T]he arrangements at issue were (1) likely authorized by the directors and most senior managers of the hospitals involved with knowledge of the risk that they might violate the anti-kickback law, (2) central to the activities through which the hospitals accomplish their exempt purposes, and (3) potentially harmful to the charitable class the hospitals were established to serve.[166]

The IRS will not generally get into an analysis of the health care law aspects of a particular arrangement, but any activity by the DOJ related to alleged false claims or violations of the anti-kickback statute has the potential to trigger an IRS audit, and if a settlement of liability for health care law violations is undertaken, a closing agreement—an agreement between a taxpayer and the IRS that resolves a tax dispute—is usually a prudent companion. Likewise, for the not-for-profit provider, any disclosure of potential perils associated with the investigation must take into account the potential loss of tax-exempt status, even though there are no known cases of loss of tax-exempt status for bonds issued to finance a hospital.[167]

Loss of exempt status may not have direct economic implications for the provider, because most not-for-profit hospitals have relatively small margins and would owe little if any income tax. The more severe problems arise in connection with the corollaries to loss of tax-exempt status: the hospital's tax-exempt bonds will be treated as taxable industrial development bonds, and the hospital is likely to become subject to state taxes such as sales and ad valorem taxes that are imposed without regard to net income—all in all an ugly picture.

## C. The Problem Summarized

As shown by the foregoing, the provider that must meet its obligations under the securities laws in the face of a government health care investigation, particularly one stemming from a sealed *qui tam* suit, is likely to feel that it is between a very large rock and a place that is not only quite hard, but rather thorny as well. The securities laws contemplate that an issuer must, in meeting whatever disclosure duties are applicable, make judgments about materiality. In any sort of litigation, particularly that involving government regulators, that judgment may have high stakes associated with it.

However, in the garden variety circumstance, an issuer facing a litigation-related disclosure decision will have been served with a complaint (or, in gloomier circumstances, an indictment) informing the issuer of the essential claims against it and providing at least an outline of the basis of such claims, and an issuer will have available to it a forum to challenge the sufficiency of such claims at an early stage. Further, ordinary litigation complaints are publicly available documents, and the issuer (1) will be aware that information about the

---

[166]*Id.* at n.16.

[167]Mark Scott, Director, Tax Exempt Bonds, Internal Revenue Service, personal communication (Jan. 28, 2002) (quoted with permission).

complaint will be available to those interested enough to look for it or will be disclosed in the media if it is sufficiently sensational, and (2) will ordinarily not be subject to potential sanctions for discussing it.

In the health care setting, in contrast, the issuer may well not be aware that a complaint is pending for some time; may not see the contents of the complaint—much less be served with it—for even longer; may be subject to broad investigational and informational demands without specific explanation; and may be told that, notwithstanding the lack of service (and thus technical lack of jurisdiction over the issuer), a court has ordered that the issuer not disclose or discuss the action and may impose sanctions on the issuer for doing so.

Further, because the extensive remedial arsenal available to the government potentially involves financial penalties greatly in excess of actual overpayments or other damages, the issuer is hard pressed to make a quantitative calculation of its likely potential exposure. Does it assess materiality based on what it can discern of the actual potential damages involved, or must it take into account the many and duplicative penalties that may be imposed on top of those damages? Going still further, where it appears that the case involves innovative and speculative theories of liability—for example, categorizing claims as "false" because they allegedly relate in some way to violations of "behavioral" statutes (such as the anti-kickback statute) or issues of quality, even where the claims relate to necessary services actually rendered—should the issuer assume the validity of those theories or discount them?

The issuer must consider whether the materiality standard is affected by the nature of the proceeding: whether it is civil, criminal, or administrative. Much of the securities case law involves disclosure of criminal proceedings. On the other hand, many health care cases present facts that may be pursued criminally, civilly, or at the administrative agency level, at the discretion of the prosecuting or investigating agency or department. Is a criminal proceeding necessarily more or less material than a civil or administrative proceeding? What about the situation where civil monetary sanctions actually exceed potential criminal fines?

Finally, what about the potential for "death penalty" sanctions, such as program exclusion or loss of exempt status? Does the existence of a statutory vehicle for such sanctions always make the underlying proceedings material, even where it appears unlikely that they would come into play?[168]

---

[168]For example, the threat of program exclusion is potentially implicated in any serious health care violation. However, it appears not to be commonly acted on in cases involving corporate entities (other than those that are effectively alter egos of individuals who themselves become excluded). *See, e.g.,* U.S. DEP'T OF HEALTH & HUMAN SERVS., OFFICE OF INSPECTOR GEN., SEMIANNUAL REPORT TO CONGRESS, APR. 1–SEPT. 30, 2006, at 18–19, *available at* http://oig.hhs.gov/publications/docs/semiannual/2006/Semiannual%20Final%20FY%202006.pdf (during the period in question, OIG imposed exclusions on 1,885 individuals and entities, but the six specific examples described involved only individuals, and only three of those examples involved program fraud); U.S. DEP'T OF HEALTH & HUMAN SERVS., OFFICE OF INSPECTOR GEN., SEMIANNUAL REPORT TO CONGRESS, OCT. 1, 2005–MAR. 31, 2006, at 19-20, *available at* http://oig.hhs.gov/publications/docs/semiannual/2006/SemiannualSpring2006.pdf (1,540 exclusions during period; five of the six specific examples provided involved individuals, and only three of those related to program fraud); U.S. DEP'T OF HEALTH & HUMAN SERVS. & U.S. DEP'T OF JUSTICE, HEALTH CARE FRAUD & ABUSE CONTROL PROGRAM ANNUAL REPORT FOR FY 2005,

All of these considerations make the evaluation of disclosure issues in the health care environment potentially much more complicated than it is in other settings. How, then, can a health care issuer make a reasonable (and defensible) determination of what it can, should, or must do when faced with a *qui tam* suit or other nonpublic investigation?

## IV. AN APPROACH TO ANALYZING AND RESPONDING TO DISCLOSURE ISSUES IN THE HEALTH CARE SETTING

When facing the question, "Should we make a public disclosure of this potential problem?" the default answer of the securities lawyer is normally, "Yes, and sooner rather than later." From a defensive perspective, there is always some merit to that position, if for no other reason than the fact that the sooner the issuer discloses a potentially adverse contingency, the sooner the issuer cuts off the potential class period for securities fraud claims. Indeed, despite the arguments suggested by the *Matthews* line of cases, many issuers may decide for various reasons to disclose the existence of an investigation well before it is clear, as a legal matter, that such disclosure is required.[169]

However, such a course of action may not always be wise, or even particularly good disclosure practice, even where issues of the statutory seal under the FCA are not involved. In *TSC Industries,*[170] the Supreme Court noted that

> [s]ome information is of such dubious significance that insistence on its disclosure may accomplish more harm than good. The potential liability for a Rule 14a-9 [relating to proxy disclosures] violation can be great indeed, and if the standard of materiality is unnecessarily low, not only may the corporation and its management be subjected to liability for insignificant omissions or misstatements, but also management's fear of exposing itself to substantial liability may cause it simply to bury the shareholders in an avalanche of trivial information—a result that is hardly conducive to informed decisionmaking.[171]

Perhaps it is rare that information concerning a government investigation is fairly characterized as "trivial" for a health care issuer, but there is still reason to be concerned that premature, ill-informed disclosure of such an event is inconsistent with the issuer's duty to its stockholders or bondholders. Any

---

*available at* http://www.usdoj.gov/dag/pubdoc/hcfacreport2005.pdf (Aug. 2006) (3,804 individuals and entities excluded in fiscal 2005, of which only 1,034 were excluded for program fraud or program-related crimes; the four specific examples provided were all individuals). In recent years, the government has entered into many seven-, eight-, and nine-figure settlements with entities without excluding those entities. Although those cases are, of course, settlements and not judgments, so that lack of exclusion is part of the negotiation, (1) most large health care fraud cases do settle, (2) the likelihood of a settlement involving an exclusion of a large entity is, in most cases, remote, because there would be no incentive for the entity to settle, and thus (3) the likelihood of exclusion's actually being an issue is arguably remote as well, except as it affects the dollar value of the settlement.

[169] As noted in Section II.A.1.a., above, for example, a fair number of issuers seem to have opted for such early disclosure in the 2006–2007 wave of stock option backdating matters.

[170] TSC Indus. v. Northway, Inc., 426 U.S. 438 (1976).

[171] *Id.* at 448–49. This statement was quoted with approval by the Supreme Court in *Basic,* which, as already noted, extended the *TSC Industries* materiality standard beyond the proxy context to Section 10(b) and Rule 10b-5. *See* Basic, Inc. v. Levinson, 485 U.S. 224, 231 (1988).

disclosure of a government investigation, particularly one implicating the exorbitant penalties available in the health care context, is likely to cause the issuer's stock price to drop, perhaps precipitously, and may cause rating agency downgrades or other adverse events affecting the issuer's bondholders.[172] Where the issuer lacks sufficient information to adequately assess and disclose the materiality of its potential exposure, disclosing a worst-case scenario (or simply indicating that the results, although potentially awful, cannot be estimated) may not provide meaningful information—conducive to making informed investment decisions—to the market, and may work an extreme, and perhaps unjustified, disservice on those who hold the issuer's stock or bonds at the time the announcement is made.[173]

In the context of a sealed *qui tam* case, of course, the issuer's situation is rendered more complex, not only by its probable lack of specific information about the details and strength of the case against it, or even the particular claims asserted, but also by the asserted requirement that it not make any disclosure while the case remains under seal. It may be questioned whether a court has the power to enforce the seal over an issuer who has not been served with a complaint, but the practical reality of the situation is that an issuer who may one day have to appear before that court to defend against the claims will not lightly make disclosure in the face of the seal. In that situation, even if the issuer believes that prompt disclosure of the matter is required or prudent, the issuer will likely conclude that it must make some effort to get relief from the seal, delaying its disclosure until that effort is resolved.

Further, although it has frequently been noted that the fact that disclosure may cause various kinds of adverse results to the issuer does not obviate the duty to make such disclosure (if such duty exists in the particular circumstance),[174] an issuer must remain sensitive to the degree to which the timing and nature of the disclosure may compromise legitimate corporate interests. An issuer that has concluded that it has a duty to disclose information concerning an investigation or suit will not want to make that disclosure in such a way that

---

[172]A rating agency downgrade will typically cause the yield demanded by bond purchasers in the secondary market to increase, thereby lowering the trading price of the bonds to the detriment of existing bondholders seeking to sell the bonds (as well as of bondholders such as insurance companies who are relying on the value of the bonds to meet statutory capital requirements, for example). Further, a downgrade may cause bondholders who are subject to limitations on the credit quality of bonds in their portfolios—for example, pension funds subject to "legal investment" limitations or mutual funds whose investment policies limit them to holding bonds with a particular minimum rating—to dump their holdings quickly into the market, thus further increasing the downward pressure on the secondary market price of the bonds in question.

[173]"Unjustified" in the sense that, if the matter were ultimately resolved without liability or with immaterial liability—a result that may be quite likely if, after investigation, the government declines to intervene in a *qui tam* suit, for example—the holders who sold their securities in the aftermath of the announcement may have incurred significant but unnecessary losses.

[174]*See, e.g.,* Roeder v. Alpha Indus., 814 F.2d 22, 25 (1st Cir. 1987) ("The securities laws do not operate under the assumption that material information need not be disclosed if management has reason to suppress it."); *In re* Par Pharm., Inc. Sec. Litig., 733 F. Supp. 668, 675 (S.D.N.Y. 1990) ("The illegality of corporate behavior is not a justification for withholding information that the corporation is otherwise obligated to disclose."); Ballan v. Wilfred Am. Educ. Corp., 720 F. Supp. 241, 249 (E.D.N.Y. 1989) ("The fact that a defendant's act may be a crime does not justify its concealment.").

its ability to defend the claim or negotiate a settlement limiting its exposure is jeopardized. That concern, perhaps, has even more immediacy in the context of a typical health care investigation, where the issuer may still lack crucial information concerning the facts and allegations of the case at the time it initially makes its disclosure.

With these considerations in mind, then, the following sections suggest an approach to analyzing disclosure duties and structuring disclosure in the health care investigation/*qui tam* litigation context, recognizing that there is no strategy that is either suitable for all situations or perfectly defensible in the cold eye of hindsight.

## A. Determining When to Disclose

### 1. What Does the Issuer Know About the Existence and Procedural Context of the Investigation or Proceeding (and How Did It Come By That Knowledge)?

Other than plaintiffs' securities litigators, whose capacity to argue from hindsight is without peer, virtually no one would argue that an issuer has a duty to disclose mere suspicions that a government agency or department is conducting an investigation or considering initiating litigation (or intervening in *qui tam* litigation of which the issuer has not been notified).[175] Health care providers in today's environment are continually subject to requests for information, records reviews, and audits by agency and government contractor personnel. Sometimes these activities are routine, sometimes they relate to investigations of others doing business or having relationships with the provider (such as pharmaceutical or equipment vendors, physicians on the provider's medical staff, and so on), sometimes they relate to generalized investigations of industry practices,[176] and sometimes they relate to inquiries or investigations concerning the provider itself. At an early stage, it may not be easy to discern which of these situations—or even some other circumstance—obtains.[177]

Even if the provider believes that audit or review activities or unusual requests for information relate to an investigation of (or potential action against) itself, in most circumstances, disclosure at this stage would be unwise.

---

[175] *See, e.g., Ballan,* 720 F. Supp. at 248 ("[The issuer] was not obligated to disclose information of which it had no knowledge or about which it could only speculate. Indeed, it would be misleading for it to do so.") (citation omitted).

[176] In that context, however, a provider/issuer in an industry where such an industry-wide investigation has become public knowledge should evaluate its position in light of the SEC's rather sweeping pronouncements in the Defense Contractors Release and the more recent announcement of its "wildcatting" enforcement initiatives, both of which are discussed in Section II.A.1.a., above.

[177] *See* Patric Hooper, *Challenges to Warrantless Searches in the Healthcare Industry,* 13 HEALTH LAW. 8, 11 (Oct. 2000) ("Seemingly, every Medicare and Medicaid reviewer, surveyor or inspector is in the fraud-busting business these days. Thus, when a [California] State Medi-Cal auditor knocks at the door of a provider, the provider cannot be certain whether the result of a 'search' will be an educational audit of the provider's billing practices, or will ultimately be the provider's imprisonment as a member of 'organized crime,' as defined by the State Legislature [under what is essentially a state criminal false claims statute relating to the California Medicaid program].").

In general, the provider is unlikely to have enough information to make such disclosure meaningful, and there are many things at this stage that could still derail or dissipate an investigation. Instead, the provider and its investors are probably best served if the provider reasonably cooperates with the (assumedly) investigatory activities and seeks to obtain further information about the specific matters at issue.

What if the provider receives a more pointed request for information (but not a demand letter, as in the 72-Hour Window Project) from, for example, an Office of Inspector General (OIG) or DOJ attorney (whether from Washington or from a local U.S. Attorney's Office)? This situation clearly requires more thought. Particularly if the request comes from the DOJ, there is a greater likelihood that a *qui tam* case is involved. However, at this stage the provider may still lack enough information to say with confidence what is at issue, much less what its materiality is. These sorts of requests may still relate to investigatory activities that are directed at persons other than the provider,[178] and they may not be focused specifically enough to allow the provider even to make a good guess at what the underlying questions are. For example, a simple, unexplained request for patient records may alert the provider that something is going on, but it will not provide much clarity as to what that something may be. In that context, it is difficult to determine what meaningful disclosure would be, much less whether there is a material issue that might require such disclosure. Similarly, the request may relate to a practice or policy that the provider feels comfortable complies with applicable laws and regulations, and the provider may be comfortable that its response will be adequate to defuse whatever the situation is. In that case, the provider may likewise be comfortable that it need not consider disclosure of the inquiry, because it may feel comfortable that its ultimate disposition will not be material.

The situation ratchets up still further if the provider receives a subpoena or civil investigative demand. The government may sometimes use such techniques, rather than voluntary requests for information, to obtain information from the provider with respect to third parties under investigation, but their use tends to suggest that it is more likely that the provider itself is a subject or a target. Although it is not uncommon for a provider/issuer to decide to make some disclosure when it receives such formal process, even a subpoena may not give the provider meaningful notice as to what is at issue or what its exposure might be. At this point, the provider may well decide that it is appropriate to defer disclosure until it takes other steps—negotiating a suspension of enforcement of the subpoena in exchange for more limited voluntary production of information, seeking to obtain more information from the issuing authority as to what its objectives and interests are, or initiating an internal investigation (if it has not already done so) to attempt to determine whether it has problems and the scope of its potential liability. The provider may also, of course, seek to challenge the validity of the subpoena, but that may entail actions that would involve a greater need for early disclosure. Where formal process is received, the provider will want to carefully analyze its particular disclosure situation,

---

[178]For example, the DOJ may be seeking information on industry practices in order to evaluate claims asserted in a *qui tam* suit against another provider.

and may want to get guidance from independent outside counsel if it has not already done so.

In any of these situations, where the provider has not been notified of or directly threatened with litigation (or an administrative proceeding), the timing of potential disclosure may be significantly affected by external and practical considerations. If, for example, the provider's initial notice of an investigation comes by way of a dawn raid by federal agents on the provider's facilities or business offices, there is a good chance that this will be picked up by the media or other external observers. In such a case, the provider will almost indisputably need to make some sort of disclosure—probably by a press release with an accompanying 8-K filing—even where it has no clear idea of what it is suspected of or what the consequences may be. Less dramatically, if the provider has chosen to cooperate with a request for information or respond to a subpoena and carrying out that plan requires informing many nonmanagement employees, outside vendors, consultants, etc., of the investigation or inquiry, the provider may determine that it is advisable to make a public disclosure in order to avoid the risk of unmanageable leaks, potential insider trading, or similar problems. Thus, even in a "pre-threat" situation, the provider must take into account all relevant factors in determining whether disclosure is advisable, even when it is not necessarily required by law.

The provider's decision (as to both disclosure and timing) becomes more complicated when it is actually threatened with litigation by the government (as in the 72-Hour Window Project demand letter scenario), and perhaps most complicated when it is notified that the government is evaluating intervention in a *qui tam* case that remains under seal. As noted earlier,[179] it may be argued that neither of those things necessarily constitutes a proceeding "known to be contemplated by governmental authorities" required to be disclosed under Item 103 of Regulation S-K or a known event or uncertainty required to be discussed under Item 303, but to the extent those items are applicable (because the actual initiation of litigation or intervention in a *qui tam* case probably still requires certain approvals that may not have been obtained at the time the provider is notified), this argument becomes an increasingly fine one to make and defend. Further, if the matter is under seal, the provider has to determine how it will reconcile the obligation of confidentiality sought to be imposed on it by the seal with any obligation of disclosure that it may conclude the securities laws impose. The decision to disclose at this stage is still not automatic, especially where the seal is in place. However, when faced with a direct threat of this nature, the provider/issuer must probably rely primarily on its evaluation of the materiality of the potential action and its determination whether it has an affirmative duty to disclose information concerning it, rather than simply assuming that it will someday be able to rest on an argument that, at this stage, it had still not been "charged" with misconduct.[180]

---

[179] See Section II.A.1.a., above.

[180] The questions of materiality and duty, of course, are relevant at any of the earlier points in the process discussed in this section. However, at those earlier points, it will normally be much easier to take and defend the position that the situation is too speculative to require disclosure than it will be when the provider has an actual demand letter or notice of a pending *qui tam* suit in hand.

## 2. *What Does the Issuer Know About the Materiality of the Investigation or Proceeding?*

At this point, the provider/issuer will want to review the information available to it to determine what it can, in good faith, conclude about the materiality of the investigation or action. Any unfriendly interest by the government in a provider's business dealings has the potential to be material, but that conclusion is not a foregone one, and several factors may influence the position that the provider should ultimately take.

### a. *What Is the Nature of the Claims at Issue?*

Because the scope of health care matters that are now addressed through the adversarial process (as opposed to being addressed through audits, reviews, and refunds, as was once the case) has grown so expansively, even cases superficially characterized as fraud encompass a wide range of scenarios, some of which are intuitively more likely to be seen as material. Where a provider is accused of violating the anti-kickback statute over a long period of time, potentially involving a substantial volume of services rendered as a result of referrals sought to be characterized as illegal, that may clearly be material. On the other hand, where the provider is alleged to have committed a violation in an isolated historical circumstance—improperly accounting for capital costs in a particular cost reporting period, for example—the materiality of that claim may be less clear. More colloquially, if the provider can resolve the claim simply by "paying the ticket" for a specific violation, as opposed to having to defend against a pattern and practice of violations (and, perhaps, substantially change its method of operations going forward), the provider may be able to reach a justified conclusion that the matter is not material, at least if the "ticket" is not too punitive.

More broadly, a case that involves classic fraud—kickbacks, billing for services not rendered, blatant upcoding, and the like—will most likely be viewed as material, even where the dollars involved are relatively small.[181] On the other hand, a case that involves alleged noncompliance with highly technical, frequently ambiguous requirements (such as, for example, the circumstances involved in the Lab Unbundling Project cases) may be less likely to be perceived at an early stage as material, even if the case seeks to describe such noncompliance as fraud.

Further, following the significant consolidation of the health care industry in the early to mid-1990s and the associated boomlet in divestitures beginning in the late 1990s, it has become increasingly common for the alleged violations at issue in a particular case to have occurred under the previous ownership and management of a predecessor or acquired entity, sometimes several transac-

---

[181]*But see* Karl A. Groskaufmanis, Matt T. Morley, & Michael J. Rivera, *To Tell or Not to Tell: Reassessing Disclosure of Uncharged Misconduct,* 1 33RD ANNUAL INSTITUTE ON SECURITIES REGULATION (Practising Law Institute 2001) (republished from INSIGHTS, June 1999), at 469–70 (internal pages 13–14) (suggesting that earlier SEC statements and dicta in *Roeder v. Alpha Indus.,* 814 F.2d 22 (1st Cir. 1987), and other cases involving the "qualitative materiality" concept "lack[] vitality today"). *Cf.* Greenfield v. Professional Care, Inc., 677 F. Supp. 110 (E.D.N.Y. 1987), discussed in Section II.A.4.a., above.

tions removed from the entity from which the government now seeks relief. Ignoring for a moment the potential financial exposure, an acquiror/issuer may determine that such a claim is not material because it is an inherited problem that is neither a reflection of the competence and integrity of current management nor related to business practices engaged in by the acquiror today.[182]

### b. Does the Issuer Have Good Defenses (and Will That Be Apparent to the Government at an Early Stage)?

Perhaps so obvious as to be overlooked, one factor in the materiality analysis is whether the issuer has a strong position that it has no liability. In some cases, the claims are just wrong—they involve an incorrect understanding of the facts, for example, or a failure to understand the applicable regulations and program policies. DOJ attorneys usually depend on information from agency or contractor personnel or on relators for their initial understanding of a case, and sometimes that information is erroneous or incomplete.[183] Where such a circumstance is apparent to the issuer, it may determine that the allegations in the case are not material.

That determination, of course, is dependent on the issuer's belief that it will be able to make the relevant facts and law known to the government early on and persuade the government of its error. The issuer may not itself have enough information to pursue that course of action at an early stage, depending on how clearly the claims have been articulated to it. Further, the issuer may not be able to persuade the government investigators or attorneys to listen to its arguments and explanations in a particularly prompt fashion. Where the issuer believes that it will prevail on the merits but may not be able to do so until the proceeding progresses well down the line, the issuer may not so readily conclude that the fact of the investigation or proceeding is not material. Similarly, if the issuer determines that it really does have a problem, this prong of the materiality analysis does not help it justify delaying or avoiding disclosure. However, the issuer should always consider whether it might, in fact, be innocent of wrongdoing and take that factor into account in determining if, when, and how to make disclosure.

### c. What Is the Potential Financial Exposure?

Many factors may go into materiality analysis, but the bottom line, in both the literal and figurative senses, is normally the expected financial impact of

---

[182] Somewhat paradoxically, however, early disclosure may be more attractive in this sort of situation. The acquiror may want to get the allegations out in the open quickly, to avoid any claim that it failed to meet its disclosure obligations, while making the argument that the problem is irrelevant to the market because it relates to acts or omissions by another entity at another time.

[183] One of the authors has personal knowledge of an investigation that was halted when the government attorney realized that the intermediary personnel who had concluded that a statutory violation had occurred had done so because they read the wrong column on a spreadsheet. *See also* U.S. Government Accounting Office, Medicare Fraud and Abuse—DOJ's Implementation of False Claims Act Guidance in National Initiatives Varies, GAO/HEHS-99-170 (Aug. 1999), at 11–13, also discussed in Section III.A.4., above [hereinafter GAO August 1999 Report] (outlining various circumstances where U.S. Attorneys' Offices had initiated Lab Unbundling Project investigations based on data later acknowledged to be flawed). It may not happen often, but it does happen.

an investigation, prosecution, or civil or administrative proceeding on the provider/issuer. If the matter will be resolved with a one-time payment that is relatively insignificant to the issuer's financial position, the issuer's conclusion that the matter was not material will probably not be successfully challenged later. If that payment is large, or if it has an ongoing impact on the issuer's financial position and results (as, for example, where the issuer will have to substantially restructure its business operations or relationships or lose significant government program reimbursement), the matter is more likely to be material.[184]

The touchstone of this analysis, of course, is the probability/magnitude balancing test articulated in *Texas Gulf Sulphur*[185] and adopted by the Supreme Court in *Basic*.[186] However, that balancing test is particularly difficult in the health care setting. The "magnitude" factor is, at least at first blush, greatly enhanced by the punitive remedies available to the government under the FCA and other statutes applicable to health care providers, as described earlier. The "probability" factor is similarly enhanced, because, simply put, health care fraud cases settle; the risk involved in litigation is too great.[187]

In fact, however, the materiality calculus may not be this simplistic. Despite the ominous specter of treble damages, which may be raised early in FCA proceedings, the government still must establish that the provider knowingly submitted a false claim, and many proceedings settle for a simple refund of overpayments.[188] Further, while the huge numbers tossed around in FCA allegations relate in large part to the arithmetic impact of per-claim penalties,[189] it appears that per-claim penalties are of significance primarily in adding

---

[184]*See, e.g.,* Roeder v. Alpha Indus., 814 F.2d 22, 26 (1st Cir. 1987) (passage quoted in Section II.A.4.a., above); Greenfield v. Professional Care, Inc., 677 F. Supp. 110, 113 (E.D.N.Y. 1987) (passage quoted in Section II.A.4.a., above).

[185]Securities & Exchange Comm'n v. Texas Gulf Sulphur Co., 401 F.2d 833 (2d Cir. 1968).

[186]Basic, Inc. v. Levinson, 485 U.S. 224 (1988).

[187]*See, e.g.,* AMERICAN HEALTH LAWYERS ASS'N, FRAUD AND ABUSE: DO CURRENT LAWS PROTECT THE PUBLIC INTEREST? A REPORT ON THE 1999 PUBLIC INTEREST COLLOQUIUM HELD JANUARY 29–30, 1999, WASHINGTON, D.C., 33–34 (1999) [hereinafter COLLOQUIUM REPORT] (colloquium participant noted that "[t]he current system [of enforcement through the FCA] almost forces the providers to settle . . . disputes rather than contest the government's demands" and stated that "the providers can't afford to defend themselves when the potential damages are that high").

[188]*See, e.g.,* U.S. GOVERNMENT ACCOUNTING OFFICE, MEDICARE—APPLICATION OF THE FALSE CLAIMS ACT TO HOSPITAL BILLING PRACTICES, GAO/HEHS-98-195 (July 1998), at 9 (of 3,000 hospitals that received demand letters in 72-Hour Window Project by April 1998, 2,400 had settled, of which 1,700 paid no damages but simply refunded overpayments); COLLOQUIUM REPORT at 19 (government panelist stated that the average settlement in 72-Hour Window Project cases was $25,000 and noted that the average FCA case settled for "a very modest amount of money"). *See also* GAO AUGUST 1999 Report at 13 (despite U.S. Attorney's Office allegations of false claims against three dozen hospitals in Lab Unbundling Project, office had subsequently concluded that one-fourth of the hospitals should not be pursued for FCA violations; in another U.S. Attorney's Office, over 40% of Lab Unbundling Project settlements involved only recovery of overpayments, despite GAO's conclusion that this office had stronger evidence than others it reviewed).

[189]*See, e.g.,* COLLOQUIUM REPORT at 34 (example demonstrating that a provider who submits 2,000 claims for $50 each can be liable for $20 million in per-claim penalties, although its maximum exposure on treble damages would be only $300,000). Note that the $20 million would be $22 million under current law.

pressure to settle and are not significant in the amount of settlements actually obtained.[190]

The conservative disclosure position, obviously, would be to take into account the maximum possible exposure in evaluating the magnitude component of the materiality calculation. However, the probability that the provider will be exposed to the maximum statutory liability will probably be quite small in most cases. Further, the issuer/provider may well be concerned that disclosing a maximum liability figure that, as a practical matter, may bear little relationship to the actual settlement value of the case may itself be misleading to investors, who may lack sufficient knowledge to evaluate what such an exorbitant number actually means. This may make the issuer's balancing test more of a balancing act, but the issuer may be justified, in the course of its materiality analysis, in at least attempting to estimate what its practically probable exposure is—in view of the nature of the claims at issue, the actual damages being asserted, its assessment of its own culpability, and the degree to which it is cooperating with the government—rather than simply considering statutory penalties that may not bear a meaningful relationship to the actual value of the case.

### d. Is the Proceeding Civil or Criminal?

Whether a proceeding is civil or criminal in nature would seem to be very relevant in determining the materiality of that proceeding, especially in view of the mandatory program exclusion that accompanies a criminal health care fraud conviction. Intuitively, it would also seem that most observers would likely consider a criminal action to be almost by definition more serious than a civil or administrative proceeding.

However, this distinction may not have much practical significance in many health care cases. As previously described, the statutory enforcement scheme provides a variety of means by which the same alleged offense can be pursued under both criminal and civil statutes, and the financial penalties associated with liability under the civil statutes can be as punitive as, or even more punitive than, fines under the criminal statutes. Further, because the government's burden of proof in civil or administrative proceedings is less demanding than it is in criminal actions (and the procedural protections for defendants are likewise lower in civil or administrative proceedings), the government may well elect to proceed under a civil statute even where it could also pursue criminal charges.[191] It also seems intuitively likely that the government may believe that a provider would be more likely to feel that it had to litigate criminal charges, and thus may believe that both the likelihood of an early settlement and the value

---

[190] *See, e.g.,* GAO July 1998 Report, at 10 (of 2,400 hospitals that had then settled 72-Hour Window Project cases, none had been assessed per-claim penalties). *See also* United States v. Krizek, 111 F.3d 934, 938–40 (D.C. Cir. 1997) (extensively analyzing government's position as to what constitutes a "claim" and remanding the case for recalculation of civil penalty from "astronomical" $81 million on actual damages of $245,392).

[191] *See, e.g.,* Robert Salcido, *The Government Unleashes the Stark Law to Enforce the False Claims Act: The Implications of the Government's Theory for the Future of False Claims Act Enforcement,* 13 Health Law. 1, 5–6 (Aug. 2001) (suggesting that the government was moving toward a strategy of pursuing FCA cases based on alleged violations of the Stark law, even where the anti-kickback statute would also apply, because the anti-kickback statute is a criminal statute).

of a settlement would be increased in a civil proceeding. Thus, although the civil/criminal distinction should not be ignored in analyzing materiality, it seems unlikely to be determinative in most health care cases.

### e. Is the Proceeding a Qui Tam *Suit at the Pre-Intervention Stage?*

Where, as increasingly seems the common case, the investigation relates to a *qui tam* suit in which the government is evaluating its position on intervention, the issuer has still further refinements to add to its materiality analysis. As discussed earlier, the government intervenes in a fairly small proportion of *qui tam* suits, and the ultimate judgment or settlement amount in a suit that the government declines is likely to be much lower than it would have been had the government intervened.[192]

Of course, in many cases where the government has declined intervention, the provider may have no notice of the case until it is unsealed and served, if it is served at all. In cases where the provider does have such notice, however, it may be able to form a judgment about the likelihood of intervention that will help it more appropriately estimate its potential exposure. If the government appears to be aggressively pursuing the investigation—scheduling meetings with the provider, submitting extensive information requests, seeking employee interviews, and so forth—the provider may be well advised to assume that the government is likely to intervene and to evaluate the case accordingly. On the other hand, if the government's inquiries are perfunctory, or if the provider is able to articulate its defenses early on and the government seems responsive to them, the provider may feel that it has a basis to discount the value of the case for materiality purposes.

In any event, the provider may believe that it cannot reasonably evaluate materiality if it has not been given the actual complaint or at least been given the specifics of the claims against it, a common situation at an early stage in a *qui tam*–related investigation. Thus, even without regard to the FCA seal, the provider may determine that it can, in good faith, defer disclosure until it has enough information to make such disclosure in an intelligent and informed manner.[193] The seal, of course, adds more difficulty to the issue, a difficulty that is discussed later.[194]

### f. Is the Issuer Pursuing a Settlement Strategy
      *or Litigating Aggressively?*

As it evaluates its position with regard to an investigation or *qui tam* suit, a provider/issuer must determine whether it intends to seek an expeditious set-

---

[192]See Section III.A.4., above.

[193]In *Basic,* the Supreme Court noted that "[w]here . . . [a corporate] event is contingent or speculative in nature, it is difficult to ascertain whether the 'reasonable investor' would have considered the omitted information significant at the time." Basic, Inc. v. Levinson, 485 U.S. 224, 232 (1988). At least at the early stage of the intervention decision, there is an argument to be made that the nature of the action and its potential consequences are contingent and speculative. *See also In re* Par Pharm., Inc. Sec. Litig., 733 F. Supp. 668, 678 (S.D.N.Y. 1990) (issuer "not obligated to speculate as to the myriad of consequences, ranging from minor setbacks to complete ruin, that might have befallen [it]" if bribery scheme were discovered).

[194]See Section IV.B.1., below.

tlement of the matter or to pursue a strategy of noncooperation, vigorous defense, and, possibly, counterattack. While the choice of strategy may not seem to have an impact on the materiality of the matter, it does seem to present at least two relevant considerations.

First, to the extent the issuer is relying on an attempt to quantify "real" financial exposure, as discussed earlier, a strategy that is aimed at an effort to respond cooperatively and settle the case may lower that exposure. As noted earlier, a settlement is unlikely to involve per-claim penalties and may involve lower (or no) damage multipliers, depending on the facts of the case and the degree to which the provider is able to successfully argue its defenses in the settlement negotiations. Further, if the case is a criminal matter, the federal sentencing guidelines provide for lower multipliers in a case where the defendant cooperates with the government and acknowledges culpability at an early stage.[195] If the provider intends to withhold cooperation and aggressively fight the matter until close to trial (or even until trial), it runs a greater risk of increased exposure.

Moreover, although not directly related to the concept of materiality, a provider that does not cooperate with the investigation and is not disposed to engage in meaningful early settlement talks is more likely to reach a procedural posture where nondisclosure is impracticable. If the provider is going to fight, it will eventually have to do so in some judicial or administrative forum, in which the allegations are likely to emerge publicly. At that point, the provider will be subject to retrospective attack for not disclosing the matter at an earlier date. Thus, unless a provider is deeply convinced that it can both fight and win, its decision to pursue an aggressive, confrontational strategy may suggest that it should look for an opportunity to make early disclosure of the allegations.

### g. What Is the Likely Market Reaction?

SAB 99[196] includes the issuer's perception of the likely market reaction to a disclosure (in the financial statement context) as one of the factors that may indicate materiality. If, as some predict, SAB 99 principles are expanded beyond the financial statement context, the issuer will need to take that into account in nonfinancial disclosures as well.

This is not a particularly helpful standard, however. In today's information-addicted market, where analysts' estimates and stock prices chase each other downward like lemmings on any adverse news, quantitatively predicting the market's reaction to a disclosure can be a highly speculative exercise. Further, the nature of the current health care enforcement environment means that news of an investigation or *qui tam* suit, in and of itself, may be a relative nonevent if the issuer is in a position to disclose enough information about it to satisfy the market that its outcome will not be disastrous. Although it is an unfortunate commentary in various ways, news that a health care provider is *not*

---

[195] *See* U.S. Sentencing Comm'n, Guidelines Manual (Nov. 2006) §§3E1.1, 8C2.5(g).

[196] SEC Staff Accounting Bulletin No. 99—Materiality (Aug. 12, 1999), *available at* http://www.sec.gov/interps/account/sab99.htm (discussed in Section II.A.4.b., above).

under some sort of investigation has developed a "man bites dog" sort of newsworthiness; news that it *is* under investigation now borders on the routine.

The standard is also unlikely to help in the context of a nonprofit organization: Given the linkage between program violations and tax-exempt status, the threat to tax-exempt status of a nonprofit organization's bond debt has to be factored into the analysis, and the tax-exempt market takes no prisoners when the subject of tax exemption comes up. The bonds immediately become "illiquid," and the "bid and ask" spread widens dramatically.

Thus, the "market reaction" analysis is, in reality, probably just a distillation of factors of the type described in the preceding paragraphs. If an issuer believes that those factors can be incorporated into a disclosure, if and when one is made, in such a way as to persuade others that the information was not material (or at least was not susceptible of a materiality determination) at any earlier date, the issuer can probably also reach a defensible conclusion that the anticipated market reaction at such earlier date would not have indicated materiality.

### 3. Does the Issuer Have a Duty of Disclosure?

It is, as noted previously, important to remember that even where information is material, there can be no liability for failure to disclose the information unless there is a duty to disclose it. An issuer may defer disclosure until such a duty arises even if the information is quite material indeed. Thus, in determining the timing of a disclosure, the issuer should first consider the circumstances that may require disclosure to be made in the particular circumstance (bearing in mind always that the issuer always—subject to the FCA seal, if applicable—retains the option to disclose information at an earlier time than is required if the issuer determines that to be a prudent or advantageous course of action).

#### a. Is There a Specific Requirement of Disclosure Under the 1933 Act or the 1934 Act?

The requirements for disclosure under various 1933 and 1934 Act forms are discussed at considerable length earlier[197] and are not usefully rehashed at this point. Again, the fundamental question is whether applicable Items of Regulation S-K require disclosure in the 1933 Act registration statement or 1934 Act report at issue, and that question is essentially resolved by the materiality determination made by the issuer under the analysis outlined in the preceding subsections.[198]

---

[197]See Sections II.A.1.–2., above.

[198]The discussion herein relates to the issuer's duty of disclosure. However, it is at least worth noting one case that suggested the possibility of liability for a corporate officer for failing to make an individual disclosure concerning misconduct in which he personally was involved. In *In re Ramp Corp. Securities Litigation*, No. 05 CIV.6521(DLC), 2006 WL 2037913 (S.D.N.Y. July 21, 2006), the court denied a motion to dismiss by defendant Andrew Brown, who had served as chairman and chief executive officer of the issuer, a troubled health care technology company that had, among other things, engaged in violations of the 1933 Act. Shortly after joining the issuer in October 2003 as its president, Brown received a "cash gift" from an advisor to certain

### b. Is Disclosure Necessary to Ensure That Other Statements by the Issuer Are Not Misleading?

Absent a specific duty to disclose information, the issuer may simply remain silent, no matter how material the information in question may be.[199] However, if the issuer undertakes to speak on an issue, it must provide enough information to cause the statements made not to be misleading in any material respect.[200] Thus, where an issuer that is the subject of an investigation or a *qui tam* suit makes affirmative statements concerning things relevant to the subject matter, the issuer may well be found to have undertaken a duty to disclose the existence of the investigation or the action, or at least to disclose the risk that it may have committed illegal acts.[201] It is even possible that such a duty may be

---

investors in the company. Brown did not inform the company's board of directors of this gift (which the court characterized as a bribe) until May 2005. In declining to dismiss the complaint as to Brown, the court noted that the company's 2004 10-K had included as an exhibit the company's code of ethics, which would have required disclosure of the bribe to the board. Brown, as chief executive officer of the company, signed a certification pursuant to Section 302 of the Sarbanes-Oxley Act of 2002 that certified that the 10-K did not contain any untrue statement of a material fact. The court found that the plaintiffs had sufficiently alleged that this certification "implied that [Brown] had complied with the terms of [the issuer's] code of ethics and thus was a misstatement of fact." *See id.* at *12–13. Thus, the *Ramp* court apparently found a positive disclosure obligation that was personal to the certifying officer, even though it is not clear that the issuer itself would have been required to disclose the bribe, both since the issuer was not aware of it prior to Brown's May 2005 disclosure and because it does not appear that the issuer made any statements that were rendered misleading by the nondisclosure of the bribe (the court's opinion did not address the issuer's liability, perhaps because the issuer was bankrupt and essentially defunct by the time of the opinion).

[199] *See* Basic, Inc. v. Levinson, 485 U.S. 224, 239 n.17 (1988) (quoted in Section II.A.4.a., above).

[200] *See, e.g., In re* Par Pharm., Inc. Sec. Litig., 733 F. Supp. 668, 675 (S.D.N.Y. 1990) ("Under [Rule 10b-5], even though no duty to make a statement on a particular matter has arisen, once corporate officers undertake to make statements, they are obligated to speak truthfully and to make such additional disclosures as are necessary to avoid rendering the statements made misleading [citing Securities & Exchange Comm'n v. Texas Gulf Sulphur Co., 401 F.2d 833, 860–62 (2d Cir. 1968)]."); *In re* Cirrus Logic Sec. Litig., 946 F. Supp. 1446, 1467 (N.D. Cal. 1996) ("If a company chooses to speak to the market on a subject, . . . it is obligated to make a full and fair disclosure to ensure that its statements are not materially misleading."); Helwig v. Vencor, Inc., 251 F.3d 540, 561 (6th Cir. 2001) ("With regard to future events, uncertain figures, and other so-called soft information, a company may choose silence or speech elaborated by the factual basis as then known—but it may not choose half-truths.").

[201] *See, e.g., Par Pharmaceutical*, 733 F. Supp. at 675–78 (describing numerous affirmative statements by issuer suggesting that its success in obtaining FDA approvals was due to its special expertise and finding jury question as to whether such statements were misleading because they did not disclose bribery scheme); Ballan v. Wilfred Am. Educ. Corp., 720 F. Supp. 241, 249–50 (E.D.N.Y. 1989) (where issuer "issued reports suggesting that its prosperity would continue . . . [it] was then obliged to reveal any 'facts' suggesting otherwise so as to make the matters disclosed not materially misleading"); *In re* MobileMedia Sec. Litig., 28 F. Supp. 2d 901, 932–33 (D.N.J. 1998) (where prospectus contained "affirmative representations which falsely assured investors [that issuer] was in compliance with applicable law . . . [t]he fact that [issuer] could face serious legal consequences as a result of . . . alleged violations is information a reasonable investor would find important," and thus failure to disclose violations could be a basis for liability). *Cf.* Roeder v. Alpha Indus., 814 F.2d 22, 26–28 (1st Cir. 1987) (upholding dismissal of securities fraud claim where complaint did not allege existence of misleading reports or statements, even though issuer did not disclose material information concerning alleged violations of law); Gallagher v. Abbott Labs., 269 F.3d 806, 810–11 (7th Cir. 2001) (upholding dismissal where plaintiffs could not successfully identify any statements that were untrue or materially misleading when made, even though defendant subsequently settled claim of regulatory violations for $100 million fine).

found where the person speaking on behalf of the issuer was not aware of the underlying facts.[202] Thus, in evaluating the duty to disclose, an issuer should take into account earlier affirmative statements concerning its compliance with laws, projections concerning its future financial performance, and so forth. It is not necessary for an issuer "to direct conclusory accusations at itself or to characterize its behavior in a pejorative manner," even if it is aware of alleged violations of law.[203] However, where the possibility of such violations is brought to its attention by an investigation, the issuer must be cautious about affirmative statements that would be made false or misleading if such violations were borne out by the investigation.

It should be noted that a real danger in this area arises if the issuer engages in reviewing and commenting on analysts' reports before their release. That practice has, presumably, diminished somewhat after Regulation FD, but it remains commonplace, and many issuers, particularly smaller ones seeking to obtain and retain analyst coverage, feel that they must engage in some level of review. The practice poses many perils for issuers, and a full description of those perils is beyond the scope of this chapter.[204] However, where an issuer goes beyond correcting inaccurate historical information in draft analysts' reports and comments on those analysts' projections, the issuer's ability to keep silent on matters known to it that may affect those projections—such as the impact of pending government investigations that may affect the issuer's future financial position—can be compromised.[205]

### c. What About Rumors?

Given the pattern of health care enforcement activity in recent years, it is common for health care issuers to be the subject of rumors concerning pending investigations, and this presents a delicate situation for an issuer. Unless the rumors are somehow attributable to the issuer, an issuer "has no duty to correct or verify rumors in the marketplace."[206] Thus, an issuer that maintains a strict policy against commenting on rumors can, absent some independent duty of disclosure, stand mute in the face of rumors, including those relating to investigations and enforcement activity. However, an issuer that chooses to speak must provide disclosure that is complete and accurate.[207] Further, an issuer that has—intentionally or unintentionally—made a materially inaccurate statement

---

[202] *See, e.g., In re* Carnation Co., Exchange Act Release No. 22,214, 33 SEC Docket 1025 (July 8, 1985) (Rule 10b-5 violation where corporate spokesman erroneously represented that no merger negotiations were under way, even though spokesman was personally unaware of such negotiations).

[203] *Ballan*, 720 F. Supp. at 249.

[204] A pre-FD overview of some of those dangers may be found at William W. Horton & F. Hampton McFadden, Jr., *Disclosure Obligations of the Newly Public Healthcare Company: Practical Strategies for the Company and Its Counsel*, 32 J. HEALTH L. 1, 20–24 (1999).

[205] *See* Elkind v. Liggett & Myers, Inc., 635 F.2d 156, 163–64 (2d Cir. 1980) ("A company which undertakes to correct errors in reports presented to it for review may find itself forced to choose between raising no objection to a statement which, because it is contradicted by internal information, may be misleading and making that statement public at a time when corporate interest would best be served by confidentiality.").

[206] State Teachers Retirement Bd. v. Fluor Corp., 654 F.2d 843, 850 (2d Cir. 1981).

[207] *See, e.g.,* Roeder v. Alpha Indus., 814 F.2d 22, 26 (1st Cir. 1987).

has a duty to correct such statement for so long as the earlier statement remains "live"—i.e., for so long as it is reasonable for investors to rely on it.[208] Thus, if the issuer goes down a path of commenting on rumors, the issuer must be prepared to make full, nonmisleading disclosure, and an issuer that has adopted a practice of denying unfounded rumors of investigations may, when the rumors arise in the face of actual, known investigations, find that it has undertaken a duty of disclosure that it might not otherwise have.[209]

## B. Determining How and What to Disclose

### 1. How Does the Issuer Deal with a False Claims Act Seal?

Where the problem at hand is an issuer's perceived obligation to disclose a matter that is the subject of a *qui tam* suit that remains under seal, the question the issuer must confront is how to reconcile the disclosure obligation with the obligations of the seal.[210] One option, of course, is to conclude that the securities laws trump the FCA and simply disclose the existence of the suit, notwithstanding the seal. While this may be a defensible position, it is unlikely to be the way to win friends and influence judges in the *qui tam* case.

A more palatable alternative may be to file a motion in the *qui tam* suit to unseal the case. Although this involves delay in making the disclosure, it would seem to demonstrate good faith on the issuer's part, and such delay may not cause harm if the issuer is careful not to make statements or take actions that would arguably require affirmative disclosure while the motion is pending. However, the government may oppose such a motion if it believes that lifting the seal would impair its ability to investigate and prosecute the action, and it is possible that the relator may oppose it as well if the relator is, as relators usually are, averse to having his or her identity made public.[211] If this course of action is pursued, it will almost certainly be desirable to give the government advance notice of the motion, in the hope of reaching a negotiated resolution of any conflicts before the court rules on the motion.

Still another alternative is to disclose key facts underlying the investigation, and perhaps even the issuer's belief that an investigation is pending,

---

[208] *See* Linda C. Quinn & Ottilie L. Jarmel, *Disclosing Bad News: An Overview for Securities Counsel*, in COUNSELING CLIENTS IN TURBULENT MARKETS & UNCERTAIN TIMES: DISCLOSURE & FINANCING ISSUES 7 (Practising Law Institute 2001), at 18–19 (internal pages 6–7); Meredith B. Cross, Denise Manning-Cabrol, & Deborah M. Wiggin, *Overview of Disclosure Obligations of Public Companies: Mandatory Disclosure, Voluntary Disclosure and Duties of Officers and Directors*, in THE ART OF COUNSELING DIRECTORS, OFFICERS & INSIDERS: HOW, WHEN & WHAT TO DISCLOSE 7, 16–17 (internal pages 8–9) (Practising Law Institute 1998).

[209] *See* Basic, Inc. v. Levinson, 485 U.S. 224, 239 n.17 (1988) (quoted in Section II.A.4.a., above).

[210] Note that there is precedent approving, in some contexts, an issuer's failure to make disclosure at a particular time because of a legal or contractual requirement of confidentiality. *See, e.g., Fluor Corp.*, 654 F.2d at 850 (lack of disclosure represented "a good faith effort to comply with the [contractual] publicity embargo"). However, that line of reasoning presumably only applies where the issuer is not making other statements that are misleading in the absence of the omitted disclosure. *See id.* at 853.

[211] This latter problem could presumably be mitigated by a partial unsealing of the case, in which the relator's identity remains confidential.

without disclosing the existence of the specific *qui tam* suit. This is certainly consistent with the many cases discussed in this chapter that hold that, while an issuer may not be required to disclose the fact of a government investigation, the issuer may be required to disclose facts relating to its potential violations of law that are the subject of the investigation. However, making that sort of disclosure meaningful is, to say the least, challenging.

Something along the lines of "We believe that our [contracts with physicians/cost reporting practices/coding practices] comply with applicable law, but we could be wrong, which could expose us to all manner of problems" is good, traditionally defensive securities lawyer language, but will undoubtedly be attacked as vague and inadequate by plaintiffs' lawyers if there is an adverse market impact when and if the case actually becomes public. "Our [contracts with physicians/cost reporting practices/coding practices] violate numerous federal regulations" falls within the category of self-accusatory disclosures characterized as " 'silly' and 'unworkable' " by the court in *Ballan*,[212] at least until such violations have been charged and proved. "We understand that our [contracts with physicians/cost reporting practices/coding practices] are under investigation for possible violations of law, and we expect to vigorously defend against such allegations" requires some context if it is to be meaningful disclosure (for example, what is the potential financial impact of the allegations? What is the scope of the claims?), and providing such context may arguably violate the seal, compromise the ability to defend the claims, or both.

In practice, where there has been no public disclosure of a suit or investigation, most issuers will probably rely on a general description of key regulatory factors applicable to their business, a description of the range of penalties available for violation of those factors, and an identification, where appropriate, of business practices that may involve particular exposure in light of those factors (reliance on joint ventures, for example), at least until they have concluded that they have enough information to make an informed materiality judgment and provide meaningful specifics to investors. Where an issuer has determined that the time is ripe to disclose a specific matter, but it is unable or unwilling to have the case unsealed, the issuer is probably well advised to disclose the existence of the investigation and as much as possible about the nature of the claims and exposure, while disclosing as little as practicable about the specifics of the sealed action itself.

## 2. By What Means Should the Issuer Make Disclosure?

Under Regulation FD, an issuer that determines to disclose material information must do so in a way reasonably calculated to lead to broad public dissemination of the information. If the issuer is a reporting company and circumstances do not require the disclosure of a suit or investigation to be made earlier than the next Form 10-K filing, 10-K disclosure provides an opportunity to put the information in the context of the issuer's total business. From a

---

[212]Ballan v. Wilfred Am. Educ. Corp., 720 F. Supp. 241, 249 (E.D.N.Y. 1989) (quoting Amalgamated Clothing & Textile Workers v. J. P. Stevens & Co., 475 F. Supp. 328, 332 (S.D.N.Y. 1979), *vacated as moot,* 638 F.2d 7 (2d Cir. 1980)).

practical standpoint, while there is no dispute that 10-K disclosure constitutes broad public dissemination, the reality of the matter is that it may take awhile for the information to be picked up by the market (particularly if, like most issuers, the issuer is a calendar-year reporting company and thus files its 10-K at the same time as the rest of the issuer world is also filing 10-Ks). This may give the issuer an opportunity (*after* the information is publicly available in the 10-K) to focus its analysts' attention on the information in a way that helps ensure that the issuer's side of the story is fully understood (always being careful not to provide material information that is not included in the 10-K disclosure, however).

Frequently, however, the luxury of waiting for the 10-K may not be available to the issuer. Where events dictate that disclosure must be made sooner rather than later (including, of course, the circumstance where the issuer has determined that it need not disclose the information until the case is unsealed, which time has now come), the issuer will need to resort to more immediate means of disclosure. This will typically take the form of a press release, which will frequently be accompanied by a simultaneous 8-K filing with the same information.[213] Where an issuer's press releases are not reliably picked up by the national press and wire services, as is frequently the case with small issuers, the issuer must probably file an 8-K to ensure that its obligations under Regulation FD are satisfied.[214]

If the event precipitating disclosure is an offering of securities by the issuer, the issuer will need to make disclosure in its 1933 Act prospectus, either in the text itself or by incorporation by reference from an 8-K or other 1934 Act report. Where the issuer makes disclosure in full in the prospectus, it is probably prudent for it also to put out a press release (or file an 8-K) in order to avoid any risk of a contention that a disclosure in a 1933 Act form (which will presumably be most actively perused by prospective purchasers in the offering) does not provide appropriately broad dissemination to the general market.

It has become increasingly common practice for corporate issuers to hold conference calls with analysts to discuss and provide additional flavor on material corporate developments shortly after they are announced through a press release or other public disclosure.[215] Conference calls can provide an issuer with the opportunity to amplify points made in its press release, ensure a uniform response to questions (as opposed to having many spokespersons answering many individual phone calls), and otherwise put a more expansive spin on its disclosure. However, where the disclosure in question relates to a government investigation or suit, an issuer is probably wiser to put as much detail as it believes appropriate

---

[213]Note that stock exchange and NASDAQ rules typically require that disclosure be made by press release, and after the adoption of Regulation FD, the New York Stock Exchange stated its position that disclosure by other means contemplated by Regulation FD, including the filing of an 8-K, did not satisfy the Exchange's requirements. *See* Quinn & Jarmel at 49–50 (internal pages 37–38).

[214]*See* Final Rule: Selective Disclosure and Insider Trading, Securities Act Release No. 33-7881, 65 Fed. Reg. 51,716 (Aug. 24, 2000), at text accompanying nn.73–74, *available at* http://www.sec.gov/rules/final/33-7881.htm.

[215]Since the adoption of Regulation FD, these conference calls are overwhelmingly open to the public, via publication of a call-in number or, more commonly, via webcast.

in its press release or 8-K and eschew the temptation to have a conference call. The risk that management personnel will convey information that may compromise the defense of the case or employ a tone that will be unhelpful for subsequent settlement discussions in a conference call is just too great. If the issuer does elect to have a call, it should under all circumstances assume that the government's representatives will be on the call, and the issuer's management personnel who are on the call should conduct themselves accordingly.

As usual, the tax-exempt municipal issuer is forced to rely on common sense, tradition, and analogy to the corporate disclosure regime in determining how to proceed with disclosure. Because Regulation FD is based on powers of the SEC under Section 15 of the 1934 Act, the regulation does not apply to municipal issuers, who are exempt from those provisions. Likewise, municipal issuers are not required to file Forms 10-K, 10-Q, and 8-K. As a result, there is no regulation (other than the omnipresent Rule 10b-5) that guides the decision to disclose, the content of the disclosure, or the method of dissemination for municipal issuers. Even so, there are some obvious points for such issuers to bear in mind. First, anything said should be accurate and should not be misleading through the omission of other information. Information that is reasonably expected to reach investors and trading markets is subject to the antifraud provisions, and the antifraud provisions are equally applicable to disclosures in the secondary market for municipal securities.[216]

Second, because the absence of equity trading makes analyst coverage unlikely for not-for-profit issuers, dissemination of information may be a real challenge. Use of the nationally recognized municipal securities information repositories mandated by Rule 15c2-12 for filing of annual reports and information concerning 11 specified "material events" is not likely to produce sufficient dispersion of information, but this method should probably be used because it is a mandated way for broad dissemination of information and can be used as a defense to any claim of selective disclosure.[217] Likewise, even though Regulation FD does not apply to municipal securities, a press release sent to financial wire services and to *The Bond Buyer* (a municipal industry periodical) is a prudent course.

Third, the issuer should probably inform certain key players contemporaneously with the release of information. These include nationally recognized statistical rating organizations that maintain ratings on the issuer's municipal securities, relevant credit and liquidity providers, and remarketing agents and investment banks that are active in the secondary market for the issuer's securities. Rating agencies and credit and liquidity providers can generally be pro-

---

[216]*See* Statement of the Commission Regarding Disclosure Obligations of Municipal Securities Issuers and Others, Securities Act Release No. 7049, 1994 WL 73628 (Mar. 9, 1994), at text accompanying nn.85–90. The 1994 Interpretive Release is also discussed in Section II.B.1., above.

[217]*See* Letter from Investment Company Institute to Martha Mahan Haines, Director, Office of Municipal Securities, U.S. Securities & Exchange Comm'n (Nov. 12, 2001), *available at* http://www.ici.org/statements/cmltr/01_sec_muni_disclose_com.html (noting, among other things, that the repository system is "inefficient and ineffective" and that it "does not meet the needs of municipal securities investors"). *See also* Mary Chris Jaklevic, *Toward Full Disclosure,* MODERN HEALTHCARE (Feb. 19, 2001), at 50–54.

vided information in advance of the actual public release on a confidential basis, but it is difficult to imagine an issuer becoming comfortable with providing such information to remarketing agents or trading desks until it is publicly available.

Finally, given the cross-linkage between health care program violations and tax-exempt status, special consideration should be given to making disclosure to the IRS, taking into account both whether to provide the information and whether to begin the process of seeking a closing agreement. Obviously, seeking a closing agreement presumes that the issuer does not expect the underlying health care claims simply to disappear.

### 3. What Should the Disclosure Actually Say?

Having made the determination that disclosure is required or advisable and that it is most appropriately made by a particular means, the issuer must, of course, actually write the disclosure. The issuer should consider the text of the disclosure well before the last minute, as the language used may affect both the issuer's defense of the case and the market's perception of the risk to the issuer's fortunes. Indeed, it has been suggested that the issuer prepare a press release very early in the process in order to ensure that it is not caught flatfooted if information concerning the investigation leaks out before the issuer has planned to make disclosure.[218]

Fraud is, as they say, an ugly word. Despite the government's recent predilection to characterize any violation of a health care regulation or standard as a fraudulent or false claim, the issuer does not have to accept and use that characterization. Many FCA cases, as discussed earlier, are based on alleged violations of highly technical and ambiguous laws, regulations, and policies. The issuer may be well served by pointing this out in its disclosure and by describing the nature of the claims in some detail. Where possible, it may be desirable to describe the specific statutes involved: "The government has alleged that we have committed technical violations of the regulations requiring that [insert specifics], and that, as a result, we have received overpayments from the Medicare program"—assuming that this is an accurate characterization—is certainly less inflammatory than "The government has alleged that we have defrauded the Medicare program." While it is important that the disclosure not be misleading, the issuer should not ignore the "MEGO factor"[219] associated with descriptions of complex and technical regulations.

The issuer should also disclose whatever mitigating facts it can point to without compromising its defense. The issuer should certainly state that it has cooperated and is continuing to cooperate with the government's investigation, if that is the case. If the issuer has conducted an internal investigation that contradicts the allegations, it may wish to say so, or it may wish at least to state that it

---

[218] *See* Karl A. Groskaufmanis, Matt T. Morley, & Michael J. Rivera, *To Tell or Not to Tell: Reassessing Disclosure of Uncharged Misconduct,* 1 33RD ANNUAL INSTITUTE ON SECURITIES REGULATION, at 467 (internal page 11) (Practising Law Institute 2001) (republished from INSIGHTS, June 1999).

[219] "MEGO" stands for "my eyes glaze over"—a not uncommon reaction in the lay reader who encounters a description of the rules governing bundled versus unbundled laboratory claims, for example.

has an internal investigation in process if that is true. If the allegations relate to acts or omissions by a previous owner or by prior management, the issuer will almost undoubtedly want to point that out. Where the government has declined to intervene in a *qui tam* case that the relator continues to pursue, the issuer will certainly want to make it clear that the government has declined the case. In the circumstance where the investigation relates purely to isolated historical circumstances, to a discontinued line of business, or to any other situation that suggests that the impact on future operations (beyond the expense of the judgment or settlement) will be slight or nonexistent, that is helpful information. Specific quantitative information on the potential exposure is, of course, helpful if it can be provided without harming the issuer's settlement position.

In that regard, if the claims involve the potential for per-claim penalties or multiplied damages, that possibility should be noted. However, it will normally be preferable to try to quantify the alleged single-damage exposure, if that is possible, and then indicate the additional liability that may be imposed if things go badly. This will give the disclosure recipient a more objective basis to assess the probable risk associated with the litigation than simply tossing out exorbitant worst-case scenarios without appropriate context.

Finally, although the principal concern of this chapter is disclosure issues that arise before a case is resolved, the issuer must also be prepared for the disclosure it will make when the case is settled, as it most likely will be. If the case is of any significance, the government will put out its own press release, which will normally describe the alleged violations in quite pejorative terms. It will be critical for the issuer to get its own side of the story out at the same time as the government's press release, if not earlier. The government will not typically allow the issuer to review its release, but it may be possible to try to negotiate the inclusion of some language regarding cooperation with the investigation and to get the government to agree to provide the issuer with a copy of its release simultaneously with its distribution. The issuer's release should focus on any mitigating factors that are available regarding future impact of the settlement and should attempt to provide as objective a view as possible of the nature of the claims that were settled in order to counteract the more inflammatory descriptions that will likely be in the government's release.

Tax-exempt issuers face slightly different considerations if resolution of the matter also involves the Internal Revenue Service. The IRS is generally prohibited by Internal Revenue Code Section 6110[220] from disclosing taxpayer information. However, the content of the taxpayer press release may be negotiated as a part of a closing agreement, and closing agreements frequently include a provision waiving the protections of Section 6110 if the taxpayer issues a press release that substantially (in the eyes of the IRS) mischaracterizes the settlement or the alleged violations.[221]

---

[220]26 U.S.C. §6110.

[221]A related sort of issue may arise in announcements relating to the settlement of an SEC enforcement investigation, as illustrated by the SEC's 2004 settlement of an enforcement action against Lucent Technologies. In that case, the SEC imposed a $25 million penalty on Lucent for lack of cooperation with the SEC's investigation. As one of the indicia of noncooperation, the SEC pointed to an interview given by Lucent's chief executive officer and its outside counsel

## C. Protecting the Disclosure Decision

Pat Dye, at the time head football coach of Auburn University, once noted that "Hindsight is 50/50."[222] As is apparent from the above discussion, the issuer's determination as to if, when, and how to disclose information concerning a government investigation is a matter of subjective judgment, usually based on imperfect and evolving knowledge of the situation, and that determination may be subject to attack by the SEC or the plaintiffs' bar after the fact. The issuer must, accordingly, consider how it can best prepare to defend its decision in the face of such an examination based on hindsight.[223]

First, it is critical that the issuer carefully control who in its organization is permitted to speak to analysts, investors, and the press and ensure that those persons are aware of the issuer's policies concerning disclosure, including when to say "no comment" and how to avoid running afoul of Regulation FD. Given the delicate assessments required in determining when and how to disclose matters relating to government investigations, it is critical that the issuer not be forced into premature disclosure by careless, inadvertent, or ill-informed remarks. Similarly, the issuer's investor relations and press relations personnel should be cautioned to report to those persons responsible for the issuer's securities disclosures any information they receive—such as reports of rumors from analysts, questions from the press about a potential investigation, and so forth—suggesting that information about the investigation is making its way into the public. The issuer will need to determine whether this information is a result of leaks originating in some way with the issuer, and it will also want to be prepared to respond in the event that the press or an analyst produces an unexpected report on the matter.

The issuer will also want to ensure that its regular periodic disclosures and other public statements do not contain information that would require disclosure of the investigation (or the facts underlying it) in order to make such disclosures not misleading. Counsel knowledgeable about the investigation should carefully review in advance the issuer's public statements concerning its compliance with laws and any business practices or relationships involved in the investigation in order to avoid the *Par Pharmaceutical*-type situation,

---

after Lucent had agreed in principle to settle the matter without admitting or denying liability. In that interview, according to the SEC, outside counsel "characterized Lucent's fraudulent booking of [a $125 million 'software pool agreement'] between Lucent and another company as a 'failure of communication'[,] thus denying that an accounting fraud had occurred." The SEC determined that this statement "undermined both the spirit and letter of its agreement in principle with the [SEC Enforcement] staff." *See* SEC Press Release 2004-67, *Lucent Settles SEC Enforcement Action Charging the Company with $1.1 Billion Accounting Fraud* (May 17, 2004), *available at* http://www.sec.gov/news/press/2004-67.htm.

[222]*See* Kevin Scarbinsky, *Kickoff's Comin' and We're Feelin' All Right*, BIRMINGHAM NEWS, July 28, 2000.

[223]It has been pointed out that such judgments in hindsight may frequently be based on an adverse market reaction after disclosure is ultimately made, without regard to whether that reaction was foreseeable based on information available at the time in question. *See* Groskaufmanis, Morley, & Rivera, at 465–67 (internal pages 9–11). Pages 463–70 (internal pages 7–14) of that article contain an excellent summary of practical considerations involved in the disclosure of uncharged misconduct, to which the analysis in this subsection is much indebted.

where glowing statements about business success directly implicate the alleged violations under investigation.[224]

As described earlier, in many cases an issuer's decision to defer disclosure relating to an investigation will be based on its then-current assessment that the matter is not material, or that it lacks sufficient information to make the materiality determination—in other words, that the possibility of a materially adverse outcome is, at the time, speculative or contingent.[225] That assessment is, by its nature, subject to change as information concerning the progress and direction of the investigation becomes available to the issuer. While remaining sensitive to issues of privilege and the potential for subsequent discoverability, the issuer should also consider establishing a paper trail concerning these assessments, or at least the facts underlying them (such as internal studies concerning the potential exposure, review of the claims at issue, and so forth). Such a paper trail may help demonstrate that, even if the failure to make disclosure at a particular time proves in hindsight to have been a poor decision, the issuer did not have the scienter necessary to support a 10b-5 claim.

In that regard, the issuer should consider periodically consulting with experienced, independent outside counsel, perhaps both securities counsel and (if different) regulatory and defense counsel advising the issuer on the matter.[226] (In that circumstance, it is of course essential that securities counsel be informed of the investigation and any facts the issuer knows that are relevant to it.) This consultation will be particularly important if the issuer is undertaking an offering of its securities in the face of an undisclosed investigation, because it will need to determine whether it has a prospectus disclosure obligation that might not otherwise arise until a future periodic report is due. While outside counsel may not be as familiar as internal counsel with either the intricacies of the regulatory structure applicable to the particular issuer or the details of the specifically relevant facts, the judgment of outside counsel with respect to both the disclosure issues and the exposure risk in the underlying matter may be perceived as less likely to be influenced by personal concerns (personal financial impact, status and security within the organization, and so on).

When it becomes aware of the investigation, the issuer will generally need to undertake some sort of internal investigation or review in order to determine both its potential realistic exposure and its defense strategy. Virtually as a

---

[224] *See In re* Par Pharm., Inc. Sec. Litig., 733 F. Supp. 668 (S.D.N.Y. 1990). See Section II.A.1.a., above.

[225] *See* Basic, Inc. v. Levinson, 485 U.S. 224, 232 (1988).

[226] In that regard, however, the issuer should be cautious about requesting written opinions from counsel, and counsel should be cautious in rendering them. Although counsel, as a matter both of professional responsibility and of enlightened self-interest, will want to give comprehensive advice concerning the legal risks involved in both the investigation or litigation itself and the disclosure issues, the issuer may find itself in an uncomfortable corner if it has received a written opinion from counsel—perhaps based on a premature or incomplete understanding of the facts—directing the issuer toward a course of action that, in the event, it does not pursue. On the other hand, carefully structured dialogues between outside counsel and the issuer's senior management team may help to establish the absence of requisite "scienter" where there is a substantial effort to determine the nature of the information available and whether the information is material.

matter of course, the issuer will want to have such investigation conducted under the direction of outside counsel and to have communications concerning it channeled through outside counsel, in order to obtain the protection of the attorney-client privilege to the greatest extent possible.[227] Such an investigation will, as it progresses, provide the issuer with a greater ability to assess the materiality of the situation, and those among the issuer's personnel responsible for fulfilling its securities disclosure obligations should stay informed of material developments and findings in the investigation in order to ensure that disclosure decisions are continually reevaluated as appropriate.

Finally, the issuer will want to consider whether it needs to impose additional limitations on trading by its officers and directors. As discussed earlier, a corporate insider trading for his own account may have a disclosure obligation that is separate and distinct, at least as a matter of timing, from the issuer's disclosure obligations. In order to avoid the risk of liability for its insiders and to avoid the risk of being forced into a premature corporate disclosure, the issuer may find it desirable to limit the market activity of those persons who are knowledgeable about the investigation (and, as well, those persons who might be presumed by their positions to be knowledgeable about it).

## V. BRIEF THOUGHTS ON INVESTIGATION-RELATED DISCLOSURE ISSUES IN OTHER CONTEXTS

The primary concern of this chapter is the analysis and handling of disclosure issues relating to government investigations and FCA suits as they affect providers who have publicly traded securities and are thus subject to ongoing disclosure obligations under the federal securities laws. However, these same issues present themselves in other contexts where disclosure may be legally or contractually required, even though the provider does not have publicly traded securities. A discussion of common-law fraud and other principles that may be applicable in such situations is beyond the scope of this chapter, but it is perhaps worthwhile to briefly outline some of those situations and some thoughts on addressing them.

### A. Venture Capital/Private Equity Transactions

After a torrid but ultimately disappointing fling with the Internet, there is some indication that the venture capital community is once again turning a bit toward the familiar but still enticing charms of health care. Venture capital or private equity investments are typically structured as acquisitions of convertible preferred stock by the venture investors pursuant to exemptions from registration under the securities laws. Those investments are commonly made

---

[227]It should, however, be noted in passing that it has become increasingly unlikely that the issuer will be able to rely on the privilege to prevent disclosure of the results of any such internal investigation, because waiver of the privilege may be seen as necessary as part of the organization's strategy to cooperate with the government in its investigation. *See generally, e.g.,* William W. Horton, *A Transactional Lawyer's Perspective on the Attorney-Client Privilege: A Jeremiad for* Upjohn, 61 BUS. LAW. 95–133 (2005), and sources cited therein.

without a formal offering document containing prospectus-like disclosure.[228] Instead, the venture investors will rely on representations and warranties given by the issuer in a stock purchase agreement, including representations and warranties concerning the absence of pending or threatened litigation and the issuer's compliance with applicable laws and regulations.[229]

Notwithstanding the lack of an offering document like those used in 1933 Act registrations or public bond offerings by exempt issuers, a venture capital investment is a securities transaction, and the issuer is subject to potential liability under Section 10(b) and Rule 10b-5, as well as to liability under common-law fraud and breach of contract theories. Thus, a provider issuing securities in a private equity transaction is subject to the same types of exposure that are discussed earlier in this chapter if the provider's disclosures in connection with the transaction are inaccurate or misleading. Thus, the provider/issuer will want to apply the same general type of analysis.

There is, however, an important difference in the venture capital setting. Where an issuer has publicly traded securities in the marketplace, the issuer must be concerned about the potential impact on the market value of its securities of the failure to make a required disclosure and of the making of a disclosure that is inaccurate or misleading. As noted previously, the issuer is potentially exposed to liability if it discloses too little, too late, as well as to liability (or at least to unfairly harsh results for its investors) if its disclosures overestimate the adverse effects of an investigation or suit. For a venture-stage issuer, however, there is no public trading market for its securities, and the issuer will not have a duty to make broad public disclosure, perhaps in the face of time pressure arising from rumors or impending press or analyst reports. Instead, the issuer will have an opportunity to present its side of the story to a presumably sophisticated audience, normally under the protection of a confidentiality agreement from the prospective investors. Thus, subject to any concerns relating to an FCA seal, a venture-stage company will probably be best served by making full and early disclosure to prospective venture investors.

## B. Loan Agreements

Banks and other institutions that lend to health care providers have become increasingly knowledgeable about, and sensitive to, the risks associated with the current health care enforcement environment. Accordingly, it is common for loan agreements with health care providers to contain representations and warranties concerning compliance with government program regulations, absence of pending or threatened litigation, and so forth. Thus, a provider under investigation is confronted with difficult disclosure decisions in that context, as

---

[228] In some cases, the venture-stage company may utilize a private placement memorandum similar to a 1933 Act prospectus, but most venture investments are made by sophisticated investors pursuant to exemptions that do not require specific formal disclosure documents.

[229] Of course, counsel also must consider the likely requirement of an opinion confirming the absence of pending or threatened claims, and the possibility that the opinion itself may become the occasion for litigation. *See, e.g.,* Dean Foods Company v. Pappashanai, 18 Mass. L. Rptr. 598 (Mass. Super. Ct. Dec. 3, 2004). For an interesting discussion of the case, see Robert Wolin, *Government Investigations and Legal Opinion Liability,* Health Law. (Aug. 2006) at 18.

well as in the securities law contexts discussed earlier. However, unlike the securities law context, there are no specific regulations governing the form and context of such disclosure, and the provider may be less worried about the prospect of a lawsuit over nondisclosure than it is about a default under the loan agreement, potentially resulting in the acceleration of indebtedness and an inability to obtain further credit. The problem is exacerbated where the provider/borrower also has publicly traded securities, because it would normally be regarded as undesirable for the issuer's loan documents to disclose material information not also disclosed in a publicly available source.[230]

The first step in managing the risks inherent in this situation is for the borrower to carefully negotiate credit agreement representations, ensuring that appropriate qualifications regarding knowledge and materiality are included. Although the concepts of materiality that have been articulated in the securities law context may or may not be persuasive in the credit agreement context, limiting the required disclosures to material matters should allow the borrower some flexibility to defend against an argument that it has breached its credit agreement representations. Similarly, where possible, the borrower should seek to limit the representations to pending actions or actions in which it has received some sort of formal process, although the lender may not be receptive to this concession.

If the borrower does not have publicly traded securities, it may well want to raise the issue at an early stage (giving due attention to a seal, if one is present). As in the venture capital situation described earlier, the borrower can sit down with its lender and attempt to explain why the problem is not as large as it may appear and why it is still a good credit risk. Even if the lender is not entirely pacified, the borrower may be able to negotiate some leeway, such as a limitation of the lender's ability to declare a default so long as the proceedings are civil in nature or the liability exposure does not exceed a certain dollar threshold or involve an exclusion.

Where the borrower has some other disclosure obligation, under the securities laws or otherwise, and has not previously disclosed the issue to its lender, it will want to disclose the information to the lender simultaneously with its public disclosure and promptly seek to ameliorate any concerns that the lender has. In that context, it should be remembered that there is an important difference between stockholders and lenders. Stockholders who have allegedly been harmed by an issuer's failure to make appropriate disclosure essentially have nothing to lose by participating in a securities fraud class action. They have already lost their money when the stock price dropped; given that a class action suit allows them a shot at getting some of it back at no additional out-of-pocket expense, most stockholders will be delighted to join in. Lenders, on the other hand, have significant incentives to try to work with the borrower to salvage the situation. No lender is enthusiastic about having a defaulted loan or a bankrupt borrower. Lenders will act aggressively to limit their exposure to a credit that has

---

[230]Indeed, given the increasingly blurry lines between commercial banks and investment banks with brokerage and money management arms, selective disclosure of material information to a bank could, in the absence of an appropriate confidentiality agreement, involve a violation of Regulation FD.

suddenly turned bad, but they typically realize that their most desirable outcome will result from working out a solution with the borrower that allows for an orderly restructuring of the debt, if that is necessary. Thus, the borrower that is confronted with the need to make an unexpected, unhappy disclosure to its lender will be best served by doing it promptly and fully and by offering realistic assurances to the lender that the present difficulties, although serious, are not disastrous for the borrower (assuming, of course, that this is the case).

## C. Merger and Acquisition Transactions

Similarly, a provider that is engaged in a merger or acquisition transaction, whether as acquiror or target, may well be confronted with the need to provide representations and warranties concerning its compliance status and the nature of pending or threatened litigation against it. Such disclosures will almost invariably be required from the target company in such a transaction, and may frequently be requested from the acquiror as well, particularly if the acquiror is offering its securities as consideration or if all or part of the purchase price is deferred.[231]

The considerations in such a circumstance are likely not much different from those the borrower faces in the bank loan situation described earlier. The provider's first focus should be to obtain appropriate materiality qualifications in the representations and warranties, in order to ensure that there is no need to disclose immaterial information. The provider may also want to carefully negotiate any language purporting to define its "knowledge" for purposes of representations and warranties and may seek to have disclosures regarding violations of laws limited to those for which it has received some sort of formal notice, rather than simply requiring it to disclose any known violations of law. The provider's ability to do this will, of course, depend on its relative negotiating leverage and the sophistication of the other party.

Where the acquiror is using its stock or other securities as consideration for the transaction, it must be mindful that Section 10(b) and Rule 10b-5 will apply to the representations it makes in the acquisition agreement. In addition, if the securities are to be issued to the target or its stockholders in a registered transaction, as in a public company merger, the acquiror will file a registration statement with respect to the transaction and will be subject to potential liability under the 1933 Act as well. Accordingly, in such a situation, the acquiror will need to analyze its disclosure duties under the principles described in earlier sections of this chapter.

Finally, as in the loan situation described earlier, where the acquiror or target, as the case may be, can disclose information to the other party without triggering other disclosure obligations, it should in most circumstances ensure that there are appropriate confidentiality protections in place and make the

---

[231] In a cash deal, where the entire purchase price is being paid at closing, the acquiror may be able to resist requests for representations and warranties concerning anything other than its due organization and existence and its ability to pay. However, in some circumstances the target may insist on such representations even in a cash deal, and, because it is awkward to protest too much on these types of subjects, the acquiror may have to give in.

disclosure with appropriate explanations of mitigating factors. Where, on the other hand, disclosure under the acquisition agreement would likely entail an obligation (whether legal or practical) to make broader public disclosure, the entity may decide to make the best case it can that disclosure is not required under the applicable representations and warranties and fight the matter out when and if it becomes necessary.

In that connection, however, a 2005 SEC report adds yet another wrinkle for a publicly traded provider under investigation that is engaged in a merger or acquisition transaction. On March 1, 2005, the SEC issued a report under Section 21(a) of the 1934 Act in connection with a settled enforcement action against the Titan Corporation, a military intelligence and communications solution provider.[232] The SEC indicated that it was issuing the Titan Report "to provide guidance concerning potential liability under [1934] Act Sections 10(b) and 14(a), and Rules 10b-5 and 14a-9 thereunder, for publication of false or misleading material disclosures regarding contractual provisions such as representations."

According to the SEC, Titan had engaged in activities constituting a violation of the Foreign Corrupt Practices Act (FCPA).[233] Thereafter, Titan agreed to be acquired by another publicly traded company, and entered into a merger agreement containing a representation that, to its knowledge, neither Titan nor anyone acting on its behalf had taken any action that would cause Titan to be in violation of the FCPA (the "FCPA Representation"). The proxy statement relating to the proposed merger described Titan's representations and warranties, including the FCPA Representation, and the merger agreement was attached as an appendix to Titan's proxy statement relating to the merger, which was filed with the SEC and disseminated to Titan's stockholders. According to the SEC, the merger agreement and the proxy statement were amended several times due to SEC and DOJ investigations of the potential FCPA investigations. However, the FCPA Representation in the merger agreement was not changed.

The SEC took the position that the continuing inclusion of the FCPA Representation in the appendix to the proxy statement (and the unchanged description of the representation in the text of the proxy statement) potentially constituted a materially misleading disclosure to Titan's stockholders, because "a reasonable investor could conclude that the statements made in the representation describe the actual state of affairs," and that Titan's failure to describe additional material facts "contradicting or qualifying the original representation" (such as the facts relating to the SEC and DOJ investigations) could violate Section 14(a) and Rule 14a-9, or, if the requisite scienter were present, Section 10(b) and Rule 10b-5. The SEC apparently focused on the existence of "specific additional material facts ... known to an issuer [or which an issuer

---

[232]Report of Investigation Pursuant to Section 21(a) of the Securities Exchange Act of 1934 and Commission Statement on Potential Exchange Act Section 10(b) and Section 14(a) Liability, Exchange Act Release No. 51283 [hereinafter Titan Report], *available at* http://www.sec.gov/litigation/investreport/34-51238.htm.

[233]Pub. L. No. 95-213, title I, §101 *et seq.*, 91 Stat. 1494, enacting 15 U.S.C. §§78dd-1 and 78dd-2 and amending 15 U.S.C. §§78m and 78ff. In addition to settling civil charges by the SEC, Titan entered a guilty plea to criminal charges relating to the alleged FCPA violations.

was reckless or negligent in not knowing]" to conclude that additional disclosure could be required in such circumstances.

This is a somewhat startling result, because (1) the proxy statement disclosure apparently did not go to the truth of the representations in the merger agreement, but merely described them and indicated that the continued accuracy of such representations was a condition to closing, and (2) subsequent public announcements and filings by Titan and the acquiror described the potential FCPA problems faced by Titan. The Titan Report does clearly focus on the fact that the merger agreement and associated disclosure were actually contained (or incorporated by reference) in a disclosure document, and expressly notes that "[r]epresentations, covenants, or other provisions of an agreement made by an issuer that are not public or disclosed to shareholders are not covered by the scope of [the Titan Report]." However, the SEC goes on to note that an issuer cannot avoid a disclosure obligation "simply because the information published was contained in an agreement or other document not prepared as a disclosure document."

It remains to be seen how the principles espoused in the Titan Report will be applied in other factual settings. However, issuers and their counsel should be aware of the SEC's view that documents not expressly prepared for disclosure purposes can nonetheless be the basis for liability under the federal securities laws where they (1) are disclosed to investors and (2) contain provisions that may be construed to be inconsistent with material facts relating to the issuer that are known to the issuer. Thus, where a health care issuer has entered into a merger or acquisition agreement that is (1) filed with the SEC and (2) contains representations concerning the lack of any investigations or enforcement activity against the issuer, and (3) the issuer subsequently becomes aware of, say, a sealed False Claims Act complaint and an ensuing government investigation, the issuer will need to carefully consider whether the Titan Report principles expose it to potential securities fraud liability if corrective disclosure is not made.[234]

## D. Research Grant Activities

The government-wide effect of an exclusion from governmental health care programs[235] means that a provider facing serious health care enforcement proceedings must also consider the potential effect of such proceedings on its research- and grant-related activities. Among other things, persons who have been debarred or suspended from participation in government programs may not receive payments, even for goods or services actually delivered or performed.[236] Further, persons seeking grants and other arrangements are required to certify, inter alia, that they are not "presently . . . criminally or civilly

---

[234]Much of the above discussion of the Titan Report appeared in somewhat different form in William W. Horton, *SEC's "Titan Report" Raises the Stakes for Disclosure of Government Investigations*, ABA HEALTH ESOURCE vol. 1, no. 8 (Apr. 2005), *available at* http://www.abanet.org/health/esource/vol1no8/index.html.

[235]*See* 45 C.F.R. §76.110(d).

[236]*See* 45 C.F.R. §225.

charged by a governmental entity (Federal, State or local) with commission of any of the offenses" enumerated in the certificate, including fraud, falsification of records or documents, or making false statements.[237] Furthermore, the participant is required to provide immediate notice if it becomes aware that the certification has become erroneous because of changed circumstances.[238] Because the certification is itself a statement made to the government, it can presumably also become the subject of a separate claim if it is false.[239] Failure to be able to certify does not lead to automatic denial of participation, so dialogue is again probably a safer course than concealment.[240]

The exclusion also bars other government contractors from using the provider as a subcontractor. As a result, academic research centers facing suspension or debarment will cause significant hardships for researchers working in their facilities, because it will not be possible for the research center to receive payment for the use of its facilities in connection with government-funded research activities—a highly unlikely outcome, no doubt, but one that may affect the recruitment of star research scientists.

### E. Private Philanthropy

The potential loss of tax-exempt status implicit in any governmental program investigation that alleges unlawful conduct may also complicate private fundraising activities for not-for-profit organizations. In addition to seeking to endow various worthy causes, donors are without doubt expecting tax deductions for their beneficence. Except in rare instances, loss of tax-exempt status would also mean loss of the tax deductions for donors. Given the possibility that the donor may make the gift by will, when the decision tends to be exceedingly final, the stakes for deciding to disclose the investigation and the associated risk may be quite high. Because there have been no reported cases of actual loss of exempt status, it may be tempting for the provider to delay disclosure on the assumption that the closing agreement will always protect innocent donors who contributed expecting simply to help the cause and had no hand in whatever bad acts led to the regulatory sanctions. However, if the donor is one who might continue to provide future support, failure to disclose may injure the trust necessary to continue the relationship.

### VI. A Sidebar: What if the Attorney and the Issuer Disagree?

While a full exploration of the issue is beyond the scope of this chapter, one question that the attorney for the publicly traded health care organization cannot afford to ignore is what his or her duties are if the attorney's conclusions regarding the issuer's obligations are different from those of the issuer's management.

---

[237]45 C.F.R. Part 76, App. A, Item (1)(c).

[238]45 C.F.R. Part 76, App. A, Instruction 4.

[239]*See, e.g.,* Cook County v. United States *ex rel.* Chandler, 538 U.S. 119 (2003).

[240]45 C.F.R. Part 76, App. A, Instruction 2.

Section 307 of the Sarbanes-Oxley Act required the SEC to adopt a regulation that would require an attorney who "appears and practices" before the SEC in the representation of an issuer to (a) "report evidence of a material violation of securities law or breach of fiduciary duty or similar violation by the [issuer] or any agent thereof, to the chief legal counsel or the chief executive officer of the [issuer]," and (b) if there is not an appropriate response (including appropriate remedial measures or sanctions) forthcoming from such officer(s), to report such evidence to the audit committee of the issuer's board of directors (or to another committee of nonemployee directors, or to the full board).[241] The SEC's initial and continuing response to this statutory requirement holds significant implications for the lawyer advising health care issuers on disclosure requirements.[242]

In November 2002, the SEC proposed rules under Section 307 of Sarbanes-Oxley that not only would have imposed a duty on a lawyer appearing and practicing before the SEC to report such evidence of a material violation "up the ladder" within the issuer, but also would have required the lawyer to withdraw from representing the issuer and disclose such withdrawal to the SEC (and to disaffirm any part of any document filed with or submitted to the SEC that the attorney prepared or assisted in preparing and reasonably believed was or might be materially false or misleading) *if,* in the lawyer's view, the issuer had not made a timely and appropriate response to such a report.[243] After considerable controversy, the SEC adopted a final rule that limited the lawyer's obligations to up-the-ladder reporting and did not require the "noisy withdrawal" contemplated by the initial proposal.[244] However, in an accompanying release the SEC continued to propose the rules originally contained in the initial proposal that would require the lawyer to withdraw and notify the SEC (or, alternatively, to require the issuer to make an 8-K filing disclosing such withdrawal and "the circumstances relating thereto") if the lawyer did not receive what the lawyer determined to be an appropriate and timely response to his or her report of evidence of a material violation.[245] Further, while the final rules did not require the attorney to make a "noisy withdrawal," they did permit the attorney to disclose confidential information to the SEC, without the issuer's consent:

---

[241] Section 307 of Sarbanes-Oxley is codified at 15 U.S.C. §7245.

[242] For a more comprehensive description of the history, status, and particulars of the SEC's rulemaking under Section 307, see William W. Horton, *Representing the Healthcare Organization in a Post-Sarbanes-Oxley World: New Rules, New Paradigms, New Perils,* 37 J. HEALTH L. 335 (2004). For other considerations concerning potential exposure for attorneys representing health care organizations, see Chapter 1 (Baumann, An Introduction to Health Care Fraud and Abuse), at Section §I.B.

[243] *See* Proposed Rule: Implementation of Standards of Professional Conduct for Attorneys, Securities Act Release No. 33-8150 (Nov. 21, 2002), *available at* http://www.sec.gov/rules/proposed/33-8150.htm.

[244] *See* Final Rule: Implementation of Standards of Professional Conduct for Attorneys, Securities Act Release No. 33-8185 (Jan. 29, 2003), *available at* http://www.sec.gov/rules/final/33-8185.htm.

[245] *See* Proposed Rule: Implementation of Standards of Professional Conduct for Attorneys, Securities Act Release No. 33-8186, *available at* http://www.sec.gov/rules/proposed/33-8186.htm.

to the extent the attorney reasonably believes necessary: (i) [t]o prevent the issuer from committing a material violation that is likely to cause substantial injury to the financial interest or property of the issuer or investors; (ii) [t]o prevent the issuer, in [an SEC] investigation or administrative proceeding, from committing perjury . . . ; suborning perjury . . . ; or committing any act proscribed in 18 U.S.C. [Section] 1001 that is likely to perpetrate a fraud upon the [SEC]; or (iii) [t]o rectify the consequences of a material violation by the issuer that caused, or may cause, substantial injury to the financial interest or property of the issuer or investors in the furtherance of which the attorney's services were used.[246]

As discussed above, the determination whether the securities laws require disclosure of an investigation or sealed *qui tam* suit, or of potential underlying wrongdoing that has not been charged, is a complex one, and one as to which reasonable lawyers and reasonable clients may differ. However, the new SEC rules raise the stakes for the lawyer who counsels in favor of disclosure if the client declines to make such disclosure.[247] If the lawyer believes not only that disclosure is the prudent course, but also that a failure to make such disclosure could be reasonably construed by another competent lawyer with knowledge of the same facts to constitute a material violation of the securities laws by the issuer, the lawyer is, at a minimum, required to report the matter up the ladder within the issuer. If the SEC adopts any version of its proposed noisy withdrawal/ reporting-out requirements, the lawyer may have further affirmative duties if the issuer persists in nondisclosure contrary to the lawyer's advice. Even under the current permissive reporting-out provisions of the SEC rules, the lawyer who continues to represent the nondisclosing issuer may be exposed to criticism, and perhaps to liability as well, once the issuer has made it clear that it does not intend to make any disclosure that the lawyer believes should be made.[248]

---

[246]*See* 17 C.F.R. §205.3(d)(2).

[247]In addition to the disclosure issue, of course, the lawyer who is aware of the substantive law violation that gives rise to the disclosure issue has duties relating to reporting evidence of that violation up the ladder within the organization, separate and apart from any violation that non-disclosure may entail, at least if the lawyer is deemed under the rule to be "appearing and practicing" before the SEC.

[248]In that regard, see, e.g., the Independent Examiner's Report Concerning Spiegel, Inc. (Sept. 5, 2003), filed in *Securities & Exch. Comm'n v. Spiegel, Inc.,* Case No. 03-C-1685 (N.D. Ill.), available as Exhibit 99.2 to Spiegel, Inc.'s Current Report on Form 8-K, dated Sept. 12, 2003. In that case, according to the Independent Examiner's filings, Spiegel did not file various 1934 Act reports because doing so would have involved filing audited financial statements containing a "going concern" qualification in the auditor's report. Both internal counsel and external securities counsel advised Spiegel's audit committee and another committee of the board on multiple occasions that the reports were required to be filed and that failure to file them exposed the corporation to various potential consequences, including the possibility of SEC enforcement action. Nonetheless, and apparently relying on advice from another law firm engaged by Spiegel's controlling shareholder to advise the company, Spiegel neither filed the required reports nor disclosed what the Independent Examiner found to be the true reason that it had not filed them. Although the Independent Examiner noted that the new SEC rules had not become effective at any relevant time, and that no version of the reporting-out/noisy withdrawal proposals had yet been adopted in any event, the Independent Examiner was sharply critical of external securities counsel for continuing to represent Spiegel in the face of such nondisclosure. It is clear that, in the Independent Examiner's view, the lawyers at least bore moral culpability for, in effect, deferring to their client's judgment after having made extensive efforts to give appropriate advice to the client and having been overruled by the client, after the client's consultation with other counsel. *See id.* at 80–84, 212.

The final scope of the SEC's rulemaking under Sarbanes-Oxley Section 307 remains to be established, as does the ultimate outcome of the public debate over the proper role of lawyers in the post-Enron world.[249] What is immediately clear, however, is that the lawyer advising a health care issuer on disclosure matters must bear in mind not only the impact of a disclosure decision on the issuer, but also the potential impact on the lawyer himself or herself if the lawyer acquiesces in the issuer's decision not to make disclosure contrary to the lawyer's advice and, in hindsight, that decision proves to have been the wrong one. What this dynamic will mean for the professional relationship between the lawyer and the client continues to be a subject of much debate.[250]

## VII. CONCLUSION: NOW WE SEE AS THROUGH A GLASS, DARKLY (BUT LATER, THE PLAINTIFF WILL CLEAR THINGS UP FOR US)

In a fairly recent Broadway musical, an exchange along the following lines occurs toward the end of the last act, accompanying the impending doom of all the remaining cast:

> *Little Sally:* What kind of a happy ending is *that?*
> *Officer Lockstock:* I told you, Little Sally, it's not that kind of a musical.[251]

This chapter began with a story, of sorts, and readers of a story may have an expectation that it will have a happy ending. However, the nature of the problems faced by providers evaluating their disclosure obligations amid the vagaries of the current health care enforcement environment makes the likelihood of a happy ending—one in which the provider can feel comfortable that its disclosure decisions are fully insulated from challenge in hindsight—as speculative and contingent as any underlying liabilities themselves may be. The various potential resolutions of an investigation, the uncertain outcome of a pre-intervention *qui tam* suit, the unpredictable reaction of the market, and the many issues that may be raised by other constituencies and stakeholders all make it difficult for a provider to be sure that it is doing the right thing at the

---

[249] In that regard, consider also the 2003 amendments to Rules 1.6 and 1.13 of the American Bar Association's Model Rules of Professional Conduct, *available at* http://www.abanet.org/cpr/mrpc/mrpc_toc.html (providing permission for a lawyer to reveal client confidences to prevent (or mitigate or rectify the effects of ) a crime or fraud committed by the client or, if the client is an organization, where the lawyer believes that such disclosure is in the best interests of the organization even where no crime or fraud is involved, in each case subject to certain requirements and conditions precedent set forth in the amended Model Rules). *See generally* William W. Horton, *Representing the Healthcare Organization in a Post-Sarbanes-Oxley World: New Rules, New Paradigms, New Perils,* 37 J. HEALTH L. 335 (2004), *passim;* Lawrence A. Hamermesh, *Up the Ladder and Out the Door? Illegal Activities, New Model Rules and Reporting Obligations,* BUS. LAW TODAY (May/June 2004) at 11.

[250] *See, e.g.,* Hearing of the Subcommittee on Capital Markets, Insurance and Government Sponsored Enterprises, Committee on Financial Services, U.S. House of Representatives, on "The Role of Attorneys in Corporate Governance," Feb. 4, 2004 (prepared statements) *available at* http://financialservices.house.gov/archive/hearings.asp@formmode=detail&hearing=274.html; ASS'N OF THE BAR OF THE CITY OF NEW YORK, REPORT OF THE TASK FORCE ON THE LAWYER'S ROLE IN CORPORATE GOVERNANCE (2006).

[251] Music & Lyrics by Mark Hollman, Book & Lyrics by Greg Kotis, *Urinetown—The Musical.* (This quote, based on memory, is paraphrased.)

right time, and any bad result makes it likely that the provider's decisions will be extensively scrutinized after the fact. Those undertaking that scrutiny will have the benefit of knowledge of facts that are frequently unclear, and sometimes even unsuspected, at the time that the provider must make those decisions.

That being the case, the provider must soldier on with the information at hand, recognizing that it is critical to assess and reassess its disclosure status based on the continually evolving nature and scope of its knowledge and the particular circumstances in which it finds itself. In that ongoing reassessment, the provider must recognize that the lines are not clear, and that the issues of materiality and duty to disclose are inextricably intertwined with the facts involved in the underlying investigation or action and the direction in which that matter seems to be heading. The analysis simply does not admit of black-letter rules, and there is case law to support or rebut almost any position that the provider might take.

In such a treacherous environment, then, the provider must integrate its disclosure analysis with its developing knowledge of the investigation or action and must recognize that its ability to defend against subsequent claims of inadequate, inaccurate, or misleading disclosure will depend largely on its ability to articulate a reasoned process that it followed in making the decision as to if, when, what, and how to disclose. That process must be informed by the case law that is out there, with its many nuances and subtle distinctions, and it must be informed by knowledge of how government investigations proceed and how they are resolved. Further, it must involve close interaction between counsel and the provider's executive management and, as applicable, investor and press relations personnel, because the dangers involved where the team is not on the same page—as to knowledge, as to strategy, and as to legal requirements—are potentially immense.

This chapter attempts to summarize a large body of relevant legal and factual considerations, and to suggest a somewhat disciplined approach to such a process. In the end, the success or failure of a challenge to a provider's decisions as to the timing and content of disclosure may stand or fall as much on the outcome of the investigation or action itself as on the "correctness" of those disclosure decisions. However, the provider that undertakes such an informed process in making those decisions will stand a much better chance of defending them than the provider that simply steps blindly into the situation.

# 10

# Controlling Fraud, Waste, and Abuse in the Medicare Part D Program*

*Larri A. Short, JD, and Richard S. Liner, JD, MPH, Arent Fox LLP, Washington, D.C.

## I. Introduction

### A. Overview

With the passage of the Medicare Prescription Drug, Improvement, and Modernization Act of 2003 (MMA),[1] Congress established a voluntary, outpatient prescription drug benefit, known as Medicare Part D. The Part D benefit makes prescription drug coverage available to all 43 million Medicare beneficiaries. According to Congressional Budget Office (CBO) estimates, Medicare would spend $46 billion on the new drug benefit in 2007 and, by 2017, Part D expenditures would reach $142 billion.[2] By all accounts, the addition of Part D constitutes the most sweeping change to Medicare since the program's inception in 1965. The enormity of this undertaking is complicated by a unique benefit design that relies heavily on effective coordination between Medicare and a number of private entities. The federal government delegates an unprecedented amount of responsibility to private industry for administrating the Part D benefit, determining the financial obligation of the Medicare program for Part D plan costs, and ensuring compliance in Part D plan operations.

The novel and complex structure of the Part D program and competition among private entities for a share of the substantial new source of revenue from Medicare prescription drug reimbursement make Part D highly susceptible to fraud, waste, and abuse (FWA). This chapter explores the incentives for FWA created by Part D, the program vulnerabilities that provide opportunities for FWA, and the significant statutory, regulatory, and subregulatory measures taken by the government to safeguard the integrity of the Part D benefit and to protect program beneficiaries from abuse.

### B. Anatomy of the Part D Benefit and the Potential for FWA

The Part D benefit establishes an economic partnership between the federal government and the private sector unlike any other in the Medicare program.[3] Under Part D, the Centers for Medicare and Medicaid Services (CMS) contracts with private health insurance companies, known as prescription drug plan "Sponsors," to provide outpatient prescription drug coverage to Medicare beneficiaries who choose to enroll in the voluntary benefit. Beneficiaries desiring Medicare coverage for outpatient prescription drugs may select from a number of stand-alone drug plans. Alternatively, they may choose a Medicare managed care plan that pairs the Part D drug benefit with the types of health care services historically covered by Medicare+Choice plans (Part C) in an

---

[1] Medicare Prescription Drug, Improvement, and Modernization Act of 2003, Pub. L. No. 108-173, 117 Stat. 2066 (2003).

[2] *See* Congressional Budget Office, *Budget and Economic Outlook: Fiscal Years 2008 to 2017* (Jan. 2007), at 58, *available at* http://www.cbo.gov/ftpdocs/77xx/doc7731/01-24-Budget-Outlook.pdf.

[3] *See* Rebecca Burke, *Fraud, Waste and Abuse Oversight in Medicare Part D Program, available at* http://www.pharmaceuticalcommerce.com/frontEnd/main.php?idSeccion=295 (Apr. 30, 2006). Note that this chapter does not present a comprehensive discussion of Part D. Rather, it briefly describes program elements from a fraud and abuse compliance perspective.

integrated, comprehensive health care program. Such plans are called Medicare Advantage Prescription Drug (MA-PD) plans. Health insurance companies offering the Part D benefit through stand-alone or MA-PD plans are referred to as plan "Sponsors" throughout this chapter. The key prescription drug FWA compliance issues facing Sponsors of both plan types generally are the same and will be discussed collectively whenever appropriate.

Although CMS contracts with private health plans to provide services under other Parts of the Medicare program, the structure of the Part D benefit is unique in several ways. First, by design, the Part D model encourages competition within the private sector. Private insurers seeking to become Sponsors must compete for contracts from CMS as well as for enrollees in their respective prescription drug plans. Some pharmacy benefit managers (PBMs) also may want to become plan Sponsors, while others may compete for contracts to provide PBM services to Sponsors. In some instances, pharmacies must compete with one another for contracts with Sponsors to serve as a "preferred provider" in a Part D plan's retail network. In other instances, pharmacies will have to compete just to become a non-preferred provider in the network, or risk losing substantial business from Part D beneficiaries. Pharmaceutical manufacturers will compete for favorable positioning of their drugs on Part D plan formularies, as well as existing commercial plan formularies, as a way to spur sales and increase market share. Enforcement authorities clearly expect efforts to gain a competitive advantage in the multibillion dollar Medicare prescription drug market to lead some unscrupulous industry players to try to "game" the system in ways both old and new to generate increased revenue from the Medicare program.[4] Defense lawyers representing Sponsors and other pharmaceutical industry players are aware of the potential dangers as well.[5]

---

[4]One Assistant U.S. Attorney indicated that the risk areas for Sponsors most likely to grab the attention of the federal prosecutors are activities that result in harm to patients, corruption of physician judgment, and theft of program money. *See Federal Justice Department Officials Say HHS OIG Work Plan Sets Top Priorities*, 10 HEALTH CARE FRAUD REP. (BNA) 731 (Oct. 11, 2006). Further, James G. Sheehan, the Inspector General for New York's Medicaid program and former Assistant U.S. Attorney for the Eastern District of Pennsylvania, said in 2006 that there is "no question" that the Medicare Part D prescription drug program will drive the enforcement agenda. *See* Keynote Speech of former Assistant U.S. Attorney and current New York State Medicaid Inspector General James G. Sheehan at the American Health Lawyers Association Conference on Legal Issues Affecting Academic Medical Centers and Other Teaching Institutions (Jan. 27, 2006), 10 HEALTH CARE FRAUD REP. (BNA) 97 (Feb. 1, 2006). Similarly, Assistant U.S. Attorney Virginia A. Gibson expressed the belief that the $2 billion paid by the drug industry for pharmaceutical fraud that occurred when Medicare covered a relatively small number of drugs will "pale in comparison" to recoveries once the Medicare drug benefit goes into effect. *See* Kirk J. Nahra, *The Sky Is Falling, the Feds Are Coming: Top 10 Tips for Protecting Part D Plans*, 10 HEALTH CARE FRAUD REP. (BNA) 78 (Jan. 18, 2006) (quoting Virginia A. Gibson, Assistant U.S. Attorney for the Eastern District of Pennsylvania).

[5]*See Monitoring, Auditing Should Be Key Focus For Part D Plans, Attorneys Say*, 11 HEALTH CARE FRAUD REP. (BNA) 202 (Oct. 19, 2006) [hereinafter *Monitoring, Auditing Should Be Key Focus*]; *Medicare Part D Drug Benefit Could Be Area Ripe for Fraud, Experts Say*, 10 HEALTH CARE FRAUD REP. (BNA) 47 (Jan. 4, 2006) (discussing opinions expressed by the defense bar that the enormous financial opportunities opening up under Medicare Part D will be a temptation to bad actors in the industry); *MMA, Pharmaceutical Pricing Top 2005 Enforcement, Compliance Concerns*, 9 HEALTH CARE FRAUD REP. (BNA) 51 (Jan. 5, 2005) (discussing concerns of defense counsel over developing fraud deterrent strategies when so little is understood about the weak spots in the program); *see also OIG Chief Counsel Cites Likely Areas of Potential Abuse*, 1 DRUG PRICING REP. & PART D COMPLIANCE, Issue 11 (Aug. 2005).

Second, in contrast to fiscal intermediaries and carriers[6] that are paid by CMS to administer the Medicare Part A and B programs, respectively, as agents for the federal government, Part D Sponsors actually assume some financial risk for the cost of the prescription drug benefit. Certain financial safeguards[7]—risk corridors,[8] risk adjustment,[9] and federal reinsurance[10]—are in place to protect Sponsors from unanticipated excessive costs. Even though beneficiaries' Part D premium payments are determined in a manner similar to that used under the Medicare+Choice program, the relationship between a sponsoring plan's initial cost estimate for the year and the plan's ultimate payment from Medicare is much more direct under the Medicare Part D program.[11] As a result, the amount Medicare is obligated to pay each Part D Sponsor is extremely sensitive to the Sponsor's initial cost projection as well as the cost data reported by the Sponsor throughout the plan year. Accordingly, any misrepresentation or misreporting of these data could effect the accuracy of Medicare payment amounts to Sponsors and potentially create a serious FWA compliance issue. Section III.A., below, provides an expanded discussion of the Part D reporting requirements and the associated risk areas for FWA.

Third, Sponsors are responsible for the design, operation, and administration of virtually all aspects of their respective Part D plans within certain parameters established by CMS. Significantly, Sponsors have flexibility in structuring and managing their plan's drug formulary as well as in designing utilization controls, medication therapy management programs, and drug safety reviews. As a result, the Medicare Part D benefit actually may vary quite a bit from plan to plan. Furthermore, Sponsors control the administration and payment of Part D claims.

---

[6]Section 911 of the MMA (Medicare Contracting Reform) mandates that the HHS Secretary replace the current contracting authority to administer the Medicare Part A and Part B fee-for-service programs with a new Medicare Administrative Contractor (MAC) authority. CMS began implementing the Medicare Contracting Reform measures in October 2005 and, as required by the statute, expects to complete the transition of all current Medicare fee-for-service contracts to the new MAC authority by 2011.

[7]For a more detailed discussion of Sponsor financial risk mitigation under Part D, see *Medicare Drug Plans and Risk Mitigation: Risk Corridors, Risk Adjustment and Federal Reinsurance*, THE PIPER REPORT, *available at* http://www.piperreport.com/archives/2006/04/risk_mitigation.html (Apr. 5, 2006) [hereinafter *Risk Mitigation*, THE PIPER REPORT.]

[8]See Chapter 6 (Rinn and Ryland, Managed Care Fraud and Abuse). For 2007, Sponsors reap all gains and bear all losses that fall within 2.5% of their expected costs (their contract bid to CMS). If actual costs exceed expected costs by more than 2.5% but less than 5%, the Sponsor is responsible for 25% of the excess cost and the federal government pays the remaining 75% of the cost overrun. If actual and expected costs differ by more than 5%, the Sponsor is responsible for 25% of the amount between 2.5% and 5% and 20% of the amount in excess of 5%. Conversely, if costs fall below expectations, then Sponsors must share the savings with the federal government based on the same risk corridors. For 2008 through 2011, the risk corridor thresholds will double and the federal share covered by the risk corridors will drop from 75% to 50% because it is assumed that, as Sponsors gain experience providing Part D coverage, they will project the annual cost of the benefit more accurately. 42 C.F.R. §423.336; *see also Risk Mitigation*, THE PIPER REPORT.

[9]42 C.F.R. §423.329(b). CMS will adjust payments to a Sponsor based on differences in expected drug spending for the beneficiaries in that Sponsor's plan using factors such as age, sex, and health status to determine the appropriate adjustment.

[10]42 C.F.R. §423.329(c). The federal government "reinsures" Sponsors for 80% of certain costs attributable to the cost of drugs for beneficiaries who have exceeded their annual out-of-pocket threshold. For additional information, see Section III.A., below.

[11]*See Risk Mitigation*, THE PIPER REPORT.

Pharmacies, typically operating through PBMs, submit claims for covered drugs directly to the Sponsors, not the Medicare program. Sponsors determine which claims are payable and, by virtue of their financial stake in the program, bear some risk for the proper administration of claims. They also must put in place customer service, beneficiary grievance, and coverage appeal programs that comport with minimum requirements established by CMS through regulations and guidance. The substantial extent of Sponsor autonomy in administering their own prescription drug plans creates significant opportunities for Sponsors to engage in abusive conduct with respect to plan marketing, beneficiary enrollment, formulary management, coverage decisions, and claims adjudication. These and other FWA compliance risk areas related to plan administration are examined in more detail in Section III.

Fourth, and particularly relevant to this chapter, Sponsors represent the first line of defense for combating FWA in the Part D program. Congress included in MMA a provision requiring Sponsors to have in place, directly or indirectly through contractual arrangements, "a program to control fraud, abuse, and waste" with respect to covered Part D drugs.[12] In the final regulations for Part D (Part D Final Rule),[13] CMS implemented Congress's mandate by requiring not only that Sponsors maintain a compliance plan, but also that their compliance plan include a comprehensive program to detect, correct, and prevent FWA.[14] Sponsors will be held accountable for the effectiveness of their compliance program and subject to sanctions for failing to address FWA within their Part D plans. This chapter devotes extensive discussion to the implementation of the FWA compliance plan requirement in Section III.D.

Despite the substantial amount of responsibility vested in private contractors, CMS retains ultimate oversight authority over the Part D benefit. Congress included in MMA a requirement that CMS audit annually the financial records of "at least one-third" of Part D Sponsors and also provided CMS with specific authority to hold Sponsors accountable for compliance with Part D regulatory requirements.[15] For certain infractions,[16] CMS has the au-

---

[12]Social Security Act §1860D–4(c)(1)(D) [42 U.S.C. §1395w–104(c)(1)(D)].

[13]70 Fed. Reg. 4194 (Jan. 28, 2005).

[14]42 C.F.R. §423.504(b)(4).

[15]Social Security Act §1860D-12 [42 U.S.C. §1395w–112]; 42 C.F.R. §423.504(d). In early 2007, CMS commenced the first series of audits for one-third of all Part D plans, which, according to CMS, would focus on the plan's compliance with random chapters of the *Medicare Prescription Drug Plan (PDP) Sponsor Audit Guide. See* Centers for Medicare & Medicaid Servs., Medicare Prescription Drug Plan (PDP) Sponsor Audit Guide (Apr. 10, 2006), *available at* http://www.cms.hhs.gov/PrescriptionDrugCovContra/Downloads/PDPAuditGuide.pdf. In addition to the Sponsor's FWA compliance program, the Audit Guide covers most areas of the plan's administration and operation, including enrollment and disenrollment, marketing, privacy and confidentiality, formulary and drug utilization management, claims processing and payment, first-tier and downstream contracts, coordination of benefits and TrOOP, licensure, financial solvency, and coverage determinations and appeals. The results of the first round of CMS audits would provide Sponsors and other Part D stakeholders with a useful blueprint for fine-tuning their compliance programs and learning how CMS intends to apply its guidance to actual conduct.

[16]*See* 42 C.F.R. §423.752. CMS may impose sanctions against a Sponsor if the Sponsor (1) fails substantially to provide to a Part D plan enrollee medically necessary services that the organization is required to provide (under law or under the contract) to a Part D plan enrollee, and that failure adversely affects (or is substantially likely to adversely affect) the enrollee;

thority to levy intermediate sanctions against Sponsors. Those sanctions include suspension of the Sponsor's marketing activities to Medicare beneficiaries, suspension of beneficiary enrollment in the Sponsor's Part D plan, and suspension of the Sponsor's payments for Part D drugs.[17] Moreover, CMS may terminate the Sponsor's contract unilaterally if the Sponsor fails to operate the Part D plan in accordance with the terms of its contract with CMS or triggers one of the termination provisions specified in the Part D Final Rule.[18] CMS may combine such administrative sanctions with civil monetary penalties (CMPs) ranging from $10,000 to $100,000 or, alternatively, use CMPs alone to punish errant Sponsors.[19] CMPs are more likely in situations that adversely affect beneficiaries. In addition, CMS may refer cases involving serious Sponsor misconduct to federal enforcement agencies for investigation and, potentially, prosecution under applicable civil and/or criminal health care fraud and abuse laws. Although CMS's intermediate sanction authority only extends to Sponsors and not to Sponsors' first-tier or downstream contractors, Sponsors that fail

---

(2) imposes on Part D plan enrollees premiums in excess of the monthly basic and supplemental beneficiary premiums permitted under MMA and the Part D regulations; (3) acts to expel or refuses to reenroll a beneficiary in violation of the provisions of this part; (4) engages in any practice that may reasonably be expected to have the effect of denying or discouraging enrollment of individuals whose medical condition or history indicates a need for substantial future medical services; (5) misrepresents or falsifies information that it furnishes (i) to CMS or (ii) to an individual or to any other entity under the Part D drug benefit program; (6) employs or contracts with an individual or entity who is excluded from participation in Medicare under certain sections of the Social Security Act (or with an entity that employs or contracts with an excluded individual or entity) for the provision of any of the following: (i) health care, (ii) utilization review, (iii) medical social work, or (iv) administrative services. *Id.*

[17]42 C.F.R. §423.750. Procedurally, before imposing sanctions, CMS must provide the Sponsor with notice, an opportunity to respond, and an informal reconsideration, consisting of a review of the evidence by a CMS official who did not participate in the initial decision to impose a sanction. 42 C.F.R §423.756. In May 2007, CMS issued a Notice of Proposed Rulemaking, 72 Fed. Reg. 23,368 (May 25, 2007), in which it proposed several modifications to the procedures for imposing intermediate sanctions on Sponsors, including a change that would completely eliminate the reconsideration step.

[18]42 C.F.R. §423.509. CMS may terminate a contract for any of the following reasons, if the Sponsor (1) substantially fails to carry out the terms of its contract with CMS; (2) carries out its contract with CMS in a manner that is inconsistent with the effective and efficient implementation of the Part D Final Rule; (3) no longer meets the requirements in the Part D Final Rule for being a contracting organization; (4) commits or participates in, by a showing of credible evidence, false, fraudulent, or abusive activities affecting the Medicare program, including submission of false or fraudulent data; (5) experiences financial difficulties so severe that its ability to provide necessary prescription drug coverage is impaired to the point of posing an imminent and serious risk to the health of its enrollees, or otherwise fails to make services available to the extent that a risk to health exists; (6) substantially fails to comply with the requirements in the Part D Final Rule relating to grievances and appeals; (7) fails to provide CMS with valid risk adjustment, reinsurance, and risk corridor related data as required under the Part D Final Rule (or, for fallback entities, fails to provide the information in the Part D Final Rule); (8) substantially fails to comply with the service access requirements in the Part D Final Rule related to access to covered Part D drugs (i.e., formulary management); (9) substantially fails to comply with the marketing requirements in the Part D Final Rule related to the dissemination of Part D plan information (i.e., marketing and promotion of the plan); (10) substantially fails to coordinate Part D coverage with prescription drug coverage under other Medicare drug benefits; or (11) substantially fails to comply with the cost and utilization management, quality improvement, medication therapy management, and fraud, waste, and abuse program requirements as specified in the Part D Final Rule. *Id.*

[19]*Id.*

to implement adequate compliance programs may be held accountable for the misconduct of their subcontractors.

In the early days of the Part D benefit, CMS exhibited few reservations about exercising its authority to sanction noncompliant sponsors. CMS imposed intermediate sanctions against Sponsors 75 times for Part D compliance violations within just the first six months of implementation.[20] Even before Part D reached its first anniversary, CMS reported issuing more than 2,800 "letters of warning" to plan Sponsors, including corrective action plan requests, notices of non-compliance, warning letters, and notices that information was being suppressed from the Medicare Drug Plan Finder.[21] Most Sponsor compliance issues related to call center performance, inaccurate data reporting, and inadequate exceptions and appeals related information.[22] In total, more than 92 percent of all Sponsors received at least one warning letter, although, in general, CMS noted that the triggering issues were resolved and that beneficiary satisfaction with the benefit was high.[23] Sponsors should expect CMS to increase the severity of its enforcement measures if they persist in noncompliant behavior after receiving notification of a violation. Moreover, CMS stated that prior performance and compliance with program requirements and guidance will be key considerations in determining whether to renew a Sponsor's Part D contract.[24]

In addition, CMS engaged a new group of contractors, called Medicare Drug Integrity Contractors (MEDICs),[25] to assist CMS with its auditing responsibilities and to oversee Sponsor activities from both a performance and a

---

[20]*See* Press Release, U.S. Dep't of Health & Human Servs., Centers for Medicare & Medicaid Servs., *Medicare Takes Steps to Improve Customer Service by Drug Plans* (June 29, 2006), *available at* http://www.cms.hhs.gov/apps/media/press/release.asp?Counter=1890. Some of these compliance violations resulted in restrictions on enrollment of new plan members and, in one case, CMS announced termination of the Sponsor's participation in the Part D program due to "a persistent pattern of failure to comply with Medicare requirements." *Id.*

[21]*See* Press Release, U.S. Dep't of Health & Human Servs., Centers for Medicare & Medicaid Servs., *Enhanced Tools Available to Help People with Medicare Improve their Health Care: Plan Performance Measures Show Further Improvement* (Sept. 21, 2006), *available at* http://www.cms.hhs.gov/apps/media/press/release.asp?Counter=1969&intNumPerPage=10& checkDate=&checkKey=&srchType=&numDays=3500&srchOpt=0&srchData=&keyword Type=All&chkNewsType=1%2C+2%2C+3%2C+4%2C+5&intPage=&showAll=&pYear= &year=&desc=false&cboOrder=date [hereinafter *Enhanced Tools Available to Help People*].

[22]*See id.*

[23]*Id.*

[24]*See* Letter from Cynthia G. Tudor, Acting Director, Medicare Drug Benefit Group (CMS), regarding Instructions for 2007 Contract Year (Apr. 3, 2006) at 6, *available at* http:// www.cms.hhs.gov/PrescriptionDrugCovContra/Downloads/2007PDPCallLetter.pdf.

[25]In October 2005, CMS contracted with eight companies to serve as the initial MEDICs: Delmarva Foundation for Medical Care, Inc.; Electronic Data Systems; IntegriGuard LLC; Livanta LLC; Maximus Federal Services, Inc.; NDCHealth; Perot Systems Government Services, Inc.; and Science Applications International Corporation. *See* Press Release, U.S. Dep't of Health & Human Servs., Centers for Medicare & Medicaid Servs., *The New Medicare Prescription Drug Program: Attacking Fraud and Abuse* (Oct. 7, 2005). In October 2006, CMS awarded additional MEDIC contracts to Science Applications International Corp., Electronic Data Systems (two contracts), and Health Integrity LLC. *See* Press Release, U.S. Dep't of Health & Human Servs., Centers for Medicare & Medicaid Servs., *CMS Announces Four New MEDIC Contracts; Says Anti-Fraud Efforts Have Saved $2 Billion* (Oct. 13, 2006).

compliance perspective.[26] MEDICS also will assist Sponsors with their own investigations of suspected FWA within their respective Part D plans. When MEDICs or CMS identify potentially illegal activities, they will convey their findings to the Office of Inspector General (OIG) for the Department of Health and Human Services (HHS) or the Department of Justice (DOJ), or both. CMS explicitly warned in the Preamble to the Part D Final Rule that "[n]othing in this regulation should be construed as implying that the financial relationships described in this final rule meet the requirements of the anti-kickback statute."[27] Accordingly, Sponsors should be aware that the threat of OIG and DOJ involvement looms over the monitoring and oversight responsibilities of the MEDICs as well as the sanctioning authority of CMS.

Sponsors also should consider that CMS may hold them accountable for the conduct of their Part D subcontractors in addition to their own conduct. The Part D Final Rule requires Sponsors and their subcontractors to certify that claims data submitted to CMS are true and accurate to the best of their knowledge and belief.[28] If a Sponsor's compliance program fails to detect and redress deceptive reporting by a first-tier contractor or downstream entity and a MEDIC identifies and reports the problem, the Sponsor could be at risk for sanctions, or even worse, referral of the matter to the OIG or DOJ. As the entity ultimately responsible for the submission to the government of all claims and cost data for its Part D plan, the Sponsor could be targeted by enforcement authorities along with the first tier contractor or downstream entity suspected of actually committing the fraud.

Furthermore, the significant number of individuals involved in the administration and operation of a Part D plan increases the universe of potential whistleblowers. Sponsors, PBMs, and pharmacies each are likely to employ individuals in a position to discover fraud or misconduct within a plan. Employees may be attracted to the possibility of sharing in a recovery based on the enormous number of claims each plan will submit to Medicare for Part D drugs. Sponsors that did little or no business with the government before Part D should

---

[26]In April 2006, CMS released a draft Part D Audit Guide, which includes the elements CMS, and in turn MEDICs, will use while conducting audits of stand-alone prescription drug plan Sponsors and MA-PD plan Sponsors. *See* Centers for Medicare & Medicaid Servs., *Medicare Prescription Drug Plan (PDP) Sponsor Part D Audit Guide, Version* 1.0 (Apr. 28, 2006) [hereinafter Audit Guide], *available at* http://www.cms.hhs.gov/PrescriptionDrugCovContra/ Downloads/PDPAuditGuide.pdf. The Audit Guide provides an outline of the areas MEDICs will test during these audits, including the FWA compliance plan. The Audit Guide specifically refers to PDBM Chapter 9 as the reference tool for auditing the Sponsor's compliance with the FWA compliance program requirement. *See id.* at 30. See also Section III.B., below. In May 2006, CMS published a response to comments from industry on the Audit Guide, *see* Centers for Medicare & Medicaid Servs., *Part D Audit Guide—Response to Industry Comments* (May 9, 2006), *available at* http://www.cms.hhs.gov/PrescriptionDrugCovContra/downloads/PartDAuditGuideResponsetoIndustryComments_05.09.06.pdf, but as of August 2007, the agency had not issued a consolidated revised version. In November 2006, CMS published a memorandum for Sponsors with general guidance regarding the Part D audit process that began in 2007. *See* Centers for Medicare & Medicaid Servs., *Final MA-PD and PDP Part D Audit Guides for Part D Program Audits* (Nov. 13, 2006), *available at* http://www.cms.hhs.gov/PrescriptionDrugCovContra/ Downloads/MemoAuditGuides.pdf.

[27]70 Fed. Reg. 4194, 4201 (Jan. 28, 2005).

[28]42 C.F.R. §423.505(k)(3).

consider that their employees now have a much greater incentive to focus on plan vulnerabilities and to look for potential causes of action.

Federal enforcement agencies have been vigorous in their investigation and prosecution of health care fraud and abuse offenses.[29] Much of the enforcement push in recent years has focused on the pharmaceutical industry.[30] The pharmaceutical manufacturer and PBM industries in particular have paid almost $3.9 billion in fines over the last six years.[31] The explosion of whistleblower actions under the federal False Claims Act over the last decade,[32] the

---

[29] Recent examples include, e.g., Press Release, U.S. Dep't of Justice, *The Scooter Store to Pay United States $4 Million to Resolve False Claims Act Allegations* (May 11, 2007); Press Release, U.S. Dep't of Justice, *SCCI Health Services & Subsidiary Pay U.S. $7.5 Million For Kickback & False Claims Act Violations* (Jan. 5, 2007); Press Release, U.S. Dep't of Justice, *Biopharmaceutical Firm Intermune to Pay U.S. Over $36 Million for Illegal Promotion and Marketing of Drug Actimmune* (Oct. 26, 2006); Press Release, U.S. Dep't of Justice, *Medtronic to Pay $40 Million to Settle Kickback Allegations* (July 18, 2006); Press Release, U.S. Dep't of Justice, *Tenet Health Care Corporation to Pay U.S. More Than $900 Million to Resolve False Claims Act Allegations* (June 30, 2006); Press Release, U.S. Dep't of Justice, *Largest Health Care System in New Jersey to Pay U.S. $265 Million to Resolve Allegations of Defrauding Medicare* (June 15, 2006); Press Release, U.S. Dep't of Justice, *Minnesota-Based Home Health Care Chain Pays U.S. $8 Million to Settle Civil Fraud Allegations* (Feb. 9, 2006); Press Release, U.S. Dep't of Justice, *HealthSouth to Pay United States $325 Million to Resolve Medicare Fraud Allegations* (Dec. 30, 2004); Press Release, U.S. Dep't of Justice, *Gambro Health Care Agrees to Pay Over $350 Million to Resolve Civil & Criminal Allegations of Medicare in Fraud and Abuse Case* (Dec. 2, 2004); Press Release, U.S. Dep't of Justice, *Adventist Health System, Hospitals, Ambulance Companies to Pay U.S. More Than $20 Million to Settle Fraud Claims* (Oct. 28, 2004).

[30] Recent examples include, e.g., Press Release, U.S. Dep't of Justice, *Bristol-Myers Squibb Pleads Guilty to Lying to the Federal Government About Deal Involving Blood-Thinning Drug* (May 30, 2007); Press Release, U.S. Attorney's Office for the Western District of Virginia, *The Purdue Frederick Company, Inc. and Top Executives Plead Guilty to Misbranding Oxycontin; Will Pay Over $600 Million* (May 10, 2007); Press Release, U.S. Dep't of Justice, *Medicis Pharmaceutical to Pay U.S. $9.8 Million to Resolve False Claims Allegations* (May 8, 2007); Press Release, U.S. Dep't of Justice, *Cell Therapeutics, Inc. to Pay United States $10.5 Million to Resolve Claims for Illegal Marketing of Cancer Drug* (Apr. 17, 2007); Press Release, U.S. Dep't of Justice, *Omnicare, Inc. to Pay $49.5 Million to United States and 43 States Medicaid Prescription Drug Fraud Allegations* (Nov. 14, 2006); Press Release, U.S. Dep't of Justice, *King Pharmaceuticals to Pay $124 Million for Medicaid Rebate Underpayments and Overcharging for Drug Products* (Nov. 1, 2005); Press Release, U.S. Dep't of Justice, *Serono to Pay $704 Million for the Illegal Marketing of AIDS Drug* (Oct. 17, 2005); Press Release, U.S. Dep't of Justice, *GlaxoSmithKline Pays $150 Million to Settle Drug Pricing Fraud Case* (Sept. 20, 2005); Press Release, U.S. Attorney's Office for the Eastern District of Pennsylvania, *AdvancePCS to Pay $137.5 Million to Resolve Civil Fraud and Kickback Allegations* (Sept. 8, 2005); Press Release, U.S. Dep't of Justice, *Schering-Plough to Pay $345 Million to Resolve Criminal and Civil Liabilities for Illegal Marketing of Claritin* (July 30, 2004); Press Release, U.S. Dep't of Justice, *Wal-Mart to Pay $2 Million for Allegedly Dispensing Partial Prescriptions & Billing U.S. Health Programs for Full Amounts* (June 25, 2004); Press Release, U.S. Dep't of Justice, *Rite-Aid to Pay $7 Million for Allegedly Submitting False Prescription Claims to Government* (June 25, 2004); Press Release, U.S. Dep't of Justice, *Warner-Lambert to Pay $430 Million to Resolve Criminal & Civil Health Care Liability Relating to Off-Label Promotion* (May 13, 2004). Further, in December 2006, Bristol-Myers announced that it had reached an agreement in principle with DOJ to pay $499 million to resolve a dispute over allegations involving the company's drug pricing and sales and marketing activities. *See Bristol-Myers Announces Agreement With DOJ Over Pricing, Will Pay $499 Million,* 11 HEALTH CARE FRAUD REP. (BNA) 22 (Jan. 3, 2007).

[31] *See* Taxpayers Against Fraud, *$3.9 Billion in Pharmaceutical Fraud Is Just the Tip of the Iceberg* (Mar. 8, 2007), *available at* http://66.98.181.12/whistle134.htm.

[32] For fiscal year 2006, DOJ reported recoveries of more than $3.1 billion in fraud and False Claims Act settlements, 72% of which came from health care fraud cases. *See* Press Release, U.S. Dep't of Justice, *Justice Department Recovers Record $3.1 Billion in Fraud and False Claims in Fiscal Year 2006* (Nov. 21, 2006).

government's focus on the pharmaceutical industry, and the tremendous amount of federal money at stake under Part D all suggest that Sponsors and the entities with which they do business likely will be the targets of investigations and prosecutions under a variety of federal fraud and abuse laws,[33] including the federal Civil False Claims Act,[34] the federal anti-kickback statute,[35] and the Civil Monetary Penalty Law.[36]

## II. The OIG's Part D Agenda

Even before Part D was implemented, the OIG began considering the potential implications for FWA. As early as February 2005, Daniel R. Levinson told the Senate Committee on Finance, during hearings on his confirmation as HHS Inspector General, that the OIG

> has undertaken an extensive strategic planning effort to identify areas of potential program vulnerability and to plan monitoring strategy. The office has developed a plan for "prudent oversight" of the Part D benefit. Later this year, it will initiate some Part D early implementation reviews that will address beneficiary protection and access issues as well as controls over the bidding and application process for drug plan sponsors. In 2006, the OIG . . . also has planned work to address Part D payments to plan sponsors (including risk corridor adjustments), employer subsidies, beneficiary protection, drug access issues, and the coordination of benefits and programs, particularly Medicaid.[37]

After Inspector General Levinson took office, the OIG and other agencies continued to assess Part D program vulnerabilities and plan ways to address program FWA. Well-known health care fraud prosecutors took to the speaker circuit to educate Sponsors, PBMs, pharmacies, drug manufacturers, and beneficiaries about perceived Part D vulnerabilities and the potential legal consequences facing those who attempt to exploit them.[38] Attorneys in the Office of

---

[33]For a full discussion of the federal FWA statutes and regulations, see Chapter 1 (Baumann, An Introduction to Health Care Fraud and Abuse).

[34]31 U.S.C. §3729 *et seq.*

[35]42 U.S.C. §1320a–7b(b).

[36]42 U.S.C. §1320a–7a.

[37]Nomination of Daniel R. Levinson, Harold Damelin, and Raymond T. Wagner, Jr. Before the United States Senate Committee on Finance, 109th Cong. 46 (2005) [hereinafter Statement of Daniel A. Levinson].

[38]At the American Health Lawyers Association Annual Meeting in June 2005, then-Assistant U.S. Attorney for the Eastern District of Pennsylvania James G. Sheehan suggested that Part D would create "a whole new category of payments and financial relationships" which will necessitate careful scrutiny by Sponsors, manufacturers, and suppliers of their operations and compliance obligations. *See Enforcement Officials Detail New Weapons, Concerns Posed by New Medicare Rx Benefit,* 9 Health Care Fraud Rep. (BNA) 575 (July 20, 2005) (reporting on the American Health Lawyers Annual Meeting, June 27–30, 2005). Sheehan expressed particular concern over program fraud and abuse that affects the more vulnerable beneficiary populations, such as those residing in institutions in which patient access to pharmacies is treated as a facility asset (e.g., kidney dialysis services, nursing home residents, Alzheimer's and psychiatric patients, and individuals suffering from chronic diseases in custodial settings). *Id.* He further suggested that prosecutors will consider using novel applications of existing federal laws,

General Counsel to the Inspector General also lectured extensively.[39] Government officials have continued to speak publicly about the potential compliance and fraud and abuse issues under the Part D program.[40]

In testimony before the House Committee on Ways and Means in March 2007, Mr. Levinson described a "strategic plan to fight fraud, waste, and abuse in Part D and to protect the health and welfare of its beneficiaries."[41] According

---

such as the Travel Act (18 U.S.C. §1952), which prohibits interstate travel or use of an interstate facility in aid of a racketeering or an unlawful business enterprise, and the Public Contracts Anti-Kickback Act (41 U.S.C. §51), which prohibits payments made, directly or indirectly, to any prime contractor or subcontractor of the United States for the purpose of improperly obtaining or rewarding favorable treatment in connection with a prime contract or a subcontract. *Id.* Although it remains an open question as to whether these laws would survive judicial scrutiny in most health care fraud cases, DOJ has alleged violations of the Public Contract Anti-Kickback Act in at least two such cases. In the AdvancePCS case, DOJ alleged that AdvancePCS, a PBM, violated the Public Contracts Anti-Kickback Act by soliciting and receiving kickbacks from pharmaceutical manufacturers in exchange for preferred treatment of drugs in contracts with health plan providers. *See* Press Release, U.S. Attorney's Office for the Eastern District of Pennsylvania, *AdvancePCS to Pay $137.5 Million to Resolve Civil Fraud and Kickback Allegations* (Sept. 8, 2005). Similarly, in a case brought against Medco, DOJ alleged that Medco, also a PBM, violated the Public Contracts Anti-Kickback Act by making improper payments to health plans to induce them to select Medco as their PBM for government contracts. *See* Press Release, U.S. Attorney's Office for the Eastern District of Pennsylvania, *U.S. Announces $155 Million Settlement of Medco False Claims Case* (Oct. 23, 2006). Of particular relevance in both of these cases, unlike the anti-kickback statute (42 U.S.C. §1320b–7b(a)), which is more commonly used in health care fraud cases, the Public Contract Anti-Kickback Act is not limited in its application to certain federal health benefit programs—namely, Medicare, Medicaid, and TRICARE. In particular, the Public Contract Anti-Kickback Act would apply to contracts related to Federal Employee Health Benefit Plans. Sheehan also cautioned Sponsors to be careful about the activities of their downstream contractors. *See Monitoring, Auditing Should Be Key Focus.* Specifically, he advised Part D plans to develop processes for identifying overpayments and underpayments at any level of the network, including the retail pharmacy and PBM levels, and to report and repay overpayments. *See id.*

[39] In June 2005, Lewis Morris, Chief Counsel to the OIG, remarked that the roll out of the Part D program would be by far the largest enforcement challenge facing the OIG. *See Enforcement Officials Detail Weapons, Concerns Posed by New Medicare Rx Benefit*, 9 HEALTH CARE FRAUD REP. (BNA) 575 (July 20, 2005) (reporting on the American Health Lawyers Annual Meeting, June 27–30, 2005). Morris voiced a specific concern about the "great potential for unlawful activities aimed at influencing which manufacturers' prescription drugs are included on the formularies that are being developed by plan sponsors," and also noted the potential for Sponsors to manipulate data related to enrollees' out-of-pocket costs in order to keep enrollees in the coverage gap (so-called "doughnut hole") where the plans have no obligation to pay for the enrollee's covered drugs. *Id.* Morris reiterated and expounded upon this sentiment during his remarks at the Seventh Annual Pharmaceutical Regulatory and Compliance Congress and Best Practices Forum, commenting that in 2007 the OIG planned to focus on Part D and, in particular, risk areas related to price comparisons between Part B and Part D, beneficiary access to drugs, adequacy of drug utilization controls, duplicate claims because of plan switches, and CMS oversight of beneficiary true out-of-pocket (TrOOP) cost calculations. *See Off-Label Drug Promotion Remains Key Concern for Federal Law Enforcers*, 10 HEALTH CARE FRAUD REP. (BNA) 837 (Nov. 22, 2006).

[40] *See CMS Says Agency Must Continue Oversight Of Marketing Efforts by Managed Care Plans*, 11 HEALTH CARE FRAUD REP. (BNA) 361 (May 23, 2007); *Medicare, Medicaid Still At-Risk to Fraud, Abuse, and Mismanagement, GAO Says*, 11 HEALTH CARE FRAUD REP. (BNA) 123 (Feb. 14, 2007); *Federal Justice Department Officials Say HHS OIG Work Plan Sets Top Priorities*, 10 HEALTH CARE FRAUD REP. (BNA) 31 (Oct. 11, 2006).

[41] Testimony of Daniel R. Levinson, Inspector General, U.S. Dep't of Health and Human Servs. Before The House Committee on Ways and Means, Subcommittee on Health and Oversight Hearing (Mar. 8, 2007), at 11.

to Mr. Levinson, the OIG's strategic plan covers five broad areas: (1) enforcement and compliance, (2) payment accuracy and controls, (3) beneficiary access and protections, (4) drug pricing and reimbursement, and (5) information technology and systems.[42] He also indicated that the OIG already had initiated investigations of Medicare Part D cases.[43] As of August 2007, however, the OIG had not completed or at least had not publicly disclosed the results of Part D investigations.

## A. OIG Work Plans

The OIG publishes an annual work plan, which describes the agency's planned studies and areas of focus for the coming year and, essentially, offers the health care community a roadmap to the compliance issues that will be at the forefront of the agency's enforcement agenda. Often, many of the areas identified in the annual plan reflect recent investigations or settlements with health care entities. Sponsors and entities that do business with Sponsors under Part D should view the work plans as strong predictors of future enforcement activity.

### 1. 2006 Work Plan

In its 2006 Work Plan,[44] the OIG identified 18 distinct areas of concern about Part D that the agency intended to study, monitor, or investigate. Interestingly, a significant number of these studies focused on the efficacy of the procedures and controls CMS had implemented to contain FWA in the Part D program. More typically, the OIG concentrates on the behavior of recipients of Medicare money (e.g., providers, suppliers, Medicare health plans), rather than CMS. Clearly, the OIG wanted to make certain that CMS corrected any deficiencies in its untested policies and procedures for Part D oversight and administration. A brief discussion of each study and, when available, the OIG's findings, follows.

#### a. CMS Program Integrity Safeguards for Medicare Drug Plan Applicants

The OIG said in its 2006 Work Plan that it would review the bid and approval process for Part D plan sponsor applicants and assess the safeguards implemented by CMS to ensure applicants are qualified to provide drug benefits under Medicare Part D.[45] The OIG planned to pay particular attention to whether the safeguards implemented by CMS are effective in identifying applicants that raise program integrity concerns.

---

[42] *See id.*

[43] *See id.*

[44] U.S. Dep't of Health & Human Servs., Office of Inspector General, Work Plan for FY 2006 (Nov. 19, 2005), *available at* http://oig.hhs.gov/fraud/docs [hereinafter 2006 Work Plan].

[45] 2006 Work Plan at 11.

### b. Beneficiary Awareness of the Medicare Part D Low-Income Subsidy

The low-income subsidy benefit[46] provides full or partial assistance with premiums and cost-sharing obligations to Medicare beneficiaries with limited assets and incomes below 150 percent of the applicable federal poverty level.[47] Unlike the situation with full-benefit dual eligible individuals who, by statute,[48] are automatically enrolled in Part D, this population must sign up for Part D and submit applications for the low-income subsidy.[49] This study plan reflects the general belief that effective outreach to low-income-subsidy individuals will be difficult even though their prescription drug needs currently are underserved. The low levels of participation by the estimated population of low-income-subsidy eligible individuals when penalty-free enrollment in Part D was scheduled to end on May 15, 2006, caused CMS to extend the deadline through the end of 2007 for these individuals.[50] The need for this extension highlights the importance of the OIG's plan to carefully analyze the effectiveness of various methods of educating beneficiaries about the availability of the low-income subsidy, assessing applicant eligibility, and encouraging subsidy participation where appropriate. Using the results of the study, CMS hopes to put in place more effective outreach programs to resolve what otherwise could become a continuing problem with the benefit.

The OIG completed this initial study of the low-income subsidy issue in the fall of 2006 and reported its findings to CMS in a memorandum, dated

---

[46] *Id.*

[47] 42 C.F.R. §§423.771–423.800. To qualify for the low-income subsidy, a beneficiary must be enrolled in a prescription drug plan or Medicare Advantage plan, have an income below 150% of the applicable federal poverty level, have assets (excluding a primary residence) that meet specific resource limitations, and live in the United States. 42 C.F.R. §423.773. For individuals with incomes between 135% and 150% of the federal poverty level, the beneficiary must have liquid resources in 2006 either less than three times the amount of resources an individual may have and still be eligible for Supplemental Social Security Income (SSI) (including the assets of the individual's spouse) or less than $10,000 (if single) or $20,000 (if married, including the assets of the individual's spouse). For individuals with incomes below 135% of the federal poverty level, the beneficiary must have liquid resources less than three times the amount of resources an individual may have and still be eligible for SSI. 42 C.F.R. §423.773. Other significant rules govern the low-income subsidy, *see generally Medicare Drug Benefit, Low-Income Subsidy, and the Beltway Expectations Game*, THE PIPER REPORT (Aug. 6, 2005), *available at* http://www.piperreport.com/archives/2005/08/medicare_drug_b_1.html. For subsequent years, the amount of resources allowable for the previous year will be increased by the annual percentage increase in the consumer price index (all items, U.S. city average) as of September of that previous year, rounded to the nearest multiple of $10. 42 C.F.R. §423.773.

[48] Social Security Act §1860D–14(a)(1)(D) [42 U.S.C. §1395w–114(a)(1)(D)].

[49] CMS already had addressed at least part of this issue, i.e., by announcing a program for the facilitated enrollment of low-income-subsidy-eligible beneficiaries. *See* Centers for Medicare & Medicaid Servs., *PDP Guidance: Eligibility, Enrollment and Disenrollment*, §30.1.5 (June 30, 2006), *available at* http://www.cms.hhs.gov/PrescriptionDrugCovContra/Downloads/DraftPDPEnrollmentGuidance.pdf. CMS views "facilitated enrollment" as similar to autoenrollment for full-benefit dual eligibles. *Id.*

[50] *See* Letter from Cynthia G. Tudor, Acting Director, Medicare Drug Benefit Group (CMS), Regarding Instructions for 2007 Contract Year (Apr. 3, 2006), at 15, *available at* http://www.cms.hhs.gov/PrescriptionDrugCovContra/Downloads/2007PDPCallLetter.pdf [hereinafter 2007 Call Letter].

November 17, 2006.[51] The OIG found that there is no way to identify the pool of beneficiaries who may be eligible for the subsidy prior to receiving a beneficiary's application for the subsidy. CMS does not have a comprehensive source of income data to accurately identify potentially eligible beneficiaries who may benefit from education and outreach concerning the low-income subsidy.[52] The OIG concluded that legislation would be necessary to allow CMS to identify more effectively beneficiaries who are potentially eligible for the subsidy and to target more efficiently and effectively outreach efforts. The OIG further noted data sharing among federal agencies, such as CMS, the Internal Revenue Service, and the Social Security Administration, has been permitted by Congress in the administration of other Medicare benefits, for instance, the Medicare Secondary Payer program.[53]

### c. Tracking Beneficiaries' True Out-of-Pocket Costs for Part D Prescription Drug Coverage

The structure of the Part D benefit requires a beneficiary to incur out-of-pocket costs (deductibles and copayments only; premiums are not considered) of $3,600 in 2006 (increased annually)[54] before he or she qualifies for catastrophic drug coverage, where copayments fall to 5 percent.[55] Even prior to the implementation of Part D, government officials had identified the gaming of true out-of-pocket (TrOOP) costs as a particular concern from the perspective of FWA.[56] Depending on the nature of the abuse, TrOOP manipulation could deny beneficiaries needed drug coverage or add excess costs to the Medicare program. If a beneficiary's actual TrOOP expenditures were skewed downward, for example, by a Sponsor's inappropriate application of coverage denials[57] for expensive therapies while the beneficiary is in the benefit's coverage gap (i.e., the "doughnut hole"), the beneficiary could be forced to do without coverage for those drug therapies and also would remain in the coverage gap longer. In the meantime, the Sponsor would avoid bearing the cost of the denied drugs while continuing to

---

[51]Memorandum from Daniel R. Levinson (OIG) to Leslie V. Norwalk (CMS), *Identifying Beneficiaries Eligible for the Medicare Part D Low-Income Subsidy*, OEI-03-06-00120 (Nov. 17, 2006), *available at* http://www.oig.hhs.gov/oei/reports/oei-03-06-00120.pdf [hereinafter LOW INCOME SUBSIDY REPORT]. CMS provided specific guidance to Sponsors on the reassignment of low-income subsidy beneficiaries into Part D plans in its "call letter" for 2008. *See* Centers for Medicare & Medicaid Servs., 2008 Combined Call Letter (Apr. 19, 2007), at 73, *available at* http://www.cms.hhs.gov/PrescriptionDrugCovContra/Downloads/CallLetter.pdf [hereinafter 2008 Call Letter].

[52]The OIG noted the Internal Revenue Service may release individual tax returns only to a person designated by the taxpayer. *See* LOW INCOME SUBSIDY REPORT. Therefore, the Social Security Administration would not have access to this information for purposes of prospectively marketing the subsidy to those beneficiaries most in need.

[53]*See id.*

[54]The annual percentage increase for each year is equal to the annual percentage increase in average per capita aggregate expenditures for Part D drugs in the United States for Part D eligible individuals and is based on data for the 12-month period ending in July of the previous year. 42 C.F.R. §423.104(d)(5).

[55]42 C.F.R. §423.104(d).

[56]*See OIG Chief Counsel Cites Likely Areas of Potential Abuse*, I DRUG PRICING REP. & PART D COMPLIANCE, Issue 1 (Aug. 2005).

[57]Beneficiary spending on drugs that are not covered by their Part D plan does not count toward TrOOP. See Section II.B., below.

collect premiums and manufacturer rebates on those TrOOP-eligible drugs purchased by the beneficiary. On the other hand, if a beneficiary's actual TrOOP expenditures were skewed upward, for example, by a Sponsor's manipulation of drug prices for a particular therapy, then the beneficiary would reach the Part D catastrophic limit quicker than he or she should. Because Medicare pays $0.80 of every $1.00 spent on drugs in the catastrophic stage of the Part D benefit, this type of TrOOP manipulation could increase payments to the sponsor, and, in turn, Medicare costs.[58]

Through this study, the OIG would examine the accuracy of tracking mechanisms put in place to assess beneficiaries' TrOOP spending through Part D's Coordination of Benefits systems. The OIG also would assess the adequacy of CMS's oversight of TrOOP tracking processes.[59]

### d. Prescription Drug Plan Marketing Materials for Prescription Drug Benefits

The OIG sought to determine whether Sponsors' marketing materials were both compliant with CMS regulations and guidelines and comprehensible to beneficiaries.[60] How Sponsors market their plans to enrollees had been identified as a high-risk area for FWA. One concern is that Sponsors would seek to reduce their overall costs by "cherry-picking" low-cost beneficiaries through marketing materials and formulary designs that were (i) more attractive to beneficiaries the Sponsor believes would use fewer and/or less costly drugs, and/or (ii) less attractive to beneficiaries projected to be high-cost enrollees. Another concern is that Sponsors would induce or trick beneficiaries, who would otherwise opt for a stand-alone prescription drug plan so they can maintain their existing physician relationships, into inadvertently enrolling in a comprehensive MA-PD plan that promises to be more lucrative for the Sponsor, but not necessarily better for the beneficiary.

---

[58] 42 C.F.R. §423.336; see also Section III.A., below, for a discussion of allowable reinsurance costs under Part D.

[59] 2006 WORK PLAN at 12.

[60] *Id.* This particular study was not intended to look at certain more egregious fraud schemes perpetrated by entities that pose as sales agents for Part D plans in order to obtain demographic and financial information from beneficiaries that may be used to steal their identities or raid their bank accounts. Complaints about such scams were received against a number of different companies during the spring of 2006 and the OIG has reportedly been investigating these allegations. *See* Press Release, U.S. Dep't of Health & Human Servs., Centers for Medicare & Medicaid Servs., *Medicare Fights Against New Schemes to Defraud Beneficiaries* (June 16, 2006); Press Release, U.S. Dep't of Health & Human Servs., Centers for Medicare & Medicaid Servs., *Medicare Beneficiaries Urged to Be on the Look-Out for Phone Scams* (Mar. 7, 2006). Kimberly Brandt, Director of Program Integrity at CMS, reported that her own grandmother was a victim of such a scheme. *See Part D Benefit, Medicaid Fraud Fighting Highlighted by HHS Inspector General, CMS*, 11 HEALTH CARE DAILY REP. (BNA) (Apr. 25, 2006). CMS responded to these reports by publishing a fact sheet for beneficiaries to alert them to such illicit practices and educate them about steps to take to avoid becoming a victim. *See Quick Facts About Medicare Prescription Drug Coverage and Protecting Your Personal Information*, CMS Pub. 11,147 (Revised June 2006), *available at* http://www.medicare.gov/Publications/Pubs/pdf/11147.pdf.

### e. Autoenrollment of Dual Eligibles into Medicare Part D Plans

Under MMA, Congress transferred primary responsibility for providing drug coverage to full-benefit dual-eligible beneficiaries from Medicaid to Medicare under Part D provisions that waive premiums and deductibles, and greatly limit cost-sharing obligations for this vulnerable population when they are enrolled in cost-effective plans.[61] To facilitate the transition from Medicaid to Medicare, MMA stipulates that full-benefit dual eligibles should be automatically enrolled in qualifying stand-alone Part D prescription drug plans and then allowed, if they wish, to change their plan selection.[62] Unfortunately, the size of the dual-eligible population, inadequate technology, miscommunications, and numerous other factors, including the preponderance of dual eligibles residing in long-term care facilities and/or with cognitive impairments, caused significant delays and confusion in the autoenrollment process. Many beneficiaries reported difficulties in obtaining drugs from pharmacies because their Medicaid drug coverage had been canceled before pharmacies were able to confirm their enrollment in Part D or their entitlement to drugs without the payment of premiums, deductibles, and standard plan copayments.[63]

The OIG intended to analyze the factors that contributed to the problems with the autoenrollment process, and to identify any further systems changes that could help prevent future difficulties as beneficiaries transition in and out of dual-eligible status. In addition, the OIG planned to evaluate data concerning the numbers of dual eligibles that were overlooked in the autoenrollment process and the numbers that switched plans after autoenrollment. Given the difficult operational issues facing long-term care facilities (and the institutional pharmacies that

---

[61] Social Security Act §1860D-14(a)(1)(D) [42 U.S.C. §1395w–114(a)(1)(D)]. Under MMA, beneficiaries who are full-benefit dual eligibles and whose income does not exceed 100% of the federal poverty limit are not obligated to pay the otherwise applicable coinsurance amount for Part D drugs, and, instead, must pay a copayment, in 2007, of $1 for generic drugs or preferred drugs that are multiple source drugs (i.e., sold by more than one manufacturer or by one manufacturer under two or more different proprietary names) and $3.10 for all other drugs. *Id.* For 2007 adjustments see also Centers for Medicare & Medicaid Servs., Office of the Actuary, Medicare Part D Benefit Parameters for Standard Benefit: Annual Adjustments for 2007 (May 22, 2006), *available at* http://www.cms.hhs.gov/MedicareAdvtgSpecRateStats/downloads/2007_Part_D_Parameter_Update.pdf.

[62] Social Security Act §1860D-1(b) [42 U.S.C. §1395w–101(b)]; 42 C.F.R. §423.34(d).

[63] *See* Press Release, U.S. Dep't of Health & Human Servs., Centers for Medicare & Medicaid Servs., *Medicare Takes Steps to Help People with Limited Incomes and Resources Take Advantage of Comprehensive Medicare Drug Coverage* (Mar. 20, 2006), *available at* http://www.cms.hhs.gov/apps/media/press/release.asp?Counter=1806; *see also Medicare Part D Drug Benefit Brings Significant Program Changes, Uncertainty*, 11 HEALTH CARE DAILY REP. (BNA) (Jan. 18, 2006). Several Medicare and Medicaid beneficiary advocacy groups have filed lawsuits against HHS and CMS relating to the efficient enrollment of dual eligibles into the Part D program. *See id.* (citing New York Statewide Senior Action Council v. Leavitt, No. 05-09549-LAP (S.D.N.Y. complaint filed Nov. 14, 2005) (dismissed Dec. 30, 2005 for lack of jurisdiction) *and* Erb v. McClellan, No. 05-CV-6201 (E.D. Pa. complaint filed Dec. 5, 2005). In March 2006, CMS reached an agreement in the *Erb* case with the Pennsylvania Health Law Project (PHLP) and the Center for Medicare Advocacy to extend the transition period for more than 110,000 Medicare and Medicaid beneficiaries in Pennsylvania, who were passively enrolled into a Medicare HMO. Under the settlement agreement, beneficiaries covered by the settlement may continue to see out-of-network providers without first obtaining a referral or a prior authorization and may also continue to obtain off-formulary drugs they were taking before January 1, 2006, without prior authorization or other obstacles, until June 30, 2006. *See Part D Drug Benefit to Extend Transition for Pennsylvania's Dual Eligibles*, 11 HEALTH CARE DAILY REP. (BNA) (Mar. 29, 2006).

serve them) due to the fact that any given facility may have residents enrolled in multiple Part D plans, the OIG's report also was expected to cover this enrollment issue with specific regard to beneficiaries in long-term care settings.

### f. Medicare Prescription Drug Benefit Pharmacy Access in Rural Areas

MMA requires that beneficiaries have convenient access to retail pharmacies and establishes minimum pharmacy access standards.[64] The OIG announced an audit of beneficiary access to retail pharmacies that dispense Medicare Part D covered prescription drugs in rural areas.[65] The study also would assess the Sponsor compliance with the minimum pharmacy access requirements.

### g. Monitoring Fluctuation in Drug Prices Under Prescription Drug Plans and MA-PD Plans

Under MMA, most beneficiaries are permitted to select a stand-alone prescription drug plan or an MA-PD plan during an annual open enrollment period. They then are locked into their chosen plan until the next plan year. Because beneficiaries are expected to base their plan selection in part on an assessment of the overall costs for the drugs they anticipate taking during the plan year, the OIG had expressed concerns about "bait and switch" activities by Sponsors.[66] Therefore, the OIG created a study to monitor patterns of drug price variations over the course of a plan year for both stand-alone and MA-PD plans.[67] Given the debate over the cost-effectiveness of using private plan partners to deliver the Part D benefit instead of allowing the government to negotiate with pharmaceutical manufacturers for discounted prices,[68] this study

---

[64] Social Security Act §1860D-4(b)(1)(C) [42 U.S.C. §1395w–104(b)(1)(C)]; 42 C.F.R. §423.120.

[65] 2006 WORK PLAN at 12.

[66] For example, inducing a beneficiary into a particular plan with a promise of a low cost-sharing tier for a particular drug and then eliminating the drug or changing its cost-sharing tier after enrollment. *See* PDBM Chapter 9 §70.1.1 (Apr. 25, 2006), *available at* http://www.cms.hhs .gov/PrescriptionDrugCovContra/Downloads/PDBManual_Chapter9_FWA.pdf.

[67] 2006 WORK PLAN at 12.

[68] *See* §1860D-11(i) [42 U.S.C. §1395w–111(i)]. MMA expressly states that HHS "may not interfere with the negotiations between drug manufacturers and pharmacies and PDP sponsors" or "require a particular formulary or institute a price structure for the reimbursement of covered part D drugs." *Id.* After the Democratic Party gained a majority in the 110th Congress after the 2006 elections, there was discussion on Capitol Hill about whether Medicare was paying too much for prescription drugs under Part D and whether the program would be better served by allowing CMS to negotiate price directly with pharmaceutical manufacturers. Within the first 100 hours of the new Congressional session, Representatives John D. Dingell (D-Mich.), Jo Ann Emerson (D-Mo.), Charles B. Rangel (D-NY), Carol Shea-Porter (D-NH), and more than 190 Republican and Democratic House members introduced the Medicare Prescription Drug Negotiation Act of 2007 (H.R. 4), which would *require* the federal government to negotiate directly with pharmaceutical manufacturers over drug prices for products covered under Medicare Part D. *See Democrats Seek Probe of Marketing by Rx Plan Sponsors, Offer New Bill*, 11 HEALTH CARE DAILY REP. (BNA) (Jan. 31, 2006). H.R. 4 passed the House by a vote of 255 to 170 on January 12, 2007. *See Medicare Rx Negotiation Bill Dies in Senate After Lawmakers Oppose Attempt at Cloture*, 12 HEALTH CARE DAILY REP. (BNA) (Apr. 19, 2007).

The Senate Finance Committee approved a similar bill (S. 3) by a vote of 13 to 8 on April 12, 2007. *Id.* Yet the advancement of this reform stalled when the Senate defeated an attempt by Senate Majority Leader Harry Reid (D-Nev.) to obtain cloture on the bill. *Id.* Without a vote for

posed an interesting question as to whether the OIG would follow past practice and compare Part D prices with government-negotiated prices available to the Department of Veterans Affairs.[69]

### h. Coordination and Oversight of Medicare Part B and D to Avoid Duplicate Payments

The OIG intended to examine whether there is sufficient coordination and oversight of Medicare Parts B and D to prevent duplicate payments for drugs.[70] The Part D benefit does not cover drugs that, as prescribed and administered or dispensed, would be covered under Medicare Part B (e.g., drugs injected or infused in a physician's office, separately billable drugs administered to dialysis patients under the end-stage renal disease benefit, drugs administered through nebulizers, etc.).[71] Although Sponsors should not be paying claims for Part B drugs, they also should not be unduly delaying access to drugs just because they may, at times, be covered by Part B.[72] Similarly, physicians and suppliers should

---

cloture, Senators opposing the bill would be able to filibuster and, effectively, prevent the bill from ever coming to the floor of the Senate for a vote. Moreover, even if both houses of Congress passed a bill, President George W. Bush promised to veto any bill allowing the Medicare program to negotiate drug prices directly with manufacturers. *Id.* Another bill (S. 250), technically alive in the Senate as of August 2007, would remove the prohibition in MMA against direct negotiations in limited circumstances. Specifically, HHS would be *required* to negotiate contracts with drug manufacturers if a drug is a single source medication without a therapeutic equivalent, and to *participate* in the negotiation of contracts with manufacturers for Part D covered drugs at the request of the plan Sponsor, for covered Part D drugs for which there is a substantial amount of Federal research funding in the development of the drug and for any comprehensive fallback prescription drug plan HHS must provide. The full text of S. 250 is available at http://frwebgate .access.gpo.gov/cgi-bin/getdoc.cgi?dbname=110_cong_bills&docid=f:s250is.txt.pdf.

Proponents of allowing the government to directly negotiate with manufacturers argue that the purchasing power of a program as large as Medicare Part D would drive down the price of pharmaceuticals. If successful, these price reductions also would trickle down to state Medicaid programs, which are entitled to the "best price" offered to any other drug purchaser. CMS has opposed this strategy, stating that that direct government negotiations are "unnecessary because experience with Part D thus far demonstrates that competition and plan negotiation are clearly working . . . [and] [w]ere the government to negotiate prices directly in an attempt to obtain lower prices, access to drugs would likely be restricted . . . . Price negotiating requires limiting access to some drugs, while promoting others in exchange for price discounts." CMS Fact Sheet, CMS Actuaries Conclude That H.R. 4 Would Have No Effect on Lowering Drug Prices (Jan. 11, 2007), *available at* http://www.cms.hhs.gov/apps/media/press/release.asp?Counter=2072&intNum PerPage=10&checkDate=&checkKey=&srchType=&numDays=3500&srchOpt=0&srchData= &keywordType=All&chkNewsType=1%2C+2%2C+3%2C+4%2C+5&intPage=&showAll= &pYear=&year=&desc=false&cboOrder=date.

[69]*See, e.g.,* Dep't Health & Human Servs., Office of Inspector General, Comparing Drug Reimbursement: Medicare and Department of Veterans Affairs, OEI-03-97-00293 (Nov. 1998), *available at* http://oig.hhs.gov/oei/reports/oei-03-97-00293.pdf.

[70]2006 Work Plan at 12.

[71]*See* CMS Draft Guidance, Medicare Part B Versus Part D Coverage Issues (July 27, 2005), *available at* http://www.cms.hhs.gov/PrescriptionDrugCovGenIn/Downloads/PartBand PartDdoc_07.27.05.pdf.

[72]The Medicare Payment Advisory Commission (MedPAC) also has considered this issue. *See* MedPAC, Public Meeting Transcript (Mar. 8–9, 2007), at 387–412, *available at* http://www .medpac.gov/transcripts/0307_allcombined_transc.pdf. On April 12, 2007, MedPAC approved three recommendations to Congress for limiting the confusion over coverage policies for drugs covered under both Medicare Part B and Part D. *See* MedPAC, Public Meeting Transcript (Apr. 12–13, 2007), at 214–248, http://www.medpac.gov/transcripts/0407_allcombined_transcript .pdf. As formally presented to Congress in its June 2007 report, MedPAC recommended that

not be billing Part B for drugs that were dispensed by a retail pharmacy and re-imbursed under Part D. Claims knowingly submitted to the Medicare Part B program for drugs covered by the Part D benefit could support a false claims case.[73]

### i. Enrollee Access to Negotiated Prices for Covered Part D Drugs

The OIG planned to examine whether stand-alone prescription drug plans and MA-PD plans are complying with the program requirement that beneficiaries have access to negotiated prices for drugs covered under Part D.[74] MMA and its implementing regulations require that enrollees have "access to negotiated prices [including all discounts, direct or indirect subsidies, rebates, and direct or indirect remunerations] used for payment for covered Part D drugs, regardless of the fact that no benefits may be payable under the coverage with respect to such drugs because of the application of a deductible or other cost-sharing or an initial coverage limit" or because they are purchased by the beneficiary in the benefit's coverage gap.[75] Given the importance beneficiaries place on premium rates in choosing a drug plan, the OIG likely wanted to ensure that, once enrolled in a plan, Sponsors actually pass through all negotiated discounts received from drug manufacturers to the beneficiaries as reductions in premiums. It would be interesting, however, to see precisely how the OIG interprets the concept of negotiated prices, particularly in light of the increased transparency required for drug prices under the Deficit Reduction Act of 2005.[76] Arguably, the study plan could be read to imply an expectation by the OIG that all price concessions should be passed through to the beneficiary. However, MMA does not go that far, requiring only that negotiated prices "*take into account* negotiated price concessions."[77] The Part D Final Rule also recognizes the right of Sponsors to retain some undefined portion of the price concessions they negotiate. The regulatory definition of negotiated prices states merely that they "[a]re reduced by those discounts, direct or indirect subsidies, rebates, other price concessions, and direct or indirect remunerations that *the Part D sponsor has elected to pass through* to Part D enrollees at the point of sale."[78]

---

Congress should (i) direct CMS to identify selected overlap drugs and direct plans to always cover them under Part D; identified drugs should be low cost and covered under Part D most of the time; (ii) allow plans to cover a transitional supply of overlap drugs under Part D under the same conditions as the general transition policy applied by CMS; and (iii) permit coverage for appropriate preventive vaccines under Medicare Part B instead of Part D. *See* MedPAC, *Report to the Congress: Promoting Greater Efficiency in Medicare,* Chapter 7 (Issues in Medicare Coverage of Drugs) (June 2007), *available at* http://www.medpac.gov/chapters/Jun07_Ch07.pdf.

[73] "If you are a PDP [Sponsor], a fraud on you is a fraud on the government." Remarks of former Assistant U.S. Attorney James G. Sheehan at the American Health Lawyers Association and Health Care Compliance Association Fraud and Compliance Forum (Sept. 26–27, 2005) (*reported in Part D Fraud Opportunities Abound: PDPs Will Be Key to Detection, Reporting,* 3 Pharmaceutical Law and Industry Rep. (BNA) 1024 (Sept. 30, 2005)).

[74] 2006 Work Plan at 12.

[75] Social Security Act §1860D-2(d) [42 U.S.C. §1395w-102]; *see also* 42 C.F.R. §423.104(g).

[76] Deficit Reduction Act of 2005 (DRA), Pub. L. No. 109-171, 120 Stat. 4, §6001 (Feb. 8, 2006), *amending* Social Security Act §1927 [42 U.S.C. §1396r–8] to require that CMS disclose (through a Web site accessible to the public) average manufacturer prices.

[77] MMA §101, adding Social Security Act §1860D–2(d)(1)(B) (emphasis added).

[78] 42 C.F.R. §423.100 (emphasis added).

Sponsors should pay careful attention to any conclusions drawn by the OIG on this matter to avoid a potentially significant compliance risk.

### j. Prescription Drug Plans' Use of Formularies

The OIG proposed to evaluate whether the Sponsors' management of their formularies complies with Part D regulations and Medicare program guidance.[79] The OIG's study would focus on three broad areas: (1) the Pharmacy and Therapeutics (P&T) committees that construct the formularies; (2) the breadth and depth of drugs included on the formularies; and (3) beneficiary management tools, including beneficiaries' rights to formulary exceptions and appeals.

CMS approves Part D formularies prior to the beginning of each plan year.[80] Most changes to a Sponsor's Part D formulary during a plan year require CMS approval. In cases in which a Sponsor intends to make a change to the formulary that is likely to adversely affect beneficiaries, such as removing a drug from the formulary or changing a drug's out-of-pocket cost to the beneficiary, CMS will approve the change only if the Sponsor exempts beneficiaries currently taking the drug.[81] CMS's formulary approval process is intended to ensure that beneficiaries have access to a therapeutically appropriate array of drugs that is not selected to entice or discourage certain types of patients. For example, formularies may be manipulated in more subtle ways to steer certain types of patients to or away from a plan, e.g., telling CMS a particular drug is included on a plan's formulary but not listing the drug on the CMS Formulary Plan Finder so that beneficiaries who take the drug would believe it is not covered under the Sponsor's plan. As a result, the OIG's study likely would assess the effectiveness of CMS oversight from an access perspective, as well as look at formulary operations from a "bait and switch" perspective.

The OIG's formulary study potentially could focus on kickback concerns as well. In the OIG Compliance Program Guidance for Pharmaceutical Manufacturers,[82] the OIG discussed the kickback risks associated with certain interactions between pharmaceutical manufacturers and P&T committee members. It also raised kickback concerns about manufacturers' payments for formulary placement and their financing of certain formulary support services. This study could afford the OIG an opportunity to probe these types of relationships in the context of Part D.

Further, if Sponsors and manufacturers have not carefully separated their Part D and commercial contracting functions, the OIG's formulary study could stumble upon pricing arrangements in which the manufacturer offers the

---

[79] 2006 WORK PLAN at 13.

[80] 42 C.F.R. §423.272(b).

[81] 42 C.F.R. §423.120(b); *see also* Letter from Abby L. Block, Director, Center for Beneficiary Choices (CMS), to Part D Sponsors, *regarding* Formulary Changes During the Plan Year, dated April 27, 2006, *available at* http://www.amcp.org/data/nav_content/Part%20D%20 Policy%20of%20Drug%20Continuity%20-%2004.27.06.pdf.

[82] 68 Fed. Reg. 23,731, 23,736 (May 5, 2003).

Sponsor a better price on drugs for the Sponsor's commercial plan(s) in return for the Sponsor's Medicare Part D business. Such a "swap" arrangement could raise concerns under the anti-kickback statute. In addition, this type of scheme allows Sponsors to conceal the price concession from Medicare, thereby artificially inflating Part D costs.

### k. Coordination Between State Pharmaceutical Assistance Programs and Medicare Part D

The OIG planned to examine the coordination between State Pharmaceutical Assistance Programs (SPAPs)[83] and Medicare Part D to determine whether SPAP-eligible beneficiaries enrolled in Part D are able to obtain needed assistance and appropriate drug coverage under the Medicare program.[84] CMS provided detailed coordination of benefits instructions, which include a section on SPAP procedures, in Chapter 14 of the Medicare Prescription Drug Benefit Manual (PDBM).[85] Further, in the 2008 Call Letter, CMS announced that, beginning with the 2008 coverage year, it would review coordinating criteria established by SPAPs for beneficiary enrollment in a Part D plan.[86] CMS will not permit SPAPs "to specify coordinating criteria of the sort that would be difficult for plans to meet" which, according to CMS, "would result in a narrow pool of preferred Part D plans into which the SPAP (when acting as its beneficiaries' authorized representative) would enroll its beneficiaries, in violation of the SPAP non-discrimination requirement."[87] In other words, SPAPs may not implement burdensome rules for enrollment in prescription drug plans that in effect would result in the SPAP "steering" its beneficiaries into a preferred plan or plans.[88]

The OIG also could address the kickback implications of certain arrangements between SPAPs and Sponsors. In a memorandum to potential Sponsors,[89] CMS explained its concerns about Sponsors or SPAPs that eliminate choice in prescription drug plans for the low-income-subsidy population by steering them toward one preferred Sponsor. CMS became aware that certain states with the authority to act as agents for their SPAP enrollees were making deals with Sponsors to move these low-income beneficiaries into the Sponsor's plan.[90] In exchange, the state would receive, either from the Sponsor or directly from

---

[83] "SPAPs provide funding for prescription drugs to eligible senior and disabled citizens in their States. A significant portion of individuals currently enrolled in SPAPs became eligible for Medicare Part D drug coverage in January 2006. SPAPs may offer wrap-around benefits to beneficiaries with Medicare Part D coverage who experience a coverage gap." *See* 2006 WORK PLAN at 13.

[84] 2006 WORK PLAN at 13.

[85] *See* Medicare PDBM Chapter 14, Coordination of Benefits, at 14, *available at* http://www.cms.hhs.gov/PrescriptionDrugCovContra/downloads/PDMChapt14COB.pdf.

[86] *See* 2008 Call Letter at 76.

[87] *Id.*

[88] *See id.*

[89] Memorandum from Leslie Norwalk, Deputy Administrator (CMS) to Potential Part D Sponsors, State Medicaid Directors, and State Pharmaceutical Assistance Programs, *SPAP Assistance for Low Income Subsidy Eligible Individuals Under the Medicare Prescription Drug Benefit* (undated), *available at* http://www.cms.hhs.gov/States/Downloads/TheMemorandumtoPotentialPartDSponsors,SMD,andSPAPs.pdf.

[90] *Id.* at 2.

the drug manufacturer, rebates or other financial considerations generated from drug sales to the low-income beneficiaries.[91] Because Sponsors are supposed to report rebate data and use rebates and other cost savings on the price of Part D drugs to reduce overall plan costs, CMS objected to the planned SPAP-Sponsor deals because they could increase costs for all Medicare beneficiaries and the Medicare program.[92] CMS also suggested that the establishment of such arrangements could violate the federal fraud and abuse laws.[93]

*l. Implementation of Required Programs to Deter Fraud, Waste, and Abuse*

The OIG announced a study to examine the mechanisms put in place by CMS to oversee these compliance programs.[94] The OIG also announced that it would evaluate whether the compliance programs established by stand-alone and MA-PD plans to deter FWA are consistent with CMS guidelines and the applicable regulations in the Part D Final Rule.

The OIG commenced this study in January 2006 by reviewing the Part D compliance plan of every Sponsor selected by CMS to determine whether each Sponsor had:

(1) developed a compliance plan that addressed all eight elements required by the MMA; and

(2) addressed in their compliance plans all of CMS's subregulatory requirements and selected recommendations regarding the eight compliance plan elements.[95]

In reviewing the compliance plans, the OIG relied on two compliance guidance documents issued by CMS: (1) a summary guidance document issued by CMS in June 2005 and (2) Chapter 9 of the Prescription Drug Benefit Manual (PDBM Chapter 9). The OIG considered whether each plan addressed the 17 requirements for establishing a Part D compliance plan that CMS included in its summary guidance, and also whether each compliance plan addressed a sampling of 11 recommendations included in PDBM Chapter 9.

The OIG completed its study in December 2006 and found that while all 79 Part D plans had implemented some form of compliance plan, only seven addressed each of CMS's 17 subregulatory requirements for a Part D compliance plan.[96] Further, only 15 plans incorporated all 11 recommendations

---

[91]*Id.*

[92]*Id.* at 3.

[93]*Id.*

[94]2006 WORK PLAN at 13.

[95]DEP'T HEALTH & HUMAN SERVS., OFFICE OF INSPECTOR GENERAL, PRESCRIPTION DRUG PLAN SPONSORS' COMPLIANCE PLANS, OEI-03-06-00100 (Dec. 2006), *available at* http://oig .hhs.gov/oei/reports/oei-03-06-00100.pdf [hereinafter 2006 OIG REPORT].

[96]*Id.* at 4. Nearly all of the deficiencies identified by the OIG related to designation of a compliance officer (and compliance committee) and establishing procedures for internal monitoring and auditing. Further, according to the report, 71 plans failed to address all of the compliance plan requirements for monitoring and auditing. *Id.*

the OIG selected from PDBM Chapter 9. The OIG reported that plans most frequently failed to address CMS's recommendations regarding fraud detection procedures, fraud awareness training, and efforts to coordinate and cooperate with CMS and law enforcement agencies.[97] The OIG also determined that 44 of the 79 Part D plans failed to include any provisions for monitoring and auditing downstream entities.[98] This finding is particularly important given the compliance oversight responsibility Sponsors have over their sub-contractors.

As a general matter, it was not entirely unexpected that the OIG would find a substantial number of Part D plans in 2006 (the inaugural year of Part D) to be out of compliance with PDBM Chapter 9. Sponsors, as well as CMS, faced significant challenges in implementing Part D. The Part D Final Rule was essentially silent on the parameters for developing a compliance plan for FWA. CMS only was able to provide Sponsors with a skeleton summary of its compliance guidance before Part D went into effect. Yet, as CMS learned from its early experience with Part D and listened to feedback from Sponsors and beneficiaries, its compliance guidance grew robust. Throughout 2006 and into much of 2007, CMS published guidance documents with regularity as it refined existing guidance and identified new issues to bring to the attention of Sponsors. At times, however, the evolution of CMS's guidance resulted in policy changes, necessitating second and sometimes third versions of the same guidance document. The difficulty Sponsors experienced in obtaining reliable guidance from CMS during the developmental stages of Part D in 2005 and 2006 almost certainly contributed to the audit results in the 2006 OIG Report.

In responding to the 2006 OIG Report, CMS acknowledged that "the short timeframe for implementing many new provisions of the [MMA] may have had an impact on how thorough documents, such as compliance plans, were."[99] For instance, the OIG found most Part D compliance plans failed to identify a specific individual responsible for compliance issues related to FWA. Yet, CMS had not established that particular requirement until well after Sponsors had to submit their compliance plans to the OIG. In fact, CMS did not publish a final version of PDBM Chapter 9 until April 2006, more than four months after the effective date for Part D. Accordingly, many Sponsors may have designated their general compliance officer to oversee FWA compliance issues without expressly stating so in the compliance plan. Given that CMS was aware of this situation, it seems unlikely that the agency would sanction a Part D plan that failed to meet all requirements for its compliance plan in 2006. In 2007 and 2008, however, Sponsors should expect CMS to enforce the Part D requirements to the full extent of its authority. Further, as the OIG completes more studies and identifies patterns of noncompliant behavior, individual Sponsors may be targeted for further investigation.

---

[97] *Id.* at 9.
[98] *Id.* at 10.
[99] *Id.*

## m. Prescription Drug Cards

The OIG had been assessing whether sufficient controls were in place to minimize or eliminate FWA in transitional assistance payments made under the Medicare discount drug card program,[100] which terminated in January 2006. Between August 2006 and January 2007, the OIG issued five reports finding that a sponsor of a discount drug card program did not have proper procedures in place to ensure that beneficiaries did not exceed their transitional assistance (TA) limits under the program, apply TA funds only to covered drugs, or pass on to beneficiaries the proper amount of rebates included in the negotiated price of the drugs.[101] In each case, the OIG found that, as a result, the sponsor received overpayments from CMS and, therefore, recommended that the sponsor reimburse CMS for the amount of the overpayment and that the sponsor implement policies and procedures, if it continues as a Part D Sponsor, to ensure that it (a) does not pay for statutorily excluded drugs with CMS funds and (b) offers negotiated prices to beneficiaries. While the drug card program has been replaced by Part D, the OIG's experience with the program allowed the agency to get a head start building a knowledge base for monitoring and enforcing compliance under Part D. Sponsors that were required to refund money to CMS as a result of the OIG's investigation into the drug card program very likely would be under close scrutiny as Sponsors of Part D plans.

---

[100]The discount drug card program was authorized by MMA to provide temporary assistance to qualified beneficiaries prior to the implementation of the Part D prescription drug benefit. Social Security Act §1860D-31 [42 U.S.C. §1395w–141]. Under the program, which began accepting enrollees in May 2004, beneficiaries whose incomes fell within certain ranges of the federal poverty level qualified for $600 federal assistance (transitional assistance) in the purchase of prescription drugs through a discount drug card. *Id.* Sponsors had asked the OIG for guidance on the application of the agency's fraud and abuse authorities to payments from drug card program sponsors to network pharmacies for "education and outreach services" in connection with the enrollment of new members. In April 2004, the OIG responded by issuing guidance that concluded payments to network pharmacies may raise anti-kickback concerns. U.S. Dep't of Health & Human Servs., Education and Outreach Arrangements Between Medicare-Endorsed Discount Drug Card Sponsors and Their Network Pharmacies Under the Anti-Kickback Statute (Apr. 8, 2004), *available at* http://oig.hhs.gov/fraud/docs/alertsandbulletins/2004/FA040904.pdf. Shortly thereafter, the OIG published a regulation specifying its authority to impose CMPs against drug card program sponsors that knowingly engaged in false or misleading marketing practices, overcharged enrollees, or misused transitional assistance funds. *See* OIG Civil Money Penalties Under the Medicare Prescription Drug Discount Card Program, 69 Fed. Reg. 74,451 (Dec. 14, 2004).

[101]U.S. Dep't of Health and Human Servs., Office of Inspector General, Report on the Medicare Drug Discount Card Program Sponsor Computer Sciences Corporation, A-06-06-00112 (Dec. 18, 2006); U.S. Dep't of Health and Human Servs., Office of Inspector General, Report on the Medicare Drug Discount Card Program Sponsor McKesson Health Solutions, A-06-06-00022 (Sept. 25, 2006); U.S. Dep't of Health and Human Servs., Office of Inspector General, Report on the Medicare Drug Discount Card Program Sponsor Medco Health Solutions, A-06-05-00066 (Sept. 25, 2006); U.S. Dep't of Health and Human Servs., Office of Inspector General, Report on the Medicare Drug Discount Card Program Sponsor aClaim, Inc., A-06-06-00014 (Sept. 25, 2006); U.S. Dep't of Health and Human Servs., Office of Inspector General, Report on the Medicare Drug Discount Card Program Sponsor Public Sector Partners, A-06-05-00062 (Jul. 10, 2006).

### n. Employer Subsidies for Drug Coverage

MMA provides a mechanism for Medicare to provide a subsidy to employers[102] that sponsor[103] qualified retiree prescription drug plans. The subsidy equals 28 percent of a retiree's allowable drug costs[104] attributable to gross retiree costs between the cost threshold ($250 in 2006 and $265 in 2007) and the cost limit ($5,000 in 2006 and $5,350 in 2007).[105] The OIG planned to assess whether CMS has implemented effective controls to ensure that only qualified sponsors receive the subsidy.[106] Employer subsidies constitute a significant expense under Part D and the OIG views the subsidies as ripe for FWA. To qualify for a subsidy, an employer self-certifies to CMS the count of qualified retirees in its plan. The employer also self-certifies that drug coverage under the subsidized retiree plan will be at least actuarially equivalent to coverage under Part D. The OIG intends to audit a sampling of employer records as part of its review.

### o. Medicare Part D Drug Benefit Payments

The OIG intended to review a sampling of Part D beneficiaries' claim files to evaluate the payment policies and procedures and the computerized payment systems established by CMS.[107] The OIG would focus on whether CMS has controls in place to ensure that (1) benefits are paid on behalf of eligible beneficiaries and (2) Medicare, as well as the beneficiaries, are paid appropriate amounts for drug coverage. Though it has conducted similar oversight reviews of other Medicare benefits, the OIG likely viewed this type of assessment as even more important in the context of Part D because of the public-private partnership approach adopted for the delivery of the prescription drug benefit, the number of different parties typically involved in the delivery of the benefit,

---

[102]In an effort to encourage employers to maintain drug coverage for certain retired employees after the implementation of the Part D benefit, MMA created the Retiree Drug Subsidy (RDS) program, which requires CMS to pay special subsidy payments on a tax-exempt basis to sponsors (e.g., private or governmental employers, labor unions) of qualified retiree prescription drug plans for each qualified covered retiree. The sponsors of these subsidy plans can receive an annual subsidy equal to 28% of specified retiree drug costs. *See* Social Security Act §1860D-22 [42 U.S.C. §1395w–132]; 42 C.F.R. §423.880.

[103]For purposes of the employer subsidy, "sponsor" means a plan sponsor as defined in §3(16)(B) of the Employee Retirement Income Security Act of 1974, 29 U.S.C. §1002(16)(B), except that, in the case of a plan maintained jointly by one employer and an employee organization and for which the employer is the primary source of financing, the term means the employer. 42 C.F.R. §423.882.

[104]For purposes of the employer subsidy, "allowable drug costs" means covered retiree plan-related prescription drug costs that are actually paid (net any manufacturer or pharmacy discounts, chargebacks, rebates, and similar price concessions) by either the qualified retiree prescription drug plan or the qualifying covered retiree (or on the qualifying covered retiree's behalf), but excludes administrative costs incurred under the plan for Part D drugs during the year, whether paid for by the plan or the retiree, including costs directly related to the dispensing of Part D drugs. 42 C.F.R. §423.882.

[105]Social Security Act §1860D-22 [42 U.S.C. §1395w–132]; 42 C.F.R. §423.886.

[106]2006 Work Plan at 13.

[107]*Id.* at 14.

the complex combination of plan payment methodologies adopted by Congress, and the rapidity with which CMS was tasked with implementing such a massive new Medicare benefit.

### p. State Contribution to Drug Benefit Costs Assumed by Medicare

The OIG has had ongoing concerns about state "gaming" of Medicaid funding mechanisms.[108] Part D provides a new opportunity for states to manipulate federal financial participation (FFP) in state Medicaid programs. MMA requires the Medicare program, under Part D, to subsidize the prescription drug costs of full-benefit, dual-eligible individuals who previously were insured for outpatient prescription drugs under a state Medicaid program. Beginning in January 2006, all states and the District of Columbia became responsible for making monthly payments to the federal government to defray a portion of the Medicare drug expenditures for these individuals.[109] This so-called "clawback" provision[110] wedges a considerable amount of money between CMS and state Medicaid agencies.[111] Several states have taken the position that the federal government has no authority to levy such a "tax" on them.[112] Given the

---

[108] In testimony before the Senate Finance Committee on States' use of Medicaid financing mechanisms and pricing of Medicaid prescription drugs, the OIG reported that "Intergovernmental transfers (IGT), one such State financing mechanism, are transfers of non-Federal public funds between local public Medicaid providers and State Medicaid agencies. Misuse of IGTs circumvents the Federal/State Medicaid partnership and increases Federal payments to States at the expense of the intended beneficiaries." *See* Press Release, Dep't of Health & Human Servs., Office of Inspector General, *OIG Reports $35.4 Billion in Savings and Recoveries* (Dec. 2, 2005). For example, audits conducted by the OIG in 2005 identified several nursing homes in which the quality of care was adversely affected because of state abuses of Medicaid funding mechanisms. *See id.* Regarding Part D, the OIG likely has concerns that states will try to continue claiming federal financial participation for full-benefit dual eligibles who received prescription drug coverage through the state Medicaid program but have now switched over to Medicare Part D.

[109] Social Security Act §1935(c) [42 U.S.C. §1396u–5(c)]; 42 C.F.R. §423.908–910.

[110] The "clawback" provision, enacted under MMA §103, obligates every state and the District of Columbia to pay to CMS a "phased-down contribution" to defray a portion of the Medicare prescription drug expenditures for individuals whose projected Medicaid drug coverage is assumed by Medicare Part D. 42 C.F.R. §423.910. The monthly state contributions for each year are based on a percentage of the projected amount the state would have had to spend to provide prescription drug coverage for the dual eligibles through its Medicaid program. Beginning in January 2006, states became obligated to pay 90% of the projected monthly per capita drug payment for all of the full-benefit, dual-eligible individuals in the state. As the 10-year phase-down progresses, the percentage drops gradually until year 10 in 2015, at which point it remains fixed at 75%. *Id.*

[111] The Congressional Budget Office (CBO) estimates the aggregate clawback payment due from the states to CMS in 2007 would be $8 billion and expects this amount to increase to $38 billion in 2017. *See* CONGRESSIONAL BUDGET OFFICE, THE BUDGET AND ECONOMIC OUTLOOK: FISCAL YEARS 2008 TO 2017 (Jan. 2007), *available at* http://mirror1.cbo.gov/ftpdocs/77xx/doc7731/01-24-BudgetOutlook.pdf.

[112] On March 3, 2006, five states—Kentucky, Maine, Missouri, New Jersey, and Texas—filed a lawsuit in the U.S. Supreme Court against HHS challenging the constitutionality of the "clawback" provision, which the states view as a direct discriminatory tax on every state and a violation of the doctrine of intergovernmental tax immunity and the system of dual sovereignty. *See "Clawback" Lawsuit Breaks New Ground; States Ask Supreme Court for Injunction,* 15 HEALTH L. REP. (BNA) 327 (Mar. 23, 2006). The states also asked the Court to grant a preliminary injunction to prevent HHS from demanding payment until the case is adjudicated. *Id.* The Supreme Court refused to take the case, stating that the case should be brought in lower court, and also rejected the states' motion for a preliminary injunction without comment. *See Supreme*

propensity of the states to look for opportunities to generate new FFP dollars, the magnitude of the clawback payments expected from the states, and some states' belief that the contribution payments are unconstitutional, the OIG's decision to monitor potential fraud and abuse in this area is not surprising. The OIG planned to assess whether states have been complying with the controversial "clawback" provision by reviewing data used to calculate states' contribution payments, the calculation of states' contribution payments, states' payment amounts, and the controls established by CMS and the states related to contribution payments.[113]

### q. Medicare Part D Risk-Sharing Payments and Recoveries

Medicare shares in a portion of a Sponsor's losses or profits within a certain risk corridor. CMS calculates risk-sharing payments or recoveries based on information reported by the Sponsors. The study ordered by the OIG would determine whether CMS and the Sponsors have established adequate controls over Medicare Part D risk-sharing payments and recoveries to ensure that (1) the plans submit accurate and timely information to CMS, (2) CMS's calculations are performed in accordance with applicable laws and regulations, and (3) payments and recoveries are made in accordance with applicable laws and regulations.[114] Failing to comply with CMS enrollment and cost-reporting requirements may affect the calculation of risk-corridor payments and recoveries and could create a significant compliance risk for Sponsors. Certainly, hospitals, nursing facilities, and home health agencies required to file cost reports

---

*Court Refuses Action on Challenge By States to Medicare "Clawback" Provision*, 15 HEALTH L. REP. (BNA) 735 (June 22, 2006).

Further, in October 2006, the National Association of State Medicaid Directors (NASMD) sent a letter to CMS on behalf of all 50 states and the District of Columbia asserting that there are "significant flaws" in CMS's calculation of the states' 2007 clawback payments that will result in higher payments, which, according to NASMD, "runs counter to [MMA's] concept of phasing down state monthly contributions." Letter from Nancy Atkins, Chair of NASMD, to Leslie Norwalk, Acting Administrator of CMS (Oct. 5, 2006), *available at* http://www.nasmd.org/ issues/docs/Part_D_Norwalk_Letter_2006_10_06.pdf. CMS responded to NASMD in February 2007 and disagreed with NASMD's assessment of the clawback calculation, commenting that, while CMS agreed that State Medicaid Directors should be more involved in Part D implementation discussions, it also believed the National Health Expenditure data constituted a reasonable basis for determining State contribution payments. *See* Letter from Dennis G. Smith, Director, Center for Medicaid and State Operations (CMS) to Nancy Atkin (Feb. 12, 2007), *available at* http://www.nasmd.org/issues/docs/CMS_Response_NASMD_on_Part_D_Claw-back_Methodology.pdf. The National Association of Governors sent a similar letter to the Secretary of HHS in February 2007. *See* Letter to The Honorable Michael O. Leavitt, Secretary of HHS, from Governors Jon S. Corzine and Jim Douglas (Feb. 12, 2007), *available at* http:// www.nga.org/portal/site/nga/menuitem.cb6e7818b34088d18a278110501010a0/?vgnextoid=dff-7450163be0110VgnVCM1000001a01010aRCRD.

[113]2006 WORK PLAN at 14.

[114]*Id.* The deadline for Sponsors to submit plan enrollment data to CMS was May 31, 2007. However, CMS found some discrepancies between its data and data submitted by certain Part D plans. Given the importance of this information to payment reconciliation, CMS extended the deadline to June 30, 2007, for plans to resubmit enrollment data initially rejected by CMS. *See* Centers for Medicare & Medicaid Servs., Memorandum, Systems Guidance for Enrollment Reconciliation for Coverage Year 2006 (Mar. 6, 2007), *available at* http://www.cms.hhs.gov/ PrescriptionDrugCovContra/downloads/MemoEnrollmentReconUpdate_03.06.07.pdf. Accordingly the OIG's study of this issue likely would be delayed until all of the relevant data were submitted to and accepted by CMS.

under Medicare Part A have found themselves facing allegations under the federal False Claims Act for analogous, inaccurate reporting.[115] Some cases involving allegations of intentional false reporting on cost reports have been prosecuted criminally and resulted in company officials serving time in jail.[116]

### r. Prescription Drug Benefit

Effective January 2006, Medicare Advantage organizations offering a coordinated care plan had to begin offering at least one plan, throughout that plan's service area, that includes prescription drug coverage under Part D. The OIG said it would examine the bidding process when a Medicare Advantage organization offers both a Part D plan and a plan with supplemental prescription drug coverage.[117] The OIG also would review the impact of the amount a beneficiary must spend on Part D covered drugs to reach catastrophic coverage of prescription drugs available under a Medicare Advantage plan and any drug benefit provided as an additional benefit.

As of the time this chapter went to press in August 2007, the OIG had completed and published its findings on only a few of the audits from the 2006 Work Plan. However, the OIG gathered additional information through careful monitoring of the early successes and failures in the implementation of Part D and through extensive communication with CMS, beneficiaries, and Congress. This intelligence facilitated the development of a more refined approach for examining Part D compliance, targeting areas believed to pose a high risk of FWA based more on observation than expectation.

### 2. 2007 Work Plan

In October 2006, the OIG released its Work Plan for 2007 (2007 Work Plan),[118] announcing several new Part D audits and the continuation or expansion of studies initiated under the 2006 Work Plan.[119] The studies planned for 2007, compared to 2006, appeared to reflect a more focused approach, concentrating on fewer issues but in greater depth. For example, four of the eight new studies identified in the 2007 Work Plan addressed aspects of the Part D Retiree Drug

---

[115]For example, in 2003, Columbia/HCA paid $250 million to resolve overpayment claims arising from certain of its cost reporting practices. *See* Press Release, U.S. Dep't of Justice, *Largest Health Care Fraud Case in U.S. History Settled HCA Investigation Nets Record Total of $1.7 Billion* (June 26, 2003).

[116]For example, in Tennessee, a man who owned a home health agency (HHA) serving Medicare beneficiaries and an agency providing private duty nursing services to non-Medicare beneficiaries was sentenced to 24 months' incarceration for failing to disclose his nursing service agency as a related party on his HHA's cost reports for years 1998, 1999, and 2000. *See* OIG Web site at http://www.oig.hhs.gov/fraud/enforcement/criminal/06/0206.html#5.

[117]2006 WORK PLAN at 14.

[118]U.S. DEP'T OF HEALTH & HUMAN SERVS., OFFICE OF INSPECTOR GENERAL, WORK PLAN FOR FY 2007 (Sept. 25, 2006), *available at* http://www.oig.hhs.gov/publications/docs/workplan/2007/Work%20Plan%202007.pdf [hereinafter 2007 WORK PLAN].

[119]Note that this discussion addresses only new studies announced by the OIG in the 2007 WORK PLAN. For a discussion of studies identified in the 2007 WORK PLAN, but which were announced initially by the OIG in the 2006 WORK PLAN, see Section II.A.1., above.

Subsidy (RDS) program, whereas the 2006 Work Plan only included one audit of the RDS program. Further, many of the audits identified in the 2007 Work Plan expanded upon ongoing studies, further underscoring the OIG's concern about particularly sensitive Part D compliance issues such as access to drugs for dual eligibles, beneficiary protections from improper marketing schemes, and drug formulary management by Sponsors, and the coordination of drug benefits under Part D and Part B. A brief discussion of each new initiative announced in the 2007 Work Plan follows.

### a. Third Party Liability Safeguards

The OIG announced in its 2007 Work Plan that it would review safeguards in place to ensure that Medicare does not inappropriately pay for Part D prescription drug claims for which a third party is liable.[120] This study would assess the effectiveness of coordination among various payors, specifically including CMS, SPAPs, insurers, employers, and all other payors of prescription drug coverage. Interestingly, this study appears to broaden the OIG's existing audit concerning the coordination between Medicare Part B and Part D by adding private payors and employers. The OIG wants to make certain that Part D does not pay for drugs that should be the responsibility of any other payor, whether public or private.

### b. Comparisons of Part D Drug Pricing

The OIG planned to conduct pricing comparisons for Part D drugs, in particular by contrasting drug prices under Part D with the same drug prices covered under Medicare Part B and, for certain drugs, with Medicaid reimbursement amounts.[121] Since the implementation of the prescription drug benefit, and increasingly since the 2006 Congressional elections, there has been much discussion among policy makers about whether Part D overpays for drugs. Some have argued that the Veterans Administration pays significantly less for drugs because it negotiates directly with pharmaceutical manufacturers over the price of the drugs.[122] At a minimum, the OIG likely wanted to make sure Sponsors' bids reflect a fair price for drugs compared with other drug benefits administered by CMS.

### c. Medicare Part D: Drug Access Through Prior
### Authorization and Exceptions

The OIG said it intended to examine controls instituted by CMS to ensure that Part D plans implement appropriate prior authorization and formulary exceptions processes.[123] The study also was to explore how policies and processes compare across plans. In the 2006 Work Plan, the OIG indicated a con-

---

[120]2007 WORK PLAN at 15.

[121]*Id.*

[122]*See, e.g.*, Alain Enthoven and Kyna Fong, *Medicare: Negotiated Drug Prices May Not Lower Costs*, National Center for Policy Analysis (Dec. 18, 2006), *available at* http://www.ncpa .org/pub/ba/ba575/ba575.pdf.

[123]2007 WORK PLAN at 16.

cern that Sponsors may engage in formulary management techniques designed to "cherry pick" less costly beneficiaries by making the plan less attractive to beneficiaries with higher prescription drug utilization rates.[124] The study identified in the 2006 Work Plan addressed P&T Committees and the construction of formularies, drugs included on formularies, and beneficiary management tools. For 2007, however, the OIG appeared more focused on prior authorization and exceptions to formulary restrictions. Sponsors should remain cognizant of this shift in focus when making coverage decisions based on prior authorization and exceptions. The OIG likely would test various formulary management policies to determine whether Sponsors have crossed a line between effective benefit management and abusive practices toward beneficiaries.

### d. Dually Eligible Hospice Patients

The OIG planned to determine the propriety of drug claims for individuals that have elected the Medicare hospice benefit, but receive prescription drug coverage under Medicare Part D.[125] Under the Part A hospice benefit, Medicare pays hospice providers an all-inclusive per diem rate that includes the cost of drugs used for pain relief and symptom control related to the beneficiary's terminal illness.[126] However, the hospice benefit does not cover drugs that may be medically necessary but are not prescribed to relieve pain and manage symptoms related to the beneficiary's terminal illness. Hospice beneficiaries who elect to enroll may obtain coverage under a Part D plan for prescription drugs that are not covered by the hospice benefit. In some cases, the same drug could be covered under either the hospice and the Part D benefit, depending on the purpose for which the drug is prescribed. Just as the OIG indicated a concern about CMS making duplicate payments for drugs covered by both Part B and Part D, the hospice benefit presents a risk that Medicare Part D could pay for drugs which have already been paid for under the Part A hospice per diem payment. The OIG intended to assess the frequency with which such inappropriate payments occur and, depending on the extent of the problem, what controls are needed to prevent duplicate payments.

### e. Part D Dual-Eligible Demonstration Project

The OIG planned to review the systems implemented by CMS to reimburse states participating in the Part D Dual-Eligible Demonstration Project. In January 2006, CMS initiated a demonstration project to reimburse states that assist dual-eligible and low-income subsidy beneficiaries to obtain Part D coverage and pay prescription drug costs for beneficiaries ineligible for Part D coverage.[127] Under the demonstration project, Medicare would reimburse states

---

[124] *See* 2006 WORK PLAN at 13.

[125] 2007 WORK PLAN at 16.

[126] 42 C.F.R. §418.202.

[127] *See* Memorandum from the Center for Medicaid and State Operations (CMS) to State Medicaid Directors and State Pharmacy Assistance Program Directors (Feb. 2, 2006), *available at* http://www.cms.hhs.gov/States/Downloads/PartDDemoSMDL.pdf.

for the difference between drug plan and Medicaid costs and for certain state administrative costs. Given the enormous difficulty CMS had transitioning dual eligibles from Medicaid to Part D, which resulted in significant delays for thousands of beneficiaries in obtaining their medication as well as high-profile, negative publicity for HHS, it is not surprising the OIG elected to review the effectiveness of this initiative. The OIG also planned to examine the states' submission of data to CMS to determine the accuracy of payments made to the states under the demonstration project.

### f. Medicare Part D Duplicate Claims

The OIG announced that it would review the controls put in place by CMS to prevent duplicate Part D claims for the same beneficiary, particularly when a beneficiary changes plans, tries to enroll in more than one plan, or tries to enroll in a plan and a retiree-subsidy covered plan.[128] Proper controls are essential, in large part, because of the risk posed by the six million beneficiaries who are dually eligible for Medicare and Medicaid permitted to change their enrollment in Part D drug plans on a monthly basis.

### g. Allocation of Employer Premiums Under the Retiree Drug Subsidy Program

The OIG intended to assess selected employers' controls to track actual "allowable retiree drug costs"[129] under the Part D RDS program.[130] Under the RDS program, Medicare makes interim subsidy payments based on actuarial estimates to employers with fully insured plans. These estimates must be reconciled with certain allowable retiree costs. Accordingly, cost data reported by employers play a critical role in determining the subsidy amount. The OIG intended to study whether RDS-reported costs are accurate and supportable, how closely interim subsidy payments approximate actual allowable costs, and the impact of the difference between interim payments and final payments to the Medicare program.

### h. Allowable Costs Under the Retiree Drug Subsidy

The OIG said it would review employer controls designed to ensure that only drugs covered under Part D and related allowable costs are included in employer interim drug cost submissions.[131] This study would evaluate whether effective systems are in place to prevent private employers from abusing the Part D benefit through false or fraudulent reporting of their covered drug costs.

### i. Actuarial Value of Retiree Prescription Drug Coverage

The OIG planned to examine selected employers' RDS plans to identify any material changes to the actuarial value of the plan since the plan's initial

---

[128] 2007 Work Plan at 16.

[129] See Section II.A.1.n., above, for a discussion of the RDS program, including a definition of "allowable retiree drug costs."

[130] 2007 Work Plan at 17.

[131] Id.

approval.[132] In addition, the OIG would assess whether any identified plan modifications affected subsidy payments to the employer and whether the employer provided CMS with the required certification that qualified retiree health coverage was at least actuarially equivalent to standard prescription drug coverage under Part D. Although Congress apparently wanted to encourage employers to maintain their existing drug plans for retirees, the OIG may suspect that some employers may skimp on coverage to drive down costs and retain the savings from the subsidy.

### j. Rebates in the Retiree Drug Subsidy Program

The OIG planned to study controls established by employers for developing estimates of the impact of expected manufacturer rebates and other price concessions on drugs costs under their RDS plans.[133] Without accurate estimates, interim payments made by CMS during the plan year will not reflect actual allowable retiree costs, which are calculated net of discounts, rebates, chargebacks, and similar price concessions[134] after the close of the plan year. The OIG said it would determine whether the employers' cost estimates are reasonable, supported, and consistently applied.

### k. Rural Pharmacy Drug Purchases

The OIG intended to compare payments made by Part D Sponsors to rural pharmacies to pharmacy costs for drugs and dispensing fees. Further, the OIG planned to review provisions of Sponsor contracts that include rural pharmacies in their networks. Though the OIG did not identify particular contract provisions it would review, this study may be a complement to an investigation announced in 2006 (although not described in the 2006 Work Plan) of beneficiary access to pharmacies in rural areas. If so, the OIG might be looking for contract provisions that could result in limitations on beneficiary access Part D covered drugs in rural areas.

### l. Evolution of Part D

Building on the wide net cast by the studies initiated in 2006, the 2007 Work Plan evidenced an evolution in the OIG's perspective on the vulnerable features of Part D. As more information about Part D becomes available to the OIG, we would expect the focus of future studies to narrow and shift, progressively, as more specific risks of FWA are identified. If the OIG adheres to past practice, audits of individual Sponsors likely will follow closely behind those work plan studies that reveal a particular program weakness. Prudent Sponsors will examine their Part D plans for signs of vulnerability to FWA based on the OIG's findings and implement changes to plan operations or revisions to their compliance programs as necessary to address weaknesses. Given the aggressive enforcement environment of the 1990s and 2000s, Sponsors and other Part D

---

[132]*Id.*
[133]*Id.* at 17–18.
[134]42 C.F.R. §423.882.

participants should view any disregard of the OIG's findings as an invitation for more expansive government investigations and *qui tam* actions.

## B. Patient Assistance Programs

The structure of the Part D benefit potentially exposes enrolled beneficiaries to substantial out-of-pocket costs. In 2006, beneficiaries enrolled in a plan offering the standard benefit were responsible for a $250 deductible, 25 percent copayments on drugs up to an initial coverage limit of $2,250, 100 percent copayments once drug costs exceeded the initial coverage limit until out-of-pocket spending reached the catastrophic coverage limit of $3,600, and 5 percent copayments thereafter.[135] Mandatory indexing of the cost-sharing levels defining the standard benefit increased the deductible to $265, the initial coverage limit to $2,400, and the catastrophic coverage limit to $3,850 in 2007.[136] Beneficiaries enrolled in plans offering an actuarially equivalent benefit to the standard benefit or in plans that provide enhanced benefits also may face significant out-of-pocket costs during a "doughnut hole" in the benefit or on expensive therapies that have been placed on a specialty tier of the plan's formulary requiring a percentage-based copayment. In 2006, some plans imposed copayment percentages as high as 50 percent on their specialty tiers. CMS's Part D formulary guidance for 2007 limited copayment percentages to 25 percent for specialty tier drugs but allowed any drug with an estimated average monthly cost of $500 or more to be placed in a specialty tier.[137]

Prior to the implementation of Part D, for drugs not covered by Medicare Part B, many pharmaceutical manufacturers offered free drugs to financially needy Medicare beneficiaries who did not have supplemental insurance with a drug benefit or who had exhausted their supplemental drug coverage. Most manufacturers with patient assistance programs (PAPs) wished to continue helping these beneficiaries with drug copayments and deductibles under Part D. Generally speaking, manufacturers hoped that any assistance they provided would count toward the beneficiary's TrOOP drug spending so that donations would wrap around the Medicare benefit and not delay the beneficiary's ability to access the Part D benefit's catastrophic coverage. They also wanted to be able to continue providing PAP assistance in the form of free drugs to hold PAP program drug expenses to the marginal cost of the drugs.

Initially, there was confusion about how PAPs would be treated for purposes of TrOOP. MMA defines the concept of "incurred costs" that count toward a beneficiary's TrOOP.[138] Those costs only include payments for the Part D deductible and required cost-sharing on covered Part D drugs. Payments for drugs that are not on formulary or that are statutorily excluded from Part D

---

[135]Social Security Act §1860D–2(b) [42 U.S.C. §1395w–102(b)].

[136]Centers for Medicare & Medicaid Servs., Office of the Actuary, *Medicare Part D Benefit Parameters for Standard Benefit: Annual Adjustment for 2007* (May 22, 2007), *available at* http://www.cms.hhs.gov/PrescriptionDrugCovContra/downloads/CY07PartDParameterUpdate .pdf.

[137]Centers for Medicare & Medicaid Servs., *Medicare Modernization Act 2007 Final Guidelines—Formularies*, *available at* http://www.cms.hhs.gov/PrescriptionDrugCovContra/ Downloads/CY07FormularyGuidance.pdf.

[138]Social Security Act §1860D–2(b)(4)(C) [42 U.S.C. §1395w–102((b)(4)(C)].

coverage do not count toward TrOOP. Further, for costs to be treated as incurred they must be "paid by the part D eligible individual (or by another person, such as a family member, on behalf of the individual)."[139] Costs paid on behalf of the individual under Part D's low-income subsidy provisions or under an SPAP count toward TrOOP as well.[140] TrOOP-eligible costs may not be reimbursed "through insurance or otherwise, a group health plan, or other third-party payment arrangement."[141]

When CMS published the Part D Final Rule, it clarified that payments for Part D deductibles and cost-sharing obligations made on behalf of an enrollee by "a natural person, corporation, mutual company, unincorporated association, partnership, joint venture, limited liability company, trust, estate, foundation, not-for-profit corporation, unincorporated organization, government or governmental subdivision or agency" could be counted toward TrOOP as long as those payments were not reimbursed through a group health plan, an individual insurance policy, or some similar third-party payment arrangement.[142]

In the preamble to the Part D Final Rule, CMS confirmed that deductible and copayment assistance provided to individuals enrolled in Part D through bona fide charities operated, like those approved in the Part B context under OIG Advisory Opinions 02-01[143] and 04-15,[144] would be counted toward TrOOP.[145] The OIG has since issued another Advisory Opinion permitting an independent charity to provide premium and copayment assistance for both Part B and Part D drugs under similar circumstances.[146]

---

[139]*Id.*

[140]*Id.*

[141]*Id.*

[142]42 C.F.R. §423.100.

[143]OIG Advisory Op. No. 02-01 (Apr. 4, 2001), *available at* http://www.oig.hhs.gov/fraud/docs/advisoryopinions/2002/0201.pdf, permits an independent charity funded by cash donations from pharmaceutical manufacturers designated for specific disease silos to provide Medigap premium or Part B drug copayment support to financially needy individuals with a covered disease who meet the foundation's financial eligibility criteria without risk of penalties under the federal anti-kickback law or the beneficiary inducement provision of the Civil Monetary Penalty Law. Because the foundation accepts patients after diagnosis regardless of their prescribed drug therapy and without regard to their choice of physician, practitioner, or supplier, permits patients to change therapy without putting their financial assistance at risk, and avoids providing patients and donors with information about each other, the OIG reasoned that the interposition of the independent charity between donors and patients prevented donors from being assured that their contributions would go to support patients on their drugs and, therefore, sufficiently mitigated any potential kickback risk.

[144]OIG Advisory Op. No. 04-15 (Nov. 5, 2004), *available at* http://www.oig.hhs.gov/fraud/docs/advisoryopinions/2004/ao0415.pdf, follows the logic of Advisory Op. No. 02-01 and permits an independent charity funded by pharmaceutical manufacturers and operated in a similar manner to provide copayment assistance to financially needy Part B beneficiaries.

[145]70 Fed. Reg. 4193, 4239 (Jan. 28 2005).

[146]Unlike Advisory Op. Nos. 02-01 and 04-15, Advisory Op. No. 06-04 (Apr. 27, 2006), *available at* http://www.oig.hhs.gov/fraud/docs/advisoryopinions/2006/AdvOpn06-04A.pdf, permits the charity to add new disease silos as funding becomes available. The charity has certified that it will define its disease categories in accordance with widely recognized clinical standards and in a manner that covers a broad spectrum of available products. In addition, new disease categories will not be defined by reference to specific symptoms, severity of symptoms, or the method of administration of drugs. The potential FWA risk posed by defining disease categories in a way that results in charitable assistance being available only for a single drug or a narrow band of drugs is discussed more fully later in this Section.

CMS also included a pointed discussion in the preamble to the Part D Final Rule cautioning that any PAP programs supported or operated by drug manufacturers to pay a Medicare beneficiary's Part D cost-sharing obligations must comply with federal fraud and abuse laws, including the federal anti-kickback statute[147] and the provisions against beneficiary inducement in the Civil Monetary Penalty Law.[148] This declaration sent a chill through the manufacturer community because Advisory Opinions 02-13[149] and 03-03[150] had concluded that manufacturers would put themselves at risk of violating the federal anti-kickback statute if they offered copayment assistance only for their own Part B drugs through a captive foundation or an internally operated PAP, respectively. Both of these Advisory Opinions reasoned that such assistance posed a kickback risk because the manufacturers were paying beneficiaries to use their drugs. The OIG expressed concerns about copayment assistance skewing clinical decisionmaking when therapeutic alternatives or generic options were available, thus increasing costs to federal health care programs and adversely impacting competition.

Calls for guidance from the OIG about how manufacturer PAPs serving Part D enrollees could be structured and operated lawfully led to the publication of a Special Advisory Bulletin on Patient Assistance Programs for Medicare Part D Enrollees in November 2005[151] (Special Advisory Bulletin). The Special Advisory Bulletin reiterated the OIG's longstanding position that manufacturers "may provide free drugs to financially needy beneficiaries, so long as no Federal health care program is billed for all or part of the drugs."[152] It encouraged manufacturers to continue offering PAP assistance to Part D-eligible individuals who elect not to enroll in the program.

The Special Advisory Bulletin also detailed two acceptable approaches that manufacturers may use to help Part D-enrolled beneficiaries with cost-sharing obligations. Not surprisingly, the first involved funding bona fide in-

---

[147]Social Security Act §1128B(b) [42 U.S.C. §1320a–7b(b)].

[148]Social Security Act §1128A(a)(5) [42 U.S.C. §1320a–7a(a)(5)].

[149]OIG Advisory Op. No. 02-13 (Oct. 4, 2002), *available at* http://www.oig.hhs.gov/fraud/docs/advisoryopinions/2002/ao0213.pdf, analyzes the fraud and abuse risks of Part B copayment assistance provided to financially needy individuals by an otherwise independent nonprofit foundation funded by a single pharmaceutical manufacturer and offering assistance only for that manufacturer's drug as if the company itself were running the program. The OIG concluded the program implicated the federal anti-kickback law because it involved paying patients to take the manufacturer's drug. The OIG noted that the program permitted the manufacturer to profit from drug sales to Medicare beneficiaries even after it incurred the cost of copayment support, relieved patients' physicians of bad debt risk, and provided the manufacturer's drug with a financial advantage over competing drugs in the market. In addition, the OIG pointed out that nonabusive alternatives for providing copayment assistance through bona fide charities were available.

[150]OIG Advisory Op. No. 03-3 (Feb. 12, 2003), *available at* http://www.oig.hhs.gov/fraud/docs/advisoryopinions/2003/ao0303.pdf, concludes that a copayment assistance program operated directly by a pharmaceutical manufacturer to provide support to financially needy patients taking the manufacturer's branded drug instead of one of several available competing generic products implicates the federal anti-kickback law for the reasons given earlier in Advisory Op. No. 02-13 (discussing a captive foundation PAP).

[151]*See* OIG Special Advisory Bulletin (Nov. 7, 2005), *available at* http://www.oig.hhs.gov/fraud/docs/alertsandbulletins/2005/PAPAdvisoryBlletinFinal-Final.pdf, *reprinted in* 70 Fed. Reg. 70,623 (Nov. 22, 2005).

[152]*See id.* at 70,625 (citing OIG Advisory Op. Nos. 02-13 and 03-3).

dependent charities offering copayment assistance programs for diseases treatable with Part D drugs.[153] The second indicated that manufacturer-operated PAPs that "furnish free outpatient prescription drugs entirely outside the Part D benefit pose a reduced risk under the anti-kickback law."[154] Under such a model, manufacturers would have to notify each beneficiary's Part D plan about the free product(s) so the plan could take steps to ensure that no Medicare payments were made for the products even though the free drugs were integrated into the plan's medication therapy management and drug utilization review programs applicable to the patient. The OIG indicated "outside Part D PAPs" should provide assistance for the whole Part D coverage year or the portion remaining after the beneficiary is first enrolled in the PAP, regardless of whether drug usage is continuous or periodic, and maintain documentation establishing that Part D was not billed. CMS published an open letter to providers on January 25, 2006, reiterating its support for the outside Part D option outlined by the OIG.[155]

The Special Advisory Bulletin concluded that the OIG did not have sufficient factual information to draw conclusions about the permissibility of institutional PAPs. Such PAPs typically involve bulk in-kind donations of drugs to hospitals or community health clinics that use the products to treat patients they determine meet the donor's financial eligibility criteria.[156] The OIG also declined to offer definitive guidance on the concept of a "coalition model" Part D PAP under which a group of manufacturers would offer copayment assistance or product discounts during the period when Part D beneficiaries are

---

[153] *See id.* at 70,627. To reduce the likelihood that a PAP would function as an improper conduit for manufacturers to provide funds to patients using their specific drugs, the OIG stated that "pharmaceutical manufacturers should not influence, directly or indirectly, the identification of disease or illness categories, and pharmaceutical manufacturers should limit their earmarked donations to PAPs that define categories in accordance with widely recognized clinical standards and in a manner that covers a broad spectrum of available products." *Id.*

[154] *See id.*

[155] *See* Centers for Medicare & Medicaid Servs., CMS Perspective on Pharmaceutical Company Patient Assistance Programs (Jan. 25, 2006), *available at* http://www.cms.hhs.gov/ hillnotifications/downloads/PAPCMSinfo 012406.pdf.

[156] The OIG subsequently published Advisory Op. No. 06-08 (June 30, 2006), *available at* http://oig.hhs.gov/fraud/docs/advisoryopinions/2006/06-08.pdf, in which it declined to impose sanctions under the federal anti-kickback statute on a free clinic that does not treat insured individuals, including those covered by Medicare or Medicaid, but that, without charging manufacturers for its services, does dispense drugs through its pharmacy on behalf of institutional PAPs sponsored by pharmaceutical manufacturers that provide free drugs to financially needy patients, including some enrolled in the Medicare Part D benefit. These Part D beneficiaries receive their prescriptions through providers that are not affiliated with the clinic but they cannot afford the cost-sharing that would be required if they sought to fill the prescription at a Part D participating pharmacy. The OIG concluded that the institutional PAPs operated by the free clinic constitute outside Part D assistance programs because the clinic does not bill any patients or payors for its services and, in fact, does not even have a billing system in place. Furthermore, the OIG noted that the clinic is not in a position to generate business for any PAP sponsor that would be payable by a federal health care program because prescriptions filled for Part D enrollees derive from care the beneficiaries receive at settings other than the free clinic. Precisely for this reason, Advisory Op. No. 06-08 does little to clarify the safeguards that would need to be in place to mitigate sufficiently the kickback risks inherent in the operation of institutional PAPs at disproportionate share hospitals and federally qualified community health clinics in a position to make referrals that benefit PAP sponsors because they regularly treat and bill for services provided to Medicare and Medicaid patients.

facing 100 percent copayments. The OIG did, however, suggest that this approach would require the participation of a large number of manufacturers, including manufacturers of both branded and generic products, to be acceptable from a fraud and abuse perspective under the federal anti-kickback statute.

The pharmaceutical industry responded to the Special Advisory Bulletin cautiously because it only characterized the risk of operating a PAP outside of Part D as "reduced." That concern was first addressed by the issuance of Advisory Opinion 06-03[157] to Schering Plough. That Advisory Opinion covers two programs that provide Part D-covered drugs free of charge to patients meeting the company's financial criteria, without sharing information with CMS or the patients regarding the value or cost of the free products. The PAPs committed to provide free products to enrolled patients from the time of enrollment to the end of the Part D plan year and they agreed to work with CMS to ensure that beneficiaries receiving PAP help would be appropriately identified to CMS and the beneficiaries' Part D plans. This process will allow the plans to conduct appropriate drug utilization and medication therapy management activities while ensuring payments will not be made for PAP-provided drugs. The value of the PAP drugs would not be counted toward TrOOP. The PAPs also said they would notify patients that PAP assistance falls outside of Part D and will not count toward TrOOP.

In addition, Advisory Opinion 06-03 acknowledges the propriety of establishing financial eligibility criteria that take into account the cost of particular therapies and the nature of the diseases those drugs treat. Here, Schering Plough offered assistance with drugs that treat cancer and hepatitis to patients with incomes below 325 percent of the federal poverty level (FPL). Patients receiving other types of Part D covered drugs must demonstrate incomes below 250 percent of the FPL. Schering Plough required Part D enrollees seeking PAP help to apply for and be rejected for the benefit's low-income subsidy and to attest that they could not find an affordable Part D plan. Finally, the company would not accept patients into its PAPs until they had already spent at least three percent of their household income on outpatient prescription drugs during the coverage year, arguing that this additional financial need test reflects the generally different levels of potential exposure to out-of-pocket health care and drug costs faced by uninsured and Part D enrollees with comparable income levels.[158] After the issuance of Advisory Opinion 06-03, a number of major pharmaceutical manufacturers announced they intended to continue providing PAP assistance to financially needy individuals who are eligible for Part D but elect not to enroll. Some also continued to serve Part D-enrolled beneficiaries who meet their PAP criteria through programs modeled on Advisory Opinion 06-03. Further, a number of more risk-averse manufacturers obtained Advisory Opinions specific to the details of their own programs distinct from Part D PAPs.[159]

---

[157] *See* OIG Advisory Op. No. 06-03 (Apr. 18, 2006), *available at* http://www.oig.hhs.gov/fraud/docs/advisoryopinions/2006/AdvOpn06-03F.pdf.

[158] The OIG notes in footnote 16 to Advisory Op. No. 06-03 that "we would likely reach the same outcome in this advisory opinion were Requestor, in the future, to eliminate the 3% test." *Id.*

[159] The OIG has published several Advisory Opinions in which it stated that it would not impose sanctions against the PAPs, as described by each of the requestors, because in each case adequate safeguards existed to mitigate the risk of abuse to the Part D program and, more

Advisory Opinion 06-03 indicates that Schering Plough was "working on" a data sharing agreement with CMS to permit its PAPs to identify enrolled Part D patients to the agency and applicable Part D plans. Neither the Advisory Opinion nor the Special Advisory Bulletin provide further details about how manufacturers should go about ensuring that Part D plans do not pay for, or count for TrOOP purposes, drugs provided free through PAPs operated outside Part D. CMS does, however, address the notification issue in various guidance documents on coordination of benefits (COB) for Part D plans (COB Guidance), most of which have been incorporated into the PDBM.[160] CMS emphasizes that the most effective way for PAPs to operate outside of Part D is to enter into a PAP-specific data sharing agreement (PAP DSA) with CMS to exchange eligibility files with CMS's COB contractor electronically.[161] Alternatively, a PAP may provide its enrollees with a notice which they would provide to their Part D plans indicating that they are receiving one or more drug products from that PAP. CMS prefers the PAP DSA approach because it permits an electronic data interchange between PAPs and CMS and is more foolproof than a manual notification process, particularly one that depends on patient participation. Further, the PAP DSA will allow the COB contractor to flag the PAP as a non-TrOOP-eligible payor for the particular covered drugs it provides at no cost to Part D enrollees. The COB contractor will make this information available to plans through the TrOOP facilitation process so that the plans may set their systems to recognize PAP drugs as part of a patient's profile while establishing system edits to prevent payments for the PAP drugs, thus keeping the drugs from affecting TrOOP and total drug spend amounts on plan prescription drug event records.[162]

In addition to defining the PAP's data exchange obligations, the December 2006 version of the PAP DSA, available on the CMS Web site,[163] would impose on the PAP certain obligations that may be unfamiliar or even troubling to manufacturers operating outside Part D PAPs. For example, the PAP DSA requires the PAP to adopt policies and procedures to ensure that the data are used and disclosed only in accordance with the authorization or consent provided by the beneficiary. The PAP also would be contractually obligated to establish administrative, technical, and physical safeguards to protect the

---

specifically, each proposed PAP would operate outside the Medicare Part D drug program, meaning that no drugs provided by the PAPs to a Part D enrollee would be billed to the Medicare program or a Part D plan, nor would the costs count toward participating beneficiaries' TrOOP costs. *See, e.g.,* OIG Advisory Op. No. 06-14 (Sept. 26, 2006), *available at* http://oig.hhs.gov/fraud/docs/advisoryopinions/2006/Adv-Opn06-14.pdf; OIG Advisory Op. No. 06-19 (Nov. 2, 2006), *available at* http://www.oig.hhs.gov/fraud/docs/advisoryopinions/2006/AdvOpn06-19E.pdf; and OIG Advisory Op. No. 06-21 (Nov. 9, 2006), *available at* http://www.oig.hhs.gov/fraud/docs/advisoryopinions/2006/AdvOpn06-21.pdf.

[160]*See* Medicare Prescription Drug Benefit Manual, Chapter 14, Coordination of Benefits (revised Dec. 19, 2006), at 49–55, *available at* http://www.cms.hhs.gov/PrescriptionDrug-CovContra/Downloads/PDMChapt14COB.pdf.

[161]*See* CMS Memorandum to All Part D Sponsors, HPMS Q&A–Patient Assistance Programs (Oct. 4, 2006), at 3 [hereinafter PAP Memorandum], *available at* http://www.cms.hhs.gov/PrescriptionDrugCovGenIn/Downloads/MemoPAPsOutsidePartDBenefit_10.04.06.pdf.

[162]*See id.*

[163]CMS's Patient Assistance Program Data Sharing Agreement (Dec. 6, 2006) is available at http://www.cms.hhs.gov/PrescriptionDrugCovContra/downloads/PAPDSA11-27-06.pdf.

confidentiality of the data and to prevent unauthorized access to data furnished under the agreement to the PAP by CMS.

Furthermore, CMS has created an attestation requirement for PAPs that choose to enter a PAP DSA with CMS (PAP Attestation). Prior to entering into a PAP DSA, an authorized representative of the PAP, who must also be an authorized representative of the company sponsoring the PAP (i.e., the drug manufacturer), must sign an attestation certifying that CMS's requirements for operating an outside Part D PAP are acknowledged and understood.[164] In particular, the PAP must certify that:

(1) its program operates outside of Part D;

(2) the PAP will ensure that each enrollee's Part D plan is notified of the drug(s) covered by its program that would otherwise be covered under Part D;

(3) by reporting PAP-covered drug(s) to the enrollee's Part D plan, the PAP is providing information the plan needs to exclude PAP assistance from the enrollee's TrOOP balance;

(4) the PAP will never submit a claim for drugs covered under its program to the enrollee's Part D plan; and

(5) any assessment by the PAP more than nominal beneficiary cost-sharing appears inconsistent with the charitable mission of a PAP.

This certification could be viewed as a statement upon which the government relies in determining payments for Part D drugs. If so, any violation of one of the certifications included in the PAP Attestation potentially could implicate the False Claims Act.

Moreover, the PAP Attestation includes an express disclaimer against any use of the PAP Attestation or the PAP DSA as evidence of the PAP's compliance with health care fraud and abuse laws. Specifically, the PAP must certify as to its understanding that neither the PAP Attestation nor the PAP DSA constitutes a finding that the particular PAP complies with all federal health care fraud and abuse laws, including the anti-kickback statute and the Civil Monetary Penalty provisions. In addition, manufacturers sponsoring PAPs should be aware the PAP Attestation requires the PAP to furnish a narrative describing the assistance program, including its eligibility criteria and how it will provide assistance and operate outside of the Part D program. The PAP must agree to update the narrative, as necessary, on a timely basis as long as its PAP DSA with CMS remains in effect.

When evaluating whether to enter a PAP DSA, manufacturers should review carefully the terms of the sample PAP DSA,[165] the PAP Attestation, and the accompanying PAP DSA User Guide[166] published by CMS. PAPs that elect

---

[164]*See* PAP Memorandum at 3. A copy of the PAP Attestation is available at http://www.cms.hhs.gov/PrescriptionDrugCovGenIn/Downloads/PAP_Attestations_rev_050207.pdf.

[165]CMS's Patient Assistance Program Data Sharing Agreement (Dec. 6, 2006) is available at http://www.cms.hhs.gov/PrescriptionDrugCovContra/downloads/PAPDSA11-27-06.pdf.

[166]CMS released a user's guide to assist PAPs that enter into a PAP DSA with the implementation and ongoing management of the information sharing process with CMS. The PAP DSA User Guide (Dec. 4, 2006) is available at http://www.cms.hhs.gov/PrescriptionDrugCov-Contra/downloads/PAP%20User%20Guide%2012-4-06.pdf.

not enter into a PAP DSA should consider implementing procedures for filing Part D plan-specific notices on behalf of each beneficiary enrolled in an outside Part D PAP program so that they can ensure that proper notices are submitted to the appropriate contact person at each enrollee's Part D plan.

## III. PART D REGULATORY REQUIREMENTS WITH SIGNIFICANT FWA COMPLIANCE IMPLICATIONS

### A. Data Reporting Requirements

The Part D Final Rule requires each Sponsor to implement an effective procedure to develop, compile, evaluate, and periodically report certain information about the operation of the plan.[167] CMS has published guidance on the Part D reporting requirements, specifying reporting timelines and data elements that Sponsors must provide to CMS (2007 Reporting Requirements).[168] Sponsors are responsible for submitting data, typically quarterly, in a specified format on a broad range of plan operational matters. Specifically, data Sponsors must report include numbers of low-income enrollees and beneficiaries who have reached the Part D coverage gap; medication therapy management programs; generic dispensing rate; grievances; redeterminations that resulted in partial reversals; P&T Committee membership and their confidentiality agreements with PBMs; transition of beneficiaries into the plan; exceptions from plan formulary and utilization management programs; appeals; call center measures; overpayments; drug manufacturer rebates, discounts, and other price concessions; long-term care rebates; licensure and solvency, business transactions, and financial requirements; and drug benefit analyses.[169] CMS will use these data to calculate payments due to the Sponsor for providing the Part D benefit and to assess Sponsor performance from an operational and beneficiary service perspective.

The Part D reporting requirements for plan cost data, in particular, raise a number of sensitive compliance issues for Sponsors as well as their contractors. The reason for this sensitivity is that CMS relies on financial information reported by Sponsors to determine the Medicare program's payment liability under Part D. Under MMA, Congress limited Sponsors' financial risk for the cost of operating a Part D plan by including a reinsurance provision under which Medicare will reinsure Sponsors for 80 percent of the drug costs of individual plan enrollees who

---

[167]42 C.F.R. §423.514. MMA authorizes CMS to require Sponsors to disclose fully any information necessary for carrying out the payment provisions of Part D. 42 U.S.C. §1395w–115(d)(2).

[168]Centers for Medicare & Medicaid Servs., *Medicare Part D Reporting Requirements: Contract Year* 2007 (Apr. 26, 2007) [hereinafter 2007 Reporting Requirements], *available at* http://www.cms.hhs.gov/PrescriptionDrugCovContra/Downloads/PartDReportingRequirements_CurrentYear.pdf.

[169]*See generally* 2007 Reporting Requirements. Note that for the 2006 plan year, CMS also required Sponsors to report data on enrollment and disenrollment in the Part D plan. CMS suspended this requirement in November 2006 and has not included it in the 2007 Reporting Requirements. *See* CY2007 Part D Reporting Requirements: Frequently Asked Questions (Apr. 26, 2007), at 4 [hereinafter 2007 Reporting Requirements FAQ], *available at* http://www.cms.hhs.gov/PrescriptionDrugCovContra/Downloads/PartDReportingRequirementsFAQ.pdf.

exceed their annual out-of-pocket threshold (i.e., enrollees who have passed through the coverage gap).[170] However, a Sponsor's "allowable reinsurance costs"[171] are limited to costs "actually paid" by the Sponsor, which means the reimbursable amount must be "net of any direct or indirect remuneration... that would serve to decrease the costs... for the drug."[172] In other words, the allowable reinsurance payment is based on the amount the Sponsor paid for the drugs after taking into account all rebates, discounts, and other price concessions from manufacturers or other entities that result in a price reduction on the cost of Part D drugs for the Sponsor. CMS pays Sponsors for allowable reinsurance costs prospectively on a monthly basis and, accordingly, once it receives the Sponsor's cost reporting information CMS must reconcile (or "true up") the amounts paid with the total amount actually owed by Medicare to the Sponsor for allowable reinsurance costs. CMS cannot calculate the true allowable reinsurance costs owed to a Sponsor until the Sponsor has reported its rebates, discounts, and other price concessions. Moreover, the data reported by Sponsors must be truthful, accurate, and complete; otherwise CMS may overpay or underpay Sponsors for allowable reinsurance costs.

Under the 2007 Reporting Requirements, Sponsors not only must report the full amount of rebates, discounts, and other price concessions on Part D drugs, but also any grant monies related to Part D business[173] and so-called "value adds" received from pharmaceutical manufacturers.[174] CMS explains a "value add" as any "gift-in-kind or other programs (e.g., coupons or disease management programs specific to a Part D Sponsor)."[175] Whereas the identification and quantification of a rebate appears relatively straightforward for reporting purposes,[176] CMS's ability to understand the effect on the Sponsor's

---

[170]Social Security Act §1860D–15(b) [42 U.S.C. §1395w–115(b)].

[171]"Allowable reinsurance costs" means the subset of gross covered prescription drug costs actually paid that are attributable to basic prescription drug coverage for covered Part D drugs only and that are actually paid by the Part D sponsor or by (or on behalf of) an enrollee under the Part D plan. 42 C.F.R. §423.308. "Gross covered prescription drug costs" means those actually paid costs incurred under a Part D plan, excluding administrative costs, but including dispensing fees during the coverage year and costs relating to the deductible. *Id.*

[172]42 C.F.R. §423.308. CMS states that remuneration includes "discounts, chargebacks or rebates, cash discounts, free goods contingent on a purchase agreement, up-front payments, coupons, goods in kind, free or reduced-price services, grants, or other price concessions or similar benefits offered to some or all purchasers... from any source (including manufacturers, pharmacies, enrollees, or any other person)." *Id.*

[173]*See* 2007 Reporting Requirements FAQ at 23. However, Sponsors have discretion in whether to report the full amount of administrative fees received from manufacturers, which CMS suggests would be determined by the terms of the agreements between the Sponsor, its PBM, and the manufacturer. *See id.*

[174]*See* 2007 Reporting Requirements at 19.

[175]*See id.*

[176]Rebate data for multiple Sponsors may not be aggregated by subcontracting PBMs for reporting purposes. CMS offers the following examples: (1) national Part D Sponsors with multiple regional plans contracting independently or through a PBM should report rebates at the level of the national Part D Sponsor, (2) regional or local Part D Sponsors, whether using subcontractor PBMs or not, should report at the Part D Sponsor-specific level, and (3) PBMs providing Part D coverage outside of a subcontractor role should report rebates at the PBM level. *See* 2007 Reporting Requirements at 18. Although rebate information must be reported by manufacturer and by drug, Sponsors are required to aggregate drug-specific rebates without regard to dosage form, strength, or package size. *Id.*

drug costs of other types of price concessions and value adds may depend on how individual Sponsors characterize the remuneration in their reporting to CMS. Accordingly, CMS requires Sponsors to submit more detailed information regarding value adds, non-rebate discounts, and other price concessions provided by manufacturers. Sponsors are instructed to describe each individual value add, non-rebate discount, or price concession, identify its monetary value, provide a justification for receipt, and list the name of each manufacturer that provided the remuneration.[177]

Furthermore, Sponsors have been told to include in their quarterly reports to CMS 100 percent of the remuneration they receive from their PBM subcontractors, including manufacturers' rebates passed through by the PBM and price concessions on PBM services.[178] The payment arrangements between Sponsors and PBMs are a primary concern to CMS from a cost reporting perspective[179] and Sponsors must take care to follow CMS's guidelines on properly accounting for those arrangements. For example, a Sponsor may contract with a PBM to negotiate rebates from pharmaceutical manufacturers on drugs covered under the Sponsor's Part D plan. In some arrangements, the PBM will retain a portion of the negotiated rebate and compensate the Sponsor by reducing its own fee for PBM services. According to CMS, such arrangements constitute a reportable price concession to the Sponsor because the reduction in the PBM's fees lowers the amount the Sponsor "actually paid" for the drugs for purposes of calculating allowable reinsurance costs.[180] In the alternative, CMS states that if the PBM remits the full amount of all manufacturer rebates to the Sponsor and bills the Sponsor directly for the full cost of its services, the charge will be an administrative cost that must be deducted from gross covered prescription drug costs.[181] Given that the calculation of gross covered prescription costs excludes administrative costs and price concessions,[182] CMS concludes that "the Sponsor should have the same gross covered prescription drug costs, and thus allowable reinsurance costs, regardless of what proportion of the PBM services are paid for directly by the Sponsor (an administrative cost) and what proportion of services are compensated through manufacturer rebates retained by the PBM (a price concession)."[183]

As a means of ensuring compliance with these reporting requirements, Sponsors should include data reporting provisions in contracts with their PBMs that mirror CMS specifications.[184] CMS even indicates that a "best practices"

---

[177] *See id.*

[178] *See* 2007 Call Letter at 10–11.

[179] *See id.*

[180] CMS assumes "for purposes of calculating allowable reinsurance costs that the value of this price concession equals the portion of the manufacturer rebates retained by the PBM." *Id.* at 11–12.

[181] Social Security Act §1860D–15(b) [42 U.S.C. §1395w–115(b)].

[182] Price concessions are excluded indirectly from the definition of gross covered prescription drug costs. Although not expressly carved out of the definition of the term, gross covered prescription drug costs only include costs "actually paid," which do not include rebates, discounts, or other price concessions. *Id.*

[183] *See* 2007 Call Letter at 11.

[184] *See id.*

approach would be to include an audit requirement in PBM contracts in addition to a 100 percent reporting requirement.[185]

Other financial relationships also may raise compliance concerns under the reporting requirements. For example, a manufacturer might offer to roll a rebate or discount on a Part D drug into the price of a non-Part D drug reimbursed by the Sponsor under a commercial insurance program. Alternatively, a manufacturer might provide the Sponsor with a grant to fund a disease management program in lieu of a discount on a Part D drug. Under either scenario, Sponsors' rebate reports will provide the government with a new level of insight into the off-invoice price concessions available from pharmaceutical manufacturers. The "value add" reports certainly will shine a spotlight on the types of price concessions that have been at the heart of a number of recent settlement agreements between major pharmaceutical manufacturers and DOJ resolving allegations of fraudulent Best Price reporting.[186] Manufacturers should recognize that Sponsors facing Part D reporting obligations may choose to characterize certain contract terms (e.g., data purchases) as "value adds" even though the manufacturer may take a different view.

Sponsors also are responsible for reporting overpayments associated with Part D benefits on a semiannual basis.[187] CMS expects occasional overpayments to pharmacies to occur as part of claims processing. That said, PBMs and other subcontractors also are potential recipients of overpayments from Sponsors. CMS has specifically identified excess fees paid to PBMs for administrative services as overpayments for purposes of this reporting requirement.[188] Reportable overpayments include both those that have been recouped and those that have been identified but not yet recouped.[189] Like data on rebates and other price considerations, CMS relies on overpayment data for calculating the actual amount Medicare owes to Sponsors and, therefore, such data is important during the reconciliation of CMS's monthly Part D payments. CMS also may use these reports as a way of ensuring that Sponsors implement effective payment oversight and overpayment recovery programs.

Because CMS relies so heavily on cost and payment data reported by Sponsors to calculate Medicare's actual Part D payment liability, Sponsors can expect a significant amount of oversight and monitoring of reporting requirement compliance. CMS may impose intermediate sanctions on Sponsors for failing to report accurately, and, depending on the nature of a reporting violation, may refer the matter to the OIG.[190] Sponsors should review the records of fraud and abuse prosecutions faced by Medicare fiscal intermediaries and carriers to get a sense of the seriousness with which the government takes intentional misrepresentations on filings used to determine Medicare payment

---

[185] *See id.*

[186] See Section I, above.

[187] *See* 2007 Reporting Requirements at 17. According to CMS, an overpayment occurs whenever a Sponsor "erroneously makes a payment in excess of the amount due and payable under the Part D drug benefit." *Id.*

[188] *See* 2007 Reporting Requirements FAQ at 20.

[189] *See* 2007 Reporting Requirements at 17.

[190] 42 C.F.R. §423.752.

obligations to contractors.[191] Fraud prosecutions of hospitals and home health agencies found to have filed inaccurate cost reports to facilitate end-of-year true-ups of reimbursement paint a similar picture.[192]

## B. Marketing Guidelines

Shortly after Part D took effect, Congress, CMS, and the OIG became aware of abusive marketing practices used by some Sponsors and their contracted agents to take advantage of beneficiaries. Sponsors could use promotional and marketing activities, as well as certain beneficiary or provider education and outreach programs, to increase plan enrollment and, in turn, their Part D payments, at the expense of the best interest of the beneficiary. As early as February 2006, Representative Fortney "Pete" Stark (D-Cal.) sent letters to both CMS and the OIG demanding an investigation of the alleged "illegal marketing practices" used by some Sponsors of Part D plans to steer beneficiaries into more lucrative Medicare Advantage managed care plans (which cover traditional Medicare services in addition to drugs and provide sponsoring insurers with larger Medicare premium payments).[193] Some Sponsors attempted to increase beneficiary enrollment in MA-PD plans over stand-alone plans by rewarding employees or contractors with bonuses for steering patients into the Sponsor's MA-PD plan instead of its stand-alone Part D plan. After a number of investigations and numerous complaints regarding this tactic, CMS issued a memorandum cautioning Sponsors that "engaging in activities that could mislead or confuse Medicare beneficiaries, or misrepresent an MA or Part D plan," is prohibited.[194] Furthermore, CMS stated that beneficiaries should not be pressured by sales agents in making plan choices and reminded Sponsors that

---

[191] *See, e.g.,* Press Release, U.S. Attorney's Office for the Eastern District of Pennsylvania, *U.S. Attorney's Office and Highmark, Inc. Enter into Unique Agreement to Address Insurers' Obligations Under the Medicare Secondary Payer (MSP) Rules* (June 19, 2006) (announcing a settlement in which Highmark agreed to pay $2,030,840 to the government and to implement a model Medicare Secondary Payor (MSP) program to resolve allegations that the Pennsylvania insurance company underpaid the amounts due for care of certain Medicare beneficiaries under the employer group health plans insured or administered by the company); Press Release, U.S. Dep't of Justice, *Blue Cross Blue Shield of Michigan Pays U.S. $24 Million to Resolve Medicare Claims Dispute* (Jan. 18, 1995) (announcing a settlement in which Blue Cross Blue Shield of Michigan agreed to pay $24 million to the government to resolve allegations that the Medicare contractor unlawfully billed the government's Medicare program for thousands of medical insurance claims that should have been paid from private insurance funds).

[192] See Section II.A.q., above.

[193] *See Democrats Seek Probe of Marketing by Rx Sponsor, Offer New Bill,* 4 PHARMACEUTICAL LAW & INDUSTRY REP. (BNA) 138 (Feb. 3, 2006). Representative Stark suggested that Sponsors were paying higher sales commissions to marketing personnel for enrolling beneficiaries into Medicare Advantage plans instead of stand-alone prescription drug plans. *Id.*

[194] *See* Memorandum from CMS Medicare Drug Benefit Group Director Cynthia G. Tudor and Medicare Advantage Group Director David A. Lewis, *Marketing Activities for Organizations Employing or Contracting with Sales Agents* (Dec. 1, 2006), *available at* http://www.dads.state.tx.us/medicare/news/2006/BrokerActivites120106.pdf [hereinafter CMS Marketing Memorandum]; *see also CMS Restates Marketing Guidance Amid Complaints of Improper Sales Agent Activities,* 11 HEALTH CARE FRAUD REP. (BNA) 10 (Jan. 3, 2007).

they are responsible for ensuring compliance among their employed, as well as independently contracted, agents and brokers.[195] CMS also provided Sponsors with a not so subtle warning that "CMS will be diligent in enforcing our regulations and policies to protect Medicare beneficiaries. We hope that your proactive measures will reduce the need for CMS to take action against organizations and sponsors for the inappropriate activities of their sales agents."[196]

In 2007, CMS took additional steps to address a marketing scheme carried out by brokers engaged by certain Sponsors to promote and sell their Medicare Advantage "private fee-for-service" plans (MA-PFFS).[197] Numerous beneficiaries lodged complaints with CMS arguing that their enrollment in a MA-PFFS plan was the result of misleading or deceptive marketing practices.[198] Apparently, some brokers seized upon the confusion experienced by some beneficiaries over the distinction between Medicare coverage under MA-PFFS plans and the more familiar, and generally well-received, Medigap supplemental coverage policies purchased under Medicare Part B.[199] Beneficiaries complained these brokers failed to explain the attributes of MA-PFFS plans and fraudulently induced them into enrolling by misrepresenting MA-PFFS plans as equivalent to a traditional Medicare fee-for-service option.[200] As a result, seven of the largest sponsors of MA plans entered into an agreement with CMS in June 2007 to suspend voluntarily all marketing of PFFS plans until "CMS certifies that the plan has the systems and management controls in place to meet all of the conditions specified in the 2008 Call Letter and the May 25, 2007 guidance issued by CMS."[201]

Though MA-PFFS plans and traditional Medical fee-for-service primary and supplemental coverage have certain features in common (i.e., beneficiary premium requirements and unrestricted choice of provider), victims of this deception would find significant differences between MA-PFFS plans and traditional fee-for-service Medicare. First, providers must accept the terms and

---

[195] *See* CMS Marketing Memorandum at 1.

[196] *Id.* at 2.

[197] A PFFS plan is a type of Medicare Advantage health plan offered by private insurers under contract with CMS to provide beneficiaries with all their Medicare benefits plus any other benefits the insurer decides to provide under the plan at an additional cost to the beneficiary. *See* CMS Web site at http://www.cms.hhs.gov/PrivateFeeforServicePlans/. In some respects, MA-PFFS plans are structurally similar to traditional fee-for-service Medicare, which may confuse some beneficiaries. For example, although Medicare subsidizes plan costs on a per member per month basis, beneficiaries pay premiums and have cost-sharing obligations as they would under Part B. *See id.* Further, beneficiaries are not limited to providers in a plan network and do not have to obtain a referral to see a specialist. *See id.* Providers furnishing services to PFFS plan enrollees are paid on a fee-for-service basis and do not bear any financial risk, as they typically would as part of a managed care provider network *See id.*

[198] Between December 2006 and April 2007, CMS reported receiving 2,700 complaints relating to plan marketing, many of which involved MA-PFFS plans. *See* Press Release, U.S. Dep't of Health & Human Servs., Centers for Medicare & Medicaid Servs., *Plans Suspend PFFS Marketing* (June 15, 2007) [hereinafter PFFS Press Release].

[199] *See* 2008 Call Letter at 51.

[200] *See* 2008 Call Letter at 51–52; *see also CMS Seeks to Protect Beneficiaries By Medicare Marketing Crackdown*, 12 BNA HEALTH CARE DAILY REP. (June 1, 2007).

[201] PFFS Press Release.

conditions of the MA-PFFS plan in order to receive payment for services rendered to plan enrollees. A provider, however, does not have to accept any or all MA-PFFS plans and may elect not to provide services to MA-PFFS plan enrollees, even if the provider participates in other parts of the Medicare program.[202] Accordingly, beneficiaries who enroll in a MA-PFFS plan may no longer have access to their provider of choice for services covered by the MA-PFFS plan. Second, Sponsors of MA-PFFS plans have flexibility in setting their plan's premiums and enrollee cost-sharing obligations. Accordingly, the cost of individual MA-PFFS plans to the beneficiary may vary and may even exceed the beneficiary's costs for the same or similar coverage under traditional Medicare Part B.[203]

In response to these beneficiary complaints, CMS issued specific guidance to Sponsors of MA-PFFS plans designed to ensure beneficiaries as well as providers are informed about the distinctive features of Medicare MA-PFFS plans. CMS divided the guidance into mandatory "marketing processes" and recommended best practices.[204] Among the mandatory marketing processes, MA-PFFS plans: (i) must provide CMS with monthly listings of all planned marketing and sales events; (ii) are prohibited from implying in marketing materials or presentations that MA-PFFS plans function as a Medicare supplement; (iii) are required to prominently display on advertisements and enrollment materials a specific disclaimer, drafted by CMS, explaining that MA-PFFS plans work differently than Medigap plans and that providers do not have to accept the plan's terms and conditions and, therefore, may be unable to treat the beneficiary; (iv) are required to include in each enrollment kit a "leaflet" that describes the plan's rules for the beneficiary and furnishes information for providers concerning the choice to accept the plan; and (v) are required to conduct outbound education and verification calls to ensure that beneficiaries requesting enrollment understand the plan rules.[205] Further, CMS provides "best practice" recommendations for Sponsors of MA-PFFS plans, which include (i) adopting language drafted by CMS for sales presentations to distinguish MA-PFFS plans from Medicare supplemental insurance, (ii) participating in the Health Plan Employer Data and Information Set (HEDIS) and the Health Outcomes Survey (HOS), and (iii) developing provider relations

---

[202] *See* Centers for Medicare & Medicaid Servs., Private Fee-For-Service—Beneficiary Questions and Answers (Feb. 10, 2006), *available at* http://www.cms.hhs.gov/PrivateFee forServicePlans/Downloads/benqa.pdf.

[203] *See id.*

[204] *See* Memorandum from Abby L. Block, Director of the Center for Beneficiary Choices (CMS), to Medicare Advantage Private Fee-For-Service (PFFS) Plans, Ensuring Beneficiary Understanding of Private-Fee-For Service Plans, Actions and Best Practices (May 25, 2007), *available at* http://op.bna.com/hl.nsf/id/sfak-73qt8w/$File/Letter%20to%20All%20PFFS%20 Plans%2005-24-07.pdf.

[205] *See id.* Outbound education and verification calls, for which CMS provides a model script, must be made after the sale, not at the point of sale, and may not be made by the same sales agent who brokered the transaction. The Sponsor must document at least three attempts to contact the enrollee by telephone within 10 days of receiving the application for enrollment. After the first attempt, if unsuccessful, the Sponsor must send the enrollee an "education letter" for which CMS also provides a model.

strategies and educational materials for use in explaining MA-PFFS plans to providers and encouraging them to participate.[206]

More generally, in the Part D Final Rule, CMS set out the broad ground rules for marketing MA-PD and stand-alone prescription drug plans to beneficiaries.[207] These rules are designed to limit gaming of the enrollment process by Sponsors. They also are intended to ensure that beneficiaries have adequate, accurate information about the plans available to them. Under the Part D Final Rule, Sponsors may not:

- Offer cash or other remuneration as an inducement for enrollment. This prohibition does not prevent Sponsors from explaining any legitimate benefits the beneficiary might obtain as an enrollee of the Part D plan.
- Engage in any discriminatory activity such as targeted marketing to Medicare beneficiaries from higher income areas without making comparable efforts to enroll beneficiaries from lower income areas.
- Solicit Medicare beneficiaries door-to-door.
- Engage in activities that could mislead or confuse Medicare beneficiaries, or misrepresent the Sponsor or its Part D plan. Sponsors may not claim that their Part D plans are recommended or endorsed by CMS, Medicare, or HHS, nor may they claim that CMS, Medicare, or HHS recommends that the beneficiary enroll in their particular plan. Sponsors may, however, indicate that their plan is approved for participation in Medicare.
- Use providers, provider groups, or pharmacies to distribute printed information comparing the benefits of different Part D plans unless they accept and display materials from all Sponsors.
- Accept Part D plan enrollment forms in provider offices, pharmacies, or other places where health care is delivered.
- Use Part D plan names that suggest a plan is not available to all Medicare beneficiaries.
- Engage in any other marketing activity prohibited by CMS in its marketing guidance.[208]

Further, CMS requires that Sponsors make marketing materials available to the disabled Medicare population as well as beneficiaries age 65 and over.[209] Sponsors also must have systems in place for confirming enrollment with beneficiaries and ensuring they understand the rules applicable to them under the plan in which they enrolled.[210]

CMS issued initial sub-regulatory guidance interpreting the Part D marketing regulations in August 2005, and then revised its guidance in November 2005, and again in July 2006 (Marketing Guidelines).[211] The extensive Mar-

---

[206] *See id.*

[207] 42 C.F.R. §423.50.

[208] 42 C.F.R. §423.50(f)(1).

[209] 42 C.F.R. §423.50(f)(2).

[210] *Id.*

[211] Centers for Medicare & Medicaid Servs., Medicare Marketing Guidelines for: Medicare Advantage Plans (MAs), Medicare Advantage Prescription Drug Plans (MA-PDs), Prescription

keting Guidelines place several limitations on the promotion and marketing of Part D plans. CMS clarified the general rule prohibiting the inducement of beneficiaries into a particular Part D plan, explaining that Sponsors may not offer prospective enrollees items of any value for the purpose of inducing them to select a particular Part D plan but may offer gifts of nominal value ($15 or less) to potential enrollees as long as the gift is provided to all eligible beneficiaries (i.e., regardless of whether the beneficiary enrolls) and is not in the form of cash or other monetary rebates (e.g., gift certificates, coupons).[212] In addition, any drawings, prizes, or promises of a free gift must be accompanied by a disclaimer that there is no obligation to enroll.[213] Sponsors may offer current enrollees certain Value-Added Items and Services (VAIS) that do not meet the definition of "benefits" under the Sponsor's Part D plan.[214] VAIS may be health-related (e.g., discounts on eyeglasses) or nonhealth-related (e.g., discounts on movie tickets). However, VAIS may not be funded by the Medicare program or advertised as endorsed by Medicare or as a part of the Medicare covered benefit. Further, Sponsors must offer VAIS uniformly to all enrollees and potential enrollees. Because Part D plans are covered entities under the Health Insurance Portability and Accountability Act of 1996 (HIPAA),[215] Sponsors should be particularly sensitive to the restrictions on marketing activities in the HIPAA Privacy Rule.[216]

The Marketing Guidelines augment the restrictions in the Part D Final Rule on the means Sponsors may use to convey their marketing message. For instance, the Marketing Guidelines establish that Sponsors may not send prospective enrollees unsolicited e-mails.[217] However, Sponsors may engage in outbound telemarketing, within the parameters of applicable privacy laws, provided they telemarket solely to provide information and not to enroll beneficiaries over the phone.[218]

The Marketing Guidelines also address CMS's concerns about communications between beneficiaries and pharmacists, physicians, or other health care providers under contract with the plan[219] about enrollment in a particular

---

Drug Plans (PDPs) and 1876 Cost Plans, (Aug. 15, 2005; Rev. Nov. 1, 2005, 2d Rev. July 25, 2006) [hereinafter Marketing Guidelines], *available at* http://www.cms.hhs.gov/Prescription DrugCovContra/Downloads/FinalMarketingGuidelines.pdf. The Marketing Guidelines define "marketing" as "[s]teering, or attempting to steer, an undecided potential enrollee towards a plan, or limited number of plans, and for which the individual or entity performing marketing activities expects compensation directly or indirectly from the plan for such marketing activities. 'Assisting in enrollment' and 'education' do not constitute marketing." *Id.* at 8.

[212]*Id.* at 118–19.

[213]*Id.*

[214]*Id.* at 110.

[215]Pub. L. No. 104-191, 104th Cong. (1996).

[216]45 C.F.R. §§164.501 and 164.508(a)(3).

[217]*See* Marketing Guidelines at 132.

[218]*Id.* at 133.

[219]As used in the Marketing Guidelines' discussion about provider promotional activities for Part D plans, "providers" generally refers to all providers contracted with the Part D plan and their subcontractors, including but not limited to pharmacists, pharmacies, physicians, hospitals, and long-term care facilities. *Id.* at 122.

Part D plan.[220] CMS notes that providers may not be fully aware of all plan benefits and costs. It suggests that providers could confuse those beneficiaries who perceive the provider as acting as an agent of the plan instead of as the beneficiary's caregiver. Further, CMS is concerned that providers may use their influence as caregivers to steer patients to one plan or another based on financial incentives available to the provider rather than the best interest of the beneficiary.[221] Accordingly, CMS offers a list of sample, appropriate and inappropriate, provider interactions with potential Part D plan enrollees. Specifically, providers who contract or subcontract with Part D plans may provide:

- The names of plans with which they contract and/or in which they participate.
- Information and assistance in applying for the low-income subsidy.
- Objective information on specific plan formularies, based on a particular patient's medications and health care needs.
- Objective information regarding specific plans, such as covered benefits, cost sharing, and utilization management tools.
- Referrals to other sources of information, such as the State Health Insurance Assistance Programs, plan marketing representatives, the State Medicaid Office, the local Social Security Administration Office, or the CMS Web site.[222]
- Printouts or information from the CMS Web site.
- Comparative marketing materials assessing plan information created by a nonbenefit/service providing third party.

In contrast, providers who contract or subcontract with Part D plans may not:

- Direct, urge, or attempt to persuade a beneficiary to enroll in a particular plan or to insure with a particular company based on financial or any other interest of the provider (or subcontractor).
- Distribute stand-alone prescription drug plan or MA-PD plan marketing materials. Instead, the provider must inform individuals where they may obtain information on all available options within the service area.[223]
- Collect enrollment applications.
- Offer inducements to persuade beneficiaries to enroll in a particular plan.
- Health screen when distributing information to patients, as health screening is a prohibited marketing activity.

---

[220]*Id.* at 122–128. The current Part D regulations and the preamble to the Part D Final Rule give the impression that CMS intended to allow pharmacies and providers to market Part D plans to beneficiaries. *See* 42 C.F.R. §423.50(f); 70 Fed. Reg. 4194, 4223 (Jan. 28, 2005). In May 2007, CMS clarified its position on this issue, explaining that it never intended to permit pharmacies and providers to engage in "marketing," as the term is defined in the marketing guidelines. *See* 72 Fed. Reg. 29,403 (May 25, 2007). Rather, CMS intended to allow pharmacies and providers to assist, more generally, with beneficiary enrollment and education. *Id.* Accordingly, CMS proposed a revision to the Part D regulations that would permit pharmacies and providers to assist beneficiaries with enrollment and education, while at the same time stating that such activities are not covered under the definition of marketing in the Marketing Guidelines. *Id.*

[221]Marketing Guidelines at 122–23.

[222]*See* http://www.medicare.gov or 1-800-MEDICARE.

[223]For example, information is available at 1-800-MEDICARE or http://www.medicare.gov.

- Offer anything of value to induce plan enrollees to select them as their provider.
- Accept compensation in consideration for the enrollment of a beneficiary.
- Accept compensation directly or indirectly from a plan for beneficiary enrollment activities.[224]

When the Second Revision to the Marketing Guidelines was published in July 2006, CMS was in a better position to refine its guidance based on Sponsor behavior during the initial Part D open enrollment period in 2005 and early 2006.[225] The revised Marketing Guidelines clarified existing policy and incorporated new policies, most notably emphasizing that Sponsors are responsible for the marketing and promotion of their plans by subcontractors (e.g., PBMs, contract sales forces) and downstream entities (e.g., pharmacies). CMS also recognized the potential for Sponsors to mislead beneficiaries regarding drug coverage and cost-sharing amounts under their Part D plans. For example, a Sponsor might use a "bait and switch" approach to induce beneficiaries to select its plan by marketing a particular drug under a lower cost-sharing tier and then change the formulary to increase enrollees' cost-sharing obligation at the next permitted opportunity (usually, at the beginning of the next plan year). Accordingly, in addition to issuing separate guidance on formulary management (discussed below), the revised Marketing Guidelines required current-year marketing materials to carry notices stating that any advertised benefit, formulary, pharmacy network, premium, or copayment could change in the following year.[226] Further, the revised Marketing Guidelines prohibited Sponsors from displaying the logos of co-branding partners on enrollee identification cards[227] and updated requirements for using call-centers,[228] marketing to special needs plans[229] and employer and union groups,[230] and included details about exceptions and appeals in marketing materials.[231]

One of the government's most significant concerns about the marketing of prescription drug plans is the use by Sponsors of performance-based employee or contractor compensation arrangements that tie earnings to the volume or value of that person's sales.[232] CMS wants to prevent Sponsors from "cherry picking" healthier beneficiaries for their plan or steering beneficiaries to one plan over another based on financial incentives from the Sponsor.[233] Not only are such activities prohibited under the Part D Final Rule and the Marketing

---

[224]*See* Marketing Guidelines at 127–28.

[225]Centers for Medicare & Medicaid Servs., 2nd Revision: Medicare Marketing Guidelines for: Medicare Advantage Plans (MAs), Medicare Advantage Prescription Drug Plans (MA-PDs), Prescription Drug Plans (PDPs) and 1876 Cost Plans (July 25, 2006), *available at* http://www.cms.hhs.gov/PrescriptionDrugCovContra/Downloads/FinalMarketingGuidelines.pdf.

[226]*Id.* at 18.

[227]*Id.* at 12. Beneficiaries reportedly have mistakenly concluded that a pharmacy chain co-branding logo on the enrollment card means covered prescriptions may only be filled by a store in the chain.

[228]*Id.* at 164.

[229]*Id.* at 115.

[230]*Id.* at 148.

[231]*Id.* at 77 and 166.

[232]*Id.* at 129.

[233]*Id.*

Guidelines, they also may raise concerns under federal fraud and abuse laws and state insurance laws. Accordingly, the Marketing Guidelines require that compensation structures must:

- Avoid incentives to mislead beneficiaries, cherry pick certain beneficiaries, or churn beneficiaries between plans.
- Provide reasonable compensation in line with industry standards and appropriately related to the value of the services rendered.
- Not reimburse marketing personnel for payments made to beneficiaries.
- Withhold or withdraw payments when an enrollee disenrolls in less than 60 days.[234]

Further, when Sponsors contract with third parties to perform marketing services, the contracts must obligate agents to comply with Part D and federal fraud and abuse laws and with CMS prescription drug plan policies, including the Marketing Guidelines.[235] Contracts with marketing agents also must stipulate commission rates and those rates should not vary with the volume or value of business generated for the Sponsor.[236]

Given the number of beneficiary complaints and outspoken concerns voiced by members of Congress over the marketing of Part D plans, CMS has taken a particular interest in the enforcement of the Marketing Guidelines. CMS has retained a contractor to increase the resources available to the agency for Part D oversight.[237] The contractor has been "secretly shopping" Part D sales and marketing events across the country and reporting to CMS about the marketing activities beneficiaries are actually encountering.[238] Information provided by the contractor will allow CMS to identify noncompliant Sponsors without necessarily having to conduct an audit or receive a complaint.[239]

Moreover, CMS began working more cooperatively with state insurance regulators.[240] Specifically, CMS worked with the National Association of Insurance Commissioners (NAIC) and the State Departments of Insurance to develop a model Compliance and Enforcement Memorandum of Understanding (MOU) that enables CMS and State Departments of Insurance "to freely share compliance and enforcement information, to better oversee the operations and market conduct of companies we jointly regulate and to facilitate the sharing of specific information about marketing agent conduct."[241] As of August 2007, twenty-six states and Puerto Rico had signed the MOU.[242]

---

[234]*Id.* at 128.

[235]*Id.* at 129.

[236]*Id.*

[237]*See* Testimony of Abby L. Block, Director of the Center for Beneficiary Choices, Centers for Medicare and Medicaid Servs. Before The Senate Finance Committee on the Medicare Prescription Drug Benefit; Review and Oversight (May 8, 2007), at 5, *available at* http://www.senate.gov/~finance/hearings/testimony/2007test/050807testab.pdf.

[238]*Id.*

[239]*Id.*

[240]*Id.*

[241]*Id.*

[242]*See* STATEMENT OF ABBY L. BLOCK BEFORE THE ENERGY AND COMMERCE SUB-COMMITTEE ON OVERSIGHT AND INVESTIGATIONS ON MARKETING OF MEDICARE ADVANTAGE PLANS (June 26, 2007), at 8, *available at* http://energycommerce.house.gov/cmte_mtgs/110-oi-hrg.062607.Block-testimony.pdf.

## C. Drug Formulary Requirements

MMA permits Sponsors to use a formulary as a drug utilization control tool, provided the formulary drug list and benefit management methods comply with certain statutory and regulatory requirements intended to protect beneficiary access to Part D drugs.[243] Sponsors may design their own plan formularies or they may adopt the therapeutic categories and pharmacologic classes developed by the U.S. Pharmacopeia (USP).[244] Regardless of the formulary structure selected, Sponsors must include at least two drugs from each therapeutic category and class of covered Part D drugs on their plan formulary.[245] Sponsors only may change a plan formulary's therapeutic categories and pharmacologic classes at the beginning of a plan year, except as CMS may otherwise approve to take advantage of new therapeutic uses or newly approved Part D drugs.[246]

If a Sponsor elects to use a formulary, MMA mandates that a P&T Committee develop and review the formulary.[247] To ensure that formulary decisions are based on clinical and not financial considerations, MMA requires

---

[243] Social Security Act §1860D–4(b)(3) [42 U.S.C. §1395w–104(b)(3)].

[244] The United States Pharmacopeia (USP) model formulary classification system is available at http://www.usp.org. CMS refers to the USP classification system as a "safe harbor" for a plan's formulary classifications. *See* Centers for Medicare & Medicaid Servs., *Medicare Modernization Act* 2007 *Final Guidelines—Formularies: CMS Strategy for Affordable Access to Comprehensive Drug Coverage* (Mar. 27, 2006), at 3 [hereinafter Formulary Guidelines] *available at* http://www.cms.hhs.gov/PrescriptionDrugCovContra/Downloads/CY07Formulary Guidance.pdf. In March 2007, CMS republished the Formulary Guidelines, with some modifications, as Chapter 6 of the Medicare Prescription Drug Benefit Manual (Part D Drugs and Formulary Requirements) [hereinafter PDMB Chapter 6], *available at* http://www.cms.hhs.gov/ PrescriptionDrugCovContra/Downloads/PDBMChap6FormularyReqrmts_03.09.07.pdf.

[245] Social Security Act §1860D–4(b)(3)(C)(i) [42 U.S.C. §1395w–104(b)(3)(C)(i)]; 42 C.F.R. §423.120(b)(2)(i). In some cases, an exception will apply for the inclusion of only one drug for a particular category or class (e.g., if only one drug exists). 42 C.F.R. §423.120(b)(2)(ii). Generally, CMS considers the requirement that a formulary include at least two drugs in each therapeutic category and class as a floor rather than an absolute standard. CMS may require more than two drugs in certain cases. *See* Formulary Guidelines at 3.

[246] Social Security Act §1860D–4(b)(3)(C)(iii) [42 U.S.C. §1395w–104(b)(3)(C)(iii)]. In accordance with CMS guidance on mid-year changes to Part D formularies, CMS must approve any mid-year change (not otherwise prohibited by MMA) that may adversely affect beneficiary access, and for certain changes, such as removing a drug from the formulary or increasing the beneficiary cost-sharing amount, the Sponsor must exempt from the change all plan enrollees currently taking that drug for the remainder of the plan year. *See* Letter from Abby L. Block, Director, Center for Beneficiary Choice (CMS) to Part D Sponsors, *regarding* Formulary Changes During the Plan Year (Apr. 27, 2006) [hereinafter Formulary Changes], *available at* http://www.cms.hhs.gov/PrescriptionDrugCovContra/Downloads/MemoFormularyChange Guidance_04.27. In addition, Sponsors are required to provide 60 days prior notice to CMS, SPAPs, prescribers, network pharmacies, pharmacists, and affected enrollees, 42 C.F.R. §423.120(b)(4), and also must post notice of the change on their Web site in a timely manner. Social Security Act §1860D-4(a)(3)(B) [42 U.S.C. §1395w-104(a)(3)(B)]. CMS generally will give positive consideration to the following types of formulary maintenance changes during a plan year: removing or re-tiering a brand name drug if an A-rated generic or multisource brand equivalent is added to the formulary at a lower cost to the beneficiary; removing a drug inadvertently added to the formulary; removing a drug that receives a "black box" warning or market withdrawal; removing or re-tiering a drug based on new clinical guidelines or information accepted by CMS; and adding utilization management necessary to effectuate other approved formulary changes, to help determine Parts B and D coverage, or to promote safe use of a Part D drug based on new clinical guidelines or information. Formulary Changes at 2–3.

[247] Social Security Act §1860D–4(b)(3)(A)(i) [42 U.S.C. §1395w–104(b)(3)(A)(i)].

that a majority of P&T Committee members are practicing physicians and/or practicing pharmacists, and at least one practicing physician and practicing pharmacist is independent and free of conflicts (e.g., financial relationships) with the Sponsor, the plan, and pharmaceutical manufacturers and has expertise in the care of elderly or disabled persons.[248] Best practice suggests that Sponsors should ask P&T Committee members to sign a conflict-of-interest statement revealing economic or other relationships with entities affected by drug coverage decisions that could influence committee decisions.[249]

In developing and reviewing the formulary, MMA requires that the P&T Committee base clinical decisions concerning the formulary on the strength of scientific evidence of clinical efficacy and standards of practice, and take into account whether including the drug on the formulary (or in a particular tier on the formulary) has therapeutic advantages in terms of safety and efficacy.[250] The P&T Committee also must annually review and approve the inclusion or exclusion of therapeutic classes in the formulary. Although the P&T Committee function is intended to insulate the formulary from financial considerations, other individuals and committees within Sponsors and PBMs may factor cost into decisions regarding a formulary's tiering structure and the number of drugs to include in each formulary category and class at or beyond the minimum number deemed acceptable by the P&T Committee.

In the Part D Final Rule, CMS established several additional responsibilities for the P&T Committee intended to protect the integrity of formulary development and management from abuses that may inappropriately limit beneficiary access to Part D drugs. Specifically, the P&T Committee must:

- Review and advise Sponsors on policies that guide exceptions and other utilization management processes, including prior authorization and step therapy requirements, drug utilization review standards, quantity limits, generic substitution, and therapeutic interchange.
- Evaluate and analyze, at least annually, treatment protocols and procedures related to the plan's formulary consistent with written policy guidelines and other CMS instructions.
- Review protocols and procedures for clinical appropriateness and for the timely use of and access to both formulary and nonformulary drug products. For example, according to CMS, a nonformulary drug may be needed when the formulary drug would cause adverse effects or would not be as effective or both, based on scientific evidence or medical necessity.
- Document in writing its decisions regarding formulary development and revision and utilization management activities.
- Meet other requirements consistent with written policy guidelines and other CMS instructions.[251]

---

[248] Social Security Act §1860D–4(b)(3)(A)(ii) [42 U.S.C. §1395w–104(b)(3)(A)(ii)]; 42 C.F.R. §423.120(b)(1).

[249] *See* Formulary Guidelines at 2.

[250] Social Security Act §1860D–4(b)(3)(B) [42 U.S.C. §1395w–104(b)(3)(B)].

[251] 42 C.F.R. §423.120(b)(1).

In March 2006, CMS issued guidelines to Sponsors and prospective Sponsors for the development and management of Part D formularies (Formulary Guidelines).[252] The Formulary Guidelines offer further protection against formulary practices by Sponsors designed to limit access or discriminate against vulnerable beneficiary populations. For example, in the Formulary Guidelines, CMS requires Sponsors to cover "substantially all"[253] of the drugs in six specific classes: immunosuppressants, antidepressants, antipsychotics, anticonvulsants, antiretrovirals, and antineoplastics. CMS expressly prohibits Sponsors from implementing prior authorization or step therapy requirements intended to steer beneficiaries toward a preferred alternative drug within these classes.[254] According to CMS, this policy is necessary to ensure that Medicare beneficiaries taking these drugs would not be substantially discouraged from enrolling in a Part D plan and to mitigate the risks and complications associated with an interruption of therapy for these vulnerable populations.

As a final check on the appropriateness of Sponsors' formularies, CMS reviews proposed plan formularies prior to the beginning of each new contract year[255] and must approve certain formulary changes before they may be made during a plan year. The Formulary Guidelines detail the factors on which CMS intends to focus during its review of plan formulary drug lists and benefit management tools (e.g., prior authorization, step therapy,[256] utilization review requirements). Specifically, CMS plans to do the following.

(1) *CMS will review plan formularies using the USP Formulary Key Drug Types*[257] *to test for outliers.*[258] Rather than review plan formularies for the purpose of ensuring that each Key Drug Type is represented by one or two specific drugs, CMS intends to use the presence of USP Formulary Key Drug Types as an "outlier test" to ensure these drug types are strongly represented on all Part D formularies.[259]

---

[252] *See* Formulary Guidelines. *See also* PDBM Chapter 6.

[253] CMS states that "substantially all" in this context means that "all drugs and unique dosage forms in these categories are expected to be included in plan formularies with the following exceptions: multisource brands of the identical molecular structure; extended release products when the immediate-release product is included; products that have the same active ingredient; and dosage forms that do not provide a unique route of administration (e.g., tablets and capsules)." *Id.* at 7.

[254] *Id.* Sponsors may consult with physicians regarding treatment options and outcomes for these beneficiaries. *Id.*

[255] 42 C.F.R. §423.272.

[256] "Step therapy" is "one method of benefit design currently used by industry for the purpose of managing costs by requiring more cost effective drugs to be used before more expensive options are prescribed." *See* Part D Final Rule at 4299.

[257] Formulary Key Drug Types are drug groups that the USP Model Guidelines Executive Committee believes CMS should look for in plans' formularies. *See* Preamble to the Model Guidelines Version 2.0, *available at* http://www.usp.org/healthcareInfo/mmg/revisions.html.

[258] *See* Centers for Medicare & Medicaid Servs., 2008 Call Letter for Medicare Advantage Orgs. (Apr. 19, 2007), at 62, *available at* http://www.cms.hhs.gov/PrescriptionDrugCovContra/Downloads/CallLetter.pdf. The 2008 Call Letter revised this guidance, which previously, under the Formulary Guidelines at 4, stated that CMS would review plan formularies to ensure that each included at least one drug from each of the Key Drug Types.

[259] *See* 2008 Call Letter at 62.

(2) *CMS will review tier placement to provide an assurance that the for-mulary does not substantially discourage enrollment of certain ben-eficiaries.*[260] Drug formularies place drugs into two or more categories, called tiers, which impose different beneficiary cost-sharing amounts on drugs included within each tier.[261] CMS recommends Sponsors use standard industry practices (e.g., tier 1 should be considered the lowest cost-sharing tier available to beneficiaries) when they develop their formulary tier structures. CMS's review will focus on identifying drug categories that may substantially discourage enrollment of certain beneficiaries by placing drugs in nonpreferred tiers in the absence of commonly used therapeutically similar drugs in more preferred po-sitions. CMS will scrutinize drugs placed on specialty formulary tiers, and has proposed a dollar threshold for 2008 of $600 per month for Sponsors' specialty formulary tiers.[262] In other words, CMS will only allow Sponsors to place drugs with a negotiated price over $600 per month in a specialty tier. CMS also has limited beneficiary cost-sharing for specialty tier drugs in the initial coverage range to 25 percent for 2008.[263]

(3) *CMS will analyze formularies to determine whether appropriate ac-cess is afforded to drugs or drug classes addressed in widely accepted treatment guidelines that are indicative of general best practices.*[264] CMS is interested in ensuring that Part D formularies provide bene-ficiaries with access to drugs commonly accepted as best practice for the treatment of certain diseases. In particular, CMS will focus on access to drugs for treatment of the following diseases: asthma, dia-betes, chronic stable angina, atrial fibrillation, heart failure, throm-bosis, lipid disorders, hypertension, chronic obstructive pulmonary disease, dementia, depression, bipolar disorder, schizophrenia, benign prostatic hyperplasia, osteoporosis, migraine, gastroesophageal reflux disease, epilepsy, Parkinson's disease, end-stage renal disease, hepa-titis, tuberculosis, community acquired pneumonia, rheumatoid ar-thritis, multiple sclerosis, and HIV.

(4) *CMS will analyze the availability and tier position of the most com-monly prescribed drug classes for the general Medicare and the dually eligible population.*[265] CMS derived a list of commonly prescribed

---

[260] *See* Formulary Guidelines at 4.

[261] In the 2008 Call Letter, CMS stated that it "expects that sponsors must assign preferred cost-sharing amounts in alignment with preferred formulary tiers." 2008 Call Letter at 67. In other words, cost-sharing amounts for a preferred tier must be lower than cost-sharing amounts for a non-preferred tier. *Id.* CMS warned that Part D "plans whose cost-sharing amounts fall above the mean will be rigorously examined under the discrimination review." *Id.*

[262] *See* 2008 Call Letter at 62; *see also* PDBM Chapter 6 §30.2.4.

[263] *See* PDBM Chapter 6 §30.2.4.

[264] *See* Formulary Guidelines at 4–5.

[265] *Id.* CMS furnishes a list of the Top Drug Classes as Appendix A to the Formulary Guidelines.

drugs from the Medicare Current Beneficiary Survey (MCBS) data from 2002[266] and the OIG's study on *Dual Eligibles' Transition: Part D Formularies' Inclusion of Commonly Used Drugs.*[267] CMS recognizes that plans will not provide identical coverage of these drug classes, but will focus its review on assuring that plans present a balanced formulary.

CMS also will consider the methods a plan uses to manage its formulary because management tools such as prior authorization, step therapy, and prescription fill limits can have a significant effect on beneficiary access to formulary drugs. CMS's review is intended to ensure that Sponsors (and applicants) and their PBMs manage the formulary in the best interest of plan enrollees, in a way consistent with existing best practices, including current industry standards, appropriate guidelines from expert organizations (such as the National Committee on Quality Assurance, the Academy of Managed Care Pharmacy, and National Association of Insurance Commissioners), and standards used in commercial drug plans widely used by seniors and people with disabilities.[268] When a plan falls outside of best practices, CMS will ask the plan to provide a reasonable justification for its practices.[269] CMS intends to compare formularies and formulary management tools proposed by different Sponsors (and applicants) to identify outliers. Outliers will be scrutinized to assess whether their formulary practices have the potential to discriminate against particular beneficiary populations. Sponsors will have to present a reasonable clinical justification for outlier formulary practices that appear to create access problems.

Collectively, the Part D formulary requirements are intended to ensure that Part D drug plans provide access to medically necessary treatments, do not discriminate against any particular types of beneficiaries, and encourage and support approaches to drug benefit management that are proven and in widespread use in current commercially available prescription drug plans.[270] CMS may refuse to renew the Part D contracts of Sponsors, or to enter into initial contracts with applicants, that fail to satisfy the formulary requirements. Additionally, Sponsors or PBMs that develop or manage their formularies in a way that advances their own financial interests at the expense of beneficiaries risk further investigation or referral to federal enforcement authorities.

---

[266] *See* Centers for Medicare & Medicaid Servs., Medicare Current Beneficiary Survey, The Characteristics and Perceptions of the Medicare Population (2002), *available at* http://www.cms .hhs.gov/apps/mcbs/PubCNP02.asp.

[267] *See* Dep't Health & Human Servs., Office of Inspector General, Dual Eligibles' Transition: Part D Formularies' Inclusion of Commonly Used Drugs (Jan. 2006), *available at* http:// oig.hhs.gov/oei/reports/oei-05-06-00090.pdf.

[268] Formulary Guidelines at 5.

[269] *Id.*

[270] *Id.* at 1.

## D. FWA Compliance Program Requirements and Guidelines

Entities that participate or do business with others that participate in a federal health benefit program often have a voluntary corporate compliance program or have at least a passing familiarity with the expected structure of such plans. CMS notes that "fraud and abuse compliance plans have been a part of private business practices since the early 1990's with the implementation of the Federal Sentencing Guidelines for Organizations of 1991" (Sentencing Guidelines).[271] In the late 1990s, the OIG began offering compliance program guidance to providers, suppliers, and other industry players, based largely on the seven elements for an effective compliance program described in the Sentencing Guidelines.[272] Private insurance companies that carried a Medicare+Choice[273] plan have operated under Medicare managed care regulations that also required compliance programs.[274]

Similarly, CMS requires Part D plans to have a compliance program that includes the traditional seven basic elements of a compliance plan:

(1) Written policies, procedures, and standards of conduct articulating the organization's commitment to comply with all applicable federal and state laws.

(2) Designation of a compliance officer and compliance committee accountable to senior management.

(3) Effective training and education of the organization's employees, contractors, agents, and directors by the compliance officer.

(4) Effective lines of communication between the compliance officer and the organization's employees, contractors, agents, directors, and members of the compliance committee.

(5) Enforcement of standards through well-publicized disciplinary guidelines.

(6) Procedures for effective internal monitoring and auditing.

(7) Procedures for ensuring prompt responses to detected evidence of misconduct and the development of corrective action initiatives in response to identified misconduct.[275]

---

[271] Part D Final Rule, 70 Fed. Reg. 4194, 4338 (Jan. 28, 2005), also discussed in Section I., above. The Federal Sentencing Guidelines for Organizations, 69 Fed. Reg. 28,994 (May 19, 2004), as amended, provide that corporations with effective compliance plans may receive preferred treatment, such as mitigated sentencing, when convicted of a federal crime, and, alternatively, prosecutors may use their discretion in pursuing criminal conduct against corporations that have an effective compliance plan. *Id.* For additional information on the Federal Sentencing Guidelines, see Chapter 7 (Baumann, Corporate Compliance Programs) and Chapter 8 (Walton, Humphreys, and Jacobs, Potential Liabilities for Directors and Officers of Health Care Organizations).

[272] All of the OIG's Compliance Program Guidance is available at http://www.oig.hhs.gov/fraud/complianceguidance.html.

[273] The Medicare+Choice program was replaced under MMA with Medicare Advantage plans, some of which offer prescription drug benefits under Medicare Part D.

[274] 42 C.F.R. §422.501(b)(3)(vi), replaced by the Medicare Advantage Final Rule, 70 Fed. Reg. 4587 (Jan. 28, 2005); *see also* OIG Compliance Program Guidance for Medicare+Choice Organizations Offering Coordinated Care Plans, published in 64 Fed. Reg. 61,893 (Nov. 15, 1999).

[275] 42 C.F.R. §423.504(b)(vi)(A)–(G).

However, unlike the compliance plan requirement under the Medicare+ Choice program, CMS imposes an additional eighth element on Part D plan compliance programs. The Part D Final Rule requires Sponsors to establish a comprehensive plan to detect, correct, and prevent fraud, waste, and abuse, and which also includes procedures to voluntarily self-report potential fraud or misconduct related to the Part D program.[276] In the Preamble to the Part D Final Rule, CMS defined this compliance role for Sponsors as requiring them to (i) implement effective fraud and abuse programs, consistent with industry standards; (ii) detect problems; (iii) make referrals to CMS or the appropriate program integrity contractor for further investigation and follow-up; and (iv) undertake corrective action.[277] Further, CMS recommended that Sponsors consider adopting a FWA compliance program similar to the one used by the Federal Employee Health Benefits Plans (FEHBP) and also require pharmacies in their network to adhere to the Code of Ethics of the American Pharmaceutical Association.[278] However, CMS offered Sponsors little other guidance in the Part D Final Rule for implementing a FWA compliance plan despite the fact that CMS believed the requirement is "crucial to the success of the Medicare Part D program and to the millions of beneficiaries who rely on these benefits."[279]

In June 2005, CMS issued a draft guidance document summarizing addressing the FWA compliance program requirements.[280] CMS confirmed three important points. First, because the Sponsor is the entity that holds the contract with CMS, the Sponsor will be responsible for the activities of its subcontractors and other downstream entities.[281] The onus will be on the Sponsors to implement a FWA compliance program that effectively monitors and controls the conduct of contracted PBMs, pharmacy networks, and other entities that perform plan functions.[282] Sponsors also will be responsible for all data submitted, directly or indirectly (i.e., through PBM contractors), to CMS. Second, Sponsors may establish separate compliance plan documents and structures to

---

[276]70 Fed. Reg. 4194 (Jan. 28, 2005). In May 2007, CMS proposed to eliminate the "eighth element" in (b)(4)(vi)(H), which CMS now views as "duplicative" and "confusing." 72 Fed. Reg. 23,368, 23,372 (May 25, 2007). CMS explained that any "effective" compliance plan already would have to include policies and procedures for preventing fraud, waste, and abuse. *See id.* Under this interpretation, a compliance plan established under the traditional seven elements would satisfy Congress's mandate in MMA that Part D Sponsors have a program to control FWA. *See id.* In reality, the proposed change would have little practical effect for Sponsors, which would remain responsible for all FWA compliance matters in their Part D plans. CMS recommended that Sponsors look to PDBM Chapter 9 for guidance when developing their compliance plans to ensure that appropriate measures are incorporated to prevent, detect, and correct fraud, waste, and abuse. *See id.*

[277]*See* Part D Final Rule at 4339.

[278]*See id.* at 4338. *The Code of Ethics* of the American Pharmaceutical Association is available at http://www.aphanet.org/pharmcare/ethics.html.

[279]*Id.*

[280]Centers for Medicare & Medicaid Servs., *Review of Sponsors' Fraud Waste and Abuse Responsibilities Summary Document* (May 31, 2005), *available at* http://64.233.161.104/search? q=cache:Knur4tkbtfoJ:www.cms.hhs.gov/pdps/fwacompliancesummary5-31-05.pdf+CMS+ fraud+%22draft+summary%22&hl= en&gl=us&ct=clnk&cd=1.

[281]*Id.*

[282]*Id.*

comply with the Part D FWA requirement or they may integrate their Part D FWA program into an existing, general corporate compliance program applicable to all company activities.[283] Third, although CMS confirmed that the Part D Final Rule does not require Sponsors to self-report FWA to enforcement authorities, Sponsors should, in CMS's view, treat self-reporting as a "critical element" of an effective compliance plan.[284] At the same time, CMS announced it would contract with MEDICs[285] to assist with program integrity oversight of Part D.

In April 2006, CMS finalized PDBM Chapter 9, entitled "*Part D Program to Control Fraud, Waste and Abuse,*" which provided much more detailed guidance to Sponsors for developing and implementing a comprehensive compliance plan for detecting, correcting, and presenting FWA in Part D.[286] PDBM Chapter 9 is intended to be scalable[287] and presenting best practice standard for developing and implementing an effective FWA compliance plan, but which is intended to be adjustable, in many respects, to fit the needs of individual Part D plans. Throughout PDBM Chapter 9, recommendations are reflected by the use of the term *should*, whereas statutory or regulatory program requirements are reflected by the terms *shall* or *must*.[288] For the sake of clarity, whenever the discussion of PDBM Chapter 9 presented below refers to a statutory or regulatory requirement, "must" or "shall" appears in bold and italics.[289]

PDBM Chapter 9 provides Sponsors with a detailed approach to building a compliance program. Identifying, understanding, and satisfying CMS's requirements and recommendations for an effective FWA compliance plan will be critical for Sponsors because they will be responsible, and to some extent liable, for any FWA that occurs within their Part D plan. If a Sponsor's compliance program fails to identify a fraud perpetrated by the Sponsor or one of its downstream contractors that later comes to the government's attention, the Sponsor will want to be in a position to assert nonetheless that its compliance program was effective because it complied with the applicable requirements and recommendations set forth in PDBM Chapter 9. A summary of the key provisions in PDBM Chapter 9 follows.

---

[283] *Id.*

[284] *Id.*; *see also* 42 C.F.R. §423.504(b)(4)(vi)(H).

[285] *See* Section I., above.

[286] *See* PDBM Chapter 9 (Apr. 25, 2006), *available at* http://www.cms.hhs.gov/Prescription DrugCovContra/Downloads/PDBManual_Chapter9_FWA.pdf, discussed in Section I., above. For additional discussion of PDBM Chapter 9, see Chapter 7 (Baumann, Corporate Compliance Programs).

[287] "While CMS regulations require Sponsors to implement a comprehensive fraud and abuse program, the adoption of the methods suggested within this chapter on how to implement a comprehensive fraud and abuse program are left to the discretion of each Sponsor based on the size, scope, and resources of its organization." PDBM Chapter 9 §20.

[288] *Id.*

[289] Sponsors may want to prioritize PDBM Chapter 9's mandatory provisions under their internal compliance monitoring and auditing protocols to ensure basic compliance. Although compliance protocols would be most effective when tailored based on individual experience, vigilant monitoring of CMS's essential regulatory requirements seems prudent.

## 1. Overview of Fraud, Waste, and Abuse

Sponsors *must* have written policies and procedures in place to identify and address FWA in the delivery of prescription drugs through the Medicare benefit at both the Sponsor and third-party (i.e., contractor) levels.[290] The relationships between Sponsors and their contractors and subcontractors have significant operational and compliance implications. Accordingly, as explained below, CMS has provided regulatory and subregulatory guidance on its interpretation of each level of contractor.

## 2. Sponsor Accountability and Oversight

Sponsors are ultimately responsible for providing the Part D benefit under their contracts with CMS,[291] even though the design of the benefit likely will require them to delegate some of their performance obligations to subcontractors,[292] including first tier entities,[293] downstream entities,[294] or related entities.[295] For program integrity purposes, CMS requires certain provisions to be included in contracts for the delegation of duties related to the Part D benefit:

(1) If a Sponsor delegates any of its Part D responsibilities to a related entity, contractor,[296] subcontractor, or pharmacy, the written arrangements *must* either provide for revocation of the delegation or specify other remedies in the event CMS or the Sponsor deems the performance unsatisfactory.[297]

---

[290] *Id.* (citing 42 U.S.C. §1395w–104).

[291] *Id.* §40.

[292] In a Notice of Proposed Rulemaking published in May 2007, CMS proposed to eliminate the more general term "subcontractor" in favor of the more specific terms "first tier entity," "downstream entity" and "related entity." 72 Fed. Reg. 29,368, 29,393 (May 25, 2007). In addition, CMS proposed to recodify these definitions in the General Provisions section of the Part D regulation to ensure the terms have the same meaning throughout the Part D regulation. Currently, these terms are defined only in Subpart K (Application Procedures and Contracts with Part D Sponsors).

[293] "First tier entity" means any party (usually, a PBM) that enters into a written arrangement acceptable to CMS with a Sponsor or applicant to provide administrative services or health care services for a Medicare eligible individual under Part D. PDBM Chapter 9 §40 (citing 42 C.F.R. §423.501).

[294] "Downstream entity" means any party that enters into a written arrangement, acceptable to CMS, below the level of the arrangement between a Sponsor and a first tier entity (e.g., a pharmacy that contracts with a PBM, which is a first tier entity). *Id.* §40 (citing 42 C.F.R. §423.501).

[295] "Related Entity" means any entity that is related to the Sponsor by common ownership or control and (1) performs some of the Sponsor's management functions under contract or delegation, (2) furnishes services to Medicare enrollees under an oral or written agreement, or (3) leases real property or sells materials to the Sponsor at a cost of more than $2,500 during a contract period (e.g., if a Sponsor is the parent company of its own in-house PBM, the PBM would be a related entity). *Id.* §40 (citing 42 C.F.R. §423.501).

[296] A "contractor" is any entity or individual that directly contracts with CMS to provide items or services, or perform tasks related to the Part D program (e.g., Sponsors, MEDICs). *Id.* §40.

[297] *Id.* (citing 42 C.F.R. §423.505(i)(4)(ii)).

(2) Contracts *must* contain specific provisions including, but not limited to, inspections, enrollee protection, Sponsor accountability, delegation, and record retention.[298]

(3) Contracts with first tier entities, downstream entities, and related entities *must* include provisions permitting ongoing monitoring by the Sponsor to assess compliance with Part D provisions. Contractors at all levels may be subject to any applicable civil and criminal laws, such as the False Claims Act or the anti-kickback statute, for fraud perpetrated by them in the administration or delivery of the Part D benefit.

PDBM Chapter 9 provides detailed recommendations for claims processing system edits that Sponsors, likely acting through their PBMs, should incorporate into their Part D plan operations to control and monitor the delivery of the prescription drug benefit.[299] It urges Sponsors to develop reports that facilitate monitoring payments, utilization, and physician prescribing patterns as well as zip code-based reports to detect doctor shopping or prescription mills.[300] Sponsors should trend pharmacy claims and other data[301] and maintain and monitor complaint files on providers.[302] These recommendations should not be surprising because they mirror the types of claims processing and program integrity functions required by CMS of the contractors (fiscal intermediaries and carriers) hired to assist with the administration of Medicare Parts A and B.

### 3. The Basics of a Program to Control Fraud, Waste, and Abuse

Sponsors *must* have an operational compliance program to control FWA.[303] Each Sponsor *must* determine what method for implementing a FWA program is best based on its size, structure, and resources.[304] CMS recommends that the Part D compliance officer be the chief overseer of the Sponsor's compliance efforts. Further, the Sponsor should be prepared to demonstrate the effectiveness of its program upon request to CMS or the MEDICs.

---

[298] *Id.* (citing 42 C.F.R.§423.505(e)(2), (i) and (j)).

[299] *Id.* §50.2.6.3.1. Suggested edits include, but are not limited to, controls on early refills; limits on the number of days before a refill is permitted; edits to prevent payment for statutorily excluded drugs; limits on the number of times a prescription may be refilled; prior authorization edits; real time contraindications; sex and age edits; therapeutic edits; limits of prescriptions for controlled substances; deceased, excluded, and suspended prescribing physician edits; deceased or disenrolled beneficiaries edits; insufficient or excessive dosage edits; step therapy edits; and edits identifying drugs provided through a PAP outside of Part D. *Id.*

[300] *Id.* §50.2.6.1.

[301] *Id.* §50.2.6.2. Sponsors should develop claims data analyses capable of identifying issues associated with inaccurate TrOOP accounting, potentially fraudulent pharmacy billing practices, and overutilization of particular drugs. Data mining and trending may assist with finding problem areas associated with plan enrollment, plan finances, or data submissions to CMS as well as operational deficiencies at the subcontractor level. *Id.*

[302] *Id.* §50.2.6.3.2.

[303] *Id.* §50.1 (citing 42 U.S.C. §1392 w–104 and citing 42 C.F.R. §423.504(b)(4)(vi)).

[304] *Id.* §50.1.

### 4. Components of a Comprehensive Program to Detect, Prevent, and Control Part D Fraud, Waste, and Abuse as Part of the General Compliance Plan Requirements

#### a. Written Policies and Procedures

Sponsors ***must*** have written policies, procedures, and standards of conduct that articulate the Sponsor's commitment to comply with all applicable federal and state standards.[305] These documents should be updated as necessary to incorporate any changes in applicable laws, regulations, and other Part D requirements. The Sponsor's policies and procedures should represent the organization's "response to day-to-day risks to help reduce the prospect of fraudulent, wasteful and abusive activity by identifying and responding to risk areas."[306] CMS also urges Sponsors to implement policies and procedures to deal with conflicts of interest. For instance, Sponsors should obtain certifications from first tier entities, downstream entities, and related entities stating they will require managers, officers, and directors responsible for the administration or delivery of Part D benefits to sign conflict of interest statements at the time of hire and annually thereafter attesting to the absence of conflicts of interest.

#### b. Compliance Officer and Committee

Sponsors ***must*** designate a compliance officer and a compliance committee accountable to senior management. To ensure proper oversight of the compliance program, a Sponsor ***must not*** delegate or subcontract control over the appointment and functioning of its compliance officer and compliance committee.[307] Although CMS requires that the compliance officer be an employee of the Sponsor and that the Sponsor retain ultimate responsibility for all compliance functions,[308] the compliance officer may delegate or subcontract his or her duties.[309] The Part D compliance officer may be the same individual as the corporate compliance officer, but CMS strongly recommends that the two positions be staffed independently.[310] Sponsors ***must*** ensure that the Part D compliance officer does not have other responsibilities that could lead to self-policing of those activities, e.g., the Part D Compliance Officer should not also be, or be subordinate to, the chief financial officer.[311] To the extent any of the duties of the Part D compliance officer are delegated to compliance staff or

---

[305]*Id.* §50.2.1 (citing 42 C.F.R. §423.504(b)(4)(vi)(A)).

[306]*Id.* §50.2.1.2. PDBM Chapter 9 contains several examples of policies and procedures for the Sponsor's FWA compliance program. *Id.*

[307]*Id.* §§40.1 and 50.2.2.

[308]*See* Letter from Cynthia G. Tudor, Acting Director, Medicare Drug Benefit Group (CMS), regarding Instructions for 2007 Contract Year (Apr. 3, 2006), at 29, *available at* http://www.cms.hhs.gov/PrescriptionDrugCovContra/Downloads/2007PDPCallLetter.pdf. In PDBM Chapter 9 §50.2.2.1, CMS further recommends that Sponsors dedicate a full-time employee to oversee the compliance program and operations for the Part D plan.

[309]PDBM Chapter 9 §50.2.2.

[310]*Id.* §50.2.2.1.

[311]*Id.*

others, the compliance officer should maintain appropriate oversight of those duties.[312] The Sponsor's governing body *must* establish a compliance committee overseen by the Part D compliance officer to advise and assist in implementation of the Part D compliance program.[313]

### c. Training and Education

Sponsors *must* provide effective FWA compliance training and education to the organization's employees, subcontractors, agents, and directors who are involved in the Part D benefit.[314]

### d. Effective Lines of Communication

Sponsors *must* have effective lines of communication between the compliance officer and the organization's employees, contractors, agents, directors, and members of the compliance committee.[315] Each Sponsor *must* establish a system that fosters effective lines of communication regarding how to report compliance concerns and suspected or actual misconduct.[316] A confidential or anonymous reporting mechanism (e.g., a compliance hotline) should be in place for those who may be uncomfortable reporting concerns directly to a supervisor or the Part D compliance officer.[317] Sponsors should "adopt, routinely publicize, and enforce a zero-tolerance policy for retaliation or retribution against any employee or subcontractor who reports suspected misconduct."[318] Sponsors *must* follow the grievance procedures in 42 C.F.R. Subpart M and operate meaningful procedures for the timely hearing and resolving of enrollees' grievances.[319] Sponsors also *must* follow the procedures for reporting enrollee complaints to CMS, as outlined in the Medicare Part D reporting requirements.[320]

### e. Enforcement of Standards

Sponsors *must* enforce their standards of conduct through well-publicized disciplinary guidelines.[321] It is likely the MEDICs will view evidence of disciplinary actions as a meaningful measure of a compliance program's effectiveness.

---

[312]*Id.*

[313]*Id.*

[314]*Id.* §50.2.3 (citing 42 C.F.R. §423.504(b)(4)(vi)(C)). PDBM Chapter 9 identifies numerous compliance issues and other subjects on which CMS suggests employees receive training.

[315]*Id.* §50.2.4 (citing 42 C.F.R. §423.504(b)(4)(vi)(D)).

[316]*Id.* §50.2.4.1 (citing 42 C.F.R. §423.504(b)(4)(vi)(D)).

[317]*Id.*

[318]*Id.*

[319]*Id.* §50.2.4.2 n.561; 42 C.F.R. §423.564. CMS published guidance on the resolution of enrollee complaints, *available at* http://www.cms.hhs.gov/PrescriptionDrugCovContra/Downloads/PDBManual_Chapter9_FWA.pdf.

[320]PDBM Chapter 9 §50.2.4.2.

[321]*Id.* §50.2.5 (citing 42 C.F.R. §423.504(b)(4)(vi)(E)).

*f. Monitoring and Auditing*

Sponsors *must* have procedures for effective internal monitoring and auditing.[322] Sponsors should develop a monitoring and auditing work plan that addresses the risks associated with the Part D benefit.[323] CMS identifies three important issues related to effective monitoring and auditing. First, Sponsors *must* include assessments of the Part D activities of their first tier entities, downstream entities, and related entities in their auditing and monitoring plans.[324] Sponsors *must* ensure that their contracts with these entities require record retention and provide rights of access to records to CMS or its designee, as well as the Sponsor.[325] Second, given that Sponsors *must not* pay for drugs prescribed or provided by a provider excluded by either the OIG or the General Services Administration (GSA),[326] Sponsors should review the OIG[327] and GSA[328] exclusion lists at least annually and have processes in place to prevent the payment of claims for services provided by excluded providers. Sponsors also *must* require the immediate removal of employees, board members, first tier entities, downstream entities, or related entities from any work, directly or indirectly, on the Part D benefit, and take appropriate corrective actions, in the event such persons or entities are on the OIG or GSA exclusion lists.[329] Third, when requested, Sponsors and their subcontractors *must* allow CMS or its designee (i.e., MEDICs) to audit financial records as well as other documents related to the administration or delivery of Part D benefits, including data relating to Medicare utilization and costs.[330] Sponsors and their contractors should cooperate in allowing CMS and/or MEDICs access to their facilities as requested.[331]

*g. Conducting a Timely and Reasonable Inquiry of Detected Offenses*

Sponsors *must* conduct a timely, reasonable inquiry when evidence suggests there has been misconduct related to payment for or delivery of prescription drugs or drug-related services under the Part D benefit.[332] CMS suggests that timely investigations should start within two weeks of an incident report. Sponsors should refer a matter to a MEDIC for review if resources do

---

[322]*Id.* §50.2.6 (citing 42 C.F.R. §423.504(b)(4)(vi)(F)).

[323]*Id.* PDBM Chapter 9 offers additional guidance on what Sponsors should include in a work plan.

[324]*Id.* §50.2.6.1.3.

[325]*Id.* (citing 42 C.F.R. §423.505(i)(2)). In May 2007, CMS proposed a revision to the Part D regulations to clarify that the access requirements applicable to Sponsors apply equally and directly to first tier, downstream, and related entities. 72 Fed. Reg. 29,368, 29,374 (May 25, 2007). CMS would expect these entities to produce documents and records related to the Part D program upon request from CMS or its designee.

[326]*Id.* §50.2.6.3.3 (citing 42 C.F.R. §1001.1901).

[327]The OIG exclusion list is available at http://www.oig.hhs.gov/fraud/exclusions/listofexcluded.html.

[328]The GSA exclusion list is available at http://epls.gov/epls/servlet/EPLSReportMain/1.

[329]PDBM Chapter 9 §50.2.1.2.

[330]*Id.* §50.2.6.3.4 (citing 42 U.S.C. §1395w–112; 42 C.F.R. §423.504(d)).

[331]*Id.*

[332]*Id.* §50.2.7.1 (citing 42 C.F.R. §423.504(b)(4)(vi)(G)(1)).

not permit timely investigation. Reasonable inquiries involve a preliminary inquiry by the Part D compliance officer or the Special Investigation Unit, if a Sponsor has one, to determine if corrective action, or a referral to enforcement authorities for potential fraud, is justified.[333]

### h. Corrective Actions

Sponsors *must* undertake appropriate corrective actions (for example, repayment of overpayments and disciplinary actions against responsible individuals) in response to violations.[334] Sponsors should, but are not required to, notify the MEDICs of potential fraud, waste, or abuse.[335] If a Sponsor does report an offense, the MEDIC may ask the Sponsor for additional information, which the Sponsor *must* furnish within 30 days, unless the MEDIC otherwise specifies.[336]

### 5. Implementing a Comprehensive Program to Detect, Correct, and Prevent Fraud, Waste, and Abuse and Procedures to Voluntarily Self-Report Potential Fraud and Misconduct

To assist with the development of the comprehensive compliance program that Sponsors *must* implement,[337] PDBM Chapter 9 provides long lists of risk areas that Sponsors should address as part of their Part D FWA program. Many of the identified risk areas are presented below.

### a. Risk Areas for Part D Plan Sponsors

Part D Plan Sponsors are at risk for the following behavior.[338]

- *Failure to provide medically necessary services* covered by law or contract, particularly if that failure adversely affects (or is substantially likely to affect) the beneficiary.
- *Marketing schemes* that achieve plan enrollments through methods that violate the Medicare Marketing Guidelines, or other federal or state laws, rules, and regulations.
- *Improper bid submissions* involving inappropriate overestimates or underestimates to manipulate risk corridors and/or payments, including

---

[333]*Id.*

[334]*Id.* §50.2.8 (citing 42 C.F.R. §423.504(b)(4)(vi)(G)(2)).

[335]*Id.* In a Notice of Proposed Rulemaking published in May 2007, CMS proposed to change the Part D regulations to impose a mandatory self-reporting requirement on Sponsors. *See* 72 Fed. Reg. 29,368, 29,373 (May 25, 2007). CMS noted in the Preamble that several highly publicized cases of Part D compliance violations did not become known to CMS until reported in the press. *See id.* Accordingly, CMS proposed to require Sponsors to establish procedures for mandatory self-reporting of potential fraud or misconduct related to the Part D program to the appropriate government authority. *See id.* at 29,393. If this proposed rule is finalized, Sponsors of Part D plans and MA-PD plans would be required to report all incidences of fraud or misconduct related to the Part D or MA program, as applicable, to the government.

[336]PDBM Chapter 9 §50.2.8.3.

[337]*Id.* §60 (citing 42 C.F.R. §423.504(b)(4)(vi)(H)).

[338]*Id.* §70.1.1.

miscalculations of administrative ratio costs within the bids (wrong service lines).

- *Payments for excluded drugs* violate the requirement that Sponsors **must** ensure they only provide coverage for "covered Part D drugs,"[339] as listed in their approved formularies, and in accordance with the coverage exclusion provisions in MMA.[340]

- *Multiple billings* for the same prescription (e.g., to Part A or B and Part D or to Medicaid and Part D).

- *Noncompendium payments*, such as payments for Part D drugs that are not for a "medically accepted indication."[341] Payments for off-label uses of Part D drugs are permitted only for a recognized medically accepted indication in the American Hospital Formulary Service Drug Information, the U.S. Pharmacopeia-Drug Information (or its successor), or the DRUGDEX Information System compendia.[342]

- *Inappropriate formulary decisions* in which costs take priority over criteria such as clinical efficacy and appropriateness.

- *Inappropriate enrollment/disenrollment actions* that result in inflated Sponsor payments (e.g., failing to effect timely disenrollment of a beneficiary from CMS systems upon beneficiary's request).

- *Appeals process handled incorrectly*, such as denying a beneficiary the right to appeal or denying a timely appeal.

- *Adverse selection* (e.g., selecting or denying enrollment based on illness profile or other discriminating factors).

- *Reporting false, inaccurate, or incomplete information* to CMS or to beneficiaries.

- *Delinquent reimbursements* to beneficiaries following a retroactive low-income subsidy determination.

- *Duplicative premiums or copayments* collected from beneficiaries.

- *Excessive premiums* charged to enrollees in excess of the basic and supplemental beneficiary premiums permitted under Part D.

- *Inaccuracies in eligibility or coordination of benefits* leading to wasteful expenditures. Sponsors, PBMs, and pharmacies should address this risk

---

[339]*Id.* (citing 42 C.F.R. §423.100). "Covered Part D drug" means a Part D drug that is included in a Part D plan's formulary, or treated as being included in a Part D plan's formulary as a result of a coverage determination or appeal, under applicable regulations, and obtained at a network pharmacy or an out-of-network pharmacy (as permitted in the Part D Final Rule). 42 C.F.R. §423.100.

[340]PDBM Chapter 9 §70.1.1 (citing 42 U.S.C. §1395w-102(e)(2)). With the exception of smoking cessation drugs, MMA excludes from coverage under Part D those drugs with restricted coverage under Medicaid pursuant to 42 U.S.C. §1937r-9(d)(2). As a result, benzodiazepines (e.g., Valium, Xanax, Halcion) are not covered by Part D. Dual-eligible beneficiaries, particularly those residing in long-term care facilities, where benzodiazepine usage is common, lost the Medicaid coverage that had been available for these drugs in most states when they were switched to a Part D plan. As a result, many state Medicaid programs are offering wrap around coverage for dual eligibles to help pay for drugs not covered under Part D.

[341]PDBM Chapter 9 §70.1.1 (citing 42 U.S.C. §1395w–102).

[342]42 U.S.C. §1396r–8; *see also CMS Clarification Regarding Part D Drugs/Part D Excluded Drugs* (Feb. 6, 2006) at 1, *available at* http://www.cms.hhs.gov/Prescription DrugCov Contra/Downloads/PartDDrugsPartDExcludedDrugs_04.19.06.pdf.

by using real-time systems to verify eligibility, available benefits, and payor status.

- *Incorrect calculation of TrOOP* that results in improper payments by CMS or beneficiaries.
- *Catastrophic coverage manipulation* to increase payments from CMS.
- *Failure to disclose or misrepresentation* of rebates, discounts, or price concessions obtained from pharmaceutical manufacturers.
- *Bait and switch pricing,* including frequent formulary changes to induce beneficiaries to sign up because they take specific drugs that are later removed from the formulary or moved to a tier with higher beneficiary copayment obligations.
- *Manipulation of low-income subsidy enrollee statistics* to receive unwarranted subsidy payments.

### b. Risk Areas for Pharmacy Benefit Managers

Pharmacy Benefit Managers must avoid the following activity.[343]

- *Payment-induced prescription drug switching* whereby a PBM or prescriber receives a payment for switching a beneficiary to another drug.
- *Unlawful remuneration* to steer beneficiaries toward a certain plan or drug, or for formulary placement.
- *Inappropriate formulary decisions*, which CMS interprets as PBMs or P&T committees making formulary decisions based on cost or financial inducements, not clinical efficacy.
- *Prescription splitting or shorting* at the PBM's mail-order pharmacy to increase dispensing fees by splitting the prescription into two bottles instead of one or to increase drug payments by furnishing the beneficiary with less than the prescribed amount while billing for the entire amount prescribed.
- *Failure to offer negotiated prices* to beneficiaries.

### c. Risk Areas for Pharmacies

Pharmacies are at risk if they engage in the following activities.[344]

- *Inappropriate billing practices,* including:
  - Incorrectly billing secondary payors to receive increased reimbursement.
  - Billing for nonexistent prescriptions.
  - Billing multiple payors for the same prescriptions, except as required for coordination-of-benefit transactions.
  - Billing for brand when generics are dispensed.
  - Billing for noncovered prescriptions as covered items.
  - Billing for prescriptions that are never picked up.

---

[343]PDBM Chapter 9 §70.1.2.
[344]*Id.* §70.1.3.

- ○ Billing based on "gang visits" (e.g., a pharmacist visits a nursing home and bills for numerous pharmaceutical prescriptions without furnishing any specific service to individual patients).
- ○ Inappropriate use of dispense as written (DAW) codes.
- ○ Prescription splitting to receive additional dispensing fees.
- ○ Drug diversion.
- *Prescription drug shorting.*
- *Bait and switch pricing.*
- *Prescription forging or altering* without the prescriber's permission to increase quantity or number of refills.
- *Dispensing expired or adulterated prescription drugs.*
- *Prescription refill errors.*
- *Illegal remuneration schemes* involving payments to pharmacies to induce beneficiaries or prescribers to switch drugs or to steer beneficiaries toward a particular Part D plan.
- *TrOOP manipulation* to either push a beneficiary through the coverage gap so the beneficiary can reach catastrophic coverage before they are eligible, or suppress TrOOP costs to keep a beneficiary in the coverage gap so that catastrophic coverage is never realized.
- *Failure to offer negotiated prices.*

### d. Risk Areas for Prescribers

Prescribers' potentially risky behaviors include the following.[345]

- *Illegal remuneration schemes.*
- *Prescription drug switching.*
- *Script mills* where the provider writes prescriptions for drugs, particularly controlled substances, that are not medically necessary, sometimes as a result of payments to the provider.
- *Provision of false prescription information* in order to justify coverage.
- *Theft of prescriber's DEA number or prescription pad.*

### e. Risk Areas for Wholesalers

Wholesalers are cautioned to avoid the following activity.[346]

- *Counterfeit and adulterated drugs obtained through black and gray market purchases.*
- *Failure to pass required pedigrees.*
- *Diversion.*
- *Inappropriate documentation of pricing information.*

---

[345] *Id.* §70.1.4.
[346] *Id.* §70.1.5.

### f. Risk Areas for Pharmaceutical Manufacturers

Pharmaceutical manufacturers must avoid the following scenarios.[347]

- *Lack of integrity of data* used to establish payment and/or determine reimbursement that can lead the Medicare program to overpay for drugs.
- *Inappropriate documentation of pricing information.* Manufacturers **must** maintain accurate and complete documentation of their pricing information.
- *Kickbacks, inducements, and other illegal remuneration,* usually in the form of inappropriate marketing of drugs; the provision of inducements to increase sales, such as payments to prescribers or pharmacies for switching; or the concealment of price concessions or offers of other payments or services to PBMs or Sponsors for placement on the formulary.
- *Formulary and formulary support activities,* which may include financial relationships with members of the P&T Committee as well as payments or other concessions to PBMs and Sponsors.
- *Inappropriate relationships with physicians,* which influence the physicians' prescriptive practices.
- *Illegal off-label promotion.*
- *Illegal usage of free samples,* which can lead to the submission of false claims.

### g. Risk Areas for Medicare Beneficiaries

CMS describes the types of FWA that beneficiaries of Part D could perpetrate, as well as examples of activity that might victimize beneficiaries. Medicare beneficiaries are at risk for the following behavior.[348]

- *Misrepresentation of status* to enroll in a Part D plan.
- *Identity theft.*
- *TrOOP manipulation* so the beneficiary can move through the coverage gap faster.
- *Prescription forging or altering.*
- *Prescription diversion and inappropriate use.*
- *Resale of drugs on the black market,* usually with the beneficiary reporting the drugs lost or stolen.
- *Prescription stockpiling,* whereby a beneficiary attempts to "game" his or her drug coverage by obtaining and storing large quantities of drugs to avoid out-of-pocket costs, protect against periods of noncoverage (e.g., by purchasing a large amounts of prescription drugs and then disenrolling), or permit resale on the black market.
- *Doctor shopping* to inappropriately obtain multiple prescriptions for narcotic painkillers or other drugs.
- *Improper coordination of benefits,* involving a failure to disclose multiple coverage policies.
- *Marketing schemes* intended to improperly enroll beneficiaries.

---

[347] *Id.* §70.1.6.
[348] *Id.* §70.1.7.

### h. Additional Vulnerabilities

PDBM Chapter 9 also lists "in addition to the above mentioned potential schemes, risks, and vulnerabilities . . . four other major areas of concern."[349]

- *Excluded Drugs.* Drugs may not be covered under Part D if they are not prescribed for a medically accepted indication.[350]
- *Parts B and D Coverage Issues.* Some drugs are covered by both Medicare Parts B and D and it is incumbent upon Sponsors to have mechanisms in place to ensure that the correct Medicare program pays for such drugs. The statutory definition of a covered Part D drug excludes any drug that, as prescribed and administered or dispensed, would be covered by Part B.[351] CMS has identified several specific risk areas associated with this program vulnerability.
- *Home infusion pharmacies* billing for self-injectable medications under Part D despite coverage under a specific Part B benefit (e.g., Epogen used by home dialysis patients).
- *Duplicate billing* to Part B and Part D (e.g., physician claims to Part B for drugs dispensed under Part D by a pharmacy pursuant to plan coverage requirements and then taken by the patient to the physician's office for administration).
- *Gaming of differential co-pays* between Part B and Part D by physicians or beneficiaries.

Sponsors should view the risk area listings as an excellent checklist for evaluating their own FWA compliance programs. They should, however, remain vigilant because other Part D vulnerabilities will become apparent as the benefit matures and plans, providers, beneficiaries, and government administrators and enforcement authorities become more familiar with the Part D program. Further, it is important for Sponsors to pay careful attention to the plan operations and transactions occurring downstream. The Part D risk areas identified by CMS target both the Sponsor level and various third-party levels involved in the administration and delivery of the Part D benefit. Many of the risk areas are listed for multiple categories of players in the prescription drug supply chain because a single program vulnerability may be exploited in different ways or victimize different parties.

The number and nature of the identified risks reflect the complexity of the Part D benefit delivery system. As a means of improving the efficiency and effectiveness of its oversight activities, CMS created a contractor (i.e., Sponsor) risk assessment tool designed to assess the level of compliance risk posed by various Part D program areas and individual Sponsors. This risk assessment tool

---

[349]*Id.* §70.2.

[350]*Id.* §70.2.3. As noted in Section III.D.5.a., above, "Covered Part D drug" means a Part D drug that is included in a Part D plan's formulary, or treated as being included in a Part D plan's formulary as a result of a coverage determination or appeal, under applicable regulations, and obtained at a network pharmacy or an out-of-network pharmacy (as permitted in Part D Final Rule).

[351]PDBM Chapter 9 §70.2.4 (citing 42 U.S.C. §1395w-102; 42 C.F.R. §423.100).

provides CMS with expanded intelligence for targeting its resources toward more high-risk contracts.[352] CMS plans to build a centralized data-driven program to store information obtained through the risk assessment tool.[353] According to CMS, oversight must include data analysis as well as regularly scheduled and targeted program compliance and program integrity audits.[354] CMS said it expected to begin using the risk assessment tool in January 2008.[355] As more details about the risk assessment tool are published, Sponsors should review and update, as appropriate, their compliance plans and relevant operating procedures to prepare for the heightened scrutiny.

## IV. REPORTING PART D FWA

Well-structured compliance programs provide the best available defense against the imposition of Part D sanctions by CMS and also mitigate the likelihood a whistleblower or government enforcement agency will file a false claims action. Prudent Sponsors will carefully monitor and audit their activities and those of their subcontractors for compliance with the Part D Final Rule and with applicable fraud and abuse authorities such as the False Claims Act, the federal anti-kickback statute,[356] and the beneficiary inducement provisions of the Civil Monetary Penalty Law.[357] However, although CMS has proposed a mandatory self-reporting requirement for Sponsors that identify fraud or misconduct in the Part D program,[358] currently such disclosures are voluntary. In PDBM Chapter 9, CMS implies that Sponsors that voluntarily self-report instances of FWA relating to the delivery of prescription drugs under the Part D program to MEDICs or CMS will receive the same benefits of self-reporting as the OIG and DOJ have accorded Medicare providers and suppliers under the OIG's Provider Self-Disclosure Protocol.[359] Essentially, this means that enforcement authorities will view voluntary self-reporting as a mitigating factor in assessing Sponsor liability, although self-reporting offers no guaranteed protection from prosecution. Self-reporting in the context of noncompliant subcontractor behavior may prove necessary in order to mitigate the risk to the Sponsor in the event a MEDIC, CMS, or the OIG identifies the problem through an audit or investigation.

Sponsors also should be aware that a failure to report certain problems or errors in the administration of a Part D plan may create a more significant risk than the unreported problem or error. For instance, Part D plans that report zero

---

[352]*See* Centers for Medicare & Medicaid Servs., 2008 Call Letter for Medicare Advantage Orgs. (Apr. 19, 2007), at 33–34, *available at* http://www.cms.hhs.gov/PrescriptionDrugCov Contra/Downloads/CallLetter.pdf.

[353]*See id.*

[354]*See id.*

[355]*See id.*

[356]Social Security Act §1128B(b) [42 U.S.C. §1320a–7b(b)].

[357]Social Security Act §1128A(a)(5) [42 U.S.C. §1320a–7a(a)(5)].

[358]72 Fed. Reg. at 29,381 (May 25, 2007).

[359]63 Fed. Reg. 58,359 (Oct. 30, 1998), *also available at* http://www.oig.hhs.gov/authorities/docs/selfdisclosure.pdf.

overpayments may make even more attractive targets for enforcement authorities than plans with reported overpayments. A Sponsor claiming it did not receive any overpayments may raise a flag because, from the government's perspective, it would be highly unlikely that a Part D plan or its PBM contractor would have no payment discrepancies at all over an entire plan year.[360] More likely, the government would believe the Sponsor failed to conduct diligent audits of claims. Sponsors should consider developing processes for identifying overpayments and underpayments at *any level* of the network, including those at the retail pharmacy and PBM levels.[361] That said, overpayments often result from routine administrative errors, which can be made by Medicare as well as the Sponsor. Noncompliance may not be the cause of the overpayment. Accordingly, Sponsors generally should be cautious about reporting the conduct of their subcontractors, as well as their own conduct, before completing a thorough internal investigation and seeking advice from counsel.

---

[360] *See Monitoring, Auditing Should Be Key Focus for Part D Plans*, 10 HEALTH CARE FRAUD REP. (BNA) 765 (Oct. 25, 2006).

[361] *See id.*

# Appendix Table of Contents*

---

*Appendix editor: Carol Poindexter, Shook, Hardy & Bacon, LLP, Kansas City, Missouri.
All appendix documents appear on the disk accompanying this volume.

# Table of Cases

# Index

*References are to chapter and section numbers (e.g., **5:** III.H.1 refers to section III.H.1. of Chapter 5). The Addendum to Chapter 2 is referenced as **2A**.*

## PLEASE READ BEFORE USING THIS CD-ROM

This is a legal agreement between you, the individual or entity using this software (the "User"), and BNA Books ("BNA"). Use of these software files ("Software") is governed by the terms of the following license agreement ("Agreement"). By proceeding to use this CD-ROM you agree to accept each of the terms, conditions, and covenants set forth herein. If you do not agree to each of the terms of this Agreement, promptly return the CD-ROM package and the accompanying items (including associated book and packaging) to BNA Books for a full refund or cancellation of all charges.